EVERYBODY'S BUSINESS

**Other books by Milton Moskowitz,
Robert Levering, and Michael Katz:**

Everybody's Business: An Almanac
Everybody's Business Scoreboard
The Computer Entrepreneurs
The 100 Best Companies to Work for in America

Also by Milton Moskowitz:

The Global Marketplace

Also by Robert Levering:

A Great Place to Work

EVERYBODY'S BUSINESS

A Field Guide to the 400 Leading Companies in America

EDITED BY

Milton Moskowitz, Robert Levering, and Michael Katz

DOUBLEDAY CURRENCY

New York   London   Toronto   Sydney   Auckland

A CURRENCY BOOK

PUBLISHED BY DOUBLEDAY

A DIVISION OF BANTAM DOUBLEDAY DELL PUBLISHING GROUP, INC.
666 FIFTH AVENUE, NEW YORK, NEW YORK 10103

CURRENCY AND DOUBLEDAY ARE TRADEMARKS OF DOUBLEDAY,
A DIVISION OF BANTAM DOUBLEDAY DELL
PUBLISHING GROUP, INC.

LIBRARY OF CONGRESS CATALOGING-IN-PUBLICATION DATA
Moskowitz, Milton.
Everybody's business / Milton Moskowitz, Robert Levering,
Michael Katz.—1st ed.
p. cm.
Includes index.
1. Corporations—Handbooks, manuals, etc. 2. Corporate culture—Handbooks,
manuals, etc. 3. Industry—Social aspects—Handbooks, manuals, etc. I.
Levering,
Robert, 1944–
II. Katz, Michael. 1945– . III. Title.
HD2741.M65 1990
338.7'4--dc20   90-38923
                                                    CIP

ISBN 0-385-26547-6
ISBN 0-385-41629-6 (pbk.)

Guide to Company Profiles

- The 400 companies profiled in *Everybody's Business* include the leading corporations in virtually every major industry.

- Within each industry, companies are ranked by size, usually by sales (assets are used in the banking and insurance industries).

- A company is listed in every industry where it competes. General Electric, for example, appears in three different sections: appliances, broadcasting, and conglomerates.

Rankings: Market standings of specific products and services, derived from information provided by the companies themselves, industry sources, or articles in the business press.

Sales and profits (or losses): 1989 figures as reported by the company or in annual compilations by *Business Week, Forbes,* and *Fortune.*

Founded: Starting year of company with an unbroken line to corporation being profiled.

Owners and rulers: CEOs (chief executive officers) and other top managers. Members of board of directors. Where possible, CEO's 1989 pay is denoted. Ownership information comes primarily from the annual proxy statement sent to shareholders.

As a place to work The company's workplace practices and labor relations gleaned from a number of sources: our own ongoing interviews with employees for future editions of *The 100 Best Companies to Work for in America,* and information provided by the company, and stories in local and national media sources.

Social responsibility: How the company has demonstrated their social concerns or lack thereof.

Global presence: What the company does outside the U.S.

Stock performance: Calculated by BARRA of Berkeley, California.

Consumer brands: Names of products and services offered by the company to consumers.

- At the end of each profile is the company's legal name, address, and phone number.

- Finally, 60 companies are singled out for special attention because of exemplary or deplorable performances in two areas, a performance that is symbolized with characters by cartoonist Ronald Searle:

Outstanding corporate citizen.

 Great place to work.

Lack of discernible social conscience.

Woeful place to work.

Contents

Alphabetic List of Companies Profiled

INTRODUCTION

Large corporations, a phenomenon of the past 100 years or so, went through the most wrenching period in their history during the 1980s. It was a decade of upheaval, characterized by multi-billion-dollar deals that would have staggered the imagination of the original dealmaker, J. P. Morgan. And it left a business landscape considerably altered from the one we presented in our 1980 edition of *Everybody's Business*. Of the 317 companies we profiled then, one half have been so radically transformed they no longer are recognizable in the form we described. Some companies—Norton Simon, Northwest Industries, Anaconda, City Investing, National Airlines, RCA—have vanished. Others—Carnation, A. C. Nielsen, American Motors, Nabisco, J. Walter Thompson—lost their independence and now belong to other companies. Some companies no longer provide the products and services their names used to stand for. General Electric doesn't make toasters anymore. Westinghouse doesn't make light bulbs. B. F. Goodrich doesn't make tires. Other companies supplying products deemed quintessentially American were transferred to the rosters of foreign-owned companies: 7-Eleven stores, *TV Guide,* Pillsbury, Firestone tires, Columbia Pictures, RCA records and TV sets, Contac cold capsules, Smith-Corona typewriters. Even the publisher of this book, Doubleday, has been sold to a German company (Bertelsmann), while an Australian firm (Rupert Murdoch's News Corp.) has purchased the publisher of the original edition (Harper & Row).

Despite the upheaval, big companies have, if anything, even more influence on American life. We've focused on the industry leaders, companies that by dominating their corners of the marketplace tend to define, for example, the foods we eat, the medicines we take, the cars we drive, the movies we see, the news of the world we read and hear. It's hard to go through a day without direct contact with many of these companies. What's more, almost one quarter of the U.S. population is economically dependent on paychecks from these 400 companies (nearly 20 million Americans are their employees and another 30 to 40 million are either dependents of employees or retirees). Millions more rely on these firms for their livelihood either through investments or their jobs at smaller firms doing business with these 400 corporations.

The thread running through the profiles of these 400 companies is change. Corporations were not only being bought and sold at an unprecedented clip, they also were restructuring themselves so one couldn't be sure from one day to the next what they did. Even their names and addresses were being changed much more frequently than in the past. More than a dozen companies in this book, from Exxon to Holiday Inns, moved their headquarters. Two companies—Burlington Northern and RJR Nabisco—moved twice. Another, Figgie, moved from Ohio to Virginia and then back to Ohio. Over 30 companies changed their names—some into bloodless acronyms like CSX, USX, NYNEX, UNISYS, Trionva, and Premark, others into more human forms like Chiquita Brands, Sara Lee, and Whitman. One company, United Airlines, changed their name twice in one year. The 1980s saw the entire telephone business change with the breakup of the Bell System. It was also the decade where suppliers of sneakers became the kings of the shoe business. In the 1980 edition of *Everybody's Business,* only 5 companies were non-American; now 35 are. In the 1980 edition, few of the chief executives of these companies were paid more than $1 million a year; in this edition, as we detail, it's commonplace. Not only has their pay skyrocketed, so has the ratio between their pay and that of the average worker in these firms. At the beginning of the decade, the top officers of American corporations were making about 40 times what was paid the average worker. By 1990 they were making over 90 times as much.

Capturing change is never easy, especially when it's ongoing, but we have tried to pin down these 400 companies at the end of climactic chapters in their lives. Even well-informed people have had difficulty keeping track of the multitude of changes that swept through the business world in the 1980s. The new *Everybody's Business* offers a roadmap to this turbulent world of big business.

Our approach—our spirit, if you will—remains as it was in the first edition. *Everybody's Business* answers—without jargon or technical language—a wide range of questions about America's leading companies. Rather than present a collection of facts and figures, we've tried to penetrate the corporate facades to delineate the distinctive characteristics and personalities of companies. Partly because we see companies as having individual personalities, we refer to them (ungrammatically) as "they" rather than "it" (because most people talk about companies in this way).

We have done our best to present a telling portrait of these companies based on the information we've been able to unearth about our sometimes reticent subjects. We welcome any insights from our readers, especially those who work for any of these firms, to enhance our next edition, scheduled for publication two years from now. Send your comments to: *Everybody's Business,* 1537 Franklin Street, Room 208, San Francisco, California 94109.

Milton Moskowitz
Robert Levering
Michael Katz

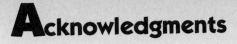cknowledgments

Everybody's Business involved a team effort of writers, editors, researchers, fact checkers, administrative whizzes, indexers, word processors, and assorted tipsters. Our masthead on the following page lists principal contributors by name. We are especially indebted to the Data Center, a remarkable research group located at 464 19th Street, Oakland, California 94612, (415) 835-4692. A nonprofit, user-supported information center with a vast collection of newspaper and periodical clippings on labor, corporate, and industry topics, they also offer a customized search service accessing electronic and paper files on subjects related to U.S. corporations and their social and business records.

To our editors at Doubleday—Harriet Rubin and Janet Coleman—we wish to express our appreciation for their support throughout the project. We would also like to extend our gratitude to the following people who made valuable contributions to the book: Jennifer Carothers, Susan P. Hymas, Okanta Leonard, Marge Lurie, Neff Rotter, Simmah Taborah.

Finally, we wish to say a special thanks to Jane Granoff of BMR and Jerald Volpe of RJ Volpe & Associates, whose production and typographical skills under extreme time pressure were invaluable.

Staff writer: Katherine Stubbs

Researchers: Harry Strharsky, Loretta Strharsky, LouAnn Aaberg

Editorial coordinator: Kristin Denham

Contributing writers: Dolly Setton, James Gibney, Jamie Stiehm, Cathy Miranker, Nancy Marx Better, Cassia Herman, Jacqueline Frost, Ray Alvarez-Torres, Susan Shepard

Assistant editor: Louis Epstein

Photo researcher: Kim Haas

Research assistants: Phyllis J. Nix, Seija Surr, Claudio Saunt

Indexer: Bonnie Galvin

Copy editor: Stephen McElroy

Word processors: Karen Chaney, Jo Simms, Grace Nichols, Wendy Shapero, Lourdes Noriega

Typography: BMR of Mill Valley, California, and RJ Volpe & Associates

Cover artist/illustrator: Ronald Searle

PART ONE:

The Almighty Consumer

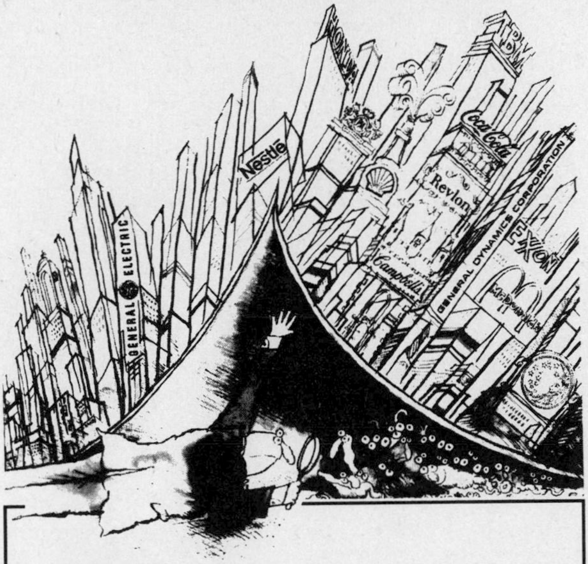

Food

- Food Packagers
- Agribusiness
- Meat & Poultry
- Specialty Foods
- Candy
- Soft Drinks
- Restaurants
- Food Wholesalers
- Supermarkets

more...

Clothing & Shelter
Clothing
Shoes
Textiles
Home Appliances
Builders & Developers
Health & Beauty

Household Products
Cosmetics
Drugs
Healthcare

Retailers
Superstores
Department Stores
Specialty Stores
Drug Stores

Automotive
Cars
Earthmovers
Tires
Car Parts
Car Rental Agencies

Fun & Games
Toys
Consumer Electronics
Movies
Hotels
Photography
Greeting Cards

Sin
Tobacco
Beer
Wines & Liquor
Gambling

The Media
Global Media Giants
Broadcasters
Newspapers
Magazines
Book Publishers
Advertising
Printers

FOOD

FOOD PACKAGERS

Somebody forgot to tell America's food packagers the 1980s were a diet-and-health conscious decade. The biggest food companies devoured each other at such a rapid rate it seemed some of them were getting indigestion in the bargain. Some of them, like ConAgra (Armour, Chun King, Banquet), got fat on what others considered leftovers. And the two biggest cigarette makers (Philip Morris and R. J. Reynolds) didn't push away from the table before gulping down what were four of the biggest food companies of 1980— Kraft, General Foods, Nabisco and Standard Brands. As a result, coming into the 1990s, the 10 largest food companies were responsible for one-third of all U.S. food shipments.

1

KRAFT GENERAL FOODS

#1 *in cheese, coffee, gelatin desserts, powdered drinks, salad dressings, ice cream, packaged meats, frozen foods*

#2 *in margarines*

#3 *in cereals*

Employees: 98,000
Sales: $23.3 billion
Profits: $1.9 billion
Founded 1903 (Kraft); 1895 (General Foods)
Headquarters: Glenview, Illinois

The Marlboro Man spent $13 billion wooing the braided Kraft cheese-and-macaroni girl. When their two companies (Philip Morris and Kraft) were joined in one of the biggest corporate marriages of the decade, the Marlboro Man at last chowed down on an all-American breakfast of strong Maxwell House coffee, a hearty helping of Oscar Mayer bacon and a bowl of Grape-Nuts (perhaps topped with a little Log Cabin syrup). As he rode the range, he could take along Velveeta sandwiches and carry some Kool-Aid in his canteen.

With 14 of the top 50 U.S. food brands, Kraft General Foods holds undisputed first place among America's food packagers. When Kraft merged with Philip Morris in 1988, they joined General Foods, which the giant cigarette maker had swallowed up three years earlier. It's hard to walk down a supermarket aisle without bumping into a product from Kraft General Foods. And you are certainly not going to go through a day without being hit by a sales message from this food combine. They spend about $1 billion a year on advertising, and 10 of the largest advertising agencies in the U.S work for them.

Philip Morris established Kraft General Foods headquarters at the Kraft home base in Glenview, 20 miles north of downtown Chicago. They immediately started looking for ways to save money by the merger. Management and salespeople in international operations were fused, and the two companies purchased raw materials together for a savings of $8 million. Three factories in the U.S. were closed, about 2 percent of the work force was fired, and many products were modified (for instance, they shrank the caps on their mayonnaise jars).

Merging food and cigarettes created some problems, however. Kraft allows employees to smoke only in private offices and certain designated areas. So, when Hamish Maxwell, chairman of Philip Morris, paid his first visit to Kraft in 1988, an employee reported this scene to the *Chicago Sun-Times*: "Before Hamish got here, they took down a lot of the no-smoking signs, and ashtrays started popping out all over the place."

History. Before they were combined in 1989, Kraft and General Foods had long histories of their own, closely intertwined with the growth of the processed foods industry. Establishing a founding date for either company is an arbitrary matter, depending, as it does, on how far back you want to go to find the birth of a predecessor company. One point is clear: Even before Philip Morris yoked them together, Kraft and General Foods were the products of an endless series of mergers and acquisitions.

For example, it's possible to go back to the years:

1765: when Dr. James Baker, a physician in Dorchester, Massachusetts, started the first chocolate factory in the New World; that was the origin of the Baker's chocolate now sold by General Foods.

1837: when Alfred Bird, a British chemist, developed a baking powder and eggless custard; that was the start of Alfred Bird & Sons, the first European company General Foods acquired (in 1947).

1882: when Joel Cheek, a Kentucky farm boy, began to make the coffee that became Maxwell House (after the Maxwell House Hotel in Nashville where it was first served).

1883: when the Mayer brothers—Oscar, Gottfried and Max—set up a retail meat market in Chicago.

1887: when P. J. Towle, a grocer in St. Paul, Minnesota, blended a table syrup from sugarcane and Vermont and Canadian maple sugars and packaged it in a log-cabin-shaped container in honor of his boyhood hero, Abraham Lincoln; that was the start of Log Cabin syrup.

1895: when Charles W. Post, a health-food addict, began selling a grain-based beverage, Postum cereal.

These enterprises are only a handful of the many roped together to form General Foods. Much of the roping was done in the 1920s when the Postum Company went on a buying spree, snapping up Jell-O, Minute Tapioca, James Baker (the chocolate maker), Franklin Baker (coconut), Calumet, Inglehart Brothers (Swans Down cake flour) and, finally, in 1929, Clarence Birdseye's company. A scientist, Birdseye had discovered how to quick-freeze food, and he had organized his businesses under the banner, General Foods, which Postum quickly adopted as their name.

Other acquisitions came later. In fact, they never stopped coming—Minute Rice (1941), Gaines dog food (1943), Kool-Aid (1953), Good Seasons salad dressing (1954), SOS scouring pads (1957) and Oven Pit barbecue sauce (1960). Three nonfood companies bought in the late 1960s and early 1970s—Viviane Woodward (door-to-door cosmetics),

WHO MAKES THE NEW FOODS?

	Number of New Products
1. Kraft General Foods	156
2. Nestlé	52
3. Campbell Soup	51
4. Unilever	47
5. Nabisco Brands	46
6. Ralston Purina	41
7. Borden	39
8. General Mills	38
9. Pillsbury	32
10. ConAgra	29

Source: *Food Engineering,* April 1990. Statistics for 1989.

Khoner Brothers (toys) and W. Atlee Burpee (seeds)—were sold off or closed in the same decade. Later General Foods got rid of the Burger Chef fast-food restaurants they bought in 1968. In the 1980s came the purchases of Oscar Mayer (1981), Entenmann's baked goods (1982) and Ronzoni pasta (bought in 1984, sold to Hershey in 1989). A year later they sold out to Philip Morris.

Whereas GF has always dabbled with technology to invent food products, Kraft began as part of the real thing: the dairy industry. However, Kraft's genealogy is just as convoluted as GF's. The company was named after James L. Kraft, son of a Canadian Mennonite farmer, who in 1903 arrived in Chicago and began selling cheese to grocers from a horse-drawn wagon. By 1914, he and his four brothers were selling 31 varieties of cheese in many parts of the country under the brand names Kraft and Elkhorn. After World War I the Krafts introduced a five-pound cheese loaf wrapped in foil and set inside a rectangular wooden box. Within a month Kraft was producing 15,000 boxes a day to satisfy demand. After 1928, the company's history is far less coherent. In that year, Kraft merged with rival Phenix Company, and then in 1930 was roped into the National Dairy Products Corporation, whose dairy firms could trace their histories back to:

1866: when William Breyer began selling ice cream in Philadelphia, and

1883: when Isaac and Joseph Breakstone opened a dairy store on the lower East Side of New York City.

For a brief period in the early 1980s, Kraft succumbed to the conglomerate craze by merging with Dart Industries, a miniconglomerate put together by a crony of Ronald Reagan's named Justin Dart. The newly renamed Dart & Kraft turned around and bought Hobart, the company that makes KitchenAid home appliances. The marriage was soon on the rocks, and in 1986 Kraft sold off most of their non-food operations to Premark International (see profile, page 145) and dropped the Dart name. In 1988, when they sold off Duracell batteries, Kraft became an all-food company for the first time in more than 30 years. Just in time to be acquired by Philip Morris.

Owners and rulers. Owned 100 percent by Philip Morris (see profile on page 313). John M. Richman, Kraft's CEO at the time of the merger, retired in 1989 with the year's biggest golden parachute—$22.4 million! Run by Kraft, rather than GF, people. Top man at KGF coming into the 1990s is Michael Miles, a marketing whiz (and ardent antismoker) who did such a good job turning around Kentucky Fried Chicken that Kraft recruited him in 1982. In 1989, Miles' successor at Kentucky Fried Chicken, Richard Mayer, followed his old boss to KGF, becoming president of General Foods USA.

As a place to work. Dreadful things used to be said about the old General Foods. Bureaucratic. Uninventive. More interested in advertising than the product itself. Constant turnover at the top. Two presidents of GF came out of Procter & Gamble and tried to implant P&G systems minus the P&G culture. Kraft has been a more stable place but not exactly swinging. From now on in, though, big brother, in the form of Philip Morris in New York, will be watching this food business closely.

Global presence. They do from 20 to 25 percent of their business outside the U.S., but neither GF nor Kraft has been a screaming success in overseas markets

Every year, *Kraft General Foods produces 1,720,000,000,000 (that is, 1.72 trillion) pounds of food, requiring 546 million pounds of soybean oil, 104 million pounds of cheese and 428 million gallons of water.*

(they lag behind Heinz, Sara Lee and CPC; and Nestlé and Unilever kill them in Europe). However, in 1990 Philip Morris gave them a big boost by acquiring the Swiss company, Suchard (coffee and candy), moving KGF closer to Nestlé in the world food standings.

Consumer brands. According to Kraft, they make 3,300 products under 850 trademarks. The following are the most well known.

Cheeses: Kraft, Cheez Whiz, Velveeta, Cracker Barrel, Casino, Harvest Moon, Knudsen, Select-A-Size, Elkhorn.

Baked goods: Boboli, Francisco, Northridge Old Country, Coon, Oroweat, Entenmann's, Freihofer's.

Barbecue sauces: Bull's-Eye, Kraft, Thick 'N Spicy. *Cereals:* Alpha-Bits, Fruit & Fibre, Grape-Nuts, Honey Bunches of Oats, Honeycomb, Post Toasties, Raisin Bran, Pebbles, Super Golden Crisp.

Coffees: Brim, General Foods International, Maxim, Maxwell House, Sanka, Yuban.

Desserts: Baker's Fudge-tastics, Cool Whip, Crystal Light, Jell-O, Baker's, D-Zerta, Dream Whip, Minute.

Dry grocery: Country Kitchen, Good Seasons, Log Cabin, Minute Rice, Oven Fry, Shake 'N Bake, Stove Top.

Frozen foods: Bird's Eye, Kraft Entrees, Foremost, Nice 'N Light, Tombstone, Budget Gourmet.

Milk: Carousel, Knudsen, Partytime.

Meats: Louis Rich, Oscar Mayer.

Dressings: Kraft, Sauceworks.

Seafood: Louis Kemp.

Snacks: Cheez Links, Mohawk.

Beverages: Postum, Country Time, Crystal Light, Kool-Aid, Tang.

Dairy and ice cream: Philadelphia Brand cream cheese, Light 'n' Lively, Sealtest, Breyers, Frusen Glädje, Knudsen, Cream White creamer.

Shortening: Richmix.

Margarine: Chiffon, Parkay.

Dressings: Miracle Whip, Seven Seas.

Bagels: Lender's.

Kraft General Foods, Inc., Kraft Court, Glenview, IL 60025; (312) 998-2000.

2

#1 *in flour milling, shrimp processing*
#2 *in poultry*
#3 *in beef production*

Employees: 49,100
Sales: $14.5 billion
Profits: $224 million
Founded: 1919
Headquarters: Omaha, Nebraska

If you go into a supermarket and walk out with a shopping cart filled with Country Pride chicken, Singleton frozen shrimp, Armour hot dogs, a Banquet frozen dinner, Chun King chow mein and Patio frozen enchiladas, you will be dining on ConAgra foods. And if you stopped at the meat department to pick up a sirloin steak or lamb chops or a pork loin, the chances are also good that these foods came to you via Con-Agra, a food powerhouse in American life even though hardly anyone has ever heard of them.

History. Amazingly, ConAgra rose to such prominence only in the 1980s. Coming into the decade, their annual sales were under $1 billion; by the end of the decade, they were closing in on $15 billion.

How they did it is no secret. They went on a shopping spree and bought 50 companies. Leading this charge was Charles "Mike" Harper, a wheeler-dealer from the breadbasket of America. He came to ConAgra in 1974 after 20 years at Pillsbury and proved adept at buying food businesses other companies either didn't want or couldn't run profitably. He lifted Banquet off RCA's hands; relieved Greyhound of Armour; acquired the Chun King, Patio and Morton frozen food businesses from RJR Nabisco; and took over the Swift Independent and Monfort meatpacking businesses. In 1990 he scooped up Hunt-Wesson foods, Swift-Eckrich meats and Beatrice cheeses for a bargain price of $1.3 billion, an acquisition that will balloon Con Agra's annual sales to $20 billion. And because they weren't wanted, Harper got them at bargain-basement prices. *Fortune* writer Bill Saporito quoted a Prudential-Bache security analyst, John McMillin, who depicted Mike Harper as follows: "The guy buys things you wouldn't pay a wooden nickel for and gets change back."

There's poetic justice in ConAgra's growth as well. People used to complain that urban corporate monoliths, with headquarters in New York and Chicago, were dominating the food industry with packaged, laboratory-produced items—a long way from the farm fields. ConAgra reverses that syndrome. They come out of the farm fields. The chain that ends on a supermarket shelf stretches back, in ConAgra's case, to huge poultry farms and cattle-feeding lots and grain elevators. They're an integrated food processor. And then there's this irony. Mike Harper left Pillsbury after the company sold out the division he headed, poultry, because they figured more money was to be made in Burger Kings than in processing and selling birds. In 1984, now in command at ConAgra, Harper bought back that same poultry business. And today, ConAgra has surpassed Pillsbury in the food business.

The company was formed in 1919 by the merger of four flour mills located in the Nebraska towns of Grand Island, Ravenna, Hastings and St. Edward. They took as their name Nebraska Consolidated Mills, and their branded flour was called Mother's Best. The company didn't break out of the state of Nebraska until 1941 when they put a flour mill into Decatur,

More than 30,000 students have graduated from McDonald's Hamburger University with a degree called "Bachelor of Hamburgerology."

Alabama, which led, in 1942, to their entry into the feed business under the Red Hat name. These feeds were made at the Decatur plant. This southern connection also brought them into the broiler business after World War II when they acquired poultry plants at Dalton, Georgia, and Athens, Alabama. Getting chickens ready to market is largely a matter of force-feeding, and Nebraska Consolidated was already supplying the feed.

The flour millers had a brief swing at glory in the 1950s when they signed on as a licensee of Hines-Park Foods to make a pancake mix under the Duncan Hines label. A pancake mix is basically flour, so Nebraska Consolidated wasn't really doing anything new. However, this was their first foray into the arena of fast-moving consumer products. And although they did very well—in the Midwest the Duncan Hines mixes were soon challenging the brand leaders, Betty Crocker and Pillsbury—Nebraska Consolidated blanched when they saw how much money was going to have to go into advertising, a business they knew nothing about. They proved to be amazingly complaisant when Procter & Gamble, looking for a way into the cake mix business, took a fancy to the Duncan Hines name and came courting. Nebraska Consolidated sold out and went back to milling flour, producing feeds and growing chickens and turkeys. In 1971, they changed their name to ConAgra, a word coined from Latin, meaning "in partnership with the land."

Disaster struck in the early 1970s when the company lost a bundle of money in commodity futures. Grain companies routinely have a forward position in commodities—e.g., a commitment to buy wheat or corn or soybeans at a set price sometime in the future—as a hedging device, not as a way to make money. The temptation is always there, however, to speculate: to attempt to guess correctly on future prices and make big profits (remember Eddie Murphy and Dan Ayckroyd in *Trading Places*?). Managers at ConAgra made some wrong guesses, and the company lost so much money they were virtually bankrupt in 1974. To the rescue, from Pillsbury in Minneapolis, came Mike Harper.

No one who knows Harper believes his appetite is sated.

The secretive Mars company refused to let M&M's appear in Stephen Spielberg's blockbuster movie E.T., *much to their later regret. Hershey's Reese's Pieces got the role instead, giving sales an enormous boost.*

Owners and rulers. Mike Harper is the boss. He and other top management people own about 7 percent of the stock. He took home a whopping $4.1 million in 1989. Harper has been on a health kick since he suffered a heart attack in 1985. He has quit smoking and drinking coffee, he watches his calorie intake carefully, and, believe it or not, he rarely eats beef. Having seen the light, he's trying to change what ConAgra does. He told *Forbes:* "We in the food industry didn't believe bad eating was our fault, because we didn't believe there was a market for healthy foods. Well, we were wrong." ConAgra now sells low-fat frozen dinners called Healthy Choice. ConAgra jumped on the oat bran fad in 1989 with both feet, tripling the amount of oat bran they milled in one year to become the biggest industrial oat miller.

As a place to work. With Harper's need to make money, ConAgra is not the greatest place in the world to work. On the chicken line in Arkansas, a 48-person team debones 65 chicken breasts a minute. In buying Armour from Greyhound, ConAgra made sure that 13 unionized Armour plants were closed first. After buying the business, ConAgra reopened the plants with a non-unionized workforce with pay scales beginning at $5.50 an hour.

Global presence. ConAgra has flour mills and feed operations in Puerto Rico, Spain and Portugal.

Stock performance. ConAgra stock bought for $1,000 in 1980 sold for $20,479 on January 2, 1990.

Consumer brands.

Meats: Armour, Swift.

Poultry: Country Pride, Golden Star, Longmont.

Deli and dairy products: World's Fare, Main Street, Miss Wisconsin, Cloverbloom.

Seafood: Singleton, Taste O' Sea, Country Skillet.

Frozen foods: Chun King, Patio, Banquet, Morton, Sensible Chef, Armour.

Grocery: Home Brand jellies and peanut butter, Maple Rich syrups.

Miscellaneous: Pfaelzer Brothers mail-order meats and gourmet foods, Geisler pet foods, Singer sewing products.

ConAgra, Inc., One Central Park Plaza, Omaha, NE 68102; (402) 978-4000.

3

#1 *in smoked sausage, frozen baked goods, pantyhose, shoe polish*

#2 *in hot dogs, bras and panties*

Employees: 93,800
Sales: $11.7 billion
Profits: $441 million
Founded: 1939
Headquarters: Chicago, Illinois

Diversity has always been the hallmark of this company, and that seems unlikely to change in the 1990s. They changed their name in 1985 from Consolidated Foods to Sara Lee, after their most well-known brand name, but the company remained as difficult as ever to define. They run a host of businesses in the U.S. and around the world, operating 177 manufacturing plants in 25 states and 23 other countries, holding it all together with a Chicago command force of 247 employees. They manufacture but they also wholesale. They also have some stores of their own. And they sell some products (Fuller Brush) door-to-door and via mail order catalogs.

In the food business, their biggest U.S. businesses are packaged meats and frozen baked goods. These products include a variety of meats with down-home names and regional appeal, including Hillshire Farm, Jimmy Dean meats, Kahn's, Rudy's Farm, Prairie Belt, Smoky Hollow and King Cotton. Sara Lee also sells Hanes and

Here is the real Sara Lee in 1990. She is the latest spokesperson for the company that was named for her in 1985.

L'Eggs hosiery, and in 1989 cornered 42 percent of the hosiery market.

Their diversity may be gleaned from some of their acquisitions during the late 1980s: Champion athletic wear in the U.S. (sweats); France's number one insecticide, Catch; Esquire shoe polish; Ty-D-Bol toilet bowl cleaner; and Ball Park Franks (600 million franks a year sold to U.S. consumers).

History. Nate Cummings, a man with little formal education, was the master chef behind the casserole now known as Sara Lee. In 1939, 43-year-old Cummings bought the Baltimore-based C.D. Kenny Company, a wholesale distributor of sugar, coffee and tea. That first purchase only whetted his appetite. After adding 11 more companies, Cummings renamed his company Consolidated Foods Corporation in 1954. Two years later, he added a tasty goody: the Kitchens of Sara Lee, named after founder Charles Lubin's one-year-old daughter. By the time Nate Cummings relinquished the president's title in 1970, he had bought more than 90 companies, including a variety of nonfood businesses, like Oxford Chemical, Electrolux vacuums, Fuller brushes, Gant shirts, Aris gloves and Tyco toys.

When CEO John H. Bryan, Jr., took over in the late 1970s, he began selling off many obscure brands—almost four dozen companies, many of them in nonfood industries. And he bought only well-known, branded consumer products companies (Hillshire Farms in 1976, Douwe Egberts in 1978, Hanes in 1979, Kiwi Brands in 1984).

Owners and rulers. The people at the top come from companies Consolidated Foods acquired. John H. Bryan, Jr., became chief executive in 1975 when he was 38. Bryan made $2.1 million in 1989. Consolidated had bought his family's Mississippi meatpacking company, Bryan Foods, in 1967. Paul Fulton, elected president in 1988, came from Hanes, which Consolidated took over in 1979.

Global presence. Sara Lee sells nearly $3 billion worth of products a year in Europe. Their Douwe Egberts company in Holland is one of the world's leading coffee roasters (number one in Belgium and the Netherlands, number two in France and Denmark), and they also sell nuts, sauces, tobacco (Amphora), tea and wines. Other leading Sara Lee brands in Europe are the Kiwi shoe polishes, Biotex detergents and Bloom insecticides. Kiwi is sold in 130 countries and in the U.S. has over 90 percent of the consumer shoe-polish market. Kiwi is Sara Lee's most widely marketed brand.

Stock performance. Sara Lee stock bought for $1,000 in 1980 sold for $15,637 on January 2, 1990.

Consumer brands.

Frozen foods: Sara Lee, Big Stick, Creamsicle, Fruitsicle, Fudgsicle, Sidewalk Sundae.

Meat packing: Emmber Brands, Jimmy Deam, Lean 'N' Tender, Gallo, Galileo, Hillshire Farm, Kahn's. Ball Park, Hygrade, Grillmaster, West Virginia.

Grocery: RB Rice, Rudy's Farm, Sara Lee, Began, Gourmet Entree, Prairie Belt, Smoky Hollow, King Cotton, MarTenn, Baked Perfect, Chef Pierre, Lloyd J. Harris, Bagel Time, Heart Fruit, Le San*Wich.

Coffee: Douwe Egberts, Royal Kona, Superior.

Personal products: Aris Isotoner, Notice.

Leatherwear: Coach.

Underwear: Hanes, Bali, A-OK, Flexnit, Not Just Another Bra, Not Just Another Panty, Something Else, Canadell, Dici, Wonderbra, L'Eggs, Sirena.

Household products: Fuller, Amtipus, Erdal, Miss Den, Odorex, Prodent, Roger Para, Tana, Ambi, Aspro, Finimal, Kiwi, Kylie, Miracle White, Tadox, Rennie, Tuxas.

Sara Lee Corporation, Three First National Plaza, Chicago, IL 60602; (312) 726-2600.

4

#1 *in dairies, pasta, canned seafood, glue, wallpapers, packaged lemon juice, bouillon*

#2 *in salted snacks*

Employees: 46,500
Sales: $7.6 billion
Profits: $61 million
Founded: 1857
Headquarters: New York City, New York

Borden still makes their original product, Eagle Brand condensed milk, but after that, nothing—not even Elsie the Cow, the company's living symbol—is sacred. Every few years the honchos at Borden inspect the products in their cow barn and decide there are plenty they can live without. Out they go. That's followed by a furious buying spree. And then, several years later, Borden cleans house again, throwing out many of the products recently acquired. So the recurring question is: What exactly is Borden? And the answer is: It depends on which year you're talking about.

Borden entered the 1980s as a chemical giant wrapped in a food package. They had a long line of food products, but they had also become one of the nation's 15 largest chemical producers, and they were making more money in chemicals than foods. At the end of the 1980s they had discarded most of their chemical business, and three-quarters of their sales were in foods (if you accept as foods such items as Wise's Cheez Doodles, Campfire marshmallows and Cracker Jack caramel-coated popcorn).

The 1980s ended for Borden just the way they began. Toward the end of 1989 Chairman Romeo J. Ventres announced he would sell 65 of Borden's 265 plants, eliminating 7,000 people from the payroll and bringing employment back to the 1980 level of 39,000.

The planned reduction would still leave Borden the world's largest dairy operator. However, they no longer make commodity cheeses that they used to distribute to grocers along with milk and ice cream. Now they make imitation cheeses like Fisher's Sandwich-Mate. Their brand-name pastas (Creamette, Prince, 17 regional brands) cornered 31 percent of the national market in 1989, and in 1990, for the first time, profits from pasta are expected to be greater than profits from dairy.

Borden still has a bunch of other products in their kitbag, including ReaLemon, Cremora nondairy creamer (no offense, Elsie), Elmer's glue and 16 different brands of wallcoverings, but you never know which one will be on tomorrow's hit list. You can only stay *au courant* by getting the latest version of a wallet-sized card listing all their products. They issue the card to employees and shareholders with this plaintive message from Romeo Ventres: "I encourage you to join with me in purchasing at least one more Borden product each week, which would add over $5 million to our annual sales."

History. Returning in 1851 from England, where he had received a gold medal from Queen Victoria for the invention of a dehydrated meat biscuit, Gail Borden was anguished by the cries of hungry babies aboard ship. Four died from drinking contaminated milk. That experience impelled Borden, an inveterate tinkerer, to experiment until he came up with a vacuum process to remove water from milk and make it safe for use over a long period of time. He called his product condensed milk, received a patent for it in 1856 and a year later started a company in New York City to make it (he was then 56).

A vocal advocate for condensed foods, Borden once declared, "I mean to put a potato into a pillbox, a pumpkin into a tablespoon, the biggest sort of watermelon into a saucer." He built his own tombstone

TOP PACKAGERS OF REGULAR COFFEES

	Market Share
Folgers (Procter & Gamble)	32.3%
Maxwell House (Kraft General Foods)	18.3%
Master Blend (Kraft General Foods)	8.2%
Hills Brothers (Nestlé)	3.4%
Yuban (Kraft General Foods)	2.4%
MJB (Nestlé)	2.4%

Source: *Advertising Age,* 17 April 1990

in the shape of a condensed milk can. Borden died in 1874. A year later his company, then called New York Condensed Milk, began selling fluid milk in New York City, delivering it by horse and wagon. In 1885 they became the first company to sell fresh milk in bottles.

By 1929 Borden was the largest food company in the nation, except for the big meatpackers, Swift and Armour. That year also marked Borden's entry into chemicals when they bought the Casein Company of America. The move was logical: Casein is a milk and cheese protein used to make adhesives.

Owners and rulers. Although Borden is a food company, they haven't had a food person running the company since 1967. Augstine R. Marusi (who became CEO in 1968) and Eugene Sullivan (CEO in 1979) were both chemical salesmen. Romeo Ventres (CEO in 1986) also came up from the chemical division. (And he's doing very well in his new position—he brought home $1.5 million in 1989.) Some 13,000 employees are shareholders. For eight months Borden was in the unique position, among major American companies, of having two blacks serve on their board of directors: Franklin H. Williams, president of the Phelps-Stokes Fund, and Wilbert J. LeMelle, president of Mercy College in Dobbs Ferry, New York.

Williams retired from the board in 1988 after 11 years of service.

As a place to work. Borden has never been known as an exciting place, and the way things are going now, you might want to ask about severance pay before signing up.

Social responsibility. Borden pioneered purchases from minority-owned companies, buying $68.9 million from them in 1988.

Global presence. They're selling Lady Borden ice cream in Japan, Adria pasta in Italy, Weber breads in Germany and Klim milk powder the world over. Borden does 22 percent of their sales outside the U.S.

Stock performance. Borden stock bought for $1,000 in 1980 sold for $13,348 on January 2, 1990.

Consumer brands.

Dairy: Borden, Hi-Calcium, Hi-Protein, Light, Lite-line, Thirstee Smash, Viva, Meadow Gold, Mountain High Yogurt.

Ice cream and frozen goods: Borden, Eagle Brand, Lady Borden, Frostick, Mississippi Mud, Juice Sticks, Glacier Bar, Turtles.

Snacks: Cracker Jack, Jays, Ranch Fries, Krunchers!, La Famous, New York Deli, Seyferts', Wise, Bravos, Cheez Doodles, Cottage Fries, Pick Ups, Ridgies, Spirals.

Pastas: Creamette, Prince, Anthony's, Bravo, Dutch Maid, Gioia, Globe A-1, Goodman's, Luxury, Merlino's, New Mill, Pennsylvania Dutch, R-F, Red Cross, Ronco, Silver Award, Vimco.

Sauces: Bennett's, Aunt Millie's, Prince.

Grocery: Klim whole milk powder, Lite-line cheeses, CheezTwo, Campfire marshmallows, Cary's maple syrup, Classico pasta sauce, Coco Lopez drink mix, Cremora creamer, Doxsee chowder, Eagle Brand condensed milk, Fisher cheese substitute, Frostee shakes, Harris crabmeat, Haviland candy, Hilton's oyster stew, Kava coffee, None Such mincemeat, Orleans and DeJean's seafood products, ReaLemon lemon juice, ReaLime lime juice, Serv, Americana, Chatsworth, Snow's chowders, Steero bouillon, Bama jams and jellies, Laura Scudder's peanut butter, Mrs. Gross soup mix, Soup Starter, Stew Starter, Chili Starter, Wyler's bouillon.

Regional foods: Borden Citrus punch (Florida), Hotel Bar butter (New York), Keller's butter (Philadelphia), Louis Sherry ice cream (New York).

Adhesives: Elmer's glue, Alphaset, Betaset, Casco, Cascophen, Cascoset, Loadmaster Resinite.

Packaging film: Proponite, Resinite, Sealwrap.

Home decoration: Krylon spray paint, Birge, Borden Home Wallcoverings, Crown, Fashion House, Foremost, Guard, James Seeman Studios, Mitchell Designs, Satinesque, ShandKydd, Sunwall 54, Sunwall 27, Sun-Tex, Sunworthy, Wall-Tex.

Borden, Inc., 277 Park Avenue, New York, NY 10172; (212) 573-4000.

5

Nestlé

#1 *in packaged foods, coffee, infant formula, chocolate (world)*

#1 *in low-calorie frozen food entrees (U.S.)*

#2 *in instant coffee (U.S.)*

#3 *in ground coffee, pet foods, chocolate (U.S.)*

Employees: 198,000 (47,000 in U.S.)
Sales: $7.06 billion (U.S.),
$33.7 billion (world)
Profits: $1.7 billion (world)
Founded: 1866
Headquarters: Vevey, Switzerland
Headquarters (U.S.): Solon, Ohio

Travel the world and you'll find Nestlé everywhere. They wrote the book on how to conduct a multinational operation. They do 98 percent of their business outside their home country, operating 392 factories on five continents. They're the world's biggest chocolate makers. They're number one in coffee. And they have become the world's largest food company, bigger even than the newly created Kraft General Foods arm of Philip Morris. Nestlé's a power in the U.S., too. After a string of acquisitions during the 1980s that netted them Chase & Sanborn coffees, Hills Bros. and MJB; Sark's coffee beans; Carnation; Pasta & Cheese; Chunky, Raisinets and Oh Henry! candies, Nestlé entered the 1990s as one of the top 10 food companies in the American market.

When Nestlé put up $3 billion in 1985 to bag Carnation (including Friskies dog food), they took over a company that had sold milk for years under the slogan "Milk from contented cows." The founding Stuart family was also contented with Carnation: *Forbes* estimated that the family was worth about $400 million in 1989.

Nestlé is not all food. In addition to running Stouffer Foods (and their Lean Cuisine business), Nestlé owns the Stouffer hotels (33 of them, including the newly acquired Stanford Court in San Francisco) and the Stouffer restaurants (72 of them, including the Rusty Scupper, J. B. Winberie and Parkers' Seafood Grill chains). They're also a player in the California wine industry, with sales of over $100 million a year under the labels Souverain, Beringer, Meridian, Deutz and Asti. They own Alcon Laboratories, a Fort Worth company that is one of the largest in the eye treatment market (both instruments to test, and drugs to treat, eyes). And finally, they are the controlling stockholder in the worldwide cosmetics business, L'Oreal, whose American arm, Cosmair, is among the top five in U.S. cosmetics.

In 1988 Nestlé became a big pasta maker by purchasing the Buitoni business from Italian entrepreneur Carlo de Benedetti. With it came a bonus: Perugina, the Italian maker of fancy chocolates. Later that year Nestlé came up with an even bigger chocolate quarry when it took over Britain's Rowntree. With it came a bonus in the U.S.: St. Louis-based Sunmark, a Rowntree subsidiary whose American firms include Sunline brands (Sweetarts, Tangy Taffy, Chewbonga), Willy Wonka brands (Nerds, Rinky Dinks, Zanies) and David & Sons (sunflower seeds, pumpkin seeds and pistachio nuts). However, not included in the deal—for the United States anyway—was Rowntree's Kit Kat bar, which Hershey makes and sells in the U.S. market under license from the English company.

History. Although Nestlé was founded in Switzerland, an American link was present from the start. After the Civil War Charles A. Page was posted to Zurich as the American consul. He hit upon the idea of making condensed milk in Switzerland (Gail Borden had been making it in America for 10 years). In 1866 Page and his brother George organized the Anglo-Swiss Condensed Milk Company (so named because they expected Britain to be their big market) at Cham, a

The average American eats 19.5 pounds of candy a year, about 3.5 pounds more than in 1980.

small town on Lake Zug in central Switzerland. That was one root of what was to become Nestlé.

The other root was forming at the same time, 120 miles away in the Swiss town of Vevey. Upset over the Swiss mortality rates (one out of five babies died in the first year of life), Henri Nestlé, a German-born merchant, artisan, and inventor, hit upon the idea of making a milk-product substitute for mother's milk. In 1867 he tried out his new product, which was milk mixed with a meal baked by a new process.

Eventually Anglo-Swiss and Nestlé became rivals, both firms making infant formula and condensed milk all over the world. Anglo-Swiss developed a famous brand name, Milkmaid; Nestlé products retained the Nestlé name even though in 1875 Henri sold his company to three well-to-do Swiss burghers. Nestlé didn't start making chocolate until 1904. In 1905 the two firms joined forces, becoming the Nestlé and Anglo-Swiss Condensed Milk Company. In 1938 Nescafe instant coffee became their first nonmilk-related product.

Social responsibility. Ever since the 1970s Nestlé has been embroiled in a controversy over the marketing in Third World countries of infant formula, of which they are the world's largest supplier. For seven years they were on a boycott list. They came off it in 1984 when they satisfied critics they were living up to, and policing their compliance with, the marketing code of the World Health Organization. In 1988 they were returned to the boycott roster, along with American infant-formula producer American Home Products, on the grounds that they continued to deluge hospitals with free samples, thereby discouraging new mothers from breast-feeding. Nestlé heatedly denied violation of any provision of the WHO code.

Another major scandal for Nestlé occurred in 1987 when it was discovered that Nestlé's baby-food subsidiary, Beech-Nut, was selling adulterated apple juice. In 1989 Nestlé sold Beech-Nut to Ralston Purina. One industry analyst told the *Wall Street Journal,* "I don't think the management of

Nestlé ever forgave Beech-Nut for selling fake apple juice and a lot of mothers never forgave Beech-Nut, either."

Consumer brands.

Chocolates/confections: Goobers, Bit-O-Honey, Chunky, Oh Henry!, Nestlé candy bars, Raisinets, Toll House, Le Confiseur (French truffles), Sunline, Perugina, Willy Wonka, Demet's, Alpine White.

Coffees/tea: Taster's Choice, MJB, Hills Bros., Chase & Sanborn, Nestea, Nescafe.

Grocery: Carnation (milk, ice cream, Instant Breakfast), Coffee-Mate, Libby's canned meats and pumpkin, Contadina sauces.

Milk products: Carnation.

Seasonings and soup: Maggi.

Drink mix: Quik.

Frozen foods: Stouffer, Lean Cuisine.

Wines: Meridian, Deutz, Souverain, Beringer, C&B Vintage Cellars, Napa Ridge.

Pet foods: Friskies, Mighty Dog, Fancy Feast, Grand Gourmet, Perform, Acclaim.

Cosmetics: L'Oreal, Lancôme, Cosmair.

Nestlé SA, Vevey, Switzerland; 41-021-924-211. Nestlé Enterprises, Inc., 5757 Harper Road, Solon, OH 44139; (216) 349-5757.

6

General Mills

#1 *in flour, cake mixes, frozen fish*
#2 *in yogurt, cereals*

Employees: 79,100
Sales: $6.3 billion
Profits: $315 million
Founded: 1928
Headquarters: Minneapolis, Minnesota

Social Conscience

It's back to the kitchen for General Mills. Coming into the 1980s they were selling

toys (Parker Bros., Kenner), costume jewelry (Monet), clothes (David Crystal, Izod, Lacoste), golf shoes (Foot-Joy), stamps and coins (H. E. Harris, Bowers and Ruddy) as well as operating stores (Eddie Bauer, Talbots, LeeWards, Wallpapers to Go). Out they went during the 1980s, all of them.

In the mid-1960s when they began to diversify, General Mills had 94 percent of their sales in consumer foods. By the late 1970s that share had fallen to 62 percent. Now that they have shucked off nearly 50 businesses, they are back to being a nearly 100 percent food company, if you count restaurants as a food business.

The restaurants now account for slightly more than one-quarter of General Mills' total sales, and the company expects them to be even more lucrative in the future. Olive Garden, a chain of Italian restaurants, had 145 restaurants in 1990, and General Mills plans to add another 250 within five years, making Olive Garden one of the fastest-growing chains in the nation. General Mills also operates the tremendously successful seafood chain Red Lobster (450 restuarants in 1990).

In the late 1980s, General Mills profited handsomely from the oat bran health craze. Led by their flagship brand, Cheerios, 40 percent of their cereals are made from oats. While Kellogg's share of the ready-to-eat cereal market stayed constant at about 40 percent, General Mills share rose from 21 percent in 1979 to 25 percent in 1989.

History. In 1928 James Ford Bell convinced six big U.S. milling companies to combine into the mammoth General Mills. From the start, the new company had two big winners: Wheaties (one of the most widely advertised products of the Depression) and Betty Crocker brand products. Their hectic diversification program began in 1964 when they bought Morton Foods (corn chips, potato chips, pork skins). A few year later, they bought Kenner Products (the Play-Doh manufacturers), Craft Master (maker of paint-by-number sets), Model Products (maker of model toys) and Parker Brothers (maker of Monopoly and other board games).

Owners and rulers. H. Brewster Atwater, Jr., became president in 1977 at age 49. Four years later he became CEO, and in

1982, chairman of the board. In 1989 Atwater took home $2.7 million. The square-jawed Atwater graduated from Princeton and received an MBA from Stanford before rising through the ranks of General Mills' marketing division. Two women are on the board of directors, Dr. Betsy Ancker-Johnson and Dr. Gwendolyn A. Newkirk.

As a place to work. Many in the business world consider General Mills' brand manager system a great training ground for a marketing career—though it's tough to get a job there in the first place. To fill these spots, General Mills interviews exclusively on college campuses. Before someone is hired, he or she typically goes to Minneapolis for two more days of interviewing. In 1988, women made up 27 percent of managers and professionals at General Mills. About 8 percent of the company's managers and professionals are minorities, and minorities comprise over 21 percent of U.S. employees. General Mills has a generous program for working parents, including job-sharing, paid maternity leave for up to eight weeks, unpaid leave for parents, childcare referral, and 80 percent coverage of adoption expenses up to $1,000.

General Mills has an art collection at the Golden Valley headquarters so large that a curator is employed to oversee it. The paintings range from traditional landscapes and portraits to abstract collages. Newcomers can pick a work of art for their own offices from a large trove in the basement of the building. Headquarters also has a barbershop and variety store. During the winter a pickup truck cruises the parking lot to jump-start cars whose batteries have died in the Minnesota cold.

Social responsibility. In 1988, the General Mills Foundation awarded over $6.9 million to nearly 600 nonprofit organizations, much of it donated because the company matches employee charity donations, two dollars for every one dollar a worker gives up to $100, and one for one thereafter. Among the social programs General Mills supports are Altcare, a nonprofit program for elderly people with chronic ailments; the Women's Economic Development Corporation, a program helping women go into business for themselves; programs to help battered wives; Planned Parenthood of Minnesota; AIDS education for teenagers; and a program to reduce infant mortality. Over $200,000 each year goes toward college scholarships for the children of employees.

General Mills has also won several awards for support of the disabled (establishing a Disability Awareness Council) and has depicted a disabled athlete on boxes of Wheaties.

In 1987, General Mills made an embarrassing mistake. Their Count Chocula cereal boxes featured Bela Lugosi in his famed role as Dracula. In the picture, Lugosi sported a six-pointed medallion that closely resembled the Star of David (the symbol of Judaism). When the boxes hit the supermarket, a number of consumers accused the company of anti-Semitism. The company altered the picture for future boxes.

Some of General Mill's earliest products are still familiar friends today.

General Mills publishes a slick corporate citizen report detailing its extensive support for philanthropic causes. And in 1981 General Mills started the "external involvement" program for employees. At the beginning of the year, each manager must state his or her plans to get involved in the community.

Stock performance. General Mills stock bought for $1,000 in 1980 sold for $9,723 on January 2, 1990.

Consumer brands.

Breakfast products: Cheerios, Wheaties, Honey Nut Cheerios, Lucky Charms, Total, Trix, Golden Grahams, Kix, Fiber One, Cocoa Puffs, Crispy Wheat 'N Raisins, Cinnamon Toast Crunch, Raisin Nut Bran, Oatmeal Raisin Crisp, Total, Oatmeal, Benefit.

Mixes and convenience foods: Betty Crocker, Bisquick, Hamburger Helper, Tuna Helper, Oriental Classics, Gorton's seafood.

Flour: Gold Medal.

Snacks and beverages: Pop Secret, Nature Valley granola, Fruit Wrinkles, Fruit Roll-Ups, Goldrush ice cream bars, Yoplait, Squeezit, the Berry Bears, Shark Bites, BacO's garnish.

Restaurants: Red Lobster, The Olive Garden.

General Mills, Inc., Number One General Mills Boulevard, P.O. Box 1113, Minneapolis, MN 55440; (612) 540-2311.

7

⊞ Ralston Purina

#1 *in pet foods, bread, batteries*

#2 *in baby food*

#3 *in cereals*

Employees: 56,500
Sales: $6.9 billion
Profits: $350 million
Founded: 1894
Headquarters: St. Louis, Missouri

In 1985 William Leach, a security analyst at the Wall Street firm of Donaldson Lufkin Jenrette, noted to the *New York Times* that Ralston Purina's animal feed business was doing poorly and that the company might therefore sell it, except

THE BREADWINNERS

Sales of Bread, Rolls and Buns

1.	Continental Baking (Ralston Purina)	$1.1 billion
2.	Campbell-Taggart (Anheuser-Busch)	$555 million
3.	Flowers Industries	$442 million
4.	Interstate Bakeries	$376 million
5.	Metz Baking	$344 million

Source: The *New York Times,* 15 October 1989. Sales are for 1988.

that "they would hesitate because there must be some sentimentality attached to it." Leach clearly didn't have a handle on William P. Stiritz, Ralston's CEO. Within a year he had sold it to British Petroleum. So he unhesitatingly axed Ralston Purina's parent business, launched when Sunday school teacher William H. Danforth started filling 175-pound sacks of grains on the St. Louis riverfront in 1894. Stiritz epitomizes the cold-eyed manager who looks at any business from the standpoint of how much it's contributing to the bottom line. Not only has he gotten rid of the foundation business, he has downplayed the rural, folksy, checkerboard symbol once so much a part of this company.

Stiritz, who took over as chief executive in 1981, spent the 1980s recasting the company that makes more dry dog and cat food than anybody else. After taking over, he sold off a passel of businesses his predecessors had bought—tuna fishing, mushroom farming, pet foods in Europe, shrimp farming, a Colorado resort (Keystone), a hockey team (the St. Louis Blues), soybean crushing. Out they all went after he announced in 1982 that the company would now concentrate on their "core" businesses, animal feeds and grocery products. In their places he brought in Eveready batteries and Continental Baking, the nation's leading bread baker (Wonder Bread) and supplier of Twinkies and Hostess cakes. So today's Ralston Purina is a creature of the 1980s, the Stiritz era. Stiritz took home $4.9 million in 1989.

History. The new era has little in common with the early days when founder Danforth led his employees in daily prayer and calisthenics. The "Purina" in the company's name was coined from an early Danforth slogan, "Where Purity Is Paramount." "Ralston" came from a Dr. Ralston, who headed a prominent health club at the turn of the century, and whom Danforth persuaded to endorse a wheat cereal. The company's checkerboard symbol was rooted in Danforth's personal experience. He grew up near a family, the Browns, whose children always wore clothes their mother had made from distinctive red-and-white checkerboard cloth. Danforth reasoned the checkerboard motif would identify his products as clearly as it had the Brown kids. Eventually it went on everything, even becoming the company's address. And Danforth himself sometimes wore a red checkerboard jacket and matching socks to the office. His book of pep-talk maxims, *I Dare You,* is still given to employees after their first year at the company. His son Donald succeeded him in 1932.

In September of 1989 Ralston bought Beech-Nut, the floundering baby food company rocked by an apple juice scandal in 1987 (it was convicted of selling adulterated apple juice). This purchase continued Ralston's expansion into the kid food market, begun with their introduction of Cookie Crisp cereal in 1977.

Stock performance. Ralston stock bought for $1,000 in 1980 sold for $10,525 on January 2, 1990.

Consumer brands.

Pet foods: Dog Chow, Cat Chow, Puppy Chow, Purina, Meow Mix, Mainstay, Bonz, Tender Vittles, Alley Cat, Happy Cat, Lucky Dog, Pro Plan.

Cereals: Chex, Dinersaurs, Ghostbusters, Cookie Crisp, Muesli.

Breads: Wonder, Home Pride.

Crackers, cakes, snacks: Ry Krisp, Hostess, Twinkies.

Baby food: Beech-Nut.

Batteries: Eveready, Energizer, Conductor.

Ralston Purina Company, Checkerboard Square, St. Louis, MO 63164; (314) 982-1000.

8

#1 *in ketchup, frozen potatoes, canned tuna, canned cat food, rice cakes, weight-reduction classes*
#2 *in vinegar, pickles*
#3 *in baby foods*

Employees: 37,600
Sales: $6 billion
Profits: $486 million
Founded: 1869
Headquarters: Pittsburgh, Pennsylvania

Most people link Heinz with ketchup in the same breath, and with good reason. Ketchup is the most widely used condiment on American tables, and Heinz has been packing it for more than 100 years. Moreover, their market position is awesome. The ketchup bottle with a Heinz label is a fixture on restaurant tables across the land, and Heinz has a 55 percent share of the business.

Of course today Heinz is more than ketchup. Like many companies, they have expanded by eating others. Heinz now makes rice pilaf mixes in Leominster, Massachusetts (Near East); corn syrups in Koekuk, Iowa (Hubinger); rice cakes in Gridley, California, and Metcalfe, Mississippi (Chico-San); and toffees in Cremona, Italy (Spelari).

Through StarKist, acquired in 1961, Heinz is the world's largest tuna packer, and it is a major producer of cat food (9-Lives). Through Ore-Ida, acquired in 1965, Heinz is the leading seller of supermarket frozen potatoes. Through Weight Watchers, acquired in 1978, Heinz sells low-calorie food items and operates weight-reduction classes in which more than 2.5 million people were enrolled in 1987. No doubt, these people were trying to take off some of the weight gained by eating Heinz foods.

History. The man after whom this company is named, and whose great-grandson is now the senior U.S. Senator from Pennsylvania, was depicted as follows by biographer Robert C. Alberts in *The Good Provider*:

> *H. J. Heinz was a small man with prodigious energy and drive. His blue eyes sparkled, his reddish muttonchop whiskers bristled, and he seemed always to move along at a half trot.... He had overpowering enthusiasms for work and success, for travel, for his family, for religious pursuits and kind deeds, for good horses and bad paintings. He liked others to enjoy what he enjoyed; so far as it is known, he is the only American industrial magnate who ever returned from Florida (in 1889) with an 800-pound alligator and installed it in a glass tank atop one of his factory buildings so that his employees might share his pleasure in the sight.*

The first of nine children born of German immigrants, Henry J. Heinz grew up near Pittsburgh in a strict Lutheran household where children who missed church were required to sit down and listen to their mother retell the minister's sermon. At age 8 he was selling produce from the family garden to other households. By 10 he had a wheelbarrow; by 12, a horse and cart.

In 1869, when he was 25, Henry formed a partnership with a friend to sell bottled food. Their first product was horseradish; then came sauerkraut, pickles and vinegar. The business went under in the panic of 1875, and Henry Heinz started over again the following year, carrying in his pocket a notebook marked "M.O.," which stood for Moral Obligations. It contained a list of all the people to whom he owed money from the bankruptcy of the previous business. He paid all these debts as his second venture succeeded, and he became known throughout the land as the "pickle king." The Heinz company bottled and sold pickles, relishes, sauces and condiments to spice up what was then a monotonous American diet. They made tomato soup and then beans in tomato sauce. In 1893, when the World's Columbian Exposition was staged in Chicago, Heinz had the largest exhibit of any American food company.

Heinz entered the 20th century as one of the nation's premier businesses, ranking as the number one producer of pickles, vinegar and ketchup; as the largest grower and processor of mustard; and as the

A *single Big Mac attack hits you with 32.4 grams of fat and 950 milligrams of sodium in a total package of 560 calories.*

fourth largest packer of olives. In all, the company made more than 200 products, giving the lie to the "57 Varieties" slogan Heinz had coined in 1892. Actually, it wasn't accurate even then—Heinz had more than 60 products in 1892—but he liked the poetic cadence of that number, and he put it on all his labels and in all his advertising. (It survives today in the company's post office box number and telephone number.) In 1900, the number went up in lights in New York City's first electric sign, at Fifth Avenue and 23rd Street. The sign was six stories high, used 1,200 bulbs and cost $90 to illuminate each night. It also had a green pickle 40 feet long. Henry Heinz was considered an advertising and merchandising genius, but he gave orders never to run Heinz advertising in Sunday newspapers so as not to violate the Sabbath.

Heinz received many awards for his model factories, including a turn-of-the-century accolade from a union leader. Harry W. Sherman, Grand Secretary of the National Brotherhood of Electrical Workers of America, attended a convention in Pittsburgh in 1899 and after visiting the Heinz plant, pronounced it "a utopia for working men."

In 1906, following publication of Upton Sinclair's novel, *The Jungle*, which exposed the grimy conditions prevailing in the Chicago stockyards, the U.S. was the scene of a hotly debated move to establish a Pure Food Act to regulate conditions in food plants. Most U.S. food processors bitterly opposed the legislation, but not Henry Heinz. He supported it, even sending his son to Washington to campaign for it.

Through 117 years of feeding Americans, the Heinz Company had a Heinz family member at or near the helm. That era ended on February 23, 1987, when Jack Heinz died at age 78. He had chaired every annual shareholders meeting for 40 years.

Owners and rulers. Anthony J. F. O'Reilly became CEO in 1979, when he was 43. He made $2.8 million in 1989. Born in Dublin, O'Reilly stands six feet, two inches tall and was a renowned rugby player in Ireland. He controls six newspapers in Ireland (60% of the national circulation), magazines in Britain, outdoor advertising companies in France, Austria and Germany, and an assortment of other Irish–based enterprises (including two castles). Only 60 people work in the Heinz world headquarters located on the 48th and 49th floors of the U.S. Steel building in downtown Pittsburgh. Heinz believes strongly in decentralization, letting managers on the firing line make their own decisions without interference from a bureaucratic headquarters. The president of Heinz U.S.A., the company's biggest unit, is David Sculley, younger brother of John Sculley, the leader of Apple Computer.

Although no more Heinzes work at H. J. Heinz, family interests still own as much as 15 percent of the company's stock, and top executives own up to another 10 percent.

As a place to work. Heinz used to be known for providing good working conditions. Even though unions have represented employees in the U.S. and Britain, Heinz has had a long record of labor peace. That family feeling began changing in the late 1980s under CEO O'Reilly, who closed factories and laid off workers. These cuts created "a mounting feeling of bile" at the company, O'Reilly admitted to *Fortune.* "There was an ever-increasing feeling of hostility among the employees. Fewer people do more work." O'Reilly tried to combat that feeling in 1988 by introducing a Total Quality Management program with teams of employees evaluating every aspect of the business, from management memos to carrots on the assembly line.

U.S. supermarkets sell about $5.9 billion worth of pet food a year. About 1,200 companies produce 3,200 different pet foods for 107 million dogs and cats.

Social responsibility. Heinz has been a bulwark of support for worthy causes in the communities where it operates, a tradition rooted in the company's history. Pittsburgh is dotted with Heinz gifts, whether at the University of Pittsburgh or Carnegie-Mellon University or any number of cultural institutions. In 1986, Heinz, alone among U.S. food processors, notified contract farmers that they would not buy crops treated with any of a dozen chemicals, including aldicarb, captan, linuron and cyanazine.

In the late 1980s, environmental groups boycotted Heinz's StarKist tuna because dolphins were being slaughtered as a side effect of commercial fishing techniques. In April 1990 when a group threatened to boycott all Heinz products, Heinz announced they would no longer buy tuna caught at the expense of dolphins. StarKist cans will now cary "Dolphin Safe" labels. That same month Heinz also responded to environmental concern about their packaging by announcing a change in the formula of squeezable plastic ketchup bottles to make recycling easier.

Global presence. Major. Heinz started doing business in Britain in 1905 and now does 40 percent of their business outside America. Heinz is one of the largest food companies in Britain as well as in Australia, where they have been manufacturing for more than 50 years (one of their current Australian entries being Heinz Spooky Spaghetti Shapes in Tomato Sauce). Early in the 1980s Heinz's non-American chief, Tony O'Reilly, noted pointedly that Heinz was currently selling to only 15 percent of the world's population. When O'Reilly talks, things happen at Heinz. By 1987, the company had new joint ventures going in Zimbabwe, China, South Korea and Thailand. The Zimbabwean and Chinese ventures were with their respective governments. The Chinese company began turning out baby food in 1986. O'Reilly pointed out to shareholders the significance of the Chinese plant: "Sixteen million infants will be born in China this year, as compared with three million in the United States." Eat your heart out, Gerber.

Stock performance. Heinz stock bought for $1,000 in 1980 sold for $14,779 on January 2, 1990.

Consumer brands.

Heinz, StarKist, Breast O' Chicken, Weight Watchers, Ore-Ida, Chico-San, 9-Lives, Amore, Kozy Kitten, Jerky Treats, Meaty Bone, Alba, Near East, Steak-umm, Skippy Premium, Vets, Sturdy, Petuna, Glamour Puss, Cardio-Fitness Centers.

H. J. Heinz Company, 600 Grant Street, P.O. Box 57, Pittsburgh, PA 15230; (412) 456-5700.

9

Campbell's

#1 *in soups, pickles, olives*

#2 *in canned pasta, spaghetti sauce*

Employees: 52,000
Sales: $6 billion
Profits: $37 million
Founded: 1869
Headquarters: Camden, New Jersey

The people working for Campbell Soup really believe soup is good for you. Campbell has cornered a whopping 80 percent of the soup market. So they thought they had a winner in the 1980s with their "Soup Is Good Food" campaign. To their chagrin, watchdogs like the Federal Trade Commission and the attorney generals of nine states chomped down on them, asserting Campbell was wrong to tell consumers that salt-laden soups are good for them. So Campbell paid $35,000 to each of the states as a penalty for false advertising and scrapped their campaign, reverting to that emotional oldie, "M'm! M'm! Good!"

Campbell frequently gets surprised this way. They're like an innocent in a slick world not of their making. They try to be modern. They do more than make soup these days. They pack pickles (Vlasic), make all kinds of frozen foods (Swanson, Le Menu) and bake expensive cookies (Pepperidge Farm). And they have moved overseas, acquiring an assortment of companies (Freshbake in England, Lazzaroni in Italy, Delacre in Belgium). But outsiders, particularly the gunslingers on Wall Street, still regard Campbell as a fuddy-duddy relic from the past.

History. Joseph Campbell, a fruit merchant, and Abram Anderson, an icebox manufacturer, started the firm to can and preserve fruits and vegetables. But it didn't take off until Dr. John Thompson Dorrance, Campbell's nephew and a brilliant chemist, joined the company in 1897. He invented condensed soup, which is simply soup minus the water. At that time three companies canned soup in America, but they couldn't achieve wide distribution because they shipped bulky, water-logged cans. Campbell's condensed product swept the nation. By 1911 they had become one of the first American companies to sell a brand-name food product from coast to coast.

In 1915, Campbell acquired Franco-American, another soupmaker. The next major purchase was made in 1955, when Omaha's C. A. Swanson, a frozen-dinner packer, came aboard. Campbell entered the baked goods business in 1961 with the acquisition of Pepperidge Farm, based in Norwalk, Connecticut. The 1970s were a decade of rapid expansion, when Campbell entered the dog food and restaurant businesses (since sold) as well as the garden, chocolate and pickle businesses, mostly by buying other companies. In 1978 Campbell acquired Vlasic Foods, the Michigan packer of pickles, relishes, peppers and sauerkraut.

The heady mood of the 1970s gave way to rocky times in the late 1980s. In 1989 they fired 2,800 people and closed four plants in the U.S., including the original plant in Camden.

Owners and rulers. Campbell's management was rocked by a nasty feud within the Dorrance family, which controls 59 percent of the stock. John ("Jack") Dorrance, Jr., headed Campbell for many years, but when he died in 1989, the Dorrance clan split into two factions. Most of Jack Dorrance's nieces (called "the dissidents" by insiders), wanted to sell the company, but another faction (Jack's children, who hold more shares) does not. In early 1990 the dissidents helped to oust CEO R. Gordon McGovern. Australian David W. Johnson, an import from Gerber, succeeded him and immediately began slashing. He laid off 14 percent of the corporate staff and put up for sale a bunch of businesses, including mushroom farms, refrigerated salads and Marie's salad dressing. Leaving no doubt where he stood, Johnson said: "The scorecard we're going to be judged on is the quarterly report." Curiously, pickle heir Robert J. Vlasic is chairman of the board of directors while John Dorrance III is chairman of the Vlasic pickle subsidiary.

As a place to work. Campbell's headquarters in Camden has an on-site child care center where 110 employee children are enrolled. The company covers 40 percent of the center's cost. They also offer adoption aid, flextime and job sharing. However, working conditions aren't so cushy in some other parts of the Campbell empire. In 1988, the Labor Department proposed a $1.4 million fine against Campbell's Pepperidge Farm plant in Downingtown, Pennsylvania. The department charged management ignored complaints when 50 plant workers were diagnosed with carpal tunnel syndrome, a wrist inflammation, resulting from the repetitive motion workers performed in packaging cookies.

Stock performance. Campbell stock bought for $1,000 in 1980 sold for $11,603 on January 2, 1990.

Consumer brands.

Campbell's, Pepperidge Farm, Swanson, Le Menu, V8, Franco-American, Prego, Mrs. Paul's, Vlasic, Milwaukee's, Open Pit, Early California, Plum & Juicy, Home Cookin', Mrs. Giles, Mrs. Kenser's, Swiss Maid, Godiva, Barringer's, Lasera, Betis, Great Starts, Bounty, Win Schuler, Domsea, Delacre, Exeter, Target, Unger, Freshbake, Groko, Nobo, Beeck, Lacroix, Gattuso, Lazzaroni, Borsari, Granny's, Devos-Lemmens, Imperial, Kwatta, Lutti, Leo, Lamy, Tubble Gum, Laforest-Perigord.

Campbell Soup Company, Campbell Place, Camden, NJ 08103; (609) 342-4800.

10

#1 *in hot cereals, pork and beans, sports beverages*

#2 *in dog food*

Employees: 31,300
Sales: $5.7 billion
Profits: $203 million
Founded: 1891
Headquarters: Chicago, Illinois

They don't bake cookies for the Girl Scouts anymore, but despite such a fall from grace, Quaker Oats managed to navigate their way through the turbulent 1980s without going through the upheavals that beset other food companies. They didn't change their name. They didn't get bought by a cigarette company. They didn't sell out to another food company. And at the end of the decade, they were in a much stronger position in the food industry than they were at the start. Virtue rewarded, or just plain dumb luck?

Quaker got rid of some businesses—chemicals, Magic Pan restaurants, Jos. A Bank Clothiers, Brookstone—and bought their way into some new businesses by acquiring Stokely Van Camp, Golden Grain, and the Gaines dog food business (although the Gaines line has floundered in recent years). The major addition, a result of the Stokely acquisition, was Gatorade, now a $300 million-plus product and the biggest brand Quaker has. They're still number one in hot cereals, the beneficiary of all the reports about oat bran being good for the heart.

History. One day in 1877, an oatmeal miller named Henry D. Seymour read an article about Quakers in an encyclopedia, and Seymour decided the religious group represented a wholesome goodness. So he named his Ravenna, Ohio, mill the "Quaker Mill," and he registered a new trademark for his products—a Quaker, dressed in sober black garb and hat. In 1891, the company combined with six competitors to become a dominant player in oat milling.

An early company leader was Canadian-born Robert Stuart, who had followed in the footsteps of his father, John Stuart, a Scottish oatmeal miller. The Scottish connection with oatmeal is strong. At one point, oats grew on one-third of all Scottish cropland. But the English and Americans were prejudiced against the stuff. A cartoon in a 1910 issue of *Cosmopolitan* showed a Yankee farmer who, after eating oatmeal, pranced around his barnyard and drank from the horses' trough.

Quaker changed popular opinion by selling rolled oats in packages instead of in bulk (making oatmeal one of the first packaged foods) and by advertising heavily. One early ad line went "Quaker Oats give you strength—strength of mind, strength of body. Then you are healthy and happy. Then you are honestly thankful." In 1925 Quaker bought the Aunt Jemima Mills of St. Joseph, Missouri. The Aunt Jemima brand name was lifted from the 1893 Chicago exposition, where a black woman using that name demonstrated a pancake flour.

In 1969 Quaker picked up Fisher-Price Toys, headquartered in East Aurora, a suburb of Buffalo, New York. An estimated 84 percent of homes with young children have at least one Fisher-Price toy. The company cranks out about 200 different toys and sells some 70 million of them a year. Several times a day, an employee circulates through the Fisher-Price plant with a tray of Quaker-made Gatorade.

In mid-1990 Quaker announced their intention to make Fisher-Price a separate company owned by Quaker shareholders, who would receive stock in the new firm. The announcement came after Fisher-Price had a bad Christmas season in 1989, losing an estimated $20 to $30 million.

Owners and rulers. Members of the Stuart family headed Quaker until 1981 when William D. Smithburg became chief executive at age 42. He had been with Quaker since 1966; before that he worked with a missile manufacturer. Smithburg took home $2.8 million in 1989.

As a place to work. Quaker's hiring practices are among the most progressive in the nation; they expressly forbid discriminating against candidates because of sexual orientation. Quaker employees who have AIDS receive the same benefits as those with other disabilities. Since 1947, a Quaker charity foundation has matched gifts from employees to schools, hospitals, youth programs and the arts. About one-third of the money goes to local United Way charities and over 25 percent for education. Quaker also supports United Student Aid Funds, guaranteeing loans to employees' children attending schools.

Social responsibility. Quaker has a deserved reputation for the quality of its products. The *Wall Street Journal* reported in 1989 that U.S. cornfields were being inundated with aflatoxin, one of the most virulent carcinogens known to science, and that it was clearly entering the food chain. Food industry responses were varied. General Mills, for example, did only random testing and didn't ask farm-

Aunt Jemima then and now.

This cartoon appears in a "Popeye the Quaker Man" comic book as part of the latest and most controversial of Quaker Oats' ads.

ers to test their own supplies until after the 1989 harvest had begun. At Quaker's mill in Cedar Rapids, Iowa (the largest cereal mill in the world), a team of lab technicians snapped into action with an expensive, complex barrage of tests to determine contamination levels. Trucks of corn were first probed with a robotic device; then samples went into the lab; and each time the corn moved within the mill, it was tested again (up to six times). Boxes of cereal were also tested at random. Quaker uses contamination standards 25 percent stricter than the FDA's.

Quaker found themselves in the middle of a controversy with the real Quakers— the Religious Society of Friends—because of an ad campaign featuring "Popeye the Quaker Man," introduced in fall 1989. In the ads Popeye saves the day by punching out his opponents. After some Quakers, including 26 Quaker children from North Carolina, complained to the company, they pulled a Saturday morning TV spot in which Popeye beats up a shark to save

Wimpy. But the company said it would use up the Popeye the Quaker Man comics already printed on thousands of oatmeal boxes. Even though Quakers are known for their adherence to nonviolence and pacifism, a spokesman for Quaker's ad agency defended the ads, telling *Business Week*, "If it is against anyone's principles to save Wimpy by bopping a man-eating shark, well, that is a major stretch."

A Quaker religious leader in Philadelphia, Elizabeth J. Foley, responded: "Would anyone advertise 'Popeye the Catholic Man' or 'Popeye the Jewish Man'?" The flap with the Society of Friends was not the first for the food company. The religious group had lobbied Congress to prevent the food company from using the Quaker name but lost the battle in 1915.

Global presence. Quaker's petfood business is the biggest in Europe. They also claim to be the number one producer of chocolate in Mexico.

Stock performance. Quaker stock bought for $1,000 in 1980 sold for $11,305 on January 2, 1990.

Consumer brands.

Cereal: Quaker, Cap'n Crunch, Oh's!, Puffed Rice, Puffed Wheat, Life, 100% Natural.

Grocery: Gatorade, Kretschmer wheat germ, Van Camp canned pork and beans, Golden Grain pasta, Noodle-Roni, Rice-A-Roni, Celeste frozen pizza, Aunt Jemima.

Pet foods: Gravy Train, Gaines Burgers, Cycle, Kibbles 'n Bits, Top Choice, Ken-L Ration.

The Quaker Oats Company, Quaker Tower, P.O. Box 9001, Chicago, IL 60604-9001; (312) 222-7111.

11

International Inc.

#1 in mayonnaise, English muffins, corn oil

#2 in peanut butter

#3 in pasta

Employees: 32,800
Sales: $5.1 billion
Profits: $328 million
Founded: 1906
Headquarters: Englewood Cliffs,
New Jersey

If they're not the dullest company around, they're close to it, beginning with their name, adopted in 1969 to replace Corn Products Company, which in turn was adopted in 1958 to replace the original monicker, Corn Product Refining Company. Their original business was corn wet-milling, the extraction from the corn kernel of starches, which have hundreds of industrial uses and can be further refined into syrups, sugars and oils. Argo corn starch and Karo syrup were two of their earliest products.

Corn Products accounted for virtually all the refined corn in the country until 1916 when their monopoly was busted. But the company, controlled by a series of crafty New York financiers, continued to be the dominant force in the industry.

Their expertise in corn refining sent them overseas after World War I. They opened corn refining mills all over Europe and Latin America and, as a result, became the most international of all U.S. food companies. They still do nearly 60 percent of their business outside the U.S. Not until after World War II did they enter the consumer foods business in a major way. The company bought the big German soupmaker, Knorr, as their answer to Campbell in the U.S. In 1958 they bought Best Foods (Hellmann's mayonnaise and Skippy peanut butter) and went on to purchase S. B. Thomas, the English Muffin producer, and Mueller, the pasta maker. The Best Foods merger meant CPC inherited an oddity—twin brands of mayonnaise. West of the Rockies, the mayonnaise was sold under the Best Foods name; east of the Rockies, the mayonnaise was sold as Hellmann's, a brand which started in New York state in 1912. CPC, afraid to tamper with consumer brand loyalty, continues to sell the mayonnaise under different names, although the packaging, ad jingles and mayonnaise itself are identical.

Such an approach clarifies Corn Products' strategy: away from corn milling and toward cachet specialty foods on a global scale—47 countries on 5 continents by the mid-1980s.

Despite the marketing of these consumer products, CPC has long been known as a company as bland as the mayonnaise they sell. They had some excitement in 1986 when corporate raider Ronald Perelman grabbed over 5 percent of CPC's shares. CEO James R. Eiszner (a Ph.D. in chemistry) responded with what has been called "greenmail." To keep control of the company, Eiszner bought back Perelman's shares for $357 million, giving Perelman a $94 million profit. CEO J. R. Eiszner made $2.3 million in 1989.

To pay off the huge greenmail debt, the company restructured, selling a number

The most heavily advertised brand name in America is McDonald's, with advertising costs of around $1 billion a year.

of their subsidiaries. Tradition went out the door as they sold their European corn wet-milling business to Italy's Ferruzzi Group for over $600 million in 1987. Eiszner also sold off Bosco chocolate syrups, Mrs. Fanning's pickles, CPC's South African subsidiary and their specialty chemicals operation. "In today's economic world," Eiszner told *Forbes* in 1987, "anything can be sold, including Hellmann's."

Stock performance. CPC stock bought for $1,000 in 1980 sold for $7,621 on January 2, 1990.

Consumer brands.

Hellmann's, Best Foods, Mazola, Skippy, Arnold (bread), Thomas' English muffins, Mueller's, Karo, Argo, Knorr, Maizena, Golden Griddle, Old London, Rit (dyes).

CPC International Inc., International Plaza, P.O. Box 8000, Englewood Cliffs, NJ 07632; (201) 894-4000.

12

Beatrice

#1 *in popcorn, Oriental foods*
#2 *in ketchup and tomato sauce*
#3 *in cooking oil, peanut butter*

Employees: 15,900
Sales: $4.3 billion (1989)
Founded: 1894

Now you see it, now you don't. Beatrice no longer exists as a company, having been dismembered, piece by piece, the parts sold to a dozen other companies. The final cut came in mid-1990 when the last remaining pieces of what was once the largest food company in the nation were about to be sold off to Conagra (see ConAgra profile on page 4)

Beatrice Foods climbed to the top of the American food tree after World War II by acquiring more than 400 companies. They entered the 1980s with sales of $7.5 billion and 88,000 employees.

By mid-decade they had ballooned even further, by acquiring their Chicago neighbor, Esmark (the old Swift meatpacking company—minus the fresh meats), which had just absorbed Norton Simon. Sales were now pushing $13 billion, employees were over the 100,000 mark, and Beatrice was in 26th place on the *Fortune 500* (up from 36th in 1980).

Until the 1984 Olympics Beatrice had never drawn attention to their corporate name, preferring to let the individual companies toot their own horns. In that year, however, they began whispering in television commercials ("You've known us all along") about the Beatrice family of brand names: Tropicana juices, Meadow Gold dairy products, La Choy Chinese foods, Swiss Miss chocolate mixes, Rosarita and Gebhardt Mexican foods, Eckrich meats, Shedd's peanut butter, Dannon yogurt, Louis Sherry ice cream, Milk Duds, Fisher nuts, Swift sausages.

But by the end of the 1980s Beatrice was once again invisible. Why? Because in 1986 the Wall Street firm Kohlberg Kravis Roberts bought Beatrice in a deal known as a leveraged buyout, and the public could no longer buy their stock through the New York Stock Exchange. Prior to doing this deal, KKR people promised Beatrice directors that they would not dismember the company. But that's precisely what they did do. To buy all the stock, KKR borrowed $8 billion. The only way to pay off the debt was to sell off parts of Beatrice. So, Beatrice-owned companies were peddled all over the place; international food operations went in one clump to investment banker Reginald Lewis' TLC Group, thereby creating the nation's largest black-owned company; Tropicana went to Seagram; company managers took over Playtex; Avis went to Wesray and was then resold to Wesray employees; Meadow Gold went to Borden.

The objective of all this shuffling was to have been a glistening profit for the people who had engineered the deal. KKR and Beatrice's chairman Donald Kelly, after investing $420 million of their own money, were looking to make a quick $3.7 *billion* for themselves. Their goal was tantamount to someone coming in and buying your $100,000 house with a down payment of $5,000, reselling it as quickly as possible for $150,000 and keeping the change.

The KKR-Kelly deal didn't work out as planned because they couldn't get the prices they wanted for the Beatrice components. When the last remnants—Hunt-Wesson, Swift-Eckrich meats, Beatrice cheeses—were sold to ConAgra in 1990, the total proceeds from all the sales came to about $9 billion, only 10 percent greater than the 1986 purchase price.

Global presence. Beatrice International, which accounted for most of their non-U.S. food operations, was sold in 1988 for $985 million.

Consumer brands.

Snack food: Orville Reddenbacher's popcorn, Snack Pack pudding.

Grocery: Hunt's tomato products, Peter Pan peanut butter, Manwich sloppy joe sauce, Wesson oil, Swiss Miss cocoa mix, La Choy oriental foods, Rosarita refried beans, Gebhardt chili.

Cheese: County Line, Treasure Cave, Pauly.

Bread: Sunbeam, Country Hearth.

Meats: Butterball, Plume de Veau, Sizzlean, Eckrich, Swift Premium Brown 'n Serve.

Audio speakers: Advent.

Beatrice Company, Two North LaSalle Street, Chicago, IL 60602; (312) 782-3820.

TOP POPCORNS

	Market Share
Orville Redenbacher (Beatrice)	36.0%
Pop Secret (General Mills)	21.7%
Planters (Nabisco Brands)	7.2%
Jolly Time	7.0%
Pillsbury	4.5%
Jiffy Pop	3.3%
Newman's Own	2.1%
Pops-Rite	1.5%

Source: Advertising Age, 24 July 1989.

13

#1 *in cereals, frozen waffles, toaster pastries, frozen pies*

Employees: 17,400
Sales: $4.7 billion
Profits: $422 million
Founded: 1906
Headquarters: Battle Creek, Michigan

Some things never change. Kellogg has been king of cereals for the entire 20th century, selling about 40 percent of all cereals in the U.S. Kellogg's Corn Flakes was invented in a Michigan sanitarium as a health food, and in the 1980s dry cereals were once again being peddled as "drugs" to fight cancer, heart disease, constipation and whatever else ails you. Dry cereal is one of the most boring foods ever concocted, hence the never-ending stream of new varieties designed to mask the dullness. During the 1980s Kellogg introduced Nutri-Grain, Crispix, Raisin Squares, Mueslix, Nut & Honey, Just Right, Nutrific, Cracklin' Oat Bran and Common Sense Oat Bran. By the end of the decade Kellogg was shipping 30 different kinds of ready-to-eat cereal. But what was their largest seller, measured by pounds sold? The original product: Kellogg's Corn Flakes. Lots of folks seem to prefer dull.

History. During the 1980s, food companies were favorite takeover targets, but Kellogg is considered invulnerable because a huge block of stock, 34 percent of the total, remains in the hands of the W. K. Kellogg Foundation, one of the nation's largest foundations. Still based in Battle Creek, the foundation was set up during the Great Depression by founder William K. Kellogg, whose signature still appears on Kellogg cereal packages.

Kellogg worked for years as the business manager of the world-famous Battle Creek Sanitarium, where his brother was chief surgeon and had the patients observe a strict vegetarian diet. To make the meatless fare more palatable, the brothers began experimenting with various foods in the sanitarium kitchens. During one such experiment in 1894, they placed some boiled wheat on a baking tin. Kellogg's brother was called away to perform an emergency operation. When the brothers returned to the kitchen the next day, they ran the wheat through a roller, expecting it to come out in sheets. What emerged instead were individual flakes, the forerunner of ready-to-eat cereals. This accidental discovery was welcomed by the patients, who loved the new wheat food. (The corn flakes were not popular at first because the kernels were tough, so W. K. Kellogg developed a tastier flake using only the grits, or heart, of the corn and adding malt.)

A master marketer, Kellogg had the company erect what was in 1911 the world's largest electric sign, at Times Square in New York. The "K" in Kellogg stood 66 feet tall. Kellogg died in 1951 at age 91. He had no heirs. At the start of the 1980s the foundation owned 54 percent of Kellogg's shares but had to sell off 20 percent to satisfy new IRS regulations. To make sure they didn't fall into unfriendly hands, the Kellogg Company bought the shares in 1984.

In 1989, Kellogg's chairman and CEO William E. LaMothe fired president Horst W. Schroeder. Schroeder, a West German, had been president for only nine months, and his abrupt, autocratic personality and ostentatious life-style (he drove a new Mercedes-Benz) ruffled feathers at Kellogg, where executives usually favor teamwork and a low public profile. In addition, Schroeder ascended at a time when Kellogg's share of the cereal market dropped from 42 percent in 1987 to 39.8 percent in 1989.

Kellogg has always had a phenomenal ability to wring profits out of sales. No other food company can match them on this count. Borden, Campbell Soup, ConAgra, General Mills, H. J. Heinz, Quaker Oats, Ralston Purina and Sara Lee all have higher sales, but Kellogg outearns them all. One reason is a heavy investment in highly efficient, automated factories. In 1989 Kellogg was building a new cereal plant in Memphis at a cost of $1.2 billion. The prototype for this factory is Building 100, which started up in Battle Creek in 1988. Kellogg used to troop visitors through their cereal plants but stopped these tours in 1986 after finding two competitors from Europe taking the Battle Creek tour. However, in 1988 they allowed *Fortune* writer Patricia Sellers to visit Building 100. Here's her report:

Each of its four floors is larger than a football field, and when you stand on the 50-yard line, peering in every direction, the degree of Kellogg's cost-cutting becomes comprehensible. Not a human being is seen. Seven days a week, 24 hours a day, computer-monitored machines perform every step of the cereal-making process, from mixing the grains to packing the boxes in cartons.

R. L. Zimmerman, a *Fortune* reader in Lexington, Kentucky, gave another reason for Kellogg's extraordinary profitability: "They are selling a nickel's worth of corn for a dollar."

$tock performance. Kellogg stock bought for $1,000 in 1980 sold for $11,016 on January 2, 1990.

Consumer brands.

Cereal: Kellogg's, All Bran, Apple Cinnamon Squares, Apple Jacks, Apple Raisin Crisp, Bran Buds, Cocoa Krispies, Common Sense, Corn Flakes, Cracklin' Oat Bran, Crispix, Froot Loops, Frosted Flakes, Frosted Krispies, Frosted Mini-Wheats, Fruitful Bran, Fruity Marshmallow Krispies, Just Right, Nut & Honey Crunch, Muëslix, Nutrific, Nutri-Grain, Pep, Pop Pro Grain, Product 19, Raisin Bran, Raisin Squares, Rice Krispies, Smacks, Special K.

Other food: Eggo waffles, Dutch Maid creamer, Croutettes bread crumbs, Whitney's yogurt, Pop-Tarts, Fearn and Culinary Classics soups, Le Gout dessert mix, Mrs. Smith's pies, Natural Juice pies, Salada teas.

Kellogg Company, One Kellogg Square, Battle Creek, MI 49016; (616) 961-2000.

14

NABISCO BRANDS INC

#1 *in cookies and crackers, nuts*
#2 *in margarine, hot cereals*

Employees: 35,000
Sales: $4.6 billion
Profits: $750 million
Founded: 1898
Headquarters: East Hanover, New Jersey

Life Savers and Camels. Oreos and Winstons. Fig Newtons and Salems. That improbable product lineup was one consequence of a series of realignments in the 1980s that saw Nabisco, one of the world's largest food packagers, join with one of the world's largest cigarette makers.

Coming into the 1980s, Nabisco was already the nation's largest cookie and cracker maker, boasting sales of $2.4 billion, good enough for 149th place on the *Fortune* 500. In 1981 they moved into the top 60 by combining with Standard Brands (Planters Nuts, Blue Bonnet Margarine, Royal puddings) to form Nabisco Brands with sales near $6 billion. Standard Brands came encumbered with some sinful products like Fleischmann's gin, Inver House scotch, Guckenheimer whiskey and Lemon Hart rums, but these were soon sloughed off along with the drugstore nostrums Nabisco had previously latched onto—Geritol, Sominex, Aqua Velva. Nabisco Brands was going to be an all-food company.

This goal was short-lived. In 1985 they ceased to be an all-food company by being swallowed by R. J. Reynolds Industries, whose main industry was tobacco but whose interests also included wine and liquor (Heublein), restaurants (Kentucky Fried Chicken) and foods (Del Monte, Hawaiian Punch, Chun King). The next four years saw constant restructurings of RJR Nabisco. Del Monte was attached to Nabisco and then separated, with headquarters first in San Francisco, then in Coral Gables, Florida. Kentucky Fried Chicken was sold to PepsiCo. In 1987, Heublein bought one of the big California wineries, Almaden, and a week later, RJR

sold all of Heublein except the food and condiment lines (A.1, Grey Poupon, Ortega) to Grand Metropolitan, meaning the Nabisco people no longer had any wine to drink with their salty crackers.

Finally, the coup de grace came in 1989. RJR Nabisco was taken private in a $25 billion buyout. You can no longer buy RJR Nabisco stock, but you can still buy their food products, though not as many as before. Because as soon as the buyout was completed, they began selling off companies to pay down the colossal debt incurred. The first ones out the door were Chun King, all the snack companies in Europe and Del Monte (both the canned and the fresh fruits).

Of course, Nabisco still sells plenty of foodstuffs, enough to rank among the largest five food companies in America. They are by far the leading maker of cookies and crackers, holding 37 percent of the cookie market and 55 percent of the cracker business. Oreo, the largest-selling cookie in the United States, accounts for 10 percent of all cookies sold. Nabisco also has the second and third largest sellers—Chips Ahoy! and Teddy Grahams. The largest-selling cracker is Nabisco's Ritz. They also have the second, third and fifth largest sellers—Premium saltines, Wheat Thins and Triscuit. Nabisco turns out these cookies and crackers in 27 bakeries across the country.

History. The name Nabisco comes from the National Biscuit Company, the firm formed in 1898 from the merger of 48 bakeries. Headed by Adolphus W. Green, a Chicago lawyer, the company invented the first package to keep biscuits fresh: a cardboard carton lined with waxed paper. Before that, crackers were shipped in, and sold out of, barrels. Green also came up with the first nationally-sold brand-name cracker, Uneeda (the name was chosen over other candidates like WantaCracker and HavaCracker). One of Green's other tasks was to bind all the regional bakeries together into a national network. His solution: massive doses of advertising.

In 1906 he moved company headquarters from Chicago to Manhattan's lower west side, where he built the largest baking center in the world. In *Out of the Cracker Barrel*, a Nabisco company history, author William Cahn described the scene:

When the wind was right, seamen and stevedores coming off the North River docks could sniff appetizing smells of Vanilla Wafers and Marshmallow Fancies. On other days, the aroma of Animal Crackers and Fig Newton Cakes contrasted sharply with the smells emanating from taverns along Ninth Avenue. "An air of innocence," one writer put it, "clings to the National Biscuit Company, as it must to any business where grown men concern themselves with a ginger snap named Zuzu."

Nabisco now fields an army of well-known brands. Dozens of companies joined National Biscuit over the years and contributed new brand-names:

- A.1. Steak Sauce, first concocted in 1820 for King George IV of England, who upon tasting his chef's creation allegedly declared, "This is A-One."
- Premium saltine crackers, which in 1876 won first prize at a Centennial exhibition.
- Grey Poupon mustard, first sold from a condiments shop in Dijon, France, in 1877.
- Cream of Wheat, invented in 1893 by a Scottish-born flour mill worker, who liked to cook the unused hearts of wheat ("middlings") and heat them in a porridge.
- Ortega Mexican foods, established in 1898 by Emile Ortega, a former California sheriff who discovered how to can green chilies.
- Planters nuts, founded in 1906 by a young Italian immigrant who ran a fruit stand. He invented a machine that automatically roasted peanuts, and he was also the first to salt them.
- Shredded Wheat, invented in 1892 by a Denver lawyer who developed a machine that pressed wheat into thin strips.
- Life Savers candies, invented in 1912 by a Cleveland chocolate manufacturer who wanted a distinctive look for his mints. They ended up looking like miniature life preservers, hence the name.

Owners and rulers. RJR Nabisco's financial wizards in New York who have the job of paying off the debt. The bearded H. John Greeniaus became chief executive officer of Nabisco brands in 1987, at age 42. Born in Canada, Greeniaus graduated

NABISCO BRANDS PRODUCTS

		Market Share
1.	Crackers	55%
2.	Cookies	44%
3.	Pet snacks	39%
4.	New products	38%
5.	Margarine	25%
6.	Mustard	19%
7.	Hot cereals	15%
8.	Mexican foods	13%
9.	Cold cereals	4%

Source: *Business Week,* 23 April 1990.

from McGill University before signing on with Procter & Gamble, J. Walter Thompson, PepsiCo and then Standard Brands (joining Nabisco Brands when Nabisco merged with Standard Brands). A tennis enthusiast and fierce competitor, Geeniaus declares, "I have no interest in winning—I hate to lose. I'll do anything not to lose." That included turning on his former mentor and boss F. Ross Johnson, the ex-head of RJR Nabisco. When Johnson told Greeniaus that his plan to buy RJR Nabisco did not include Greeniaus, Greeniaus promptly sent confidential documents to RJR Nabisco's board that set in motion the battle over the sale of the company. Greeniaus won—he kept his job while Johnson was ousted.

As a place to work. RJR Nabisco is one of the few places around where you can tell your friends you don't know whom you will be working for next year. Shortly after privatization, the internal magazine at Nabisco told employees to follow these guidelines: "Treat every spending decision as if it were *your* cash.... From pencils to packaging, strive to have supplies delivered 'just in time' for them to be used.... Collect receivables as soon as possible. Pay bills as late as possible. Sometimes it's worth it to pass up a discount if it enables the Company to keep its cash longer. There is no such thing as 'petty' cash. In today's environment, cash is king." Welcome to our newly private company.

Social responsibility. Since being submerged in various corporate entities during the 1980s, Nabisco, as a corporate citizen, has about disappeared from public sight. No longer are they a major presence in philanthropy.

Global presence. The sale of cookie and cracker operations in Britain, France and Italy wiped out Nabisco's international presence. Those companies had sales of $1.2 billion in 1989.

Consumer brands.

Beverages: Snap-E-Tom.

Biscuit products: Almost Home, Apple Newtons, Baker's Own, Bakers Bonus, Barnum's Animals, Biscos, Blueberry Newtons, Bugs Bunny, Cameo, Cherry Newtons, Chips Ahoy!, Chips 'n More, Pinwheels, Cookie Break, Fig Newtons, Heyday, Ideal, Lorna Doone, Mallomars, Mystic Mint, Nabisco National, Nilla, Nutter Butter, Oreo, Pantry, Social Tea, Strawberry Newtons, Super Heroes, Better Blue, BetterCheddars, Better Nacho, Better Swiss, Nips, Tid Bit, Chicken in a Biskit, Crown Pilot, Dandy, Doo Dads, Escort, Great Crisps!, Holland, Honey Maid, Meal Mates, Oysterettes, Premium, Ritz, Royal Lunch, Sea Rounds, Sociables, Teddy Grahams, Triscuit, Twigs, Uneeda, Vegetable Thins, Oat Thins, Waverly, Wheatsworth, Wheat Thins, Comet, Chipsters, Harvest Crisps, Mister Salty, Nab, Easy Cheese, Suddenly S'Mores, Toastettes.

Candy: Beechies, Beech Nut, Bonkers, Bubble Yum, Care-Free, Fruit Strip, Life Savers, Merchens, Pearson, Planters, Cocktails, Pom Poms, Breath Savers.

Grocery products: A.1., Blue Bonnett, Brer Rabbit, Oreo ice creams, College Inn, Shredded Wheat, Cream of Rice, Cream of Wheat, Davis, Dromedary, Egg Beaters, Escoffier, Nabisco, Fleischmann's, Fruit Wheats, Grey Poupon, My-T-Fine, Ortega Mexican, Toastettes, Regina, Royal, Spoon Size, Team, Vermont Maid, Wright's.

Ice cream: Life Savers, Oreo.

Nabisco Brands, Inc., 100 Deforest Avenue, East Hanover, NJ 07936; (201) 682-5000.

15
WHITMAN

#1 *in Mexican food, mufflers*
#2 *in soups*

Employees: 24,600
Sales: $4 billion
Profits: $191 million
Founded: 1885 (Pet)
Headquarters: Chicago, Illinois

They could have named the company Old El Paso or Progresso or Midas, but they opted for the sweetest brand name in their line-up, Whitman, after the best-selling one-pound box of candy in the nation, Whitman's Sampler. The Whitman name was adopted on December 1, 1988, to replace IC Industries, a name adopted in 1975 to replace Illinois Central Railroad. They had been trying for a long time to get rid of the railroad but could never find a buyer. Finally, on the first day of 1989, the railroad was spun off to shareholders as a separate company (Illinois Central Transportation), and Whitman was free at last to concentrate on selling Midas mufflers, Progresso soups, El Paso Mexican foods, Downyflake frozen waffles, canned Underwood ham and other bits and pieces they had latched onto in their desperate flight from railroading. (They entered the food industry in 1978 when they bought St. Louis-based Pet Inc., whose original business was condensed milk.) One of Whitman's main activities, accounting for 13 percent of sales, is bottling and distributing Pepsi-Cola in 11 North Central states (they own 80 percent of the bottling operation; PepsiCo owns the other 20). In 1989 they bought Van de Kamp frozen foods.

Whitman got a new boss in mid-1987: a big ex-marine, Karl D. Bays, who had been on IC's board. Bays had also been chief executive of another Chicago-area company, American Hospital Supply Corp., which he tried to merge into Hospital Corp. of America, only to be outmaneuvered by Baxter Travenol, which took over AHS. Bays was known as a hands-on manager, and he certainly knew how to motivate his people. In the fall of 1987 he summoned 23 top managers to a meeting at which he handed each of them an envelope. Inside the envelope was a stock award the board of directors, at his behest, had just voted. The awards covered 1.2 million shares worth $37 million, and they were to be distributed to the managers in annual installments over the next five years. Coupled with the gifts was Bays' request that managers cut costs by $50 million. They stormed out of that meeting and within days came up with $80 million worth of savings, part of which came from firing 900 employees. "We're trying to get our executives to think and act as if they owned the company," said Bays. He obviously succeeded. Bays' tenure was cut short in late 1989 when he dropped dead from a heart attack on his return from a European business trip. He was succeeded by 62-year-old James W. Cozad, who had been vice chairman and chief financial officer at Amoco.

Consumer brands.

Pet, Accent, Old El Paso, Progresso, Hain, Hollywood, Las Palmas, Van de Kamp, Midas.

Stock performance. Whitman stock bought for $1,000 in 1980 sold for $0000 on January 2, 1990.

Whitman Corporation, One Illinois Center, 111 East Wacker Drive, Chicago, IL 60601; (312) 565-3000.

16

#1 *in bananas*

Employees: 43,000
Sales: $3.8 billion
Profits: $68 million
Founded: 1871
Headquarters: Cincinnati, Ohio

Here's the first company to put a brand name on fresh fruit. Their Chiquita bananas are market leaders, not just in the U.S. but in Europe and the Far East. They hold 40 percent of the $3.1 billion world-wide banana market. And because that labeling ploy has worked so well, they now apply those pressure-sensitive Chiquita labels to pineapples, melons and grapefruits. Plus they have a line of Chiquita fruit juices. Chiquita is a powerful brand name, so much so that in early 1990, the company changed their name from United Brands to Chiquita Brands. However, bananas remain the meal ticket. Chiquita sold 4.4 billion pounds of them in 1987, up 25 percent over 1977. Americans, paranoid about their health, are scarfing up 25 pounds of potassium-rich bananas per person every year. And for people who don't care about their health, Chiquita will supply them with cholesterol-rich meats. They pack bacon, hams, hot dogs, steaks, salami, and various luncheon meats under a variety of labels—John Morrell, Rath Black Hawk, Bob Ostrow, Scott Peterson and Nathan's Famous are some of them. (It's an atypical year when there aren't strikes or other labor disputes at the John Morrell plants.)

History. Chiquita's parentage is the old United Fruit Company, longtime exploiter of the Central American "banana republics." Based in Boston for nearly 100 years, they changed their name to United Brands and became part of an eclectic, New York–based conglomerate assembled in the late 1960s and early 1970s by a former rabbinical student, Eli Black. A socially conscious businessman, Black improved housing and working conditions on the company's banana plantations. Then, in 1975, he smashed the window in his office on the 44th floor of New York's Pan Am building and leaped to his death. A week later it was disclosed he had paid $1.25 million into a Swiss bank account on behalf of the president of Honduras in exchange for a $1-a-box banana export tax reduced to 25 cents. Two weeks later the government of Honduras fell, and the company's stock hit its lowest level of the century.

During the interim two brothers, Seymour and Paul Millstein, New York real estate operators, ran the company, but the power behind the throne was the reclusive Cincinnati financier, Carl H. Lindner, who took complete control in 1984. He installed himself as chairman, put his son Keith in charge of Chiquita and moved the headquarters to Cincinnati, where he nursed the company back to financial health. Lindner's 65 percent control is exerted through his privately owned insurance company, American Financial Corp.

Stock performance. Chiquita stock bought for $1,000 in 1980 sold for $4,000 on January 2, 1990.

Consumer brands.

Foods: Chiquita, Brander, California Natural, Chico, Clover, Cremelado, Don Paco, Numar, Petite 150.

Meats: John Morrell, Nathan's Famous, Tobin's First Prize, Hunter, Tom Sawyer, Krey, Krey Gourmet, Peyton, Buckboard, Rath Black Hawk, Partridge, Rodeo, Scott Peterson, Bob Ostrow, EZ Cut, Table Trim, Golden Smoked.

Chiquita Brands International, Inc., One East Fourth Street, Cincinnati, OH 45202; (513) 579-2115.

17

Pillsbury

#1 in refrigerated dough, frozen pizza
#2 in pancake mixes, flour
Employees: 16,000
Sales: $2.4 billion
Founded: 1869
Headquarters: Minneapolis, Minnesota

The Pillsbury doughboy was punched out in the 1980s—and this Minneapolis flour miller also lost their American citizenship. It wasn't the first time. In 1889 the 20-year-old company fell into the hands of an English financial syndicate, although the Pillsbury family regained control in 1923. When Pillsbury fell to the British again, in 1988, the buyer was Grand Metropolitan, the world's largest wine and spirits company, and they intend to poke the doughboy until he learns how to make more money in the food business.

Grand Met paid $5.7 billion for Pillsbury, whose sales broke down 58 percent foods, 42 percent restaurants. The restaurants were the problem. Pillsbury took a $144 million reduction in profits in 1988 because of restaurants that had to be sold off or upgraded. Thrown out of the Pillsbury family were Godfather's Pizza and the Bay Street, Quik Wok and Key West restaurant chains. Pillsbury's biggest restaurant operation, Burger King, opened their 5,000th U.S. restaurant in 1988, but the hamburger chain was taking a severe beating from the industry leader, McDonald's. Grand Met decided to take no chances with letting Americans who had already botched the job continue to run the show. They took Burger King under their own wing rather than keeping it as part of Pillsbury, and they brought in their own people—Ian Martin to head up Pillsbury in Minneapolis and a pub operator, Barry Gibbons, 43, to run Burger King out of Miami. The Grand Met people are cocky. A former executive describes them "as the most arrogant bunch of bastards I've ever met."

The new kids on the block lived up to that assessment by immediately selling off Van de Kamp and Bumble Bee seafoods (Bumble Bee was sold less than a year after it had been purchased) and three different restaurant chains: Steak and Ale, Bennigan's and Azteca. Steak and Ale and Bennigan's were sold because of laws prohibiting liquor manufacturers from operating restaurants that also sell liquor.

Pillsbury still has plenty of goodies left, including some big brands: Green Giant, Joan of Arc, Totino's, Jeno's, Hungry Jack. And they still make their original product, Pillsbury flour.

The company got their start by investing in an innovative machine that milled hard spring wheat into fine white flour. Founder Charles A. Pillsbury put up $10,000 for an interest in a Minneapolis flour mill. Some of his money came from an uncle, John S. Pillsbury, who later served three terms as governor of Minnesota and was regarded as the father of the University of Minnesota.

Consumer brands.

Pillsbury flour, prepared doughs, dessert mixes, Joan of Arc and Green Giant vegetables, Totino's, Jeno's, Hungry Jack, Haagen-Dazs.

The Pillsbury Company, Pillsbury Center, 200 South Sixth Street, Minneapolis, MN 55402; (612) 330-4966.

18

Land O'Lakes, Inc.

#1 *in butter.*
Employees: 5,830
Sales: $2.4 billion
Profits: $34 million
Founded: 1921
Headquarters: Minneapolis, Minnesota

The largest U.S. butter supplier is not Borden or Kraft or any other private dairy-based company. It's a farm cooperative, Land O'Lakes, which makes one out of every three sticks of butter sold in the U.S. And butter was the cooperative's point of departure. They created the Indian maiden symbol in 1924, and their butter soon became widely known as a quality product, the gold standard of the dairy industry. The co-op soon branched out into milk, cheese, turkey, eggs, canned and frozen foods—and margarine. For years Land O'Lakes had touted butter's superiority over margarine. When other dairy people criticized Land O'Lakes for producing margarine, the co-op shot back with the message, "It takes a butter company to give you the taste you really want in margarines."

In 1989, 45-year old Jack Gherty was named president and CEO. Gherty is no farmer. He joined the company straight out of the University of Wisconsin, where he earned degrees in business, law and industrial relations. Land O'Lakes is owned by farmers and ranchers in 15 states and is governed by a 36-member board of farmers and local co-op managers. They have a joint

An old window display of America's number one butter maker.

venture with Cenex, a St. Paul–based farm supply cooperative.

C*onsumer brands.*

Dairy products: Land O'Lakes, Lean Cream sour cream, Natural Dairy Blend, Cocoa Classics mix, 100% Natural sauces.

Animal feed: Litterwean, Littermilk.

Land O'Lakes, Inc., P.O. Box 116, Minneapolis, MN 55440; (612) 481-2222.

AGRIBUSINESS

Agribusiness giants like Cargill and Continental Grain are middlemen in the food chain between the farmer and the world marketplace. Relatively unknown to the world at large, the best window on their operations is Dan Morgan's Merchants of Grain, *published in 1979. Morgan noted there what is still true in 1990:*

> *Most large American companies today take the view that they have some responsibility to account to the public, to disclose and explain their actions. This is not the prevailing view among the five major grain companies. The code of secrecy that applied in 1844 has not only been perpetuated but fortified as the control of the major companies became centralized in the hands of a few people. The result is often suspicion, reticence—and arrogance.*

1

#1 *in grain trading, soybean crushing, egg production, cotton trading*

#2 *in meatpacking*

#3 *in corn milling, wheat milling*

Employees: 53,710
Revenues: $43 billion
Founded: 1865
Headquarters: Minneapolis, Minnesota

Hardly anyone outside the farm belt has heard of Cargill, but nearly everyone inside it knows about them. When a farmer harvests a crop—corn, wheat, soybeans—Cargill is waiting to receive it. They will buy it, store it, process it or sell it in markets around the world. They have 330 grain elevators (capable of holding 400 million bushels of grain) to store all the wheat and corn they buy. They handle about one-quarter of all U.S. grain exports.

In addition to traditional grain trading, Cargill now operates in at least 50 different lines of business and in many different parts of the world. They're making steel and squeezing oranges in Texas, raising chickens in Britain and trading cotton in India and Tanzania. And the whole show is run by managers ensconced in a 63-room replica of a French chateau on the outskirts of Minneapolis.

From the humble beginnings of this 1870 grain warehouse in Calmar, Iowa, evolved Cargill's largest export elevator in Reserve, Louisiana. Costing more than $50 million to open in 1977, its annual capacity exceeds 300 million bushels of grain.

Although they're one of the largest companies in the nation, they are often called an "invisible giant" because they are privately held, with no public stock offering. That relieves them of having to disclose salient features of their operations. As a result, what we do know about Cargill is pieced together from trade magazine stories, infrequent interviews granted to reporters, Dun & Bradstreet credit rating reports, investigative articles, gossip and sheer guesswork. At one point, in the mid-1980s, the company was forced to disgorge some information in a prospectus issued in connection with a European debt offering. A year later Chairman Whitney MacMillan, great-grandson of founder W. W. Cargill, told a *Forbes* reporter: "We didn't realize the reporting requirements. If we did, we wouldn't have done it."

History. The company started in 1865 with one grain warehouse in Conover, Iowa, operated by William Cargill, the son of a retired Scottish sea captain who had settled his family on a Wisconsin farm. As the western wheat fields opened up with the coming of rail lines after the Civil War, William Cargill and his brothers were

there with the right product: grain elevators or warehouses to store the crops. They opened elevators in the Iowa, Wisconsin and Minnesota farm fields. William Cargill made his headquarters in La Crosse, Wisconsin, where he lived across the street from another Scottish Presbyterian family, the MacMillans. His eldest daughter married John High MacMillan in 1895, and his eldest son also married a MacMillan. The Cargills and the MacMillans have ruled this grain company ever since.

History was on their side. The need to store crops became crucial as farm population declined while farm output, spurred by technology, soared. The situation was made to order for the middleman, and Cargill became the biggest middleman of them all.

Trading in grain has led to trading other commodities—cocoa, cotton, metals. As Whitney MacMillan told *New York Times* reporter Steven Greenhouse: "We stick to our knitting like Procter & Gamble. How many soaps does P&G make? In a sense they're all the same. Can you tell me the difference between trading soybeans, cotton and rubber? They're all soaps to us."

And they've been successful traders. In 1978 they put $75 million on the table to outbid Omaha's ConAgra and acquire MBPXL, the nation's second largest meat packer. As Dan Morgan pointed out in *Merchants of Grain*, Americans "eat steak cut from animals fattened on Cargill grain in Cargill feedlots and slaughtered in a Cargill packing house." And it can be seasoned with Leslie salt, another business Cargill bought in 1978 for $30 million.

While many U.S. farmers endured hard times during the 1980s, Cargill went about their business accumulating companies and modernizing and expanding old facilities. Their revenues exploded from $2.2 billion in 1971 to $11 billion in 1976, $28.5 billion in 1981 and $32 billion in 1986. Also during those years Cargill expanded from a grain trader to a processor of the commodities they bought. It made sense. If you have all that corn in your elevators, why not mill it and produce animal feed and corn sweeteners? And as long as you're producing feed, why not buy feedlots and raise cattle? And then, why not slaughter the cattle and pack beef? And if you have all those

soybeans, why not crush them and produce oils? Of course, it takes money to put up all those plants, and Cargill has it.

From published reports, it appears that during this decade Cargill bought, among other entities, a steel mill in Texas, a molasses trading operation, a New York coffee importer, a Dutch cocoa processor, a metals trader, Ralston Purina's soybean business, a couple of meatpacking plants and a fertilizer plant in Tampa.

Owners and rulers. Cargill's riches are divided among 38 members of the two families who built and sustained the company from the beginning, the Cargills and the MacMillans. Four of nine company directors are Cargills or MacMillans. One is named Cargill MacMillan, Jr. The two families own all the voting shares of stock, but some nonfamily senior managers own nonvoting stock. Cargill is a moneymaking machine, but they pass on only 3 percent of their profits to the owners. The rest goes back into the business. Whitney MacMillan, great-grandson of founder Will Cargill, runs the company, but he was not immediately anointed chairman. Far from it. He went through the tough Cargill management trainee program in 1951, and only 26 years later, in 1977, did he get the CEO job. *Forbes* dubs him "an unknown" because in keeping with company tradition, he is loath to reveal anything about himself, or Cargill, to the press. But, says a retired executive in the industry, MacMillan is worth his salt; he "got there through ability." The most memorable thing MacMillan told the *New York Times* in a rare interview was: "Food has become such an interesting issue in the nation and the world."

As a place to work. If you're interested in learning how to be a grain trader, head straight for Minneapolis—and Cargill. They're known as the training ground for the whole industry. Dwayne Andreas passed through Cargill and later transformed Archer-Daniels-Midland into an agribusiness giant and Cargill competitor.

Social responsibility. Cargill never craves the spotlight but they're so big they often can't avoid it. In the mid-1980s they aroused the wrath of American farmers, whom they buy from and sell to, by planning to import 25,000 tons of Argentine wheat. Cargill said they could land the

Argentine grain in New Orleans at $6 to $10 less per ton than wheat from American farms. After heated protests by farm groups, Cargill backed down and sold the Argentine wheat elsewhere. One of the protesters was Texas Agriculture Commissioner Jim Hightower, who said:

> It's an insult to the farmers of America who have been the bread and butter of Cargill for years. We'll come right back at them. The American farmer won't sit around and buy their Nutrena feeds, their seeds, their Burros Mills pancake flour. And he might even turn off "Prairie Home Companion" on Saturday nights and go out organizing other farmers.

In December 1989, in response to complaints from the United Food and Commercial Workers International Union, Excel (Cargill's meatpacking subsidiary and the third largest meatpacker in the nation) agreed to a program to reduce repetitive-motion injuries in the workplace. Workers on meatpacking assembly lines are prone to a disease called carpal tunnel syndrome in which wrist nerves are severely damaged.

In a rare display of gregariousness, Cargill sponsored "Prairie Home Companion" on public radio stations from its inception in 1975 to 1988 when host Garrison Keillor left. The total underwriting cost over those years was close to $1 million. For Cargill, chickenfeed.

G*lobal presence.* This is what Cargill is all about. They buy and sell goods from 800 locations on six continents.

C*onsumer brands.*

Honeysuckle white turkeys, Excel beef, Nutrena feeds.

Cargill Incorporated, Box 9300, Minneapolis, MN 55440; (612) 475-7575.

2

#2 *in grain trading*

Employees: 12,000
Sales: $13.5 billion
Founded: 1813
Headquarters: New York City, New York

Second only to Cargill in worldwide trading of commodities like grain and oilseeds, Continental Grain retrenched during the 1980s when agricultural exports slumped. They also had a change of guard at the top, the first such in 44 years. When Donald L. Staheli, a native of Hurricane, Utah, succeeded Michel Fribourg as CEO in 1988, it marked the first time in 175 years that someone named Fribourg had not headed the firm, whose business begins when farmers sell their crops.

Like Cargill, Continental functions as a middleman, buying grain from farmers and other dealers and selling it to customers around the world. They have trading posts at 200 locations in 58 countries and control about 20 percent of world grain trade. Also like Cargill, Continental has moved beyond trading to process some of the agricultural products they buy and store. They crush soybeans, produce animal feeds and pet foods, mill flour, turn out broiler chickens and pack beef and pork.

Also like Cargill, Continental Grain is a privately held company about which little is known—even less than Cargill. It would appear, though, that during the 1980s, as Cargill continued to expand, buying companies and building plants here, there and everywhere, Continental did some streamlining. They sold their bakeries (Arnold and Oroweat) and closed down their commodities brokerage house, ContiCommodity, terminating 500 employees. ContiCommodity had sought customers with this come-on: "Would the possibility of yields of 25–35 percent per year interest you?" They ended up being sued by 160 customers who alleged fraud and misrepresentation.

When he stepped down as chief executive in 1988, Michel Fribourg was 74 and planned to continue with the company as an advisor. This came as no surprise because he is believed to own 90 percent of the stock, worth over $800 million. And the Fribourgs will probably furnish another CEO one day. One of the group heads at Continental Grain is Michel Fribourg's son, Paul, who was 36 in 1990.

History. The business was founded in Belgium by Simon Fribourg, Michel's great-great-grandfather. Their first major international deal came in 1848, during a drought in Belgium, when Simon's son traded several sacks of gold for large stocks of Ukrainian wheat. The Fribourgs became influential during the latter half of the 19th century as Europe began to change from a rural to an industrial economy, with people increasingly working at a distance from their food sources. By 1900 England was growing only a fraction of the wheat it consumed, and the Fribourgs filled the gap. The Fribourgs reorganized their business as Continental Grain after World War I, establishing a U.S. subsidiary in Chicago. In 1940, when German armies overran Belgium and France, the Fribourgs fled, regrouping in New York after World War II.

According to Dan Morgan in *Merchants of Grain*, the Fribourgs have had a lot of success in trading grain with the Soviets:

> The mysterious, aristocratic Michel Fribourg was just the kind of archetypical capitalist who perfectly fitted the old Communist stereotype and had the same strong personal authority as did the people at the top of the Soviet bureaucratic hierachy.

Although Continental Grain keeps to itself, Michel Fribourg didn't mind writing an *op-ed* piece for the *New York Times* in 1986 in which he urged a free trade policy for agriculture that would eliminate government farm support programs. Fribourg said the U.S. should join with other food-exporting countries in a global pact to end farming subsidies:

> Neither the United States nor any other nation can singlehandedly end this self-defeating cycle of excessive and artificial supports, subsidies, surpluses and trade barriers that are primarily increasing the amount of food produced for Government storage while saddling taxpayers and consumers with costs exceeding the total benefits received by farmers.

Continental Grain wants to see that food stored in their elevators.

Continental Grain, 277 Park Avenue, New York, NY 10172; (212) 207-5578.

3

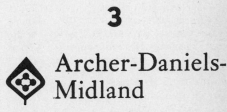

Archer-Daniels-Midland

#1 *in vegetable oils, corn processing, corn sweeteners, ethanol*

#2 *in flour milling*

Employees: 9,000
Sales: $8 billion
Profits: $425 million
Founded: 1902
Headquarters: Decatur, Illinois

They call Dwayne Andreas the "Soybean King," and with good reason. Archer-Daniels-Midland, the company he heads, crushes more soybeans than anyone else, and Andreas is a tireless proselytizer for the soybean as the answer to world hunger. He has also proved himself a dynamo at running a business and making friends with politicians, not only Republicans (like Tom Dewey and Robert Dole) and Democrats (like Tip O'Neill and Hubert Humphrey), but political leaders around the world, including Mikhail Gorbachev. The *Wall Street Journal* wrote that Andreas may well have eclipsed Occidental Petroleum's Armand Hammer as "Moscow's favorite American businessman." Brought up on a farm in a Mennonite family (no movies, no bright clothing, no newspapers or magazines on Sundays), Andreas was recruited to ADM in 1965.

The sleepy descendant of a clutch of small midwestern companies that made farm products, ADM was then based in Minneapolis. Andreas moved the headquarters to Decatur, Illinois (the "Soybean

Capital of the World," whose residents can listen to WSOY and WSOY-FM). There, he literally transformed ADM into an agribusiness giant rivaling, in some areas, the company he used to work for, Cargill. ADM's sales have multiplied 10-fold under Dwayne Andreas. They market the crops of 20 farmer-owned cooperatives, operate 118 processing plants, buy 5 million bushels of grain and oilseeds a day, maintain 102 grain elevators and move goods around in 8,900 rail cars and 400 tank and trailer trucks.

The peripatetic Andreas flits around the globe in one of ADM's Falcon jets. He almost never writes letters or memos, preferring to maintain constant contact with his empire by phone, whether he is in the air, in a car, or in a golf cart. (There's a phone in the golf cart that accompanies him on his daily round on the links.) Others at ADM are used to Andreas' fast-paced style. Company president James R. Randall, who shares a secretary with another executive, told *New Yorker* writer E. J. Kahn: "People around here make money instead of writing reports or going to meetings."

Andreas has made a lot of money at ADM. His 7 million shares of stock were worth over $200 million in 1990. And others in his family own about 7 percent of ADM's stock. His son Michael (whose godfather was Hubert Humphrey) and two nephews, Martin and Allen, are officers at ADM. His brother Lowell is on the board as was another brother who served until age 79 when he became a director emeritus. Andreas also brought to the ADM board Robert Strauss, former national Democratic party chairman, and Happy Rockefeller, widow of former Vice President Nelson Rockefeller. Mrs. Rockefeller sold Andreas his Fifth Avenue co-op apartment in New York City. (Andreas also owns an apartment at the Waldorf-Astoria as well as homes in Bal Harbour, Florida, and Decatur.)

Though he turns 73 in 1990, Andreas has no intention of retiring. He told Kahn: "I have too much still to do. A third of all the business in the world is my kind of business, and the longer you're in it the more things you see that need to be done. When you see that they're not done, you get very uneasy, and the next thing you know you're trying to do them yourself."

ADM profits handsomely from government subsidies of corn sweeteners and soybeans. During the 1988 presidential campaign, both candidates wanted to increase support for a corn product called ethanol, a grain alcohol used to make a gasoline substitute called gasohol. ADM produces 75 percent of the nation's ethanol; in 1989 alone, they produced 630 million gallons and received federal and state tax exemptions totalling about $504 million. In early 1990, ADM and a group of farmers and Congressmen were fighting for tax breaks for a gasoline additive, ETBE, containing 40 percent ethanol. Some critics claim the tax breaks are a form of "corporate welfare" for ADM.

G*lobal presence.* Processing plants in Canada, the United Kingdom, West Germany and Holland.

S*tock performance.* ADM stock bought for $1,000 in 1980 sold for $4,388 on January 2, 1990.

Archer-Daniels-Midland Company, 4666 Faries Parkway, Decatur, IL 62526; (217) 424-5200.

4

Staley

#2 *in corn refining, high fructose corn syrup*

Employees: 9,100
Sales: $1.1 billion
Profits: $57 million
Founded: 1898
Headquarters: Decatur, Illinois

At Decatur, Illinois, in the heart of the Midwest farm fields, where in 1929 this corn-based company put up a 14-story headquarters building that became known as the "Castle in the Cornfield," the people at Staley are still trying to figure out what hit them in the 1980s. Donald E. Nordlund, a hard-nosed lawyer who had become the first non-Staley family member to run this corn processor, was determined to leave his mark. He discontinued Staley's corn-based grocery products (Sta-Puf, Sta-Flo, Staley syrups), sold off the soybean-crushing business and spent $330 million to acquire CFS Continental, a major food distributor of foods to restaurants. The company's name was changed to Staley Continental, and Nordlund, tired of looking at cornfields, moved the headquarters to the old CFS Continental base in Rolling Meadows outside Chicago, from where he directed the acquisition of six other food distribution outfits, including a Chicago-based company, HAVI, that supplied hamburger buns to McDonald's.

Moving into 1988, Staley Continental was grossing $3.4 billion a year (more than double the 1980 revenue), with two-thirds of those sales coming from food service. McDonald's alone accounted for $500 million in revenue. But in 1988 Tate & Lyle, the big British sugar company, decided they wanted Staley. Nordlund shopped around for another bid, couldn't find one and finally accepted the Tate & Lyle offer of $1.5 billion. Tate & Lyle's plain-speaking chairman, Neil M. Shaw, said that in the negotiations Nordlund and his aides were mainly concerned about getting their "golden parachutes," which Tate & Lyle had disparaged in a court filing as "a web of enrichment devices" that were "grossly excessive and wholly unjustified." In the end, Tate & Lyle paid them, and Nordlund walked away with $2.6 million.

The British quickly sold off the food service businesses to Sysco, changed the name of the company back to A. E. Staley Manufacturing Company and returned the headquarters to Decatur, where they were once again in the corn-refining business with sales roughly about what they were in 1980. Only now they were British-owned and the head of the company was Larry H. Cunningham, an American.

Staley's new corporate owners, Tate & Lyle, have a long history. Founder Sir Henry Tate was the donor of Britain's Tate Gallery. His descendant Henry Saxon Tate is the last family member on the board. The Lyles, who ran the firm for years, turned the firm over to Earl Jellicoe in 1978. He joined the board after being forced out of leadership in the House of Lords because of a sex scandal. Before picking up Staley, Tate & Lyle bought the American sugar giant Amstar, makers of Domino and Sweet 'n' Low.

A. E. Staley Manufacturing Company, 2200 Eldorado Street, Decatur, IL 62525; (217) 423-4411.

MEAT AND POULTRY

Americans are eating less beef. The milestone year was 1987 when, for the first time, poultry (chicken and turkey) consumption rose to the top—78.2 pounds per person, compared to 75.7 pounds for beef. What haven't changed much since Upton Sinclair wrote his muckraking novel, The Jungle, are the working conditions in meatpacking and chicken slaughterhouses. In a 1987 report New York Times reporter William Glaberson wrote:

> *Modern machinery has changed the look and the sound of a packing house. But the meatpacking industry, which employs 100,000 people, remains the most hazardous industry in America. Meatpackers work in extreme heat or refrigerated cold, often standing shoulder to shoulder, wielding hones, knives and power saws. Grease and blood make the floors and the tools slippery. The roar of the machines is constant. Occasionally, an overpowering stench from open bladders and stomachs fills the air. The workers cut themselves. They cut each other. They wear out their insides doing repetitive-motion jobs. They are sliced and crushed by machines that were not even imagined when Sinclair published his book in 1906.*

1

#1 *in meatpacking*

Employees: 22,000
Sales: $9.1 billion
Profits: $35 million
Founded: 1960
Headquarters: Dakota City, Nebraska

Workplace

They are the biggest slaughterers and processors of cattle and hogs in the nation, and they doubled their sales during the 1980s. They send their boxes of beef and pork to supermarket chains, restaurants, meat wholesalers and companies making finished meat products. They also seem to mangle the people who work for them, if one reads through the unending stories appearing in the nation's press over the past two decades recounting IBP's fights with labor unions, the Labor Department and the Occupational Health & Safety Administration.

Formerly known as Iowa Beef Processors, this company revolutionized the meatpacking industry. Occidental Petroleum acquired them in 1981, and in 1987 Oxy sold off 49.5 percent of the company for $408 million. IBP stock is now listed on the New York Stock Exchange.

History. Currier J. Holman, a slaughterhouse butcher turned independent cattle dealer, founded the company with Andy Anderson in 1960. While Holman managed the firm, Anderson came up with the innovative, efficient meatpacking system that has made IBP a leader in beef processing. Traditionally, cattle were shipped live to stockyards in major urban centers such as Chicago. Under Anderson, the company built slaughterhouses in small towns in the heart of America's beef country. Iowa Beef sidestepped the problems of shipping live animals and avoided paying big-city wages by putting their plants in places like Denison, Iowa; West Point, Nebraska; and Emporia, Kansas. They established a private radio network to coordinate cattle purchases from ranchers and feeders in the Midwest and Northwest and delivery to the nearby slaughterhouses. Their slaughterhouses became highly mechanized steak factories. After an animal is slaughtered, its carcass moves through the plant on conveyor belts while laborers perform specialized tasks that reduce it to boxed, plastic-wrapped cuts of beef. The meat is then shipped to supermarket chains, meat brokers, wholesalers and restaurant and hotel chains.

Although innovative, IBP has never had a nice-guy image. Holman and Iowa Beef were convicted in 1974 of conspiring with a Mafia figure to bribe their way into New York City, the world's largest meat market, by paying off butchers' union officials and supermarket executives. The *Wall Street Journal* reported that Iowa Beef's "history is laced with criminals, gangland figures, civil wrongdoers, brazen conflicts of in-

From 1917 to 1948 the two largest food companies in the nation were the Chicago meatpackers Armour and Swift.

terest and possible violations of antitrust and labor laws. Floating in and out of the scene are people engaged in vicious beatings, shootings and fire-bombings." In 1974 *Forbes* characterized the company as follows: "At Iowa Beef, getting into trouble is a way of life. So is making money."

IBP's reputation as industry trailblazer suffered during the 1980s. They have fallen behind in the latest trend in the business, "branded beef," wherein meatpackers build brand loyalty by identifying their own products in the stores. In the past IBP delivered boxes of generic beef to supermarkets, which then packaged it and passed it on to the customer. Now that's going to change, says the company brass. To add to their problems, increasingly health-conscious Americans started eating less red meat and more poultry.

As a place to work.   Don't work for IBP if you've grown attached to your hands. There's always the risk one might get chopped off in the assembly line, but an even greater risk is that your hands might get crippled by various nerve disorders: carpal tunnel tendonitis or "trigger finger syndrome." Take your pick. As many as one out of five meatpacking workers (industrywide) are afflicted with hand injuries, because the repetitive work they do can numb nerves, making it impossible to lift, flex or grip. Some might say that just goes with the job, but in 1988, OSHA decided IBP job practices made this occupational hazard significantly worse and fined the firm a whopping $3.1 million for failing to take steps to reduce nerve injuries among workers. Such steps would have included such simple measures as slowing down the assembly line, rotating jobs or redesigning tools. IBP is also known for high turnover, low wages in depressed farmbelt towns and bitter fights with unions, most memorably a violent lockout at their Dakota City plant in 1986. Only 4 of their 17 plants are unionized, partly because IBP recruits a migratory workforce of Hispanic and Southeast Asian immigrants. In all, IBP operates 11 beef and 6 pork plants.

Social responsibility.   IBP's credibility sank lower than the *Titanic* during the 1980s. Their top executive, CEO Robert Peterson, got caught lying to a congressional committee about their record-keeping practices, and excused himself by saying, "It was inaccurate [testimony], but it wasn't perjury." When IBP was fined $2.6 million in 1987 for failing to report more than 1,000 on-the-job injuries, Assistant Secretary of Labor John A. Pendergrass commented, "This is the worst example of underreporting injuries and illnesses to workers ever encountered by OSHA." During the 1988 presidential campaign, several candidates singled out IBP as a symbol of corporate greed. Bruce Babbitt called it a "monument to everything shabby and backward in the American economy, not only because the company lies and cheats, but because it believes its employees are the problem and not the solution." Toward the end of the 1980s, some thought they detected signs that IBP was trying to clean up their public act. *Business Week* called it "remarkable" when IBP recognized the United Food and Commercial Workers (UFCW) union at their plant in Joslin, Illinois. The same year, 1988, IBP worked out a deal with OSHA under which they paid only $975,000 out of the $5.7 million in fines they picked up in the previous two years. In return, IBP hired experts to set up an in-house research project to study repetitive-motion injuries.

Stock performance.   IBP stock bought for $1,000 in 1980 sold for $889 on January 2, 1990.

IBP, Inc., Dakota City, NE 68731; (402) 494-2061.

2

#1 *in chicken*

Employees: 34,100
Sales: $2.9 billion
Profits: $104 million
Founded: 1935
Headquarters: Springdale, Arkansas

Dressed in his khaki work clothes, Don Tyson may look like an Arkansas bumpkin, but he's a tough corporate fighter with blood on his hands. His company slaughters 17 million chickens every week and 1 million pigs a year. Tyson is the largest producer of chickens in the nation. In 1989 they outbid a much bigger food company, ConAgra, for Holly Farms. Both ConAgra and Holly Farms were also major chicken producers. So this 10-month fight was for leadership in the poultry business, and Don Tyson, son of the company founder, was not about to lose it. Despite the preference Holly's management had for ConAgra, Tyson persisted.

Old Tyson hands weren't surprised. They had been saying all along, "If Don wants it, he'll get it." It wasn't as if he was new to corporate takeovers. Since 1961 he has bought 14 companies with 27 processing plants. Tyson Foods began the 1980s with sales of $390 million and emerged doing close to $4 billion. The combination of Tyson with Holly created a company that controlled 25 percent of the chicken market, with sales equal to the combined sales of the next three producers (ConAgra, Gold Kist and Perdue).

History. In 1935, a slender Arkansas farmer named John Tyson bought 500 chickens, loaded them on a truck and took them to Chicago. He made a profit of $235 and started his own chicken business. The company depended on outside suppliers until 1958 when their Springdale, Arkansas, chicken plant was built. Tyson Foods went public in 1963. After Tyson bought Holly Farms in 1989, they trimmed away that company's non-chicken business, selling the flour milling and bakery division (Dixie Portland Flour Mill, White Lily Foods) to a subsidiary of Archer-Daniels-Midland Company. Holly Farms was in business before John Tyson had ever laid eyes on a chicken, in 1887 as the Grenada Cotton Compress Company in the state of Mississippi. This down-home company, later renamed the Federal Company, slowly evolved into a cotton producer, flour miller and feed manufacturer by 1968, which was when they bought Holly Farms Poultry Industries, one of the first of the chicken "factories."

Owners *and rulers.* Don Tyson took over the firm in 1967 at age 36, when his father and stepmother died in a car crash. Don Tyson is no jet-setter; the only time he leaves Arkansas is to go on a business trip, or to go marlin fishing. *Forbes* estimates his wealth at $375 million. His younger brother Randal choked to death on a cookie in 1986, leaving his widow with company stock worth about $290 million. Although the company is fond of stating that they lead all *Fortune* 500 companies in percentage of stock owned by employees (20 percent), directors and officers own 14.7 percent of those shares, leaving only 5.3 percent for the remaining 25,000 Tyson people. And Tyson has two classes of stock, A and B, the distinguishing difference being that B class has 10 votes, A class one. Don Tyson owns 99.9 percent of the B class stock. He also believes in paying himself a handsome stipend: $2.5 million in 1988.

As *a place to work.* Tyson is a down-home Arkansas company that talks incessantly about the people who work there, featuring them (and their thoughts) in annual reports and internal publications. Executives are expected to wear khaki farm clothes. They are a virulently antiunion company, believing their policies are fair enough to keep unions out. Less than 7 percent of their workforce is organized, and employees at a number of plants have voted down union membership. Tyson no longer calls employees "employees." They call them "Tyson people." They have encouraged share ownership by allowing Tyson people to allocate up to 10 percent of their wages to buy stock, and Tyson provides a match up to 5 percent. Before their purchase by Tyson, Holly

Farms had enacted one of the most far-reaching stock option programs in American business, extending to all employees the right to have options usually reserved for top executives.

G*lobal presence.* Small but they're beginning to target international markets. They have joint ventures going in Canada and Mexico, and in 1988 they doubled their export sales to $122 million. Their biggest overseas market is Japan, where Tyson became the first nationally advertised chicken brand.

S*tock performance.* Tyson stock bought for $1,000 in 1980 sold for $36,697 on January 2, 1990.

C*onsumer brands.*

Tyson, Holly Farms, Chick 'n Quick, Weaver.

Tyson Foods, Inc., 2210 West Oaklawn, Springdale, AR 72764; (501) 756-4000.

3

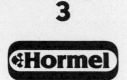

#4 *in meatpacking*

Employees: 8,000
Sales: $2.4 billion
Profits: $71 million
Founded: 1891
Headquarters: Austin, Minnesota

Hormel, the company that brings you Hormel chili and Dinty Moore beef stew, is a corporate hero to some for taking on the workers in their hometown and crushing them the way they compress ham into their world-famous product, Spam. It seemed an unlikely place for it to happen, but Austin, in Southeast Minnesota near the Iowa border, became the scene for the most bitter, prolonged strike of the 1980s, the aftershocks of which will probably still be reverberating in 1991 when Hormel marks their centennial.

When Hormel entered the 1980s, Austin, Minnesota, seemed a picture-perfect company town. Nearly 10 percent of Austin residents worked for Hormel, and one-third of the company's shareholders lived there. The Hormel annual meeting was a big social event, attended by hundreds. At the 1980 meeting they gave away a $4 package of Hormel meats to each attendee. And a sign on Austin's outskirts declared, "The good life is here to stay."

The picture was shattered in 1985 when Hormel decided to cut workers' base wage 23 percent, to $8.25 an hour. About 1,400 unionized workers left the plant in protest. During a nasty 13-month strike, tension ran so high between strikers and nonstrikers that the National Guard was called in. "It's split families, it's split friends," one Austin resident told the *New York Times.* The strike cost Hormel $2 million, but the company still clocked record profits of $39 million for the 1986 fiscal year. The strike collapsed when the local union was drummed out of the international union for refusing to end the strike. The international then ended the strike and negotiated a raise in the base wage to $10.70 an hour over a three-year period. Meanwhile, many strikers had been replaced, and some may never return to work at Hormel.

During the 1980s, when Americans bought less beef and pork and began eating more chicken and fish, Hormel took the hint. "Our consumers didn't know what to do with a 3-pound pot roast—and they didn't want to know," observed CEO Richard Knowlton. By 1983, Hormel (which in 1926 was the first packer to can ham) was selling catfish snacks and fillets and three years later introduced turkey products (they bought Jennie-O Foods in 1986). Even the famous Spam—introduced in 1937, and for years the world's largest-selling brand of canned meat—got a new image. Hormel began experimenting with a low-salt, low-fat, low-sugar product called Spam Lite.

The Hormel Foundation, set up by George Hormel (who founded the company in 1891), currently owns 45 percent of the company. An employee pension plan owns an additional 12 percent.

S*tock performance.* Hormel stock bought for $1,000 in 1980 sold for $10,878 on January 2, 1990.

Consumer brands.

Hormel, Black Label, Spam, Cure 81, Curemaster, Di Lusso, Dinty Moore, Frank 'N Stuff, Homeland, Light & Lean, Little Sizzlers, Mary Kitchen, Range Brand, Super Select, Wranglers, Broiled & Browned, Top Shelf, Jennie-O, Traditions, Farm Fresh.

Geo. A. Hormel & Company, 501 16th Avenue N.E., P.O. Box 800, Austin, MN 55912; (507) 437-5737.

SPECIALTY FOODS

Some 8,000 new food products are introduced every year, angling for space on a supermarket shelf. Most fall by the wayside, but hope springs eternal. Everyone's aim is to field a product that will find a special niche—as has Lipton in tea, Gerber in baby foods, Ocean Spray in cranberries, Frito-Lay in snacks.

1

#1 *in snack foods*

Employees: 28,000
Sales: $4.2 billion
Profits: $821 million
Founded: 1933
Headquarters: Plano, Texas

Here's the king of the snack food business. They operate 40 plants across the U.S., turning out a variety of salt-laden products that are the bane of health food fanatics. They're so good at what they do they account for one-eighth of all U.S. snack food sales. Frito-Lay's top six products are Doritos tortilla chips (retail sales of $1 billion in 1988), Ruffles potato chips (retail sales of $800 million), Lay's potato chips ($700 million), Fritos corn chips ($500 million), Chee-tos cheese-flavored snacks ($400 million) and Tostitos tortilla chips ($200 million). That's a lot of crunching.

Within the business world, Frito-Lay is almost as famous for their sales force as they are for their products. They have a route sales force of 10,000 people, many of them unionized, who not only get the product to the stores but also live and die to please the customer. This crew doesn't just deliver bags of Doritos. They stock them on the shelves for the supermarket. And they make frequent runs to make sure the chips are always fresh. It's not unusual for a Frito-Lay salesperson to restock a store two or three times on a busy weekend. This service ethic is reinforced by rules and high commissions for the route force. In his book, *The Marketing Edge*, Harvard Business School professor Thomas Bonoma described how a Frito salesman, Jess Pagluica, "took the time to 'flex' each bag of Fritos…, smoothing out the wrinkles so that the display would look better."

History. Frito and Lay were two separate companies begun in the Depression. The Frito part began when a Texas ice-cream maker, Elmer Doolin, stopped for lunch in 1932 at a small San Antonio cafe that was selling 5-cent packages of corn chips. When he asked where the chips came from, he was directed to a local Mexican who was willing to sell the corn-chip recipe for $100 to return to his native land. Doolin borrowed the money and started the Frito business out of his own home. His mother, Daisy Dean Doolin, cooked the batches of chips in the kitchen. That same year, Herman Lay began selling potato chips in the Nashville area for an Atlanta potato-chip manufacturer. Ten years later, when the Atlanta company was having financial problems, Lay bought them out and began selling Lay's potatos chips.

The two companies merged in 1961, only four years before PepsiCo bought Frito-Lay with dreams of couch potatoes sitting in front of TV sets munching chips and downing six-packs of Pepsi. It was a vision realized. Wayne Calloway, now CEO of PepsiCo, previously served as head of Frito-Lay. He once said about Frito-Lay: "Sales to service' is stamped on everyone's underdrawers around here."

Global presence. Attached to Frito-Lay is PepsiCo Foods International, which accounts for 28 percent of Frito-Lay's sales. They operate 31 plants and have 16,000 employees, marketing 100 brands of snack foods in more than a dozen countries. Their largest international market is Mexico, where they make Sabritas potato chips and sweets like hard candy and gum. In Canada they have teamed up with Hostess. They recently invaded Italy, India, Turkey and South Korea, where they introduced Lay's potato chips and Chee-tos snacks. They figure the whole world is ready for salted snacks. Maybe it is.

Consumer brands.

Snack food: Fritos, Doritos, Tostitos, Ruffles, Chee-tos, Lay's.

Cookies: Grandma's.

Frito-Lay, Inc., 7701 Legacy Drive, Plano, TX 75024; (914) 253-2000.

2

#1 *in tea, dry soup mixes*

Employees: 5,000
Sales: $1.4 billion
Profits: $125 million
Founded: 1914
Headquarters: Englewood Cliffs, New Jersey

This company introduced the English to packaged tea! They took tea out of upper-class drawing rooms and turned it into a beverage for the masses. After converting many Americans to tea drinking, they disappeared in their mother country. Today, Lipton is an arm of Britain's biggest consumer products company, Unilever, but their entire business is in the U.S., where they operate independently of other Unilever companies. Aside from tea, Lipton has a number of other businesses—Wish-Bone salad dressings, Lawry's seasonings, Good Humor ice cream, Knox gelatin, Sunkist fruit snacks, Wyler's beverage mixes (acquired from Borden in a trade for Pennsylvania Dutch noodles). Tea is still Lipton's mainstay. They make half of all tea consumed in America.

History. Sir Thomas Lipton, the familiar face on Lipton's tea packages, won the hearts of Americans for his repeated attempts to win the America's Cup yacht race between 1899 and 1930. Lipton never won the Cup, but like Charlie Brown and the kite, millions loved "Sir Tea" for being a good sport, always ready to try again. Just before Lipton's death in 1931, Will Rogers wrote a letter to the *New York Times*, suggesting everyone chip in to buy a cup for

Sir Thomas Lipton provided affordable tea to Britain's masses, as illustrated by this 1890 advertisement.

"the world's most cheerful loser," and thousands of donations poured in, enough to commission a cup crafted by Tiffany's.

Lipton was born of good grocer stock in Glasgow. At 15 he crossed the Atlantic, seeking his fortune, and worked at odd jobs—as a fireman in Charleston, a tobacco harvester in Virginia, a grocery clerk in New York. He admired the American "go-get-it" attitude, as he called it, and went home, determined to import it to Scotland. Soon he had the most successful grocery business in Glasgow, with 20 stores, known for their inventive advertising—a drawing of an orphan pig, sad because his family had "gone to Lipton's."

His Americanized entrepreneurial spirit was further moved when Lipton spotted a bargain in tea. Telling his staff he was going on vacation, Lipton sailed for Ceylon, now Sri Lanka, in 1891 and bought up every last tea plantation he found there. He then dispensed with the teak chests in which tea was traditionally sold, and put tea in tins and packages to preserve freshness. And he made sure everyone knew the tea they were drinking was Lipton's by plastering his name on the package and all over Glasgow's streets. Lipton then moved to London, where he became a man about town. He became friendly with Prince Edward, who encouraged him to make the challenge for the America's Cup. In 1898 Queen Victoria knighted him, making Lipton, Sir Thomas.

The company Lipton built expanded steadily through the century. In 1940, they took their first step away from tea and started selling dry soup mixes. In 1952 Lipton boosted their tea business by introducing the "Flo-Thru" tea bag. In the 1950s Arthur Godfrey, the famous radio host, plugged for Lipton. One day Godfrey read a listener's letter that suggested a strange concoction: mixing Lipton's onion soup mix with sour cream and eating it with potato chips. That day, California Dip, as we know it, was born, and Lipton's onion soup sales took off.

By now Lipton is a senior citizen of New Jersey. They were in Hoboken for 44 years before moving in 1963 to Englewood Cliffs overlooking the George Washington Bridge.

Owners and rulers. Unilever owns Lipton 100 percent, but they develop their own managers. After Unilever bought the company in 1937, they looked for an American to run the business. A help-wanted ad in the *New York Times* drew over 500 applicants, one of whom was a Borden salesman, Robert Bartly Small-wood. He headed Lipton until 1958 when he was succeeded by W. Gardner Barker, who had negotiated Lipton's first acquisition, Wish-Bone, in 1957. Barker ran the company for the next 20 years. In 1988, Blaine R. Hess, a veteran of 25 years with Lipton, took over.

As a place to work. Every afternoon at 2:30, tea and cookies are brought around the halls of the headquarters, keeping alive the British custom of "teatime" in at least this one patch of corporate America. In their plants, Lipton is experimenting with a program called "Excelling Through Teamwork," which involves management giving feedback on employee suggestions, whether or not they are accepted, to demonstrate they're listening.

Global presence. They cover the U.S. and let Unilever take care of the rest of the world.

Consumer brands.

Lipton teas, iced tea, soups and side dishes; Cup-a-Soup; Wyler's; Sunkist Fun Fruits; Wish-Bone salad dressings; Knox gelatin; Equal (artificial sweetener); Lawry's Seasoned Salt; Good Humor ice cream.

Thomas J. Lipton, Inc., 800 Sylvan Avenue, Englewood Cliffs, NJ 07632; (201) 567-8000.

3

McCORMICK

#1 *in spices and seasonings*

Employees: 7,600
Sales: $1.2 billion
Profits: $136 million
Founded: 1889
Headquarters: Hunt Valley, Maryland

They're an old-fashioned company making old-fashioned products—spices, seasonings, flavorings. McCormick dominates the spice business, selling about 43 percent of all seasonings bought in stores. That's more than double the amount sold by number two, Durkee French Foods. Nowadays, because Americans are eating more prepared foods and frozen dinners, spice companies rely more on sales to companies making packaged foods. Only one-third of McCormick's sales come from supermarkets. The rest comes from firms supplying restaurants or to big food packagers (like ConAgra or Nabisco Brands).

McCormick imports paprika from Morocco, ginger and cinnamon from China, vanilla beans from the Malagasy Republic. They're the world's biggest producer of dehydrated garlic and onions. And you can see their wares in the spice section of your supermarket. In the eastern part of the U.S., the spices carry the McCormick label, in the West, the Schilling brand name, a reflection of McCormick's 1947 acquisition of San Francisco-based A. Schilling, a spice house founded in 1881.

McCormick retains a filial affection for Baltimore, their hometown even though they moved to the suburbs and in 1988, just as they were about to celebrate their centennial, sold their historic Light Street building overlooking Baltimore harbor (despite community protests). Grandnephew of founder Willoughby McCormick, chairman and CEO Charles P. McCormick, Jr., who is called "Buzz" inside the company, told employees and shareholders the sale of McCormick's properties in Baltimore "does not mean we are abandoning or deserting the city of Baltimore. The city is our birthplace, and I promise you we will continue to make our presence known."

McCormick navigated their way through the turbulent 1980s escaping various threats. They repelled a takeover attempt by the Swiss chemical giant, Sandoz. Then they were found to be "cooking the books" to make profits look better than they really were. As a result, in 1982, for the first time in their history, they placed outsiders on their board. However, company executives still dominate the board, and it continues to be all-male. All the officers of McCormick are male as well. More than half the company's stock is owned by the McCormick family and current and retired employees.

The McCormicks and management control half of the voting shares. If you are a shareholder, you'll always know when the annual report is in the mail because it comes scented. In 1987 the pages were scented with a buttered-cinnamon flavor, in 1988 it was apple-pie spice.

New employees are still handed copies of the book written 40 years ago by Buzz McCormick's father with the unlikely title, *The Power of People.* His legacy continues in the form of "Multiple Management" boards. Each of the 13 boards functions like a junior board of directors for the company's major operating divisions. They parallel the divisional boards composed of key executives within each part of the company. While the divisional boards concentrate on administration, the Multiple Management boards analyze and offer solutions to a wide variety of nuts-and-bolts problems.

When introduced in 1932, the boards immediately dealt with some basic employee concerns. Time clocks were eliminated in the factories, and today McCormick's hourly employees don't clock in except when working overtime. The boards also established a buddy system, now called a "sponsorship" program, whereby a new employee is introduced to others throughout the company by an old hand.

Stock performance. McCormick stock bought for $1,000 in 1980 sold for $6,984 on January 2, 1990.

Consumer brands.
McCormick, Schilling, Club House spices and seasonings, Season All, Cake Mate decoration products, Parsley Patch seasoning and sauces, Gilroy seasonings.

McCormick & Company, Inc., 11350 McCormick Road, Hunt Valley, MD 21031; (301) 667-7301.

4

Gerber

#1 *in baby foods*

Employees: 14,700
Sales: $1.1 billion
Profits: $93 million
Founded: 1901
Headquarters: Fremont, Michigan

In 1927 Mrs. Dan Gerber (the company never identifies her by *her* name) complained to her husband about the chore of straining peas for their newborn baby. So Dan, whose father happened to own a cannery in Fremont, Michigan, started to strain the peas for his baby at the plant. Before long he was doing it for millions of babies. Today, Gerber—still based in Fremont—packs 165 varieties of cereals, fruits, juices and "main dish" combinations, and they control 70 percent of the market they invented: baby foods.

Gerber used to snipe at competitors Heinz and Beech-Nut with the slogan, "Babies are our business—our *only* business," but they had to drop that after buying into insurance, toys, day-care, furniture, clothing and trucking. However, they've had a hard time making anything but baby foods work. In recent years they shucked off the trucking, furniture and toy subsidiaries.

The Gerbers are no longer active in day-to-day management, but they still control close to 20 percent of the stock. Dan Gerber, a writer, is on the board, however. The board had to go outside the company in 1987 to recruit Australian David W. Johnson as CEO. He succeeded Leo D. Goulet, who died suddenly of a heart attack. Johnson didn't stay long, however. In 1989 he accepted the job as CEO of Campbell Soup. He was suc-

In 1928, artist Dorothy Hope Smith submitted this unfinished drawing to Gerber authorities for initial approval. The rough sketch was found to be so appealing that it became the company's trademark.

ceeded by 42-year-old Alfred A. Piergallini, who holds an MBA from the University of Chicago and was a senior vice president at Carnation before moving to Gerber. Gerber has been on every list of likely takeover targets posted during the past 15 years.

Gerber took some flak in 1986 after a widely publicized report of glass found in a baby food jar. Shortly after that stonewalling, William L. McKinley left the chief executive's post. In 1989 they came out with Gerber Baby formula, made by Bristol-Myers. Because infant formulas have been so controversial in recent years, Gerber uses ads admitting that breastfeeding is in the best interest of the baby. Gerber made up for a lot of their recent bad press when, in 1990, they made a special baby food called MBF for one customer—a severely allergic 15-year-old boy. The company had stopped making MBF (made of beef hearts, sesame oil and sugar) in 1985 because of declining sales. When they discovered that the boy, Raymond Dunn, Jr., would die without it, Gerber decided to allot one-quarter of the production space at their research center to make the special formula. Gerber

research director, George Purvis, explained: "People here are working on this on their own time."

Stock performance. Gerber stock bought for $1,000 in 1980 sold for $13,898 on January 2, 1990.

Consumer brands.

Gerber, Buster Brown childrenwear.

Gerber Products Company, 445 State Street, Fremont, MI 49412; (616) 928-2000.

5

#1 *in cranberries, fruit juices*

Employees: 2,200
Sales: $873 million
Founded: 1930
Headquarters: Plymouth, Massachusetts

Ocean Spray and cranberries are synonymous and not merely because of slick advertising. This grower-owned cooperative harvests, juices, packages, promotes, distributes and sells nearly all the cranberries in the U.S. Unlike the early days when most cranberries were sold for Thanksgiving and Christmas feasts, over 70 percent of Ocean Spray's present sales are from juices. Because of health-conscious consumers, sales have jumped 1,500 percent since Cranapple juice first appeared on supermarket shelves in 1967. Ocean Spray now sells more than 16 juices and juice drinks in more than six different containers, including the popular paper bottle. By 1981, Ocean Spray had become the biggest U.S. seller of canned and bottled juice drinks.

History. The Pilgrims and Indians probably didn't eat cranberries when they sat down to their first Thanksgiving dinner. There was not enough sugar around to sweeten the bitter berries. Colonists later found a use for the cranberries that grew wild in New Jersey and on Cape Cod. They concocted a potent libation of cranberries, water, oatmeal and rum.

Cranberries were largely ignored as a cash crop until the late 19th century when growers discovered the advantages of flooding the cranberry marshes, or bogs. The berry vines grow deep roots and thrive in acidic soils, and water protects the berries from frost. Harvesters cover the bogs with several feet of water and drive a machine called an "egg beater" across the plants. The beater churns the water and loosens the berries that are then scooped up for processing. About 80 percent of all cranberries are harvested this way.

Early in the 20th century, growers found a market for their berries. A Boston lawyer named Marcus Urann, also known as the "Cranberry King," developed a cranberry sauce recipe that could be cooked in large vats and preserved in tins. The first can of cranberry sauce went on the market in 1912 under the Ocean Spray name.

From the start Ocean Spray was a cooperative venture, owned by Massachusetts growers. In 1930, they merged with similar co-ops in Massachusetts and New Jersey. In 1940, Wisconsin growers joined up and a year later, Oregon and Washington growers signed on. They pooled their cranberries and for 30 years were satisfied with selling their fruit canned or fresh during the holiday season.

But their modest success did not last. In 1959, a cancer scare almost wiped out the fledgling cooperative. Two weeks before Thanksgiving, the government announced that an herbicide called amino triazale, used by many growers to kill poison ivy, caused cancer in laboratory rats. Frightened grocers pulled the cranberries from their shelves and sales crashed. Subsequent business was so bad that some growers complained they couldn't give their berries away. "We were jolted into trying to find another use for our crop," said Ocean Spray grower Jay Normington. Desperate growers turned to marketers for help. They lured Hal Thorkilsen away from cigarette maker Philip Morris and swallowed his advice to turn their crop into juices. "It was not a popular recommendation," Thorkilsen recalled.

However, their investment in new processing plants paid off. In 1974, Ocean Spray placed 916th in the *Fortune* list of the top 1,000 companies. A decade later, the cooperative was in the top 500.

Ocean Spray avoided the competitive orange juice market, dominated by Coca-Cola's Minute Maid and Beatrice's Tropicana, and instead concentrated on selling their own fruit mixed with blueberries, apples, apricots, raspberries and whatnot. They sold the juices with the slogan "It's good for you, America." In 1976, the company branched out into grapefruit juice by allying with citrus growers from Florida's Indian River region. Five years later, Ocean Spray helped pioneer the highly successful paper bottle, an aseptic container that fits neatly into a lunch box. Ocean Spray entered the chilled section of the supermarket with Crantastic, a multijuice drink, and pushed further into the blended juice market in 1983 with a guava-lemon drink called Mauna-La'i. Their only lemon was Cranprune, a cranberry and prune juice mixture.

Owners and rulers. Ocean Spray is owned by 650 cranberry and 125 citrus growers in Massachusetts, New Jersey, Florida, Wisconsin, Texas, Washington and Canada. The cranberry and citrus operations are kept separate; neither shares in the profits of the other. But all other costs, including marketing and distribution, are handled as if they were line extensions of the same market group. Harold Thorkilsen retired as president and CEO in 1987, and John S. Llewellyn, Jr., succeeded him.

As a place to work. Ocean Spray employees often see their names in print. The company newsletter, "Ocean Spray Life," regularly publishes announcements of births, weddings, retirements, promotions and even the fishing triumphs of some 2,200 workers. Employees are also encouraged to speak out in the newsletter's "Letters to the Editor" column. Benefits include a retirement plan to which Ocean Spray contributes 50 cents on every dollar employees tuck away in the plan. Ocean Spray paid $368,000 into it in 1987.

Social responsibility. In 1988, Ocean Spray pleaded guilty to illegally dumping cranberry peelings and acidic waste into a Massachusetts river and sewer system from 1983 to 1987. Under the Clean Water Act, the company was fined $400,000 for

21 misdemeanor charges; Ocean Spray also donated water-treatment equipment worth $100,000 to Middleboro, Massachusetts.

Global presence. Ocean Spray is strictly a domestic producer, but their drinks and sauces are sold in almost 40 countries.

Ocean Spray Cranberries, Inc., 225 Water Street, Plymouth, MA 02360; 617-747-1000.

CANDY

If Americans are off on a health kick, it hasn't interfered with their candy consumption. In 1980 the average American ate 15.7 pounds of candy a year; by 1990 intake was nearing 20 pounds. The dollar figures were even better because the price of a candy bar escalated during the decade from 25 cents to 45 cents (50 cents in some cases). Two companies, Hershey and Mars, dominate this $8 billion industry, accounting for nearly 40 percent of sales and an 80 percent share of the entire market.

1

Hershey Foods Corporation

#1 *in chocolate and candy*

#2 *in pasta*

Employees: 12,000
Sales: $2.4 billion
Profits: $171 million
Founded: 1900
Headquarters: Hershey, Pennsylvania

Social Conscience

Hershey is, perhaps more than any other company except Coca-Cola, an American institution. They make an innocent product, chocolate, and their candy bars are sold in tens of thousands of places across the country: movie theaters, groceries, drugstores, five-and-dimes, tobacco shops, candy stores, vending machines. In all, more than 1 million stores sell Hershey products. To make their milk chocolate, Hershey buys milk from 1,000 farms that graze 50,000 cows to supply the company's needs. Every day, Hershey uses enough milk to supply all the people in a city the size of Salt Lake City. Hershey is also the nation's largest single user of almonds.

These days, Hershey is still an American institution, but they are also very canny operators. In 1989, CEO Richard Zimmerman declared, "We think of ourselves as a manufacturer of food products,

Milton Hershey and one of his "boys".

not just chocolate products." Hershey is now the number two maker of pasta in the U.S. (Borden is first), selling under the brand names Ronzoni, San Giorgio, P&R and American Beauty. And they get rid of whatever doesn't work. In August 1989, they sold off the floundering Friendly restaurant chain for $375 million.

In the 1980s, Hershey relished the sweet taste of success. In 1980, they had just over 15 percent of the U.S. confectionery market; in 1988, they had 20.5 percent. They purchased their way to this impressive showing, beginning with the 1986 purchase of Dietrich for $100 million (Dietrich makes Luden's Cough Drops, Mellomints, 5th Avenue candy bars, Queen Anne chocolates). In July 1989, Hershey edged into first place in the candy business (ousting longtime rival Mars) when they paid $300 million for the American division of Cadbury Schweppes (Peter Paul Almond Joy, Mounds and York Peppermint Patty brands). Hershey now sells 9 of the 20 top-selling candy products.

In addition to the Hershey line of chocolate products, they sell Reese's Peanut Butter Cups (as a result of a 1963 acquisition), Kit Kat wafer bars and Rolo chocolate-covered caramels (via a 1970 licensing agreement with Britain's

Rowntree Mackintosh) and Y&S licorice (via a 1977 acquisition).

History. Hershey Foods is the legacy of one man, Milton Snavely Hershey, who grew up in the Pennsylvania Dutch country of Mennonite farmers, where the highest virtues were hard work, religious devotion and simplicity. Apprenticed at age 15 to a candy maker in Lancaster, Pennsylvania, at 19 he was off—first to Philadelphia, then to Denver, Chicago, New Orleans, and New York, all the while practicing the candy trade. At the 1893 Chicago Exposition, Hershey spotted an innovative chocolate-making machine from Germany. He bought the machinery and toted it to Pennsylvania, where he began making chocolate-coated caramels. The caramels were made with a fresh milk recipe he picked up in Denver, Colorado. According to an official company biography, Milton Hershey "lived in small drab houses and worked in bleak basement kitchens for long hours each day." All of Lancaster, including his mother, was surprised then when he came home with a bride, the beautiful Catherine Sweeney of Jamestown, New York, whom he had met in a candy shop where she was employed. They were married in the rectory of New York's St. Patrick's Cathedral in 1898, when Hershey was 41 years old.

In 1900, Hershey sold his profitable candy business, the Lancaster Caramel Company, for $1 million. But by 1905 he was back in the candy biz with a factory 30 miles from Lancaster in the town where he was born, Derry Church—renamed Hershey in 1906. By 1911 Milton Hershey's new company was selling $5 million worth of chocolate a year.

But Milton Hershey was interested in creating more than a chocolate company. He had been reared on the Mennonite precept that money was not to be used for personal gratification. In 1909 he and Mrs. Hershey, who were never to have children, founded and personally financed the Milton Hershey School for orphaned boys. The first classes were held in the farmhouse where Hershey had been born. ("Every time I see these boys playing on the lawn," Milton Hershey once said, "I think of the time when I roamed these fields as a barefoot boy.")

In 1918 the prosperous chocolate company was donated to a trust for the school.

TOP CANDY BARS

	Sales
Snickers Bar (Mars)	$440 million
Reese's Peanut Butter Cups (Hershey)	$350 million
M&M's Peanut Chocolate Candies	$320 million
M&M's Plain Chocolate Candies	$310 million
Kit Kat (Hershey)	$160 million
Hershey's Milk Chocolate with Almonds	$155 million
Milky Way Bar (Mars)	$150 million
Hershey's Milk Chocolate	$145 million
Crunch (Nestlé)	$125 million
Butterfinger (Nabisco Brands)	$115 million

Source: The *Wall Street Journal*, 29 March 1989. Sales are for 1988.

In effect, the orphanage owned the Hershey company (and it is still the largest shareholder). Meanwhile, the town of Hershey grew under the benevolent prodding of its founder. Milton Hershey built a planned community, homes were built and rented or sold to Hershey workers. In 1927, 20 percent of the Hershey company's stock was sold to the public, and the Hershey shares were listed on the New York Stock Exchange.

The Great Depression was a motivator for Milton Hershey. While his business associates were concerned about conserving assets, Hershey wanted to put unemployed people to work. On a hill overlooking the town a grand luxury hotel, patterned after a Mediterranean resort, went up. Near the hotel an extensive rose garden was planted; today it covers more than 23 acres. Five golf courses were created, making Hershey the "golf capital of Pennsylvania." A Romanesque community center was erected to house the Hershey Public Library and two

theaters. The Hershey Museum of American Life was opened, featuring collections of native American, Eskimo and Pennsylvania German artifacts. A sports arena with seating for 10,000 was built; the Hershey Bears, a professional hockey team, play there; and the Ice Capades were born on the Hershey rink in 1940. Finally, in 1939 the Hershey Park Stadium was completed as a setting for college football games, concerts, rodeos and other outdoor shows; it seats 16,000, considerably more than the total population of Hershey (then or now).

Milton Hershey died on October 13, 1945, exactly one month after his 88th birthday. One of Hershey's legacies was his refusal to advertise. "Give them quality," he said. "That's the best kind of advertising." That long tradition ended on July 19, 1970, when a full-page ad for Hershey's syrup ran in 114 newspapers. With candy-consuming youngsters growing up in front of a TV tube, Hershey felt they could no longer afford not to toot their own horn. In 1988, they spent $298 million on advertising, making Hershey the 35th largest advertisers in the U.S.

Owners and rulers. The Hershey Trust Company, which operates the orphanage Milton Hershey founded, remains the dominant shareholder but in recent years has been reducing holdings. They're now down to 31 percent of all the common stock. However, the trust retains effective control of the company by holding 99 percent of the Class B shares, which have 10 votes per share.

As a place to work. Hershey provides a good, clean environment for their employees. They are not paid fabulously (there has never been a union at Hershey), but the company takes care of their people with above-average benefits. The workforce is predominantly white, and no females work in the upper ranks of the company.

Social responsibility. Good citizenship is something Milton Hershey built into the core of this company, and it's reflected most dramatically in the town of Hershey, which still depends heavily on its corporate patron. Hershey is also careful about the kind of promotion they direct at children, and has been an industrial leader in providing nutritional information on labels.

The Milton Hershey School admitted girls for the first time in 1978, and two years later the company placed their first woman on the board of directors.

G*lobal presence.* Minimal—in 1988 only 2 percent of Hershey sales were from ouside the U.S. and Canada.

S*tock performance.* Hershey stock bought for $1,000 in 1980 sold for $12,589 on January 2, 1990.

C*onsumer brands.*

Candy products: Hershey's, Reese's, Krackel, Kit Kat, Mr. Goodbar, Whatchamacallit, After Eight, NibNax, Y&S licorice, Marabou, Rolo, Peter Paul Almond Joy, Mounds, York Peppermint patty, 5th Avenue, Queen Anne, Mellomints, Luden's Cough Drops.

Pasta: San Giorgio, Ronzoni, Delmonico, Skinner, P&R (Procino-Rossi), American Beauty.

Other: Cory Food Service.

Hershey Foods Corporation, 19 East Chocolate Avenue, Hershey, PN 17033; (717) 534-4200.

2

#1 *in rice*
#2 *in candy*
#3 *in pet food*

Employees: 22,000
Sales: $8.5 billion
Founded: 1911
Headquarters: McLean, Virginia

According to *Forbes*, the Mars family fortune is worth $5.2 billion. According to *Fortune*, it's worth $12.5 billion. That's a big spread, but none of the Mars family is about to set us straight. Mars is a privately held company, controlled by the Mars family, and they are notoriously secretive. No plant tours. No annual report. No information whatsoever is presented to the public except in advertising, where Mars spends about $400 million a year to tout their brands. However, even at the low estimate, the Mars family fortune is one of the biggest in the world. You probably would never have guessed there was so much money in a Snickers bar.

Of course, Mars is more than Snickers, the top-selling candy bar in the U.S. They make 100 million M&M's *every day*. They make a dozen other candy bars, including 3 Musketeers, Twix, Milky Way and Starburst; they own one of the leading rice brands, Uncle Ben's; and they compete in the pet food market under the Kal Kan label. They are also a major force in Europe, especially Britain. Ten years ago their sales were estimated at $1 billion. Now they are estimated at over $8 billion. Not a bad decade.

H*istory.* In 1911, Frank C. Mars and his wife Ethel cooked up big batches of buttercream candies in the kitchen of their home in Tacoma, Washington. The candies were so popular they decided to open a candy factory. In 1920 they moved to Minneapolis and began trying to create the ultimate candy bar. His first try was a number called the Mar-O-Bar, but no one bought it. He struck gold with his second try—Snickers. The bar became popular as a treat in hot weather (the first Snickers had no chocolate coating). Mars was on a roll. That same year, his son Forrest suggested making a candy bar with malted milk and chocolate. Milky Way was an instant hit.

Father and son didn't get along, however. Tensions finally led the father to hand his 30-year-old son $50,000 to go overseas and to produce Mars' candy abroad. Forrest promptly set up business in Britain where he became wildly successful by making Milky Way's chocolate coating sweeter and selling packaged pet foods. Forrest returned to the U.S. in 1940 and founded his own company, named after a candy product he masterminded: M&M's. (To get the name, Mars combined the first letter of his last name with the first letter of the last name of a close associate, Bruce Murrie.) Mars' genius extended to other foods as well. He introduced a line of pet foods and developed a rice-processing technique that led to the mega-hit product, Uncle Ben's rice. Famous for his temper tantrums (he once threw candy bars at a window during a business meeting), Forrest Mars forced even the highest-level executives to

TOP GUMS

	Market Share
Wrigley	46.5%
Warner-Lambert	29.5%
Nabisco Brands	17.5%
Other	6.5%

Source: The New York Times, November 1988.

punch a time clock. He once told employees, "I'm a religious man. I pray for Milky Way. I pray for Snickers." In 1964 Forrest merged his company with his father's, and the family was well on its way to becoming one of the richest in America.

Forrest retired from Mars in 1973 but started yet another candy business, named after his late mother—the Ethel M. Candy Co., producing liqueur-flavored chocolates. Like his own father, Forrest later sold the company to his two sons. Forrest now lives in what has been described as Howard Hughes–like seclusion in a penthouse over his candy factory in Las Vegas. There are few known photographs of him. His own aversion to publicity extends to company executives, who are forbidden to have their pictures taken for publications.

Owners and rulers. Forrest's twin sons, Forrest, Jr., and John Mars, rule the roost as co-presidents. Forrest, Jr. (aged 59 in 1990), runs the candy division, while John (54) runs the rest of the Mars food empire, such as their pet food and Uncle Ben's rice divisions. Like his father, Forrest, Jr., is known for his temper tantrums and also for taking his socks and shoes off during office meetings. His more subdued brother was trained as an engineer. The only known pictures of them are from their Yale yearbook.

The brothers are not considered as capable as their father. From all reports, they suffer a severe case of sibling rivalry, constantly competing for control of the company. Yet neither is liked or respected by the rank and file. "Neither of these guys is equipped to run a multi-billion-dollar company," a former Mars manager told Fortune. Some consider each man a liability, but in different ways. John, says another former executive, "sees people as a necessary evil. If he could run the company without them, he would." Forrest, the temperamental twin, is undergoing a huge divorce settlement that could, according to Fortune, cause a partial breakup of the company.

As a place to work. The company is called "the Kremlin," and no outsider knows exactly what goes on inside. But even so Mars is an egalitarian employer. Everyone, from executives to floor moppers, punches a time clock. The workers are called "associates." The company brochure brags, "No one at Mars has an office. No one." Instead, managers and staff alike sit in wagon-wheel arrangements in an open-plan space so everyone can see what everyone else is up to. Everyone eats in the same company dining room, where they can sample snacks fresh from the assembly line.

One union report claimed Mars "employees are encouraged to feel like members—though not necessarily an adult member—of a 'big Mars' family." Their wages and working conditions are excellent, so much so that union officials have given up trying to organize Mars workers. But apparently a feeling of frustration is spreading through the ranks, especially among managers, at being held back from trying anything new through most of the 1980s. That tide may have turned in 1989 when Hershey took the lead in the candy market. Mars reacted vigorously by introducing new products, such as peanut butter M&M's and Milky Way Dark (dark chocolate and vanilla nougat).

The company's plants are reputed to be so clean they would pass the most thoroughgoing inspection. "Their dog food plants are cleaner than some hospitals I've been in," an advertising executive told Fortune. The company brochure says, "If you could visit [our plants], we know you'd be impressed."

Social responsibility. Mars caused a public furor in 1976 when they suddenly stopped making red M&M's. A consumer outcry followed, demanding to know why. The answer: the FDA banned Red Dye No. 2 that year, after finding it caused cancer in rats. So Mars promptly pulled red M&M's off the market "to avoid consumer confusion and concern." So they said.

The catch: Mars had never used Red Dye No. 2 in making their famous red M&M's. But apparently they thought the public couldn't absorb that information without making a dent in sales, so they took the drastic step of dumping the popular red M&M's altogether for the next 11 years. Finally, after a trial Christmas run, Mars brought back the red M&M's in 1987, to their customers' delight. But why then and no sooner? "We decided that there was such a large popular demand for it that we ought to bring it back," is all the company's PR person would say in response to queries.

Consumer brands.

Candy: Snickers, M&M's, Bounty, Mars, Milky Way, Kudos, Holidays, Skittles, Starburst, Twix, 3 Musketeers, Balisto.

Ice cream: Dove, Rondos.

Foods: Uncle Ben's, Combos.

Pet foods: Kal Kan, Whiskas, Sheba.

Mars Inc., 1651 Old Meadow Rd., Westgate Park, McLean, VA 22102; (703) 821-4900.

3

Wm. **WRIGLEY** Jr. Company

Wrigley enticed his buyers with unusual premiums such as this 4'9" thermometer (above) and a 10" Wizard cigar lighter (below).

#1 *in chewing gum*

Employees: 5,600
Sales: $993 million
Profits: $106 million
Founded: 1892
Headquarters: Chicago, Illinois

A throwback to another era, Chicago's Wrigley chewing gum company held to their monomaniacal agenda during the 1980s. In an age when companies make numerous products, they concentrate on one. In an age of mergers, they remain single. In an age of slick, irreverent advertising, they persist in simple, virginal commercials à la the twins in the Doublemint campaign ("double your pleasure"). In an age of absentee owners, they're still controlled by the founding family. And in the 1980s the one outside link the family had—to the Chicago Cubs—was disconnected. So it's now back to bedrock: chewing gum.

Ironically, founder William Wrigley, Jr., gave gum away before he sold it. A gregarious salesman, at age 16 Wrigley was riding a horse-drawn wagon from town to town in Pennsylvania, selling his father's soap to retailers and giving away a box of baking soda to go with it. The gum was a gimmick, something he threw in with the baking soda.

Wrigley was 29 in 1891, when he came to Chicago from Philadelphia with $32 in his pocket. A year later he switched from soap to gum, and by 1910 Wrigley's Spearmint was America's biggest-selling gum. At the same time, Wrigley was setting up gum companies abroad—first in Canada (1910), then in Australia (1915) and Great Britain (1927).

After Wrigley died in 1932, his son Philip took over and ran the company until his death in 1977. During World War II, when ingredients of the usual quality weren't available, Wrigley continued to make gum, using what they could get. But they refused to put their name on this inferior product. As owner of the Chicago Cubs and their stadium, Wrigley Field, Philip Wrigley refused to allow home games at night. Only in 1988, after the team had been sold to the *Chicago Tribune*, did the field finally get night lighting.

For over 75 years, Wrigley made only three kinds of gum: the familiar Doublemint, Spearmint, and Juicy Fruit. In 1974 Wrigley came up with something new for the first time in 59 years—Freedent for denture wearers. The next year they introduced Big Red, a cinnamon-flavored gum. Wrigley refused to make sugarless gum until 1977, when they finally brought out Orbit. (Unfortunately, British researchers later discovered Orbit's main sweetener, xylitol, was a carcinogen.) The next year they gave us a soft bubble gum, Hubba Bubba. Extra, a sugar-free gum introduced in 1984, has now passed Warner-Lambert's Trident.

In 1988 Wrigley was chomping on 46.5 percent of the $2.5 billion a year gum market. In 1989, they bought Reed Candy (sales: $10 million).

William Wrigley, grandson of the founder, has been president and CEO since he was 28 in 1961. Wrigley owns a quarter of the common stock; he's worth over $500 million, putting him high on the Forbes 400 list of the richest Americans. Yet, in 1989 William Wrigley earned a relatively modest sum for a CEO: $679,000. He has prevented the company from diversifying, instead focusing on expanding the market for gum.

Stock performance. Wrigley stock bought for $1,000 in 1980 sold for $11,112 on January 2, 1990.

Consumer brands.

Wrigley's Spearmint, Doublemint, Juicy Fruit, Big Red, Freedent, Extra, Hubba Bubba, Big League Chew, Bubble Tape.

Wm. Wrigley Jr. Company, 410 North Michigan Avenue, Chicago, IL 60611; (312) 644-2121.

4

Tootsie Roll Industries

#1 *in lollipops*

Employees: 1,330
Sales: $179 million
Profits: $20 million
Founded: 1896
Headquarters: Chicago, Illinois

They make 10 million Tootsie Rolls a day, plus a variety of other jaw-breaking, tooth-destroying candies like Mason Dots, Bonomo Turkish Taffy and Charms lollipops. Between Tootsie Roll Pops and Charms, they make more than half of the 3 billion lollipops licked each year in the U.S. It all added up in 1989 to sales of $179 million on which the company netted $20 million after paying salaries and taxes. The leaders are the husband-and-wife team of Melvin (he's chairman) and Ellen (she's president) Gordon. They own almost 60 percent of the shares. Ellen Gordon inherited Tootsie Roll Industries from her father, William Rubin, who bought the company in the 1930s. "Tootsie Roll" was the nickname of the daughter of an Austrian candy maker who immigrated to the U.S. and began making the candy in 1892. The Gordons keep a low profile. They sometimes don't even bother to attend the company's annual meeting (they already know the news).

Headquartered on the West Side of Chicago, Tootsie Roll hews to some old-fashioned ideas. They have no long-term debt. They don't spend much money on advertising. They're not interested in anything but the candy business. And they have no plans to sell out to a larger company. In fact, they intend to hand control over to their four daughters—an investment banker, an engineer, a doctor and a Harvard student. They have to compete for the sweet tooth, but as Mrs. Gordon says: "No one else can make a Tootsie Roll."

Stock performance. Tootsie Roll stock bought for $1,000 in 1980 sold for $21,082 on January 2, 1990.

Consumer brands.

Tootsie Roll, Tootsie Pop, Tootsie Bubble Pop, Tootsie Pop Drops, Tootsie Roll Flavor Rolls, Mason Dots, Cella's chocolate covered cherries, Charms Blow Pops.

Tootsie Roll Industries, 7401 S. Cicero Avenue, Chicago, IL 60629; (312) 838-3400.

SOFT DRINKS

Compared to their parents, the Baby Boomers are a bunch of teetotalers. Since 1980 wine sales have declined slightly, beer sales are up a little, hard liquor sales are down by more than 10 percent, milk is about even, tea is down—and soft drink sales (measured by quantities guzzled) are up 30 percent.

1

#1 *in soft drinks*
#2 *in orange juice*

Employees: 19,900
Sales: $9 billion
Profits: $1.7 billion
Founded: 1886
Headquarters: Atlanta Georgia

The Coca-Cola Company likes to collect "gee-whizzers." And they have to keep updating them because of soaring sales. In the 1970s they estimated that if all the Coca-Cola ever consumed by the human race were poured over Niagara Falls, the falls would flow at their normal rate for 8 hours and 57 minutes. A decade later, this figure was 23 hours and 21 minutes.

Even more amazing is that in 1886 when Coca-Cola was introduced, they sold an average of nine drinks a day that year. In 1988, according to the "gee-whiz" collectors in Atlanta, Coke was served 560 million times every day of the year. They're incorrigible, these Coca-Cola statisticians. They've also let us know that all the Coke consumed in 1980 would fill one of the towers of the New York's World Trade Center 80 times from the ground to the 110th floor or fill 213,000 Olympic-sized swimming pools. They go on and on. If all the Coke ever consumed were placed in the old 6 1/2-inch bottles, there would be 2.4 trillion bottles that, laid end to end, could wrap around the earth 11,863 times, reach the moon 1,237 times or stretch one-third of the way to Saturn. Give up?

TOP POPS
(What Makes America Fizz)

		Market Share
1.	Coca-Cola Classic	20.0%
2.	Pepsi-Cola	18.5%
3.	Diet Coke	8.2%
4.	Diet Pepsi	5.2%
5.	Dr Pepper	4.3%
6.	Sprite (Coca-Cola)	3.6%
7.	Mountain Dew (Pepsi)	3.4%
8.	Seven-Up	3.1%
9.	Caffeine Free Diet Coke	2.0%
10.	RC Cola	1.6%

Source: *Beverage World*, March 1989.

The point is, Coke is very big—the biggest beverage in the world except for water. And despite what seemed to be an incredible blunder in the 1980s—changing the Coke formula to more closely resemble Pepsi's—Coca-Cola not only survived this gaffe, they thrived. So much so that some people suspected it was all a planned maneuver. There are now seven different versions of Coke—Coca-Cola Classic, New Coke, Caffeine-Free Coca-Cola, Cherry Coke, Diet Cherry Coke, Diet Coke, and Caffeine-Free Diet Coke. Added to the Coca-Cola lineup are Sprite, Mr. Pibb, Fanta, Fresca and Mello Yello.

Coke did other things before the 1980s—Minute Maid orange juice, regional coffees and wines (now sold)—but during this past decade they moved boldly into the entertainment business. In 1982, Coca-Cola bought Columbia Pictures for about $700 million, to which they added Tri-Star Pictures in 1987. Poor Columbia. Coke hired and fired three studio chiefs in five years, and presided over one of the biggest movie debacles of the 1980s—the mega-flop *Ishtar*. But don't cry for Coke. They sold the whole works to Sony for $3.4 billion in 1989.

History. John Styth Pemberton, an Atlanta pharmacist who fooled around with patent medicines, invented Coca-Cola in 1886. Some of his other concoctions were Triplex liver pills, Globe of Flower cough syrup, Indian Queen hair dye, Gingerine, Extract of Styllinger (a blood medicine) and French Wine Coca. One day, Pemberton decided to brew a batch of special syrup in a big iron pot in his backyard. He used sugar, water, a host of flavorings (which chemists later identified as cinnamon, nutmeg, lime juice, vanilla, guarana and glycerin, among others). Pemberton also added a "secret" ingredient, believed to be a flavoring mixture derived from coca leaves (with the cocaine removed) and cola nuts. The result was dubbed Coca-Cola—and Pemberton claimed it could cure headaches, sluggishness, indigestion and throbbing temples resulting from overindulgence.

Two years later, Pemberton died and his business changed hands several times, ending up with another Atlanta pharmacist, Asa Candler. Candler promoted Coca-Cola as a nostrum (he himself took it for his headaches and dyspepsia) but quickly realized its potential as a soda fountain drink. He poured money into advertising: Painted Coca-Cola signs went up on barns, trays, Japanese fans, bookmarks and glasses. By 1895 Coke was sold in every state and territory in the country.

Asa Candler made the syrup but didn't bottle it. In 1899 he signed a contract giving two lawyers the rights to bottle Coca-Cola in the entire U.S. for one dollar. The lawyers were the middlemen, buying the syrup from the Coca-Cola Company and reselling it to local bottlers. This franchise system continues today (although the largest bottler, Coca-Cola Enterprises, Inc., is now 49 percent owned by Coke).

In 1919 the Candler family sold the company to financier Ernest Woodruff for $25 million (it was the largest financial transaction that had ever taken place in the South).

In 1923, Ernest's son Robert Winship Woodruff, 33, took over. (He retired in 1955 and died in 1985). A marketing genius, Woodruff used massive amounts of advertising to elevate a 5-cent soft drink into a national symbol as significant as baseball and hot dogs. Few employees actually were needed to manufacture the syrup; most were in market research and sales, busy establishing the Coca-Cola mythology. Deloney Sledge, longtime advertising director of Coca-Cola, once said, "It was a religion... The product has some kind of strange characteristic.... I think it's symbolism. I don't know why, I've spent up to 50 years now trying to figure it out."

During World War II, "Mr. Bob" (as Robert Woodruff was known) boldly declared: "We will see that every man in uniform gets a bottle of Coca-Cola for 5-cents wherever he is and whatever it costs." General Dwight D. Eisenhower, a Coke fancier, agreed. While competing soft-drink companies watched helplessly, Coca-Cola bottling plants were set up near all battle fronts. When the war was over, Coca-Cola had 64 overseas bottling plants in place, most of them ferried over at the expense of U.S. tax payers. Coke jingles over the years have been the terse "Drink Coca-Cola" in 1886, to the 1988's "Can't Beat the Feeling." In 1982 Coke established their first corporate licensing department, stamping the Coke trademark on beach towels and posters. Two years later they licensed Coke sportswear for men, women and children.

Owners and rulers. Fayez S. Saofim holds 8.4 million shares of Coca-Cola, which in early 1990 were worth $483 million. Financier Warren Buffet held even more: his 6.3 percent of Coke's stock was worth more than $1 billion. In 1981, at age 49, Cuban-born Roberto C. Goizueta (pronounced Goy-SWET-ah) became CEO and chairman of Coca-Cola. Goizueta holds a degree in chemical engineering from Yale and started at the Coca-Cola Bottling Co. of Havana when he was 22, working his way up through the ranks. He is a hard-driving chain-smoker. In 1982 he told Sky magazine, "I'm in favor of *legends,* and particularly the Coca-Cola *legend.* However, I'm even more in favor of the Coca-Cola *ledger* which shows growing profits." Goizueta is certainly aware of his own pocketbook. In 1989 he pulled in $10.8 million, making him the best-paid of the CEOs of *Forbes'* Super-50, their list of the 50 largest companies. Iowa-bred Donald R. Keough, Coke's president and chief operating officer, isn't short on cash either. He was the ninth on *Business Week*'s list of the highest paid non-CEOs in 1989 when he took home a total of $6.19 million. Goizueta flushed out the last Candler (Asa's grandson Charles Howard, Jr.) from the board by instituting a mandatory retirement age for directors. In 1989, there was one woman (Anne Cox Chambers) on the board of directors and two minorities; one is CEO Goizueta and the other is Donald McHenry, the former U.N. ambassador, who is black. Of the company's top officers, 12 are women and 9 are minorities. In 1988, the company decided to build a Coke museum in Atlanta, filled with memorabilia and free samples of Coke products.

As a place to work. Coke has a benevolent reputation. Minorities are strongly represented throughout the company, for example. When Goizueta took over as chairman, the firm experienced a corporate cultural revolution. Aggressive merchandising became the name of the game, and developing management talent was one of Goizueta's priorities, including recruiting young people for top corporate spots.

Social responsibility. A social and cultural bulwark of Atlanta. Coke used to be the second-largest employer in South Africa, until 1986 when they "disinvested." However, Coke continues to be the best-selling drink there and, as critics charge, the bottlers continue to bottle the Coke syrup.

Global presence. You better believe it. Coke is sold in 160 countries, and the company earns 75 percent of their profits outside the U.S. In 1989, they sold 47 percent of the soft drinks worldwide.

Stock performance. Coca-Cola stock bought for $1,000 in 1980 sold for $10,385 on January 2, 1990.

Consumer brands.

Coca-Cola, Coke, Sprite, Hi-C, Five Alive, Minute Maid, Fanta, Mr. Pibb, Fresca, Mello Yello.

The Coca-Cola Company, One Coca-Cola Plaza, N.W., Atlanta, GA 30313; (404) 676-2121.

2

#1 *in salted snacks, chicken, pizza, and Mexican restaurants*

#2 *in soft drinks*

Employees: 250,000
Sales: $15.2 billion
Profits: $901 million
Founded: 1919
Headquarters: Purchase, New York

Pepsi-Cola has been playing second fiddle to Coca-Cola for the entire 20th century. However, they're a very *big* fiddle whose sound grew louder and louder during the 1980s. Pepsi fired some big guns at Coke during this decade—Michael Jackson, Mike Tyson and (in a very brief burst) Madonna—but in the end Coca-Cola remained number one. Coke sells about 40 percent of all soft drinks, Pepsi about 30 percent.

But PepsiCo, parent company of Pepsi-Cola, is more than soft drinks. In fact, during the 1980s, when they nearly tripled their sales, they became a company of three equal parts: soft drinks (Pepsi, Mountain Dew), snacks (Frito-Lay) and restaurants (Kentucky Fried Chicken, Pizza Hut, Taco Bell).

To keep this engine in motion, PepsiCo employs 250,000 people, more than 10 times as many as Coca-Cola (restaurants are labor-intensive), operates more than 100 manufacturing plants, controls more than 1,000 bottlers and runs more than 6,000 restaurants.

History. In the 1890s, inspired by an Atlanta pharmacist's success with Coca-Cola, imitators popped up everywhere, keeping the patent lawyers busy. In New Bern, North Carolina, another pharmacist, Caleb D. Bradham, concocted a cola syrup he called Pepsi-Cola. He dropped the drugstore business entirely by 1902, and a year later registered the Pepsi-Cola name. By 1909 there were 250 Pepsi bottlers in 24 states. Bradham advertised: "Pepsi-Cola is the Original Pure Food Drink—guaranteed under the U.S. Gov't. Serial No. 3818. At all soda fountains, 5 cents a glass—at your grocer's, 5 cents a bottle."

Bradham went broke after World War I, and Pepsi changed hands a lot, finally ending up during the Depression in New York City as an appendage of the Loft candy shop chain. Enter Walter Mack, who in the early 1940s made Pepsi the number two soft drink in America. Mack headed Pepsi-Cola from 1938 to 1951, and used memorable advertising jingles to promote Pepsi. For instance, in pushing Pepsi's 12-ounce bottle (versus Coke's classic 6-ounce size), the company used lyrics writen to an old English hunting song, "D'ye Ken John Peel":

Pepsi-Cola hits the spot
Twelve full ounces, that's a lot
Twice as much for a nickel, too
Pepsi-Cola is the drink for you.

During the 1950s, Pepsi stopped emphasizing cheap price and began representing themselves as the beverage for "those who think young": the Pepsi Generation. In 1957, Donald M. Kendall became head of Pepsi-Cola's international division and began a long-standing relationship with consumers in the Soviet Union (he got Nikita Khrushchev to knock back nine bottles of Pepsi during his debate with Richard Nixon at the 1959 Moscow Trade Fair). Kendall, who later became Pepsi's chief executive, said: "If we can get the Soviet people to enjoy good consumer goods, they'll never be able to do without them again."

Owners and rulers. D. Wayne Calloway took over the top post from Donald Kendall in 1986, after a stint running Frito-Lay. The two men's personal styles couldn't be more different. Kendall, CEO for 21 years, was a forceful, charismatic personality who liked globe-trotting with his pal Richard Nixon. Calloway, a soft-spoken southerner with a background in finance, melts into the background more than Kendall ever did. But few doubt Calloway's managerial competence. One Harvard Business School professor said, "It was amazing how he could get all these terribly ambitious people with big egos pulling in the same direction." In 1989, Calloway earned $1.5 million.

Pepsi's highly visible number two, Roger Enrico, who likes to take potshots at Coca-Cola in the press, wrote a book, *Cola Wars*, published in 1986. Pepsi's board includes General Motors' CEO Roger Smith and lawyer Robert Strauss, former head of the Democratic Party. The lone woman on the board is Sharon Percy Rockefeller, whose father and husband were both U.S. senators. Kendall once introduced her at an official function as "a very attractive girl."

As a place to work. Pepsi is a place where stars shine brightly for a while, and then burn out. A place where "there are a lot of great jobs, but very few careers," in the words of a former manager. People are promoted fast but pay a price for advancement. Sales and marketing managers are expected to meet ambitious growth goals every year and are evaluated by the results they deliver. Pepsi's corporate culture breeds competition more than it nurtures and develops people. As a result, they have unusually high turnover, even among top management. Senior executives stay in their jobs, on average, only 18 months.

An internal study in 1984 showed many managers felt stressed and under-appreciated. Pepsi responded by changing their company tune a little. Instead of basing pay only on results, they also took into account how well managers developed careers other than their own. In general, they tried to inculcate a new culture of "niceness" at Pepsi, where people take the time to give each other positive feedback.

This strategy was extended to make workers at Pepsi feel appreciated, too. In 1989, Pepsi made history by announcing a "Sharepower" stock-option program open to all employees who work at least 30 hours a week. This program is a first among huge corporations, which usually reserve stock-option plans for senior executives only. CEO Calloway told the *Wall Street Journal* that this was a way of saying "you are important" to every employee. "This says that in spades."

Pepsi hasn't been afraid to try new ideas on the factory floor, either. At Frito-Lay, they are experimenting with "work teams," a system where groups of workers set their own goals for the day, do their own inspection, learn more than one job and manage themselves.

Thanks to ex-CEO Kendall, Pepsi has a sculpture garden outside the headquarters in Purchase, New York, that is considered one of the best corporate art collections in the country. Kendall chose and positioned the pieces himself, which include works by Alexander Calder, George Segal and Alberto Giacometti.

Social responsibility. Pepsi attracted unwanted attention in 1982 when a scam was uncovered involving branches in Mexico and the Philippines that overstated profits by $73 million. Four years later, one of their bottling executives was indicted for price-fixing.

On the up side, Pepsi committed itself to spending $150 million purchasing goods and services from minority firms between 1984 and 1989. They don't have any investments, property or employees in South Africa, but they provide products there.

In 1985, Pepsi started a highly successful youth literacy program called "Book It!," the largest program of its kind. But some of PepsiCo's social programs have been criticized as thinly veiled product promotions, especially Frito-Lay's Parque de la Amistad, which donates money for playgrounds in Hispanic communities, while encouraging children to eat large quantities of Frito-Lay snacks. Pepsi has a generous scholarship program for children of employees. In 1989, six vice presidents and two chief financial officers of divisions were women.

Global presence. In spring 1990, Pepsi signed a $3 billion accord with the Soviet Union to barter their soft drink in exchange for the Soviet Stolichnaya vodka and at least 10 Soviet tankers and freighters. Pepsi's bottling network in the Soviet Union will double as a result, and Pepsi will eventually be available there in cans (rather than just in bottles). The *New York Times* called it the largest deal in history between an American company and the Soviet Union. Pepsi has been sold in the Soviet Union since 1974, and the Soviets have paid for the drink by bartering Stoli. Because U.S. law keeps restaurant owners out of the liquor business and Pepsi is the biggest restaurant owner in the world, Pepsi has sold the Stolchinaya to importers abroad. Pepsi also has two bottling plants in China.

Stock performance. PepsiCo stock bought for $1,000 in 1980 sold for $10,652 on January 2, 1990.

Consumer brands.

Beverages: Pepsi, Diet Pepsi, Mountain Dew, Slice, Diet Slice, Mirinda.

Snacks: Fritos, Lay's, Ruffles, O'Grady's, Munchos, Chee-tos, Doritos, Tostidos, Funyuns, Bacon-ets, Grandma's Cookies.

Restaurants: Pizza Hut, Taco Bell, Kentucky Fried Chicken.

PepsiCo, Inc., Purchase, NY 10577; (914) 253-2000.

RESTAURANTS

Americans now spend close to half their food dollars eating out, creating a huge industry. In numbers of players, here's the biggest business of them all. More than 300,000 eating and drinking places operate in the U.S., and they employ more than 6 million people. And although this is one of the last provinces of the mom-and-pop operator (7 out of every 10 restaurants do less than $500,000 a year, and half of them are owned by a single person or partnership), the fast-food revolution Ray Kroc ignited when he started McDonald's in 1955 has transformed this industry. There are now more than 100,000 fast-food establishments in the country, and they take in more than one-third of the dollars spent in restaurants.

1

#1 *in fast-food restaurants*

Employees: 176,000
Sales: $6.1 billion
Profits: $727 million
Founded: 1955
Headquarters: Oak Brook, Illinois

The question is: How many McDonald's restaurants can the world absorb? During the early and mid-1980s they opened 500 new ones every year. In 1988 new store openings went to 602 and in 1989 to 650, or 1 every 14 hours. And they see no reason why they can't continue this pace. By 1990 this metronomic expansion had brought their worldwide total to 11,000 restaurants in 51 countries, including Hungary, Yugoslavia and the Soviet Union. McDonald's figures they serve 22 million people a day. On any given day in the U.S., they serve 6 percent of the population. They took 33 years to build 10,000 restaurants, but they think they'll build the next 10,000 in only 18 years.

McDonald's is, in short, the biggest restaurant business the world has ever seen. They have sold more than 70 billion hamburgers. They buy 7.5 percent of America's potato crop. They own 60 percent of their U.S. restaurants sites, making them the nation's biggest owner of commercial real estate. More than 8 million Americans have worked for McDonald's at one time or another. McDonald's is the first employer of 1 out of every 15 Americans. They spend $1 billion a year on heart-tugging advertising, making McDonald's the single most advertised brand in the world.

McDonald's has only one business, and they manage it with machinelike precision. They worry as much about keeping the bathrooms clean as they do about the texture of the french fries and the thickness of the milk shakes. This is a franchise business—McDonald's owns only one-quarter of the restaurants—and getting a franchise is not easy.

Hamburgers are still the mainstay, but the average McDonald's today has a 33-item menu that includes chicken (they're the world's second largest retailer of chicken after Kentucky Fried Chicken), salads, decaf coffee and sausages—and in 1990 they were experimenting with a new pizza cooked in 5–1/2 minutes.

History. Ray Kroc was a 52-year-old all-purpose salesman when he met Maurice and Richard McDonald in 1954. The McDonald brothers ran a hamburger stand in the Los Angeles suburb of San Bernardino. Kroc was selling the Prince Castle Multi-Mixer, a contraption that could make six milk shakes simultaneously. The McDonalds ordered eight of them. Max Boas and Steve Chain report in their book *Big Mac* that Kroc wanted a firsthand look at an operation that found it necessary to make 48 milkshakes at the same time.

McDonalds failed miserably in the U.S. market when they created a pork sandwich called McRib, but in West Germany it was a great success.

Amazed at how popular the joint was, Kroc estimated the stand was doing $250,000 worth of business a year—as customers lined up at the window under a pair of garish golden arches to order ready-made hamburgers and french fries kept warm under heat lamps. On the second day he knew them he approached the brothers about franchising the operation. They were leery of this fast-talking salesman from Chicago, with his bow tie, roomy suit and brilliantined hair. But Kroc was persistent, and the brothers finally gave in. Kroc headed back to Illinois and opened his first McDonald's in Des Plaines, near Chicago—and the McDonald's empire began. In 1961, Ray Kroc convinced 12 investors (including Princeton University and Swarthmore College) to lend him $2.7 million to buy out the McDonald brothers. In 1984, Ray Kroc died at age 81. But even beyond the grave, he makes his personality felt. At company headquarters in Oak Brook, there is a video exhibit called "Talk to Ray," where one can ask Kroc's opinion on a variety of matters. There are videotapes of Kroc in later life spouting off on talk shows (like "Donahue") and tapes he made of himself for company archives.

Owners and rulers. It's fairly common at McDonald's to work your way up from an entry level job; over half of all corporate executives never got a college degree. Michael R. Quinlan, aged 45 in 1990, who is chairman, CEO and president of McDonald's, began his career there when he was 18, working part-time in the mailroom. In 1989, Quinlan's total compensation was $1.1 million. Chairman Fred Turner, who was a door-to-door salesman before he joined the company at 23, flipping burgers, has come up in the world. In 1989, he earned $1.4 million. McDonald's USA President Edward H. Rensi, aged 46 in 1990, went to work there when he dropped out of college. Several other officers began their careers behind the grill, as did over half of operations executives and restaurant managers. In 1988, employees owned about 9 percent of McDonald's shares and Roy Kroc's widow, Joan, owned about 7.2 percent. In 1984, 40-year-old Bob Beavers became the first black member of McDonald's board of directors. He began at the company in

1963 at a wage of $1 an hour and made milkshakes.

As a place to work. McDonald's has a strong array of benefit programs—profit-sharing, an investment savings plan, a free physical exam every other year (if under 35; every year if you're older) and a three-month sabbatical after 10 years' service. But critics charge the company exploits teenagers and those at the lowest levels of the operation. Contrary to popular belief, they do pay burger flippers more than the minimum wage—about 84 cents more in 1988. Still, McDonald's represents a dead-end job for most workers. The most telling statistic is that the annual turnover rate at the typical McDonald's is 180 percent, meaning that two workers quit or were fired in the course of a year for every restaurant job.

McDonald's is the largest employer of minority youth in the nation; 25 percent of management is minority, and 48 percent is female. About 20 percent of franchisees are minorities.

Social responsibility. McDonald's made *Multinational Monitor*'s list for "The 10 Worst Corporations of 1988" because their "nonbiodegradable, nonrecyclable, petrochemical styrofoam" pollutes the environment. The company makes over 1.6 billion cubic feet of styrofoam trash every year, and so far they show no sign of switching to different packaging. However, in October 1989, McDonald's announced plans for a large-scale, $16 million recycling project. Customers will be asked to throw used plastic hamburger containers into designated trash baskets; the containers will then be taken to local recycling centers, owned by McDonald's and eight other plastic producers (including Chevron Chemical and Dow Chemical).

McDonald's has also been criticized for the high-fat and high-cholesterol content of their food. In April 1990, the National Heart Savers Association took out full-page ads in newspapers around the nation, accusing McDonald's of "poisoning" America with high-cholesterol, high-fat foods. In response, McDonald's announced they would experiment with vegetable oil instead of unhealthy beef tallow when cooking french fries, use a low-fat mix for milk shakes and post nutritional data for all their products in all their restaurants. The firm also threatened legal action against newspapers that published the National Heart Savers Association ad again, calling the ad "reckless" and "malicious."

McDonald's does give a great deal of money to high-profile charities like the Special Olympics, muscular dystrophy and the Ronald McDonald houses (lodging for parents of hospitalized children, a

McDonald's got its start at this octagonal store in San Bernardino, California. The two McDonald brothers, Maurice and Richard, ran the popular business.

highly praised project the company founded in 1974).

Global presence.   One important reason McDonald's can keep opening more than 600 new restaurants a year is that it's a big world. These days 40 percent of the openings are overseas. Of the 11,000 restaurants in place in early 1990, about one-quarter were outside the U.S. But the non-U.S. restaurants contribute one-third of total system sales. Biggest outpost by far is Japan, with more than 600 McDonald's restaurants (called "Ma-ku-do-na-ru-do"). When they opened in Yugoslavia in March 1988, McDonald's broke an opening day record as 6,000 customers poured into the Belgrade store with the golden arches. That record lasted until January 1990 when the biggest McDonald's in the

Tale of the Drake

Drake Bakeries, a 104-year-old company based in Wayne, New Jersey, invented Devil Dogs and Yankee Doodles, pastries that have lined the stomachs of many youngsters growing up in the Northeast. Their history also mirrors the development of the U.S. food industry:

1888   Newman E. Drake, a bakery machinery salesman, develops a pound cake in his home oven.

1896   Drake opens a bakery, Drake Baking, to make his pound cake.

1899   The Drake bakery was bought, along many other bakeries, by the company that became Nabisco. But Newman Drake was retained to run the bakery.

1900   Newman Drake's four sons form their own company, Drake Brothers Bakery. They made a slab pound cake in Wallabout Market, Brooklyn.

1913   Drake has their first $1 million year, making cakes in Brooklyn and Boston.

1923   Devil Dogs—cream-filled chocolate cakes that look like hot dogs—are introduced.

1929   Drake buys Yankee Cake Co. of Providence, Rhode Island, bringing into Drake's lineup Yankee Doodles, cream-filled chocolate cupcakes. Drake's annual sales: $6.6 million.

1930   Newman Drake dies at age 70.

1933   Sales, hit by the depression, drop to $3.3 million. Borden begins to acquire stock.

1946   Borden buys Drake. Arthur W. Drake, Newman's son, stays on as vice president.

1954   Arthur Drake retires—the last Drake to work for the bakery.

1961   A new product: Ring Dings.

1964   Fruit Doodles, forerunner of Drake pies, introduced.

1970   Drake moves to Wayne, New Jersey.

1980   Sales top $100 million.

1985   Borden puts Chris Christodoulou in charge of Drake.

1986   Borden sells Drake to Continental Baking (Wonder Bread, Twinkies) division of Ralston Purina.

1987   Drake Bakeries sold to partnership that includes management. Chris Christodoulou becomes president.

1988   Drake celebrates centennial of their pound cake.

1989   Drake distributes their cakes on the West Coast for the first time. ∎

world, a three-story, 27-cash-register, 900-seat affair, opened in Moscow's Pushkin Square, serving, on their first day, 20,000 Russians lusting for a big Mac.

Stock performance. McDonald's stock bought for $1,000 in 1980 sold for $8,000 on January 2, 1990. McDonald's first sold stock to the public in 1965. Anyone who bought 100 shares then for $2,250 would have stock worth $594,880 at the start of 1990.

McDonald's Corporation, McDonald's Plaza, Oak Brook, IL 60521; (708) 575-3000.

2

#2 *in hamburger chains*

Employees: 41,000
Sales: $5.7 billion
Founded: 1954
Headquarters: Miami

The Burger King chain of 6,000 restaurants in 33 countries steamed into the 1990s flying the Union Jack. They passed into British hands in 1989 when the food-and-drink giant, Grand Metropolitan, bought Pillsbury, owner of Burger King since 1967.

Change was nothing new. Under Pillsbury, Burger King went through eight presidents, six chairmen and at least a dozen advertising themes. If customers couldn't figure out what Burger King stood for by watching—and listening to—their advertising pitches, they could when they visited one of the restaurants, found during the 1980s to be, in the words of the *New York Times*, "often dirty, to have slow service and offer food of uneven quality." Grand Met's solution was to send one of their British aces, 42-year-old Barry Gibbons, to Burger King's pink headquarters in Miami to cope with the American fast-food eater. "Neutron Barry" had been running restaurants and pubs for Grand Met in Britain and on the European continent. One of his first acts

was to fire one-third of the headquarters and field staff.

Although he's British, Gibbons probably won't use one of his predecessor's tactics. Jeffrey Campbell headed Burger King from 1983 to 1987 during a slump in sales (they were in a slump right through the 1980s). And according to *The Transformational Leader,* by Mary Anne Devanna, shortly after he took over, Campbell summoned top aides to a revival-type meeting at the end of which he asked everyone to remain silent and think about whether they were up to the challenge of turning Burger King around—and as they mulled over this question, the theme music from the British-made movie, *Chariots of Fire,* cascaded into the room. Pumped up, the Burger King honchos pressed forward, shook Campbell's hand and promised him they would come through. For a brief period they did, but then it was back to dirty bathrooms and inconsistent delivery.

In the mid-1980s Campbell spent millions on a short-lived campaign centered around a fictional character called "Herb," whose claim to distinction was that he had never eaten in a Burger King. The idea was to "get the Herbs of the world to realize what they are missing by not visiting Burger King." Herb failed—and Burger King's market share continued to decline during the second half of the 1980s. Although they are still the number two hamburger chain, their cash registers don't ring as frequently as McDonald's. In 1988 average sales at a McDonald's were $1.6 million; at Burger King, $980,000. Although McDonald's owns about one-quarter of the restaurants in their system, Grand Met (like Pillsbury before) owns only 15 percent.

Franchisees—those who own and run the local Burger King restaurants—are therefore much more powerful at Burger King than they are at other fast-food companies, and they were happy to see the British arrive. They felt Pillsbury never gave them the support they needed. In his first year at the helm Gibbons closed 76 derelict restaurants, remodeled 300 of the company-owned stores, hired a new marketing chief, replaced the advertising agency with two agencies and uncorked a $200 million ad campaign keyed to the enigmatic theme, "Sometimes You've

Gotta Break the Rules." In the opinion of many observers, Burger King hasn't had a winning ad campaign since their first one in 1958: "Home of the Whopper."

Grand Met will need more than clever ads to compete with McDonald's. Not only does McDonald's have a much larger ad budget, they have much more control over their franchisees than does Burger King. Perhaps part of Burger King's problem is inadequate franchisee training. At Burger King, a new owner need only go through 50 hours of training, but at McDonald's a new restaurant manager undergoes 2,000 hours of unpaid training at another McDonald's restaurant before spending two additional weeks at the company's Hamburger University. Even so, Grand Met's new marketing chief, Gary L. Langstaff, gathered his troops around him toward the end of 1989 and told them: "Don't look back anymore. We're a brand new company."

Burger King Corporation, 17777 Old Cutler Road, Miami, FL 33157; (305) 378-7011.

3

Kentucky Fried Chicken

#1 *in chicken restaurants*

Employees: 141,800
Sales: $5 billion
Founded: 1955
Headquarters: Louisville, Kentucky

You can smell a Kentucky Fried Chicken place a long way off—the odor of chicken in batter soaking in grease: a vegetarian's nightmare. And you can get that whiff in a lot of locations: about 7,600 going into the 1990s. Some 2,700 of those restaurants were outside the U.S. Indeed, the biggest KFC restaurant, a three-story affair seating 512 customers, can be found in Beijing's Tiananmen Square, scene of the Chinese government's brutal crushing of the student revolt in June 1989. Opened in 1987, to the tune of *haodao yun shouzhi* ("so good you can suck your fingers"), the Beijing KFC set a new world record in

their first year, using 350,000 chickens. The second biggest Kentucky Fried Chicken outlet is in London's West End, near Marble Arch. This London KFC has potted plants and cane chairs with a seating capacity of 220. They used 250,000 chickens in their first year.

Considering the favorite American fast food is hamburger, Kentucky Fried has done all right in their home country, too, although they have had four different owners. The U.S. restaurants serve more than 800 million meals a year, going through more than 300 million chickens. According to the company lore, if all the KFC chickens consumed around the world were laid head to claw, they would stretch 281,784 miles or circle the earth at the equator more than 11 times.

Kentucky Fried Chicken was founded by Colonel Harland Sanders, a seventh grade dropout, when he was 66 years old. His secret was a blend of 11 herbs and spices. The company took off quickly. It was always a franchise business in which local businesspeople owned the stores. In 1964 Colonel Sanders sold out to John Y. Brown (Kentucky's future governor) and Nashville businessman Jack Massey (cofounder of Hospital Corporation of America) for $2 million. In 1971 wine-and-spirits supplier Heublein bought KFC for $275 million. In 1982, Heublein became part of R. J. Reynolds, which sold KFC to PepsiCo in 1986 for $845 million. At PepsiCo, KFC is part of a restaurant entourage that includes Pizza Hut and Taco Bell. Of the 7,600 KFCs in operation, PepsiCo owns 1,900. In the fast-food industry KFC ranks fourth measured by number of outlets (behind McDonald's, stablemate Pizza Hut and Burger King) but sixth measured by annual sales per store: $597,000. The average McDonald's grosses $1.6 million a year. People are just not coming into Kentucky Fried Chicken for breakfast.

Colonel Sanders was employed as an ambassador for the chain until his death in 1980. The colonel didn't like anyone messing with his original recipe, however. When the chain introduced Extra Crispy fried chicken, he said it tasted like it had been dipped in wallpaper paste. When Colonel Sanders died at the age of 90, his body lay in state in the Kentucky state capitol rotunda. The Colonel was a

Colonel Harland Sanders thought KFC's Extra Crispy chicken tasted like it had been dipped in wallpaper paste.

strict father, according to his daughter Maggie Sanders. "He would tie me to a tree, and I would be tethered with a big long rope like a dog on a clothesline," she told the *Miami Herald* in 1987, recalling her early childhood. Sanders willed his daughter franchised stores in the state of Florida.

Kentucky Fried Chicken, P.O. Box 32070, Louisville, KY 40232; (502) 456-8300.

4

#1 *in pizza restaurants*

Employees: 85,000
Sales: $2.5 billion
Profits: $208 million
Founded: 1958
Headquarters: Wichita, Kansas

Meet the world's largest user of mozzarella: Pizza Hut, a wholly owned subsidiary of PepsiCo (guess which cola they serve?). This is the biggest pizza business in the world, fueled by a voracious American appetite: 8 pounds per person a year. Lumbering into the 1990s, Pizza Hut had 6,000 red-roofed restaurants in the U.S., and they were serving more than 250 million pizzas a year, or about one-fifth of the $13 billion pizza market. In addition, they had opened more than 1,000 Pizza Huts in 53 other countries, including 2 in Moscow. To keep these restaurants in cheese, Pizza Hut buys over 125 million pounds of mozzarella a year, the yield from 1.2 billion pounds of milk or the yearly contribution of 125,000 cows.

While they expanded via the franchise route, Pizza Hut keeps more units for themselves than other fast-food chains. They own nearly half of the U.S. restaurants—that's close to 3,000—which makes them the biggest owner of restaurants in the world. Pizza Hut was originally a place where you came to eat pizza or took it home to eat. However, after Domino's built the second biggest pizza chain in the business by catering to the couch potato's desire to have the pizza come to the house, Pizza Hut ordered up their own delivery trucks (and drivers), and by early 1990 half of their restaurants sent speeding vans over hill and dale with hot pizza.

Pizza Hut was started in Wichita, Kansas, in 1958 by two college students, Frank and Dan Carney. Frank was 19, Dan 25. Their first restaurant did so well they

POP WARS

Coke Sellers	Pepsi Sellers
McDonald's	Pizza Hut
Burger King	Taco Bell
Wendy's*	Kentucky Fried Chicken
Hardee's	Wendy's*
Little Caesar's Pizza	Shakey's Pizza
Domino's Pizza	Subway Sandwiches
Denny's	Ground Round

* Wendy's is split between Coke and Pepsi until January 1991 when they go exclusively into the Coke camp.

Source: *The Wall Street Journal*, 2 May 1990.

opened two more in Wichita by February 1959, and licensed their first franchisee in Topeka. They sold stock to the public in 1969, by which time they had more than 300 restaurants, and then in 1977 they sold out to PepsiCo for $300 million.

The Carney brothers left the business, but Pizza Hut's headquarters remained in Wichita, where various executives have been imported to fight the pizza wars. Latest to take the helm was Steve Reinemund, who came aboard in 1985 from Marriott's Roy Rogers chain. One of his preoccupations is cutting turnover, which is high among both employees and restaurant managers in the fast-food business. In 1988 he reported he had reduced "our unit manager turnover to less than the industry average."

While Pizza Hut was happy in 1989 to relay to their troops the *Wall Street Journal* report that New Yorkers were rejecting Domino's pizzas as being "bland" and "homogenized" as if they "came out of a factory," they somehow neglected to tell them about the August 1986 article in *Harper's* wherein a Santa Fe attorney told a tale of woe involving two clients who crunched down on Pizza Hut pizzas laced with shards of glass and a metal washer.

In late 1989, Pizza Hut found they had to defend their territory against McDonald's, which was test-marketing McDonald's pizza in Evansville, Indiana. Pizza Hut took out a series of ads in the local papers, berating McDonald's with slogans like, "If you're looking for great

pizza, make no Mcstake." Pizza Hut's public affairs director warned that if McDonald's started dishing out pizza across the nation, they will "be in for the fight of their lives."

Pizza Hut, Inc., 911 East Douglas, P.O. Box 428, Wichita, KS 67201; (316) 681-9000.

 **5**

#1 *in pizza delivery*

Employees: 60,000
Sales: $2.5 billion
Profits: $5 million
Founded: 1960
Headquarters: Ann Arbor, Michigan

If the 1980s belonged to any company, it was Domino's Pizza. They started out the decade with fewer than 500 stores and ended it with more than 5,000. Originally an Italian dish, pizza has emerged from some unlikely places in the U.S. Pizza Hut, the largest pizza chain, came out of Wichita, Kansas. Domino's, the second largest, came out of Ypsilanti, Michigan, launched in 1960 by Tom Monaghan, whose father died when he was four years old. His mother then shipped young Tom to a series of grim foster homes and a Catholic orphanage. Ellen Stern, profiling

Tom Monaghan, founder of Domino's Pizza posed with pieces from his Frank Lloyd Wright collection.

Monaghan in the July 1989 *GQ*, detailed his relationship with his mother:

> When he was in the seventh grade, she retrieved him, only to dispatch him to a foster family on a farm, where he baled hay, milked cows, drove tractors, read about Abraham Lincoln by the light of a gas lantern. At 16, he borrowed her car and she had him thrown in jail. And when he was 17, with no provocation whatsoever, she condemned him to a detention home. He has forgiven everything but this.

After a stint in the Marine Corps, Monaghan, then 22, began delivering newspapers. He then bought a newsstand in downtown Ann Arbor before joining with his brother, Jim, to buy a pizzeria in Ypsilanti. (His brother checked out of the business after eight months.) From the beginning Monaghan's idea was not to serve people in the pizzeria but to bake the pizzas and deliver them. His first customers were college students and military personnel. His idea triumphed, aided by the Domino's pledge: If your pizza is not delivered within 30 minutes of your call, you can deduct $3 from the bill.

Domino's has become the world's largest pizza deliverer, accounting for 53 percent of the pizza delivered in the U.S. They sold 230 million pizzas in 1988, using 125 million pounds of cheese, 178 million pounds of flour, 24 million pounds of pepperoni and 87,000 cans of anchovies. Their 5,000 restaurants—1,400 of them company owned—rang up sales of $2.3 billion in 1988.

Domino's has made Tom Monaghan a multimillionaire—*Forbes* estimated his wealth at $480 million—and his success has let him indulge his passions. He owns 200 classic cars, including a 1931 Bugatti Royale he bought for $8 million; five boats; three planes; and the Detroit Tigers baseball team, which he bought for $53 million in 1983, just in time for the Tigers to win the World Series the following year. He rarely watches the team play, however. Monaghan also owns the world's largest collection of Frank Lloyd Wright objects. He once said, "I believe you're a better person, morally, if raised in a well-designed house. And if it's a Frank Lloyd Wright house, well, that's best of all."

Monaghan, who dropped out of seminary and considers himself a failed priest, often speaks aloud to the Virgin Mary ("Mary's my buddy," he told *Forbes*) and to Sister Berarda, his grade school teacher who died many years ago. At Christmastime, Monaghan has put up thousands of lights around the headquarters' parking lot depicting gift-bearing kings, camels and angels. In 1989 the extravaganza cost $1 million and drew nearly a half-million people causing horrendous traffic jams and infuriating local residents.

The Domino headquarters outside Ann Arbor is evidence of Monaghan's whimsy; it contains a pen of sheep (so that visitors may pet the animals), a train set, a 1903 Cadillac and a bronze statue, without a face, called *Self-Made Man*. There is also a Domino's Pizza Catholic chapel at headquarters. Monaghan plans to begin constructing a new company headquarters in 1990; the building will be tilted 15 degrees (the Leaning Tower of Pisa in Italy is tilted 5 degrees) and a chapel will be on the top floor.

In the latter part of the 1980s, as Domino's outlets proliferated, two discordant voices were raised. Some complained that deliverers drove their cars so rapidly to meet the 30-minute guarantee that they were involved in an unusually large number of accidents. Domino's denied this. The other complaint came from the National Organization for Women, which urged women to boycott the chain because Monaghan was a big contributor to antiabortion groups. The dispute with NOW is turning ugly. Monaghan told *Business Month*: "The NOW people are full of lies and viciousness." Jan Ben-Dor, president of the Michigan NOW chapter, responded: "The Domino's headquarters is a thicket of sexism, cultism and intrigue. He's a self-defeating, tragic figure. There are people who are mad at him for just about everything. He even ruined the Tigers—and you have to work really hard to lose the support of baseball fans. Besides, his pizza tastes like cardboard." Monaghan isn't worried:

> *Look, 10 percent of our customers are never going to buy a pizza from Domino's because of my stand on abortion, and another 10 percent are not going to buy pizza from anyone else because of my stand. The 80 percent in the middle are indifferent; all I've done with them is create more awareness for the product, so Domino's comes out ahead.*

Tom Monaghan owns 97 percent of Domino's (long-term employees own the other 3 percent). In 1989 he created a stir among "Dominoids," as Monaghan refers to his employees, by letting it be known he might be interested in selling the company so he could devote his time to philanthropy and public service. He turned over day-to-day company management and the presidency to 40-year-old David Black but had made no further moves to sell out by mid-1990.

Domino's Pizza, Inc., Prairie House, Domino's Farms, 30 Frank Lloyd Wright Drive, Ann Arbor, MI 48106; (313) 930-3030.

TOP 10 FAST-FOOD CHAINS

Average Annual Sales per U.S. Unit

1.	McDonald's	$1.6 million
2.	Burger King	$984,000
3.	Hardee's	$920,000
4.	Wendy's	$759,000
5.	Taco Bell	$589,000
6.	Arby's	$610,000
7.	Kentucky Fried Chicken	$597,000
8.	Pizza Hut	$510,000
9.	Domino's Pizza	$485,000
10.	Dairy Queen	$408,000

Source: Technomic, Inc., and company reports for 1989.

6

#3 *in hamburger chains*

Employees: 42,000
Sales: $1.1 billion
Profits: $24 million
Founded: 1969
Headquarters: Dublin, Ohio

When R. David Thomas opened his first Wendy's in Columbus, Ohio, in 1969, naming it after his eight-year-old daughter, McDonald's already had 1,200 restaurants. So who needed another hamburger chain? Thomas, who began working in restaurants when he was 12, saw an opening for a folksy place that emphasized old-fashioned values. He promised to cook hamburgers to order, and he put carpets, Tiffany-style lamps and bentwood chairs in his restaurant. When Wendy's celebrated their 20th birthday in 1989, they had 3,700 restaurants (one-third of which they owned) to the 10,000 flying the McDonald's flag. Whereas the average McDonald's took in $1.6 million annually, the average Wendy's rang up

$759,000, lagging behind Burger King, Hardee's and Jack in the Box.

And somewhere along the way Wendy's appeared to have lost their *raison d'être*. They enjoyed a brief moment of glory in the mid-1980s with the campaign that asked, "Where's the beef?" That brought customers into the stores where they found, according to the *Wall Street Journal*, "poor service, messy tables and inconsistent quality." James W. Near, president of Wendy's (and named CEO in 1989), conceded the company "didn't watch the stores as carefully as they should have."

Wendy's has restaurants in all 50 states, with the biggest concentration in the Midwest (Ohio still has more stores than any other state: 289 at the start of 1989). They also have 250 restaurants in 17 other countries. The franchised restaurants (two-thirds of the total) pay Wendy's a royalty of 4 percent on sales.

As Wendy's limped into the 1990s (their profits in 1988 and 1989 were lower than in 1980), the flagship product was still the hamburger, but they were offering less expensive versions such as a 99-cent junior bacon cheeseburger and taking advantage of new trends with an all-you-can-eat SuperBar featuring salads, Mexican food and pasta. They were also experimenting with accepting Visa cards, a move the company characterized as "a willingness to explore and test contemporary ideas."

In 1989, still unsure about what theme to adopt in their advertising, Wendy's brought back founder R. David Thomas in a series of TV commercials in which he said, "Our hamburgers are the best in the business, or I wouldn't have named the place after my daughter." Wendy herself is an off-screen voice in some of these commercials.

Thomas retired from an active management role in 1982, but he continued in the post of senior chairman of the board and remained the company's largest stockholder—7.7 percent of the shares worth $40 million in 1990. Thomas is a rags-to-riches story. Born in 1932 in Atlantic City, he never knew his father or mother. His adoptive mother died when he was five, and his adoptive father married four more times, moving from state to state. Thomas never went beyond 10th grade. He began working as a waiter in a Knoxville restau-rant when he was 12 and as a busboy in the Hobby House restaurant in Fort Wayne when he was 15. He was later a cook at the Hobby House, whose owner, Phil Clauss, was one of the early franchisees of Colonel Harland Sanders. In 1962 Clauss took over four failing Kentucky Fried Chicken carryouts in Columbus and promised Thomas 45 percent of the action if he could turn the stores around. He did, opened four new outlets in Columbus and then sold all the restaurants to KFC for $1.5 million. He had a brief fling with Arthur Treacher's Fish & Chips before starting Wendy's at 257 East Broad Street in downtown Columbus. He began selling franchises in 1973. One of his first franchisees was James Near, who brought Wendy's into West Virginia and Florida during the 1970s.

$tock performance. Wendy's stock bought for $1,000 in 1980 sold for $2,238 on January 2, 1990.

Wendy's International, Inc., 4288 West Dublin-Granville Road, Dublin, OH 43017; (614) 764-3100.

FOOD WHOLESALERS

Food wholesalers are companies that get food to local groceries. Classic middlemen, standing between the food manufacturer and the store that sells to consumers, the wholesalers have thousands of trucks plying the nation's highways. The grocery wholesale field experienced the same wave of mergers and consolidations that has washed over other parts of the economy. At the start of the 1980s the top 10 wholesalers handled 20 percent of the business; now they do over 40 percent. And the top two, Fleming and Super Valu, control more than 20 percent, up from 7 percent a decade ago.

1

Fleming Companies Inc.

#1 *in food wholesaling*

Employees: 23,700
Sales: $12 billion
Profits: $80 million
Founded: 1915
Headquarters: Oklahoma City

Supermarket shoppers probably never stop to wonder: "How did all this food get here?" Fleming is a big part of the answer. They're the nation's largest grocery wholesaler, delivering food to 5,200 stores in 36 states. Their fleet of 5,000 trucks traveled more than 100 million miles last year. They not only deliver to stores but also pick up food from suppliers, which they store in 38 cavernous warehouses they maintain. They're a sophisticated business (nearly all Fleming trucks are equipped with on-board computers), and a huge one, as their sales volume attests.

Grocery wholesaling is also more than just a pickup-and-delivery business. Stores that Fleming supplies are offered a wide variety of support services, including advertising assistance, computerized order entry and shelf management systems and employee training programs.

Fleming also leases retail space, provides financing to store owners and sells them insurance. To better compete against the big grocery chains, independent store owners have grouped themselves into voluntary associations. Fleming is at the heart of a number of these voluntary groups, to wit: IGA, Piggly Wiggly, United Supers, Thriftway, Big T, Shop 'n Bag, Value King, Minimax, Food 4 Less and Sentry. Fleming licenses stores to use those names and, in some cases, owns the stores themselves.

Part of the Fleming service is to supply goods under their own labels. If you're in a store carrying such brands as Bonnie Hubbard, Sentry, Marquee, Montco, Good Value and Rainbow, you're looking at goods Fleming supplied.

Fleming leaped to the top during the 1980s. Coming into the decade, they had sales of $2.5 billion and 7,500 employees (the company calls its people "associates," never employees); those figures have about quadrupled. And this quadrupling came from gobbling up other wholesalers: McClain, 1981; Waples-Platter, 1982; American-Strevell, 1982; Giant Wholesale, 1983; United Grocer, 1984; Associated Grocers, 1985; Godfrey, 1987; Malone & Hyde, 1988. The last acquisition vaulted them ahead of rival Super Valu.

The growth has not been without strain. In 1989 the Teamsters, who represent warehouse workers and truck drivers, strung picket lines around 15 Fleming distribution centers across the country. The dispute centered over wage concessions Fleming demanded to keep the company's pay rate equal to the scale the Teamsters negotiated for a competing wholesaler. The strike lasted six months, affected 4,000 workers, and nicked company profits by $11 million.

In 1989 not a single female held any of the 71 officer positions in the company, nor was there a single woman serving on the board of directors. As of early 1989, 89-year-old Ned Fleming (son of the founder) still held the title of Honorary Chairman of the Board; he had been on the board of directors since 1922. In 1990 his stock was worth $30 million. E. Dean Werries, who has spent his career with the firm, was named president and CEO in 1981.

Nearly half of Fleming's business comes from new superstores or warehouse markets, like the one shown above.

Stock performance. Fleming stock bought for $1,000 in 1980 sold for $4,779 on January 2, 1990.

Fleming Companies, Inc., 6301 Waterford Blvd., Oklahoma City, OK 73126; (405) 840-7200.

2

#2 *in food wholesaling*

Employees: 37,700
Sales: $11 billion
Profits: $142 million
Founded: 1870
Headquarters: Eden Prairie, Minnesota

"We want to make people rich." That's the gospel preached by Michael W. Wright, a lawyer and ex-University of Minnesota football star who took com-

mand of this Minnesota-based grocery wholesaler in 1981 when he was 42 and presided for the rest of the decade over a spectacular growth. The people he was talking about were his customers, who own and operate supermarkets. Super Valu stocks their shelves and offers to help them in any area of merchandising, from store layout to advertising, so that they can contend with the big chains. Moving into the 1990s, Super Valu was servicing over 3,000 stores in 33 states, concentrated in the Midwest, South and West. They also own Shopko, a chain of 98 department stores.

As in any business, you win some and you lose some. Super Valu lost the $300 million Albertson's account in the Pacific Northwest in 1988, but they also added some 300 new accounts, including Red Owl groceries in Minnesota, Wisconsin and three other states. A wholesaler often does more than just fill orders. They can float new retailing concepts. In the 1980s Super Valu opened discount warehouselike supermarkets called Cub, franchising most of them to independent owners but operating some themselves. So as not to irritate their regular customers, Super Valu opened the Cubs where the grocers they serve "have little or no market base." A smaller version of the Cub stores is County Market, intended for small cities and towns. There were 100 of these at the start of 1990. In 1985 Super Valu forgot that wholesaling had been the secret of their success. They got back into retailing when they bought Food Giant, a floundering supermarket chain of 57 stores based in Atlanta. By 1988 they had closed 16 of the stores and sold off 33 more. "When we stick to traditional wholesale operations, we do well," CEO Michael Wright admitted to *Forbes* in 1988.

Acquisitions fueled much of Super Valu's growth during the 1980s. They bought seven other wholesalers. But other big wholesalers were buying, too. Super Valu reigned as the nation's largest grocery wholesaler until late 1988 when the Fleming Companies in buying Malone & Hyde overtook them.

Stock performance. Super Valu stock bought for $1,000 in 1980 sold for $6,018 on January 2, 1990.

Super Valu Stores, Inc., 11840 Valley View Road, Eden Prairie, MN 55344; (612) 828-4000.

SUPERMARKETS

The number of food stores in the U.S. has declined steadily over the past 50 years, replaced by cavernous, self-service supermarkets. The nation's 30,000 supermarkets represent less than 20 percent of the total number of food stores, but they do 75 percent of the sales. The average supermarket carries 25,000 items. However, it's a big country, and no supermarket chain has established a national presence. However, regional chains are strong. The top 10 chains control about one-third of the business. Considerable industry restructuring occurred during the 1980s. Of the top 10 national chains in 1980, only one—Winn-Dixie—came through the decade unscathed.

1
American Stores

#1 *in supermarkets*

*Employees: 167,700
Sales: $22 billion
Profits: $118 million
Founded: 1891
Headquarters: Salt Lake City, Utah*

Their name isn't on any of the supermarkets they operate, and American Stores likes it that way. Known for their secrecy, they were operated out of Salt Lake City for years by Sam Skaggs, a man known as "The Wizard," who quietly amassed a $400 million family fortune by building the land's biggest supermarket empire. While competitors Safeway and Kroger fought over the number one position by expanding their own stores, American Stores became a national powerhouse by buying up regional supermarket and drug chains. As a result, shoppers buying groceries in a Skaggs supermarket in Dallas, a Star market in Boston, a Jewel store in Chicago or a Lucky market in Los Angeles are all customers of this company.

American Stores moved into the 1990s with 1,917 stores in 39 states, nearly double the number they had in 1980. They sell food and drugs under various retail guises: food stores, combination drug/food stores, drugstores, super drug centers. Their latest acquisition, Lucky

Stores, pushed then passed Kroger to become the number one supermarket operator in the country. On the drugstore side, they are among the five largest chains in the U.S.

American Stores has two hallmarks—tenacity at the top, decentralization at the bottom. Chairman L. S. "Sam" Skaggs pursued Jewel Companies for two decades, initially by trying to talk the directors into a merger. He failed, so when he saw the opportunity, Skaggs launched an unfriendly takeover in 1985. Similarly, the Lucky purchase took two years, lots of money ($2.5 billion) and a protracted fight with California's attorney general who thought it would inhibit competition. To settle this dispute, American Stores had to sell 152 Alpha-Beta and nine Lucky stores in California.

Theoretically, a company running a lot of stores benefits by having a national name, one that's the same from state to state. American Stores' entry here is Osco, which means drugstore in 25 states. In 1986 they moved to establish a greater national presence for Osco by changing the name of their Sav-on stores in California and Las Vegas to Osco. However, the name never caught on with shoppers, so in 1988 the Osco name came down—and Sav-on went back up.

History. The name "Skaggs" looms large in the history of American retailing. Skaggs family members were responsible for, or had strong connections to, at least six major store chains: Safeway, Osco, Longs, Skaggs, PayLess and Albertson's.

The patriarch of the family was S. M. Skaggs, a Baptist minister who opened an 18-by-32-foot grocery store in American Falls, Idaho, in 1915. Skaggs built sales volume by taking a small profit on his merchandise. His credo, "He who serves best, profits most," was drummed into the heads of his six sons, all of whom were to make their marks in retailing—one founded Safeway, another founded the Osco drug chain and another created the PayLess drug chain.

At one time four of the Skaggs brothers worked in the Safeway organization (M. B. was chairman from 1926 to 1934), and in 1939 one of them joined with a Safeway district manager, A. J. "Joe" Albertson, to open a giant new store in Boise, Idaho, designed as a one-stop shopping center for foods and drugs. The operation was called Skaggs-Albertson. Later on, they parted company, Skaggs taking the drug stores, Albertston the food stores. Skaggs senior died in 1950, and his son, L. S. "Sam" Skaggs, then 26, took over the drug chain and remained in command for the next 39 years.

From headquarters in Salt Lake City, he expanded the Skaggs Companies into a powerful force in retailing drugs and groceries. In 1979 he merged Skaggs with Philadelphia-based American Stores, taking not only the corporate name but the Acme supermarkets in the East and the Alpha Beta supermarkets in the West. In 1984, he acquired the biggest supermarket operator in Chicago, Jewel, whose entourage included the Osco drug chain (founded by another Skaggs family member), the Montana-based Buttrey stores and the Boston-based Star markets.

Owners and rulers. The Skaggs family controls 21 percent of the company's stock. Sam Skaggs, who holds 12 percent of the shares, left day-to-day operations to his managers while he spent his time on grand strategy. Reaching the mandatory retirement age of 65 in 1988, he became chairman, where he intends to serve until at least 1992. Jonathan L. Scott, an old hand at running big supermarket chains, succeeded him as CEO. He formerly served as CEO of Albertson's (he was once married to Joe Albertson's daughter) and A&P. L. S. Skaggs' wife, Aline, is a board member, as is L. Tom Perry, a high-ranking member of the Mormon Church.

Stock performance. American Stores stock bought for $1,000 in 1980 sold for $7,631 on January 2, 1990.

Consumer brands.

Jewel food stores (Illinois, Michigan, Indiana, Iowa), Jewel Osco (Florida), Skaggs Alpha Beta (Arkansas, Kansas, New Mexico, Texas, Oklahoma), Buttrey Food and Drug (Idaho, Montana, North Dakota, Utah, Washington, Wyoming), Acme (mid-Atlantic), Lucky Stores (California, Nevada), Alpha Beta (Nevada), Star Market (Massachusetts, Rhode Island), Osco and Sav-on (New England, Midwest, Southwest and California).

American Stores Company, 5201 Amelia Earhart Drive, Salt Lake City, UT 84116; (801) 539-0112.

2

#2 *in supermarkets*

Employees: 170,000
Sales: $18.8 billion
Loss: -$16 million
Founded: 1883
Headquarters: Cincinnati, Ohio

They're still the tough guys of the grocery industry. They'll play hardball with competitors, cutting prices to the bone to maintain their market share, and they'll bench employees, closing stores rather than raise wages. In the 1980s they defended their turf with ferocity, not only fending off corporate raiders but also passing Safeway to become the nation's top supermarket operator until they themselves were surpassed by American Stores at the end of the decade.

Kroger's turf extends to 29 states in the Midwest, South and West where they operated 1,235 supermarkets and 958 convenience stores at the start of 1990. The supermarkets account for 90 percent of sales. The convenience stores operate under the names Turkey Hill (Pennsylvania), Tom Thumb (Florida and Alabama), Time Saver (Louisiana), Quick Stop (California), Loaf 'N Jug (Colorado, Oklahoma and New Mexico) and Mini Mart (Wyoming, Montana, Colorado, Nebraska, and North and South Dakota), and together represent the fourth largest convenience store operation in the nation.

Kroger edged ahead of Safeway in 1983 when they were celebrating their centennial. They did it by acquiring Kansas City-based Dillon Companies, which brought the King Soopers, City Market, Fry's, Quik Stop, Kwik Stop and Time Saver stores into the Kroger tent.

Kroger doesn't like to play second fiddle. In many major cities—Cincinnati (their hometown), Dayton, Atlanta, Memphis, Indianapolis—they are the dominant grocer. When they can't get their own way, they'll pull out. In 1984, when they couldn't get unions to give them wage concessions, they closed down their 45 supermarkets in Pittsburgh, eliminating 1,500 jobs.

In late 1988, a feared corporate raider (the Haft family of Washington, D.C.) tried to buy Kroger, offering $4.3 billion. In short order, another raider, the Wall Street investment house of Kohlberg Kravis Roberts, came in with a $4.6 billion bid. KKR had recently bought Safeway in a similar scenario. Kroger spurned both the Hafts and KKR. Instead, in a move that would frighten away any raider, Kroger borrowed $5 billion to pay shareholders a onetime dividend of $40 a share. They also issued bonds that saddled them with interest payments of $500 million a year, but they retained their independence.

History. The chain's tough-guy personality can be traced to founder Bernard H. Kroger. The son of immigrant German shopkeepers, Kroger spent several years selling coffee and tea door to door from wagons. The owners of the Imperial Tea Co. of Cincinnati offered their 21-year-old salesman $12 a week and a 10 percent share of the profits if he would manage their failing enterprise. He accepted, fired everyone except the delivery boy, and began to work 16-hour days, with the help of a new cash register and cashier (innovations at that time). Peevish, cranky and irascible, Kroger was known as a particular and demanding buyer, weeding out merchandise until the store's inventory was up to his quality standard. His customers became devoted. At the end of the first year Imperial Tea had made a $3,000 profit; Kroger asked for a one-third share of the company, was refused and stalked out to form his own company.

By 1885 Kroger's Great Western Tea Co. had four stores in Cincinnati, and he began placing what were the first grocery ads in daily newspapers. His wagons and stores were painted fire-engine red, and while his competitors laughed, the customers flocked in. The competitors stopped laughing when Kroger began purchasing by the carload and underselling them with loss leaders, another Kroger first. At the time, Kroger figured the overhead in his original store to be 4 percent: $4 for himself, $1 for rent and $1 for expenses on sales of $150 a day. In 1899 his wife and son died, and Kroger plunged ever more deeply into his business life, becoming obsessed with success. Kroger was loud and erratic, with a temper that could explode at the slightest transgression. Managers would be fired on the spot for a dirty window or floor.

Kroger expanded into mail order and manufacturing. In 1902 Great Western Tea was renamed Kroger Grocery and Baking, and 40 stores were flying the Kroger name. Kroger was the first grocer to operate his own bakery, selling his bread for 2 1/2 cents a loaf. He was also the first grocer to bring a meat department into a grocery store, and he fought a long battle with his butchers to prevent them from short-weighting and stealing. As Kroger expanded across Ohio, he steadily bought out his competition. In 1928, at age 68, he sold all his holdings just before the crash, retired to Palm Beach, Florida, and took up golf.

Owners and rulers. Lyle Everingham, head of the company since 1978, started with Kroger as a produce clerk more than 40 years ago. He has a reputation for being a quiet, almost taciturn man, but insiders say he's a strong-willed and determined leader. He proved it during the hectic days of 1988 when, with the help of Goldman, Sachs, he repelled the Haft and KKR raids. The special dividend paid to shareholders enriched him (he got $10 million in cash) and other senior managers but Everingham also cut employees in by offering stock options to everyone. As a result, employee ownership of Kroger jumped to 35 percent.

As a place to work. Struggling under its new debt, Kroger lopped more than 4,000 people from their payroll in the late 1980s, but *Wall Street Journal* reporter Susan C. Faludi credited them with serving their employees far better than Safeway. She pointed out that Kroger gave more generous severance packages (up to 9 months pay, compared to Safeway's maximum of 8 weeks), improved their profit sharing plan (Safeway stopped contributing to its plan) and launched an incentive bonus plan that reaches down to secretaries. The bottom line, though, is that Kroger sold 100 stores while Safeway sold 1,100 and today, Faludi notes, Kroger "supports 60,000 more workers than Safeway."

Stock performance. Kroger stock bought for $1,000 in 1980 sold for $15,576 on January 2, 1990.

Consumer brands.

Kroger, Dillon's, Fry's, City Markets, King Soopers, Quik Stop, Kwik Stop, Time Saver.

The Kroger Co., 1014 Vine Street, Cincinnati, OH 45201; (513) 762-4000.

3

#3 *in supermarkets*

Employees: 107,000
Sales: $13.6 billion
Profits: $31 million
Founded: 1926
Headquarters: Oakland, California

Workplace

Companies are masters at putting a good face on disaster, and Safeway qualifies as one of the most adept at this maneuver. During the 1980s they dropped from first to third in the supermarket industry, sold or closed 1,100 of their 2,100 stores including all of them in five states and in the largest grocery market in the U.S. (Los Angeles), withdrew from the international field (except for Canada), cut 75,000 people from the payroll, and then insisted they were much better off.

Why such gyrations? The company was sold to a Wall Street investment firm and the chain's top managers in mid-1986. Prior to that time, Safeway Stores was owned by stockholders who could buy or sell their shares on the New York Stock Exchange. To avoid a takeover, Safeway's management hooked up with the investment firm Kohlberg Kravis Roberts (KKR) to buy the stock from all the public shareholders for $4.3 billion and revert to private ownership. That saddled the

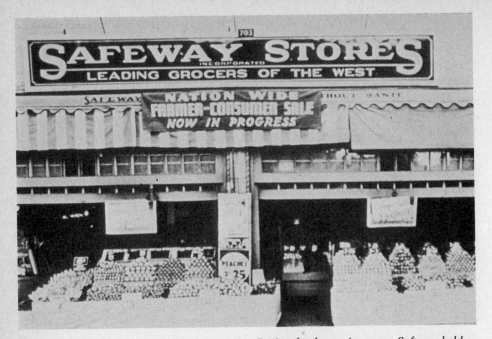

During the depression years, Safeway held special sales to help farmers push their slow moving crops. In 1936 this Safeway store in Los Angeles, California, emphasized oranges, signifying the reciprocity between the store and California farmers.

supermarket chain with long-term debt of $4.6 billion (up from $1.4 billion). And to bring down that debt they sold supermarkets in Kansas, Utah, Oklahoma, Texas and southern California; the Liquor Barn stores in California and Arizona; and all their stores in Britain. As a result, Safeway's sales, $20 billion in mid-decade, retreated to what they were at the start of the 1980s: $13.6 billion.

Even a slimmed down Safeway is big. Entering the 1990s, they had 1,117 supermarkets, almost half of them superstores (averaging 43,000 square feet and carrying 45,000 different items), all in the western U.S. and Canada, except for 150 stores in the mid-Atlantic region around Washington, D.C. They have stores in both Alaska and Hawaii. Their biggest concentration is in northern California, where they have more than 200 stores and where they are headquartered in a nondescript, warehouse-looking building in Oakland hard by the Nimitz Freeway. To supply their stores, Safeway operates 12 giant distribution centers and delivers with a

truck fleet that includes 859 tractor-trailer combinations (plus another 1,737 trailers). They also run 56 manufacturing facilities, including 11 fluid milk plants, 9 bakeries, 8 ice cream plants and 4 cheese plants. Safeway sells 3,400 items under their own brand names, such as Lucerne, Cragmont, Town House and Bel-Air, and these private label goods bring in 15 percent of total sales. In exiting southern California, Safeway acquired, in exchange for their 162 stores, 35 percent of the stock of Vons, the number two supermarket operator in the big Los Angeles market.

Safeway has never inspired much love or affection among their customers, but they do know how to run big stores and are quick to latch onto trends others start. In recent years they have expanded the size of their stores and added bakeries, delicatessens, plant shops, salad bars and pharmacies. They have the muscle to do almost anything. For example, their markets now carry 350 produce items over the course of a year (up from 130 a few years ago). Seven out of every 10 Safeways are open 24 hours a day. Nearly all of them have optical scanners at the checkout counters.

Employees forced to leave the company after the 1986 buyout may not agree, but Chairman Peter Magowan insisted the KKR-management purchase was a great success, enabling Safeway to become a much stronger company by eliminating weak operations and middle- and upper-management people making high salaries. And looked at from a strictly financial perspective, it was successful. In 1989 Safeway made more profits on $14 billion of sales than on $20 billion in 1986. And in late April 1990 Safeway became a publicly held company again as they sold off 10 percent of their stock, which is again traded on the New York Stock Exchange. KKR owned 74.5 percent of the company after the sale of 10 million shares to the public; the management group, 9.3 percent.

History. Wall Street has been intimately linked to the history of Safeway since 1926. Like American Stores, Safeway's roots can be traced to 1915 when S. M. Skaggs opened his grocery store in American Falls, Idaho. The Baptist minister's eldest son, M. B. Skaggs, extended the original grocery store to a western chain that by 1926 encompassed 428 units in the 10 states. That year Skaggs' United Stores merged with a southern California chain of 322 stores using the Safeway name. Charles Merrill of the Wall Street investment house of Merrill Lynch negotiated the merger.

Merrill stayed in the background, however, as Safeway continued to grow under M. B. Skaggs' successor, Lingan A. Warren, who took company reins in 1934. A crusty grocery man, Warren was known throughout the industry as a principled crusader. He fought repeated battles on behalf of his customers: waging war against trading stamps, against dairy/government agreements that fixed the price of milk and against couponing by manufacturers (Warren thought they should cut prices rather than issue coupons). Though Safeway grew during Warren's reign, his policies didn't yield high profits. He was replaced in 1955 by Merrill Lynch's Robert A. Magowan, who had married Charles Merrill's daughter, Doris. Their son Peter became Safeway's CEO in 1978.

Safeway was riding high as America's biggest grocery chain in 1986 when they were hit by the favorite Wall Street game of the 1980s. The ensuing drama had all the elements of a Hollywood movie like *Wall Street*: a villain, the well-known corporate raiders, Herbert Haft and his son, Robert, and a white knight in Kohlberg Kravis Roberts, who saved the day for Safeway's top managers. It began when Haft started buying up Safeway stock, putting the company "in play," that is, up for sale. That sent shudders down the spines of Safeway's top managers, who feared, justifiably, that if Safeway was taken over, it would be dismembered—and they would lose their jobs. So they arranged with KKR to take Safeway private with a higher bid, thereby giving the Hafts a short-term profit of $160 million—and Safeway's top managers stayed in place and did their own dismembering of the company they had built up.

Owners and rulers. KKR and investors in their buyout fund got control of Safeway with an investment of only $175 million. On top of that, KKR pocketed a fee of $60 million from Safeway for arranging the buyout and has a management consulting agreement with them that paid $590,000 in 1987 and $726,000 in 1988. The management in place before the buyout still runs Safeway. Magowan and 20 other top executives came away from the deal with options to buy up to 10 percent of Safeway stock for $2 a share. When Safeway went public, these shares were worth more than five times what they paid for them. In 1989, Peter Magowan pulled down a salary of over $1.2 million; the other four top officers averaged between $450,000 and $600,000.

As a place to work. The buyout cost Safeway their good reputation as an employer. Their SOS motto—"Safeway Offers Security"—became a grim reminder of how drastically the company changed in just a few short months. All told, more than 75,000 Safeway employees lost their jobs, though many were rehired by the new owners. Elsewhere there were plenty of horror stories: one man was fired a month after his wife was diagnosed with cancer. Twenty-year veterans were told, with no warning, to clear out their desks and to be gone by noon. Simple niceties were spared; one long-time employee complained that her supervisor "didn't say 'thank you,' or 'I'm sorry,' or anything." As one ex-employee put it: "No new products. No new stores. No new divisions. A few men got a lot richer—and that's about what it boils down to." When asked about the unceremonious disposal of one-third of his former work force, CEO Peter Magowan said only, "There was a strong urgency to put the whole unpleasant matter behind us as soon as possible." Magowon got help from unions, which traded wage hikes for some measure of security for the remaining jobs. In 1989 Safeway's cost per employee was $14.85 an hour, up only 21 cents over 1986. Of Safeway's 107,000 employees, 100,000 are covered by union contracts.

Social responsibility. After the buyout, Safeway cut its charitable contibutions by almost a third. However, after the October 1989 earthquake in Northern California, they diverted truckloads of bottled water, baby formula and batteries to the hardhit Watsonville area and matched $100,000 of customer donations to the Salvation Army.

Global presence. It was wiped out by the KKR-management buyout.

Safeway Inc., Fourth and Jackson Streets, Oakland, CA 94660; (415) 891-3000.

4

#4 *in supermarkets*

Employees: 83,000
Sales: $11.1 billion
Profits: $147 million
Founded: 1869
Headquarters: Montvale, New Jersey

In 1979, when German grocery store magnate Erivan Haub bought control of the slumping A&P supermarket chain, a Wall Street wiseacre quipped, "Do you think we finally put one over on the Germans?" No such luck. Haub installed James Wood, an Englishman, at the helm of what was once the largest grocer in the U.S. and by 1990 a very different looking A&P had made such a strong comeback that Wood was now talking about being number one again. Unlike their competitors, A&P has no debt. They had already become the top grocer in the New York metropolitan area and were number one or two in Philadelphia, Detroit, Toronto, and Milwaukee. The Germans had put one over on the Americans.

The new A&P wears different disguises. Rather than staying with one name, Wood bought regional chains and came up with new names for old stores, so the company now sells groceries under many banners. More than 200 A&Ps in the Mid-Atlantic states were converted to the SuperFresh name, operating a "Quality of Work Life" program enabling employees to share in productivity gains. If you shop in New York, you're patronizing A&P if you go to Food Emporium or Waldbaum's. In Detroit, Farmer Jack is now an A&P-owned chain. Other A&P-owned groceries are Kohl's in Wisconsin, Dominion in Toronto (A&P does 20 percent of their sales in Canada) and J. Bildner & Sons in Boston. Some of these stores are upscale, some right down the middle, others discount food outlets. A&P will try anything. They opened an A&P Food Bazaar on New York's Union Square and a gigantic Futurestore in Atlanta. They have warehouse stores under the Sav-A-Center name. For A&P, the A&P name is no longer important. Only half their stores carry the A&P name. They're trying to be all things to all people. In the words of James Wood, "Our product is a store."

Wood has been well paid for this comeback, including a bonus of over $25 million. Haub can afford it. His family owns Tengelmann Warenhandelsgesellschaft, the largest supermarket chain in Europe, and the family is one of the richest in the world, worth an estimated $5 billion. Tengelmann was founded four generations ago as a coffee shop in the Ruhr river town of Muelheim, where the firm is still headquartered. Because of the low social status accorded German retailers, Haub's great-grandfather didn't want the store to be named after himself, so he named it after one of his salesmen, Emil Tengelmann. Known as a quiet man, Erivan Haub has spent a lot of time in the U.S., starting in the early 1950s when he worked for a year as a management trainee with Jewel supermarkets in Chicago and another year with Alpha Beta in California. His three sons were born at a family estate in Tacoma, Washington. Haub told *Forbes*: "One reason I enjoy working in the U.S. is that the supermarket business is much more highly thought of there."

History. In buying control of A&P (Haub now owns just over 50 percent of the shares), Haub was buying one of the legends of American retailing history. The chain was founded in New York City by George Huntington Hartford with the pompous name of The Great Atlantic and Pacific Tea Company. The front of the original store on Vesey Street was painted with "real vermillion imported from China," with touches of gold leaf. The cashiers' cages resembled miniature Chinese pagodas. In the center of the store a large cockatoo squawked "welcome," and on Saturday nights a band played free. A&P grew because they undersold their competition, especially in the early years of this century when they introduced 7,500 "cash-and-carry" economy stores in a three-year period. These were one-person operations having all the same goods in the same location. George Hartford's son John boasted he could walk blindfolded into any store and find the beans.

A&P survived the threat of the new supermarkets during the 1930s by closing down small operations and opening hundreds of their own supermarkets. In 1970 A&P was still America's biggest grocer—a position they'd held since the turn of the century. But with competitors like Safeway and Kroger nipping at its heels, A&P engaged in a series of desperate cost-cutting moves to boost sales. Morale dropped. Stores became dirty. One manager said that "while the crud kept mounting,... it got to the point where we not only had dirt, we had dirty dirt." Customers fled in droves, sometimes abandoning their shopping carts in the aisles because checkout lines were so long. When the Germans took over in 1979, A&P had dropped to third place and was still falling.

Stock performance. A&P stock bought for $1,000 in 1980 sold for $7,203 on January 2, 1990.

Consumer brands.

A&P, The Food Emporium, Waldbaum's, SuperFresh, Dominion, Kohl's, A&P Sav-A-Center, A&P Futurestore, A&P Food Bazaar.

The Great Atlantic & Pacific Tea Company, Inc., 2 Paragon Drive, Montvale, NJ 07645; (201) 573-9700.

5

#5 *in supermarkets*

Employees: 89,000
Sales: $9.5 billion
Profits: $147 million
Founded: 1925
Headquarters: Jacksonville, Florida

A southern company slow to change, Winn-Dixie runs the biggest supermarket business in the Sunbelt, operating more than 1,200 stores in 13 states stretching across the southern tier of the country from Florida to Texas. Their main base is Florida, where they have 470 stores. In addition to selling groceries, they have 27 plants that turn out a lot of the foodstuffs sold in their stores: coffee, tea and spices; soft drinks; cookies and crackers; bread and cakes; frozen pizza; detergents; jams, jellies and salad dressings; sausages and luncheon meats; peanut butter; milk, ice cream, butter and eggs.

Prior to the 1980s, Winn-Dixie had a formula that worked well—if you were a stockholder. They would have nothing to do with labor unions. Nor did they pay much attention when other supermarket chains added pharmacies, delis and in-house bakeries. They stuck to the food business. They didn't build giant, cavernous stores. And it was hard to fault them. They boasted one of the highest profit margins in the supermarket industry.

This comfortable existence ended during the 1980s. Other supermarkets—Publix, Kroger, Albertson's, Food Lion, Bruno—began moving onto their turf with bigger stores and lower prices. Winn-Dixie, not used to this kind of attack, responded slowly. The number of stores they had in 1990 was about the same they had in 1984. But profits in 1990 were also the same as they were in 1984. Meanwhile, total sales and number of employees had increased, meaning profit margins deteriorated. Soon Winn-Dixie may no longer be king of the hill in Dixie.

Headquartered in dusty offices in Jacksonville, Florida, Winn-Dixie clings to a Confederate past. The *Dixie* in Winn-Dixie's name is the key to this company's outlook—southern and paternalistic. In 1925, W. M. Davis borrowed $10,000 to open his first grocery store in Lemon City, Florida. Nine years later, his four sons took over. The company was called Table Supply until 1955 when they changed their name because they wanted to "Win Dixie." The Davis brothers were fond of buying their competitors, which they did left and right until 1966 when the FTC prevented them from buying another store for 10 years—for antitrust reasons. The Davis family remains active in the chain's management. The Davis brothers were all on the job until the youngest, Tine Wayne Davis, died in 1980 at age 66. During the 1980s the other brothers stepped back, though longtime chairman, James Elsworth Davis, who stepped down in 1983 at age 76, and Artemus Darius Davis are still on the board. James' son, A. Dano Davis is now chairman (in 1989 he earned a relatively modest $526 thousand), and A. D.'s son, Robert, chairman from 1983 to 1988, is now vice chairman. Tine Wayne Davis, Jr., is a director. The family owns 38 percent of the company and is reputed to be worth nearly $1 billion.

Winn-Dixie follows some unique practices. For example, in the financial summary that runs in the annual report they list the average number of shareholders they have in stores. This number declined from 39 in 1984 to 32 in 1988. Amazingly, they still pay shareholders a cash dividend *every* month. And they are big on dividends at Winn-Dixie. In 1989 they increased their monthly cash dividend from 16 cents to 16-1/2 cents. That was the 45th consecutive year in which the dividend payout was raised, a record for New York Stock Exchange-listed companies. So, if you happen to own one share of Winn-Dixie stock, the company puts a 25 cent stamp on an envelope every month to send you 16-1/2 cents.

S*tock performance.* Winn-Dixie stock bought for $1,000 in 1980 sold for $6,496 on January 2, 1990.

Winn-Dixie Stores Inc., 5050 Edgewood Court, P.O. Box B, Jacksonville, FL 32203; (904) 783-5000.

6

THE SOUTHLAND CORPORATION

#1 *in convenience stores*

Employees: 47,000
Sales: $7.9 billion
Founded: 1927
Headquarters: Dallas

The world's biggest convenience store chain—7-Eleven—was up for grabs early in 1990. They faced two choices: declare bankruptcy or sell out to the Japanese. They picked the Japanese. It marked the end of a long financial struggle for Southland, one that began in 1987 when the Thompson brothers (sons of the founder) borrowed some $4.9 billion to buy the company stock from other shareholders. They promptly sold off a number of side businesses including their original business (ice). But the debt was too much. Aside from being saddled with the mountain of debt the buyout incurred, Southland was confronted with new competition in the form of gasoline stations adding mini-groceries and supermarkets staying open later and later (many of them 24 hours). Thus, the creator of another American-born institution fell into foreign hands.

With nearly 7,000 stores, 7-Eleven is the nation's largest food chain in terms of number of units. But 7-Elevens are not grocery stores in the conventional sense. They're the modern world's version of the corner mom-and-pop grocery— where people go to pick up a few items between time-consuming trips to the supermarket and pay higher prices for the convenience. Besides grocery items like bread, milk, packaged meats, canned goods and cereal, they sell such items as money orders (more than anyone except the post office), comic books, beach and picnic paraphernalia, flashlight batteries and pantyhose. They also do a brisk business in prepared food and drink, notably sandwiches, coffee, hot chocolate and, of course, Slurpees, a frozen syrup concoction available only at 7-Eleven. Two of their biggest sellers are beer and cigarettes.

During the 1980s, 7-Eleven stopped selling *Playboy* and *Penthouse* to appease Christian fundamentalists, who accused them of peddling pornography. The 7-elevens had been the largest sellers of those magazines. They made up for it by adding Oscar Mayer hot dogs, videocassettes and lottery plays.

History. When Joe C. Thompson was a high school student in Dallas during the First World War, he spent his summers loading blocks of ice onto horse-drawn wagons. After school he joined the ice firm and soon came up with the idea of selling chilled water melons off the ice docks. The first ice-cold watermelons sold in Texas became an immediate hit. But the idea that made Thompson's fortune was that of a dock manager at Thompson's Southland Ice Company. In the summer of 1927, "Uncle Johnny" Green started a brisk sideline to the ice business, selling bread, milk and eggs. The convenience store business was born.

Soon the company was running a string of convenience stores from their ice docks. Called Tote'm Stores, their trademark was an Alaskan Indian totem pole displayed outside. In 1946 they changed the name of the stores to 7-Eleven, because they stayed open from 7 A.M. to 11 P.M. (although in later years most stores would be open 24 hours a day). In 1947 there were 74 stores; at Joe Thompson's death in 1961, 600.

Southland's troubles began in 1983 when they bought Citgo Petroleum, the country's largest independent refiner and marketer, from Occidental for a total of $777 million. It was the wrong time to get into the refinery business. The very next year Citgo reported a pretax loss of $50 million. In January 1985, Southland cut Citgo's output in half, fired 850 workers

E*very beat of your heart (one second) Phillip Morris/Kraft General Foods produces 3 pounds of margarine, 8 jars of mayonnaise, 5 1/2 pasta dinners–and 16,666 cigarettes.*

and replaced Citgo's president. The next year they sold half of Citgo to the Venezuelan national oil company for $290 million.

After the Thompsons took Southland private in 1987, they sold off their entire dairy operation (milk, ice cream, frozen goods); the Reddy Ice Division (block and processed cocktail ice); the food, chemical and preservatives factories in Chicago, Dallas and New Jersey; their electronic and mechanical equipment company; 400 Chief Auto Parts stores; and their snack food operations (Pate Foods, El-Ge Potato Chip and Keystone Pretzel).

Owners and rulers. Joe Thompson, who ran Southland until his death in 1961, probably wouldn't have approved of all the panic. His two sons John (as president) and Jere (as vice president) took the helm on his death. In 1986, 60-year-old John resigned as CEO and was succeeded by 54-year-old Jere. John stayed on as chairman of the board, and 46-year-old Joe C. ("Jodie") Thompson, Jr., became a director. When John and Jere were boys, their father had put them to work sweeping floors and washing trucks—at less than 30 cents an hour. The brothers are known for their political conservatism and are practicing Catholics. One Christmas in the mid-1980s, Jere erected a crèche on the front lawn of the family's rambling mansion, which featured Santa cradling the Christ child.

Ito-Yokado, the new Japanese owners, have been running the 7-Elevens in Japan since 1973. From a single store in downtown Tokyo, Ito-Yokado has built the chain to more than 4,000 stores that feature box lunches and rice balls and are reported to serve 127 million bowls of instant ramen noodles a year. Ito-Yokado also owns supermarkets and department stores in Japan, doing more than $12 billion a year in sales, and is said to be Japan's most profitable retailer. When

Southland was selling off stores in 1989 to help pay off their debt, Ito-Yokado bought the firm's 58 stores in Hawaii, partly because of complaints from Japanese tourists about the stores being run down. "Many Japanese go to the United States and Hawaii, and if they see a bad 7-Eleven it is not good for us," a company spokesman in Tokyo explained to the *New York Times*. According to the terms of the deal, the Thompsons will be allowed to keep 15 percent of their stock while 10 percent will be given to the bondholders. Some bondholders opposed the sale to Ito-Yokado, arguing the Japanese only had to put up $400 million to get 75 percent of the company. Considering that the Thompsons spent more than 10 times as much ($4.9 billion) four years earlier to buy the company, the bondholders had a good point. But by 1990, the Thompsons may have had little choice.

As a place to work. Southland franchises almost half of all their 7-Eleven stores, but it's not a system for free spirits, as Southland is the Big Brother of franchisers. Applicants are attracted by the surprisingly low initial fee—about $20,000. In exchange for that fee, Southland trains you, gives you a fully equipped and stocked 7-Eleven store and maintains the building and equipment. You're accountable for the rest—and you have to pay Southland a hefty chunk of all profits, ranging from 52 percent to 63 percent. If profits fall too low, they can shut you down in 72 hours. "Essentially, we're managers with the responsibility of owners," one franchisee complained in 1989.

Social responsibility. In 1984 Southland was convicted of conspiring to defraud the IRS. They were fined $10,000. This hurt Southland's image, but it also hurt sales in two states—Iowa and Oregon—where laws forbid felons to sell liquor. Southland launched a vigorous lobbying campaign, and within three days the legislatures in both states had changed their laws. In 1985 Southland paid a $100,000 fine to the Environmental Protection Agency for a chemical leak at a plant in New Jersey. Southland has also been accused numerous times of discriminating against black franchisees, but the company stoutly denies all charges.

Consumer brands.

Convenience stores: 7-Eleven, Quik Mart, Super-7.

Food: Deli Shoppe sandwiches, Casa Buena and Sonritos burritos, Italini pizzas, Aunt Bea's cookies, Smiley's sandwiches, Slurpees.

The Southland Corporation, 2828 North Haskell Avenue, Dallas, TX 75204; (214) 828-7011.

7

Albertsons®

#7 *in supermarkets*

Employees: 53,000
Sales: $7.4 billion
Profits: $197 million
Founded: 1939
Headquarters: Boise, Idaho

The youngest of the big supermarket chains (only 50 years old in 1989), Albertson's has spread from their Boise, Idaho, base to 17 western and southern states where they operate more than 500 stores that are the envy of the grocery industry because of their ability to squeeze profits out of sales. In an industry where earning a penny on every sales dollar is considered the norm, Albertson's nets two pennies. For 19 straight years, their sales and profits have increased. Each unit makes a profit—or it's sayonara. Store managers earn bonuses every year, based on their store's profit. In 1988, for example, Albertson's paid out $27 million in bonuses to 3,800 managers; it is not unusual for a store manager to make upwards of $100,000 a year. No unions represent employees, and to keep labor costs down, no Albertson's has more than five service departments—a pharmacy, deli, fish and meat department and bakery. The typical Albertson's store is very large (between 35,000 and 65,000 square feet), located in a small city or in the suburbs (where land is cheap) and doesn't stock specialty food items. As one analyst told

Forbes: "When you see their stores, it's just like Wal-Mart, nothing impressive. But that's what's impressive."

The company was started by a former Safeway district manager, A. J. "Joe" Albertson, who was 83 years old in 1989 and still controlled about 17 percent of the stock, worth about $440 million in 1990. Albertson's current CEO is Warren McCain, aged 64, who earned $1.05 million in 1989.

S*tock performance:* Albertson's stock bought for $1,000 in 1980 sold for $14,737 on January 2, 1990.

Albertson's Inc., 250 Parkcenter Blvd., Boise, ID 83726; (208) 385-6200.

8

WHERE SHOPPING IS A PLEASURE

Publix super markets, inc.

#1 *among Florida supermarkets*

Employees: 57,000
Sales: $4.8 billion
Profits: $86 million
Founded: 1930
Headquarters: Lakeland, Florida

Workplace

Publix refuses to expand beyond their home state, but they have become one of the top 10 grocers in the nation by becoming the biggest in the Sunshine State—Florida. Their formula is simple. They try to live up to the company slogan emblazoned on each store's facade: "Publix: Where shopping is a pleasure." A national magazine once dubbed Publix "the Tiffany of the food store business." According to a rival grocery store executive: "[Publix] has spent more to give the impression that [their] stores are marble palaces while ours aren't quite that nice." Founder George Jenkins' first supermarket, built in Winter Haven in 1930,

was hailed as the most up-to-date store in the nation with such pioneering ideas as shopping carts, wide aisles, self-service meat and produce departments and air conditioning. But what really attracted shoppers from miles around were the electric-eye doors, which Jenkins had first seen at New York's Pennsylvania Station. Publix has kept on innovating—they were first in the nation to install electronic scanning devices in all their stores (1981).

Yet it's more than outward appearances and new gadgets that make Publix so unusual. Publix also believes that the company should be a place "where working is a pleasure." Publix employees work for themselves because the chain is one of the country's largest employee-owned companies. Employees have been entitled to buy stock since Jenkins opened his first store, and a number have retired as millionaires because of the huge rise in the value of Publix stock over the years. Publix employees are paid hourly wages comparable to their counterparts at other Florida chains, but they earn more because of a generous profit-sharing program. Twenty percent of a store's profits are distributed to employees every quarter. There's a genuine family feeling at Publix despite the size. Virtually all company officers started at the bottom. Every time a new Publix store opens, top management officials welcome new employees at an opening night banquet. And the officers stay the next morning to work shoulder-to-shoulder with the newcomers stocking the shelves and bagging groceries. In early 1990, 82-year-old George Jenkins stepped down as chairman of the board and was succeeded by his son, 38-year-old Howard, who is also CEO.

Publix Super Markets, Inc., Box 407, Lakeland, FL 33802; (813) 688-1188.

CLOTHING & SHELTER

CLOTHING

Trying to figure out six to nine months ahead what clothing people may want to buy is not easy. And that may explain why the clothing industry doesn't have many corporate giants. The biggest companies in the field—Levi Strauss, Liz Claiborne and VF—rely heavily on well-established brand names. In 1980, $6.2 billion worth of clothing was imported into the U.S.; by 1987, imports were well over the $20 billion mark. This business still relies on people sitting behind sewing machines. In this country, the two biggest employment centers are New York City and Los Angeles (accounting for about one-quarter of the 1 million employees in the industry).

1

#1 *in clothing*

Employees: 32,000
Sales: $3.1 billion
Profits: $272 million
Founded: 1850
Headquarters: San Francisco, California

Social Conscience

They're the original. The Levi's trademark ranks with Coca-Cola and McDonald's and Johnnie Walker in that select group of brand names enjoying worldwide recognition. Since they went into business 140 years ago, Levi Strauss has sold more than 2 billion pairs of jeans, becoming in the process the world's largest clothing maker. Today, they make casual wear other than jeans—pants, shirts, jackets, children's wear, women's sports wear—but jeans remain the core business, accounting for about half of the company's $3 billion-plus in sales. By 1990 they were turning out about 100 million pairs a year, which would mean one out of every five jeans-wearers sports Levi's.

While they continue to be the preeminent jeans maker and still enjoy a reputation as one of the most socially responsible companies in America, Levi Strauss in 1990 was not the same company they were in 1980. In the middle of the decade the Haas family that has ruled this enterprise since their founding in 1850 reversed a move made 15 years earlier and returned the company to private—that is, the family's—ownership. All the public shareholders were paid off, Levi Strauss stock left the New York Stock Exchange, and Robert D. Haas, CEO and great-great-grandnephew of founder Levi Strauss, didn't have to worry anymore about quarter-to-quarter performance or presentations to Wall Street security analysts.

The reversion to 100 percent private ownership came with other changes. To shrink the company to fit a declining jeans market and to help pay off the debt going private incurred, Levi's closed 41 plants in the U.S., automated factories to reduce their labor force, slashed the white-collar ranks and thereby ended up cutting their total payroll from 48,000 to 31,000.

Levi Strauss has been trying for a long time to lessen their dependence on jeans. During the 1980s they entered a dozen new fashion businesses, either by acquisition or licensing agreements, including a Perry Ellis America collection, Oxford dress suits, a line of career women clothing by designer Alexander Julian, Resistol hats and athletic wear with the brand name of Olympic marathoner Frank Shorter. They bought Koret sportswear and Britannia jeans. By 1988 every one of those businesses, except Britannia, had departed Levi Strauss. Toward the end of the decade they hit paydirt with Dockers, a line of casual cotton pants for Yuppies who have outgrown jeans. Selling in the $35 to $40 range, Dockers' sales were approaching $500 million, which means that if they were broken out as a separate company, they would rank as the seventh or eighth largest clothing maker in the U.S.

These 19th century miners were actually fashion pioneers, helping to make the button fly and shrink-to-fit denim jeans into American classics.

History. Levi Strauss, a German-Jewish immigrant, came out to San Francisco from New York in 1850 when he was 20 years old. He planned to sell dry goods, especially tent canvas, to California gold-miners. It turned out that no one wanted to buy tents, so Strauss used the canvas to make pants, which the miners dubbed Levi's. A Nevada tailor named Jacob Davis discovered a way to repair the ripped pockets on pairs of Levi's. He wrote to Levi Strauss and described his modification: "The secratt of them Pents is the Rivits that I put in those Pockets." After Davis' modification, the company was soon turning out a model that has remained virtually unchanged to the present day: the "501 Double X blue denim waist overall"—501 being the lot number, Double X the term for heavyweight denim. The jeans were "guaranteed to shrink, wrinkle and fade." The two notable changes in the jeans were the elimination of a copper rivet in the crotch (be-cause cowboys crouching over campfires were burned that way) and the elimination of rivets on the back pockets (schools complained the rivets scratched school furniture). According to legend, miners, farmers and cowboys made each pair fit perfectly by putting them on when they were new and jumping into a watering trough. When the pants dried, they fit.

Levi Strauss, a bachelor, died in 1906 and left the bulk of his $6 million estate to four nephews: Jacob, Sigmund, Louis and Abraham Stern. The Sterns and their descendants (among them the Haases) established the company's humanitarian reputation. When the great 1906 earth-quake leveled San Francisco, destroying the Levi Strauss facilities, the company continued to pay their 350 employees. And the firm offered low- or no-interest loans to retail merchants whose stores had been wiped out.

Owners and rulers. The Haas family's ownership of Levi Strauss increased from

According to the Oxford English Dictionary, *the word* jean *derives from* Genoese *and originally meant twilled cloth made in Genoa. Denim got its name from the city of Nimes, in southern France, where the cotton fabric was originally produced. Originally called serge de Nimes, the British corrupted it to denim.*

40 percent to 92 percent in 1985 when they paid $1.6 billion for the company shares. The buyout was funded with so-called junk bonds and the Haas family put very little of their own money into the deal—a group led by San Francisco's Wells Fargo Bank lent $1.45 billion. The leader of this deal, and an important minority shareholder, was San Francisco investment banker, Hellman and Freidman. Fifteen years earlier, Warren Hellman (who was working for Lehman Brothers at the time) managed the deal that took Levi's public. Despite the huge debt they've taken on, Levi's has not resorted to the wholesale restructurings that have followed similar buyouts during the 1980s. In 1988, Levi Strauss announced their U.S. employees would be given the option to buy stock in the company.

As a place to work. In the 1960s and 1970s Levi Strauss was a scruffy place, not too big on formality. They had a sense they were changing the world. Today, they're a more "corporate" place, run by managers who have been to graduate business schools, but they try to hew to the old values. Now they even let headquarters people come to work in jeans. They moved their headquarters from downtown San Francisco in the early 1980s after deciding that being located in a high rise in the Embarcadero Center complex was inconsistent with their character as a "treetop company." They bought some land in an area near the waterfront and built themselves a low-rise complex. In the 1980s they also adopted a mission statement that stresses their aims to "make a fair profit," maintain a "workplace of people with different backgrounds, ideas and opinions" and conduct their business in an ethical manner. In 1990 Levi's closed one of their three sewing plants in San Antonio, Texas (and their second largest in the U.S.), throwing 1,100 people out of work. Average wage in the plant, which made Dockers pants, was $5.57 an hour. Levi's moved this production to the Dominican Republic, where the average wage is closer to $1 an hour. But Levi's has gotten plant-closing down to such a fine art (they had plenty of experience in the 1980s) that they took very little flak, even in San Antonio, for this shutdown, because of excellent severance packages. However, Louisa Hernandez, district manager of the Amalgamated Clothing Workers, was not impressed: "Levi is like any other company. They will look to see where they can make the most money."

Social responsibility. In their home territory, the San Francisco Bay Area, Levi Strauss is a very visible presence. They're in the forefront of private support for community services and cultural activities, and many people, not distinguishing between the family and the company, connect them with the Oakland A's, the baseball team that won the World Series in 1989. The A's are owned by Walter A. Haas, Jr., honorary chairman of Levi Strauss and father of CEO Robert Haas, and the club itself has a strong community outreach program of its own. Levi's allocates 2.5 percent of pretax profits to charitable contributions, well above the average in the corporate world. They have led in rallying support for persons with AIDS. They also encourage and support employee volunteerism through community involvement teams. In 1989 the Haas family gave $15 million to the School of Business Administration at the University of California at Berkeley, which promptly changed its name to the Walter A. Haas School of Business, after the father of Walter, Jr. It was the largest single donation ever made to Cal-Berkeley.

Global presence. With 15 plants and 7,800 employees over seas, they do about one-third of their business, more than $1 billion a year, outside the U.S. Levi's jeans are sold in more than 70 countries. A licensee makes them in Hungary, and they can't wait to get into Russia and China. Although they went private in the U.S., their Japanese subsidiary sold stock to the public in 1989 in an offering so much in demand that one-fifth of the company fetched $100 million. Japan is now the only place in the world where the public can buy stock in a Levi Strauss entity. Levi's used to be proud to point out that while they had developed a major international business, the goods they sold in the U.S. were made there too. That will change now although the company said in early 1990 that 90 percent of Levi's jeans and 75 percent of all garments sold in the U.S. were still being made here. However, Peter Thigpen, senior vice president of the company, said what no Levi Strauss official would have said 10 years ago: "American consumers value high quality, style and price—and don't care too much where the garments come from."

Consumer brands.

Levi's, Britannia, Dockers.

Levi Strauss & Company, Levi's Plaza, 1155 Battery Street, San Francisco, CA 94106; (415) 544-7222.

2

VF CORPORATION

#1 *in jeans*

Employees: 44,000
Sales: $2.5 billion
Profits: $176 million
Founded: 1899
Headquarters: Wyomissing, Pennsylvania

Most people think Levi Strauss, the inventor of blue jeans, is the largest jeans manufacturer. But they're not anymore. The volume leader is VF, which stands for Vanity Fair, the brand name for a line of lingerie. VF backed into the jeans business in 1969 when the people running the company became a little nervous on hearing feminists talk about burning bras. At the time VF made nothing but lingerie. So they bought H. D. Lee, maker of Lee jeans, which they turned into the number two brand behind Levi's. Then, in the mid-1980s VF bought

Blue Bell, maker of Wrangler, Rustler and Girbaud jeans. The four-brand combination lifted them a notch above Levi Strauss. Lee, which celebrated their centennial in 1989, is the big brand, accounting for 13 percent of the jeans market and 25 percent of VF's total sales.

The Blue Bell purchase also brought them Jantzen swimwear and sportswear brands as well as the Red Kap and Big Ben work clothes and uniform businesses.

VF bought two other companies in the 1980s: Bassett-Walker, maker of knitted, fleeced sweats, shorts and other garments known as "activewear," and Modern Globe, a company that supplements VF's original business—they make women's cotton underwear, men's underwear and T-shirts. Modern Globe owns the Lollipop brand name, but most of their products turn up under store labels.

The jeans industry began to fade in the 1980s, sales plummeting from a peak of 516 million pairs in 1981 to 400 million pairs in 1988. In 1988, to perk up sales of Lee jeans, VF started distributing them in discount stores, like Target and Venture, where VF sells Wrangler and Rustler brands. Instead of increasing sales, the move lowered the quality cachet of Lee jeans—and sales dropped alarmingly. May department stores dropped all Lee jeans.

History. Vanity Fair originated in 1899 as the Reading Glove & Mitten Manufacturing Company, maker of silk gloves. They branched into silk stockings and lingerie in 1914. Lee started in 1889 as a wholesale grocery in Salina, Kansas, where Henry David Lee sold canned foods to other stores. By the turn of the century, Lee was also selling furniture, hardware, school supplies and clothing. He began making his own overalls, jackets and dungarees in 1911. Lee was quite a designer. In 1913 he invented the overall or "Lee Union-All" to keep his chauffeur's uniform clean while he changed a tire. He was the first to put a zipper fly in cowboy pants, the first to use slider fasteners on work clothing and the first to put a center crease in jeans.

Owners and rulers. Laurence Pugh became president of VF in 1980 when he was 47—straight from Beatrice, where he ran the Samsonite division. He became chairman and CEO in 1983. In 1989, he earned $1.2 million. Robert Gregory, Jr., a lawyer, is president. He took over VF's Lee division in 1979 when he was 36. A trust for the descendants of John Barbey, the founder of Vanity Fair, owns 17 percent of the company.

As a place to work. VF is always looking for ways to cut costs, and the people who work for them are usually the prime target. The quest for cheap labor took them to the nonunion South starting in 1937. In the late 1980s, they shut down 15 Wrangler sewing plants, 5 Lee plants, 2 Lee distribution centers, 1 Jantzen and 1 Bassett-Walker plant.

Global presence. VF does 12 percent of their jeanswear sales ($1.4 billion in 1988) outside the U.S. Lee jeans have been made in Northern Ireland for more than 40 years. They derive only 2 percent of their U.S. sales from imported garments.

Stock performance. VF stock bought for $1,000 in 1980 sold for $17,118 on January 2, 1990.

Consumer brands.

Jeans: Lee, Wrangler, Rustler, Girbaud.

Lingerie & sleepwear: Vanity Fair, Lollipop, Modern Globe.

Sportswear: Jantzen, JanSport, Bassett-Walker, BW, Sturdy Sweats, Willis & Geiger, Skeets, Cotton Works, Pepsi Apparel America.

Work clothes: Red Kap, Big Ben by Wrangler.

Outdoor gear: JanSport.

V.F. Corporation, 1047 North Park Road, Wyomissing, PA 19610; (215) 378-1151.

3

Liz claiborne

#1 *in women's sportswear in department stores*

Employees: 5,578
Sales: $1.4 billion
Profits: $165 million
Founded: 1976
Headquarters: New York City, New York

Liz Claiborne's first line of clothes hit the department stores in 1976 just as the burgeoning cadre of working women began chafing against the suit-and-floppy-bow-tie look that seemed de rigueur when they first entered corporate America. With businesslike yet chic clothes, Liz Claiborne became an overnight hero to the fashion-starved professional.

Claiborne clothes have the cachet of a designer label, but they're actually mass-produced, reasonably priced and up-to-date rather than avant-garde. Founder Claiborne doesn't think of herself as a fashion innovator. "I don't make the news with new fashion trends," she once told *Newsweek.* Her successors are trying their best to maintain the Claiborne formula intact.

History. The preeminent clothier for career women wouldn't have had a career herself if her father had had his way. He was a banker from an old New Orleans family, posted in Brussels when Elizabeth was born in 1929. He roused her interest in art with trips to museums and cathedrals and let her study painting at Académie des Beaux Arts in Paris. But as Claiborne told *Cosmopolitan,* "My father was of the old school. His view was, 'A woman's place is in the home.' A little painting was fine. But not a career."

Strong-willed like her father, Claiborne entered a *Harper's Bazaar* design contest while vacationing in New Orleans in 1949. When she won, she refused to go back to Europe. So her father handed her $50, and that was that.

She nonetheless cherishes family history—she is a direct descendant of William C. C. Claiborne, Louisiana's governor during the War of 1812. When a 1958 movie called *The Buccaneer* showed the pirate Jean Laffite, played by Yul Brynner, cavorting with Governor Claiborne's daughter at a time when the girl would actually have been 3, not 20 years old as portrayed, Liz and her family considered a lawsuit but later dropped the idea.

Claiborne made a name for herself on Seventh Avenue, New York's design enclave, at Jonathan Logan, where she spent 16 years designing moderately priced junior dresses. She and her second husband Arthur Ortenberg, a veteran clothing executive, toyed with the idea of being their own bosses before 1976. But they waited until their kids, two from his previous marriage and one from hers, were college-age before risking $50,000 in savings and $200,000 borrowed from friends and family on a company of their own.

Even before her clothes started to sell, Claiborne's reputation helped give the company status. And because her founding partners were also experts in their areas—Leonard Boxer in manufacturing and Ortenberg's college roommate Jerry Chazen in marketing—they had the contacts to line up favorable overseas suppliers and prestigious sales outlets from the start.

Claiborne called her customers "Liz Ladies" and worked hard to find out what they wanted—and what price they were willing to pay. A full-time crew travels the country to get firsthand information about the Liz Lady's taste. Every week, the marketing department analyzes what customers buy at a cross section of stores, and projects what they'll want several months hence. Armed with that information, Claiborne responds to the consumer better than any other clothing company, in *Fortune*'s estimation. Liz Claiborne supplies stores with new clothing more frequently than other companies, six collections a year instead of the traditional

Liz Claiborne, founder and, until 1989, head of the popular women's apparel company that bears her name.

four. As a result, customers can find something new whenever they go shopping. They can find summer Claiborne clothes in July, for example, when other makers traditionally switch to fall fashions. The company is currently opening their own stores, called "Liz" and "First Issue," stocked entirely with Liz Claiborne clothing. At the end of 1989, there were 25 First Issue stores.

Claiborne's 14 designers create clothes that fit real women, not the impossibly thin models in magazines. They use fabrics that won't permanently wrinkle if they're jammed in a suitcase. And they keep Claiborne clothes affordably priced by using independent suppliers in Hong Kong, Taiwan, Korea, Sri Lanka, the Philippines and 10 other countries. They get 88 percent of their product from outside the U.S. Claiborne owns no factories.

Claiborne's functional style has paid off. Her clothes are carried in 9,000 department and specialty stores. They are the number one brand among some 15 million women. Her stockholders used to give her standing ovations at annual meetings. *Fortune* has named her one of the 50 most interesting businesspeople. And *Forbes* ranked Claiborne as one of the 800 most powerful bosses in America, an elite that included only one other woman.

O*wners and rulers.*   Claiborne and her husband retired in 1989, leaving the running of the firm to Jerry Chazen. Claiborne still sits on the board as a director. She owns 4 percent of the stock, worth about $100 million.

A*s a place to work.*   Claiborne was as particular about her midtown Manhattan offices as she is about her clothing. The result is a businesslike yet friendly atmosphere. The walls are white, her favorite color, so that designers won't be distracted from the fabrics at hand. The internal telephone directory lists employees alphabetically—by first name.

After juggling work and childrearing as a young designer, Claiborne tried to make things easier for her employees. Her New Jersey distribution and administrative operations contain an employee day-care center. And through the charitable Liz Claiborne Foundation, she helped finance a day-care center in Chinatown, where many of New York's garment factories,

and some of her own suppliers, are located. Women are well represented in key company jobs. One-third of Claiborne's senior managers are women, and 6 of 21 executive officers are women. About 62 percent of employees are women, and 40 percent of senior management is female.

G*lobal presence.*   With 88 percent of manufacturing done overseas in 15 countries, Claiborne has branch offices in Hong Kong, Taipei and Manila to act as go-betweens for headquarters and their contractors. Sensitive to criticism they're taking jobs away from Americans, Claiborne is working with the International Ladies Garment Workers Union to import offshore techniques. They're setting up a jeans factory in New York's Chinatown to be staffed by union workers and run by one of Claiborne's Hong Kong manufacturers.

S*tock performance.*   Liz Claiborne stock bought for $1,000 in 1980 sold for $26,095 on January 2, 1990.

C*onsumer brands.*

Liz Claiborne, Lizsport, Lizwear, Lizkids, Claiborne (for men), Dana Buchman.

Liz Claiborne, Inc., 1441 Broadway, New York, NY 10018; (212) 354-4900.

4

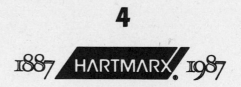

#1 *in men's clothing*

Employees: 22,500
Sales: $1.3 billion
Profits: $23 million
Founded: 1887
Headquarters: Chicago, Illinois

Brand-name tailored clothing is what this company is all about. Lodged here is the greatest collection of brand names in the clothing industry: Hart Schaffner & Marx (the original company name, changed to Hartmarx in 1983), Christian Dior, Hickey-Freeman, Austin Reed, Kuppenheimer, Nino Cerutti, Pierre Cardin, Gleneagles, Jaymar-Ruby are some of them. Hartmarx is the largest producer of men's clothing in the United States. Harry Hart, his brother-in-law Marcus Marx and Joseph Schaffner started out with a clothing store on Chicago's State Street. They can point to a string of industry firsts. They were the first company, in 1897, to run a national advertisement for men's clothing, featuring Hart Schaffner & Marx suits and overcoats priced between $10 and $30. They were one of the first clothing companies to recognize labor unions. They were the first to blend wool and synthetics in men's suits. In the early years their salesmen—nattily dressed in silk toppers, spats and walking sticks—sold finished garments to retailers from as many as 20 wardrobe trunks.

As of 1990, Hartmarx was still synonymous with quality, controlling 25 percent of the "high-end"—read expensive—suit market. But the company also owns 440 stores, operating under three dozen names and accounting for half the firm's sales. These stores were losing money, and profits were down. Part of the problem was an ambitious restructuring begun in 1985 by then-CEO Richard Hamilton. The retailing operations were linked up to a computer center at the Chicago headquarters. The total cost: $30 million. The restructuring was designed to save about $12 million as about 500 jobs, or 30 percent of retail staff, were eliminated. The idea sounded great, but the restructuring was a disaster. In 1986, Hamilton abruptly resigned as CEO. His replacement was Harvey A. Weinberg, whose purchase of the lackluster Raleighs chain in 1988 for $35 million has also contributed to Hartmarx's problems.

Stock performance. Hartmarx stock bought for $1,000 in 1980 sold for $3,902 on January 2, 1990.

Consumer brands.

Mens's apparel: Hart Schaffner & Marx, Hickey-Freeman, Intercontinental, Austin Reed, Nino Cerutti, Pierre Cardin, Gleneagles, Jaymar-Ruby, Kuppenheimer, H. Oritsky.

Women's apparel: Country Miss, Lady Sansabelt.

Specialty retailing: Wallachs, Baskin, Hastings, Jas. K. Wilson, Silverwoods, F. R. Tripler.

Hartmarx Corporation, 101 North Wacker Drive, Chicago, IL 60606; (312) 372-6300.

SHOES

Who would have thought, 10 years ago, that sneaker manufacturers would become the kings of the shoe industry? But during the 1980s Americans went wild for athletic footwear, putting them on not just to play tennis and basketball but to go to work and even to social functions. They became fashion statements. As a result, we now have an athletic footwear industry pushing $6 billion a year in sales, with Nike and Reebok contributing $2 billion each. Sneaker mania has also decimated shoe manufacturing in the United States. Most of our sneakers are made in South Korea.

1

#1 *in athletic shoes*

Employees: 3,800
Sales: $2.0 billion
Profits: $212 million
Founded: 1968
Headquarters: Beaverton, Oregon

Nike was born as a supplier of athletic shoes, and this preoccupation with performance, rather than fashion, has held true for more than a quarter century, lifting the company into the premier position in the American footwear industry.

When sprinter Carl Lewis won four gold medals at the 1984 Olympics, he was wearing Nikes. When Joan Benoit won the first women's Olympic marathon, she was shod in Nikes. In all, 58 athletes at the 1984 Olympics wore Nike shoes, and they captured 65 medals. Tennis brat John McEnroe became a spokesman for Nike, pushing not only their shoes but also sweats and other apparel. High-flying Michael Jordan, star of the Chicago Bulls, floats through the air on a pair of Air Jordans crafted by Nike. And toward the end of the 1980s, in one of the most celebrated commercials of the decade

In 1957, the future cofounders of Nike, coach Bill Bowerman and track star Phil Knight confer at the University of Oregon track.

(sneakers commercials now have a life of their own), the versatile Bo Jackson made the point that Nikes show up wherever games are played.

Nike's sales exploded during the 1980s, topping the $2 billion mark by 1989, 10 times what they were at the start of the decade. Nike's sales also include sports clothing and accessories like athletic bags. And in May 1988 they bought Cole-Haan, maker of dress and casual shoes for men, women and children.

Nike is not a manufacturer. The millions of sneakers they have sold come from plants in other countries, none of them Nike owned. South Korean producers supply Nike with two-thirds of their footwear. Nike's best-sellers are basketball shoes (18 percent of total sales in 1988), followed by running shoes (14 percent) and children's shoes (8 percent).

History. Nike was born on the cinder track at the University of Oregon. That's where Bill Bowerman, one of the top running coaches in America, met Phil Knight, a hotshot runner on Bowerman's track team. Coach Bowerman's hobby was designing faster, lighter running shoes, which he handcrafted for his world-class team. "He figured carrying one extra ounce for a mile was equivalent to carrying something like an extra thousand pounds in the last 50 yards," Knight once told the *New York Times*. In 1962, young Knight moved on to the Stanford Business School, with his coach's passion for lightweight athletic shoes still on his mind. At Stanford, Knight wrote a research paper arguing that high-tech, low-priced running shoes could be made in Japan and successfully merchandised in the U.S. Knight soon went to Japan and wangled a distribution deal with a Japanese athletic-shoe manufacturer, Onitsuka Tiger Company. Blue Ribbon Sports, Nike's predecessor, was born when Bowerman and Knight each kicked in $500.

Knight stored the shoes, called "Tigers," in his father's basement and distributed them at local track meets. During the 1960s, Blue Ribbon Sports gained a cult following among serious runners, who favored models like "the Cortez," "the Boston" and "the Marathon"—the first running shoe with a lightweight nylon upper. Coach Bowerman continued to tinker with designs—like the "waffle" sole, created by dripping rubber onto a waffle iron. In 1971, they adopted the "Swoosh" trademark, the now-familiar Nike logo of a curved strip on the side of the shoe, and introduced the brand name Nike (after the Greek goddess of victory). After a dispute with Onitsuka Tiger in 1972, they contracted out to other Asian factories. That same year, Bowerman coached the U.S. Olympic track and field team. Blue Ribbon Sports officially changed their name to Nike in 1978.

Owners and rulers. Founder Philip Knight is still firmly in control. Of the two classes of stock, A and B, he owns 90.4 percent of the Class A shares, worth $760 million. These holdings put him high on

Forbes, 1989 list of the 400 richest Americans. The Class A stock elects 75 percent of the board, whose members in 1990 included cofounder William Bowerman and Jill K. Conway, former president of Smith College.

As *a place to work.* A lot of jocks used to work at Nike. More professional managers run the show these days. In his 1988 report to shareholders, Knight proudly pointed out that all of the vice presidents listed in the 1981 annual report had left the company. All employees participate in a profit-sharing plan funded by the company, whose 1988 contribution was $3 million. Stock options are available only to "key employees."

Global presence. Nike sells their products in 60 countries, and 20 percent of their sales occur outside the U.S. They use the Japanese trading company, Nissho Iwai, as their sales agent.

Stock performance. Nike stock bought for $1,000 in 1981 sold for $5,952 on January 2, 1990.

Consumer brands.

Nike, Cole-Haan.

Nike Inc., 3900 Southwest Murray Boulevard, Beaverton, OR 97005; (503) 641-6453.

Buster Brown and his dog Tige comprised a popular traveling show during the Brown Group's early days.

2

Brown Group, Inc.

#1 *in shoes made in U.S.*

Employees: 29,000
Sales: $1.8 billion
Profits: $34 million
Founded: 1878
Headquarters: St. Louis, Missouri

Brown is the nation's largest shoe manufacturer, turning out more than 20 million pairs a year or about 8 percent of U.S. output. But they import three times as many shoes—60 million pairs a year, mostly from Taiwan and mainland China. Part of the St. Louis business scene for more than 100 years, Brown owns numer-

ous brand names in the shoe industry: Naturalizer (the top-selling women's shoe), Life Stride, Connie, Fanfares and Buster Brown are some of them.

In their early life Brown was content just to make shoes. Now they sell them as well—in their own stores, in stores owned by others and in department stores where they lease and operate the shoe department (with 800 such leaseholds they are the largest operator of leased footwear space in department stores). Their shoes show up in nearly 10,000 stores across the country, of which they own about 1,000, including the Regal and Famous Footwear chains. And, of course, they're always experimenting with new store ideas. They started the Castleby men's stores in the late 1980s and soon had more than 130 of them operating in shopping centers. It's not unusual to find Brown shoe outlets competing against one another in the same community.

During the 1980s Brown learned to stick to cobbling. Because shopping mall operators like to sign up companies that can fill a lot of slots, Brown had branched into different kinds of stores: Cloth World (fabric stores), Meis (family clothing stores), the Linen Center (linens, curtains), Etage (beauty products, fashion accessories). By decade's end Brown had jettisoned all of these except Cloth World. In the mid-1980s, they also closed 12 of their 31 shoe factories. They also exited other businesses: Hedstrom bicycles, Gerry outerwear,

Tempo western clothes. In 1983 Brown earned $67 million after taxes. Six years later they earned half that. The big growth in footwear came from athletic shoes, which Brown Group does not supply.

History. New England was the shoe capital of the nation in 1878 when 25-year-old George Warren Brown founded the company in St. Louis. At that time men's and women's shoes were essentially the same—black, boring and functional. The only shoemakers in St. Louis made custom boots for the very rich. Brown realized the Midwest needed locally made, mass produced shoes—and not just any shoes, a special line of fashionable "fine lady's shoes." Brown's idea was a smashing success. One of the company's most famous lines originated in 1904, when they bought the rights to a newspaper comic strip character named Buster Brown, now known to generations of children and their parents by the familiar logo of a boy and his dog. In the early years of this century, the company hired 20 midgets and 20 small dogs to play "Buster" and "Tige" in touring shows—promotional skits performed in local theaters, department stores and shoe stores.

Owners and rulers. B. A. Bridgewater, Jr., took over the company in 1979 at age 45. He has an MBA from Harvard and spent two years in the Office of Management & Budget under Richard Nixon. The head of the Brown Shoe division is Richard W. Shomaker. One woman, Joan F. Lane, is on the board of directors; she is a former chairman of the board of trustees of Smith College and is now assistant dean of the School of Humanities and Science at Stanford University.

Stock performance. Brown Group stock bought for $1,000 in 1980 sold for $5,069 on January 2, 1990.

Consumer brands.

Naturalizer, Life Stride, Connie, Fanfares, Buster Brown.

Brown Group. Inc., 8400 Maryland Avenue, St. Louis, MO 63105; (314) 854-4000.

3

Reebok

#2 *in athletic shoes*

Employees: 2,250
Sales: $1.8 billion
Profits: $175 million
Founded: 1979
Headquarters: Stoughton, Massachusetts

Social Conscience

As athletic shoes (the new name for sneakers) became a fashion statement, Reebok rode the crest of the wave. They had more to do with establishing this trend than any other company, sensing early on that women didn't want to go to aerobic classes in just any old shoe. And when women and men began showing up for work in athletic shoes, Reebok was home free. Their sales sprinted, incredibly, from $900,000 in 1980 to $1.8 billion (i.e., $1,800,000,000) in 1989, one of the most spectacular spurts in the history of American business.

Even though sales appear to qualify them for the *Fortune* 500 (number 1989 had sales of $500 million), Reebok doesn't make the grade because, like Nike, they don't really make *anything*. To be listed in the *Fortune* 500, a company must derive at least 50 percent of sales from manufacturing. Outside contractors produce all of Reebok's shoes. Their 2,250 employees are engaged primarily in selling the shoes. Reebok gets some 60 percent of their shoes from South Korea and 20 percent from Taiwan. One big South Korean producer filled 30 percent of the company's requirements, nearly 2 million pairs of shoes a month.

In the $5 billion athletic shoe market, Reebok and Nike swapped the lead during the 1980s. Reebok edged Nike in 1986, based largely on their stylish image, only to fall behind at the end of the decade as Nike emphasized performance. *Sporting Goods Intelligence* put Nike's share of the market at 24.8 percent, Reebok's at 22.7 percent. As 1990 opened, Reebok was hoping their $170 inflatable shoe, "The Pump," would return them to the top spot. The verdict was still out on whether athletic shoes are something you wear when you're exercising and performing or whether they're simply part of a life-style. It's also unclear where you buy your shoes. If cachet means much for future sales, Reebok may be in trouble. One store chain, *Woolworth's* Foot Locker, accounts for 20 percent of their sales.

Using 1980s' profits, Reebok bought a clutch of companies: Avia (another line of sneakers), Rockport (casual shoes), Frye (boots) and Boston Whaler (motorboats). Frye was sold off in 1989. They also bought U.S. rights to Ellesse, a line of upscale, Italian-designed sportswear. The plot is to make Reebok more than a shoe seller. Their aim, in the words of Chairman Paul Fireman, is to become "a consumer company dealing with consumer leisure-time products."

History. Young Joseph and Jeffrey Foster, grandsons of the inventor of spiked track shoes, took the Reebok name from the African gazelle—whose spirit, speed and grace were qualities the young men wanted in their new company's shoes. The British brothers learned their trade at the family company, the elite athletic shoe manufacturer J. W. Foster and Sons. Reebok shoes were rarely seen on American soil before 1979. That year, a boyish sports equipment salesman, Paul Fireman, was at an international sales conference where the British shoes caught his eye. He bought U.S. distribution rights. The first Reeboks to hit American stores were three extremely expensive running shoes (at retail prices that were then unheard of—$60).

But Reeboks didn't take off until 1982, when Fireman had an inspiration—a fashion-conscious athletic shoe for women. He called it an "aerobic" shoe. That year, he introduced two women's shoes— "Freestyle" and "Energizer"—and sales exploded. Their surge was fueled by other popular Reebok models designed for tennis, walking, running, volleyball and cycling. In 1986, they introduced shoes for toddlers called "Weeboks."

Owners and rulers. Pentland Industries, the British company from which Reebok sprang, announced in 1990 that they wanted to sell their 32 percent stake. Chairman Paul Fireman (who turned 46 in 1990) and his wife, Phyllis, own another 14.5 percent, worth $380 million, placing him on the *Forbes* list of the 400 richest Americans. In addition, Fireman was the eighth highest paid CEO in America during the 1980s, earning a total of $54.4 million. In 1989 alone he raked in $14.6 million, making him *Business Week*'s fifth highest paid CEO for the year.

As a place to work. Reebok grew so much so fast that the company lacked a formal corporate structure until 1987. That was when president C. Joseph LaBonte took a get-tough attitude. His program led to discontent among many Reebok employees, as well as within the Reebok dealers network, because they no longer had a voice in the design of new products. LaBonte left in 1989.

Social responsibility. In 1988, Reebok gave $10 million to sponsor the Amnesty International "Human Rights Now!" concert tour. After the tour they established the Reebok Human Rights Award to recognize people under the age of 30 who "have advanced the cause of human rights around the world."

Global presence. In 1989, they sold 15 million pairs of shoes outside the U.S., racking up sales of $240 million. They are now the number one brand in Canada, Australia, New Zealand, Hong Kong and Singapore. Reeboks are now also sold in the Soviet Union. Fireman predicts international sales of $1 billion by the mid-1990s.

Stock performance. Reebok stock bought for $1,000 in 1980 sold for $5,694 on January 2, 1990.

Consumer brands.

Shoes: Reebok, The Pump, Avia, Rockport.

Motorboats: Boston Whaler.

Apparel: Ellesse, Reebok Sport.

Reebok International Ltd., 100 Technology Center Drive, Stoughton, MA 02072; (617) 341-5000.

4

U.S. Shoe

Employees: 46,000
Sales: $2.5 billion
Profits: $51 million
Founded: 1931
Headquarters: Cincinnati, Ohio

A funny thing happened to U.S. Shoe at the end of the 1980s. In keeping with the tenor of the times ("get the most for the shareholders"), they put themselves up for sale. And found out no one was really interested in buying them. U.S. Shoe is another one of those shoemakers that expanded into various store operations that line shopping malls: Casual Corner, Ups 'N Downs, Caren Charles, Petite Sophisticates, LensCrafters—in all, they have about 1,800 locations (not counting their shoestores).

In offering U.S. Shoe for sale, Chairman Philip G. Barach learned buyers were only interested in two pieces of the company—the original business, footwear, and the fast-growing LensCrafters chain. He then made a deal with Merrill Lynch to sell the shoe business for $425 million, but the deal fell through. So Barach went back to running the company, paying particular attention to boosting LensCrafters, which was selling $500 million a year in eyewear to elderly customers. As *Business Week* put it, "Barach's strategy is to cash in on the graying of America." And who should know better than U.S. Shoe how to do this? Sitting on their 10-member board of directors are 90-year-old John O. Toor (a retired company chairman), 84-year-old Daniel G. Ross (senior partner in a New York law firm) and 83-year-old John F. Lebor (director of Carlisle Retailers). Four other directors were also over 65.

In early 1990, the hard-driving Barach, head of U.S. Shoe for 25 years, stepped down as CEO—surprising everyone in Cincinnati. One former executive said, "I thought the only way he would leave would be in a box." Barach was only 59, but he'd had a heart attack in 1978 and bypass surgery in 1983. He stayed on as chairman to oversee the work of the new CEO, Bannus B. Hudson, who spent 18 years with U.S. Shoe's Cincinnati neighbor, Procter & Gamble.

The company's headquarters on the edge of Cincinnati has been described as spartan. They operate with a staff of just 64 people. U.S. Shoe's 1988 annual meeting was held in the company cafeteria.

Stock performance. U.S. Shoe stock bought for $1,000 in 1980 sold for $9,063 on January 2, 1990.

Consumer brands.

Shoes: Red Cross, Joyce, Selby, Pappagallo, Amolfi, Capezio, Cobbies, David Evins, Easy Spirit.

Apparel stores: Casual Corner, Ups 'N Downs, Caren Charles, Petite Sophisticate.

Eyewear: LensCrafters.

U.S. Shoe, One Eastwood Drive, Cincinnati, OH 45227; (513) 527-7000.

5

#3 *in athletic shoes*

Employees: 1,000
Sales: $600 million
Profits: $57 million
Founded: 1984
Headquarters: Los Angeles, California

Adorned with fringes, bedecked with lace, studded with rhinestones and available in a rainbow of colors, L.A. Gear's high-top athletic shoes were the hip statement for teenage girls in the late 1980s. Launched in mid-decade, L.A. Gear did to Reebok what Reebok had previously done to Nike: taking away customers who wanted to wear more stylish athletic shoes—without necessarily being athletic. While Reebok and Nike shoes sprinted out of sporting goods stores, L.A. Gear shoes made their big run in department stores and women's shoe stores.

Before the end of the decade, L.A. Gear hit $600 million a year in sales, exploded into the hottest stock on the New York Stock Exchange and slipped past Converse into third place in the athletic shoe business—all a tribute to their entre-

U.S. sneaker sales doubled between 1983 and 1988.

preneurial founder, the reclusive Robert Y. Greenberg, who had had no previous experience in selling shoes. Greenberg is actually a hair stylist by training. He attended hair styling school in California, opened five salons in the Boston area and over the years has sold wigs, roller skates, and he reportedly made $3 million in 90 days selling E. T. shoelaces. He owns one-quarter of the stock, worth $80 million in mid-1990.

Coming into the 1990s, L.A. Gear was sprinting for the $1 billion sales level with fewer than 1,000 employees. Like Nike and Reebok, their shoes are made in South Korea and Taiwan. But they spend a lot on promotion. In 1989 they hired Los Angeles Laker star Kareem Abdul-Jabbar to front for their men's athletic shoes, and then signed on superstar Michael Jackson.

Working out of L.A. Gear's anonymous nine-building headquarters near the beach, Greenberg plots to bring out more L.A. Gear sportswear (currently the company has a small line of T-shirts, jeans and wristwatches). L.A. Gear became successful by catering to affluent teenage—"Valley"—girls. Now Greenberg hopes to appeal to young men with "performance" shoes for basketball and running. He expects to overtake Nike and Reebok by 1994 on his way to building "the biggest brand name in the world." A true Hollywood story.

Stock performance. L.A. Gear stock bought for $1,000 in 1986 sold for $10,500 on January 2, 1990.

Consumer brands.

L.A. Gear.

L.A. Gear, Inc., 4221 Redwood Avenue, Los Angeles, CA 90066; (213) 822-1995.

6

INTERCO

#1 *in men's dress shoes, U.S.-made sneakers*

Employees: 25,000
Sales: $1.4 billion
Loss: -$59 million
Founded: 1911
Headquarters: St. Louis, Missouri

Interco did a good imitation of shooting themselves in the foot while engaging in fancy financial two-stepping, the fad of the 1980s. Originally known as the International Shoe Company, they changed their name to Interco after assembling a motley collection of other businesses that included clothing companies, clothing stores, junior department stores, discount stores and home improvement centers. Buying became a way of life for them starting in the mid-1960s. In the early 1980s after buying Ethan Allen furniture company as well as Broyhill and Lane, they became the world's largest furniture maker. A string of retail furniture channels—some freestanding, others inside stores—boosted sales.

By 1988 they had pumped themselves up to sales of $3.2 billion a year, sporting such brand names as Florsheim, Thayer-McNeil, London Fog, Big Yank, Clipper Mist, Sergio Valente, Le Tigre and Abe Schrader, along with such store names as Central Hardware, Sky City, Fine's and United Shirt. At that point, defining Interco was difficult (shoes accounted for only one-quarter of revenues). The Rales brothers of Washington, D.C.—Steven, 37 in 1988, and his younger brother, Mitchell, 32—decided they would impose some definition by taking over the company. Backed by the junk bond house of Drexel Burnham Lambert, the Rales brothers bid $2.5 billion for Interco. They planned to keep the furniture business and sell off most of the rest.

Interco's management defeated this bid by a massive restructuring masterminded by the newly formed Wall Street investment banking house of Wasserstein Perella. In effect, they "saved" Interco (at least their jobs) but ended up dismembering the company anyway, leaving the shareholders worse off than if the Rales' bid had been accepted. Although their bid failed, the Rales made a $75 million profit from selling their stock back to the company.

The Interco that moved into the 1990s was a shrunken version of the old Interco. Sales had been chopped in half. The company had been stripped of most of their clothing business and general merchandise stores, as well as the operation once considered their jewel, Ethan Allen furniture—most of them at distress prices. The businesses Interco now considered "core" (meaning they didn't want to sell them) were the two furniture companies, Broyhill and Lane (both bought during the 1980s), Converse (the athletic shoe company acquired in 1986) and the old mainstay, Chicago-based Florsheim Shoe, which includes both manufacturing and selling through Florsheim and Thayer-McNeil stores. And it was unclear whether Interco would be able to hold onto these businesses because of the crushing debt ($1.15 billion in loans) they had taken on to pay shareholders a huge dividend.

The one bright spot for Interco appeared to be Converse, but they took a beating in 1989 when sales of their green canvas shoes evaporated. Converse ranks number four in the still-growing athletic gear industry, behind Nike, Reebok and L.A. Gear. Converse can also claim to be the largest U.S. sneaker manufacturer (because the other three companies import, rather than make, shoes). Interco's president and CEO, Richard B. Loynd, was chairman of Converse when Interco bought it.

S*tock performance.* Interco stock bought for $1,000 in 1980 sold for $844 on January 2, 1990.

C*onsumer brands.*

Furniture: Broyhill, Lane.

Shoes: Converse, Florsheim, Thayer, McNeil, Winthrop.

Interco Incorporated, 101 South Hanley Road, St. Louis, MO 63105; (314) 863-1100.

7

Edison Brothers

Employees: 16,300
Sales: $1.1 billion
Profits: $55 million
Founded: 1922
Headquarters: St. Louis, Missouri

For years no one much cared what happened at Edison Brothers. Dull and conventional, Edison Brothers operated a number of undistinguished chains, selling sensible shoes to the middle-aged and low-priced clothing to young men. The company was founded in 1922, when five Edison brothers (Harry, Mark, Sam, Simon and Irving) started selling shoes in St. Louis. Unlike other shoe companies, they never went into the manufacturing end of the business. They remained a family-run, inbred operation for 65 years, and Edison descendants still hold about 30 percent of the company's stock.

Things began to change in the late 1980s under chairman Andrew Newman (who is married to an Edison) and president Bernard Sneider, a Harvard MBA. Newman shifted the company's emphasis from shoes to clothing—specifically, menswear. In 1986 shoe sales accounted for two-thirds of Edison Brothers' sales; by 1989 they contributed only half. In the meantime, Newman and Sneider had recast clothing chain Jeans West as JW—featuring a wide variety of casual clothing in addition to their own brand of jeans for young men. They also expanded their Oak Tree chain—which sells lower-priced designer clothing for men—and pushed the trendy 5–7–9 Shops. And in 1987 they bought the J. Riggings menswear chain of 209 stores (aimed at the khaki-and-sport-jacket Yuppie crowd) for $44 million and then quickly added 100 new J. Riggings stores in malls around the nation. They now have, through their various chains, 2,300 stores across the country.

Another big change: Edison Brothers used to hang on to ailing chains for years. Under Newman, the company closed down a number of shoe stores and spent $20 million in 1987 to create a hipper, upscale look at the remaining shoe stores (Chandlers, Bakers, Leeds, Burts, the Wild Pair and Sacha London). Wild Pair became Edison Brothers' showpiece. Located in suburban malls, the shoe stores have successfully courted younger customers with trendy accessories, more daring styles and high-tech decor (complete with closed-circuit TVs showing music videos).

Stock performance. Edison Brothers stock bought for $1,000 in 1980 sold for $4,970 on January 2, 1990.

Consumer brands.

Shoe stores: Bakers, Burts, Chandlers, Leeds, Sacha London, Wild Pair.

Clothing stores: JW, J. Riggings, 5–7–9 Shops, Oak Tree.

Edison Brothers Stores, Inc., 501 Broadway, St. Louis, MO 63102; (314) 331-6000.

TEXTILES

A textile mill today is a marvel of high technology, driven by electronic sensors, robots and high-speed looms, producing yarns and fabrics that end up not just as sweaters and pants but as bandages, filters, masks, carpets and tire cords. And the center of this industry remains in the South. Three states—Georgia, North Carolina and South Carolina—account for more than 60 percent of textile mill employment. But much of the change within the industry during the 1980s took place hundreds of miles north, on Wall Street. Thirteen of the 15 largest firms in the industry were either bought by other companies (as happened to J. P. Stevens) or went private (a group bought all the stock so the public can no longer buy shares on a stock exchange). The result was invariably the same: Textile companies were ripped apart like a piece of cloth caught in a chainsaw. Case in point: After buying Burlington Industries, Wall Street banker Morgan Stanley sold off or closed down half the mills of what was in 1980 the largest U.S. textile company.

1

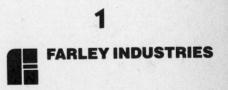

FARLEY INDUSTRIES

#1 *in men's underwear*
#2 *in textiles*

Employees: 51,000
Sales: $3.9 billion
Founded: 1976
Headquarters: Chicago, Illinois

Social Conscience

At the start of 1985 hardly anyone had heard of Bill Farley. Five years later he sat atop a debt-laden pyramid that qualified, for the moment anyway, as the nation's largest textile-and-apparel combination, with sales of nearly $4 billion, more than Milliken or Levi Strauss.

E *very year the U.S. produces enough tea bag strings to circle the equator 67 times.*

There was only one problem. Farley also had debts of $4 billion—and interest payments of $1.5 million a day. Not surprisingly, many people were asking if he'd be able to pay off the debts he had incurred in taking over companies that put the shirts on our backs, the sheets on our beds and the socks on our feet. A lot of them were betting he would fail, especially after the collapse in early 1990 of his main backer, Drexel Burnham Lambert. But the wise money had bet against Farley in the past, and lost.

Farley and such players as Donald Trump and Michael Milken symbolized the 1980s. Starting with nothing, he borrowed huge amounts of money to buy out a succession of companies whose managements thought they could crush him like a fly on a wall. He not only turned the tables on them but once in control showed these managements the door. He then sold off parts of those companies to reduce his debt enough so backers would then lend him more money to buy other companies. Ambition still not satisfied, in 1988 he seriously entertained the idea of running for the U.S. presidency. Bill Farley thinks big.

His textile-apparel empire, as 1990 opened, included a flock of well-known brand names such as Gold Toe socks; Martex towels; sheets, linen and other household fabrics sold under the names Lady Pepperell, Ralph Lauren, Laura Ashley, Pierre Cardin and Gloria Vanderbilt; Fruit of the Loom and BVD underwear; and Lucchese, Dingo and Acme boots.

History. How Farley came to control all these brands is a story of derring-do. Born in 1942 in an impoverished Rhode Island mill town, where his father was a postman, Farley won a scholarship to Bowdoin College. After graduating, he wandered through Mexico, earning money by selling encyclopedias. His wanderlust satisfied, Farley took a law degree from Boston College and then tried his hand at investment banking with

Lehman Brothers, where he discovered his true love. "I enjoy buying companies," he told *Business Week*. "No one ever told Americans that they have to stop at a certain point."

Bill Farley started his buying spree in 1976 when he bought Anaheim Citrus Products for $1.7 million with only $25,000 of his own money (he borrowed the rest). Using the same tactic, he picked up Baumfolder, maker of paper-folding machinery; the metals division of NL Industries; and Condec, a defense and electrical company. In 1985, Farley entered the big leagues when he paid $1.4 billion for the Chicago–based conglomerate, Northwest Industries. Farley rapidly carved up and sold off large chunks of the company. One that he didn't sell was the Union Underwear Company, maker of Fruit of the Loom underwear, the number one maker of men's underwear and one of the top five U.S. sock makers. Farley changed the name of the company to Fruit of the Loom and put this brand name on sports clothes and women's underwear and featured himself in ads for activewear. He sold 36 percent of Fruit of the Loom to the public, and shares of the company now trade on the New York Stock Exchange.

In 1989 Farley bet even bigger chips with a down-and-dirty takeover of West Point–Pepperell, a huge textile conglomerate. Formed in 1963 by the merger of two textile companies, West Point–Pepperell has roots in the 19th century. The West Point mill was started in Georgia after the Civil War by two brothers, LaFayette and Ward Crockett Lanier, both Confederate Army veterans. Succeeding generations of the Lanier family carried on with the business, continuing to run the show after West Point merged with Pepperell, a Yankee textile company founded in 1850 and based in Biddeford, Maine. West Point–Pepperell was very successful over the years—so much so that in 1988 they paid $1.2 billion for J. P. Stevens, maker of fabrics for clothing and home furnishings. J. P. Stevens had been number two in the textile industry and the number one enemy of organized labor—as dramatized in the 1979 film *Norma Rae*, starring Sally Field. West Point–Pepperell then sold off Stevens' carpet and industrial fabrics plants to Odyssey partners for $530 million.

West Point–Pepperell was the kind of gem that catches Bill Farley's eye. But the company didn't want to be bought. Joseph L. Lanier, Jr., a fourth-generation Lanier running West Point, told the *New York Times*: "We are going to fight Farley until hell freezes over, and then we are going to fight him on the ice." But Lanier underestimated Farley's relentlessness. Even though the Georgia House of Representatives tried to block his bid by passing an anti-takeover measure, in the end Farley conquered West Point. He won by agreeing to pay shareholders $58 a share (far more than their stock had been selling for on the New York Stock Exchange) at a cost of $1.56 billion in cash and a commitment to take on another $1 billion in West Point debt.

Farley then resorted to his usual tactic of auctioning off chunks of his empire to raise the cash to complete the deal. He sold off Cluett Peabody, maker of Arrow Shirts, but that sale wasn't enough to complete the West Point stock purchase. He only had enough money to buy 95 percent. Worse, he couldn't count on his usual source of financing, the investment bank of Drexel Burnham Lambert, which had promised to raise the money for the takeover. When Drexel went out of business in early 1990, Farley was squeezed. He couldn't raise the money to buy the remaining 5 percent. He therefore couldn't complete his deal and was exploring other financial maneuvers to get himself out of the mess. *Business Week* suggested "Farley may be hanging by one clothespin." Hanging in the balance was one of the nation's largest textile manufacturers.

O*wners and rulers.* A square-jawed caricature of the self-made man, Farley used to stop whatever he was doing promptly at 5 P.M. each day to work out. A minority owner of the Chicago White Sox, he has even worked out with that team during spring training. A relentless overachiever, he uses a private jet to reach appointments jammed into his 16-hour work days or to reach his homes: a Chicago lakefront apartment, a Colorado ski lodge, a house in Maine. One of Farley's favorite subjects is Bill Farley. When workers at one company met him for the first time, they expected to hear his plans for their future. Instead they heard his life story. *Business Week* noted that "Farley's self-absorption is almost a religion." His abortive run for the 1988 Democratic presidential nomination included campaigning in Iowa. But he dropped out when he decided he couldn't take the flak for his three failed marriages and the disclosure that he has an illegitimate daughter.

A*s a place to work.* Farley practically force-feeds his health consciousness to employees. He bans cigarette machines from his factories, and each plant is fitted with athletic facilities of some sort, from running tracks and weight rooms to tennis courts and ball fields. Visitors to Farley's office often are served herb tea. Such idiosyncrasies can be annoying to the more sedentary among Farley's troops. He has been known, for instance, to begin management meetings with calisthenics.

S*tock performance.* Fruit of the Loom stock bought for $1,000 in 1987 sold for $1,724 on January 2, 1990.

G*lobal presence.* He has enough trouble in the U.S. without tackling the rest of the world.

C*onsumer brands.*

Underwear: Fruit of the Loom, BVD, Screen Stars, Gold Toe.

Linens: Eileen West, Lady Pepperell, Liberty of London, Martex, Tastemaker, Utica.

Boots: Acme, Dingo, Lucchese.

Farley Inc., 233 S. Wacker Drive, 6300 Sears Tower, Chicago, IL 60606; (312) 876-1724.

2

Milliken

#1 *in textiles*

Employees: 14,000
Sales: $2.5 billion
Profits: $200 million
Founded: 1865
Headquarters: Spartanburg, South Carolina

One of America's largest family fortunes resides in this spinner and weaver of textiles. How big they really are is unknown because Milliken is privately owned by the same family that started the

Sixteen percent of all sweaters imported last year came from China, where clothing workers make as little as $500 a year. China ranks as America's third largest supplier of clothing and textiles, behind Hong Kong and Taiwan.

company 125 years ago—and they won't open their books to outsiders. The estimates above come from *Forbes*, which managed in 1989 to wangle an interview with Roger Milliken, grandson of the founder, on the promise that they would talk only about industry issues. Every time reporter Alyssa A. Lappen asked a question about the company, Milliken would snap: "You've crossed the line."

However, enough is known to place Milliken & Co. at the very top of the U.S. textile industry. They reached that pinnacle during the 1980s when the old industry leaders—Burlington, J. P. Stevens, West Point–Pepperell—were restructured and pared down. Milliken's 57 plants, all high-tech marvels, turn out fabrics for swimsuits (Lycra), clothes and tablecloths (Visa), tires (they supply braided polyester cord to Michelin) and uniforms. According again to *Forbes*, they sell nearly half of the acetate and acetate blends used in coats and women's outerwear, one-quarter of all automotive fabrics and one-third of the stretch fabrics used in sportswear.

Milliken is also a tiger about product quality, attention to customer needs and research. In the bargain they're rabidly antiunion and zealously protariff to keep out imports. Their rallying of employees into teams that work to improve quality and solve customer problems has made them a hero to management guru Tom Peters. He dedicated his 1987 bestseller, *Thriving on Chaos*, to Roger Milliken.

The Milliken mills have spun so much gold that three family members—Roger, his brother Gerrish and his cousin Minot—all made the *Forbes* roster of the 400 richest Americans. Roger, in 1989, was said to be worth $1.4 billion; Gerrish, $900 million; and Minot, $450 million. In addition to the textile business, the Milliken family owns 100,000 acres of Maine timberland, where

the company started out, and 41 percent of Wilmington, Delaware–based Mercantile Stores, operator of 81 department stores in the South and Midwest (including Jones, Joslins, McAlpin's, Gayfers, Castner Knott and J. B. White).

History. Like many other textile companies (Textron and J. P. Stevens, to name two of the biggest), Milliken & Co. was born in New England. Seth Milliken joined with William Deering in 1865 to start a fabric company in Portland, Maine. Deering later left to start a farm equipment company that became one of the founding companies of International Harvester in 1902, while Seth Milliken took the business to New York City where he also collected money that was owed to various textile mills. In that position he began buying up mills that were in financial trouble. Seth's son, Gerrish, continued that tradition, buying up failing mills in the South during the depression.

Roger Milliken succeeded his father as company head after World War II, and he is credited with building Milliken into the giant they are today. He was 74 years old in 1990 and showed no signs of slowing down. He visits as many plants as he can, and he spends a lot of time with customers. Watching him in motion in 1989, *Forbes* reporter Alyssa Lappen wrote: "he still works 90 to 100 hours a week."

Owners and rulers. There are 200 shareholders, most of them Milliken family members. Roger, his brother Gerrish and his cousin Minot control more than half of the stock. However, Roger's second in command in 1990 was a nonfamily member, Thomas Malone, who became president in 1984. *Forbes* reported that managers at the company "seem to almost universally dislike" Malone. Even though the Millikens remain firmly in control, there's some dissension in the family ranks. The seven children of Joan Milliken Stroud, Roger's late sister, own about 15 per cent of the stock—and they began to make noises in the 1980s about getting fatter dividends and having more say in running the company. And, as the decade was running out, some of them, in what may be the forerunner of a nasty family squabble, sold a small number of shares to Erwin Maddrey and Bettis

Rainsford, founders of Delta Woodside Industries, a Milliken & Co. competitor.

As a place to work. In 1956 workers at a Milliken plant in Darlington, South Carolina, voted to join the Textile Workers Union. The next day Roger Milliken closed the plant. And he spent the next 24 years fighting charges of unfair labor practices, finally agreeing in 1980 to pay $5 million to the Darlington workers who had lost their jobs. Milliken has automated his plants, trying to do with as few workers as possible. However, those on the payroll are well paid. They are also recruited for Roger Milliken's crusade for quality and customer service. Milliken himself is a workaholic and expects managers to work 60-hour weeks. To get ahead here, you have to live and breathe the business. But then you get a chance to work for a man dubbed by *Forbes* as "one of the great businessmen of the modern era."

Social responsibility. Roger Milliken is a rightwing Republican who supports conservative think tanks like the Heritage Foundation. According to former South Carolina Governor Jim Edwards, "Richard Nixon would not have been President and Ronald Reagan would not have been President were it not for Roger Milliken." Milliken set aside his distaste for labor unions to join with them in the "Crafted with Pride in U.S.A." campaign to get consumers to buy American-made clothes and fabrics. He was stunned in 1985 when Ronald Reagan vetoed legislation that would have helped roll back imports from Hong Kong, South Korea and Taiwan. "Our industry," he said, "has learned a grim lesson. We can no longer rely on the promises of this administration." Milliken believes "we are sacrificing our industrial base on the altar of free trade, a god no other nation worships."

Global presence. Not major but Milliken does have eight plants outside the U.S. Milliken yarn is being spun in Britain, France and Belgium.

Milliken & Co., Milliken Road, Spartanburg, South Carolina 29304; (803) 573-2020.

3
⊞ Burlington Industries

#1 *in fabrics for clothing*

Employees: 28,000
Sales: $2.2 billion
Losses: $23 million
Founded: 1923
Headquarters: Greensboro, North Carolina

The nation's textile titan dethroned themselves during the 1980s. The largest U.S. textile company coming into the 1980s, Burlington had cut themselves almost in half by 1990. The truncated Burlington had also been transformed in one other important respect. Previously publicly owned, its shares traded on the New York Stock Exchange, Burlington now found themselves the ward of a Wall Street investment banker, Morgan Stanley, with none of their shares in the hands of the public.

What happened to Burlington was a story typical of the decade's fancy financial shenanigans. In 1987, New York investor Asher B. Edelman joined with a Canadian company, Dominion Textile, to mount a takeover of Burlington. Burlington's management immediately spurned the Edelman-Dominion bid as "hostile," charging outsiders would dismember the company. Burlington's top executives may have also regarded the bid as hostile because they had no assurance they would keep their jobs. Ergo, Chairman Frank Greenberg cut a deal with the investment banking house of Morgan Stanley, which raised $3 billion to outbid the outsiders. The result: Stockholders were paid cash for their shares, leaving Burlington to start out their new life under private ownership. The Greenberg management then did what they had accused Edelman-Dominion of plotting: They dismembered the company to pay down the debt.

Burlington closed or sold 35 of their 83 plants in North Carolina, South Carolina and Georgia. Among the businesses dumped were industrial fabrics, Burlington Prints, Masland carpets and interior trim for cars, precision fabrics, glass fabrics and blended fabrics. They also dumped 16,000 employees, and sales went from $3.2 billion to $2.2 billion. And lo and behold, the debt was reduced by 45 percent. The sale that brought in the most money was Burlington's state-of-the-art denim plant in Erwin, North Carolina, which went for $205 million to—surprise—Dominion Textile, the erstwhile Canadian bidder. This buy vaulted Dominion into the top tier of U.S. denim producers, which is precisely the outcome Burlington had warned against in asking a judge to bar the Edelman-Dominion bid. Explaining the sale, Greenberg said: "We would have chosen not to have been in this situation, but my job is to be concerned about Burlington's perpetuity."

With all the cutbacks, Burlington remained a giant in the textile industry. They are the world's largest producer of finished fabrics, both knitted and woven, for clothing. Men's suits, women's dresses, sweaters and children's wear are all fashioned from Burlington fabrics and yarns. No one, for example, turns out as much worsted—a staple of fine men's suits—as Burlington. And they're still a leading maker of denim for jeans. Burlington also ranks number one in drapery fabrics and mattress ticking and number two in upholstery fabrics. And they're one of the leading carpet makers under the names Lees and Burlington. Most of their customers are other companies— suit makers, jeans producers, drapery manufacturers. They have 22,000 U. S. customers. The largest of these accounted for 7 percent of sales; the 10 largest, 22 percent.

History. In 1923, J. Spencer Love persuaded the citizens of Burlington, North Carolina, to buy stock to help him finance a new mill there. The mill was christened Burlington, after the town, but times were rough because the mill produced cotton products that were going out of style. Love turned to a new fiber called rayon. And then Burlington thrived—even through the Great Depression, with the help of cheap labor in the South. They gobbled up mills that others were forced to close.

The 1950s brought even greater growth through the purchases of well-known textile companies such as Pacific Mills and Klopman Mills. In 1960 Burlington bought James Lees & Co., a Philadelphia carpet maker founded in 1854.

Spencer Love, architect of this growth, was described by his successor, Charles F. Myers, as follows: "He had secretaries in his office and secretaries at home. When he came off the tennis court, he had a secretary waiting and he would go right to work dictating." In 1962, when he was 65, Love died of a heart attack after playing tennis.

During the late 1970s and early 1980s, Burlington spent $2 billion on cutting-edge technology for Burlington plants. Unfortunately, that investment was for apparel production, where cheap imports made it extremely difficult to turn a profit—no matter how high-tech the plant. The era of big spending at Burlington had ended by 1988, when new CEO Frank Greenberg told *Business Week* magazine, "We are less chivalrous and romantic and more prudent."

Owners and rulers. Frank S. Greenberg became CEO in 1986 at age 57, just in time to face the takeover threat. Morgan Stanley owns a majority of the voting stock and occupies three of the five board seats. Greenberg and Donald R. Hughes hold the other two seats. According to a *Business Week* report in late 1988, Burlington executives "will soon get a chance to buy a 14 percent stake." Nonmanagement employees will own another 16 percent through an employee stock ownership plan that replaced a profit-sharing plan. The expectation, of course, was that before long Burlington would sell stock to the public, enabling Morgan Stanley and the Burlington execs to make a killing. As of mid-1990, that had not happened.

As a place to work. In 1987, CEO Frank Greenberg told *Look*, Burlington's employee publication, that "machines did not make Burlington what it is today—people made Burlington the world's leader in textiles.... Burlington is like an extended family." A year later, he added, "when threatened with harm from outside forces, a family unites and disagreements are forgotten." Greenberg's cutbacks and sellouts have eliminated 16,000 members of the Burlington "fam-

A *mericans use 50 pounds of textile products per year, about four times the world average.*

ily" (though many of them kept their jobs with those who purchased their plants). Burlington's executives, however, still call the company's upscale Greensboro headquarters "the garden club," although even they have felt the crunch—6 of Burlington's top 13 executives took early retirement after the buyout. Burlington still maintains offices in their skyscraper on New York's Avenue of the Americas for the CEO and a marketing staff.

Global presence. Overseas sales account for less than 10 percent of Burlington's total output.

Burlington Industries, Inc., 3330 West Friendly Avenue, Greensboro, NC 27410; (919) 379-2000.

4

#1 *in sheets and pillowcases*
#3 *in textiles*

Employees: 23,600
Sales: $1.9 billion
Profits: $65 million
Founded: 1887
Headquarters: Fort Mill, South Carolina

Social Conscience

Unlike other big textile makers, Springs stuck to their knitting, avoided any financial hanky-panky during the 1980s and ended the decade stronger than ever. Springs makes sheets, pillowcases, bedspreads, draperies, window blinds and a wide range of finished fabrics sold to other manufacturers. Their leading brand names include Springmaid, Wondercale, Pacific, Ultrasuede and Graber.

Coming into the decade, Springs (then known as Springs Mills) was making frozen foods under the Seabrook and Snow Crop labels, but they exited that business in

1981. And in 1985 they reinforced their central, and original, business by acquiring M. Lowenstein for $265 million. Lowenstein brought 19 plants, 9,000 employees and the Wamsutta brand name into the Springs profile.

History. In 1887, Captain Samuel Elliott White decided he was sick and tired of seeing northern industrialists make money from cotton grown in his beloved South. So he persuaded 16 friends to help him build a textile factory in his home town of Fort Mill, South Carolina. While many other southern cotton mills floundered, Captain White's flourished on the strength of the Fort Mill community. They were behind him all the way.

Leroy Springs, who married Captain White's daughter and was one of the original investors, eventually took over from the elderly man. He was succeeded in 1931 by his only child, Elliott White Springs, known as "The Colonel." Possibly the most colorful character American industry has produced in this century, the Colonel built Springs Mills into one of the largest textile firms in the nation, using a sexually suggestive ad campaign in the prudish years following World War II. Ads featured risqué young women and outrageous double entendre copy, using words like "ham hamper" and "lung lifter" to describe undergarments and mottos like "Protect Your Assets." The daring language and illustrations got Springs Mills a lot of sales and publicity, though *Life* and the *Saturday Evening Post* rejected the ads as too racy. The Colonel and his son-in-law, H. William Close, were fond of wearing shirts with prints of the "Springmaids"—pretty young women featured in the ads. Close took over after the Colonel's death in 1959. Seven years later, Springs sold stock to the public for the first time.

Owners and rulers. In an age of corporate raiders, Springs remains safe because the founding family controls nearly 60 percent of the stock. However, only one family member, Crandall Close Bowles, daughter of H. William Close, held a seat on the board in 1990, and none of them appear to be active in management. Professional managers now run Springs. Walter Y. Elisha, formerly vice chairman of the Chicago-based Jewel supermarket

About 5,000 attended this 1983 meeting of the Springs 25 Year Club at the company's 102-acre employee park near Lancaster, South Carolina.

chain, reigned as CEO throughout the 1980s. In 1985 he brought in W. Paul Tippett, former chairman of American Motors Corp., as president. Elisha and Tippett were fraternity brothers at Wabash College in Crawfordsville, Indiana.

As a place to work. Textile companies have long been regarded as crummy places to work—low wages, unhealthy plant conditions and unfeeling managements— but Springs has been an exception. The founding family, perhaps paternalistically, brought profit-sharing, medical insurance and low-cost hot meals to their plants well before such benefits were adopted by other weavers. Fort Mill has a 102-acre recreation area, Springs Park, and the company maintains Springmaid Beach on the Atlantic Coast as a low-cost vacation retreat for employees. Of their 37 plants, 24 are located in South Carolina, where Springs is the largest manufacturing employer.

Social responsibility. Considered a model corporate citizen, Springs has long been a generous supporter of schools, hospitals and other community services in the Carolina communities where their mills are located. However, their image suffered in early 1990 when CBS's "60 Minutes"

reported that Will Close, a young scion of the founding family, had been arrested several times for possession and distribution of cocaine but had not been jailed although a plant worker with even less evidence against him had been sent to prison on a first arrest. The implication was that family connections kept Close out of jail even though Springs had dedicated themselves during the 1980s to making their plants drug-free and had cooperated with law enforcement agencies in investigations at two of their mills that resulted in arrests and jail terms for employees. Every job applicant is now drug-tested.

Global presence. International business represents only 3.8 percent of total sales. Springs has one plant in England and one in Belgium.

Stock performance. Springs Industries stock bought for $1,000 in 1980 sold for $6,308 on January 2, 1990.

Consumer Brands.

Springmaid, Wamsutta, Ultrasuede, Skinner, Pacific, Performance, Fashion Pleat, Custom Designs, Pacific Silvercloth.

Springs Industries, Inc., P.O. Box 70, Fort Mill, SC 29715; (803) 547-3774.

HOME APPLIANCES

In 1916, 60 companies made washing machines. Today, only five are left. In 1973, home appliance makers employed 161,000 people. Today, this work force is below 95,000. These downturns accelerated during the 1980s even as appliance shipments went up, from 30 million to nearly 50 million, because of automation and imports. In the appliance industry (makers of refrigerators, dishwashers, washing machines, dryers, ranges and ovens), companies joined forces with each other both in this country and abroad. A major reason for the international push is that the American market is saturated. Refrigerators can be found in 99 percent of American homes, washing machines in more than 70 percent, microwaves in more than 50 percent and dishwashers in 48 percent. Appliance makers have to look elsewhere to find buyers for their wares.

1

GENERAL ⊛ ELECTRIC

#1 *in major appliances*
Sales: (major appliances): $4.7 billion
Profits: $490 million
Founded: 1878
Headquarters: Louisville, Kentucky
[For a full profile of GE, see page 555.)

General Electric is a huge conglomerate involved in plastics, aerospace and broadcasting, but most of us know them as a maker of home appliances. Although appliances accounted for only one-tenth of General Electric's sales, GE is the number one maker of home appliances in the nation. They no longer make small household appliances (toasters, irons, coffeemakers) or even any consumer electronic goods like radios, TVs, VCRs and tape recorders. (The small items bearing the GE name are made by other companies that have bought the right to use it.) However, GE continues to supply the big stuff: refrigerators, dishwashers, washing machines and dryers, ranges, microwave

ovens. And in this arena, called "major appliances" or "white goods," GE maintained through the 1980s the first-place ranking Chairman Jack Welch insists on holding. Welch has decreed that if a product isn't either number one or number two, it's a candidate for expulsion from the GE ranks.

General Electric's major appliance division avoided resorting to imports by a massive investment in automated plants. In the 1980s GE spent $1 billion to automate their Appliance Park in Louisville. One result was the dishwasher plant there now turns out more units with fewer workers—and the end product improved so much customer complaints declined. GE also made one of their biggest investments ever in a new manufacturing facility—$120 million to build an automated plant in Columbia, Tennessee, to produce rotary compressors for refrigerators. Along with the plant, GE established a training center where workers learn the skills they need to operate a sophisticated, high-tech plant.

GE makes appliances in 14 plants in eight states although the biggest production site, by far, is Louisville where 12,500 people are employed at Appliance Park. While GE is intent on defending their "core manufacturing" business, not all the appliances carrying the GE name are made in their U.S. plants. For example, microwave ovens and room air conditioners are supplied from overseas plants of other companies. In their book, *The Silent War*, Ira Magaziner and Mark Patinkin provide a graphic description of how GE decided to give the Samsung company of South Korea an order for microwave ovens:

In 1983, it cost GE $218 to make a typical microwave oven. It cost Korea's Samsung only $155...Assembly labor cost GE $8 per oven; Samsung only 63 cents. The differences in overhead labor—supervision, maintenance, setup—were even more astounding: for GE it was $30 per oven; for Samsung, 73 cents. GE was spending $4 on materials handling for each oven; Samsung, 12 cents. The biggest area of difference was in GE's line and central management—that came to $10 per oven. At Samsung it was 2 cents. What the companies got for their money was the most disturbing figure of all. Samsung workers were paid less but delivered more. GE got *four units per person each day. Samsung got nine.*

In June 1983 GE began buying small and midsize microwaves made in Japan and Korea. Two years later they stopped making microwaves in the U.S. Today, Samsung in Korea makes every microwave oven carrying the GE name—and Samsung is now the world's largest maker of microwave ovens.

Because the microwave oven had never been a big product for GE, it was not a difficult decision to make. Refrigerators are another story. They are central to GE— hence the big investment in automated plants in the U.S. If you ever read that GE refrigerators are being assembled abroad, you'll know the game is over.

General Electric clearly believes they know something about making refrigerators, washers and other home appliances. In 1988, after acquiring the factories of the Roper Corp., GE reactivated the RCA name rival Whirlpool once used on their appliance line. So now there's a full line of RCA home appliances in stores, courtesy of GE. And GE has still a third line, Hotpoint—appliances that look suspiciously like GE models but sell for less. Finally, GE has signaled they will be a global player in appliances by buying a 50 percent stake in the European appliance business of Britain's General Electric Company (no relation).

The first big project, a new refrigerator model begun in 1986, turned into a fiasco, however. GE believed they could annihilate the competition with a new refrigerator design. Everything seemed to work perfectly at first. The huge compressor plant in Tennessee cranked out one compressor every six seconds—more than one million in the first year of operation. Unfortunately, refrigerators with the new compressors broke down in people's homes, and GE had to replace more than one million defective units by 1990, costing the company more than $450 million. The replacements came from overseas— Singapore, Japan and Italy. According to a detailed account of the debacle in the *Wall Street Journal*, some engineers spotted the flaw before the compressors went into production. But their supervisors and managers didn't listen because they were under so much pressure from above. As one engineer said, "It would have taken a

TOP VACUUM CLEANERS

		Market Share
1.	Hoover	35%
2.	Eureka	22%
3.	Whirlpool	10%
4.	Singer	10%
5.	Kirby	8%
6.	Electrolux	5%
7.	Regina	4%
8.	Other	6%

Source: Appliance, September 1989. A total of 10.6 million Vacuum cleaners were sold in 1988.

lot of courage to tell [GE chairman] Welch that we had slipped off schedule."

Consumer brands.

GE, Hotpoint, RCA, Monogram.

General Electric Appliance Division, Appliance Park, Louisville, KY 40225; (502) 452-4311.

2

Whirlpool
CORPORATION

#1 *in washing machines*
#2 *in major appliances*

Employees: 39,400
Sales: $6.2 billion
Profits: $187 million
Founded: 1911
Headquarters: Benton Harbor, Michigan

A "rust belt" manufacturer of home appliances, Whirlpool has managed not only to survive more than three-quarters of a century but also to outlast or outpunch such appliance giants as Westinghouse, Frigidaire and Kelvinator. This staying power enabled Whirlpool to become the nation's second largest supplier of home appliances: washing machines, dryers, ranges, dishwashers, refrigerators, freezers, trash compactors, microwave ovens. According to a company estimate (and you wonder who did the counting), more than 100 million Whirlpool products are in use today in homes and businesses.

Only General Electric, a much bigger company, outsells Whirlpool in appliances. But unlike GE, Whirlpool's life begins and ends with appliances, not entirely by choice. Whirlpool could simply never make a go of it in other businesses they tried—TV, space heaters, electronic organs, kitchen cabinets.

The prime reason they're still making appliances is that they had a steady meal ticket in Sears, Roebuck, their main customer for more than 70 years. Sears sells appliances made by Whirlpool under the Kenmore name. However, this long relationship is on the wane. Whirlpool sells more and more products under their own name and names they've recently acquired: KitchenAid and Roper. Meanwhile, Sears now stocks other brand-name appliances such as the GE line next to Whirlpool-made Kenmores. The figures tell the story. In 1970, Sears accounted for two-thirds of Whirlpool's sales; by 1980, 50 percent and by 1990, 36 per cent.

During the 1980s Whirlpool managed to position themselves as a giant of the industry and a global player in a league whose contenders include General Electric, Maytag, Electrolux of Sweden and Bosch-Siemens of West Germany. In acquiring the KitchenAid appliance business from Dart and Kraft, they added an upscale line to confront Maytag. After a tussle with General Electric, they won the right to use the Roper name on ranges and other appliances. And they forged a trans-Atlantic alliance with Philips of Holland. "Our vision can no longer be limited to our domestic borders because national borders no longer define markets," said David R. Whitwam, chairman.

By the year 2000 Sears, Roebuck might just be a tiny blip on a Whirlpool computer screen.

History. In St. Joseph, Michigan, brothers Fred and Lou Upton, and their uncle, Emory Upton, set up the Upton Machine Company in 1911 to make an electric motor-driven wringer washer. The Uptons also bought a nearby ailing company that made toy trucks, guns and air rifles. They sold this business in 1928, by which time they saw the washing machine was more than a fad.

LIFE EXPECTANCY OF MAJOR APPLIANCES

Refrigerators	17 years
Freezers, standard	16 years
Humidifiers	13 years
Microwave ovens	11 years
Water heaters, gas	11 years
Dishwashers	10 years
Vacuum cleaners	10 years
Color TVs	8 years
Shavers	4 years

Source: Appliance, September 1989.

The symbiotic relationship with Sears began in 1916 when the Chicago mail-order house contracted with the Uptons for the supply of two washers to be listed in the Sears catalog under the Allen name. By 1925 the only washing machines Sears sold came from the Uptons—and the business was growing because Sears was opening up stores. In 1929, to meet that demand, the Uptons merged with the Nineteen Hundred Washer Company, a firm founded in Binghamton, New York, in 1898. The Upton name was dropped in favor of Nineteen Hundred Corporation. At their formation, they were the world's largest washing machine maker, and remained number one, thanks to Sears.

Sears, Roebuck was still the Nineteen Hundred mainstay in 1948 when the decision was made to market a washing machine under the Whirlpool name. By 1950 the Whirlpool line had done so well—sales in the first year reached 87,000 units—that the brand became their corporate name.

Over the next 20 years Whirlpool evolved from a washing machine manufacturer to a full-line appliance house. Two of their major employment centers—refrigeration plants in Evansville, Indiana, and Fort Smith, Arkansas—were formerly operated by International Harvester and Norge, respectively. Whirlpool's appliances output zoomed from 3.3 million in 1961 to 6 million in 1967, to 9.8 million in 1973. But it was all a little confusing. Still a little insecure about the Whirlpool name, the company adopted the brand name, RCA Whirlpool, after acquiring the Estate range and air-conditioning divisions of RCA in 1955. They used the RCA name until 1966. Not counting the Philips business, Whirlpool now makes appliances under four names: Whirlpool, Kenmore, KitchenAid and Roper.

Whirlpool needs to make a variety of appliances because dealers like to offer a full line of appliances from a company. In addition, about 25 percent of all appliance sales derive from sales to builders, who install appliances in homes they build (the home buyer usually has no choice). And you're not likely to see a new house equipped with a General Electric refrigerator and a Whirlpool dishwasher. A package deal is usually made.

O*wners and rulers.* In 80 years Whirlpool has had only five CEOs. The first was Lou Upton, who served nearly 40 years before retiring in 1949. The next was Bud Gray, in charge from 1949 to 1971; he made Whirlpool a full-line appliance company. He was followed by John Platts, who rose to the top from the factory floor and was succeeded in 1982 by another up-from-the-ranks leader, Jack Sparks. Sparks spent 46 years with Whirlpool, starting off on the assembly line in 1940 at 30 cents an hour. His final earnings, in 1987, were $1 million. David R. Whitwam, current chairman, president and CEO, is a sales executive who joined Whirlpool in 1968 after getting a degree in economics from the University of Wisconsin. He is the first college graduate to head the company since Bud Gray. Stephen Upton, son of founder Fred Upton, retired as senior vice president for communications in 1988. He was the last Upton to play an active company role. In 1980, two Sears officials sat on the board. Now, none do.

S*ocial responsibility.* The last of Whirlpool's four plants in the St. Joseph–Benton Harbor area was closed in 1987, and fewer than 1,000 people now work at the headquarters there. But Whirlpool is not about to abandon their hometown. They plan to convert the 80-acre plot that held the plants into a $70 million resort-and-office

A 1920s washing machine made by Upton, which was later to become Whirlpool Corporation.

TOP AIR CONDITIONERS

	Market Share
1. Electrolux (WCI)	21%
2. Fedders	20%
3. Whirlpool	18%
4. Matsushita	10%
5. Emerson Quiet Kool	9%
6. Carriet	6%
7. Friedrich	5%
8. Amana	3%
9. Addison	2%

Source: Appliance, September 1989. A total of 4.6 million air conditioners were sold in 1988.

complex that will include a new office-and-engineering building for themselves, a retail shopping area, a 300-room hotel and a 400-slip marina. For St. Joseph and Benton Harbor, Michigan, Whirlpool is going to remain a major presence.

Global presence. Whirlpool does only 12 percent of sales outside the U.S., but that's going to change. As the company told stockholders in 1988, "the U.S. represents only about 25 percent of the worldwide potential for major appliance sales." The springboard is the deal with Philips, the second largest appliance seller in Europe and a global operator. Whirlpool paid $350 million for 53 percent of Philips' appliance business, with an option to buy the remaining 47 percent by 1991. The deal could make Whirlpool the largest appliance company in the world.

Stock performance. Whirlpool stock bought for $1,000 in 1980 sold for $5,528 on January 2, 1990.

Consumer brands. Whirlpool, KitchenAid, Roper, Inglis, Kenmore.

Whirlpool Corporation, Benton Harbor, MI 49022; (616) 926-5000.

3

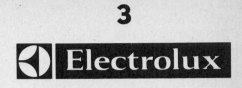

#1 *in major appliances (world)*
#3 *in major appliances (U.S.)*

Employees: 147,000 (19,350 in U.S.)
Sales: $11.6 billion ($3.4 billion in U.S.)
Profits: $239 million
Founded: 1919
Headquarters: Marietta, Georgia

Electrolux, a Swedish company, swept into first place in the world appliance business by vacuuming up companies in Italy, the U.S. and Britain. The Swedes took over Zanussi in Italy (1984), White Consolidated Industries (1986) and Regina vacuum cleaners (1989) in the U.S., and part of Thorn in Britain (1987). And that was after they'd already roped in more than 300 companies in 40 countries between 1970 and 1985.

As a result, there's hardly a home appliance that Electrolux doesn't make—and sell—under a list of brand names a yard long. Among the U.S. brands Electrolux owns are: Frigidaire, Kelvinator, White-Westinghouse, Gibson, Eureka, Elna, Tappan, O'Keefe and Merritt. One name is missing from that roster: Electrolux. The Swedes don't have the right to their own name in the American market because of some wheeling and dealing in the 1960s.

History. Axel Wenner-Gren, a fabled Swedish entrepreneur, came up with the idea of a lightweight vacuum cleaner that could be trundled from room to room—and went into business with it right after World War I. He combined the names of two Swedish companies, Electron and Lux, to arrive at a brand name. His salesmen rang doorbells all over Sweden, an invasion of privacy later exported to the U.S. and other countries. Wenner-Gren planned from the start to build an international business. He wanted to vacuum the entire world. By 1930 he had Electrolux subsidiaries operating in 30 countries. A resourceful and indefatigable promoter, he even persuaded Pope Pius XI to let Electrolux clean the Vatican for a year, an idea that generated a lot of publicity.

Electrolux of Sweden lost control of Electrolux in the U.S. in 1968 when they sold their 38 percent interest to Consolidated Foods, whose corporate name is now Sara Lee. Six years later the Swedes changed their minds about the American market and acquired National Union Electric, maker of Eureka vacuum cleaners. The original Electrolux company was now fielding another vacuum to battle the Electrolux. The U.S. is the only country in the world where the Swedes don't own the Electrolux brand. (In 1987, Sara Lee sold off Electrolux to the firm's division managers.)

Electrolux's $740 million takeover of Cleveland-based White Consolidated Industries in 1987 was the biggest foreign acquisition ever made by a Swedish company. White, founded in 1866, was originally a sewing machine manufacturer. They were a small outfit (sales of $20 million) until a frenetic Ed Reddig became chairman in 1957 and set about buying up other companies. In the 1960s and 1970s White became a dustbin for discarded appliance lines: Gibson (dumped by Hupp), Franklin (dumped by Studebaker), Kelvinator (dumped by American Motors), Westinghouse (dumped by Westinghouse), Philco (dumped by Ford) and Frigidaire (dumped by General Motors).

The Swedes now own the entire dump, the third largest appliance maker in the U.S.

Consumer brands.

Refrigerators, air conditioners and house-hold appliances:
White-Westinghouse, Kelvinator, Gibson, Frigidaire, Tappan, O'Keefe and Merritt.

Vacuum cleaners: Eureka, Regina.

Air conditioners and other accessories for recreational vehicles: Dometic, DuoTherm.

Sewing machines: Husqvarna, White.

Outdoor products: Poulan, Pioneer/Partner.

Electrolux, 1 Lux Backen, Stockholm, Sweden; 46 (8)-738 6000.

Electrolux Corp., 2300 Windy Ridge Parkway, Marietta GA 30067; (404) 933-1000.

4

MAYTAG

#3 *in washing machines*
#4 *in major appliances*

Employees: 26,000
Sales: $3.1 billion
Profits: $132 million
Founded: 1893
Headquarters: Newton, Iowa

Maytag's bucolic, earnest, stick-to-your-knitting scenario was rewritten completely during the 1980s. Maytag began the decade as an Iowa innocent. Sales were so small—$370 million a year—that they didn't qualify for the *Fortune* 500. But there wasn't a cent of debt on the books. And the washing machines and dryers Maytag made enjoyed such a good reputation for trouble-free operation they charged top dollar for them. Maytag reliability also made it possible for the company to launch their "lonely repairman" advertising campaign starring actor Jesse White.

In those days Maytag made their products only at plants in Newton, Iowa, where company headquarters are, and in Hampton, Iowa, 90 miles away. Maytag employed people who came from farm communities and who brought with them a work ethic. The employees took pride in the quality of the products coming out of those plants. And every one of those products carried the same brand name: Maytag.

Such an approach translated into a financial bonanza. In 1979, on sales of $369 million, Maytag earned $45 million *after taxes*, double the profit usually extracted from a dollar of sales in the appliance industry. So what more could a company want? In the context of today's corporate and financial landscapes, considerably more. It was consolidation time in the appliance industry—you couldn't make just a couple of appliances, you had to have a full line. And you couldn't be satisfied with just the American market—you had to think and act globally. Sitting in Newton, Iowa,

Maytag could see what was happening and decided they could not afford to opt out. They either joined the parade or risked becoming a sitting duck for a corporate acquisitor.

Maytag joined the parade. In quick succession, they bought Hardwick Stove (1981), Jenn-Air (1982), Magic Chef (1986) and Hoover (1989). By the end of the 1980s, Maytag was no longer a simple Iowa company making a handful of appliances. They were making just about every major appliance there was to make, as well as soft drink vending machines (Dixie-Narco) and dollar-bill changers (Ardac). They were operating plants in eight states and eight other countries and were selling products under the brand names Admiral, Hardwick, Hoover, Jenn-Air, Magic Chef, Norge—and yes, of course, Maytag. When they entered the decade, Maytag didn't make refrigerators; now they make them under six different brand names. And for the first time in more than 50 years, Maytag borrowed money. They closed out the 1980s with a half a billion dollars of long-term debt on their books. Welcome to the modern world.

History. Born and reared in the Iowa cornfields, Maytag is still headquartered where they began—Newton, 40 miles east of Des Moines. Four men, one of them F. L. Maytag, founded a firm in 1893 to make farm implements. In 1907, during one of those periodic slumps that afflict the farm business, they decided to start a sideline. They began making a hand-cranked wooden tub washer, the Pastime, to ease the burden of washing clothes. Also in 1907, F. L. Maytag became the sole owner.

Maytag's contraption was improved over the years. The wringer washer came out in 1909, an electric motor-powered model in 1911, a gasoline engine-powered machine in 1914 (a boon to farm homes not yet electrified), an aluminum tub washer in 1919. But Maytag's big breakthrough was the Gyrafoam washer of 1922. Until that time washers were designed with a lid having a dolly with pegs on its underside. By cranking the dolly clothes were dragged through the tub water. The Gyrafoam put a vaned agitator on the bottom of the tub—and forced water through the clothes. The new design was an instant winner and put Maytag on the national map. In the next two years they rose from 38th position in

TOP MICROWAVES

Samsung	17%
Goldstar	17%
Sharp	15%
Matsushita	12%
Sanyo	12%
Litton	6%
Electrolux (Tappan)	6%
Raytheon (Amana)	5%
Maytag (Maggie Chef)	3%
Toshiba	2%
Whirlpool	1%
Others	4%

Source: Appliance, September 1989. A total of 10.8 million microwave ovens were sold in 1988.

the washing machine industry to number one—and agitator action became an industry standard. With that success, Maytag abandoned the farm equipment business. In 1925 Maytag sold stock to the public and had their shares listed on the New York Stock Exchange. By 1927 they had sold 1 million washers.

Two sons of founder F. L. Maytag guided the company in the interwar period. L. B. Maytag served as president from 1920 to 1926, when he was succeeded by his brother, E. H. Maytag, who died in 1940. E. H. Maytag's son, 29-year-old Fred Maytag II, then took the reins.

During World War II Maytag stopped making washers and produced components for airplanes, tanks and other military equipment, resuming wringer washer production in 1946. The first automatic washers were made in 1949—and in 1953 Maytag began making dryers. In 1962, after three generations of Maytags, the first non-Maytag family member became company head.

Maytag added dishwashers in 1966 and food waste disposers in 1968.

Maytag lays claim to a long line of technological firsts and practiced employee involvement in the work place long before anyone heard of a Japanese quality circle. The company's position as a quality producer was reinforced by a 1980 survey showing:

- Maytag produced the longest lasting automatic washer.
- Maytag had the lowest percentage of washers that were scrapped or junked.
- Maytag was the washer with the lowest average number of service calls.
- Maytag owners spent less on service or repairs than owners of all other brands.
- Maytag had the longest time period to the first service call.
- Owners ranked Maytag first in dependability.

Heady stuff. But right after that survey was taken, Maytag charged out of Iowa and began buying up other appliance companies, ready to take their place on the world stage. When it was all over, Maytag ranked 146th in the 1989 *Fortune* 500. CEO Daniel Krumm, who presided over this dramatic growth, knows it's not the same Maytag. Interviewed by *Forbes* reporter Kerry Hannon in early 1989, Krumm said:

> *"I feel so removed from what's going on. I miss the old Maytag. Everything was so clear then. You built the very best products and didn't worry too much about the price. Goodness gracious, I didn't realize how easy my life was." And he added: "You have to deal with what the world gives you."*

Owners and rulers. The Maytags no longer run the company bearing their name, and no surviving family member owns even as much as 5 percent of the stock. The last Maytag to play a role here was L. B. Maytag, grandson of the founder, who retired as a director in 1988 because of ill health. Maytag, who was then 62, ran Frontier Airlines from 1958 to 1962 and then led National Airlines until they merged with Pan Am in 1979. Another of the founder's grandsons, Fritz Maytag, founded the Anchor Steam beer company in San Francisco.

Maytag has strong roots in Iowa. Robert D. Ray, a former Iowa governor, was elected to the board in 1983, and many

TOP COFFEE MAKERS

		Market share
1.	Mr Coffee	22%
2.	Black & Decker	18%
3.	Wear-Ever/Proctor-Silex	15%
4.	N.A.P. (Norelco)	10%
5.	Braun	8%
6.	Krups	6%
7.	Hamilton Beach	4%
8.	Regal	3%
9.	Others	14%

Source: Appliance, September 1989. A total of 12.7 million coffee makers were sold in 1988.

Maytag executives are only one generation away from an Iowa farm. And although actor Jesse White may be more well known to the public than CEO Daniel J. Krumm, Krumm was celebrating his 37th year with Maytag in 1990, the past 16 as CEO (he also serves as chairman). He joined the company as a sales analyst.

The issue for Maytag in the 1990s is whether the acquisition binge of the 1980s will erode their Iowa culture. Because Maytag stock was used to buy companies, the largest shareholders are now outsiders. As a result of the Hoover purchase, Lester Crown and/or members of his family became the company's largest stockholders, with a little over 5 percent of the shares. Lester Crown is scion of the Henry Crown Chicago-based financial empire, one of the biggest in the U.S. The Crowns are also the largest shareholders in General Dynamics. The second largest Maytag shareholder, with less than one-half of 1 percent of the stock, is S. B. Rymer, Jr., who sold Magic Chef to Maytag in 1986.

As a place to work. Maytag has often been held up as a model of harmonious management-labor relations. As far back as 1947 they initiated a work simplification program that encouraged employees to contribute their own ideas on cost savings and productivity improvements. The company is known for having the best employee suggestion program in American industry. In 1987, nonsupervisory employees turned in a total of 6,346 suggestions—an average of 3 per employee—and more than 2,700 were implemented. Maytag awards up to $7,500 for these ideas. In 1987, the awards totaled $200,322. The United Auto Workers represent Maytag's Newton employees. In June 1989, Maytag established an Employee Stock Ownership Plan that will own about 3 percent of outstanding shares.

Global presence. Prior to the Hoover acquisition, negligible. But that was the whole point of the Hoover takeover: to thrust Maytag into the international arena. Although Hoover's vacuum cleaners are well known in the U.S., overseas units also make washers, dryers, dishwashers and refrigerators. Of Hoover's $1.4 billion in sales, 60 percent came from outside the U.S. Hoover is particularly strong in Britain and other Commonwealth countries. Initially Maytag bid for Hoover's non-U.S. business. Rebuffed, they bought the whole company.

Stock performance. Maytag stock bought for $1,000 in 1980 sold for $5,590 on January 2, 1990.

Consumer brands.

Maytag, Magic Chef, Hoover, Jenn-Air, Admiral, Hardwick, Norge, Dixie-Narco.

The Maytag Company, 403 W. 4th Street N., Newton, IA 50208; (515) 792-8000.

5

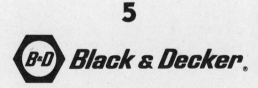

Black & Decker.

#1 *in power tools*

Employees: 28,200
Sales: $3.6 billion
Founded: 1910
Headquarters: Towson, Maryland

Old images die hard. To most people, Black & Decker still means power tools—drills, saws, sanders, grinders. These tools are small, lightweight and portable. Many are cordless. The typical Black & Decker product can be found in the basement or garage of a do-it-yourselfer's home. One even made it to the moon. On the *Apollo 15* mission in 1971, astronauts took along a Black & Decker battery-operated drill to scrape up samples of the moon's surface.

All right, that's what Black & Decker *used* to stand for. And although they're still kings of the power tool business, they transformed themselves during the 1980s.

Black & Decker entered the decade with sales of $1.2 billion, 60 percent of it overseas. They emerged with almost $4 billion, 55 percent of it outside the U.S. In 1980 they had 18,500 employees; by decade's end, over 28,000. They started the 1980s as a homogenous company making many different products, nearly all of them related to the power tool trade. They emerged from the 1980s making toasters, blenders, food processors, locks, adhesives, faucets and golf club shafts, among many other products. Power tools account for about half their sales whereas household products contributed another third. The rest is split between outdoor products and service parts.

Black & Decker grew fat itself by becoming a player in the takeover games that raged in the 1980s. First, they took over the housewares division General Electric no longer wanted to mess with. So if you're looking for a GE toaster oven to replace the one that just died in your kitchen, you'll find it under the Black & Decker name. The same goes for irons, blenders and a score of other small appliances formerly bearing the GE logo. In 1989, Black & Decker bought an industrial mainstay of old New England, Hartford-based Emhart, which brought Kwikset locks, Pfister faucets and True Temper lawn and garden tools (and golf club shafts) into the house—and about doubled Black & Decker's size.

The 1980s also marked the passage of Black & Decker from a family-oriented company with a well-defined mission to a faceless corporation with roving eyes. Not until 1975 did they have a CEO who was not a Black or a Decker. And when the 1980s began, Alonzo G. Decker, Jr., who always made a point of talking to as many employees as possible, had just stepped down as chairman. The chief architect of the new Black & Decker is Nolan D. Archibald, lured away from Beatrice Foods in the mid-1980s to bring Black & Decker into the modern world. He closed seven plants, chopped 2,000 people from the payroll and set about finding new partners. A six-foot, five-inch former basket-ball star at Utah's Weber State College, Archibald received a good education at Beatrice in how to revitalize family companies that turn into big corporations. Archibald is a Mormon, and he worked in seven different cities before coming to the Baltimore metropolitan area where Black & Decker is based. His wife, Margaret, bore him a son in each of those cities. In Baltimore, she gave birth to their first girl.

To lure the 42-year-old Archibald to Black & Decker in 1985, the company crafted a compensation-and-benefits package that included an interest-free loan of $500,000, repayable in five annual installments. Black & Decker also agreed to pay Archibald an annual performance bonus of $100,000 for five years, even if he leaves the company. Archibald holds the titles of chairman, president and CEO—in case anyone wondered who's in charge here.

Stock performance. Black & Decker stock bought for $1,000 in 1980 sold for $1,146 on January 2, 1990.

Consumer brands.

Black & Decker, Emhart, Molly, Lawn Genie, Drip Mist, Viking, True Temper, GardenAmerica, Kwikset, Price Pfister.

Black & Decker Corporation, 701 East Joppa Road, Towson, MD 21204; (301) 583-3900.

6

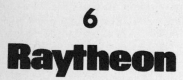

Raytheon

#5 *in major appliances*

Employees: 7,900
Sales: (appliances): $1.1 billion
Profits: $41 million
Founded: 1934 (Amana)
Headquarters: Lexington, Massachusetts

The Speed Queen coin-operated washers found in laundromats, the Amana Radarange microwave ovens restaurants use and the Modern Maid ranges and ovens installed in new homes are all Raytheon products. An aerospace company doing more than half their business with the Pentagon, Raytheon has been trying for a long time to make it in appli-

THE COST OF RUNNING YOUR APPLIANCES

Appliance	Average Energy Cost* (per year)
Water heater	$450
Refrigerator (manual defrost)	$45
Refrigerator/freezer (frost free)	$120
Freezer (manual defrost)	$75
Freezer (frost free)	$135
Air conditioner (Central)	$60
Air conditioner (one room)	$60
Range	$60
Clothes washer (includes water heating)	$90
Clothes dryer	$70
Dishwasher (includes water heating)	$70
TV (color)	$25
Lights (household total)	$25-50

*These energy costs are based on electricity price of 7.5 cents per kWh.

Source: The *Wall Street Journal,* 8 December 1987.

ances. The parent, founded in 1922 as American Appliance Company, intended to make refrigerators. They switched instead to radio tubes. At the end of World War II, as a by-product of their work in supplying radar systems to the military, they stumbled onto the idea of a microwave oven. In 1945, a Raytheon engineer put a bag of popcorn in front of a microwave, a key element of radar. The kernels popped as if they were over a fire. Company president Marshall immediately saw the commercial possibilities, and the company quickly named their invention

The first Raytheon Radarange microwave ovens were sold to restaurants and hospitals during the 1950's. The cost: $3,000.

the Radarange. But Raytheon's expertise was in technology, not in selling consumer goods. So the microwave oven remained an idea until the big weapons contractor bought Amana Refrigeration in 1965.

Amana was run by the Amana Society, founded by a religious sect that emigrated to Iowa from Germany in the 19th century. Amana was a rare creature in corporate America: a cooperatively owned and operated company based on the credo that "each member is to bear his burden, according to his ability, for the common good of the community." George Foerstner, a member of the colony, began making refrigerators in 1934, and he was still running the business when Raytheon president Tom Phillips approached him in 1965. Foerstner acknowledged the company had grown too large for him to manage alone, and he agreed to sell out to Raytheon, so long as he remained company head. Amana got a much-needed infusion of capital, and Raytheon got a first-rate consumer appliance company that could market the

microwave oven invention. By the early 1970s, the Radarange was in kitchens across the country.

Few vestiges of the original communal society are left, but the main Amana plant remains in Amana, Iowa, 20 miles southwest of Cedar Rapids, where it now functions as a subsidiary of the company making the Hawk, Patriot, Sparrow, Sidewinder and Stinger missiles.

Raytheon has also bought two other appliance makers, Caloric and Speed Queen. The Glenwood and Sunray appliances come from Caloric; Speed Queen makes the Marathon line of washers and dryers.

Stock performance. Raytheon stock bought for $1,000 in 1980 sold for $2,803 on January 2, 1990.

Consumer brands.

Amana, Caloric, Speed Queen, Radarange, Glenwood, Sunray, Modern Maid, Huebsch.

Raytheon Company, 141 Spring Street, Lexington, MA 02173; (617) 862-6600.

BUILDERS & DEVELOPERS

In a country where big business is supposed to be boss, home building remains the province of small, local companies. Over 93,000 home builders operate, and not one is really national in scope the way a food company or appliance maker is. The 100 largest home builders supply only 15 percent of the market. The average contractor has fewer than 10 employees. A host of companies sell products to the building industry, and they too tend to be small, except for the giant lumber producers and other suppliers such as Honeywell (thermostats) and American Standard (plumbing). Real estate developers, however, are getting bigger and bigger. The 1980s saw Donald Trump buy the Plaza Hotel, Japan's Mitsubishi Estate buy Rockefeller Center and Detroit's Al Taubman buy the huge Irvine Ranch in southern California. It was a swinging era for real estate developers whose stock in trade has always been leverage—in effect, buying property without putting up much, if any, of your own money and reselling at enormous profit down the road.

1

Honeywell

#1 *in thermostats*

Employees: 68,100
Sales: $6.1 billion
Profits: $604 million
Founded: 1885
Headquarters: Minneapolis, Minnesota

In 1989 Honeywell said they would do what antiwar activists had been demanding they do for 21 years: get out of the defense business. It wasn't exactly a moral decision. Honeywell had posted an unexpected loss of $435 million in 1988, largely because of problems with military contracts. And so they restructured the company for the sixth time since 1984. In addition to selling their defense and marine systems, which produced torpedoes, land mines and mortar shells, Honeywell planned to eliminate 4,000 jobs, nearly 1,000 at the corporate level.

Defense business accounted for 20 percent of Honeywell's sales.

The goal of the latest restructuring was to bring in enough money to reward Honeywell's long-suffering shareholders who've had to sit through one debacle after another, from antiwar protesters disrupting annual meetings to Honeywell management making a mess of things. A major revamping took place in 1986 when Honeywell exited the computer business. They had previously bought General Electric's computer operations with the aim of becoming a major player in this field.

Another foul-up in the 1980s was the purchase of Sperry's aerospace business from Unisys. They paid $1 billion for a business that quickly lost money on several military contracts. Honeywell sued Unisys for $350 million, charging them with overstating the assets and income of the business they sold to Honeywell. Outsiders wondered why Honeywell took 18 months to discover these problems.

In any case, entering the 1990s, Honeywell was once again about to create a "new Honeywell," one that returned them to their core business of control systems. They make electronic automation and control systems for homes, commercial buildings and factories; six out of every seven single-family U.S. homes have at least one Honeywell device—a thermostat, electronic air cleaner or security system.

History. Honeywell began with a gizmo called the "damper flapper"—an automatic temperature controller for coal-fired furnaces—that tinkerer, gadgeteer, inventor Albert Butz came up with in 1883. Two years later he and his investors began to manufacture the damper flapper in Minneapolis. William R. Sweatt dominated much of the firm's early history by investing $1,500 in the venture in 1891 and gathering in all the stock in 1902. His son, Harold Sweatt, succeeded him in 1934.

The only competition Sweatt's firm had was Honeywell Heating Specialties of Wabash, Indiana. Although both companies were flourishing, they each had patents blocking the other from expansion. Mark Honeywell and William R. Sweatt were arch rivals, but they merged their companies in the 1920s.

Some anti-weapons demonstrators in front of Honeywell's corporate headquarters on October 24, 1983, when over 400 were arrested.

Honeywell began to expand just before World War II. They entered the world of military contracts by making precision optical equipment for submarine periscopes and artillery sights used during the war. Then experimental work in electronics led to the development of the first successful autopilot in 1941. They set up an aeronautical division in 1949 and got serious about making guidance systems for planes and missiles. Once when their electronic engineers needed ceramic transducers, they simply bought a one-person ceramics company that produced the necessary piece. Honeywell entered the field of fire detection and alarm systems in 1957.

Their attempts to become a power in the computer industry got off to an inauspicious start in the mid-1950s, and not until the end of the '70s did their subsidiary, Honeywell Information Systems, begin to turn a profit.

Owners and rulers. James Renier, a chemist-turned-CEO, has been running Honeywell since 1987 when he was 57 years old. Renier, a Minnesotan, joined Honeywell in 1956 as a research scientist and has taken turns running all their various branches: aviation, controls, defense, computers. Cleaning out the computer branch earned him the nickname "Neutron Jim," as in the neutron bomb. Renier cut so many jobs, said a colleague, that "all the buildings were there. It's just the people who were gone." Renier may be one of the few *Fortune* 500 CEOs who has raised five children on his own, after his first wife died of cancer in the early 1970s. That experience, he has said, put things in a new perspective. Now he leaves work early enough to spend time with his family, and, as he puts is, "If you have a wife dying... there isn't a damn thing that can bother you as much. If something goes haywire at Honeywell, you say: 'So what? We're here to fix it.'"

As a place to work. As Honeywell plunged into the red in 1988, one employee complained to the *Wall Street Journal* that "the only trademark we've ever had is mediocrity." In the mid-1980s, Honeywell had a reputation for infighting between engineers and salespeople and for thwarting the creative spirits in their midst. Now "quality circles" are a feature of work at Honeywell, where employees meet every week or so to discuss ideas for improving efficiency. They credit these circles with reducing absenteeism and turnover. CEO Renier is also a believer in retreats, where managers and coworkers get away and relate to each other in the wilderness. Honeywell generally gets high marks as an employer for women. The Honeywell Women's Council, organized to address the needs of female employees, had a worldwide meeting in 1988. They also have a committee charged with singling out talented women, minority and handicapped employees and promoting them to responsible positions.

Social responsibility. Nearly 2,000 people have been arrested in nonviolent civil disobedience demonstrations held at Honeywell's corporate headquarters since 1982. Led by community activist Marv Davidov, the Honeywell Project was formed in 1968 in reaction to the news that Honeywell, which many people regarded as a benign manufacturer of thermostats, was the chief supplier of the brutal fragmentation bombs that tore people apart during the Vietnam War. The project donated a $35,000 settlement from a civil suit against Honeywell and the FBI for harassment to the American Friends Service Committee's "Shovels for Laos Project," to help clean up unexploded cluster bombs that still maim and kill Laotian peasants.

In 1989, Honeywell was implicated in a Pentagon procurement fraud scandal when a former Navy engineer admitted he'd accepted $75,000 in bribes from Honeywell between 1982 and 1984. In exchange, he said he provided Honeywell with information about Pentagon electronics and computer contracts.

Global presence: They do nearly one-quarter of their business outside the U.S.

Stock performance. Honeywell stock bought for $1,000 in 1980 sold for $2,860 on January 2, 1990.

Honeywell Inc., Honeywell Plaza, Minneapolis, MN 55408; (612) 870-5200.

2

American Standard Inc.

#1 in plumbing fixtures
#2 in air conditioning

Employees: 34,100
Sales: $3.7 billion
Loss: $46 million
Founded: 1881
Headquarters: New York City, New York

The company that claims to have made one out of every five toilets in the non-Communist world was flushed from public view toward the end of the 1980s. After a series of seemingly endless mergers going back more than 100 years, American Standard became the target of a takeover bid in January 1988. Appliance and toolmaker Black & Decker offered $56 a share for American Standard stock then selling for $34 a share. American Standard resisted the offer, which Black & Decker increased to $77 a share. To escape Black & Decker's clutches, American Standard agreed in March 1988 to be acquired by the investment banking house, Kelso & Co., whose founder, Louis O. Kelso, devised the employee stock ownership plans many companies adopted in the 1980s. The Kelso company paid $78 a share, or $2.5 billion, to take over American Standard, a world leader in plumbing fixtures, air conditioning and air brakes. The buyout saddled American Standard with a couple of billion dollars of debt, forcing them into "Operation Selloff." They sold their railway signaling business, their Steelcraft steel door business, their fluid power business and their railway braking business. Perhaps the most poignant sale was their landmark New York City headquarters at 40 West 40th Street across from the New York Public Library. The Art Deco skyscraper was immortalized in the 1927 Georgia O'Keeffe oil painting, Radiator Building. The 25-story building was sold to a Japanese company wanting to convert it to a hotel.

However, debt-laden American Standard remained a powerful company, operating 80 plants around the world, turning out Ideal-Standard plumbing fixtures, Trane air-conditioning systems for buildings and factories and Westinghouse air brakes for trucks. They're also beholden to their lenders. In 1989 they had to pay interest totaling nearly $300 million, and that wiped out all their profits for the year.

History. The "American" half of the name comes from American Radiator, a company founded in 1881 in Buffalo to make equipment for steam and hot-water heating of buildings. In 1899, New York banker J. P. Morgan consolidated just about all U.S. heating equipment companies under the American Radiator name.

The "Standard" comes from Standard Sanitary, created in 1899 with the merger of two plumbing supply companies, Ahrens & Ott of Louisville and Standard Manufacturing of Pittsburgh. Standard Sanitary was famous for enameled cast-iron plumbing fixtures, and for pioneering the one-piece lavatory, claw-foot and built-in bathtubs and the single tap for hot and cold water.

In 1929, the two companies combined to form the American Radiator & Standard Sanitary Corporation. In that same year they bought C. F. Church, the nation's leading maker of toilet seats (thereby consolidating their hold on the bathroom). They were among the first to embrace advertising, becoming a client of Batten, Barton, Durstine & Osborn during the early years of this century. They sought always to identify their bathroom products as symbolic of a higher standard of living. In the 1970s they were still running ads describing the bathroom "as the most important room in your home.... It's the only room where a guest can lock the door and judge so much about you—your taste, your character, and your life style."

In the 1960s, though, they decided to come out of the bathroom and use the profits from vitreous china to diversify. They went into real estate and home building. They had Majestic fireplaces. They bought Mosler Safe and a check-printing company. The strategy didn't work. They sold off most of these companies in the late 1970s and early 1980s. In 1984 they bought one they kept: Trane Air Conditioning, now the largest business American Standard has, accounting for more than half of sales.

Owners and rulers. The big winners in the Kelso takeover were the veteran American Standard managers who not only held their jobs but reaped rich rewards. In 1989, when American Standard lost money, CEO Emmanuel A. Kampouris was paid a salary of $980,000. His number two, Nicolas M. Georgitsis, received $680,000. The top managers were also given an opportunity to buy 8 percent of the stock, the purchase of which the company is subsidizing. In 1989 Kampouris and Georgitsis collected $337,500 each (on top of salaries) as "bonuses" for buying stock. Bonuses to all executives buying stock came to $2.4 million. And those "thank you for buying our stock" bonuses continue through 1995. In addition, these top managers participate in an ESOP (employee stock ownership plan) holding 19 percent of the shares.

Coming into the 1990s, a Kelso & Co. partnership owned 68 percent of American Standard's shares—and a 14 percent interest in this partnership was held by Hoxan Corp., a Japanese distributor of American Standard products. Shigeru Mizushima, president of Hoxan, holds a seat on the American Standard board.

As a place to work. The buyout solidified the gulf between top managers and the rest of the employees, ironic in view of Louis Kelso's philosophy that employee stock ownership is the way to motivate and properly reward workers. The 8,400 factory employees at American Standard are covered by 34 different union contracts—and these workers got no stock. The ESOP covers only salaried people, and even here it's skewed to the top. Stock is allocated on the basis of 3 percent of compensation. Ergo, Emmanuel Kampouris, with his near $1 million salary, gets $30,000 worth whereas a nonunion employee earning $30,000 gets $900 worth.

Global presence. American Standard operates in 26 countries and does nearly half their business outside the U.S. They are particularly strong in Europe, where they have seven plants making bathtubs, toilets and other plumbing products. In Europe and Brazil they are the largest maker of air brakes for heavy trucks.

Consumer brands.

Air conditioning: Trane, American-Standard, Tyler.

Plumbing: American-Standard, Ideal-Standard, Standard.

American Standard Inc., 1114 Avenue of the Americas, New York, NY 10036; (212) 703-5100.

3

Armstrong

#1 *in flooring and ceilings*

Employees: 25,600
Sales: $2.5 billion
Profits: $188 million
Founded: 1860
Headquarters: Lancaster, Pennsylvania

The country's leading maker of floor coverings (they introduced linoleum in 1908), and one of the largest makers of ceilings and furniture (they own North Carolina's Thomasville), Armstrong is as American as corn-on-the-cob, and clings to a bygone innocence. While changes ruled the business world during the 1980s, the company once known as Armstrong Cork (they changed their name in 1980) tried to stay true to what they call "family-oriented, middle-American values." They did buy more than a dozen companies—the biggest the ceramic tile-maker American Olean (sales: $200 million)—and they greatly expanded their overseas operations (now 25 percent of sales); but Armstrong World Industries of 1990 did not differ markedly from Armstrong Cork of 1980. In Lancaster employees still gathered at Christmastime to sing carols in the auditorium of the red-brick schoolhouselike building that is headquarters. The company even has their own Christmas carol, "A Holiday Wish." Also, Armstrong was still promulgating the operating principles adopted in 1960 when the company celebrated their centennial. These principles bind Armstrong people "to maintain high moral and ethical standards" and "to reflect the tenets of good taste and common courtesy."

Armstrong's flavor wafts up from the pages of *Armstrong Today*, an employee magazine they have been publishing for over 50 years. Two issues during the 1980s paid special tribute to employees who had served in the Vietnam and Korean Wars. Another featured the exploits of children of employees: eight-year-old Chivas Clark made "the principal's honor roll in both the first and second grade" and "won the 50-yard dash at his school's field day"; nine-year-old Lauren Hoover was 1987 May Queen of Maytown, Pennsylvania; 14-year-old Gillian Shearer was ranked one of the top 50 women chess players in the U.S.

Armstrong looks for people who fit this mold—not so much the "brightest people" as those who have "a positive attitude."

New single marketing trainees make their home at the Armstrong Manor where they are expected to absorb the company's unique values.

And here's where they get them from: Penn State, Grove City (Pennsylvania), Virginia Polytechnic Institute, Indiana University, University of Delaware, Lehigh, Syracuse University, University of Tennessee, Drexel University and Purdue. Those colleges, in that order, were where Armstrong recruited the largest number of employees during the 1980s. Not an Ivy League school in sight. And once people come to Armstrong, they stay.

Harry A. Jensen, CEO from 1978 to 1983, retired from the board in 1988 after 48 years of service. Joseph L. Jones, his successor, joined Armstrong in 1947 and was still on the board in 1989. And William W. Adams, who became chief executive in 1988, joined Armstrong in 1956 fresh out of Iowa State University. All three were also graduates of Armstrong Manor, a remodeled farmhouse outside of Lancaster where, since the 1920s, newly hired sales trainees spend three months getting inculcated with Armstrong values before starting their careers.

Armstrong has even had the same advertising agency, BBDO, since 1917— and Mary Joan Glynn, one of two women on the board, is a senior vice president of BBDO. Some people think Armstrong's character reflects their surroundings: they are based in the heart of the Pennsylvania Dutch country, where Amish farmers lead simple, hardworking lives, eschewing cars, computers and other trappings of modern civilization. However, Armstrong has moved considerably beyond that base. They have 73 plants in 21 states and 20 more in 11 other countries, and they spread the Armstrong philosophy throughout the company.

It's a philosophy that did not impress the Belzberg family of Canada. Noted real estate operators and corporate raiders (they are among the richest people in North America), the Belzbergs bought 11.5 percent of Armstrong in 1989, and waged an expensive proxy fight to take over the company in mid-1990. Armstrong responded by lobbying the Pennsylvania legislature to pass a strong anti-takeover law. They also got out of the low-profit carpet business and induced some veteran employees to take early retirement, efforts to show shareholders management had their interests at heart. Armstrong defeated the Belzberg proxy fight (winning three of the four contested

seats), and the Belzbergs sold all their Armstrong stock—at a loss of $16 million.

Stock performance. Armstrong World Industries stock bought for $1,000 in 1980 sold for $6,920 on January 2, 1990.

Armstrong World Industries, Inc., P.O. Box 3001, Liberty and Charlotte Streets, Lancaster, PA 17604; (717) 397-0611.

4

Trammell Crow Company

#1 *in real estate developers*

#1 *in homebuilding*

Employees: 12,324
Sales: $1.6 billion
Founded: 1948
Headquarters: Dallas, Texas

Trammell Crow, the name of a man and a company, came out of Texas after World War II to become the largest real estate developer in the U.S. The company he built from scratch now towers over other real estate operators and qualifies as the U.S.'s only truly national developer (with offices in more than 100 cities). Trammell Crow has built skyscrapers, warehouses, garden apartments, huge trade marts, single-family homes, hotels, hospitals and shopping centers. They have changed the Dallas skyline, but their hand can be seen in cities across the country: Peachtree Plaza in Atlanta, the Embarcadero Center in San Francisco, the International Mall Promenade in Miami, One Renaissance Square in Phoenix, Minnetonka Corporate Center in Minneapolis. They have 350 office buildings in 50 cities, and they own or manage 160 shopping centers.

In addition to managing their own properties, Trammell Crow performs this task for other property owners. They are the largest landlord in the country. They have also become the nation's largest home builder, with 90,000 residential units in more than 50 cities. More than 100,000 people live in Trammell Crow–built homes or apartments. They have 35 hotels (if it bears the name "Wyndham" it's a Trammell Crow property). And through all this meteoric growth,

Trammell Crow has retained a nice guy aura, the opposite of the greedy real estate salesmen portrayed in David Mamet's play *Glengarry Glen Ross*. At least it's difficult to find anyone who has harsh words about Trammell Crow, including people who leave to start their own businesses.

History. Trammell Crow was born in Dallas in 1914, one of eight children. His father, a bookkeeper of modest means, couldn't send him to college so Crow studied accounting at Southern Methodist University night school while working at odd jobs. He did a stint at a big accounting firm, Ernst & Ernst, before shipping out as a Navy commander during World War II. Discharged, he took over his wife's struggling wholesale grain company.

But running the Doggett Grain Company failed to satisfy him, and by age 34 he was restless. He noticed the Ray-O-Vac battery company, which was leasing space in Doggett's warehouse, needed a new site. So in 1948 Crow borrowed $40,000, built a warehouse and leased half of it to the battery company. Soon he was on a roll in Dallas, lining up customers and constructing warehouses left and right. After a while, he started building on "speculation"—wherever he anticipated a need, even before he had guaranteed customers. His good name and scrupulous business dealings were the banks' only guarantee the unleased buildings would yield money. Although buying with debt was risky, it paid off handsomely—especially since Trammell Crow did not sell his warehouses but merely leased them and charged higher and higher rents. And his warehouses were attractive, with lots of windows and landscaped lawns and plants outside.

Until the mid-1950s, Crow had only two employees and was building in Dallas, Atlanta and Denver. Then Crow began taking on partners to help him build "trade marts," huge structures devoted to exhibiting products for wholesalers in a particular industry, like the Dallas Homefurnishings Mart (now the Dallas Market Center). These marts had the trademark Trammell Crow touches: attractive interiors, outdoor sculpture and landscaping. In the early 1960s, Crow started on his "centers," buildings grouped together for utility yet harmoni-

TOP 10 BUILDING SUPPLY/ HOME CENTERS

		Sales
1.	The Home Depot	$2.74 billion
2.	Lowe's Companies	$2.65 billion
3.	Builder's Square	$2.00 billion
4.	Payless Cashways	$1.90 billion
5.	Hechinger Co.	$1.20 billion
6.	Grossman's	$1.10 billion
7.	Home Club	$1.00 billion
8.	Wickes Lumber*	$1.00 billion
9.	84 Lumber	$800 million
10.	Wickes Companies*	$675 million

*These two companies were originally part of the same firm.

Source: Lowe's 1989 Annual Report.

ous in design, like the Peachtree Center in Atlanta and the Embarcadero Center in San Francisco. By 1971, Trammell Crow and his partners owned over $1 billion worth of real estate. He did hit rough sledding during the real estate slump of the 1970s and sold off many properties.

In early 1990, Crow was forced to look for a sugar daddy to avoid defaulting on loans. The problem was a poor real estate market, particularly in the Southwest where Crow has many properties. As had happened before when Crow had faced similar credit squeezes, the company pulled another rabbit out of the hat by getting the real estate subsidiary of Equitable Assurance to put up a whopping $456 million to refinance 150 properties.

Owners and rulers. The largest real estate empire in the nation was built largely on the force of Trammell Crow's charismatic and energetic personality. "He believes that persistence is far more important than genius," one of his partners told *Inc.* "Never, never, never give up—that's his motto." Another added that Crow "thinks of himself as a manufacturer of a product—space."

According to one Crow associate, "More than anybody else in American business, Trammell Crow has developed his life around this notion of partnership."

Trammell Crow is owned by their partners, each of whom owns a percentage of each project they build. In recent years, the company management has become less free-form and more hierarchical. In 1977, legal and financial control was given to a board of partners, headed by Managing Partner J. McDonald "Don" Williams, then 35—and often cited as Crow's successor. Trammell Crow himself turns 76 in 1990 but has no retirement plans. He did, however, surrender daily operations in the mid-1970s, and now reigns as the company's resident visionary and father figure, remaining "a managing partner." An avid sculpture collector, Crow entertains guests on his 151-foot yacht and owns Crow Farms and a wildlife refuge, both in Texas.

As a place to work. Trammell Crow's 230 partners (1988) are chosen carefully. Crow described his unique criterion to *Inc.*: "I ask myself if he's a nice person, a good human being, someone you like to see coming into the room. Has he got any brains? Is he disciplined and eager enough to get up in the morning without an alarm clock?" To be a partner, it also helps to have an MBA from Harvard, Stanford, or another prestigious business school. Everybody who becomes a Crow partner starts at the bottom. They get a low flat salary; further income coming from commissions and property ownership. Many partners are millionaires. Even nonpartners—from attorneys to secretaries and file clerks—share in the rewards through an employee profit-sharing trust; the partners set aside a 10 percent ownership stake in every third or fourth property the company develops. Income from that property is then put into the trust. Each year a nonpartner can expect an amount equal to as much as 75 percent of his or her annual income to be placed into his or her trust account.

Social responsibility. In the early 1960s, Trammell Crow began turning slums into architectural showpieces. "We have three words in our company that we use to describe our function," Crow told *Fortune*. "The words are: To do good. That means *good* buildings, *good* support for our lessees, *good* civics, *good* morals, and having a *good* time." And he told *Development* that "there is a responsibility to the city, to

everyone, responsibility to the future, responsibility to ourselves, to do things as well as they can be done."

Global presence. In 1988, Trammell Crow had offices in five European countries and Hong Kong, and has built trade marts in Brussels and Japan.

Trammell Crow Company, 2001 Bryan Tower, Suite 3200, Dallas, TX 75201; (214) 742-2000.

5

Trump

#1 *in Atlantic City casinos*

Employees: 25,000
Sales: $1.4 billion
Founded: 1923
Headquarters: New York City, New York

When the news broke in February 1990 that Donald Trump had left his wife, Ivana, and was seeking a divorce, his picture adorned the cover of *Playboy*, where he told interviewer Glenn Plaskin that a display of wealth is a "good thing" because it "shows people that you can be successful.... It's very important that people aspire to be successful." Trump, who was born rich (his father built apartment buildings in Brooklyn and Queens), magnanimously flaunted his wealth all through the 1980s, buying and developing properties in New York City and Palm Beach, becoming the biggest croupier in Atlantic City and dashing in and out of the stock market to make quick killings in shares of companies rumored to be takeover targets. *Forbes* estimates his wealth at $1.7 billion.

In 1982 Trump opened Trump Tower, the glitzy complex of stores, offices and residences at Fifth Avenue and 56th Street where the Trump family was ensconced in a three-story condo at the top. In 1985 he bought the 20-acre, 118-room Marjorie Merriweather Post mansion in Palm Beach. Outmaneuvering Holiday Inns and Hilton, he bought his way into the Atlantic City gambling scene with two casino hotels, Trump Plaza and Trump's Castle (Trump puts his name on everything he touches). Then he bought another Atlantic City gambling den, Resorts International, which he quickly sold, at a profit, to Merv

Griffin while keeping for himself Taj Mahal, the opulent hotel-casino then under construction. When opened in 1990, the onion-domed, 42-story Taj Mahal became the tallest building in New Jersey. With a casino the size of two football fields, it has 3,000 slot machines and 167 gaming tables. On opening day, April 2, 1990, $925,000 was bet in eight hours. Trump calls his Taj Mahal the "eighth wonder of the world." In 1988, Trump bought the Plaza Hotel in New York City for $400 million and the Eastern Air Shuttle for $365 million (renamed of course the Trump Shuttle). Meanwhile, Trump had time to write, with Tony Schwartz, the best-selling *The Art of the Deal*.

Humility is not Donald Trump's strong point. Reviewing his book, *Fortune* described him as "the leading egomaniac in American business" and "the finest example we have of materialism, ambition and self-love among the baby-boomers." In 1988 Paul Goldberger, *New York Times* architectural critic, said Trump "is tailor-made for a time in which aggressive private developers have taken over many of the functions of the public sector, a time when the very idea of the public realm has been put aside, when greed and power are celebrated and selfishness triumphs over the common weal." A year later *Time* came to the same conclusion, depicting Trump as "a symbol of an acquisitive and mercenary age."

None of this criticism phases Donald Trump. When Glenn Plaskin of the *New York Daily News* mentioned to him that there were one or two things he doesn't have yet—a TV network, the New York Yankees, the U.S. presidency—Donald Trump responded: "Worthy goals for me, I agree 100 percent."

Donald Trump's empire was built on debt—for example, he bought the Plaza Hotel without putting up any money of his own—and in mid-1990 he found himself in the same position as a Visa cardholder who couldn't meet the monthly interest payments, except that with Trump the figures are so much bigger. In May 1990 he paid banks $2.1 million interest on his *personal* lines of credit. In June, however, he couldn't meet an interest payment due to bondholders who loaned him money to buy Trump's Castle in Atlantic City. A group of 70 banks rescued him with a new loan package of $65 million but they were tough on him. One of the conditions of the new loan was that Trump had to cut his personal spending from $583,000 to $450,000 a month.

The Trump Organization, 9 West 57th Street, New York, NY 10019; (212) 832-2000.

6
Helmsley

Employees: 13,000
Sales: $1.4 billion
Founded: 1955
Headquarters: New York City, New York

Workplace

Harry Helmsley, one of the biggest U.S. real estate operators, would have probably remained an obscure character, unknown to anyone outside his field, if he hadn't divorced his wife of 33 years in 1971 and married a high-powered real estate broker, Leona Roberts. She pushed him into the Manhattan social whirl and into such indulgences as a 10-room duplex (equipped with an indoor pool) atop the Helmsley-owned Park Lane Hotel, a Palm Beach condo and a 28-room mansion on 26 acres in Greenwich, Connecticut (price tag: $8 million). Previously, Helmsley had lived in a modest one-family house in a New York suburb, and was known in real estate circles as a frugal operator, a landlord who would "take a schlock property and run it as a schlock property forever." After marrying Leona, Helmsley moved into the hotel business, installing her as the "Queen" of this turf, which included the luxurious Helmsley Palace and the Harley (their first names combined).

In 1989 the Helmsleys were indicted for tax evasion, accused of buying all kinds of expensive baubles—a $2,000 gown, a $210,000 mahogany card table, a $45,000 silver clock—and charging them to the hotels as business expenses. Stories quickly surfaced of how Leona tyrannized employees. One ex-employee called her a "bird of prey." Another said the Helmsley home in Greenwich was a "boot camp for servants." The *Miami Herald* reported that "people were waiting on line to testify against this woman." The case became fodder for Johnny Carson joke writers and prompted a cover story in *People* magazine that was headlined: "GREEDY GREEDY GREEDY." Harry, 80 years old in 1989 and reportedly suffering from a stroke, was excused from standing trial. After a nine-week jury trial his wife was convicted of tax evasion and 33 felony counts and sentenced to four years in prison.

Harry Helmsley began his real estate career in 1925 (when he was 16) as a $12-a-week clerk. Over the years, using real estate syndication (where you get other investors to put up money), he assembled a portfolio of properties encompassing 50 million square feet of commercial space (including the Empire State Building), 50,000 apartments (including the giant complexes, Parkchester in the Bronx and Fresh Meadows in Queens, both developed originally by insurance companies) and 13,000 hotel rooms. His primary company is Helmsley-Spear, whose name appears on many Manhattan buildings. Buildings carrying the Brown Harris Stevens name are also Helmsley properties. With a fortune estimated at $1.7 billion, Harry placed 25th in the 1989 *Forbes'* ranking of the richest Americans. The *New York Daily News* ranked Leona Helmsley as one of New York's 10 pushiest women.

Helmsley-Spear, Inc., 60 East 42nd Street, New York, NY 10165; (212) 687-6400.

7
CENTEX

#1 *in home building in Dallas, Chicago*
#1 *in construction in Florida*
#4 *in home building*

Employees: 4,500
Sales: $2 billion
Profits: $59.5 million
Founded: 1950
Headquarters: Dallas, Texas

Centex builds homes—single-family homes, townhouses and condominium complexes—in 20 metropolitan areas, stretching from Seattle and southern California on the West Coast to Washington, D.C., and Miami on the East Coast and running from Texas up into Minnesota and Illinois. Centex is one of the few home builders with a national presence, a reach attained by buying up local companies. To sell some 6,000 homes a year, Centex offers their own financing. Centex homes range in price from the low $50,000 to about $420,000 (average $94,000). More than half have been sold to first-time buyers. Although Centex is big in home building, more than half their sales come from general construction projects. Centex also makes gypsum wallboard, mixes cement in three plants and operates a general construction business.

History. Centex began as a small construction company in Dallas. The Murchisons, a family of Texas oil millionaires, acquired a controlling interest in the firm in 1955. Their contribution was not so much money as cosigning power. They agreed to stand behind the loans Centex made. Under the direction of Frank M. Crossen, a former real estate loan officer who joined Centex in 1956, the company used this borrowing power to the hilt, becoming the largest home builder in Dallas and then buying builders in other parts of the country. During 1987 Centex crews were building the $81.3 million Ben Taub Hospital in Houston; the $70.6 million Grand Floridian Hotel at Lake Buena Vista, Florida; and a $45.4 million parking garage in Orlando, Florida. In 1989, Centex continued work on their

Six out of 10 modern homes are built with fireplaces.

largest-ever construction project, the $172 million Veterans Administration Medical Center in Houston, Texas. They also completed their fourth project for Disney parks—the $47 million Caribbean Hotel in Orlando's Disney World (they also built Cinderella's Castle there).

Centex brought to home building a hard-nosed philosophy: Standardized materials were used, production schedules had to be met and flashy salesmanship sold homes. Centex enforces this philosophy by bringing to newly acquired units their own managers. Centex also uses nonunion labor wherever they can (and in most places they can). Most of their employees are temporary workers. When the houses are up, they are out of jobs. Centex does have a strong managerial core, well rewarded and transferred to different units with the Centex philosophy.

Home building is a boom-and-bust business, but Centex has managed to even out the troughs. They have never lost money. During the 1980s they went from a $1 billion to a $2 billion company.

The financially troubled Murchisons gradually reduced their holdings in Centex until, in 1987, they were out completely. The biggest Centex stockholder today is Equitable Life Assurance, the nation's third largest life insurance company. They held a 10 percent stake in Centex in 1990—a far bigger source of cosigning power than the Murchisons.

Stock performance. Centex Corporation stock bought for $1,000 in 1980 sold for $1,748 on January 2, 1990.

Centex Corporation, 3333 Lee Parkway, P.O. Box 19000, Dallas, TX 75219; (214) 559-6500.

HEALTH & BEAUTY

HOUSEHOLD PRODUCTS

According to Dr. V. W. Greene, professor of environmental health at the University of Minnesota, people fantasize too much about the "good old days," which were, he argues, marked by "devastating epidemics, filth-borne disease, infant mortality, and early death of young adults." Dr. Greene got off these remarks in the mid-1980s in a monograph, Cleanliness and the Health Revolution, *funded by the Soap and Detergent Association. A gigantic industry has been built on getting rid of dirt and insects—and academics like Dr. Greene provide a philosophical justification for these companies. Dr. Greene compiles a table showing 38 diseases, from amebic dysentery to yaws, "whose transmission is mitigated by personal hygiene," and he has a wonderful chart showing a direct relationship between soap consumption and infant mortality. Yes, the greater the soap consumption, the lower the infant mortality. So let's hear it for Procter & Gamble, Unilever, et al.*

1

#1 *in soaps and detergents; toothpastes; shampoos; disposable diapers; fabric softeners; cooking oil; sinus, cough, cold remedies; toilet tissue and paper towels*

#2 *in advertising, coffee, cake mixes*

Employees: 77,000
Sales: $21 billion
Profits: $1.1 billion
Founded: 1837
Headquarters: Cincinnati, Ohio

Every household in America is likely to have a Procter & Gamble product: a detergent (Tide, Cheer, Dash, Bold), a toothpaste (Crest, Gleem), a shampoo (Head & Shoulders, Prell, Vidal Sassoon), a food or beverage pack (Folgers coffee, Duncan Hines mixes, Fisher nuts, Jif peanut butter) or a personal care item (Pampers, Oil of Olay, Always, Secret). Indeed, an early 1980s' study showed 95 percent of American homes had at least one P&G product—a penetration no other company achieved. And P&G products tend to be winners. In 1989 their brands held first place in 21 of 40 product categories in which the company competed, and they ranked second or third in most others.

Their two most important products, from the sales standpoint, are Pampers and Luvs disposable diapers. They bring in close to $2 billion annually. Credit P&G research in coming up with the first disposable diaper that worked. P&G's research and development budget (at $650 million in 1988) is bigger than the comparable budgets at Lockheed, McDonnell Douglas and Monsanto, and nearly 10 times as great as the research budget at longtime rival Colgate-Palmolive. P&Gers are known for zealous attention to product quality and readiness to invest for the long term. P&G's research yielded Tide, the detergent that displaced soaps. They funded research proving fluoride's (and therefore Crest's) ability to prevent cavities. And in the late 1980s they formulated the first zero-calorie fat substitute—olestra, made of sucrose polyester. Olestra looks and tastes just like fat but according to Procter & Gamble can actually *reduce* cholesterol.

Beyond their vast physical presence, P&G products occupy nooks and crannies in our minds too because of a massive advertising onslaught: over $1.5 billion a year. These dollars buy a seemingly endless barrage of TV commercials. If a product can't be advertised, it doesn't belong in the P&G stable.

P&G's character remained largely intact during the turbulent 1980s. They did buy their way into a medicine chest full of health care products and greatly expanded their business outside the U.S. As a result, sales more than doubled. But

Procter & Gamble commissioned Norman Rockwell to do a series of paintings for Crest ads in the 1950s.

these changes did not bring, as they have at other companies, a dilution of a culture that stresses old-fashioned values of "integrity, doing what's right for the long-term, respect for the individual and being the best in what we do." P&G was 153 years old in 1990, and it has seen a fair amount of change.

History. The culture originates with founders William Procter, a British candlemaker, and James Gamble, an Irish soapmaker, who joined their businesses in Cincinnati in 1837, at the suggestion of their father-in-law (Procter and Gamble were married to sisters). Both were raised in religious families. Both were frugal and scrupulously honest. They were known to reimburse customers who overpaid. When they went into business, Cincinnati had 18 other soap- and candle-makers. P&G was the only one to survive. By the Civil War, they were the largest company in Cincinnati, and they still are.

This pure P&G image came into question during the 1980s, when some said their corporate trademark, the "Moon and Stars" symbol stood for satanism or a sign the company had been taken over by the "moonies" (followers of Rev. Sun Myung Moon and his Unification Church). P&G considers the mark their "symbol of quality" and went to great pains to quash the rumors. The "Moon and Stars" was, in fact, registered as the company's trademark in 1882, the same year the first advertisement appeared for a "floating" soap called Ivory, depicted as "99 44/100 % Pure." Procter's son, Harley, came up with this brand name one Sunday morning in 1879 during a church reading of the 45th Psalm: "All thy garments smell of myrrh, and aloes, and cassia, out of the ivory palaces whereby they have made thee glad." The soap floated because a workman left a stirring machine on too long, resulting in a batch of soap laced with air bubbles. That soon became the standard way of making Ivory, the first in a long and seemingly never-ending line of well-advertised P&G brand names. P&G began competing with itself in 1923 when they pitted Camay beauty soap against Ivory.

Few companies can lay claim, as P&G can, to a spirit, a way of operating, more than 150 years old. No Procters or Gambles serve in the company anymore, but their traditions have been carried forward by several generations of earnest mid-westerners intent on preserving the culture. The first time neither a Procter nor a Gamble was president of P&G occurred in 1930 when William Cooper Procter, grandson of the founder, stepped aside for Richard Redwood Deupree, who had joined the company as an office boy in 1905. Procter's advice to Deupree was: "Always try to do about what's right. If you do that, nobody can really find fault." Procter & Gamble was already, at that point, a substantial company. Annual sales of $200 million made them one of the 25 largest manufacturers in the nation.

A superior pay-and-benefit package is also part of the P&G tradition. Barney Krieger, P&G's first employee, stayed with the company for 47 years. Employees were given Saturday afternoons off in 1885. A profit-sharing plan (believed the first in American business) was started in 1887, followed two years later by an employee stock purchase program. Medical insurance was provided in 1915, the eight-hour day in 1918, the five-day work week in 1933.

Coming out of World War II, P&G was basically a soap and detergent company. They then invaded, successfully, a series of new markets: toothpastes (Gleem and Crest), hair care (Prell and Head & Shoulders), foods (Duncan Hines mixes, Jif peanut butter), paper (Charmin, Bounty), disposable diapers (Pampers), coffee (Folgers) and frozen juices (Citrus Hill).

In the 1980s P&G entered health care and cosmetics by buying Richardson-Vicks (Clearasil, Nyquil and other cold remedies), Norwich-Eaton (Pepto-Bismol, Chloraseptic), G. D. Searle's nonprescription drugs (Dramamine, Metamucil), Squibb's suncare line (Bain de Soleil) and Noxell (Cover Girl, Clarion, Noxzema). At the end of the decade P&G ranked first in sales of over-the-counter drugs. Less successful was their soft drink invasion. They bought Crush International (Crush orange drink and Hires root beer) in 1980, failed to boost sales and put the company up for sale in 1989. But they haven't given up on beverages. In 1989 they bought Sundor, the sixth largest maker of fruit beverages (Sunny Delight citrus punch, Speas Farm apple juice, Texum grape fruit juice), and in 1990 the Hawaiian Punch business of

RJR Nabisco. That same year they picked up Fisher nuts from Beatrice Foods.

P&G's most embarrassing corporate moment was the 1980 retreat from the tampon field when they stopped making, and recalled from the marketplace, Rely tampons after the product had been linked to Toxic Shock Syndrome (TSS) in menstruating women. Ironically (an irony lost on P&G), the company's legendary obsession with bringing out superior products may, in this case, have been their undoing. P&G sought to trump Tampax by making Rely superabsorbent. And although the cause of the widespread out breaks of TSS in 1980 was never precisely determined, one strong school of thought implicated the superabsorbent fibers in Rely as a perfect incubator of strep bacteria. P&G didn't wait around for the final answer. They yanked the product from the market in September 1980, beating the FDA to the punch. Two years later a jury in Cedar Rapids, Iowa, directed Procter & Gamble to pay $300,000 to the family of Pat Kehm, a Rely user who died of toxic shock syndrome two weeks before P&G issued their recall. It was the first time in P&G's history that one of their products had been found responsible for the death of a customer. P&G still makes a feminine napkin, Always.

Owners and rulers. No person owns as much as one-half of 1 percent of the stock. Employees, through profit sharing and employee stock ownership plans, own 20 percent. The people who run P&G are, to a man (there were no women officers in 1989), veteran P&Gers steeped in the culture. Chairman John Smale's 1988 compensation of $2 million ranked him 101st on the roster of the 800 highest-paid corporate executives. Smale was CEO from 1981 until January 1990 when 59-year-old Edwin L. Artzt became chairman of the board and CEO. Artzt is known for his aggressive style; he has read *The Leadership Secrets of Attila the Hun* and told *Fortune,* "Winning is the only result that matters." His nickname at P&G was the Prince of Darkness because of his quick decisions—arriving at a division, making sweeping changes and then moving on. "I'm a wrecking crew. If it doesn't work right, I break it down and build it up again."

As a place to work. Superior. In addition to *The 100 Best Companies to Work for in America,* P&G makes every "best" list around: best companies for blacks *(Black Enterprise),* women *(Savvy),* working mothers *(Working Mother).* Their training is so good many use it as a springboard for top management positions in other companies. It's no longer de rigueur to wear white shirts, but P&G is not to be mistaken for a hang-loose place. If you have a glass of wine during lunch, don't go back to work because P&G doesn't want you making decisions under the influence of alcohol. P&G is trying these days to be more of a "tough guy," denying, for example, that they guarantee lifetime employment. But they still come off as a company where the individual employee is valued, not just regarded as a cog in a wheel. One policy remains intact: P&G doesn't recruit from other companies. You are expected to start here in an entry-level position and work your way up. And if you do leave, don't try to come back. P&G does not rehire deserters.

Social responsibility. Every fund-raiser in Cincinnati knows the first stop has to be the P&G headquarters anchoring the downtown area. "In my experience," said Hamilton County Commissioner Robert A. Taft II in 1987, "every time that we've had to go after the community for support or assistance, Procter & Gamble has been there." P&G contributes both money and people. In a count done in the late 1980s, P&G people were serving on the boards of 112 of the 117 member organizations of United Way in Cincinnati. Environmental groups recently discovered Dawn dishwashing liquid not only cuts through grease—it also cuts through oil and helps contain oil spills. Forthwith, Procter & Gamble began donating cases of Dawn to help cleanup efforts after major oil spills. Procter & Gamble is also looking for ways to recycle disposable diapers, such as using the plastic outer layer for garbage bags and the padding for cardboard boxes and insulation. If you ever have questions or complaints about a P&G product, you can call the 800 number usually displayed on the packaging. Procter & Gamble began testing an 800 number in 1974 and by 1981, every product type (food, health care) had its own. The company gets over 800,000 such calls a year.

Global presence. Strong. P&G has 60 plants overseas and sells in 140 countries.

In 1980, they did just over one quarter of their sales outside the U.S. In 1990, the figure was approaching 40 percent—and P&G looks for it to reach 50 percent during the 1990s.

Stock performance. Procter & Gamble stock bought for $1,000 in 1980 sold for $5,725 on January 2, 1990.

Consumer brands.

Laundry products: Tide, Cheer, Dash, Bold, Gain, Oxydol, Solo, Era Plus, Biz, Bounce, Downy, Ivory Snow, Dreft.

Cleaners and dishwashing products: Cascade, Liquid Ivory, Joy, Dawn, Comet, Spic 'n Span, Mr. Clean, Top Job.

Skin care products: Secret, Sure, Lava, Ivory, Camay, Safeguard, Zest, Coast, Bain de Soleil, Wondra, Oil of Olay, Clearasil, Noxzema.

Paper and personal hygiene products: Pampers, Luvs, Pufs, Bounty, Charmin, White Cloud, Attends, Always.

Hair care products: Head & Shoulders, Prell, Ivory, Lilt, Pert Plus, Vidal Sassoon, Pantene.

Oral care products: Crest, Gleem, Denquel, Scope, Fixodent, Fasteeth.

Health care products: Vicks, Sinex, Chloraseptic, Victors, Norwich aspirin, Dramamine, Icy Hot, Metamucil, Pepto-Bismol, Formula 44, Nyquil.

Foods: Puritan, Crisco, Pringles, Jif, Duncan Hines, Fisher nuts.

Beverages: Folgers coffee, Citrus Hill fruit juices, Sunny Delight, Speas Farm, Texum, Lincoln, SunSip, Hawaiian Punch.

The Procter & Gamble Company, 391 East 6th Street, Cincinnati, OH 45201; (513) 983-1100.

2

Unilever PLC

#1 *in margarine, spaghetti sauce, tea, dry soups*

#3 *in detergents*

#4 *in toothpastes*

Employees: 24,000 (291,000 worldwide)
Sales: $35.3 billion (worldwide),
$8.8 billion (U.S.)
Profits: $1.5 billion (worldwide),
$133 million (U.S.)
Founded: 1895 (U.S. branch)
Headquarters: Rotterdam/London
(worldwide), New York (U.S.)

Unilever is the benign face of British and Dutch imperialism, seeing their earthly duty as improving the lot of mankind by making people look and feel cleaner. Their stock-in-trade is the everyday, inexpensive, household item—a stick of margarine, a bar of soap, a tea bag, a package of dry soup, a can of shortening, an ice-cream bar, a box of detergent. By almost any measure (sales, profits, assets, number of products, number of employees, geographical scope of operations), Unilever is the world's largest producer of such items. The title "World's Largest Consumer Goods Company" belongs to them. Most of us use at least one of their products every day. You become one of the countless Unilever customers when you buy a bar of Dove soap, a box of Lipton tea bags, a package of Imperial margarine, a jar of Ragú spaghetti sauce, a tube of Aim toothpaste or a flask of Passion, Elizabeth Taylor's perfume.

Simultaneously British and Dutch, Unilever maintains dual headquarters in London and Rotterdam, controlling more than 500 companies. In the U.S., a New York-based holding company, Unilever U.S., rides herd over five main offshoots: Lever Bros., operating from the sleek Lever House on Park Avenue; Thos. J. Lipton, across the Hudson River in

Englewood Cliffs, New Jersey; Chesebrough-Pond's, headquartered in the New York suburb of Greenwich, Connecticut; Van Den Bergh Foods, based in New York; and National Starch & Chemical, domiciled in Bridgewater, New Jersey.

The U.S. became a much more important market for Unilever in the 1980s. Coming into the decade, they did only 11 percent of their business in North America (the U.S. and Canada); today, American companies account for 22 percent. U.S. sales tripled. A key factor was the 1986 purchase, for $3.1 billion, of the Chesebrough-Pond's business. That swung a new phalanx of brands into their armada, including Vaseline, Cutex, Pond's and all the Prince Matchabelli fragrance lines (Cachet, Verve, Aviance, Wind Song). In 1989 they also picked up Elizabeth Arden, Fabergé and Calvin Klein cosmetics, plus three more fragrances: White Shoulders, The Baron and Most Precious.

History. Unilever was formed in 1930 by the transnational merger of two giants, Lever Brothers of Britain and the Margarine Union of the Netherlands. It put under one roof a fats and oils cartel whose operations spanned the globe. The Dutch side of the business was created by Anton Jurgens and Simon van den Bergh, originally butter traders who deserted to margarine after its invention in 1869. The British side was the work of William Hesketh Lever, the son of a wholesale grocer who started a company in 1885 to make and sell a packaged soap called Sunlight at a time when most soaps were coarse and sold in long, anonymous blocks cut to a customer's order.

An indefatigable promoter with a curiosity that knew no national boundaries, Lever became the world's largest soap seller and extended his business into a variety of fields and every country he could find on the map. His operations included African and Asian plantations to grow needed raw materials and shipping lines to transport them.

Lever entered the U.S. in 1895, opening an office in New York to import Sunlight and Lifebuoy soaps. For the first half of the 20th century Lever Bros.–USA was led by an accountant, Francis Countway, who presided over a period of great growth

WORLD'S TOP 10 COSMETICS COMPANIES

	Company	Country	Wholesale Sales
1.	L'Oréal	France	$4.3 billion
2.	Unilever	Britain & Netherlands	$4.0 billion
3.	Shiseido	Japan	$2.8 billion
4.	Avon	U.S.	$2.2 billion
5.	Revlon	U.S.	$2.1 billion
6.	Kao	Japan	$1.5 billion
7.	Procter & Gamble	U.S.	$1.4 billion
8.	Estée Lauder	U.S.	$1.3 billion
9.	Bristol Myers	U. S.	$1.3 billion
10.	Beiersdorf	W. Germany	$1.1 billion

Source: The *New York Times*, 23 July 1989.

powered by two bellwether brands, Lux toilet soap and Rinso soap powder. He advertised these products assiduously. For Americans growing up in the 1930s, the "Lux Radio Theatre," produced by the J. Walter Thompson agency from a Hollywood office, was a Monday night ritual, spreading the fiction, "Nine out of 10 movie stars use Lux toilet soap."

In buying Pepsodent toothpaste in 1944, Lever got more than a new product line. They also got their next leader, Charles Luckman, an architect by training but a born salesman. Luckman garnered many accolades for Lever by commissioning Skidmore, Owings and Merrill to design a Park Avenue headquarters gracious in its use of open space on the ground floor. Completed in 1952, two years after Luckman had left Lever, the 24-story glass and stainless steel structure was later saluted as "one of the three most significant buildings in the past 100 years of architecture in America."

From 1950 to 1980 Lever Bros. floundered under various managers, most of them Americans recruited from other companies. They responded slowly to the detergent revolution ushered in by the Procter & Gamble brand, Tide. Occasional advertising successes, such as Wisk's "Ring around the collar," failed to stem the decline. By 1980 they were grossing $1 billion annually and remitting zilch to London/Rotterdam because profits were nonexistent. The British and Dutch then came up with a brilliant strategy: to shape up the U.S. company, send in non-Americans—like Englishman Michael Angus, who was back in London in 1990 as chairman of the British company. As the 1980s drew to a close, Lever Bros. was making money again. And true to their European heritage, they had, by picking up discarded brands and launching new ones, become the largest U.S. margarine seller. Lever's margarine tub includes Imperial, Shedd's, Krona, Mrs. Filberts, Promise and "I Can't Believe It's Not Butter."

Owners and rulers. One hundred percent owned by the Unilever Group, which operates as a single entity even though the two parent holding companies are incorporated in two different countries: Unilever N.V. (Netherlands) and Unilever PLC (Britain). American investors own 15 percent of the Dutch company. Samuel C. Johnson, chairman and owner of S. C. Johnson & Son (see profile, p. 000), has an interesting perspective on Lever in the U.S. He told an interviewer that when Lever moved headquarters from Boston to New York and put up their much acclaimed Park Avenue building, "the company realized a great dream...but was never the same company after the move because management ended up hiring people who didn't understand the traditional culture of the company."

As a place to work. Comfortable. Lever has not been known as a demanding employer. They're also a window on the rest of the world. Employees are very much aware of being part of a huge multinational operation. The *Financial Times* once called Unilever "the nearest thing British commerce has to civil service."

Social responsibility. Unilever is proud of their economic and social contributions in the Third World. They're not conspicuous for their social involvement in the U.S.

Global presence. They may not be in Albania, but there aren't too many countries where they don't have something for sale.

Stock performance. Unilever stock bought for $1,000 in 1980 sold for $11,731 on January 2, 1990.

Consumer brands.

Dental care: Aim, Close Up, Pepsodent.

Fragrances: Aviance, Hero, Elizabeth Taylor's Passion, White Shoulders, Wind Song.

Hair care: Rave.

Skin care: Pond's, Vaseline.

Other personal care products: Aziza, Cutex, Q-Tips.

Margarine: Imperial, Promise, Country Crock, Shedd's, Krona, Mrs. Filbert's, I Can't Believe It's Not Butter.

Tea: Lipton. Soup: Lipton.

Sauces and dressings: Ragú, Wishbone.

Other foods: Sunkist Fruit Snacks Adolph's Tenderizers, Mrs. Butterworth's Syrups, Lawry's.

Laundry detergents and softeners: All, Surf, Wisk, Final Touch, Snuggle.

Dishwashing detergent: Sunlight.

Personal washing: Dove, Shield, Lux, Caress.

Unilever U.S., 10 East 53rd Street, New York, NY 10022; (212) 906-4694.

3

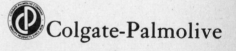Colgate-Palmolive

#1 *in liquid soap, liquid dishwasher detergent*

#2 *in toothpaste, detergents*

Employees: 24,700
Sales: $4.7 billion
Profits: $204 million
Founded: 1806
Headquarters: New York City, New York

Colgate's products—Colgate toothpaste, Fab and Fresh Start detergents, Irish Spring soap, Palmolive liquid detergent—are, of course, familiar brands in the American marketplace, but to fully understand this company's clout, you have to go to Buenos Aires, Caracas, Rome, Paris or Bangkok. Although based in New York City, Colgate-Palmolive does two-thirds of their business outside the U.S. and derives less than 10 percent of their profits from U.S. sales.

No wonder Colgate people harp these days on being a "global marketer," introducing products with a view toward their potential in the worldwide market rather than in any one country. To some extent, they're making the best of a bad situation. Colgate has been whipped so soundly by Procter & Gamble in the American market they might as well look to their laurels abroad. Once the king of the U.S. toothpaste market, Colgate was upended by P&G's fluoride brand, Crest. In laundry detergents, P&G brands outsell Colgate's by a margin of better than 3-to-1.

Colgate maintains a 75-acre research center at Piscataway, New Jersey, from which cynics say nothing of worth has ever emerged. Among the launches of the 1980s were Maniac, a teen fragrance line; Fresh FeLiners, a deodorant liner for cat litter boxes; and Hill's W/D, a canned high-fiber formula for overweight dogs. As the decade closed, the company, undaunted by a long string of new product failures, was masochistically preparing to put the Colgate name on a new line of over-the-counter drugs—aspirin, laxatives, cough remedies, cold tablets, antacid, dandruff shampoo, all products P&G already makes.

Colgate spent the 1980s undoing what they'd done in the 1970s when they bought more than 20 companies that had them running two fast-food chains (Lum's and Ranch House) and making Carolina rice, Hebrew National hot dogs, Etonic running shoes, Bancroft tennis rackets, Helena Rubenstein cosmetics, Curad bandages, Bike athletic supporters, Victoriaville hockey sticks. All these were sold off as Colgate decided, in those well-worn words of corporate restructuring, "to concentrate on our core business." As a result, Colgate's sales were static in the 1980s although payroll lightened dramatically. Colgate entered the 1980s with 56,600 employees and exited with 24,700.

History. Old age does not necessarily render a company venerable. Colgate has been making soap since 1806 when 23-year-old William Colgate opened a "Soap, Mould & Dipt Candles" factory and shop two blocks from where New York's World Trade Center stands today. In other words, Colgate is older than Procter & Gamble and Unilever but has never developed the strong culture these two main

rivals have. They simply got off to an early start in supplying two products that became bathroom fixtures: soap and toothpaste. Colgate began selling toothpaste, in jars, in 1877. Toothpaste in a tube—Colgate Ribbon Dental Cream—debuted in 1908. And Colgate's hugely successful Palmolive soap was introduced in 1898 by a Milwaukeean, B. J. Johnson, who named it for the oils he used. It has ranked as one of the world's top-selling bar soaps for the entire 20th century.

Colgate's strength was—and is—their penetration of overseas markets, which began in 1913. The two flag bearers overseas have been Palmolive soap and Colgate toothpaste. Palmolive soap, in particular, has always had a worldwide appeal, especially in Latin countries. European sales are nearly double those in Latin America, but the Latin American units contribute far more profits than Europe—indeed, sometimes double and triple.

Colgate management has been characterized by one-man rule. Only three men ran the firm in the forty years before 1980. The third was David R. Foster, who embarked on the disastrous adventure in diversification. Take, for example, the Mission Hills golf course outside Palm Springs, California, the site of the annual Dinah Shore women's golf tournament Colgate sponsors. One year the greens did not play well, so Foster had Colgate buy the property for $5.5 million to ensure proper upkeep (and the stocking of Colgate soaps in the locker rooms).

After Foster was fired in 1979, nearly all the companies he had acquired were sold, including Mission Hills (where Foster had bought a retirement home). And Colgate sought a buyer for a year and virtually gave away Helena Rubenstein cosmetics to get rid of it.

Owners and rulers. Because of such poor performance over so many years, Colgate was, during the 1980s, on the top of everyone's takeover list. It never happened, perhaps because even would-be raiders blanched when they examined Colgate's record as a consistent breather of P&G's exhaust. Directors and officers own a little more than 1 percent. The biggest holding, 11 percent, is an employee stock ownership plan. Jersey City–born Reuben Mark, who prefers to be called "Reuben" rather than Mr. Mark, became CEO in 1984. Confronted with criticism that Colgate has a short-term outlook, Mark said: "You can't judge us on what only happens here; 68 percent of our business is done overseas."

As *a place to work.* Colgate has long been known for internal bickering, antipathy to the press and inability or unwillingness to develop an organization that brought out the best in people. Among the epithets hurled at Colgate over the years have been "dull," "stodgy," "reclusive," "hierarchical," "scared of its own shadow." Looking the company over in 1986, the *New York Times* concluded: "Excitement has always been in short supply."

Social responsibility. In 1985, after purchasing a 50 percent interest in a Hong Kong–based company, Hawley & Hazel, Colgate came under scathing criticism in the U.S. for allowing the company to continue to market a toothpaste named "Darkie," whose symbol was a black-faced minstrel in a top hat (patterned after Al Jolson's jazz singer). Religious orders represented by the New York–based Interfaith Center on Corporate Responsibility expressed shock that Colgate would "be associated with promoting racial stereotypes in the Third World." At first Colgate maintained that Darkie, a popular toothpaste in Taiwan and other Asian markets, was "not racially offensive in the areas where it is sold." However, after more than three years of protests, Colgate announced in early 1989 that the Darkie name would be phased out in favor of a new name, "Darlie," and the offensive symbol would be changed to a man of "ambiguous race" wearing a top hat. However, as of March 1990, they still hadn't made this change—and Cardiss Collins, an Illinois congresswoman, threatened Colgate with a boycott.

In 1987 Mark announced Colgate would close their oldest plant, located in his hometown of Jersey City. In its place is rising a 34-acre, $2 billion commercial and residential complex from which Colgate expects to derive a steady stream of money. Beats fighting Procter & Gamble.

Global presence. Massive. To Colgate-Palmolive, the U.S. is an undeveloped country.

Stock performance. Colgate-Palmolive stock bought for $1,000 in 1980 sold for $7,317 on January 2, 1990.

"Darkie" toothpaste, one of many consumer products whose symbol was a black-faced minstrel wearing a top hat. Unlike its predecessors, this product is still available in certain Asian markets.

Consumer brands.

Toothpastes and mouthwashes: Colgate, Ultra-Brite, Dentagard, Fluorigard, Viadent.

Soaps and detergents: Palmolive, Cashmere Bouquet, Softsoap, Irish Spring, Ajax, Octagon, Dynamo, Fab, Fresh Start, Axion.

Hair care: Halo, Palmolive.

Miscellaneous: Sterno cooking fuel, Hill's pet products, Princess House crystal.

Colgate-Palmolive Company, 300 Park Avenue, New York, NY 10022; (212) 310-2000.

4

#1 *in insecticides, shaving preparations, furniture care, floor care*

#3 *in hair care, hand lotion*

Employees: 11,500
Sales: $2.5 billion
Founded: 1886
Headquarters: Racine, Wisconsin

Social Conscience · Workplace

While the takeover wars raged during the 1980s, S. C. Johnson stayed above the fray. They celebrated their centennial in 1986 by rededicating themselves to staying the course they had traveled during the previous century: Remain a family-owned company, develop useful products that are "environmentally sound" and give employees a sense of being in a family that cares about them.

Though the company keeps a low profile, they spend more than $100 million a year advertising some two dozen familiar household products, among them Pledge furniture polish, Future and Brite floor-care products, Raid insecticides, Glade air freshener, Curel hand lotion and Edge shaving gel.

History. Samuel Curtis Johnson began selling parquet floors out of a Racine hardware store in 1886. After customers asked for help in preserving the wood, Johnson mixed up batches of paste wax and sold it to them. By 1898, wax sales had topped the flooring sales, and the future course of the company was set. Johnson was an early advertiser. They ran their first national ad in 1888, and by 1927 they were spending $1 million a year to advertise Johnson's liquid and paste waxes in the leading women's magazines. For 15 years, from 1935 to 1950, Johnson Wax sponsored one of the most popular programs on radio, "Fibber McGee and Molly."

Intertwined with the growth of the company was a concern for employees, reflected in programs well ahead of their time. Paid vacations were offered in 1900, profit sharing in 1917, a pension plan in 1934 and hospital insurance in 1939. The statement the company quotes and requotes is one Herbert Fisk Johnson, son of the founder, made at a profit-sharing speech on Christmas Eve, 1927 (to this day, a Johnson family member reviews the year and hands out profit-sharing checks just before Christmas): "The goodwill of the people is the only enduring thing in any business. It is the sole substance. The rest is shadow."

Waxes led to many offshoots—varnishes, enamels, polishers, cleaners, stainers—all variations of the same theme. Great-grandson Samuel C. Johnson joined the company in 1954 after graduating from Cornell. He created a new products department and in 1956 launched Johnson's first nonwax product, an insecticide called Raid, an improvement on previous bug killers in that it didn't smell like kerosene. Soon it was the company's biggest-selling brand and paved the way for others.

The most successful launch outside Raid was Edge shaving gel, introduced in 1970. Johnson had the temerity to challenge Gillette, the dominant shaving company, and won a place for Edge (present annual sales: $300 million).

Because they're a private company, S. C. Johnson need not release any financial information. Outsiders therefore have no sure way of knowing how the company is doing. But it seems as if the 1980s were stagnant. Few successful new products were launched, and Johnson ended the decade looking very much as they had in 1980.

They did lose one of their longtime symbols, Johnson Wax. As the decade closed, the company became "SC Johnson Wax," with "Wax" in muted outline rather than the old block letters. That was the transitional phase. In 1990, "Wax" was dropped entirely so the company is now S. C. Johnson. The company justified the change by saying there were negative connotations to having wax in their name when they made so many different products. So ended a 100-year tradition.

Owners and rulers. Raymond F. Farley, who joined Johnson in 1951 and who formerly headed up international operations (he also did six years in Tokyo), was named president in 1980, the third time a non-Johnson has held that post, and became CEO in December 1988. Chairman Samuel C. Johnson, great-grandson of the founder, was 62 years old in 1990 and owned 60 percent of the stock; other family members own the rest. All four of his children—Curt, 35; Helen, 33; Fisk, 32; and Winifred, 31—work in the company. Johnson, who likes everyone to call him Sam, is certain about the advantages of family ownership. It imparts stability, he says, when everyone in the company "knows clearly who is the owner and who will still be the owner five or 10 years hence"; they know that "we are not going to change direction capriciously." It's also like a poker game, he points out, with the public company required to "expose many of its cards almost from the start" whereas the private company "doesn't even have to show much of its hand when the moment of truth finally arrives.... As a result, your competitors have little idea of how strong you are, where your problems might be, or even if you're winning." According to *Forbes*, Sam's stake in the company is worth $690 million.

As a place to work. Just about everyone in Racine knows that S. C. Johnson is the best place in town to work. A super benefit package. A 147-acre park open to Johnson families that includes a huge in-

The S.C. Johnson Company began as a parquet flooring manufacturer. Assembled here is an early production crew and examples of their craft.

door recreation center and a separate Aquatic Center. Remote resort facilities that can be rented for vacations. No executive washrooms, executive cafeterias or executive limousines. No general layoff in the history of the company.

In 1984, when Samuel C. Johnson was visiting with employees at the British plant at Frimley Green, 40 miles outside of London, he found some of them concerned about their future and wondering how they fitted into this American company. It happened that 1984 was the 70th anniversary of the British subsidiary (the company's first overseas unit, established by Samuel Johnson's grandfather), and so Johnson hit upon a happy way to mark it. He closed the plant for a week, chartered a Boeing 747 and flew the entire British work force, 480 people, to the U.S. They went first to Johnson headquarters in Racine, where they were put up in hotels, toured the company's facilities and were feted at a banquet. On one night employees in Racine picked up the British guests and brought them to their homes for dinner. Before flying back to England, the British employees spent two days sightseeing in New York City. The company took all of them to dinner at the World Trade Center.

Of course, if you do it for one, you have to do it for the next one. Three years later, when the Australian subsidiary was celebrating their 70th anniversay, Sam Johnson flew the 230 Aussie employees to the U.S. for a week. They spent five days in Racine and two in Los Angeles.

It's worth a visit to Racine to see the grand headquarters created in the late 1930s by Frank Lloyd Wright. Especially notable is The Great Workroom, an open, light, airy, undivided office expanse that includes original furniture Wright designed. Visting there in 1987, *New York Times* architectural critic Paul Goldberger depicted this space as having the "dignity of a church and the order of a cloister...a space that ennobles workers as few spaces built in our time have done."

Social responsibility. Since the 1940s Johnson's policy has been to allocate 5 percent of U.S. pretax profits to worthy causes. In overseas companies, the guideline is 3 percent of pretax profits (and it was once 25 percent in South Africa). This policy is in keeping with the company's mission that "no matter where it is in the world, every place where we do business should become a better place because we are there." In 1975, well before it became a major environmental issue, Johnson stopped using fluorocarbons in aerosols because they might damage the Earth's ozone layer. Racine, company birthplace, has been a special beneficiary. Johnson has played a central role in redeveloping the downtown and lakefront areas, meanwhile preserving historic buildings.

Global presence. Major. Johnson has subsidiaries in 45 countries, making and selling the same kind of products offered in the U.S. International accounts for 60 percent of sales. Of 11,500 employees, 8,000 are overseas—and they receive benefits (such as profit sharing) similar to the ones provided in the U.S.

Consumer brands.

Furniture and floor care: Johnson waxes, Brite, Step Saver, Future, Clean 'n Clear, Klear, Glo-Coat, Glory, Klean 'n Shine, Complete, Jubilee, Pledge, Favor, Duster Plus.

Laundry soil and stain remover: Shout.

Air fresheners: Glade.

Insecticides: Raid.

Insect repellent: Off!

Personal products: Edge shaving gel; Curel and Soft Sense skin lotions; Halsa, Agree and L'Envie shampoos and conditioners; Check-Up and Zact toothpastes; Aveno skin care soaps, bath oils and lotions; Rhuli anti-itch, antipain gels and sprays; Cramer's athlete's foot remedy and topical pain reliever (for muscular aches).

S. C. Johnson & Son, Inc., 1525 Howe Street, Racine, WI 53403; (414) 631-2000.

5

PREMARK
INTERNATIONAL

#1 *in food storage containers*

Employees: 24,000
Sales: $2.6 billion
Profits: $78 million
Founded: 1986
Headquarters: Deerfield, Illinois

Here's a true child of the 1980s, a company made up of discards reassembled under a name nobody every heard of or understands. And Premark's character has yet to be formed. Having had three different owners in 10 years, the companies that add up to Premark have a right to feel shaky. Premark's businesses include:

- Tupperware (Orlando, Florida)—plastic food storage containers sold via the infamous Tupperware parties
- Hobart (Troy, Ohio)—equipment found in the back of restaurants and supermarkets: Hobart scales and food mixers, Vulcan ovens, Wolf ranges
- Wilsonart plastic laminates (Temple, Texas)—decorative coverings for tabletops, cabinets, walls and other surfaces
- West Bend appliances (West Bend, Wisconsin)—pots and pans, cordless irons, Borg scales, Precor home exercise equipment
- Sikes ceramic tile (Lakeland, Florida)

Premark was created in 1986 when Kraft Foods decided to break up the casserole they'd baked earlier in the decade. Feeling a little bored by cheese, in 1980 Kraft bought Dart Industries (Tupperware, Wilsonart, West Bend and Duracell batteries), adding Hobart to the kettle a year later. The whole potage was called Dart & Kraft, Dart standing for Justin Dart, a wheeler-dealer friend of Ronald Reagan who'd fashioned his conglomerate out of the old Rexall Drug company.

Justin Dart died in 1984. By 1986 Kraft was tired of variety. Back to cheese. So they got rid of all the businesses bought in 1980 and 1981. The KitchenAid part of Hobart went to Whirlpool. The Duracell battery business was sold off to an investor group formed by Kohlberg Kravis Roberts. And the rest, the "cats and dogs,"

were yoked together as Premark International under the direction of Warren Batts, whom Kraft recruited from Mead Paper to run the Dart side of the business. Batts set up shop in the Chicago suburb of Deerfield, not far from Kraft headquarters.

And why the name, Premark International? Premark stands for "premier trademarks" (in a million years you wouldn't have guessed that). And International represents 30 percent of the business outside the U.S. In fact, a lot of Americans might be surprised to learn that Tupperware does two-thirds of their sales overseas. Of the 325,000 people out there selling Tupperware, 235,000 are in 35 countries outside the U.S. The latest information from Premark is that every year there are 3.5 million Tupperware parties. And the people who attend them probably never heard of Premark International.

Stock performance. Premark stock bought for $1,000 in 1986 sold for $1,682 on January 2, 1990.

Consumer brands.

Food storage containers: Tupperware, Modular Mates, Wonderlier and Servalier bowls, Counterparts containers.

Toys: Tuppertoys.

Food equipment: Adamatic, Foster, Hobart, Stero, Tasselli, Vulcan, Wolf.

Decorative products: Hartco flooring products, Pattern-Plus wood-flooring system, Wilsonart laminates, Lokweld adhesives.

Consumer products: Premiere Cookware, West Bend housewares.

Premark International, 1717 Deerfield Road, Deerfield, IL 60015; (708) 405-6000.

6

#1 *in bleach*

Employees: 4,800
Sales: $1.4 billion
Profits: $145 million
Founded: 1913
Headquarters: Oakland, California

Bleach is bleach, a chemical compound, and according to *Consumer Reports* the only difference in the bleaches found on supermarket shelves is price. If that's so, the marketplace is completely irrational. Clorox bleaches, generally the highest-priced ones on the shelves, dominate the market, accounting for about 60 percent of sales. And it's been that way for a long time.

Mighty Procter & Gamble was so impressed with Clorox's clout they bought the bleach company in 1957, operating them as a subsidiary for the next 10 years while the Federal Trade Commission sought to undo the merger in the courts. In 1967 the case reached the Supreme Court, which agreed with the FTC that antitrust laws had been breached. P&G, the ruling said, was big enough to get into the bleach business on their own; they didn't have to buy the biggest player in the field.

P&G therefore set Clorox free, and the company resumed operations as an independent company in January 1969. Heading up the company were P&G-trained people. They had one product: Clorox liquid bleach. Still the king of the market.

The one-product company is an anomaly in today's world, and soon Clorox set about buying companies and launching new products. Bleach profits eased the way. Not everything they bought worked out (restaurants, foods and paints flopped), but 20 years later no one could call them an all-bleach company. Their lineup included Formula 409 spray cleaner, Hidden Valley Ranch salad dressings, K.C. Masterpiece barbecue sauce, Kingsford and Match light charcoal bri-

quets, Liquid-plumr drain opener (their first acquisition), Soft Scrub liquid cleanser and Fresh Step, an odor-controlling cat litter (whenever a cat steps on the litter, a fragrance is released).

And still, with all these additions, the bleach business brings in 60 percent of profits. Procter & Gamble never took the FTC's advice about entering the bleach business to compete with Clorox. But in the late 1980s the P&G alumni heading up Clorox decided they would go after their "father" with a Clorox detergent. P&G responded with a new version of the number one detergent, Tide with Bleach. By 1990 Clorox Super Detergent was selling in almost half of the country and holding 4 percent of the market. Clorox has plenty of money to spend on promoting the detergent because they net twice as much money as P&G on every sales dollar. Thank heavens bleach buyers don't read—or listen to—*Consumer Reports*.

Headed by Chairman and CEO Charles Weaver, Clorox gained their independence from Cincinnati (P&G headquarters)—but now find themselves looking to Düsseldorf, home of Henkel, the giant West German chemical and household products company, which owns 23 percent of the Clorox stock. Two Henkel representatives, Hans-Dietrich Winkhaus and Ursula Fairchild, hold seats on Clorox's board. A member of the Henkel family, Fairchild is a professional photographer.

Clorox has been a good corporate citizen in their hometown of Oakland. They supported a development center for disadvantaged youths, launched the city's first "adopt-a-school" program and contributed close to $100,000 to strengthen city child-care services.

Stock performance. Clorox stock bought for $1,000 in 1980 sold for $12,747 on January 2, 1990.

Consumer brands.

Household products: Clorox 2, Liquid-plumr, Formula 409, Clorox Pre-Wash, Soft Scrub, Tilex.

Charcoal: Kingsford, Match Light. Cat litter: Fresh Step.

Paint: Olympic, Lucite.

The Clorox Company, 1221 Broadway, Oakland, CA 94612; (415) 271-7000.

7

#1 *in plastic housewares*

Employees: 7,960
Sales: $1.3 billion
Profits: $116 million
Founded: 1920
Headquarters: Wooster, Ohio

Plastics are the folk art of the 20th century, and if anyone has mastered this art, it's Rubbermaid. They mold plastic resins into an incredible number of rubbery shapes to serve a wide variety of mundane functions (and they're available in assorted colors). Every household or office has Rubbermaid products: sink drainboards, dustpans, wastepaper baskets, laundry hampers, trays, Gott ice chests, Little Tikes toys, outdoor furniture, food storage containers, clipboards, file dividers, mats (for the bathroom or office chair), Con-Tact shelf liners, plates, planters—the list is endless. Plastic is, after all, infinitely moldable. (Little Tikes even molds an 800 telephone number into each of their toys for consumer questions or complaints.)

Rubbermaid began life in 1920 as the Wooster Rubber Company of Wooster, Ohio. They made balloons. In 1934, their president, James Caldwell, came up with the idea of a rubber dustpan—and that swept them into housewares. Their brand name, Rubbermaid, became their corporate name in 1957.

Rubbermaid was transformed in the 1980s, and that had a lot to do with the return of a hometown boy, Stanley Gault. Gault was born in Wooster in 1926. His father was, in fact, one of the local businessmen who founded Wooster Rubber (but sold his interest in the company shortly after Stanley's birth). Gault stayed in Wooster, living at home, right through his 1948 graduation from the College of Wooster. He married a girl from a nearby town and began his career as a General Electric sales trainee in Cleveland, 50 miles north of Wooster. Gault rose at GE to senior vice president of industrial electronics and components, and in 1979 was in the running to succeed Reginald Jones as CEO. He had also, in 1978, joined Rubbermaid's board of directors. When the GE promotion didn't come through, Gault jumped ship for Rubbermaid. In 1980, he was installed as CEO. Back in his hometown after 32 years.

Aided by a crew of GEers who followed him to Wooster, Gault pushed Rubbermaid to plasticize the world. A demanding boss, he fired 10 percent of the white-collar staff and set the company off on a new product craze. They have a new rule at Rubbermaid (similar to one at 3M): 30 percent of sales must come from products introduced during the last five years. That means, of course, an unending flow of new items. Gault boasted proudly in 1989 that in the previous five years Rubbermaid had introduced 1,000 new products. One of them: a step-on version of their traditional wastebasket "for those who want a covered basket." Rubbermaid took 67 years to reach sales of $1 billion (in 1987). Gault has $2 billion targeted for 1992.

Gault's Rubbermaid excels at squeezing profits out of plastics. One reason: high prices. Another: a lean work force. During the 1980s Rubbermaid sales quadrupled while the number of employees didn't quite double. Profits zoomed to a level seven and eight times that of 1980. In 1985, Rubbermaid became the smallest company ever to make *Fortune's* annual roster of the "10 Most Admired Corporations," a ranking based on a poll of executives.

Stock performance. Rubbermaid stock bought for $1,000 in 1980 sold for $12,704 on January 2, 1990.

Consumer brands. Rubbermaid, Gott, Contact, Little Tikes.

Rubbermaid Inc., 1147 Akron Road, Wooster, OH 44691; (216) 264-6464.

8

#1 *in contact lenses*

Employees: 12,000
Sales: $1.2 billion
Profits: $114 million
Founded: 1853
Headquarters: Rochester, New York

It's hard to visualize Bausch & Lomb without thinking about the eyes. They began as an eyeglass store. They introduced Ray-Ban sunglasses in 1937. And they invented soft contact lenses. But Bausch & Lomb began a major life change in 1982, when Chairman Daniel E. Gill began selling off eye-related products—including the opthalmic frames, lens, lab and industrial instrument businesses (microscopes and computerized drafting equipment). B&L then began buying into other technologically sophisticated and health-oriented businesses, such as Voroba Hearing Systems, the hearing aid manufacturer; and the Dental Research Company, maker of the tremendously successful Interplak electronic toothbrush. In 1984, they earned the dubious distinction of being the largest supplier of virus-free mice and rats for laboratory research when they bought the Charles River Breeding Laboratories. Bausch & Lomb still remains a formidable eye company, making contact lenses, lens solutions, sunglasses and binoculars. And in the late 1980s they came up with SeeQuence, disposable contact lenses that can be removed and thrown away like a razor or pen.

History. John Jacob Bausch came to the U.S. from Germany in 1849 as an impoverished immigrant. Four years later, he had to borrow $60 from his friend Henry Lomb to save his optical goods shop in Rochester, New York. In return, he promised Lomb a partnership in the business. Financial security came with Bausch's

---

Whatever Happened To...Norton Simon Inc.?

In 1980, this company made so many consumer products that it was able to boast: "At least one of our brands is used in 9 out of every 10 American households." Norton Simon, a West Coast entrepreneur and art collector, formed the company in 1968 by merging various businesses he had acquired over the previous 25 years into an entity that bore his name. The hodgepodge included Hunt (tomatoes), Wesson (oil), Canada Dry (soft drinks and liquor), McCall (magazines, printing plants, sewing patterns) and Ohio Match. Having given the company his name, Simon then retired from the business, selecting his successor David Mahoney, a Bronx-born adman. Mahoney added other bits and pieces—Max Factor cosmetics, Avis Rent-A-Car, Old Fitzgerald bourbon—and then presided over the dissolution of the company. In 1983, Norton Simon Inc. disappeared into the bowels of the Chicago meatpacker-turned-conglomerate, Esmark, which a year later disappeared into the larder of Beatrice Foods, which has since dismembered itself. Max Factor was sold to Revlon. Avis was sold to its employees. Canada Dry soft drinks were sold to Dr Pepper. Most of the Canada Dry liquor business (Johnnie Walker Scotch, Tanqueray gin) went to Schiefflin. The McCall pattern company was sold and resold. The McCall publishing arm *(McCall's, Working Woman, Working Mother)* is now 50 percent-owned by Time Warner. Hunt, Wesson and Orville Redenbacher popcorn are now part of ConAgra. The Norton Simon name graces a splendid art museum in Pasadena. ∎

invention of eyeglass frames made out of a hardened rubber called Vulcanite, a less costly and more durable material than the gold-filled metal or horn-rim frames then in use. From there, the firm moved into microscopes, telescopes and binoculars. In 1912, Bausch & Lomb also became the first U.S. firm to produce large quantities of optical glass, which until then had been a European import.

But what really brought B&L into the public eye was Ray-Ban sunglasses. In 1929 the U.S. Army Air Corps asked them to develop nonglare glasses for pilots. The lenses, named Ray-Ban because they reduced ultraviolet and infrared rays, soon were standard issue. Offered to the public in 1936 for the then-princely sum of $3.75 (several times more expensive than any other shades), they were sold as Anti-Glare glasses. One year later, the name was changed to Ray-Ban. The teardrop frames known as Aviators became Ray-Ban's all-time bestsellers, worn by flyboys, playboys and Old Soldiers like General Douglas MacArthur. Still, sales of all sunglasses were languishing by 1982, when B&L paid Unique Product Placement of Burbank $50,000 to put Ray-Bans on the faces of film and TV stars on camera. The previous year, their Wayfarer brand had sold a mere 18,000 pairs. Four years later, after they were seen perched on the noses of the likes of Don Johnson and Bruce Willis, they sold 826,000 pairs. And when Tom Cruise donned his Aviators for the 1986 movie *Top Gun*, B&L sold 1.5 million pairs—not bad for a product unchanged since its debut 50 years earlier.

By the early 1980s, the company that had come up with innovations like Cinemascope for the movies (which won them a special Oscar) and lenses for the Polaris missile guidance system came down with myopia. "Instead of concentrating on developing new products," observed *Business Week,* B&L "was spending most of its time improving old ones." True, for three years after the 1971 introduction of soft contact lenses B&L controlled 100 percent of the market. But they began treating customers arrogantly, even charging $25 to show optometrists how to fit new lenses. Before long, others jumped into the fray. As one competitor put it, "We won many of our customers from Bausch because it was so hated."

Owners and rulers. The single largest stockholder in 1985 was Manning & Napier Advisors Inc., a Rochester investment advisory firm holding 7.6 percent of B&L's stock. The last Bausch on the board was Carl L. Bausch, nephew of the founder and former chairman of B&L (1956–1959). He retired in 1978.

The current chairman, Daniel E. Gill, joined B&L as a group vice president in 1978. *Fortune* describes him as "an accountant keenly interested in the bottom line…[and] worried about short-term profits." His own, they should have added. Buried in Bausch & Lomb's 1987 proxy statement is a compensation package for Gill that adds up to a packet. In 1986, he received nearly $2 million: a salary of $701,478; a bonus of $260,000; and stock options worth $850,000. Gill also has low-interest company loans worth $379,534. Should Gill and the company part ways without mutual assent, he gets three times his base salary and bonus.

As a place to work. Gill is trying to inspire Bausch & Lomb's staid scientists by setting up what are called "tiger teams" to come up with new products. According to *Business Week,* "groups…composed of scientists from different disciplines meet in a special room at the R&D center dubbed the 'tiger den,' or at local pubs. If an idea developed by a team goes to market, the members will be rewarded with cash or stock options." The teams have "really fired things up around here," says one B&L research chemist. "People aren't afraid to bring forth ideas, and management's saying, 'We're behind you.'"

Social responsibility. In 1986, the FDA warning about possible complications arising from improper use of extended-wear contact lenses scared off many consumers. In 1988, the drug manufacturer Pharmafair (a B&L subsidiary purchased in 1987) was forced to recall the entire year's production of an opthalmic solution because it failed FDA standards.

Global presence. Expanding. In 1984, sales overseas comprised a mere 17 percent of total sales; by 1989, 40 percent. Much of the growth came from targeting consumers in Latin America, Europe and Asia. For instance, B&L's popular plastic sunglasses were designed for American faces and didn't fit most Japanese, who disliked B&L's

metal-framed alternative. In 1987, the glasses were redesigned for the Japanese market and sales skyrocketed.

Stock performance. Bausch & Lomb stock bought for $1,000 in 1980 sold for $4,448 on January 2, 1990.

Consumer brands.

Sunglasses, binoculars, and telescopes: Bausch & Lomb, Ray-Ban, Sensitive Eyes, Bushnell.

Contact lenses and eyecare solutions: Bausch & Lomb, The Boston Lens, Soflens.

Toothbrushes: Interplak. Hearing aids: Voroba.

Bausch & Lomb Inc., One Lincoln First Square, P.O. Box 54, Rochester, NY 14601; (716) 338-6000.

COSMETICS

People make fun of cosmetics, rolling their eyes over the prices at which these beauty products sell. Yet, sell they do — like crazy, year after year: currently $3 billion a year in skin care treatments, over $4 billion in fragrances. Cosmetic and fragrance houses were sold and resold during the 1980s, accompanied by frenzied launches of new brands, among them Elizabeth Taylor's Passion, Cher's Uninhibited, Calvin Klein's Obsession. And who can forget the fragrance commercials on television? Humorist Stan Freberg, who admits to wearing Aramis and Aqua Velva, told Advertising Age:

> *For a guy who distrusts advertising on sight, I amaze myself that I'm always suckered in one more time by a cologne ad. The left brain is saying, "This is just some copywriter trying to bludgeon your senses," and the right side says, "Will I be beating women off with a stick?"... Once a woman sold me on a perfume at Bloomie's. She said her boyfriend wore it—and you'll love it! I brought it home and my wife said, "Who sprayed the Raid?"*

1

The Gillette Company

#1 *in shaving, toothbrushes*

#2 *in ballpoint pens*

Employees: 30,000
Sales: $3.8 billion
Profits: $284 million
Founded: 1901
Headquarters: Boston, Massachusetts

Here's a company that can honestly claim to have changed the face of the world. Every day men all over the world stare into a mirror and shave the hair off their faces. They're not all using a Gillette razor, but enough of them are to give this com-

No. 775,134.

PATENTED NOV. 15, 1904.

K. C. GILLETTE.
RAZOR.
APPLICATION FILED DEC. 3. 1901.

NO MODEL.

A diagram of King Gillette's first safety razor patented in 1904.

pany a 60 percent share of the $2.4 billion worldwide market for shaving products.

Gillette has held this leadership position for the entire century, and they maintain it by bringing out new razors that take more expensive blades that have to be continually replaced: It's a variant of the perpetual money-making machine. Their latest ploy is Sensor, a razor that allegedly gives closer shaves through spring-mounted blades that follow the facial contours. (After 90 years, they've finally got it down.) Sensor was introduced in the U.S. and Europe in 1990 with a promotional budget of $175 million. Gillette has never been stingy when it comes to advertising.

In addition to razors and blades, Gillette makes men's and women's toiletries, including Foamy shaving cream; one of the best-selling deodorants, Right Guard; toothbrushes (Oral-B); and hair products like Toni and Silkience. They also market Paper Mate ballpoint pens, Liquid Paper correction fluid, German-made Braun household appliances and electric shavers.

In the 1980s Gillette accomplished something many other companies found impossible to do: They maintained their independence. In the latter half of the decade they repelled a series of raiders who thought the company ripe for picking. To do it they took on a heavy load of debt.

History. Although the name Gillette is now synonymous with the scraping of faces, to 1895 America it meant socialism. King C. Gillette, the inventor of the first safety razor, was first known for his ideal-

TOP HAND-HELD HAIR DRYERS

	Market Share
1. Conair	50%
2. Windmere (Save-Way)	12%
3. Clairol	7%
4. Sunbeam	7%
5. N. A. P. (Norelco)	6%
6. Gillette	6%
7. Others	12%

Source: Appliances, September 1989. In 1988 19.5 milion hand-held hair dryers were sold.

istic 1894 book, The *Human Drift,* which set forth a sweeping plan for a worldwide utopia under a single enormous corporation. Gillette even went so far as to set up The Twentieth Century Corporation.

Then in 1895 the 40-year-old bottle-cap salesman had a flash of inspiration. After trying repeatedly to put an edge on his straight razor with a leather strap, Gillette came up with the idea of a rigid-handled safety razor with replaceable blades. He carved a rough prototype out of a block of wood and showed it to friends, but not until 1901 did the idea finally became a metal reality—thanks to a Boston inventor and machinist, William Nickerson. The two men formed the American Safety Razor Company that same year and convinced a number of wealthy Bostonians to back them.

The company quickly established a reputation for marketing brilliance by peddling "Service Set" shaving kits (3.5 million razors and 36 million blades) to doughboys going off to fight World War I. When the soldiers returned, they were confirmed Gillette customers. During the 1920s Gillette embarked on a series of promotional campaigns that sealed the fate of the straight razor. Under the motto "Shave and Save," banks across the country gave away a Gillette razor to every new depositor. Hotels, restaurants and service stations gave away razors at their opening day ceremonies. And one enterprising merchant sold 100,000 boxes of marshmallows by packing a free Gillette razor in each one.

Gillette became a major radio sponsor of sporting events in the 1930s and carried that tradition over to television. They sponsored the 1939 World Series for $100,000 (that wouldn't buy a minute of World Series time now), and quickly followed with the Orange and Sugar Bowl football games and the 1940 Kentucky Derby. In 1941 the company began sponsoring dozens of sporting events, advertised as Gillette's "Cavalcade of Sports." Also in 1941 they initiated their long association with professional boxing— and its overwhelmingly male audience— by sponsoring the Joe Louis–Billy Conn heavyweight championship fight.

Gillette had no serious competition for male faces until the early 1960s when Britain's Wilkinson Sword introduced a stainless steel blade that lasted longer than Gillette's carbon steel ones. Wilkinson grabbed a good chunk of the market before a mortified Gillette roared back with their own stainless steel blades, burying Wilkinson with superior marketing guns. And in 1990 Gillette mopped up by acquiring Wilkinson's U.S. business. Gillette's major threat in the 1970s and 1980s came from France's Bic, a challenger on three fronts: disposable ballpoint pens, disposable lighters and disposable shavers. Bic forced Gillette into the disposable razor business (Good News) and out of the disposable lighter business (Cricket). In these businesses competition revolved around price, not an arena in which Gillette feels comfortable.

In the mid-1980s Gillete became the target of two takeover raids. The first raider was the tenacious conqueror of Revlon, Ronald O. Perelman. Gillette bought off Perelman using what was criticized as $34 million in "greenmail," that is, giving him a higher price for his shares than they were selling for on the stock market. In exchange, Perelman agreed not to mount another takeover before 1996. Also in 1986 Coniston Partners gained 6 percent of Gillette's shares and tried to get four seats on the board of directors. Gillette bought back their shares, and Coniston profited $13 million on the deal. The proxy fight was nasty. Gillette hired two ex-CIA agents to dig up dirt on Coniston, but they found nothing. A federal judge later ruled Gillette ran a misleading ad about Coniston, implying notorious Swiss financier Tito Tettamanti controlled the firm. To beat back these takeover attempts, Gillette took on $2 billion worth of debt. They also fired 2,400 employees—about 8 percent of their work force—to save money.

Owners and rulers. Colman Mockler, Jr., named CEO in 1976 when he was 46, hails from Missouri, received his BA and MBA from Harvard and started at Gillette as assistant to the controller. A devout Christian (he attends a monthly prayer breakfast with Raytheon's chairman Thomas Phillips and Digital Equipment's president Kenneth H. Olsen), Mockler drives himself to work. He speaks publicly only at the company's annual meeting.

Social responsibility. In 1987, Gillette closed their animal testing laboratory in Rockville, Maryland, after protests over the inhumane treatment of animals in product testing there. In 1989, Gillette agreed to remove a carcinogen found in their Liquid Paper formula and paid $300,000 in fines.

Global presence. Gillette is a name recognized the world over. They sell their products in 200 countries, manufacture at 61 plants in 28 countries and do 63 percent of their sales outside the U.S. Of their 30,000 employees, fewer than 10,000 work in the U.S. In 1987 they bought the Waterman pen company of France.

Stock performance. Gillette stock bought for $1,000 in 1980 sold for $11,382 on January 2, 1990.

Consumer brands.

Shaving appliances: Gillette, Braun.

Shaving cream: Foamy.

Hair care: Silkience, White Rain, Adorn, Toni, Lustrasilk.

Pens: Waterman, Papermate, Flair.

Facial care: Aapri.

Correction fluid: Liquid Paper, Mistake Out.

Deodorants: Right Guard, Soft and Dri.

Toothbrush: Oral-B.

The Gillette Company, Prudential Tower Building, Boston, MA 02199; (617) 421-7000.

2
Avon

#1 *in cosmetics*

Employees: 28,500
Sales: $3.3 billion
Profits: $54.6 million
Founded: 1886
Headquarters: New York City, New York

"Ding, dong, Avon's falling." That was Avon's story during the 1980s. They peaked in the early 1970s after their network of door-to-door sales representatives—called Avon Ladies—had established the company as the world's largest supplier of cosmetics and toiletries. With no need to spend a ton of money on advertising and promotion, as Revlon did, they became the darlings of Wall Street. Between 1950 and the early 1970s the price of Avon shares increased over one hundred fold. But in the late 1970s the tide turned against them. And in the 1980s they were overwhelmed. Almost everything they tried came a cropper.

For years the company eased their sales reps into American homes by running an advertising campaign that featured a ding-dong chime, "Avon Calling." In recent times, however, the Avon Lady found no one home when she rang doorbells. Women were out working. And few women entering the work force wanted to be an Avon Lady.

For the company, these inexorable social trends had dire consequences. They sold less. And they had trouble recruiting sales reps.

Avon dealt with change by shopping around. They bought four different health care companies in the 1980s. By the end of the decade they were all sold. Two fragrance acquisitions—Valentino and Parfums Stern—were also sold, and a third, Giorgio, lingered because Avon couldn't get the right price for it.

Avon's troubles attracted outsiders who thought they could straighten out the company. In mid-1990 an investment partnership called Chartwell Associates emerged as Avon's largest shareholder, owning 20 percent of the shares.

Chartwell partners include May Kay Corp., the Fisher real estate family of New York and oil heir Gordon Getty.

H*istory.* Avon was 100 years old in 1986. They'd come a long way since book salesman, David H. McConnell, began giving away perfume to customers in the 1880s. He noticed a funny thing. People seemed to prefer the fragrances to the books. So in 1886, when he was 28, McConnell and his wife, Lucy, began making fragrances. They called their business the California Perfume Company, although it had nothing to do with California. McConnell used the name because of the glowing tales he'd heard about California in letters from a former employer. The McConnells turned out their fragrances in a musty warehouse near Wall Street. Avon has always been a New York City–based company.

The first Avon Lady was Mrs. P. F. E. Albee, who went door to door selling McConnell's Little Dot Perfume Set. She also recruited other women to this sales crusade, thereby developing for McConnell the sales idea that fueled Avon's success, as well as altering the image of the sales reps from itinerant peddler to friendly neighbor. She died in obscurity in 1914.

The California Perfume Company introduced in 1928 a new line of products, including a toothbrush and talcum powder, to which they gave the name, Avon, after the Stratford-upon-Avon birthplace of Shakespeare. The corporate name became Avon Products in 1950, just as the company took off on their spectacular post–World War II spurt.

After they stalled in the 1970s, Avon decided they had better get into other kinds of businesses. In 1979 they bought Tiffany's, whose famous flagship jewelery store was catty-cornered from their headquarters on 57th Street; they sold them in 1984. They bought Mallinckrodt, a St. Louis–based chemical and hospital supply company, in 1982 and sold them in 1985. They bought Mediplex, a nursing home operator, in 1986, and sold them in 1988. They bought Foster Medical, a home health supplier in 1987, and you guessed it, sold it in 1989. They bought Retirement Inns of America in 1987 and sold them in 1989.

Ergo, entering the 1990s, Avon was back where they were at the beginning of the 1980s—except that they owed a lot of money and weren't sure about the future of their original business. In 1989, when they reported a 1988 loss of $405 million, they tried to buck up the spirits of their hapless shareholders by reminding them: "The world of beauty is a timeless world. Adornment of the face and body began before recorded history and persisted through the millennia... Fashions change, but the fundamental truth does not: When people look good, they feel good about themselves." Now if only Avon makes it to the 21st century...

O*wners and rulers.* Two outsiders steered Avon into one disaster after another in the 1980s. Hicks Waldron, a General Electric engineer who had been CEO of Heublein, was installed as the boss in 1982. He bought an apartment at Trump Plaza (one of seven residences he owned), from where he could walk to work. Avon paid the $6,400 monthly maintenance and agreed to buy back the apartment from him when he retired, which he did in 1988. Waldron's heir apparent, John S. Chamberlin, who joined Avon in 1985 from the Lenox china company, quit in early 1988. James Preston was elected president and CEO in 1988 and chairman in 1989, when he was 55. His first moves were to sell off businesses Waldron had bought and announce the heart-warming news that he was cutting costs by more than $100 million by 1991. "It's becoming very apparent that Avon has been living far beyond its means," said Preston. Translation: Heads would roll because of management's mistakes.

And what of the founding family? Edna McConnell Clark, born in 1886, the year her father started the California Perfume Company, died in 1982 at 96. Her son, Hays Clark, formerly an Avon officer, was still an Avon director in 1990 when he owned 2.8 percent of the shares, worth about $60 million in January 1990. In 1990, two women were on the board: Ernesta G. Procope, president and CEO of E. G. Bowman Co., the nation's largest minority-owned insurance brokerage firm; and Cecily Cannan Selby, a professor of science education at New York University.

A*s a place to work.* Indirectly, Avon is the world's largest employer of women, with some 1.5 million active Avon Ladies, 425,000 of whom are in the U.S. These sales reps are independent contractors and not agents or Avon employees. To become an Avon Lady, a woman pays a franchise fee, for which she receives a starter kit of products and, if she is selling in the U.S., a territory of approximately 100 households. The rep sells door to door from catalogs and samples, writes up orders and sends them to an Avon distribution center. When Avon delivers the order to her, she delivers it to the customer and collects payment on the spot. The Avon Lady receives no salary or stipend from the company, only a commission. Not surprisingly, the annual turnover rate of Avon Ladies is somewhere between 100 and 150 percent.

Among the full-time staff, the female representation is also strong (75 percent). The company has won awards and recognition for advancement of women and minorities. They claim to have more women in management than any *Fortune* 500 company. Four of 17 corporate officers are women. Three of the 15 members of the board of directors are female. On the other hand, poor performance has resulted in sharp cutbacks. Entering the 1980s they had 14,000 U.S. employees; exiting, 10,000. One of the top female executives is Phyllis Davis, head of the U.S. sales force. She is the younger sister of the Burke brothers: James Burke, CEO of Johnson & Johnson during the 1980s, and Daniel Burke, president of Capital Cities/ABC and an Avon board member.

Social responsibility. One of the legacies of Avon's success is the Edna McConnell Clark Foundation, which Mrs. Clark established in 1950 to "help those least helped by the established institutions of society." With a $200 million endowment, the foundation gives annual grants ranging from $10 to $15 million, targeting such areas as prison reform, disadvantaged youth and mental illness. Because of their willingness to take risks, the foundation won high marks from foundation watcher Waldemar Nielsen, who called them "a refreshing contrast to the dullness and conformism of many foundations." This risk taking was demonstrated by their selection in 1977 of former Haverford College president John Coleman as their third president. Coleman has become a media hero by taking sabbaticals to dig ditches, spend time in prison and wander the streets of New York City as a derelict to find out how the other half lives.

During the 1980s animal-rights groups trained their guns on Avon, trying to get them to halt the use of animals to test products—and in 1989 they succeeded when the company said they would no longer use animals in their laboratories.

Global presence. Impressive—and a lifesaver. About half of Avon's sales are now outside the U.S. And the overseas business is growing faster than the American side. They are big in Britain and Japan. More than 1 million Avon Ladies sell for them outside the U.S. Nearly two-thirds of their full-time employees are overseas.

Stock performance. Avon stock bought for $1,000 in 1980 sold for $1,968 on January 2, 1990.

Consumer brands.

Avon cosmetics, skin-care products, jewelry, ornaments and collectibles.

Perfume: Giorgio.

Avon Products, 9 West 57th Street, New York, NY 10019; (212) 546-6015.

THE TOP MEN'S SHAVERS

	Market Share
1. Norelco	52%
2. Remington	30%
3. Braun	12%
4. Matsushita (Panasonic)	2%
5. Schick	1%
6. Others	3%

Source: *Appliance*, September 1989. In 1988 7 million men's shavers were sold.

3

REVLON

#2 *in cosmetics*

Employees: 42,000
Sales: $2.47 billion
Founded: 1932
Headquarters: New York City, New York

They are, more than ever, the General Motors of the beauty business, offering lipsticks, fragrances, skin-care creams and other cosmetics under a bewildering variety of brand names in all kinds of outlets, from upscale department stores like Neiman-Marcus and Bloomingdale's to lowbrow stores like K mart and Walgreen's. However, to return to what they'd once been, Revlon underwent a traumatic change of life during the 1980s.

They entered the decade under the cool, methodical management of Michel Bergerac, who had taken the helm in 1975 after the death of founder Charles Revson. Bergerac didn't have the passion for cosmetics Revson did. He put Revson's bust into a closet and built up the pharmaceutical side of the business, which he thought had more promise and usefulness. By 1985 health care products—Tums, Oxy acne remedies, contact lens solutions, medical diagnostic equipment—accounted for two-thirds of sales. Meanwhile, their cosmetics business was losing ground—and that opened the takeover door for Ronald A. Perelman, a 41-year-old Philadelphian who had discovered, with the help of Drexel Burnham Lambert, how to use junk bonds to take over companies.

In a bruising battle in which he was consistently portrayed as the "bad guy," Perelman took Revlon away from Bergerac with a $1.8 billion bid, besting such heavyweights as Judge Simon H. Rifkind (a Revlon board member), attorneys Martin Lipton and Arthur Liman and investment banker Felix Rohatyn. Bergerac left with a consolation prize of $36 million, and Revlon belonged to Perelman. He took Revson's bust out of the closet, sold off the health care companies and returned Revlon to their roots as a flamboyant maker and seller of cosmetics and fragrances. In 1987,

not wanting to share Revlon with anyone, he privatized the company, buying out all the public shareholders.

When he took over Revlon, sales were $1 billion. By decade's end, Perelman's Revlon had sales over $2.5 billion, and he was being saluted for restoring the glamour and luster to the Revlon name. He did it, to some extent, by adding cosmetic and fragrance lines others discarded: Max Factor, Halston, Charles of the Ritz, Germaine Monteil and Alexandra de Markoff. As a result, Revlon charged into the 1990s as a powerhouse.

History. The history of the American cosmetics industry is dominated by iron-willed, tyrannical leaders like Helena Rubenstein, Elizabeth Arden, Max Factor and Estée Lauder. Revlon's founder may have been the most eccentric of them all.

Charles Revson founded the Revlon nail enamel company with $300 in 1932. Although he had two partners (his older brother Joseph, and the source of the letter "L" in Revlon, Charles Lachman), Revlon was Revson's baby right from the start. Until he died at age 68 in 1975, Revson lived for Revlon. For years he pushed his nail polish salon by salon, until he had a near monopoly on beauty parlor sales. He expected the same dedication from his employees. He thought nothing of holding meetings until 2 A.M. or calling his chemist late Sunday night for three hours.

Revson expanded into the lipstick market with the famous slogan "Matching Lips and Fingertips," and created a style women had to have. His infallible eye for color, packaging and advertising produced such landmark ad campaigns as "Fatal Apple" and *"Fire and Ice."* Revson did blunder occasionally, once with the idea for a male genitalia deodorant called Private.

Along the way, Revson "chewed up executives the way some people chew vitamins," as one former employee reported. He himself said, "All I demand is perfection," according to Andrew Tobias' biography of him, *Fire and Ice.* Charles Revson hired and fired receptionists to go with the changing decor of his offices, cussed out employees, and pretended to sleep during presentations. His goal was to dominate, a legacy alive and well under Perelman.

Owners and rulers. Rather than a rags-to-riches story, Ronald Perelman's road to unimaginable wealth has been the classic story of the 1980s—a trip from riches to even greater riches. Perelman's father was a multimillionaire, and Perelman spent his 20s learning corporate finance in his father's firm, a small Philadelphia conglomerate. He then set out on his own by going to New York loaded with cash. In 1989, 11 years and several buyouts later, *Forbes* named Perelman the fifth richest American, with a fortune of $2.75 billion, all at the ripe age of 46. According to *Financial World,* Perelman may double his fortune by 1994 by having bought from the government five bankrupt S&Ls at a fire-sale price in 1988.

Perelman's road to Revlon was paved with a series of smaller acquisitions made through the 1980s: Consolidated Cigar (maker of Muriel), a licorice extract producer and Technicolor, which puts the color in Hollywood movies. These companies may seem strange bedfellows, but Perelman says they have a common denominator. All are "free of any fashion, free of any fad." He bought these firms via what's known as the leveraged buyout, which allows him to acquire multimillion-dollar companies without putting up much money of his own. With the help of the junk bond wizards at Drexel Burnham Lambert, Perelman borrowed huge amounts of money. For collateral he used the value of the company he was buying—in much the same way the value of a house operates as collateral in getting a mortgage.

Perelman on Perelman: "I am very tenacious." Associates agree, especially the one Perelman hounded for two years before convincing him to run his cigar company. He's known for making as many as 15 bids for a company he wants, so the 5 he made for Revlon didn't depart from his customary way of doing business. He made two passes at Gillette during the 1980s.

A devout Jew, Perelman's second wife is Claudia Cohen, a TV entertainment reporter, age 37. Revlon's board of directors includes former Secretary of State Henry Kissinger; former First Lady, Nancy Reagan; actress Audrey Hepburn; and Ann Getty, wife of oil heir Gordon P. Getty.

Social responsibility. In June 1989, a group calling themselves People for the Ethical Treatment of Animals told Revlon they would hire airplanes on the East and West Coast, to trail banners declaring

U. S WOMEN'S FRAGRANCE MARKET

		Market Share
1.	Avon	19.5%
2.	Estée Lauder	12.5%
3.	Unilever	12.4%
4.	Revlon	11.6%
5.	Chanel	6.0%
6.	Cosmair	5.6%
7.	Other	32.4%

Source: The New York Times, 24 September 1989.

"Revlon and L'Oreal kill animals." Two weeks later, Revlon announced they would no longer test their products on animals nor buy from companies that did.

Consumer brands.

Fragrances and cosmetics: Charlie, Jontue, Norell, Ciara, Intimate, Bill Blass, Princess Marcella Borghese, Ultima II, Moon Drops, Alexandra de Markoff, Charles of the Ritz, Jean Naté, Germain Monteil, Jeanne Gatineau, Lancaster, Prestige Fragrances Ltd., Claude Montana, Laura Biagiotti, Maroc, Revlon (some products), Visage Beauté, Almay, Carrington, Enjoli, Eterna 27, European Collagen Complex, Forever Krystle, Max Factor, Scoundrel, Tatiana by Diane Von Furstenberg, Trouble, Xi'a Xi'ang.

Beauty care and treatment products: Flex, Care for Kids, Clean & Clear, Aquamarine, Mitchum, Natural Wonder, Colorsilk, Roux.

Men's grooming products: Halston, Hugo Boss, Chaz.

The Revlon Group, 767 Fifth Avenue, New York, NY 10022; (212) 572-5000.

4

Estée Lauder

#1 *in department-store makeup sales, department-store skin-treatment sales (Estée)*

#3 *among beauty product companies, overall in makeup sales*

Employees: 10,000
Sales: $1.9 billion
Founded: 1946
Headquarters: New York City, New York

When President and Mrs. Reagan entertained the Prince and Princess of Wales, Princess Diana asked for three guests: Robert Redford, Bruce Springsteen and Estée Lauder. Chances are, the queen of cosmetics patted the royal cheek. Perhaps she even pressed a perfume sample into Diana's hand. It's an instinct with Estée. All her life, she's been making women up, dispensing advice and giving away samples, confident that gifts inspire sales. That's how she built Estée Lauder, Inc., into the world's largest family-owned beauty company.

The key to her company's success in the beginning was their focus on well-heeled customers—often middle-aged and older women. Many cosmetic companies sell their products at discount and drug stores. Not Estée Lauder, whose products are available only in top department and specialty stores with their more affluent customers. During the 1980s, Estée Lauder owned more than one-third of department store counterspace, where they pushed products under the names Estée Lauder, Clinique, Aramis and Prescriptives. This means that although Estée Lauder sells only about one-tenth of all beauty products, they ring up more than one-third of all the women's beauty aids sold in department stores—and one-quarter of the men's cosmetics sold there. Another key to Estée Lauder's success was their emphasis on "clinical" skin care—a pseudoscientific approach that had salespeople wearing white coats and using devices resembling slide rules (to "analyze" the customer's skin-care needs). They used this approach for their Prescriptives line, launched in 1979 (unprofitable until 1987).

During the mid-1980s, as European companies (L'Oreal, Unilever) introduced even more expensive cosmetics lines, Estée Lauder became a mid-priced product—associated with the middle class. And "if you're in the middle, you're nowhere," Leonard Lauder (Estée's son and company president) told *Forbes.* "You're neither the value line nor the prestige line." Thus, in early 1990, the company upped prices by as much as 50 percent. Likewise, product names, Private Collection perfume for example, are meant to convey a cachet of exclusivity. Leonard Lauder tried to revamp the company's chaste, older-woman image in 1989 by hiring sexy Czech model Paulina Porizkova to embody the Estée Lauder woman. "I don't want the teenyboppers. I want young, independent women who can afford my products and are upmarket in their attitudes and sense of style," he said.

History. For years, people speculated that America's cosmetics queen had been born in a Hapsburg castle and grown up as some sort of countess. Estée (pronounced Es-ty) did nothing to dispel that notion until 1985, when Lee Israel's unauthorized biography promised to reveal her secret past. Not to be upstaged, Estée beat the author to press with a hastily dictated autobiography. She revealed she was born Josephine Esther Mentzer in the New York City borough of Queens, lived over a hardware store, divorced her husband Joseph Lauder in 1939 and remarried him four years later.

Estée recalled her mother as a Hungarian beauty, her father as a dapper horseman from Czechoslovakia. She claims to have spent hours brushing her mother's hair and devising facial treatments for her, plus arranging the window displays in her father's hardware store. She found her calling when a Hungarian uncle showed her how to concoct face cream. She named it Super-Rich All Purpose Cream, slathered it experimentally on family and friends and cooked up variations in her kitchen as a young bride and mother.

Estée's hobby turned into a business at the House of Ash Blondes, a Manhattan beauty parlor where she would get her "blondness renewed." When owner Florence Morris complimented her on her complexion one day, Estée whipped out her creams and cosmetics and made up the woman's face on the spot. In return, she was invited to run the beauty concession at a new salon. Before long, Estée was operating in two salons—and wherever else she happened to be. At hotels where she vacationed, she'd do makeovers by the pool. Her converts later would invite her to their homes, where Estée would make up their friends, sell cosmetics and get more invitations.

Estée broke into department-store sales in 1946 when Saks Fifth Avenue ordered $800 worth of cosmetics. She and her husband shut down their beauty-salon concessions to fill the order, cooking up skin creams on the gas burners of their "factory"—a former restaurant on Central Park West. While he set up more business-like manufacturing, she hit the road, visiting department stores all over the country to persuade more of them to rent counterspace to her. "Estée Lauder came in without an introduction, forty years ago," department-store magnate Stanley Marcus of Nieman-Marcus told writer Kennedy Fraser for a *New Yorker* profile of Estée. "Barged her way in. She was a cyclone on the selling front. She'd outsell me any day."

With Estée's first perfume, Youth Dew, her business took off. In pre–Youth Dew days, women rarely bought perfume for themselves—it was a gift. Estée changed that in 1953 by making Youth Dew a bath oil that could also be dabbed on as perfume, correctly guessing its duality would encourage women to buy perfume as readily as bath oil. It became, at that point, the best-selling perfume in the world.

Estée made her way up in society, not just business, by patting makeup on people's faces. "Mrs. Lauder is such a nice person," the late Princess Grace once told an interviewer. "I don't know her very well, but she keeps sending all these things." With personal assets at $233 million, she entertains lavishly at houses in New York City, Long Island, Palm Beach, the French Riviera and London's Eaton Square. She has counted Nancy Reagan, the late Duchess of Windsor and the widow of the Aga Khan among her friends.

No one is too famous or too ordinary to escape her attentions. After being introduced to Jeanne Kirkpatrick, Estée bluntly told the former UN delegate she looked all wrong and proceeded to talk to her about makeup. She urged waiters clearing up after a pep talk for Texas employees to take leftover samples for their wives and girlfriends. When she was well into her 70s (her exact age is secret), Estée manned a counter at Saks Fifth Avenue to spray her latest scent on ladies' wrists. Of course, Estée can't glad-hand everyone. But she's seen to it that no woman can walk into a department store without seeing her gift-with-purchase promotions: Buy one Estée product, get a kit of other ones free. Those giveaways inspire half the sales at Estée Lauder counters.

Estée expects her sons, their wives and their children to live and breathe the beauty business the way she has. Estée's rivals—Elizabeth Arden, Helena Rubenstein, Germaine Montel, Max Factor, Charles of the Ritz—have all been swallowed up by big public companies. "They're all gone now, the people who founded the great companies of beauty," Estée says in her autobiography, *Estée: A Success Story.* "The personal love and involvement are gone; they're companies now, not a family's heart and soul. It won't happen at Estée Lauder."

As the company's creative genius, Estée usually has the first, and always the last, word on everything. Her instincts haven't always met with quick success, however. Clinique lost $20 million over four years before breaking even. Aramis was a dud when launched in 1964. And a scent named Soft Youth Dew was completely upstaged by Yves Saint Laurent's Opium perfume. But her family was willing to weather missteps and work with Estée's products until they took off—a stick-to-itiveness they say a publicly owned company couldn't have. Withdrawn from the market, repackaged and reintroduced as a skin-treatment product line, Aramis became the best-selling collection of toiletries for men in department stores.

Owners and rulers. Estée and her family own and run the company—with the help of the thousands of makeup artists and beauty advisers they employ behind cosmetics counters in department stores around the world. Until his death in 1983, Estée's husband headed up manufacturing. Her elder son Leonard has been president since 1972. (He was first pressed into service at age 10, collecting profits from her beauty parlor concessions. While he was in college and the Navy, she sent him copies of all the Lauder business correspondence.) Her younger son Ronald served as a marketing executive for 17 years before becoming assistant defense secretary and later ambassador to Austria

TOP WOMEN'S SHAVERS

	Market Share
1. Remington	38%
2. Norelco	22%
3. Schick	11%
4. Matsushita (Panasonic)	11%
5. Braun	4%
6 Clairol	4%
7. Wahl	2%
8. Other	8%

Source: Appliances, September 1989.
In 1988 1.9 million women's shavers were sold.

and candidate for mayor of New York City in 1989. Leonard's wife Evelyn launched the company's sales training program and named the allergy-tested Clinique line of products. And grandson William left Macy's to join the family business.

As a place to work. Estée Lauder, Inc., is headquartered in New York's General Odors Building since the Revlon Group is also a tenant. Belying Estée's sedate decor—blue elevator banks, blue walls, blue carpets, blue-and-white overstuffed sofas in the reception area—is an atmosphere of secrecy and intense political sparring over product names, packaging and advertising. But her lieutenants always yield to Estée's intuition. "I think up names in the middle of the night," she told *New Yorker* writer Kennedy Fraser. "I call up my son Leonard and say, 'Please have it registered immediately.'"

Global presence. In 1960, Estée Lauder began selling internationally, starting in London's famous Harrod's department store. Now they do about half their sales overseas and have a cosmetics plant in Belgium. Estée had a difficult battle to woo haughty European stores. When she first approached the Galleries Lafayette in Paris, the buyer said he didn't need Youth Dew, he had Chanel. Undaunted, Estée got friendly with a salesgirl and accidently-on-purpose spilled some Youth Dew in front of her counter. For two days, so Estée tells the story, customers exclaimed over

the fragrance. Eventually the buyer overheard and was himself won over.

Consumer brands.

Cosmetics: Estée Lauder, Clinique, Prescriptives.

Perfume: Estée, Beautiful, White Linen, Cinnabar, Azuree, Youth Dew, Aliage, Private Collection.

Men's toiletries: Aramis, Devon, JHL.

Estée Lauder, Inc., 767 Fifth Avenue, New York, NY 10153; (212) 572-4200.

5

IFF

#1 in fragrances
Employees: 4,200 (1,360 in the U.S.)
Sales: $870 million
Profits: $139 million
Founded: 1909
Headquarters: New York City, New York

Ever wonder how your soap became fragrant or how the flavors got into your yogurt? Here's an answer. International Flavors & Fragrances, a company based in the heart of New York City, directly across from CBS News, concocts hundreds of different fragrances and flavors and sells them to companies like Revlon, Estée Lauder, Unilever, General Foods and Colgate-Palmolive for use in their products. They are the perfumer for the perfume companies. IFF does their concocting in 23 laboratories in 20 countries, using organic chemicals and natural ingredients such as essential oils and concentrates derived from fruits, vegetables, flowers and animal products. Their main U.S. research center is at Union Beach, New Jersey, where in 1986 they were fined $5 million by the state's Environmental Protection Department for contaminating ground water. In 1989 IFF reported they were spending nearly $15 million to comply with regulations covering discharges from their facilities.

IFF can afford it; they're one of the most profitable companies around. In 1988 they earned $128 million on sales of $839 million, thereby netting considerably more than such companies as Hormel ($60 million), Black & Decker ($97 million), Mack Trucks ($32 million), Zenith ($12 million) and National Steel ($88 million), all of whom had revenues more than *double* IFF's. Who needs heavy manufacturing?

IFF fragrances and flavorings go into lipsticks, after-shave lotions, perfumes, colognes, air fresheners, soaps, detergents, soft drinks, candies, baked goods, drugs, dairy products, alcoholic beverages and tobacco. Their business breaks down 64 percent fragrances, 36 percent flavorings. Their top 30 customers bring in 52 percent of sales. They do 72 percent of all business outside the U.S.

Descendants of the founding Van Ameringen and Haebler families still control more than one-quarter of the stock, and one Van Ameringen still sits on the board. Former Chairman Henry G. Walter, Jr., who once said, "Our business is basically sex and hunger," holds about 10 percent of the shares. A surprise holder of 6 percent is the State Farm Mutual Automobile Insurance Company. They know a good thing when they smell it.

Stock performance: IFF stock bought for $1,000 in 1980 sold for $4,975 on January 2, 1990.

International Flavors and Fragrances, Inc., 521 West 57th Street, New York, NY 10019; (212) 765-5500.

6

#1 *in skin creams*

Employees: 2,000
Sales: $522 million
Profits: $51 million
Founded: 1917
Headquarters: Hunt Valley, Maryland

A little blue jar of cold cream can carry you a long way. In 1989 it carried Noxell into the arms of Procter & Gamble, which bought the family-owned enterprise for $1.3 billion. Noxell will now serve as P&G's entry into the cosmetics business. It's not a bad match. P&G is the Harvard of advertising, and Noxell spends more money on advertising than on paying their 2,000 employees. The annual ad budget, promoting Noxzema and drugstore cosmetics sold under the Cover Girl and Clarion lines, runs to $135 million whereas total payroll costs are about $80 million. Even after spending one-quarter of their sales dollar on advertising, Noxell manages to bring home after-tax profits representing 10 percent of sales, which may indicate how little it costs to make these beauty products. Still around—and still a strong seller—is the original product, Noxzema, or as the company prefers, Noxzema Medicated Skin Cream, still packaged in a blue jar.

In 1914 George Bunting, a 44-year-old pharmacist, concocted a mixture of clove, eucalyptus, lime, menthol and camphor in the back room of his Baltimore drugstore to come up with a new skin cream. A customer reported it cured his eczema, which prompted the brand name, Noxzema ("no eczema"). Bunting formed the Noxzema Chemical Company in 1917 to make and sell the cream, which was soon being promoted as a treatment for sunburn, acne, blemishes and chapped hands as well as a shaving cream. Noxell (they adopted this name in 1966 when they moved their headquarters to a suburb north of Baltimore) have remained largely true to their original calling: supplying products that improve a person's looks.

They did have a few sidelines P&G may or may not retain—Lestoil household cleaner (just what P&G needs, another detergent) and Texas-made Caliente chili. Both of these were acquired.

Noxell had a notable record as a corporate citizen. They no longer test their products on rabbits; instead, they use a tissue culture technique. They belonged to the Baltimore Five Percent Club, binding them to contribute 5 percent of pretax profits to worthy causes (the average in corporate America is 1 percent). This policy was instituted by George L. Bunting, Jr., who became CEO in 1973 and was around to sell the company to Procter & Gamble in 1989. He is the grandson of founder George Bunting, who died in 1959 at the age of 89.

Consumer brands.

Cover Girl, Clarion, Noxzema, Rain Tree.

Noxell Corporation, 11050 York Road, Hunt Valley, MD 21030; (301) 785-7300.

DRUGS

The pharmacy may occupy only a small section of the drugstore, but that's where the big money lies. Sales of ethical drugs (the industry term for doctor-prescribed medications) dwarf sales of over-the-counter remedies. This will come as no surprise to anyone who recently had a prescription filled.

The 1980s saw a wave of big mergers as drug makers tried to summon up more research power for their dollar. Some of the mergers reflect the increasingly international nature of the business (sickness knows no borders). SmithKline of Philadelphia merged with Beecham of London, and the Swiss firm of Hoffman-LaRoche bought a majority of California's Genentech. Of the world's top 10 drug makers, two (Ciba-Geigy and Sandoz) are Swiss, two (Hoechst and Bayer) are German, two (Glaxo and SmithKline Beecham) are British and the remaining four (Merck, Bristol-Myers Squibb, Pfizer and American Home Products) are American.

1

#1 *in prescription drugs*

Employees: 33,200
Sales: $6.6 billion
Profits: $1.5 billion
Founded: 1668
Headquarters: Rahway, New Jersey

Social Conscience | Workplace

One thing you can say right away about Merck: They know what they're about. Merck is in the business of finding drugs that cure illnesses and save lives. They take a long-term view of their mission. They avoid fads.

Those ideas turned the 1980s into Merck's decade. Entering it with a tenuous grip on first place in prescription drugs, they emerged with an iron grip, holding in their medicine chest 18 drugs, each of which enjoyed worldwide sales of more than $100 million a year. Fourteen of the 18 were pharmaceuticals introduced since 1978. No company in the drug industry has ever held that many big winners in their hand at the same time or fielded such a rapid-fire series of successful new drugs.

Merck's name is not widely known by the general public because they don't make consumer products. Their name is on the pill bottle you pick up from the pharmacist. Their biggest selling drug of the 1980s was Vasotec, a treatment for congestive heart failure. Only introduced in 1985, by 1988 it was the first Merck drug to reach annual sales of $1 billion. Another big winner was Mevacor, a cholesterol-lowering drug introduced in late 1987. Still another power drug is ivermectin, which Merck developed in 1975 to treat parasites and ticks in cattle, sheep and other livestock; it became the world's top-selling animal health product. Ivermectin also turned out to be the first effective treatment for "river blindness," a parasitic infection afflicting 18 million people in tropical areas of Africa, the Middle East and Latin America.

Merck owes such success to what everyone in pharmaceuticals agrees must be done: research. Merck invested $755 million in research and development in 1989, more than 10 percent of total industry research expenditures. For each employee, they spend $20,900 on research. Success in pharmaceuticals also takes patience. Mevacor resulted from three decades of research and a $125 million investment. Finally, more than money, success depends on the right people in the labs. Here too Merck excelled, providing the cultural environment that attracts top scientists. Merck's CEO through the second half of the 1980s was a research scientist, Dr. P. Roy Vagelos.

During the 1980s, when many drug makers were intent on combining with other companies, Merck went their own way, although in 1989 they began a joint venture with Johnson & Johnson to develop and market over-the-counter drugs.

Together, Merck and Johnson & Johnson field products like Pepcid, an antiulcer treatment Merck developed, and Mylanta antacid, one of the nonprescription drugs they picked up from ICI Americas, the U.S. subsidiary of Britain's Imperial Chemical Industries. The same year, Merck announced a deal with Du Pont to market drugs to treat hypertension. As a result of such tactics, Merck more than doubled their sales and tripled profits. They displaced IBM as the most admired company in the nation on the annual Fortune poll of executives. And they advanced to seventh place on *Business Week's* roster of the most valuable companies. So Merck rode out of the decade with a market value (the value of all stock) of $27.5 billion, roughly the same as General Motors, a company 20 times their size.

History. The world has two drug companies operating under the name Merck. One is E. Merck of West Germany; the other, Merck & Co. of the U.S., is more than three times as big as the German Merck. Although they are no longer related, the two Mercks have a common ancestry, dating to 1668 when Friedrich Jacob Merck bought an apothecary, At the Sign of the Angel, in Darmstadt, Germany. The pharmacy became a factory in 1827, benefitting from Heinrich Emmanuel Merck's friendship with another Darmstadt resident, Justus von Liebig, the father of organic chemistry. Their initial products were the alkaloids morphine, codeine and cocaine. By 1855, when Heinrich Emmanuel died, chemical compounds bearing the E. Merck name were sold all over the world.

Two years after this death, a Darmstadt chemist, Theodore Weicker, arrived in the U.S. to represent Merck. He was to play a pivotal role in the American pharmaceutical industry, first at Merck and then at Squibb. George Merck, 24-year-old grandson of Heinrich Emmanuel, joined Weicker in the U.S. in 1891 and together they put down roots here, buying 150 acres in New Jersey at the turn of the century and starting alkaloid production in 1903. Merck is still based at Rahway. Weicker and Merck split up in 1904. Weicker, with the backing of his wealthy father-in-law, Lowell Palmer, bought control of E. R. Squibb. (His grandson, Lowell Weicker, later represented Connecticut in the U.S. Senate.)

When the U.S. entered World War I in 1917, George Merck was in the uneasy position of running a company largely owned by his relatives in the enemy country. Without prodding, he turned over to the Alien Property Custodian the 80 percent interest his German cousins owned. As a result, after the German defeat the Merck shares were sold to a friendly investment group with the understanding that George Merck would remain in control. When he died in 1926, control fell to his son, George W. Merck. The German and American Mercks were never reunited, although they agreed in 1932 to exchange technical information, a pact dissolved in World War II (and never resurrected).

A Harvard chemistry graduate, George W. Merck established a a large, modern research laboratory at Rahway and recruited some of the nation's top biologists and chemists to work there. They pioneered during the 1930s in vitamin synthesis. In World War II George Merck was assumed to be enough of an American patriot to head up a Pentagon research effort to develop deadly disease strains to offset any biological warfare attacks by Germany or Japan.

After the war, Merck scientists, working in the new field of steroid chemistry, developed cortisone, hydrocortisone and dexamethasone, all prime agents in the treatment of rheumatoid arthritis. Although these discoveries enhanced Merck's reputation, antibiotics and new hormone drugs were ushering in a new era after World War II. Heretofore, Merck's core business had always been the sale of chemical compounds to other companies, especially drug makers. Now customers were developing their own compounds and selling them under their own brand names. The prescription drug business was exploding. Merck joined that explosion in 1953 when they merged with Philadelphia's Sharp & Dohme, an old pharmaceutical house rooted in an apothecary opened in Baltimore in 1845. Sharp & Dohme salespeople called on doctors and druggists. Merck could now market drugs under their own name through the newly established pharmaceutical division, Merck Sharp & Dohme.

George W. Merck died in 1957, the last Merck to head the company. He left in place a philosophy emphasizing basic research and long-term investment. He put it this way: "Medicine is for the patients. It is not for the profits. The profits follow, and if we have remembered that, they have never failed to appear. The better we have remembered it, the larger they have been."

Owners and rulers. Albert W. Merck, George Merck's son, took his seat on Merck's board in 1961 when he was 40. In 1989 he was still the largest single shareholder, although his holdings, 583,000 shares worth $35 million, amounted to only one-seventh of 1 percent of all the shares. Four of Merck's 16 directors are physicians. One of these is CEO Roy Vagelos, a legend in his own time. As a boy Vagelos waited tables and did dishes at his parents' luncheonette, six blocks from Merck headquarters in Rahway. Vagelos' sister married a Merck chemist. After graduating from medical school at Columbia and interning at Boston's Massachusetts General, Dr. Vagelos became a researcher. He headed the biological chemistry department at Washington University of St. Louis in 1966 when Merck asked him to "come home." He set in motion the research that yielded the bonanza of new drugs in the 1980s. Vagelos, 60 in 1990, has stated that before he steps down he wants Merck to develop drugs in every major disease category. In 1989 he told the *Financial Times:* "My dream is to be like Bell Laboratories in its heyday. It was so large and could work on so many things, and things so way out that they would not pay off for years... I'm talking about pure basic research." Vagelos went a long way toward fulfilling his personal financial dream when in 1989 he pulled down a hefty $6.8 million, making him the 14th highest paid CEO in *Business Week's* annual survey.

As a place to work. Merck's reputation as a superior workplace—they have long been the best payer in the drug industry—survived a 15-week strike by unionized employees in 1985. Merck didn't mind being a top payer, but they sought, and gained, some relief from signing on new workers at wage scales, in some cases, 75 percent above the industry average. Three years later a new contract was signed with no fuss. Merck's payroll costs, as a percentage of sales, are the highest in the

THE BILLION-DOLLAR DRUGS

Prescription Drugs

		Annual Sales
1.	*Zantac* (Glaxo) for ulcers	$2.0 billion
2.	*Capoten* (Bristol-Myers Squibb) for hypertension, congestive heart failure	$1.15 billion
3.	*Vasotec* (Merck) hypertension, congestive heart failure	$1.10 billion
4.	*Tagamet* (Smith-Kline Beecham) for ulcers	$1.0 billion

Source: *The New York Times*, 11 October 1989.

pharmaceutical industry. On the scientific side, Merck is regarded as a mecca for ambitious researchers because of the high caliber of people and the collegial spirit found at the 210-acre, landscaped, campuslike headquarters at Rahway. A 1988 employee poll showed that 85 percent believe Merck a better place to work than other companies they know. In 1990, Merck named Judy C. Lewent Chief Financial Officer. She is one of the few women to hold such a high-ranking position at a Fortune 500 company.

Social responsibility. Merck has a long legacy of social responsibility, derived from a sense of how their business impacts directly on public health. They have been generous with their discoveries: In the 1940s they made streptomycin available to all comers and recently decided to make their "river blindness" drug, Mectizan, available free of charge for as long as it is needed. Similarly, in the race to find a cure for AIDS, Merck has led the research efforts and in 1987 disclosed to everyone else in the field their early findings on the critical role played by the protease enzyme in replication of the HIV virus. Peggy Johnston, director of the federal AIDS drug discovery program at the National Institute of Allergy and Infectious Disease, said Merck's contribution was "the difference between blindly trying a lot of keys in a lock and having a picture of the inside of the lock's tumblers." Also notable is Merck's absence

from the ranks of drug companies hauled before regulatory agencies and/or courts for shoddy research and nondisclosure of major side effects of drugs.

Global presence. Major. Merck manufactures drugs in 24 countries and does nearly one-half of sales outside the U.S. Their share of the worldwide market for prescription drugs has been estimated at 3.95 percent, ranking them number one, ahead of Britain's Glaxo, Switzerland's Ciba-Geigy and Germany's Hoechst.

Stock performance. Merck stock bought for $1,000 in 1980 sold for $8,433 on January 2, 1990.

Merck & Co., Inc., P.O. Box 2000, Rahway, NJ 07065; (201) 594-4000.

2
 SQUIBB

#1 *in hair coloring, orthopedic implants*
#2 *in prescription drugs, infant formula*
#3 *in painkillers*

Employees: 53,700
Sales: $9.2 billion
Profits: $747 million
Founded: Bristol-Myers: 1887
Squibb: 1858
Headquarters: New York, New York

Heart failure being the biggest cause of death in the U.S., it's somehow fitting that heart medicine helped spawn the biggest merger in the history of the American drug industry. Squibb doubled sales in the 1980s largely on the strength of a $1 billion-a-year heart drug, Capoten. Meanwhile, (Bristol-Myers makes Bufferin and Excedrin, both of which contain asperin.) Bristol-Myers reaped the dividends from a medical study showing aspirin to be effective in preventing a second heart attack. Bristol-Myers and Squibb concluded that together they could make beautiful music. In 1989 they combined forces.

As recently as 1988 such a merger seemed unlikely. That year Squibb's Richard M. Furlaud had boasted in a *New York Times* interview that Squibb's single-minded concentration on prescription drugs gave them a competitive advantage. "We're not in animal health, not in proprietary drugs [products sold on TV instead of via prescription pads], not in candies or chewing gum," he said. "We've put all our eggs in one basket." Less than a year later Furlaud yoked Squibb to a company whose interests include coloring women's hair (Clairol), unclogging drainpipes (Drano) and flogging headache remedies on TV.

Why? Simply because Furlaud and his close friend, Richard L. Gelb of Bristol-Myers, believe the combined research arms of the two companies will yield potent new medicines. Although best known for their well-advertised home remedies and beauty aids, Bristol-Myers also makes anticancer drugs, antibiotics and the tranquilizer Buspar. They are testing an AIDS vaccine called Peptide T and have been given exclusive marketing rights from the federal government. During the 1980s they used some of the big bucks earned from hawking Bufferin and Excedrin to build a state-of-the-art $160 million research center at Wallingford, Connecticut. Ailments of the aged are targeted at Wallingford. Squibb contributes a research arm strong in the cardiovascular field. Together, Bristol-Myers and Squibb plan to invest $575 million a year in research, the industry's biggest research budget outside of Merck.

Developing new drugs is important in this industry. Squibb's experience with their blood pressure pill, Capoten, introduced in the early 1980s, is illustrative. Capoten became one of the world's top selling drugs, accounting for 40 percent of Squibb's 1988 revenues of $2.5 billion. Bristol-Myers Squibb wants more Capotens.

History. For Squibb, becoming part of Bristol-Myers represented the fourth major realignment of the company in 131 years—and once again they preserved not only their name but also their reputation as a responsible medicine maker. Squibb seems irrepressible. For Bristol-Myers, acquiring Squibb was right in character. The sum of many parts, they have been buying other companies for over 100 years.

In the jumbled histories of these two companies, Dr. Edward Robinson Squibb stands out as a heroic figure. Born into a Philadelphia Quaker family in 1819, Squibb developed the first safe, reliable ether for use in surgical procedures. In 1858, after service as a Navy doctor, he set up a lab in Brooklyn to make ether and other drugs. By century's end Squibb's name stood for high-quality products doctors could depend on. Dr. Squibb was a teacher, researcher, stickler for high standards and fighter against quack drugs.

This reputation clung to the company long after Dr. Squibb died in 1900 and E. R. Squibb & Sons went through a series of gyrations. In 1905, the company was sold to German-born chemist Theodore Weicker and his father-in-law, Lowell Palmer. Then, in the 1950s, Squibb became part of a jerry-built conglomerate, Olin Mathieson (guns, chemicals, perfumes, aluminum). And then, in 1968, Squibb was liberated from the Olin Mathieson contraption by a bright lawyer, Richard Furlaud, who felt he had to shore up the company by bringing in candies, gums and mints (Beech-Nut Life Savers) and cosmetics and perfumes (Charles of the Ritz–Lanvin).

Twenty years later Furlaud was still at the helm but had jettisoned Beech-Nut and Ritz-Lanvin and was reaping the rewards of investing bubble gum profits into basic pharmaceutical research that had led to such hits as Capoten. Furlaud unhesitatingly credited the born-again Squibb as being "the outgrowth of the uncompromising integrity and dedication to quality of Dr. Squibb." A year later Furlaud steered that integrity into Bristol-Myers.

Meanwhile, Bristol-Myers had thrived with such advertising jingles as: "Ipana for the smile of beauty, Sal Hepatica for the smile of health." Anyone listening to the radio in the 1930s will remember that line, delivered in stentorian tones on the Fred Allen and Eddie Cantor shows. These two were the ace products of Bristol-Myers, a company founded in 1887 by William McLaren Bristol and John Ripley Myers, two recent Hamilton College graduates who knew nothing about pharmaceuticals but bought an ailing drug company located in the town (Clinton, New York) where they'd gone to college. Their first successful nostrum was Sal Hepatica, a mineral salt laxative. (People have always been constipated.) Their second winner was Ipana, a toothpaste made with a disinfectant. Other drugstore products followed: Vitalis (promoted as the favorite of barbers on "Mr. District Attorney"), Bufferin (first of the buffered aspirins) and Ban roll-on deodorant (introduced nationally in 1955 on "The Arthur Godfrey Show").

Figuring they knew their way around an advertising budget, the Bristol-Myers people set out to buy companies whose products they could then promote to stardom. Their most fateful purchase, in 1959, was Clairol, a company Lawrence Gelb and his wife founded at a time when the social standing of hair coloring was not far removed from that of pornography. Bristol-Myers bought Clairol for $22 million four years after their sales took off under the stimulus of a famous ad campaign: "Does she…or doesn't she? Hair color so natural only her hairdresser knows from sure!" With Clairol came not just a new line of products but the two sons of the founders, Richard and Bruce Gelb, both graduates of the Harvard Business School. Richard became president of Bristol-Myers in 1967, by which time Clairol was the biggest product in the house. In 1972 he was elected CEO, a position he still held in 1990.

A succession of other companies followed Clairol into Bristol-Myers: Drackett (Windex, Drano, O'Cedar mops), Mead Johnson (infant formula and children's vitamins), Westwood (Keri skin-care products, PreSun), Zimmer (orthopedic implants). Bristol Laboratories, a Syracuse company acquired during World War II, put them in the prescription drug business. A leading producer of antibiotics, Bristol later developed a broader line of pharmaceuticals, especially chemotherapeutic agents to combat cancer and the cholesterol-lowering drug, Questran. In the 1980s Bristol Labs became Bristol-Myers' most important business. Prescription drug sales tripled, paving the way for the $12 billion merger with Squibb.

Owners and rulers. The two "Dicks"—Gelb and Furlaud—put together the 1989 merger and remain in charge, Gelb as chairman and CEO, Furlaud as president in charge of pharmaceutical operations. At the merger, Furlaud was 66, Gelb 65. Gelb's younger brother, Bruce, retired in 1989 to become director of the U.S. Information Agency. Dick Gelb's premerger holdings of 1 million shares were worth $50 million. He received a cool $3.5 million in salary and stock in 1989. Furlaud's Squibb holdings translated to $27 million of Bristol-Myers stock. In addition to his 1988 $1.5 million pay package, Furlaud was paid $400,000 in deferred vacation pay to make up for the six months of vacation time he didn't take over the previous 18 years. Squibb's president, Jan Leschly, resigned after the merger and was awarded a so-called golden parachute worth $5.4 million.

As a place to work. Premerger, Squibb and Bristol-Myers were both regarded as good places to work, especially Squibb, where Richard Furlaud instilled a strong spirit around the quest for new medicines to attack life-threatening diseases. In 1988 Squibb named Denise Palmieri to the newly created position of ombudsperson to handle and investigate employee complaints. Squibb announced there would be no layoffs as a result of the Bristol-Myers Squibb merger. At Bristol-Myers, the proportion of women and minorities in management positions quadrupled between 1968 and 1988.

Social responsibility. Bristol-Myers has had a long-standing battle with regulatory agencies over claims made for Bufferin. The latest came with the trumpeting of claims about aspirin helping to curb heart attacks. The Bristol-Myers unit, Mead Johnson, has also had problems over promotion of their infant formula, Enfamil. In 1989 Bristol-Myers earned the wrath of the medical community for a joint venture with Gerber in which a baby formula Bristol-Myers makes was marketed as Gerber Baby Formula. Doctors were incensed by this direct consumer appeal. Previously, baby formulas were advertised only through the medical profession. Doctors complained the new drive would discourage breast-feeding. At least four hospitals, including those at Johns Hopkins and Yale, stopped using Enfamil in their nurseries.

Global presence. Squibb was more of an international operator than Bristol-Myers, doing 52 percent of their sales outside the U.S., compared with 29 percent for Bristol. The combined companies do 29 percent of their business overseas.

Stock performance. Bristol-Myers Squibb stock bought for $1,000 in 1980 sold for $8,529 on January 2, 1990.

Consumer brands.

Analgesics and cold remedies: Bufferin, Excedrin, Comtrex, Congesprin, Nuprin, 4-Way.

Personal care products: Clairol, Miss Clairol, Clairesse, Final Net, Loving Care, Nice 'N Easy, Sea Breeze, Highlighters, Pazazz, Color Play, Ultresse, Ban, Keri, Presun, Vanish, Theragran.

Household products: Drano, Windex, Vanish, Behold, Endust, Renuzit, Twinkle, O'Cedar, Bowl Brite.

Bristol-Myers Squibb, 345 Park Avenue, New York, NY 10154; (212) 546-4000.

3

SmithKline Beecham p.l.c.

#1 *in clinical laboratories, antacids, acne remedies*

#2 *in antiulcer drugs*

#3 *in prescription drugs, toothpaste*

#4 *in animal health products*

#5 *in cold remedies*

Employees: 63,000
Sales: $7.5 billion (worldwide)
Profits: $780 million
U.S. sales: $2.5 billion
Founded: SmithKline: 1830
Beecham: 1850
Headquarters: Brentford, England

It's dangerous to mix drugs, except if you're a drug company. Then the more the better. Two companies—one U.S. based, the other in Britain—stumbled into the future in 1989 by merging forces. This trans-Atlantic marriage created Smith-Kline Beecham, which ranked, for at least a week, as the world's second largest prescription drug maker (behind Merck), second largest over-the-counter drug maker (behind American Home Products) and fourth largest maker of animal health products (behind Hoffmann–La Roche, Rhone-Poulenc and Pfizer). The Bristol-Myers Squibb merger, announced immediately after the SK-Beecham nuptials, dropped this Anglo-American hybrid to third place in prescription drugs.

The American partner in this merger was stuffy Philadelphia drug house, SmithKline Beckman, best known to con-sumers for Contac cold capsules and to doctors (and their ulcer patients) for the prescription drug Tagamet. The British partner was the eclectic British pill house, Beecham, known for a host of nostrums in England (Bovril, Marmite, Horlicks, Eno's salts) and best known to American con-sumers for popular home remedies like Geritol, Sominex, Tums, Massengill douches, Aqua-Fresh toothpaste and to doctors (and their patients) for the antibi-otics Augmentin and Amoxil.

The merger capped a series of misad-ventures by both companies. Beecham and SmithKline collapsed into one another's arms like two drunks trying to hold each other up.

The merger was a classic case of the tail wagging the dog. The Beecham name may come last but that's where ultimate con-trol resides. Beecham did the acquiring, not SmithKline. Headquarters are in England, not Philadelphia. And the CEO of the combined shebang is Robert Bauman, not Henry Wendt. Consolation: Bauman is an American.

History. So many strands were inter-twined to create SmithKline Beckman and the Beecham Group it's difficult to see anything beyond the knots. Neither com-pany had, before the 1989 merger, a clear-cut mission or an overriding culture.

Originally a Philadelphia apothecary, SmithKline supplied quinine to U.S. troops during the 1846 war against Mexico, spirits of ammonia to U.S. troops during World War I and amphetamines—Dexedrine and Dexamyl—to a lot of wired Americans just after World War II. They heard about an allergy drug developed by the French com-pany, Rhone-Poulenc, and brought it to the U.S. as the tranquilizer, Thorazine. It en-abled mental hospitals to discharge thou-sands of patients during the 1950s.

SmithKline used to pretend they were choosy about bringing out new products, being interested only in drugs that made "a definite contribution to medicine," an ap-propriate stance for a company whose re-search laboratories rarely discovered any new drugs. Tagamet, the first drug capable of healing peptic ulcers, was discovered in SmithKline's British labs and caught the company by surprise. Earlier they had al-most pulled the plug on this research, and when Tagamet was introduced in 1976 they never dreamed it would turn out to be a barnburner. In five years Tagamet sales exceeded SmithKline's *total* 1975 revenues. By the end of the 1980s Tagamet was accounting for one-fourth of SmithKline's sales of $4.3 billion and one-half of the profits of $570 million.

That was the good news. The bad news came in triplicate: SmithKline had no drugs in the pipeline to follow Tagamet; their number two drug, the blood pressure medicine Dyazide, had a patent expiration in 1987 (opening the door to generic substitutes); and Britain's Glaxo began to eat SmithKline's lunch with a new ulcer medication, Zantac. SmithKline was the only major drug company failing to market an important new drug in the 1980s. The one drug they did bring out, Selacryn, had to be hastily withdrawn after reports of deadly side effects.

SmithKline bought their way into other problems. In 1982, flush with Tagamet profits, SmithKline gave $1 billion worth of their stock to buy a highly regarded California-based company, Beckman Instruments. Arnold O. Beckman, who founded the company in 1935, invented such devices as the pH meter, enabling chemists to measure the acidity or alkalinity of a solution, and the spectrophotometer, enabling researchers to illuminate samples and measure the emerging light to determine the substances present. These instruments revolutionized laboratory work in chemistry and biology. After SmithKline bought Beckman, the instruments company went into decline, spurred in part by Medicare changes that led hospitals to cut back on their diagnostic equipment. In 1989, Arnold Beckman, then 88, said he regretted selling the company. He accused SmithKline of not giving Beckman the resources they needed. In combining with Beecham, SmithKline sheared off the Beckman name and sold off the Beckman businesses.

Beecham, SmithKline's savior, is a relic from 19th century England. Thomas Beecham, the eldest of seven children of a farm laborer, sold a laxative to constipated Britons that he called Beecham's Pills. He ran his first ad for the pills in 1859. By 1900 his factory in the Merseyside city of St. Helens was turning out 1 million pills a day to meet the demand stoked by omnipresent advertising keyed to the line, "worth a guinea a box." The Beecham family faded from the scene in the early part of the 20th century (one of them, the grandson and namesake of the founder, became a world-famous orchestral conductor), but the company bearing their name plodded on, buying one business after another without much discrimination. Gin, whiskey, wines, glue, perfumes, cosmetics, toothpaste, hair shampoo, milk delivery, soft drinks, canned and frozen foods and, of course, drugs were all part of the picture as recently as the mid-1980s.

The pharmaceutical business—especially antibiotics—was Beecham's lifesaver. Amoxil, a broad-spectrum antibiotic, is one of the most frequently prescribed drugs in American medical practice. Augmentin, another antibiotic, also sells well. During the 1980s Beecham sold off more than a dozen companies, finally giving up on cosmetics and perfumes and wines and spirits altogether. But they kept all the drugs.

The U.S. has always been a mystery to Beecham. They came here with two of their big British brands, Brylcreem hair dressing and Macleans toothpaste, and had their head handed to them. To be more of a presence in the American market, Beecham wrote checks totaling $500 million during the 1980s to buy businesses whose brands include Aqua Velva, Geritol, Sominex, Tums and Oxy.

Beecham was so disoriented during the 1980s that the board of directors, led by Lord Keith of Castleacre, fired the CEO, Sir Ronald Halsted. Lord Keith said that for the first time the board was looking over the companies Beecham owned and asking: "Do we really want to be in that business?" They looked all over Britain and Europe for a new chief but couldn't find one. So they went to the U.S. and recruited, for $1 million a year, Robert P. Bauman, the 55-year-old deputy chairman of Textron, who began his career with General Foods, selling Maxwell House coffee to Philadelphia grocers.

Bauman introduced American-style management to Beecham. The top 4,000 managers now face regular performance reviews. And there's a plan of attack. When he was being interviewed for the Beecham job, Bauman asked Lord Keith: "Can I see your corporate plan?" Lord Keith supposedly replied: "That's part of the problem. We don't have one." Bauman has a plan. Three years after he was hired, he made his big American play by getting Beecham to buy SmithKline Beckman.

Owners and rulers. The shots are clearly being called from London by Bauman. After taking over he brought in 30 new senior managers, 11 of them from outside Beecham. Beecham and SmithKline each contributed nine members to the new board of directors. One who made the transition to the new company was SmithKline's black director, Donald F. McHenry, former U.S. ambassador to the United Nations. One who did not was public relations operative Linda Godsen Robinson, whose husband, James Robinson III, CEO of American Express, helped to set up Squibb's merger with Bristol-Myers.

As a place to work. Who knows what's in store at a company formed by such unstable characters? *The Economist* once depicted Beecham as "bureaucratic, inflexible and secretive." A scientist once described SmithKline Chairman Henry Wendt as a "numbers man" who wouldn't "know a molecule if he fell over one." The immediate speculation was that SmithKline Beecham would eliminate at least 10,000 people from the payroll.

Social responsibility. Neither SmithKline in the U.S. nor Beecham in Britain has won high marks for philanthropy. They stand in sharp contrast to Arnold Beckman, who after selling his company to SmithKline emerged in the 1980s as one of the biggest benefactors of scientific research in America, giving away $75 million in 1985 alone through his private foundation. SmithKline was disgraced in the 1980s for rushing a blood pressure drug, Selacryn, into the marketplace one

month after receiving reports about liver damage among users. In an indictment brought by the Justice Department, SmithKline pleaded guilty to 34 counts of failing to make timely reports about the drug's side effects to the FDA. SmithKline was given two years' probation and ordered to pay $100,000 to a child abuse program. Three company executives were sentenced to 200 hours each of community service. Selacryn, on the market less than a year, was linked to 36 deaths.

Global presence. The whole point of this merger was to create a company that could be a contender in a worldwide market for drugs. Prior to the merger, SmithKline did 40 percent of their sales overseas, and Beecham did 25 percent of their sales in the U.S.

Consumer brands.

Contac, Tums, Aquafresh, Aqua-Velva, Geritol, Sucrets, Massengill, Vivarin, Calgon, ClingFree, Lectric Shave, N'ice, Sominex, Oxy, Orafix, Liquiprin.

SmithKline Beecham, Brentford, Middlesex, TW8 9BD, England; 1-560-5151

SmithKline Beecham, One Franklin Plaza, P.O. Box 7929, Philadelphia, PA 19101; (215) 751-4000.

4

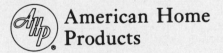

American Home Products

#2 *in over-the-counter drugs*
#4 *in prescription drugs*

Employees: 51,100
Sales: $6.7 billion
Profits: $1.1 billion
Founded: 1926
Headquarters: New York, New York

Social Conscience

To help sell their blood pressure-lowering drug, Inderal, available only by prescription, American Home Products worked out a deal with American Airlines frequent flier program: For every patient a doctor starts on this drug, she or he receives 1,000 miles credit.

It's a simple, patriotic-sounding name—American Home Products—but most Americans have never heard of this company even though they've probably used one of their products. AHP's familiar lineup includes the heart drug Inderal, the menopausal treatment Premarin, the headache remedies Anacin and Advil, the infant formula SMA, the cold pill Dristan, the nasal clearer Primatene, and the canned pastas sold under the Chef Boyardee label. AHP doesn't cosy up to customers. They don't put their corporate name on packages. They don't provide an 800 telephone number for consumers. And although they rank as the nation's 27th largest advertiser, with a 1988 expenditure of $393 million, AHP doesn't spend a dime promoting American Home Products. They may be the only company of their size to get along without a corporate public relations department. This behavior prompted one writer to describe their motto as: "Walk softly and carry a big ad budget."

AHP's passion for anonymity springs from a long-held belief that corporate image polishing doesn't sell products. Are hemorrhoid sufferers more likely to buy Preparation H if they know American Home Products makes it? In any case, in financial terms their approach works. No one in the drug industry, outside of Merck, makes as much after-tax profit as AHP. And one record they are very proud of is that through 1989 sales, profits and dividends paid to stockholders had increased for 37 consecutive years.

They did make a minor adjustment in the 1980s. Previously, when people called the New York headquarters, switchboard operators answered with the telephone number. Now they respond, "American Home Products."

Otherwise, it was business as usual for AHP during the 1980s. They bought several companies (Wheatena and Maypo cereals, Today contraceptive sponges, Sherwood medical devices entered the lineup). They sold off some (Brach candies and Ecko pots and pans) and in early 1990 announced they would sell their household products companies. But they remained true to themselves. They didn't go along with the crowd and seek out a megamerger partner. They entered and ended the decade without a cent of long-term debt.

History. AHP's past is murky because the company sheds no light on it. No history of the company, authorized or unauthorized, exists. Anniversaries are never celebrated. They treat their history the way they treat their product ingredients: "It's nobody's business but ours." It is known American Home Products was organized in 1926 as a blend of nostrum makers. One of the companies had been selling Hill's Cascara Quinine, another a medicine called Petrolager, another Freezone (still an AHP brand). Once AHP was formed, business strategy was to buy up other companies with products easily promoted to a gullible public.

That strategy accelerated after Alvin George Brush took the helm in 1935. An accountant who had been running the Dr. Lyon's toothpaste business, Brush bought 34 companies. Into the fold came Anacin, Black Flag, 3-in-One oil, BiSoDol, Kolynos toothpaste, G. Washington coffee and Clapp's baby foods, among other products.

AHP's most important buy, Wyeth Laboratories, was a virtual gift. Wyeth was born in that "cradle of pharmacy," Philadelphia, in 1860. During the 1920s control was in the hands of Stuart Wyeth, an eccentric bachelor who spent a good part of his time cavorting in Paris, where he died in 1929. He left the company to his alma mater, Harvard, which hadn't a clue what to do with the business and happily unloaded it for virtually nothing in 1932. AHP knew exactly what to do with the firm: Wyeth became the foundation of their prescription drug business. In the 1940s AHP bought another prescription drug company, Ayerst.

We do know a bit about AHP's sales because the Securities and Exchange Commission forces them to disclose the breakdown—and the latest split shows prescription drugs account for 48 percent of the total, compared to 40 percent at the start of the 1980s. They have been criticized for being stingy about putting money into research. Their biggest seller of the 1980s, Inderal, did not come out of AHP labs. After drugmaker A. H. Robins entered bankruptcy proceedings, weighed down by claims brought by women who had used the Dalkon Shield IUD, AHP made a beeline for the sunken assets, outbidding two other operators. AHP paid $700 million worth of stock and set up a $2.4 billion fund to pay off Dalkon Shield claimants. A. H. Robins swung into AHP prescription drugs with annual sales of $100 million and popular over-the-counter products such as Robitussin cough syrups, Chap Stick and Dimetapp cold remedies—precisely the kind of products AHP loves to peddle to the American public.

The household products they agreed to sell to Beckitt & Coleman for $1.2 billion—Black Flag insecticides, Easy-Off oven cleaner, Sani-Flush, among others—accounted for $700 million of sales.

Owners and rulers. Tight-fisted Puritans who hang on for a long time. Alvin Brush ran the company for 30 years. In 1965 he passed the baton to William F. Laporte, a reclusive figure whose banker father had been Brush's close friend. Laporte, according to one report, tape-recorded every conversation he had (none with journalists because he never talked to them). In 1986, 48-year-old John R. Stafford, a lawyer, became CEO (1989 pay: $3.7 million). He has looking over his shoulder the two previous bosses, Laporte and Culligan (CEO, 1981–1986) who remained on AHP's board. Aside from this trio, the AHP board has only eight other directors, none of them a physician or scientist, all of them white. William Wrigley, head of the chewing gum company, has been a director since 1981. And there always seems to be a "Hearst" seat. John R. Miller, CEO of the Hearst Corp. (the publisher of *American Druggist*), held it for 12 years, and in 1988 Miller's successor, Frank A. Bennack, Jr., took it.

As a place to work. AHP runs a tight ship. No corporate jets, no lavish expense accounts. Managers are under the gun to reach profit goals—or else. One former employee told *Fortune* writer Susan Fraker: "It's a lousy place to work. But it's a great place to invest your money."

Social responsibility. For nearly 30 years AHP has battled with government regulatory agencies (principally the Federal Trade Commission) and competitors (Bristol-Myers, Sterling Drug, Johnson & Johnson) over claims made for various products. Much of the litigation had to do with charges of deceptive advertising for Anacin. AHP doggedly promoted Anacin for over 20 years as having "the pain reliever doctors recommend most" (never disclosing they were talking about aspirin) or as being "stronger" than regular aspirin (never disclosing the extra strength resulted from Anacin's containing 23 percent more aspirin than a regular aspirin tablet). The word *aspirin* was always taboo in AHP advertising (even though it had to be specified, in small print, of course, on the package). Until recently. Now that studies have indicated aspirin's efficacy as a heart attack preventive, AHP seems ready, after 70 years, to admit Anacin is basically aspirin. AHP has also come under fire because they market baby formula as a breast-milk substitute in the Third World—and distribute free samples to hospitals, thereby discouraging new mothers from breast-feeding. Several groups are currently boycotting AHP as a result. The Interfaith Center of Corporate Responsibility called AHP "the most unresponsive of the U.S. infant formula manufacturers" on this issue.

Global presence. They trail behind other drug makers in overseas penetration. With plants in 22 countries, AHP does 31 percent of their business outside the U.S.

Stock performance. American Home Products stock bought for $1,000 in 1980 sold for $6,402 on January 2, 1990.

Consumer brands.

Foods: Chef Boyardee pasta and pizzas, Mama Leone's Pasta Supreme, Gulden's mustard, Jiffy Pop popcorn, Franklin Crunch 'n Munch, Dennison's chili, Luck's country style beans, Ranch style beans, G. Washington's seasonings and broth, Wheatena, Maypo.

Infant formula: SMA, S-26, Nursoy.

Over-the-counter drugs: Advil, Anacin, Anacin-3, Arthritis Pain Formula, Momentum, Trendar, Dimetapp, Robitussin, Dristan, Viromen, Primatene, BiSoDol, Riopan, Anbesol, Dermoplast, Preparation H, Quiet World, Sleepeze, Compound W, Freezone, Neet, Outgro, Youth Garde.

Contraceptives and pregnancy tests: Clearblue, Clearplan, Semicid, Today.

Personal care: Chap Stick, Denorex.

American Home Products Corp., 685 Third Avenue, New York, NY 10017; (212) 878-5000.

5

#1 *in eyedrops, men's fragrances, citric acid*
#3 *in animal health (world)*
#5 *in prescription drugs*

Employees: 41,500
Sales: $5.7 billion
Profits: $681 million
Founded: 1849
Headquarters: New York, New York

During the 1980s Pfizer advanced into the first tier of the pharmaceutical industry. No longer regarded as an uncouth outsider, Pfizer's growth was fired by the development of new blockbuster drugs, ending a heavy dependence on antibiotics. During the decade, Pfizer introduced Feldene, a once-a-day pill for arthritis suffererers, and Procardia, an antiangina agent. These two drugs accounted for nearly one-fifth of Pfizer's revenues. Such is the power of drugs gaining the confidence of physicians. But antibiotics were still Pfizer's biggest class of drugs, accounting for sales of $835 million in 1989. Their biggest brand was Unasyn.

Driven by an appetite for other companies, Pfizer also makes and sells products that can be advertised directly to consumers. They own the companies that bring you Visine, Ben-Gay, Barbasol and the Coty fragrances. Of course, not everything works all the time. One of their 1987 flops was Equalactin, a drug touted as an effective remedy for *both* diarrhea and constipation. And that was followed by a 1988 flop, Mexicali Musk, a Coty fragrance packaged in a tequila-look-alike bottle with a plastic worm inside. Pfizer's marketing whizzes thought it would appeal to fanciers of Mexican food and spirits.

History. In 1849, two German immigrants, cousins Charles Pfizer and Charles Erhart, began experimenting in their Brooklyn laboratory. Pfizer had spent time at an apothecary in Ludwigsburg, and Erhart was a confectioner. They blended those skills in making their first product, a sugar-cone-wrapped dewormer. During the last half of

the 19th century and well into the 20th, Chas. Pfizer & Co. of Brooklyn turned out a variety of chemical compounds—iodines, tartars, boric acids and camphor—mainly sold to other companies.

Pfizer began producing citric acid in 1870, refining it from citrate of lime imported from Italy. A component of citrus fruits, citric acid is an incredibly versatile product, used as a flavoring agent in foods, beverages and drugs; as a dissolving agent in industrial processes; as a cement remover; as a plating agent. But not until the 1920s did Pfizer find out how to ferment citric acid from molds. They then built deep fermentation tanks to produce the acid. Aside from making Pfizer the world's largest supplier of citric acid, this tank production method had serendipitous consequences. Penicillin was a 1928 discovery but remained a laboratory curiosity until World War II when the U.S. government challenged companies to come up with a way of mass-producing it. Pfizer's fermentation tanks proved to be the ticket. By war's end Pfizer was making half the world's penicillin.

But penicillin wasn't the financial bonanza you might imagine. Other companies soon figured out how to make it themselves. So Pfizer, a little miffed, collected 135,000 soil samples from around the world in the search for a new antibiotic. They isolated a broad-spectrum antibiotic, oxytetracycline, and in 1950 they made a bold decision that was to transform the company. Instead of selling the drug in bulk to established pharmaceutical companies, as they had been doing for 100 years, Pfizer put their own brand name, Terramycin, on the antibiotic and began promoting directly to the doctors who had to prescribe it.

A *mericans gulp down 80 million aspirin tablets per day. The British prefer aspirin in powdered form, stirred into water. Scandinavians like coated tablets, while Italians go for effervescent aspirin. The French favor suppositories.*

Because the Pfizer name was unknown to the medical profession, Pfizer felt they had to do something spectacular. And they did. They mounted razzle-dazzle promotions that included production of their own magazine bound into the *Journal of the American Medical Association* as a paid advertisement. Pfizer spent $7.5 million to promote Terramycin, an unheard of sum in those days. Between 1952 and 1956 Pfizer became the largest advertiser in medical journals. They gave medical students summer jobs. They sent physicians gifts of pillows and golf balls imprinted with Pfizer brand names. In 1961, they moved their headquarters from Brooklyn to Manhattan, bringing them closer to their advertising agencies.

Other drug companies looked with disdain on this flamboyance, regarding Pfizer as an undignified interloper in their business. But it worked. Physicians now know who Pfizer is. And as they brought out more drugs and bought more than a dozen companies, Pfizer rose steadily in the industry ranks. When Pfizer started out after World War II, the pantheon of the so-called ethical drug industry consisted of Eli Lilly, Merck, Upjohn, and Parke, Davis. Of that group, only Merck is now bigger than Pfizer.

Owners and rulers. The Pfizers and Erharts are long gone from the scene (most of the later generations preferred playing to working), and the company has evolved into a modern, faceless corporation whose shares are widely scattered among pension funds and the like. No individual holds more than two-tenths of 1 percent of the stock. Business or engineering types rather than medical people have traditionally managed Pfizer. No physicians sit on the board. John McKeen, a chemical engineer from Brooklyn, became CEO in 1950 and ran the show until 1965. He was succeeded by John Powers, Jr., a laywer whose father went to work for Pfizer in 1909. Powers, who built up the international side of the business, recruited Edmund T. Pratt, Jr., an ex-IBMer, from the Pentagon—and Pratt has operated the company with military precision since 1972. He received nearly $2 million in 1989 for his work. Pratt's number two since 1972 is an MIT chemist, Gerald D. Laubach, who received over $4.4 million in pay in 1989.

THE PAINKILLER MARKET

Total Annual Sales: $2 Billion

Acetaminophen (40% Of Total)

	Market Share
Tylenol	30.0%
Panadol	2.0%
Others	8.0%

Aspirin (40% Of Total)

	Market Share
Bayer	7.0%
Excedrin	7.0%
Bufferin	4.5%
Anacin	5.0%
Others	16.5%

Ibuprofen (20% Of Total)

	Market Share
Advil	12.0%
Nuprin	3.5%
Medipren	2.5%
Others	2.0%

Source: *Business Week*, 29 August 1988.

As a place to work. In their early days Pfizer hired only German immigrants for their Brooklyn plant. In 1920 they introduced a year-end bonus plan that awarded $10 to employees with 10 years or more service, $5 to those with 5 to 10 years, $3 for 1 to 3 years, and $2 for employees with less than a year's service. Pfizer has usually been ruled by a strong man at the top. Only recently have Pfizer scientists achieved recognition. That Merck's chief financial officer is a woman cuts no ice with CEO Pratt, who said: "Why would any woman choose to be a chief financial officer rather than a mother?"

Social responsibility. Always quick to advertise, Pfizer embarked in the 1980s on an image-burnishing campaign identifying the company as "one of your partners in health care." Ads offered medical advice—how to spot symptoms of angina, for example—and recommended, of course, that readers consult their doctors. The campaign was launched after a study showed that when presented with the name, Pfizer, only 1 out of 100 persons over age 35 could say what the company is or does. After spending $16 million in two years, they lifted that awareness to 2 percent.

After years of protests, Pfizer withdrew the Bjork-Shiley heart valve in 1986 after it had been linked with the deaths of more than 100 persons. In 1982, the FDA excoriated Pfizer for misleading promotion of their heart medicine, Procardia, alleging "untruths, partial truths and omitted information." One of Pfizer's recently acquired drugs, Plax dental rinse, came under sharp attack in 1989 for claims that it "removed 300 percent more plaque than brushing alone." After competitors complained to the Better Business Bureau, Pfizer stopped making this claim on TV. It remained on bottles until Pfizer used up their supply.

Global presence. May be more well known outside the U.S. Pfizer has been doing half their business abroad since 1964. The last two CEOs came from the international wing.

Stock performance. Pfizer stock bought for $1,000 in 1980 sold for $4,904 on January 2, 1990.

Consumer brands.

Ben Gay, Visine, Barbasol, Unisom, Desitin, Rid, Warming Ice, Stetson, Lady Stetson, Iron, Sand & Sable, Plax, !ex'cla-ma'tion...

Pfizer Inc., 235 E. 42nd Street, New York, NY 10017; (212) 573-2323.

6

Bayer USA

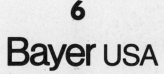

#1 in hangover remedies, scouring pads

Employees: 165,000 (U.S.: 29,600)
Sales: $23 billion (worldwide) U.S. sales: $5.4 billion)
Profits: $154 million (U.S.)
Founded: 1863
Headquarters: Pittsburgh, Pennsylvania

Bayer doesn't make Bayer aspirin—at least not in the U.S. One of the Big Three of the German chemical industry (BASF and Hoechst are the other two), Bayer does make such all-American products as Alka-Seltzer, One-A-Day vitamins, Flintstone chewable vitamins for kids and S.O.S. scouring pads. These products were part of Miles Laboratories of Elkhart,

Indiana, a company Bayer bought for $250 million in 1978.

Bayer (pronounced buyer) is insinuated into American life in a lot of other ways, to the point where their U.S. company now ranks 91st on the *Fortune* 500. Their Pittsburgh-based Mobay subsidiary is the nation's largest producer of polyurethane, a versatile chemical having a variety of end uses, including automobile bumpers, shoe soles and foam insulation for refrigerators and freezers. Their Agfa Corp., based in Ridgefield Park, New Jersey, rides herd over half a dozen companies, including one producing a full line of photographic films and another, Compugraphic, a major supplier of electronic, cold-type systems for the print industry.

But drugs remain a core business for Bayer. Using Miles as a base, Bayer expanded their U.S. drug operations during the 1980s. They introduced several new prescription drugs, including the antibiotic Cipro and the heart medication Adalat, and built a spanking new research center at West Haven, Connecticut. Bayer is one of the world's leading drug developers and likes to point out they hold more patents, 150,000, than any other company in the world. Aspirin was invented in a Bayer laboratory at the turn of the century—and Bayer remains the world's largest producer of it. But after Germany lost World War I, Bayer's U.S. properties were auctioned off, and they lost the right to use their own name in the American market. To this day, Bayer aspirin in the U.S. belongs to Sterling Drug, now part of Eastman Kodak. But in 1986 Bayer of Germany reached an agreement with Sterling allowing them to use their name in the U.S. on industrial products (but not the use of the Bayer cross trademark appearing on every Bayer box). They also got permission to use it as the master name for their U.S. holding company, Bayer U.S.A., headquartered in Pittsburgh along with Mobay (this name is an amalgam of Monsanto and Bayer—Monsanto was originally a 50-50 partner but has since sold their interest to Bayer).

Their biggest (with 16,500 employees) and most visible U.S. company, Miles was founded in Elkhart in 1884 by a general practitioner, Dr. Franklin Miles, who concocted, and sold to his patients, a sedative called Dr. Miles Nervine. Alka-Seltzer was invented at the local daily, the *Elkhart Truth* (the only paper in the world to carry this name outside of Moscow's *Pravda*), where reporters used to down a mixture of aspirin and bicarbonate of soda to ward off colds. Hearing that no one at the *Truth* caught the flu during the epidemics of 1918 and 1927, Andrew Hubble Beardsley, Miles' leader during the 1920s, had a chemist formulate a tablet of aspirin, bicarbonate of soda and citric acid—and they began promoting it to Americans in 1931. Their timing couldn't have been better. The U.S. emerged from Prohibition in 1933, and Alka-Seltzer was there to take its place as the antidote for hangovers.

Now it all belongs to Bayer, inventor of aspirin, backer of Adolf Hitler, operator of a plant outside Auschwitz and born-again leader in the world chemical industry.

Consumer brands.

Alka-Seltzer cold medicines; One-A-Day, Flintstone, and Bugs Bunny vitamins; S.O.S. cleansers; Cutter insect repellents.

Bayer AG, 5090 Leverkusen, West Germany.

Bayer USA, 500 Grant Street, Pittsburgh, PA 15219; (412) 394-5554.

Miles Inc., P.O. Box 40, Elkhart, IN 46515; (219) 264-8111.

7

#1 *in insulin therapy, antibiotics*

Employees: 27,500
Sales: $4.2 billion
Profits: $940 million
Founded: 1876
Headquarters: Indianapolis, Indiana

Of all the drug companies, Eli Lilly has probably changed least. They're conservative midwesterners who don't rattle easily. When the 1980s began, Richard D. Wood, born and raised in Indiana (always an advantage at Eli Lilly), held the positions of chairman, president and CEO. In 1989 he was still occupying these offices,

taking home $2.6 million for the year. In completing 40 years of service with Eli Lilly, Wood joined 55 other employees in that class. At the decade's start 18 percent of Eli Lilly's stock was held by the Lilly Endowment, one of the largest private foundations in the nation and a great benefactor of Indianapolis and Indiana (there's probably not a school in the state without a Lilly-donated lab or library). At the decade's end 18 percent of the stock was still held by the Lilly Endowment, whose trustees include top executives of the company and descendants of Colonel Eli Lilly, a Civil War veteran (9th Indiana Cavalry) who started mixing elixirs in downtown Indianapolis in 1876.

Although they're no longer the industry sales leader, Eli Lilly remains an important medicine maker. Nine of their prescription drugs each generated sales of more than $100 million in 1988. Among them were the antibiotics Ceclor, Keftab and Keflex; the antidepressant Prozac; the heart drug Dobutrex; and Humulin, human insulin produced by biosynthesis (gene-splicing). Eli Lilly orginally made their mark as a world-class drug company in the 1920s when they learned how to extract insulin from the pancreases of slaughterhouse animals, thereby prolonging the lives of millions of diabetics. Even today Lilly racks up sales of nearly $500 million dollars a year in insulin and other diabetic care drugs.

The 1980s were not without trauma for Eli Lilly. In 1985 they pleaded guilty to criminal charges of failing to report numerous deaths and injuries associated with the use of their arthritis drug, Oraflex, withdrawn from the U.S. market in 1982 only three months after its introduction. Lilly was fined $25,000. Toward the end of the decade Lilly refused to provide the State Department with their herbicide tebuthiuron, sold under the names Spike and Grassland. The government's plan was to spray the herbicide on coca plants growing in the Andean region of Peru. Tebuthiuron is a powerful, root-active herbicide that renders the soil sterile so that no crops can be grown. Lilly said this proposed use was indiscriminate and inappropriate. The State Department promptly branded Lilly AWOL in the war on drugs. In 1989 Eli Lilly combined their agricultural chemicals division with Du Pont's herbicide division, creating an entirely new company called Dow Elanco, headquartered near Lilly in Indianapolis. Dow owns 60 percent of the company and Lilly owns the rest.

Unlike many of their competitors, Lilly let the 1980s slide by without trying to buy, or merge with, other drug companies. But they have, through acquisitions, become a major player in medical instruments. The defibrillators ambulance rescue crews use to treat cardiac-arrest patients are very likely to have come from Lilly-owned Physio-Control. Cardiac Pacemakers, Advanced Cardiovascular Systems, IVAC Corp. and Devices for Vascular Intervention are other Lilly companies.

Wall Streeters laughed in 1970 when Lilly paid $37 million to buy the Elizabeth Arden cosmetics business, then taking in $65 million a year amd losing money. What do a bunch of Hoosiers know about selling beauty products? By 1986 Lilly appointed managers had boosted Arden's sales to $400 million. In 1987 Lilly sold the business to Fabergé for $700 million. The money went into research for new drugs.

Stock performance. Eli Lilly stock bought for $1,000 in 1980 sold for $6,498 on January 2, 1990.

Eli Lilly & Co., Lilly Corporate Center, Indianapolis, IN 46285; (317) 276-2000.

8

Warner-Lambert
COMPANY

#1 in cholesterol-lowering drugs, mouthwashes, allergy remedies, drug capsules, cough drops, breath mints

#2 in chewing gum, razors

#3 in antacids

Employees: 33,500
Sales: $4.2 billion
Profits: $413 million
Founded: 1856
Headquarters: Morris Plains, New Jersey

The people who make Junior Mints, Rascals and Sugar Babies lent a helping hand to scientists crafting a new cholesterol-lowering product. In 1988 Warner-Lambert introduced Cholybar, a cholesterol-lowering drug packaged as a candy bar. Available by prescription only, Cholybar followed on the heels of another cholesterol-lowering drug, Lopid, which rang up sales of $200 million for Warner-Lambert in its first year on the market. Cholybar was the ideal product to emerge from a company that traffics in prescription medicines and candies.

Warner-Lambert likes this kind of synergy. They sell sugar-laden confections like Pom Poms and Charleston Chew! while pointing out that their sugarless Trident gum will help candy eaters "fight dental decay." Warner-Lambert's business splits roughly three ways: one-third in prescription drugs; one-third in over-the-counter nostrums (Benadryl, Rolaids, e-p-t, Sinutab, Efferdent); and one-third in gums (Dentyne, Chiclets, Bubbaloo), mints (Certs, Clorets), candies, shaving products (Schick) and the Tetra pet-care line (food for aquarium fish and, as of 1988, reptiles). Outside of prescription drugs, Warner-Lambert's biggest selling product is Halls cough drops: $215 million a year. Second is Listerine at $150 million. Third is Rolaids at $85 million. Warner-Lambert stands to do well even if their own brands slump. More than 100 billion gelatin-coated drug capsules are swallowed every year by patients around the world; Warner-Lambert supplies half of the empty capsules. And as the 1990s began, they had high hopes for a new starch-based, allegedly biodegradable plastic, Novon.

How this motley collection came to be assembled under one banner is a convoluted story going back to the opening of a pharmacy by William R. Warner in Philadelphia in 1856. More than 100 different companies have gone through this meat grinder in 140 years. Among the men who contributed fresh meat were Jordan Wheat Lambert (he began making Listerine in St. Louis in 1884), Hervey C. Parke and George S. Davis (they built the Detroit drug house, Parke, Davis, which Warner-Lambert absorbed in 1970), Henry and Gustavus Pfeiffer (two brothers who bought the Warner company in 1908), Colonel Jacob Schick (inventor of the magazine repeating razor) and Elmer H. Bobst (who took charge of the company in 1945 when sales were only $29 million).

Many products whose names once resonated in the American marketplace are no longer made by Warner-Lambert. They include Hudnut–Du Barry cosmetics, Lactona toothbrushes, Cool-Ray sunglasses, O! Henry candy bars, Good 'n Plenty licorice bits and Smith Brothers cough drops. Others are still made by the company but unadvertised: Sloan liniment, Bromo-Seltzer.

Buying and selling companies remains a Warner-Lambert specialty. In 1978 they paid $243 million to buy Entenmann's baked goods business, selling it off four years later to General Foods for $315 million. And in 1982 they paid $468 million for a medical technology company, IMED, maker of intravenous pumps, selling it off for $162 million (and a whopping loss) in 1986.

Warner-Lambert's biggest expense is advertising. In 1988, they spent $259 million on research and $880 million on advertising and promotion. They rank as the nation's 13th largest advertiser. Warner's top two executives, Chairman J. D. Williams, and President M. R. Goodes, paid themselves into the million-dollar club in 1989, with incomes of $1.8 million and $1.3 million respectively.

Stock performance. Warner-Lambert stock bought for $1,000 in 1980 sold for $8,799 on January 2, 1990.

Consumer brands.

Listerine, Listermint, Halls, Efferdent, Rolaids, Benadryl, Benylin, Caladryl, Anusol, Lubriderm, Sinutab, e.p.t., Tucks, Gelusil, Schick, Trident, Dentyne, Certs, Bubblicious, Clorets, Chiclets, Chewels, Rascals, Sugar Babies, Bubbaloo, Pom Poms, Charleston Chew!, Beeman's, Clove, Black Jack, Tetra.

Warner-Lambert Company, 201 Tabor Road, Morris Plains, NJ 07950; (201) 540-2000.

9

⌀ Schering-Plough

#1 *in asthma drugs, suntan lotions, foot care*

Employees: 21,900
Sales: $3.2 billion
Profits: $471 million
Founded: 1851 (Berlin)
1929 (New York City)
Headquarters: Madison, New Jersey

Schering-Plough unites two strains—one (Schering) German, the other (Plough) from the streets of Memphis; one specializing in drugs sold only by prescription, the other in drugstore items hawked in every available medium including TV and billboards. The result is a delicate balancing act. While one arm assaults consumers with pitches for Coppertone suncare lotion and Fiber Trim diet pills, the other arm is busy working in the laboratory on new compounds they hope will attack cancer, heart disease and AIDS. Traditionally, Schering-Plough's strength is in allergies and dermatology. In 1987 they ploughed $250 million into advertising and $250 million into research.

Schering-Plough is admired for their skill or luck at finding hot-selling drugs. In the 1960s they scored with Meticorten, a drug for arthritis sufferers. Outdistanced in that field, they then came up with the broad-spectrum antibiotic Garamycin, which carried them through the 1970s. In the 1980s they had winners in Proventil and Theo-Dur, two asthma treatments, plus—by virtue of buying Key Pharmaceuticals—the two sustained-release heart drugs, K-Dur and Nitro-Dur.

Schering-Plough chopped payroll by 4,500 in the 1980s but doubled their research budget. They also exited the cosmetics field. In 1989 they sold their European cosmetic companies (Rimmel and Chicogo) to Unilever; in 1990, Maybelline went to the investment banker Wasserstein Perella.

A tangled history accompanied Schering-Plough into the last decade of the 20th century. Schering, founded in Berlin in 1851, began selling their diphtheria antitoxin in the U.S. in 1894. They abandoned America during World War I, returning afterwards to make a laxative, Saraka, and female sex hormones in that favorite nesting place of drug companies, New Jersey. In World War II Schering's U.S. assets were seized by the Alien Property Custodian, which held them for the next 10 years while a lawyer, Francis Brown, ran the business. In 1951 Schering was sold at auction and became a publicly held company.

They became a peddler of over-the-counter goods in 1971 when they merged with Plough, Inc., of Memphis. In 1908, when he was 16, Abe Plough mixed up a batch of cottonseed oil, camphor and carbolic acid, bottled it and sold it door-to-door as Plough's Antiseptic Healing Oil. That was the start of a business whose products eventually included St. Joseph's aspirin, Di-Gel anatacid and Solarcaine sunburn lotion, in addition to Maybelline cosmetics and Coppertone. Those were the *successful* ones. Many others died. Abe Plough bought more than two dozen companies. He regularly spent 25 cents of every sales dollar on advertising. And he became so impressed with the power of advertising he bought a clutch of radio stations. When Abe Plough died in 1984, at age 92, flags in Memphis flew at half-mast.

Schering-Plough's leaders during the 1980s were Robert Luciano, a lawyer (chairman and CEO), and Richard Kogan, a financial executive (president). They were both born in the Bronx, a situation you are not likely to find at any other company profiled in this book. Their 1989 salaries weren't bad for two boys from the Bronx either. Luciano took home $2.5 million; Kogan, $1.4 million.

S*tock performance.* Schering-Plough stock bought for $1,000 in 1980 sold for $8,142 on January 2, 1990.

C*onsumer brands.*

Dr. Scholl's, Coppertone, Solarcaine, Tropical Blend, Fibre Trim, Stay Trim, Drixoral, Di-Gel, Correctol, Feen-A-Mint, Chlor-Trimeton, Coricidin, Tinactin, Afrin, A&D Ointment, St. Joseph's, Dura-Soft, Aquaflex, Ocu-Clear.

Schering-Plough Corporation, One Giralda Farms, Madison, NJ 07940; (201) 822-7000.

10
CIBA–GEIGY

#3 *in prescription drugs (world)*

Employees: 88,750 (world); 19,000 (U.S.)
Sales: $12.5 billion (worldwide)
U.S. sales: $3 billion
Profits: $905 million (worldwide)
Founded: 1758
Headquarters: Ardsley, New York

When this Swiss company introduced their arthritis drug, Voltaren, in the U.S. in 1988, they pulled out all the stops in a publicity campaign. All-time baseball great Mickey Mantle, an arthritis sufferer, showed up at a Voltaren press conference and appeared on NBC's "Today" show to bat for the drug. The Food and Drug Administration hit the ceiling. Voltaren is a prescription drug, and the FDA said Ciba-Geigy was out of line in dispensing medical advice to consumers in this direct manner. The FDA's criticism didn't hurt Voltaren, which quickly captured 11 percent of the arthritis drug market.

Criticism is not new to Ciba-Geigy, one of Switzerland's "Big Three" drug houses (Hoffmann–La Roche and Sandoz are the other two). They have been involved in one hassle after another over their marketing practices and the untoward effects of their drugs and insecticides. In Japan a medication they distributed to treat diarrhea apparently caused a degenerative neurological disease that killed 1,000 people. In Egypt they tested an insecticide, Galecron, by getting six Egyptian boys to stand barefoot in a cotton field as it was sprayed. In 1989, their epilepsy drug, Tegretol, was found to cause an unexpectedly high rate of birth defects. In 1985 the state of New Jersey hit them with a $1.4 million fine for dumping hazardous wastes at three landfills near their Toms River dyestuffs plant, which they subsequently closed.

Ciba-Geigy is the largest dyestuff producer in the U.S. and the world. They rank among the world's five largest chemical companies. They place second in the production of insecticides and pesticides. They rank third in prescription drugs. They were formed in 1970 by the merger of two large Swiss chemical companies each having

A *typical physician receives five or six calls every day from drug company sales reps.*

11

Upjohn

#1 *in baldness drugs*

Employees: 20,600
Sales: $2.9 billion
Profits: $176 million
Founded: 1886
Headquarters: Kalamazoo, Michigan

large pharmaceutical components—Geigy, founded in 1758, and Ciba, founded in 1884. Geigy invented DDT, and the Geigy scientist who headed this research, Dr. Paul Muller, received the Nobel Prize in 1948. Ciba pioneered in steroid chemistry and mind-altering drugs.

Ciba-Geigy does one-third of their business in the U.S., most of it a result of acquisitions. You'll recognize them in the drugstore as Softcolor and Vision Care contact lenses, Nupercainal ointment, Privine nasal spray, Doan's pills, Fiberall laxative, Sunkist vitamins, the diet aid Accutrim. And if your prescription is for Estraderm (a menopausal product delivered via a patch attached to the skin); Ten-K, a potassium supplement; Transderm-Nitro (another patch product, this one for the heart); or Tegretol, an antiepileptic, you're getting a Ciba-Geigy drug. They are big on sustained-release patches through their association with the California company, Alza, which invented this delivery system. When Alza was foundering in the 1970s, Ciba-Geigy rescued them with direct cash infusions.

Another American company Ciba-Geigy owns is Funk Seeds.

Ciba-Geigy, Ch-4000, Basel, Switzerland; (41) 61-361-110.

Ciba-Geigy Corp., 444 Saw Mill River Road, Ardsley, NY 10502; (914) 478-3131.

At last, there is some hope for the bald. While competitors introduced drugs to treat heart disease, AIDS and ulcers, the big news at Upjohn during the 1980s was the launching of Rogaine, a product to grow hair on bald heads. It was a bizarre turn for a company ranked as one of America's leading medicine makers for more than 100 years. Upjohn pioneered in steroid research that led to cortisone and other hormone-based drugs, introduced the first oral drug for diabetics and became a major antibiotic supplier. Upjohn's brand of ibuprofen, Motrin, rose to the top tier of the prescription drug sales chart in the 1970s. And in the 1980s Upjohn had two new prescription winners in the tranquilizer Xanax and the sedative Halcion (although in 1989 the ABC news program "20/20" reported harmful side effects from these drugs—everything from memory loss to addiction—and sales of Halcion dropped 21 percent; of Xanax, 9 percent).

Of major drug companies, none recycles more of the sales dollar into research than Upjohn—13.8 percent in 1988. But the development of Rogaine shows that once you start messing around in the laboratory, you never know what will happen. Upjohn began experimenting in 1958 with a chemical compound that seemed to have promise as an antacid. It proved to be ineffective. However, one study showed it lowered blood pressure in laboratory animals. By 1968 Upjohn scientists had isolated a chemical agent they called minoxidil, which the company prepared to market as an antihypertensive under the brand name, Loniten. In 1971 came another wrinkle. Researchers noted unusual hair growth in some patients taking minoxidil. By 1979, when the Food and Drug Administration approved the marketing of Loniten as an antihypertensive, Upjohn was already testing minoxidil as a treatment for baldness. More than 4,000 patients were treated, confirming that, applied topically, it could grow hair on some scalps, especially on the heads of younger men. In 1988 the FDA approved the drug as the only prescription drug in America effective in treating baldness in men. Upjohn brand-named it Rogaine (Regaine in most foreign markets).

Rogaine got off to a shaky start. It doesn't work for all men, it's not easy to use and it's expensive (at least $50 a month). In addition, Upjohn had the tricky problem of promoting a prescription drug for a condition that's not exactly life threatening. Upjohn anted up an ad budget of more than $20 million to advise balding men to consult their doctor about using Rogaine. Expected to be a blockbuster, Rogaine was limping along in 1989 at a sales pace of $4 million a month.

Upjohn's Asgrow Seed Company is one of the world's leading suppliers of vegetable (peas, beans and sweet corn) and agronomic (hybrid corn and sorghum, and soybeans) seeds. Upjohn sells throughout the world, doing 40 percent of their business outside the U.S.

Upjohn is the last of the big drug companies where the founding family retains a strong influence. Indeed, when Dr. Theodore Cooper succeeded Ray T. Parfet, Jr., as CEO in 1987, it marked the first time the company had not been headed by an Upjohn family member (either by direct descent or marriage). Upjohn family members hold 3 of the 14 board seats. Two sons of Ray Parfet are executive officers. When the company first sold stock to the public in 1958, Upjohn family members retained 60 percent of it. Their holdings today are estimated at 10 percent of the total. The early Upjohns tended to be doctors, and although that's not true of the new generation, physicians still play important roles here. Of six CEOs over 104 years, four have been doctors. Dr. Cooper, a surgeon, was formerly dean of Cornell's medical school. Two other physicians, Drs. Mark Novitch and William N. Hubbard, Jr., are directors. Daryl F. Grisham, head of Chicago's Parker House

Sausage Company, became Upjohn's first black director in 1988.

Along with the continuing family influence is the continuing umbilical-cord relationship with Kalamazoo, Michigan, the company birthplace. Upjohn's contributions to Kalamazoo are everywhere—parks, schools, redevelopment projects, support for social service agencies. They're the largest employer in the greater Kalamazoo area, and their 8,300 employees account for over 20 percent of worker earnings in Kalamazoo County. Upjohn's centennial gift to Kalamazoo, in 1986, was a $2 million grant for the establishment of the Kalamazoo Area Mathematics and Science Center, open to public and nonpublic high school students.

Stock performance. Upjohn stock bought for $1,000 in 1980 sold for $6,662 on January 2, 1990.

Consumer brands.

Kaopectate, Cheracol, Cortaid, Unicap, Haltran, Motrin IB. (The ibuprofen sold by Bristol-Myers under the Nuprin label is supplied by Upjohn.)

The Upjohn Company, 7000 Portage Road, Kalamazoo, MI 49001; (616) 323-4000.

12

⊕ Sterling Drug

#1 *in aspirin*

Employees: 21,000
Sales: $2.5 billion
Founded: 1901
Headquarters: New York, New York

The maker of Bayer aspirin, Phillips' Milk of Magnesia ("Mom knows best") laxative, d-Con rat poison and prescription heart medicines (Inocor and Primacor) now belongs to Eastman Kodak. The photography giant bought Sterling for $5.1 billion in 1988 to foil a takeover attempt by Swiss drug house, Hoffmann–La Roche. Kodak's goal is to have Sterling rank among the nation's 10 largest—and the world's 20 largest—pharmaceutical companies by

Ewing M. Kauffman, founder of Marion Laboratories, is co-owner of the Kansas City Royals baseball team. The company is named after Kauffman—his middle initial stands for Marion.

meeting. *Sterling News*, the company newsletter, captured the scene:

> *It was visually striking, done on three huge floating screens. The information appeared, paragraph by paragraph, on a center screen. When Harry finished discussing a paragraph, it moved to a different screen, until eventually the entire document formed a single entity, on one screen.*

> *In a conclusion accompanied by many oohs and ahs, a laser reproduced Harry's signature across the document, symbolic of an impressive personal commitment to the new Winthrop credo. The response was overwhelmingly positive. The end of Harry's presentation was accompanied by much applause and many cheers.*

Consumer brands.

Over-the-counter drugs: Bayer, Panadol, Phillips Milk of Magnesia, Stri-Dex, Neo-Synephrine, pHisoDerm, Campho-Phenique, Haley's M.O., Midol.

Household products: Lysol disinfectant, d-Con rodenticide, Love My Carpet, Beacon wax, Mop & Glo, Thompson Water Seal, Minwax and Formby treatments for wood surfaces.

Personal care: Ogilvie home permanents, Tussy deodorants, Dorothy Gray cosmetics, Chubs towlettes.

Sterling Drug, 90 Park Avenue, New York, NY 10016; (212) 907-2000.

the year 2000. To do so, they'll have to change a culture that hasn't generated many breakthrough products. Sterling's chief, John Pietruski, and his lieutenants left the company soon after the takeover.

Sterling acquired their most successful product, Bayer aspirin, as a result of Germany's defeat in World War I. The German chemical company, Bayer, invented aspirin, but during the war the Alien Property Custodian seized their U.S. assets. After the war, they were auctioned off, and Sterling was the high bidder. To this day, the U.S. and Canada are the only countries in the world where the Bayer does not have the right to sell, under their own name, the product they invented.

In 1989, a year after Kodak acquired them, Sterling's prescription drug arm, Winthrop Pharmaceuticals, adopted a credo emphasizing ethical conduct. Harry Shoff, Winthrop's president, said it resulted from his sense that "something was missing in his organization," and he soon realized the missing ingredient was "an articulated value system." Shoff unveiled the credo at a Winthrop national sales

13

MARION LABORATORIES, INC.

Employees: 4,000
Sales: $2.3 billion
Founded: 1950
Headquarters: Kansas City, Missouri

Workplace

One of the best places to have worked in 1989 was Marion Labs. Nearly one-tenth of their work force became instant millionaires when they were taken under the wing of Dow Chemical. Most of the rest of the staff did well, too, as the average Marion worker's stock in the company was worth three-quarters of a million dollars.

Before Dow came along, Marion Labs had prospered by a business strategy that involved the marketing of drugs others developed and a humanistic philosophy that valued employees. The strategy and philosophy were the ideas of Ewing M. Kauffman, who founded the company in 1950, and gave the firm his middle name. His first product was a calcium supplement made from crushed oyster shells.

Most pharmaceutical companies are proud of their research laboratories, which they regard as the key to finding new drugs. Prior to the 1980s, Marion spent little or nothing on original research, reformulating compounds already discovered and then doing a good job of selling their merits to doctors. Their first consumer product, introduced in 1978, was the heartburn remedy, Gaviscon.

Marion Labs hit the jackpot in the 1980s with two drugs licensed from a Japanese company, Tanabe Seiyaku. One was Cardizem, a heart drug that prevents calcium deposits from clogging arteries. The other was Carafate, an antiulcer drug. Both were sensational sellers, and Marion quintupled sales. During the late 1980s doctors were writing more than 1 million prescriptions for Cardizem every month. In 1989 Cardizem accounted for 59 percent and Carafate 22 percent of Marion's $930 million in sales.

Success of this kind does not go unnoticed. In 1989, Dow Chemical, struggling to build up a pharmaceutical business of their own, descended on Kansas City with an offer that could not be refused. Dow merged their pharmaceutical division, Merrell Dow, into Marion to create a new company, Marion Merrell Dow, in which Dow Chemical holds two-thirds of the stock. In return, Dow showered Marion shareholders with payments that may, by 1992, exceed $5 billion.

Unlike many takeovers, this deal was one in which Marion's 3,400 associates (they were never called employees) shared in the spoils according to the Kauffman doctrine: "Those who produce shall share in the results." Every associate at Marion was a stockholder, either through the profit-sharing plan or through exercising stock options available to *everyone* who worked there—not just to the top executives, as is the case at Dow and nearly all other companies. Not only that, the employee profit-sharing plan, at the time of the Dow offer, held about 7 million shares or 5 percent of the company. The Dow offer increased the value of those shares to $250 million or $735,000 per associate (of course, individual accounts varied). About 300 of the 3,600 associates saw their accounts jump over the $1 million mark as a result of the merger. Anyone with the firm more than 20 years stood to gain at least $500,000. Kauffman, who owned one-quarter of Marion Labs, came out of the deal a billionaire, worth an estimated $1.3 billion. One of his interests is baseball; he owns 50 percent of the Kansas City Royals.

Marion Merrell Dow entered the 1990s with sales of $2.3 billion. Among the prescription drugs Merrell contributed to the new company were Seldane, a potent antihistamine, and Lorelco, a cholesterol-lowering drug. They also make Nicorette, a drug to help smokers kick the habit.

Stock performance. Marion Merrell Dow stock bought for $1,000 in 1980 sold for $48,535 on January 2, 1990.

Consumer brands.

Nicorette, Gaviscon, Debrox, Gly-Oxide, Citrucel, Cepacol.

Marion Merrell Dow, Inc., 9221 Ward Parkway, Kansas City, MO 64114; (816) 363-4900.

14

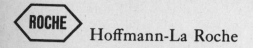 Hoffmann-La Roche

Employees: 50,200 (17,800 in U.S.)
Sales: $6 billion (world),
$2.2 billion (U.S.)
Profits: $520 million (Worldwide),
Founded: 1896
Headquarters: Basel, Switzerland
U.S. Headquarters: Nutley, New Jersey

Although they're Swiss, Roche—the name this company goes by—has a mighty position in the American market. They do one-third of their business in the U.S., employ 7,000 more people in the U.S. than New Jersey neighbor Warner-Lambert; and in 1990 they moved to enlarge their presence by agreeing to pay $2.1 billion for 60 percent of Genentech, the leading biotechnology firm. Two of the most successful drugs ever marketed, the tranquilizers Librium and Valium, were invented in Roche's laboratories at Nutley, New Jersey. They are the world's foremost producers of vitamins. No matter which brand of vitamins you buy, Roche probably supplied them in bulk. The same goes for the vitamins in your breakfast cereal.

Roche is a familiar name to American doctors. Their sales force calls on doctors regularly with news about Roche's 50 prescription drugs, including ulcer remedy Zantac and acne treatment Accutane. Glaxo, the British drug company, developed Zantac and turned the U.S. marketing over to Roche—with sensational results (SmithKline's Tagamet was clobbered). When marketing Accutane in 1982 they warned doctors the drug should not be taken by pregnant women because of the possibility of birth defects. Nevertheless, 73 cases of birth defects associated with the use of Accutane were reported—and Roche was sued in a number of courts across the country. One Mississippi woman was awarded $1 million in 1989 (Roche is appealing this verdict), but most of the suits have either been dismissed or won by the company.

Doctors also know Roche for their network of clinical laboratories that test blood and urine samples. Roche's is the second largest lab network in the nation (SmithKline has the largest). Roche also does AIDS and substance-abuse testing. And if you're involved in a paternity suit, the chances are good a Roche lab will do the tests. They run the world's largest such service.

Until recently it was very difficult for anyone to buy stock in the parent company. The shares, listed only in Switzerland, traded at the rich price of $100,000 per share. So-called baby shares, one-tenth of a regular share, were created and they traded at $10,000 a share. However, in 1989 Roche split the shares 55-to-1, and it soon became possible to buy a share for a measly $2,500. Of course these are not voting shares. Those are mostly still held by the founding Hoffmann family and their in-laws, the Sachers.

Roche has a child-care center for their employees at the gates of their plant in Nutley. They were one of the first companies in America to have one.

F. Hoffmann–La Roche & Co., CH-4002, Basel, Switzerland (Roche has a government post office on the premises); 41-61-271-1122.

Hoffmann–La Roche Inc., 340 Kingsland Street, Nutley, NY 07110; (201) 235-5000.

15

#1 *in nonprescription drugs*
Sales: $1.5 billion
Founded: 1837
Headquarters: Cincinnati, Ohio
(See also Procter & Gamble profile,
page 133.)

Procter & Gamble entered the drug field during the 1980s—and by mid-decade were claiming first place in the sales of over-the-counter remedies (products that can be bought without a prescription). It took P&G three bites and nearly $2 billion to reach this position. First, in 1982, they bought Norwich Eaton, a pharmaceutical house being divorced from Morton Salt. Their two mainstays were Pepto-Bismol and Chloraseptic (lozenges and spray for sore throats). In 1985, P&G made two more acquisitions: G. D. Searle's over-the-counter drugs (Metamucil, Dramamine and Icy Hot), and Richardson-Vicks, whose lineup included cold remedies sold under the Vicks name (Nyquil, Formula 44, VapoRub, Sinex) and the world's top selling acne fighter, Clearasil. P&G even has a small prescription drug component whose products include Peridex mouthwash for gum disease and Didronel for osteoporosis. Also, P&G is either lucky or prescient. Metamucil was the leading bulk fiber laxative when P&G acquired it. But new medical studies are now showing the fiber used in Metamucil, psyllium, also results in "significant" reductions in cholesterol.

Consumer brands.

Vicks, VapoRub, Sinex, Formula 44, Nyquil, Chloraseptic, Norwich, Dramamine, Icy Hot, Metamucil, Pepto-Bismol, Percogesic, Clearasil, Fixodent, Fasteeeth.

Procter & Gamble, 391 East 6th Street, Cincinnati, OH 45201; (513) 562-1100.

16

Employees: 10,000
Sales: $1.3 billion
Profits: $303 million
Founded: 1944
Headquarters: Palo Alto, California

Here's a company that owes their existence to the birth control pill, even though in recent years they have relied primarily on an arthritis drug.

The pill was the brainchild of a motley group of chemists toiling in the unlikely locale of Mexico City. It all began in 1944, with an astonishing discovery by Russell E. Marker, a chemist from Penn State.

Using the black, lumpy root of vines growing wild in Mexican jungles, Marker isolated a chemical that could be converted into the female hormone, progesterone. He packed 4½ pounds of it (market value at that time: $160,000) into two jars, wrapped them in newspaper and brought them to two European scientists at the Laboratorios Hormona in Mexico City. The three men promptly founded a company, Syntex, to produce the hormone. The name came from combining the "synt" in chemical synthesis and the "ex" from Mexico.

For years Syntex scientists (refugees from Hungary, Germany and Austria) synthesized human hormones and sold them in bulk to American and European pharmaceutical companies. In 1956 Syntex obtained a valuable patent for a progesterone compound that became the active ingredient in the first birth control pills. Although Chicago's G. D. Searle beat Syntex to the market in 1960 with an oral contraceptive called Enovid, Syntex licensed their idea to Johnson & Johnson, which then marketed the Ortho-Novum birth control pill. In 1964, Syntex finally began selling their own pill, Norinyl. By 1966, over 5 million American women were using oral contraceptives. On Wall Street, Syntex's stock became a shooting star. A share bought for $11 in 1962 cost $190 in 1964. In 1969 over half of all Syntex's revenues came from its oral contraceptives.

The dark side of Syntex's dependence on The Pill came in the early 1970s, when many women shunned oral contraceptives after widespread reports of adverse side effects. But Syntex was saved from extinction by another megahit—the 1976 introduction of the arthritis drug Naprosyn. The drug lifted Syntex over the $1 billion sales mark, making them the first major drug player west of the Mississippi.

By the late 1980s, over half of Syntex's sales and profits were coming from Naprosyn and Anaprox, a similar compound. Because the patent on Naprosyn runs out in 1993, some observers believe Syntex is headed for a replay of earlier woes—being too dependent on one drug. So the company has been busily churning out other products—like Cardene, an antihypertensive, and Cytovene, an antiviral agent. In addition to medicines for humans, Syntex makes animal health products and diagnostic systems.

They have a convoluted corporate history. Three famous scientists—George Rosenkranz, a Hungarian-born chemist, Carl Djerassi, a Vienese-born chemist, and Alejandro Zaffaroni, a Uruguayan-born biochemist—played key roles. Rosenkranz remained at the helm of the company in Mexico City for many years while Djerassi and Zaffaroni established the Syntex laboratories (and later operating headquarters) in Palo Alto, California, near Stanford University. However, the legal headquarters of Syntex is Panama City because that's where the company was incorporated in 1958 after the Wall Street investment banker Charles Allen gained control. Djerassi and Zaffaroni later left Syntex to found two other drug companies, Zoecon and Alza.

Syntex has a reputation as a pleasant place to work. Women make up about half the work force, and Syntex offers a near-site child-care center. At the Palo Alto facility, research takes place amidst gorgeous paintings, sculpture and tapestries. The location has become famous for an art gallery and extensive art collection (about 200 pieces, scattered throughout the Palo Alto grounds—including a sculpture of a seated woman by Henry Moore), valued at over $1 million.

Albert Bowers, an English chemist, became CEO in 1981, and Paul E. Freiman succeeded him in 1989. Freiman, with a degree in pharmacy from Fordham University, joined Syntex in 1962 as a medical representative. Syntex treats their head honchos royally. The year before Bowers retired, he was the 13th-highest-paid CEO in the nation, with $7.8 million, and another $2 million for his last year. It should be noted, however, that in 1989 Syntex also had seven women making more than $100,000 a year and 296 making over $50,000. The biggest shareowner is still Allen & Co., which held 6 percent of the stock in 1990.

S*tock performance.* Syntex stock bought for $1,000 in 1980 sold for $12,670 on January 2, 1990.

Syntex Corporation, 3401 Hillview Avenue, Palo Alto, CA 94304; (415) 885-5050.

17

Genentech, Inc.

#1 *in biotechnology*

Employees: 1,800
Sales: $383 million
Profits: $44 million
Founded: 1976
Headquarters: South San Francisco, California

Founded in 1976 by a venture capitalist, Robert A. Swanson, and a microbiologist, Herbert W. Boyer, Genentech emerged in the 1980s as the leader of the infant biotechnology industry, developing drugs by gene-splicing or recombinant DNA technology. They sold their initial products to other companies—human insulin to Eli Lilly and alpha interferon to the Swiss company Hoffmann–La Roche. In 1990 Genentech agreed to be bought out by Hoffmann-La Roche.

The first product Genentech sold on their own was Protropin, a human growth hormone that prevents dwarfism. Introduced in 1985, Protropin rang up sales 1988 of $111 million. A drug of much greater potential, Activase, made a much-heralded debut in late 1987 when the FDA approved it. About 80 percent of heart attacks are caused by clots that shut off blood flow to the heart. Activase is a clot dissolver known as a TPA drug, a gene-spliced version of the human body's tissue plasminogen activator. Given within five hours after the onset of a heart attack, it dissolves clots and saves lives. In its first year, Activase had sales of $188 million, and Genentech claimed it was "now established as a basic treatment for heart attack." But a subsequent study found Activase, at $2,200 a dose, was no more effective than another drug, streptokinase, at $200 a dose. Activase sales in 1988 were $151 million, $100 million less than Genentech had confidently predicted. When the FDA okay for Activase came through, Swanson (who continues as chairman of the board and CEO) awarded options on 100 shares of Genentech stock to all 1,700 employees.

At the start of the 1990s Genentech had in their research pipeline new formulations that could be effective against AIDS and various cancers. Genentech believes they're the wave of the future. They predict that by the century's end "most new pharmaceuticals will be touched in their development by biotechnology." Competitors have, of course, surfaced. Some 200 companies are now engaged in biotechnology, four-fifths of them started since 1980.

In 1989, Genentech built a $1 million on-site day-care center at their South San Francisco headquarters. Called the "Cadillac of child-care centers" (the company claims it's the largest corporate day-care center of its kind in the nation), the center can be used by 258 children, has 13 classrooms, 60 teachers and 4 administrators. Genentech subsidizes 50 percent of the costs of the center.

Stock performance. Genentech stock bought for $1,000 in 1980 sold for $2,427 on January 2, 1990.

Genentech, Inc., 460 Point San Bruno Boulevard, South San Francisco, CA 94080; (415) 266-1000.

HEALTHCARE

By almost any measure this industry is America's biggest. According to the Health Care Financing Administration, national expenditures on health care soared over the $500 billion mark in 1988. That's equivalent to $2,000 for every man, woman and child in the country. To put it in perspective, note that such expenditures were about $75 billion in 1970.

Companies such as Abbott Laboratories and Johnson & Johnson have been selling products to hospitals and doctors for over 100 years—and they're still doing well. But they represent only a small fraction of the health-care industry, composed mostly of small firms, private doctors and hospitals. The biggest component is, of course, hospital care. Nearly 40 percent of the money is spent there.

1
Baxter

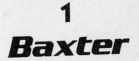

#1 *in supply of products to hospitals, intravenous solutions, kidney dialysis machines*

Employees: 64,000
Sales: $7.4 billion
Profits: $446 million
Founded: 1931
Headquarters: Deerfield, Illinois

It's not enough to be the top supplier of products to hospitals. Baxter wants people to know their name. This colossus of the health care industry was created in 1985 when Baxter Travenol Laboratories acquired a bigger Chicago-area neighbor, American Hospital Supply Corp. Four years later, in a plaintive appeal for attention, Baxter took big ad space in the *Wall Street Journal* declaring: "We're I.V. solutions. Diagnostic products. And critical-care devices. We're in the operating room. The emergency room. The hospital pharmacy. In fact, we provide 65 percent of everything a hospital needs."

Most people haven't heard of Baxter because they sell nothing directly to those who eventually use, or benefit from, their products: patients. Of course the next

Baxter's 1985 acquisition of American Hospital Supply created a unique situation for employees of NDM Corp., a Dayton, Ohio, maker of electrodes used in heart monitoring. NDM was acquired by AHS on the morning of November 25, 1985. Two hours later the Baxter-AHS marriage became official. So the 320 Dayton employees—plus 12 in Puerto Rico—worked for three different companies on the same day.

time you're wheeled into an operating room, you might notice Baxter supplied the surgical instruments and the trays they rest on, the gloves the nurses wore, even the surgeon's gown. And when you're wheeled out, you might look up and see the plastic bag of intravenous solution being injected into your veins via a catheter—Baxter probably supplied all of that too. And when you're well enough to sit up and eat macaroni-and-cheese, that too may have been provided by Baxter.

By their own count, Baxter has an arsenal of more than 120,000 health care products. Many of these—intravenous solutions, kidney dialysis machines, blood collection equipment—are made by Baxter at more than 40 U.S. plants (and another 40 in 22 other countries). Other products are made by some 800 companies whose products Baxter distributes from 79 U.S. warehouses. About 70 percent of Baxter's sales come from their own products. More than half of sales come from hospitals, the rest from physicians, pharmacists, nursing homes, clinics, patients being cared for at home. In addition to hardware, Baxter develops management programs to help their customers (hospitals) get a better handle on running their businesses.

History. The two companies united in a shotgun marriage in 1985 spent a good part of their earlier lives scrapping with one another. Both were Chicago companies whose origins go back to the 1920s.

American Hospital Supply was founded in 1922 by five men who saw a

business opportunity in the improvement of service to hospitals. The key founder was Foster G. McGaw, who began selling surgical instruments the day after he graduated from high school. Under his direction AHS developed a sales force catering to the special needs of hospitals. McGaw, son of a Presbyterian minister, used to say: "From the beginning I was careful about the type of salesman I hired. If he wasn't the type of person I wanted in my house as a guest, he was out."

In 1928, Dr. Donald Baxter, a Chicago physician, developed the Vacoliter, an intravenous solution packed in a glass container. Up to then, hospitals had prepared their own I.V. solutions, but they were of uneven quality and not always reliable. In 1931, Baxter joined with surgeon Ralph Falk to form a new company to make Vacoliters. A year later Foster McGaw signed them up as a client of AHS.

They were good for each other during those dark days of the depression. AHS gave Baxter an entree to hospitals. And the Vacoliter was a tonic to AHS, accounting by 1940 for one-half of their $1.2 million in sales.

However, there was plenty of friction along the way, inspired partially by a convoluted financial structure that saw one company, Don Baxter Inc., responsible for sales in 11 western states whereas another company, Baxter Labs, had the rights to sell the I.V. solutions in 37 eastern states. AHS, as distributor, was somewhere in the middle—and everyone was jealous of everyone else. Lawsuits were filed, and AHS, after acquiring Don Baxter Inc., made an unsuccessful stab at merging with Baxter Labs. Meanwhile, another Chicago-area company, Abbott Laboratories, took advantage of the infighting to take over first place in sales of intravenous solutions.

The love-hate relationship between AHS and Baxter Labs ended in 1964. Baxter began distributing through their own sales force. And AHS began making their own I.V. solutions.

With that record of hostility, it's no wonder the two Chicago neighbors—Baxter in the western suburb of Deerfield, AHS in the northern suburb of Evanston—came to blows again 21 years later. By this time, under the forceful command of Karl Bays, Appalachian-born son of a railroad engineer, ex–Marine Corps officer and holder of an MBA from Indiana University, AHS was logging annual sales of $3.5 billion—about twice the size of Baxter Travenol, whose CEO was another ex–Marine Corps officer, Vernon L. Loucks, Jr., son of a well-to-do Chicago lawyer, Yale graduate and holder of an MBA from Harvard. Loucks was a protege of William Graham, the University of Chicago–educated lawyer who turned Baxter into a billion-dollar company after World War II.

Karl Bays had a plan in 1985. He wanted to fold AHS into Hospital Corp. of America, the nation's largest operator of hospitals. He thought it would be a great fit. Vernon Loucks thought otherwise. Uninvited, he submitted a $3.8 billion bid for AHS, clearly a better offer than HCA's. Bays resisted, describing Baxter as a company that had performed poorly, until his board forced him to accept Loucks' offer. There was no question as to who was acquiring whom. AHS headquarters in Evanston was sold and before long nearly all the top executives of AHS, including Bays, had left.

Foster McGaw, who retired as AHS chairman in 1980, lived to see it all. He died on April 16, 1986, five months after the acquisition of the company he had founded. He was 89.

Baxter's aggressive moves in the 1980s vaulted them from sales of $1.3 billion to $7.4 billion at the decade's end. It was quite a bit to digest—and in early 1990 they began to regurgitate some of it. Loucks announced Baxter would sell or close 21 plants, lay off 6,400 workers and dispose of businesses whose sales totaled $140 million. Baxter had to slim down, he explained, so that they could help their "customers meet their objective of providing high-quality health care while controlling costs."

Owners and rulers. Vernon Loucks, 55 in 1989, took over as CEO in 1980, succeeding William Graham, who, at age 78, was still on the board in 1990. Loucks was paid a hefty $2.4 million in 1989. Loucks played wide receiver on Yale's football team, and one of his first picks for the board was Clinton Frank, former adman and all-time Yale football great. After Frank left the board, the late A. Bartlett Giamatti, former Yale president and then a commissioner of major league baseball,

joined the board. About half of Baxter's stock is owned by 350 institutions—banks, insurance companies and pension funds. Of the 88,000 individual shareholders, about 5,800 are Baxter employees. The biggest of these holdings: 3 million shares worth about $60 million held by Ralph Falk II, son of the surgeon who cofounded the company. Falk's holdings represented 1.3 percent of all the shares.

As a place to work. Merging two different cultures was rough, but Baxter has carried it off with a minimum of disruption and pain. Baxter employees have access to good benefits, including profit sharing, subsidized child care and flexible work schedules. Baxter also maintains a strong affirmative action program. In 1988, one out of three officials and managers was a woman, and minorities held 9.1 percent of those positions. Michele J. Hooper, a black who joined Baxter in 1976 after getting her MBA from the University of Chicago Business School, was promoted seven times in her first eight years at the company. In 1989 she was president of Baxter's Canadian subsidiary.

Social responsibility. Given the products they make, it's easy for Baxter to get into trouble. But the company has an excellent product safety and reliability record. In mid-1990, Baxter was accused of violating the U.S. antiboycott law. Baxter had a factory in Israel, where they produced intravenous fluids; as a result of this Israeli presence, the Arab League blacklisted them. In 1989, Baxter quietly sold the Israel plant and agreed to a joint venture with the Syrian government to build an intravenous fluids plant in Syria. Baxter was suddenly off the Arab blacklist, but then pro-Israeli groups were questioning whether Baxter had cooperated with the Arab blacklist—and hence violated American law. The Baxter Foundation gave away $3 million in 1988, and Baxter has announced that by 1993 they will increase their charitable giving to 2 percent of pretax profits, putting them into the upper echelon of corporate givers.

Global presence. Twenty-two percent of sales are outside the U.S. Baxter is the largest single supplier to Britain's National Health Service.

THE JURY OF BABIES
Does Declare
JOHNSON'S BABY POWDER
THE BEST FOR THE TOILET

One of Johnson & Johnson's ads that appeared repeatedly in the major home magazines just after World War I.

S*tock performance.* Baxter International stock bought for $1,000 in 1980 sold for $2,543 on January 2, 1990.

Baxter International, 1 Baxter Parkway, Deerfield, IL 60015; (312) 948-2000.

2

Johnson & Johnson

#1 *in painkillers, feminine sanitary napkins, adhesive bandages, baby-care products*

#3 *in suncare, tampons*

Employees: 82,200
Sales: $9.7 billion
Profits: $1.1 billion
Founded: 1886
Headquarters: New Brunswick, New Jersey

Workplace

There's something almost too good to be true about Johnson & Johnson. They make products associated with healing (Tylenol, Band-Aids, surgical dressings) and softness (Johnson & Johnson baby powder and shampoo). Their sales and profits go up year after year. They have a credo that ranks their responsibilities—customers first, employees next, shareholders last. They give employment to more people than anyone else in the health care business. They're loyal to their hometown. Their products sell in every corner of the world. They're always among the most admired companies in America, no matter who is doing the admiring—from Wall Street analysts to social responsibility gadflies.

So what's the catch? Maybe there isn't any. J&J is simply a superb example of a type of American management that knows how to handle change and diversity. And they do it through a highly decentralized operation. Johnson & Johnson is not so much one company as a collection of 171 companies in 54 countries bound together by a thread of common values and goals. Most of their companies have their own board of directors.

J&J's mettle was tested in the 1980s. In 1982 a madman decided to use their number one product, Tylenol, as a vehicle for mass murder. Capsules laced with cyanide killed eight people in the Chicago area. Johnson & Johnson's chairman, James Burke, acted quickly and decisively. Every package of Tylenol capsules—31 million—was recalled from the marketplace and destroyed. Four years later the nightmare recurred when another person, this time in upstate New York, died from a cyanide-laced Tylenol capsule. Once again J&J withdrew all the capsules. Only this time they went one step further. They banned the use of capsules in the packaging of any of their products because they were so easy to tamper with. Three years later they came out with Tylenol packaged in gelcap—called a caplet, it looks like a capsule but it isn't. It's a one-piece, solid package with a smooth gelatin covering.

H*istory.* In the 1870s, British surgeon Sir Joseph Lister identified the principal cause of infection in hospitals: airborne germs. Lister recommended that all operating rooms, patients and medical staff be frequently sprayed with a fine mist of carbolic acid. His sterilization methods were too complex and cumbersome for most American hospitals.

Robert Wood Johnson thought he had a better idea. In 1885, nine years after hearing one of Lister's speeches, Johnson formed a partnership with his two brothers, James Wood and Edward Mead Johnson. In a former wallpaper factory in New Brunswick, New Jersey, the brothers began making individually wrapped, antiseptic surgical dressings—an absorbent cotton-and-gauze dressing that could be mass-produced and shipped in quantity to big-city hospitals or to doctors in Podunk. During the 1890s Johnson & Johnson began to experiment with dry heat and steam to make a bandage that was not only antiseptic but also sterile. They slowly evolved a process of repeated sterilization during production, and by

1897 they were using the new technique on catgut sutures. (That same year Edward Mead Johnson left to form his own company, Mead Johnson, now a subsidiary of Bristol-Myers Squibb).

Demand for the sterile bandages increased dramatically in the early 20th century. In 1910 James Wood Johnson succeeded his brother as president, and the company branched out into other products, the most famous being the Band-Aid, an easy-to-apply adhesive bandage for consumer use developed in 1920. A newlywed J&J employee, Earl Dickson, invented the bandage after his wife kept burning and cutting herself. The product soon became standard issue in first-aid kits.

In 1932, Robert Wood Johnson (son of the founder) took over the company. Later known as the General because of his World War II career as a brigadier general, Johnson established policies that persist

The J&J Credo

We believe our first responsibility is to the doctors, nurses and patients, to mothers and fathers and all others who use our products and services. In meeting their needs everything we do must be of high quality. We must constantly strive to reduce our costs in order to maintain reasonable prices. Customers' orders must be serviced promptly and accurately. Our suppliers and distributors must have an opportunity to make a fair profit.

We are responsible to our employees, the men and women who work with us throughout the world. Everyone must be considered as an individual. We must respect their dignity and recognize their merit. They must have a sense of security in their jobs. Compensation must be fair and adequate, and working conditions clean, orderly and safe. We must be mindful of ways to help our employees fulfill their family responsibilities. Employees must feel free to make suggestions and complaints. There must be equal opportunity for employment, development and advancement for those qualified. We must provide competent management, and their actions must be just and ethical.

We are responsible to the communities in which we live and work and to the world community as well. We must be good citizens—support good works and charities and bear our fair share of taxes. We must encourage civic improvements and better health and education. We must maintain in good order the property we are privileged to use, protecting the environment and natural resources.

Our final responsibility is to our stockholders. Business must make a sound profit. We must experiment with new ideas. Research must be carried on, innovative programs developed and mistakes paid for. New equipment must be purchased, new facilities provided and new products launched. Reserves must be created to provide for adverse times. When we operate according to these principles, the stockholders should realize a fair return. ∎

at the company today. Because he favored political involvement, some Johnson & Johnson executives took leaves of absence and went into state and local politics. Because he often said, "Make your top managers rich and they will make you richer," many J&J officers have retired as millionaires. And, because he believed in decentralization, J&J began buying companies and setting them up under autonomous bosses.

People have a hard time classifying today's Johnson & Johnson in the usual business categories. They're a consumer products company, with 40 percent of sales derived from products like Tylenol, Stayfree pantyliners, Band-Aids, Reach toothbrushes and Johnson's baby products (which adults also use). They are big in pharmaceuticals—birth control pills, the antianemia drug Eprex, the acne treatment Retin-A, the leading antidiarrheal prescription drug Imodium. And they have a huge professional division selling items like surgical dressings, sutures, medical instruments and even gowns to hospitals and doctors. Walk around a hospital—and J&J is everywhere. They are also a heavy in the world of advertising, ranking 20th in the land in 1988 with an expenditure of $468 million. You know them from their most heavily advertised product, Tylenol, but they are also the force behind those strident "Step up to the Mike" TV pitches for Micatin, an athlete's foot remedy. In 1989, in a match seemingly made in heaven, J&J joined with Merck to form a company that will bring to the marketplace drugs adapted from previous winners in the prescription field. The merger united J&J's promotional artifice with the laboratories of the world's top prescription drug producer. Watch your pharmacy, and TV screen, for further developments.

J&J is tremendously successful at almost everything they do. But they don't always win. In 1979 they paid $74 million for a nearly bankrupt company called Technicare, which manufactured a barrage of electronic and computer devices used in diagnosing diseases. But the products were criticized as too sophisticated for radiologists to use, and in the next five years, Technicare lost $110 million. J&J sold it at a huge loss in 1986. They also tried, and failed miserably, to gain a foothold in disposable diapers.

Owners and rulers. It's not easy to fill the shoes of someone the *New York Times* once called a "legend" because of his handling of the Tylenol disaster. But that was precisely the task Ralph Larsen took on when he replaced retiring James Burke as J&J's CEO in 1989 at age 50 (Burke's brother is now president and CEO of Capital Cities/ABC). A Brooklyn-born son of a Norwegian immigrant, Larsen joined J&J straight out of college. He made his mark by helping turn Tylenol into a megahit but was upset when Burke didn't reward him with a big promotion. So Larsen quit and worked for rival Becton-Dickinson for two years before Burke lured him back to J&J in 1983. J&J has a high-powered board of directors, including a former chairman of Exxon, as well as GM's Roger Smith and Capital Cities/ABC's Thomas Murphy. Two women also have seats on the board—Joan Ganz Cooney, head of the company that produces "Sesame Street," and Ann Dibble Cook, social service director at the University of Chicago's Lying-In Hospital. The biggest stockholder is the Robert Wood Johnson Foundation, with 8.4 percent of the stock.

As a place to work. General Johnson was a pioneer in providing good wages, shorter work days and clean factories. The company's humanist philosophy, "Our Credo," was recently updated in response to the concerns of working parents. J&J added the line: "We must be mindful of ways to help our employees fulfill their family responsibilities," and backed it up with a galaxy of new benefits—including an on-site child-care center at the New Brunswick headquarters, unpaid personal leave up to one year, pretax salary set-aside for dependent care and support for alternative work options.

Social responsibility. When General Johnson died in 1968, he left the bulk of his estate, $1.2 billion, to the Robert Wood Johnson Foundation, making it the second largest foundation in the country and the largest one devoted to health care.

Global presence. Half of sales—and more than half of profits—are derived outside the U.S. Of 82,000 employees, 48,000 work overseas. One of their prime drug companies is Belgium's Janssen Pharmaceutica.

Stock performance. Johnson & Johnson stock bought for $1,000 in 1980 sold for $5,776 on January 2, 1990.

Consumer brands.

Dental care: Reach toothbrush, Prevent toothbrush, ACT fluoride rinse.

Health care: Band-Aid, Red Cross, Steri-Pad, Tylenol, Sine-Aid, Medipren, Sundown sunblock, Piz Buin sunblock, Micatin athlete's foot remedy.

Personal care: Johnson & Johnson baby shampoo, oil and powder, Stayfree pads, Sure and Natural, o.b. tampons, Modess, Carefree, Serenity guards, Assure!, Silhouettes, Shower to Shower powder.

Contraceptives: Gynol II, Delfen foam.

Pregnancy test: Fact Plus.

Johnson & Johnson, One Johnson & Johnson Plaza, New Brunswick, NJ 08903; (201) 524-0400.

3

⊐ABBOTT

#1 *in medical diagnostic equipment, infant formulas*

Employees: 39,800
Sales: $5.4 billion
Profits: $860 million
Founded: 1888
Headquarters: Abbott Park, Illinois

Crucial to the practice of modern medicine today is the blood test—and Abbott Labs has emerged as the leading maker of diagnostic equipment to analyze blood samples. That's quite a comeback for a company that was flattened in the early 1970s because of shipments of contaminated intravenous solutions.

Increasingly, blood is being analyzed to detect all kinds of substances, legal and illegal, and Abbott rides high on the trend. They developed the first diagnostic tests for AIDS and hepatitis. Their Vision desktop blood analyzer can deliver results for routine blood tests in eight minutes—and it

screens for 24 different conditions representing 90 percent of the blood chemistry tests that a physician typically needs.

It's good they developed this $1 billion sideline because in their original business, pharmaceuticals, Abbott has dropped far back in the pack, ranking somewhere between 10th and 20th among U.S. drug producers. They remain the leading producer of the antibiotic, erythromycin, which they introduced in 1952, and their other prescription drugs include the clot-buster, Abokinase, and the anticonvulsant Depakote. And still in their medical bag is the 55-year-old anesthetic, sodium pentothal (the drug famous for making criminals talk). Abbott also makes a wide range of nutritional products, and their two infant formulas, Similac and Isomil, hold 50 percent of that market. Abbott does 35 per cent of their sales outside the U.S. and has a working partnership with Japan's largest drug producer, Takeda.

Based 40 miles north of Chicago's Loop, not far from where they were founded in 1888, Abbott almost went down for the count in the 1970s. They had developed a $50 million product, the artificial sweetener Sucaryl, which had to be pulled from the market after the FDA banned all cyclamates as possible cancer-causing agents. Abbott is still trying to get this ban rescinded. Much more serious was the 1971 recall of 3.4 million bottles of intravenous solutions after the discovery that some were not properly sealed. The solutions were blamed for the deaths of nine persons. Abbott eventually pleaded no contest to a conspiracy charge, paying a fine of $1,000. The incident cost Abbott their leadership in the intravenous market (they have never regained it), not to speak of the dent it put in their image as a health care provider.

If the 1970s were the nadir for Abbott, the 1980s were a renaissance as the company turned their high-tech hospital and laboratory products into a $2.3 billion business, accounting for nearly half of total sales. Abbott nearly tripled sales and quadrupled profits during the 1980s, rising from 197th on the *Fortune* 500 to 90th.

Credit for this comeback went to Robert A. Schoellhorn, the latest in a long line of aggressive, domineering CEOs who have led Abbott into battle, beginning with Dr. Wallace Calvin Abbott, a physician who had more fun peddling drugs than treating patients. A chemist, Schoellhorn arrived at Abbott in 1973 after 26 years with American Cyanamid. He became CEO in 1979, at which time he told an interviewer, "My hobbies are mainly my business." His reign has been marked by the departures of his seconds-in-command. James L. Vincent quit as president in 1981; he became chairman of Biogen Inc. in Cambridge. Kirk Raab quit as president in 1985; he became president of Genentech in South San Francisco. In the summer of 1989 Jack W. Schuler quit as president, citing "differences in philosophy" with Schoellhorn.

Schoellhorn then had the tables turned on himself. Upset with his ouster of Schuler and apparent inability to line up a successor, Abbott's board of directors fired Schoellhorn in December 1989. Then, in a highly unusual action, Schoellhorn sued the company for wrongful dismissal, asking the court to reinstate him. That suit unleashed a vigorous counterattack by Abbott, one that included charges of fraudulent conduct by their former chairman during much of the 1980s. The company said Schoellhorn had "repeatedly misappropriated Abbott corporate assets [like the company jet] for his personal use" and "submitted false expense reports." Abbott also let it be known that within days of his dismissal, Schoellhorn had exercised 253,022 stock options giving him an instant profit of $9.3 million. Schoellhorn said he had been the victim of an "ambush" by outside board members. Among the outsiders sitting on the Abbott board were the heads of Borg-Warner, Communications Satellite Corporation, Humana hospital chain, Household International (HFC finance), Quaker Oats, Ameritech and the Baylor University Medical Center.

Schoellhorn was replaced by vice chairman, Duane L. Burnham, who earned $1.3 million in the number two post in 1989.

Stock performance. Abbott Labs stock bought for $1,000 in 1980 sold for $8,327 on January 2, 1990.

Consumer brands.
Nutritional foods: Similac, Isomil, Pedialyte, Ensure.

Personal care: Clear Eyes, Murine eye care products, Selsun Blue shampoo, Tronolane hemorrhoidal treatments, Faultless rubber sundries.

Abbott Laboratories, One Abbott Park Road, Abbott Park, IL 60064; (312) 937-6100.

4

 HCA Hospital Corporation of America

#1 *in hospitals*

Employees: 45,000
Sales: $ 4.1 billion
Founded: 1968
Headquarters: Nashville, Tennessee

They thought health care could be packaged, delivered and sold the way McDonald's sells hamburgers. So in 1968 three Nashville entrepreneurs—Thomas Frist, Sr., a successful heart surgeon, his son, Thomas, Jr., and Jack Massey, a cofounder of the Kentucky Fried Chicken business—organized Hospital Corporation of America to operate hospitals that would make money. It wasn't long before they were the world's largest operator of hospitals, doubling sales every three years and running more than 400 health care facilities, including a handful outside the U.S.

Then came the 1980s—and it all came apart, leaving a very different HCA at decade's end.

First came new Medicare rules setting ceilings on what the government would pay for medical procedures. Then came HCA's abortive attempt to take over American Hospital Supply Corporation. And throughout the decade HCA faced criticism that they were more interested in making money than healing patients. To deflect this criticism, HCA has sponsored the Thomas F. Frist Humanitarian Award since 1972—given annually to a hospital administrator "whose life mirrors the humanitarian spirit" of Dr. Thomas Frist, Sr.

In the closing years of the decade, HCA shrank. First they sold off 104 acute-care hospitals to HealthTrust Inc., formed by HCA employees (mostly management). The conflict of interest between healing and business was clear in Wall Street comments that HCA was getting rid of the "deadwood." That left HCA with 82 general hospitals, 53 psychiatric hospitals and management contracts to operate more than 200 other hospitals. Then, in 1989, HCA retreated entirely from the stock market, when the company was bought for $4.5 billion by a group of investors led by their top managers, headed by cofounder Dr. Thomas Frist, Jr., a physician who has never practiced medicine.

Frist prefers to be called "mister" rather than "doctor," to preserve his reputation as a businessman. After graduation from medical school, Frist was drafted into the Air Force—at the height of the Viet Nam War—and when he came back two years later he was itching to do one thing: make money. As he explained to an interviewer for *Health*: "Doctors can certainly enjoy a good standard of living, but after they educate their children and pay their taxes... I don't know many who accumulate tremendous wealth. So you must do it outside the practice of medicine." In 1968 Frist and his father (an internist-cardiologist) joined with Jack Massey (who bought Kentucky Fried Chicken from Colonel Sanders and took the firm public) to found HCA. Thomas Frist, Sr., is still a member of the board of directors, with the unusual title of Chief Medical Officer. Thomas Frist, Jr., became chairman in 1985, when he was 47. For Frist, the hospital business is a business like any other. "Though we say we're a health company, we're really a thousand different businesses: we're one of the largest operators of restaurants, drug stores and computer services in the country," Frist proudly told *Health*.

Frist is now free to wring as much profit as he can out of the business of taking care of sick people—without having to worry about the prying eyes of stock analysts or public health activists.

Hospital Corporation of America, One Park Plaza, Nashville, TN 37203; (615) 327-9551.

RETAILERS

SUPERSTORES

At the top of the retail trade are five superstores—Sears, Roebuck; K mart; Wal-Mart; J. C. Penney; and Dayton Hudson. Each rings up more than $12 billion worth of sales annually. Together they have more than 5,000 stores carrying a variety of names (Western Auto, Pay Less Drugs, Sam's Wholesale Clubs, Thrift Drug and Walden's are some of them). With the exception of Dayton Hudson, their flagship stores continue to be their primary outlets. These five operators employ more than 1.3 million people. They can, and do, open new stores all the time, remodel old ones and change merchandise mixes. Prior to the 1980s, Sears stocked only their own brands. Now they carry Levi's jeans and Sony TV sets. K mart and J. C. Penney have both tried to go upscale. Dayton Hudson used to be the nation's leading bookseller and jewelery store chain, but they sold those businesses, bought Marshall Field and expanded Mervyn's from 50 to 220 stores, Target from 65 to 400. And Wal-Mart? They only multiplied sales by 10 times during the 1980s on their way to a certain first place in retail sales in the early 1990s.

1

#1 *in retailing*

Employees: 510,000
Sales: $53.8 billion
Profits: $1.5 billion
Founded: 1886
Headquarters: Chicago, Illinois

Americans still shop at Sears—by the millions—but their stores no longer dominate the retail scene the way they once did. Discount operators like K mart and Wal-Mart have captured customers from the big general merchandise chains, as have new specialty stores (The Limited, Nordstrom, Circuit City). As they came through a very difficult decade, fraught with realignments, Sears, Roebuck had two landmark events to face in the 1990s.

First, both K mart and Wal-Mart will pass Sears in store sales: a trend that built through the 1980s. Sears, Roebuck will still be the bigger company, but only because there is so much more to Sears than stores. Second, by 1993 Sears will have relocated their headquarters, and 6,000 employees, from Chicago, their hometown since 1887. Their 110-story skyscraper, the world's tallest building, was sold in mid-1990. They're moving to Hoffman Estates, a town of 45,000 people 30 miles northwest of Chicago.

It's possible—but unlikely—that Sears will hold on to their leadership position. In 1986, when they celebrated their centennial, 51-year-old Edward A. Brennan, who had followed his father, uncles and grandfather into Sears, was named CEO. He said then: "We're not looking back. We are the premiere retailer in the world. We intend to stay that way." But the next four years witnessed a further weakening of Sears as a retailer for the masses. By the decade's end, Sears, Roebuck was earning nearly twice as much from their Allstate Insurance operations as they were from store and catalog sales.

One thing is sure: they stand for much more than the 847 department stores carrying their name in all 50 states. They have more than 100 paint and hardware stores plus more than 100 catalog outlet stores. And they now own a string of specialty stores: Western Auto, Eye Care Centers, Sears Business Systems Centers, Pinstripe Petites. Their Allstate Insurance unit insures more automobiles and homes than any other company except State Farm. Their catalog business takes in more than $3 billion a year. They also take in about $3 billion a year in interest charges on customer accounts—a profit center they found so exciting they launched their own all-purpose credit card, Discover. In 1981, Sears found two other ways to make money on money: They bought Coldwell Banker, one of the nation's largest residential real estate bro-

Edward A. Brennan runs Sears, Roebuck, while his brother Bernard (see page 213) is in charge of archcompetitor Montgoery Ward.

kers, and Dean Witter, one of the nation's largest stockbrokers.

In short, Sears, Roebuck remains a commanding presence in the American economy. They're the largest employer in the country after General Motors. And no one employs more women than Sears, Roebuck.

History. The guiding genius behind Sears was a supersalesman named Richard Warren Sears, who in 1886 left his job as telegraph agent at a railway station to start the R. W. Sears Watch Co. in Minneapolis. In 1887 he headed for Chicago, and hired Alvah Roebuck from Indiana as a watch assembler and repairman. Sears expanded into diamonds (sold on the installment plan), and then added jewelry. He published the first Sears catalog in 1887, with a version of what was to become Sears' famous money-back guarantee.

The catalogs grew rapidly. By September 1893 the 196-page catalog carried sewing machines, furniture, dishes, clothing, harnesses, saddles, guns, wagons, buggies, bicycles, shoes, baby carriages and musical instruments. And they had adopted a name that was to stick: Sears, Roebuck & Co. In 1895, Roebuck, in ill health, sold out to his partner for $25,000. Sears brought in Julius Rosenwald, a former clothing supplier. Rosenwald organ-

ized the business side of things while Sears wrote spectacular ad copy for the catalog. According to *Counters and Catalogues* by Boris Emmet and John Jeuck, Sears was a superactive, brilliant promoter who worked from 7 A.M. to 11 P.M., showing up nearly every morning "with all his pockets bulging with ideas he had scribbled down, advertisements he had written, plans he had outlined." A banker once said Sears could sell a breath of air.

The company's main customers in those days were midwestern farmers. Jealous merchants attacked the catalog, calling the company "Rears and Soreback" or "Shears and Rawbuck." But by 1908, the year Rosenwald became president, Sears had surpassed their nearest competitor—Montgomery Ward—by millions of dollars in sales. And they had established an enormous base of goodwill. *Counters and Catalogues* reports how customers used to write Sears, Roebuck to ask advice on family matters, to report on crop and weather conditions or just to let the firm know they were getting along all right ("recovered from the accident when the mule kicked me and broke my right arm, so I couldn't write sooner").

In the early 1920s, Rosenwald accurately perceived the population shift from rural to urban centers. He changed Sears' emphasis from mail-order business to retail stores for city dwellers. The first Sears store opened in 1925. In 1928 General Robert Elkington Wood became president. The General (as employees always called him) had been quartermaster for the construction of the Panama Canal, then quartermaster for the Army during World War I, and finally an executive at Montgomery Ward, before joining Sears. He was the single most dominant personality in the company's history. A reactionary (one writer called him a "political Neanderthal"), he headed the isolationist America First organization before World War II. And in the 1950s, he was a financial backer of Senator Joseph McCarthy. Observing the automobile's rise, General Wood decided to locate Sears stores outside cities, in open spaces with plenty of room for parking. He also led the company's expansion into Latin America and built up chains of stores in the American South and West.

In the 1960s Sears began losing big chunks of business to other chains and suffered a severe identity crisis. After a decade of soul-searching, alternately raising prices to seem more fashionable and then slashing them like a discount house, Sears realized they weren't cut out to be Bloomingdale's or K mart. They moved into their 110-story headquarters in 1973, and in 1978 announced, "We are not a store for the whimsical or the affluent. We are not an exciting store. We are not a store that anticipates. We reflect the world of Middle America."

During the turbulent 1980s, as Sears fought desperately to keep their place in American life, they retreated from practices once considered sacrosanct. They introduced national brand names into their stores. They sold off stock they owned in companies that supplied them with merchandise. They opened self-contained stores within their stores à la the boutiques found in department stores. In 1989 they closed their stores for two days and reopened them with great fanfare to demonstrate that instead of sales they would have low prices every day, a move K mart greeted by pointing out they'd been doing this for 27 years.

Owners and rulers. Edward A. Brennan, named chairman in 1986 at the age of 51, joined Sears in 1956 to sell ties and underwear. He hails from a long line of Sears workers—both parents, a grandfather and two uncles worked for the company—and his younger brother Bernie is CEO of rival Montgomery Ward. The burly Brennan grew up in a broken home in an Irish-Catholic suburb outside of Chicago, wearing Sears clothing and playing football. He is known as the consummate bureaucrat and is obsessively neat—his computer is hidden behind a painting in his office. Brennan rewarded himself with $2.5 million in 1989 (the CEO of Sears' Dean Witter subsidiary, P. J. Purcell, took home $2 million).

Three women are on the board of directors: Sybil Collins Mobley, a black who is Dean of the School of Business at Florida A & M University; Norma Pace, President of ECAP Associates; and Nancy Clark Reynolds, Vice Chairman of Wexler, Reynolds, Fuller, Harrison & Schule, Inc. Institutions like insurance companies and pension funds own roughly half of

Sears' shares. The Sears profit-sharing fund owns 15 percent; under a new Employee Stock Ownership Plan employees will soon own 21 percent of Sears. The biggest individual shareholder is Edgar B. Stern, Jr., a descendant of Julius Rosenwald and a director since 1958. He owns 282,000 shares (worth about $11 million in 1990), less than 1 percent of the total.

As a place to work. Sears used to be regarded as a great place to work because the profit-sharing fund, invested heavily in Sears stock, provided lush payouts to people with long service. But the fund has been a poor investment in recent years and employees have become disgruntled. Salespeople in two New Jersey stores, unhappy over reductions in base pay, even launched an organizing drive for the Office and Professional Employees International Union. Sears won a victory in the mid-1980s when a federal judge dismissed a six-year-old case charging them with excluding women from jobs where sales commissions are earned. Sears has consistently maintained they're in the vanguard of equal employment opportunity. Their work force has certainly changed. Minority representation jumped from 8 percent in 1966 to 27 percent in 1988. Sears reported that in 1988 women held 39.6 percent and minorities 13 percent of positions classified as "officials and managers." Those percentages increased sharply during the 1980s.

Social responsibility. Sears has one of the biggest philanthropy budgets in American business, well over $25 million a year. They are also one of the largest buyers of goods and services from companies owned by minorities and women: $254 million in 1988. But they've been involved in continual scrapes over their advertising. In 1988 New York City's Department of Consumer Affairs accused Sears of running "misleading and deceptive" ads—for example, urging consumers to "hurry" and order a $34.98 carpet-cleaning service by September 26 and then running a similar ad a month later ("Hurry! Call by October 25."). In 1989, *after* announcing their every-day low-price policy, they ran ads offering items at a special price until a deadline day—for example, $58.88 for an AT&T answering machine "good through April 1." So much for "low everyday" pricing.

G*lobal presence.*   Limited to Canada and Mexico, where Sears has about 100 stores and some 1,600 catalog sales offices. Total international sales in 1988 were $3.7 billion. Sears failed abysmally in the 1980s with an attempt to establish a worldwide trading company patterned after the powerful Japanese trading companies (Mitsui, Mitsubishi, Sumitomo). Sears World Trade was formed in 1982 under the direction of Roderick M. Hills, former chairman of the Securities and Exchange Commission. After he was fired in 1984, Sears hired Frank Carlucci, former deputy director of the Central Intelligence Agency (and later Secretary of Defense), to run the trading company—with no great success. Sears World Trade was disbanded in 1986.

S*tock performance.*   Sears, Roebuck stock bought for $1,000 in 1980 sold for $3,703 on January 2, 1990.

C*onsumer brands.*

Sears stores, Allstate insurance, Dean Witter Reynolds financial services, Discover credit card, Coldwell Banker realty.

Sears, Roebuck and Co., Sears Tower, Chicago, IL 60684; (312) 875-2500.

2

#2 *in retailing, bookstores*

Employees: 360,000
Sales: $29.7 billion
Profits: $740 million
Founded: 1897
Headquarters: Troy, Michigan

K mart, whose basic proposition has always been to save customers money, entered the 1990s on the threshold of supplanting Sears, Roebuck as the nation's largest retailer. However, even as they were about to move into first place, K mart began fiddling with the strategy adopted in 1962 to displace Kresge variety stores with K mart discount centers. Tired of being de-

picted as a ticky-tacky house of polyester, they now seek a more upscale aura.

Joseph Antonini, appointed CEO in 1987 and sometimes described as the "Lee Iacocca of retailing," said the new K mart will cater to "life-style needs." He explained K mart will now give customers more choices "instead of just carrying all cheap stuff." The centerpiece of this strategy was to hire Martha Stewart as "lifestyle and entertaining" consultant. Stewart, author (*Weddings and Entertaining*) and lecturer on gracious, upper-class living, began plumping for K mart as the 1980s ran out, in commercials showing how she used K mart products to renovate her 150-year-old Connecticut farmhouse and introducing a new line of sheets and pillowcases carrying her name.

This means local K marts look different today than they did 10 or even 5 years ago. For starters, they're brighter and better organized, with clearly marked sections for clothing, "home care," kitchenware and even financial services. Instead of being strewn on tables, clothing is hung on racks, and shoes now come in boxes. What you can buy at K mart these days also represents a dramatic departure from their days as a bargain basement store. More brand names—everything from Cuisinarts to Danskins to Bill Blass chocolates—are stocked on Kmart's shelves. Lest anyone fear the old K mart is gone for good, they still offer their own low-priced line of merchandise. Their famous "bluelight specials" continue with a flashing light beaming on sale items and a loudspeaker blaring "Attention K mart shoppers!" These reminders of the old K mart may be why some image-conscious clothiers, like Levi Strauss, are not yet believers in the new K mart and refuse to sell clothes there.

K mart is more than their 2,275 K marts (700 of which will be remodeled by 1995, at a cost of $1.3 billion). They also operate Waldenbooks, the number two bookseller in the nation (1,139 stores in 50 states); Pay Less Drug Stores (254 drugstores, mostly in the West); and Builders Square (118 home-improvement enters in 21 states). They also operate Office Square and Sports Giant. And as the 1990s dawned they were moving into other retail avenues. They have linked up with Bruno's, a supermarket operator in the

Southeast, to develop hypermarkets under the American Fare name; they own 51 percent of Marko, an operator of warehouse club stores; and 100 percent of PACE, a Colorado-based chain of 41 warehouse clubs ranking fourth in this field (behind Price Club, Costco and Sam's Wholesale Club division of Wal-Mart).

History. When Sebastian S. Kresge, Kmart founder, closed all his five-and-dime stores for an hour on the day Frank Woolworth died in 1919, he was acknowledging his indebtedness to the granddaddy of the variety store. Kresge treaded in Woolworth's footsteps when he took his life's savings and, with J. G. McCrory, bought a Memphis, Tennessee, store in 1897. The partners opened a second store in Detroit a year later. As aggressive then as now, they owned 150 dime stores with annual sales of over $12 million when they incorporated in Michigan in 1916 as S. S. Kresge.

Sebastian Kresge was a notorious penny-pincher. According to Waldemar A. Nielsen in *The Big Foundations*, Kresge was married three times, but "his first two wives divorced him, each citing his stinginess as a major complaint. He would wear a pair of shoes until they literally fell apart; when the soles got too thin, he would line them with newspaper. He gave up golf because he could not stand to lose the balls." He explained his hobby of beekeeping: "My bees always remind me that hard work, thrift, sobriety, and earnest struggle to live an upright Christian life are the first rungs of the ladder of success." By the time Sebastian Kresge stepped down as president in 1929, the chain had 600 variety stores in the U.S. He remained chairman of the company until 1966, a month before his 99th birthday, and died four months later.

The man credited with creating the highly successful K mart concept is Harry B. Cunningham, who quit his job as a newspaper reporter in Harrisburg, Pennsylvania, to become a Kresge store manager and ultimately company president in 1959. He built the first K mart in 1962 in a Detroit suburb, then blitzed the country, opening more than a hundred a year, usually as free-standing stores not associated with shopping centers. During 1976 Kresge launched an unprecedented 271 K marts. To acknowledge that big discount houses had become the backbone of their business, Kresge's directors recommended to the 1977 annual meeting that the company's name be changed to K mart Corp. What ensued was an emotional debate. Stanley Kresge, the founder's son and former company chairman, rose and told the meeting he was "not pleased with the change," and later explained to the *Wall Street Journal*, "We've been successful...with the Kresge name, and the company name should relate to the founder." But the directors won the vote. A teetotaler, Stanley Kresge donated his stock to charity shortly before his death in 1985 after learning that some K mart stores were selling beer and wine.

Owners and rulers. K mart stock has been a favorite of institutional investors (like insurance companies and corporate employee pension funds), who own more than two-thirds of the shares. Company directors and officers own less than 1 percent. CEO Antonini's 1988 holdings of 25,000 shares were worth $1 million. In 1989 Antonini earned $899,000. Two blacks—Los Angeles radio station owner and ex–Green Bay Packer football great Willie Davis and Ford automobile dealer David Harper—and two women, Nabisco marketing executive Ellen R. Marram and Berry College president Gloria M. Shatto, sit on K mart's board.

As a place to work. K mart rarely promotes from the outside, and most of their top managers have never worked for another company. The last two CEOs, Bernard Fauber and Antonini, began their K mart careers as stockboys. Until the 1980s K mart didn't recruit at graduate business schools, preferring to hire and train college graduates. That's changing. Store employees are not unionized. In 1989 more than 130,000 employees were enrolled in a savings plan under which they were allowed to salt away up to 16 percent of their salary, with K mart matching the first 6 percent with 50 cents for every dollar the employee saved. (The company contribution buys K mart stock.)

Social responsibility. K mart has never been known for innovative or substantial philanthropic activities. With free-standing stores usually located on a highway between here and there, K mart isn't really part of any community. Giving is under 1 percent of pretax profits. Their biggest grant of the 1980s was $2 million to endow a marketing chair at Wayne State University. The Kresge Foundation, set up by the founder, is one of the 10 largest foundations in the country, with assets of almost $1 billion.

Global presence. Owns 22 percent of Coles Myer, the largest retailer in Australia (where there are 125 K marts). Also owns 150-store Canadian discount chain, Bargain Harold's.

Stock performance. K mart stock bought for $1,000 in 1980 sold for $3,282 on January 2, 1990.

Consumer brands.

K mart, Waldenbooks, Builders Square, Pay Less Drugs Northwest, Bargain Harold's (Canada), Jupiter/Kresge, Office Square, Sports Giant, American Fare.

K mart Corporation, 3100 West Big Beaver Road, Troy, MI 48084; (313) 643-1000.

3

WAL-MART

#3 in retailing

Employees: 247,500
Sales: $25.9 billion
Profits: $1.1 billion
Founded: 1962
Headquarters: Bentonville, Arkansas

Workplace

The shooting star of retailing, Wal-Mart Stores soared right to the top during the 1980s by combining a simple strategy with rigorous attention to detail, a streak of down-home southern evangelism and the charisma of Sam Walton, who never stopped telling associates ("employee" is taboo at Wal-Mart) they could accomplish miracles and that the company's success was due entirely to them.

The strategy was clear-cut: Sell goods at low prices; concentrate on brand-name merchandise; always have products in stock (which meant having a distribution center within a day's truck drive of every store); offer friendly service (greet every customer with a "Welcome to Wal-Mart" and never argue with someone returning an item); stay out of big cities; go into small towns (under 50,000 population) or into the perimeters of major metropolitan areas. Too simple? A secret formula? No. Wal-Mart told everyone what they were doing. And any competitor was free to check out a Wal-Mart store. And every year there were more of them to check out.

Wal-Mart's execution was superb. Fanning out from Bentonville, Arkansas, in the foothills of the Ozarks, they advanced in concentric circles, putting down stores (and distribution centers behind them) and selling a wide variety of household goods, clothes, personal-care items, drugs, jewelry, toys, garden supplies—all under such banners as: "We Sell for Less" and "Everyday Low Prices." By mid-1990 they had about 1,500 stores in only 29 states (including their first ones in California and Pennsylvania). They were about to become number one in retailing, but nearly half of all Americans didn't even know what a Wal-Mart is (although they will soon).

In 1980, when the first edition of this book was published, Wal-Mart wasn't even profiled. They were too small—the 39th largest store operator in the country, based on sales. In 1990 they were nearing sales of $30 billion a year, pointing to $60 billion by 1994. The retailing industry has never seen anything like the Wal-Mart phenomenon.

In addition to Wal-Mart discount centers, the company operates 105 membership-only Sam's Wholesale Clubs in 21 states, 4 Hypermarkets (each the size of five football fields), 14 Dot discount drug stores in 4 states and 8 Wal-Mart Supercenters (combination general merchandise and grocery store).

History. In 1940, 22-year-old Sam Walton took a management trainee position at J. C. Penney in Des Moines, Iowa. At Penney, Walton found he had a knack for retailing. He learned there to call employees "associates" and to refer to managers as "partners." By 1945, Walton was ready to run his own store—and when a franchised Ben Franklin store became available in Newport, Arkansas, he took it on.

By 1959, Walton was operating nine Ben Franklins and was the largest franchisee in the chain. Then Sam Walton got his brainstorm: Why not turn Ben Franklin stores into a discount chain, specializing in low prices not merely occasionally, but *every day*? When the owners of the Ben Franklin system turned him down, Walton struck out on his own. In 1962, he opened his own discount store, called Wal-Mart Discount City, in Rogers, Arkansas. In 1970 company shares were first sold to the public.

Owners and rulers. Sam Walton, aged 72 in 1990, stepped down as Wal-Mart CEO in favor of David Glass in 1988. CEO Glass took home a whopping $6.8 million in 1989, making him the second-highest paid CEO on *Forbes* Super 50 list of the 50 biggest companies. Walton has continued as chairman and chief cheerleader. Wal-Mart stock rose so much during the 1980s that for four consecutive years beginning in 1985 Sam Walton stood at the top of the annual *Forbes* roster of the 400 richest Americans. He was down-listed to 18th in 1989 only because the magazine decided it was appropriate to split the fortune among the Walton family members—Sam, his three sons and daughter. Each was therefore ranked 18th with $1.8 billion. The family company, Walton Enterprises, owns 38.5 percent of Wal-Mart's stock. Sam Walton is not a flamboyant or publicity-seeking billionaire. He has turned down repeated invitations to appear on CBS's "60 Minutes." He works out of a plain, drab office. He never took a salary higher than $325,000 a year. He brought onto the Wal-Mart board Robert Kahn, a San Francisco Bay Area management consultant who functions as the social conscience of the retail industry. His presence says a lot about what Wal-Mart stands for. No hanky-panky. No gifts accepted from vendors. No exorbitant salaries. No false advertising.

As a place to work. The wages aren't high, but Sam Walton has instilled in his employees a spirit of partnership through constant stroking, a profit-sharing plan invested largely in Wal-Mart stock (almost the best investment anyone could have made in the 1980s), bonuses tied to profit goals and reduction of shrinkage (merchandise lost through thievery, either by employees or customers) and a stock purchase program partially subsidized by the company. And anyone who's ever been to a Wal-Mart annual meeting in Bentonville knows this approach: The annual show is like a high school football pep rally. CEO David Glass likes to describe the Wal-Mart culture as one where ordinary people can become overachievers. Neither women nor minorities are prominent in the Wal-Mart management hierarchy, however.

Social responsibility. Wal-Mart has been so successful not everyone likes to see them come to town, especially other merchants. Kenneth Stone, an economist at Iowa State University, conducted a study which found that after a Wal-Mart opened up, local merchants—stores selling groceries, hardware, shoes, toys, clothing—suffered, many of them even forced out of business. A study conducted at the University of Misouri came to the opposite conclusion, finding everyone benefits from a Wal-Mart, but then Wal-Mart funded the Missouri study with a $10,000 grant. In 1989 a referendum to stop a new shopping mall anchored by a Wal-Mart was put to a vote in Iowa City; it lost, 4,669 to 3,954. Wal-Mart insists they're a good corporate citizen wherever they operate and that opposition to their stores is frequently inspired by inefficient storekeepers. Wal-Mart encourages associates to volunteer for community service and supports such efforts by grants of up to $2,000 to groups in which associates are active.

Wal-Mart even makes believers out of hardened security analysts on Wall Street. In 1989, after the *New York Times Magazine* ran an article describing how Wal-Mart drove local merchants out of business in Independence, Iowa, Margaret A. Gilliam, retail security analyst at First Boston, protested in a letter to the editor that was never published. Gilliam wrote, "Wal-Mart deserves accolades for bringing low-cost merchandise to people struggling to make ends meet in small communities in the Farm Belt and Oil Patch."

Global presence. Zero. Strictly American—and proud of it. In 1985 Sam Walton launched a "Buy American" crusade, offering to work with American manufacturers to "bring production back to our shores." He promised, in effect, to buy American-made goods that were competitive in price and quality with imports. In 1989 Wal-Mart reported that as a direct result of this program 41,000 jobs had been created or saved and more than $1.7 billion worth of orders had gone to domestic companies that otherwise would have been placed offshore. Two examples: Wal-Mart used to buy stacking chairs from Taiwan; now, thanks to a $459,000 commitment from Wal-Mart, the chairs come from Flanders Industries of Fort Smith, Arkansas. In 1983 Wal-Mart imported most of their dress shirts; today 50 percent come from U.S. plants. In 1988 Japan's Sanyo was ready to close their TV set plant in Arkansas after Sears, Roebuck stopped buying receivers made there. The plant stayed open because Wal-Mart came through with a contract. Wal-Mart stores were selling a 25-inch Sanyo color set for $289 in 1989.

S*tock performance.*   Wal-Mart stock bought for $1,000 in 1980 sold for $43,283 on January 2, 1990.

C*onsumer brands.*

Wal-Mart, Sam's Wholesale Club, Hypermarket.

Wal-Mart Stores, Inc., Bentonville, AR 72716; (501) 273-4000.

4

JCPenney

#1 *in clothing stores*

Employees: 194,000
Sales: $16.1 billion
Profits: $802 million
Founded: 1902
Headquarters: Dallas, Texas

When U.S. athletes enter the 1992 Summer Olympic Games in Barcelona, they'll be dressed in uniforms designed and supplied by J. C. Penney. This is an appropriate symbol for a company with roots deep in American life and stores in all 50 states as well as Puerto Rico. They have been around for the entire 20th century, and are still going strong. During the 1980s they didn't merge with another company or buy another company or take themselves private in a leveraged buyout. And although their longtime rival, Sears, Roebuck, was aging fast, Penney remained, more or less, on course as the store for middle America.

But it's not because they stayed the same. During the 1980s Penney made a wrenching effort to shed their frumpy dime-store image and put on a hip, new, fashion-wise face. They ejected from their stores hardware, appliances, radios and TVs, sporting goods, lawn-and-garden supplies, automotive products and photographic departments. In their place, as *Advertising Age* put it, "are clothes, clothes and more clothes." By 1990 82 percent of Penney's total sales was in clothes.

One major stumbling block to this overhaul was the elitism of clothing designers. Prestigious brand-name manufacturers—Calvin Klein, Liz Claiborne, Ralph Lauren—won't deal with Penney. And when Levi Strauss agreed to sell through J. C. Penney in 1981, social climber Macy's dropped Levi's like a hot potato. But Penney's was undeterred. Today's J. C. Penney ranks as the country's largest fashion-oriented department store, selling more men's suits and women's fashions than any rival.

Penney's new advertising slogan, "You're looking smarter than ever, J. C. Penney," is meant to inspire confidence. But not everything has been rosy in recent years. In 1988 Penney's $100 million home-shopping television service was an acknowledged disaster: "We underestimated the complexity of it all," a company spokesman told the *Wall Street Journal*.

In a big change from the 1950s when most of them were in small towns, 80 percent of Penney's 1,350 stores are located in suburban malls. In recent years Penney spent $1 billion to renovate 700 stores, throwing away shopping carts, ripping out worn, tiled floors and installing carpets and parquet walkways. Penney owns the 434-store Thrift Drug chain, and in the late 1980s were experimenting with free-standing store concepts outside of Penney: Units, contemporary knitwear stores; Portfolio Interiors, upscale furniture outlets; Tazio, private label cosmetics; Details, a bed-and-bath shop. Also a candidate for this treatment is Mixit, a sportswear boutique they opened in more than 100 stores.

History. James Cash Penney believed in preparation, hard work, honesty, confidence in people, spirit—and above all, the practical application of the Golden Rule. He named his first store the Golden Rule, and from the time this store opened in Kemmerer, Wyoming, in 1902 when he was 27, until he died at 95, he never stopped trying to merge profits and ethics. He was pretty good at both.

In opening his first store, this son of a Primitive Baptist minister in Missouri insisted on cash-only sales. People said it couldn't work, but Penney was undaunted. He kept the store open from 7 A.M. until late at night, slashed overhead and prices and offered a money-back guarantee. His formula proved popular, and before long Penney was dreaming of a chain of stores throughout the Rockies.

Penney had a novel plan for expansion. He helped store managers accumulate enough money from their earnings to buy a one-third partnership in a new store. By 1910 J. C. Penney had 14 Golden Rule Stores and eight partners (all of whom had started as clerks). Three years later Penney and his partners met in the Salt Lake City headquarters where J. C. drafted the "Penney Idea," a seven-point code of business ethics. He invented the Affirmation Ceremony for store managers, who swore an Oath of Obligation (later changed to Oath of Affirmation) in which they not only pledged their loyalty to the company but also made a personal commitment to a life of "honesty, integrity, and moral leadership both within and outside the company." This ceremony takes place every few years, when managers who have been with Penney for over five years are initiated. Penney would have no employees, only "associates," trusted people who never had to be bonded. They would wear pins that said, "Honesty, Confidence, Service, Cooperation." The J. C. Penney Company would be more than a place to earn money; profits and responsibility would be shared.

The company expanded rapidly. By the early 1950s, they had a store in every state because J. C. Penney and his associates

James Cash Penney opened this Golden Rule dry goods store in Kemmerer, Wyoming, in 1902. The Golden rule stores were incorporated as J. C. Penney company in 1913.

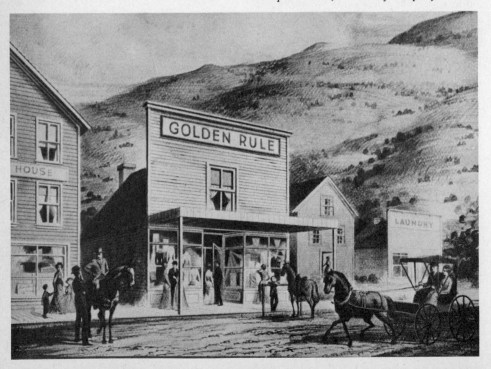

had opened an average of one new store every 10 days for 40 years. In 1958 they allowed credit card purchases for the first time (against the founder's advice), and in 1962 they opened a nationwide catalog service. A few years later, they entered the world of multinationals by buying the 87-store Sarma chain in Belgium. (They sold the Belgian operation in 1988.) They branched out to new enterprises in the mid-1960s, buying drugstore chains and insurance companies, and moved from New York's tacky west side to the 45-story Penney Building on the Avenue of the Americas, where they had neighbors like Exxon, Time Inc. and CBS.

In 1988 Penney moved their headquarters to Dallas, leaving behind 2,100 of 3,300 New York employees. The reasons were primarily economic: Penney will save $60 million a year. The company received $350 million for their New York City building. But the move had its drawbacks. Experienced buyers were lost in the shuffle, and the new Dallas recruits fumbled the ball. At Christmas 1988, inventories were gone before the buying season ended.

Unlike Montgomery Ward, Penney remains committed to the catalog business. Recent Penney catalogs weighed in at four pounds and more than 1,200 pages. Annual catalog sales exceed $3 billion. They have nearly 1,900 catalog sales offices.

Owners and rulers.   Penney's associates (employees) still have a big stake in the company. Through profit sharing or retirement plans, they own 22.8 percent of the company. Penney's board includes such corporate heavyweights as Walter Wriston, former head of Citicorp; Clifton Garvin, former head of Exxon; and current or former top officers of AT&T, Warner-Lambert, Eastman Kodak and Ryder. Also on the board are Vernon E. Jordan, former president of the National Urban League, and Juanita Kreps, Jimmy Carter's Secretary of Commerce.

As a place to work.   The founder's principles are alive and well. Employees are expected to subject every policy to the company's 1913 code-of-conduct test: "Does it square with what is right and just?" Such maxims flow from the mouths of longtime Penney Associates. And the company assures newcomers that "people

join our company with the expectation that they will retire from our company. And it's our commitment to do our best to make that possible." The company promotes from within, offers intensive in-house training and has one of the strongest benefit programs in retailing. Full benefits are extended to part-timers who work 20 hours a week.

Penney's is known for having a family atmosphere. Relatives are encouraged to come and work where their father, mother, sister or brother worked—or works. William R. Howell, Penney's CEO, is the son of a Penney store manager; the number two man, Robert Gill, is also the son of a former Penney executive.

Social responsibility.   Penney had a philanthropic budget of $18.4 million in 1988. They have long been a bulwark of support for voluntarism—encouraging associates to be active in community organizations (these groups are eligible for automatic grants from Penney) and recognizing outstanding community volunteers outside the company through their annual Golden Rule awards. For 1988 they reported buying $263 million worth of goods and services from 1,487 minority-owned suppliers. Like Sears, Penney buys all the merchandise they sell—they manufacture nothing. They claim 75 percent of those goods come from U.S. manufacturers.

Stock performance.   J. C. Penney stock bought for $1,000 in 1980 sold for $8,716 on January 2, 1990.

Consumer brands.

J. C. Penney, Mixit, Units, Portfolio, Thrift Drug Stores, Amanda Fielding.

J. C. Penney Company, Inc., 14841 North Dallas Parkway, Dallas, TX 75240; (214) 591-1000.

5

Dayton Hudson Corporation

#5 *in retailing*

Employees: 135,000
Sales: $13.6 billion
Profits: $410 million
Founded: 1881
Headquarters: Minneapolis, Minnesota

Social Conscience

If you grew up in Minneapolis, you know the most elegant department store in town is Dayton's. If you grew up in Chicago, you know it's Marshall Field, the *grande dame* of State Street. And if you grew up in Detroit, you know it was the rambling, cavernous, 49-acre Hudson's (closed during the 1980s). All three of these store companies are over 100 years old, and their founding families are no longer active in their affairs. And all three now belong to Minneapolis-based Dayton Hudson, one of the new giants of American retailing. Dayton Hudson reigns over 700 stores in 36 states. Not counting food stores, they're the nation's fifth largest retailer behind Wal-Mart, K mart, Sears and J. C. Penney.

Dayton's started the Target discount stores from scratch in 1962. In 1969 they took over Hudson's and in 1978 Mervyn's, a California-based specialty store featuring moderately priced clothing. In 1990, for $1 billion in cash, they bought Marshall Field, creating a Midwest department store empire. Dayton's has 17 stores, Hudson's 20 and Field's 24.

The 400 Target stores in 32 states constitute Dayton Hudson's biggest business. They bring in half the company's revenues. The second biggest is Mervyn's now up to 220 stores in 13 states, mostly in the western U.S. They bring in about one-quarter of sales. And then come the department stores with about $3 billion in annual revenues.

The last member of the Dayton family to head Dayton Hudson was Kenneth Dayton, grandson of the founder. He stepped down as chairman in 1977. And during the 1980s he and his brother Bruce left the board of the company. Professional managers now run Dayton Hudson. The era of the family-owned department store is over.

The merchants who run the show do it dispassionately. During the 1980s they sold off the B. Dalton bookstore chain they'd started (bookstores have never made great profits), the Diamond's department stores in Arizona and Nevada, the John A. Brown department stores in Arizona, a clutch of jewelry store chains (Shreve's, Jessop, C. D. Peacock, J. E. Caldwell, Charles W. Warren) and the Lechmere appliance chain in New England they'd earlier acquired.

Dayton Hudson has long enjoyed a reputation for social responsibility because they contribute 5 percent of pretax profits to charity, a policy the Daytons started and one continued by the Daytonless management. That record helped them in 1987 when Herbert Haft and his son Robert (the Dart Group of Washington, D.C.) were considering a takeover of Dayton Hudson. The Minnesota Legislature, called into special session by Governor Rudy Perpich, promptly passed a tough antitakeover bill, requiring, among other things, that an acquiring company be barred for five years from selling off any company assets acquired. That won the day; no takeover attempt was made. So social responsibility pays. Washington, D.C., writer James K. Glassman had another view. Writing in *The New Republic*, he implied that the Dayton Hudson people were largely interested in preserving their jobs and don't mind giving away the shareholders' money to charitable causes. He said the Hafts, if they had taken over Dayton Hudson, "would undoubtedly continue donating $20 million a year to charity. It's a small price to pay for owning a legislature."

Stock performance. Dayton Hudson stock bought for $1,000 in 1980 sold for $7,699 on January 2, 1990.

Consumer brands.

Mervyn's, Hudson's, Dayton's, Target, Marshall Field.

Dayton Hudson Corporation, 777 Nicollet Mall, Minneapolis, MN 55402; (612) 370-6948.

THE OLD-FASHIONED FULL-LINE DEPARTMENT STORES

The 1980s were open hunting season on the old, gracious, wide-aisled department stores as they came under siege from raiders of various nationalities and with various motives. They also had to defend their turf against invasions by new specialty stores honing in on a particular area: The Limited in trendy women's wear, the Gap in casual wear, Circuit City in consumer electronics, Crate & Barrel in home accessories. It was a turbulent period. Among the department stores changing hands were Marshall Field, Saks Fifth Avenue, Lord & Taylor, Foley's, I. Magnin, Bloomingdale's and Filene's. Among the stores closing their doors were B. Altman, Gimbel's, Liberty and Bonwit Teller. Peter J. Solomon, a New York investment banker who follows the retail industry, summed it up this way: "Department stores are at the end of their life cycle and have to be reinvented. People are more sophisticated. They don't want to go out and wander around department stores anymore. Department stores are no longer the dominant form of retailing, although, when good, they still have a tremendous amount of capital, muscle and drawing ability."

1
MAY

#1 *in department stores*

Employees: 125,000
Sales: $9.6 billion
Profits: $498 million
Founded: 1988
Headquarters: St. Louis, Missouri

Jewish immigrants from Europe founded or developed many of America's early department stores (Filene's, Macy's, Gimbel's, Rich's)—and May was one of them. The founders were David May and his three brothers-in-law, Louis, Moses and Joseph Shoenberg, who opened a store under the May name in Denver in 1888 after having been merchants in the Colorado mining camps around Leadville. May developed the concept common today, but not so in the 19th century, of the department store group in which one company owned different outlets in different cities.

Among the department stores May brought into the fold were Famous-Barr in St. Louis, Kaufmann's in Pittsburgh and Meier & Frank in Portland, Oregon. The May Company of Los Angeles, successor to A. Hamburger & Sons, was the setting for the Mary Livingston department store skits on Jack Benny's long-running radio program.

In 1911 May became the first department store company to be listed on the New York Stock Exchange. They began paying a cash dividend to shareholders every quarter and have not missed one since. Few companies have paid quarterly dividends for a longer period.

The turbulent 1980s were turbulent for May, too. David C. Farrell, perhaps the only Antioch College graduate ever to become head of a major American corporation, presided over the firm. Farrell, who started working at Kaufmann's in Pittsburgh as part of his Antioch work-study program and never worked at another company, took the helm at May in 1979 when he was 46. Still there at the end of the 1980s, he had more than tripled sales by a series of acquisitions that transformed May into one of the giants of U.S. retailing. Entering the 1990s they had 13 companies operating 297 department stores in 29 states and the District of Columbia.

Farrell's first buy, in 1979, was Volume Shoe Corporation, the nation's largest operator of self-service shoe stores under the name, Payless ShoeSource. When acquired, Volume had 739 stores in 32 states. By 1980s end they had more than 2,600 stores in 43 states. May's biggest acquisition, Associated Dry Goods, came in the mid-1980s and swung into their column Lord & Taylor (one of the oldest U.S. department stores) and J. W. Robinson's of Los Angeles, among others. In 1988, as fallout from the Campeau purchase of Federated Department Stores, Farrell brought Filene's of Boston and Foley's of Dallas into the May fold. Mean-

while, shuffling and reshuffling was constant. They sold the Horne's department stores to permit some competition in Pittsburgh. They changed O'Neil's department stores in Ohio to May, and they sold the L. S. Ayres department stores in Cincinnati and Kentucky. The Goldwaters department stores in Arizona became part of Robinson's, and four Hahne's department stores in New Jersey were converted to Lord & Taylor's.

At one time, May seemed to be bidding to become a major discount operator. They started the Venture discount stores from scratch, and in buying Associated Dry Goods they picked up Caldor's and the deep discount clothing chain, Loehmann's. By the 1980s end, however, they were all sold or ticketed to be sold. May went back to their roots: department stores. Previously, they had a reputation as a well-run operator of dowdy stores for middle-income Americans. By buying Lord & Taylor, May seemed to be entering a more upscale, high-fashion league—but they promptly got rid of many of the European labels while introducing moderately priced apparel (a move critics called "May-o-nnaising" Lord & Taylor). They are expected to be a bidder for other department stores. They want to be the king of the full-line department store business.

Stock performance. May stock bought for $1,000 in 1980 sold for $9,134 on January 2, 1990.

Consumer brands.

May, Foley's, Filene's, Lord & Taylor, Kaufmann's, J. W. Robinson's, Payless ShoeSource, Venture, Sibley's, G. Fox, Hecht's, Meier & Frank, Goldwater's, Famous-Barr, L.S. Ayres.

May Department Store Company, 611 Olive Street, St. Louis, MO 63101; (314) 342-6300.

2

CAMPEAU

CORPORATION

#2 *in department stores*

Employees: 99,000
Sales: $10.4 billion
Loss: $1.1 billion
Founded: 1953
Headquarters: Toronto, Canada

Briefly, in the late 1980s Robert Campeau, an aggressive, daredevil Canadian real estate developer, seemed about to end up as the largest operator of department stores in the U.S. He owned, as 1989 dawned, 250 stores in 28 states, including such stellar attractions as Bloomingdale's, Abraham & Straus, Rich's, Jordan Marsh and Burdine's. Pretty good for someone who had absolutely no experience in department stores. However, in early 1990, Robert Campeau no longer controlled the company bearing his name, and the American department stores he'd bought were operating under the protection of the bankruptcy court. His fall was a morality tale of high-yield debt in the 1980s.

History. Campeau became a hotshot department store operator in two big bites. First, in 1986, he bought New York–based Allied Stores, the fifth largest U.S. department store group. Allied entered the 1980s running 16 different store chains, among them Jordan Marsh, Joske's, Bon Marché, Donaldson's, Bonwit Teller and Stern's. Campeau was so pleased with this purchase that in 1988 he swallowed Cincinnati-based Federated Department Stores, besting R. H. Macy by bidding $6.6 billion, most of which he borrowed from friendly Canadian investors and banks (getting even for the American financial pillaging of Canada). Federated was the largest U.S. department store group, running 17 different store chains, among them Bloomingdale's, Abraham & Straus, Lazarus, Rich's, Filene's and Sanger-Harris.

At this point Campeau was staring at debt of $11 billion, but he was number one in department stores in the U.S. But before he could get Sears, Roebuck in his sights, he had to lighten some of that debt load. From the Allied Stores stable he sold venerable Brooks Bros. to Britain's largest department store operator, Marks & Spencer, and the Ann Taylor women's fashion stores to the managers who had been running this chain. And from the Federated bunch he quickly peddled seven divisions for $4 billion. Filene's and Foley's went to May Department Stores, I. Magnin and Bullock's went to Macy's. Gold Circle, Children's Place and MainStreet were also sold off. But Campeau still couldn't meet his interest payments.

The stores Campeau bought have long been part of the fabric of American urban life. Brooks Bros. made the suit in which Abraham Lincoln was assassinated. Lazarus has been part of the texture of life in Cincinnati since 1830. And it's said southerners are as chauvinistic about Rich's as they are about *Gone with the Wind*. Morris Rich had put planks across the red clay mud to encourage customers into his first store in Atlanta, opened just two years after Sherman's Union army leveled the city during the Civil War. Some still remember that during the depression, when Atlanta wrote bad checks to pay its schoolteachers, Rich's cashed them at full value for the teachers, no purchase necessary. I. Magnin's made their reputation as the provider of post–Gold Rush luxury in San Francisco, a tradition that continues today as Magnin's caters to the society matrons of Pacific Heights and Hillsborough. Bloomingdale's opened in 1872 as a good neighbor to the conservative, middle-class families of Third Avenue and 59th Street in Manhattan. But in the 1960s, Bloomie's became synonymous with jet-setting chic. Bloomie's influence was preserved in celluloid in a scene from *Annie Hall*. "Sometimes I wonder how I would stand up to torture," muses Diane Keaton. "You?" Woody Allen retorts. "The Gestapo would take away your Bloomingdale's charge card and you'd tell them everything."

All this history appeared lost on Robert Campeau, who seems never to have shaken the sense of being an outsider, a poor-boy-made-good—even after conquering the worlds of Canadian, and more recently, American business. He had 13 siblings (only 7 of whom survived early childhood) and grew up in a small mining town in Ontario. He dropped out of school after the eighth grade and got a job at an International Nickel mine using the baptismal records of a dead brother to pass as a 16-year-old. Campeau entered real estate by building his own house, and selling it before moving in when someone offered him twice what it cost him to build. He was off and running, constructing subdivisions and apartment buildings for housing-starved World War II veterans. At one time, Campeau had built more than 20 percent of the housing stock in Ottawa. He became a skiing buddy of Prime Minister Pierre Trudeau, and while his fellow French-Canadian was in office, Campeau became the builder of choice for new government office complexes.

But even after he built the largest real estate development company in Canada, the English-speaking Canadian business establishment still snubbed him. Campeau's personal life contributed to the disdain. While still married to his first wife and unbeknownst to his three children, Campeau started a second family with his mistress. He married her after she'd given birth to two illegitimate children. At one point, he had filed lawsuits against or was being sued by three of his six children in disputes over the family fortune. In 1980, when Campeau tried to buy Royal Trust Co., a blue-blooded financial firm, several English-speaking businessmen broke securities laws to block his takeover. "The friends in the club got together to keep me out," Campeau explained to Fortune. After that shock, Campeau set his sights on the U.S. where, he believed, "it doesn't matter who you are."

Campeau soon proved himself to the American business establishment by perfecting the art of corporate raiding—the ultimate business sport of the 1980s. Campeau had Wall Street in awe over his tactics in winning Allied Stores in 1986. After meeting opposition from Allied's board, Campeau withdrew his original offer. A few minutes after this apparent withdrawal, Campeau purchased nearly half of Allied's shares through a stockbroker in Los Angeles (Jeffries) in a tactic called the "street sweep." At the time, this was the largest single block of stock ever traded. (The ensuing uproar led to a tightening of stock-trading regulations effectively preventing such a "street sweep" in the future.) In his highly publicized 1988 raid on Federated Department Stores, Campeau beat out Macy's, further enhancing his reputation.

But Campeau had won pyrrhic victories. In addition to the $11.7 billion in debt the buyouts incurred, Campeau paid his investment bankers and lawyers fees of $400 million. Less than a year after Campeau's face had graced the cover of the New York Times Magazine, his empire began to unravel. He just couldn't pay the mountain of debt he'd incurred to win control of his retailing empire. So he asked for a $250 million cash infusion from Paul and Albert Reichmann, owners of the huge Toronto-based Olympia & York real estate development company. The Reichmanns immediately relieved Campeau of his role as head of the company but let him keep the title of chairman. Campeau even lost the title in the futile last-ditch efforts to keep the company from filing bankruptcy. In a postscript on the bankruptcy filing, the New York Times editorialized:

> Any corporate executive can figure out how to file for bankruptcy when the bottom drops out of the business. It took the special genius of Robert Campeau, chairman of the Campeau Corporation, to figure out how to bankrupt more than 250 profitable department stores. The dramatic jolt to Bloomingdale's, Abraham & Straus, Jordan Marsh and the other proud stores reflects his overreaching grasp and oversized ego.

Owners and rulers. In the wake of the bankruptcy filing, G. William Miller, a former Secretary of the Treasury, was named chairman and CEO of the holding company for Campeau's U.S. retailing operations. Allen Questrom, former head of Neiman-Marcus, became CEO of the two store groups—Federated and Allied. But the real power at Campeau became Toronto's Reichmann family. Their Olympia & York realty company is the world's biggest landlord. Among other properties, they own the headquarters housing ITT, American Brands and Harper & Row in New York City, as well as nearly 50 million square feet of real estate in Boston, Hartford, Dallas, Miami, Los Angeles, San Francisco and elsewhere.

As a place to work. After Campeau took over, few thought of making a career with any of these stores. Campeau himself was known for his "Ivan the Terrible management style." Shortly after buying Allied, he fired more than 600 of 1,000 corporate staff employees and laid off 2,000 of the 40,000 store workers. Campeau started swinging the axe at the old Federated stores before the ink was dry on his purchase deal in 1988. At Goldsmith's, Campeau quickly zapped 600 of the 2,500 employees, including all the top executives and the administrative and buying staffs. Predictably, morale plummeted with sales clerks telling the *Wall Street Journal* that they were "very unsettled."

Social responsibility. None.

Consumer brands.

Bloomingdale's, Maas Brothers, The Bon Marché, Abraham & Straus, Jordan Marsh, Burdine's, Rich's, Goldsmith's, Lazarus, Ralph's Supermarkets (southern California).

Campeau Corporation, Suite 5800, 40 King Street West, Toronto, Ontario M5H 3Y8; (416) 868-6460.

3

MACY★S [★]

#1 in New York department stores, northern California department stores

Employees: 78,000
Sales: $7 billion
Loss: $54 million
Founded: 1858
Headquarters: New York, New York

Although they have a major presence in only three metropolitan areas—New York, San Francisco and Atlanta—Macy's is probably the most well known department store in the country. And that remains true even though they receded from Wall Street's view in the 1980s when their top executives borrowed a potful of money to pay out all public shareholders and take Macy's private. So people can still shop in Macy's, they just can't own any of it. That's because Chairman Edward Finkelstein wanted Macy's all for himself and his buddies. Coming into the 1990s, the privatized Macy's was operating 90 full-line department stores branching out from three main trunks in New York City, Newark and San Francisco. They were also the new owners of the I. Magnin and Bullock's stores on the West Coast.

Macy's is well known for various reasons. Their enormous, 11-story store covering a city block on New York's 34th Street is a must visit for tourists—by some accounts it's the largest store in the world. Macy's has sponsored the annual Thanksgiving Day parade in New York since 1924—and millions now watch it on TV every year. And it's difficult to get through a Christmas period without a televising of the film, *Miracle on 34th Street*, inspired by the Macy Santa Clauses. Finally, Macy's is also well known to department store managers across the country. Families owning local department stores used to send their sons and daughters to Macy's to learn all about buying and selling merchandise. That was before the family-owned stores became targets of the big chains.

History. The company's name comes from Rowland Hussey Macy whose family had lived on Nantucket Island, Massachusetts, for eight generations by the time he was born in 1822. At age 15 he shipped out to sea on a whaler, where he was tattood with a red star (later adopted as a Macy's trademark). On his return Macy opened the first of his doomed dry goods stores in Boston; two years later he wrote the final entry in his account book: "I have worked two years for nothing. Damn, Damn, Damn, Damn." Macy tried and failed to find gold in California and then flopped at six other retail ventures. Finally, in 1858, he established a store in lower Manhattan (on 14th Street near Union Square) that took off.

The store thrived under Macy's four-point plan: (1) sell at fixed, marked prices, (2) sell for less, (3) buy and sell for cash only (credit cards were added in 1939) and (4) advertise heavily. By 1888, the store's founding fathers (including Macy) were all dead and the store passed into the hands of three men who had run the store's china department: Lazarus Straus and his two sons, Isidor and Nathan. The family moved the store uptown to the present location on Herald Square and started Macy's expansion in the New York metropolitan area and across the country. Isidor eventually became a U.S. congressman and a casualty on the *Titanic*. The Straus family remained in control until 1968.

In the early 1970s, Edward Finkelstein—a Harvard graduate who went through his Macy's baptism by fire in New York and Newark—transformed Macy's California division into the company's biggest moneymaker by a radical upscaling. Macy's was known for most of their history as a store for the unwashed masses. Finkelstein changed Macy's into a more elegant store featuring designer names, expensive culinary products and merchandise carrying much higher prices. It worked, and in 1974 he was brought home to New York to work the same magic there. He is credited with transforming the Herald Square store from a "grim warehouse" into "New York's ultimate loft." The early 1980s were golden years for Macy's—and Finkelstein. Merchandise leaped off Macy's counters into customers' arms. Sales and profits were the highest in the company's 100-year history. Macy's was once again king of New York retailing. But then came the mid-1980s and a wave of takeovers in retailing. Finkelstein decided to act before Macy's became a target. He reasoned that the people who had accomplished the turnaround at Macy's deserved to own the store—literally.

Finkelstein wasn't content with merely doing a good job as a well-paid business executive (an annual salary of $780,000, plus generous stock grants, perks and a New York apartment). He saw the chance to make a bundle for himself and his cronies by taking Macy's private in what is known as a leveraged buyout. By using Macy's various assets (especially real estate) as collateral, Finkelstein and other Macy's executives teamed up with GE Credit and other investors to buy all the stock from the public share holders. In the bargain, the executives picked up 19 percent of the company stock with minimal personal investment. In his riveting account of the takeover, *Macy's for Sale*, Isadore Barmash writes: "It was as if the brightest boy in the class, the one who earned all the A's and received all the awards on Class Day, suddenly announced he was buying the school." For his part, Finkelstein was clear about his own motives. Echoing the atmosphere of the greedy decade, Finkelstein recounted how he had recently seen another executive who'd earned nearly $40 million from another leveraged buyout:

> *Recently, I ran into Michel Bergerac, who had just sold Revlon and who I think is just counting his money now. I told him how grateful we were to him.... All of them got such great deals in remuneration that it changed the whole executive remuneration environment. It made all of us—and all the young people—become very money-minded. And that's what we have to make sure to engender as a motivation.*

In 1988, as Macy's struggled to make interest payments on the huge debt they'd acquired because of the leveraged buyout, the retailer laid off hundreds of employees in the New York area. Despite the huge debt load, Macy's tried to buy Federated Department stores that year but lost a much publicized battle to Campeau. Considering that the Campeau stores went bankrupt a year later, perhaps Macy's was lucky to have lost.

Entering the 1990s, Macy's had 90 stores, nearly all of them now carrying the Macy's name. The 14 Davison's stores in Atlanta were renamed Macy's. The 23 Bamberger's stores in New Jersey were also renamed Macy's. And on the West Coast they were consolidating their newly acquired Bullock's and I. Magnin operations.

Macy's board includes some big names: Henry Kissinger, real estate developer Alfred Taubman and CBS Chairman Laurence Tisch.

Consumer brands.

Macy's, Bullock's, I. Magnin.

R. H. Macy, 151 West 34th Street, New York, NY 10001; (212) 695-4400.

4

Montgomery Ward

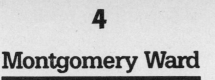

#4 *in department stores*

Employees: 67,200
Sales: $5 billion
Profits: $139 million
Founded: 1872
Headquarters: Chicago, Illinois

It would be an understatement to say the 1980s were climactic times for Montgomery Ward. For starters:

♦ The company emerged as a privately held firm after a 14-year stay as a ward of Mobil Oil.

♦ They discontinued the business that created the company—mail-order catalogs.

♦ They closed more than 100 stores and revamped the rest to concentrate on four areas—home furnishings, apparel and jewelry, automotive and electronics and appliances.

Their new leader, Bernard F. Brennan, came to Ward's in 1985 when Mobil Oil executives were in despair, having kept alive "The Monkey Ward" through $609 million worth of cash transfusions since 1974. In picking the then 46-year-old "Bernie" Brennan, Mobil was turning to a man with retailing in his blood. His elder brother, Edward Brennan, heads Sears, Roebuck. Both his parents, several uncles, and his grandfather were loyal Sears workers. Bernie himself worked in a Sears warehouse during high school and joined Sears the day after his college graduation. According to insiders, Bernie left in 1976 because of tension with older brother Edward.

Once in command at Ward's, Brennan shut down the unprofitable $1.2 billion catalog operation, and killed the Jefferson Ward discount chain, closing 133 stores. To counter what *Forbes* called a "polyesters 'r' us" image, Brennan began emphasizing name brands and the latest fashion trends, hiring 250 apparel specialists to upgrade Ward's dowdy merchandise. He transformed the Montgomery Ward general merchandise store into a store made up of four "boutiques." These separate

stores—Electric Avenue, Home Ideas, The Apparel Store (includes The Kids Store and Gold 'N Gems) and Auto Express—can be found under one roof. Different Montgomery Ward stores offer different combinations of specialties. In Tucson, Arizona, the stores are together on one site but have separate entrances—like a mini-mall. In 1987, the first free-standing, single-specialty store—Electric Avenue—was built in California. Montgomery Ward is now opening a number of other single-specialty, free-standing stores, pitting them against champion specialty retailers like Circuit City for electronics and The Limited for clothing. Brennan also moved the New York buying office to Chicago. Montgomery Ward operates in 39 states—where they run 325 stores, 133 product service centers and 26 distribution centers.

From all reports, Brennan is a harsh taskmaster. He holds meetings during the evening and over the weekend (meetings have been known to last for 16 hours). In his first three years as CEO, he took only a few days vacation. He is known for his explosive temper and impatience with bureaucracy, often firing employees with-

Bernard F. Brennan is reshaping Montgomery Ward while his brother Edward (see page 197) is guiding Sears, Roebuck.

out notice. "I expect results," he once told the *Los Angeles Times*. "My tolerance level of failure is not very high."

There's no denying Brennan has brought positive results. In 1987 Ward reported $130 million in profits on $4.6 billion in sales, and the next year he executed a leveraged buyout of the company with the help of General Electric Capital Corporation, the financial services arm of General Electric. Brennan and GECC paid $1.5 billion in cash and assumed $2.3 billion in debt. Part of the deal involved the sale of Ward's credit card operation to GECC. The transaction made Brennan a very rich man and put him in firm control of the company he had turned around.

When he sold Ward's catalog division, Brennan cut loose a piece of American history begun in 1872 with young Aaron Montgomery Ward, a traveling salesman for a Chicago-based dry goods firm. Each day, in a horse and buggy, he visited little country stores. He observed that farmers were entirely dependent on their local country stores, stores often selling goods at great profit to their owners. Everyone involved in the transaction—the whole saler, retailer, jobber and merchant—took a piece of the action. The exploited farmer had nowhere else to turn for staple goods. Ward had an idea: cut out those middlemen and pass the savings on to the consumer. The large-scale mail-order store was born. The famous Montgomery Ward catalog (or "Wish Book," as it was popularly called) evolved into a piece of enduring Americana: a bound book complete with woodcut illustrations and an index. It went from a 24-page pocket-sized booklet in 1874 to a two-pound, 544-page catalog in 1893.

Although Ward started in the mail-order business 15 years before Sears, they lost the lead early in this century. In 1924, Ward's directors turned down General Robert E. Wood's suggestion to open retail outlets. Wood, then a Ward's vice president, quit, joined Sears and led that company's expansion into retail sales. Ward's was left behind as Sears became the dominant force in U.S. retailing. Now an ex-Sears man is leading the charge at Ward. He was planning to open 35 new stores and hire 10,000 people in 1990.

Montgomery Ward, Montgomery Ward Plaza, Chicago, IL 60671; (312) 467-2025.

SPECIALTY STORES

Here's an industry-invented term under which you find stores with a single product line: clothing (Nordstrom), electronics (Tandy), computers (ComputerLand), do-it-yourself (Lowe's). Three stores—Woolworth's, Melville and The Limited—own different types of specialized stores in addition to their flagship outlets. Each has its own niche and distinctive culture. We're also including here the nation's leading deep-discount, members-only store (the Price Club) and one of the country's most successful purveyors of outerwear and other clothing (L. L. Bean) through mail-order catalogs.

1

#1 *in specialty retailing*

Employees: 132,000
Sales: $8.8 billion
Profits: $329 million
Founded: 1879
Headquarters: New York, New York

Say Woolworth and you immediately think of the five-and-dime variety store. And today's Woolworth Corporation *is* like a variety store. Just as the old five-and-dime set out counters filled with notions—candy, lipsticks, pencil cases, toys, pocketbooks, thimbles, yarns—the new Woolworth provides variety by fielding a zillion stores specializing in—well, you name it: shoes, men's suits, children's apparel, athletic equipment, women's clothes, costume jewelery, discount drugs, home furnishings. Woolworth has become the master store crafter. They still run the familiar F. W. Woolworth variety stores (1,140 in 1989), but they have more Kinney shoe stores (1,815) and nearly as many Foot Lockers (1,017). Coming into the 1980s, they had stores operating under 7 names; into the 1990s, 43 different names (more than 8,000 stores). In 1988 they opened an astounding 1,100 stores or a store every eight hours. They now own more stores than any other company in

TOP FIVE
SPORTING GOODS CHAINS

		Sales
1.	Herman's	$700 million
2.	Thrifty (Big 5, MC, Gart Bros., Browns, Dave Cook's, Mages)	$635 million
3.	Oshman's	$305 million
4.	Sportmart	$165 million
5.	Champs (Woolworth)	$88 million

Source: DSN research, 1989.

the world. (McDonald's has more stores but owns only one-quarter of them.) And they still haven't stopped. This store-crazy company wants to be the king of the shopping malls. The U.S. has some 1,400 shopping malls. Woolworth wants to be in every mall with 5 to 10 stores. Among Woolworth's many offshoots are Mathers, Susie's, Afterthoughts, Athletic X-Press, Richman, Champs and Woolworth Express (a scaled-down version of the big Woolworth's, ticketed for 2,000 units by the year 2000).

Woolworth's chairman and CEO, Harold E. Sells, started in retailing in 1945 as an assistant store manager with Kinney Shoe Corp., which Woolworth bought in 1963. A native of Ozark, Arkansas, Sells played a key role in refashioning Woolworth's during the '80s—including the closing of the Woolco discount stores (Woolworth's unsuccessful response to K mart) and a strategic concentration on opening specialty stores. Also during the decade, Woolworth sold their holdings in their British subsidiary, though the company still owns and operates a variety of stores, including F. W. Woolworth, in Canada, Germany and Australia.

History. In selling their stake in the British operation, Woolworth was cutting a link with their past dating from 1909 when founder Frank Winfield Woolworth opened his first British stores—called "Three and Sixpence" stores. Frank Woolworth's first venture, The Great Five Cent Store, opened in Utica, New York, in 1879, failed because of a poor location, but Woolworth opened a new store in Lancaster, Pennsylvania, just 10 days

later. There he sold toys, police whistles, kitchenware—all for 5 cents or less.

The Lancaster store caught on, and Woolworth upped his price limit to 10 cents. "As soon as we added 10-cent goods to the line," he later wrote, "we took away part of the 5-cent store's charm—the charm of finding only one price on a counter, and only one price in the store. But as long as we kept the 5-cent goods on one side of the store and 10-cent goods on the other, the charm was not entirely lost."

Frank Woolworth changed the name to Woolworth's 5¢ and 10¢ Store. He admired the red color of A&P grocery stores, and painted his storefronts the same color, adding the firm's full name in gold letters: F. W. WOOLWORTH Co. Since the company first sold stock to the public in 1912, they have never failed to pay quarterly dividends.

The famous Woolworth Building in New York City was completed the next year; at the time it was the tallest in the world. President Woodrow Wilson pressed a telegraph key on April 24, 1913, to light the building. Called the "Cathedral of Commerce," the 792-foot Gothic skyscraper remains Woolworth's headquarters. Frank Woolworth personally paid the $13.5 million construction costs in cash and installed himself in a 24th floor marble office that was a detailed replica of the Empire Room of Napoleon Bonaparte's palace in Compiègne, complete with an oil portrait and life-size bust of Napoleon. When he finished a day's work as the Napoleon of American commerce, he went home to his 30-room mansion on Fifth Avenue, where he had installed an enormous pipe organ that played great musical works at the flick of a switch and displayed on the wall an illuminated portrait of the composer.

When Woolworth died in 1919, five days short of his 67th birthday, his empire encompassed 1,081 Woolworth stores, with annual sales of $119 million. He left a fortune worth $60 million. A granddaughter, Barbara Hutton, eventually inherited about one-third of the estate and made headlines by marrying Georgian Prince Alexis Mdivani, German Count Court Haugwitz Hardenberg Reventlow, movie star Cary Grant, Lithuanian Prince Igor Troubetzkoy, Dominican playboy Porfirio Rubirosa, German Baron

Gottfried von Cramm and Laotian Prince Doan Vinh Na Champassak.

In spring and summer 1988, on its 75th anniversary, the Woolworth Building in New York City was opened to visitors. Thousands of residents and tourists viewed a huge memorabilia exhibit in the lobby. The outside of the building was illuminated from the 27th to the 60th story.

Stock performance. Woolworth stock bought for $1,000 in 1980 sold for $8,477 on January 2, 1990.

Consumer brands.

> Woolworth, Woolco, Kinney Shoes, Foot Locker, Lady Foot Locker, Kids Mart, Mothers, Carimar, Afterthoughts, Susie's, Athletic X-Press, Williams the Shoemen, Richman, Champs Sports, Anderson-Little, Sportelle, Fredelle, Randy River, Moderna, Der Schuh, Robinson's, Northern Reflections, Raglans, Footquarters, Rubin, Canary Island, Little Folk Shop, Woolworth Express, Frame Scene, Herald Square Party Shop, Kids Foot Locker, The Rx Place, Live Wire, Ashbrooks, U.B. Anywear, Face Fantasies, Lewis, Fun + Fashion, Activeworld, Cotton Supply Company.

Woolworth Corporation, 233 Broadway, New York, NY 10279; (212) 553-2000.

2

MELVILLE CORPORATION

#1 in shoe retailing

Employees: 98,500
Sales: $7.6 billion
Profits: $398 million
Founded: 1892
Headquarters: Rye, New York

Stanley P. Goldstein had some mighty big shoes to fill when he became Melville's chairman and CEO in 1987. His predecessor, Frank Rooney, had run the nation's biggest shoe seller for nearly a quarter century and was considered by many to be a retailing genius. When Rooney took over in the mid-1960s, the Thom McAn shoe store chain, long Melville's mainstay, was faltering under the founding family's leadership. Although his father had been in the shoe business and he himself was a shoe designer, Rooney didn't believe the

world began and ended with shoes. He took Melville out of the cities and into suburban shopping malls where he filled as many slots as possible with new stores. And not just shoe stores but clothing stores, toy stores, discount stores and drugstores.

Rooney's strategy yielded rich returns for Melville and made them proprietor of over 6,000 stores, including the shoe departments they run in 2,400 K marts, 990 Thom McAns, 560 Chess Kings (young men's clothes), 775 Kay-Bees (toys), 350 Marshalls discount stores, 500 Wilson's leather shops and 790 CVS drugstores. Stanley Goldstein came out of CVS, (Consumer Value Stores). In fact, he, along with his brother and a friend, founded CVS in Lowell, Massachusetts, in 1963 with one store. By 1969 when Rooney scooped them up for $12 million worth of Melville stock, there were 42.

Goldstein remained CVS president and moved up in the Melville hierarchy until he reached the top at age 53. A self-effacing native New Englander, Goldstein told *Business Week* in 1987, "I am not the genius merchant. I ask good questions and encourage a style where people work closely together." Goldstein was paid $1.2 million in 1989.

Sitting on Melville's board is Frank Melville, grandson of the company founder. His grandfather, also named Frank, went into the shoe business because his prospective bride didn't care for his former occupations as cowboy, sailor and stagecoach driver. So in 1882 Frank became a shoe clerk, earning $11 for a 92-hour week. Soon he established himself as a traveling wholesaler, and after one of his customers skipped town without paying for a shoe shipment, Frank took over the man's three shoe stores in New York and started the Melville Shoe Company in 1892.

Frank's son, Ward, was the real force behind the company's success. He made two excellent decisions: enter shoemaking by merging with the manufacturing firm of his World War I commanding officer, and create what became the famous Thom McAn shoe brand (by shortening a Scottish golf pro's name). The first Thom McAn opened in New York in 1922, offering black or brown men's shoes for $3.99. Five years later they had 370 stores across the country. But the sensible black shoe

TOP FIVE MEMBERSHIP WAREHOUSE CLUBS

		Sales
1.	Price Club	$4.0 billion
2.	Sam's (Wal-Mart)	$3.8 billion
3.	Costco	$1.9 billion
4.	PACE	$1.2 billion
5.	BJ's Wholesale Club	$800 million

Source: DSN research, 1989.

didn't wear well into the fashion-conscious 1950s, and in 1964 the Melvilles turned to Francis C. Rooney to bring them into the modern world.

Stock performance.   Melville stock bought for $1,000 in 1980 sold for $9,077 on January 2, 1990.

Consumer brands.

Apparel: Marshalls, Chess King, Free Fall, Wilson's, Berman's, Tannery West, Accessory Lady.

Footwear: Thom McAn, Fan Club, Smart Step, B.O.Q.

Drug, health and beauty aid: CVS Drug, Freddy's.

Toys: Kay-Bee Toy & Hobby, Toy World, Play Things.

Domestics: Linens 'n Things.

Furniture: This End Up, Prism.

Wall decor: Prints Plus.

Melville Corporation, One Theall Road, Rye, NY 10580; (914) 925-4000.

3
PRICE CLUB®

#1 *in warehouse retail stores*

Employees: 12,545
Sales: $4.9 billion
Profits: $117 million
Founded: 1976
Headquarters: San Diego, California

You are in a warehouse, standing on concrete floors; the air is sweltering. All around you are industrial-strength gray metal shelves stocked with familiar goods packaged in mammoth quantities—huge drums of soy sauce, 10-gallon tubs of Hershey's chocolate sauce, paper cups in jumbo packages of 10,000. The rows seem to extend for miles; shelves are stocked two stories above your head. Welcome to the Price Club, the world's first warehouse retail store. No frills, no service, no credit cards, no decor, no air-conditioning, no advertising. Just lots of stuff, big and cheap.

These "barebones giant emporiums," as *California* magazine called them, mark up all items about 9.5 percent, compared with 30 percent for most discount stores and 50 percent for most full-service department stores. Of course, this kind of shopping can be rugged, and buyers are urged to stay alert to dodge the forklift trucks manuevering through the aisles. To shop at the Price Club, you must be a member. To qualify, you have to be a business or an individual with a business license ($25 a year fee) or be employed in the public sector or work for a hospital, utility or transportation company ($15 a year fee). Today more than 50 Price Clubs operate in eight states. More than half are in California. The others are in Arizona, New Mexico, Connecticut, New Jersey, New York, Virginia and Maryland.

History.   Sol Price was a crusading liberal lawyer in San Diego who found law didn't offer enough action, so in 1953 he founded the Fed-Mart discount chain, a combination mass-merchandising operation and supermarket chain, that he built into a giant discounter. According to a former colleague, "Sol has a real social conscience—he believed this business could be conducted with considerable benefits to consumers."

In 1975 he sold control of Fed-Mart to a German retailer, Hugo Mann. The sale left Price with a five-year management contract as president and CEO, but he and Mann locked horns at the first board meeting. At the second meeting Price was fired and management changed the locks on his office. Seven months later he was back in business with the Price Club.

Owners and rulers.   For years, Sol Price ran the business himself, with the help of his son, Robert. Now he is chairman emeritus and Robert has taken over as CEO, president and chairman of the board.

Price's 10 percent ownership, worth $200 million, qualifies him for the *Forbes* list of the 400 richest Americans. But he was paid a modest (by American CEO standards) $249,000 in 1989.

As *a place to work.* More than 90 percent of employees are warehouse personnel. The Clubs in California, Maryland, Connecticut, and New Jersey operate under labor union contracts. The Price Club is extremely proud that they've never had an employee strike or lockout and boasts of excellent employee relations. Anyone thinking of working for the Price Club should also know the company is tightly disciplined. Sol Price monitors all the Price Clubs and visits one every day. "Some of my employees consider me an SOB," he says. "I do criticize... I get upset when my managers say they're going to train a new employee. You train a dog, you teach a person."

Global presence. The Price Club has a joint Canadian venture with five clubs in Quebec and one in Ontario.

Stock performance. Price Club stock bought for $1,000 in 1982 sold for $12,247 on January 2, 1990.

Consumer brands.

Price Club.

The Price Company, 2657 Ariane Drive, San Diego, CA 92117; (619) 581-4600.

Charles Lazarus, founder of Toys 'R' Us, was the highest paid corporate executive in America during the 1980's. He took home a total of $156 million.

4

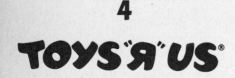

#1 *in toy stores*

Employees: 35,900
Sales: $4.8 billion
Profits: $321 million
Founded: 1948
Headquarters: Paramus, New Jersey

People used to shop for Christmas toys at department stores, Woolworth's and other general merchandise retailers. Then Charles Lazarus invented a whole new concept: toy supermarkets. He revolutionized the toy business, creating one of the great successes of modern retailing. In 1990 Toys 'R' Us was operating 404 self-service toy stores in 41 states and 74 foreign stores. These stores are big, averaging about 43,000 square feet, stocked with 18,000 toys sold at discount prices. No one can compete with them in terms of selection. Toys 'R' Us has been such a smash hit they commanded 25 percent of U.S. toy sales by 1990, but founder Charles Lazarus is still not satisfied. He wants 50 percent of the market—plus the rest of the world. He's also going after the children's wear market with over 150 Kids 'R' Us stores. His wife, psychiatrist Helen Singer Kaplan, calls him a "retail junkie."

The toy business is notoriously unstable for manufacturers. They never know what's going to sell. In 1987, two companies, Coleco and Worlds of Wonder, went belly up, and General Mills fled the business by getting rid of Kenner-Parker toys, bought later by Tonka. One toy company executive said to *Business Week*: "The toy companies did poorly, and Toys 'R' Us did great. Something in the equation is not working out." Toys 'R' Us really calls the tune. A manufacturer has to pay them a fee to get a product featured in the store's newspaper circular.

Retailing is supposed to be a low-margin business where profits are counted in pennies. But someone forgot to tell Charles Lazarus that. Toys 'R' Us regularly nets close to seven cents on the sales dollar—*after* taxes. Almost unheard of in the store business.

History. In 1948, World War II veteran Charles Lazarus converted his father's bicycle repair shop in Washington, D.C., into a children's furniture store. Lazarus soon realized cribs and diaper-changing tables are one-time purchases, but toys are constantly replaced. So he renamed his store the Baby Furniture & Toy Supermarket (re-christened Toys 'R' Us in 1957). The first store thrived, and three more were opened before Lazarus sold the company to Interstate Stores in 1966. In 1974, Interstate went bankrupt and Lazarus came back to rescue his company.

Lazarus organized his toy stores like supermarkets—displaying a vast array of toys and brands in warehouse-sized buildings and emphasizing consistently low prices, not sales. Stores were located off the main highway, near a shopping center. Computerized cash registers kept track of inventory, reporting what was hot and what was not. In 1983, Lazarus duplicated this formula, launching Kids 'R' Us: stores selling upscale clothing for kids (J. G. Hook, Izod-Lacoste, Calvin Klein) at prices about 30 percent less than the manufacturer's suggested retail price. Kids 'R' Us featured tony carpeted floors, neon signs, fun-house mirrors, TVs showing music videos and a play area.

Owners and rulers. Lazarus has rewarded himself well for his efforts. In fact, the $156 million he earned during the 1980s made him the most highly paid American executive of the decade. But the largest owner, with nearly 14 percent of the shares, is Petrie Stores.

As a place to work. Although Toys 'R' Us has a reputation as a one-man company, Lazarus has groomed young executives, giving them a large measure of independence. He thought Cabbage Patch Kids wouldn't catch on, but his merchandising people disagreed and bought lots of the dolls anyway—much to his relief. They promote entirely from within. And they claim to have made a dozen employees millionaires through a generous stock purchase program.

Global presence. They now have 74 stores overseas and have shaken up the British toy industry with the Toys 'R' Us concept. Next target: Japan. The company plans to have four to six stores there by 1991. In 1989, they entered into a joint venture with McDonald's (80 percent owned by Toys 'R' Us and 20 percent by McDonald's), whereby McDonald's will help locate Toys 'R' Us sites in Japan in exchange for permission to open fast-food outlets at the toy stores.

Stock performance. Toys 'R' Us stock bought for $1,000 in 1980 sold for $21,341 on January 2, 1990.

Consumer brands.

Toys 'R' Us.

Toys 'R' Us, 461 From Road, Paramus, NJ 07652; (201) 262-7800.

5

THE LIMITED, INC.

#5 *in specialty retailing*

Employees: 59,900
Sales: $4.6 billion
Profits: $347 million
Founded: 1963
Headquarters: Columbus, Ohio

When Leslie Wexner opened his first store, he wanted to limit the clothing to one line: women's sportswear. Before his Limited chain appeared in malls across the nation, women looking for sportswear had to search through department stores or pricey boutiques. Wexner's particular genius was to narrow his selection to specific clothing targeted at a specific consumer. The first Limited store opened in 1963, and Wexner's formula worked like a charm. In 13 years he had 100 stores, by 1990 over 750. And that was just the Limited.

During the 1980s, Wexner duplicated his formula many times. What the Limited did for women's sportswear, Victoria's Secret does for lingerie—an entire store devoted to lacy panties and bras. Wexner bought this chain of 4 stores in 1982; seven years later he had 353 "Vickie's" stores (as executives have nicknamed the chain). Wexner targeted overweight women when he purchased Lane Bryant in 1982. He threw out the frumpy frocks and started selling style, telling *Fortune* that "Big women are just like every other woman. They read the same books, watch the same TV, and fall in love with Burt Reynolds just as fast. They want to look like their smaller friends." In the six years after Wexner bought the chain, the number of Lane Bryant stores tripled.

Wexner's stores are guns aimed at very specific targets. In 1980 he started Limited Express—sportswear for younger women along with a smattering of men's wear; now there are over 400 of these stores. In 1985 he went after low-income women by acquiring the 67-year-old Lerner chain and high-income women by latching onto the upscale Manhattan shop, Henri Bendel, which he then moved into Chicago, Boston and Columbus. Wexner closed out the decade by snatching Abercrombie & Fitch, a 25-store chain offering clothing and eccentric baubles for the rich and idle.

Result: Leslie Wexner moved into the 1990s with an armada of over 3,000 stores. Merchandise comes from 6,300 suppliers around the world; over 40 percent of the clothes are made outside the U.S. But although many of the labels on these clothes boast of their foreign origins, no one "designer" creates the Limited look and many of the "European" designs (the pseudo-Italian Forenza, the pseudo-Australian safari Outback Red line) were made in Turkey, China and Hong Kong.

Leslie Wexner was born in 1937, the son of Russian immigrants. His father managed clothing stores and opened a store in Columbus called Leslie's (after his son). Wexner went to work at the store after dropping out of law school at Ohio State, but soon quarreled with his parents. He wanted the store to focus on hot-selling sportswear items, but they maintained a wide variety of merchandise. So Wexner borrowed $5,000 from his aunt and opened his own store. His parents later joined him at the Limited. Stock was first offered to the public in 1969; Wexner's dad was listed as chairman and his mom

was secretary. Wexner has been president and CEO of his company since the founding, and became chairman in 1985. His stock is worth $2 billion, making him one of the dozen richest people in America (salary: $1.7 million).

A bachelor, Wexner has a close relationship with his mother Bella. Still on the Limited's board, Bella lives near his house and has an office at company headquarters. Wexner told *Fortune* his mother was his inspiration and that they discuss matters once or twice a week. He also said he agreed with notorious womanizer Charles Revson (founder of Revlon):

What do women want? Anything they don't have. Every woman already has enough clothes to last 100 years. You have to sell excitement. Revson said women all hope they get laid, and I agree. They're sensuous. They're different from men. They dress to please men. You're not selling utility. That's why uptight women stockbrokers will put on a G-string when they get home. Like Revson said, we're selling hope in a bottle.

Wexner is known as the "Jewish Rockefeller" of his hometown, Columbus, because of his numerous charitable donations there—the most visible of which is the Wexner Arts Center (he chipped in $25 million of the $43 million cost). He has also made sizable contributions to the Wexner Research Center at the Columbus Children's Hospital, the Heritage House (a retirement home for Jewish people) and the Columbus United Way.

Stock performance. The Limited stock bought for $1,000 in 1980 sold for $70,151 on January 2, 1990.

Consumer brands.

Stores: Limited, Limited Express, Limited Too (children), Lingerie Cacique, Express, Victoria's Secret, Lerner, Lane Bryant, Lerner Woman, Abercrombie & Fitch, Henri Bendel.

Catalogs: Brylane, Victoria's Secret Catalogue.

The Limited Inc., Two Limited Parkway, P.O. Box 16000, Columbus, OH 43216; (614) 479-7000.

6

Tandy

#1 *in electronics stores*

Employees: 37,500
Sales: $4.3 billion
Profits: $304 million
Founded: 1899
Headquarters: Fort Worth, Texas

Tandy has been called the "Rodney Dangerfield of the consumer-electronics business," meaning, of course, they just don't get respect. Their vital statistics should inspire respect. They run 7,000 Radio Shack stores, selling more than 2,000 products, everything from extension cords, antennas, telephones and TVs to fax machines, computers and laser printers. They sell more than 100 million batteries a year and enough electrical wire to rope the globe 15 times. But, and here's the rub, the typical customer comes in and buys a couple of sockets for $5. In a high-tech world, Radio Shack has a low-tech image. Tandy makes highly regarded computers. In the 1980s they ranked just behind IBM and Apple as a supplier of personal computers. But their hardware-store image clings to them. As a result, they haven't penetrated the biggest market for personal computers: businesses. Not many corporate puchasing agents put Radio Shack on a short list of prospective suppliers.

Tandy tackled that problem head-on in the late 1980s. They remodeled the Radio Shack stores and introduced new nomenclature. Radio Shack now calls itself The Technology Store. And Tandy Corp. now calls itself America's Technology Answer. On top of that, in 1988 Tandy acquired Silicon Valley's GRiD Systems, a leading maker of top-of-the-line laptop computers, and they quickly established GRiD as the focal point for their attack on the corporate market. Tandy-made computers are now being sold to companies under the GRiD label.

It's ironic that a low-tech image adheres to one of the last of the Mohicans: an American company making high-tech products in the U.S. Of their 34 manufacturing plants, 28 are located in the U.S. What's more, in the late 1980s, the company inked agreements to make desktop computers for Digital Equipment and personal computers for Japan's Matsushita, the world's largest consumer electronics company.

The Matsushita deal is a milestone: A Japanese giant contracting with an American company to supply a high-tech product the Japanese will then sell in the American market under their own name. What a switch! Tandy's president, Texan John Roach, summed it up: "We think we can be America's preeminent consumer electronics company. Of course, there aren't many others trying, so we may win by default."

History. Mr. Lucky was the name Charles Tandy used over the CB radio in his sleek black Lincoln. Lucky, indeed: In a few years in the early 1950s Tandy turned his family's business, a small Fort Worth leather store founded in 1899 into a nationwide chain of leathercraft and hobby stores. But it wasn't really all luck; under Tandy's simple country-boy veneer lay a marketing genius.

His next goal was to branch out from his leathercraft business. He tried oil wildcatting, real estate and even a Texas department store in attempts to branch out from the core business. Nothing clicked until 1963, when he bought Radio Shack. To just about everyone else the Boston-based chain of nine electronics stores, with a mail-order business carrying $800,000 in unpaid bills, looked like a dry well. Tandy went into action. He cut back Radio Shack staff and aggressively pursued delinquent accounts. He was a firm believer in advertising ("If you want to catch a mouse, you have to make a noise like a cheese," Tandy said).

Charles Tandy's ideas and phenomenal energy put Radio Shack on the map—or rather, all over the map. From 1968 to 1973 the number of Radio Shacks jumped from 172 to 2,294. In 1973 alone, Tandy opened some 600, nearly 2 stores per working day. Despite enormous success, Tandy remained, until he died peacefully in his sleep in 1978, the "good ole boy." His office was in a coveted ground floor suite (once a Christian Science reading room); he answered his own phone; and his door was never closed to employees. Today, an eight-foot-tall bronze statue of Charles Tandy (with a foot-long cigar be-

The 8-foot tall bronze statue of Charles Tandy holding a foot-long cigar stands on the grounds of the Tarrant County Courthouse in Forth Worth.

tween the fingers of his right hand) stands in downtown Fort Worth, Texas.

Owners and rulers.　John V. Roach was behind Tandy's first push into the personal computer market in 1976, and he became CEO in 1981 at age 42. *Fortune* described him as a "big, tall Texan known for his charm," but by the mid-80s, when personal computer sales lagged, one associate called him "a thin-skinned prima donna—sharp with subordinates and hard to live with."

As a place to work.　Encouraging employees to invest in the company, Charles Tandy told them, "Stick with me and I'll make you rich." Sixty employees who bought company stock became millionaires. Tandy still has a Corporation Stock Purchase Program, where all employees can put between 1 and 10 percent of monthly income into Tandy stock. The company matches between 40 and 80 percent of the employee contribution. Approximately 75 percent of employees participate and own about 25 percent of the company. *Business Week* reported that in 1986 Tandy aggressively recruited at colleges and brought 200 well-scrubbed graduates to Fort Worth for three days of intensive training. The goal: a well-educated sales force. Within a year, all 200 had quit because competitors paid three times as much. In 1986, trying to upgrade their image with quick fixes, Tandy told all salespeople at Radio Shack computer centers to clean up their act; beards had to be shaved and white shirts with red ties were required.

Global presence.　In 1986, Tandy created a separate company called InterTan (owned by Tandy shareholders) to distribute Tandy products in Europe. After acquiring the Victor microcomputer and the Micronic hand-held computer from Sweden's Datatronic AB, Tandy gained access to a network of 2,700 distributors in Sweden, France, Britain, Germany, Switzerland, Holland, Norway, Denmark and Austria.

Stock performance.　Tandy stock bought for $1,000 in 1980 sold for $5,348 on January 2, 1990.

Consumer brands.

Radio Shack, Tandy, Archer.

Tandy Corporation, 1800 One Tandy Center, Fort Worth, TX 76102; (817) 390-3700.

7

nordstrom

#7 *in specialty retailing*

Employees: 26,500
Sales: $2.7 billion
Profits: $115 million
Founded: 1901
Headquarters: Seattle, Washington

Even before they opened their first East Coast store in 1989, Nordstrom was famous inside the retailing industry. Retailers traveling on the West Coast used to drop into Nordstrom to see if what they'd heard was true. And usually they found it was. This store prospers by emphasizing one of the oldest shibboleths of retailing: The customer comes first. And because so many stores do not, Nordstrom shines.

The company started in 1901 as a shoe store, founded in Seattle by a Swedish immigrant, John W. Nordstrom. His three sons turned their father's modest business into the nation's largest shoe chain. Nordstrom was strictly a shoe business until 1963 (the year John Nordstrom died), when they bought Best Apparel, a Seattle-based clothing store. In 1966 they added a Portland retail fashion outlet, Nicholas Ungar. The company sold stock to the public in 1971 and four years later had 11 stores in three states (Washington, Oregon and Alaska).

By 1985, Nordstrom had ousted Saks Fifth Avenue to become the nation's leading specialty fashion retailer—one specializing in fashion and nothing else. By 1988 Nordstrom had 48 stores in six western states and Virginia. Although Nordstroms are still primarily located in the West, they're moving eastward with two stores in the Washington, D.C., area and one that was scheduled to be opened in Paramus, New Jersey, in fall 1990. Stores are also slated for Chicago and Maryland.

When you walk into one of Nordstrom's 59 stores (43 Nordstroms, 10 clearance stores and 6 Place Two stores for younger customers), their formula for success is obvious. Stores feature marble and polished wood, piano players at baby grands (usually willing to take requests) and huge dressing rooms. They try to stock every size and color of an item—a holdover from their days as a shoe store. And the shoe department remains Nordstrom's centerpiece. They offer sizes to fit every foot, meaning some stores carry 100,000 pairs of shoes. In toto, the Nordstrom stores carry an inventory of 3.5 million pairs of shoes. Left in boxes, they would make 33 stacks each the size of Mt. Everest.

Nordstrom's hallmark is customer service, also a holdover from the shoe business. As the company points out, "Selling shoes is the epitome of one-to-one service—nowhere else in the fashion business will you find a salesperson on his or her knees in an effort to please the customer."

New Nordstrom employees are handed a statement summing up the company's philosophy. It reads, "Welcome to Nordstrom. We're glad to have you with our Company. Our Number One goal is to provide outstanding service. Set both your personal and professional goals high. We have great confidence in your ability to achieve them. NORDSTROM RULES: Rule No. 1: Use your good judgment in all situations. There will be no additional rules."

Nordstrom employees ("Nordies") go the extra mile, and they tell tales to prove it. They go out of their way to thank customers, including thank-you notes; they telephone customers when merchandise arrives; they give refunds cheerfully, sometimes on goods bought at another store. They might warm up customers' cars on cold days. To keep the sales force in this hyped-up state, Nordstrom holds daily team-spirit rallies. Devoted Nordies are as loyal as they are eager to please. In 1988, when Nordstrom opened a new store in Tyson's Corner, Virginia, 200 experienced Nordies moved cross-country at their own expense, eager for a shot at management jobs opening up there.

However, it appears Nordstrom's excellent reputation for customer service may sometimes come at the price of worker exploitation. In 1989, disgruntled employees in Washington state complained to the United Food and Commercial Workers Union that hourly wage earners were not being paid for overtime and were expected to perform a host of extra services for free—such as attending mandatory meetings, doing paperwork, making personal deliveries and writing customer correspondence after hours. These complaints were amplified in February 1990, when the *Wall Street Journal* published a scathing front-page exposé of employee conditions. But Nordies were quick to defend the company. Hundreds of them staged rallies in front of stores in Seattle, San Francisco, San Diego and Orange County, California, and at the offices of the *San Francisco Examiner*—holding big signs scrawled with phrases like "We Love Nordstrom" and "We Love Our Job." "We want to set the record straight that we're not being slave driven," one worker told the *San Francisco Chronicle*. In early 1990, the Washington State Department of Labor and Industries ruled Nordstrom had violated the state's Minimum Wage Act and must compensate employees for back wages. Nordstrom set aside $15 million to cover such claims and for the first time in their history, announced a drop in annual profits.

Three of the founder's grandsons, known as "Mr. Jim, Mr. John and Mr. Bruce," run the company along with John McMillan, a brother-in-law, and Robert Bender, a close friend of the Nordstroms. The family owns about 40 percent of the stock, worth $1.4 billion in 1990. In the late 1980s the Nordstrom family sold their 51 percent stake in the Seattle Seahawks football team for $99 million. Of the 16 top officers outside the board of directors, 8 are women.

Stock performance. Nordstrom stock bought for $1,000 in 1980 sold for $15,461 on January 2, 1990.

Consumer brands.

Nordstrom, Place Two.

Nordstrom Inc., 1501 Fifth Avenue, Seattle, WA 98101; (206) 628-2111.

8

#1 *in building supply stores*

Employees: 15,000
Sales: $2.6 billion
Profits: $75 million
Founded: 1946
Headquarters: North Wilkesboro, North Carolina

Workplace

Lowe's runs the nation's largest chain of building supply stores—those glorified lumber yards selling everything from hammers to TVs to two-by-fours. But unless you live in the Southeast, chances are good you have never heard of them. Their 306 stores operate in cities and small towns in 20 states rippling out in concentric rings from their headquarters in western North Carolina. They go as far south as Florida, as far west as west Texas and as far north as Indiana, Ohio and southern Pennsylvania. Like Wal-Mart, they prefer small towns. So you'll find Lowe's stores in places like Prattville, Alabama; Pine Bluff, Arkansas; Kissimmee, Florida; Whitesburg, Kentucky; Marble Falls, Texas; Teays Valley, West Virginia; and Zebulon, North Carolina.

In the past, Lowe's supplied lumber and materials to home builders. Now, with baby boomers and yuppies on their hands, they have to think about what's going inside those homes. In 1978, builders and contractors accounted for 59 percent of Lowe's sales. Ten years later that percentage was exactly reversed, with do-it-yourselfers now ringing up 59 percent of Lowe's sales. Lowe's had anticipated that baby boomers would eventually buy into the American dream of owning a home. The company's 1986 annual report noted, with some relief, that "flower children didn't grow up to live in trees after all, but settled down and bought houses made of lumber instead." Aware most boomers were nesting in what Lowe's calls "used homes," they concentrated on capturing these new customers by doubling floor sales space for everything from light fixtures to VCRs to wall coverings to ready-to-assemble furniture to hot tubs.

History. Lowe's started life as a hardware store in North Wilkesboro in 1946. The owner, Carl Buchan, set up a system to buy building materials directly from the manufacturer, at wholesale prices, and then discount them to individual customers. It sounds simple now, but nobody had ever done it that way before. Buchan planned for expansion from the start, and his first stop was Sparta, North Carolina.

By 1960, Lowe's had expanded to 13 stores in three states, mainly serving professional builders. That was also the year Buchan died, at 44, having barely begun to realize his dream of building his business into "the largest and most successful of its type in the world, owned and controlled by those who have built it."

Buchan was one of the first entrepreneurs to implement the idea that workers should share in a company's wealth. People still tell about the time Buchan approached a store manager and asked him what he saw in front of him. The manager said, "A damaged water pump, a dented refrigerator, and windows with broken glass." Buchan replied, "What I see is money—my money—because I paid for all that broken stuff. Before the year is out, we're going to have a plan so part of that will belong to you and the other employees. Then when you look, you'll see money, too."

Buchan's plan became the Profit Sharing Plan and Trust, which, after his death, took control of half of Buchan's stock. Through the 1960s and 1970s, this plan became famous when national magazines ran stories about how Lowe's employees retired rich. In 1975 there were stories about a $125-a-week warehouseman who retired with $660,000; a truck driver, with $413,000; and two store managers with $3 million each. These employees were direct beneficiaries of the enormous growth Lowe's went through during that period: from 13 stores in 1960 to 150 stores in 1976. During the 1970s, Lowe's standardized store design, and oriented themselves toward the do-it-yourselfer, the trend they capitalized on with a vengeance during the next decade.

Owners and rulers. Although Lowe's shares trade on the New York Stock Exchange, the Employee Stock Ownership Plan owned 31 percent of all shares at the start of 1990. This percentage keeps going up because the company buys shares each year to deposit in the plan for each employee's account. The 1988 contribution came to 13 percent of an employee's annual pay. The employee pays nothing. Lowe's is one of the largest employee-owned companies in the nation, and Chairman Robert Strickland and CEO Leonard Herring are prominent evangelists for profit sharing and employee stock ownership. When he was in the U.S. Senate, representing Louisiana, Russell B. Long was a tireless promoter of employee stock ownership plans and helped rewrite the tax code to make it advantageous for companies to establish such plans. After he left the Senate in 1987, Lowe's put him on their board.

As a place to work. The number of employees more than doubled during the 1980s and thanks to the stake they have in the company, Lowe's people tend to be loyal, committed workers. Those who were aboard in 1980 saw the value of their shareholdings triple.

Stock performance. Lowe's stock bought for $1,000 in 1980 sold for $4,955 on January 2, 1990.

Consumer brands.

Lowe's.

Lowe's Companies, Inc., P.O. Box 1111, North Wilkesboro, NC 28659; (919) 651-4000.

9

Employees: 500
Sales: $2 billion
Founded: 1976
Headquarters: Pleasanton, California

ComputerLand was invented by William H. Millard, who grew up poor in east Oakland, California, and who realized in the late 1970s that once computers were mass-produced (he was one of the first personal computer manufacturers), stores would be needed to sell and service them. The chain he started became the largest in the field. ComputerLand started as "Computer Shack" but Radio Shack forced a name change in 1977. Entering the 1990s, 749 ComputerLands were open in 34 countries—473 of them in the U.S. ComputerLands sell IBMs, Apples, Compaqs and other personal computer brands, with sales to businesses accounting for 87 percent of volume. All the ComputerLand stores are owned by local franchisees. ComputerLand Corp., headquartered near San Francisco, buys the computers for the stores and provides them with technical and service support. In return, they take 5 percent of sales (once upon a time 8 percent).

Bill Millard, a disciple of Werner Erhard's est philosophy, never got to stay around to savor this success. He fled to the South Pacific island of Saipan after losing a bitter court battle over a $250,000 note that he had signed in 1976 when he was hard up for cash. The note was convertible into a 20 percent share of any company Millard started or owned. When the noteholders sought to do exactly that, Millard stonewalled them. They took him to court and in 1985 won not only a judgment but also an award of $141 million in damages. In 1987 Millard flew in from Saipan to sell his controlling interest in ComputerLand to the Wall Street investment house of E. M. Warburg, Pincus & Co. Early in the 1980s *Forbes* had estimated Millard's 96 percent stake in ComputerLand was worth $1 billion. At one point, the noteholders were so tired of fighting Millard they agreed to sell it to him for $300,000. Millard stubbornly turned down the offer. According to *Forbes*, that cost him dearly. When Millard finally did sell, his take was only $75 million.

ComputerLand has been racked with so many changes in management and operating practices it's a wonder they survived to the 1990s. At one point, franchisees revolted at the 8 percent royalty, which was later scaled down. They also objected when Millard threw out Ed Faber, responsible for the chain's early development. In the late 1980s they went through several other upheavals, finally entering the 1990s under the direction of William Y.

Tauscher, formerly head of the drug wholesaler, FoxMeyer, and a major investor in ComputerLand. The six foot, six inch, 250 pound Tauscher, a Yale graduate, plans to spruce up the company and then sell stock to the public.

C*onsumer brands.*

ComputerLand.

ComputerLand Corporation, 5694 West Las Positas, P.O. Box 9012, Pleasanton, CA 94566; (415) 734-4000.

10

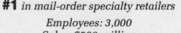

#1 *in mail-order specialty retailers*

Employees: 3,000
Sales: $580 million
Founded: 1912
Headquarters: Freeport, Maine

Until 1980, L. L. Bean was a thriving but relatively unknown maker of outdoor equipment and clothing. Then came Lisa Birnbach's *Official Preppy Handbook*. The best-seller may have been written tongue-in-cheek, but many readers took it seriously. When the *Handbook* called Bean "nothing less than prep mecca," would-be preppies responded by making the pilgrimage to Bean's store in Freeport, Maine. Those who stayed at home ordered merchandise from one of Bean's seasonal catalogs. All told, sales in 1981 shot up 42 percent. By the mid-1980s, sales were going up at a less astronomical 12 percent, but Bean's popularity is still high. And Freeport itself has become the site of retail outlets for dozens of designers and manufacturers—from Ralph Lauren to Laura Ashley. After the Atlantic Ocean, Bean's Freeport store (open 24 hours a day, 365 days a year) is Maine's second biggest tourist attraction, drawing an average of 2.5 million visitors each year.

H*istory.* Leon Leonwood Bean was a man who took his business personally. According to grandson Leon Gorman, who now runs the company, when L. L. heard a product failed, "he'd write the customer, return his money, enclose a trout knife, invite him fishing, or do anything else to make the matter right." Bean's first product—the Maine Hunting Shoe—was a flop. Ninety of the first 100 pairs he sent out fell apart. L. L. refunded the purchase price. He also sent follow-up letters offering a new, improved boot. Persistence paid off. In 1986, L. L. Bean, Inc. sold 266,771 pairs of the rubber-soled, leather-topped shoes. They remain the centerpiece of the million catalogs the company mails out each year.

To sell his boot, L. L. targeted holders of Maine hunting licenses. Thus began one of the first experiments in direct-mail merchandising. Since only nonresidents needed licenses, L. L.'s first buyers were East Coast lawyers, doctors and businessmen who spent their free time tramping through the Maine woods. Bean became their guide to the Maine outdoors. "This is the shirt I personally use on all my hunting and fishing trips," went a typical ad from one of the first catalogs. The reliable products and firm, friendly advice made Bean known not only for his honesty but for a quirky thriftiness. But L. L. was no born businessman. Before starting the company (when he was 39), L. L. had unsuccessfully sold soap and worked in a creamery. He saw his firm as a meal ticket, not a money-maker. After sales hit $2 million in the early 1960s, Bean was content to let things sit. "I'm eating three meals a a day," he said, "and I can't eat four."

Grandson Leon Gorman had a bigger appetite. When he took over the firm after L. L.'s death in 1967, the average employee age was 60, files and letters were stashed in cardboard shirt boxes and mailing labels (over one million of them) were typed by hand. Gorman began hiring MBAs, commissioning customer surveys and installing computers. Sales rose from $4.8 million in 1967 to $30 million in 1975. But as they did, the company's character changed. Gorman wasn't like his grandfather. He told W. R. Montgomery, author of *In Search of L. L. Bean*: "If I were in another business, I probably wouldn't care much about hunting or fishing, but I'm learning fast." More and more space in the catalog was devoted to women's wear. Much to their embarrassment, the company won a Coty fashion award in 1975.

Bean's customers still include hunters, fishers and men like the chief supply officer of the Israeli army, who bought 80 pairs of Maine Hunting Shoes, 300 pairs of socks and 100 green chamois shirts after the Yom Kippur War. Yet, closer to the mark these days is Jackie Kennedy Onassis (gum shoes and firewood carriers). Between 1978 and 1984, almost 70 percent of Bean's new customers were women, and their two most effective magazine ads ran in *The New Yorker* and *The New York Review of Books*.

Bean's Freeport outlet may look something like a Maine country store with its pine paneling, stuffed moose heads, and canoes on the ceiling, but the resemblance ends there. Other Maine country stores aren't cited in Harvard Business School case studies and don't need an IBM 3084 computer with 500 terminals to do inventory, handle postal orders and send customers letters with quaint misspellings for that "personal" touch.

Owners and rulers. L. L. Bean Inc. is privately owned by L. L. Bean descendants. Although Gorman reports he receives one or two offers a month to buy the company, so far nothing has come of them. A granddaughter, Linda Bean-Jones, unsuccessfully ran for Congress as a Republican from Maine in 1988.

As a place to work. Old man Bean paid his workers a nickel above minimum wage. No one retired because there were no retirement benefits. Today, there is a retirement plan, as well as benefits that include a gym, a bonus of up to 15 percent of annual pay, tuition write-offs and free use of sporting equipment. Annual turnover is 5 to 7 percent, not including temporary workers Bean hires during the Christmas season.

Social responsibility. According to Gorman, Bean gives 2 to 3 percent of pretax earnings to charity or conservation organizations. In recent years, that has included $500,000 to the Appalachian Mountain Club and $1 million to the Maine Medical Center for a new wing.

Global presence. The only place outside Freeport where you can buy Bean's merchandise off the shelf is in Japan, where Bean has a deal to sell selected Bean goods in Sony retail stores.

L. L. Bean, Inc., Freeport, ME 04033; (800) 221-4221.

DRUGSTORES

If you've been in a drugstore lately, you know they sell more than drugs. In fact, if you live in a state that allows it, you are just as likely to pick up a fifth of Scotch at your drugstore as you are a bottle of aspirin. And you aren't going to find many drugstores with soda fountains anymore. However, the pharmacy still brings in the big bucks. Prescription drugs account for anywhere from one-third to 40 percent of sales in the typical drugstore. This retail field has proved impervious to national chains. The big players tend to be regional. Longs is a dominant store in northern California, Eckerd is big in Florida, Rite Aid is strong in the Northeast. The only chain close to being national is Walgreen. Because so many independent drug stores exist, McKesson's role is crucial. They are, by far, the nation's leading drug wholesaler. McKesson doesn't operate any stores. They get the product to the stores—something they've been doing for over 150 years through some bizarre and precarious circumstances.

1

M Kesson

#1 *in drug wholesaling*

Employees: 15,800
Sales: $7.6 billion
Profits: $106 million
Founded: 1833
Headquarters: San Francisco, California

Social Conscience

They have few employees, considering their hefty sales (Honeywell and Borden, with comparable sales, have 76,000 and 46,000 employees, respectively), but that's easily explained. McKesson hardly makes anything. And they don't run any stores (Melville and Albertson's, two store operators with sales comparable to McKesson's, have 96,000 and 50,000 em-

ployees, respectively). McKesson is primarily a drug wholesaler, standing squarely in the middle of the equation between manufacturer and retailer. They deliver some 120,000 products other companies make, everything from prescription drugs to over-the-counter hemorrhoid remedies, to more than 14,000 independent drugstores, 3,000 chain stores (mostly with fewer than 50 stores) and 2,500 hospitals. Drug wholesaling is a $20 billion-a-year business— and McKesson owns 27 percent of it (nearly twice the share of the number two wholesaler, Bergen Brunswig). McKesson is the only wholesaler with a national reach, and their warehouses are computerized so pharmacy reordering is almost as automatic as withdrawing cash from a bank teller machine. More than 3,000 independent pharmacies are closely tied to McKesson through a Valu-Rite voluntary program under which McKesson acts as chain headquarters, supplying them with private label drugs and providing merchandising services to help them compete.

McKesson used to be Foremost-McKesson, an unwieldy conglomerate that sold milk and other dairy products, built homes, distributed chemicals, ran industrial parks, made spaghetti and wholesaled wines and spirits—in addition to distributing drugs. They quit all those activities during the 1980s and stripped Foremost (the dairy business) from their name. McKesson ranked as the nation's largest distributor of wines and liquors (they also owned some of the producers) when they left that field in 1988. They saw the handwriting on the wall: Alcoholic beverage sales were fizzling while bottled water sales bubbled. One of the residues of the Foremost business is bottled water, which McKesson sells in California, Arizona, Nevada and Texas under the Alhambra, Sparkletts and Crystal names. They also own 83 percent of Armor-All (products to protect car finishes).

History. McKesson has one of the most unbelievable company histories in America. Events began innocently enough, when John McKesson, scion of an old colonial family, opened a drugstore in Manhattan in 1833. In 1840 he took on a partner, Daniel Robbins, and changed the company name to McKesson-Robbins. They quickly became one of the most prestigious drug firms in the world, largely on the merits of their gelatin-capsule quinine pills. In 1929, Robbins' son sold the company to an ambitious man, F. D. Coster.

Coster was as crooked as a dog's hind leg. His real name was Philip Musica, son of a Neapolitan barber-turned-importer who brought Italian cheese and olive oil into New York. When shipments arrived, Philip went down to the docks and bribed the customs weigher to certify Musica's imports weighed less than the scales showed. The family prospered, moved to Brooklyn's fashionable Bay Ridge section and became leaders of the Italian community—until 1909, when father and son were arrested. Philip took the rap, paid a $5,000 fine and served five months of a one-year sentence at Elmira Reformatory.

Upon his release, Philip convinced his father to go into the hair-exporting business, shipping human hair overseas to wig makers, and the family prospered again. By 1913 they had $500,000 in bank loans, all supposedly secured by the company's stock of long, valuable hair. But when Philip went off in search of another loan, a bank investigator discovered that the hair in the Musica warehouses consisted of worthless ends and short sizes. Detectives burst into the Musica home in Bay Ridge. They found no Musicas, but they did find the valuable hair under the floor boards. They nabbed Philip and his father in New Orleans just as their getaway ship was about to cast off. Philip again took the blame and served three years in New York jails. He was released in 1916 and worked for the D.A.'s office as an undercover stool pigeon named William Johnson, specializing in informing on German spies. He went into the poultry business during the war, and was indicted for suborning perjury in a murder case in 1920. But Musica was never again convicted and never served another day in jail.

In the early 1920s he reemerged as Frank B. Costa, president of Adelphi Pharmaceutical Company of Brooklyn, ostensibly makers of hair tonic. Adelphi was actually a profitable bootlegging front, but Musica/Costa became so intimidated by his brawny partner, Joseph Brandino, that he closed it down. He turned up again in 1926 as head of Girard & Co., another hair tonic firm with a sizable clientele of nonexistent companies. Using these phony accounts as collateral, he borrowed his way into a position where he could buy McKesson-Robbins as Frank Coster, businessman.

He headed McKesson for 13 years, and by 1938 was listed in *Who's Who,* although two-thirds of his biography was phony. McKesson's sales seemed to grow steadily until the treasurer noticed no cash ever seemed to emerge. It was eventually revealed Coster had stolen almost $3 million (some used to pay off Brandino, who was threatening to reveal him). In the end, Coster/Musica shot himself and McKesson-Robbins was humiliated by the ensuing publicity.

In 1967, McKesson was purchased—against their will—by Foremost, a dairy firm named after James Cash Penney's prize bull.

Owners and rulers. The biggest chunk of stock—18 percent of all the shares—is lodged with an employee stock ownership plan. Individual employees have the right to vote the shares credited to them. The next biggest chunk, nearly 10 percent, was held in early 1990 by an investment management firm, Delaware Management. Professional managers run McKesson. Alan Seelenfreund, who rose through the financial side of the company, became chairman and CEO in 1989, succeeding an abrasive ex–grocery store executive, Thomas W. Field, Jr. Seelenfreund holds a PhD in management science from Stanford.

Social responsibility. During the 1980s McKesson earned a reputation as a company receptive to community needs. On the occasion of their 150th birthday, they sponsored a nationwide tour of the San Francisco Symphony. They sharply increased charitable contributions, giving more than $2.5 million annually, well over 1 percent of pretax profits. They contributed $10 million to the McKesson Foundation so it would not be dependent on annual company bequests. And they encouraged employees to volunteer their time and services through a grant program that steers company contributions to organizations in which McKesson people are active and through an annual awards program for outstanding employee community service.

Global presence. Virtually none, but in 1990 they gained control of Canada's largest drug wholesaler, Medis Health and Pharmaceutical.

Stock performance. McKesson stock bought for $1,000 in 1980 sold for $4,700 on January 2, 1990.

Consumer brands.

Bottled water: Alhambra, Sparkletts, Crystal.

Car finish: Armor-All.

McKesson Corp., One Post Street, San Francisco, CA 94104; (415) 983-8300.

2

Walgreens

#1 *in drugstores*

Employees: 47,400
Sales: $5.6 billion
Profits: $158 million
Founded: 1901
Headquarters: Deerfield, Illinois

The company that invented the chocolate malted with ice cream and originated the drugstore soda fountain is the closest thing we have to a national drugstore chain. They don't sell milkshakes anymore, and 12 percent of current sales come from liquor, wine and other beverages, but they're still the old Walgreen company.

You won't find a Walgreen's everywhere. They're conspicuous by their absence from the Pacific Northwest and the Southeast (except for Florida)—but coming into 1990 they were operating 1,525 stores in 28 states and the District of Columbia. Three states—Illinois, Florida and Texas—have 46 percent of their stores. In 41 of their top 50 markets, they rank either first or second. And they're highly computerized. If a senior citizen moved from Florida to California, the pharmacist would quickly be able to locate her prescription drug history. The pharmacy accounts for one-third of Walgreen's sales.

Walgreen's is quintessentially midwestern. They aren't slick. They compete in pricing but they don't scream the way a

Rite Aid does. They treat their employees as family.

Born in Chicago at century's turn, Walgreen retains a filial affection for their hometown. Even today, with stores from coast to coast, the Chicago metropolitan area accounts for 18 percent of total sales. In 1989 they were planning to open 17 new Chicago stores, where people sometimes say they have "a store on every corner."

During the 1980s Walgreen doubled their number of stores in a constant struggle to keep the chain up to date. In the five years ended August 31, 1988, they opened 460 new stores, acquired another 102 (the biggest chunk being the 66-store Medi Mart chain in the Northeast), closed 87 stores and remodeled 375 others. Walgreen doesn't just sell products—they also make them. In 1988, the company made and packaged 400 private-label health and beauty products. They also develop film in five photo-processing studios. The 1980s also saw the end of Walgreen's long-standing interest in the Mexican retailer, Sanborn's, and they exited the restaurant business as well, selling the Wag's chain to Marriott.

History. In 1901, Charles R. Walgreen, son of a Swedish immigrant, opened a drugstore on Chicago's south side. A pharmacist, he made many of the drugs so he could charge low prices. Walgreen became a chain in 1909 with the purchase of a second Chicago store. Then came Charles Walgreen's own brand of "double-rich" ice cream served at a fountain connected to the store. The fountain survived the winter by becoming a soup-and-sandwich shop serving food Charles' wife, Myrtle, prepared. That was the start of Walgreen's restaurant business, and the origin of the drug store soda fountain, for which Walgreen's became famous. A replica of the fountain they had in their Times Square store was featured in the 1955 motion picture, *My Sister Eileen*.

The third store opened in 1911—and the numbers just kept growing. Walgreen became a household word in Chicago during the 1920s. The founder died in 1939 and his son, Charles R. Walgreen, Jr., succeeded him. His task after World War II was to convert the chain into a self-service operation.

TOP FIVE DRUGSTORE CHAINS

	Sales
Walgreen	$4.8 billion
American Drug Stores (Skaggs, Osco, Sav-on)	$3.1 billion
Eckerd	$2.9 billion
Rite-Aid	$2.8 billion
Revco	$2.4 billion

Source: *Chain Store Age Executive*
August 1989.

Owners and rulers. The Walgreens hang in there. Charles R. Walgreen III, grandson of the founder, was elected to the board in 1963 when he was 28. He became president in 1969 and chairman in 1976, a post he still held in 1990. Like his father and grandfather, he is a registered pharmacist (1989 salary: $1 million). In February 1990, 48-year-old L. Daniel Jorndt was named president. He joined the company as a pharmacist. The Walgreens seem not to have retained any substantial stockholdings in the company. In 1988 Charles R. Walgreen III was listed as the owner of 471,000 shares (then worth about $14 million), seven-tenths of 1 percent of the total. In other respects as well, Walgreen is true to their Chicago roots. The entire board of directors consists of Chicagoans. Walgreen got their first female director in 1987 with the election of Marilou M. Hedlund, senior vice president of the big public relations firm, Hill & Knowlton.

As a place to work. The family tone at Walgreen is evident in the pages of their 1988 Annual Report: Its cover features a San Antonio store manager and his three sons bathed in sunlight. The boys are wearing baseball uniforms and the manager sports a proud grin. Walgreen likes to emphasize they're the land of opportunity and explosive growth, where cashiers become executives. In 1989, Walgreen's had 4,246 pharmacists, and they project 7,000 by 1993. They also projected that by 1993 they would need over 1,000 new store managers, over 2,000 executive assistants and 6,500 management trainees.

Social responsibility. Walgreen was the first drug chain to put prescription drugs in child-proof containers—long before it was required by law. They also supported the substitution of low-cost generic drugs for brand-name formulations. Yet, as President Fred Canning told the Walgreen employee magazine, "We don't need to be the cheapest place in town.... Surveys show that convenience, not price, is the motivating factor for shoppers, especially those 50 years and older."

Global presence. Their only business outside the continental U.S. is in Puerto Rico, where they operate 25 stores.

Stock performance. Walgreen stock bought for $1,000 in 1980 sold for $14,264 on January 2, 1990.

Consumer brands.

Walgreen.

Walgreen Co., 200 Wilmot Road, Deerfield, IL 60015; (708) 940-2500.

3

#2 *in drugstores*

Employees: 28,900
Sales: $3.1 billion
Profits: $103 million
Founded: 1962
Headquarters: Shiremanstown, Pennsylvania

No one has more drugstores than Rite Aid, a hard-nosed, combative operator of 2,350 stores in 22 states and Washington, D.C. Rite Aid specializes in brightly lit small stores (average size 6,500 feet), crammed with low-priced drugs and health and beauty aids—many carrying Rite Aid labels. As *Forbes* describes them, Rite Aid "caters to the middle class, and below. The stores are located...mostly in low-rent strip malls and in low-income areas. Rite Aid units flourish in the small, dying steel towns outside Pittsburgh, like McKeesport, and in poor coal towns like Logan, West Virginia."

Scrappy and successful. That was the image Rite Aid enjoyed—until May 1,

1989, when the *Wall Street Journal* published a front page article detailing a scandal involving Rite Aid's president, Martin L. Grass, son of founder Alex Grass. Ohio law enforcement officials had videotaped Grass allegedly bribing a member of the Ohio pharmacy board (the board had fined Rite Aid for a number of infractions, one of which was that Rite Aid had allowed nonpharmacists to handle prescription drugs). Rite Aid's stock remained depressed for a year after the incident. In 1990 an Ohio state judge threw out all bribery charges against Grass and the company, citing lack of hard evidence.

Rite Aid has also been in the middle of a fight over third-party reimbursement of prescription drug purchases. Health insurance plans have been trying to reduce pharmacy reimbursements, and Rite Aid has fought these moves in state after state. These third-party payments now account for nearly half of prescription drug sales, and Rite Aid is in no mood to see prices shaved, even though they are known as the most profitable operator in the drugstore field.

In 1988 Preston Robert Tisch, president of Loews Corp. and brother of CBS president Laurence Tisch, returned to the Rite Aid board after service as U.S. Postmaster General. He replaced Richard L. Thornburgh, former Governor of Pennsylvania, who became Attorney General in the Bush cabinet. The Grasses allowed they would miss Thornburgh but "recognize the significance of his new position."

In addition to operating drugstores, Rite Aid runs 72 ADAP auto parts stores in 5 New England states, 48 Encore bookshops in 5 mid-Atlantic states, and 168 Concord dry cleaners in 10 southeastern and midwestern states. They also own a business that supplies plasma for use in therapeutic and diagnostic products. In 1989, they bought Circus World Toys, operator of 190 toy stores. The same year they sold their 46.8 percent interest in Super-Rite Foods, the original business from which Rite Aid sprang.

S*tock performance.* Rite Aid stock bought for $1,000 in 1980 sold for $6,234 on January 2, 1990.

C*onsumer brands.*

Rite Aid, ADAP, Encore, Concord, Circus World Toys.

Rite Aid Corp., Railroad Avenue & Trindle Road, Shiremanstown, PA 17011; (717) 761-2633.

AUTOMOTIVE

CARS

American automakers had a bumpy ride during the 1980s. At decade's start, the Big Three—General Motors, Ford and Chrysler—held 77 percent of the U.S. market; they emerged with 67 percent. Chrysler absorbed a fourth company, American Motors. One by one Japanese automakers moved into the U.S. with manufacturing plants. In 1980, Japanese cars had 20 percent of the U.S. market; by decade's end, 26 percent. In California, their share is 40 percent. The Honda Accord was the best-selling car model in the U.S. during 1989. A 1989 survey of car owners by research firm J. D. Power & Associates found two-thirds of American motorists under age 45 prefer Japanese cars to American ones. These trends led acerbic British weekly, The Economist, to predict the Big Three may not survive to the next century—at least not in their present forms. The Economist said: "A truth has become self-evident: Detroit's Big Three are staring death in the face."

1

#1 *in automobiles, robots, diesel locomotives, defense electronics, data processing*
#2 *in trucks, mortgage banking*
#7 *in defense contracting*
Employees: 775,100
Sales: $126.9 billion
Profits: $4.2 billion
Founded: 1908
Headquarters: Detroit, Michigan

General Motors spent the 1980s closing plants, replacing factory hands with robots, substituting computers for white-collar workers, entering the arena of elec-tronic weaponry and juggling their books so they could buy up GM stock and continue to pay fat dividends. However, observers can't remember a single GM car of the 1980s that drew kudos from car buffs or ordinary car buyers. For years they made luxury V-8s with the subliminal message "Big is better," and were blindsided by the small car invasion from Japan. Not to be discounted, however, is inertia. GM ended the decade atop lists that rank corporations by their size. Their 1989 sales of $126,974,300,000 topped nearest contender, Ford, by $30 billion. The stats meant that every day of the year GM sold about $348 million worth of cars and other products.

The 1980s at GM constituted the Roger Smith Era, after Detroit-born Roger Bonham Smith, an accountant who became CEO in 1981 after a rise through the ranks from the finance side of the business. Always on the corporate staff, he had never worked for any of the car divisions. No one expected him to shake things up. But after taking command, Roger Smith tried to teach the elephant to dance. He bought Ross Perot's Electronic Data Systems in 1984 to make GM a powerful factor in computerized data processing systems (EDS' biggest customer is GM). He bought Hughes Aircraft in 1985 to enter the aerospace business, hoping space-age technology would help GM to build better cars (GM's Delco electronics wing was folded into Hughes). Also in 1985, Smith announced GM would launch a sixth car line, Saturn, to take a place alongside Chevrolet, Buick, Pontiac, Oldsmobile and Cadillac (the first Saturns were to roll out in summer 1990). In the mid-1980s Roger Smith could do no wrong. The business press hailed him as an innovator who was placing his personal imprint on GM.

However, it's a fickle world. By 1980s' end, GM had problems with their new businesses, their market share had nosedived and Ford Motor was being hailed as the industry's technological leader (for their aerodynamically styled cars) and profit leader (they made more money than GM in 1986, 1987 and 1988). Roger Smith suddenly fell out of favor.

Cadillac sales plummeted when GM shortened the cars by two feet in 1984. The next year, when engineers added tail fins, fender skirts and nine extra inches, sales soared 36 percent.

The *Wall Street Journal* headlined that GM was "Plagued with Drop in Morale." A former speechwriter for Smith, Albert Lee, wrote a book, *Call Me Roger*, purporting to tell how Roger Smith had "transformed the industry leader into a fallen giant." And in 1989 journalist Michael Moore took aim with a scathing film entitled *Roger & Me*, depicting GM chairman Roger Smith as an unfeeling bureaucrat who had abandoned GM's hometown—Flint, Michigan.

History. Although the acquisitions of the Roger Smith Era were impressive because of their size (Hughes Aircraft alone had sales of over $5 billion), they didn't really represent a new departure for GM. General Motors has been accumulating companies since their founding in 1908 by William C. Durant, a supersalesman with grandiose ideas. In fact, former buggymaker Billy Durant formed GM just to acquire other automakers. His base was Buick Motor, which he'd been running since 1904. He quickly brought over two dozen companies into the GM tent—parts suppliers as well as car builders such as Oldsmobile, Oakland and Cadillac (named for the French explorer who founded Detroit in 1701). If he'd had his druthers (and all the money in the world), Durant would have bought up every car company and parts manufacturer he could find. He made a good try at it anyway. Among those that got away were Ford, Goodyear Tire and Willys-Overland. Among those that didn't were vehicles bearing the now extinct marques of Rapid, Welch, Ewing, Elmore, Rainier, Reliance, Marquette and Cartercar.

A risk-taker ever alert for the next opportunity, Durant overextended himself and lost control of his company to eastern bankers in 1910. Never mind, he organized a new combination of car companies—Mason, Republic, Little, Sterling, Monroe, Chevrolet—and in 1916, with the backing of the du Ponts, Durant regained control of General Motors. Once again he was off on a buying spree. He bought the Scripps-Booth and Sheridan car companies, Fisher Body, Frigidaire, Dayton-Wright Airplane, Samson Tractor and a bunch of important parts makers: Dayton Engineering Laboratories (Delco), Remy Electric, New Departure Manufacturing and Hyatt Roller Bearing. With Delco came Charles F. Kettering, inventor of the self-starting ignition system. With Hyatt came Alfred P. Sloan, a management wizard.

This time Durant's reign lasted four years, twice as long as the last time. Caught in a vicious squeeze on Wall Street after borrowing millions of dollars to buy GM shares, Durant was rescued by people he despised, the bankers at J. P. Morgan. The Morgan interests and the du Pont family took firm control of GM, and Billy Durant was once again, in 1920, forced to leave the company he'd founded.

The du Ponts reorganized GM, and Alfred Sloan shaped the firm into a colossal global enterprise. Sloan reigned as president from 1923 to 1937 and as chairman until he retired in 1956 at age 80. His memoirs, *My Years with General Motors*, published in 1963, set forth his philosophy and became a bible for business executives trying to run a great big company. Borrowing from the German Army, Sloan created a divisional organization giving line managers operations responsibility while staff committees at the top set policies and long-term goals.

Whereas Henry Ford was content to make a black car that would serve a buyer for a lifetime, Sloan introduced the annual model change and different cars for different folks: "Chevrolet for the hoi polloi, Pontiac for the poor but proud, Oldsmobile for the comfortable but discreet, Buick for the striving, and Cadillac for the rich." In his book, Sloan recalled how GM passed Ford to become the nation's number one automaker. What Ford failed to realize, Sloan observed, was that the demand for cars for basic transportation would soon be met. "When first-car buyers returned to the market for the second round," he wrote, "with the old car as a down payment on the new car, they were selling basic transportation and demanding something more than that in the new car. Middle-income people, assisted by the trade-in and installment financing, thus created the demand not for basic transportation but for progress in new cars, for comfort, convenience, power and style. This was the true trend of American life and those who adapted to it and met that need got the business."

Such consumer devotion paid rich dividends. The car changed the way Americans live—and that car more often than not was a GM make. By 1936 GM was the largest company in the land, and was to hold this position through most of the next 54 years. GM also financed the American dream, setting up General Motors Acceptance Corp. to lend money to buyers of GM cars. In addition to financing car sales, GMAC became the nation's second largest mortgage banker. In recent years GMAC has occasionally made more money than the car divisions. As of 1989, loans outstanding totaled $74 billion, making GMAC a bigger lender than every commercial bank in the nation except Citicorp (but not as big as rival Ford).

GM is trying new strategies. They joined with Toyota to operate a car manufacturing plant in Fremont, California, on a 50-50 basis, so GM could learn more about making small cars in a cooperative work environment. Still, GM's U.S. market share continued to fall (from 44.5 percent in 1981 to 34.5 percent in 1989). Roger Smith's reaction, when pressed by a *Financial Times* reporter, was: "Where is GM today? We're number one in the world—right? We account for one out of every five cars produced worldwide—right? Now, where is America's TV industry? Where is the steel industry? I don't think GM has done too badly."

Owners and rulers. The Supreme Court forced the du Pont Company, which controlled about one-quarter of GM shares, to sell their shares in 1962. GM has 2 million stockholders who also own GM Class E and GM Class H shares, issued with the purchases of Electronic Data Systems and Hughes Aircraft. Institutional investors own 40 percent of the shares; directors and officers own less than two-tenths of 1 percent. Roger Smith was the biggest single stockholder among the directors and officers, holding 39,000 shares worth $1.5 million. In 1988, when GM had record profits despite a decline in market share,

Smith's pay went up 55 percent to $3.7 million. Meanwhile, GM's 470,000 salaried and hourly workers received profit-sharing checks averaging $265 apiece. A major flap ensued when GM announced they were doubling Smith's pension. In a page one story, *USA Today* quoted a local UAW president, who said: "I don't think anyone is worth $1.1 million for retirement." Smith retired in August 1990 and was succeeded by 56-year-old Robert Stempel, the first engineer to lead the company in many years. After stepping down as Secretary of State in 1989, George Shultz returned to the GM board, joining such luminaries as Anne L. Armstrong (chairman of the President's Foreign Intelligence Advisory Board), James H. Evans (former chairman of Union Pacific), Walter A. Fallon (former chairman of Eastman Kodak), John J. Horan (former chairman of Merck), Edmund T. Pratt, Jr. (chairman of Pfizer), John G. Smale (former chairman of Procter & Gamble) and Dennis Weatherstone (chairman of J. P. Morgan).

As a place to work. Working for GM used to be a sure ticket to a secure, well-paid, lifetime job. No more. During the 1980s General Motors cut employment in automotive operations by more than 100,000. In 1987, GM set a goal: reduce costs by $10 billion by 1990. A big chunk of those savings were made in the bloated bureaucracy called salaried employees. The salaried staff was decreased by 40,000, resulting in $2 billion savings. With all these cutbacks, GM still provides more jobs for people than any other company. More people work for GM than live in San Francisco. Even so, employees are not too highly valued. In their book, *The Big Boys*, Ralph Nader and William Taylor describe how GM ignored employee reports that cancer rates were abnormally high in the company's wood-model and machine-tool plants in the Detroit area.

Social responsibility. In 1953, President Eisenhower nominated Charles E. Wilson, GM's president, to be Secretary of Defense. At his confirmation hearing in the U.S. Senate, Wilson amazed Senators, and much of the public, by saying he could see no conflict arising as a result of his being a GM stockholder because he always felt that "what was good for our country was good for General Motors, and vice versa.

Our company is too big. It goes with the welfare of the country." Consumer activist Ralph Nader has tilted with GM for a quarter century, charging GM is more concerned with GM's own well-being than the safety and health of their customers and the American public in general. GM even has critics inside the house. John Z. De Lorean, the most flamboyant executive vice president GM has ever had, quit in 1973 and painted a vivid picture of a stultifying bureaucracy. Before leaving he wrote a memo citing GM's "lack of social responsibility," noting: "In no instance, to my knowledge, has GM ever sold a car that was substantially more pollution free than the law demanded—even when we had the technology." The Rev. Leon H. Sullivan (originator of the Sullivan principles to combat apartheid in South Africa) became GM's first nonwhite director in 1971, and he voted against management and in favor of proxy resolutions asking the company to terminate all sales and licensing agreements in South Africa. Ross Perot, who sold his company, Electronic Data Systems, to GM in 1984, quickly developed into an in-house critic. He fired off salvos like these: "Get rid of the 14th floor [the GM executive suite]. Get rid of the private dining rooms and chauffeured limos and heated garages. Get rid of everything that separates people." "You hate your customers, you hate your dealers, you hate your workers and your shareholders, you even hate each other—how can you have a bright future?" In December 1986 Roger Smith paid Perot $742 million to go away.

Global presence. GM does 16 percent of their sales abroad and holds 18 percent of the worldwide automobile market. In 1989, GM sold 11.2 percent of the passenger cars bought in Western Europe, marketed under the names Opel and Vauxhall. GM owns 33 percent of Isuzu, 5 percent of Suzuki and has partnerships going with Toyota, Daewo in Korea and Fujitsu-Fanuc (now Fanuc Ltd.), the big Japanese robot maker. And GM recently bought the British luxury sports car maker Group Lotus PLC and a 50 percent interest in Sweden's Saab.

Stock performance. General Motors stock bought for $1,000 in 1980 sold for $3,209 on January 2, 1990.

Consumer brands.

Buick: Century, Electra, LeSabre, Reatta, Regal, Riviera, Skylark.

Cadillac: Allante, DeVille, Eldorado, Fleetwood, Seville.

Chevrolet: Camaro, Caprice, Cavalier, Celebrity, Beretta, Corsica, Corvette, Lumina, Geo, Astro/Safari, S-10 Blazer, S-15 Jimmy, Suburban.

Oldsmobile: Calais, Cutlass, 88 Royale, 98 Regency, Toronado, Silhouette.

Pontiac: Bonneville, Firebird, Grand Am, Grand Prix, Le Mans, Sunbird, Trans Sport.

General Motors, 3044 West Grand Blvd., Detroit, MI 48202; (313) 556-5000.

2

#1 in trucks
#2 in automobiles, savings & loans
#3 in tractors

Employees: 358,900
Sales: $96 billion
Profits: $3.8 billion
Founded: 1903
Headquarters: Dearborn, Michigan

Ford's character has been shaped by the family whose name is on one out of every five cars and trucks on American highways. Ford has always had a more quirky, less predictable business approach than GM. They have gone through violent swings in performance, accompanied by upheavals in the executive suite as the ruling Ford family shuffled their prime ministers. The pendulum swung wildly in the 1980s, a climactic decade that Ford entered in deep gloom and exited in euphoria. This decade was also the first of the century in which the CEO wasn't a Ford family member.

Figuring people are always going to need money, Ford built up an amazing presence in financial services during the 1980s. Like GM, Ford has a finance arm, Ford Motor Credit, to finance the purchase of their cars—currently $55 billion in loans outstanding. But beyond that,

Ford now owns the nation's second largest savings and loan, San Francisco–based First Nationwide, with 350 branches in 13 states (acquired in 1985 and buttressed later on with bankrupt thrifts picked up at bargain prices), San Francisco–based U.S. Leasing, which leases big equipment like planes and computers (acquired in 1987) and the Associates, a Dallas-based small loan company with a network of offices throughout the country (acquired from Paramount Communications for $3.4 billion in 1989). Result: Ford Motor entered the 1990s with a loan portfolio of $115 billion. Only one other financial institution, Citicorp, is bigger. This interest in making money by dealing in money has sapped Ford's interest in other sidelines. As 1990 got under way, they had their communications satellite business (Ford Aerospace & Communications) on the auction block and were exploring a joint venture with Italy's Fiat that would include their New Holland farm equipment business.

History. A legend in his own time, Henry Ford introduced the assembly line to make cars, doubled employee wages so workers could buy the cars they were making and kept car prices low to give ordinary folks a chance to get behind the wheel. In the process he created one of the world's great manufacturing companies. He also became the richest man in the U.S. But he was, to the end, an eccentric loner. A populist, he hated bankers and Jews (in his mind, synonomous). He revered his mother, who died when he was 12, but rarely had anything to do with his brothers and sisters. He distrusted his business associates and had an uneasy relationship with his only son, Edsel, who died of cancer in 1943. And before he died in 1947, at age 83, he nearly ruined the company that bore his name. He died a month after the death of General Motors founder William C. Durant (who ended up penniless).

Whereas Durant was an inspirational salesman, Ford was a hardworking farmboy who became entranced early in his life with machinery. He was born in 1863 on a farm 10 miles outside Detroit, in a village called Dearborn. Ford put Dearborn on the world map by making it the headquarters of his automobile company.

The automobile was not an American invention, but here it reached its apotheosis. Between 1900 and 1910 more than 500 automakers began production in the U.S. One of them was the Ford Motor Company, formed in 1903 when Henry was 40. Ford built his first car in 1896, but two other companies founded to develop his cars had already failed. This time the investors got their money back in a year: The company sold 658 Model As, for $750 apiece, each sale generating a profit of $150.

Ford worked through the alphabet, naming new cars (although not all versions reached the market). His next hit was the Model T, debuting in 1908. It was a spirited classy-looking automobile, with a suspension system that could handle rural America's rough roads and an "ability," as biographer Robert Lacey put it, "to inspire affection in its drivers." The Model T ushered in the automobile age in America. More than 10,000 were sold in the first year. Ten years later more than half the world's cars were Model Ts. By

Ford Motor's first truck, the one-ton Model TT, introduced July 27, 1917.

the time the line was shut down in 1928, more than 15 million had been sold. Henry Ford fed this demand by bringing the car's price down. The Model T originally sold for $825; then for $440 in 1914 and $345 in 1916. And as he reduced the car's price, Ford boosted worker wages. He stunned the business world in 1914 by announcing a minimum wage of $5 a day, more than double the existing minimum for auto workers. The move made Ford a national hero and shielded him from the criticism of muckrakers.

While he was being hailed as an industrial messiah, Ford was doing an exquisite job of squeezing out the investors who had put him in business. He wanted nothing less than 100 percent control, achieved in 1919 by paying $105.8 million to seven stockholders whose original investment was $41,500. Henry Ford no longer had any use for them. He considered stockholders "parasites."

The deterioration of Ford Motor began after Henry Ford no longer had to answer to anyone but himself. His son, Edsel, joined the company, but Henry was never able to share power with him. In fact, as numerous biographers have detailed, Henry Ford humiliated and intimidated his son. At General Motors, long-time president Alfred Sloan used installment plans to attract low-income buyers; Ford refused to sell on credit. Sloan fielded different lines of cars and introduced the annual model change; Henry Ford insisted that "we cannot conceive how to serve the customer unless we make him something that...will last forever. We want the man who buys one of our products never to have to buy another." Thanks to the Model T, Ford continued to lead the automotive pack through the early 1920s. In 1923, when Henry Ford celebrated his 60th birthday, Ford turned out 2.1 million cars, good enough for 57 percent of the American market and 50 percent of the world market. But that was Ford's peak year. Never again were they to dominate again, not even with the new Model A, a six-cylinder car introduced in 1927. In the 1930s General Motors pulled steadily ahead, and even Chrysler began to outsell Ford. While Alfred Sloan was bringing professional management to GM, Henry Ford, to son Edsel's shame and horror, was giving more and more power

THE WHEELER-DEALERS
(or Who Keeps America Rolling)

		Market Share
1.	GM (U.S.)	35.1%
2.	Ford (U.S.)	24.6%
3.	Japanese automakers	21.9%
4.	Chrysler (U.S.)	13.8%
5.	European automakers	3.4%
6.	Korean automakers	1.2%

Source: *Automotive News*,
5 February 1990.

to his chief detective, Harry Bennett, who ruled a group of thugs and fought organized labor's efforts to unionize the Ford work force. World War II was a savior for the company: Ford went to work for the Pentagon and became the third largest military contractor of the war years.

If Ford's first 42 years were dominated by the founder, Henry Ford, the next 35 were the province of his grandson, Henry Ford II, who never forgave his grandfather for the way he treated Edsel. The reins of power were handed over on September 20, 1945, when Henry Ford bowed to pressure applied by his wife, Clara, and Edsel's widow, Eleanor, and resigned from the presidency in favor of his grandson.

Only 28 years old, Henry Ford II ("the Deuce") stocked the company with management talent, some imported from General Motors—and a block of it was the "Whiz Kids," a team of 10 ex-Air Force systems people headed by Charles B. "Tex" Thornton. Two Ford Motor Company presidents—Robert McNamara (President John Kennedy's defense secretary) and Arjay Miller—emerged from this group.

Henry Ford II saw his role clearly: modernize Ford, make it more like GM. At the same time, he inherited a *family* role. That was *his* name on the company door. In that sense, Ford would always be different from GM. To make sure no one missed that point, Henry's two younger brothers came into the company, Benson as head of the Mercury Division, William Clay to develop a new luxury model to compete with Cadillac: the Continental Mark II.

The founding family retained tight control. In 1978, Henry Ford II, Ford chairman, fired Lee Iacocca, Ford president.

Iacocca had 32 years with the company, but Henry Ford disliked him intensely and told the board: "It's me or Iacocca." Iacocca was out—the vote was unanimous. Iacocca was later to describe Henry Ford II as a "spoiled brat," saying he acted "like his grandfather," as if the company was his to do with as he pleased.

In 1979, with Iacocca out (he became CEO of Chrysler), Henry Ford II stepped down as CEO and in 1980 surrendered the chairmanship, replaced by a veteran Ford manager, Philip Caldwell. It was the first time in the company's history a Ford family member did not hold that position. Henry Ford II could look back on a 34-year reign whose milestones included selling stock to the public for the first time, introduction of the Thunderbird and Mustang models, the flop of the Edsel, the Pinto disaster, Ford's rise in Europe into the top tier of the European auto industry and the company's general expansion as an employer of 160,000 to one employing 518,000 and from one turning out 900,000 vehicles a year to one producing 6.5 million.

Ford's fortunes were at a low ebb when Henry Ford II relinquished the scepter. Still fresh in the public's mind was the Pinto controversy: Its rear-end fuel tank had a nasty tendency to go up in flames when hit from behind. Ford paid out millions to settle lawsuits over Pinto fires. Meanwhile, imports at the start of the 1970s, 1.2 million cars, hit 2.2 million in 1979. And Ford cars, boxy and unimaginative, were taking a beating in the marketplace, with the company's market share falling to an all time low of 16.5 percent. Between 1980 and 1982 Ford lost $3.3 billion.

However, those misfortunes were reversed in the 1980s as Ford—first under Caldwell and then under Donald E. Petersen, an engineer elected chairman in 1985—became the shooting star of the U.S. automotive industry. With the introductions of the Taurus and Sable in December 1985 (three months later than planned), Ford seized the styling leadership from GM. Ford's market share shot up to 22 percent and the company made more money than GM for the first time since the 1920s.

Henry Ford II remained on the board until his death on September 29, 1987, at age 70. The *Wall Street Journal* said he "was probably America's most famous businessman." Ford CEO Donald Petersen said, "He was born to lead, and he fulfilled his destiny."

Owners and rulers. Ford has two classes of stock—A and B. The B shares represent 8 percent of the total number of shares, but have 40 percent of the votes. And all the B shares are in the hands of Ford family members. When he stepped down as CEO in 1979, Henry Ford II said there are "no crown princes in Ford Motor Company" and that "ownership of B stock is no passport to a top position in Ford, either on its board of directors or its management." In 1989, William Clay Ford, the youngest and last living grandson of Henry Ford, stepped down as vice chairman, leaving the company without a Ford family member in a top management position for the first time in their history. However, young people with the Ford name are making their way through the company ranks. Edsel B. Ford II, son of Henry II, and William Clay Ford, son of the vice chairman who retired in 1989, were elected to the board in 1988. Edsel, 41 years old in 1990 and general sales manager of the Lincoln-Mercury division, was still far from the top rung, as was his cousin, William Clay Ford, Jr., 33 in 1990. In early 1990 the younger William Clay Ford appeared to be the heir apparent; he was named strategy director for the automotive group. The new chairman and CEO in 1990 was Harold "Red" Poling, aged 64 (1989 pay: $3.2 million), who made his reputation at Ford as a cost-cutter. His predecessor, Petersen, made $7.1 million in 1989, his last year. Two women are on the board of directors: Marian S. Heiskell, member of the Sulzberger family (owner of the *New York Times*), and Ellen R. Marram, president of the Nabisco Biscuit Company.

As a place to work. Thanks to forging a new partnership with their work force in the 1980s, Ford has more gung-ho feeling in their plants than GM. Ford has been featuring assembly line workers in their commercials, and in 1990 when they introduced the Escort to the press in 21 cities, members of the United Auto Workers were on hand with management and PR people to "tell about their commitment to quality and their new partnership with

Ford." However, the company also chopped their U.S. labor force from 261,00 in 1978 to 180,000 in 1987. Ford's average hourly pay in 1987, including benefits, was $28.88, about the same as GM, but Ford's profit sharing was far better. In 1988, profit-sharing payouts averaged $3,700 per worker; in 1989 they were $2,800 per employee. GM had a profit-sharing payout averaging $265 per employee in 1989—and that was their first payout since 1985.

Social responsibility. Fords produced in the 1980s generally won high marks, but the company continued to live with the nightmare of pre-1980 automatic transmission cars that slip into reverse after drivers believe they've shifted into park. Complaints and lawsuits charged that 26 million Ford cars and trucks had unsafe transmissions. As the *Wall Street Journal* put it in an exhaustive 1988 report, "Between 1977 and 1980, the company that put America on wheels stood accused of producing an entire decade of cars that were killing and injuring people." Ford changed the transmission design in future models but steadily denied previous cars were unsafe. A recall was demanded, but on the last day of 1980 Transportation Secretary Neil Goldschmidt settled the case by having Ford agree to send a letter and dashboard sticker to 23 million owners of vehicles made between 1970 and 1979, warning that before leaving the car they should shift into park, set the brake and turn off the engine. Critics alleged Ford got off lightly because the government feared that stronger action, such as a recall, might have sunk the then-struggling company. In any case, the controversy raged into the 1980s, with damage claims against Ford mounting to $600 million by 1988. And in a tragic overtone, Douglas R. Dixon, a Ford engineer who suggested in a 1971 memo that Ford look into the functioning of its transmissions, jumped to his death from a hospital window in 1985. His wife later sued Ford, charging the company had harassed her husband when he refused "to perjure himself" in legal depositions representing parties suing Ford over the transmissions.

In 1990, Ford had 260 black-owned dealerships, considerably more than GM or Chrysler.

Global presence. A major player on the world automotive scene. Ford has plants in Britain and West Germany, consistently ranking among the top five European automakers. More than one-third of their vehicle sales and over half of employees are outside the U.S. Ford's share of the world car market is 14 percent; the truck market 17 percent. They produce more cars and trucks than GM outside the U.S. and Canada. Ford owns 25 percent of the Japanese automaker, Mazda, 10 percent of the South Korean automaker, Kia, and 75 percent of the British luxury sports car maker, Aston Martin. And in November 1989, Ford bought the British luxury car maker, Jaguar. To bolster Jaguar's high-performance reputation, in 1992 the company will release a limited edition (no more than 350) of the Jaguar XJ220—priced at $464,000.

Stock performance. Ford Motor Company stock bought for $1,000 in 1980 sold for $9,641 on January 2, 1990.

Consumer brands.

Ford: Escort, Festiva, LTD Crown Victoria, Mustang, Probe, Taurus, Tempo, Thunderbird, Aerostar, Bronco, Econoline, F-Series, Ranger.

Lincoln-Mercury: Continental, Mark VII, Town Car, Cougar, Grand Marquis, Sable, Topaz, Tracer.

Ford Motor Company, American Road, Dearborn, MI 48121; (313) 845-8540.

3

CHRYSLER CORPORATION

#3 *in U.S. automaking*
#11 *in world automaking*

Employees: 121,900
Sales: $34.9 billion
Profits: $359 million
Founded: 1925
Headquarters: Detroit, Michigan

It's probably fair to say that if not for Lee Iacocca, there wouldn't be a Chrysler anymore. Fired by Henry Ford II as president of Ford Motor in 1978, Iacocca quickly hooked up with Chrysler and saved the company from going under.

He did it in a highly visible manner, arguing successfully in Congress for a government loan guarantee, fulminating on numerous platforms against the Japanese car invaders, writing an autobiography that became one of the best-selling books in the history of publishing and appearing repeatedly in TV commercials as salesman for the Plymouth, Dodge and Chrysler cars. In the 1980s Lee Iacocca became a folk hero and there was even talk of his becoming a presidential candidate in 1988. It was a bravura performance that preserved Chrysler's position as the third largest U.S. car and truck maker, a position reinforced in 1987 by the purchase of American Motors, which swung the Jeep and Eagle lines into the Chrysler column.

Chrysler entered the 1990s making 2.3 million cars and trucks annually, double the output of 10 years ago. Iacocca's biggest hits of the decade were the Dodge Caravan and Plymouth Voyager minivans and the LeBaron convertible (while the less successful Omni and Horizon lines were discontinued in early 1990). However, his major accomplishment was transforming Chrysler into the low-cost industry producer. He closed 20 plants and removed more than 100,000 people from the payroll. In his book, modestly entitled *Iacocca*, he proudly pointed out that in 1979 Chrysler needed to "sell 2.3 million cars and trucks just to break even... But now, through the combined effort of a lot of people, we had reduced our break even point all the way down to 1.1 million."

In 1990 Iacocca was still trying to sell cars by berating the Japanese, claiming that Chrysler made better products. The made-in-America pitch was falling on deaf ears. One out of four American buyers chose a Japanese make. Only 1 out of 11 picked a Chrysler car. To raise money, Iacocca sold off Chrysler's tank division, thereby removing the company from the roster of major defense contractors. Like General Motors and Ford, Chrysler has also learned the secret of making money on money by beefing up their financial services. They bought E. F. Hutton's commercial leasing and lending unit and Bank of America's network of small loan offices (FinanceAmerica). And in 1989, they bought the fifth largest car rental company, Thrifty. In the late 1980s Chrysler was selling 25 percent of their cars to rental agencies.

History. Iacocca's Chrysler is the survivor of a host of American automotive pioneers. The company was formed in 1925 by Walter P. Chrysler, a railroad man (like his father) who fell in love with cars at the Chicago Auto Show of 1908, where he invested his $700 life savings plus borrowed funds of $4,300 to buy a gleaming, ivory-white, red-cushioned Locomobile touring car. Three years later Chrysler was in Flint, Michigan, running the Buick plant for General Motors. He did so well, expanding Buick's production to 150,000 cars a year, that he became head of manufacturing for the entire GM shebang being assembled by wheeler-dealer Billy Durant, who paid Chrysler $500,000 a year. But Durant's erratic, seat-of-the-pants management didn't suit the methodical Chrysler, who quit in 1920.

Chrysler, a fix-it man if there ever was one, then went to Toledo, Ohio, to revitalize sagging Willys-Overland before taking over another slumping automaker, Maxwell Motor, where he, along with three young engineers, developed a high-compression, six-cylinder automobile that could zip along at 50 miles an hour. Chrysler put his own name on the car and the company, which moved in 1926 from 27th to 5th place in the auto industry.

Chrysler became one of the Big Three of the industry in 1928 when they absorbed Dodge, founded by the Dodge brothers, John and Horace, both of whom had died in 1920's influenza epidemic. The Dodges were among the original investors in Ford Motor. In fact, they built the engines, transmissions and axles for the original Model A.

Walter Chrysler built a company known for engineering excellence. Among Chrysler's early contributions were automatic spark control, the oil filter, torsion-bar suspension and rubber-mounted engines (to eliminate vibrations). During the depression, with a lineup that included Plymouth, DeSoto and Dodge, Chrysler passed Ford to take over second place behind GM. A symbol of the company's rising star was the 77-story, Art Deco Chrysler Building, completed in 1930 at 42nd Street and Lexing-

Though Chrysler cars are born in the USA, Bruce Springsteen rejected Lee Iaccoca's $12 million offer to sing their praises, just as he's turned down all the other corporate bosses who wanted a piece of the Boss's name.

ton Avenue in New York City, reigning for a short while as the tallest building in the world. (The Empire State Building went up in 1931.)

Walter Chrysler died in 1940—and the company was never the same. After World War II Chrysler drifted, living on their reputation and ruled by one incompetent managerial group after another. Market share skidded from 21 percent in 1952 to 9 percent in 1979. Iacocca said he found the company being "run like a small grocery store" with "no overall financial controls." Through most of the 1970s Chrysler was soaked in red ink.

Things were so bad that shortly after Iacocca took over he found he was running out of cash. With the support of the United Auto Workers, he launched an all-out drive to get the government to guarantee $1.5 billion in loans. Congress approved the bailout in June 1980—and by the end of 1982, helped by a drop in interest rates, Iacocca had Chrysler making money again. It was, to be sure, a slimmed-down Chrysler. Iacocca won the day in Washington, D.C., by arguing that the loan guarantee would save jobs. But in the zeal to bring costs down, thousands of jobs were eliminated. In 1977, Chrysler had a payroll of 250,000; five years later, 80,000. On July 13, 1983, with a great flourish, Iacocca held forth at a press conference where he announced Chrysler was repaying the government-guaranteed loan *seven years in advance.* "We at Chrysler borrow money the old-fashioned way," he said. "We pay it back."

The humdrum K-cars Chrysler unveiled in the 1980s—Reliant, Aries, Dodge 600, LeBaron, the New Yorker—didn't win applause from automotive buffs, but they were better made than the Aspens and Volares of the previous decade. Iacocca sold them by wrapping them in the American flag—while step-

ping up imports of compact cars from Mitsubishi sold under the Colt name ("the only Japanese you need to know"). Also helping to sell the cars was a five-year warranty on major components.

One of the provisos of the government loan guarantee was that Chrysler sell their Gulfstream jet (considered an unnecessary executive perk). The jet was sold. Six years later Iacocca got even. He bought Gulfstream Aerospace, the company that makes this plane. But, alas, four years later he had to sell it—for $825 million—to raise badly needed cash.

The acquisition of American Motors brought into the Chrysler garage a company whose history includes pioneers who rubbed elbows with Walter Chrysler himself. American Motors was formed in a 1954 merger of Nash, named for Charles W. Nash, who worked at General Motors alongside Chrysler; and Hudson, founded in 1909 with money put up by the Detroit department store owner, Joseph L. Hudson. AMC had bought the Jeep line in 1970 from Kaiser Industries, which had acquired it from Willys-Overland after World War II. If you've been paying attention, you'll recall that Walter Chrysler saved Willys-Overland from going under in the 1920s.

O*wners and rulers.* Lee Iacocca and his cronies from Ford are in charge here. Among the ex-Ford people who came to Chrysler were Gerald Greenwald, Robert Lutz, Bennett Bidwell and Frederick Zuckerman. Heir apparent in 1989 was Greenwald, but he left in 1990 to head an employee group trying to buy United Arilines.

Iacocca's pay has generated a lot of publicity since he agreed to work for a dollar one year when they got the government loan. But he also took lots of stock options, bringing his compensation to $11 million in 1985 and $20.6 million in 1986. In 1987 ($20 million compensation) and 1988 (almost $18 million), Iacocca was the highest-paid U.S. executive. In 1988, the United Auto Workers negotiated a new contract prohibiting Chrysler from paying cash or stock bonuses to executives in any year in which the union's 60,000 members do not receive profit-sharing payments. That meant no bonuses for Chrysler's executives in 1989. Iacocca still took home $3.8 million that year.

As a place to work. Now a much smaller workplace, Chrysler has become the industry's low-cost producer, but workers don't share in profits the way their counterparts at Ford do, nor do they hanker to be stockholders. At Ford in 1988, the average payout was $3,700, compared to $720 at Chrysler. An Employee Stock Ownership Plan was set up at Chrysler in 1980 as a proviso of the federal loan guarantee. By 1985 the plan held 13 million shares of Chrysler stock worth $443 million. The company had contributed all the shares. The plan was then terminated and the stock distributed to 88,000 employees. When Chrysler offered to buy the shares, more than 60,000 employees cashed in rather than hold their shares for the long term. A year after buying American Motors, Chrysler decided to close the oldest automobile assembly plant in the U.S.—the AMC plant at Kenosha, Wisconsin. After fighting for nine months to keep the plant open, the UAW negotiated an agreement with Chrysler that provided generous benefits for the 4,000 employees to be laid off. It was called the "most costly plant closing agreement in history." In 1990, white-collar employees were also feeling the crunch—8 percent of their jobs are being eliminated through layoffs and early retirement.

Social responsibility. The federal Occupational Safety & Health Administration fined Chrysler $1.5 million in 1987 for health and safety violations at their Newark, Delaware, assembly plant, including worker exposure to hazardous levels of lead and arsenic. It was the stiffest penalty OSHA ever imposed on a company. Also in 1987, it was disclosed that Chrysler was selling cars already driven by executives for as much as 400 miles (with the odometers disconnected). Iacocca took out ads to apologize for the practice, admitting it was "a lousy idea. That's a mistake we won't make again at Chrysler." In 1989, Chrysler signed an agreement with the National Association for the Advancement of Colored People (NAACP) to increase the number of blacks working throughout the company. That year, 10 percent of Chrysler management was black; the company has a goal of 19 percent by 1994. Chrysler also agreed to increase the number of minority-owned dealerships by 7 percent.

Global presence. Puny. Chrysler does more than 95 percent of their business in the U.S. and Canada. In 1986, they sold the 12.5 percent stake they had in French automaker, Peugeot, a holding acquired in 1978 when Chrysler sold their European subsidiaries to the French company. Chrysler does own 12.1 percent of Mitsubishi Motors and has a 50-50 partnership with the Japanese company in a new auto plant at Normal, Illinois, producing 240,000 compact cars a year. Chrysler also owns the Italian luxury automaker, Lamborghini, and a minority interest in another Italian auto company, Maserati.

Stock performance. Chrysler stock bought for $1,000 in 1980 sold for $7,784 on January 2, 1990.

Consumer brands.

Spirit, Jeep, Eagle, Acclaim, Shadow, Sundance, Voyager, Caravan, Town and Country.

Chrysler Corp., P.O. Box 1919, Detroit, MI 48288; (313) 956-5741.

4

TOYOTA

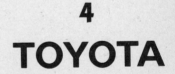

#1 *in Japanese manufacturing, Japanese automaking, U.S. imported cars*

#3 *in world auto industry*

Employees: 91,790
Sales: $61 billion (World), $10 billion (U.S.)
Profits: $2.6 billion
Founded: 1926
Headquarters: Toyota City, Japan
U.S. Headquarters: Torrance, California

In many parts of the West—the San Francisco Bay Area, for example—Toyota models such as the Corolla and Tercel are more familiar than Buicks and Pontiacs. It's a sign of how much a part of American life this Japanese car company has become. Toyota was in the vanguard of the Japanese car invasion of the U.S. and has ranked number one in imports since 1975, when they passed Volkswagen. Now they also make cars in the U.S., turning out Camrys at a new plant in Georgetown, Kentucky, and Corolla FXs and Chevy Novas at the NUMMI plant they operate with General Motors in Fremont, California. In the late 1980s Toyota was selling 1 million cars and trucks a year in the U.S., about 7.3 percent of all cars sold in the U.S. So many Toyotas roll on American roads—more than 7 million—that in 1988 the company sold more than $1 billion worth of parts and accessories.

The whole roadshow—parts, accessories and cars—was run by a network of 1,100 franchises, giving Toyota the strongest dealer organization of any foreign automaker. They have adapted to American ways in other respects, too, investing $270 million a year in advertising (38th largest advertiser in the U.S. in 1988). And they endowed a foundation, the Toyota USA Foundation, with $10 million. It gives annual grants of at least $500,000 to nonprofit organizations in the fields of education, health, culture and community affairs.

In Japan, where they sell one out of every three cars and trucks, Toyota relishes their country bumpkin image. They are based not in sophisticated Tokyo but in a rural backwater midway between Osaka and Tokyo. Toyota takes very good care of their workers in Japan, with high wages and lavish benefits. They've long been known as the most efficient automaker in the world. And their cars have a reputation, in the U.S. and Japan, for going and going.

Toyota Motor Corp. is the largest entity in a labyrinth of 14 interlocking companies known as the Toyota Group. They own pieces of one another. The original company was Toyoda Loom, founded in the early part of this century by a Japanese inventor, Sakichi Toyoda. He developed the first Japanese power loom, and his success in making textile machinery enabled his son, Kiichiro, to enter the automaking business in the 1930s. To run the company, he recruited the people who had been running GM operations in Japan.

Kiichiro's son, Dr. Shoichiro Toyoda, was sent as a young man to open the American market. He remembers struggling on American roads to drive a Toyopet, a hopelessly underpowered car shipped here in 1968 and quickly withdrawn. Those days seemed long gone by 1989, when Toyota introduced their ultra luxury Lexus line with a sticker price of $35,000. The Lexus outsold Nissan's Infiniti by 3-to-1, but 8,000 had to be recalled after reports that the cruise control mechanism was sticking, the brake light covers were warped, and the batteries flawed.

A roly-poly man with a humorous glint in his eye, Dr. Toyoda became company president in the 1980s (his uncle, Eiji Toyoda is chairman). In 1988, when Toyota's U.S. dealers held their annual convention in Nashville, Dr. Toyoda and his wife, Hirodo, were decked out in full western regalia.

The U.S. is very important to Toyota. Of the 60 million cars they've produced, 11 million were sold here. Toyota's share of the world car market is 9.4 percent. Toyota is also the world's largest forklift producer. They're opening a forklift plant in 1990 near Columbus, Indiana, home of Cummins Engine.

Stock performance. Toyota Motor Corp. stock bought for $1,000 in 1980 sold for $7,634 on January 2, 1990.

Consumer brands.

Corolla, Tercel, Celica, Supra, Camry, Cressida, Land Cruiser, Van, 4Runner, Lexus.

Toyota Motor Corp., 1, Toyota-cho, Toyota City, Aichi Prefecture 471, Japan; (0565) 28-2121.

Toyota Motor Sales, 19001 S. Western Avenue, Torrance, CA 90509; (213) 618-4000.

5

HONDA MOTOR CO., LTD. TOKYO, JAPAN

#1 *in motorcycles*
#3 *in Japanese automaking*
#4 *in U.S. automaking*
#8 *in world automaking*

Employees: 79,200
Sales: $27 billion
Profits: $572 million
Founded: 1948
Headquarters: Tokyo, Japan

TOP 10 CAR MODELS OF 1989

		Sales
1.	Accord (Honda)	362,707
2.	Taurus (Ford)	348,061
3.	Escort (Ford)	333,535
4.	Corsica/Beretta (GM)	326,006
5.	Cavalier (GM)	295,715
6.	Camry (Toyota)	257,466
7.	Civic (Honda)	235,452
8.	Tempo (Ford)	228,426
9.	Sentra (Nissan)	221,292
10	Grand Am (GM)	202,815

Source: Automotive News, 8 January 1990.

Honda is the maverick of the Japanese auto industry. When Soichiro Honda decided, after conquering the motorcycle market, that he wanted to make automobiles, Japan's Ministry of International Trade & Industry (MITI) told him Japan didn't need another car company. Honda ignored the advice, introduced his first car in 1962 and became the biggest Japanese company started since the Second World War. In 1970, when American companies had all but concluded a catalytic converter was needed to control polluting emissions, Honda introduced their zippy Civic, equipped with a new engine, the CVCC, that yielded clean exhaust. When nearly everyone had conceded the Japanese were primarily masters of the small, economical car ("basic transportation," with no frills), Honda whipped out the Accord, described by automotive writer Brock Yates as a "milestone car" because it showed the Japanese were "capable of mass-producing automobiles that rivaled the quality once considered to be the exclusive property of Mercedes-Benz, BMW, and Porsche." And when a lot of people—in Japan and the U.S.—were saying American workers couldn't build a good automobile, Honda proved them wrong by opening the first Japanese auto assembly plant in the U.S. at Marysville, Ohio, where in 1982 they began turning out Accords indistinguishable from the ones produced in Japan. In 1989, the Accord became the top-selling car in America, selling 362,707 cars beating out second-place Ford Taurus at 348,061.

By getting a jump on their Japanese rivals, Honda became both the fourth largest U.S. car producer (behind GM, Ford and Chrysler) and the fourth largest seller (the combined sales of their imports and their Ohio output moved them ahead of Toyota and Nissan). Honda sells 7.6 percent of the cars sold in America. And Honda pioneered on another front: exporting Accords made in Ohio to Japan where they enjoyed a certain foreign cachet—and were soon outselling Ford and GM combined.

Soichiro Honda has been called "the Henry Ford of Japan." He never went to college, nor did his sidekick, Takeo Fujisawa, a cofounder who managed the administrative and sales sides of the business while Honda worked in the machine shop. A feisty character, Honda also knew when to step down. In 1973, when he was 66 and Fujisawa 62, both men retired from day-to-day management, leaving the company in the hands of younger people, none of whom is a relative. In an interview with a Japanese journalist, Honda explained his departure by saying he was losing his sexual prowess ("Great leaders love sex, and I am not a great leader anymore") and his ability to drink ("For entertaining customers and employees, presidents should be able to drink more"). In 1989, Detroit paid Soichiro Honda the ultimate compliment: He became the first

Japanese auto executive to be initiated into America's Automotive Hall of Fame.

Of their $27 billion in sales, 53 percent is derived from the U.S. and Canada. Honda holds 50 percent of the U.S. motorcycle market. They assemble motorcycles at Marysville (the bike plant came before the car factory)—and in 31 other countries. Aside from bikes and cars, they make pumps, generators and lawn mowers.

S*tock performance.* Honda stock bought for $1,000 in 1980 sold for $5,449 on January 2, 1990. Honda is the only Japanese automaker whose shares are traded on the New York Stock Exchange.

C*onsumer brands.*

Accord, CRX, Prelude, Acura, Integra, Legend.

Honda Motor Ltd., 1-1, 2-chome, Minami-Aoyama, Minato-ku, Tokyo 107, Japan; (81) 3-423-1111.

American Honda Motor, 100 W. Alonda Blvd., Gardena, CA 90242; (213) 327-8280.

6

#5 *in world automaking*

Employees: 130,000
Sales: $39.5 billion
Profits: $812 million
Founded: 1911
Headquarters: Tokyo, Japan

The most somber faces ever to stare out from an annual report appear in the ones issued by Nissan, Japan's second largest automaker. It's as if the executives were warned not to smile. A scowl seems to be the accepted facial expression. The deadly serious tone is in keeping with Nissan's history, a company known for rigidity and a highly politicized bureaucracy. David Halberstam captured Nissan's insensitivity in his 1986 book, *The Reckoning.* He describes a shouting match that took place in 1980 between

T*he number of new car dealerships in the U.S. decreased from around 46,000 in 1950 to about 25,000 in 1990.*

Nissan's chairman, the unsmiling Takashi Ishihari, and Douglas Fraser, then president of the United Auto Workers.

"Your problem in America," said Ishihari, "is of your own making... Nobody wants to work." Fraser retorted: "You wouldn't understand America because you're such an undemocratic man, and you come from so undemocratic a country."

Ishihari's opinion of American workers notwithstanding, in 1983 Nissan began making small pickup trucks at a new plant in Smyrna, Tennessee. Later they began assembling Sentra passenger cars there as well. Smyrna plant capacity will double by 1992 to 440,000 vehicles a year—and at that size will be the largest auto assembly plant under one roof in the U.S.

Initially, the Tennessee plant won high marks for teamwork and an egalitarian style. However, reports soon surfaced of burn out on a fast-moving assembly line, and the United Auto Workers called an election to unionize. The union lost. Honda's plant at Marysville, Ohio, is also nonunion—but the UAW knows they haven't a chance of winning an election there.

Toyota and Nissan used to run neck-and-neck in their home market, but Toyota now has a wide lead, outselling Nissan by nearly 2-to-1. In the American market Nissan has also faltered, trailing Honda as well as Toyota.

Nissan has always had a hard time naming their cars. They called their first car the Dat (the first letters of the founders' names). Then it became Datson. And then Datsun. In 1981, after 20 years of promoting the Datsun name ("We are driven") in the U.S., the top honchos in Tokyo decided to phase that out in favor of the corporate name, Nissan, an abbreviation of "Japan Industries." The American dealers were aghast but Tokyo held to its decision. After spending hundreds of millions of dollars to establish the Nissan name, the company polled Americans in 1988 and found the Datsun name was still better known. So Nissan switched adver-

Performing more than just autobody work, these Nissan employees gather daily for calisthenics at their plant in Smyrna, Tennessee.

tising agencies, handing their account to Chiat/Day of Los Angeles, which came up with an image-building campaign, "Nissan: Built for the human race," with designers and engineers sitting around extolling their designs. The dealers hated it. That was followed in 1989 and 1990 by a $100 million ad campaign, created by the Boston agency Hill, Holliday, Connors, Cosmopolis, introducing Nissan's new $38,500 luxury car, the Infiniti. The campaign was remarkable for TV commercials that whispered and featured scenes of natural beauty without showing the car itself. The ultimate in soft sell, the campaign flopped in the marketplace. In the first three months of 1990 Infiniti's sales totaled 3,695, trailing far behind Toyota's new luxury model, Lexus.

Nissan is the most multinational of all Japanese car companies, operating assembly and production plants in 21 countries. In 1989 they turned out 2,930,000 cars and trucks, a shade behind Volkswagen (2,948,000).

In addition to cars and trucks, Nissan makes rocket motors and other aerospace gear, textile machinery, forklifts and boats.

Stock performance. Nissan stock bought for $1,000 in 1980 sold for $4,075 on January 2, 1990.

Consumer brands.

Sentra, Pulsar, Stanza, Maxima, 300ZX, 240SX, Axxess, Hardbody, Pathfinder.

Nissan Motor, 17-1, Ginza 6-chome, Chuo-ku, Tokyo 104-23, Japan; (03) 543-5523.

Nissan Motor, P.O. Box 191, Gardena, CA 90247; (213) 532 3111.

7

#4 *in Japanese automaking*
#5 *in auto imports*
#11 *in world automaking*
Employees: 28,000
Sales: $16.8 billion
Profits: $164 million
Founded: 1920
Headquarters: Hiroshima, Japan

Based in the atom-bombed city of Hiroshima, where they were founded in 1920 as a cork producer, Mazda turns out 850,000 cars a year in Japan. Since 1987, they have been turning out 340,000 cars a year at a plant in Flat Rock, Michigan, where the United Auto Workers represents 3,100 workers. Mazda is the only Japanese company to have accepted UAW representation from the start, but, according to many critics, Mazda has the worst relations with their American workers (white-collar and assembly-line) of any Japanese-owned auto plant in America. Four top American managers quit from 1988 to 1989. A union worker at the Flat Rock plant complained, "If you get injured at work, you better have a witness and you better have gotten hit by a car."

Rebounding from the rotary engine disaster of the 1970s, Mazda now ranks as Japan's fourth largest automaker. Since 1979 Ford Motor has owned 25 percent of the firm, and Mazda makes Ford's front-wheel Probe at the Flat Rock plant. Mazda holds 2 percent of the U.S. auto market. Their top seller is the low-priced 323 series, but they had a runaway seller in 1989 with the stylish convertible, the MX-5 Miata, designed at Mazda's research and development center in California. The Miata is part of Mazda's new strategy to create a more upscale—and memorable—image. The campaign began when Mazda's marketing division discovered, much to their consternation, that Americans had a "very vague perception of Mazda" and that Mazdas were the least recognized of major Japanese cars (a sort of silent sibling to Nissan, Toyota and

Honda). The name, Mazda, is derived from the founding Matsuda family.

Consumer brands.

Mazda 323, 626, MX-6, 929, RX-7, Miata, Protege, MPV.

Mazda Motors, 3-1, Shinchi, Fuchu-cho, Aki-gun, Hiroshima 730-91, Japan; (082) 282-1111.

Mazda Motors of America, 7755 Irvine Center Drive, Irvine, CA 92718; (714) 727-1990.

8

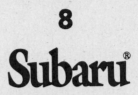

#7 *in import car sales*
Employees: 1,130
Sales: $1.7 billion
Losses: $42 million
Founded: 1968
Headquarters: Cherry Hill, New Jersey

Popular in New England and California (and the official cars of the U.S. Olympic ski teams since 1976), the Japanese-made Subaru automobiles have engendered a fierce loyalty among owners even when the cars break down. There's something about a Subaru that says "sturdy," "tough," "rugged." Subaru's forte has been four-wheel drive. Half the U.S. sold Subarus have four-wheel drive. In 1989 Americans bought 150,000 Subarus, making the car the seventh most imported, right behind Volkswagen.

The Legacy sedans and wagons are Subaru's entry in the mid-priced car market ($11,000 to $19,000). The Legacy is the largest car Subaru has ever made. According to one industry analyst, "If the Legacy fails, no more Subaru." That's because Subaru sales have been steadily declining; in 1986, 183,242 were sold; three years later, only 150,000. One reason is the rising yen. Another is that consumers are overlooking Subaru's classic draw, the four-wheel-drive, in favor of sturdier vehicles, like the Jeep Cherokee.

Made by Fuji Heavy Industries, Japan's seventh largest automaker, Subarus have been distributed in the U.S. since 1968 by

Subaru of America, currently through 800 dealers. Unlike other import car distributors, Subaru of America was not completely manufacturer-owned—in fact, you could have gotten rich investing modest sums in Subaru of America's stock. But that all changed in 1990 when Fuji decided to buy up the 49.6 percent of shares they didn't already own.

In 1989 Fuji Heavy joined with another Japanese automaker, Isuzu, to open a manufacturing plant in Lafayette, Indiana. There, Isuzu trucks and Subaru sedans will be built on the same assembly line.

Stock performance. Subaru stock bought for $1,000 in 1980 sold for $3,926 on January 2, 1990.

Consumer brands.

Subaru, Legacy, Justy, Loyale, XT/XT6.

Subaru of America, Inc., 2235 Route 70 West, Cherry Hill, NJ 08002; (609) 488-8500.

PERSONS PER CAR

U.S.	1.9
Australia	2.3
W. Germany	2.5
France	2.6
Italy	2.8
U.K.	3.4
Spain	4.4
Japan	4.5
E. Germany	6.0
Brazil	15.0
Mexico	16.0
U.S.S.R.	26.0
Taiwan	27.6
S. Korea	104.9
Nigeria	125.0
China	10,200.0

9

#1 *in European automaking*

#4 *in world automaking*

Employees: 251,000
Sales: $35 billion
Profits: $523 million
Founded: 1937
Headquarters: Wolfsburg, West Germany

A creation of Adolf Hitler, Volkswagen ranks as a world automotive power, but not on the basis of their U.S. presence. When the Volkswagen Beetle was phased out (more than 5 million were sold in the U.S.), Americans switched their allegiance to the Japanese. As a result, Volkswagen's share of the American market was sliced from 7 percent in 1970 to 2 percent in 1989.

It didn't help—in fact it seemed to hurt—that VW was the first foreign company to open an assembly plant in the U.S. An abandoned Chrysler factory at New Stanton, Pennsylvania, began turning out

Rabbits in 1978. But American motorists turned an emphatic thumbs-down on the car. On top of that, VW had labor problems at the plant. A group of black employees filed a racial discrimination suit—and one member of the group, an assistant personnel manager, was then found dead, an apparent suicide. He left a note saying Volkswagen had pressured him not to join the suit, using as leverage sexual harassment charges earlier brought against him. After 10 years of losses and embarrassments, VW closed the plant in July 1988, leaving them free to boast about their "German engineering."

Adolf Hitler launched the Volkswagen company to bring to life a dream of the legendary German automobile designer, Ferdinand Porsche, whose name now graces another car. Porsche always wanted to build a sturdy, inexpensive car for the masses, an idea his former employer, Daimler-Benz, never bought. Hitler bought the idea and created a factory town, Wolfsburg, in Lower Saxony to carry it out. But starting World War II distracted him from automaking. Not until after the war—and after the British and Americans expressed no interest in the Wolfsburg plant—did Volkswagen, "the people's car," come rolling out to become the most successful model in automotive history. In 1978, when the U.S. plant was opened, Wolfsburg stopped making the Beetle, or bug, by which time 19 million had been produced, topping the 15 million Model T's Ford made. By 1990, 21 million Beetles had been made.

The Beetle's demise did not prevent Volkswagen from becoming the top European car company and a major player in many other world markets, save for the U.S., where they experienced more anguish in 1987 and 1988 when Audi owners complained their cars inexplicably leaped forward. Volkswagen bought Auto-Union, maker of the Audi, from Daimler-Benz. In 1986, VW acquired control of Spain's largest auto producer, SEAT (Sociedad Española de Automoviles), moving their annual output over the 3 million mark for the first time. Also in 1986, VW and Ford merged their automotive operations in Argentina and Brazil in a new company called Autolatina, which has 15 plants with an annual capacity of 900,000 vehicles, 75,000 employees and sales of $4 billion. Volkswagen owns 51 percent of Autolatina.

Only the U.S., the world's largest automobile market, remains an enigma for Volkswagen.

Consumer brands.

Cabriolet, Jetta, Vanagon, Golf, Corrado, Passat, Audi, Fox.

Volkswagen, PO Box 3180, Wolfsburg 1, West Germany; (49) 5361-90.

Volkswagen of America, P.O. Box 3951, 888 W. Big Beaver, Troy, MI 48007; (313) 362-6000.

10

VOLVO

#1 in Swedish manufacturing, Swedish automaking

#18 in world automaking

Employees: 78,614
Sales: $14.2 billion
Profits: $680 million
Founded: 1926
Headquarters: Gothenburg, Sweden

Long the car of choice with university professors, urban liberals and the affluent

upper-middle class, sturdy Swedish-built Volvo grew more popular in the 1980s. Volvos were selling about 100,000 units a year in the late 1980s, up dramatically from the 50,000 sold in 1978. The company making Volvo is Sweden's largest company—and they do more than make cars. They're the world's third largest maker of heavy-duty trucks (vehicles weighing over 16 tons), and through a series of acquisitions have become Sweden's second largest food supplier. Charismatic Pehr Gyllenhammar (pronounced Pare YULE-en-hommer), who believes in stirring up the juices, has headed Volvo since 1971. "An organization without conflict is dying," he once said.

Gyllenhammar has built an auto plant without an assembly line (teams of workers put together the entire car), forged alliances with General Motors, Renault and Clark Equipment, sold Volvo stock through the Swedish post office and had Volvo stock listed in eight countries outside Sweden (including the U.S.) so 12 percent of the shares are now held outside the mother country. Gyllenhammar has become one of the most well-known international business figures. He organized the European Business Roundtable (heads of 29 big European companies), and he sits on the boards of 8 other companies, including United Technologies and Hamilton Oil in the U.S.

Volvo sponsored the National Football League's trip to Sweden in 1988 when the Minnesota Vikings battled the Chicago Bears. Throughout the televised game, Volvo's blue and white banners were visible. Sponsorship of sports events (primarily men's professional tennis and sailing regattas) is one way Volvo targets their average car buyer. According to the company, in 1988 the average Volvo buyer was 37 years old, worked as a manager or professional, was married and had an average household income of $54,300.

Stock performance. Volvo stock bought for $1,000 in 1985 sold for $2,544 on January 2, 1990.

Consumer brands.

Volvo.

Volvo AB, S-405 08, Gothenburg, Sweden; (46) 31-590000.

Volvo of America, P.O. Box 915, Rockleigh, NJ 07647; (201) 767-4535.

11

DAIMLERBENZ

#1 *in German manufacturing, heavy truck production (world), German defense contracting, diesel engine car manufacturing (world)*

Employees: 308,000
Sales: $40.6 billion
Profits: $3.4 billion
Founded: 1886
Headquarters: Stuttgart, West Germany

What's wrong with making cars? Especially sleek, luxury automobiles admired the world over for their performance and appearance? Well, nothing, except that something happens to companies when they get big. They want to dabble in all sorts of other businesses rather than stick to what they originally did. That's Daimler-Benz's story in the 1980s. Parallelling recent moves of General Motors in the U.S., this German producer of the Mercedes-Benz vehicles decided to drive up other alleys.

After 99 years of doing nothing but make automotive products, Daimler-Benz went on a buying spree, acquiring control of MTU, West Germany's largest jet engine maker; Dornier, a producer of commuter planes, rockets, satellite parts and medical equipment; and AEG, a giant electronics outfit making everything from computers to vacuum cleaners and typewriters. Still not sated, D-B then went after Messerschmitt-Bolkow-Blohm, the largest West German aerospace company (helicopters, fighter planes) and owner of 38 percent of Europe's Airbus Industrie consortium. The shopping spree made Daimler-Benz the largest company in Europe, excluding the two oil giants, Shell and British Petroleum. As if that were not enough, in early 1990 the company went into a frenzy of joint ventures. They will make jet engines with Pratt & Whitney

(owned by United Technologies); helicopters with Aerospatiale of France (the joint venture creates the world's second-largest helicopter manufacturer); everything from aerospace equipment to electronic products with Mitsubishi; and lorries and railway cars with East German firms. Whew.

Daimler-Benz is where the car was born. It's not clear whether Karl Benz or Gottlieb Daimler invented it. Both were working, 30 miles apart, in their own workshops, and both turned out a motorized vehicle in 1886—yet the two never met. Daimler died in 1900, Benz in 1925. In 1902, Daimler registered a new trademark: Mercedes. The name originated when a part-time Daimler salesman, Emile Jellinek, the son of a Bohemian rabbi, began racing cars (a turn of the century fad). It was common to race under a pseudonym, and Jellinek chose the name of his 11-year-old daughter, Mercedes. He made several suggestions to designers at Daimler, and agreed to order 36 of these new cars—provided they bore the nameplate Mercedes. In 1911, another trademark was registered: the three-pointed star, symbolizing the three places where Mercedes engines were used (land, water and air). Daimler and Benz merged in 1926.

Mercedes-Benz passed Cadillac as the world's top-selling luxury car in the early 1970s. However, Daimler-Benz executives bridle at the term *luxury car*. An executive once lectured a reporter, "For us, luxury lies in building a car that we think is right." All Mercedes-Benz cars are made in Germany—and there's no "Chevrolet" in the lineup. The smallest car, the 190, called the "baby Mercedes," carries the lowest sticker price: $29,000.

Mercedes has done well in the U.S. market. They sold 53,000 cars here in 1980, peaked at 99,000 in 1986 and then dropped to 85,000 and 84,000 in 1988 and 1989. (The U.S. accounts for about one-sixth of their car sales.) And they work hard to maintain the

Privileged Rolls-Royce customers often wait for over six months for the delivery of their luxury cars, which cost them an average of $160,000 each.

WHERE THE WORLD'S CARS ARE MADE

Country	Annual Car Production
1. Japan	7.8 million
2. U.S.	7.1 million
3. W. Germany	4.4 million
4. France	3.0 million
5. Italy	1.8 million

resale value of their cars. In 1989 they introduced 12- and 24-month warranties on all *used* Mercedes cars bought from any one of 431 U.S. dealers.

Fifty-nine-year-old Edzard Reuter was elected Daimler-Benz chairman in 1987. He's a member of West Germany's Social Democratic Party (imagine a liberal Democrat reaching the top at General Motors), and fellow Social Democrats have criticized him for wanting to create a European aerospace giant under the Daimler-Benz banner. Reuter's reply, given to *New York Times* reporter Steven Greenhouse, was: "There is no law that big is beautiful or small is beautiful. But if you are in a position where you have to compete globally, size is indispensable." So there.

The company's two largest stockholders are Deutsche Bank (holder of 28 percent of the shares) and the Kuwait Investment Office (14 percent).

Consumer brands.

Mercedes.

Daimler-Benz, P.O. Box 600202, D-Stuttgart 60, West Germany; (49) 711-17-0.

Mercedes-Benz of North America, One Mercedes Dr., Montvale, NJ 07645; (201) 573-0600.

12

MITSUBISHI

#5 *in Japanese automaking*
#12 *in world automaking*

Employees: 38,000
Sales: $17 billion
Profits: $164 million
Founded: 1937
Headquarters: Tokyo, Japan

An offshoot of the powerful Mitsubishi Group (one of Japan's giant trading companies), Mitsubishi Motors entered the U.S. one inch at a time, beginning in 1971 when Chrysler bought 15 percent of Mitsubishi and started selling their cars under the Chrysler name (Colt). Problems surfaced when Mitsubishi started competing with Chrysler in 1982, selling identical cars in the U.S.—under the Mitsubishi name. By 1987 they were selling 67,000 cars in the U.S. Mitsubishi and Chrysler have an uneasy relationship (Chrysler's Lee Iacocca is always railing against the Japanese). But the companies joined forces to build an auto plant in the heart of Illinois near the towns of Bloomington and Normal. In 1989, Mitsubishi made 500,000 V-6 engines for Chrysler. In early September 1989, Chrysler owned 21.8 percent of Mitsubishi; by month's end, Chrysler had sold off about half the stock for $592 million. Chrysler now owns a mere 12.1 percent of the Japanese firm.

Consumer brands.

Starion, Cordia, Tredia, Mirage, Galant, Precis.

Mitsubishi Motors, 2-6-3 Maranouchi, Chiyoda-ku, Tokyo 100, Japan; (81)-3-210-2121.

Mitsubishi Motor Sales of America, Inc., 6400 West Katella Avenue, Cypress, CA 90630; (714) 372-6000.

EARTHMOVERS

If you want to blast through a mountain or move a mound of earth or plow a field, you don't have a wide range of equipment options. The two world-class American companies in construction and farm equipment are Caterpillar Tractor and Deere. They're both midwestern companies that grew out of the farming business. And they both went through hard times in the 1980s.

1

⊞ CATERPILLAR

#1 *in crawler-tractors, earthmoving and off-highway construction machinery*

Employees: 60,800
Sales: $11.1 billion
Profits: $497 million
Founded: 1928
Headquarters: Peoria, Illinois

Hailed at the start of the 1980s as a paragon of U.S. industry, a world champion that could hold their own against all comers, Caterpillar was humbled during the decade into a series of retrenchments that left them leaner and, so far as their employees were concerned, meaner. Under attack by the Japanese giant, Komatsu, Caterpillar held on to their position as the world's leading producer of earthmoving equipment but went through the biggest upheaval in their history. They closed 9 plants, completely overhauled the remaining 30, cut their work force from 90,000 to 60,000, introduced new machinery and moved aggressively into foreign markets. During the 1980s they relocated half their factories outside the U.S.

This transformation was accompanied by a fair amount of anguish. In 1982 and 1983 Cat's unionized workers went out on strike for seven months, one of the longest walkouts a major American corporation ever endured. Cat had made money for 50 years. Then, in 1982, they lost money— $180 million—and from 1982 to 1984 lost almost $1 billion more. Not until 1988 did they surpass 1980's sales.

Cat's machines are all painted Caterpillar's trademark butterscotch yellow. They are used the world over to clear jungles and reshape mountains and as road graders and scrapers, tractors, bulldozers, backhoes, forklifts, loaders, excavators and dump trucks. In recent years demand has shifted from the huge machines—selling for as much as $530,000 each—to smaller machines like tractor-mounted backhoes for house building, road repair and sewer installation.

History. Caterpillar's roots are in California's Sacramento Valley, where Benjamin Holt hit on the idea of running a tractor on crawler tracks rather than on iron wheels that sank into California's muddy farmland. The crawler track, which allowed big, clumsy equipment to move over the dirt easily, was dubbed the Caterpillar. It inspired the 1915 British invention of the armored tank. When World War I ended, the U.S. Army gave their tanks to states and counties to use in road construction work.

Holt's company drifted after the war, burdened by debt and facing strong competition from Best Tractor, another California firm. In 1925 a San Francisco stockbroker proposed a merger between the two, and in 1928 the Caterpillar Tractor Company was born. Headquarters were moved to Peoria, Illinois, to be closer to farm customers. Soon the company's new president, Raymond Force, decided there was more growth potential in the earthmoving and construction businesses, and the company began to concentrate their efforts there. Force's decision to expand into foreign markets helped Cat weather the depression. Between 1929 and 1933—the time of the first Soviet five-year plan—Caterpillar sold the Soviet Union $18 million worth of equipment.

Caterpillar also began to acquire a reputation for homespun management under Force, a reputation his successor, Louis Neumiller, cemented. Cat became known as a place where traditional values matter, where fancy degrees and prestigious schools were less important than on-the-job training. Neumiller's "industrial version of the Boy Scout law," as *Fortune* called it in 1963, consisted of homey axioms on duty and honesty. A sample: "There is but one Caterpillar and wherever it is, you will find it reaching for high levels of integrity, achievement and quality—standing first and foremost for the rights and dignity of the individual and wishing to make association with the Company a life-satisfying experience."

Owners and rulers. George Schaefer, a Kentucky native who described himself as an "old bookkeeper," ran Cat from 1985 to the summer of 1990 when he was succeeded by Donald Fites, a civil engineer from Indiana's Valparaiso University who has worked for Cat all over the world (he speaks German, Japanese and Portugese).

As a place to work. In 1987, Cat employees in Uddingston, Scotland, were laid off and made their rage public. The 850 workers staged a sit-in at the Cat plant that lasted 24-hours a day for 14 weeks. The former employees built a 75,000-pound crawler tractor and painted it pink instead of yellow. They then drove the tractor, nicknamed the "Pink Panther," through Glasgow in a protest parade—complete with bagpipe music.

After years of slimming down and massive layoffs, Cat has slowly started hiring again.

The United Auto Workers and Caterpillar established a profit-sharing plan for employees and a program called the Employee Satisfaction Process to involve blue-collar workers in decision making and quality improvement. Workers are organized into teams to handle multiple tasks on a variety of machines and take responsibility for the parts they produce. In 1988, the UAW signed a three-year agreement with Caterpillar, including a 3 percent wage increase for each year, cost-of-living adjustments and job security provisions.

Global presence. One of the largest U.S. exporters, they do half their sales overseas. In 1989 one-quarter of their profits came from Brazil. One-third of their employees work in 15 plants in seven different countries. They also have new partnerships with foreign companies—Daewoo in Korea and a Norwegian company are making forklift trucks for them, and they recently joined forces in a project with India's Hindustan Motors.

Stock performance. Caterpillar stock bought for $1,000 in 1980 sold for $1,415 on January 2, 1990.

Caterpillar Inc., 100 N.E. Adams Street, Peoria, IL 61629; (309) 675-1000.

2

#1 *in farm equipment*

Employees: 38,600
Sales: $7.5 billion
Profits: $410 million
Founded: 1837
Headquarters: Moline, Illinois

Just about everybody likes John Deere: their dealers, the farmers who use their green equipment (tractors, combines, planters, hay balers), their employees, the other people who live in towns where Deere has plants, Wall Street analysts, institutional investors and reporters. During the bruising 1980s they needed all the love they could get. It was Deere's toughest decade since the Great Depression of the 1930s.

While the rest of corporate America was off on a wild binge of acquisitions, mergers and leveraged buyouts, the world's largest farm equipment maker was fighting for life. Farmers were mired in a deep recession as world crop production exceeded consumption. U.S. farm exports in wheat, soybeans, cotton and coarse grains (corn, oats, barley, sorghum) plunged. Many farmers were driven off the land. As a result, not many farmers were in the market for new equipment. In 1989 the farm equipment industry sold 9,111 combines, compared to 32,246 in 1979.

The slump pulverized Deere. After a decade (the 1970s) when sales quintupled, they saw sales decline 25 percent by the mid-1980s. For two years, 1986 and 1987, they lost money. They slashed their work force from 65,000 employees in 1979 to 39,000 by 1989. And yet in 1989, they were still capturing more than 40 percent of the farm equipment market and registering the highest profits in their 153-year history.

In addition to farm machinery, Deere makes construction equipment (bulldozers, loaders and excavators) and lawn and garden equipment (small versions of their big tractors).

History. John Deere was an enterprising Vermont blacksmith who in 1837 moved to Grand Detour, Illinois, and invented the first self-cleaning steel plow. The plow was curved to one side, enabling it to cut a clean furrow slice without frequent stops to scrape off the dirt. John Deere (the man and the company) became, in the words of Wayne G. Broehl, Jr., in his painstaking *John Deere's Company*, "an authentic American folk hero." In later years, Deere made a combine that harvested and shelled ears of corn right in the field through a corn head, an attachment resembling a giant hair clipper that scrapes individual kernels off the ears and cuts harvesting time by hours. Deere also introduced the first hay cuber, which cuts and compresses hay into one-by-two-feet blocks—perfect for cows. Over the years, John Deere's successors (all Deeres by blood or marriage) invented the first automatic wire-tie hay baler, to package and tie hay bales, and the first bale ejector, to toss the bales into a wagon. A major architect of Deere's success was William Hewitt, CEO from 1955 to 1982. Hewitt courted the "Cadillac market" (the top 20 percent of farmers who earn most of the cash income), led Deere overseas, and decentralized operations to the point where each factory became responsible for design, testing and manufacturing.

The company's most valuable asset has been their relationship with midwestern farmers. During the Great Depression, Deere continued to extend credit to their customers on their most expensive equipment, although it took years to collect. The policy resulted in repeat business and

fervent loyalty. In the words of the *Wall Street Journal*, Deere enjoys an "almost mystical bond" with farmers.

They remained the farm equipment leader during the turbulent 1980s, although they faced tougher competition from Tenneco's JI Case, which absorbed the International Harvester lines in 1985. Case came out of the 1980s doing better than $5 billion a year.

Deere publishes a popular magazine for farmers, *The Furrow*, founded in 1896 and currently published in 12 languages.

Owners and rulers. In 1982 Robert A. Hanson, a Moline native and a lifetime Deere employee, became the first non-Deere family member to head the enterprise (1989 pay: $2.1 million). He was succeeded in 1989 by Hans Becherer (born of German immigrants), who rose through John Deere international. During a stint in Germany he fired nearly one-fifth of the key managers. During the 1980s restructuring he fired many more in Moline. Deere stock is a great favorite of institutional investors, such as pension funds and insurers. At one point in the mid-1980s they owned 88 percent of all the shares (down to 74 percent in early 1990).

As a place to work. Deere has generally enjoyed friendly relations with their unionized work force, particularly in comparison to the adversarial conditions that prevailed at Caterpillar and the old International Harvester, but the strains of the 1980s weakened those bonds. Cutting the payroll by 40 percent didn't endear

Deere's trademark for their bicycle line, 1896.

management to employees, and the antagonism was evident in 1986 and 1987 when workers shut down Deere plants in a walkout lasting 163 days. The strike ended in workers concessions, including a wage freeze. In 1988 the UAW negotiated a new contract that included the first wage increase since 1981 (current average wage: $16 an hour) and a guarantee that none of the 13,500 factory workers would be laid off.

G*lobal presence.* Hewitt ended Deere's insularity and set the company on an international course, cajoling and badgering old midwest hands who had never been out of the country to get some plane tickets and see the rest of the world. By 1990 Deere had a $1.7 billion business overseas (23 percent of sales), operating tractor factories in Germany, Spain and Argentina; farm implement factories in Australia, France, Germany and South Africa; and an engine factory in France.

S*tock performance.* Deere & Company stock bought for $1,000 in 1980 sold for $2,204 on January 2, 1990.

Deere & Company, John Deere Road, Moline, IL 61265; (309) 765-8000.

TIRES

The U.S. tire industry went through a cataclysmic change during the 1980s. Coming into the decade, the industry consisted of six major producers: Goodyear, Firestone, Uniroyal, Goodrich, General and Armstrong. Those marks are still around, etched into rubber on your car, but by decade's end nearly all of them had new owners.

Continental A.G., the West German tire company, bought the General Tire business. Japan's Bridgestone grabbed Firestone. Italy's Pirelli took over Armstrong Rubber. Uniroyal and Goodrich combined into one company, then Uniroyal Goodrich was bought by France's Michelin in 1990.

That left one company in American hands: Goodyear.

1

#1 *tires (U.S.)*

Employees: 111,500
Sales: $10.9 billion
Profits: $189 million
Founded: 1898
Headquarters: Akron, Ohio

In 1990, for the first time in 74 years, Goodyear Tire & Rubber was run over by a competitor. Though still the leading U.S. tire maker, with about one-third of the market, Goodyear has fallen behind France's Michelin in the race for world's tire champion. Being number two in anything was a humbling experience for Goodyear, a company that wore the title, "world's largest tire company," with a great deal of swagger. In the rubber industry, Goodyear's nicknames have justly been "the Brute" and "the Gorilla" because Goodyear plays hardball. They have put more tires on more vehicles than any other company in the world—and they didn't do it by being nice. For years, Goodyear opposed federal safety standards. While the rest of the world rode on radial tires (widely acknowledged to offer supe-

Tire making at Goodyear, 1908.

rior performance and a longer life than bias-ply tires), Goodyear stubbornly resisted producing them until the early 1970s.

Goodyear started out making bicycle tires. They began making airplane tires in 1909 when there were only 100 planes in the U.S. When the Apollo reached the moon in 1971, it landed on Goodyear tires. A multinational giant, they operate 43 plants in the U.S. and 44 overseas. And although they now fill most of their requirements with synthetic rubber, they still own six rubber plantations. In addition to 2,000 kinds of tires, they make a wide range of chemical and plastic products, including hoses, belts, foams, resins, PVC films, shoe soles, vinyl laminates and roofing materials. And, of course, they still operate the high-visibility fleet of Goodyear blimps, although they no longer make them.

They no longer make blimps because of a bruising takeover battle in the mid-1980s with the elegant, consummate Anglo-French raider, Sir James Goldsmith. Goodyear fought off his advances, but at a stiff price, taking on $4.7 billion in debt to buy back stock from Goldsmith and other shareholders and selling off a bunch of operations, including recently acquired oil and gas interests, Goodyear Aerospace (the blimp maker) and Goodyear Farms, a 12,000-acre spread 18 miles from downtown Phoenix.

In the early 1980s Goodyear also began building a 1,750-mile pipeline, jingoistically called the All-American Pipeline, designed to carry crude oil from California to Texas refineries. In testifying before Congress during his takeover foray, Gold-

smith called the pipeline a "wholly lunatic idea," saying Goodyear should stick to making tires. In the ensuing restructuring, the pipeline was ticketed to be sold, but no one wanted to buy it. Goodyear finally completed the pipeline, at an estimated cost of $1.4 billion, in 1989—and a trickle of oil began flowing through it.

History. When Frank Seiberling and his brother Charles started their rubber company in Akron in 1898, they named it after the discoverer of vulcanized rubber, Charles Goodyear. With the Seiberlings selling and MIT graduate Paul Litchfield in charge of production, Goodyear became the largest U.S. tire maker by 1916. But Frank Seiberling, whom associates affectionately called "Little Napoleon," was ignorant of finance. He brought the company to the brink of ruin in the brief depression that followed World War I. The New York investment banking firm Dillon, Read & Co. stepped in, reorganized the company and booted out the Seiberling brothers. The company thrived by selling harder than competitors. During the Great Depression, when many dealers were wiped out, Goodyear opened their own company stores. Later, when tires with obscure brand names began to erode profits, Goodyear made off-brand tires they sold through subsidiaries Kelly-Springfield and Lee Tire. They also made the Atlas brand tires several oil companies sold.

One of the castoffs of the 1980s was Goodyear Farms in Arizona, where the company began cotton farming in 1916, eventually building around it a company town called Litchfield Park (named after

Paul W. Litchfield, Goodyear Tire's chairman for three decades). Included in the sale was the Wigwam, which began as a company hotel and then became a posh watering hole for the wealthy.

Owners and rulers. In 1989, 58-year-old Thomas H. Barrett became CEO, succeeding Robert Mercer. A Kansas native often described as "plain-spoken," Barrett joined the company when he was 23, fresh out of Kansas State College. He was paid nearly $1 million in 1989.

As a place to work. Goodyear used to boast that they were run by men who grew up within sight of Akron's smokestacks, in the heart of the world's Rubber Capital. But the smokestacks are gone now, as are the glory days of manufacturing in Akron, Ohio. In the late 1970s and early 1980s, all the tire factories were abandoned and many were torn down. Goodyear's manufacturing division joined an industry exodus to the South and Southwest (where taxes and labor costs were lower). Goodyear's Akron facilities now house white-collar workers in administration and research.

Social responsibility. Goodyear began an aggressive program to recruit minority dealers in the early 1980s. In 1987 they reported 122 dealerships were owned by minorities and women. For every dollar an employee contributes to a college or university (up to $2,500), Goodyear will kick in $2.

Global presence. Strong. They have plants in 26 countries and derive 40 percent of their sales and more than half their profits overseas.

Stock performance. Goodyear Tire stock bought for $1,000 in 1980 sold for $5,625 on January 2, 1990.

Consumer brands.

Goodyear, Eagle, Atlas, Lee, Kelly-Springfield.

Goodyear Tire & Rubber Company, 1144 East Market Street, Akron, OH 44316; (216) 796-2121.

2

#2 tires (U.S.)

Employees: 18,500
Sales: $2.2 billion
Founded: 1870 (Goodrich), 1892 (Uniroyal)
Headquarters: Akron, Ohio

Years of blowouts culminated in the 1980s in the amalgamation of two of the biggest U.S. tire producers: Uniroyal and Goodrich. The only question was: Can two losers yield a winner? As the decade ended, the answer seemed to be: no. They were about to be consumed by Michelin, thereby shifting world tire leadership from the U.S. to France.

Uniroyal Goodrich was created in August 1986 by patching together the tire operations of Uniroyal Inc. and B. F. Goodrich. These two companies had developed other businesses—chemicals particularly—that were making money while tire making was not. So both were happy to dump the businesses that were their birthrights. Freed of tires, Uniroyal could concentrate on products like Alar, a chemical that keeps apples looking red and ripe even though they've been around for a while. And Goodrich could pay full attention to PVC (polyvinyl chloride), a plastic used in pipes, flooring, bottles and many other products. (See B. F. Goodrich profile on page 530.)

Coming into the 1980s, Uniroyal was the number three tire maker and Goodrich number four. Their merger moved them into the number two slot behind Goodyear. But looks are deceiving. They ranked so high because of one customer: General Motors. Uniroyal has long been GM's preferred tire. However, such sales aren't easy money. Auto companies drive a hard bargain, and if you don't like the price, they can always find another supplier. The real money comes from selling tires to motorists who are replacing old ones, and that's where Uniroyal and Goodrich flounder, accounting for 2.5 percent and 4 percent, respectively, of the

In the winter of 1839, Charles
Goodyear accidentally invented
vulcanized rubber when he dropped
sulfur and crude rubber on his stove.

replacement market. Their combined share in 1980 was at least 15 percent.

History. Goodrich was the first Akron rubber company, founded in 1870 by Dr. Benjamin Franklin Goodrich, a Civil War surgeon from upstate New York who went into business because he didn't think he could support his wife properly in the medical profession. They were on a train to Chicago to seek advice from a rich relative on relocating the Hudson River Rubber Company, a business Goodrich had bought into, when a stranger told him Akron had great possibilities. Akron, then served by two railroads, had another one coming. "Mary, get your bonnet on," cried the young entrepreneur. They got off at the next stop—considerably short of Chicago—and before the century's turn Akron was the center of the world's rubber industry. B. F. Goodrich was known as the brains of the tire industry. In 1896 they became the first company to produce tires for the new "horseless carriage." Three years later, Goodrich came up with rubber-wound golf balls, which revolutionized the game. In 1939, they became the first company to produce synthetic rubber. Uniroyal's early history is a little less inspiring. The United States Rubber Company came to life in 1892 as the "rubber trust," a product of the great monopolistic era of American business. Charles R. Flint combined nine of the leading makers of rubber footwear into U.S. Rubber. They controlled 70 percent of the market, but had little in common save for a desire to throttle competition. They took 25 years to decide to market all their footwear under the brand name Keds. In that same year, 1917, four tire companies, then part of U.S. Rubber, began selling their products under a common brand name, U.S. Royal.

U.S. Rubber eventually captured 30 percent of the tire market, helped enormously by General Motors, which elected to put Royals on half the cars they built. However, it wasn't exactly a competitive bidding situation. During the 1920s the du Ponts, then the controlling owners of GM, began investing in U.S. Rubber, eventually accumulating 30 percent of the shares. GM bought their paint from du Pont and their tires from U.S. Rubber—for the same reason. And they got such a good price on the tires that in some years they filled two-thirds of their tire needs from U.S. Rubber.

But the GM–du Pont connection sowed the seeds for future disaster. With a voracious customer such as GM in their pocket, U.S. Rubber had little incentive to modernize plants, improve products or figure out how to sell replacement tires. After World War II they began to have serious problems with product quality. Enough tires were failing on the road that highway patrol officers would write letters to the company saying they couldn't help noticing that many flats and blowouts they saw on the turnpike were happening to Royals. By this time company headquarters had shifted to New York City, far from the tire plants. Executives changed the company name to the more modest Uniroyal in 1967. It didn't help. During the 1970s the company sold off many of their operations—golf balls, fire hoses, Keds footwear among them. Many observers suspected the only reason they held onto their tire business was that no one would be crazy enough to buy it.

B. F. Goodrich's decline was in some ways a sadder story. They continued being the tire industry's innovator. They made the first commercial tubeless tire and were the first rubber company to back the radial tire as a superior product. But with all these credits, Goodrich was rarely able to convert laboratory breakthroughs into marketplace successes. They were beaten to the draw again and again by Goodyear and Firestone, both of which set up the retail networks needed to sell replacement tires in America.

By the 1980s then, Goodrich was ready, along with Uniroyal, to say good riddance to tires. And so they did.

Owners and rulers. Michelin.

As a place to work. Disappearing.

Global presence. Before being snapped up by Michelin, Uniroyal Goodrich operated only on American soil. Now, they'll answer to the French.

S*tock performance.* Uniroyal Goodrich stock bought for $1,000 in 1980 sold for $3,468 on January 2, 1990.

Uniroyal Goodrich Tire Company, 600 South Main Street, Akron, OH 44318; (216) 374-2805.

3

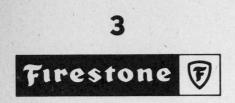

#3 *in tires*

Employees: 55,000
Sales: $11.7 billion
Profits: $67 million
Founded: 1900
Headquarters: Akron, Ohio

Organized at century's turn, Firestone Tire & Rubber hit the 1990s a crippled orphan adopted by the Japanese, with survival to the year 2000 in doubt. As Firestone Tire, that is. In 1950, when the company was 50, McGraw-Hill published a slavishly adulatory history, *The Story of Firestone*, by Alfred Lief, who sanctimoniously drew this moral:

> *The industrial eminence of The Firestone Tires & Rubber Company stands out as a great American story. Here, in a country which abhors cartels, which encourages initiative, provides opportunities, and rewards those who perform their social function well, the vision and vigor of a single man have created a tower of strength for all the American people.*
>
> *The company to which he gave his name is keeping the faith. The sons and associates of Harvey S. Firestone, and the men and women whom they in turn have trained, have by their works given assurance that this name will persist as a symbol of service to mankind.*

By 1980, those words were hollow. Firestone, long the nation's second largest tire maker (largely from being Ford's chief supplier since 1906), had lost credibility as a reliable manufacturer and responsible corporate citizen. They made illegal political contributions at home and abroad, and they had to recall 10 million

Firestone 500 steel-belted radials in 1978 or the government would step in because 500s were blowing out and 27 people were dead. Firestone family members were no longer active in the company.

In that crisis, they brought in John J. Nevin from Zenith to perform surgery. And he did. During the 1980s Nevin closed 11 of Firestone's 17 plants in the U.S. and Canada, sold off nontire businesses like plastic resins, car seat belts, truck wheels and polyurethane foam; chopped employment from 107,000 to 55,000; and moved corporate headquarters from Akron to Chicago (where he lived).

Then, in 1988, he administered the coup de grace, selling the entire company to Japan's Bridgestone for $2.6 billion. The sale consolidated Bridgestone's hold on third place in the world tire market, behind Michelin and Goodyear. The Japanese said Firestone would operate separately from Bridgestone, with headquarters again in Akron. Bridgestone, whose tires enter the U.S. on cars made in Japan, entered the U.S. market in 1983 when they began making truck tires at an old Firestone plant in La Vergne, Tennessee, near a new Nissan assembly plant.

Firestone, Bridgestone's new American subsidiary, operates a network of 1,500 sales and service centers across the U.S. But Firestone's forte has been selling not replacement tires but original equipment rubber on new automobiles. They supply more tires to GM and Ford than any other tire maker. In 1987, nearly half the tires they made went onto new cars and light trucks. In fact, in 1987 Firestone supplied tires for 20 percent of GM cars and trucks. But that long-standing relationship ended in 1988 when the Japanese moved in; GM bid sayonara to Firestone tires. Firestone has been Ford's chief tire supplier for most of this century. They also make tires in Spain, France, Portugal, Italy, Argentina, Brazil and Venezuela. In early 1990, Nevin retired as chairman to become a university professor, his lifelong dream. He was replaced by 55-year-old George W. Aucott, who was already CEO. Aucott signed on with Firestone in 1956 as a time study engineer.

Newsweek once said the name Bridgestone "sounds more like a domestic cottage cheese than a Japanese tire maker." The company name derives from

THE WORLD TIRE MARKET

	Company	Where Based	Sales Share
1.	Michelin	France	22%
2.	Goodyear	U.S.	18%
3.	Bridgestone	Japan	17%
4.	Continental	W. Germany	7.5%
5.	Pirelli	Italy	7%
6.	Sumitomo	Japan	6%
7.	Yokohama	Japan	5%
8.	Toyo	Japan	3%
9.	Other		14.5%

Source: The *New York Times,*
11 February 1990.

founder Shojiro Ishibashi. Ishibashi means stone (*ishi*) and bridge (*bashi*)—and when the company started to make tires in 1931 there were only 40,000 cars in Japan. So Ishibashi translated his name into English and reversed the order to make it "more acceptable internationally." Of course, now they could change the name to Firestone.

Bridgestone-Firestone Inc., 1200 Firestone Parkway, Akron, OH 44317; (216) 379-7000.

4

MICHELIN®

#1 *in tires (world)*
#2 *in tires (U.S.)*

Employees: 120,000
Sales: $8.6 billion
Profits: $384 million
Founded: 1863
Headquarters: Paris, France

The Michelin mystique is the envy of the industry: a name synonymous with high-quality, premium tires. Unlike Firestone, they have not been associated with horror stories involving tire failure. Their perfor-mance has permitted the company to claim that children are safer riding on Michelins. And because of this reputation they can charge top dollar. Now, in addition to this pristine image, France's Michelin can add another leaf to their wreath: They're the world's largest tire maker, and number two in the U.S.

They rolled into first place in 1990 by—for Michelin—an unusual route: they absorbed top competitor Uniroyal Goodrich. Heretofore, Michelin hasn't grown by buying other companies. On the contrary, their growth has flowed from a zealous, single-minded devotion to one product: the rubber tire. Michelin pioneered this product. Edouard Michelin invented, in 1891, the removable pneumatic tire. They put it first on a bicycle. They were the first to put it on a carriage, then on a car and then on a truck. In 1906 they invented the first removable rim and the first inflatable spare tire. They made the first tubeless tire in 1930. And after World War II they developed the radial tire, invading the U.S. when the American rubber makers resisted retooling their factories to make radials. Michelin forced Goodyear into production of radials, the tire now standard car equipment.

Michelin has allowed themselves very few diversions from tire making. One is the publishing of maps and travel and restaurant guides. This business was started in 1900, and Michelin is now one of the world's largest publishers of road maps and travel guides. Their *Guide Michelin* is the arbiter of French haute cuisine.

History. Michelin began in a machine shop. Until the invention of the bicycle tire in 1891, the company produced a small variety of rubber products and had only a dozen employees. In 1898, André Michelin created the roly-poly man who has become Michelin's jolly advertising symbol. The original poster came about after the Michelins saw a stack of tires at an exhibition, and one of them remarked, "If it had arms, it would look like a man." A cartoonist put arms on the stack, presenting him in a poster with the slogan, "Nunc est bibendum" (Latin for "Now is the time to drink"). Monsieur Bibendum was shortened later to Bib, and became Michelin's mascot. Roadsides in France are dotted with his likeness giving speed limits and other travel information.

Owners and rulers. Through all this heady growth, Michelin has remained very much a family business. There are no Goodyears, Goodriches, Seiberlings or Firestones in the tire business anymore. But there are certainly Michelins. Those who know François Michelin, head of the company, call him Le Roi Michelin. He is Edouard Michelin's grandson and in 1990 was 64 years old. The Michelin family controls up to 40 percent of the shares and more than half of shareholder votes.

As a place to work.   Everywhere Michelin has gone, they have encountered labor troubles, so they build factories in areas where unions are weak, such as the American South. François Michelin once said, "The presence of a union in a company merely reflects the inadequacy of the bosses." They are notoriously secretive about their research and factories, paternalistic toward their workers, and obsessive about their product—which until the Uniroyal Goodrich purchase was just one type of tire: radials.

Global presence. A worldwide company with more than 80 percent of production outside of France.

Michelin, 30 avenue de Bretail, 75341 Paris, France; (33) 1-45-63-0101.

Michelin Tire Corp., P.O. Box 19001, Greenville, SC 29062: (803) 458-5000.

CAR & TRUCK PARTS

You may never think about it when you get a new car, but many of its parts come from companies other than the automobile manufacturer. The same goes for trucks. Motor vehicle manufacturers depend on outside suppliers. This market, known as the "original equipment" market, is served by the likes of Dana, Eaton, Cummins Engine—giants in their own right. But they're giants closely tied to their customers. When automobile and truck makers catch a cold, the companies in this chapter contract pneumonia.

1

#1 *in truck parts*

Employees: 38,500
Sales: $5.2 billion
Profits: $132 million
Founded: 1903
Headquarters: Toledo, Ohio

This "Rust Belt" manufacturer of truck and car parts has a lot of fans. In business circles, they're regarded as a well-managed company. Outside the business world, they're regarded as a good place to work. They hung on to this reputation right through the 1980s, even when they had to lay off thousands of employees as a result of downturns in the automotive industry, to which they are inextricably linked.

Dana's fortunes generally rise and fall with truck sales. Two salient sets of statistics tell the story. One: They do one-quarter of their sales in front and rear axles for highway vehicles, primarily trucks. Two: Ford and GM account for 15 percent and 10 percent, respectively, of total sales.

They do have thousands of other customers, and they do make many other vehicle components, including gaskets, seals, pistons, piston rings, filters (oil, air, fuel) and universal joints (their first product). And some of these products find their way into passenger cars, but Dana's main focus is the truck manufacturer. Paradoxically, customers like Chrysler, Caterpillar and Deere are also their main competitors because they, too, make axles and engine parts. Dana also competes against independent suppliers of vehicle components (independent in that they are not part of any automotive company). The major ones are Bendix (part of Allied Corp.), Borg-Warner, Budd (part of Germany's Thyssen), Eaton, Rockwell, Sealed Power, Parker-Hannifin and TRW. Measured by sales of components, Dana is larger than all of these independents.

Dana buys 400,000 tons of steel a year to feed 90 U.S. plants. Their home state, Ohio, has the most plants, but the two biggest ones are Spicer Axle in Fort Wayne, Indiana, and Parish Frame in Reading, Pennsylvania.

History. The Fort Wayne plant is named for the founder of the company, Clarence Spicer, a Cornell engineering graduate who, in 1902, developed a universal joint—or driveshaft—to deliver power to a vehicle's rear axle. At the time, automobiles worked almost the same way as bicycles, using sprockets and chains to convey power from the front axle to the rear axle. Spicer saw that a driveshaft would do the same thing more efficiently. He dubbed his invention the "Spicer universal joint," and soon built an experimental car to try out his invention. It worked. Spicer left Cornell and started making and selling his universal joints in a Plainfield, New Jersey plant. When car manufacturers (Peerless, Pierce Arrow, Winton) switched to universal joints, Spicer's small operation struggled desperately to meet demand—and to fend off competition.

In 1914, Spicer's business was saved by the money and enthusiasm of Charles A. Dana, a well-heeled prosecuting attorney from New York City. At 33, Dana had already been elected three times to the New York State Legislature and was president of the New York and New Jersey Water Company. Dana was born into a famous New England family (Richard Henry Dana wrote *Two Years Before the Mast* and second cousin Charles A. Dana was editor of the *New York Tribune*). After giving Spicer some much-needed cash, Dana climbed aboard as adviser. Two years later, he was company president, a post he held until 1948 by which time the firm was named after him. In 1928, the company moved from New Jersey to Toledo, Ohio.

Owners and rulers. Gerald B. Mitchell, who went to work for Dana as a machine operator when he was 16 (he dropped out of high school), became CEO in 1979 and remained in that post until 1989 (1989 pay: $1.6 million). His successor as CEO is Southwood J. Morcott, aged 52 in 1990. Morcott graduated from Davidson College and joined the company as a sales engineer in 1963. Dana's board is composed entirely of white males.

As a place to work. In the late 1960s, president René McPherson set about making Dana a great place to work. He pushed an employee stock plan, abolished time clocks and established "Dana University," a training program for employees who want to rise in the company. Most Dana plants have a small company store with dozens of items bearing the Dana logo, from baseball caps, t-shirts and sweat suits to shoehorns, golf balls and bumper stickers. Some 70 percent of employees hold Dana stock. Dana's corporate headquarters in Toledo—a red brick building—resembles a structure from the restored colonial Williamsburg in Virginia. The pieces of furniture in the reception room, dining room and boardroom are 18th century antiques.

Global presence. Dana does 25 percent of sales outside the U.S. and earns 31 percent of profits abroad. They operate plants in 27 countries.

Stock performance. Dana stock bought for $1,000 in 1980 sold for $3,250 on January 2, 1990.

Dana Corporation, 4500 Dorr Street, Toledo, OH 43614; (419) 535-4500.

2

E·T·N

#2 *in truck parts*

Employees: 38,300
Sales: $3.7 billion
Profits: $225 million
Founded: 1911
Headquarters: Cleveland, Ohio

This pillar of the Cleveland industrial establishment—their 28-story Eaton Center at 12th and Superior is a notable feature of downtown Cleveland—tried in the 1980s to transform themselves into a high-tech company. They put astronaut Neil Armstrong on their board in 1981 and charged into space. The mission was perilous, however, and by decade's end they were rededicating themselves to what they have always done: make components—transmissions, axles, clutches, brakes—for heavy-duty trucks (not quite as exciting as their earlier project, building a landing station for the space shuttle).

Eaton traces their ancestry to a Danish immigrant named Viggo V. Torbenson, who patented a rear axle for trucks. By 1911 he was ready to manufacture the axles but needed a backer. He found one in Joseph Oriel Eaton, a colorful 38-year-old entrepreneur. Son of a Hudson River School painter famous for his portraits of the rich and famous (Herman Melville, Abraham Lincoln), Eaton attended Williams College and then drifted around until he linked up with Torbensen to cofound the Torbensen Gear and Axle Company in Bloomfield, New Jersey. They built seven axles that year—by hand.

Eaton was no mechanic. He was unable to drive a car. He tried once (it was an early electric model) and promptly crashed into a wall. But he was in charge of selling the axles and financing the company, and he accurately predicted that trucks would be in high demand. In 1914, Eaton moved the company to Cleveland, then calling itself the nation's "automotive capital." Eaton went on to buy several auto parts and motor companies before his death in 1949. He was unrelated to another Cleveland Eaton, Cyrus S. Eaton, with whom he was often confused.

The early 1980s saw Eaton go through what they themselves called "Operation Shrink." They sold a number of businesses, including forklifts and hoisting equipment, and closed nine plants, including the "mother" plant, opened in Cleveland in 1920 to make axles for trucks. From a high of 170 plants and 63,000 employees in 1979, they slimmed down to 40,000 employees and 140 plants in 1983.

Eaton's infatuation with high tech began when they bought the electronics company, Cutler-Hammer, in 1979, the same year they unloaded a previous acquisition, the Yale & Towne lock business (for five years the company was even called Eaton Yale & Towne). Milwaukee-based Cutler-Hammer brought Eaton into the electronic controls business, making such products as switches, relays and circuit breakers, as well as into the sophisticated defense electronics business via a Cutler-Hammer arm called AIL (Airborne Instruments Laboratory), based in Deer Park, New York. AIL was formed after World War II by scientists who had worked together during the war on detecting German submarines and jamming radio-borne guided missiles. When Ronald Reagan resurrected the B-1 bomber project, AIL came away with a huge subcontract to build a radar-jamming system for the giant plane. At the start of the 1980s AIL had sales of $100 million. Seven years later revenues were up to $900 million. But for Eaton, the truck parts supplier in Cleveland, the growth was troublesome and profitless. In 1986 the Air Force complained the electronic system Eaton's AIL division designed didn't work. Intended to foil enemy radar, it was prone to jamming itself. In 1988, Eaton announced they were exiting defense electronics, Chairman and CEO James R. Stover explaining: "Simply put, we must get bigger in defense electronics or get out, and we think our resources are better applied in other businesses." A few months later the Air Force terminated their contract with AIL "for default" and demanded the return of $39 million.

Meanwhile, Eaton, looking more and more like the *old* Eaton, maintains 140 locations on six continents, selling transmissions and engine components to the world's leading truck makers. Their number one customer is Ford, whose purchases accounted for 21 percent of 1988 vehicle component sales. Nothing Eaton makes is sold to consumers except Golf Pride golf club grips, which they make at Laurinburg, North Carolina.

Stock performance. Eaton stock bought for $1,000 in 1980 sold for $4,720 on January 2, 1990.

Consumer brands.

Golf Pride golf club grips.

Eaton Corporation, Eaton Center, Cleveland, OH 44114; (216) 523-4736.

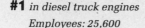

#1 *in diesel truck engines*

Employees: 25,600
Sales: $3.5 billion
Losses: $6.1 million
Founded: 1919
Headquarters: Columbus, Indiana

Social Conscience

A maverick company based in southern Indiana, Cummins Engine builds diesel engines for trucks, takes their social responsibilities very seriously and emphatically rejects the philosophy that ran like a litany through the 1980s: A company's primary mission is to maximize shareholder value. In his 1983 report to share holders, Chairman Henry B. Schacht described the company's goal as "being fair and honest and doing what is right even when it is not to our immediate benefit." That took some courage since the previous two years had seen sales slide and profits drop. Five years later, in an interview with the *Wall Street Journal*, Schacht was singing the same tune. Schacht told the *Journal* that those contending the sole

managerial responsibility is to maximize short-term value are wrong. That too took courage. Cummins Engine was in the red $14 million in 1988, yet the company gave more to charity that year than all but 95 of the *Fortune* 500 companies. In 1989, when Hurricane Hugo ravaged the South Carolina coast, Cummins quickly donated engines and generators. "Nobody," said Schacht, "stopped to say, 'Hey, we aren't making any money.'"

Such is Cummins' reputation for quality that their engines are offered by every major builder of heavy-duty trucks in the U.S., even by companies building their own engines. During the 1980s Cummins began making and selling other truck components and power systems so that by decade's end one-third of sales was coming from products other than diesel engines. At the same time they faced stiff price competition from Japanese diesel makers. Nissan and other Japanese engine builders began offering engines priced 20 percent below the Cummins' new product. Cummins slashed prices and then costs to meet the competition. As a result, they were still making half of all diesel engines—but profits were decimated. In 4 of the 10 years of the 1980s, there were no profits: Cummins lost money.

Cummins' benevolence doesn't extend to keeping unneeded employees on the payroll. To reduce costs, 4,000 people were laid off or offered early retirement during the 1980s in Columbus, the town Cummins has beautified over the years by commissioning public buildings by world-class architects like I. M. Pei and Richard Meier, a school designed by Caudill Rowlett Scott and a golf course by Robert Trent Jones. Cummins' corporate headquarters, opened in the mid-1980s and designed by Kevin Roche and John Dinkeloo, is a white, airy, two-story structure extending for three blocks in the middle of town. The company used to employ 1 out of every 10 Columbus workers. But Cummins has assured the town's residents they would never desert Columbus for low-paying labor markets in other parts of the country.

Cummins Engine is so well regarded because of the J. Irwin Miller family. Clessie L. Cummins, a chauffeur for Miller's great uncle, Will G. Irwin, developed a diesel engine both economical and dependable—and with the backing of Irwin, a Columbus banker, he set up the company bearing his name. J. Irwin Miller took the reins in 1937, holding them until 1977 as he built Cummins into a preeminent maker of diesel engines and a benefactor not only of their hometown but of various social causes as well. Miller's rule was that Cummins would allocate 5 percent of pretax profits for charitable contributions every year (the maximum deduction then allowed by the IRS). To integrate Cummins' ranks, he recruited some 100 black managers and trainees to come to Columbus between 1965 and 1973.

Two Ivy League graduates, both in their mid-40s when the decade opened—Schacht (Yale, Harvard Business School) and James A. Henderson (Princeton, Harvard Business School)—remained in command at Cummins as chairman and president, respectively, during the rocky 1980s. They both live on the same street in Columbus. The family patriarch, J. Irwin Miller, rescued the company in 1989 after the British conglomerate, Hanson Industries, had acquired almost 10 percent of Cummins' stock. Miller stepped in and bought Hanson's shares for $72 million (they had paid only $57 million for them), paying a premium of $5 million over the current market price. Miller's son, William, who holds a seat on the Cummins board, said: "We ate the premium. It was not a very '80s thing to do."

"Cummins has a fantastic future," the 80-year-old Miller told the *Wall Street Journal* in 1989, "because it isn't just factories, machines and cash. It's outstanding people who take intense pride in their work and their community."

Those sentiments were not shared by the aggressive New Zealand investor, Sir Ronald Brierly, whose Hong Kong–based conglomerate, Industrial Equity (Pacific), bought nearly 15 percent of the stock by early 1990 and filed suit in an Indianapolis Federal Court, charging the purchase of the Hanson stock the previous year was a "sweetheart" deal that enriched the Miller family at stockholders' expense. For a while a major battle seemed to be brewing: When Industrial Equity's chairman showed up at Cummins' annual meeting in April to confront Schacht, the New Zealander was subpoenaed to testify in a suit Cummins had brought charging Industrial Equity with violation of securities laws. A month later, the foreigners threw in the towel, agreeing not to buy any more Cummins stock for 10 years. "We got tired of it," an Industrial Equity spokesman told the *New York Times*. "[Cummins management is] deeply entrenched. Shareholders should be concerned."

In mid-1990 Cummins picked up three friendly investors when they sold 27 percent of their stock—at a substantial premium over the market price—to Ford Motor, Tenneco and Japan's Kubota. (All three are tractor makers.)

Stock performance. Cummins Engine stock bought for $1,000 in 1980 sold for $2,435 on January 2, 1990.

Cummins Engine Company, Inc., 500 Jackson Street, Columbus, IN 47201; (812) 377-5000.

Cummins Engine's headquarters, designed by Kevin Roche, is one of the buildings that make Columbus, Indiana (population 30,000) an architectural oasis.

4

#4 *in automotive parts*

Employees: 68,000
Sales: $2.2 billion
Founded: 1928
Headquarters: Chicago, Illinois

A leading supplier of automotive parts (axles, carburetors, transmissions), Borg-Warner had their gears stripped during the 1980s. Samuel Heyman, head of the chemical giant GAF, drew a bead on the company. To escape his clutches, Borg-Warner management worked a deal with Merrill Lynch in 1987 to pay off all the shareholders and privatize the company in a $4.2 billion buyout (almost $1 billion more than Heyman was bidding). Saddled now with a crushing debt burden, Borg-Warner spent the rest of the decade selling off chunks of the industrial-and-services empire they had meticulously assembled since the end of World War II. The biggest piece that left the house, and perhaps the most profitable part of the whole company, was the chemical business, which included the ABS hard plastics that have replaced steel and other metals in car bodies, telephones and appliances. General Electric snapped them up for $2.3 billion in 1988. The sale knocked Borg-Warner's annual revenues down from $3.6 billion to $2.2 billion, leaving them with scaled-down automotive parts operations (mainly manual transmissions, wheel drive systems, automotive chains, electronic controls for the chassis, turbo chargers and friction products) and an army of security guards and armored cars they provide to banks, factories and offices under the Burns International and Wells Fargo banners. Borg-Warner, with their building on Michigan Avenue, facing Grant Park and Lake Michigan, was for a long time a prominent member of the Chicago business establishment. They contributed mightily to city charities, schools and cultural groups. After the 1987 buyout, though, these activities ceased as Borg-Warner dropped from sight. James Beré was chairman and CEO in 1990, at the ripe age of 67.

Borg-Warner Corporation, 200 South Michigan Avenue, Chicago, IL 60604; (312) 322-8500.

CAR & TRUCK RENTERS

No one rents cars like Americans. They rent them by the day, the week and the month—and if the renters are companies, they lease car and truck fleets over much longer periods. Such rental revenues have been estimated as high as $10 billion a year.

Most car rentals are done by businesspeople on the road. And most car rental business is done at airports. A lot of small companies rent cars—they cluster around airports—but the bulk of the business is done by big renters. According to a 1987 estimate, over 5,000 car rental companies were operating in the U.S., but the top four, Hertz, Avis, Budget and National, controlled 90 percent of the business. Just like the cars they rent, the major companies in this field seem to be always changing hands. Not one firm had the same owner in 1990 that they'd had in 1980. Indeed, Avis was sold six times during the 1980s.

1

#1 *in truck leasing*

Employees: 43,700
Sales: $5.1 billion
Profits: $52 million
Founded: 1933
Headquarters: Miami, Florida

Most of us think of Ryder as the company that rents those yellow trucks to do-it-yourself movers. But that's only a small part of their business. Ryder has grown fat and rich by taking advantage of a modern business proclivity. Many companies simply don't want to tie up their money in big equipment purchases. For example, a company might need a truck fleet to run their business. But that doesn't mean they have to buy them. That's where Ryder

comes in. They'll lease a truck fleet to that company, which can then deduct rental payments on income tax returns. Ryder not only leases those trucks, they maintain them for the company—and will even show the company how to get the best use out of them. The 300 trucks that roll every day for the *Chicago Tribune* are Ryder-owned vehicles the newspaper leases. Ryder also leases jet aircraft although they're not so big in this business as they are in trucks. One Ryder company overhauls and services jet engines.

So in renting trucks to ordinary consumers, Ryder ranks number two to U-Haul. But their leasing business makes them a much bigger outfit than U-Haul. And Ryder *owns* all those leased trucks—more than 150,000 vehicles, the world's largest truck fleet.

Their expertise in running fleets has put them into the school bus business as well. They now have 6,900 buses serving 320 school districts in 15 states. They're number two in this business to Laidlaw, but they hope to capture the top spot in the early 1990s. Ryder is nothing if not confident.

Their expertise in getting materials from one point to another has put them into another business: transporting cars and trucks from factories to dealerships. They're number one in this carriage business, carrying 6 million vehicles a year.

The architect of Ryder's growth is Tony Burns, who took over as CEO in 1983 at age 40. A devout Mormon, Burns joined Ryder in 1974 as a financial planner after nine years with Mobil Oil. When he arrived, the company was on the verge of bankruptcy under the leadership of founder James Ryder. Ryder had started the company in 1933 with a black Model A Ford truck hauling cement blocks to a construction site. He soon discovered he could make more money leasing trucks to others. The firm grew slowly until 1949 when they won a contract to operate the Minute Maid orange juice company's fleet of 109 refrigerated trucks. This brought Ryder out of south Florida into a service network throughout the country. In 1968 Ryder launched their most familiar service, the consumer rental operation called One Way. But in the early 1970s the company overexpanded, and bankers pushed James Ryder out the door. He started a competitor, Jartran (a word derived from James R. Ryder Transportation), which went belly up in 1982. Ryder's growth has created many new jobs. Employment has more than doubled since Burns took over in 1983.

Stock performance. Ryder System stock bought for $1,000 in 1980 sold for $3,562 on January 2, 1990.

Ryder System, Inc., 3600 N.W. 82nd Avenue, Miami, FL 33166; (305) 593-3726.

2

#1 *in car rentals*

Employees: 30,000
Sales: $2 billion
Founded: 1918
Headquarters: Park Ridge, New Jersey

"We're number one, we're number one." That was Hertz's battle cry as they entered the 1990s, a theme they drummed like a tom-tom in their messages to the public and to employees. Hertz was the first company to rent cars, and they've been the leader ever since, despite multiple changes in ownership.

In the U.S., Hertz rents cars from 1,800 locations. They have another 3,000 locations in 120 other countries. They maintain a fleet of 400,000 cars and trucks, by far the largest fleet in the car rental industry.

Hertz is therefore the largest single customer Detroit has. When they buy, they buy big—100,000 cars at a shot. They don't keep cars for more than a year, and that brought Hertz into another business. They sell their old cars at lots all over the country, making Hertz the nation's largest used car dealer. And it's more than just a sideline business. Used car sales can mean the difference between a profit and a loss for the company.

Walter L. Jacobs, a 22-year-old Chicago car salesman, started what became Hertz in 1918. His inventory consisted of a dozen Ford Model T's. Within five years Jacobs was renting 600 cars and taking in $1 million a year. He then sold the company to John Hertz, the Yellow Cab ty-

coon, staying on to run the business. Jacobs established an important precedent. Since then car rental companies have been sold and resold.

John Hertz, for example, sold the business bearing his name after only two years. General Motors bought the company in 1925, adopting the name GM Hertz Drive-Ur-Self. Not many people were renting cars during the depression, but GM hung on to the business until 1953 when they sold it back to—yes, you guessed it—John Hertz. And founder Walter Jacobs was still running the company. (He was one of the few people in the country who knew *how* to run a car rental business.) Hertz sold stock in the company to the public—and Hertz shares were listed on the New York Stock Exchange—in 1954. Walter Jacobs, amazingly, continued to run the company until he stepped down as CEO in 1960. (In addition to being the maven of the car rental business, he was one of the nation's top contract bridge players.)

Renting cars became a big business after World War II, especially with the rise of air travel. People getting off planes wanted to have their own wheels. More often than not Hertz supplied those wheels. But it's a tricky business. You have to buy all those new cars on credit, you have to keep them in good shape, and then you have to know how to get rid of them. And there aren't too many people like Walter Jacobs who know that business, which might account for the seemingly endless changes of ownership.

In 1968 Hertz was bought by RCA, a company that made television sets and owned the NBC broadcasting network. RCA sold Hertz in 1985 to United Airlines, which had this Technicolor dream: Passengers on United flights descend to the baggage area to pick up their bags, move over to the Hertz counter to rent cars and speed downtown to another United property, a Westin hotel. It was a good pipe dream but fell apart in two years.

In 1987, as UAL Corp., the parent of United Airlines, changed their name to Allegis and back to UAL and fired their CEO, the Hertz business was once again on the move. Frank Olson, who had been running Hertz, was tapped to head the airline company, where his assignment was to sell off assets. Having worked at

Hertz for a long time, he knew that business well—and quickly sold Hertz for $1.3 billion. The buyers were Ford Motor Company and a group of Hertz executives headed by Frank Olson. Ford took 80 percent, the Hertz group 20 per cent.

Of course Hertz never stays long in one place. Before the 1980s ended, Ford sold 25 percent of Hertz to the Swedish car maker, Volvo, and 5 percent to a West German bank. That reduced Ford's stake to 50 percent. Hertz now buys all their cars from—yes, you guessed it—Ford.

Not long after Olson's return to Hertz, he had to contend with the fallout from a nasty scandal. In their aggressive money making Hertz managers had been systematically overcharging customers and insurance companies for auto repairs. It led the company to the dubious distinction of this first place: Hertz was slapped with the largest fine ever imposed on a corporation for criminal fraud.

The Hertz Corporation, 225 Brae Boulevard, Park Ridge, NJ 07656; (201) 307-2510.

3

#2 *in car rentals*

Employees: 14,000
Sales: $1.1 billion
Founded: 1946
Headquarters: Garden City, New York

For more than a quarter century, Avis told us they try harder because they're number two. Soon, Avis may have to abandon that slogan. They're poised to overtake archrival Hertz. At the beginning of the 1980s, Hertz had 41 percent of the rental car business to Avis' 23 percent. By decade's end the difference was only 2 percentage points (30 to 28). Avis already earns more profits than Hertz (and has since 1984). And Avis is number one in Europe (a position held since 1973).

Losing their underdog status would be a major change for Avis. After World War II, Hertz and other rental car agencies had only downtown locations. Warren E. Avis, a Ford dealer in Detroit, came up with the idea of renting cars at airports and opened his first location at Detroit's Willow Run Airport, and then a second one at Miami International. The idea caught on, forcing Hertz and others to follow suit. Airport car rentals now account for 80 percent of the business. Avis operates over 100,000 vehicles, most of them made by GM and Chrysler. By 1990, Avis agencies could be found in over 4,700 locations (1,200 of them in airports), in 142 countries.

In 1962, under Robert C. Townsend's reign, Avis introduced their long-lived advertising slogan—"We're only No. 2. We try harder." Glorifying Avis' underdog status suited Townsend. He delighted in playing the role of corporate maverick, even writing a best-selling satire on the sacred cows of corporate America. The title said it all: *Up the Organization: How to Stop the Organization from Stifling People and Strangling Profits.* Avis also pioneered in the 1970s with the Wizard computer system, linking reservations offices and rental counters. Avis has long been the field's most technologically advanced company and even today spends more on data processing than for any other division in their budget.

Avis has not only been an underdog for most of their existence, but a stray dog. Eight years after founding the company, Warren Avis sold it to New England investor Richard S. Robie. That was the first of 11 sales over the next 33 years. Other owners include a veritable who's who of American financial wheeler-dealers and conglomerates: Lazard Frères (1962), ITT (1972), Norton Simon (1977), Esmark (1983), Beatrice (1984), Kohlberg Kravis Roberts (1985) and Wesray (1986). Finally, in 1987, Avis' employees bought the company themselves for $1.75 billion, through one of the largest ESOP (employee stock ownership plans) stock purchases in the nation's history.

Shortly after the buyout, Avis's ad agency (Backer Spielvogel Bates) launched a major campaign with TV spots and full-page magazine and newspaper ads trumpeting the ownership change: "At Avis Inc., our employees are acting like they own the place"; and "Now when you rent from Avis Inc., you can deal directly with the owners" were two of the pitches. Several studies of Avis employees indicate they overwhelmingly approve of the change, especially because the company now solicits suggestions and opinions.

Leading the employee-owners is Joseph Vittoria, Avis' president since 1982. According to Vittoria, "My whole philosophy about business is that if you treat someone correctly and properly, chances are you'll get a good day's work out of them." Vittoria has personal reasons to upend Hertz. Hertz's chairman Frank Olson demoted Vittoria twice during Vittoria's tenure at the competitor. When Vittoria left Hertz to join Avis, he took 15 key employees with him. Hertz then sued Vittoria trying to force him out of his Avis job. The suit failed, but bad blood continues between the two companies.

Avis, Inc., 900 Old Country Road, Garden City, NY 11530; (516) 222-3000.

4

#3 *in car rentals*

Employees: 5,540
Sales: $512 million
Profits: $86 million
Founded: 1958
Headquarters: Chicago, Illinois

While Hertz and Avis have been battling for the number one position in the rental car business, Budget has been quietly gaining on both of them. Starting the decade a distant fourth, Budget passed National by 1987 and now has an eye on number two. (For those who keep track of such things, Budget is number one in Hawaii, Canada and Australia.) Over 3,550 Budget agencies operate worldwide; 1,240 in the U.S.

From the outset, Budget catered to people renting for pleasure rather than business. Founded by Morris Mirkin in a Los Angeles storefront, they were aptly named, with rates of $4 a day and 4 cents a mile when Hertz and Avis were charging $10 a day and 10 cents a mile. Today, more than half of Budget's customers (55 percent) rent for personal uses. At Hertz and Avis, business renters make up 70 percent of sales.

Budget rental locations were originally concentrated in downtown and suburban locations rather than at airports. Today, although they still have more urban/sub-

One of Budget Rent-a-Car's original outlets, 1958.

urban locations (including 93 Sears stores) than any competitor, Budget now does over two-thirds of their business at more than 700 airports. In the late 1980s, Budget decided to buy back the agencies they had franchised, and rent the 173,000 vehicle fleet themselves. They opened their first counter inside an airport in 1968, the same year the company was bought by Transamerica, a San Francisco–based insurance company that once owned United Artists along with a variety of other unrelated businesses. In 1986, Transamerica sold Budget to a managerial group and the investment banking firm of Gibbons, Green, van Amerongen. Less than a year later, the investors sold 28 percent of their shares to the public for about $41 million, making Budget a publicly traded company for the first time. Leonard T. Green, Lewis W. van Amerongen and one of their associates got three of the six seats on the board of directors.

In 1988, Gibbons, Green, van Amerongen bought Budget back for $333 million—a deal financed by the Ford Motor Company, which supplies over half of Budget's vehicles. The company head is Clifton E. Haley, who's been with Budget since 1977.

Budget Rent-a-Car Corporation, 200 North Michigan Avenue, Chicago, IL 60601; (312) 580-5000.

FUN & GAMES

TOYS

This business is not for the fainthearted. Predicting what kids want (and will convince their parents to buy) is a perilous way to make a living. Toy companies are always falling by the wayside. While toy sales doubled during the 1980s, General Mills fled the business, selling off their Kenner and Parker companies. So did MCA, setting LJN Toys adrift. Hasbro absorbed Milton Bradley, and in early 1990 Quaker Oats decided to liberate Fisher-Price.

These days most toys come from Hong Kong, Taiwan and South Korea—and the decade's biggest hit, Nintendo hand-held video games, roared in from Japan, moving into one out of every five American homes and capturing 80 percent of the home video game market.

1

HASBRO® TOYS

#1 *in toys, board games, baby bibs*

#2 *in preschool toys*

Employees: 8,300
Sales: $1.33 billion
Profits: $92 million
Founded: 1923
Headquarters: Pawtucket, Rhode Island

In a business notorious for a high fatality rate—toy companies on top of the world one Christmas find themselves in bankruptcy court the following Christmas—Hasbro has stayed on the kids' winning side year after year after year. They make perennial favorites: Lincoln Logs, Tinker Toys, Raggedy Ann, Mr. Potato Head, Candyland, Yahtzee and G.I. Joe, plus nearly 500 other toys, board games and puzzles. Nearly one of every seven toys sold in the U.S. comes from Hasbro. The name stands for Hassenfeld brothers. Although the business is now publicly owned, Hasbro is still run by the third generation of the founding family.

History. The original Hassenfeld brothers, Henry and Hillel, were Polish Jewish emigres who started selling fabric remnants in Providence, Rhode Island. They also sold cloth-covered pencil boxes and zippered cloth pouches filled with pencils, compasses, protractors and other school supplies. In 1935, when their pencil suppliers raised prices, the Hassenfelds started making pencils. (Now an independent company, that branch of the business, Empire Pencil, is the nation's largest pencil maker.) Henry's son Merrill suggested making toys in the 1940s—initially paint sets, crayons and doctor and nurse kits—to fill in slack times for school supplies.

As a toymaker, Hasbro has cashed in on America's wars. Inspired by the blitz, they made junior air-raid warden kits with dummy gas masks and flashlights. They introduced G.I. Joe in 1964, just in time to capitalize on the escalation of the Vietnam War. But they didn't want to risk too close an association with current events. So the 11½-inch figure and his enemies reflected a historical mishmash. Joe was equipped as a World War II soldier. His enemy dolls were a World War I German infantryman with an Iron Cross and a Japanese soldier from 1941. In two years, Hasbro sold over 8 million G.I. Joes. When antiwar sentiment (inspired by the Vietnam conflict) and competing characters (Kenner's Six Million Dollar Man and Ideal Toy's Evil Knievel) slowed G.I. Joe sales, Hasbro turned him into an "adventurer" with a "Kung Fu grip" and "atomic bionic limbs." In 1976, they scrapped him altogether, but brought him back in the early 1980s, after the Iranian hostage crisis, as a terrorist fighter. In 1988 he was the best-selling toy in the nation with sales of $200 million for Joe and his paraphernalia—by which time about 200 million Joes had been sold.

Merrill had his day with G.I. Joe and in the late 1970s put his two sons, Stephen and Alan, in charge of the business, letting them learn by their mistakes. They started a gourmet cookware line that failed after termites munched their way through a warehouse full of wooden salad bowls. They backed a monster toy called Teron the Terrible that flopped. Critics began calling Hasbro, "Has been." And then they had family troubles. Uncle Harold ran the pencil business, which produced reliable profits while the erratic toy business soaked up investments in new products. After Merrill died in 1979, the uncle and his nephews were at each other's throats. As a result, they divorced. Harold took Empire Pencil out of Hasbro.

The Hassenfeld brothers—Stephen and Alan—finally came into their own during the 1980s. While competitors were chasing fads like video games and Cabbage Patch dolls, Hasbro cleaned up with prosaic items like My Little Pony, a pastel horse with a combable mane, and GLO Worm, a stuffed doll whose face lights up when it's hugged. They also scored big with TransFormers, a line of transformable robots and vehicles. And they had old favorites like Tinker Toys. Not many who saw it are likely to forget the Eddie Murphy pre-Christmas skit on "Saturday Night Live" in which he advised parents not to buy their kids anatomically incorrect dolls like Ken but to stick to tried-and-true winners like Mr. Potato Head (a Hasbro toy).

When other toy companies found the going too tough, the Hassenfelds always picked up the pieces. In 1983 they bought Knickerbocker Toy (Raggedy Ann dolls) and Glenco Infants (the top maker of baby bibs). In 1984 they bought Milton Bradley, the biggest supplier of board games, maker of Playskool toys and home of one of America's oldest toys, Lincoln Logs, created in 1916 by John Lloyd Wright, son of architect Frank Lloyd Wright. In 1986 Hasbro also acquired Child Guidance (Busy Fire Truck and Sesame Street toys) from CBS. And in 1989, after competitor Coleco Industries hit the skids, they bought them and picked up the Cabbage Patch dolls, the runaway best-seller of the mid-1980s, and the board games Scrabble and Parcheesi.

No wonder by the end of the 1980s Hasbro Industries had an iron grip on first place in the toy industry. Of course, toymakers are forever burying their mistakes. One toy Hasbro discarded at the end of the 1980s was Maxie, a doll trotted out with great fanfare in 1988 to compete with Mattel's Barbie.

Owners and rulers. The Hassenfelds control one-third of the stock. Before his

EMPERORS OF TOYLAND

		Sales
1.	Toys 'R' Us	$3.6 billion
2.	Child World (Cole)	$800 million
3.	Kay-Bee (Melville)	$780 million
4.	Lionel Leisure (Kiddie City, Playworld, Toy Warehouse)	$409 million
5.	Greenman Brothers (Circus World, Playland)	$177 million

Source: DSN research, 1989.

death in 1989 at 47, Stephen owned 9.4 percent worth $100 million. The next biggest shareholder is Time Warner, which got one-fifth of Hasbro's stock in exchange for Knickerbocker Toy. The public owns the rest.

The business has a distinct family flavor even though outside executives far outnumber Hassenfelds. Alan took over as chairman after his brother's death from pneumonia. Stephen and Alan shared a house on the Rhode Island coast and drove to work together in Stephen's Targa. Alan's mother Sylvia, a company director, is consulted before new toys are put into production.

As a place to work. The eight original Hasbro employees were all relatives of Henry and Hillel Hassenfeld, and when the brothers started hiring outsiders they treated them like family too. They invited employees to weddings and bar mitzvahs, handed out Hanukkah gifts and slipped extra cash to families in trouble. With 8,300 employees, Hasbro is too big for that now. But some of that ambiance survives. Senior vice presidents often come to work in jeans. Stephen used to call top executives on their birthdays.

The Hasbro style was a shock to Milton Bradley managers, who found themselves transported from a plush Federal-style building in Springfield, Massachusetts (furnished with elegant colonial furniture), to strikingly plain offices, one of which is in a converted supermarket in Pawtucket, Rhode Island.

Social responsibility. Hasbro offended mental-health groups by describing one of the new G.I. Joe enemy figures, Zartan, as an "extreme paranoid schizophrenic with multiple personalities." They wound up apologizing, changing the description and donating money to mental-health research.

Hasbro clashed with the city of Chicago after they announced plans to close the Playskool factory there and lay off 680 workers in 1984. Playskool had previously promised to improve the factory and expand the work force after receiving $1 million in industrial development bonds in 1980. Chicago sued Hasbro, and in January 1985 Hasbro agreed to keep the factory going a year longer than planned and help find new jobs for Playskool workers and a nonprofit tenant for the factory. But nine months later, ex-employees complained to *The Neighborhood Works* newsletter that over half the work force was still unemployed. An unidentified Hasbro spokesman told the newsletter, "Sure there are problems and people may still be unemployed. But who else [among Chicago employers who laid off workers] is doing anything?"

Stock performance.   Hasbro stock bought for $1,000 in 1980 sold for $60,790 on January 2, 1990.

Consumer brands.

Toys: G.I. Joe, TransFormers, Jem, Raggedy Ann, Mr. Potato Head, GLO Worm, Lincoln Logs, Tinker Toys, My Little Pony, Real Baby, Yakity Yaks (Bingo the Bear and Montgomery Monkey), Wuzzles, Watchimals, Kid Sister, My Buddy, Inhumanoids, Playskool toys, Teach Me readers, Mickey Mouse Talking Phone, Romper Room toys.

Games and puzzles: Candyland, Chutes and Ladders, Bed Bugs, Scruples, Game of Life, Yahtzee, Battleship.

Baby equipment: Tommee Tippee cups.

TV shows: "Romper Room," "Bowling for Dollars."

Hasbro, Inc., 1027 Newport Avenue, Pawtucket, RI 02861; (401) 431-8697.

2
Mattel

#2 *in toys*

Employees: 11,000
Sales: $1.2 billion
Profits: $80 million
Founded: 1945
Headquarters: Hawthorne, California

In 1959 Mattel introduced the most successful toy the industry has ever seen, the Barbie doll. Barbie is a big consumer of clothes and accessories, and Mattel became a big consumer too, using the profits Barbie generated to buy other companies and launch new businesses. Before you knew it, Mattel was running the Ringling Bros. & Barnum Bailey circus, Shipstad & Johnson's Ice Follies, Western Publishing (the largest publisher of children's books) and a new line of electronic toys, including the Intellivision videogames. All these businesses were sloughed off during the early 1980s as Mattel decided to turn the clock back and become—surprise—a toymaker. Especially a Barbie maker.

Barbie has stood the test of time. Since 1959 more than 500 million Barbies have been sold, enough to circle the world 3½ times. According to Mattel, 90 percent of girls aged 3 to 11 own at least one Barbie. During 1988 they were selling Barbies at the phenomenal rate of 54,000 a day. And, of course, the dolls are just the beginning. They need clothes. Mattel introduces 100 new Barbie outfits every year (although the best-seller is always the wedding gown). Since 1959 Mattel has gone through 75 million yards of fabric, making them the fourth largest maker of women's garments in the U.S. And that gave Mattel an idea. They're now planning a line of Barbie clothes for children—in other words, for Barbie's owners.

Barbie accounts for about half of Mattel's total business. Others have introduced Barbie clones, but they all failed. Hasbro, the nation's largest toymaker, copied the idea in the 1980s, first with Jem and then with Maxie. They both flopped. Gary Jacobson, a security analyst at the Kidder, Peabody brokerage house, said:

Barbie doll through the years (left to right) 1989 SuperStar Barbie, 1977 Barbie, 1968 Barbie and the original Barbie of 1959.

"It's very difficult to compete against Barbie. She's up there with Mickey Mouse, Coke and Nike."

Barbie is also an international seller. Mattel gets 70 percent of sales outside the U.S. No toys are made in the U.S.; they come mainly from China, Malaysia and Mexico.

History. Ruth Handler, youngest of 10 children of Polish immigrants, was a secretary at Paramount Pictures in Los Angeles when she married Elliott Handler, an industrial designer, who went into the picture-frame business. In 1945 he found himself with a lot of extra frame slats, so the Handlers joined with buddy Harold Matson to make toy furniture. The name Mattel came from combining Matson's last name with Elliot's first name. By 1955 they were raking in $6 million. That year, the Handlers introduced toy burp guns, which took off when they ran ads all year long on Walt Disney's TV hit, "The Mickey Mouse Club." The Handlers used their new brand name, Mattel, with the slogan, "You can tell it's Mattel, it's swell."

Mattel's big hit came in 1959, when Ruth Handler devised a doll that looked like a buxom teenager. As she later explained to the *New York Times*: "If a little girl was going to do role playing of what she would be like at 16 or 17, it was a little stupid to play with a doll that had a flat chest. So I gave it beautiful breasts." Barbie, as the doll was christened, soon had a boy friend, Ken, and they both had extensive wardrobes (that were bought separately). Another Mattel winner was a talking doll, Chatty Cathy.

Sales boomed and by 1965, Mattel was doing more than $100 million a year and they were number one in the toy industry. Their stock was listed on the New York Stock Exchange. In 1968 they introduced another spectacular seller, Hot Wheels, miniature model cars.

Things soured in the 1970s, when Mattel's plant in Mexico burned, a shipping strike in the Far East cut off their toy supply and the Handlers—to avoid reporting a sales drop—doctored their books. In 1978 they were each fined $57,000 and given 41-year jail sentences—which were suspended with the proviso that the Handlers do community work. The judge told them: "The crimes each of you committed, in the opinion of this court, are exploitive, parasitic and I think disgraceful to anything decent in this society." The Handlers sold most of their Mattel stock in 1980, and Ruth Handler started Ruthton, a company making prosthetic breasts for mastectomy patients.

Owners and rulers. After the Handlers departed, Mattel was taken over by Arthur Spear, who stepped down when he reached 65. For a brief period, the company was run by a committee. In early 1987, International Division head John W. Amerman was named chairman and CEO. In 1986, Mattel had lost $8.3 million and their number one position in the toy industry to rival Hasbro. White-haired Amerman snapped into action. The next year, Mattel closed 40 percent of their manufacturing plants and decided to focus on

There are 3.2 billion words that can be made out of all the possible seven-letter combinations you could get playing the game of SCRABBLE. About two million SCRABBLE boards are sold annually.

core products rather than a slew of trendy toys. The Wall Street investment house, Warburg, Picus owns 20 percent of Mattel.

Stock performance. Mattel stock bought for $1,000 in 1980 sold for $2,847 on January 2, 1990.

Consumer brands.

Barbie, See 'N Say, Hot Wheels, Li'l Miss Makeup, Li'l Miss Dress Up, He Man, Boglins, Cherry Merry Muffin, P.J. Sparkles, Disney toys.

Mattel, Inc., 5150 Rosecrans Avenue, Hawthorne, CA 90250; (213) 978-6635.

CONSUMER ELECTRONICS

Just about every American home has a TV. Many have two or three. The U.S. has two radios for every man, woman and child in the country. At the start of the 1980s the VCR, or videocassette recorder, was virtually unknown. By decade's end, a VCR could be found in more than 60 million homes—and stores selling and renting tapes (a business where an advanced degree is not necessary) had surfaced everywhere. American companies missed out on this boom. General Electric abandoned consumer electronics and sold RCA to the French. By the end of the 1980s, consumer electronics stores featured wall-to-wall displays of products made by non-U.S. companies. The one exception was Zenith, last of the American TV set makers to hang in there.

1

Matsushita Electric

#1 *in consumer electronics (world), VCRs, TVs, stereo systems, radios*

Employees: 198,000
Sales: $42 billion (World), $5 billion (U.S.)
Profits: $1.4 billion
Founded: 1918
Headquarters: Osaka, Japan

A common misconception is that every Japanese company is like every other Japanese company. There's as much truth to that as the syllogism that General Electric is the same as IBM and Westinghouse and Hewlett-Packard. Matsushita had their origins in a simple product, a double-ended socket. Founded by one man, Konosuke Matsushita, a grade school–dropout who attached to the mundane business of manufacturing a spiritual significance, Matsushita was not part of a *zaibatsu*, the financial trusts (Mitsubishi, Mitsui, Sumitomo, Yasuda) that dominated Japanese business prior to World War II. Unlike Sony, which made their mark in overseas marketing, or Hitachi and Toshiba, prime suppliers of heavy electrical equipment to industrial customers, Matsushita's base is the Japanese con-

FOREIGN TV SETS BORN IN THE U.S.

Company	U.S. Plant	TVs Made Each Year
Goldstar	Huntsville, AL	1,000,000
Hitachi	Anaheim, CA	360,000
JVC	Elmwood Park, NJ	480,000
Matsushita	Franklin Park, IL	1,000,000
Mitsubishi	Santa Ana, CA, and Braselton, GA	685,000
Philips	Greenville, TN	2,000,000
Samsung	Saddle Brook, NJ	1,000,000
Sanyo	Forrest City, AR	1,000,000
Sharp	Memphis, TN	1,100,000
Sony	San Diego, CA	1,000,000
Thomson (RCA/GE)	Bloomington, IN	3,000,000
Toshiba	Lebanon, TN	900,000

Source: Electronic Industries Association, 1988.

sumer. And unlike their big electronic rivals in Japan, Matsushita's home base is Osaka, not Tokyo (Osaka, more like Chicago than New York, has long been a commercial center).

Americans may never learn how to pronounce this name—it's Mot-SOOSH-ta—but consumers shopping for a TV or videocassette recorder or stereo system don't have any trouble getting their tongues around the Matsushita brand names: Panasonic, Quasar, Technics. Their fourth brand is National, a name used mostly in Japan and other Asian markets. You may also be buying a Matsushita product without knowing it. VCRs sold in the U.S. under the General Electric, Magnavox, Sylvania and J. C. Penney names come from Matsushita factories.

Matsushita makes a product line that will not stop. GE's Jack Welch insists on making only products that rank first or second in their categories, but Matsushita makes everything. Americans are familiar with Matsushita's audio and video products, but in Japan the Panasonic, Technics and National names appear on a multitude of home appliances: toasters, vacuum cleaners, refrigerators, fans, food processors, washing machines, rice cookers, irons, air-conditioners, kerosene heaters, bread bakers. Beyond that, they now make a wide range of industrial products, office machines and basic electronic components: light bulbs, batteries, telephones, computers, semiconductors, laser printers, robots. By their own count Matsushita makes over 14,000 products.

Matsushita entered the 1980s with sales of $10 billion and emerged with sales of $40 billion. Unbelievable. Some of that growth reflects appreciation of the yen against the dollar but most of it was a sales explosion. Little of it reflected mergers or acquistions.

With more than 40 percent of sales outside Japan, Matsushita makes more and more of their products overseas. Japan has 110 Matsushita factories. The rest of the world has more than 70. Eight of them are in the U.S., turning out TVs, microwave ovens, cellular phones, VCRs, electronic pagers and car audio systems, among other products. Matsushita became a U.S. manufacturer in 1974 when they took over the Franklin Park, Illinois, plant where Motorola had been making TVs under the Quasar name. Motorola was delighted to exit that business; Matsushita was happy to get into it. A milestone was reached in June 1988 when Matsushita exported from Franklin Park to Japan a shipment of 27-inch wood-encased color TVs bearing the Panasonic name. Matsushita is the world's leading video maker: so far over 100 million TVs and over 50 million VCRs.

Another milestone was reached in March 1989 when Matsushita did what few Japanese companies have ever done: appoint an American, Richard A. Kraft, to be second in command of North American operations. Kraft worked for Motorola before Matsushita bought the Franklin Park plant in 1974.

Matsushita's U.S. payroll was 9,200 in 1989 and is expected to hit 12,000 by 1992. They aim to be a good corporate citizen in the U.S. They have set up a $10 million foundation, endowed $1 million chairs at MIT, Stanford and the Harvard Business School and pledged to donate one-tenth of 1 percent of U.S. sales to nonprofit groups (about $5 million in 1989).

It's behavior the founder would have approved. In 1932, when his company was 14 years old, he gathered his employees around him to tell them he thought the mission of business should be to eliminate poverty. Konosuke Matsushita died on April 17, 1989, at age 94, leaving an estate valued at $1.5 billion, reportedly the biggest personal estate ever left in Japan. Matsushita's son-in-law, Masaharu Matsushita, was company chairman in 1989 (according to a Japanese custom, he has assumed his wife's last name since she has no brothers). President and CEO was Akio Tanii, graduate of an industrial high school, who emphasizes "human electronics." Tanii told *Fortune*: "We've always been manufacturers. Now we have to be socially minded. We have to invest in culture, not just technology, and we have to do it all over the world."

Stock performance. Matsushita stock bought for $1,000 in 1980 sold for $7,685 on January 2, 1990.

Consumer brands.

Panasonic, Technics, Quasar, National.

Matsushita, 3-2, Minamisemba 4-chome, Minami-ku, Osaka 542, Japan; (81) 6-282-5111.

Matsushita, 1 Panasonic Way, Secaucus, NJ 07094; (201) 348-7000.

2

#1 *in electric razors, light bulbs (world)*

#2 *in world electronics industry, light bulbs (U.S.)*

#3 *in TVs, records (world)*

Employees: 293,300
Sales: $30 billion (World), $6 billion (U.S.)
Profits: $414 million
Founded: 1891
Headquarters: Eindhoven, Netherlands

Some of the great modern electronic inventions—the audio cassette, the videocassette recorder and the compact disk player—emerged from this giant Dutch company. But one would never know it from their U.S. standing, where their corporate name is not a household word, as it is elsewhere in the world. Cornelius van der Klugt, who became Philips CEO in the mid-1980s, acknowledged as much by observing, "When you say Philips in the United States, people think it is spelled with two *l*s and is in oil." Philips wants to change that impression. They're the world's leading maker of light bulbs (their first product), and in 1983 they bought the Westinghouse lighting business in the U.S. Timid about using their own name, they continued to sell the bulbs under the Westinghouse name. Then, in 1985, they took the plunge, launching a series of humorous TV commercials promoting *Philips* light bulbs.

They took an even bigger plunge when they bought the 42 percent of their American arm, North American Philips (NAP), they didn't already own. NAP, seller of

Norelco shavers and Magnavox, Sylvania and Philco audio and video products, was set up during World War II to protect the Dutch company's U.S. assets. They operated under a peculiar charter enabling them to function independently with an American management even though ultimate control rested in the Netherlands. In fact, Philips suffered the embarrassment of having their American satellite, NAP, opt for the VHS standard Matsushita developed for VCRs, thereby spurning the V-2000 system their Dutch parent developed. In 1987 Philips ended this nonsense by buying up all the NAP shares and integrating the American outpost into their worldwide operations.

Philips is the largest European electronics company; their brands include Pye in Britain and Grundig in Germany. They employ nearly 300,000 people in 60 countries. Their product lineup is enormous. If it plugs into a wall socket, chances are good Philips makes it. In the late 1980s they ranked as the world's largest producer of color TVs. In the American market, their brand, Magnavox, ranks third behind RCA and Zenith. They are the world's third largest record producer through their 80 percent–owned Polygram, whose labels include Decca, Deutsche Grammophon, Mercury, Island, A&M, London and Verve. Their Norelco brand is stamped on half of the electric shavers sold in the U.S.

They have also been a leading producer of major appliances like refrigerators and washing machines, but in 1988 they sold 53 percent of this business to Whirlpool, which wants to become a global player in appliances. Philips is providing them with that access. Philips will celebrate their centennial in 1991, a year before the start of the European Common Market. They're prepared to take on the Japanese in any market, including the U.S., and they have been critical of American companies that buy electronic components from Japan instead of making them in their own factories. Van der Klugt put it this way in a 1989 interview with *Barron's*: "Every dollar you pay for Japanese goods holds 10 cents with which they will make the bullets that will kill you." Philips knows what they're talking about. Philips' patents enabled Sony to get into the consumer electronics business.

THE COLOR TV MARKET

		Share
1.	Thomson (RCA/GE)	12%
2.	Zenith	12%
3.	Philips (Magnavo Sylvania, Philco, Philips)	11%
4.	Sony	6%
5.	Sears	5%
6.	Sharp	5%
7.	Matsushita (Panasonic, Quasar)	5%
8.	Mitsubishi	4%
9.	Emerson	3%
10.	Toshiba	3%
11	Others	24%

Source: Appliance, September 1989. In 1988 20.2 million TVs were sold.

Van der Klugt was ousted in 1990 when profits slid. He was replaced by Jan D. Timmer, head of the consumer electronics division, who immediately announced he would cut 10,000 jobs.

Stock performance. Philips N.V. stock bought for $1,000 in 1980 sold for $4,033 on January 2, 1990.

Consumer brands.

Shavers: Norelco.

Audio and video products: Sylvania, Philco, Magnavox.

Records: Decca, Deutsche Grammophon, Mercury, Island, A&M, London, Verve.

Philips N.V., 5621 BA Eindhoven, Netherlands.

North American Philips Corp., 100 East 42nd St., New York, NY 10017; (212) 697-3000.

3

TOSHIBA

#1 *in laptop computers*
#4 *in TVs (world)*

Employees: 120,000
Sales: $29 billion (World), $4 billion (U.S.)
Profits: $924 million
Founded: 1875
Headquarters: Tokyo, Japan

A superpower in world electronics, Japan's Toshiba—world's fourth largest TV set maker, fifth largest semiconductor supplier—does 15 percent of their sales in the U.S., where they make VCRs, TVs and microwave ovens (in Lebanon, Tennessee); assemble their top-selling laptop computer (in Irvine, California); and have joint ventures going with a bunch of companies, including Westinghouse, Motorola, LSI Logic and General Electric (Toshiba is often called the "GE of Japan"). You name it and Toshiba makes it, everything from nuclear reactors, elevators, CAT scanners and electric locomotives to light bulbs, juicers, electric fans and Auto Sweepy, a robot programmed to clean and scrub floors.

By now most people have probably forgotten a 1987 incident in which it was disclosed that Toshiba, through a 50.8 percent–owned subsidiary, Toshiba Machine, had illegally shipped milling tools to the Soviet Union, enabling the Russians to deaden the sound of submarine propellers, making them more difficult to detect. Congressmen gathered on the White House lawn to sledgehammer Toshiba products, and the U.S. Senate, in an unprecedented act, voted 92-to-5 to ban all Toshiba products from the American market for five years. The sanctions that finally emerged from Congress were far less onerous and while Toshiba's top two executives resigned over the furor, the company did not seem to suffer any long-term consequences. In 1988, after Orel Hershiser pitched the Los Angeles Dodgers to a World Series title, Toshiba signed him up to promote their copiers. In 1989, just as U.S. trade sanctions against Toshiba were about to be lifted (sanctions cost the company $240 million in 1988 alone), they were back in hot water. Toshiba admitted providing Libya with electronic equipment for a chemical weapons plant. Company officials claimed they believed the Libyan plant would be used to desalt seawater and the shipments did not violate export laws.

In the pecking order of Japanese industry, Toshiba ranks as the fifth largest manufacturer. They're number three in electronics (behind Matsushita and Hitachi). They've long had a reputation as a technically proficient but boring company. Headed by Joichi Aoi, president and CEO, Toshiba is a tiger when it comes to research, investing well over a billion dollars a year in their laboratories. In 1988, they secured 750 patents from the U.S. Patent Office. Only one other company—Hitachi—received more (907).

Consumer brands.

Toshiba.

Toshiba Corporation, 1-1 Shibaura, Minato-ku, Tokyo 105, Japan; 81-3-457-2104.

Toshiba America, 82 Totowa Rd., Wayne, NJ 07470; (201) 628-8000.

4

SONY

#2 *in records*
#3 *in TVs*

Employees: 79,000
Sales: $20 billion (World), $7.4 billion (U.S.)
Profits: $720 million
Founded: 1946
Headquarters: Tokyo, Japan

Sony is the most well-known Japanese brand name in America, and Sony's cofounder, Akio Morita, is the most well-known Japanese businessman in America. Sony's hallmark is the development of high-quality miniaturized consumer electronic products—transistor radios, tape recorders, Walkmans, compact disks, camcorders—that perform as well or better than their bulkier predecessors. Cultivation of the American market has always obsessed Sony, witness the gigantic steps taken in the 1980s: buying CBS Records from CBS Inc. for $2 billion and then shelling out over $4 billion for Columbia Pictures. A billion here, a billion there, Sony has the yen. They are well on their way to becoming a colossus of the entertainment world.

Coming into the 1990s, Sony was doing a third of their sales in America. Aside from Honda, no other Japanese company is that dependent on the U.S. Sony established their first U.S. branch office in 1958. In 1961 they became the first Japanese company to sell stock to American investors, raising $4 million in a public offering. In 1970 they became the first Japanese company to secure a listing on the New York Stock Exchange. In 1970 they began assembling TVs in San Diego, the first Japanese company to produce receivers in the U.S. Sony recently announced purchase of a plant in Pennsylvania (once belonging to Volkswagen) to make Sony TVs. Morita boasts the Sony name is so well known to Americans that they didn't have to advertise for employees—word-of-mouth brought them in. Modesty is not one of Morita's hallmarks. He is fond of lecturing Americans on their shortcomings. One of his opinions is that Americans have too high a regard for the underdog.

History. Akio Morita *is* Sony. A flamboyant jet-setter, he was born in Nagoya, Japan, in 1921. Although his family had a successful sake-brewing business, Morita was more interested in music as a child—he even made an electric phonograph when he was a schoolboy. During World War II, Morita served in the Japanese Navy where he met and befriended Masaru Ibuka, an engineering genius who owned an electronics research company. They teamed up in 1946 with Ibuka's father-in-law to form Tokyo Tsushin Kogyo (Tokyo Telecommunications Engineering).

One of Ibuka's first products was a device that converted a standard radio receiver into a shortwave set. In 1950, Tokyo Tsushin became the first Japanese company to produce a tape recorder. It was so new no one in Japan knew how to use it, and it fell to supersalesman Morita to scare up customers. In 1953, Tokyo Tsushin paid $25,000 to Western Electric for the use of the American company's transistor technology, and four years later, they introduced a pocket-sized transistor

TOP 10 CONSUMER ELECTRONICS STORES

Retailer	1989 Sales
1. Radio Shack	$2.97 billion
2. Kmart	$2.48 billion
3. Sears, Roebuck	$2.06 billion
4. Circuit City	$1,37 billion
5. Service Merchandise	$1.25 billion
6. Silo	$610 million
7. The Federated Group	$253 million
8. Trader Horn	$160 million
9. Lowe's	$120 million
10. Rose's Stores	$120 million

Source: Lowe's 1989 Annual Report.

radio. (It was actually slightly larger than a shirt pocket, so they had special shirts made with outsized pockets for their salesmen). The radio was a hit, and the first product to carry the Sony brand name. Morita explained how they came up with the name: "We wanted a short name for our products, an international name that would sound the same all over the world. So Mr. Ibuka and I worked together, checking many, many dictionaries, and we found two terms, *sonus*, a Latin word meaning sound, and sonny boy. So we thought: We are a group of *sonny boys* in the sonus business. So we combined *sonus* and *sonny* and came up with Sony." In 1958 Sony became the corporate name.

Sony suffered some setbacks in the early 1980s. Their Betamax videocassette recorder lost out to the VHS system fielded by JVC and Matsushita, even though Sony had invented the VCR. Sony admitted defeat in 1988 when their new line of videocassette recorders were designed to use VHS tapes. That year they also introduced the Video Walkman, a tiny VCR weighing 2½ pounds, with a 3-inch TV screen. In the 1980s, Sony also came out with the Watchman, a hand-held TV. The company's newest product is a minilaser disk—which Morita calls "the compact disk of tomorrow"—holding 20 minutes worth of songs. Such spectacular technological advances come at a cost:

Sony devotes 10 percent of earnings to research and development.

In 1988, Sony gave notice they were moving into Silicon Valley when the company established a subsidiary in Palo Alto, California. The reason: Sony's latest push into computer work stations. The first three such attempts failed—Americans will buy Sony electronics but not Sony computers. Sony is now selling two cloned computer models to U.S. scientists and engineers (based on the Sun computer made by Sun Microsystems). In early 1990, Advanced Micro Devices sold a San Antonio, Texas, factory to Sony for $55 million, and in exchange Sony agreed to share advanced semiconductor manufacturing technology. It is Sony's first American microchip plant. (Sony makes $1 billion worth of chips a year for their own products.)

Owners and rulers. The biggest owner is the Morita family. The Morita's original family business (which still makes sake) owns nearly 10 percent of Sony. In 1989, Norio Ohga succeeded Morita as CEO. A former opera singer, Ohga came to Morita's attention when he told him how bad Sony's tape recorders were. Sony has arranged for Ohga to conduct an orchestra.

As a place to work. In 1989, a disillusioned former Sony employee named Gary Katzenstein wrote a book called *Funny Business* describing his time at Sony in Tokyo. Katzenstein had many complaints: a rigid hierarchy (any problems were to be taken to your direct superior), stifling paternalism (you are assigned a partner to eat lunch with), and constant surveillance in the company dormitory, where a caretaker watches your every move.

Social responsibility. Some critics blasted Sony's acquisition of Columbia Pictures, the biggest Japanese takeover of a U.S. company, as the sale of an American legacy. But Akio Morita told a Japanese reporter: "If I were to tell Michael Jackson to change the way he sings, he would call me stupid. The same goes for movies. It's simply out of the question to buy [America's] soul." Former President Ronald Reagan had a different view. While visiting Japan on a speaking engagement (for which he was paid $2 million), Reagan told a Japanese audience that Sony's purchase of Columbia might "bring back decency and good taste" to American movies.

Stock performance. Sony stock bought for $1,000 in 1980 sold for $8,267 on January 2, 1990.

Consumer brands.

Sony, Betamax, Trinitron, Walkman, Watchman, Video 8, Epic, Columbia, CBS Masterworks, Columbia Pictures.

Sony Corporation, 9 West 57th Street, New York, NY 10019; (212) 371-5800.

Sony Corporation, 7-35, Kitashinagawa 6-chome, Shinaga-ku, Tokyo 141, Japan; (81) 3-448-2111.

5

Thomson

#1 *in TVs (U.S.)*

#2 *in defense electronics (world)*

#3 *in TVs (world)*

Employees: 104,000 (world), 17,000 (U.S.)
Sales: $12.5 billion (World), $3 billion (U.S.)
Profits: $78 million
Founded: 1893
Headquarters: Paris, France

The French government owns the largest piece of the U.S. market for TVs. Weird as it sounds, that was the result of a 1987 transaction that saw the French company, Thomson SA, acquire the consumer electronics business of General Electric. Included in that business were all the audio and video products carrying the RCA and GE names: TVs, radios, VCRs, stereos, tape recorders. The most important of these lines are TVs—the RCA brand was the number one seller in the American market, with a market share of 16 percent, and GE makes added another 3 or 4 percent. RCA receivers are turned out at the world's largest TV set plant—a 40-acre factory at Bloomington, Indiana, with an annual capacity of more than 3 million units.

A company with origins in the end of the last century, Thomson was nationalized by the French government in 1982 and remains a 100 percent state-owned chattel. However, Thomson does not operate under a stodgy, government bureaucracy, which was exactly how their previous capitalist owners ran the firm. To run the sprawling, money-losing conglomerate that Thomson had become, making everything from light bulbs to computers, the Mitterand government selected Alain Gomez, grandson of a Spanish anarchist, reformed Marxist, ex-paratrooper and graduate of the Harvard Business School: in short, a firebrand. He whipped Thomson into a profit-making, fighting multinational, cutting manufacturing businesses from 23 to 2 (consumer electronics and defense electronics) and setting up a sideline, a currency-trading bank that sometimes makes more money than the manufacturing end. Intent on beating the Japanese in consumer electronics, he bought television companies in half a dozen countries, including Telefunken in Germany and Ferguson in Britain. When GE's Jack Welch approached him to take over Thomson's medical electronics business, Gomez asked for a swap: medical electronics for GE's consumer electronics. Welch's reaction was: "He wants to sell TV sets against the Japanese? Give it to him." And so Gomez—and by proxy, France—took over a faltering American business GE was unwilling to defend. It represented virtually the last nail in the coffin of U.S. consumer electronics. The only American-owned company left is Zenith—and they're not a world player. Depending on which estimate you see, Thomson is now third or fourth in the world in consumer electronics.

Thomson's U.S. invasion completed the decimation of a company called RCA, founded in 1919 by General Electric. General David Sarnoff (made a brigadier general during World War II) presided over an independent RCA for more than four decades and was responsible for a policy that may have been the company's undoing. Rather than expand overseas with their own plants, bringing electronic technology to the rest of the world, RCA licensed their patents to foreign manufacturers, and was content to collect royalties. As biographer Kenneth Bilby noted, "To a greater degree than any other company, RCA revered the patent... The decision had been made to license the world rather than sell RCA products to consumers." In the end, of course, the Japanese companies with RCA licenses came to the U.S. to beat RCA at their own game.

In 1985, RCA was bought by the company that founded it. GE, it turned out, was more interested in NBC than making TVs—hence the 1987 deal with Thomson. RCA, prior to being acquired by GE, operated under their 1919 U.S. Navy–dictated charter provisions: Foreigners could own no more than 20 percent of the shares and no one except U.S. citizens could hold seats on the board. It should make for pretty interesting reading these days in Paris.

Consumer brands.

RCA and General Electric TVs, VCRs, radios, stereos, tape recorders.

Thomson Consumer Electronics, 600 North Sherman Drive, Indianapolis, IN 46201; (317) 267-5000.

Thomson Consumer Electronics, Cedex 66, 92050 Paris, France.

6

#2 *in TVs*

Employees: 32,500
Sales: $1.5 billion
Losses: $68 million
Founded: 1923
Headquarters: Glenview, Illinois

In 1960, 27 American companies were making TVs. By 1989 one was left: Zenith, a stubborn Chicago company that has fought the foreign invaders on every front, in the marketplace, in the halls of Congress and in legal battles right up to the Supreme Court. General Electric, Admiral, RCA, Magnavox, Motorola, Philco and Sylvania have all either left the field or had their TV brands bought by foreign companies. In 1980 a lot of people thought Zenith was a goner. Their share of the U.S. market plunged during the 1980s from 20 to 12 percent, and their CEO, Revone Kluckman, died suddenly of a heart attack in 1983—and yet they emerged from this decade in stronger shape than anyone ever thought they would be.

A $65 million purchase made in 1979 helped Zenith navigate the turbulent

1980s. That was the price they paid Schlumberger for Heath, a maker of kits for ambitious people who want to put together their own radios, stereos or computers. Being a TV set maker, Zenith already knew how to make monitors (computer screens)—and presto, they became a maker of personal computers. Nearly everyone was making computers in the early 1980s, but Zenith outlasted most of them by targeting the U.S. government as their prime customer—the military, the IRS, the Postal Service. It was a winning strategy. By the end of the 1980s Zenith was the largest maker of IBM-compatible laptop computers. Computers were accounting for about half of Zenith's sales, about $500 million of which were computer sales to the U.S. military. The architect of this resurgence was Jerry K. Pearlman, an abrasive manager who came up through the finance side of the business. He succeeded Kluckman as CEO when he was only 44. Pearlman is now president, CEO and chairman.

During the mid-1980s, as TV sales plunged, Zenith racked up three consecutive years of losses. The computer business was doing fine, and so there were incessant calls from Wall Street for Zenith to get out of consumer electronics. But they didn't know Jerry Pearlman. Zenith's heritage is consumer electronics, and they don't want to get out of it. Instead, as the 1980s drew to a close, Zenith decided to sell their *computer* business to the French company, Groupe Bull, for $511 million and charged into the future with high definition television (HDTV), where they're already a leader. Pearlman has a deal with AT&T for joint research into HDTV, and he also sought U.S. government funding for HDTV research to foil the Japanese.

Zenith began making radios in Chicago in 1919 and by the 1930s was the leading maker of portable radios. Their official name remained Zenith Radio until 1984, when it was changed to Zenith Electronics. In 1939 they went on the air with the nation's first all-electronic TV station, W9XZV. They introduced their first TVs in 1948. This company likes to make TVs. They just used computers as a way to get back to what they were born to do.

S*tock performance.* Zenith stock bought for $1,000 in 1980 sold for $1,429 on January 2, 1990.

C*onsumer brands.*

Zenith.

Zenith Electronics Corporation, 1000 Milwaukee Avenue, Glenview, IL 60025; (312) 391-7000.

MOVIES

The number of movie tickets sold has remained remarkably stable, at a little over 1 billion a year, over the past 25 years. That's down a lot, of course, from the 4 billion sold in the pre-TV days of 1946, but the movie industry isn't suffering. First, the average ticket price is now $5. Second, videocassettes have let Hollywood studios tap a rich stream of new revenues. Toward the end of the 1980s they were earning more money there than at the box office. Almost everyone wants to be in the entertainment business, often for reasons having nothing to do with money. So turmoil was constant during the 1980s. Two film studios—Columbia Pictures and Twentieth Century-Fox—changed hands twice. Warner Bros. became part of the company publishing Time and Fortune. Metro-Goldwyn-Mayer and United Artists went through multiple ownership and management changes. Refugees from Paramount Pictures took over Walt Disney—and Paramount did so well their name went up in lights, replacing Gulf & Western in the corporate title. (Paramount originally took their name from an apartment building on New York City's upper West Side.)

1

The ꞌꞌ Walt Disney ꞌꞌ Company

#1 *in theme parks*

Employees: 43,000
Sales: $4.8 billion
Profits: $729 million
Founded: 1923
Headquarters: Burbank, California

Soviet journalist Vladimir Voina probably had it right. Visiting Disneyland for the first time in 1990, he called it "a metaphor for America," adding: "Where else would someone build an industry based on happiness?" Disney's happiness business exploded during the 1980s under the aggressive management of a new leader, Michael D. Eisner, who became Mickey Mouse's boss in mid-decade in the wake of a bruising takeover battle. Eisner soon had Mickey working harder than ever. In 1988, when the mouse was 60, Eisner had him blowing out candles everywhere as Disney put up $100 million to celebrate his birthday. Eisner pushed hard on all three Disney fronts—theme parks, movies and merchandising Disney characters—to score a quantum leap in financial results: Disney's profits soared from $100 million in 1984 to $700 million in 1989.

In *theme parks*, Eisner more than doubled the admission charge—to $32.75 for adults, $26.40 for children (age three to nine)—at Disney World in Orlando, Florida. He also opened three new separately ticketed attractions—the Disney-MGM Studio Theme Park, Typhoon Lagoon and Pleasure Island—and began covering the rest of the huge Orlando site with hotels and a convention center, including a 900-room Grand Floridian Beach Resort, modeled after the 19th-century Victorian resorts. Theme park revenues crossed $2 billion in 1988 and zoomed to $2.6 billion in 1989, accounting for nearly 60 percent of Disney's revenue. Theme park attendance is also spectacular. From its founding in 1955 until 1990, about 300 million people visited the Disneyland in Anaheim (only 250 million people live in the U.S.). Eisner has also modified Disney's puritanism. Restaurants at Disneyland now serve beer and wine at night, and guards no longer halt same-sex dancing (after three gay men sued and accused park officials of discrimination based on sexual orientation).

In *films*, Eisner also changed the culture. Commitment to family-type entertainment still exists—they cite *The Little Mermaid* as an example—but a week after joining Disney from Paramount Pictures, Eisner recruited Jeff Katzenberg from Paramount as studio head. They quickly signed Paul Mazursky to make *Down and Out in Beverly Hills* (camouflaged under the Disney label, Touchstone). Released in 1985, it was the first R-rated movie in the company's history. In 1986 they released *Ruthless People*, starring Bette Midler, described by critics in terms never before applied to a Disney movie: "raunchy," "rude," and "vulgar." Eisner's movies—*The Little Mermaid, Three Men and a Baby, Who Framed Roger Rabbit, Good*

Morning Vietnam, Dead Poets' Society, Pretty Woman—sold tickets. In 1988 Disney scaled the heights: first ever top slot in box-office sales.

In *consumer products*, Eisner more than tripled sales to over $400 million, opening Disney stores in shopping malls, expanding mail-order catalog sales by buying Childcraft from Grolier and purchasing a TV station, KCAL in Los Angeles. He extended licensing to cover over 16,000 products sold in some likeness to a Disney character. He also brought in a new cast of characters by acquiring Henson Associates, bringing Miss Piggy, Kermit the Frog, Gonzo and Fozzie Bear into the Disney lineup.

Eisner is even creating Disney architecture. He has commissioned world-famous architects—Michael Graves, Frank Gehry, Arata Isozaki, Antoine Predock, Robert A. M. Stern—to design fanciful structures to fit into a Disney–Mickey Mouse setting. Twin hotels, the Swan and the Dolphin (designed by Graves), opened at Disney World in 1990, are the first in this series that will eventually encompass 20 hotels and office buildings (including the new Disney headquarters in Burbank) in three cities and on two continents (Euro Disneyland in France will have a Hotel New York). Eisner is determined to "Disneyize" the world. "If your eye sees something," he says, "your feet will follow." Even the critics are bowled over. Paul Goldberger, *New York Times* architectural critic, said: "No company has ever tried to market serious architecture to the masses the way Disney is now doing. That is why, whatever the buildings turn out to be like, there can be no doubt that Disney is a force to be reckoned with in architecture in the last decade of the 20th century—a corporate patron like none other, past or present."

History. Walt Disney grew up on a small farm in Missouri where his father was a member of the Congregational Church and a socialist. Walt's first cartoon business, in Kansas City, went bankrupt. So in 1923 he set out for Hollywood, where his older brother Roy was turning out silent comedies in a garage. With a small animation staff, Walt made the first Mickey Mouse cartoon (*Steamboat Willie*) in 1928. After a long string of cartoon shorts, including *The Three Little Pigs*, which contained the first hit song from a cartoon ("Who's Afraid of the Big Bad Wolf"), Disney made an animated feature film. The result, in 1937, was *Snow White*, the first blockbuster hit for Disney Productions, followed by other blockbusters: *Pinocchio, Fantasia* and *Bambi*.

From 1932 to 1942, Disney won eight Oscars. Walt Disney himself worked as story editor, idea man and decision maker. Although people believed he was a brilliant cartoonist, he was actually a terrible artist. He was unable to draw Donald Duck or any of his other famous charac-

Include Me out: More Sayings of Sam Goldwyn.

Samuel Goldwyn, Polish-born producer who founded one of the Hollywood studios that went into Metro-Goldwyn-Mayer, never quite mastered the English language although he lived in the U.S. for 80 years. He was famous for his malapropisms, known as "Goldwynisms"—hilariously mangled expressions, mixed metaphors and syntactical blunders. Here are some examples:

"You've got to take the bull by the teeth."

"You need Indians you can get them right from the reservoir."

About his film *Edge of Doom*: "This is a simple story of a boy who wants a fine funeral for his mother, so he kills a priest."

"I'm no Polly Alder."

"Tomorrow we shoot whether it rains, whether is snows, whether it stinks."

"I'm sticking my head in a noose." ∎

Source: The New York Review of Books, 18 May 1989.

Disney Chairman Michael Eisner meets with the cast of Disneyland, 1984.

ters, according to author Richard Schickel in *The Disney Version*.

Behind the scenes of this family entertainment company was fraternal rivalry—and hatred. While Walt tended the creative side, Roy managed the company's business end. Roy saw himself as the cautious brake to his younger brother's wild enthusiasms. They fought constantly. For years they didn't speak to one another, and the company divided into "Roy" and "Walt" factions. In *Storming the Magic Kingdom*, his 1987 account of the stormy takeover battle of the mid-1980s, John Taylor related how Roy would tell stories of young Walt wetting the bed they shared while growing up. "He'd pee all over me," said Roy, "and he's still doing it." Walt's version went this way: "I pissed on him then and I'm pissing on him now." The fraternal rivalries survived their deaths (Walt in 1966, Roy in 1971) into the next generation—and almost broke up the company in the 1980s.

Roy E. Disney, Roy's son and Walt's nephew, left the company in 1977 but stayed on the board until 1984. He was frustrated at being treated as "the idiot nephew" by the "Walt" faction. Three weeks after Roy resigned from the board a larger stockholder surfaced: Saul Steinberg, chairman of Reliance Group Holdings, whose hobby was raiding companies and walking away with a profit when they bought his shares at a premium, a tactic known as "greenmail." Steinberg had accumulated 6.3 percent of Disney's shares and several months later was bought out, at a greenmail profit of $31 million. Roy Disney then formed an alliance with Bass Brothers of Fort Worth, Texas, the largest Disney stockholder.

Ron Miller, Walt Disney's son-in-law, was ousted—and Roy Disney and the Bass Brothers gave the top spot to Eisner, a 42-year-old hotshot from Paramount. As a balance wheel, Frank Wells, former president of Warner Brothers, was brought in as Eisner's number two. The Eisner-Wells team was a shot of adrenaline. By decade's end, they'd put together such a string of victories Disney was making more money than any other company in the entertainment business. Revenge has no doubt been sweet for the Roy Disney clan.

O*wners and rulers.* The old Disney company was a WASP enclave in Hollywood. Now management is largely Jewish. Roy Disney has sold most of his Disney stock and neither he nor his attorney, Stanley Gold, hold board seats anymore.

THE TOP 10 THEME PARKS

Theme Park	City	Annual Visitors
1. WaltDisney World	Orlando, FL	30.0 million
2. Disneyland	Anaheim, CA	13.3 million
3. Universal Studios (MCA)	Universal City, CA	5.1 million
4. Knott's Berry Farm	Buena Park, CA	4.0 million
5. Sea World of Florida (Anheuser-Busch)	Orlando, FL	4.0 million
6. Sea World of California (Anheuser-Busch)	San Diego, CA	3.6 million
7. Kings Island	Kings Is, OH	3.2 million
8. Cedar Point	Sandusky, OH	3.2 million
9. Six Flags Magic Mountain	Valencia, CA	3.2 million
10. Busch Gardens (Anheuser-Busch)	Tampa, FL	3.1 million

Source: *Money*, May 1990.

The Sid Bass group in Fort Worth still holds the biggest chunk of stock (18 percent). As part of the deal bringing Eisner to the company, Walt's daughter, Sharon Disney Lund, took a board seat. She holds 1.65 percent of the stock. Eisner and Wells have been well rewarded for turning Disney around. In 1988 Eisner was the highest-paid executive in American business, with total compensation of $40 million. In 1989 he made $9.5 million, ranking ninth among all CEOs in pay. He was the fifth highest-paid CEO in America for the decade 1980–1989. Over the three-year period, 1987–1989, Wells made $86 million in pay and long-term compensation awards. Even Disney's number three executive, chief financial officer Gary Wilson, made $64 million over those three years (Wilson resigned those posts in 1989 but remains to advise the board). While Walt Disney grew up in modest circumstances in Kansas, Eisner grew up rich on Park Avenue. In the 1989 Disney annual report, he tells shareholders how his three children are doing. Sidney Sheinberg, president of MCA, calls Eisner "an egomaniac."

As a place to work. No longer a "family company," Disney is known now as a "Yuppie concentration camp." In a line quoted all over Hollywood, Jeff Katzenberg said: "If you don't come in on Saturday, don't bother to come in on Sunday." The old Disney company used to insist employees traveling on company business fly first class to compensate them for being away from their families. Now they fly coach. Eisner's Disney has a Hollywood reputation for frugality. They don't pay top dollar—either to stars or lower-level employees. The cherubic-looking Eisner used a strike by unionized employees at Disneyland to gain the right to use part-timers and reduce labor costs. With some of those bucks, they are completing a new headquarters in Burbank, California, featuring large statues of Doc, Dopey, Happy, Grumpy, Sneezy, Sleepy and Bashful holding up the fifth floor (some neighbors are complaining about the architectural design).

Social responsibility. Disney's contribution to society is making people happy through films, amusement parks and Mickey Mouse sweatshirts. Michael Eisner would like to bury the world in Disney paraphernalia. He once had a cornfield planted in the shape of Mickey Mouse's head so people flying over it would be reminded of Mickey though they were nowhere near a Disney amusement park. The giant amusement park in Orlando, covering 43 square miles, is Disney's most successful effort at what they call "imagineering" (imagination plus engineering). Disney World has made this central

Florida city the world's most popular tourist destination, attracting 30 million visitors a year. In 1965, Orlando had a population of 30,000; today, it's 650,000. Orlando has more hotel rooms, 70,000, than any other city in the world. Disney employs 31,000 people there, double the payroll of the number two employer, aerospace company Martin Marietta. In March 1990, Disney created a new corporate position, vice president of environmental policy, because of allegations that workers at Walt Disney World's Discovery Island were mistreating and killing vultures (Disney was fined $10,000).

Global presence. Disney is known the world over. When the late Emperor Hirohito of Japan visited the U.S., he went to Disneyland to meet with Mickey Mouse. Nikita Khrushchev threw a temper tantrum when he couldn't get into Disneyland. And after the Socialists triumphed in France in 1982 and brought François Mitterand to power, the government approved a Euro Disneyland outside Paris. The Disney company owns 49 percent of Euro Disneyland, scheduled to open in 1992. They collect a 10 percent royalty on admissions to the Disneyland in Japan. They get only 15 percent of sales from abroad, but it's a big world—and Michael Eisner's ambition is boundless.

Stock performance. Walt Disney stock bought for $1,000 in 1980 sold for $11,409 on January 2, 1990.

Walt Disney Company, 500 Buena Vista, Burbank, CA 91521; (213) 845-3141.

2

MCA

Employees: 17,400
Sales: $3.27 billion
Profits: $192 million
Founded: 1924
Headquarters: Universal City, California

More than any other Hollywood company, MCA stands for corporate power. MCA's origins are found in Music Corpo-

ration of America, once the biggest agents in the entertainment business, and are reflected in their 15-story headquarters in the San Fernando Valley, known as "the black tower" or "tower of fear." MCA is certainly the most "corporate" of the Hollywood companies—a place where executives dress in suits and ties, a place that doesn't change hands every other year, a place where more is going on than just movies. MCA has divisions that publish books (Putnam, which had many best-sellers during the 1980s), send out mail-order catalogs and operate over 400 stores (Spencer Gifts), press records, publish music and provide all the visitor amenities at California's Yosemite Park. In addition, their black tower overlooks Hollywood's biggest tourist destination (the Universal Studios Tour), they operate a television station in the New York metropolitan area (WWOR) and they own 50 percent of Cineplex Odeon, North America's second largest movie theater chain.

The film divisions, Universal Pictures and Universal TV, account for about half of revenue. Universal is where Steven Spielberg started, and he gave Universal their two biggest hits of the 1980s: *E.T.* and *Back to the Future.* They hit a dry spell in mid-decade, backing one of the greatest flops in the history of motion pictures, *Howard the Duck,* but rebounded in 1989 with *Parenthood, Back to the Future II* and *Born on the Fourth of July* to capture second place in box-office receipts.

MCA was started by Jules C. Stein, who put himself through the University of Chicago medical school by playing "schmaltzy" violin and saxophone. Stein and his band began getting more gigs than they could do themselves. So he started booking other bands into clubs and charging the bandleaders a commission. Business boomed. Stein got his MD but found a career in the music business more exciting, and lucrative, than ophthalmology. In 1924, with $1,000, he founded Music Corporation of America. By the early 1930s Stein had a flourishing national talent agency.

In 1936 he signed on 22-year-old Lew Wasserman ("the biggest, toughest Jew I could find," said Stein) as national director for advertising and public relations. Wasserman had been a bouncer in a Chicago speakeasy run by the Purple Gang. MCA moved to California in 1937, where

Wasserman was the first agent ever to get stars a percentage of a movie's earnings instead of a straight salary. Wasserman was as tough as nails; he often summed up his management philosophy with the anecdote that if you kicked your dog every day and then one day didn't kick it, it would wonder why you stopped loving it. After World War II, MCA controlled half the top-name stars and earned a fat 10 percent commission. In 1946 Stein made Wasserman, at age 33, president of MCA. By the mid-1950s MCA was the nation's biggest producer of TV shows, which over the years have included "The Virginian," "Rockford Files" and "The Six Million Dollar Man." In 1966 they merged with Decca, the company that owned Universal, and began producing major films, such as *Jaws*, *The Sting* and *The Deer Hunter*.

MCA is still run by the aging Lew Wasserman as chairman and CEO, and Sidney Sheinberg as president and chief operating officer. Sheinberg—who hails from Corpus Christi, Texas, and earned a law degree from Columbia—hates Michael Eisner, head of Disney studios (he calls him an "egomaniac" who has "a failure of character"). In 1989, Sheinberg earned a whopping $7.9 million.

When MCA founder Jules Stein died in 1981, his pallbearers were Jimmy Stewart, Cary Grant and Ronald Reagan—just sworn in as president. Reagan's ties with MCA go way back. In 1952, when he was president of the Screen Actors Guild, Reagan exempted MCA from the rule that agencies could not produce shows *and* represent actors. In return, MCA hired Reagan to host "GE Theater."

MCA is big, and getting bigger. They are into records (15 percent of the U.S. market after buying Geffen Records in 1990 for $545 million—making David Geffen the largest MCA shareholder with 9 percent of the stock). Even the national park system is not safe from their grasp. In 1973, MCA started operating in California's Yosemite. They now run all the lodging places and restaurants there despite complaints from conservationist groups. The MCA subsidiary operating at the park, the Curry Company, has annual revenues of $85 million and pays the government a mere $635,000 in license fees. And Universal Studios in Hollywood is such a moneymaker MCA wants to create a chain. Universal Studios in Orlando, Florida, opened in 1990, and plans are afoot for parks in Japan and Europe.

Stock performance. MCA stock bought for $1,000 in 1980 sold for $4,240 on January 2, 1990.

MCA Inc., 100 Universal City Plaza, Universal City, CA 91608; (213) 985-4321.

3

Paramount Communications Inc.

Employees: 11,800
Sales: $3.5 billion
Profits: $1.4 billion
Founded: 1912
Headquarters: New York City, New York

Paramount Pictures, the studio that gave us Gary Cooper, Jeanette MacDonald and Claudette Colbert, was Hollywood's hottest studio during the 1980s, turning out a string of hits like *Raiders of the Lost Ark*, *Beverly Hills Cop* and *Fatal Attraction*, signing stars like Eddie Murphy and producing a strong TV series lineup whose shows included "Family Ties," "Cheers" and "Entertainment Tonight." For most of the decade Paramount ranked first or second in box-office receipts. They were first in three of those years and stayed on top despite the departure of Barry Diller, who was in charge of Paramount's resurgence after the studio was acquired by Gulf+Western Industries (recently rechristened Paramount Communications). His lieutenants included Michael Eisner, Jeff Katzenberg and Dawn Steel. They all left during the 1980s—Diller to run Twentieth Century-Fox for Rupert Murdoch and Eisner to run Walt Disney. Katzenberg (and 17 other Paramount people) joined Eisner at Disney, and Steel went to Columbia Pictures. Without missing a beat, Paramount installed a marketing whiz, Frank Mancuso, as the film studio head, and he continued to turn out hits.

History. When it came to companies, Charles G. Bludhorn, an Austrian immigrant, was like a kid in a candy store. He wanted everything he saw. Under the banner of Gulf+Western, a name he selected

ALL-TIME MOVIE BLOCKBUSTERS

Theatrical Rentals*	
The Teens/'20s	
1. The Birth of a Nation	$10. million
2. The Big Parade	$5.1 million
3. BenHur (MGM)	$4.6 million
4. The Singing Fool (Warner Bros.)	$4.0 million
The '30s	
1. Gone with the Wind (MGM)	$79.4 million
2. Snow White and the Seven Dwarfs (Disney)	$61.8 million
3. Pinocchio (Disney)	$33.0 million
4. Fantasia (Disney)	$28.7 million
5. King Kong (RKO)	$5.0 million
The '40s	
1. Bambi (Disney)	$47.3 million
2. Cinderella (Disney)	$41.1 million
3. Song of the South (Disney)	$29.2 million
4. Samson and Delilah (Paramount)	$11.5 million
5. The Best Years of Our Lives (Goldwyn)	$11.3 million
The '50s	
1. The Ten Commandments (Paramount)	$43.0 million
2. Lady and the Tramp (Disney)	$40.2 million
3. Peter Pan (Disney)	$37.6 million
4. BenHur (MGM)	$37.0 million
5. Around the World in 80 days (United Artists)	$23.1 million

Theatrical Rentals*	
The '60s	
1. The Sound of Music (Fox)	$79.7 million
2. Love Story (Paramount)	$50. million
3. Doctor Zhivago (MGM)	$47.3 million
4. Butch Cassidy and the Sundance Kid (Fox)	$46.0 million
5. Airport (Universal)	$45.2 million
The '70s	
1. Star Wars (Fox)	$193.5 million
2. The Empire Strikes Back (Fox)	$141.6 million
3. Jaws (Universal)	$129.5 million
4. Grease (Paramount)	$96.3 million
5. The Exorcist (Warner Broso)	$89.0 million
The '80s	
1. E.T. The Extra-Terrestrial (Universal)	$228.6 million
2. Return of the Jedi (Fox)	$168.0 million
3. Batman (Warner Bros.)	$150.5 million
4. Ghostbusters (Columbia)	$130.2 million
5. Raiders of the Lost Ark (Paramount)	$115.6 million

*In real dollars, not adjusted for inflation.

Source: Variety, 2 May 1990.

because he owned an auto parts supplier based on the Gulf of Mexico whose markets were mainly in the West, he grouped a wild assortment of unrelated companies. The entourage included the nation's largest cigar maker (Consolidated Cigar), one of the largest clothing manufacturers (Kayser-Roth), zinc mines, sugarcane fields in the Dominican Republic, concrete plants, the New York Rangers and the New York Knicks (Madison Square Garden), racetracks, mattresses (Simmons), consumer loan offices (Associates First Capital Corp.), book publishers (Simon & Schuster, Pocket Books), movies and TV films (Paramount Pictures).

Bludhorn died suddenly of a heart attack in February 1983 and was succeeded by one of his lieutenants, Martin S. Davis, a Bronx-born high school dropout who had come up through the movie side of the business (Paramount).

Davis proceeded to dismantle what Bludhorn had assembled. Bludhorn bought more than 100 companies. Davis sold 65 of them, and cut payroll from 113,000 to 19,000. And in 1989 he changed the name of the company to Paramount Communications.

The name change underlined Davis' determination to narrow the company's scope to entertainment (Paramount, Madison Square Garden) and publishing (Simon & Schuster, Prentice Hall). The newly christened Paramount Communications has nothing to do with the Gulf of Mexico, doesn't look to the West and eschews manufacturing. They just want to produce more hit movies and TV sitcoms, publish more authors like Harold Robbins and field more players like Patrick Ewing for the New York Knicks. Meanwhile, they wouldn't mind gobbling up some magazines, book publishers and radio-TV stations.

That's precisely what Davis was up to at the end of the 1980s when he tried to take over Time Inc. He had the financial muscle for this lunge because he had just raked in $3.5 billion from the sale of the Gulf+Western loan company, Associates First Capital Corp., to Ford Motor. But his bold takeover effort failed. Time preferred to go ahead with their long-planned merger with Warner Communications, although Davis' move forced them to switch from an exchange of stock to a purchase of Warner by Time (so the deal didn't have to have stockholder approval). Davis' bid was doomed in a landmark ruling by the Delaware Supreme Court, which said boards of directors, looking to a company's long-term interests, had a right to say no to a hostile bid without consulting the shareholders, who, in this case, might have preferred Paramount's all-cash bid. It was a victory for the board of directors, and management, over the great unwashed mass of stockholders.

In any case, Martin Davis retired to lick his wounds, waiting for the next opportunity to expand his entertainment-and-publishing empire. At least he knows what business he is in.

Owners and rulers. Paramount's board of directors includes George Weissman, former chairman of Philip Morris; J. Hugh Liedtke, the pugnacious CEO of Pennzoil; former Florida Senator George A. Smathers; and—the lone woman—Grace J. Fippinger, who became the first female officer in the Bell System when she was elected secretary and treasurer of New York Telephone in 1974. The directors voted Davis the princely 1988 income of $15 million, making him the third most highly paid CEO in America that year. In 1989 he made a meager $11.6 million.

Paramount Communications Inc., 15 Columbus Circle, New York, NY 10023; (212) 373-8000.

4

Sales: $1.1 billion
Profits: $120 million
Founded: 1935
Headquarters: Los Angeles, California

Once every decade a blockbuster movie bails out Twentieth Century-Fox, a major Hollywood studio formed in 1935. In the 1960s it was *Sound of Music*. In the 1970s it was *Star Wars*. Both rank among the all-time best-selling motion pictures. Alas, in the 1980s no such savior appeared—and the studio legendary movie mogul Darryl F. Zanuck built dropped to the bottom of the heap in Tinsel Town.

Zanuck had formed the Twentieth Century Company in 1933 with Joseph M. Schenck, then head of United Artists (and later sent to prison). Two years later they merged with Fox film, founded by William Fox. Twentieth Century-Fox entered the 1980s with a star-studded (Sylvester Stallone and Dolly Parton) flop, *Rhinestone*, and moved on to further disasters. They did have some winners. In 1982 they distributed one of the decade's most tasteless films, *Porky's*, and they later scored with *Die Hard*, *Working Girl* and *Wall Street*. But in 1989, despite releasing 17 movies, their share of box-office receipts had sunk to 6 percent, making the studio seventh among the eight major studios. This was lousy showing despite the leadership of Barry "Killer" Diller, who failed to work the magic he'd used to turn Paramount Pic-

One billion film tickets (give or take 10 percent) have been sold every year since the late 1960s.

tures into a powerhouse with a long string of box-office hits.

Twentieth Century-Fox also went through two ownership changes in the 1980s. Denver oilman Marvin Davis bought the studio in 1981, hired Diller as head and then sold the firm in 1985 to Australian Rupert Murdoch, who spent the decade gearing his umbrella company, News Corp., to become a global all-media octopus. In summer 1989, Murdoch brought in Joe Roth, an independent producer, to head the studio. The 41-year-old Roth is the first film director to head a major studio in 50 years (Ernst Lubitsch led Paramount Pictures in the 1930s). Roth soon began production on 25 movies, including *War of the Roses*, a box-office hit.

Roth's predecessor, Barry Diller, whose interests lay more in television, went on to chair Fox Inc., where he's creating a powerful fourth television network, the Fox Network (to compete with ABC, NBC and CBS). The Fox network produces such hits as "The Simpsons" (the most popular show in the nation among 12- to 24-year-olds), "Married...With Children" and "The Tracey Ullman Show," and made much of their revenue by selling shows to local stations (their tabloid-news show, "A Current Affair," earns the company $25 million a year in syndication). Unlike the Big Three networks, which the FCC prohibits from syndicating their shows, Fox is allowed to both produce shows and sell reruns as long as their offerings stay below 15 hours a week. Diller was also riding herd over the seven TV stations Murdoch had acquired during the 1980s.

Twentieth Century-Fox, 10201 West Pico Boulevard, Los Angeles, CA 90035; (213) 277-2211.

5
MGM 🦁

Employees: 830
Sales: $880 million
Profits: $80 million
Founded: 1919
Headquarters: Culver City, California

Two of Hollywood's most venerable studios, Metro-Goldwyn-Mayer and United Artists, were batted about like shuttlecocks during the 1980s, ending the decade in limbo, their cultures all but destroyed. Swinging the racket was dealmaker Kirk Kerkorian, whose hobby is buying, selling, rebuying and reselling the same properties, usually making a handsome profit coming in and going out. By all accounts he has absolutely no interest in movies themselves. They're just vehicles. According to Aaron Latham, writing in *Manhattan, Inc.* in 1988, Kerkorian "systematically looted two of Hollywood's greatest golden-age studios." Also according to Latham, during the time he owned these movie companies Kerkorian made only one suggestion about the business: When United Artists was looking for a new James Bond to replace Roger Moore, Kerkorian wondered why they couldn't cast Eddie Murphy.

Kerkorian bought control of MGM, the maker of *Gone with the Wind* and *The Wizard of Oz*, for $70 million in 1969 and then used the film company as a vehicle to open the MGM Grand hotels and casinos in Las Vegas and Reno. In 1980 he divided the company into two parts, MGM Grand (the casinos) and Metro-Goldwyn-Mayer Film. In 1981 he bought United Artists, the company D. W. Griffith, Charlie Chaplin, Douglas Fairbanks and Mary Pickford started, for $380 million from Transamerica and combined UA with Metro-Goldwyn-Mayer to form MGM/UA Entertainment. In 1986, in a classic Kerkorian deal, MGM/UA was sold for $1.5 billion to Ted Turner, who sold the UA segment back to Kerkorian for $480 million. But Turner found himself overextended and before the year was out he also sold most of MGM back to Kerkorian; the only part Turner kept was MGM's

Leo the Lion—readying for his debut roar for MGM, 1924.

3,000-film library. So once again the firm was MGM/UA, now 80 percent Kerkorian's. During the 1980s, they made some box-office winners—*Rain Man, Moonstruck* and *Baby Boom*—but the company languished through the latter part of the decade, losing money while their market share slid to 8 percent.

At the beginning of the 1980s, when Kerkorian combined UA with MGM, it appeared he was creating a company that could have been the biggest player in the industry. Instead, after hiring and firing a series of studio heads, Kerkorian saw MGM/UA slide to next to last among the major Hollywood companies. They lost money in 1987 and 1988. As the decade ended, Kerkorian was cooking up new deals. He announced two but both fell through. At Christmas 1989 the company had no box-office winners in the theaters. Their most valuable assets, as the decade ran out, were the UA film library, including all the James Bond and *Rocky* movies, and Leo the Lion who roars at the start of every MGM film. Kerkorian had stripped away most of the other assets—the real estate, the props from old movies, the record arm, the distribution company. What he had to sell was the nostalgic value of two of the greatest names in motion picture history: MGM and United Artists.

History. A lot of history exists in those names. Three separate companies merged to form Metro-Goldwyn-Mayer in 1924. Metro was the property of Marcus Loew, a New Yorker who converted vaudeville theaters and nickelodeons into 5-cent movie houses. To ensure a steady film supply, Loew bought a Hollywood production company called Metro Pictures in 1920.

Samuel Goldwyn was born Samuel Gelbfisz in Warsaw in 1879. He immigrated to America as Samuel Goldfish and started a movie company with Cecil B. DeMille but was kicked out after three years. He founded another movie company in 1916 with two Broadway producers, Edgar and Arch Selwyn. By combining their last names, they came up with the name for the business: Goldwyn Pictures. Sam, tired of "goldfish" jokes, liked the name so much he took it for his own. Goldwyn was squeezed out of his company again, in 1922. Although he produced 70 movies over the next 35 years, he was never part of MGM.

The third company source was Louis B. Mayer, a Russian immigrant who started a production company in 1918. When Metro-Goldwyn-Mayer was formed, Louis B. Mayer became production chief (a slot he held until 1951). MGM was soon famous for their movie stars, a virtual Who's Who of Hollywood. They owned Hollywood production facilities and a chain of movie theaters. But in 1949, the government forced them to sell off the theater chain.

The MGM glory days lasted until the 1950s, when television grabbed viewers' attention. In July 1969, they were at their lowest point financially, giving Kirk Kerkorian his chance. Kerkorian, the son of an Armenian immigrant, served as a cargo pilot during World War II. He is notorious for shunning publicity.

In spring 1990 Kerkorian found a new potential buyer in Italian financier Giancarlo Parretti, who got his foot into Hollywood's door in 1988 by gaining control of bankrupt Cannon Group, since renamed Pathé Communications. Pathé bid $1.2 billion for MGM/UA, backed by a $600 million bridge loan from Warner Bros. But then *Business Week* revealed Parretti's long history of police problems in his native Italy, including a recent conviction (under appeal) for "fraudulent bankruptcy," resulting in a three-year prison sentence. Parretti reacted to this story by telling an Italian journalist: "The Jews have ganged up on me, and since they control *Business Week*, they unleashed it against me. The fact is that the Jews don't like the idea that I represent the first Catholic communications network." Later, Parretti denied making these remarks.

Even if the deal falls through, it would make a great movie.

Stock performance. MGM/UA stock bought for $1,000 in 1986 sold for $1,042 on January 2, 1990.

MGM/United Artists Communications, 10202 West Washington Boulevard, Culver City, CA 90230; (213) 836-3000.

6

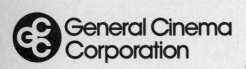 General Cinema Corporation

#2 *movie theaters*

Employees: 25,100
Sales: $1.99 billion
Profits: $948 million
Founded: 1922
Headquarters: Chestnut Hill, Massachusetts

They used to say the real profit in movie theaters was at the popcorn stand. Considering popcorn's price nowadays, that's easy to understand. In early 1990 moviegoers were buying popcorn at 310 theaters General Cinema operated in 33 states. These theaters had 1,445 screens (the one-screen theater is a relic) and took in about 7 percent of the $1.2 billion annual admis-

sions at movie houses. Popcorn is only one of the profitable sidelines General Cinema has developed.

They started to bottle soft drinks in 1968, and in 20 years were bottling 8.3 percent of all the Pepsi-Cola produced in the U.S., 6.3 percent of all the Dr. Pepper and 3.2 percent of all the 7-Up. They were also the original developer of the Sunkist orange drink, which they sold to R. J. Reynolds. And they made a pile of money buying into Smirnoff vodka distiller Heublein before R. J. Reynolds acquired them.

In 1989, they sold all their soft drink bottling operations to PepsiCo for $1.7 billion, the highest price ever paid for a beverage bottler. And the sale left General Cinema with a mountain of cash to play with. They were already playing around with a 60 percent stake in the Neiman-Marcus Group, whose businesses include the Neiman-Marcus, Bergdorf Goodman and Contempo Casual stores. On top of that, General Cinema came into the 1990s owning a 17 percent slice of the soft drink–confectionery combine, Cadbury-Schweppes, an investment the British company certainly did not welcome (no matter how many candy bars they sold at General Cinema theaters).

Showing movies was Philip Smith's original business. In 1922 he bought Boston's 3,000-seat National Theatre. In 1935 he opened the first drive-in theater. (The company name, when they first sold stock to the public in 1960, was General Drive-in Corp.) In 1947 Smith opened the first theater in a shopping mall; in 1961 the first twin theater, forerunner of today's multiscreen house.

Richard A. Smith, son of the founder, joined the company in 1946 after graduating from Harvard. In his post as vice president for corporate development, he put General Cinema into other businesses while extending the movie theater chain. In a policy dating to their drive-in days, General Cinema refuses to screen X-rated movies.

"Nothing within General Cinema is sacred," Smith once said, meaning if the price is right, anything is for sale—presumably even the foundation business, movie houses. When Richard Smith (now chairman and CEO) says General Cinema operates to enhance shareholder value, he's talking about himself, and his family. The Smith family owns 30 percent of

General Cinema stock, making them worth $400 million. In listing Smith among the 400 richest Americans, *Forbes* described him as a "philanthropist, golfer, tennis player, 'a private man who has no ego need for publicity.'" In 1989, his pay came to $1.05 million. Richard Smith's son, Robert A. Smith, joined the company after graduating from Harvard Business School in 1985. He was elected to the board in 1989.

Stock performance. General Cinema stock bought for $1,000 in 1980 sold for $10,519 on January 2, 1990.

General Cinema Corporation, 27 Boylston Street, Chestnut Hill, MA 02167; (617) 232-8200.

HOTELS

The hotel industry went on a building binge during the 1980s. They started the decade with about 2 million rooms to rent, and ended it with close to 3 million. And then they worried about filling all those rooms with paying guests. According to some insiders, most of those new hotel rooms were added to create losses for investors to deduct on tax returns. The 1980s saw a proliferation of hotels catering to travelers with special needs: the upscale, pamper-the-guest, "don't-ask-the-price" hotel (Four Seasons, Ritz-Carlton); the economy, "just-the-essentials" hotel (Fairfield Inn, Hampton Inn, Rodeway); the all-suites, "give-me-some-room" hotel (Embassy Suites, Courtyard); extended stay hotels (Marriott's Residence Inns). Some companies—Ramada, Holiday and Hilton—were clearly more interested in casinos than hotels. Ramada sold all their hotels (except the ones with casinos) to a Hong Kong group. Holiday sold all the Holiday Inns to a British brewer. And Hilton tried, but failed, to sell the entire company.

1

#1 *in hotel management, institutional restaurants*

Employees: 229,800
Sales: $7.5 billion
Profits: $177 million
Founded: 1927
Headquarters: Washington, D.C.

A hardworking Mormon family turned the simplicity of serving others into the U.S.'s biggest hospitality company. From humble beginnings, the Marriotts have left their mark on the American scene with a string of upscale hotels catering to the business traveler.

Holiday Inn has more hotels than Marriott, three times as many. But Holiday Inn is primarily a franchiser—they license other people to run the hotels. And al-

The 520-room Warsaw Marriott, the first hotel in Eastern Europe to be managed by a western company.

though Marriott does franchise some units, they are primarily a hotel operator. No company manages as many hotel rooms as they. Marriott also leads the pack when it comes to cash flow. Holiday Corp. takes in $1.5 billion annually; Marriott collects $7.5 billion.

Finally, Marriott employs more people than anyone else in the hospitality business. More than 200,000 people were working at Marriott's 4,000 different units in 1989. In fact, Marriott now ranks as the eighth largest U.S. employer.

Founded in 1927 as a root beer stand, Marriott opened their first hotel in 1957, grew steadily and really took off in the 1980s. The company entered 1980 with 65 hotels and 21,000 rooms to rent, double what they had in 1974. By 1985, when company founder J. W. Marriott died, they had 65,000 hotel rooms. Entering 1990, they had 539 hotels and 134,000 rooms (each of these rooms contained a Gideon Bible, a Book of Mormon and a biography of J. W. Marriott, Sr.).

Feeding people is a longtime Mariott activity. They used to feed them in planes

but they sold that business during the 1980s, and in 1990 they began selling their restaurant chains: Roy Rogers, Bob's Big Boy, Allie's and Hot Shoppes. However, they kept their hand in the kitchen through the operation of cafeterias in factories, offices, hospitals and college campuses. During the 1980s, Marriott bought Saga, a major food service outfit, and Host International, a food and merchandise chain operating at 52 airports, mostly in the U.S. These two purchases allowed Marriott to boast they're the world leader in contract food services.

Marriott also provides housekeeping and custodial services and operates over 100 "travel plazas" by the side of the highway. These complexes boast a combination of national-brand restaurants, like Pizza Hut and Nathan's Famous, and gift shops, like Bloomingdale's Express.

Like other hoteliers, Marriott now provides different types of hotels to offer something for everyone. They now have five hotel divisions: Marriott, Marriott Suites, Residence Inn, Courtyard by Marriott and Fairfield Inn. Marriott hotels are full-service hotels, and rooms go for a pretty penny ($85 to $225 a night); Courtyard Hotels are mid-priced ($49 to $88); Fairfield Inns are economy hotels (at $30 to $40 a night); and Residence Inns are equipped for longer stays. In 1989, Marriott opened the first of their "lifecare-facility" condominiums for the affluent elderly: giant developments boasting luxury accommodations and a variety of options for the aged, including 24-hour emergency call buttons and a nursing staff for those needing it.

With all the expansion, Marriott remains Marriott. They run a hands-on operation, with J. W. ("Bill") Marriott, Jr., visiting at least 100 hotels a year to see they're run according to the book (in 1989 he had to cut back on this schedule after open-heart surgery). Marriott has a squeaky clean operation. They believe in Mom and apple pie. They don't believe in labor unions. Seventeen of Marriott's hotels are located abroad, including ones in Warsaw, Hong Kong and Panama City (when the U.S. invaded Panama in 1989, 40 guests at the Panama Marriott were taken hostage but were later released). Mormon beliefs have so far kept Marriott out of Las Vegas and Atlantic City.

History. The company ethos was captured by a *Washington Post* writer, Richard Cohen, who said:

> If it is impossible to distinguish between Marriott, the corporation, and Marriott, the family, it is similarly impossible to separate the Marriotts from their faith and heritage. They are Mormons who came east from the tiny settlement of Marriott, Utah, stark cattle and sheep country north of Salt Lake City. What they brought with them was a vision of America that dances in red, white and blue colors and testifies to their faith that man was created in the image of Pat Boone.

In 1927, newlyweds John Willard Marriott and the former Alice Sheets moved to Washington, D.C., from their native Utah. The couple opened a franchised A&W Root Beer Stand, which did well during the summer months; during the winter, the Marriotts converted the stand into a Hot Shoppe, serving chili con carne and hot tamales. The recipes were borrowed from a cook at the Mexican embassy.

Soon the Marriotts were running a string of Hot Shoppes in the Washington metropolitan area—and raising a family. They went into the airline catering business in 1937 with a contract to service Eastern Airlines flights. Marriott built their first hotel, the Twin Bridges Marriott at Arlington, Virginia, in 1957.

J. W. "Bill" Marriott, Jr., began working in Hot Shoppes restaurants when he was in high school and continued to do so when he attended the University of Utah. He became president of Marriott Hot Shoppes, Inc. in 1964 when he was 32, and succeeded his father as CEO in 1972. Asked once about his social life, Bill Marriott replied, "I don't have a social life. Friendship is an investment and friendship takes a lot of time. My priorities are the church, the family, and the business. After that I have very little time left over."

Owners and rulers. The Marriotts. Of eight board members, three are Marriotts (including Alice C. Marriott, widow of the founder).

As a place to work. Marriott is known to have an antiunion stance. San Francisco Mayor Art Agnos refuses to hold city functions at the San Francisco Marriott because of the company's policy.

Global presence. Marriott hotels can be found in 26 countries outside the U.S. They operate 3 percent of the world's hotels.

Stock performance. Marriott stock bought for $1,000 in 1980 sold for $10,053 on January 2, 1990.

Consumer brands.

Marriott.

Marriott Corporation, Marriott Drive, Washington, D.C. 20058; (301) 897-9000.

2

The Sheraton Corporation

#2 *in hotels*

Employees: 125,000
Sales: $773 million
Profits: $113 million
Founded: 1937
Headquarters: Boston, Massachusetts

Sheraton, the most international of all the hotel chains, opened new properties in 1989 in the British West Indies, Botswana, Gibralter, Indonesia, Malaysia and Mauritius, thereby extending their reach to 70 countries. By 1990 more than 22 million people a year were checking into 500 Sheraton hotels, resorts and inns. There's a Great Wall Sheraton in Beijing (one of five Sheratons in China); a Tel Aviv Sheraton; one in Sofia, Bulgaria; a Cairo Sheraton (one of the few Sheratons with a casino); and a Sheraton Regency in Jackson, Mississippi (where Nigerian potentate, Chief Igbinedion J. B. Benin, stayed in 1988 when his son, Bright, received a Master's in economics from Jackson State University). Sheraton is Hawaii's largest hotel operator, with 13 hotels on the five islands, ranging from the 1,900-room Sheraton Waikiki in Honolulu (largest hotel in the Sheraton network) to the 500-acre Princeville on Kauai.

Since 1968 Sheraton has been a wholly owned subsidiary of ITT, where they have thrived. From 170 hotels they went to 500; from 49,000 guest rooms to 135,000; and from 12 countries to 70. The Sheraton hotels are a mix of owned, managed, leased and franchised properties. Of the 500 operating in early 1990, 298 were run by owners Sheaton franchised.

Sheraton headquarters remain in Boston, the chain's home base for over 50 years. Cofounders Ernest Henderson and Robert Moore bought their first hotel, the Stonehaven in Springfield, Massachusetts, in 1937. Their second acquisition, in 1939, was a small Boston residential hotel called the Sheraton which had an electric rooftop sign proclaiming the name. To remove the Sheraton sign would have cost more than the hotel's purchase price. So Henderson and Moore prudently adopted Sheraton as the chain's name. The Sheraton Corporation was the first hotel chain listed on the New York Stock Exchange. In 1949, Sheraton bought two Canadian hotel chains, their first foray outside the U.S. Fifty years later, Sheraton embarked on the first Soviet-American hotel venture in Moscow. Two hotels are planned for the city; the first will be built on Gorky Street, a mere mile from Red Square.

Sheraton Corporation, Sixty State Street, Boston, MA 02109; (617) 367-3600.

3

#1 *in rooms to rent*

Employees: 5,000
Sales: $1.4 billion
Founded: 1952
Headquarters: Memphis, Tennessee

Holiday Inn motels gained fame as uniquely American icons: a lodging place for families, neither upscale nor downscale, and as predictable as mashed potatoes. Holiday Inn motels are still comfortable and mid-priced, but they're no longer American.

In 1989, British brewer Bass bought the Holiday Inn chain, consisting of 1,455 hotels in North America and another 150 overseas. Holiday Corp. itself owns fewer than 100 of these inns—the rest are owned and operated by franchisees. Bass moved Holiday Inn's international headquarters from Memphis to Atlanta (Holiday Inn USA remains in Memphis).

Seasoned Holiday Inn guests always knew exactly what to expect when they spotted the big, green sign: a room with two double beds, wall-to-wall carpeting, color TV, air-conditioning, six towels, three washcloths, two bars of soap, a spare roll of toilet paper, a sanitized strip on the toilet seat, 24-hour switchboard service, a restaurant and a swimming pool. From the start Holiday Inn aimed at the broad middle of the market, which accounted for their initial success and has caused their downfall in the 1980s. In 1987 and 1988, demand for expensive luxury hotels for the wealthy and specialty suites for business travelers and the elderly grew by 10 percent, as did demand for very cheap economy motels. But no one, it seemed, wanted to go to mid-priced "hotels" (Holiday Inn stopped using the word motels). Demand grew by only 2.2 percent in 1987 and 1988.

History. The God-fearing southern Baptists who founded this company would never have believed one day they'd be dealing blackjack hands. Holiday Inn had their genesis on a miserable vacation in 1951. Kemmons Wilson, a Memphis real estate developer, took his family on a holiday to Washington, D.C. Along the way they stayed in a succession of roadside tourist courts, the kind of fleabag motels catering to traveling salesmen and clandestine lovers. Convinced Americans would flock to a clean, moderately priced, family-oriented motor hotel, Wilson returned to Memphis and put his building experience to work.

In 1952, he opened a 120-room motel on Memphis' outskirts, naming it after a movie he had just seen, *Holiday Inn*, the Bing Crosby—Fred Astaire film that introduced the Irving Berlin songs, "White Christmas" and "Easter Parade." The hotel was like no other in the area, boasting a swimming pool, free ice, free parking, a dog kennel—and every room had a bath. What's more, children under 12 could stay for free in their parents' room. Within a week every room was being rented every night.

Wilson quickly opened three more Holiday Inns on highways leading into Memphis, and began spinning dreams of a national chain. He called upon another go-getter, Wallace E. Johnson, dubbed "the Henry Ford of the home building industry." In 1953, Wilson and Johnson invited 75 home builders from across the country to hear their franchise pitch. They found plenty of takers, and Holiday Inns, all predictable but reliable, soon began sprouting along interstates.

Wilson and Johnson invented motel franchising, where others would actually own and operate the hotels but pay for using the Holiday Inn name, logo, and reservations system. The franchising concept enabled the chain to grow rapidly and shoot right to the top of the industry. The 100th Holiday Inn opened in 1959; the 500th in 1964; the 1,000th in 1968. Spurring development was a Holiday Inn Innkeeping School, where franchisees learned how to run a Holiday Inn–style hotel; this course preceded Holiday Inn University, established at Olive Branch, Mississippi, in 1973. The first non-U.S. Holiday Inn opened in 1960 in Montreal, the forerunner of others in Canada. The first European Holiday Inn opened in Leiden, Holland, in 1968.

Hard times hit during the Arab oil embargo of 1973–1974, bringing a steep decline in car travel and motel use. Holiday Inn's stock nosedived, a development that pained Roy E. Winegardner, a pioneer Holiday Inn franchisee who then owned 7.5 percent of Holiday Inn stock. Winegardner hastened from Cincinnati to Memphis, where he became vice chairman of the company, and he brought along his lawyer, Harvard-trained Michael E. Rose, who took over as senior vice president for hotel development. In the next five years the Winegardner-Rose team purged all the old Holiday Inn managers, replacing them with recruits from top business schools and companies like Procter & Gamble.

Company founder Wilson retired in 1979, leaving Winegardner and Rose in control. They quickly exercised that control, jettisoning the Trailways bus subsidiary in 1979 and acquiring Harrah's in 1980. In 1982, they sold off Delta Steamship Lines. As a sign that the company was now more than Holiday Inns, the corporate name was changed in 1985 to Holiday Corp.

The entry into gambling signaled the burial of the original Holiday Inn culture—marked by such idiosyncrasies as opening management meetings with a prayer, requiring innkeepers to post the location and hours of local church services, providing chaplains "on call" for guests and prohibiting bars in Holiday Inns until the early 1960s. A number of Holiday Inn veterans left and L. M. Clymer quit as president in 1978, citing "my overriding regard and respect for my Lord Jesus Christ."

⋅ The miscalculation that let Bass gain a foothold in Holiday Inns occurred in 1986, when CEO Rose moved to foil a takeover by giving shareholders a onetime cash dividend of $65, for which the company borrowed $2.4 billion, including $100 million from Bass. In exchange Bass gained 10 percent of the company's stock. Three years later, Holiday's management agreed to sell the chain to Bass. But CEO Rose and his cronies kept for themselves the crown jewels—the five Harrah's hotel/casinos in Nevada and Atlantic City. Rose formed a new company, called Promus, which now runs the Harrah's casinos as well as three other smaller hotel chains formerly under the Holiday umbrella—Hampton Inns (180 economy hotels), Embassy Suites (94 hotels offering guest suites—a bedroom plus a separate living/dining/work area) and Homewood Suites (10 hotels with fully equipped kitchens for extended stays).

As a place to work. In a recent annual report, the company featured, on the cover and on inside pages, their employees, noting: "There are very few secrets in the hotel industry. Because amenities, services and facilities are easy to duplicate, the one thing that truly distinguishes one hotel company from another is its people." One distinguishing feature of top management at Holiday Corp. was that many came from other companies. Stephen F. Bollenbach, chief financial officer, came to Holiday in 1986 from Marriott. David P. Hanlon, president of Harrah's Atlantic City, joined the company in 1984 from Caesar's World. Duane E. Knapp, vice president of strategic marketing, moved to Holiday in 1986 from Westin Hotels. Ben C. Peternell, head of human resources, came to Holiday in 1986 from American Hospital Supply Corp.

G*lobal presence.* Of the 1,600 hotels in the Holiday Inn chain, over 200 are located abroad.

S*ocial responsibility.* A disproportionate number of hotel fires have occurred in Holiday Inn properties. According to a 1987 *Wall Street Journal* report, Holiday Inn accounted for 29 percent of rooms available in the nation's top 10 chains but suffered "39 percent of the fires, 55 percent of the deaths, 37 percent of the injuries and 36 percent of the damage." In response to the fires, Holiday beefed up their fire-safety and fire-prevention facilities, including installation of sprinklers in public areas and smoke detectors in corridors and rooms.

S*tock performance.* Holiday Corporation stock bought for $1,000 in 1980 sold for $20,842 on January 2, 1990.

Holiday Corporation, 1023 Cherry Road, Memphis, TN 38117; (901) 762-8600.

4

HILTON

#3 *in hotels*

Employees: 38,500
Sales: $954 million
Profits: $110 million
Founded: 1919
Headquarters: Beverly Hills, California

Hilton Hotels, one of the major U.S. hotel chains, marked time during the 1980s while the courts tried to unravel the will left by founder Conrad N. Hilton, who died in 1979 at 91. The conflict over the will was argued in one court after another during the 1980s until Conrad's son Barron finally won a favorable 1988 ruling giving him voting power over 25 percent of the stock—and for

the first time he felt in control of the company bearing his name.

He exercised control by trying to sell the hotel chain. For over a year, Hilton Hotels was in limbo, the center of intense speculation while the price of their shares tripled in value on the New York Stock Exchange. Instead of selling when the stock was at its highest point, and several potential buyers were interested, Barron Hilton and the board waited. They waited too long, and the stock plummeted. *Business Week* called it "A case study on how to botch a deal." In early 1990, Barron Hilton took the company off the auction block and returned to square one: running a hotel business.

That business, in 1990, resembled what it was in 1980—a hotel company where the big kick comes from gambling. Of the nearly 300 hotels flying the Hilton flag, 222 of them are franchised to other owners. Hilton has nothing to do with operating them, but they get a cut of the room rentals for lending their name. Only eight hotels, including the Waldorf-Astoria in New York, the Palmer House in Chicago and the Hilton in Las Vegas, are company owned. And Hilton operates 38 more under management agreements with the owners. In this last group are some of the world's great destination hotels, such as the 2,500-room Hawaiian Village (biggest hotel in Hawaii); the 1,890-room San Francisco Hilton (biggest hotel in the city); the 2,120-room New York Hilton (biggest hotel in the city); the 1,200-room Fontainbleau in Miami; and the 579-room Beverly Hilton in Beverly Hills (owned by entertainment mogul Merv Griffin).

Impressive as this hotel armada is, the big cannons are shot by the Hilton casinos in Nevada, which account for more than half of company income. The Las Vegas Hilton has 3,174 rooms; and the Flamingo, also in Las Vegas, has 2,927 rooms. The Reno Hilton has 603 rooms. In 1989 and 1990 Hilton doubled their Nevada gambling space by building restaurant-and-casino combinations in Las Vegas and Reno. Plus a new 2,000-room hotel on the Colorado River in Laughlin. The expansion turned Hilton into the largest Nevada employer.

Gambling has been so good to Hilton it was no surprise in 1985 when they opened a hotel outside the U.S., on the Gold Coast of Queensland, Australia, that

Since 1980 the price of the average U.S. hotel room has doubled to about $60.

it held a casino. This hotel bore the name Conrad International, which will also go up on other properties—in Mexico, Hong Kong, Turkey, among other places—the company plans to open in the 1990s. This is actually the second time around in the international arena for Hilton. They were the first U.S. company to build hotels overseas, using the Hilton name, but in 1967 they sold Hilton International to Trans World Airlines, which resold the chain 20 years later to the British gaming company, Ladbroke. As a result, Hilton hotels operating outside the U.S. have nothing to do with Hilton Hotels operating within the states. But who knows, what with Ladbroke's and Barron Hilton's common interest in gambling, they might sit down at the poker table sometime in the 1990s and play "winner take all."

History. Conrad Hilton, Barron's father, was born on Christmas Day, 1887, and educated at the New Mexico School of Mines. He started his hotel chain in 1919, with partners L. M. Drown and Jay Powers when they bought the old Mobley Hotel in Cisco, Texas. In his vivid autobiography, *Be My Guest* (which used to be distributed in Hilton hotel rooms), Hilton told how in 1922 "an ex-partner, a crazed fellow, [shot] down in cold blood" Major Powers. Powers was coming out of an elevator of the Dallas Waldorf when a man shot him once, through the temple.

Hilton's specialty was renovating old hotels, nicknamed "dowagers," which he restored with tender care. In the early 1940s, he met actress Zsa Zsa Gabor. "I theenk I am going to marry you," she told him at their first meeting. Hilton laughed, but four months later he joined her at the altar and lost his rights to Roman Catholic communion because of an earlier divorce. The marriage didn't last, however, as Connie was disgusted by Zsa Zsa's cosmetic rituals which he complained in his autobiography "could have been the rite of an ancient Aztec temple." But Zsa Zsa boasted later that she'd won over God.

She'd find him on his knees praying, saunter past in a black negligee, and say, "Take your choice, Him or me." She said she won every time, but Hilton divorced her and comforted himself by buying the Waldorf-Astoria (he was so obsessed with owning the ritzy hotel he carried a picture of "her" in his wallet for years, until buying it in 1950). He also purchased the Statler chain.

In his entire career, Hilton took only one vacation and that only for one month. The thrice-married Hilton died at age 91 in the good graces of the Catholic Church.

Stock performance. Hilton stock bought for $1,000 in 1980 sold for $7,109 on January 2, 1990.

Consumer brands.

Hilton, Conrad International, Waldorf-Astoria, Palmer House.

Hilton Hotels, P.O. Box 5567, 9336 Civic Center Drive, Beverly Hills, CA 90209; (213) 278-4321.

5

#1 *in number of hotels*

Employees: 1,100
Sales: $600 million
Profits: $60 million
Founded: 1946
Headquarters: Phoenix, Arizona

Best Western International, which doesn't own a single hotel, likes to call itself "the world's largest lodging chain." And by number of hotel properties—3,300 (compared to 1,600 for Holiday Inns)—they are. Most Best Westerns are small; in terms of numbers of rooms, Best Western ranks second (255,000 to Holiday's 318,000). Best Western differs from other innkeepers in that they're a nonprofit association of independently owned and operated hotels, motor inns and resorts. Proprietors join up by agreeing to abide by standards meticulously spelled out in a "rules and regulations" book. A swimming pool is required, a restaurant must be on premises or within 500 feet, each room must have a direct-dial phone, bathrooms must have "good quality terry cloth" towels, check-in services should be available 24 hours a day. Every Best Western unit is inspected twice a year and must pass a quality control test. Those that fail have 90 days to clean up their act. A member can quit at any time (and bring down the sign).

A typical Best Western Inn has 100 rooms, pays an entrance fee of $15,500, and then has annual membership costs of about $26,000 a year. In return, the member uses the Best Western name and benefits from an advertising campaign and a reservations system that may account for as much as one-quarter of room sales. In their Phoenix headquarters, Best Western employs about 1,000 people at peak time (summer). There are two reservations centers (reached via an 800 number); one at Phoenix, the other at Wichita, Kansas. Since 1981 Best Western has also operated a reservations center inside a prison—at the Arizona Center for Women, a minimum-security jail in Phoenix; it handles 3.6 percent of incoming telephone calls. More than 8 million calls for reservations or information were received in 1989. Free for the asking is an annual Best Western Road Atlas & Travel Guide that lists, describes and rates every unit in the U.S. and Canada along with road maps covering all of North America. Best Western distributes over four million of these guides annually.

Social responsibility. More than 400 people die every year in hotel fires, which led in 1989 to introduction of a bill in Congress that would require hotels more than three stories high to install sprinklers in every room. Best Western International was quick to oppose it. CEO Ronald Evans said: "We support public safety. But this is the sort of thing the local building codes should handle. The federal government shouldn't be policing this."

Global presence. At the end of 1988 Best Western had 1,859 U.S. units—and 1,442 in 37 other countries. There is a Best Western in every state. The big growth is expected in the international arena. By the early 1990s Best Western expects to have 4,000 units, with 50 percent of them abroad.

Best Western International, 6201 N. 24th Parkway, Phoenix, AZ 85064; (602) 957-4200.

PHOTOGRAPHY

The number of color pictures amateur photographers took doubled during the 1980s. And at decade's end, 354 million cameras were in use around the world. That should have been good news to Eastman Kodak, leading supplier of film used in those cameras, but were they satisfied? No. They were quick to point out that "three of every four households in the world still do not have a camera in use."

In any case, while these shutterbugs were snapping away during the 1980s, the two leading American photographic companies—Kodak and Polaroid—spent the decade snapping at one another and eliminating thousands of employees from their payrolls. "Say cheese!"

1

#1 *in photography*

Employees: 141,500
Sales: $18.4 billion
Profits: $529 million
Founded: 1880
Headquarters: Rochester, New York

The 1980s were in many ways a negative for Eastman Kodak, longtime king of photography. They lost on so many fronts it looked like they'd never find their way out of the darkroom. They made a wrong bet on disk cameras (which never really caught on though they've sold 25 million of them). They almost missed the big swing to 35 mm cameras (though they now sell more 35 mm automatics than anyone else). They entered the instant camera market just as it declined and then lost a patent infringement suit to Polaroid, leaving them on the hook for a settlement expected to be well over $1 billion. The judge also ordered them to close down their instant camera business and to recall all models in the marketplace (both in stores and in the hands of users). While still dominant in the U.S. film market, Kodak lost market share to Japan's Fuji, which had captured 10 percent of the business by decade's end.

Ravaged by these setbacks, Kodak went through four different restructurings during the 1980s, and 18,500 people left the company through a combination of early retirements and dismissals. In December 1989, Kodak announced another 5,000 jobs would be eliminated. In Rochester, New York, Kodak was no longer regarded as the employer who would hire your children. And on Wall Street, where their yellow boxes were once regarded as perpetual moneymaking devices, they no longer inspired such awe—profits declined from $1.1 billion in 1980 to $529 million in 1989.

Those setbacks mask Kodak's power. For 50 billion photographs are taken around the world every year (85 percent of them in color), most of them on Kodak film. Even with the inroads Fuji made, Kodak came into the 1990s with 80 percent of the U.S. film market and 60 percent of the worldwide market. In addition, Eastman Kodak now does almost 40 percent of sales outside of photography. They make more than 25,000 products: including industrial chemicals, fibers, plastics (they're the leading supplier of resins used in plastic soft drink bottles), copiers, high-speed duplicators (their Color Edge model turns out full-color images at the rate of 23 copies a minute), printers, optical scanners and electronic systems that print newspapers and magazines at the push of a button.

Kodak also has long had a foot in health care through X-ray equipment and other imaging devices, but in 1988 they carved out a much bigger place when they paid $5.1 billion to scoop up Sterling Drug, maker of Bayer aspirin, Phillips' Milk of Magnesia, prescription drugs Demerol and Talwin and household products Lysol and d-Con insecticides. As a result, Kodak now has a health science wing bringing in $4 billion a year, ranking them among the country's top dozen pharmaceutical companies. Beyond that, they have bought pieces of various biotechnology companies.

History. As a young bank clerk in Rochester, George Eastman decided in the late 1870s to take a Caribbean vacation. A coworker suggested he take pictures of his

Thomas Edison (right) used one of George Eastman's (left) first Brownie cameras to invent the motion picture camera shown here.

trip, so Eastman bought a photographic outfit—only to discover he would need a packhorse to carry it all: enormous camera, heavy tripod, light-tight tent, glass plates and tanks, chemicals and a water jug. So instead of vacationing, Eastman began reading up on photography and experimenting in his mother's kitchen with new techniques. By 1880, he developed a way to make dry plates, eliminating the cumbersome equipment needed in wet-plate photography. That year, he rented a loft in Rochester and began making dry plates commercially. In 1884, he astounded the photographic world with a new product: film in rolls, with a roll holder adaptable to almost every camera on the market. Four years later, Eastman introduced the Kodak camera, a light, portable device that sold for $25 and came with enough film for 100 pictures. When you finished the roll you sent it, camera and all, with $10, to Rochester, where the film was developed and printed and new film inserted. The name Kodak was Eastman's invention, arrived at by trying many word combinations starting and ending with K. He explained: "The letter 'K' had been a favorite with me—it seems a strong, incisive sort of letter." George Eastman was a straitlaced Victorian bach-

elor who went on to become a major philanthropist after his company succeeded. In 1932, at age 77, after asking his doctor precisely where his heart was located, the ailing Eastman went home and calmly shot himself. His suicide note read: "To my friends. My work is done. Why wait? G.E."

Eastman Kodak always focused on the amateur end of the photography market, introducing the first Brownie camera in 1900, which sold for $1 and used 15-cent rolls of film. In 1923 Kodak introduced a home-movie camera, projector and film. The company became masters at marketing photography—advertising not just film but memories. Other successful products followed: in 1935, Kodachrome, amateur color film; in 1951, the Brownie hand-held movie camera; in 1963, the Instamatic camera, with film in a foolproof cartridge (no more loading the camera in the dark); in 1972, the Pocket Instamatic, a miniature version. But the company's major oversight was in the instant camera market, which Kodak executives thought was just a fad. After Polaroid came out with instant color film, Kodak tried to develop an instant camera of their own; when they did, Polaroid sued them for patent infringement and won.

O*wners and rulers.* To get to the top at Kodak, a technical degree is essential. Colby H. Chandler, latest in a long line of engineers, became CEO in 1983 (1989 pay: $1.48 million) and was succeeded in 1990 by Kay R. Whitmore, a chemical engineer. It also helps to be a man: of Kodak's 53 officers in 1989, only one was a woman. Nearly half of Kodak's shares are held by more than 500 institutional investors. The only big block of stock held in 1989 consisted of 6.1 million shares (less than 2 percent of the total) in the Employees' Saving & Investment Plan.

A*s a place to work.* Since their founding, Kodak has never had unions, but after the layoffs of the 1980s, the International Union of Electrical Workers tried to move in and demand more job security for Kodak employees. But the union has failed to win a vote to represent Kodak's workers. Kodak does have an employee-protection plan in case of a corporate takeover—a written guarantee that terminated workers will get severance pay, health and insurance benefits and help in finding a new job. Such wide "parachutes" are rare—usually only top executives receive them. The parachute is designed to make the company less attractive to raiders. In 1990, the once-paternalistic Kodak (their nickname was "Father Yellow") recalculated the generous employee wage dividend to save money—and the net result is employees will get much less. But the benefits are still superb; and the company still has an Employee Center, which holds a 20-lane bowling alley, a pistol range and a 2,500-seat theater. In the city of Rochester, Kodak employs 45,000. Blacks make up one-quarter of Rochester's population but less than 5 percent of Kodak's managers.

S*ocial responsibility.* Kodak gives away about $20 million a year, including substantial support to schools serving minority students. They withdrew totally from South Africa in 1987, declaring "no Kodak unit worldwide will be permitted to supply products to South Africa." In the late 1980s ground water in communities abutting Kodak Park were found to be polluted by chemicals. Kodak quickly paid cleanup costs and guaranteed the value of all homes in the nearby communities for 10 years. In 1989, Kodak announced they would recycle plastic film containers and steel film cassettes (they use about 750,000 pounds of plastic every year).

G*lobal presence.* Kodak's yellow boxes are familiar sights around the world. They get more than 40 percent of revenue outside the U.S., which means non-American business now tops $7 billion a year. Kodak manufactures in 13 countries. They make photographic products (cameras and film) in Australia, Brazil, Canada, England, France, Germany, Ireland and Mexico.

S*tock performance.* Eastman Kodak stock bought for $1,000 in 1980 sold for $3,025 on January 2, 1990.

C*onsumer brands.*

Kodak.

Eastman Kodak Company, 343 State Street, Rochester, NY 14650; (716) 724-4000.

2

≡ Polaroid

#1 *in instant cameras*
Employees: 11,500
Sales: $1.9 billion
Profits: $145 million
Founded: 1937
Headquarters: Cambridge, Massachusetts

Social Conscience

People don't buy instant cameras the way they used to. The 9.4 million Polaroid sold in 1978 represents a peak they may never reach again (Kodak sold another 4.9 million instant cameras that year). In 1989 (when Kodak was no longer making instant cameras) Polaroid sold only 3 million. When your principal product gets clobbered in this fashion, you find other things to do and/or you chop costs. Polaroid traveled both those routes during the 1980s. They began making other products, most of them allied to their expertise in instant photography, and they halved their work force.

By decade's end, Polaroid, a much leaner company, was selling blank videotapes (for use in VCRs), conventional film (going head to head with Kodak and Fuji) and various commercial and industrial applications of instant photography (medical diagnostic procedures, identification systems for security, accident pictures for insurance agents). The decade's biggest victory was defeating Kodak in the courts in a copyright infringement case. How much they will get was still unclear in early 1990, but it was expected to be hefty, possibly over $1 billion. The victory left Polaroid holding a monopoly in a dwindling market.

The decade's biggest change was learning to live without Edwin H. Land, who retired from the company he founded.

History. While an 18-year-old undergraduate at Harvard in 1928, Edwin Land discovered a method for polarizing light—essentially, eliminating rays in a light beam unless they were traveling on a single plane, thus reducing glare. His process involved polyvinyl alcohol sheets. Thinking of obvious applications in the auto industry, Land dropped out of school to pursue his experiments. Nine years later Land perfected his process, and in 1937 founded Polaroid. But automakers discovered polarized sheets (used in visors and headlights) deteriorated in heat. So Polaroid began making sunglasses instead. Business boomed during World War II with the manufacture of goggles, glasses and filters.

After the war, Land was ready with a new product. During a 1943 vacation in New Mexico with his family, he snapped a photo of his three-year-old daughter. When she asked how long it would take to see the picture, Land got the idea of developing and printing a photograph inside the camera. In 1947, the Polaroid Model 95 was born. It weighed more than four pounds, produced sepia-toned pictures of varying quality in 60 seconds, and retailed for $90. It was an instant success.

Land's basic process has remained unchanged. *Time* described it this way: "A negative inside the camera is exposed and then brought into contact with a positive print sheet. Both are then drawn between a pair of rollers, which break a tiny pod of jelly-like chemicals that spread across the sheet, producing a finished product in

seconds." In 1950 Land introduced black-and-white instead of the usual sepia-toned photos; in 1960, 15-second pictures; in 1963, color film and film cartridges; and the biggest innovation came in 1972 with the debut of the SX-70—an inch-thick, seven-inch-long, fold-up job. The film itself was thin and the color picture developed outside the camera, before your very eyes. And the picture never faded, even after light exposure for long periods.

Land's major flub came in 1977, when he brought out a movie camera that produced instant movies—but the show lasted only 2½ minutes, had no sound and the picture was grainy. On top of all this, the public wasn't interested in home movies any more.

Owners and rulers. In 1989, to make it difficult for corporate raider Roy Disney to take over the company, Polaroid instituted an Employee Stock Ownership Plan. Employees now own 14 percent of Polaroid, and each employee has a right to vote his or her shares. They used this power in 1988 to elect an employee representative to the board of directors. Polaroid has always been a great favorite of institutional investors such as big insurance companies and mutual funds. In late 1989, they owned 75 percent of all the Polaroid shares. Dr. Land sold all his shares during the 1980s. Atlanta-born I. MacAllister Booth, who holds both engineering and MBA degrees, became CEO in the mid-1980s (1989 pay: $637,000). Of the 13 board members in 1987, 5 were academics, 2 from MIT, which adjoins Polaroid in Cambridge. Polaroid may also be the only board on which Digital Equipment's Ken Olsen sits (he's another MITer). And another board member is Yen-Tsai Feng, librarian at Harvard College.

As a place to work. Polaroid was an early leader in equal employment opportunities and began subsidized daytime child care for working parents in 1971. The company also has an extraordinary emphasis on continuing education. They pick up 100 percent of the tuition for job-related courses employes take—and they themselves offers a variety of courses, everything from basic English to blueprint reading and statistics. Although major cutbacks occurred throughout the

1980s, the company has offered generous severance plans—as in 1985, when they set aside a $30 million reserve to cover costs, up to a maximum of 30 months' pay.

Social responsibility.   Polaroid has always been an exemplary citizen in terms of minority employment and support of community services. In 1987 they won the Corporate Conscience Award of the Council on Economic Priorities for contributing 4 percent of pretax profits to charity. Polaroid matches employee contributions (up to $500) on a 2-for-1 basis. Polaroid left South Africa in 1977, the first among major U.S. corporations to leave in response to that country's apartheid policies.

Global presence.   Polaroid has distribution in 100 countries, and 45 percent of sales are abroad. In 1989, Polaroid agreed to a joint venture with three Soviet partners to sell cameras in the Soviet Union; soon, there will be a Polaroid retail outlet in Moscow.

Stock performance.   Polaroid stock bought for $1,000 in 1980 sold for $4,349 on January 2, 1990.

Consumer brands.

Polaroid.

Polaroid Corp., 549 Technology Square, Cambridge, MA 02139; (617) 577-2000.

GREETING CARDS

For a small industry (the U.S. Census Bureau counts up only 154 companies), it spews out tons of paper: more than 7 billion cards a year wishing people all manner of good luck and good health and love and happiness, especially during the Christmas season and on Valentine's Day. Three companies, Hallmark Cards, American Greetings and Gibson Greetings, make 80 percent of all cards. Hallmark, the pride of Kansas City, alone makes 40 percent. But this number one standing did not shield them from the traumas of the 1980s. They would have appreciated a "get well" card.

1

#1 *in greeting cards, crayons, Spanish-language TV networks*

Employees: 20,000 (plus 10,000 part-timers)
Sales: $2.5 billion
Founded: 1910
Headquarters: Kansas City, Missouri

Workplace

Americans already send more than 7 billion greeting cards a year—about 28 for every man, woman and child. How many more can they possibly send? Hallmark Cards, controling about 40 percent of this business, butted their heads against this wall during the 1980s, and it made for a major headache.

For one thing, card sales went flat. That was the first bad news. Then Hallmark tried to develop new card lines, prompting some smaller companies to charge them with stealing designs. One company ran ads in the trade press headlined, "Hallmark Hall of Shame." Another sued Hallmark, and won.

The White House Christmas card, 1989, one of 18,000 card designs Hallmark produced that year.

To lessen their dependence on greeting cards, Hallmark bought half a dozen companies during the 1980s, with mixed success. In 1984, they bought Binney & Smith, the maker of Crayolas—and that was a winner. They make 2 billion Crayolas a year, 4 out of every 5 crayons sold in the U.S. In 1988 they acquired 10 Hispanic television stations, the Univision Inc. network, and those have been losers (so far). In early 1990, Hallmark bought Dakin Inc., a manufacturer of stuffed animals and toys (for several years, Hallmark had distributed Dakin stuffed animals through their stores).

The decade was also marked by the tragedy of two skywalks collapsing into the lobby of the Hyatt Regency Hotel in Kansas City, killing 114 people. The hotel is one of the centerpieces of Hallmark's Crown Center development.

As an indication of their confusion, Hallmark switched advertising agencies three times in the 1980s after having one agency, Foote, Cone & Belding, for 37 years. They sacked their next agency, Young & Rubicam, because they felt that Y&R's campaign for AT&T's long-distance telephone service, "Reach out and touch someone," posed a conflict with their message, "When you care enough to send the very best." The $40 million account then went to Ogilvy & Mather for four years before moving in 1989 to Leo Burnett, which came up with a secondary theme, "Hallmark has a way to make somebody's day."

The Burnett agency was given the job of positioning Hallmark's new line of "To Kids with Love" cards. These are non-occasion (why wait for a holiday or birthday?) cards adults are supposed to send to kids aged 7 to 14.

Hallmark turns out more than 11 million greeting cards a day in 20 languages, none of them indulging in any black humor. They maintain the world's largest creative staff (they passed Walt Disney during the 1980s)—some 700 artists, designers, stylists, editors and photographers who each year produce 14,000 different designs. Hallmark has three main lines—the Hallmark label; Ambassador, introduced in 1959 to supply outlets such as supermarkets and drugstores; and Shoebox Greetings, identified as "an itty bitty division of Hallmark" on their products. An unabashed trafficker in sentiment, Hallmark says they follow public taste. "Our market," comments a vice president (in a considerable understatement), "is not avant-garde. We are living in an age of pronounced sentimentalism."

But Hallmark today has become more than greeting cards. About half of revenue comes from wrapping paper and ribbon, keepsake albums, crystal and pewter figurines, commemorative plates, diaries, novel bath products, arty accessories, calendars, Christmas tree ornaments and gift books—natural spinoffs of the main business. Hallmark products are sold in over 21,000 retail outlets, including 6,000 independently owned Hallmark card shops (the company itself only owns 18, used primarily for test-marketing).

Since 1951, Hallmark has sponsored "Hallmark Hall of Fame" TV shows. These 90-minute dramas, often based on important literary works and featuring distinguished actors, have been praised as "an oasis in television's wasteland." The shows have gained only mediocre ratings (figures telling how many people are watching), but the company insists they will continue to sponsor them. "The Hall of Fame" is aimed less at selling cards than at promoting Hallmark as a quality name.

History. At the turn of the century, 9-year-old Joyce Clyde Hall started working in a Nebraska bookstore to help support his mother, sister and brothers. One of the things he sold was picture postcards. Imported from Germany and England, the cards were a fad at the turn of the century. Greeting cards as we know them today didn't exist; there were only postcards and elaborate, prohibitively expensive valentines and engraved Christmas cards.

Three companies account for about 80 percent of all greeting card sales. Hallmark is the leader with 40 percent of the market, followed by American Greetings Corp. with 35 percent and Gibson with 11 percent. About 300 small companies account for the rest, including one called "Too Cool to Be on Earth."

Joyce Hall quit school at 15 and a few years later went to Kansas City to seek his fortune. In 1910 he started a wholesale business in postcards, engraved Christmas cards and valentines. His older brother Rollie joined him in 1911, and they began selling greeting cards another firm made. Within five years they owned an engraving company and were making their own greeting cards. The first two Hallmark cards were marketed in November 1915. In 1926 they introduced decorative gift wrap and ribbon to replace the brown wrapping paper and plain red and green tissue then commonly used.

After World War II Hallmark grew explosively, fueled by Joyce Hall's innovations—as the *Wall Street Journal* put it, "his near-obsession with promoting an image of quality." Besides developing a variety of gift products, "Mr. J. C." (as he was known by employees) devised new display racks for greeting cards, which until the 1950s had been sold from drawers. The racks not only helped customers to choose but also helped stores to reorder.

J. C. Hall turned the reins over to his son Donald in 1966. A self-effacing man, Donald Hall professionalized company management as they grew 10-fold over the next two decades. During his tenure, Hallmark added Christmas tree ornaments to their line; bought the Trifari, Krussman & Fishel fashion jewelry maker; and Binney & Smith, makers of Crayola crayons. The jewelry business was sold in 1988.

Also while Donald was president Hallmark suffered the worst setback in their history. On July 17, 1981, two skywalks collapsed into the lobby of the Hyatt Regency Hotel in Kansas City, killing 114 people and injuring 216 others. Hallmark owns the hotel property located near company headquarters in the Crown Center—a 21-square block area that also contains another luxury hotel, office buildings, a 250-unit apartment complex, 60 shops and 20 restaurants, six movie theaters, a children's theater and a 10-acre central plaza with an ice-skating rink and an outdoor cafe. The Crown Center has won praise for its architecture, and the $500 million project is said to have helped revive the city's decaying downtown area. After several years of bad publicity and lawsuits, Hallmark has recovered from the hotel disaster. In 1988 they marked the center's 20th anniversary by breaking ground for a new 240,000 square foot office tower designed by I. M. Pei.

Owners and rulers. Donald Hall was still chairman in 1990, but he had turned the job of president and CEO over to Irv Hockaday, a Princeton graduate and lawyer. *Forbes* called lawyer Hockaday "an experienced conglomerator" because of his 12 years with Kansas City Southern Industries, a railroad company he moved into data processing, insurance and TV broadcasting. For Hallmark, Hockaday's biggest deals to date have been the purchases of Univision, the largest Spanish-language TV network, as well as TV stations that broadcast in Spanish in San Francisco, Miami, New York, Los Angeles and six other cities.

The Hallmark family still holds two-thirds of the stock; an employee profit-sharing trust the remainder. The family's ownership is divided among J. C.'s three children—company chairman Donald, whose share *Forbes* estimated to be worth $560 million; Barbara, who has worked for years with company artists on card designs, owning stock worth $285 million; and Elizabeth, inactive in the company, also with stock worth $285 million. The Hall family is noted for living modestly and keeping a low profile.

As a place to work. In 1975 the Hall family began selling their stockholdings to the employee profit-sharing trust, explaining they wanted all Hallmark people "to participate in the ownership of the company." This arrangement has proved a boon to employees, with the equivalent of as much as 11 percent of an employee's annual salary being put into the trust

fund. When employees retire or leave, they can withdraw their personal account from the fund, giving many lucky retirees thousands of dollars worth of profit-sharing money alone. Hallmark still has a family atmosphere: Donald Hall carries his own tray in the company cafeteria and frequently attends elaborate 25th anniversary celebrations for individual employees. Employees point with pride to being a "Hallmarker." About 34 percent of Hallmark managers are women, and women make up 10 percent of upper-level managers. Hallmark has a confidential counseling program for employees—the company will pick up the cost of four sessions with psychologists (who treat problems such as chemical dependency, stress, marital discord and grief). As of July 1, 1990, Hallmark banned smoking in company offices, warehouses and cars. The company will meet half the cost for employees attending stop-smoking clinics.

Social responsibility. In 1987, Blue Mountain Arts, a greeting card publisher, sued Hallmark, claiming Hallmark had been imitating their designs with the Personal Touch line of cards. In the course of the legal battle, one Hallmark lawyer admitted, "We copied. We imitated. We emulated." The company later disavowed that admission but, in 1989, the Supreme Court agreed with Blue Mountain and ordered Hallmark to stop marketing the Personal Touch cards. Blue Mountain was also awarded an undisclosed sum. Hallmark also agreed to give Blue Mountain equal access to Hallmark card stores. Hall Family Foundations is the largest charitable giver in Kansas City; in 1987, it donated $9 million to the area, loaned a collection of Henry Moore sculptures (valued at $16 million) to the Nelson-Atkins Museum of Art and donated $1.7 million for a sculpture garden at the museum.

Global presence. Hallmark sells cards in 100 different countries and derives 20 percent of sales from overseas operations.

Consumer brands.

Greeting cards: Hallmark, Ambassador, Shoebox Greetings.

Crayons: Crayola.

Toys: Dakin.

Hallmark Cards, Inc., 2501 McGee, Kansas City, MO 64108; (816) 274-5111.

SIN

TOBACCO

Cigarette companies are doing all right, even though U.S. cigarette consumption went down steadily during the 1980s. Consumption peaked in 1981 when 633 billion cigarettes were sold, but by decade's end annual consumption was below 525 billion cigarettes. In the 1950s over half of American men smoked; today, fewer than 30 percent do. The companies are surviving because cigarette prices went up over 50 percent during the decade and, whereas fewer Americans are smoking, consumption is rising in Third World countries. Cigarettes still yield handsome profits. Investor Warren Buffett explained: "I'll tell you why I like the cigarette business. It costs a penny to make. Sell it for a dollar. It's addictive. And there's fantastic brand loyalty."

1

PHILIP MORRIS
COMPANIES INC.

#1 *in cigarettes, food, advertising*
#2 *in beer*

Employees: 156,000
Sales: $39 billion
Profits: $2.9 billion
Founded: 1847 (Philip Morris), 1903 (Kraft),
1895 (General Foods)
Headquarters: New York City, New York

You can now smoke, eat and drink your way through the day with Philip Morris. If you stubbed out a Marlboro in a mound of Jell-O, you would be looking at an all–Philip Morris dish. Likewise, if you made an Oscar Mayer bologna sandwich with a Claussen pickle on the side and downed it with a Miller draft beer.

Today's Philip Morris is the product of two blockbuster acquisitions of the 1980s.

The first, on November 1, 1985, saw Philip Morris, the nation's largest cigarette producer, acquire General Foods, the nation's second largest food company, for $5.7 billion—cash on the barrelhead. The merger was the biggest nonoil one in U.S. business history, *up to that time.* Three years later, on December 7, 1988, Philip Morris paid $13 billion to acquire Kraft, America's largest food company.

The result is a new holding company, Philip Morris Companies, now the nation's largest maker and seller of consumer products. No company puts as many products on your local supermarket shelves as Philip Morris. And with all those products to sell, they've also become the nation's largest advertiser, with an annual ad budget over $2 billion, even though they're forbidden to promote cigarettes on radio or TV.

Prior to buying General Foods, Philip Morris was the least diversified of all the tobacco companies. With the Kraft acquisition, nontobacco sales now contribute over 50 percent of total revenues. But cigarettes still account for over 60 percent of profits (only 5 other companies on the *Fortune* 500 earn more money). The Marlboro brand is the world's best-selling cigarette, accounting for 25 percent of the entire U.S. cigarette market, and throwing off more cash each year than the entire Kraft food stable. Smokers around the world pay an estimated $9.4 billion a year to buy Marlboro cigarettes. If Marlboro were broken out as a separate company, they would rank 50th on the Fortune 500. The Marlboro man, a wind-burned cowboy featured in ads, is now so widely known many Marlboro ads don't even mention the product—they merely show him smoking a cigarette, accompanied by the phrase, "Come to where the flavor is." Cigarette profits have enabled Philip Morris to become our largest food supplier. In 1990, when they moved to acquire Switzerland's Suchard with $3.8 billion of cigarette profits, Philip Morris challenged Nestlé for first place in the world food industry.

History. "Philip Morris, Esquire, Tabacconist and Importer of Fine

Seegars," opened a shop on London's Bond Street in 1847 and began making his own cigarettes seven years later. In 1870 he introduced the Cambridge, Oxford Blue and Oval brands. When he died in 1873, his brother and widow took over the company, and in 1894 sold the firm to William Curtis Thomson.

Philip Morris prospered under Thomson. In 1901 a royal decree made them tobacconist for King Edward VII, and the following year, playing on the royal endorsement, they began selling their brands in the U.S. By 1919 Philip Morris had been taken over by American stockholders, and 10 years later they began making cigarettes in the U.S. at a plant in Richmond, Virginia.

Their big break came in 1930 when, in the midst of the Great Depression, the successors of the old Tobacco Trust, led by R. J. Reynolds, upped their prices. Philip Morris, Brown & Williamson (another firm of English origin) and several smaller companies countered with economy brands. Philip Morris' major economy brand was Philip Morris itself, and in 1933 they promoted it with one of the most successful ad campaigns in cigarette history. They found a midget bellhop named Johnny Roventini working in the lobby of the Hotel New Yorker, gave him a page's uniform and a tiny pillbox hat set at a rakish tilt and put him on the radio to "Call for Philip Morris." Soon Johnny's picture and famous line were on billboards and magazine ads across the country, establishing the low-priced Philip Morris brand as a major industry player.

After World War II Philip Morris picked up the Continental Tobacco Company and plants in Louisville, Kentucky. But a deal they made in 1954 did more for the company than any other single event in their history. They bought Benson & Hedges, maker of Parliament cigarettes. And with the company came Joseph Cullman III.

Born and raised in New York, and a third-generation member of an American tobacco-growing family, Cullman brought to Philip Morris a marketplace sensitivity that became the company's hallmark. In three years he was president, making decisions that shaped the industry for the next two decades. Cullman directed the Marlboro marketing in the mid-1950s when it was transformed from a women's cigarette into a macho brand sold in a fliptop box. When the brand wheeled into New York City with the slogan "flavor, filter, fliptop box," marketing history was made: It captured first place in 30 days. That phenomenal success gave Cullman and the group of hard-charging executives he gathered around him a taste of blood they never forgot. As they moved up from the rear of the industry, they became intent on knocking off the guy on the next rung of the ladder. They did it first in cigarettes, moving from sixth to first place, and then, after acquiring Miller Brewing in 1970, they did it in the beer business, moving from seventh to second place.

In 1978 Cullman was succeeded as CEO by George Weissman, a New Yorker who graduated from a now-extinct high school for brainy kids, Townsend Harris Hall. Weissman, who started out in PR, made important contributions in two areas. He spearheaded the international expansion, and set in motion a social responsibility program that turned Philip Morris into a major arts patron. (After he retired, Weissman became chairman of New York's Lincoln Center for the Performing Arts.)

When they're not selling cigarettes and beer, Philip Morris is building homes. They developed Mission Viejo, one of the largest communities in California's Orange County. However, not everything they touch turns to gold. After their success with Miller beer, Philip Morris bought 7-Up in 1978 and took a run at Coca-Cola. But the vaunted Philip Morris marketing prowess couldn't gain any market share for 7-Up—and in 1986 the business was sold.

When it comes to cigarettes, however, Philip Morris has the right touch. Year by year the number of U.S. cigarette smokers declines and fewer cigarettes are sold. But Philip Morris bucks that trend by increasing their market share every year. That share, in 1990, was 42 percent.

It remains to be seen whether the Marlboro magic can rub off in the food business. General Foods has certainly been a sluggish performer. Since Philip Morris acquired them, their flagship coffee brand, Maxwell House, has lost ground to Procter & Gamble's Folgers while the Post cereal line has lost out to Kellogg's and General Mills. If there's anything Philip Morris hates, it's losing. As they put it,

"Settling for second-best is not part of the Philip Morris personality."

Perhaps that's why Kraft was acquired—to shape up General Foods. The top people at the new subsidiary, Kraft General Foods, are Kraft veterans. Chicago-based Kraft put up only a token defense against the Philip Morris lunge. Very early on Chairman John Richman vetoed an idea to fight back by tarring Philip Morris as a "merchant of death." Kraft really just wanted more money, and Philip Morris obliged. Puff, puff—and all that Velveeta and Philadelphia Cream Cheese joined the Philip Morris bandwagon.

Owners and rulers. Insurance companies, pension funds, bank trust departments and mutual funds are the major holders (75 percent) of Philip Morris stock. The big commercial banks also have a major stake because Philip Morris, at the end of 1986, had debt of $16 billion on their books (up a little from the $2.5 billion they owned in 1980). All the directors and officers hold less than 1 percent of the shares. That crew's leader in 1989 was Scottish-born, Cambridge-educated Hamish Maxwell, 63, who came up through the international ranks. Maxwell's family has been in the tobacco business for four generations. In 1990 he had heart bypass surgery. The infighting at Philip Morris is fierce. You climb to the top on the backs of others. One habit is common to virtually all top company executives: smoking. One exception: 50-year-old Michael A. Miles who succeeded John Richman as CEO of Kraft General Foods. Miles is an intense workaholic, reports for work at 6 a.m. and doesn't smoke. He joined Kraft in 1982 as president.

As a place to work. If you smoke, this is probably a good place to work. You will be among fellow addicts, and you'll get a free carton of cigarettes every week. If you're the hyper, superachieving type, you'll do well here too. This company is always on the prowl. A new employee told *Fortune* that the corporate culture can be summed up as "Screw it; get it done." Resting on their laurels is not their style. Benefits at Philip Morris are good. The company is also a leader in the employment and promotion of minorities, which is only fair since blacks smoke more than whites.

Social responsibility. Philip Morris rates a zero for corporate conscience if you consider all the lung-cancer deaths health authorities link to smoking. Antismoking activists were outraged at Philip Morris' $60 million ad campaign celebrating the bicentennial of the Bill of Rights. In response to the TV ads, hundreds of thousands of viewers requested free copies of the Bill of Rights, which were mailed with a letter from Philip Morris CEO Maxwell. Philip Morris paid the National Archives $600,000 to use their name in the ads, prompting Harvard law professor Laurence Tribe to write, "Some things just should not be for sale. If Philip Morris rented the front steps of the White House, citizens would be outraged. It is just a short step from the White House to the National Archives." On the other hand, they're a major source of support for minority and women's organizations, and their arts support led the *Wall Street Journal* in 1988 to anoint them as "a 20th-century corporate Medici, probably the art world's favorite company. More than two decades of tax-deductible beneficence has given Philip Morris access to presidents and prime ministers, kings and queens."

Global presence. Very big. Marlboro is the world's largest selling cigarette, and Philip Morris claims 6 percent of world cigarette sales of 4.2 trillion units. In more than 25 countries, including France, Germany, Italy, Mexico and Sweden, Philip Morris brands control over 15 percent of the market. The big breakthrough of the 1980s was getting their cigarettes into Japan and Taiwan. The Japanese and Chinese populations have an extremely high percentage of smokers.

Stock performance. Philip Morris stock bought for $1,000 in 1980 sold for $13,821 on January 2, 1990.

Consumer brands.

Cigarettes: Marlboro, Benson & Hedges, Merit, Virginia Slims, Parliament, PM, Alpine, Cambridge, Players.

Beer: Miller, Meister Bräu, Milwaukee's Best, Löwenbräu, Sharp's, Leinenkugel, Lite.

Wines and coolers: Lindemans, Matilda Bay (imported from Australia).

Philip Morris Companies, 120 Park Avenue, New York, NY 10017; (212) 679-1800.

2

#1 *in cigarettes (worldwide)*
#3 *in cigarettes (U.S.),*
auto insurance (U.S.)

Employees: 300,000; 50,000 in U.S.
Sales: $26.6 billion (World), $6.25 (U.S.)
Profits: $1.7 billion (U.S. profits: $535
million)
Founded: 1902
Headquarters: London, England

This company is at home anywhere in the world where people smoke. And if they don't smoke, B.A.T will be happy to show them how. In the early part of this century B.A.T hooked the Chinese on cigarette smoking. Now the world's most prolific smokers, the Chinese make their own cigarettes today, but elsewhere B.A.T factories are ubiquitous. They operate 90 cigarette plants in more than 40 countries. Every day smokers around the world light up 1.5 billion B.A.T-made cigarettes. No company sells more cigarettes than B.A.T Industries. Their estimated share of the world market (not counting China and the Soviet Union) is 20 percent.

B.A.T was born a multinational. American Tobacco Company of the United States and Imperial Tobacco Company of Britain decided not to fight each other when they could divide up the world between them. So they agreed America would stay out of the British market and Imperial would stay out of the U.S. market—and together they formed British-American Tobacco to contaminate the rest of the world with cigarettes. From their inception then, this company had a mandate to bring cigarette smoking to people the world over except in Britain and the ·U.S., both of which were declared off bounds.

In one of those historical ironies, the offspring—now an independent company—became bigger than the two parents. The Supreme Court broke up the American Tobacco monopoly in 1911. Imperial Tobacco grew fat and lazy in their

home market—and is no longer a leader there. Meanwhile, B.A.T (they shortened their name and perversely refused to put a period after the T) prospered in Brazil, Germany, South Africa and many other countries where they sell such brands as Lucky Strike, Kent, Player's, Pall Mall and Benson & Hedges. In 35 countries one of their brands is the number one seller.

Also, the original covenants no longer apply. B.A.T can now operate anywhere they wish. They entered the U.S. in 1927 by acquiring Brown & Williamson, then a small player in the cigarette field. B.A.T built them up to third place in the American market, doing 12 percent of the business through such brands as Kool, Raleigh, Richland, Viceroy and Barclay.

The bad news about the cancer-cigarette connection has not deterred B.A.T from their central mission in life, but they have, like other tobacco companies, hedged their bets by getting into some smoke-free businesses: insurance, paper and stores. In 1989, when sales were approaching the $30 billion level, B.A.T attracted the attention of the elegant Anglo-French corporate raider, Sir James Goldsmith, who accumulated 2.3 percent of the shares in an opening salvo. B.A.T successfully fought him off by selling huge chunks of their nontobacco businesses. They got $1.1 billion for Chicago retailing giant Marshall Field, $1.5 billion for the Saks Fifth Avenue stores and $110 million for the J. B. Ivey department stores in the Carolinas and Florida. Next to go were paper makers—Wiggins Teape in Britain, Appleton Papers in Wisconsin—and the John Breuner furniture stores and furniture rental business, an 18-store chain acquired with Marshall Field.

These selloffs reduced B.A.T's sales, but their cupboard is not exactly bare. Aside from cigarette companies, they own the Farmers Group, the third U.S. largest car and home insurer (acquired in 1988 after a knock-down-drag-out fight). And they have 40 percent control of Montreal-based Imasco: Canada's biggest cigarette purveyor (Player's, Du Maurier) and operator of the 3,175-unit Hardee's restaurant chain in the U.S. and of drugstore chains in Canada (Shoppers Drug Mart) and the U.S. (Peoples Drug). Wherever you go in the world, B.A.T will have businesses like these. Cigarettes throw off a lot of money, which then has to be attached to something.

For all their size and power, B.A.T has remained a low-profile company. B.A.T's 60-year old chairman, Patrick Sheehy, runs a decentralized operation from a nondescript headquarters not far from London's Victoria Station.

Stock performance. B.A.T Industries stock bought for $1,000 in 1980 sold for $12,759 on January 2, 1990.

Consumer brands.

Cigarettes: Kool, Richland, Capri, Barclay, Raleigh, Viceroy, Belair.

BATUS Inc., 2000 Citizens Plaza, Louisville, KY 40202; (502) 581-8000.

B.A.T Industries PLC, 50 Victoria St., London SW 1H ONL, England; 44-1-222-7979.

3

RJR

#2 in cigarettes

Employees: 60,000
Sales: $14.0 billion
Founded: 1875
Headquarters: New York City, New York

Not every corporate leader gets his picture on the cover of Time alongside the headline: "A Game of Greed." F. Ross Johnson, president of RJR Nabisco, found himself there on November 28, 1988. Two days later Johnson was deposed, and the company he headed was sold for $25 billion in the biggest—and most highly publicized—takeover in business history.

The pawn in this story was RJR Nabisco. Their host of brand names—built up over many years—made this company worth fighting over. RJR Nabisco is one of the world's largest consumer products companies. Every day they sell 80 million packages of their products. Many of these are cigarette packages—Winston, Salem, Camel. Their Reynolds Tobacco unit is the nation's second largest cigarette producer. Other packages hold cookies and crackers—Oreo, Chips Ahoy!, Ritz, Triscuit. Their Nabisco Brands unit is the nation's largest cookie and cracker maker. As Ross Johnson used to say, "Some genius invented the Oreo. We're just living off the inheritance."

Johnson believed in living well on that corporate inheritance. Bryan Burrough and John Helyar, authors of a book on the RJR takeover, Barbarians at the Gates, toted up the baubles of the good life. RJR Nabisco's top 31 executives made a total of $14.2 million a year, an average of $458,000. All managers, even the lowliest supervisor, got company cars and country club memberships. Johnson's two maids were on the company payroll. Johnson maintained an RJR Air Force, a fleet of 10 planes and 36 corporate pilots. Johnson also put a host of jocks on the RJR Nabisco payroll, including Don Meredith (at $500,000 a year), Jack Nicklaus ($1 million a year) and Frank Gifford ($413,000 a year plus an office and apartment in New York City). One of Johnson's favorite sayings was, "A few million dollars are lost in the sands of time."

Happy-go-lucky Ross Johnson put RJR Nabisco up for sale in 1988. And like everything else he had done in his business career, he treated it as a lark. The 1980s had certainly proved his playground. Born in Winnipeg, Canada, the son of a hardware salesman, Johnson began the decade as CEO of Standard Brands (Planters nuts, Fleischmann's margarine, Royal puddings, Chase & Sanborn coffee). In 1981 he merged the company into Nabisco, creating the nation's fourth largest food company. Nabisco was considered the senior partner, but in three years Johnson had snared the CEO's job. In 1985 he merged Nabisco Brands into RJR Industries, a much bigger company, and within a year he was the CEO there. He then angered almost everyone in North Carolina by moving the headquarters from Winston-Salem to Atlanta because he just couldn't stand small-town living. "You keep running into the same people over and over," he said. "You had a town of 140,000 people where you've got 17,000 people working for the company and 10,000 retirees, and you can't breathe."

In October 1988, two years after becoming CEO and a year after moving to Atlanta, Ross Johnson told the startled company directors that because the stock market didn't place a high enough value on RJR Nabisco stock, the only way to reward shareholders would be to sell the company—to himself and other RJR Nabisco managers. The Wall Street firm of Shearson Lehman Hutton agreed to raise $17 billion to pay stockholders $75 a share ($4 higher than the stock had ever traded). Down the road, the Johnson-led management team could have come away with as much as 20 percent of the stock in the new company. And if everything else worked according to plan, they would make something like $2.5 billion in five years by selling off parts of the company—without putting up any money of their own. These terms led many to believe—and say, as *Time* did—that Ross Johnson was trying to steal the company. They never expected anyone else to enter the bidding at such a high price. They were wrong. The Wall Street investment firm of Kohlberg Kravis Roberts did enter the bidding and after six weeks came away with the prize, RJR Nabisco, for $109 a share or roughly $25 billion. Johnson left the company clutching a $53 million golden parachute (severance pay reserved for top executives). And the investment bankers who worked on the deal pocketed more than $400 million for their efforts.

So KKR now owned RJR Nabisco. And they went back to selling cigarettes and cookies—and getting rid of companies to pay off the massive debt. Cigarettes, in particular, needed serious attention since archrival Philip Morris' brands were clob-bering Reynolds' brands. Entering the 1980s, Reynolds Tobacco was in first place with 33 percent of the cigarette market. By 1990 they had dropped to second place with 28 percent of it. Not to worry, though, cigarette prices had about doubled—and tobacco was still bringing in 70 percent of RJR Nabisco's profits. Moreover, while cigarette sales were declining in the U.S., they were soaring overseas.

History.   Richard Joshua Reynolds fostered the legend that he began life as a barefoot, illiterate farmboy. In fact, Reynolds attended both college and business school before using family money to build a factory in Winston, North Carolina in 1874. By 1887 he was marketing 86 brands of chewing tobacco, some named for girlfriends. In the 1890s, Reynolds was forced to sell two-thirds of his company to rival James ("Buck") Duke of the American Tobacco Trust. Reynolds got $3 million and remained active in the business. When the Supreme Court broke Duke's monopoly in 1911, Reynolds regained his company, ready to lead tobacco users from chewing to smoking.

Mulling over package designs for his new Kaiser Wilhelm cigarette shortly before the First World War, he had second thoughts: "I don't think we should name a product for a living man. You never can tell what the damn fool will do." So he named it Camel, to play up the Turkish tobacco content, and illustrated the pack with a portrait of Ol' Joe, a camel in the

The Camel smoke-ring billboard was a Times Square landmark from 1941 to 1966.

Barnum & Bailey circus. By giving away free cigarettes to American doughboys in France, the company created a whole generation of loyal Camel smokers. Within 10 years of Camel's introduction nearly half the nation's smokers were puffing on them. The famous slogan, "I'd walk a mile for a Camel," was created in 1921. (After the Second World War, they boasted in ads that "More doctors smoke Camels than any other brand.")

Reynolds died in 1918, and no relatives went into the business (his favorite nephew, Richard S. Reynolds, went off to start an aluminum foil factory, which later became Reynolds Metals). The firm lived on, ushering in the filter era with Winston in 1955, when many smokers were beginning to suspect cigarette smoke might be unhealthy. And they got a lot of mileage from their ungrammatical advertising slogan, "Winston tastes good like a cigarette should." When researchers established clear links between cigarette smoking and lung cancer in the 1960s, R. J. Reynolds moved into other businesses—food (Del Monte and Chun King), shipping (Sea-Land) and oil (Aminoil). In 1970, they changed their name to R. J. Reynolds Industries. In 1982, they bought Heublein, a big alcohol distiller and restaurant manager (Kentucky Fried Chicken). RJR sold Heublein to Grand Metropolitan soon after the Nabisco merger.

Owners and rulers. KKR, the banker, controls the show. Their game is to trim the debt by selling off companies, cutting costs and increasing profits so investors in the deal can reap a handsome return on their money. To see this job is done well, KKR hired Louis Gerstner, president of American Express, as CEO of RJR Nabisco. To entice him away from American Express, they gave him $15 million for signing on, a five-year contract averaging $2.6 million a year, a guaranteed pension of $444,300 a year and stock options making him the largest single individual holder of RJR stock. Gerstner, who had a home in Greenwich, Connecticut, didn't even have to relocate to Atlanta. He moved RJR Nabisco headquarters to New York City so they could be near the people who put up all the takeover money. RJR Nabisco is now headquartered at 9 West 57th Street—the same building as KKR. Gerstner dismantled the RJR Air Force, selling seven of the corporate jets as well as more than a dozen corporate apartments and homes. However, they couldn't find a buyer for their lavish Atlanta hangar.

As a place to work. Until partygoer Ross Johnson arrived, Standard Brands was a very dull company, with a bunch of tired products and penny-pinching bosses. He turned the firm into a free-wheeling place. Nabisco, a very successful company, was the epitome of a staid, unimaginative octogenarian. When the two companies combined, some wags said it was "as if Hell's Angels had merged with the Rotary Club." R. J. Reynolds used to be a paternalistic company with a southern culture, although, even before Johnson, the top brass reserved for themselves the privileges of rank. They were the pride of Winston-Salem, North Carolina. As they entered the 1990s, RJR Nabisco was no place for big spenders. They were pulling in their belts, squeezing out profits to pay off the bankers. Over 2,300 jobs were eliminated, about one-sixth of Reynolds' total. A former Reynolds employee in Winston-Salem said: "Imagine you lived in this great old house. You grew up in it, and all your happy memories are in it, and you take special care of it for the next generation. Then one day, you come home to discover it's been turned into a brothel. That's how I feel about RJR."

Social responsibility. Aside from the notoriety around the 1988 buyout, RJR Nabisco is never far from the limelight because many people regard their main product as a killer. In 1990 they withdrew a new cigarette brand, Uptown, aimed at blacks, after Dr. Louis W. Sullivan, Secretary of Health & Human Services, blasted this ploy as "slick and sinister." Mark Green, newly appointed Commissioner of Consumer Affairs for New York City, appealed to Gerstner to halt the promotion of cigarettes to youth, telling him (in case he didn't know): "Your industry finds itself in the ironic position of killing off your own consumers. A thousand times a day or 40 times an hour, there's a funeral because someone was addicted to smoking." R. J. Reynolds used to be a great benefactor of Winston-Salem and the Piedmont region of North Carolina. When Johnson moved the headquarters to

Atlanta, he told a reporter he wasn't going to "support every organization from the United Way to the Seven Jolly Girls Athletic Club Bean Bag competition." But once Gerstner was CEO he committed $30 million over five years to improve the learning environment in schools throughout the country by supporting a variety of innovative programs.

In 1987 Reynolds Tobacco ran an ad in Japanese newspapers apologizing for shipping cigarettes laced with excessive amounts of herbicide residue (as if the tobacco wasn't lethal enough by itself). The shipments came right after Japan caved in to American pressure to open their markets to foreign-made cigarettes. The executive of another U.S. tobacco company said: "We need this like a hole in the head."

Global presence. They sell cigarettes in 160 countries—and business is booming—but they lag far behind Philip Morris, whose international tobacco sales are triple Reynold's non-U.S. sales. They were the largest cookie baker in Europe and the number one potato chip maker in Britain prior to the 1988 buyout, but these businesses were among the first sold to pay down the debt. In 1989 French company BSN paid RJR Nabisco $2.5 billion for cookie and cracker companies in France (Belin), Italy (Saiwa) and Britain (Jacobs Club, Huntley & Palmer) plus the potato chip and snack businesses of two British companies, Walkers and Smiths. RJR Nabisco also snagged $44 million for cookie companies in India and Pakistan and $77 million for food businesses in Spain and Portugal.

Consumer brands.

Cigarettes: Winston, Salem, Camel, Doral, Magna, Vantage, More, Ritz, Chelsea.

RJR Nabisco Inc., 9 West 57th Street, New York, NY 10019; (212) 446-5600.

4

American Brands, Inc.

#1 *in golf balls, staplers*
#3 *in liquor*
#5 *in cigarettes in U.S.*

Employees: 48,100
Sales: $7.2 billion
Profits: $631 million
Founded: 1904
Headquarters: Old Greenwich, Connecticut

Social Conscience

From the company name, it's difficult to tell what they do. And perhaps American Brands doesn't know either. During the 1980s they sold off over half the companies they owned coming into the decade. Among the discards were Sunshine biscuits, Mott's applesauce, Jergens lotion, Roi-Tan cigars, Hydrox cookies and Pinkerton security guards.

What's left is the core business, cigarettes, and an assortment of nontobacco businesses—Jim Beam bourbon, Swingline staplers, Wilson Jones loose-leaf binders, Master padlocks, Titleist golf balls, Foot-Joy golf shoes, Franklin Life Insurance. These firms were added to disguise the company's basic mission: selling cigarettes. Shortly after they began adding these nontobacco entities, in 1970, the company changed their name from American Tobacco to American Brands. The trouble is, American Brands is like the 80-year-old man who has been smoking all his life. By that time the only thing that tastes good is cigarette smoke.

It's easy to become addicted to the profits cigarettes generate. Even though their share of the U.S. cigarette market has tumbled since 1965 from 35 percent to 7 percent (their two major brands, Pall Mall and Lucky Strike, were done in by filter-tips), American Brands continues to derive two-thirds of their profits from tobacco. And those profits are sizable. In 1988, only 79 other U.S. companies

UP IN SMOKE: THE TOP TEN CIGARETTE BRANDS

Brand	Company	Market Share
1. Marlboro	Philip Morris	26.5%
2. Winston	RJR Nabisco	9.1%
3. Salem	RJR Nabisco	6.2%
4. Kool	Brown & Williamson	6.0%
5. Newport	Lorillard	4.8%
6. Camel	RJR Nabisco	3.9%
7. Benson & Hedges	Philip Morris	3.8%
8. Merit	Philip Morris	3.8%
9. Doral	RJR Nabisco	3.6%
10. Virginia Slims	Philip Morris	3.2%

Source: *Advertising Age,* 4 December 1989.

earned more than the $580 million American Brands netted after taxes.

American Brands is the only U.S. tobacco producer still deriving over half of sales from cigarettes, and the only U.S. tobacco company deriving over half of their cigarette sales overseas. That's because in 1968, when they were allegedly reducing their dependence on tobacco, they scooped up British cigarette maker, Gallaher, which went on to take first place in the lungs of English smokers.

In 1988, American Brands was the target of a controversial lawsuit in Lexington, Mississippi: The family of a man who died of lung cancer charged American Brands' Pall Mall cigarettes were laced with pesticides, herbicides and toxic substances.

Smokers usually drink too, and American Brands likes this combination. "Cigarettes, Whiskey and Wild, Wild Women" goes the old folk ballad. In 1987, as health activists began to target liquor in a manner reminiscent of the anticigarette crusades, American Brands paid $585 million to enrich their Jim Beam stable with Old Grand-Dad bourbon, DeKuyper cordials, Windsor Canadian whiskey and Gilbey's gin and vodka. These additions mean American Brands ranks third in the U.S. and seventh in the world in distilled spirits.

At the end of 1987, American Brands became a takeover target by a company called E-II Holdings, which consisted of discards from the old Beatrice Foods empire: Waterloo Industries (tool storage products), AristoKraft (kitchen cabinets), Day-Timers, Vogel Peterson (office furniture), Samsonite (luggage) and Martha White (foods). American Brands repelled this attack by using the "PAC-man defense"—they turned around and swallowed E-II for $2.7 billion. They retained E-II's hardware and office supply brands, but sold the rest to Rapid-American.

American Brands likes to live dangerously. But not in New York City, where they've been headquartered for as long as anyone could remember without leaving much of a trace in the form of philanthropic contributions to the city's well-being. In 1987, American Brands moved their headquarters to Old Greenwich, Connecticut, closer to the homes of their top executives, many of whom have come from outside the tobacco business. William J. Alley, chairman and CEO, formerly headed up Franklin Life Insurance; Thomas C. Hays, chief operating officer, rose through the ranks of the discarded Andrew Jergens Company, as did Robert L. Austin, chief administrative officer; and John T. Ludes, head of international tobacco operations, came from Acushnet, American Brands' golf ball unit.

Stock performance. American Brands stock bought for $1,000 in 1980 sold for $7,648 on January 2, 1990.

Consumer brands:

Cigarettes: Carlton, Tareyton, Lucky Strike, Pall Mall.

Distilled spirits: Jim Beam, DeKuyper, DeKuyper Peachtree, Windsor Canadian Supreme, Gilbey's, Kamchatka, Old Grand-Dad, Old Taylor, Old Crow, Beam's Choice, Beam's Black Label, Chateau, Baron Von Scheuters, Beam's 8-Star Blend, Dark Eyes, Canada House Canadian, Spey Royal, Vat 69 Traditional, Vat 69 Gold, King George IV, Talisker, Boissiere, Kamora, Aalborg Akvavit, Fletcher and Oakes, Australian Outback, CocoRibe.

Athletic shoes: Foot-Joy.

Golf clubs, balls and clothing: Acushnet.

Staplers, glue guns, riveters: Swingline.

Locks: Master Lock.

Cutlery products: Case.

Cookware, kitchen tools and carpet sweepers: Prestige.

Office supplies: Wilson Jones.

American Brands, Inc., 1700 East Putnam Avenue, Old Greenwich, CT 06870; (203) 698-5000.

5
Lorillard

#4 *in cigarettes*

Employees: 4,250
Sales: $1.6 billion
Profits: $368 million
Founded: 1760
Headquarters: New York City, New York

Thanks to young black smokers, Lorillard is going great guns. Their Newport cigarettes became very popular among young blacks during the 1980s. In 1980, Newport ranked 18th in sales, but by decade's end Newport was the 5th best-selling American cigarette, available in 12 different versions. Newport's success (one-half of Lorillard's total sales) enabled Lorillard to hit fourth place in the tobacco industry (passing American Tobacco).

The family behind all the cigarettes is the Tisch clan, who bought Lorillard in 1968. The Tisch brothers, Laurence and Preston (he prefers Robert), operate the Loews Corporation (named after an old movie theater chain). Loews is a conglomerate that owns (or controls) a number of companies, including CBS, Bulova Watch, Loews Hotels, CNA Insurance—and Lorillard. The Tisches hold powerful positions in many companies; Laurence Tisch is CBS chairman (Loews owns 25 percent of the broadcasting company). In 1989, Laurence's 40-year-old son, Andrew, was named chairman and CEO of Lorillard. Ironically, Andrew doesn't smoke. He's a health fanatic and has run three New York City marathons.

Lorillard traces their history to 1760 when an 18-year-old French immigrant, Pierre Lorillard, began selling snuff in New York City. They don't make snuff anymore, nor do they sell chewing tobacco. In 1988 the Tisches sold off Beech-Nut, Big Red and Havana Blossom chewing tobaccos. In addition to Newport, Lorillard offers the popular Kent, True and Triumph cigarettes. But Lorillard has made a few mistakes—in fact, during the 1980s many brands bombed. Stubbed out in the ashtray were such brands as Max, Rebel, Maverick, Heritage, Bistro, Satin and Harley Davidson. Their oldest brand, Old Gold, can still be found in some tobacco shops but is no longer advertised. In 1989, Lorillard came out with a cigarette targeted at young women: Spring Lemon Lights— lemon-flavored cigarettes.

Consumer brands. Newport, Kent, True, Triumph, Old Gold, Spring Lemon Lights.

Lorillard Inc., 666 Fifth Avenue, New York, NY 10103; (212) 841-8500.

6

#1 *in smokeless tobacco*

Employees: 3,300
Sales: $670 million
Profits: $191 million
Founded: 1911
Headquarters: Greenwich, Connecticut

Some people consider wadding tobacco into your mouth and chewing it a disgusting habit. Some medical authorities consider it dangerous, a contributor to mouth and throat cancer. In 1986, acting on those suspicions, the U.S. Congress required warning labels on smokeless tobacco products (snuff and chewing tobacco) and banned their advertising on radio and TV. But UST (which changed their name in 1987 from United States Tobacco) understandably, doesn't share those opinions. Their smokeless tobacco brands, Copenhagen and Skoal, are obscenely profitable products. They cost little to make, allowing UST to clear 46 cents on every dollar of sales *after* all operating costs. They are three times as profitable as tobacco rival Philip Morris. UST has garnered 85 percent of the moist snuff market. UST considers these attacks unfair. They point out Copenhagen snuff has been part of American culture since 1822 and (raising the specter of class war) that their customers are "adult males who work on farms and in factories, coal mines, and industries such as lumber, steel, or energy, where smoking may be inconvenient or not permitted." And UST knows how to reach their customers. Rather than dropping a wad on advertising in magazines and newspapers, UST sponsors rodeos, monster truck shows and tractor pulls. By some estimates, almost 6 percent of the American population uses smokeless tobacco.

Health authorities fight on just because of such statistics. They've also pointed out smokeless tobacco is a fad among teenage boys; in 1986, the Surgeon General's Advisory Committee reported 16 percent of males 12 to 25 had used smokeless tobacco within the previous year. And sometimes they win. In 1987, citing concerns about public health, the government of Hong Kong banned sales of smokeless tobacco there (despite UST's comprehensive campaign against the ban). Shortly after that, New Zealand banned smokeless tobacco. UST's chief defender in the late 1980s, on "60 Minutes" and in other forums, was their president, former Miami Dolphins linebacker, Nicholas A. Buoniconti. Buoniconti resigned in 1989, and chairman and CEO Louis F. Bantle added the title of president.

Among other products UST sells (none anywhere near the profit producer smokeless tobacco is) are wines from Washington and from California's Napa Valley, pipe tobaccos imported from the Netherlands, pipes, pipe cleaners and (a product popular in both the Appalachian Mountains and the streets of Berkeley, California) cigarette papers.

Stock performance. UST stock bought for $1,000 in 1980 sold for $17,704 on January 2, 1990.

Consumer brands.

Smokeless tobacco: Copenhagen, Skoal, Select.

Pipes: Dr. Grabow, Mastercraft.

Pipe tobaccos: Borkum Riff, Amphora.
Pipe cleaners: Dill's.

Cigarette papers: Zig-Zag.

Wines: Chateau Ste. Michelle, Columbia Crest, Conn Creek, Villa Mt. Eden.

UST Inc., 100 West Putnam Avenue, Greenwich, CT 06830; (203) 661-1100.

BEER

With their mania for health, Americans cut down on beer consumption during the 1980s. But the trend since the 1960s—the big brewers getting more and more of the market—continued inexorably.

In 1960, the five biggest brewers—Anheuser-Busch, Schlitz, Pabst, Falstaff and Carling—sold only one-third of the beer Americans consumed.

In 1970, the Big Five—Anheuser-Busch, Schlitz, Pabst, Coors and Schaefer—had 51 percent of the market.

In 1980, the five biggest beer sellers—Anheuser-Busch, Miller, Schlitz, Heileman and Pabst—took down 75 percent of the market.

In 1989, the Big Five—Anheuser-Busch, Miller, Stroh, Coors, and Heileman—controlled about 90 percent of the beer business.

1

ANHEUSER-BUSCH COMPANIES, INC.

#1 *in beer*
#2 *in bread*
#2 *in theme parks*
#5 *in salted snacks*

Employees: 41,600
Sales: $9.5 billion
Profits: $767 million
Founded: 1860
Headquarters: St. Louis, Missouri

Anheuser-Busch brews beer, and they are one tough hombre. Everything they do reinforces this "don't mess with me" stance: the Clydesdale horses, the screaming A-and-Eagle symbol in use since 1872, the upbeat "king of beer" Budweiser commercials, the T-shirts emblazoned "I'm a Miller killer." This toughness paid off in the 1980s when U.S. beer sales were flat as day-old brew. In fact, on a per capita basis, they declined slightly. In that market, there's only one way to get ahead, and

A-B was equal to the task. In 1979, they brewed 47 million barrels of beer, taking 28 percent of the market; in 1988, 78 million barrels, for 41 percent of it. In 1989, they had 43.2 percent. Take that! Pow, pow!

The largest brewer in the world (they have 12 U.S. breweries) currently markets 12 brands of beer. In the late 1970s Anheuser-Busch began offering low-calorie light beers in addition to the old standards (Budweiser, Michelob and Busch). In 1984, in response to health concerns, they introduced LA, a low-alcohol beer. Anheuser-Busch also markets a dark beer, Michelob Classic Dark, and Elephant Malt Liquor, an import. But Budweiser reigns supreme. The King of Beers is still the best-selling beer in the world and accounts for 25 percent of the U.S. beer market. Anheuser-Busch beers are bottled in brown bottles because sunlight changes beer's taste in minutes. Their "Beechwood Ageing" slogan refers to wood chips floated in the beer during the brewing process.

Besides beer, A-B takes in money from food, theme parks and baseball. Their Campbell Taggart subsidiary bakes bread under the names Colonial, Rainbo, Kilpatrick's, Earth Grains, Family Recipes, Grant's Farm and Roman Meal. They operate 45 bakeries and 14 manufacturing plants in 19 states. Another subsidiary, Eagle Snacks, produces bar food—peanuts, chips and crackers. They now rank fifth nationally in salted snacks. A-B's theme park business has grown rapidly since 1959 when they opened Busch Gardens next to their Tampa brewery. Dubbed The Dark Continent, more than 500 uncaged African big-game animals roam the acreage in natural habitats. Other A-B theme parks include Adventure Island (a water park also located in Tampa), Busch Garden's The Old Country (a park styled on 17th-century Europe located in Williamsburg, Virginia) and Sesame Place (a futuristic play park for children in Langhorne, Pennsylvania). In 1988, 6 million people attended these parks. Anheuser-Busch tripled theme park business in 1989 by buying seven parks, including four Sea World parks (and the rights to Shamu, the killer whale). Anheuser-Busch has owned the St. Louis Cardinals baseball team since 1953. Twenty years

earlier the company bought a team of purebred Clydesdale horses. These horses, hitched to four-ton antique beer wagons, frequently appear in parades, festivals, rodeos and state fairs. They are stabled near the mother brewery in St. Louis.

History. Eberhard Anheuser, a St. Louis soap maker, took over a failing brewery in 1860, but his son-in-law, German immigrant Adolphus Busch, deserves the credit for making the firm a success. Busch perfected the Budweiser's formula, which imitated the light beer brewed in the Bohemian town of Budweis. Busch guessed correctly that many drinkers would prefer the light brew to the heavy beers then marketed. As the beer's popularity surged, the company even had two songs commissioned: "Budweiser's a Friend of Mine" in 1907, and the preposterous "Under the Anheuser Bush" a few years later. A second beer, Michelob, was introduced in 1896 but remained a draught-only beer until the 1960s, when it became the first of the superpremium brands.

Anheuser-Busch's biggest survival challenge came not from other competitors but from Prohibition. When the Volstead Act closed breweries in 1920, August Busch, the founder's son, struggled to keep the company alive. He turned from beer to yeast, refrigeration cabinets, bus and truck bodies, corn and malt syrup and soft drinks—all the while lobbying to have Prohibition repealed. When repeal finally came in 1933, Anheuser-Busch had trucks of beer ready to roll to the bars of St. Louis. But the struggle had taken its toll. In poor health, August Busch shot himself to death in 1934. He was succeeded by his elder son, Adolphus Busch II, who died childless in 1946. Next in line was his brother, August A. Busch, Jr., known as Gussie. A hard-driving salesman, Gussie used to whistle-stop the U.S. in an 86-foot stainless-steel private railroad car with a wood-paneled office, a sitting room, four conference rooms, kitchen, bar and plenty of Budweiser. At home he would entertain wholesalers, retailers and saloonkeepers at his 34-room French Renaissance chateau set on 220 acres of rolling land outside St. Louis. There, visitors could stroll quietly in the formal gardens; view the 350-yard fence made entirely of Civil War rifle barrels; or

THE BEER MARKET

Brewer	Market Share
1. Anheuser-Busch	41.1%
2. Miller	21.3%
3. Stroh	10.7%
4. Coors	8.6%
5. Heileman	8.0%
6. Others	10.3 %

Source: Beverage Industry Annual Manual, 1989/1990.

see the bison, North African mountain sheep and rare deer in his private wildlife park. After retiring in 1975, Gussie remained active as president of the St. Louis Cardinals. To cheer his team to victory, he would regularly ride into the Cardinals' Busch Stadium in a wagon pulled by Clydesdale horses, waving a red cowboy hat.

Gussie's son, August A. Busch III, had been in training for his father's job since the day he was born. "Five drops of Budweiser from an eyedropper were the first things in my mouth when I was a few hours old," he told *Fortune* when he took over the top spot in 1975. "Father had arranged it with the doctor, to Mother's dismay." Augie, as he's known, brings with him a whole set of modern management skills, but doesn't have his father's personal flair. However, in the mid-1970s, when Miller Brewing, newly acquired by Philip Morris, began to make a run at the A-B flagship brand, Budweiser, the company's leader, August A. Busch III, said: "Tell Miller to come right along, but tell them to bring lots of money." In the mid-1980s, when Coors entered the New York metropolitan market, A-B supplied wholesalers with a 300-page "Coors Defense Plan" and made available extra funds to sponsor events such as Hispanic parades.

Owners and rulers. Busch family members are believed to own at least 25 percent of the stock. Gussie Busch died at age 90 in 1989. At his death he owned 12.5 percent of the company, worth over $1.3 billion. Chairman August A. Busch III's son, August A. Busch IV, works in the company. Through most of the 1980s the A-B board included two women—Vilma S. Martinez, a Los Angeles attorney and former head of the Mexican-American Legal Defense Fund; and a black, Sybil C. Mobley, dean of the business school at Florida A&M University.

As a place to work. Everyone who works for the brewery is entitled to two free cases of beer a month. If you work in the St. Louis headquarters, you'll feel part of history. Three buildings have been designated historical landmarks. The Brew House has been brewing beer since 1892. And some company executives have offices in the grade-school building August Busch, Jr., attended as a child. The Clydesdale stables, which date from 1885, are located in St. Louis, Missouri; Merrimack, New Hampshire; and Romoland, California. Over half of A-B's employees are represented by unions, 12,300 of them by the Teamsters, and their labor relations are generally good. Brewery workers get top scale. The last strike A-B had was in 1976 when they toughed out the Teamsters in a 95-day walkout. They also toughed out Jessie Jackson in 1982 when the civil rights leader demanded A-B sign a pledge to hire more blacks and buy from more black-owned companies. A-B said with an 18 percent minority work force, they had nothing to be ashamed of.

Social responsibility. In 1987, two top sales executives were arrested for taking kickbacks. They were fired—along with company president Dennis Long. A-B has faced mounting criticism for promoting beer to young people. Particularly controversial was the Budweiser ad campaign featuring the Budweiser bullterrier Spuds McKenzie—"the original party animal." T-shirts depicting Spuds became popular among young children and adolescents. In response the brewery started public service "Know When to Say When" campaign. In 1989 they spent $30 million on public service commercials, many of which discouraged viewers from driving after drinking. On the other hand, Anheuser-Busch spends $635 million a year on advertising to encourage people to drink their beers.

Global presence. Small, but that's expected to change in the 1990s as A-B opens a theme park in Barcelona, Spain, which will be their opening wedge in penetrating the beer market there. Watch for the St. Louis brewer to acquire European breweries, returning to their German roots. Budweiser is now sold in Britain and Japan.

Stock performance. Anheuser-Busch stock bought for $1,000 in 1980 sold for $13,010 on January 2, 1990.

Consumer brands.

    Beers: Budweiser, Michelob, Busch, Bud Light, Michelob Light, Natural Light, LA, Michelob Classic Dark, King Cobra.

    Imports: Carlsberg, Carlsberg Light, Elephant Malt Liquor.

    Baked goods: Colonial, Rainbo, Kilpatrick's, Earth Grains.

    Other food products: El Charrito, Eagle Snacks, Cape Cod.

Anheuser-Busch Companies, One Busch Place, St. Louis, MO 63118; (314) 577-3314.

2

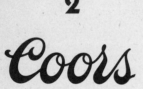

#4 *in brewing*

Employees: 10,600
Sales: $1.8 billion
Profits: $13 million
Founded: 1873
Headquarters: Golden, Colorado

Run by a vocal, right-wing family, Coors came out of the closet during the 1980s. Prior to 1980, Coors beer was found only in the western states. Now it's available in the entire U.S. (and even brewed under license in Japan by Asahi and in Canada by Molson). Before 1980, all Coors beer was brewed and packaged in the world's largest brewery (fed by 60 underground springs) at Golden, Colorado, 20 miles west of Denver. Soon, Coors beer will also be brewed in Shenandoah, Virginia—forcing the company to abandon their powerful slogan, "Brewed with Pure Rocky Mountain Spring Water." Entering the decade, Coors had two brands, Coors and Coors Light; by 1990, nine.

Once upon a time, Coors didn't have a marketing department. "We thought we

The first commercial brewery in the U.S. was opened in 1632 by the Dutch West India Company in lower Manhattan.

were doing the retailers a favor to bring beer to them," said Peter Coors. "We got arrogant." In the early 1980s, they had a shoestring advertising budget under $30 million, nowhere near the budgets of rivals Anheuser-Busch and Miller. As the 1980s closed, Coors was shelling out over $200 million, and had bumped up their share of the beer market to 9 percent (from 7.5 percent in 1980). Coors passed Heileman to take over fourth place in the industry behind Anheuser-Busch, Miller and Stroh (a brewer they almost acquired). Their best-selling brand: Coors Light. Of the 16.3 million barrels brewed in 1988, 10.4 million were Coors Light.

History. Adolph Herman Joseph Coors came to the U.S. in 1868 to avoid the German draft. After working at odd jobs in the East, he came to Colorado to start his brewery in 1873. In 1929, he died under mysterious circumstances—falling out of a hotel window. He was succeeded by his son, Adolph Jr., who was succeeded by his sons—Adolph III, William and Joseph. In 1959, Adolph III was kidnapped and killed. Coors got through Prohibition by using their plant to make near beer and malted milk. Coors became a cult beer in the 1960s and 1970s as thousands of people, including former President Gerald Ford and ex–Secretary of State Henry Kissinger, smuggled cases back East for their own consumption. Paul Newman and Clint Eastwood even demanded Coors on their movie sets. Part of the appeal came from the beer's light, clean taste. It's unpasteurized beer and uses no preservatives. So, Coors must be shipped refrigerated.

The distinction of being the first city outside of Golden to brew Coors beer goes to Memphis. Coors took over the Stroh's brewery there on September 1, 1990.

Coors is committed to developing the company's nonbeer side. "If Adolph Coors Co. became an energy or ceramics company with a brewery division, that wouldn't bother me at all," William Coors

The Coors boys (standing L to R) Joe Jr., Pete, (seated L to R) Jeff, Joe Sr., and Bill.

said in 1987. In addition to ceramics, coal and natural gas, Coors is involved in aluminum technology and recycling.

Owners and rulers. Although you can purchase Coors stock, the Coors family has a stranglehold on 30 percent of the nonvoting shares and owns all the voting shares. The elder statesmen at Coors are brothers William (Bill) and Joseph, grandsons of the founder. They serve on the nine-member board, along with Joseph's three sons: Joseph Jr., Jeffrey and Peter. The youngest of Joseph's three sons, Peter, heads Coors Brewing Company. Bill Coors, 74, has been chairman of the firm since 1970, and in 1989 resumed the title of president—replacing Joseph Jr. Joe Coors, Sr., is vice chairman.

Thirty-six family members still live in the valley surrounding the brewery and have engaged in enough internal squabbling and power plays to provide TV scriptwriters with enough material to fill a whole season's worth of "Dynasty," "Dallas" and "Falcon Crest" combined. Countless episodes could be devoted to Joe's eldest son, Joe Jr., who was disinherited and exiled for 10 years for marrying too young (he was in college at the time). Joe Jr. didn't get back into his father's good graces for years, even after what he called divine intervention. He claims God spoke to him when he was on the 16th hole of a San Diego golf course: "Suddenly I heard this voice saying to me—I can't explain it clearly," he told the *Los Angeles Times*, "but it was just so real, and I knew it was

God. And He said, 'Go home. Go home.'" Unimpressed, his father and uncle sent him away again. Joe Jr. was eventually taken back into the fold and now heads the company's ceramics division. Joe Jr. credits his return to the influence of his mother, Holly, a fervent born-again Christian fundamentalist like her five sons. In an ironic twist the TV soap opera writers would love, Joe Sr. has become the family's black sheep after running off with his younger mistress to live in the wine country of Northern California.

While all this was going on, two of Joe's sons conducted a coup when they heard their uncle was considering bringing in an outsider to run the business. Before any of their brothers knew about it, Pete and Jeff had themselves appointed to run the brewing company. J. R. Ewing would have been proud.

As a place to work. Coors attracted the undying enmity of organized labor by breaking a strike and then getting newly hired workers to vote out the union in early 1980. The AFL-CIO responded with a consumer boycott that lasted until 1987 when Peter, as the brewing division's new president, negotiated a union settlement. No sooner had the AFL-CIO faded from the picture than Teamsters union organizers were talking with the Colorado workers. Jeff Coors expects a big fight: "What else should we do? Just give 'em the keys to the place? Is that what you do? It's just like inviting the Russians in to take over America."

Social responsibility. Coors is a family many Americans love to hate. Their outspoken, conservative views have led, in addition to boycotts by organized labor, boycotts by women, gays, blacks and Hispanics. The family's loudest voice is that of vice chairman Joseph Coors, Sr. He achieved considerable notoriety by testifying during the nationally televised Iran-Contra hearings about his donation of a $65,000 airplane to Lt. Oliver North's scheme to help the Nicaraguan contras. Joe's vocal opposition to the Equal Rights Amendment precipitated a boycott against Coors sponsored by the National Organization of Women. Joe's less well-known brother Bill, company chairman, alienated blacks by telling an assembly of black businesspeople in 1984 that "one of the best things [slave traders] did for you was drag your ancestors over here in chains." To make sure not to miss possible Hispanics in the audience, he added that descendants of wetbacks should also be thankful even though their ancesters had to swim the Rio Grande to get to America. Keeping the family tradition alive, Joe's son Peter posed for National Rifle Association magazine ads in hunting garb while holding a rifle under the headline, "I'm the NRA."

During the 1980s, Coors did a lot of damage control among black and Hispanic organizations by giving them money, pledging to buy from minority organizations and improve their record on minority hiring and promotions. As a result, most of the boycotts were dropped. Coors also has been active in the fight against illiteracy, pledging $40 million in 1990.

Stock performance. Adolph Coors Company stock bought for $1,000 in 1980 sold for $1,888 on January 2, 1990.

Consumer brands.

Beers: Coors, Coors Light, Coors Extra Gold, Herman Joseph's Original Draft, Herman Joseph's Light, Killian's Red draft, Keystone, Keystone Light, and Winterfest, "a special holiday beer offered between mid-November and early January."

Adolph Coors Company, Golden, CO 80401; (303) 279-6565.

3

STROH

#3 *in beer*

Employees: 7,000
Sales: $1.5 billion
Founded: 1850
Headquarters: Detroit, Michigan

Peter Stroh, great-great-grandson of the founder, used to boast this Detroit-based beer maker is "the only major brewery in America where the family still makes decisions." August A. Busch III or Joe Coors might quibble with this claim—as their families still own sizable chunks of stock in their companies—but there's no gainsaying Stroh's assertion that among the majors, Stroh is the last of what used to be many 100 percent family-owned breweries. Stroh took 128 years to introduce a second beer. They waited even longer before they expanded sales beyond the Great Lakes states. But when they realized the national brands could drive them out of business, Stroh shed their traditional caution and expanded. In two years, 1981 and 1982, they became the nation's third largest beer maker by swallowing up F&M Schaefer and Jos. Schlitz. And they almost gave up their independence in 1989 by merging with Coors, a union that came a cropper at the last moment. A few months later they wanted to buy out Heileman.

Change suits Chairman Peter W. Stroh just fine. He originally wanted to join the CIA for a life of adventure, but an accident sidelined him three days after he got his security clearance. While recuperating, his father died, and he was recruited into the family business instead. With 17 brands, Stroh now has beers to suit all pocketbooks, plus light beers for the diet-conscious and upscale labels to balance their traditional blue-collar brew. Instead of one antiquated hometown brewery, they have modern plants around the country. And most of their beers are now available to a larger, national audience.

TOP 10 IMPORTED BEERS

	Brand	Country	Pints
1.	Heineken	Netherlands	52.3 billion
2.	Corona Extra	Mexico	27.9 billion
3.	Beck's	W. Germany	16.9 billion
4.	Molson Golden	Canada	16.7 billion
5.	Labatt's Blue	Canada	9.7 billion
6.	Moosehead	Canada	9.2 billion
7.	Amsted Light	Netherlands	7.7 billion
8.	Tecate	Mexico	5.5 billion
9.	St Pauli Girl	W. Germany	4.0 billion
10.	Fosters	Australia	4.6 billion

Source: *Impact,* 1989.

History. The Stroh family has been making beer since the late 1700s when Johann Stroh offered homemade brew to guests at his inn in Kirn, Germany. His grandson Bernhard took the tradition to America when he fled the revolution of 1848 and opened a small brewery in Detroit. Great-grandson Julius introduced the brewing process that made Stroh distinctive—fire-brewing. The technique uses a direct flame to heat the brewing kettles, rather than steam. And instead of the big steel vats most brewers use, Stroh uses relatively small copper kettles. Somehow, this approach affects beer's flavor, or so the family believes. They still fire-brew Stroh's, Stroh Light and Signature, their superpremium brand. They're the only major brewery to use the process.

Although Stroh prospered as the automobile industry grew, they sold beer relatively close to home. Around Detroit, they were the working-class favorite. In the 1970s with the Big Three automakers taking a beating from the Japanese, Detroit was not the cars-and-bars city it had once been. Stroh didn't sell in the most promising places to boost sales: the West and Sunbelt, where the population was young and growing. The solution Peter Stroh opted for was going national. As he told *Business Week,* "It was either grow or go."

If Stroh was a long time making the decision, they moved fast when they did. They added Stroh Light in 1978 and expanded Stroh's market to 17 states by 1979. Stroh used the acquired Schaefer/Schlitz breweries and distributors to put their own beers into national circulation in 1984. But with an advertising budget one-fourth Anheuser-Busch's, they tend to spend their money on "overlooked" sports on cable TV where their ads won't be hopelessly outnumbered by the two industry leaders. The "Alex the dog" commercial that introduced Stroh's to a non-Midwestern audience had retailers clamoring for posters of the canine star. In 1989 Stroh dropped the Alex ads in favor of ones featuring chairman Peter Stroh.

Owners and rulers. Stroh is owned by 27 descendants of Bernhard Stroh. Three of them, including Peter, work at the company. Since Stroh's beginnings, only two outsiders have run day-to-day operations. The current president, Roger T. Fridholm, is one of them. Stroh has recruited outsiders—most of them from companies with lots of marketing savvy, like Heublein, PepsiCo and Procter & Gamble—since the late 1960s. And the beer wars being what they are, Peter Stroh told the *Princeton Alumni Weekly* in 1985, "We can all envision circumstances under which someone who is not a member of the family might take over."

As a place to work. Stroh closed their original hometown brewery in 1985, throwing 1,159 people out of work. They kept the goodwill of former employees, however, with a $1.5 million placement program, plus $30 million in severance pay and benefits. Among their efforts, Stroh spent $100,000 to renovate an old school as a job search center and gave ex-employees unlimited free telephone calls, both professional and personal. A year after the plant closed in May 1985, all 180 managers had new jobs and 98 percent of the blue-collar workers did, too.

Consumer brands.

Beers: Stroh's, Stroh's Light, Signature, Piels Draft Style, Piels Lights, Schaefer, Schaefer Light, Goebel, Schlitz, Schlitz Light, Schlitz Malt Liquor, Schlitz Red Bull, Old Milwaukee, Old Milwaukee Light, Erlanger, Primo, Silver Thunder.

The first privately endowed women's college, Vassar, was founded by brewer Matthew Vassar in 1861.

Coolers: White Mountain Cooler.

Juice-and-soda: Sundance.

Imports: König, Barbican.

The Stroh Brewery Company, 100 River Place, Detroit, MI 48207; (313) 446-2000.

4

HOUSE OF HEILEMAN ®

#5 *in beer*

Employees: 7,500
Sales: $1.2 billion
Profits: $48.3 million
Founded: 1853
Headquarters: La Crosse, Wisconsin

You could say the 1980s were exciting for this Wisconsin brewer—and that would be an understatement. They made a stab at buying Schlitz—and were shot down. Antitrust officials also scuttled Heileman's inital attempt to take over Pabst. In 1983, however, they approved a deal giving Heileman three Pabst breweries and the Weinhard and Lone Star brands. Heileman then put their muscle behind local and regional brews acquired in previous years (Heileman bought 13 breweries between 1960 and 1980), so that by mid-1987 Heileman was selling 47 different beers and holding on to fourth place in the industry, up from sixth in 1980. Their principal brands were Old Style, Rainier, Schmidt, Lone Star, Henry Weinhard's, Carling Black Label and (their one national brand) Colt 45. Then, in September 1987, they sold out—not to another American beer company but to a pugnacious Australian empire builder, Alan Bond, whose sailboat, *Australia II*,

had captured America's Cup in 1983. Bond paid $1.3 billion for the brewery founded in 1853 by German immigrant Gottlieb Heileman.

The chubby Bond, who left school at 14 to make money, appeared the perfect marriage partner for Heileman. Bond pushed out Russell G. Cleary as chairman in 1989. Cleary had been with Heileman since 1971. Notorious for his pugnacity, Cleary reveled in pushing strong local beers, thumbing his nose at the big brewers and their national brands. "We don't give a damn what anybody thinks," he once told a *Forbes* reporter. Cleary used to finish his day at Heileman headquarters at La Crosse, Wisconsin, by knocking back brews with workers at the company bar. To reward salesmen, he gave out replicas of Thompson submachine guns. "Look, I'm an ornery guy," he told another reporter.

Alan Bond also likes to play the tough guy, getting his kicks, as *Business Week* said, from "proving the rest of the world wrong." In addition to his audacious capture of the America's Cup, the first time in 132 years the New York Yacht Club had been defeated, Bond went after companies all over the globe, building an empire spanning many industries (brewing, broadcasting, publishing, mining, hotels, real estate) and many countries (Australia, the U.S., Britain, Hong Kong, Chile). And even though he owed $7 billion, he was enjoying life. By decade's end, however, Bond's empire began to unravel. Strapped for cash, he couldn't meet interest payments—and creditors pressed for a restructuring of his companies (one embarrassment for Bond came in early 1990, when Sotheby's foreclosed on a loan Bond had taken to buy Van Gogh's *Irises* for $53 million—then the highest price in history paid for a painting).

Heileman was caught in Bond's maelstrom. In 1980 they had shipped 19 million barrels, but only 13 million in 1989, falling to fifth place in the industry. Their top seller, Old Style, was bumped from first place in the Chicago market. In 1988, Heileman sold off all nonbrewing businesses: snack foods, bakery products (Holsum bread) and machine products. Bond's right-hand man in the sell-off was Heileman's new president, 43-year-old Murray S. Cutbush, who'd helped Bond buy Heileman in the first place. An Aussie by birth, Cutbush is a CPA by training. It still wasn't clear—in mid-1990—whether Bond would hang on to Heileman or whether parts of the firm would be sold off to meet bankers' demands. One suitor who announced designs on Heileman in mid-1990 was Detroit's Stroh Brewery.

The 1990s can only be anticlimactic.

Consumer brands.

Beers: Old Style, Special Export, Blatz, Carling Black Label, Rainier, Rainier L.A., Rainier Ale, Milwaukee 1851, Schmidt, Rheingold, Duquesne, Ortlieb, Tuborg, Wiedemann, Red White & Blue, Stag, Sterling, Henry Weinhard's Private Reserve, Henry Weinhard's Dark, Weinhard's Ireland Style Ale, Lone Star, Heidelberg, Grain Belt, Falls City, Iron City, National Premium, Hacker-Pschorr Brau, Moravia, Moravia Dark, plus 20 light-beer versions of these labels.

Malt liquors: Colt 45, Champale, Mickeys, Black Label 11-11.

Nonalcoholic malt beverages: Kingsbury, Schmidt Select, Zing, Metbrau, Black Label.

Coolers: Champale Cooler, Fireside Cooler.

Sparkling mineral water: La Crois, Cold Spring.

G. Heileman Brewing Company, 100 Harborview Plaza, La Crosse, WI 54601; (608) 785-1000.

WINES & LIQUOR

Drinking is going out of style in the U.S. During the 1980s Scotch, gin, bourbon and vodka sales were down, and blended whiskey sales were about chopped in half. The only drink holding its own was rum.

At decade's start, the wine industry, centered in California, was euphoric about rising consumption and looked forward to sales doubling in the 1980s. Instead of increasing, sales of table wine declined about 10 percent. And not just California wines were hit. Imported wines also suffered a bruising sales drop.

The alcoholic beverage industry is clearly worried about the increasing publicity of the serious health and social problems alcohol abuse causes. (Alcohol is the second leading preventable cause of death, after smoking.) In a 1989 address before the annual marketing seminar sponsored by the industry newsletter Impact, Seagram executive Edgar Bronfman, Jr., said the industry faces the "most hostile environment" since Prohibition. Bronfman added, "In Americans' minds, alcohol is more and more linked to the use of illegal drugs," and the industry's task therefore is to "restore the belief that the responsible use of our products is one of life's pleasures."

1

Grand Metropolitan

#1 *in retail sales of eyecare products (worldwide), wine and spirits (worldwide), vodka (worldwide)*

#2 *in British dairy foods, gin (worldwide), Scotch (worldwide)*

#4 *in British brewing*

Employees: 137,000
Sales: $14.6 billion
Profits: $823 million
Founded: 1934
Headquarters: London, England

Most Americans have never heard of this company, which emerged during the 1980s from a British base of pubs, distillers, dairies and betting parlors to become a world giant in food and beverages. On the other hand, most Americans have heard of Burger King restaurants, Smirnoff vodka, Alpo dog food and Pillsbury flour, all of which Grand Metropolitan owns—although they began by running seedy British hotels.

Sir Maxwell Joseph, a British financier, created Grand Met. In 1926, the 16-year-old Joseph went to work at a London real estate agency. He set up his own agency in 1931, and was believed to be the youngest real estate agent in Britain. Joseph began empire building after World War II, when he bought a series of rundown hotels in London, the provinces and abroad. In 1962, he named his company Grand Metropolitan Hotels (shortened to Grand Metropolitan in 1972 after buying hundreds of companies).

When Joseph died in 1982, Stanley Grinstead, an avid horse-racer, led the company. In 1986, he was replaced by Allen Sheppard, who remained CEO and chairman through the decade. Sheppard, son of a railway worker, led Grand Met through a dizzying frenzy of activity. In 1985, Grand Met acquired Dallas-based Pearle Health Services, which now operates more than 1,300 U.S. optical stores. In 1987, they paid $1.3 billion to buy Heublein (the Smirnoff vodka producer) and Almaden vineyards. In the next year, they sold the classy Meurice Hotel in Paris; bought the Vision Express and U.S. Eye+Tech stores; sold (for $750 million) Pepsi-Cola bottling plants in Fresno, California, and Columbia, South Carolina; gained exclusive rights to run off-track betting in Malaysia; sold to the Japanese (for $2 billion) the Inter-Continental hotel chain bought (for $500 million) in 1981 from Pan American World Airways; purchased the Wienerwald spit-roasted chicken restaurants (231 of them) in Germany and the Spaghetti Factory restaurants (5 of them) in Switzerland; and acquired the William Hill betting shops in Britain (which with the Mecca parlors they already owned, made Grand Met the largest legal bookmaker in Britain, with more than 1,700 shops). Wow! In 1989, they picked up (for $5.8 billion) the Pillsbury company of Minneapolis (although the Bumble Bee tuna and Van de Kamp seafood units were sold). That year

they also acquired the Christian Brothers winery in California's Napa Valley.

The family lineup never stays the same here. In 1990, Grand Met sold their retail betting shops in Britain, pocketing a profit of $823 million, and put one of their U.S. businesses, Alpo dog food, up for sale.

Grand Met's stated aim is to rank among the world's top six companies in three areas: food, alcoholic beverages and retailing. They became number one in spirits in 1987, the acquisition of Heublein vaulting them ahead of Seagram. And although Burger King is far behind rival fast-food king McDonald's, the firm contributes a whopping 15 percent of Grand Met's profits. Other Grand Met businesses are less flashy, but ubiquitous—such as American Water Works, the U.S.'s largest private water company.

In contrast to their businesses, which encourage people to drink and gamble, Grand Met emphasizes social responsibility. In Britain, they support regeneration of inner cities and youth training. They belong to the Per Cent Club, whose members donate a minimum of one-half of one percent of pretax profits "to the benefit of the community." Grand Met notes overseas units "are required to act with the highest degree of integrity, both in complying with local laws and in trying to work in sympathy with the economic and social aims of the host country."

Consumer brands.

Food: Pillsbury, Green Giant, Totino's, Jeno's, Hungry Jack, Joan of Arc, Haagen-Dazs.

Drinks: J&B, Bailey's, Malibu, Smirnoff, Popov, Gilbey's, Bombay, Croft, Lancers, Black Velvet, Metaxa, Christian Brothers, Delaforce, Almaden Vineyards, Sambvca Romana, Archer's, Agua Libra, Cinzano, Absolut, Grand Marnier, Cointreau, Amaretto di Saronno, José Cuervo, Beaulieu, Mouton Cadet, Dos Equis, Foster's, Moosehead, Arrow, Finlandia, Pernod, Inglenook.

Retailing: Pearle Vision Center, Burger King.

Grand Metropolitan, 11-12 Hanover Square, London W1A 1DP, England; (44)-1-629-7488.

Grand Met USA, 100 Paragon Drive, Montvale, NJ 07645; (201) 573-4000.

2

Seagram

#1 *in hard liquor, orange juice, wine coolers*

#2 *in cognac*

Employees: 17,600
Sales: $4.5 billion
Profits: $711 million
Founded: 1924
Headquarters: Montreal, Canada
U.S. Headquarters: New York City, New York

What do you do when your main product is falling out of favor? For Seagram, the answer is: "Pass the juice and soda—and thank God for Du Pont."

Seagram supplies some of the most well-known liquor brands in the nation— V.O., 7 Crown and Chivas Regal, to name a few. They have cornered 15 percent of the U.S. market for spirits, 37 percent of the wine coolers sold in America, and after their 1988 purchase of Martell, Seagram became the world's second largest cognac producer. They own distilleries and wineries in Europe, including Mumm, one of France's biggest champagne houses. Despite all this, and much to the founding family's dismay, whiskey sales plummeted during the 1980s. Seagram, which entered the decade as the largest maker of distilled spirits, seemed to accept the verdict of the marketplace. They bought Tropicana juices and Soho natural sodas while unloading many of their U.S. wineries (Paul Masson, Taylor California Cellars, Taylor, Great Western and Gold Seal Vineyards). They sold 17 of their venerable brands, including the entire vodka lineup (Sam Bronfman, Seagram's late founder, would have been ecstatic; he snobbishly disdained vodka all his life). Meanwhile, thanks to their position as 24 percent owner of Du Pont, they sat back and collected fat dividend checks. Du Pont now accounts for 80 percent of Seagram's profits.

History. The word *bronfan* means "brandy" in Yiddish, so perhaps it was fated when Yechiel Bronfman fled Czarist anti-Semitism in Russia and came to Canada in 1889, he would become a liquor distributor. His sons, Samuel and Allan, started selling booze by mail order during World War I. Although every Canadian province except Quebec was dry at the time, a legal quirk allowed liquor sales through the mails. In the early 1920s, liquor was legalized in the provinces, and Sam and Allan went into the distillery business. In 1927, they bought out the much larger Joseph E. Seagram & Sons, adopted the name, and opened for business the next year.

At that time, Prohibition was still in effect in America, and smuggling whiskey across the border was big business. During Prohibition, the Bronfmans sold whiskey to bootleggers, who then shipped it to America. Years later, Samuel Bronfman told *Fortune*, "Of course, we knew where it went, but we had no legal proof. And I never went on the other side of the border to count the empty Seagram bottles." After Prohibition's repeal, Seagram had an advantage over U.S. competitors: warehouses full of aging whiskey. Bronfman's old mail-order business had taught him the value of brand names. Until the mid-1930s Americans relied on local brands. In 1934 Seagram introduced Seagram's 5 Crown, which soon became Seagram's 7 Crown. Seagram blended whiskeys were a great success, and by 1938 Seagram topped the liquor business. But beginning in the 1950s and 1960s, Seagram was faced with an ongoing problem: American tastes were shifting away from whiskey, toward lighter beverages.

Faced with steadily declining U.S. alcohol consumption, Seagram has had to get into other fields. Their first major nonalcoholic business venture came in the 1960s, with the purchase of several oil and gas concerns (sold for a hefty $2.3 billion in 1980). In 1980, by virtue of their holdings in the Conoco oil company, which Du Pont bought, Seagram became the 19 percent owner of the nation's largest chemical producer. It's not the same chemistry as whiskey, but the quarterly dividend checks are regular—and ample: $263 million in 1990 for a stake that has been enlarged to 24 percent.

Owners and rulers. The Bronfmans own 38 percent of Seagram. The family empire was built largely by Samuel (Mr. Sam) Bronfman, whose colossal temper tantrums were legendary (he was famous for hurling objects at underlings almost every day). Mr. Sam was an influential force at the company until his death in 1971. The Bronfman clan has their share of sibling rivalry. Mr. Sam sqeezed brother Allan (and his two sons) out of the company by naming his son Edgar CEO in the late 1960s. Edgar was still CEO in 1990 but the rising star was his son, Edgar Jr., named president in 1989 at age 34. Because he is the younger son (older brother Sam runs the Seagram Classics Wine Co.) and never attended college, Edgar Jr. seemed an unlikely choice for successor. He is known as a member of the Hollywood jet set (he had a stint as a film producer, although his movies were bombs). At 24, Edgar Jr. eloped with a black actress, to whom he had been introduced by singer Dionne Warwick. When he was 27 he sailed into his father's company, knowing little about the business. Seven years later he was chief operating officer.

Social responsibility. In an era sensitive to alcohol abuse, Seagram ruffled feathers in the late 1980s by launching a "frequent drinker" promotion for their Chivas Regal scotch brand. By sending in two labels from Chivas Regal bottles, drinkers could upgrade their seating on Trans World Airlines flights. Aside from critics who challenge anything encouraging more drinking, one ad agency executive noted: "It's really bizarre. Chivas has an image of something you would savor, rather than guzzle." Edgar Bronfman has close ties to Israel and is a prominant fund-raiser for that country.

Global presence. Headquartered in Montreal (but really run out of New York), Seagram has affiliated companies in 27 countries. They do 39 percent of sales in Europe and 12 percent in other countries outside the U.S. And in those countries where whiskey is not yet a bad word, they are pushing their spirits. Four Roses, just about dead in the U.S., is a big seller these days in Japan.

Stock performance. Seagram stock bought for $1,000 in 1980 sold for $8,329 on January 2, 1990.

Consumer brands.

Whiskey: Crown Royal, Seagram's V.O., Seagrams "83," Seagram's Five Star, Lord Calvert, 7 Crown, Kessler, Calvert Extra.

WHERE AMERICANS GET THEIR IMPORTED WINE

		Market Share
1.	Italy	43.7%
2.	France	29.9%
3.	Germany	9.9%
4.	Portugal	5.1%
5.	Spain	2.0%
6.	Other	9.4 %

Scotch whiskey: Chivas Regal, Royal Salute, Passport, Glenlivet.

Gin: Seagram's extra dry, Boodles, Burnett's.

Rum: Myers, Captain Morgan.

Cognac: Martell.

Wines: Sterling, Monterey Vineyard, B&G, Mumm Champagne, Domaine Mumm, Cuvée Napa.

Wine coolers: Seagram's.

Soda: Soho.

Vodka: Wyborawa.

Cordials/liqueurs: Leroux.

Fruit juice: Tropicana.

The Seagram Company Ltd., 1430 Peel Street, Montreal, Quebec, Canada H3A 159; (514) 849-5271.

The Seagram Company Ltd., 375 Park Avenue, New York, NY 10152; (212) 572-7462.

3

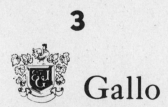

Gallo

#1 *in wine*

Employees: 2,950
Sales: $1 billion
Founded: 1933
Headquarters: Modesto, California

In the wine industry, people joke that Gallo spills more wine than anybody else sells. Even though the label doesn't say Gallo, if your wine is from Modesto, California, you can be sure you're drinking a Gallo product. Modesto is the Gallo outpost—situated south of the more well-known wine regions of Napa and Sonoma valleys. In 1980 Gallo was the largest wine maker in the world, accounting for about one-quarter of the American market. At decade's end, Gallo was still the largest wine maker in the world, and had about 30 percent of the American market. When the 1980s began, Gallo was a private company—the public held no shares. When the 1980s were over, Gallo was still a private company. When the 1980s began, Gallo was owned and run by Ernest and Julio Gallo (70 and 69 years old, respectively), the two brothers who had founded the company right after Prohibiton ended. In 1990, the two brothers, 10 years older, were still running the winery. At the decade's start wine snobs looked down on Gallo for producing cheap jug wines and heavily fortified sweet wines (Thunderbird, Ripple, Night Train) that were favorites of Skid Row derelicts. By the end of the 1980s Gallo was turning out varietal wines that had won the praise of wine experts, and had halted distribution of fortified wines in Skid Row areas.

Gallo is the only major California winery having no tasting room. Their winemaking plant at Modesto looks more like an oil refinery, with its steel holding tanks. Visitors aren't welcome, and Gallo is often reluctant to talk with the press. They made an exception in 1985 when a *Fortune* reporter was granted an interview with the Gallos. The brothers were then infuriated at some of the items in the article—for example, that their father chased his sons across a field with a shotgun before killing himself. The Gallos promptly canceled $650,000 of advertising in Time Inc. publications.

History. Ernest and Julio Gallo were born near Modesto and grew up working their father's small vineyard during Prohibition. In 1933, just before repeal, their father shot and killed their mother and then took his own life. The brothers decided to take their small inheritance (about $6,000) and produce their own commercial bulk wine—learning how to make it from two pamphlets Ernest found in the local library. While Julio pressed the grapes and made the wine, Ernest hopped a flight for Chicago and sold a distributor a contract for 6,000 gallons at 50 cents apiece. He continued east and

eventually found enough distributors to buy the company's entire production. The Gallos profited $34,000 their first year. They plowed it back into equipment, as they did with their second-and third-year profits, until they were finally large enough in 1940 to buy bottling companies in Los Angeles and New Orleans.

After the war Gallo was one of the first wineries to automate, cutting production costs to the bone. They were the first winery to hire research chemists, to abandon traditional wooden storage barrels in favor of stainless steel ones, and to computerize operations. Their salespeople were aggressive with dealers—offering a month's free wine supply in exchange for a good store display. Gallo also became known as a great training ground, and former Gallo people have long held top positions in the wine industry. The most influential factor in establishing Gallo as the nation's premier wine maker has been Ernest's uncanny knack for predicting consumer tastes. For years Gallo researchers knew ghetto blacks bought 40-proof white port and cut the obnoxious aftertaste by adding lemon juice. At Ernest's instructions, they came up with Thunderbird (white port and citric acid) in the late 1950s. The product has been a staple of ghetto drinkers and winos ever since. Ernest also created the pop wine craze of the late 1960s and early 1970s. Julio, as an experiment, had carbonated the company's slow-selling Boone's Farm apple wine in 1969. When sales skyrocketed, Ernest ordered different varieties and flavors. By 1972, when the pop wine boom peaked, Gallo was selling six of the top entries, and 16 million cases to their competitors' mere 2 million. At that point Ernest shrewdly figured the market had topped off and plunged his pop wine profits into promoting dry table wines like Hearty Burgundy, which some wine connoisseurs rated one of the finest wines ever produced in its price range. In the mid-1970s Gallo introduced a line of fine varietals—a move that kept them one step ahead of competitors.

Ernest's prowess continued during the wine cooler fad of the mid-1980s. Gallo pushed their own brand, Bartles & Jaymes, to first place with an ingenious advertising campaign created by the San Francisco agency of Hal Riney & Partners. The *tates pay back only 50 percent of the money they take in from lotteries, whereas slot machines return 90 percent and casino tables almost 97 percent.*

ads featured two folksy fictional characters, Frank Bartles and Ed Jaymes, usually sitting on their front porch. Frank (in real life an Oregon farmer) and the inscrutable Ed (a California contractor) faded from the scene during the late 1980s as consumer tastes shifted to more upscale varietal wines (wines made from a single type of grape). In 1987, Hal Riney resigned the account. Gallo is known as the toughest client in advertising; they have gone through 17 ad agencies in 33 years.

Consumer brands.

Coolers: Bartles & Jaymes.

Table wine: Carlo Rossi, Gallo, William Wycliff, Polo Brindisi.

Sparkling wine: André, Ballatore Spumante.

Low-priced wines: Thunderbird, Boone's Farm, Spañada/Tyrolia, Night Train.

Dessert wines: Gallo Dessert, Gallo Livingston Cellars.

Vermouth: Gallo Vermouth.

Brandy: E&J Brandy.

E. & J. Gallo Winery, Modesto, CA 95353; (209) 579-3111.

GAMBLING

Gambling became the rage in America during the 1980s. Eleven more states opted for lotteries to raise money, bringing the total to 33. (Until 1964 lotteries were illegal in the U.S.) Atlantic City became a gambling resort, attracting 32 million visitors in 1989. Las Vegas clocked 23 million. Donald Trump, Merv Griffin, Holiday Inn and Ramada all decided they wanted to run casinos. While all-time baseball great Pete Rose was ejected from organized baseball over allegations of illegal betting, gambling was becoming a legitimate business, doing openly what people used to be arrested for. Relying on figures industry sources provided, Business Week estimated Americans wagered $240 billion annually and said that "today gambling outlets are almost as ubiquitous and well-patronized as convenience stores." The biggest chunk of that $240 billion annual betting orgy, $161 billion, is put down in the casinos of Nevada and New Jersey. Bally is the biggest company in this industry—but Donald Trump is coming on strong.

1

#1 *in gambling, health clubs, slot machines*

Employees: 33,000
Sales: $2.1 billion
Profits: $26 million
Founded: 1931
Headquarters: Chicago, Illinois

Visualize two scenes. One, a crowded, smoke-filled casino where little old women with gray hair sit mesmerized in front of electronic slot machines, pumping coins into them and continually yanking down the handles of the one-armed bandits. Two, a sleek, carpeted health club where lithe, Spandex-garbed men and women work out on exercise machines or gyrate to the deafening music of an aerobics class.

These two worlds are Bally. They're the nation's largest casino operator—and they make slot machines. They're also the nation's largest healthclub operator—and they make exercise equipment.

Gambling exploded during the 1980s, and Bally, the company with the biggest stake in this pastime, rolled snake eyes. Coming into the decade, Bally made slot and pinball machines and operated amusement arcades where you could find your teenager playing video games. (Those were the glory days.) Coming out of the decade, Bally was operating four big casino hotels, two in Atlantic City, one in Las Vegas and one in Reno; and more than 300 health clubs bearing such names as Jack LaLanne, Vic Tanny, Holiday Health, Scandinavian and Vertical Club. They were also supplying video poker machines to U.S. military bases and lottery ticket machines to 14 states. Bally claims to supply 70 percent of the "instant winner" lottery tickets in the U.S. Although their sales tripled in the 1980s, profits were smaller. Being a croupier is not as easy as you think.

History. Raymond J. Moloney organized Lion Manufacturing in Chicago in 1931 to make coin-operated devices—pinball machines and vending machines. His big seller was a pinball machine he'd invented and called Ballyhoo, after a popular humor magazine of the times. The Ballyhoo was so successful he sold over 50,000 of them. In 1937 he began making slot machines, a gambling device invented by a San Francisco native, Charles Fey, in 1897. Slots are computer-driven today, but Fey's original Liberty Bell design has stood the test of time. Players pull a lever causing three drums in a cabinet to revolve, with the machine paying off when the same symbols line up in a row.

Fey's business never moved beyond California. And 40 years after their founding Lion wasn't doing too well either because slot machines were illegal in most states. In 1949 they stopped making them altogether. Moloney died in 1958, and William O'Donnell, Lion's sales manager, put together a syndicate to buy the company. In that syndicate were people with close ties to Mafioso leader Gerardo Catena. Catena was, in fact, a silent partner in the company that bought Lion in 1963. The newly organized Lion immedi-

ately came out with the Money Honey slot machine, the first slot to use an electrical payout mechanism triggered when a player hit a winning combination—coins would cascade out of the machine and hit a metal tray, producing an electrifying sound in the casino. It's still a feature of today's slot machines. As Bally points out, they could make a durable plastic hopper to catch the coins, but it wouldn't produce the metal-clanging *sound* so much a part of the casino environment.

Lion changed their name to Bally, after their pinball machine, in 1968, and they sold stock to the public the following year. They became the largest slot machine supplier to Las Vegas casinos. Slots pay out to players about 85 percent of the money they collect. That leaves a nice bundle for the casinos, and in the 1970s Bally decided they would like to cross over and become a casino operator, too. This decision was inspired by New Jersey's plan to convert seedy Atlantic City to the "Las Vegas of the East."

For many years, Bally was accused of having illegal underworld connections. Bally underwent umpteen investigations during the 1970s—by Nevada and New Jersey, the Securities and Exchange Commission, the Justice Department and various other law enforcement agencies in the U.S. and abroad. The upshot was William O'Donnell had to leave the company he had built and put his stock (then 7.3 percent of the total) into a trust. Bally was then allowed to open their Park Place casino in Atlantic City in 1980.

During the 1980s, Bally used gambling profits to buy other businesses. In 1981 they bought Six Flags amusement parks and in 1983 their first health clubs. Then they picked up more casinos—in 1986 the MGM Grand Hotels in Las Vegas and Reno (their names changed to Ballys) and in 1987 the Golden Nugget casino-hotel in Atlantic City (now called the Bally Grand). If there was a grand design to this expansion, it was never made clear, not even to the people running Bally. At one point or another during the 1980s, Bally announced their intention to sell several of their businesses. For various reasons—1987's stock market crash, inability to find buyers, refusal of New Jersey gaming regulators to accept Drexel Burnham Lambert as an underwriter—the only one they sold off was Six Flags, in 1987.

Donald Trump, New York real estate wheeler-dealer, accumulated 9.9 percent of Bally's stock in 1987, complaining about the way the company was run. To get rid of him, Bally bought back his stock at a premium. Trump made a quick profit of $25 million, which he invested in Atlantic City casinos to compete against Bally. By the end of the 1980s Bally found themselves competing against 11 other Atlantic City casinos.

Owners and rulers. Presiding over this chaos is chain-smoking (he admits to no personal interest in the health clubs) Robert E. Mullane, a Harvard Business School graduate who joined Bally in 1971 and became CEO in 1979 after the shotgun departure of O'Donnell. He was still CEO in 1990 when he was 57 (1988 pay: $1.8 million). Top managers at Bally are well rewarded. In 1983, when they bought the Health & Tennis clubs, Bally agreed to pay cofounders Roy Zurkowski and Donahue L. Wildman salaries of $2 million a year—each. Casino boss Richard Gillman has a base salary of $2.2 million a year, plus bonuses. In 1988 he made $4.4 million. Former Apollo astronaut James Lovell was elected to Bally's board in 1986.

As a place to work. Bally introduced employee town meetings at their Bally Grand casino in Atlantic City and opened a new employee dining room at the Las Vegas Bally. Benefits include a profit-sharing plan for all salaried employees and a savings plan that includes a 50 percent company match up to 6 percent of pay.

Social responsibility. In response to numerous critics of gambling and lotteries, Bally points out graciously that lotteries fund social programs and services. In 1988 they sponsored an exhibit, "The Legacy of Lotteries," at the Chicago Public Library and the Illinois State Museum to show the many causes lotteries have supported in American history, from raising money for George Washington's Continental Army to funding Harvard and Dartmouth colleges. In their 1988 annual report they reported to shareholders that the winner of a $55 million jackpot in the Florida lottery set up a foundation "to provide shelter for the homeless, help the elderly, feed the hungry and protect abused women and children."

Global presence. The whole world likes to gamble, but Bally has been slow to export their expertise. However, in early 1990 they decided to put up $50 million to buy one of London's posh gambling clubs, the Clermont.

Stock performance. Bally stock bought for $1,000 in 1980 sold for $462 on January 2, 1990.

Bally Manufacturing Corp., 8700 West Bryn Mawr Avenue, Chicago, IL 60631; (312) 399-1300.

THE MEDIA

GLOBAL MEDIA GIANTS

The 1980s saw the emergence of the multinational media company. For American motion picture companies—and TV film producers (often one and the same company)—the international arena has always been a major source of revenue. But the power to disseminate information and entertainment is now being concentrated in companies whose products are varied (newspapers, magazines, records, films) and whose audiences are worldwide. And one feature of this new era is the rise of non-American companies. Two major world media enterprises—News Corp. and Bertelsmann—are Australian and German, respectively. Indeed, the prime reason cited for the end-of-the-decade merger of Time Inc. and Warner Communications was the need for a strong American company to operate globally.

1

TIME WARNER INC.

#1 *in movies, magazines, records pay TV*

#2 *in cable TV networks, book publishing*

Employees: 26,800
Sales: $7.6 billion
Losses: $256 million
Founded: 1923 (Time), 1917 (Warner)
Headquarters: New York City, New York

Workplace

In a fitting epitaph to the dealmaking 1980s, Time Inc. merged with Warner Communications in early 1990 to create—until the next merger—the world's largest media empire. Among their other offerings, Time Warner brings us *Mad* and *Fortune* in magazines; HBO and Cinemax in pay TV; Little, Brown, and Book-of-the-Month Club in book publishing; Warner Bros., Reprise, Atlantic and Elektra in music publishing; *Driving Miss Daisy, National Lampoon's Christmas Vacation,* and Bugs Bunny in movies.

The new Time Warner was composed of bizarre counterpoints. Time Inc., bastion of Ivy Leaguers, was marrying a company managed by people with New York street smarts. Time, stronghold of print journalism, was embracing a company whose forté was entertainment (movies and records). The deal was paid for with borrowed money (Time Warner has $11 billion worth of long-term debt), a tactic the heads of both companies had deplored just before the merger. And while technically Time acquired Warner, many observers saw the merger as a triumph for Steven J. Ross, Warner's silver-haired boss who, in addition to the millions he had already pocketed during his reign, now received $193 million as a payout for his stock benefit plans.

Time Warner represented the end of the publishing empire established and built by a missionary's son, Henry R. Luce, and his Yale buddies. Luce's buttoned-up style is a far cry from this brave new breed of conglomerate—as is evident in their new corporate logo (a stylized eye and ear) and in Time Warner's first, highly unconventional annual report to shareholders. It features neon-bright colors, photo collages and an eccentric layout of varying typefaces, charts, illustrations and quotations (including one by Jack Nicholson as the Joker in *Batman*). In the report, Time Warner declares, "Every one of our businesses is highly successful, ranking first or second in its category."

Their businesses are mind-boggling in size and scope. Time Warner has the biggest and most prestigious portfolio of magazines in America—25 magazines (including 4 weeklies, no other publisher has more than 1), with a worldwide readership of 120 million. In March 1990 they purchased Lane Publishing, and added *Sunset*, a monthly magazine distributed in 13 Western states. Time Warner captures 20 percent of all advertising money spent on magazines (in 1989 their magazines *Time, Sports Illustrated* and *People* were the top three carriers of advertising). They're also the second largest book publisher—selling over 45 million books in 1989. Warner Bros. is number one in VCR movie rentals (thanks in part to *Batman,* 1989s highest grossing film), and produced 19 percent of the movies rented in 1989. Warner Bros. was also the number one film studio four times during the 1980s, and has been among the top three studios for the last seven years. They're the nation's second-largest cable operator (systems in 35 states). In pay TV, they operate the largest and oldest service (HBO, with 325,000 subscribers). They're the largest producer of TV programs (18 shows under the Warner and Lorimar banners, accounting for 20 percent of network prime time during 1989, including "Murphy Brown," "Dallas" and "China Beach"). They're number one in music publishing, and Warner Music is the largest record company on the planet. Some of Time Warner performers are Michael Jackson, Madonna, U2, George Michael and Prince.

History.   Henry Robinson Luce, born in Tengchow, China, in 1898 to a missionary, was sent to the U.S. for schooling (Hotchkiss and Yale). At Yale he collaborated with a classmate, Briton Hadden, to start the newsweekly, *Time,* in 1923. They began with $86,000, raised through friends and classmates. Luce ruled the company until his death in 1967. "Henry Luce was a Calvinist and a conservative," said David Shaw of the *Los Angeles Times,* "and his view of the world was *Time's* view of the world—morally, socially, intellectually and, most important of all, politically." *Time's* punchy prose style and jumbled word order changed the voice of American journalism. Writers strung out adjectives (Huey Long was "button-nosed, pugnacious, curly-headed, loose-jawed, incredible"), coined new words (G.K. Chesterton was a paradoxbund, the U.S. drugstore omnivenderous), and helped themselves to other languages (kudos from Greek, tycoon from Japanese). In the late 1980s *Time* began letting correspondents write their own stories rather than having their notes and observations rewritten into *Time*-ese by the New York editors. Among

the publications assembled in *Time's* empire were *Fortune* (Luce founded it in 1930), *Life* (Luce bought it in 1936), *Sports Illustrated* (launched in 1954), Time-Life Books, *Money* (begun in 1972), *People* (started in 1974), Book-of-the-Month Club (acquired in 1977).

The Warner brothers, who started the company of the same name, did not have Luce's privileged background. They were part of what has been called the Jewish army that invented Hollywood in the early years. The Warners emigrated from Poland (Louis B. Mayer emigrated from Lithuania; Lewis Selznick from Russia; William Fox from Hungary; Carl Laemmle from Germany). Jack Warner and his brothers Sam, Harry and Albert set up a traveling theater show in Ohio. From the theater business the brothers moved into making and distributing movies. By 1917 Sam and Jack Warner were turning out slapstick comedies in Los Angeles. They soon got a reputation as a Hollywood studio concerned with serious political and social themes, usually in simple, low-class settings. They also gave the world Bugs Bunny and Rin-Tin-Tin and some immortal Bogart classics, including *The Maltese Falcon* and *Casablanca.* But the film studio went into financial and artistic decline in the 1950s, and by 1969 the movie operation was defunct. The company at that point consisted primarily of two record companies, Warner/Reprise and Atlantic Records (famous for promoting black artists like Ray Charles).

Enter Steven Ross, who rapidly revamped Warner Brothers. Born in Brooklyn and educated at a two-year vocational school, Ross sold trousers in the garment district before marrying the heiress of a funeral home fortune. Ross built an empire out of funeral homes, parking lots and building maintenance before buying Warner Brothers. Under his guidance, the company had two of the box-office smashes of the 1970s: *The Exorcist* and *All the President's Men.*

Owners and rulers.   Steve Ross was the second highest paid CEO in America in 1989 (hauling in $34.2 million) and the second highest paid CEO of the decade ($84.6 million from 1980 to 1989). Ross, aged 62 (in 1990), shared the chairmanship and CEO slot with Time's CEO, J. Richard Munro until May 1990. Munro was replaced then by 50-year-old Nicholas J. Nicholas. Nicholas and Ross will rule as co-CEOs for five years, after which Nicholas is slated to become the sole CEO.

As a place to work. Steve Ross has a reputation for wining and dining the Hollywood crowd, and he is famed for being lavish with money and affection. Warner's top people have a loyalty to the company unusual in the entertainment industry. Time Inc. had the reputation for being insular and inbred, comfortable for insiders but somewhat intolerant of outsiders. Vice Chairman Gerald Levin told the *New Yorker,* "*Time* has what we call an immunologic system, and it rejects them [outsiders]." Before 1986, *Time's* journalists were so coddled and pampered that others in the company referred to the division as "the plantation."

Social responsibility. No one has ever detected a philanthropic impulse in Steven Ross, but Time Inc., being founded by a missionary's son, has always stressed what they called "a commitment to make a difference as well as a profit... in everything we do—not only in the ideas and products we send into our customers' homes, but also in the active corporate role we play in the community." One of *Time's* major efforts in recent years was Time to Read, a program to stamp out illiteracy. Over half of Time Warner's American employees are female and 24 percent are minorities.

Global presence. The Time Warner combo creates an *American* media giant capable of competing in world markets against the likes of Australia's News Corp. (Rupert Murdoch), Germany's Bertelsmann, and France's Hachette. Time Warner's international reach comes from the Warner side. Thanks largely to their film and music businesses, Warner was doing 40 percent of their sales abroad, and they claimed to be "the United States' largest exporter of entertainment." Time Inc.'s non-U.S. sales were negligible, derived largely from international editions of *Time.* In a message to shareholders in 1989, Ross speculated that the Chinese and Russians would surely welcome products from Steven Spielberg, Madonna and Clint Eastwood. In March 1990, Time Warner announced they'd pulled off a post-cold war coup: a contract

to build multi-screen movie theaters in Moscow and Leningrad. The movie theaters, 19 screens in all, will open sometime in 1991.

Stock performance. Time Warner stock bought for $1,000 in 1980 sold for $7,880 on January 2, 1990.

Time Warner Inc., 1271 Avenue of the Americas, New York, NY 10020; (212) 522-1212.

Time Warner, Inc., 75 Rockefeller Plaza, New York, NY 10019; (212) 484-8000.

2

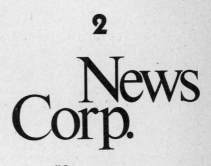

News Corp.

#4 *in broadcasting*
#5 *in magazines*

Employees: 28,300
Sales: $6.4 billion
Profits: $125 million
Founded: 1952
Headquarters: Sydney, Australia

At home on three continents and comfortable in gutter journalism or high-fashion magazine publishing, Rupert Murdoch rules an empire that encompasses newspapers, magazines, TV, motion pictures, records, books and printing. He's an authentic media baron, the latest in a 20th century line that includes William Randolph Hearst, Time Inc.'s Henry Luce and Britain's Lord Beaverbrook.

Operating through his Australian-based holding company, News Corp., the Australian-born Murdoch owns newspapers controlling half the circulation in Australia's major cities. In Britain, where he was schooled at Oxford, Murdoch papers control roughly one-third of the national press. In the U.S., he owns *TV Guide,* TV stations in six major markets and a Hollywood motion picture company, Twentieth Century-Fox. In Hong Kong, he has the largest English-language daily, the *South Morning Post.* He runs a global book publishing operation—Harper & Row in the U.S., Collins in Britain—that rings up annual sales of over $1 billion.

He stitched it all together in about 20 years with an expenditure of $5 billion, most of it borrowed. News Corp. sailed into the 1990s with debt of over $7 billion.

Murdoch owns the *Times of London*, arguably the world's most prestigious English-language paper. He also owns the *Sun*, a British national daily, and *News of the World*, a Sunday paper—arguably, two of the world's raunchiest newspapers. The *Sun* prints pictures of bare-breasted females on page 3. When Britain fought with Argentina over the Falkland Islands in 1982, the *Sun*'s front page blared: STICK IT UP YOUR JUNTA.

Obviously, eclecticism is Rupert Murdoch's trademark. In the U.S., he launched a lurid tabloid, *The Star*, and then put up $3 billion to buy a family magazine, *TV Guide*, which alternates with the *Reader's Digest* as the nation's largest circulation magazine. Tomorrow he is just as likely to buy *Penthouse* as *The Smithsonian*. He also reshuffles the deck frequently, unlike the Newhouses, who have never sold or folded a magazine. In 1990 Murdoch agreed to sell *The Star* to their chief competitor on supermarket checkout lines, *The National Enquirer*.

After coming to the U.S., Murdoch bought a passel of newspapers. Then he became infatuated with TV, forcing him (because of regulations prohibiting ownership of newspapers and stations in the same city) to sell off the *Chicago Sun-Times*, which a veteran staffer said he had "sodomized," and the *New York Post*, which he failed to turn around despite an injection of British tabloid journalism featuring front-page headlines like "Leper Rapes Virgin," "Shoot Mom for 50 Cents" and "I Slept with a Trumpet." Columnist Alexander Cockburn said Murdoch's selling the *Post* was like "Dracula selling his coffin." He also sold the *Village Voice* and his half-interest in *Elle*. Murdoch still owns the *Boston Herald* and his original U.S. newspaper, the *San Antonio Express-News* in Texas. With the purchase of *TV Guide*, he picked up the *Daily Racing Form*, the original Annenberg family paper. In 1989, about one-third of Murdoch's sales came from newspapers;

15 percent each from magazines and movies; 10 percent from TV.

History. The Murdoch empire began with a threadbare evening newspaper, the *Adelaide Sun* in Australia, which he inherited after his father died in 1952. Murdoch was then 21. His father was Sir Keith Murdoch, a distinguished Australian journalist who had helped build a powerful newspaper group radiating from the *Melbourne Herald* but had ended up owning very little of the enterprise. Murdoch vowed he would not repeat his father's mistake.

Beginning in Australia, where he bought newspapers and got into other businesses (airlines, betting parlors), and continuing in Britain and the U.S., Murdoch delighted in shaking up the powers that be. He never bought the conventional wisdom, showed a great tolerance for risk taking and was unpredictable.

Murdoch became an American citizen in 1985 to conform to FCC rules. He bought, for $1.5 billion, John Kluge's six Metromedia TV stations (in New York, Los Angeles, Chicago, Dallas, Houston and Washington, D.C.)—and U.S. citizenship is required for such ownership. Also in 1985 he bought the Twentieth Century-Fox studio, and in 1987 parlayed this combination into a fourth TV network, Fox Broadcasting, which targeted young people with shows that introduced a new level of vulgarity into TV programming. Murdoch is always pioneering. In Europe he pinned his TV hopes on a satellite program service, Sky Television.

Murdoch has a dozen U.S. magazine properties, including *New York*, *Soap Opera Digest* and *Travel Weekly*. After Si Newhouse fired Grace Mirabella as *Vogue*'s editor in 1988, Murdoch called her up and backed her in a new magazine, *Mirabella*, to compete with *Vogue*.

Competitors never know where Rupert Murdoch will strike next. And he himself admits he operates without any grand strategy.

Owners and rulers. Murdoch's company, News Corp. Ltd., trades on the New York Stock Exchange, but the Murdoch family company, Cruden Investments (named for the Melbourne country house where he grew up), owns 44 percent. Tied into News Corp. are 50 percent holdings in Ansett Airlines, Australia's largest private airline; a 5 percent stake in Reuters (a worldwide newswire but more importantly, a major supplier of electronic information on financial markets); an 18 percent interest in the British publishing house Pearson (*Financial Times*, *The Economist*, Viking, Penguin); and minority interests in assorted other enterprises. At one time they even owned 35 percent of an Australian company that runs bingo games and football betting parlors.

As a place to work. Exciting. Murdoch is not interested in boring publications—and he's a very visible, or audible, presence, even with his vast holdings. It's not unusual for the London editor of *News of the World* to get a transatlantic call from Murdoch to discuss the headlines in next Sunday's paper. In Britain he toughed out printing unions by opening a high-tech plant outside London, signing a contract with a union representing electricians.

Social responsibility. In the mid-1980s Murdoch appeared before the American Newspaper Publishers Association to lecture American publishers about going over the heads of their readers. The public, he has said, "certainly has no duty to support newspapers. It's the duty of publishers to provide the type of newspaper the public wants to read."

Global presence. In the mid-1980s News Corp. divided up one-third Australian, one-third British and one-third American, but the tilt is now toward the U.S. In 1990, they bought a half interest in two Hungarian newspapers.

Stock performance. News Corp. stock bought for $1,000 in 1985 sold for $5,085 on January 2, 1990.

The News Corporation Limited, 2 Holt Street, Correspondence Box 43245 G.P.O., Sydney, Australia 2001; (02) 288-3000.

The News Corporation Limited, 1211 Avenue of the Americas, New York, NY 10036; (212) 852-7000.

3
Bertelsmann

#1 *in book clubs*
#3 *in records*

Employees: 42,000
Sales: $6 billion
Founded: 1835
Headquarters: Guetersloh, West Germany

Dedicated to the proposition that cultural goods now cross borders freely, Bertelsmann rocketed to a premier position on the world media scene by extending their German base in publishing, music and printing around the world. Indeed, before the 1989 Time Warner merger, Bertelsmann, based on sales, was the world's top media/entertainment company.

Few Americans recognize their name but their U.S. properties are well known: RCA and Arista in records, Doubleday (publisher of this book), Bantam and Dell in book publishing, the Literary Guild, Doubleday Book Club and Mystery Guild book club, *Parents* and *YM* magazines and a string of printing plants across the country. Bertelsmann's Brown Printing, based in Waseca, Minnesota, prints 140 magazines—including *Time, Fortune* and *Business Week*. Another unit, Offset Paperback Mfrs., based in Dallas, produces one of every five paperback books printed in the U.S. Among the Bertelsmann best-sellers of the late 1980s were the Bill Cosby and Lee Iacocca autobiographies and Stephen Hawking's *A Brief History of Time.* Iacocca's book was the best-seller of the decade, selling more than 7 million copies. Whitney Houston, Placido Domingo and Bruce Hornsby & the Range all record for Bertelsmann labels.

History. The man behind the modern Bertelsmann is Reinhard Mohn, who came home from World War II to find his family printing business in ashes and ruin. The original business, founded in 1835 by Mohn's great-great-grandfather, Carl Bertelsmann, printed hymnals and prayer books. But book clubs, not hymnals, powered Mohn's empire in the beginning. In 1950, he started Germany's first book club, Lesering (2 million members by 1958). Mohn then moved on to record clubs. During the 1960s, he went international with his book and record clubs, spreading them through Europe and Latin America.

In 1969, Mohn edged into the magazine business by acquiring a minority stake (later augmented to 75 percent) in Gruner & Jahr, publisher of *Geo*. In 1979, he entered book publishing by purchasing 51 percent of U.S. paperback publisher Bantam Books; Mohn bought the remainder of Bantam in 1981 and became owner of America's largest paperback house. In 1979, Mohn bought Arista Records from Columbia Pictures and in 1986 Bertelsmann became the world's third largest record producer (behind CBS and Warner) by boosting their stake in RCA's record division from 25 to 100 percent.

Another 1986 purchase was Doubleday & Company for $475 million. Doubleday prints books under many imprints, including Dell, Delacorte, Dial, Anchor and Laidlaw, and operates several book clubs (the biggest, the Literary Guild) and bookstores. Bertelsmann's purchase did not seem like a good buy; Doubleday had long been the butt of many industry jokes. Their books were so poorly printed that a former employee once said you could always tell a Doubleday book because "it feels so rotten." As of early 1990, Doubleday was losing money in their book club and printing businesses. Membership in the book clubs dropped by 50 percent from 1987 to 1990, and a costly restructuring of the printing business meant closing three of the company's four printing factories. CEO Alberto Vitale abandoned Bantam/Doubleday/Dell in favor of rival Random House. Doubleday's president, Nancy Evans, resigned; the president of Doubleday Book and Music Clubs also resigned, as did an executive editor and two senior executives at the book clubs.

Owners and rulers. Reinhard Mohn spent two years at an American prisoner of war camp in Kansas, and he looks at his time in America as a formative influence. While detained, he "quickly realized the American concept of individual freedom was more than just a platitude," and learned that "the greatest management

teachers in the world [were] ... the Americans." In particular, Mohn was impressed by Alfred Sloan of General Motors, who preached the gospel of decentralized management. Someone who has watched Mohn over the years described him to *The Economist* as "the sort of man from whom you could buy a used car with confidence, but who will probably persuade you to buy two new ones instead." Mohn, who turns 69 in 1990, owns 89 percent of Bertelsmann stock. He remains chairman of the supervisory board (he retired as CEO in 1981), still having a say in how the company is run. But the man calling the shots day-to-day is CEO Mark Woessner, Mohn's next-door neighbor. He was behind Bertelsmann's great westward expansion in 1986 when they bought Doubleday and RCA records.

As a place to work. Bertelsmann treats top executives as entrepreneurs, giving them a lot of freedom over their piece of the pie, and linking pay to their success in racking up their division's profits. This hands-off philosophy extends to the creative side, too. "You have to understand what creative people are like, what egos they have," the music head group told the *Wall Street Journal.* "You should not have many business people above them." Rank and file employees also have some stake in the company fortunes, because all employees benefit from a profit-sharing plan. Sounding like an American fresh out of a Megatrends seminar, Woessner talks about creating a "dialogue-intensive corporate culture." He succinctly sums up their style this way: "Hire the best people, give them a lot of freedom to perform and pay them a lot." Company headquarters remains in Guetersloh, the rural Westphalian town in the north of Germany where Mohn was born; it's a 1½ hour drive from the nearest airport.

Social responsibility. Bertelsmann's publications range from the left-leaning German magazine *Stern* to *Capital*, the German equivalent of *Fortune*. Editorial independence is part of the company creed, since, as Woessner noted once, "a monolithic media company can be dangerous."

Global presence. The book clubs have 22 million members in 22 countries. They have 37 magazines in five countries. Sales break down one-third in Germany, another third in the rest of Europe and a third in the U.S.

Bertelsmann Aktiengesellschaft, Carl-Bertelsmann-Strasse 270, Postbox 5555, D-4830 Guetersloh 100, West Germany; (49) 05241-80-0.

BROADCASTERS

Operating a radio or TV station has been called a license to print money, but even so, broadcasting is fraught with problems. It is, first of all, a crowded field: the U.S. has over 10,000 radio stations and over 1,300 TV outlets (as against 1,650 daily newspapers). Second, it's a regulated business, governed by the rules of the Federal Communications Commission, which limit the number of broadcasting stations in the hands of one owner (currently, no company can own stations reaching more than 25 percent of the U.S. population). The networks get around this restriction by linking independently owned stations. The 1980s saw all three of the major broadcasting networks—NBC, CBS and ABC—change hands plus the launch of a fourth network, Fox Broadcasting. The perennial problem networks faced is coming up with hit shows, not as easily solved as you may think. Of the 23 new shows aired in fall 1989, 13 were promptly canceled. Still another problem for broadcasters is declining viewership. The audience for network shows went down steadily during the 1980s, as more people watched cable or rented videos or simply left their screens dark. But that didn't seem to affect the cost of commercials. In 1990 the cost of a 30-second commercial on the 25th Super Bowl reached a new high: $850,000. In 1989, advertisers spent $27 billion to buy TV time and $8 billion on radio commercials.

1

Capital Cities/ABC, Inc.

#1 *in broadcasting*
#12 *in magazines*
#15 *in newspapers*

Employees: 19,800
Sales: $5 billion
Profits: $486 million
Founded: 1941 (ABC), 1954 (Capital Cities)
Headquarters: New York City, New York

What do the TV shows "Roseanne" and "Wonder Years" have in common with fashion magazines *W* and *M,* the cable sports network ESPN, the trade magazine *Hog Farm Management* and the *Kansas City Times?* They all come to us courtesy of this sprawling company, Capital Cities/ABC, created smack in the mid-1980s when the boa constrictor (Cap Cities) enveloped the elephant (ABC). It was a birth midwifed by one of our time's celebrated investors, Warren Buffett, who in 1986 put up $518 million of the $3.5 billion purchase price, giving him an 18 percent stake in the new company, an interest that more than doubled in value by 1990, making him $600 million richer (on paper).

Buffett is a media buff, and in Cap Cities/ABC he holds the largest stake in one of the largest U.S. media companies. They own 8 TV stations, including KABC–Los Angeles, WABC–New York and WLS–Chicago; 21 radio stations (11 AM, 10 FM); 7 daily newspapers and 77 weeklies and shopping guides; 80 trade publications and magazines, including *Prairie Farmer, Women's Wear Daily, Institutional Investor, Compute!* and *Los Angeles Magazine;* a religious book publisher, Word Inc.; and varying slices of three major cable TV programming services—80 percent of the sports channel ESPN, 38 percent of the Arts & Entertainment Network and one-third of Lifetime (women's lifestyle). And of course they operate the ABC Television Network, which knits together 222 stations reaching 99 percent of U.S. households, and the ABC Radio Network, with 2,100 affiliates across the country.

The network has been somewhat of a drag. ABC has rarely risen to the commercial success or the editorial respect the two other major networks, CBS and NBC, command. To some extent, that's the old image. In the 1980s, Roone Arledge, who had established ABC as a power in sports coverage, did the same in network news. Peter Jennings and Ted Koppel brought new luster to ABC News. But somehow ABC still connotes number three in broadcasting (even when they're not).

Cap Cities, before gobbling up ABC, was known as the most coldly efficient miner of profits in the media world. In buying ABC, their main interest was TV stations in large cities, known affectionately as "cash cows." But they had to take the network to get the stations. And after taking control, they put John Sias in

Whatever Happened To...RCA?

Originally Radio Corp. of America, RCA pioneered radio broadcasting in the United States under the leadership of General David Sarnoff. They launched the National Broadcasting Company (NBC) network in 1926, entered the record business in 1930 and became the first company to market a television set. After World War II, RCA advanced to the ranks of the top 50 corporations by buying a variety of unrelated businesses—lending (C.I.T. Financial), frozen entrees (Banquet), publishing (Random House), carpets (Coronet) and car rentals (Hertz). More than 100,000 people worked for RCA. In the 1980s all these businesses were sold off, culminating in 1986 with the sale of RCA itself to General Electric for $6.4 billion. Hertz was sold to United Airlines and then to a partnership of Hertz managers and Ford Motor. Random House became part of the Newhouse publishing emporium. The RCA consumer electronics business (TV sets, VCRs) was sold to a French company, Thomson. The RCA record business was sold to the German publisher, Bertelsmann. RCA Global Communications (the original business) was sold to MCI. The NBC radio network was sold to Westwood One. All the NBC-owned radio stations were also sold by GE. The RCA operations that remained at General Electric are the NBC television network, five NBC-owned TV stations and the defense electronics divisions. The RCA name was rubbed off the 30 Rockefeller Plaza building in Rockefeller Center. Now it's called the General Electric Building. ∎

By the time the average child leaves high school, he/she will have witnessed 18,000 simulated murders on TV.

charge of the ABC TV network. Sias had headed up publishing properties at Cap Cities and wasn't even fond of TV. "I find it a real chore" to watch, he told *New York Times* reporter Geraldine Fabrikant. "My attention span just can't take too much of it."

History. Capital Cities/ABC represents the blending of two different cultures, although the dominant strain is Cap Cities. Even the old name, American Broadcasting Company, has been junked.

The American Broadcasting Company was founded in 1941 by government edict. At the time NBC had two radio networks, the Red and the Blue, and the FCC ruled one would have to be sold. So the Blue network, carrying NBC's less popular programs, was sold for $8 million to Edward Noble, heir to the Life Savers mint candy fortune, who renamed the firm the American Broadcasting Company. Twelve years later, ABC was near death. They owned five stations, had only eight network affiliates and were losing money. A savior came along in the form of Leonard Goldensen, a lawyer who headed up Paramount Theatres, a spinoff, by government decree, from Paramount Pictures. He bought ABC for $25 million worth of Paramount stock and retained Paul Lazarfeld, a Columbia University sociologist, to arm him with an appropriate strategy for ABC. With CBS and NBC already entrenched in many small cities and rural areas having only one or two stations, Lazarfeld advised Goldensen to go after young people living in urban centers. That strategy saw the light of the screen in 1955 with the western "Cheyenne," followed by "Maverick," "Lawman" and "Colt .45." "We selected in every case," Goldensen once explained, "young, virile men and young, attractive women in order to attract the younger families of America." ABC stuck to this formula for three decades, reaching their zenith in the late 1970s with the shows intellectuals loved to hate: "Laverne & Shirley," "Bionic Woman," "Charlie's An-

gels." ABC topped the audience ratings in the late 1970s, but hit bottom again in the mid-1980s with a string of losers like "Finder of Lost Loves" and "Jessie." Leonard Goldensen was still in command, at 79, when he sold out to Capital Cities in 1986.

Cap Cities was founded in 1954 when Frank Smith and seven other investors, one of them famed newscaster Lowell Thomas, launched a company to buy and operate radio and TV stations. Their first two stations were in Albany, New York, and Raleigh, North Carolina—hence the name, Capital Cities. Thomas Murphy, the son of a New York judge who was a crony of Frank Smith, signed on as station manager in Albany and became company head in 1964 after Smith died. His alter ego, Daniel Burke, joined Cap Cities from General Foods in 1961, becoming president in 1972. Murphy and Burke bought more radio and TV stations, adding publishing properties to the mix in 1966 with the acquisition of Fairchild Publications. Their biggest newspaper buy was the *Kansas City Star* in 1977.

Murphy and Burke are neither broadcasters nor publishers by inclination or training. What they brought to Cap Cities was business discipline. They ran a lean operation out of New York City, leaving day-to-day management of stations and newspapers to the people running them. At the time of the ABC purchase, Cap Cities had a headquarters staff of 36 people. They had no public relations department, no personnel department.

One Cap Cities hallmark is an ability to make an awful lot of money. And while they're known for being hands-off operators, woe to managers who don't meet sales and profit goals. *Advertising Age* columnist James Brady, once publisher of Cap Cities-owned *Women's Wear Daily,* said: "Cost-cutting and profitability and the bottom line aren't everything at Cap Cities; they're the only thing."

Owners and rulers. Since the mid-1980s Warren Buffett has been the biggest stockholder, but Cap Cities has been a "Tom and Dan" show for about 20 years—Tom is Thomas Murphy and Dan is Daniel Burke. Tom went to Harvard Business School with Dan's brother, James Burke (recently retired as CEO of Johnson & Johnson). They have been chairman and president of Cap Cities since 1972. In early 1990 Murphy gave up the CEO post to Burke. Both are known as tough negotiators. They were paid about $1.2 million each in 1989. Before becoming CIA director in the Reagan administration, the late William Casey was a Cap Cities director. Murphy, Casey and another Cap Cities board member, Thomas M. Macioce, were members of the Knights of Malta, described by the newsletter, *Left Business Observer*, as "a secretive international club of rightwing ruling class Catholics whose U.S. members include William Buckley, Alexander Haig, Lee Iacocca, William Simon and J. Peter Grace, chair of W. R. Grace & Co., whose board is full of Knights." Blacks and women made it onto the Cap Cities board for the first time in 1988 with the election of MIT professor Frank S. Jones and Ann Dibble Jordan, former social service director at the University of Chicago's medical school.

As a place to work. After they took charge of ABC in 1986, 1,200 heads rolled. They've had bitter fights with labor unions at their newspapers. The AFL-CIO placed them on a "Dishonor Roll of Labor Law Violators." Donald Kummer, an official of the American Newspaper Guild, said of Murphy: "If I ever get to hell, I know I'll meet him there." In 1987 Cap Cities began testing all job applicants for drug use, the only broadcaster to do so. In 1986 they considered sending a team of drug-sniffing dogs through the offices of their Kansas City newspapers.

Social responsibility. In 1988 Cap Cities/ABC supported the Drug-Free America campaign by donating $27 million worth of newspaper space and broadcast time for messages, although no one believes they bumped paying advertisers from these slots. ABC's coverage of the 1984 Olympic Games was so slanted in favor of American athletes it drew an official rebuke from the International Olympic Committee. An ABC official retorted: "We cover, as all nations do, the medal winners, and we don't feel we should be in a position of apologizing for what the Americans are doing. They're cleaning up and that's what we are covering."

Global presence. Virtually nil. They own 25 percent of a European cable TV programming service.

Stock performance. Capital Cities/ABC stock bought for $1,000 in 1980 sold for $11,831 on January 2, 1990.

Capital Cities/ABC, 77 West 66th Street, New York, NY 10023; (212) 456-7777.

2

#2 *in broadcasting*

Employees: 6,100
Sales: $3.3 billion
Profits: $410 million
Founded: 1926
Headquarters: New York City, New York

One of the symbolic acts of the 1980s was the renaming of 30 Rockefeller Plaza in New York City. Previously known as the RCA Building, it became the GE Building, a reflection of General Electric's $6.3 billion purchase of RCA in 1986. And with RCA came the National Broadcasting Company (NBC), the oldest of the broadcasting networks, long headquartered at 30 Rock. Now, at 11:30 P.M. on Saturday nights, when you hear, "Live from New York, it's Saturday Night," you'll know it's coming from the GE Building. GE moved their own manager, Robert Wright, into the top spot at NBC to replace departing hero Grant Tinker. It's GE's company and they can do what they want with it. David Letterman, whose show originates in the GE Building, wondered whether the next move might be a "miniseries on the development of the toaster oven."

By capturing NBC, General Electric became the proprietor of the hottest TV network. They took over first place in prime-time audience ratings in 1985 and held it through the rest of the decade. NBC also owns six major TV stations, including WNBC–New York, WMAQ–Chicago and KNBC–Los Angeles.

It wasn't always that way. Coming into the 1980s, NBC was dead last. Fred Silverman was then president—he had previously worked his magic at both CBS and ABC but nothing clicked for him at NBC. The nadir came on January 16, 1982, when the NBC nighttime programs garnered the lowest audience share—6.5 percent of homes—in TV history. Brandon Tartikoff, NBC's program chief, analyzed the situation this way:

I compared the networks to department stores. I thought the problem with NBC was that we had no identity. Like if you're in New York, and you want a great suit, you go to Saks Fifth Avenue, and you know you'll get a great suit. But if you want a vacuum cleaner, you go to Korvettes. Our problem was that we were up against CBS, the gray suit, the class act, the traditional network, and ABC, the bubble gum, vacuum cleaner, Top Forty television network. And then there's NBC. It's this hodgepodge—a network that didn't know what it was, that didn't have any identity.

Tartikoff said he presented this theory to Fred Silverman, who responded: "Well, that's all very interesting, but the problem with NBC is we don't have any hits. A couple of hits will change everything."

And *after* Silverman left, replaced by Grant Tinker, the hits cascaded in: "Cheers," "Family Ties," "The Bill Cosby Show," "St. Elsewhere," "The A Team," "Hill Street Blues." And NBC roared to the top, ahead of CBS for the first time in decades. GE bought in at the top.

Some thought GE, whose heritage was electrical appliances, might dump NBC. No way. Instead they dumped RCA's electronic manufacturing business—TV and radio sets, VCRs, record players—and held on dearly to NBC, now riding the crest of the wave in TV. Because they're hidden within GE, NBC's figures often don't get the public spotlight. But the fact is, their sales of $3.6 billion in 1988 topped CBS' revenues by nearly $1 billion.

History. General Electric played an instrumental role in the creation of NBC more than 70 years ago. After World War I, the federal government was paranoid about new technology falling into the hands of foreign powers. In 1919 Acting Secretary of Navy Franklin Delano Roosevelt urged GE to set up a new company, Radio Corporation of America, to buy out the British-owned Marconi Wireless Telegraph Company. Along with the deal came David Sarnoff, the key figure in building RCA into a huge communications empire and parent of the National Broadcasting Company. An immigrant from a Jewish ghetto in Russia who grew up on the lower east side of Manhattan, Sarnoff dropped out of school after the eighth grade and went to work as a wireless operator for Guglielmo Marconi, inventor of the wireless telegraph. Sarnoff was on duty in 1912 when a very weak signal came over the experimental wireless station atop the Wanamaker building in New York: "S.S. Titanic ran into iceberg. Sinking fast." For 72 hours Sarnoff stayed at his post copying down the names of the 800 survivors.

When Marconi's company was Americanized seven years later, Sarnoff was in charge. Some GE insiders tried to get rid of the uneducated immigrant, but Sarnoff held on. He was full of then-revolutionary ideas about broadcast stations and what he called "radio music boxes" (which he presciently believed would bring news and entertainment into the home). RCA soon began making radios, and in 1926, when there were 5 million radio sets in use in America, Sarnoff launched the NBC network. His original idea was to have the network serve as a public service vehicle. He never dreamed it would carry advertising. RCA owned two radio stations in New York, WEAF and WJZ, and they served as the flag ships for two NBC networks: the Red and the Blue, named for the colors of the grease pencils engineers used in drawing up the station interconnections. The Blue network, connecting stations GE and Westinghouse owned, was the forerunner of ABC.

So David Sarnoff spread his company, RCA, over the entire field—he made the equipment (radios and then TV sets), he owned stations and he had a network that carried programs nationwide. An engineer by training, he was more interested in the hardware than the entertainment

Female TV correspondents reported 22 percent of the stories at CBS, 14 percent at NBC and 10 percent at ABC, according to a 1989 Washington Post survey of the three major television networks.

side of the business. RCA developed the first TV set (shown at the New York World's Fair in 1939), introduced the first black-and-white set for sale (in 1946) and the first color set (1950).

NBC pioneered in color television (leading them to adopt the peacock as their emblem) and under the stimulus of an unorthodox, ex-advertising man, Sylvester L. "Pat" Weaver, they introduced programming to the early morning ("Today") and late evening ("Tonight") hours, but they rarely played the TV game as well as Bill Paley's CBS. Kenneth Bilby, who worked at RCA for many years and who wrote a biography of Sarnoff, *The General,* published in 1986, concluded RCA's founder and builder could never really come to terms, temperamentally, with NBC. He couldn't understand the star system and he "could never comfortably fit NBC into his family of RCA technologies." Bilby said Sarnoff was disturbed that a comic "could reap hundredfold the financial rewards of a Vladimir Zworykin, whose inventions made the medium of television possible. Discussing this imbalance once at a small staff meeting, he labeled it "an indictment of the economic values in our society."

Unsurprisingly then, NBC usually languished far behind CBS. Sarnoff died in 1971 at age 80. Under the leadership of his son, Robert Sarnoff, RCA turned into a miniconglomerate (Hertz cars, Coronet carpets, Banquet frozen foods, Random House books), but diversification didn't work. The board dismissed Sarnoff in 1975, and RCA drifted aimlessly for the next six years, a period coinciding with NBC's plunge to the depths. In 1981, the board recruited as CEO Thornton F. Bradshaw, president of Atlantic Richfield and a longtime RCA director, and in the next four years he staged a stunning comeback at RCA—and at NBC (where he brought in Grant Tinker). RCA was then earning $340 million on $10 billion in revenues, but Bradshaw decided that wasn't big enough in this age of global giants, and so he entered into talks that led to the GE acquisition. On February 13, 1986, nearly 1,000 stockholders, many of them loyal to the old Sarnoff regime, gathered at the Marriott Marquis in Times Square to vote on the merger. For three hours angry shareholders denounced the management for "selling us out," for "killing the company," "for obliterating the name RCA." All to no avail. Two years later GE sold the RCA consumer electronics business to Thomson S.A. of France. The business they kept, the jewel of the company, was NBC. David Sarnoff never understood the TV network. Now GE will put their imprint on the company.

Owners and rulers. NBC belongs entirely to General Electric, and GE people run the place. In an interview in *Rolling Stone,* Brandon Tartikoff, now president of NBC Entertainment, told how worried he was after the GE purchase because no one from GE called him. Finally, after months and a gentle suggestion from a mutual friend, Jack Welch, chairman of GE, did call and asked Tartikoff to dinner. When he returned home beaming after the dinner, his wife, Lilly, said, "You're in love, I can tell." Tartikoff said: "Lilly, he wants to win as much as I do."

As a place to work. Job security was never a hallmark of NBC—and it's no better under GE. One of GE's first actions was to cut 300 people from the NBC payroll. In 1987, 2,800 unionized newswriters and technicians went on strike for months in a dispute over whether management should use more temporary workers and nonunion crews. Robert E. Mulholland, an industry spokesman and a former NBC president, noted the network functioned fine while the strike was on, making it clear the network "can operate successfully with far fewer employees." In 1990, when NBC replaced popular "Today" show co-anchor Jane Pauley with Deborah Norville (supposedly because Pauley, at 39, was getting too old), viewers protested loudly, prompting industry wags to describe NBC's new policy: "If it isn't broke, break it."

Social responsibility. After GE took over, they threatened to move NBC out of New York City to New Jersey, saying such a move would save tens of millions of dollars a year. In the end, they relented, especially after the city of New York came through with nearly $100 million in tax breaks. Robert Wright, NBC's CEO, said they still would have saved money by trekking across the Hudson River but this was outweighed by other factors. NBC has been based at 30 Rock since 1933. "Fifty-four years is a long time," said Wright. "And in fact if you polled the NBC people, there is an awful lot of strong attachment to that location. We felt that had a value, hard to put dollars on, but a real value." Mayor Ed Koch said: "NBC's decision shows that the peacock can have both brains and beauty."

Global presence. Tiny but NBC is expected to benefit from GE's determination to be a global player. They're already gearing up on the cable front.

National Broadcasting Company, 30 Rockefeller Plaza, New York, NY 10112; (212) 664-4444.

3

CBS

Employees: 6,700
Sales: $3 billion
Profits: $297 million
Founded: 1926
Headquarters: New York City, New York

After the 1980s, CBS will never be the same. Although they underwent many changes in the previous 55 years (who remembers they once *made* TV sets?), strong continuity was the thread of those decades, and it came from the top, where the founder, William S. Paley, ruled. CBS was the class act in American broadcasting. Not only did they make the most money, but they also had an aura of integrity defined by the luminaries of their news division: Edward R. Murrow, William Shirer, Charles Collingwood, Eric Sevareid, Walter Cronkite. They were, hands down, the best at what they did.

It all unraveled in the 1980s. One by one, CBS was stripped of their nonbroadcast operations: books, magazines, toys, Steinway pianos and other musical instruments, stereo stores, even records (where Columbia Records ranked number one in the world). By decade's end, sales were more than $1 billion below what they were at the start of 1980, nearly $2 billion lower than the 1984 figure. From a payroll of 38,000, CBS went to 6,500. And, most significantly, Bill Paley was no longer the guiding force. The new leader was Laurence A. Tisch, a fiendish bridge player and stock market player. Because he owned 25 percent of CBS through his Loews holding company, the firm was now his candy store. And like a lot of candy store owners, he's obsessed with costs. Big cuts were made in the CBS staff in the late 1980s, especially in the news division. Bureaus were closed, correspondents fired. Bill Moyers left for the Public Broadcasting System, where he felt he had the freedom to do better work. Diane Sawyer left for ABC. And the revolving door never stopped revolving at the "CBS Morning News" show. One of the latest to leave was coanchor Kathleen Sullivan, a recruit from ABC. She was dismissed after referring to CBS as the "Cheap Broadcasting System."

CBS had hunkered down to what they like to call their core business: 5 TV stations (in New York, Chicago, Los Angeles, Miami and Philadelphia), 20 radio stations (12 FM, 8 AM), a TV network with 215 affiliated stations and a radio network with 410 affiliates. The stations threw off enormous profits, but the TV network was in disarray in the Tisch era. In the decade's last three years, the network ran third behind NBC and ABC in prime-time audience ratings. The only CBS show to place in the Top 10 was "60 Minutes," a 21-year-old program. The highest ranking CBS entertainment program was "Murder, She Wrote," which followed "60 Minutes" on Sunday night—and it was 6 years old in 1990. And up against ABC's "America's Funniest Home Videos," it was beginning to falter. For a company shaped by Bill Paley, who had a golden touch in program selection, it was almost unbelievable.

The Network's "CBS Evening News" began the decade with avuncular Walter Cronkite in the anchor seat and ended with the intense Dan Rather, who figured

On an average night in 1989, 69 percent of America was tuned in to one of the major networks. In 1980, before the rise of cable, the figure was 90 percent.

Laurence A. Tisch, President and CEO of CBS since 1987 and chairman of Lowes Corporatoion.

in a series of bizarre events, notably the September 11, 1987, moment in Miami when in a fit of pique about CBS coverage of the U.S. Open tennis tournament running into his time, he walked off the set, leaving a blank network screen for six minutes. It will go down in history as one of TV's great gaffes.

As CBS headed into the 1990s, Larry Tisch's strategy was not clear. Would CBS merge with Walt Disney? With Cable Network News? The only major commitment Tisch had made, as of mid-1990, was to sports. CBS made three winning, blockbuster bids: $543 million for the 1992 Olympic Games (summer and winter), $1 billion for NCAA basketball and $1.1 billion for major league baseball.

History. In 1928, William Paley invested in the struggling 22-station Columbia Broadcasting System, just two years after it was founded. He was backed by his father, a Russian Jewish immigrant who made his fortune in the cigar-making business in Philadelphia. Paley knew little about radio's technical side. His genius lay in sales, and he realized the key to radio's success was large audiences. Paley decided to give his programming free to local radio stations (known as CBS affiliates) so long as they agreed to surrender any part of their schedule for sponsored network shows. Paley could then guarantee advertisers millions of people coast to coast would hear their plugs. Within a decade CBS expanded to 114 stations, and the company's sales went up 20-fold.

The young radio network's ratings grew throughout the 1930s. Comedians like Fred Allen and singers like Bing Crosby and Kate Smith took over the evening CBS time slots, while daytime audiences were held spellbound by a series of family dramas sponsored by soap companies (the first soap operas). But not until after World War II did CBS begin to win the majority of the prime-time audience away from arch rival NBC. In 1947, William Paley launched the "Paley raids" against NBC, luring away radio stars Amos 'n' Andy, George Burns and Gracie Allen, Jack Benny, Red Skelton, and Edgar Bergen and Charlie McCarthy with offers of high salaries and tax breaks. These stars soon became hits in TV, and CBS topped the ratings for years to come, setting the standards in entertainment and news coverage. Their dominance continued into the 1970s with "M*A*S*H," "All in the Family" and "Mary Tyler Moore." And whereas they were taking huge sums of money from advertisers, their confrontational news show, "60 Minutes," struck terror in the hearts of corporate PR people who were told Mike Wallace was on the line. In the words of David Halberstam, writing in *The Powers That Be*, Bill Paley was for fifty years

the supreme figure of modern broadcasting, first in radio and then in television. Very simply, he merchandised more products for more different companies than anyone in the history of mankind. His was one of the staggering success stories of the American twentieth century ... Bill Paley ... combined the prime energies of American huckstering with the explosive new potential of American technology.

That hegemony ended, however, in the 1980s, a decade in which takeovers were the rage—and CBS could hardly escape attention. First a conservative political group whose members included Senator Jesse Helms expressed an interest in taking over CBS to end what they considered the company's leftist ideology. Then Ted Turner, founder of Cable News Network, said he'd like to take over CBS. And behind the scenes, Gannett, the nation's largest newspaper chain, was maneuvering to buy the firm. In that heady atmosphere, where CBS was on the front pages of newspapers regularly, CEO Thomas Wyman saw Larry Tisch as a white knight or protector. Through his holding company, Loews, Tisch began accumulating CBS shares. He was given a board seat. Wyman thought he had a friend and supporter. In the end, which came in 1986, Tisch teamed up with Bill Paley to throw Wyman out of the company and take over as CEO of CBS.

Owners and rulers. In two words, Larry Tisch, who was 67 in 1990. He became CEO in 1986, replacing Thomas Wyman (ousted by the board after he proposed Coca-Cola acquire CBS). Wyman was retired at $400,000 a year for the rest of his life. For his efforts in 1989, Tisch was paid $1.3 million. A very brainy man (he enrolled at New York University when he was 15), Tisch is that rarity, a CEO of two companies. He also heads Loews Corp., where he was paid a salary of $246,000 in 1989. A conglomerate built up by the Tisches from some seedy New Jersey hotels, Loews owns cigarette maker Lorillard (see profile page 000), 95 percent of watchmaker Bulova, 82 percent of CNA Insurance and, not so incidentally, 25 percent of CBS. Larry's brother, Preston R. Tisch, also sits on CBS' board. Bill Paley still held the figurehead position of chairman and he was, next to the Tisches, the biggest shareholder, with 8 percent of the stock. Paley will turn 90 in 1991.

As a place to work. The tension that has always existed between "Black Rock," CBS headquarters on 52nd Street off the Avenue of the Americas, and the CBS Broadcast Center on West 57th Street, where the news division is based, escalated during the 1980s. In 1987 unionized newswriters walked a picket line that Dan Rather, the $2 million-a-year anchor, joined on occasion to show his solidarity. Don Hewitt, producer of "60 Minutes," tried to organize a group to *buy* CBS News. And after the big news division cutbacks in 1987, when more than 200 people were fired, Dan Rather and CBS producer Richard Cohen (later fired) signed an op-ed piece that ran in the *New York Times* that concluded:

Let's get one thing straight. CBS Inc. is not a chronically weak company fighting to survive. CBS Inc. is not on the skids. CBS Inc. is a profitable, valuable Fortune 500 corporation whose stock is setting new records. But 215 people lost their jobs so that the stockholders could have even more money in their pockets. More profits. That's what business is all about.

It's hard to think of another company where dissent of this kind would be aired publicly.

Social responsibility. Being on the firing line comes with this territory. In 1982, General William Westmoreland, onetime commander of the U.S. forces in Vietnam, filed a $120 million libel suit against CBS as a result of a documentary, "The Uncounted Enemy," in which he was portrayed as the leader of a conspiracy to misrepresent enemy troop counts. The suit came to trial in 1984 but was settled on terms considered a CBS victory: Westmoreland got no money, only a public statement by CBS acknowledging his "long and faithful service" to the country and denying any intent to show him as disloyal or unpatriotic. Later in the decade CBS fired their sports prognosticator, professional gambler Jimmy the Greek, after he said black athletes had a genetic

The average TV household watched about 7 hours of TV every day in 1988. TV is regarded as the major source of news by 66 percent of the public.

advantage because of their thick thighs and hips. And in early 1990 they suspended "60 Minutes" commentator Andy Rooney for two weeks because of disparaging remarks about gays and blacks that were attributed to him in a gay newspaper.

Global presence. Except for news bureaus in major world capitals (they were about to open one in Berlin in 1990), CBS has no business abroad.

Stock performance. CBS stock bought for $1,000 in 1980 sold for $5,200 on January 2, 1990.

CBS Inc., 51 West 52nd Street, New York, NY 10019; (212) 975-4321.

4

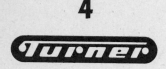

#1 in cable news

Employees: 3,300
Sales: $1.1 billion
Losses: $28 million
Founded: 1970
Headquarters: Atlanta, Georgia

Ted Turner, the flamboyant yachtsman who was born in Cincinnati, grew up in Savannah and made his business mark in Atlanta, has been put down many times as an impractical visionary. But he had critics singing a different tune at the end of the 1980s when he titled an annual report, "Realizing the Vision." By that time he had become the largest supplier of programs to cable TV. His company, Turner Broadcasting System, which collected revenues of $54.6 million in 1980, soared over the $1 billion mark in 1989. A big part of the realized vision was Cable News Network (CNN), the 24-hour all-news channel Turner launched in 1980, reaching 1.7 million cable homes in the U.S. By 1980s' end CNN was reaching 53.8 million U.S. homes (plus six million more in 89 other countries), generating revenues of $250 million and gaining respect as a prime source of instant coverage of big news events.

Turner Broadcasting System runs a five-ring circus:

1. Two 24-hour news channels, CNN and Headline News Service, which present updated programs every half hour.

2. Two entertainment channels, the so-called Super Station, TBS, an Atlanta UHF channel whose programs are satellite-beamed to cable systems across the country; and TNT, a cable network Turner launched in 1988 with a showing of Gone with the Wind.

3. Syndication and licensing, which relies heavily on the world's largest inventory of old movies (Citizen Kane, Wizard of Oz, Casablanca among thousands of other titles), cartoons and shorts ("Bugs Bunny," "Tom & Jerry," "Popeye") and TV programs ("The Muppet Show," "Fraggle Rock"). Turner assembled this inventory in 1986 when he bought MGM/UA. This purchase put him so deeply in hock he had to sell back the studio right away, but he kept the library of 3,700 feature films (MGM, RKO and pre-1950 Warner Bros.). And he then infuriated many people in the entertainment industry by colorizing classic black-and-white films.

4. Sports: Turner owns the Atlanta Hawks basketball team and the Atlanta Braves baseball team (that's why their games are always on TBS), both of which lost money right through the 1980s. All-time baseball great Hank Aaron plays a triple role as director of player development for the Braves, director of community relations for Turner Broadcasting and a member of Turner's board.

5. Real estate: Turner owns the Omni International Hotel and office complex in downtown Atlanta, where both Turner's and CNN's headquarters are based, and the Omni Arena, where the Hawks play.

Turner Broadcasting floats on a complicated financial structure hardly anyone can understand without poring over pages of abstruse accounting legerdemain. That structure includes different classes of stock and various kinds of I-O-Us, one of which is called LYON for Liquid Yield Option Notes due in the year 2004 (Zero Coupon—Subordinated). Ted Turner clearly controls the show, but other big players in the cable TV industry got their incestuous hooks into the company in 1987. By bailing out Turner from the debt-

TOP 10 CABLE NETWORKS

		Subcribers (in millions)	Owners
1.	ESPN	54.8	Capital Cities/ABC (80%), RJR Nabisco
2.	CNN	53.8	Turner Broadcasting System
3.	TBS	52.1	Turner Broadcasting System
4.	USA	50.8	Paramount Communications, MCA
5.	Nickelodeon	49.7	Viacom
6.	MTV	49.3	Viacom
7.	Nashvile	48.3	Gaylord Broadcasting Network
8.	C-SPAN	48.0	Nonprofit co-op of cable industry
9.	Family Channel	48.0	CBN, Tele-Communications
10.	Lifetime	47.0	Capital Cities/ABC, Viacom, Hearst

Source: Wall Street Journal, 19 March 1990.

laden ship he was sailing, they acquired a considerable ownership in his company.

Turner Broadcasting System has Class A stock, each share of which has one vote—Ted Turner owns 80.7 percent of these shares; Class B stock, each share of which has one-fifth of a vote—Ted Turner owns 8.8 percent of these shares; and Class C preferred stock, each share of which has two-fifths of a vote—Denver-based Tele-Communications, the nation's largest operator of cable TV systems (and therefore an important Turner customer), owns 38 percent of these shares while, Time-Warner, the second largest operator of cable TV systems and a major program supplier (and therefore both a customer and Turner competitor) owns 32 percent of these C shares, and another cable TV operator, United Cable, owns 8.9 percent of them. To complicate matters further (if you're still following this), the Class C holders can convert their shares into Class B stock—and if they did, they would own over half of this class. And representatives of all these companies hold seats on the Turner board. When all is said and done, when it comes down to voting power, Ted Turner still holds 55.3 percent of the votes.

And Turner's ship still sails on a sea of debt. Annual interest payments in the late 1980s were over $200 million a year. In other words, over 20 percent of revenue went to pay debt interest. But a little debt never scared Ted Turner, a sailor who successfully defended the America's Cup in 1977. In 1980 he appeared on the CBS program, "60 Minutes," to explain his vision of a TV news channel that would reach into every corner of the world. Later on, in mid-decade, he tried to buy CBS. An inveterate gambler, Turner once drank a bottle of Chivas Regal Scotch in 10 minutes to win a bet. In 1989 *Forbes* ranked him 19th on their roster of the 400 richest Americans, with estimated wealth of $1.76 billion.

Stock performance. Turner Broadcasting System stock bought for $1,000 in 1987 sold for $2,103 on January 2, 1990.

Turner Broadcasting System, Inc., P.O. Box 105366, Atlanta, GA 30348; (404) 827-1000.

NEWSPAPERS

Newspapers remain a powerful force in American life, but they're not nearly as strong as they once were. To be sure, they still collect more advertising dollars than any other medium (more than $31 billion in 1989), but circulation is stagnant (except on Sundays), and newspaper publishers have to be concerned about studies showing only one of three persons between the ages of 18 and 29 read a newspaper every day. As the decade closed, longtime Washington Post news executive Richard Harwood painted this picture: "The problem is quite simple. People are getting out of the habit of buying or reading newspapers. Since 1970 the number of adults in the United States has increased by 34 percent, the number of households has increased by 41 percent and the circulation of daily newspapers has been absolutely stagnant, increasing by less than 1 percent."

1

GANNETT

#1 *in newspapers*

#7 *in broadcasting*

Employees: 36,800
Sales: $3.5 billion
Profits: $398 million
Founded: 1906
Headquarters: Arlington, Virginia

The nation's largest newspaper chain was once derided as a buyer of "small Mom and Pop dailies in one-newspaper towns" or as "a chain of small monopolies." In the 1980s Gannett set out to show they could operate in big cities, too. In mid-decade they outbid other publishers for the *Louisville Courier-Journal* ($305 million), *Des Moines Register & Tribune* ($165 million) and *Detroit Evening News* ($717 million). But their most audacious move was the 1982 launch of a new national newspaper, *USA Today*. Newshounds dismissed the paper as the "McPaper of fast-food jour-

nalism," and Wall Street security analysts saw it as a sure fire money-loser. However, *USA Today* hung in there and by the decade's end had reached a paid circulation of 1.8 million, second only to the *Wall Street Journal;* 1990 is expected to be their first profitable year. Moreover, their bright graphics, lavish use of color, weather maps, easy-to-grasp charts and tables have had a strong influence on their more stodgy brethren in the newspaper business. *USA Today* also became an indelible part of the landscape itself through the placement of 135,000 vending machines on America's streets and highways, machines artfully designed to serve as mini billboards for the 50-cent product.

Coming into the 1990s, Gannett was publishing 124 newspapers (83 dailies) in 36 states and territories as well as a Sunday supplement, *USA Weekend,* carried by more than 300 newspapers. Every day over 6 million copies of these papers are sold. During the 1980s their broadcast operations expanded to encompass 16 radio and 10 TV stations. They lease outdoor advertising sites in 11 states, and they own the pollster, Louis Harris & Associates. By almost any measure—sales, profits, total paid circulation, number of employees—Gannett is the country's largest newspaper publisher. But not in number of Pulitzer Prizes won for journalistic excellence. Longtime CEO Allen Neuharth had no interest in Pulitzers because they're given for "news that's bad and sad."

History. This empire began when Frank E. Gannett merged four small papers in upstate New York in 1906. At his death in 1957, Gannett had accumulated 30 newspapers and a string of radio and TV stations. Gannett became a media powerhouse in 1978 when they swallowed Arizona-based Combined Communications (CCC), which owned 7 TV stations, 13 radio stations, and the country's second largest outdoor advertising business (billboards).

Allen Neuharth, the colorful CEO who built Gannett's empire during the 1970s and 1980s, was once asked how to pronounce the company name—*Gan*nett or Gan*nett.* "The emphasis," he answered, "is on the net." It certainly was during Neuharth's years, when the bottom line, net profits, motivated most choices. During Neuharth's 19 years heading Gannett,

Two decades ago, about 95 percent of households received a daily paper as compared to 65 percent in 1988.

he spent almost $1.5 billion buying 69 daily newspapers and grabbing 16 TV stations, 29 radio stations (some of which had to be sold to meet FCC regulations) and the billboard business. He also moved Gannett's headquarters from Rochester to the Washington, D.C., area.

Owners and rulers. The *Wall Street Journal* called Allen Neuharth (Gannett's president from 1970 to 1979, CEO from 1973 to 1986 and chairman from 1979 to 1989) "journalism's most flamboyant personality." Once, when executives at *USA Today* had exceeded the paper's budget, Neuharth invited them to a mysterious meeting in Cocoa Beach, Florida. There, Neuharth held a "Last Supper." He sat at a long table, dressed as Jesus Christ, in a flowing robe, wearing a crown of thorns with a large wooden cross behind him. The message to his employees: Shape up, or this is the last supper. The incident was detailed in his best-selling book *Confessions of an S.O.B: A Maverick C.E.O. Reveals How You Can Outfox Your Enemies, Outcharm Your Friends, Outdo Yourself And Have a Helluva Lot of Fun!* The book, published in 1989, is peppered with Neuharth's advice and memories and includes testimonials from his two jilted ex-wives, his son and his daughter. After retiring, Neuharth continued as a $200,000 a year consultant and columnist at *USA Today*. Perhaps his lasting influence on Gannett was to alter their board. He wrote in *Confessions of an S.O.B.*, "I inherited a board of twelve white males, most from the East and most golf-playing buddies of my predecessor.... When I retired as chairman sixteen years later, the board had four women, three minorities, and was representative of the country from New York to Hawaii." One of those female board members is former First Lady Rosalyn Carter. Neuharth's replacement, John J. Curley, became CEO in 1986 at age 47 and chairman in 1989, when he took home $1.3 million. Curley's style is more low-key and cerebral than Neuharth's. Curley was the first editor of *USA Today*. Peter Prichard, current editor of *USA Today* and author of *The Making of McPaper*, observed, "Al likes limos and corporate jets. John is happy with taxicabs and bicycles."

As a place to work. Gannett has the best record in the newspaper business in the hiring and promotion of women and minorities. At *USA Today*, women hold 52 percent of all jobs, minorities 24 percent. Blacks are managing or executive editors at three dailies, publishers at four others. Gannett has a reputation for opposing unions. A mere 20 percent of employees at Gannett newspapers are unionized. Employees at Gannett's *Burlington Free Press* in Vermont voted for a union in 1989 to fight for higher wages and better health benefits.

Social responsibility. Gannett bought the *Detroit Evening News* in 1986 and then went head-to-head with Knight-Ridder's *Free Press* (where Neuharth once worked). Both were losing money, so they invoked the Newspaper Preservation Act to combine their business operations (printing, advertising, circulation) and share profits 50-50 for the next 100 years. After many years in the courts, the Supreme Court approved the deal, ending competition in the Motor City.

Global presence. Nil until *USA Today*, printed via satellite in Hong Kong, Singapore and Switzerland and distributed in 50 countries.

Stock performance. Gannett stock bought for $1,000 in 1980 sold for $5,585 on January 2, 1990.

Gannett Company, 1100 Wilson Boulevard, Arlington, VA 22234; (703) 284-6000.

2

TIMES MIRROR

#2 *in newspapers*
#14 *in magazines*

Employees: 28,500
Sales: $3.5 billion
Profits: $298 million
Founded: 1886
Headquarters: Los Angeles, California

The fattest U.S. newspaper (actress Barbara Bain once sued them, charging a paper hurled toward her doorstep killed her dog), the *Los Angeles Times* was the springboard for this publishing company. Times Mirror's interests now include six other newspapers, including *Newsday* in the New York metropolitan area, the *Baltimore Sun* and the *Hartford Courant;* eight traditionally male-oriented magazines, including *Field & Stream, Home Mechanix, Outdoor Life* and the *Sporting News;* cable TV operations in 11 states; specialty book publishers (art, medical, law and business); and four TV stations. However, newspapers are, by far, the biggest business, accounting for $2 billion in revenue—and by this measure Times Mirror is second only to Gannett in newspaper publishing.

The *Los Angeles Times* is more than a flagship paper. They dominate their metropolitan area in way that no other daily does, even more so since the demise of Hearst's *Los Angeles Herald Examiner* in November 1989. That casualty boosted *Times* circulation by 90,000 to 1.2 million; and, in combination with a 50,000 circulation loss by beleagured *New York Daily News,* established the *Los Angeles Times,* for the first time, as America's largest metropolitan daily newspaper. (Only the two national dailies, the *Wall Street Journal* and *USA Today,* have higher circulations.) On Sundays the *Los Angeles Times* circulation is 1.5 million, making it the second largest Sunday paper in the country (the *New York Times* is first with 1.7 million). The *Los Angeles Times* covers an area as far north as Santa Barbara and as far south as San Diego, and delivers 75 percent of their papers directly to homes—the highest proportion of any major daily in the country. (Who knows how many dogs they kill?)

During the 1980s the *Times Mirror* threw in the towel in two cities where the competition was intense, selling off the *Dallas Times-Herald* and the *Denver Post.* It's much easier to run a monopoly paper. However, Times Mirror did wheel their Long Island–based paper, *Newsday,* into the trenches in New York City, battling the *New York Daily News* (stealing their columnist Jimmy Breslin) so successfully that the mother paper across the country scrambled into first place among metropolitan dailies.

History. General Harrison Gray Otis was a Civil War hero who joined the fledgling *Los Angeles Times* in 1881, bought a piece of it the next year and picked up the rest in 1886. Meanwhile Harry Chandler, a sickly young man from New Hampshire who had come to southern California for his health, had gotten hold of the city's newspaper circulation routes. Chandler helped Otis wipe out the rival *Tribune* by getting his newsboys to "forget" to deliver it, then cemented the partnership by marrying the general's daughter.

Between 1881 and 1886 Los Angeles' population grew from 5,000 to 100,000 and the Otis-Chandler family amassed a fortune in real estate. The paper experienced a bitter strike in 1910, when the Times building was bombed and 20 people killed. The general was fiercely anti-union and used the paper to attack the 40-hour work week, saying workers would use their spare time in "the only diversions they know—pool, poker, drinking and petty agitation." In the 1930s *Time* magazine branded the *LA Times* "the most rabid labor-baiting, Red-hating paper in the United States." For many years the *LA Times* was a staunch supporter of conservative politicians, including Richard Nixon, and was considered the quintessential mouthpiece of the Southern California establishment.

All that changed in 1960, when Otis Chandler—great-grandson of General Otis—became publisher at age 32. He hired some of the country's best journalists, including liberal easterners, and upgraded the paper's image by winning a series of Pulitzer Prizes. Through a number of well-timed acquisitions, Otis Chandler built a $2 billion, newspaper-based publishing empire, Times Mirror. The Mirror part of the name comes from an afternoon paper started in 1948 and abandoned 14 years later.

From 1979 to 1984, CEO Robert Erburu (Otis Chandler's successor) went on an ill-fated spending spree, shelling out $1.2 billion for properties that included the *Hartford Courant,* the *Denver Post,* five TV stations, forest products and cable TV. In the next three years, Times Mirror had to sell off 17 properties for a total of $1.1 billion.

Some purchases stuck. In 1986 they bought the *Baltimore Sun* for $600 million, the largest sum ever paid for a daily paper. They checked out of general book publishing by selling New American Library and checked into textbook publishing (mostly business books) by acquiring Richard D. Irwin for $135 million. Other Times Mirror interests include 20 percent of newsprint producer Publishers Paper and 7 percent of the McClatchy newspaper chain (the *Bee* papers in Sacramento, Fresno and Modesto).

Throughout the 1980s, Times Mirror lavished care and money on their beloved *Los Angeles Times,* spending $600 million on new equipment that resulted in an easier-to-read format in October 1989.

Owners and rulers. During the 1980s, Chairman Otis Chandler gradually phased himself out of the company his family had run since 1881. Robert F. Erburu was named CEO in 1981 at age 51. The son of a Basque shepherd, he attended Harvard Law School and joined Times Mirror in 1961. Erburu picked up $1.6 million in 1989. In September 1989, 55-year-old David Laventhol, a veteran of the New York City newspaper wars *(Herald Tribune, World Journal Tribune, Newsday),* was named publisher and CEO of the *Los Angeles Times.*

The Chandler family, through a trust, owns 33 percent of outstanding shares; officers, directors and other insiders own another 9 percent.

As a place to work. The *LA Times* is a huge, faceless, nonunion bureaucracy where the infighting can be fierce. Wages and benefits are good but the ambiance could never be mistaken for the one in *The Front Page.* They've always been the forefront of computer technology—and they prize efficiency. The other side of the coin is blandness. They have an elegant executive dining room that is nonalcoholic.

Social responsibility. The *Los Angeles Times* has long catered to upscale readers in the outlying suburbs, and is perceived as ignoring Los Angeles' poorer minority residents. "We had the choice of doing nothing or following our readers into pockets of middle- and upper-middle-class affluence. The alternative, of course, would have been to adjust to the changing demo graphics of our home turf—to become a Third World paper," Otis Chandler told *California* magazine in 1982.

Stock performance. Times Mirror stock bought for $1,000 in 1980 sold for $5,283 on January 2, 1990.

Times Mirror Company, 220 West First Street, Los Angeles, CA 90012; (213) 237-3700.

3
Newhouse

#3 *in magazines*
#4 *in newspaper*

Employees: 19,500
Sales: $2.9 billion
Founded: 1922
Headquarters: New York City, New York City; Newark, New Jersey

Everyone has heard of one of their properties—*The New Yorker, Vogue,* Random House, *Parade,* to name a handful—but few people outside the media world have heard of the Newhouse family, whose holding company, Advance Publications, is the nation's 4th largest newspaper chain, 3rd largest magazine publisher, largest publisher of general books and 14th largest cable TV operator.

Advance is strictly private. Newhouse family members, headed by Si and Don, sons of founder Sam Newhouse, own all the stock. They aren't required to issue financial reports, and they don't. They also keep a low profile in their personal lives. They're not socialites, and their names don't pop up in gossip columns.

Newspapers comprise the biggest part of the Newhouse empire, generating revenues estimated at $1.7 billion in 1989. They operate 26 daily papers—most of them monopolies—in 22 cities, including the original paper, the *Staten Island Advance*. The biggest of these papers is the *Newark Star-Ledger,* and with circulation of 458,000, it's the largest newspaper in New Jersey and the 16th largest in the U.S. Newhouse papers have a combined circulation of 3.1 million. Other states where they have the largest papers are Ohio (*Cleveland Plain Dealer*), Oregon (*Portland Oregonian*) and Louisiana (*New Orleans Times-Picayune*).

Newhouse also plays a strong role in numerous other American newspapers through ownership of the Sunday supplement *Parade,* which, thanks to its distribution in 333 newspapers, claims circulation of 35,300,000 (a full-page color ad costs $421,400).

As far as newspapers go, the Newhouses stood pat during the 1980s. They didn't buy a single paper during the decade. One paper, the *Globe-Democrat* in St. Louis, ceased publication, absorbed by the *Post-Dispatch* in a deal giving the Newhouses a share of the profits.

A window on the Newhouse fortune was opened slightly during the 1980s when the IRS initiated one of the largest tax disputes in U.S. history, claiming taxes due on the estate of the founder, Samuel Newhouse, who died in 1979 at 84. The Newhouses had filed a return estimating taxes due at $48 million. The IRS said the figure was more like $600 million, plus another $300 million in penalties. In early 1990 the courts found in favor of the Newhouses. *Forbes,* in their 1989 roster of the richest Americans, placed the Newhouse fortune at $5.2 billion. *Fortune* has estimated the Newhouse wealth at $7.5 billion.

History. Samuel I. Newhouse (or "S. I." as he was known) was born in 1895 to Jewish immigrant parents, the eldest of eight children. He left school before he reached 15, and the diminutive Newhouse (he was 5 feet, 2 inches tall) landed a job with magistrate Hyman Lazarus in Bayonne, New Jersey. Lazarus took over the *Bayonne Times* as payment for a bad debt and told Newhouse (then 17) to "take care of it until we get rid of it." Newhouse

revived the paper by cutting costs and stimulating local advertising (Hyman Lazarus later died of complications from poison ivy). Newhouse also put quite a few relatives on the payroll.

In 1922 Newhouse bought the *Staten Island Advance* for $98,000. This small paper in the smallest of New York City's five boroughs became the cornerstone of the Newhouse empire. Profits from that begat the *Long Island Press* in 1932, the *Newark Star-Ledger* in 1933 and many others in the coming years. The Newhouse papers weren't crusaders or prize-winners, but solid business properties that got that way through cost cutting and keeping up with technological advances. Newhouse's philosophy allowed each paper to maintain editorial integrity.

After S. I. died, his two sons, S. I., Jr. (Si) and Donald, took over, keeping the company in family hands. At one point 64 Newhouse cousins, brothers, in-laws and other assorted relatives were on the payroll. *Forbes* described the operation as "half early Rothschild, half corner grocery store." Donald serves as president of Advance Publications and looks after the newspapers and broadcasting operations (cable TV systems in 17 states). Si is Advance chairman and oversees the books (they bought Random House in 1980) and the magazines (including the *New Yorker,* bought for $200 million in 1985, and *Vanity Fair,* a 1983 relaunch of an old magazine).

Owners and rulers. In 1990, Si Newhouse was 62, his brother Donald 60. They're close collaborators—and until recently were closemouthed with the press. The Newhouses' names rarely appear in their publications; Si's name appears in several Condé Nast publications, but not in the *New Yorker.* They inherited their father's nepotism. *Fortune* reported that when the Newhouses were asked why they didn't buy the *Chicago Sun-Times,* a family member replied, "No relatives available to run it." Si and Don both prepped at Horace Mann, attended Syracuse University (neither finished) and live two blocks away from each other on Manhattan's upper east side. Si Newhouse arrives at work each morning at 4:30 a.m.

As a place to work. Newhouse newspapers are notorious penny pinchers. In the glamorous world of magazines, though, the Newhouses spend with the best of them. In 1989, the *New York Times Magazine* characterized Si Newhouse's Condé Nast magazine empire as follows: "Glamour and celebrity are the coin of the realm, editors are stars and Britannia rules the waves. In their glossy journals, they are purveyors of gossip and celebrity." They poured tens of thousands of dollars into reviving *Vanity Fair,* paying top dollar to writers. The Newhouses are hands-on managers—that is, they watch the bottom line carefully—but they're rarely visible. Many employees of Newhouse publications have never met the Newhouses themselves. The Newhouses respect the culture of a property—the *New Yorker* and Random House, for example—but won't hesitate to make top-level changes: replacing William Shawn as editor of the *New Yorker* and deposing Robert Bernstein as head of Random House.

Newhouse has no corporate headquarters. Si Newhouse has offices at Condé Nast, 350 Madison Avenue, New York, New York 10017; (212) 880-8800. Donald can be reached at the *Newark Star-Ledger,* Star Ledger Plaza, Newark, New Jersey 17101; (201) 877-4141.

4

TRIBUNE COMPANY

Employees: 17,100
Sales: $2.4 billion
Profits: $242 million
Founded: 1847
Headquarters: Chicago, Illinois

August 8, 1988, was a historic day, one that, in the minds and hearts of many Chicagoans, will live in infamy. On that day the lights went on for the first time at Wrigley Field, the pristine, ivy-trellised ballfield on Chicago's north side, where the hapless-but-beloved Chicago Cubs play. The Cubs were the last major league team to install lights in their park. And diehards, who believe baseball is meant to be played in the sunlight, felt it a desecra-

> **I**n Washington, D.C., 87 percent of people with incomes over $75,000 read the **Washington Post** on a given day, while only 48 percent of people with incomes below $25,000 read it.

tion. Some Chicagoans even went to court in a futile effort to block the electrification.

The decision to play night baseball at Wrigley Field was not made by an absentee owner. On the contrary, the Tribune Company, publisher of the *Chicago Tribune* for more than 150 years, made it. Sentiment had no place here. This was a business decision, and it was quickly justified. The Cubs played seven night games at Wrigley Field in 1988 and set a season attendance record.

The decision to illuminate Wrigley Field was emblematic of change at the Tribune Company. Once the home of cantankerous, opinionated newspapers, run by people who owned them, the firm has evolved into a modern, faceless, corporate media power, intent on the bottom line. Their two most famous properties are the *Chicago Tribune* and the *New York Daily News,* the nation's seventh and fourth largest dailies, measured by circulation size. The Tribune Company publishes four other dailies, operates six TV and five radio stations, produces and distributes such high-quality TV programs as "Geraldo" (a coventure with Investigative News Group) and "The Joan Rivers Show" and owns two Canadian paper mills which sell half their newsprint to the Tribune newspapers.

History. Joseph Meharry Medill, a Canadian-born lawyer, put his stamp on the *Tribune* in the 19th century, and his grandsons, Robert Rutherford McCormick and Joseph Medill Patterson, carried into the 20th century a tradition of personal journalism intertwined with political passions. Medill, an abolitionist, arrived in Chicago in 1855 and promptly became part-owner of the *Chicago Tribune,* which played a major role in Abraham Lincoln's election to the presidency. The *Tribune* of those days was not one to mince words. It derided Lincoln's predecessor, James Buchanan, as an "imbecile old creature"; started a daily column, "Progress of Treason," to describe events unfolding in the South; and organized recruits for the Union Army (two of Medill's brothers were killed in the war). When Lincoln wondered whether he should be aiming for the vice presidency, Medill told him: "It's the presidency or nothing. Else you may count the *Tribune* out. We are not fooling away our time and science on the vice presidency."

Medill's two grandsons, Colonel McCormick and Captain Patterson (both fought in World War I), codirected the *Tribune* until 1925 when Patterson went off to New York to run the *Daily News,* which he founded in 1919. Under Bert McCormick, the *Tribune* became a bastion of right-wing ideology, a bitter opponent of Franklin D. Roosevelt (represented as one of the four horsemen of the Apocalypse, the other three were Mussolini, Stalin and Hitler), a strong defender of Senator Joseph McCarthy and Anglophobic (despite, or because of, Bert McCormick's having grown up in England when his father was attached to the U.S. delegation there). Editorial opinions seeped into the news columns, and the *Trib* also had a penchant for simplified English ("thru" instead of "through," "nite" instead of "night," "philosofy" instead of "philosophy"). When the *Tribune* was 100 years old in 1947, *Time* put Col. McCormick on the cover, calling the *Tribune* the "most widely feared and hated" paper in the nation, despite the paper's daily circulation of 1 million (720,000 today).

In the meantime, Capt. Joe Patterson in New York had no desire to replicate the *Chicago Tribune.* A socialist in his youth, he did not share his cousin's xenophobia (the *Tribune* masthead carried the cry, "My Country Right or Wrong"). Patterson's *New York Daily News* was a populist paper, not so much in politics as in raciness, down-to-earth language, pictures, crisp captions and humorous, punchy headlines: a paper for the masses. Patterson also brought comic strips to newspapers—"Dick Tracy," "Little Orphan Annie," "Moon Mullins" and "Gasoline Alley"—which became part of American pop culture. The *News* and the *Tribune* ran them and also syndicated them nationally.

Owners and rulers. The two cousins died after World War II, Patterson in 1946, McCormick in 1955, with no surviving Pattersons or McCormicks to take over the direction of the papers. However, under the terms of Col. McCormick's will, voting control was vested in a trust whose trustees were largely *Chicago Tribune* executives. Shares in the Tribune Company were first sold to the public in 1983, but company insiders (some involved in an Employee Stock Ownership Pan) control 35 percent of the votes. Great-great-granddaughter of founder Joseph Medill, Kristie Miller, a reporter for the *News-Tribune* in La Salle, Illinois, was elected to the *Trib* board in 1981. The La Salle paper is owned by the Miller family. Stanton R. Cook, CEO from 1974 until May 1990, was succeeded by 61-year-old C. T. Brumback. Cook took home $2.2 million in his last full year at the helm.

As a place to work. The Tribune Company's newspapers have a history of adversarial labor-management relations. At the end of the 1980s the Tribune management squared off against the 3,000 unionized workers at the *New York Daily News* in a struggle that some observers felt might mean the end for the 70-year-old feisty tabloid.

Social responsibility. Col. McCormick invented the term Chicagoland to describe the Chicago metropolitan area, and the Tribune Company remains a Chicago institution. The entire board of directors is composed of Chicagoans. The Medill School of Journalism on the Northwestern campus in Evanston was founded by the company in 1925. In that same year an enduring symbol of the company's Chicago presence was completed: Tribune Tower, a 36-story, Gothic building on North Michigan Avenue near the Chicago River. An imposing, medieval structure facing the gleaming white towers of the Wrigley Building across the street, Tribune Tower was built with an exterior of limestone and lead and an interior featuring travertine marble, solid mahogany and oak, along with bronze statuary. It's one of Chicago's many architectural gems, and certainly one of the most elegant buildings ever to house a newspaper office. Not surprising then that in 1981, when the Wrigley family decided that, for tax reasons, the Chicago Cubs had to be sold, the Tribune Company across the street emerged as the logical buyer. That was a sentimental decision (worth $20 million). Six years later the Tribune Company managers looked at the bottom line and lit up Wrigley Field.

Stock performance. Tribune stock bought for $1,000 in 1983 sold for $3,665 on January 2, 1990.

The Tribune Company, 435 N. Michigan Avenue, Chicago, Illinois 60611; (312) 222-9100.

5

KNIGHT RIDDER

#3 *in newspapers*

Employees: 21,200
Sales: $2.3 billion
Profits: $247 million
Founded: 1974
Headquarters: Miami, Florida

Knight-Ridder papers will never be found next to tabloid rags at the supermarket checkout. While Gannett was buying newspapers and broadcasting stations during the 1980s, Knight-Ridder papers were winning Pulitzer Prizes, reducing the number of papers they publish and selling their TV stations. From 1980 to 1990 Knight-Ridder papers captured 33 Pulitzers, bringing their total to 56 (the *New York Times* has won more but no newspaper *chain* has won as many as Knight-Ridder). They entered the 1990s with 29 daily newspapers, 3 less than they had in 1980. Twelve papers have circulations over 100,000. Three, the *Detroit Free Press, Philadelphia Inquirer* and *Miami Herald* rank among the nation's 20 largest. The average weekday circulation of all the Knight-Ridder papers was close to 4 million in 1989, second to Gannett's 6.3 million.

Knight-Ridder had problems in the mid-1980s. The four biggest papers (*Miami Herald, Philadelphia Inquirer, Detroit Free Press* and *San Jose Mercury News*) accounted for a staggering 55 per-

cent of company revenues—and all were struggling. The *Inquirer* had a paperwide strike, the *Herald's* circulation plummeted, the *Free Press* had lost $74 million in four years, and the *Mercury News* was reeling from a slump in Silicon Valley.

But Knight-Ridder is fighting back. They're making an interesting bet on computerized data bases from which they can sell information. And in 1989 they decided to sell their TV stations and two newspapers (the *Star-News* in Pasadena, California, and the *Post-Tribune* in Gary, Indiana). Meanwhile, they plunked down $355 million to buy Lockeed's Dialog Information Services.

History. Two wealthy newspaper families, the Knights and the Ridders, established this chain in 1974. John S. Knight and younger brother, James, built up the larger and more prestigious half of the merger from the *Akron Beacon Journal,* a paper inherited from their father, Charles Landon Knight. In 1937 the brothers bought the *Miami Herald,* which became the pride of the chain. The brothers bought more papers in Detroit, Chicago, North Carolina, Georgia, Kentucky and, in 1969, Philadelphia (the *Inquirer,* which they revamped into one of the nation's most respected papers). John Knight, who died in 1981, is said to have improved every paper he purchased, setting high standards that survived at Knight-Ridder after his death. He was a vocal advocate of quality journalism, and he believed the reading public would pay to read good reporting. He also believed Knight-Ridder should function as a holding company, allowing each newspaper in the chain to maintain a degree of independence.

While C. L. Knight was buying his first paper in Akron, Herman Ridder was running the *Staats-Zeitung,* the leading German language newspaper in the U.S., which he'd purchased in 1892. His three sons, Bernard, Victor and Joseph, took over the paper on their father's death in 1915. At the time of the merger with Knight, the Ridders owned 18 dailies in Minnesota, South Dakota, Washington, California, Indiana, Michigan and Colorado. "The Ridders could have been selling shoes. They were much more interested in the bottom line than the Knights," a reporter at the Ridder-owned

San Jose Mercury News told the *Washington Monthly*.

Owners and rulers. In 1988, 52-year-old James Batten was named CEO (1989 pay: $1.1 million). Taking Batten's place as president was 47-year-old P. Anthony Ridder, great-grandson of Ridder's founder. In September 1989, Batten became chairman when 68-year-old Alvah Chapman stepped down. James L. Knight, 80, owns 10.2 percent of the common shares, worth about $270 million in early 1990. The three Ridders on the board (Bernard and Eric, grandsons of the founders, and Tony, the great-grandson) own about 4 percent of shares. Company officers and directors of the company control 40 percent of the stock.

As a place to work. Many journalists consider Knight-Ridder a good place to work. When other publishers fill high-level jobs, Knight-Ridder people are often on the top of the list. Two company vice presidents of the company are women. One notable K-R defector was Al Neuharth, who left to head rival chain Gannett. When Knight-Ridder emerged as the only newspaper chain in *The 100 Best Companies to Work for in America* in 1984, CEO Alvah Chapman said the accolade was better than winning a Pulitzer Prize.

Stock performance. Knight-Ridder stock bought for $1,000 in 1980 sold for $5,688 on January 2, 1990.

Knight-Ridder, One Herald Plaza, Miami, FL 33132; (305) 376-3800.

TOP 10 NEWSPAPERS BY CIRCULATION

Newspaper	Circulation
1. *Wall Street Journal*	1,935,866
2. *USA Today*	1,460,494
3. *Los Angeles Times*	1,210,077
4. *New York Daily News*	1,180,139
5. *New York Times*	1,149,683
6. *Washington Post*	824,282
7. *Chicago Tribune*	740,713
8. *Newsday* (New York)	711,264
9. *Detroit Free Press*	639,767
10. *San Francisco Chronicle*	569,257

Source: Advertising Age, 7 May 1990.

6

The New York Times

#1 *in Sunday newspapers*

Employees: 10,700
Sales: $1.8 billion
Profits: $267 million
Founded: 1851
Headquarters: New York City, New York

The *New York Times,* also known as "the good gray lady," is an American institution if there ever was one. The *Times* has been called the most important newspaper in the U.S. *and* the world, the first paper many U.S. presidents and foreign heads of state reach for in the morning, not to speak of nervous playwrights who want to see if their new work will be around for a while or close the next day, or authors who want to see if their book made the *New York Times* best-seller list, or survivors who want to see if their recently departed loved one made the obituary page. The *Times* is a newspaper of record, one that carries out their mission with pomposity. As the *New Yorker* said in 1990, "If Spinoza's God were to edit a newspaper, it might read like the *Times*." Through 1990 they had won 61 Pulitzer Prizes for excellence in daily journalism (more than any other newspaper)—but no comic strip has ever graced their pages. And like all institutions, they're the object of a lot of hostility. Newshounds complain the *Times* covers Afghanistan better than the Bronx.

Milestone after milestone was passed in the 1980s. In 1983 the New York Times Company crossed the $1 billion sales mark for the first time. In 1985 *Times* average daily circulation exceeded 1 million for the first time. And by decade's end, the *Times* was printing a national edition by satellite at eight different locations so that subscribers in San Francisco, Chicago, Dallas, Miami and other cities could pick up copies on their doorsteps, sometimes before New Yorkers were able to buy their papers. Average daily *Times*

Iphigene Sulzberger, matriarch of The New York Times, *died in February, 1990.*

circulation, coming into 1990, was 1.1 million, of which 190,000 represented national edition circulation. On Sundays the *New York Times* is the biggest newspaper with a circulation of 1.7 million—300,000 from the national edition.

The New York Times Company also expanded their media holdings considerably during the 1980s. Entering the decade with 9 newspapers, other than the *Times*, they emerged with 35. In 1985 alone they spent $400 million to buy five dailies and two TV stations (they now have five TV outlets). At decade's end, they exited the cable TV business but acquired *McCall's* to bring their magazine properties to 15 (the biggest is *Family Circle*). They also own two New York radio stations, WQXR, AM and FM.

History. By mid-19th century seven papers called the *New York Times* had been published, and each had died. The eighth, started in 1851 by journalist Henry J. Raymond and banker George Jones, stuck. The *Times* was, from inception, a paper for businessmen and an organ for the new Republican Party. (Raymond, known as the Godfather of the Republican Party, gave the keynote address at the party's 1856 convention.) Their coverage of the Civil War and their postwar exposes of corruption in the Tammany Hall-Boss Tweed administration made the *Times* a

popular, and highly successful, paper but they lost ground steadily in the 1880s and early 1890s after switching to the Democrats and losing readers to the new muckraking journals of Pulitzer (the *World*) and Hearst (the *Journal*). After the financial panic of 1893, *Times* circulation fell to 9,000. By 1896 they were $300,000 in debt and losing $2,500 a week. Adolph Ochs, who borrowed $75,000 from bankers to buy the paper, came to the rescue.

Ochs was the son of German Jews who had come to Tennessee to escape persecution. He bought his first paper, the *Chattanooga Times*, in 1878 when he was 20. (The Chattanooga paper is still in the Ochs family but is not part of the Times Company.) After buying the *New York Times*, Ochs set the paper on a new course. He cleaned up the typeface, added Sunday sections, adopted the slogan, "All the news that's fit to print" and reduced the price from 3 cents to a 1 cent (at a time when Hearst and Pulitzer were charging 2 cents for their papers). Circulation climbed to 75,000 by the turn of the century. The Ochs-owned *New York Times* had to be financially competitive to survive, but was not about to get into screaming matches with Hearst and Pulitzer. The *Times* was not going to be a paper for the masses. Ochs expanded coverage of financial news and began listing the names of store buyers who came to New York to shop, a move—as David Halberstam pointed out in *The Powers That Be*—that "helped make the *Times* the paper of the retail fashion business." British journalist Martin Walker said of Ochs: "His support had come from the bankers, and the *Times* became a bankers' paper." Or, as Halberstam recounts, "Ochs wanted nothing that would shock or offend or cause controversy. Since he could not win a segment of the market by being lively, he would win by being serious." And serious is what the *Times* became, a paper of record. "A dull record perhaps," said Halberstam, "but that did not bother Ochs, he liked a dull paper, and he did not mind if people thought him a bit dull as long as they treated him with respect." Many of his strictures remain. *Times* reporters still refer to men as "Mr." and women as "Mrs." or "Ms."—with the exceptions of criminals and athletes.

New York City once had a dozen daily newspapers and the *Times* has outlasted all of them but two—the *Daily News* and the *Post,* both of which have been struggling to stay alive. And the same family controls a much fatter, much more prosperous and influential newspaper, the base of an expanding media company. The New York Times Company began buying other media properties during the 1970s. They established their national edition during the 1980s. They're still headquartered in the same location on West 43rd Street, where Adolph Ochs put up a new building and printing plant in 1904. He convinced the city fathers to name the nearest crossroads Times Square.

Owners and rulers. Descendants of Adolph Ochs own 22 percent of the A shares, which trade on the American Stock Exchange, and 78 percent of the B shares, which elect 9 of the 14 directors. The *Times* has never had a publisher who was not a member of the founding family. Arthur Hays Sulzberger, who married Adolph Ochs' daughter, Iphigene, ran the paper from 1935 to 1961, when the job passed to Arthur's son-in-law, Orvil Dryfoos. When Dryfoos died two years later, Adolph's grandson, Arthur Ochs Sulzberger (known as Punch because of his boyhood habit of hitting his sister Judy), stepped into the publisher's seat at age 37. He presided over the evolution of the Times Company into a modern corporation and was still CEO in 1990. His son, A. O. Sulzberger, Jr., aged 38 in 1990, was promoted from assistant publisher to deputy publisher in 1989, at which point his name was moved next to his father's on the paper's masthead. The matriarch, Iphigene Ochs Sulzberger, died in 1990 at 97. She had been, successively, the wife, mother-in-law and mother of four *Times* publishers. Mount Iphigene in Antarctica was named for her by Admiral Richard Byrd. It overlooks Sulzberger Bay.

As a place to work. With a staff of 1,000, the *Times* employs more reporters and editors than any other paper in the world. The city room on West 43rd Street is a sea of humanity. Personal journalism it's not. But for all the bureaucracy and vicious interoffice politicking, any ambitious journalist still wants to work here. And funny things can happen. Russell Baker can end up writing a humor column on the op-ed page, and for more than 20 years an ex-society page reporter, the late Phil Dougherty, ran a highly personalized advertising news column that rarely failed to contain a subtle dig at the people, and industry, he was writing about.

Social responsibility. The *Times* is conscious of being a paper for the white upper class. In a 1990 address to a meeting of Hispanic journalists, newly elected Managing Editor Joseph Lelyveld said the health of metropolitan dailies must be linked to the health and development of minority communities in their circulation area, and he added it was incumbent on newspapers to cover "their communities as an ongoing concern and not simply as zones of violence." Lelyveld conceded the *Times* doesn't shine in community service. He noted that in covering the Happy Land nightclub fire in the Bronx that killed 85 people in early 1990, the *Times* benefitted from having two Spanish-speaking reporters. Had the disaster occurred two years earlier, the *Times* would have had none.

Global presence. One-third interest in the *International Herald Tribune,* a 40 percent stake in three Canadian newsprint mills and the biggest staff of international correspondents in the world of journalism.

Stock performance. New York Times stock bought for $1,000 in 1980 sold for $8,329 on January 2, 1990.

New York Times Company, 229 West 43rd Street, New York, NY 10036; (212) 556-1234.

7

DOW JONES & COMPANY, INC.

#1 *in daily newspapers*

Employees: 9,400
Sales: $1.7 billion
Profits: $317 million
Founded: 1882
Headquarters: New York City, New York

They like to describe their audience as "Main Street America" but their fortunes have much more to do with another street: Wall Street. They're a household word because the Dow Jones Industrial Average, composed of 30 stocks they pick, is the most widely used barometer of stock market action. And of course they publish the *Wall Street Journal,* a national daily with the highest circulation of any U.S. newspaper. *Journal* circulation peaked at 2.1 million in 1983. By the decade's end it still sold more copies than any other newspaper, but circulation had dipped to 1.8 million. Undaunted, Dow Jones continued to expand the paper's coverage (three sections now instead of one), increase the price (now 50 cents on newsstands, $129 a year by subscription), launch more regional editions (now 12) and raise advertising rates ($95,000 to buy a full page in the national edition). In the late 1980s, when the securities industry was traumatized, the *Journal's* advertising declined sharply. Rate increases helped keep revenues up but profits lagged.

The *Wall Street Journal* is the heart and soul of the Dow Jones Company, accounting for about 70 percent of revenues, but DJ does have other businesses, notably *Barron's,* a weekly paper chock full of stock tips, a string of 23 dailies in nine states, most of them in small towns like Stroudsburg (Pennsylvania), Hyannis (Massachusetts), Santa Cruz (California) and Chapel Hill (North Carolina). They also supply financial information to brokerage houses, banks, insurance companies, pension funds and foreign exchange traders via their news service, known as the Broadtape; their database known as News/Retrieval; and Telerate, which goes head-to-head with Reuters in delivering computerized market information investors need instantly. Dow Jones operates overseas, but they've yet to make it there the way they have at home. The European edition of the *Wall Street Journal* had a circulation of 43,000 at the end of 1987, the Asian edition 35,000. During the 1980s Dow Jones gave up on book publishing and cable TV.

Descendants of founder Clarence Barron continue to control the voting shares of the company. Barron bought the business in 1902 from founders Charles H. Dow and Edward D. Jones, who had started their own financial news service 20 years earlier. Their office was in a basement on Wall Street—right behind a soda fountain. Dow's job was to cover the news, taking shorthand notes on his shirt cuffs. The two young men then wrote by hand, bulletins called the *Customer's Afternoon Letter.* In 1889, they bought a small press and started the *Wall Street Journal.* Barron started *Barron's Weekly* in 1921. He died in 1928.

In 1932, when the *Journal* was 50 years old, their circulation was 28,000, and remained at that level through the depression when the paper was not preferred reading at the White House or at other newspaper offices, unlike today. The ultimate triumph of the *Wall Street Journal* is a tribute to a succession of editors, beginning with Barney Kilgore in 1941, who were perceptive enough to realize business is affected by more than just business news. They made the *Journal* a wide-ranging paper, of catholic interests. Kilgore's admonition to reporters was: "Don't write banking stories for bankers. Write for the banks' customers. There are a hell of a lot more depositors than there are bankers." He also waged war against clichés. In 1945 he tacked up a notice on the bulletin board that said: "If I read 'upcoming' in the *Wall Street Journal* once more, I'll be 'downcoming' and someone will be 'outgoing.'"

The *Wall Street Journal* has been, in their own way, a maverick. Clarence Barron once became so angry with Sinclair Oil he refused to list the company's stock in the paper or on the Dow Jones ticker. In the 1950s General Motors canceled all their *Journal* advertising because the paper printed sketches of new cars before they were introduced. In 1984 Mobil Oil canceled all $500,000 of their advertising because the *Journal* reported that Mobil's chairman, Rawleigh Warner, Jr., had awarded his son-in-law shares in a real estate transaction. The *Journal* had previously reported that the son of Mobil's president, William Tavoulareas, received questionable management fees (totaling $1.67 million) as a result of his Mobil connection. Mobil stopped sending press releases to the *Journal* and refused to respond to telephone inquiries from *Journal* reporters. The *Journal* has also opened their pages to viewpoints other than their own. In the late 1980s the *Journal's* op-ed page became a pulpit for radical, left-wing writer Alexander Cockburn.

Finally, the *Wall Street Journal* has influenced the quality of business journalism in general, clearly for the better. The *Journal* has succeeded in part because daily papers had defaulted on coverage of the business scene. Their financial pages were mostly unreadable to the uninitiated. The *Journal* demonstrated that writing about business didn't have to be dull.

In 1984, however, the *Journal's* "Heard on the Street" columnist, R. Foster Winans, was accused of insider trading. Winans was leaking information to traders before his column hit the stands. The traders could then correctly anticipate and exploit market fluctuations because Winans' column was so widely read by Wall Street. Winans was fired, and in 1985, was sentenced to 18 months in prison, a $5,000 fine and five years probation.

Chairman and CEO Warren J. Phillips (aged 64 in 1990), son of a Manhattan garment maker, joined the *Journal* as a copyreader after being rejected by Columbia University's Graduate School of Journalism. He became managing editor when he was 31. He was paid $1.3 million in 1989.

Stock performance. Dow Jones stock bought for $1,000 in 1980 sold for $6,023 on January 2, 1990.

Dow Jones & Company, Inc., 200 Liberty Street, New York, NY 10281; (212) 416-2000.

8

The Washington Post

#2 *in newsweeklies*

Employees: 6,300
Sales: $1.4 billion
Profits: $198 million
Founded: 1877
Headquarters: Washington, D.C.

How long can the *Washington Post* live off Watergate? In 1990, 16 years after the paper's investigative stories helped turn a president out of office and then yielded the book and film, *All the President's Men,* the *Post* was still basking in the reflective glory of that event and their central role in it. Still, the *Post* stirs the juices. Some New Yorkers, weaned on the *New York Times,* swear the *Post* is a better newspaper. But some people in Washington, D.C., where the paper is published, swear the *Post* is elitist, anti-union, antiblack and antifemale. What's not in dispute is the *Post's* dominant position in the nation's capital, a dominance greatly enhanced in 1981 when their main competitor, the *Washington Star,* folded. That did wonders for *Post's* circulation, which zoomed from 627,000 to 780,000, and for profits, which jumped from $32 million to $200 million. (The closest thing to a *Post* competitor in Washington now is the ultraconservative *Washington Times,* with one-eighth of the circulation of the *Post,* edited by Arnaud de Borchgrave, who used to work for the Post Company's *Newsweek.*

As some have observed, the *Post* became more conservative as they became richer. In a 1986 appraisal, the *Wall Street Journal* described the *Post* as "settling down," with "flashy writing and erratic highs and lows" giving way to "a solid, if duller, consistency" and the editorial page tilting "back toward the center." *Post* columnist Haynes Johnson said, "The *Post* is more sober, more careful, less bold."

The *Post* is often mentioned in the same breath as the *New York Times* and *Wall Street Journal* as one of the country's most important dailies. But unlike those two papers, the *Post* is strictly a local paper, not too visible outside the District of Columbia except in the New York news-

Katherine Graham, Chairman of the board of the Washington Post, is the only female CEO of a Fortune 500 Company.

rooms of TV networks. Their circulation in the nation's capital ranks them as the nation's sixth largest newspaper and the monopoly profits the *Post* generates enable them to support other activities, notably *Newsweek*, the perennial number two to *Time* in news magazines. The Washington Post Company also owns the *Herald,* a daily paper in Everett, Washington; four television stations; cable systems with 420,000 subscribers; the Stanley H. Kaplan Educational Center, which gives kids cram courses to pass standardized tests like the SAT; and Legi-Slate, a computerized data base tracking congressional and regulatory actions.

Katharine Graham, whose father, Eugene Meyer, bought the *Post* at a bankruptcy auction in 1933, took command of the company in 1963. In 1979 she relinquished the publisher's position to her son, Donald E. Graham, while she continued as chairman and CEO of the Washington Post Company. She was the first woman ever to head a *Fortune* 500 company, and she has been called the "most powerful woman in America." In 1987, when her children hosted a black-tie dinner to celebrate her 70th birthday, guests included Secretary of State George Shultz,

former Secretary of State Henry Kissinger, Sony Chairman Akio Morita, Chancellor Helmut Kohl of West Germany, newspaper moguls Rupert Murdoch, Otis Chandler and Arthur O. Sulzberger and the former British prime minister, Sir James Callaghan (now Lord Callaghan of Cardiff). The press was barred from covering the party. In early 1990, the Post Company began selling shares on the New York Stock Exchange; these shares have limited voting rights. Katharine Graham's daughter, Elizabeth Graham Weymouth, recently joined the company; but first she had to get a job offer from a competitor (which she did).

Stock performance. Washington Post stock bought for $1,000 in 1980 sold for $14,952 on January 2, 1990.

The Washington Post Company, 1150 15th Street Northwest, Washington, D.C. 20071; (202) 334-6600.

9
Thomson

#1 *in number of U.S. newspapers, Canadian newspapers, retail merchandising in Canada*

Employees: 60,000
Sales (World): $8 billion, (U.S.): $1.2 billion
Founded: 1934
Headquarters: Toronto, Canada

They buy newspapers and magazines the way some people eat popcorn. In 1988 Thomson spent $400 million to buy 11 U.S. newspapers, bringing their U.S. total to 116 dailies and 4 weeklies, up dramatically from the 64 dailies they had in 1980. Gannett and Knight-Ridder reach more people with their papers but no one owns as many newspapers as Thomson. As of early 1990, they controlled about 200. And not just in the U.S. In their home country, Canada, Thomson has a string of 40 dailies and 12 weeklies, including the country's largest daily, the *Toronto Globe & Mail.* Their papers account for 25 percent of total newspaper circulation in Canada. In Britain, they publish 61 newspapers, including the venerable *Scotsman* in Edinburgh. They're the largest regional newspaper publisher in Britain. In the U.S., their papers are located primarily in small towns. For instance, in early 1990 they blitzed Ohio, Wisconsin and Indiana, snapping up 15 news papers—including the Phoenix Publications' 9 Ohio non-dailies (serving tiny Ohio towns like Niles, Newton Falls and Hubbard), 2 Ohio daily newspapers, 2 Indiana dailies (the *Terre Haute Tribune-Star* and the *Anderson Herald Bulletin*) and 2 Wisconsin dailies.

Thanks to such acquisitiveness during the 1980s, Thomson became a major publisher of magazines, newsletters, journals, directories, books and other informational carriers aimed at business, professional and technical audiences. In their American inventory are such successful publications as *American Banker,* the *Journal of Taxation, Medical Economics, Official Railway Guide* and *Traffic World.* In Britain, Thomson owns the world-famous Jane's Publishing, the giant of military publishing. Best known for their 15 definitive annuals such as *Jane's Fighting Ships, Ward's Automotive Handbook* and *All the World's Aircraft,* they also publish a slew of newsletters and magazines. Their main competitor was Swiss-based, Interavia S.A., so in 1987 Thomson bought Interavia. The combined Jane's-Interavia operation issues over 500 different publications a year. Thomson once tallied how many different publications they owned—and the list came to well over 10,000. Thomson also controls Canada's biggest retail merchandiser, Hudson's Bay (operator of The Bay department stores; Zeller's, a discount department store chain; and the Simpson's chain) and a British travel firm.

History. It all began with Roy Herbert Thomson, son of a Toronto barber, who was born in 1894 and dropped out of school at 14. He worked at office jobs, as a farmer and an auto parts distributor before starting his own radio station, CFCH, in 1930, with a secondhand transmitter. About then Thomson had a revelation: Money could be made by selling advertisers something as intangible as airtime. He borrowed money and bought two more stations, and in 1934 bought a run-down weekly newspaper, the *Timmins Press.* A year later he converted it to a daily—the first of 11 such conversions. He wasn't interested in the editorial product, only the business side, where the money

was made. Soon he was publishing more newspapers in Ontario than anyone else, and branched out into other fields—trucking, insurance, furniture, shoe polish and Toni home-permanent kits. He bought papers in the U.S. (starting with the St. Petersburg, Florida, *Independent*), Scotland (he bought The *Scotsman* and then emigrated to Scotland) and England (the Kemsley newspaper chain and the *Times* of London). The Queen made him Lord Thomson of Fleet. He joined an oil-drilling consortium John Paul Getty led and made millions.

Owners and rulers. After Roy Thomson died, his son Kenneth assumed the title of Lord Thomson of Fleet—and the company went on a wild buying spree in the U.S., buying up hundreds of trade publications that serve particular professions and industries. Although he is one of the richest men in the world, Lord Thomson lives simply. He flies coach and often eats cheese sandwiches at his desk. In late 1989, Ken Thomson's son, David, aged 32, sold most of his holdings in the family company (worth about $95 million) to his father, giving Ken Thomson 68.4 percent ownership of Thomson Corp. and 77.3 percent of Hudson's Bay. David Thomson, heir to his father's title, is an art connoisseur and is chairman and CEO of the Simpson's Ltd. chain.

Social responsibility. Some publishers advance a political point of view. Others pioneer new journalistic forms. And others strive to improve the quality of their publications. Thomson doesn't fall into any of those camps. The culture at Thomson is making money. They just happen to be in the media business. After his father died, Ken Thomson sold one of the world's most prestigious papers, the *Times of London,* to Rupert Murdoch because the paper wasn't making enough money—and besides, Ken Thomson preferred living in Toronto to London (he moved headquarters from Britain to Canada). Bruce V. VanDusen, editor of Indiana's *Kokomo Tribune* before it was sold to Thomson in 1981, reported that after takeover the Thomson people instituted efficiency measures such as counting up the number of stories and photographs per staffer that appeared in the paper. The initial count showed the

Tribune was running 2 stories and 0.49 photographs per staffer, way out of whack with ratios on other Thomson papers, where the average was 7.7 stories and 1.2 photos per staffer. In 1988, when *Advertising Age* ranked media companies based on how much profit they squeezed out of sales, Thomson Newspapers ranked second among all companies and first among newspaper publishers.

The Thomson Corporation, 65 Queen Street West, Toronto M5H 2M8 Canada; (416) 864-1710.

MAGAZINES

This may be the electronic (that is, visual) age, but magazines still boomed during the 1980s. According to one estimate, more than 2,500 new magazines were launched between 1980 and 1989. Two new ones appeared for every one that disappeared. Most of them were specialized publications aimed at a particular audience but many were general consumer magazines, others were city magazines, still others were entertainment magazines. It was a decade of tremendous ferment. Walter Annenberg sold TV Guide to Rupert Murdoch for $3 billion. The founders of Reader's Digest died—and the company that publishes the Digest decided to sell stock to the public for the first time. The New Yorker was sold to the Newhouses. The New York Times bought McCall's. CBS got out of the magazine business and the French publisher, Hachette, became the owner of a dozen American magazines, including Elle, Woman's Day and Road & Track. The Newhouses resurrected Vanity Fair, Frances Lear used her divorce settlement from Norman ("All in the Family") Lear to start Lear's and Hugh Hefner relinquished the CEO post at Playboy to daughter Christie Hefner. Hearst bought Esquire, and Rolling Stone bought Us. The Newhouses bounced Grace Mirabella as editor-in-chief of Vogue, and Rupert Murdoch stepped in quickly to back her in a new magazine, Mirabella, Vogue's competition.

1
Hearst

Employees: 15,000
Sales: $2.0 billion
Founded: 1887
Headquarters: New York City, New York

William Randolph Hearst's death in summer 1951 at age 88 marked the end of an era. Neither his sons nor his grandchildren carried on his flamboyant tradition. But the Hearst properties survive today as a powerful, professionally-managed media empire, ranking as the 2nd largest magazine publisher, 11th largest newspaper chain, 11th largest TV station operator

BEST-SELLING CONSUMER MAGAZINES

		Circulation
1.	Modern Maturity	21.4 million
2.	Reader's Digest	16.3 million
3.	TV Guide	15.9 million
4.	National Geographic	10.9 million
5.	Better Home and Gardens	8.0 million
6.	Family Circle	5.5 million
7.	Good Housekeeping	5.2 million
8.	McCall's	5.1 million
9.	Ladies' Home Journal	5.0 million
10.	Woman's Day	4.7 million

and 10th largest radio station owner. Hearst is also a major factor in book publishing (Morrow, Avon, Arbor House) and newspaper syndication (King Features). Hearst properties include *Cosmopolitan, Good Housekeeping, Harper's Bazaar;* WCVB-TV, Boston; WBAL-AM, Boston; the *Houston Chronicle* and the flagship paper where the empire started, the *San Francisco Examiner,* self-styled "monarch of the dailies."

History. In 1897, William Randolph sent *New York Journal* correspondent Frederick Remington to Havana to keep his eye on the growing unrest among Cuban rebels fighting for freedom from Spain. After days spent idling in a Havana hotel, Remington grew bored and wired his boss: "Everything is quiet. There is no trouble here. There will be no war. I wish to return." Hearst replied: "Please remain. You furnish the pictures and I'll furnish the wars." Through his "penny press" (Hearst dropped prices and enlarged headlines), Hearst had the power to dictate war and peace and to make or break politicians—and he used it. Without Hearst, Theodore Roosevelt and Franklin Delano Roosevelt may have never ascended to the presidency, and the U.S. may never have gone to war with Spain.

Hearst's rise as a media baron began in 1887 when his wealthy father, George, who struck it rich from the fabled Comstock silver lode, gave him the *San Francisco Examiner.* Hearst was soon running bigger headlines than San Franciscans had ever seen, and he went on to build the most massive newspaper chain in America. At one point, he owned 33 papers, most often in big cities. By the mid-1920s, he also owned seven magazines, and was the world's biggest user of paper. Hearst's flamboyant life inspired Orson Welles' movie classic *Citizen Kane.* But when Hearst died in 1951 the glamour had faded and his publishing empire was shrinking. Richard E. Berlin, who went on to run the Hearst empire during the 1950s and 1960s, merged or dumped money-losing newspapers in New York, Detroit, Boston, Chicago, San Francisco, Milwaukee and Pittsburgh. Frank A. Bannack, Jr., who became CEO in 1979, reversed the selling process, buying magazines, TV stations, cable systems, newspapers and book publishing houses. *Redbook, Esquire* and the *Houston Chronicle* were added to the Hearst family during the 1980s.

Owners and rulers. In his 125-page will, Hearst left the publishing empire in the family's name, but deliberately kept corporate control from his five sons. Hearst split the company stock into thirds—leaving two-thirds to two charitable foundations and the other third to his sons and their heirs. As a result, nonfamily company executives have the voting majority on company boards.

Global presence. Hearst's British subsidiary publishes seven magazines including *Good Housekeeping* and *Cosmopolitan*.

The Hearst Corporation, 959 Eighth Avenue, New York, NY 10019; (212) 649-2000.

2

Reader's Digest

#1 *in monthly magazines*

Employees: 7,400
Sales: $1.9 billion
Profits: $171 million
Founded: 1922
Headquarters: Chappaqua, New York

Reader's Digest is the world's most widely read magazine and has been so for a long time, but the 1980s took a toll. In 1981 cofounder DeWitt Wallace died at 91. Three years later his wife and cofounder, Lila Acheson Wallace, died at 94. From Chappaqua, New York, where the *Digest* is headquartered (their mailing address is nearby Pleasantville), there were protestations nothing would change. But of course things did. Before the decade's end the *Digest* had bought four other magazines—*Travel-Holiday, The Family Handyman, 50 Plus* and *American Health*—and announced that for the first time in their history shares in the publishing company would be sold to the public.

Even before the Reader's Digest Association went public in 1990, Chairman George V. Grune had pushed through a series of changes signaling the company would change forever. Grune, an ex-marine, offered early retirement to almost 300 employees, sold off a number of subsidiaries, folded the 40-year-old Japanese edition and cut employment from 10,000 to 7,400. His moves were all part of a new profit-oriented strategy that distressed some old-time Digesters used to a family way of operating. In 1988 Lila Wallace's museum-like offices were converted into offices for editors. Deputy Editor-In-Chief Fulton Oursler, Jr., resigned, telling

NEWHOUSE MAGAZINES

Magazine	Circulation
1. *Glamour*	2,190,027
2. *Mademoiselle*	1,283,242
3. *Self*	1,229.791
4. *Vogue*	1,202.471
5. *Gourmet*	806,304
6. *Traveler*	753,381
7. *GQ*	669,923
8. *Vanity Fair*	652,310
9. *The New Yorker*	613,275
10. *HG*	601,112
11. *Woman*	518,943
12. *Bride's*	387,252
13. *Details*	50,000

Source: *Newsweek*, 1 May 1989.

Forbes: "This is a symbol of the dispossession of the *Digest's* origins by current management. An institution that loses a sense of its origins may find that its destiny deteriorates."

Grune's pedantic answer: "We're capitalizing on our past strengths to move into new markets and to better position ourselves for future growth."

Those past strengths began with the *Digest,* the pocket-sized magazine published in 39 editions and 15 languages, reaching 100 million people each month (17 million circulation in the U.S.). The *Digest,* in turn, has generated a mailing list (55 million strong in the U.S., including present and past subscribers) that has made the company a giant in two other areas: book publishing and record distribution. In 1989, 59 percent of the company's sales came from books and home entertainment; 32 percent came from *Reader's Digest;* and 6 percent came from three special interest magazines—*The Family Handyman, New Choices* and *Travel-Holiday.* About 53 percent of company sales come from Europe. The company condenses books the way they do articles—and Reader's Digest Condensed Books sold 21 million copies in 10 languages in 1989. They're masters of the art of condensation, proudly quoting a com-

*Presentation of one of the first shares of
Reader's Digest nonvoting stock.*

ment made by Jack Higgins, whose novel, *The Night of the Fox,* was digested: "When I read the condensed version of one of my books I am always astonished because I can't figure out what you've actually cut out." The *Digest* has published books from scratch, too. Three of them—*How to Do Just About Anything, ABC's of the Human Body* and *Household Hints and Handy Tips*—each sold 1 million copies in the first 30 days after they were offered. The *Digest* is also a world leader in the marketing of music. Since 1959 they have sold over 400 million records, tapes and compact discs. Unlike other magazines, which farm out order-taking to outside firms located in Des Moines and other places, the *Digest* handles their own mail. They employ over 1,000 people in their computerized data-processing center, where each day they process over 100,000 orders, deposit $2 million in customer payments, log about 500,000 sweepstakes responses (the *Digest* invented this way of selling subscrip-

tions) and print and distribute more than 2 million letters

In years past, the company was famed for being tenderly paternalistic toward the Digesters, as employees call themselves. Times have changed, In 1986, the company ended the subsidized bus service— the 16 vehicles which for a small fee would transport about 350 employees from 50 different towns to and from work. Headquarters is still in a Georgian-style building in Chappaqua. The facility is graced with paintings by Chagall, Utrillo, Matisse and Degas, a collection *Fortune* called "the corporate world's most valuable French impressionist and postimpressionist art." Employees can still opt to use plots of ground for gardening, are allowed to take four 4-day weekends a year and don't have to work on Fridays in May ("May is such a pretty month," the Digesters say). One employee doing well in the new *Reader's Digest* is CEO Grune. He earned nearly $1.5 million in salary and bonuses in 1989, received $5 million in cash when stock was sold to the public in 1990 and holds another $6 million in stock.

While the Reader's Digest Association is changing, they're unlikely to tamper with the upbeat "God-Country-Family" formula that has worked so well for the magazine started by the Wallaces (both children of ministers) in Greenwich Village in 1922 on $1,300 of borrowed funds. They didn't accept advertising in their U.S. edition until 1955—and didn't permit any ads for cigarettes, liquor, drugs and other products they found distasteful. In early 1990, however, their French subsidiary announced that they would publish a new magazine for families, which is no big surprise; the surprise is this will be a financial magazine, designed to help families with money matters (it's the first such magazine to be published by *Reader's Digest,* and the first magazine created since the company sold shares to the public). In 1990, with a paid circulation of 17 million, *Reader's Digest* was still one of the U.S.'s largest selling magazine, still carrying the uplifting articles that once prompted Thornton Wilder to describe the *Digest.* as "a magazine for bores, by bores about bores."

The Reader's Digest Association, Inc., Pleasantville, NY 10570; (914) 241-5159.

BOOK PUBLISHERS

Publishing books is no longer a cottage industry, but it still has vestiges of that heritage. Companies still publish books that have no hope of making money. They still don't have a clear idea of which books will sell and which ones won't. The basic constraint of the business is that most Americans never buy a book. Publishers therefore rely heavily on best-sellers to carry the rest of the list. Textbooks—bought by school systems—are also major profit makers. The wave of mergers that began in the 1970s continued unabated into the 1980s. Among the publishing houses acquired by other firms during the decade were: Random House (by Newhouse); William Morrow (Hearst); Bantam Doubleday Dell (Germany's Bertelsmann); Macmillan (Britain's Maxwell); Prentice-Hall (Simon & Schuster); Harper & Row (Rupert Murdoch); New American Library, Addison-Wesley and E. P. Dutton (Pearson); Times Books, Crown and Schocken (Random House); Grolier (France's Hachette).

1

S I M O N   S C H U S T E R

#1 *in book publishing*

Employees: 9,000
Sales: $1.3 billion
Profits: $2 million
Founded: 1924
Headquarters: New York City, New York

The *real* money at Simon & Schuster is not made with the steamy novels of Harold Robbins and Jackie Collins, but with tax guides and textbooks. And Simon & Shuster has made a beeline for it. More than any other big publisher, they're dedicated to the bottom-line. In the immortal words of Richard Snyder, who created the modern Simon & Schuster, "Publishing is an act of commerce."

This money-making potential attracted the attention of conglomerate Gulf + Western Industries, which bought Simon & Schuster in 1975 for $11 million. At the time, Simon & Schuster was small potatoes—sales of $40 million. By 1989, Simon & Schuster was racking up sales of $1.3 billion, and if separated from parent Paramount Communications (Gulf + Western Industries' new name), S&S would sell for upwards of $2 billion—2,000 times what they cost 15 years earlier.

That phenomenal growth reflects Simon & Schuster's transformation from a trade publisher (popular fiction and nonfiction) to publishing juggernaut. Founded in 1924 by Richard L. Simon and Lincoln (Max) Schuster, their line of popular fiction and nonfiction eventually gave way to a flood of textbooks and a raft of newsletters, books and other information products for professional, technical and business markets. To be sure, Harold Robbins and Jackie Collins are Simon & Schuster stalwarts, but the books that bring in the money reliably, year after year, without the need for million-dollar advances, are the J.K. Lasser tax guides. Another big S&S winner is *Government by the People* (Burns, Peltason and Cronin); now in its 13th edition; it has been the top-selling college government textbook since the 1950s. Trade books are only 6 percent of sales at S&S.

S&S remolded themselves during the 1980s by buying over two dozen companies. The two biggest were: Esquire Inc., publisher of elementary and high school textbooks, for $180 million; and Prentice-Hall, a combination textbook and business information publisher, for $710 million. Ginn and Silver Burdett, also textbook houses, were scooped up during the 1980s as well.

Whereas educational and professional books represent their biggest business, Simon & Schuster hasn't the dull, gray image of a McGraw-Hill. Their reputation is still defined by their trade book activities. This house has always lived and died by best-sellers. Their first title was a crossword puzzle book; they founded the first successful paperback imprint, Pocket Books; and they're still known for aggressiveness. In the publishing industry people refer to S&S as "Dick Snyder's sharkpool," after Richard Snyder, who's been in command since the 1975 Gulf + Western acquisition. Snyder is known as an abrasive boss who rules by fear and ridicule. Michael Korda, one of his chief

THE TOP TEN PUBLISHERS

		Sales
1.	Simon & Schuster	$1.1 billion
2.	Time Warner	$891 million
3.	Harcourt Brace Jovanovich	$880 million
4.	Reader's Digest	$800 million
5.	Bertelsmann	$745 million
6.	McGraw-Hill	$600 million
7.	Random House	$595 million
8.	Maxwell (Macmillan)	$593 million
9.	Encyclopedia Británica	$590 million
10.	Thomson	$475 million

Source: BP Reports, 1990.

lieutenants, once said: "We sell books, other people sell shoes. What's the difference?" Writer Helen Dudar once reported S&S doesn't like to use the word, *literary,* to describe a book; they prefer, "It's a good, solid commercial work." Writing in *Manhattan Inc.* in 1984, John Taylor said that "at Simon & Schuster they brag that they will publish any piece of trash if it will sell." One of the hard-driving editors at S&S—a match for Dick Snyder—was Joni Evans. Snyder hired her in 1974 and married her in 1978 on a lunch break (they spent their honeymoon at Simon & Schuster). She launched her own imprint, Linden Press, and then became president of S&S's trade book division in 1985. In 1986 the Snyder-Evans marriage broke up— and the following year Evans joined Random House as a top editor.

Simon & Schuster, 1230 Avenue of the Americas, New York, NY 10020; (212) 698-7000.

2

Harcourt Brace Jovanovich

#1 *in textbooks*

Employees: 10,700
Sales: $1.3 billion
Profits: $104 million
Founded: 1919
Headquarters: Orlando, Florida

Harcourt Brace Jovanovich is the nation's largest textbook publisher—first in textbooks for elementary and high schools, second in college texts—but no one has ever quite figured them out except to conclude that for 35 years, from 1954 to 1989, they did what William Jovanovich wanted them to do. He became CEO in 1954, soon establishing a one-man reign that frightened away any publishing people hankering after independence. Not that he cared. He never, for example, joined the industry trade group, the Association of American Publishers. Born to Yugoslav immigrants in a Colorado coal camp, Jovanovich began his career as a textbook salesman and editor. He also has written six books, including five novels. In 1970, he added his name to Harcourt Brace and began to shape the company according to his whims. He entered the theme park business by acquiring Sea World. He bought a specialized magazine publisher of over 60 titles. He bought two TV stations. He thumbed his nose at the New York publishing fraternity by moving HBJ's headquarters to Orlando, Florida, in 1984, where he later fielded two more recreation parks, one a baseball and amusement park close to HBJ's new headquarters. Meanwhile, he shored up the textbook business by spending $500 million to buy Holt, Rinehart & Winston from CBS in 1986, an acquisition that included W. B. Saunders, a leading medical text publisher. And that was a year after he bought Federal Home Life Insurance, leading HBJ into the ranks of the top 100 life insurers.

Having more than doubled sales during the early 1980s, Jovanovich was not about to sit still in 1987 when British publisher Robert Maxwell made a $2.2 billion bid for HBJ. He foiled that takeover attempt by going deeply into hock to pay shareholders a onetime cash dividend of $40. That stopped Maxwell, but left HBJ with huge interest payments that wiped out profits and sent HBJ's stock plunging from $18 to $5 a share. To raise cash, the trade magazines were sold off. At the end of 1988, 68-year-old Jovanovich relinquished the CEO's post to Ralph Caulo. And then, in 1989, in a humiliating retreat from previous pledges, HBJ sold all the theme parks—the Sea Worlds, Cypress Gardens, Boardwalk & Baseball—to Anheuser-Busch for $1.1 billion. That brought the company, still deep in the red, back to their core business of publishing, with insurance the only side line.

History. Alfred Harcourt and Donald Brace were fed up with the conservative style of their employer, publisher Henry Holt. In summer 1919, the two young men founded Harcourt, Brace & Company. The very next year they had a winner on their hands—economist John Maynard Keynes' famous *Economic Consequences of the Peace*. Soon the firm branched out into fiction and poetry. In the 1920s their roster of distinguished authors included Sinclair Lewis, Carl Sandburg, Virginia Woolf, T. S. Eliot and E. M. Forster. They also published an extensive line of textbooks.

Owners and rulers. William Jovanovich, who owns only 2 percent of the company, stepped down as chairman of the board in 1990 and was replaced by John S. Herrington, former U.S. Secretary of Energy. In December 1989, his 40-year-old son, Peter, became CEO, replacing Ralph Caulo. (Peter's elder brother, Stefan, showed no interest in the business.) Peter Jovanovich, a Princeton graduate, spent eight years at Macmillan, eventually heading their trade division. He joined his

Viking Penguin, publisher of *Salman Rushdie's* **The Satanic Verses,** *spent $3.4 million on security in the year after Iran's late leader, Ayatollah Khomeini, issued a death warrant for the author, who then went into hiding.*

The Publishers Inside the Publishers

BANTAM DOUBLEDAY DELL (Bertelsmann)

Bantam
Bantam Classics
Loveswept
Bantam New Age Books
Doubleday
Anchor Books
Currency
Image
Galilee
Spy Books
Foundation
Crime Club
Double D Western
Dell
Laurel
Delacorte Press
Delta

HARPER/COLLINS (News Corp.)

Harper & Row
Cornelia and Michael Bessie Books
Edward Burlingame Books
Icon Editions
Perennial Library
Torchbooks
Colophon
Thomas Y. Crowell

HEARST

Arbor House
William Morrow
Beech Tree Books
Silver Arrow
Quill Paperbacks
Avon Books
Camelot

HOUGHTON MIFFLIN

Houghton Mifflin/Seymour Lawrence
Ticknor & Fields
The American Heritage Library

MACMILLAN (Maxwell Communications Corp.)

Free Press
Collier Books
Charles Scribner's Sons
Atheneum
Rawson Associates

PEARSON

Viking
Penguin
Stephen Greene/Pelham
Arkana
Michael Joseph
Frederick Warne
Addison-Wesley
New American Library
Signet
Mentor
Plume
Meridian
NAL Books
Onyx
E. P. Dutton
Dutton
William Abrahams Books
Obelisk

PUTNAM BERKLEY GROUP (MCA)

G. P. Putnam's Sons
Perigee Books
Ace/Putnam
Philomel Books
Grosset & Dunlap
Platt & Munk
Playland Books
Sandcastle Books
Berkley Publsihing Group
Berkley
Jove
Charter
Ace

RANDOM HOUSE (Newhouse)

Knopf
Random House
Vintage
Pantheon
Times Books
Villard
Crown
Harmony Books
Clarkson N. Potter
Orion
Balantine/Fawcett/Del Rey/Ivy
Available Press
Epiphany
Gold Medal
Fawcett
Columbine
Crest
Fodor's

(cont.)

The Publishers
Inside the Publishers

SIMON & SCHUSTER (Paramount)
> Fireside
> Linden Press
> Simon & Schuster
> Touchstone
> Summit Books
> Prentice Hall
> Betty Crocker Cookbooks
> H. M. Gousha
> Mobil
> Arco
> J. K. Lasser
> Webster's New World
> Pocket Books
> Archway
> Minstrel
> Washington Square Press
> Poseidon Press

TIME WARNER
> Little, Brown
> Warner Books
> Time-Life Books

Source: Publisher's Weekly,
6 January 1989.

father's company in 1980 and went on to head the college textbook and professional lines. In 1990, HBJ directors included Virginia B. Smith, former president of Vassar College; and three men whose work Harcourt has published, including former Senator Eugene J. McCarthy.

Stock performance. Harcourt Brace Jovanovich stock bought for $1,000 in 1980 sold for $5,657 on January 2, 1990.

Harcourt Brace Jovanovich, C Harbor Drive, Orlando, FL; (417) 345-2000.

3

#1 in business magazines
#2 in textbooks

Employees: 14,600
Sales: $1.8 billion
Profits: $40 million
Founded: 1888
Headquarters: New York City, New York

Without McGraw-Hill, we would know a lot less about the business world. From their 1888 inception their mission has been to supply information about industries—mainly to people working in those industries. And that remains their core operation. They publish 33 magazines for different industries and professions, and they supply directories, newsletters, consulting reports, rating services and other informational vehicles for people working in construction (F. W. Dodge and Sweet's), finance (Standard & Poor's), commodities (Platt's), computers (Osborne) and the law (Shepard's). The basement of their building (at 1221 Avenue of the Americas in New York City) contains one of the country's most complete business bookstores. Their flagship publication, Business Week, started in 1929 (two months before the stock market crash), is the world's most widely read business magazine, carries more advertising pages than any other American magazine (4,586 during 1988) and logs more advertising revenues ($227 million in 1988) than all but five other magazines (Time, TV Guide, Sports Illustrated, People and Newsweek).

During the 1980s, under the direction of new Editor-In-Chief Stephen B. Shepard, Business Week became more sprightly, both in appearance and content. The same could not be said for the rest of McGraw-Hill, which remained a "gray" company not celebrated for enterprise or imagination—hence recurring rumors they were ripe for a takeover. They're one of the nation's largest textbook publishers, and they strengthened that position during the

1980s by acquiring Random House's college textbook division. As the decade closed, they struck a deal with Macmillan (recently bought by England's Robert Maxwell) to combine their elementary, secondary and vocational education businesses into a joint venture, Macmillan/McGraw-Hill School Publishing. With sales of $440 million, the company ranked second only to Harcourt Brace Jovanovich in textbooks. As part of this deal, Maxwell promised not to make a hostile bid for McGraw-Hill for the next 15 years.

McGraw-Hill, once the publisher of novelist Vladimir Nabokov, no longer publishes novels or popular nonfiction. They abandoned so-called trade book publishing in 1989 to concentrate on textbooks. But they continue to own four TV stations (in Denver, Indianapolis, San Diego and Bakersfield, California).

Members of the founding McGraw family still play roles here, although a non-McGraw, Joseph L. Dionne, ran the company for most of the 1980s. McGraw family members are believed to hold over 15 percent of the stock. Curently, the most involved McGraw is Harold W. McGraw III, called Terry, whose father, Harold W. McGraw, Jr., was CEO before Dionne and who became chairman emeritus in 1988 when he reached mandatory retirement age of 65. Terry McGraw, 41 in 1990, served as president of two divisions during the 1980s, apparently on his way to the top of the firm founded by his great-grandfather, James H. McGraw, with a publication called *Street Railway Journal.*

S*tock performance.* McGraw-Hill stock bought for $1,000 in 1980 sold for $5,459 on January 2, 1990.

McGraw-Hill, Inc., 1221 Avenue of the Americas, New York, NY 10020; (212) 997-2000.

4

RANDOM HOUSE

#1 *in adult trade books*

Employees: 3,020
Sales: $595 million
Founded: 1925
Headquarters: New York City, New York

Random House is the most well-known book publisher in the U.S. To some extent, that's the result of the visibility of their former leader, Bennett Cerf, a fixture on the TV program, "What's My Line?" for 17 years. But it also reflects their standing in the industry. They have published many of America's finest writers: William Faulkner, Eugene O'Neill, Sinclair Lewis, Robert Penn Warren, John O'Hara, Truman Capote. Their Modern Library imprint made available classic works in inexpensive, hardbound editions. Year in and year out they've been the most successful publisher of what the industry calls trade books, meaning novels (they publish James Michener, Robert Ludlum and Norman Mailer), juvenile books (they publish the Dr. Seuss and Babar stories), cookbooks, biographies, popular reference books and other nonfiction intended for a general audience. For five straight years (since 1985), Random House had more books on the *New York Times* best-seller lists than any other publisher. And in early 1990 they had three of the top five best-selling nonfiction books—the two Robert Fulghum treatises, *It was on Fire When I Lay Down on It* and *All I Really Need to Know I Learned in Kindergarten* (both published under their Villard imprint), and Nancy Reagan's *My Turn.* They're a big commercial house with a literary reputation, and they're known for their collegial operation. They attract employees who love books.

As a major manufacturer of words, they are also watched closely by other wordsmiths. In 1989, when Robert Bernstein stepped down as head of Random House, the news appeared on the *New*

York Times front page. Of course, in this case there was also the question, never fully answered, of whether Bernstein, then 66, had walked or been pushed by Random House's owner, S. I. Newhouse, Jr. A week later, Newhouse replaced Bernstein with Alberto Vitale, who'd been running Bantam Doubleday Dell for Germany's Bertelsmann. (In "trade" books, Bantam Doubleday Dell ranks second to Random House.)

Random House is more than just Random House. Their imprints include Villard, Ballantine, Del Rey, Vintage, Pantheon and Knopf. When Newhouse replaced William Shawn as editor of the *New Yorker,* he went to Knopf to find Shawn's successor, Robert Gottlieb. Over the years Random House has proved a hospitable home for wayward publishers. In the 1980s they brought four publishers into their home: Times Books (formerly at the *New York Times*), Fawcett (formerly at CBS), Vanguard (one of the oldest independents) and Crown (publisher of Judith Krantz, Dominick Dunne and Jean Auel). Random House also entered the toy business during the 1980s, first buying Warren

Alberto Vitale current head of Random House, former head of Bertelsmann's Bantam's Doubleday/Dell.

Toys in Lafayette, Indiana; and then introducing two new board games, Backwards and Quizzard.

History. Twenty-seven-year-old Bennett Cerf regularly asked his boss, publisher Horace Liveright, to sell him the Modern Library. And Liveright (who was quite fond of Cerf) regularly threw him out of the office. But one day in 1925 the flashy, fast-living Liveright suddenly demanded, "What will you give me for it?"

That was the start of Random House. Liveright was publishing some of the greatest writers of the time, but Modern Library, inexpensive hardbound editions of classic books, was his bread and butter. Cerf and his friend Donald Klopfer bought the line (112 titles at the time) for $215,000 and recovered their investment in two years. In 1927 they decided to start publishing luxury editions of books chosen "at random." When they told their artist friend Rockwell Kent about the new name, Random House, he immediately sketched a logo—a house half-cottage, half-mansion. Cerf and Klopfer ran the business with apparently uninterrupted good fellowship (for decades they had facing desks and shared the same secretary) until Cerf's death in 1971. He was a major public figure—a television celebrity, author of a humor column carried by hundreds of newspapers and subject of a 1966 *Time* cover story.

Random House grew slowly. They provoked, and won, the most famous censorship case in the history of U.S. publishing (James Joyce's *Ulysses,* cleared of obscenity charges in 1933). After Liveright died, Cerf signed his two premier authors, Eugene O'Neill and Robinson Jeffers.

In 1959 they went partially public (selling 30 percent of stock to the public) and began buying other houses: in 1960 Alfred A. Knopf (which included Vintage paperbacks) L. W. Singer (textbook publishers) and Pantheon. In 1973 they purchased Ballantine Books. Random House began to look less like a cottage and more like a sprawling, moneyed estate. RCA noticed and bought Random House for $38 million in 1966, ostensibly to marry electronics with publishing. RCA then sold Random House to Newhouse Publications in 1980 for about $70 million.

As a place to work. At Random House people like to see themselves as "guardians of culture." Everyone at Random House, from receptionists and messengers to the most senior editors, seems interested in books. It's a great atmosphere, and one resulting in a much lower turnover rate than at most other big publishing houses. Pay, as in the rest of publishing, is low compared with other industries, but Random House claims to pay higher than their competitors. In the late 1980s, under Bernstein's reign, 15 Random House editors made more than $100,000 a year.

Social responsibility. With Alberto Vitale, an accountant by training, now in command, the era of gentility may have run its course at Newhouse's Random House. First to feel the heat was Pantheon, known for publishing provocative, highly intellectual books. Pantheon's sales account for a mere 2 percent of Random House's revenue. Despite their literary reputation, Pantheon had been losing money for several years (in 1989, $3 million). "Why should Pantheon be allowed to lose a ton of money? If you're selling 1,500 copies of a book and printing 7,500, you don't need to have been to Harvard to know you're in trouble," Vitale told the *New York Times.* In early 1990, Vitale forced out André Schiffrin as Pantheon's managing director. Five senior Pantheon editors resigned in protest, and the issue quickly became a well-publicized cause-célèbre. Writers picketed in front of Random House, and longtime Random House author James Michener weighed in with a three-page tirade against the apparent insensitivity of the Newhouse-Vitale regime to the house's traditional literary values. In accepting the prize for best fictional work at the National Book Critics Circle awards ceremony, E. L. Doctorow declared his publisher, Random House, had "disfigured itself."

Global presence. Random House extended their reach overseas in 1987 when they bought one of Britain's leading book publishers, the group known as Chatto, Virago, Bodley Head & Jonathan Cape. They publish Iris Murdoch and Graham Greene, whose nephew, Graham C. Greene, headed the British publisher when they sold out to the Americans.

Random House, 201 East 50th Street, New York, NY 10022; (212) 751-2600.

5

Pearson

Employees: 28,000
Sales: $2.6 billion
Profits: $485 million
Founded: 1844
Headquarters: London, England

An eccentric English company, Pearson has been called "a collection of rich men's toys." And what a collection they've assembled. In addition to several top American publishers (Viking, Penguin, New American Library, Addison-Wesley, Longman), Pearson combines fine English china (Royal Crown Derby, Minton, Royal Albert); plumbing fixtures (Doulton); investment banking (Lazard Frères); historic British tourist attractions (Madame Tussaud's, Warwick Castle, the Chessington Zoo); and a host of publishing interests including the *Financial Times,* 50 percent of *The Economist;* a chain of provincial newspapers in Britain; several dozen shopping newspapers on Florida's west coast; a majority interest in the French financial newspaper, *Les Echos;* a 22 percent stake in the leading Dutch medical and scientific publisher, *Elsevier;* and numerous British publishers (Longman, Penguin, Hamish Hamilton, Michael Joseph, Pitman).

Pearson's American operation puts them among the top 10 U.S. publishers. One of their houses, Viking, published Salman Rushdie's *Satanic Verses,* which, with an assist from the late Ayatollah Khomeini, became a best-seller on both sides of the Atlantic, but even so, Pearson said the book had no major financial impact on the company.

Viscount Blakenham, descendant of the first Lord Cowdray (whose original name was Weetman Pearson), became Pearson's CEO in 1978 and chairman in 1983. Cow-

Last year $15 billion worth of books were sold in America and $4 billion in Britain. In each country 50,000 new titles were published.

dray family members are believed to hold about 20 percent of the shares. Rupert Murdoch is the next biggest shareholder, with an 18 percent stake. Directors include Colgate's CEO Reuben Mark and Volvo's CEO Pehr Gyllenhammar.

Pearson Plc., Millbank Tower, London SW1P 4QZ England; (071) 828- 9020.

6

Houghton Mifflin Company

#3 *in textbooks*

Employees: 2,149
Sales: $368 million
Profits: $24 million
Founded: 1832
Headquarters: Boston, Massachusetts

Here's the last of the tweedy American book publishers where English majors from Mount Holyoke work for substandard wages and a chance to grapple with "literature." They're the only major publisher that's still independent and only publishes books. They're proud to have been the publisher of Winston Churchill, John F. Kennedy, Franklin D. Roosevelt and Rachel Carson. They publish about 150 adult hardcover titles and 100 children's titles each year, but their bread and butter is schoolbooks. Over three-quarters of sales come from textbooks, reference materials (such as the *American Heritage Dictionary*) and educational software. The rest is brought in by popular fiction and nonfiction trade books (i.e. sold in commercial bookstores) or business software. Houghton Mifflin's two main subsidiaries are Chicago-based Riverside Publishing (printer of textbooks, including the classic *Riverside Literature Series*) and New York-based Ticknor & Fields (publisher of fiction and nonfiction). In 1989, Houghton Mifflin announced plans to buy Victor Gollancz, a private British publishing house. The match was a good one. Founded by Sir Victor Gollancz in 1928, they've published a long list of famous writers, in-cluding Arthur Koestler, George Orwell, Dorothy L. Sayers and Nadine Gordimer.

One of Houghton Mifflin's ancestors was Henry Houghton, a young Vermonter who in 1852 opened a printing factory inside a former poorhouse. The plant, on the banks of the Charles River in Cambridge, Massachusetts, led Houghton to call his operation Riverside Press. Houghton printed books for the famous publishing house, Ticknor & Fields—publisher of Longfellow, Emerson, Thoreau, Hawthorne, Twain, Stowe and Holmes, as well as Britishers Dickens and Tennyson. Houghton soon took on a younger partner, George Mifflin (who led the company after Houghton's death). In 1880, Houghton, Mifflin merged with Ticknor & Fields and became Houghton, Mifflin & Company.

Since 1973 Harold Miller has led Houghton Mifflin. He joined the company as a sales rep in 1950, and serves on the boards of the American Antiquarian Society and Bank of New England. According to insiders, working at Houghton Mifflin is like Harvard in one respect—it's tough to penetrate the ivy walls, but once you're in, you're in for life. Houghton Mifflin offers generous medical benefits, pension and saving plans, educational assistance, an excellent public transportation program and college scholarship programs for employees' children.

Houghton Mifflin narrowly escaped a takeover attempt in 1978. When Western Pacific Industries began buying up the company's stock, the management swung out with the "Vanishing Author" defense—getting longtime Houghton Mifflin authors John Kenneth Galbraith and Arthur Schlesinger among others to sign public letters, threatening to jump ship if their publisher was taken over. The tactic worked, and for 11 years Houghton Mifflin stayed out of the Wall Street fray. In 1989, the Robert M. Bass Group accumulated 5.6 percent of Houghton's shares, leading to speculation of takeover. Board directors hold 10 percent of the stock, and the Wall Street house Warburg, Pincus owns 6.2 percent.

Stock *performance.* Houghton Mifflin stock bought for $1,000 in 1980 sold for $5,711 on January 2, 1990.

Houghton Mifflin Company, One Beacon Street, Boston, MA 02108; (617) 725-5000.

ADVERTISING

In no country in the world does advertising play such a prominent—other words, "intrusive," "annoying," "destructive" come to mind—role as it does in the U.S. And during the 1980s this cacophony, which most Americans accept as background noise, became even more strident. Money spent on advertising increased from $50 billion a year at the decade's start to $123 billion in 1989. The major producers of these commercial messages are advertising agencies, invisible to the public even though the ads and commercials they turn out have become familiar patches on the culture. The big ad agencies got bigger during the 1980s and were reconfigured through mergers that created global mega-groups, two of them British-controlled. Only 4 of 1980's top 10 agencies are still independent. Although ad agencies spend billions, they're not major employers. All the agencies in the country (perhaps as many as 10,000) employ 130,000 people—Marriott has more employees. The advertising agency business, developed in the U.S. and copied around the world, now breaks down in three different ways. One is the megagroup, essentially a collection of giant agencies, all owned by the same holding company but each functioning under its own name, with its own offices and clients: Saatchi & Saatchi, WPP, Interpublic, Omnicom. Two is the diversified independent agency, exemplified by Young & Rubicam: one main agency with different arms (each with its own name) for specialized functions (public relations, medical advertising, sales promotion). And three is the old-style ad agency exemplified by Leo Burnett: one agency, one name, one set of clients—what you see is what you get.

1

SAATCHI & SAATCHI COMPANY PLC

Employees: 14,000
Sales: $1.6 billion
Losses: $131 million
Founded: 1970
Headquarters: London, England

One of the first advertising pieces to go up on the Berlin Wall in 1990 was a huge banner declaring: "Saatchi & Saatchi: First Over the Wall." It was a foretaste of the western-style advertising East Germans would soon be exposed to, and typically Saatchi & Saatchi led this invasion. They're a brash, British, bulldozing advertising agency. When the Berlin Wall went up in 1961, Saatchi & Saatchi didn't exist. As it came down, Saatchi & Saatchi could claim the title, "world's largest advertising agency." Except they're not just one advertising agency. They're a collection of agencies with different names, offices and clients. There are even agencies within agencies. Saatchi & Saatchi owns the entire shebang. They put the shop together during the 1980s, moving around the world (especially in the U.S.) and buying up ad agencies. Their philosophy was it's "good to be big, better to be good, but best to be both."

As a result, wherever advertising goes on in the world, Saatchi & Saatchi is found. In early 1990 they—that is, the agencies they own—had 14,000 people working in more than 300 offices in over 60 countries handling about $11 billion worth of client advertising.

S&S's two main arms are Saatchi & Saatchi Advertising Worldwide (SSAW) and Backer Spielvogel Bates (BSB). Each runs a worldwide network of offices. Each has their own set of clients. In worldwide standing of advertising agencies, SSAW ranks second (to Japan's Dentsu); BSB fourth. To organize these two networks, Saatchi & Saatchi submerged 19 different ad shops. Many once independent agencies are now subsumed in one of these two entities; among them: Ted Bates, Compton Advertising, Campbell-Mithun, William Esty, Dancer-Fitzgerald-Sample, AC&R Advertising, Rumrill Hoyt, Kobs & Draft.

THE UNFORGETABLE '80s

Every month from 1982–1989 Gallup (The pollsters) asked 1,000 people which ads of the previous month first came to mind, with these results:

		Number of mentions
1.	Coca-Cola	3,709
2.	Pepsi	3,081
3.	McDonald's	2,223
4.	Miller/Miller Lite	1,708
5.	Budweiser/Bud Lite	1,496
6.	Ford	1,365
7.	Wendy's	1,323
8.	Chevrolet	909
9.	Burger King	734
10.	California Raisins	688

Source: Advertising Age, 1 February 1990.

Some, Ted Bates and Dancer-Fitzgerald, no longer have their own nameplates. Others, AC&R, Klemtner, Campbell-Mithun, function under their own names although they belong to one of the Saatchi & Saatchi arms.

Although Saatchi & Saatchi owns agencies everywhere, they do about half their business in the world's biggest advertising market: the U.S. If you're outside the advertising business, you may not know the names of these agencies, but you certainly are familiar with their work, the commercials that constantly interrupt TV programs: Miller Lite beer, Tide detergent, Ivory soap, Comet cleanser, Snickers, Cheerios, Campbell Soup, L'Eggs, Tylenol, Uncle Ben's rice and Betty Crocker's pancake mixes.

By organizing parallel agencies under common ownership, Saatchi & Saatchi got around the industry taboo that prohibits an agency from handling competing clients. Ergo, in a variation of the Chinese Wall pattern prevailing in banking, where one hand supposedly doesn't know what the other hand is doing, they do the ads for both Toyota (SSAW) and Hyundai (BBS).

Their game plan worked well until the end of the 1980s when they suffered financial indigestion due to overeating. As a holding company, Saatchi & Saatchi had bought a lot of other companies besides advertising agencies—consultants in public relations (Rowland), market research (Yankelovich, Skelly & White), compensation-and-benefit programs (Hay), design (Siegel & Gale)—and that strategy (clients from one part of the house would use another part) was backfiring. After nine years of explosive growth (profits zipped from $2 million in 1980 to $80 million in 1988), Saatchi & Saatchi lost money in 1989, forcing them to regroup. The consulting companies were put up for sale and an outsider—Frenchman Robert Louis-Dreyfus, former head of a major international research company (IMS)—was installed as CEO. That meant the Saatchi brothers, Maurice and Charles, were no longer in command of the mega-advertising agency group they'd built.

History. In 1947, the Saatchi family fled anti-Semitism in Baghdad, Iraq—taking with them their two sons, four-year-old Charles and two-year old Maurice. They settled in London. Young Charles was an abysmal student; one of his former teachers told Ivan Fallon (*The Brothers: The Rise & Rise of Saatchi & Saatchi*) that Charles "was the sort of boy who made you wonder what would ever become of him." Charles dropped out of school at 17 and bummed around America, dreaming of making Hollywood films. He returned to London, and in 1970 with brother Maurice founded a fledgling ad agency, Saatchi & Saatchi.

Success was not immediate. In the early years, Charles used to grab strangers off the street to make the office look busy when clients came to visit. He once impersonated a janitor to avoid a client. By reputation, Charles is the eccentric, antisocial brother while Maurice is slightly more affable, making an occasional appearance in front of clients and investors.

The Saatchis propelled themselves to the top by bold advertising and a bold business strategy. They did the ads that helped the Conservative Party defeat Labour and bring Margaret Thatcher to power. A poster they did for the Conservatives left the impression the Labour Party platform was identical to the Communist Party's. One ad they did for the Health Education Council showed a man with a bloated stomach, the headline asking, "Would You Be More Careful If It Was You That Got Pregnant?" They did the futuristic British Airways commercials, one of which showed the entire island of Manhattan moving across the Atlantic Ocean. Their business strategy was global—they represented themselves to clients as neither British nor American but international, an agency treating the world as if it "were a single entity." As a result, they ended up serving Procter & Gamble in 34 countries, Gillette in 15, Johnson & Johnson in 20, British Airways in 50.

The Saatchis, who sold stock to the public in 1977, also became relentless acquisitors, helped by a back-office numbers cruncher, Martin Sorrell, who left the agency in mid-decade to do his own thing (see WPP, page 000). The initial S&S presence in the U.S. was Compton Advertising, a good choice because Procter & Gamble was one of Compton's longtime clients. The Saatchis reached the top in 1986 when, in rapid succession, they scooped up three sizable agencies: Ted Bates (3rd in the U.S.), Dancer-Fitzgerald-Sample (16th) and Backer & Spielvogel (24th). The Backer Spielvogel Bates agency that emerged from this reshuffle was headed by Carl Spielvogel, who began his career as advertising news columnist for the *New York Times,* sat at Marion Harper's side as he built Interpublic Group and then left to form his own shop with an important foundation account: Miller Lite beer. In what must have been an epiphany for him, in 1989 Backer Spielvogel Bates moved into fourth place in worldwide agency standings, passing McCann-Erickson, the agency he left the *New York Times* to join.

After the spate of acquisitions in 1986, a small New York ad agency ran an ad identifying itself as a "non-Saatchi & Saatchi agency."

Owners and rulers. Robert Louis-Dreyfus, who has a fiercesome reputation as a costcutter, is in charge but the Saatchi brothers still hold 7.3 percent of the stock. A mysterious American investment manager, Southeastern Asset Management, held 13 percent of the shares in early 1990.

As a place to work. Fun, but if you're looking for job security, this is the wrong place.

Stock performance. Saatchi & Saatchi stock bought for $1,000 in 1984 sold for $1,294 on January 2, 1990.

Saatchi & Saatchi Co., 80 Charlotte Street, London W1A 1AQ, England; (44) 1-930-2161.

Saatchi & Saatchi Co., 767 Fifth Avenue, New York, NY 10022; (212) 755-0060.

2
WPP Group

Employees: 21,000
Sales: $1.6 billion
Profits: $32 million
Founded: 1985
Headquarters: London, England

That the initials of the second largest company in the advertising business, WPP Group, stand for Wire & Plastic Products tells you a lot about today's industry. Run by British financial wizard Martin Sorrell (graduate of Cambridge and Harvard Business School), WPP includes two pillars of the advertising establishment— J. Walter Thompson (JWT) and Ogilvy & Mather. Their acquisition by WPP (in 1987 and in 1989, respectively) stunned the advertising agency business. Both were hostile takeovers—opposed, that is, by the managements of JWT and Ogilvy— and they were mounted by a company, WPP, that had never previously engaged in the ad agency business. Suddenly, the British upstart was the number two player.

Coming into the 1990s, WPP was the shell for more than 40 operating companies. They had 645 offices in 55 countries. They handled over $10 billion worth of advertising a year. Half of their business was in the U.S., one-quarter in Britain. In capturing JWT, Martin Sorrell gained possession of one of the venerable forces in advertising—the oldest U.S. agency and the largest agency in the world for much of this century. JWT has relationships going back 50 years or more with such leading advertisers as Ford Motor, Kraft Foods, Eastman Kodak and Lever Bros.

Ogilvy & Mather, Sorrell's other big prize, is a modern legend, thanks in large part to founder David Ogilvy, who at first was appalled at the WPP bid—he called Sorrell "an odious little jerk"—and later,

WHERE THEY PUT THEIR ADS

		Money Spent on Ads
1.	Newspapers	$32.4 billion
2.	TV	$26.9 billion
3.	Yellow pages	$8.3 billion
4.	Radio	$8.3 billion
5.	Magazines	$6.7 billion
6.	Billboards	$1.1 billion

Source: Advertising Age, 14 May 1990.

after the acquisition was a done deed, accepted a position as honorary chairman. Ogilvy, who started his agency from scratch after World War II, was responsible for a series of memorable ads: the man with an eyepatch for Hathaway shirts, Commander Whitehead for Schweppes quinine water, the long headline over a large block of copy—"At 60 miles an hour the loudest noise in this new Rolls-Royce is the electric clock." Among Ogilvy's major clients in multiple offices across the world are American Express, Seagram, Shell Oil, Polaroid and Unilever.

In *Advertising Age's* annual ranking of the world's top ad agencies, Ogilvy & Mather ranked sixth in 1989, JWT eighth. The JWT purchase also brought into the WPP fold the world's largest public relations firm, Hill & Knowlton, whose 1989 fees were $170 million.

Like Saatchi & Saatchi, which Sorrell helped to build, WPP is more than a collection of advertising agencies. They also own companies offering market research, public relations, package design, corporate image-making and sales promotion. In fact, the actual placement of advertising in media accounted for only one-half of WPP's revenues at the start of 1990.

History. WPP's history is mostly that of their two main components: JWT and Ogilvy & Mather. After all, in 1989, when JWT was celebrating their 125th birthday, WPP was all of 4 years old. WPP's founder, Martin Sorrell, is, like the Saatchis, British. And also like the Saatchis, Sorrell is Jewish, an irony for an agency like J. Walter Thompson, which eschewed Jews during their formative years. James Walter Thompson was 20 when he joined a small Manhattan ad agency as a bookkeeper

after the Civil War. Fresh from the marines, Thompson turned out to be a terrific salesman. He was one of the first to pitch housewives, saying his inspiration came from the following rhyme:

God bless our wives, they fill the hives
With little bees and honey,
They smooth life's shocks, they mend
our socks,
But don't they spend the money!

In their early years JWT vied with Philadelphia's N. W. Ayer for leadership in the agency business. JWT pulled ahead in the 1920s.

After World War I the Ivy League colleges began to send graduates into the advertising business, and Thompson took more of them than anyone else. The class of 1919 was said to be the first to send more graduates into advertising than banking. One of the 1919 recruits at J. Walter Thompson was novelist John P. Marquand, who struggled for two years writing copy for Rinso soap and U.S. Rubber tires before deciding advertising was not for him.

Stanley and Helen Resor, who bought the firm in 1916 and ran the agency from 1916 to 1960, turned testimonial advertising into a powerful tool. In 1926, the Queen of Spain testified for Pond's cold cream. They introduced Lux toilet soap in 1925 and used movie stars to establish it as a leading brand. They were the first to use fine photography in advertisements. Up to then illustrators had dominated advertising art with wash drawings and pen-and-ink sketches. Edward Steichen, the famous photographer, did his first work for Thompson in 1923: a close-up of hands peeling potatoes for a Jergens lotion ad. The slogan was, "Housework never yet spoiled the beauty of a woman's hands."

The Resors and their accomplices had a way of doing business all their own. Their style was nondirective management: no tables of organization, no heads of departments, no list of rules handed out to newcomers. Someone once brought Resor an organizational chart with neat boxes connected by lines. "Looks fine," Resor reportedly said, "but erase the lines." He felt the best way to teach people anything was by example—if you stayed around Thompson long enough and watched carefully, you would, by osmosis, learn what to do and how to do it. This philosophy was carried to such an extreme the bathrooms in the New York office were purposely not labeled "men" and "women," the idea being you would soon find out which was which (although it sometimes played havoc with visitors).

A turning point came in 1960 when Shell Oil, a client for three decades, fired Thompson (and went to Ogilvy & Mather). That was the year Resor, then 81, finally relinquished the CEO's title. The new CEO, Norman H. Strouse, together with show business type Dan Seymour, began to dismantle the old structure. New technology could no longer be ignored and a big computer was installed. Also, "men" and "women" signs went up on the bathroom doors, and in 1969 the company went public and was soon listed on the New York Stock Exchange.

In their first 100 years, J. Walter Thompson had only four presidents. They had four more in their next 10 years. One of the remarkable aspects of Thompson's first 100 years was that their growth was achieved without buying other companies. But in the 1980s it was a different story, symbolized by the formation of a holding company, JWT Group, which owned a number of different entities before they were acquired by the equally impersonal WPP Group.

If JWT represented some quintessentially American qualities (at least early on), Ogilvy & Mather had a decidedly British lineage. David Ogilvy was born near London in 1911. His mother was Irish, his father Scottish. A big influence on his early life was Mark Twain's *Adventures of Huckleberry Finn*, which he read in boarding school. Expelled from Oxford, he spent time in the kitchen of a Paris hotel before coming to America where he worked for researcher George Gallup and the British embassy (during World War II) and then bought a tobacco farm in the Amish country of Pennsylvania. In 1948, when he was 37, he set up an ad agency in New York backed by two of London's leading agencies, Mather & Crowther and S. H. Benson (where mystery writer Dorothy L. Sayers had worked—it was the model for the agency backdrop in *Murder Must Advertise*).

By 1953, after the Hathaway and Schweppes "image" campaigns, Ogilvy

was already being hailed by trade magazine *Printers' Ink* as one of "the great advertising writers of all time." At first the Ogilvy shop was known for "snob appeal" advertising in the *New Yorker*. Later on, with the addition of clients like Maxwell House coffee, Shell Oil and American Express, they climbed steadily into the topmost ranks of the U.S. advertising business. And David Ogilvy became well known in his own person, especially after his 1963 book, *Confessions of an Advertising Man*, which became the best-selling book on advertising ever published (over 1 million copies have been sold). The book helped the agency get more business, and made him, as historian Stephen Fox noted (in *The Mirror Makers*), "the only advertising man with a substantial reputation outside the trade." Ogilvy & Mather sold stock to the public in 1966, becoming the fifth ad agency to do so. J. Walter Thompson followed suit three years later, making both of these U.S. agencies vulnerable to Martin Sorrell's raids in the 1980s.

Owners and rulers. Martin Sorrell worked behind the scenes at Saatchi & Saatchi from 1977 until 1986, manipulating the numbers that enabled the Saatchis to buy agencies all over the globe. He was the financial mastermind of these deals. Then, in 1985, he decided to do it on his own. His first company, WPP, was based in Kent, England. They made shopping carts, an innocent enough vehicle for the purchases he was soon to make. The Saatchis were among WPP's initial investors. As late as 1987, they still held 6.9 percent of WPP. In early 1990, WPP's biggest shareholder was a British media operator, Michael Luckwell, who held 5 percent of the stock.

As a place to work. Under Burt Manning, who returned to lead Thompson after the WPP acquisition, JWT has become a born-again producer of eye-catching advertising, and a desirable place to work. Ogilvy, on the other hand, has had a series of defections by top creative people. *Business Week* reported in 1990 that the agency's "creative culture has been eroded by new managers and a greater emphasis on cost-cutting."

Global presence. WPP is interested in acquiring advertising agencies and related companies anywhere in the world. Their aim, like the Saatchis', is to serve clients worldwide.

Stock performance. WPP Group stock bought for $1,000 in 1987 sold for $1,561 on January 2, 1990.

WPP Group, 27 Farm Street, London W1X 6RD, England; 1-408-2204.

WPP Group, 420 Lexington Avenue, New York, NY 10017; (212) 867-1000.

3

THE INTERPUBLIC GROUP OF COMPANIES, INC.

Employees: 14,800
Sales: $1.2 billion
Profits: $71 million
Founded: 1911
Headquarters: New York City, New York

Interpublic was polygamous before Saatchi & Saatchi was even born. Their original idea, in the 1950s when they were known as McCann-Erickson, was to have an umbrella company own a group of advertising agencies, each operating under a separate name, with individual offices and clients. In that way they hurdled one of the main obstacles to agency growth: client conflict, that is, doing ads for two competing companies. It worked well for Interpublic; they became the mightiest power on the American advertising scene (number two worldwide), and were copied slavishly by the Saatchis and Martin Sorrell of WPP to fuel their meteoric ascents during the 1980s.

The 1980s were spectacular for the Interpublic agencies, too. They more than tripled the amount of advertising they handled, ending the decade serving more than 4,000 clients in 220 offices located in 80 countries. The two main agencies in Interpublic's family are McCann-Erickson, world's fifth largest advertising agency; and Lintas:Worldwide, ninth largest. They create and place advertising for many of the world's leading advertisers, including Coca-Cola, General Motors, Exxon, Gillette, Nestlé, Unilever, RJR Nabisco and—as of 1989—IBM.

McCann-Erickson and Lintas both operate worldwide. Wherever Coca-Cola is sold, they're likely to be advertised by a McCann-Erickson office. McCann offices in 10 countries handle 28 other clients. In 32 countries McCann-Erickson ranks among the top five ad agencies. Wherever there's a Lintas office, there's Unilever business. Lintas was originally Unilever's house agency (Lever International Advertising Service).

This house of advertising agencies solved the problem of client conflicts. In the U.S., two Interpublic agencies work for General Motors—McCann for Buick, Lintas:Campbell-Ewald for Chevrolet—while a third, Los Angelesbased Dailey & Associates, does Honda's advertising.

Interpublic has ventured beyond the ad agency business. In 1989 they bought 49 percent of Freemantle Inc., Europe's largest supplier of TV game shows.

History. McCann-Erickson, mother of the Interpublic companies, was founded in 1930 when two successful agencies— H. K. McCann and Alfred Erickson— merged. The McCann shop dated from 1911 when the Supreme Court broke up the Standard Oil Trust. Harry McCann was Standard Oil's ad manager, and he opened his own agency. Exxon (formerly Standard Oil of New Jersey) is a client to this day. McCann-Erickson led a successful, if dull, life as a run-of-the-mill New York ad agency until 1948. That year, a tall 31-year-old from Oklahoma, Marion Harper, became president. Harper, who rose through the research side, had a dream: He wanted to build a communications empire. During the 1950s, he began buying businesses (10 companies in 13 years, starting with Marschalk & Pratt in 1954). He also reeled in some big fish as clients: the domestic Coca-Cola account in 1956 and GM's Buick account in 1959 (for which he gave up the Chrysler account).

Marion Harper's real genius became apparent in 1961. He knew the main obstacle to agency growth was the "client conflict" problem. Two clients who competed against each other in the same industry or product line did not want to use the same ad agency. For example, Kellogg would be wary of the agency representing Nabisco.

So Harper created a holding company to control a number of ad agencies while maintaining each agency's distinct identity. In 1961, Harper revealed his masterpiece: Interpublic, an umbrella corporation comprising 22 separate companies (11 of which were ad agencies). The different agencies in Interpublic were kept physically separate, reassuring clients their secrets would not be shared with competitors. Marion Harper became president, chairman and CEO of the new company, and headed the firm until the board of directors ousted him in 1967. Interpublic had become too big for Marion Harper to control and was being eaten alive by overhead. Harper's buying spree included a service arm that was pruned back during the financial troubles of the late 1960s (including a conference center doubling as a dude ranch, two company planes, a charter air service and a cattle farm). But Harper's legacy continued. Interpublic went on to buy other agencies, and in the 1980s his ideas were copied by British upstarts who beat Interpublic at their own game.

Owners and rulers. Since 1980, Interpublic's chairman and CEO has been Philip H. Geier, Jr., aged 56 in 1990. When he took the helm, Geier told *Advertising Age* he was "tough as nails but soft as a cuddly bear." He holds a master's in marketing and finance from Columbia, and joined McCann in 1958 as a trainee. Top agency officials own 8 to 9 percent and all employees hold 16 to 17 percent, though ownership extends only to approximately 300 key employees. A group called the Development Council, composed of the 140 top agency people, not only gets long-term rewards based on company profits, but is also entitled to "supplementary health and dental insurance." In other words, the guys who can most afford it don't have to pay medical insurance premiums.

Social responsibility. Stanford University removed Interpublic stock from their portfolio because of the company's involvement in South Africa. Interpublic owns three South African ad agencies and although many of their clients (GM included) have left, Interpublic refuses to leave. In arguing against a shareholder resolution urging withdrawal, Interpublic cited as one of their accomplishments in South Africa the creation of ads featuring black and white models.

Stock performance. Interpublic stock bought for $1,000 in 1980 sold for $8,040 on January 2, 1990.

The Interpublic Group of Companies, Inc., 1271 Avenue of the Americas, New York, NY 10020; (212) 399-8000.

4

Omnicom

Employees: 11,400
Sales: $1 billion
Profits: $47 million
Founded: 1986
Headquarters: New York, New York

Three leading American ad agencies, succumbing to the Saatchi & Saatchi prescription "big is beautiful," combined forces in 1986 to create Omnicom. Roped into this corral were BBDO International (once called Batten, Barton, Durstine & Osborn), 6th largest U.S. ad agency; Doyle Dane Bernbach (they spearheaded the post–World War II creative revolution on Madison Avenue), 12th largest; and Needham Harper (roots in Chicago), 16th largest. The three-way merger created the world's fourth largest mega-agency group. They entered the 1990s handling more than $8 billion worth of advertising for clients through 260 offices in 50 countries.

Omnicom's two main components are BBDO Worldwide, whose clients include Pepsi-Cola, Apple Computer, Du Pont, Gillette, Polaroid and Dodge; and DDB Needham (after the merger these two agencies were blended into one), whose clients include Volkswagen, Bristol-Myers, Mobil, Seagram, Johnson Wax and Michelin. A third segment, Diversified Agency Services, became a catchall for ancillary service companies and specialty advertising agencies not fitting into BBDO or DDB Needham. In 1989, Omnicom paid $200 million to buy Britain's 10th largest advertising agency, Boase Massimi Pollitt (BMP), and then had to sell BMP-owned New York agency Ammirati & Puris.

THE BIG SPENDERS ON
TV ADS IN 1989

		Money Spent
1.	General Motors	$443.4 million
2.	Procter & Gamble	$408.8 million
3.	Philip Morris	$388.6 million
4.	Kellogg	$297.7 million
5.	McDonald's	$245.4 million
6.	RJR Nabisco	$230.8 million
7.	Anheuser-Busch	$207.4 million
8.	Unilever	$197.3 million
9.	Ford Motor	$175.7 million
10.	Sears, Roebuck	$85.9 million

Source: Advertising Age, 12 March 1990.

Managing all these pieces required great tact and diplomacy, and in 1988 Omnicom secured the perfect CEO, Bruce Crawford, who'd been general manager of the Metropolitan Opera in New York. For Crawford, it was back to home base. Prior to going to the Met in 1986, he'd been chairman of BBDO. Anyone who could deal with Luciano Pavarotti could certainly handle the prima donnas of the advertising world. Crawford made $300,000 a year at the Met. At Omnicom he makes $800,000.

Stock performance. Omnicom stock bought for $1,000 in 1986 sold for $3,385 on January 2, 1990.

Omnicom Group, 909 Third Avenue, New York, NY 10022; (212) 935-5660.

5

Young & Rubicam

Employees: 11,000
Sales: $758 million
Founded: 1923
Headquarters: New York City, New York

This advertising agency invented the Excedrin headache—and then lost the account when Bristol-Myers moved their business to another agency. Young & Rubicam also devised the acclaimed "Wings of Man" campaign for Eastern Airlines during the 1960s, but lost that account too; in the 1980s they were producing strident commercials for Carl Icahn's airline, TWA. In the 1950s Y&R fielded one of advertising's most humorous campaigns, featuring Bob & Ray as Bert & Harry for Piel's beer; admen loved the advertising but Piel's expired anyway.

The ad agency business is a flighty affair but sometimes there's longevity, too. Y&R does the Bill Cosby commercials for Jell-O—and the agency has had this account (General Foods) ever since Raymond Rubicam and John Orr Young left the stodgy N. W. Ayer agency in 1923 to open their own shop. In 1926, when they moved offices from Philadelphia to New York (at the behest of General Foods), they took space at 285 Madison Avenue between 38th and 39th Streets—and they're still there. They've been doing the advertising for Johnson & Johnson's baby powder and baby oil since 1928, Metropolitan Life Insurance since 1937 and Lipton Soup since 1938.

Ray Rubicam's dictum to the troops was, "Resist the usual," and during their first 30 years Y&R was known as an agency where eccentric creative types flourished. Hardly any top managers had a college degree. However, Y&R was also the agency that plucked George Gallup out of academia in the 1930s and brought him to New York to research how the public reacted to advertising. The agency flourished during the Great Depression—they did ads for Arrow shirts, Gulf Oil and Four Roses; they invented Elsie the cow as a symbol for Borden; and they emerged from World War II as one of the four big shops of the business, along with J. Walter Thompson, BBDO, and McCann-Erickson.

But somewhere along the way Y&R lost their reputation as a hot creative agency. They remained big, but their work was now seen as workmanlike but dull. They ignored a lot of the fads. They didn't go all out to win awards ("We believe creativity should be measured by the cold, gritty eye of the marketplace, not by the vibes you get in a screening room"). They didn't sell stock to the public. They didn't join with other agencies to create a mega-group. They meandered along until 1970 when Edward Ney took over as CEO. He transformed Young & Rubicam into a supermarket of services by acquiring agencies specializing in different areas. Into the

Y&R fold came Sudler & Hennessey, a leading agency for prescription drug companies; Wunderman, Riccotta & Kline, a top direct-mail agency; and Marsteller, an agency big in industrial advertising with a wing, Burson-Marsteller, that ranked as the world's second largest public relations firm (J. Walter Thompson's Hill & Knowlton is first). Cato Johnson, a sales promotion agency, also became part of Y&R. These acquisitions pushed Young & Rubicam to the top of the U.S. advertising agency rankings in 1981, a position they retained through the 1980s. Y&R's advertising accounts are split roughly 50-50 between the U.S. and the rest of the world. They had 127 offices in 44 countries, including Moscow's first ad agency. Among their worldwide clients were Adidas, Colgate-Palmolive, AT&T, Du Pont and Unisys. Ed Ney was succeeded as chief executive in 1985 by 47-year-old Alexander Kroll, an ex-pro football player, who continues as chairman and CEO. After George Bush was elected president, Ney was named U.S. ambassador to Canada.

The agency closed out the 1980s on the losing end of three court cases, an unusual occurrence for Y&R, which has long maintained a low profile. Actress Bette Midler sued them—and won $400,000—after a Y&R commercial for Mercury used a voice-over mimicking her voice. WPP sued them—and won $7 million—after Y&R helped several top executives of Lord, Geller, Federico, Einstein set up a new agency in which Y&R held a 49 percent interest (with the aim apparently of landing the IBM account the executives previously handled). And finally, in the early days of 1990, Young & Rubicam pleaded guilty, and paid a $500,000 fine, to settle charges brought by the Justice Department that the agency had conspired to bribe a Jamaican government official to obtain the account of the Jamaica Tourist Board, for whom they created the visually stunning 1980s' "Come Back to Jamaica" campaign. Y&R paid the fine—and sailed into the 1990s, still the largest agency in the land.

Young & Rubicam Inc., 285 Madison Avenue, New York, NY 10017; (212) 210-3000.

6

LEO BURNETT COMPANY, INC.

#1 *in advertising under one name*

Employees: 5,200
Sales: $428 million,
$263 million
Founded: 1935
Headquarters: Chicago, Illinois

Workplace

They do the heart-tugging ads for McDonald's, United Airlines, Kellogg's Corn Flakes and Hallmark Cards. They invented the Marlboro Man for Philip Morris, the lonely repairman for Maytag, Charlie the Tuna and Morris the Cat for H. J. Heinz and the Jolly Green Giant for Green Giant peas. These ads come from America's heartland, Chicago, where the Leo Burnett agency was born and where they stubbornly insist on doing all their U.S. work. The four largest advertisers—Philip Morris, Procter & Gamble, General Motors and Sears, Roebuck—are all Leo Burnett clients.

Burnett is proud of *not* being a New York ad agency. Leo Burnett came from St. Johns, Michigan, and worked as a reporter on the *Peoria Journal* before beginning his advertising career with Cadillac in Detroit. From the beginning, his company's symbol was a hand reaching for stars, his explanation being: "If you reach for the stars, you may not always get one, but you won't come up with a handful of mud either." Leo Burnett proudly remains a privately owned company, with no shares held by anyone outside the agency. They treat employees well (they travel first class on airlines, get fat profit-sharing checks and every August 5, the day the agency was founded, they get $1 for every year the agency has been around). Burnett is proud, too, of giving away more than

The Leo Burnett Co. introduces the Jolly Green Giant in 1935.

500,000 apples a year, in a tradition dating to their founding. Every Burnett reception room everywhere in the world has a bowl of apples free for the taking. Finally, Burnett is proud of keeping the founder's name on the door, even though he died in 1972, to remind them of his warning to remove his name when they start being more concerned with size and money than with advertising quality. They were so proud that in 1989 when they moved into a new Chicago skyscraper they *own*, they named the building for him. In 1989 Burnett also swept into first place in the U.S. ad agency business, measured by advertising done by an agency under a single name. What this means, simply, is that more advertising is produced under the Leo Burnett name than under any other agency name. Young & Rubicam ranks first in U.S. advertising, but that's the result of combining the advertising done by 10 other agencies they own.

Leo Burnett Company, Leo Burnett Building, 35 Wacker Drive, Chicago, IL 60601; (312) 220-5959.

PRINTERS

In an age of big corporations, printing remains the province of small businesses. The Bureau of the Census estimated in the mid-1980s that the U.S. had nearly 30,000 commercial printers with 495,000 employees (or about 15 persons per establishment). In practice, of course, many small print shops have far fewer than 15 employees. In recent years laser printers and computerized processes controlling everything from teletypesetting to presses have revolutionized the industry. Desktop publishing has put enormous printing power in the hands of individuals. Newspapers have their own printing presses, but all the major magazines use outside printers—and the biggest of these is Chicago's nonunion R. R. Donnelley & Sons, with a 125-year tradition of high-quality work.

Among the casualties of the 1980s were financial printers, companies that serve Wall Street with the reams of papers needed in takeovers, mergers and offerings of stock and debt securities. In the first part of the decade, when takeovers were the rage, they did very well. But when the balloon burst at decade's end, these printers ruptured too. Two of them, Sorg and C. P. Young, went under.

1

R.R. Donnelley & Sons Company

#1 *in printing industry*
Employees: 26,100
Sales: $3.1 billion
Profits: $222 million
Founded: 1864
Headquarters: Chicago, Illinois

If you drive down Chicago's Lake Shore Drive, heading south from the Loop, you'll soon come across the R. R. Donnelley printing plant, a little beyond

Soldiers Field and at the same exit as the giant convention center, McCormick Place. That's also the headquarters of Donnelley, the world's largest printer. Their Chicago roots are deep. They've been printing at that location for over 100 years. Today, they run 25 U.S. plants, printing 250 magazines and 165 million books a year. They print *Time*, *Newsweek*, *TV Guide* and the *New Yorker*. Their 10 largest customers bring in 25 percent of their sales.

Donnelley extended their reach during the 1980s into financial printing, telephone directories, sales catalogs and computer manuals. As the decade ended, they agreed to pay $570 million to acquire another big printer, Meredith/Burda, jointly owned by Iowa's Meredith Publishing and Germany's Burda family. If antitrust lawyers in the Justice Department approve the acquisition, Donnelley's sales will move over $3.5 billion, more than triple what they were in 1980.

Donnelley is proud to be a nonunion printer. They also read what they print. They print the West Coast magazine *Sunset*, but refuse to print *Playboy* (also headquartered in Chicago), because they don't approve of the content. On the other hand, they don't mind printing those advertising inserts that clog up Sunday newspapers. In 1987, they started up a large factory in Reno, Nevada, to produce such inserts for retailers like Kmart and J. C. Penney. In 1988, they opened the world's largest telephone directory printing press, in Lancaster, Pennsylvania.

Donnelley has also placed a big bet on financial printing—prospectuses, annual reports and other financial documents. They aim to become "the number one financial printer in the world." During the 1980s they built or bought financial printing facilities in New York City, Singapore, Hong Kong and Tokyo, all linked by satellite.

History. A Horatio Alger aura surrounds the Canadian-born company founder, Richard Robert Donnelley. According to company history, while learning his trade in Ontario during the 1850s, "he used to end his prayers at night by asking the Lord to make him a good printer."

In 1864, Donnelley moved to Chicago to become a partner in a printing firm associated with a large publishing house. Seven years later, the firm of Church, Goodman and Donnelley was destroyed by the Great Chicago Fire of 1871. Undaunted, Donnelley went to New York with $20 in his pocket and persuaded investors to back him in another company, which got off the ground in 1873. First called Lakeside Publishing and Printing, the firm was reorganized as R. R. Donnelley and Sons in 1882. Their national landmark plant on Lake Michigan has two signs: R. R. Donnelley and Sons and, in smaller letters, Lakeside Press.

The Donnelley family has always been closely involved with the business, from the time R. R.'s wife, Naomi, wrote a cookbook when the company needed something to print. One of R. R.'s sons, Reuben, started a publishing company. The Reuben H. Donnelley Corporation, now a subsidiary of Dun and Bradstreet, publishes the *Chicago Yellow Pages*—which are, you guessed it, printed by R. R. Donnelley and Sons.

Another son, T. E. Donnelley, took the company reins in 1899. His major coup was landing the *Time* account in 1927, when the magazine was no more than a promising curiosity. Legend has it Donnelley went to Cleveland to call on Henry Luce, and after several late-night bargaining sessions, they hammered out a printing agreement. To meet the terms, Donnelley had to build new presses and operate at a loss—a risk T. E. felt was worth taking. He was right. Their work for *Time* brought them *Life* in 1936—and that sealed their reputation as a high-quality printer.

Owners and rulers. Various Donnelley family members own about 19 percent of the company worth $665 million at the start of 1990. Gaylord Donnelley, R. R.'s grandson, the largest individual shareholder, owns about one-quarter of the family fortune. Donnelley's board includes two family members, Gaylord Donnelley, an honorary director, and James Donnelley, R. R.'s great-grandson, who runs the financial printing arm of the empire. Donnelley's chairman, CEO and president is John R. Walter, aged 43 in 1990, who was paid $773,000 in 1989.

As a place to work. Donnelley has been an open shop—that is, a nonunion workplace since 1908, after a series of labor disputes slowed production. Their aversion to unions is spelled out in the employee handbook: "Because we want to deal with employees as individuals, we hope they will not join unions." Donnelley pays wages competitive with union levels, and claims their benefits are the best in the printing industry. They stress in-house training. The company apprentice school still teaches the printing craft to nearly 1,200 Donnelley journeymen—a term they say includes women.

S*ocial responsibility.* In 1989, a former sales rep at Donnelley pled guilty to conspiracy and perjury, mail and wire fraud during the period from 1986 to 1988. Because Donnelley prints *Business Week* magazine at their plants, the employee read about stock tips in the "Inside Wall Street" section of the magazine—before the issue hit newsstands. The employee bought and sold securities based on the privileged information.

G*lobal presence.* Donnelley owns a large subsidiary in England, Ben Johnson and Company, Ltd., that prints, among other products, the *Sunday Times Magazine* and the British Yellow Pages.

S*tock performance.* Donnelley stock bought for $1,000 in 1980 sold for $9,406 on January 2, 1990.

R. R. Donnelley & Sons Co., 2223 Martin Luther King Drive, Chicago, IL 60616; (312) 326-8000.

2

#1 *in check printing, ATM transaction services*

Employees: 16,800
Sales: $1.3 billion
Profits: $153 million
Founded: 1915
Headquarters: St. Paul, Minnesota

Checks from one bank often look a lot like checks from another bank because they are printed by the same company: Deluxe. This company supplies over half of the 40 billion checks Americans write every year. Computers were supposed to usher in the checkless society, but so far no one has told Deluxe about it. So many banks rely on Deluxe because they're speedy. They receive more than 400,000 check orders a day and ship 97.1 per cent of them within two days—the same two-day turnaround ordered by founder W. R. Hotchkiss.

Hotchkiss started Deluxe after inventing a press that could print three business checks to a page. He's still quoted in the company's annual report, and Deluxe keeps an old-fashioned touch, despite 70 highly automated plants.

If a customer wants checks in one day instead of two, for instance, a yellow "promise slip" attached to the order must be initialed, dated and timed by everyone who touches the order. The numbers Deluxe intones biblically are not profits and sales, but 97.1 percent on-time delivery and 99.6 percent error-free figures.

Deluxe does do a few other things besides printing checks. They print business forms, provide software for ATMs and identify deadbeats for banks through a verification service. These other businesses now account for 30 percent of sales.

This company likes to promote from within. Five of the six senior officers have worked for Deluxe for at least 25 years. CEO H. V. Haverty was paid a relatively modest $597,000 in 1989.

According to *Business Week,* Deluxe's "most valuable asset is a highly productive, nonunion work force that has never suffered a layoff...and has a traditionally high morale." After one year of employment at Deluxe, a worker qualifies for the Employee Stock Ownership Plan.

S*tock performance.* Deluxe stock bought for $1,000 in 1980 sold for $10,501 on January 2, 1990.

Deluxe Corporation, 1080 West County Road F, Post Office Box 64399, St. Paul, MN 55164; (612) 483-7358.

PART TWO

The White Collar Corps: Serving Business and Office

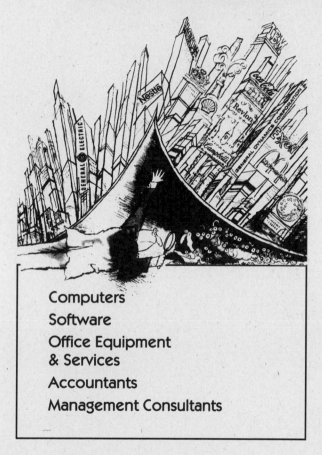

Computers

Software

Office Equipment
& Services

Accountants

Management Consultants

COMPUTERS

First there were the mainframes, big, hulking machines kept in air-conditioned rooms, accessible only to technicians who knew which buttons to push. Then came minicomputers, putting power behind scientists and engineers working in big companies and academic institutions. And then—in the 1980s—came personal computers: desktop machines with more power and speed than the old mainframes. Computers still aren't a household artifact, like a TV but they're everywhere in the business world—and the industry supplying them is explosive. The field is strewn with the remnants of companies that tried and failed to gain a foothold.

IBM ended the 1980s where they held at the start: undisputed leader. The 1980 runners-up didn't fare as well. Honeywell exited the business. Burroughs and Sperry Rand combined to form Unisys. Control Data lost their way. But spectacular newcomers emerged. Apple Computer made the Fortune 500 in just five years—a record until Compaq came along in 1983 and made it in three.

People who write about this industry are always predicting a shakeout. That's because (1) they don't know what will happen and (2) this industry is still forming.

1

#1 *in computers*

Employees: 385,200
Sales: $62.7 billion
Profits: $3.8 billion
Founded: 1911
Headquarters: Armonk, New York

Workplace

Not even IBM was immune to the turmoil of the 1980s. No one had the temerity to target International Business Machines for a takeover—they would've had to raid Fort Knox to do that—but "Big Blue" lost some of their dominance. They used to *be* the computer industry. Now they have to share power. Competitors are here to stay, especially in personal computers and workstations, where IBM was beaten to the punch by smaller, more nimble players.

However, don't pass the tin cup for IBM yet. They made more money after taxes, $51 billion from 1980 through 1989, than any other company in the world. And throughout the decade they held onto their ranking as the nation's most valuable company, based on stock market worth. At the start of 1990 their shares were worth $62.4 billion, more than twice the value of General Motors'.

Big Blue sells hardly anything directly to consumers. Nevertheless, IBM rates as one of the world's best known brand names. Say IBM and most people will say "computer." The explosive computer age has spawned hundreds of new companies like Apple and Compaq, plus strong efforts by older companies like AT&T and Hewlett-Packard, along with entries from Japan, Germany, Italy and France. Yet IBM, the model for rip-offs and imitators, the target of a host of detractors, has stayed on top, seemingly impossible to dislodge. People argue over the source of this resilience. Some attribute it to a culture that preens itself on *excellence*. Others say it's superior *sales* power rather than superior technology. And still others say it's simply a case of monopoly power. But for now the U.S. government doesn't think so. Ronald Reagan's Justice Department abandoned an antitrust complaint against IBM pursued for 13 years by other administrations. Reagan's people said they had no case, that IBM had won their place at the top fair and square.

IBMers used to joke the initials stood for "I've Been Moved." That was no joke in the late 1980s, as Big Blue cut jobs and shuffled staff all over the country. From 1986 until the restructuring is over in 1991, IBM's work force will have decreased by 21,000, 19 U.S. factories will have closed and 29,000 employees will have changed jobs—without IBM violating their long-standing no-layoff policy. Big Blue is being revamped. Profits went down in 1985 and 1986, the first two consecutive drops since the Great Depression. CEO John Akers' responded with his bureaucracy-busting "Just Say No" campaign—so named to encourage employees to think for themselves, become more entrepreneurial and refuse unwise orders from upper-level management. Akers told *Business Week* in 1988, "We're trying to change the habits of an awful lot of people. That won't happen overnight, but it will bloody well happen."

IBM declared 1987 "The Year of the Customer." They'll now come to an office and service all the equipment, no matter whose name is on it. In TV commercials, a character exclaims, "That's not the IBM I used to know." Also, in response to customer complaints, IBM started developing applications software to integrate various elements of their product line— PCs, minicomputers and mainframes.

The numbers at IBM are always big, almost mind-boggling. In 1988 only 105 U.S. manufacturing companies collected as much revenues—$4.4 billion—as IBM spent on research and development. During the 1980s scientists in four IBM research laboratories won Nobel Prizes. (They were Gerd Binnig and Heinrich Rohrer, physicists at IBM's lab in Zurich, Switzerland, who invented a new type of atomic microscope; and J. Georg Bednorz and K. Alex Mueller, physicists at the same Swiss lab, who discovered a new form of superconducting material.) IBM spends $1 billion a year just on employee training.

History. This enormous worldwide operation was built by one of the world's least-sophisticated denizens, a New York farmboy named Thomas J. Watson. In the 1890s, Watson worked as a traveling organ salesman, a sewing machine salesman and a peddler of phony building company stocks (although he was unaware of it at the time). At the turn of the century, he went to work for John Patterson's National Cash Register Company in Dayton, Ohio, where he became their top salesman. In 1912 Watson found himself indicted, along with Patterson and 27 other NCR officials, for antitrust violations (such as sabotaging competitors' machines). They were convicted. Watson and Patterson were each sentenced to a year in jail. Much has been written about whether the case was politically motivated or whether Watson had

THE 10 MOST CHARITABLE COMPANIES

Company	Philanthropic Contributions
1. IBM	$135 million
2. AT&T	$60 million
3. General Motors	$55 million
4. Hewlett-Packard	$50 million
5. Exxon	$49 million
6. RJR Nabisco	$48 million
7. General Electric	$39 million
8. Merck	$36 million
9. Ford Motor	$32 million
10. Du Pont	$31 million

Source: Across the Board, May 1990.

merely been a dupe in one of Patterson's typically overly aggressive sales schemes. Regardless, Watson never served time. An appeals court ordered a retrial, then Dayton was hit by a huge flood. NCR played such a heroic role in the disaster relief that further prosecution of the heroes was politically unthinkable. Patterson went on to fire his protégé Watson in 1913 over a relatively minor dispute about sales strategies.

Watson recovered from his shock and in 1914 took over Computer Tabulating-Recording Company, located near his old hometown, Elmira, New York. The company had begun by selling an electrical punch-card accounting system (developed for the 1890 census) and had branched out into scales, meat slicers and adding machines. Sales were slow and the company needed a wiz salesman like Watson, who more than doubled sales to $10 million by the early 1920s. In 1924, he changed the company name to International Business Machines. Under Watson's leadership, THINK signs sprouted in company offices, closets and washrooms, and salesmen would gather each morning for pep talks. Churchlike behavior was required. So were dark suits and white shirts. Smoking was forbidden on company premises. Watson even commissioned a company songbook with titles like "Ever Onward" and "Hail to the IBM." Sample lyrics:

Our voices swell in admiration;
Of T. J. Watson proudly sing.
He'll be ever our inspiration,
To him our voices loudly ring.

Watson headed the company until his death in 1956 at age 82. He was succeeded by his son, Thomas Jr., who led IBM into the computer age and articulated the Watsonian beliefs in a series of lectures he gave at Columbia Graduate Business School in 1962. Watson named the three cornerstones of IBM's philosophy as respect for the individual, customer service and excellence in everything that's done. He said he 'believed "the most important single factor in corporate success is faithful adherence to those beliefs." If you're an IBMer, you *will* believe.

In the 1920s and 1930s IBM totally dominated the market for time clocks and punch-card tabulators. In the 1930s and 1940s they pioneered the electric typewriter. So when IBM entered the computer market in the early 1950s, their established sales force already knew what businesses needed for information processing and accounting. From the start, then, they designed computers to fit customer needs. In short order IBM completely dominated the computer market, pushing out would-be competitors like RCA and GE. They were as close to a monopoly as there was in the American economy.

IBM weakened in the mid-1970s and 1980s as more powerful computer chips made it easier for small machines to do the job previously done by big IBM mainframes. In the mid-1970s, competitors arose in the form of minicomputer makers such as Digital Equipment and Data General. Then came personal computers like Apple's.

Big Blue introduced their first personal computer in 1981, blending parts others made under the IBM name. The chip came from Intel. The operating system came from Mirosoft. Most of the disk drives were supplied by Tandon. SCI Systems made the circuit boards. Epson made the printer. When critics said the IBM PC had nothing technologically new, IBM said: "Great! That was the best news we could have had. We actually had done what we had set out to do." And the IBM name was magical. They soon took over first place in personal computers. But nothing pre-

vented others from setting up a factory to compete with IBM. And many did. The computer market once again resembled a free-for-all. By 1988 IBM's share of the personal computer market had dropped to 16 percent. Makers of IBM clones, led by Compaq, had twice that share. IBM's share of the mainframe business slid from 70 percent to 53 percent. Clearly, IBM would never again command the lion's share.

IBM being IBM, people are always ready to write about the company even though the company gives them no encouragement or help. During the 1980s five books analyzing IBM appeared, from the fawning to the accusatory. In 1981 came Robert Sobel's competent history, *IBM: Colossus in Transition*. In 1986 came the laudatory account, *The IBM Way*, by ex-IBM salesman Buck Rodgers, and the damning indictment, *Big Blue: IBM's Use and Abuse of Power*, by Richard Thomas DeLamarter, an economist who had worked at the Justice Department when it was pursuing IBM on antitrust charges. In 1988 came *Blue Magic*, by writer James Chposky and publisher Ted Leonsis, describing IBM's crash program to produce a personal computer and then their abuse of the people who did the job. And in 1989 came the dreary *Beyond IBM*, by ex-IBMer Lou Mobley and consultant Kate McKeown. IBM had nothing to say about any of these books. But as the decade was closing, CEO John Akers expressed the hope that in the 1990s a new IBM might emerge, one that "has a sense of humor" and "doesn't take itself as seriously as perhaps it did in the past."

Owners and rulers. IBM has had four CEOs since Thomas Watson, Jr., stepped down in 1971 after having a heart attack: Vincent Learson, tough and abrasive (his favorite movie was *Patton*); Frank Cary, described by Robert Sobel as cold and

The first electronic digital computer, dating from the 1940s, contained 18,000 vacuum tubes and filled a large room. Today's desktop computers can perform calculations in less than a second that would have taken the early computers 5 hours.

IBM's founder, Thomas J. Watson, required
these "THINK" signs in every corporate office.

efficient ("just like the computers his firm was turning out"); John Opel, another product of IBM's sales training program but warmer than his predecessor; and John Akers, who took over in 1985 when he was 50. Akers played hockey at Yale and was a jet fighter pilot for the navy. One former IBM employee told the *Wall Street Journal*, "This is a Navy fighter pilot who knows how to pull the trigger." In 1989, he made $1.8 million, which placed him 100th on the roster of America's most well paid CEOs. IBM's board in 1990 included three ex-cabinet members: Harold Brown (defense), William T. Coleman, Jr. (transportation), Nicholas deB. Katzenbach (attorney general). Combined director shareholdings amount to less than half of 1 percent of all shares. Pension funds and insurance companies like IBM stock. Some 1,700 of these institutions own about half of IBM's 580 million shares. IBM also has an army of individual shareholders, 788,000, of whom nearly 200,000 are employees.

As a place to work. One of the best. Good pay, super benefits, and a no-layoff policy. Even in the late 1980s when Akers began closing plants and hacking away at IBM's bureaucracy, no one was fired. The payroll was pared by normal attrition and attractive early retirement packages. IBMers working in plants ticketed for closing were offered transfers to other IBM plants. IBM makes all the "best" lists best for women (20 percent of management), best for working mothers (up to three years leave to care for a new child), best for the disabled (IBM employs thousands of disabled persons and has redesigned equipment to suit their needs), best for blacks (when *Black Enterprise* compiled their roster of powerful, black U.S. executives, three were IBMers: Curtis J. Crawford, vice president-personal computers; Ira D. Hall, assistant treasurer; and Gerald D. Prothro, vice president-data systems).

Social responsibility. No one in the corporate world gives away more money and equipment to nonprofit groups than IBM—$135 million in 1988, double the donations of number two giver, AT&T. For every dollar an employee contributes to a college or university, hospital or arts group, IBM matches it with a $2 contribution—up to $5,000. Employees active in a nonprofit community group may request, and automatically get, an IBM contribution to that group. An employee may also take a year's *paid* leave to work for a community service organization; more than 1,000 IBMers have done so since 1971.

IBM withdrew from South Africa in 1987 under conditions that did not satisfy church groups represented by the Interfaith Center on Corporate Responsibility. A new company was set up, functioning as IBM's exclusive sales representative and employing 1,500 persons (nearly one-quarter of them non-white). The company is barred from selling IBM equipment to "South African police, military or apartheid-enforcing agencies," but activists charged any IBM computer sales in South Africa prop up apartheid. In 1989 over 60 IBM black employees joined with religious groups to demand the company cease all sales to South Africa. The employees noted the company agreed to take no action against them. A proxy resolution presented at the annual meeting in 1989 garnered 14.5 percent of the shares, the highest vote ever received by a resolution IBM management opposed.

Global presence. IBM means computer outside the U.S. as well as inside. Over half of sales and nearly 75 percent of profits come from overseas operations. IBM does $20 billion worth of business in Europe—$10 billion in the Far East (primarily Japan).

Stock performance. IBM stock bought for $1,000 in 1980 sold for $2,181 on January 2, 1990.

International Business Machines Corporation, Armonk, NY 10504; (914) 765-1900.

2

#2 *in computers*

Employees: 123,700
Sales: $12.9 billion
Profits: $876 million
Founded: 1957
Headquarters: Maynard, Massachusetts

Workplace

They prefer to be known as Digital, but most people still call the company DEC (pronounced deck). Whatever you call them, Digital Equipment Corp. is the biggest company started in the U.S. after World War II. They make computers, especially minicomputers operating in networked systems to help offices and factories move products and paper. Digital was an early proponent of the strategy now embraced by everyone in the computer industry: A computer company's mission is to help customers tie all their information together. Digital's VAX system did precisely that, and during the 1980s they doubled their market share, mostly at the expense of industry leader IBM.

DEC's sales quintupled during the 1980s, a function of a line of powerful minicomputers that solve business problems—and a revved-up sales force that responded to the messianic messages of company founder Kenneth H. Olsen. Digital is New England's answer to IBM and Silicon Valley. For a large company, they're famous for their lack of strong structure. And they have a religiosity imparted by Olsen, who grew up in a fundamentalist family. He once referred disparagingly to Wall Street analysts by pointing out that a falling stock price is not "trouble," adding: "Trouble is when your kids take dope."

Digital goes their own way. Unlike IBM, their salespeople are salaried rather than on commissions. Olsen insists on that because he believes commissions make salespeople "work hard for the order, but not so hard for the people who gave you the order." Olsen has also held to a no-lay-off policy even when orders were down sharply. During the late 1980s, when Digital's orders were down or flat, the company instituted a wage freeze and an attractive severance program to induce people to leave voluntarily—but they fired no one. The severance offered to 700 employees in New England featured payouts of 40 to 104 weeks of pay, depending on length of service.

Digital entered the 1990s second to IBM in revenue earned from computers and computer services. But IBM remained five times as big as DEC. The relationship between IBM and DEC is seen in different ways at different times. In 1986, Olsen told the *Financial Times* that "we are committed to giving people an alternative to IBM. It is really our social obligation to the world, and no one else is going to do it." However, in 1988 Olsen told the *New York Times*: "Our position in the world has changed quite a bit. We've been working awfully hard to look just like IBM." And to prove it, at the end of 1989 Digital began pushing their mainframe computers, introducing machines priced from $1.2 million to $3.9 million, sharply lower than IBM models of comparable power. IBM holds 70 percent of the $40 billion mainframe market—but Digital said their mainframe, the VAX 9000, is unlike previous mainframes "because extraordinary cost, complexity and inflexibility [take that, IBM] are not part of Digital's computing style."

History. DEC's world headquarters are in the same old textile mill where they started out in 1957. Olsen, a research scientist at MIT, persuaded a Boston venture capital group to invest $70,000 in his scheme to make modules for minicomputers. As Olsen tells the story, the venture capitalists made several suggestions: "First, they suggested that we not use the word *computer* because *Fortune* said no one was making money in computers, and no one was about to. Second, they suggested that five percent profit wasn't enough... So, we promised ten percent. Lastly, they suggested, promise fast results because most of the board is over eighty."

Olsen made a profit the first year out. He attributes his success to carving a busi-

There were 3 employees when Digital Equipment started in 1957 in this old converted woolen mill. Today there are more than 3,000 employees in this complex, and another 120,700 worldwide.

ness plan "in our head and in our heart. If your [plan] is not so simple you can remember every line…you don't know what you want." From the start, he says, he tried to recreate the environment of an MIT lab, later expressed in a management style the *Wall Street Journal* characterized as "Don't get organized. Don't manage. Don't control. Just let it happen." Others called it "controlled chaos." For instance, a grapefruit was once passed around during a meeting; only the person holding the grapefruit was allowed to speak.

Sometimes the freewheeling style succeeded, as when DEC put out a wide range of minicomputers, of different sizes, that worked well together. Sometimes it didn't. When DEC played catch-up in the personal computer business in the early 1980s, they designed three different PCs, all were marketed and none was compatible with any other. Confused customers weren't sure which to buy, and so didn't buy any.

Throughout their history, DEC has avoided taking on long-term debt because Olsen hates borrowing and believes "hav-

ing a few million dollars cash in the bank is much nicer than being heavily in debt." DEC has nearly $2.7 billion in the bank, but shareholders don't see any of it since DEC doesn't pay dividends. (Their stock has skyrocketed in value over the years, however.) Olsen insists, sooner or later, DEC is going to need the money "just to supply products."

Owners and rulers. Founder Kenneth Harry Olsen is the only CEO Digital has ever had. Unassuming and a little Puritanical, Olsen has put his stamp on the company. He owns about 2 percent of DEC's shares, worth more than $200 million in early 1990. His 1989 compensation (salary and bonus) was $950,000, ranking him 375th among corporate CEOs (even though DEC ranks 27th on the *Fortune* 500). Olsen believes in a tight board of directors: Only seven members, and he's the only Digital person on the board. The longest serving director is Dorothy E. Rowe, retired treasurer of American Research & Development (the venture capital firm that put up Digital's seed money).

As a place to work.   Like IBM, they make all the "best" lists—one of the *100 Best Companies to Work for in America* (Levering, Moskowitz, Katz), one of the 25 best companies for blacks (*Black Enterprise*), one of the *Best Companies for Women*, (Zeitz, Dusky). The Labor Department gave Digital an award for their affirmative action program. One striking proof of their concern for employee safety was a study carried out in 1986 after a number of women working on a semiconductor line in Hudson, Massachusetts, had miscarriages. The study confirmed this hazard (without pinpointing *why*)—and as soon as the first results were reported, Digital encouraged women of child-bearing age to switch to other jobs. They also quickly shared their findings with other members of the electronics industry.

Social responsibility.   Thanks to a donation from Digital, the World Health Organization in Geneva now has a computerized worldwide electronic mail service. And for the same reason, the Opera House in Sydney, Australia, has a computerized ticketing system. During the late 1980s DEC doubled their philanthropic budget, going from $13 million (in cash and equipment) in 1986 to $26 million in 1988. They regularly give more than 1 percent of pretax profits, placing them in the top tier of generous corporate donors. Employees have a say in grants made at the local level.

Global presence.   Strong, especially in Western Europe. Digital entered the 1990s doing 55 percent of business abroad. Digital has 50,000 overseas employees.

Stock performance.   Digital Equipment stock bought for $1,000 in 1980 sold for $2,389 on January 2, 1990.

Digital Equipment Corporation, 146 Main Street, Maynard, MA 01754; (617) 493-5350.

3

 HEWLETT PACKARD

#3 *in computers*

Employees: 91,000
Sales: $12.3 billion
Profits: $809 million
Founded: 1939
Headquarters: Palo Alto, California

Workplace

The father of Silicon Valley, Hewlett-Packard used to be known as a company of engineers making products for other engineers. The quintessential HP product is their hand-held calculator for scientific types. Introduced in 1972, it rendered the slide rule obsolete. Their products generally carried high prices. So the word used to be that HP stood for "high prices."

This elitist stance was abandoned in the 1980s as HP scrambled for a place in the fast-moving computer industry. In May 1989 they entered the lucrative workstation market when they bought Apollo Computer. They still make a variety of testing and measuring devices, such as calculators and monitors at the bedsides of intensive-care patients, but they also supply computer products, from mini-computers and laptops to disk drives and printers. Their laser jet printer, introduced in 1984, became the most successful product in Hewlett-Packard's history. By 1988 they'd shipped 1 million of them.

Not until 1978 did sales of computer products outsell testing and measuring devices. By 1990 computer products accounted for two-thirds of HP's total sales. The first top-level management change in HP's history also came in 1978, when John A. Young became CEO. It also marked the first time the company had not been headed by one of the two co-founders: William Hewlett and David Packard. The pre-1978 HP concentrated on making good products, counting on their quality to win the day. The new HP has to get their hands dirty figuring out what customers

Bill Hewlett meets with his co-founder, Dave Packard, shortly after his discharge from the Army after World War II.

need and then fighting other companies like IBM and DEC for sales orders.

However, HP has held to the values that built the company and made them a model for the rest of Silicon Valley. They still don't resort to mass layoffs. They still come to work in jeans and open shirts. They practice an easy informality. And they have many offshoots. More than a dozen companies, including Tandem, Apple, 3Com and Sydis, have roots in Hewlett-Packard.

History.   In 1934, two electrical engineers fresh out of Stanford took what turned out to be a most important fishing trip in the Colorado mountains. Discovering they had much in common, William Hewlett and David Packard talked about starting their own company some day. Five years later, they put up $538 and went into business in a garage in Palo Alto, where they built a low-priced device to measure sound frequencies. Walt Disney bought eight of them to make *Fantasia,* and the fledgling company was off to a solid start. At first HP was no more than a little lab, where Bill and Dave, as the two are known, developed various products to measure sound and light waves for engineers and scientists. In the early years, their wives worked at other jobs so that they could keep their enterprise afloat.

World War II turned the little lab into a little company. Government orders poured in, and HP had nearly 100 employees by 1943. Hewlett and Packard refused to accept large "hire-and-fire" government contracts because they didn't want to hire people—and then have to lay them off at the end of the contract. They also instituted profit sharing and made stock available to employees, enabling many HPers to leave the company as millionaires. MBWA—management by walking around—is another HP practice widely copied. In the 1960s, HP became one of the first companies to introduce flex-time.

In the 1970s, HP's hottest product was the scientific hand-held calculator. Bill Hewlett was convinced people would like a powerful calculator small enough to fit into a shirt pocket. Despite a marketing study showing people wouldn't buy it, Hewlett had his engineering team begin the design by measuring his shirt pocket. According to company lore, their most popular product of the 1980s—the laser jet printer—began in typical HP style: an informal conversation in a hallway.

Owners and rulers.   Although Hewlett and Packard have both stepped aside (Packard was still chairman of the board in 1990), they remain the largest stockholders. In 1989, the 77-year-old Packard held 16.6 percent of the shares, the 76-year-old Hewlett 11.5 percent, making each of them billionaires. In 1987, two sons of the founders joined the board, although they don't work for the company. Walter B. Hewlett, holder of 7.2 million shares, started the Center for Computer Assisted Research in the Humanities. David Woodley Packard, former professor of ancient Greek at UCLA, heads the Packard Humanities Institute, founded to support basic research in the humanities. He holds 204,000 shares. Both sons were 47 when they were first elected to the board. Packard's money also built the Monterey Aquarium in California.

CEO John Young, an Idaho-born engineer with an MBA from Stanford, started with HP in 1958. He was 58 in 1990. He earned $2.7 million in 1989.

As a place to work. A model for others. HP has no time clocks and follows one of Bill Hewlett's dictums: "Men and women want to do a good job, a creative job, and if they are provided the proper environment, they will do so." HP has good pay, profit sharing, vacation retreats, awards 10 shares of stock every time you complete 10 years of service. The one negative, heard from women, describes HP as a male engineer's domain.

Social responsibility. HP gives more than $50 million a year in cash or equipment, especially to educational institutions and communities where they have plants. Employee contributions are matched dollar for dollar. They sold their South African company in 1989. The company's success led to the creation of two of the country's biggest foundations: the William and Flora Hewlett Foundation and the Lucille Packard Foundation.

Global presence. When HP celebrated their 50th birthday in 1989, 109 ambassadors from overseas units came to Palo Alto to take part in the festivities, which included a dinner with founders Bill Hewlett, David Packard and the board of directors. A gathering of 300 people also witnessed the dedication of the garage where Hewlett and Packard started out as a California historic landmark and "the birthplace of Silicon Valley." The employees selected to come to the U.S. were, for the most part, elected by their fellow employees. They represented 32 countries. In 1988 HP did 53 percent of their business abroad, the first time that foreign sales topped the domestic total. And they take pride in exporting the HP culture as well as their technological know-how.

Stock performance. Hewlett-Packard stock bought for $1,000 in 1980 sold for $3,354 on January 2, 1990.

Hewlett-Packard Company, 3000 Hanover Street, Palo Alto, CA 94304; (415) 857-1501.

4
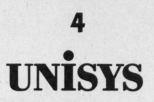

UNISYS

#4 in computers

Employees: 87,700
Sales: $10.1 billion
Losses: $639 million
Founded: 1886 (Burroughs); 1910 (Sperry); 1986 (Unisys)
Headquarters: Blue Bell, Pennsylvania

Unisys is not exactly a household word. But then they don't sell anything to households. And besides, the name is new, concocted in 1986 to stand for the company created by the merger of two computer manufacturers, Burroughs and Sperry. Burroughs and Sperry both sold mainframe computers, head-to-head with industry leader IBM. The Burroughs machines were sold under the Burroughs name, Sperry's under the Univac label. Their total market share was minor. After the merger they scrapped their old names and began selling Unisys computers. Together, they hoped to gain the critical mass needed to grapple with IBM.

As they entered the 1990s, the verdict was still out on whether W. Michael Blumenthal, architect of this merger, would be able to pull it off. At first many pundits likened the merger to the marriage of two losers. "It's like merging the *Lusitania* with the *Titanic*," said one researcher. However, as Blumenthal whipped the new company into shape, discarding assets and employees by the thousands, embracing At&T's Unix as an operating standard to oppose IBM's, acquiring Silicon Valley's Convergent Technologies and emphasizing over and over again what everyone else in the computer industry was harping on—don't sell hardware, meet customer needs—opinion in the late 1980s shifted. Perhaps Unisys had, as *Forbes* put it, "a clear sense of where they were going." Unisys was talking a confident game. They publish an upbeat newsletter for their employees, "INFO," and in 1989's first issue they proclaimed this was "the year it all must come together." Nine months later they shocked Wall Street analysts by announcing a restructuring that would eliminate 8,000 more employees and result in a third-quarter loss of $648 million. "The actions we are taking this quarter, though painful and expensive, will significantly enhance our profitability and cash flow in the 1990s," said Blumenthal, whistling in the dark.

History. Until they disappeared under the Unisys umbrella, Burroughs was distinguished as one of the few computer companies with a history stretching back more than a decade, indeed a full century. In 1885 St. Louis inventor William Seward Burroughs filed for a patent on a machine he felt would revolutionize the business world—the adding machine. Burroughs toiled away night and day to perfect his invention. According to his business partner: "Everyone but Burroughs was ready to quit. Yet the inventor himself was undaunted, demonstrating his contempt for imperfection by tossing 50 machines, one by one, out a second-story window."

Burroughs eventually reached perfection, an adding machine that didn't make mistakes. His vision was that "someday, there will be one of these machines in every city bank in the land...that means over 8,000 machines sold." The Burroughs company had sold 1 million adding machines by 1926. Most of their customers were banks, accountants, businesses, and insurance companies. A Japanese businessman visiting the U.S. in 1909 wrote: "I was struck when I saw the sacred power of God in the adding machine made by the Burroughs Adding Machine Company."

Perhaps Sperry's history is not so inspiring as Burroughs', but they can lay claim to being the world's first computer company. In 1946 two scientists at the University of Pennsylvania—J. Presper Eckert, Jr., and John W. Mauchly—built a cumbersome room-sized machine called Eniac. A few years later, the two inventors sold out to Remington Rand, which introduced the computer under the Univac name in 1951. In 1955 gyroscope maker Sperry Corp. bought the Univac division.

Burroughs was also an early entrant in the mainframe computer business, introducing their first model in 1956. But the two companies followed very different paths. Sperry specialized in selling big computer systems to the defense, airline, and communications industries, whereas Burroughs kept with its traditional base of

Walter Cronkite (standing right) used the world's first electronic computer, Univac I, to predict the outcome of the 1952 presidential election. The computer was developed by Dr. J. Presper Eckert (standing left) for the corporation now called Unisys.

PERSONAL COMPUTER MARKET

Computer	Market Share
1. IBM	21.7%
2. Apple	13.2%
3. Zenith	7.2%
4. Compaq	7.1%
5. N.E.C.	5.1%
6. Tandy	3.9%
7. Epson	3.4%
8. Hewlett-Packard	3.1%
9. Toshiba	3.1%
10. Packard-Bell	2.6%
11. Wyse	1.9%
12. Leading Edge	1.7%
13. Other	26.0%

Source: Datapro Reasearch, June 1990.

banks and financial firms (IBM outdistanced both firms).

Owners and rulers.   Mike Blumenthal "radiates authority," says a retired Burroughs executive. Part of his inner strength may be attributed to his childhood. With his family, Blumenthal escaped at age 13 from Nazi Germany. He spent his teenage years in Shanghai, where he earned one dollar a week cleaning laboratory equipment. Blumenthal once said that later when he met "people who sat behind big desks...in my mind's eye, I'd say, 'I wonder how well you'd do in Shanghai?' Some wouldn't have done too well."

Blumenthal arrived in the U.S. at 21 with $60 in his pocket and only a rudimentary command of English. Nine years later, he was the proud possessor of a PhD in economics from Princeton, where he then taught. He then began shuttling between academia, business and government. During both the Kennedy and Johnson administrations, Blumenthal served as a tough trade negotiator. He became chairman of Bendix, a post he left to become Jimmy Carter's Treasury Secretary. In that position, his toughness became a liability; he left the administration after only two years. Blumenthal was paid

$6.5 million in 1989. He was succeeded as CEO by 48-year-old James A. Unruh, a North Dakotan, who worked for Memorex before Burroughs took them over in 1981.

As a place to work.   Integrating two different cultures is a tough job. Burroughs, after five years of Blumenthal leadership, was a button-downed place. Sperry was notorious as a laid-back place where managers could do almost anything and not get fired. To integrate the two cultures, Blumenthal brought in psychologists to minister to the troops. That must have been soothing to the thousands of employees who were dismissed after the merger.

Social responsibility.   Unisys' biggest customer, accounting for 25 percent of sales, is the U.S. government—and like other defense contractors, they have been involved in corrupt practices. Managers in the weapons division (the Sperry side of the business) apparently overcharged the army for computer work by as much as $10 million. Blumenthal assured shareholders the company was cooperating fully "to bring the wrongdoers to justice." Unisys sold their South African subsidiary in 1988 but then conceded a European distributor would continue to supply Unisys products to the divested company. As a result, a number of church groups submitted a proxy resolution to the 1989 annual meeting asking all economic relationships with South Africa be terminated "until apartheid ends." It rolled up 23.3 percent of the votes cast.

Global presence.   They inherited a big international business. Unisys sells in 100 countries, doing nearly half their sales abroad. They have 49 major facilities abroad, concentrated in 11 countries: Australia, Brazil, Canada, France, Germany, Italy, Mexico, the Netherlands, Sweden, Switzerland and the United Kingdom.

Stock performance.   Unisys stock bought for $1,000 in 1986 sold for $907 on January 2, 1990.

Unisys Corporation, P.O. Box 500, Township Line and Union Meeting Roads, Blue Bell, PA 19424; (215) 542-4011.

5

#5 *in computers*

Employees: 58,000
Sales: $6 billion
Profits: $412 million
Founded: 1884
Headquarters: Dayton, Ohio

If parts of Dayton, Ohio, look like a ghost town today, it's because the city's onetime largest employer, National Cash Register, now known as NCR, pulled a Rip Van Winkle and almost missed the future. Born a maker of cash registers, they plodded along for years making the chunky machines that rang up sales in stores around the world. But the electronic revolution ushered in after World War II somehow failed to penetrate NCR's Dayton fortress until it was almost too late. The company teetered on the brink of collapse in the early 1970s when the board imported William S. Anderson, head of NCR Japan, to straighten things out. The British-born Anderson (who spent World War II in a Japanese prison camp) did. He moved NCR into the mainstream computer business, firing thousands of people in the process. He also brought in his successor, Charles E. Exley, Jr., from Burroughs.

The company known as National Cash Register—Anderson changed the name to NCR in 1974—once employed 90,000 people, most of them in Dayton. NCR now has 60,000 employees. And only 5,000 people work in Dayton, where headquarters remain. And despite Anderson's strategies, NCR is no longer the force it was when John H. Patterson built National Cash into a powerhouse during the early years of the 20th century.

Not so lovingly known as the "autocrat of the cash register," John Henry Patterson didn't invent the cash register (known then as a "thief catcher"); but he practically invented American salesmanship, sales quotas, the first formal sales training manual and one of the world's first company-sponsored sales training schools. Patterson built a model plant where as Big Daddy he pioneered industrial welfare benefits for employees: showers, lockers, swimming pools, hot lunches, medical care and inspirational lectures. Women employees were taught how to manage their homes, and children of employees were taught how to save their money, how to chew their food and how to avoid scattering germs when they sneezed. His sales force was sent out to cover the country with cash registers. His "never take no for an answer" tactics paid off—by 1910 his company was doing 90 percent of the country's cash register business. Patterson only wondered why he wasn't getting the other 10 percent. He almost went to jail trying to get that last ten percent: He was convicted of an antitrust violation in 1913 but never served his one-year prison sentence because of political reasons. Patterson also invented the slogan "THINK," later popularized by his protégé Tom Watson at IBM.

Patterson was a presence in Dayton. He was credited with saving the city from flooding in 1913. Two business leaders who came out of National Cash were Thomas Watson, IBM founder, and Charles F. Kettering of General Motors (another Dayton economic mainstay). Patterson left his mark in Dayton: Patterson Boulevard, a Patterson statue and Wright-Patterson Air Force Base. But after he died in 1922, National Cash went to sleep, sated on the money they were raking in from register sales.

Today's NCR is a shadow of the old National Cash—"a colorless, phlegmatic corporation that's an also-ran in the computer business but still a major factor in the banking and retail fields where their cash registers were once supreme. Today, they're the largest producer of ATMs, those machines that let bank customers extract cash from their accounts. NCR has installed more than 50,000 of them. And they are also a leading supplier of terminals used by tellers and cashiers. And they are bigger overseas than they are in the U.S., getting 59 percent of sales and 77 percent of profits abroad. In 1989, NCR pulled out of South Africa, selling their operations to Allied Electronics Corp.

In the 1980s, under Exley's direction (and assisted by President Gilbert Williamson), NCR began promoting a stakeholders' concept emphasizing that in addition to their responsibilities to shareholders, NCR would manage their business to fulfill responsibilities to employees, suppliers and communities where they operated. Too bad, the commitment came too late for Dayton.

Stock performance. NCR stock bought for $1,000 in 1980 sold for $4,449 on January 2, 1990.

NCR Corporation, 1700 South Patterson Boulevard, Dayton, OH 45479; (513) 449-2000.

6

#2 *in personal computers*

Employees: 12,700
Sales: $5.3 billion
Profits: $438 million
Founded: 1977
Headquarters: Cupertino, California

A Greek tragedy played itself out in the California sun at Apple Computer in the 1980s. The scenario had two California youths, barely out of their 20s, get financial backing to start a company to make a product industry leader IBM saw no need to make: a personal computer. It was a big success, leading IBM to change their mind, and the product spawned a new company, Apple Computer, pledged to making products that would make the world a better place. One of the founders,

Steve Wozniak, decided corporate life was not for him, and he dropped out with his millions and was last seen building a cave at his home. The other founder, Steve Jobs, recognized his lack of business experience and hired a headhunter to find somebody who knew how to run a company. They found John Sculley, who was enticed away from Pepsi-Cola by the challenge that perhaps he ought to be doing something more with his life than selling sugared water. Sculley pulled up stakes in the East and arrived in Silicon Valley with his pressed jeans, ready to work and espousing Apple values. In two years he decided Steve Jobs, Apple's founder, was an obstacle to the company's progress. And so Jobs was sent packing with all his millions, part of which he used to start another computer company, NeXT. And by decade's end, John Sculley was master of all he saw at Apple, having dispatched just about all the people who defined the values Apple said they wanted to uphold.

With sales pushing $6 billion at the beginning of the new decade, Apple had progressed from maverick to established member of what is still one of America's fastest-growing industries. In the early years, rock-and-roll music played in the halls, and meeting rooms were named after the Seven Dwarfs and the deadly sins. That changed with the arrival of John Sculley, known around Apple as "the guy from corporate America." Sculley rapidly positioned himself as the feel-good guru, the sincere CEO. In 1990, he told *Business Month* magazine, "There's a tribal bond among us all—this feeling that if you cut your finger, you ought to bleed in the six

Steve Wozniak and Steven Jobs with their first personal computer, the Apple I.

colors of the Apple logo." The blood image is painfully appropriate. By 1990, with more firings on the horizon, idealism and employee bonding seemed to be just so much New Age chatter. In February, numerous employees wrote scathing letters to Sculley on the company's electronic bulletin board and then sent their comments to the *San Jose Mercury News*. Much of their rage was directed at Sculley himself, and at the cushy perks given to top execs. Sculley took home $9.5 million in 1988; $6 million in 1989. "The executives are in it for themselves, not the world, not the employees, not even the shareholders," one anonymous employee wrote. The profit-sharing plan has been revised numerous times since Sculley took over—and each revision has reduced the employees' share. One employee wrote, "No more bites in my Apple!!!"

As the turbulent 1980s closed, Apple was involved in a major drive to sell their computers to businesses. Apple's computers are not only incompatible with IBM's, but there are also no Apple clones, (cheaper, nearly identical models). So, Apple computers, like the Macintosh, are high priced. Apple's draw is that their machines are "friendlier" (easier to use) and fun.

The Apple of the 1990s is a more button-downed company. They retain many of the early Apple features—wonderful benefits such as sabbaticals, on-site daycare, profit sharing, stock options for nearly everyone—but the tone is different. Kevin Sullivan, who came to Apple from Digital Equipment to head up human resources, put it this way to *Fortune*'s Brian O'Reilly: "As we move from countercultural to mainstream, all that California stuff doesn't mean as much. My 81-year-old mother shouldn't have to like surfing before she can consider using a Macintosh."

Stock performance. Apple Computer stock bought for $1,000 in 1981 sold for $2,132 on January 2, 1990.

Apple Computer, Inc., 20525 Mariani Avenue, Cupertino, CA 95014; (408) 996-1010.

7

#3 *in personal computers*

Employees: 7,800
Sales: $2.9 billion
Profits: $333 million
Founded: 1982
Headquarters: Houston, Texas

"**A**nything IBM can do, we can do better." That was the rallying cry of this start-up computer company, which jumped into the field after IBM introduced their first personal computers in 1981. Compaq's strategy was simple: produce better versions of the very computer IBM was making. Their first entry was a portable computer (hence the corporate name, Compaq), which IBM wasn't even making. They sold 53,000 in the first year. They then fielded lightweight, powerful desktop computers. All were IBM-compatible machines, meaning they could run the same software programs designed for IBMs. Compaq became the king of the IBM clones. Their product came to be known as the "BMW of personal computers."

The venture capital firm of Sevin Rosen financed Compaq, which was then staffed largely by engineers who followed Joseph R. "Rod" Canion out of Texas Instruments. Canion led Compaq into the *Fortune* 500 roster faster than any company in history after sales topped $500 million in 1985. In 1987 sales went over the $1 billion mark—no company had ever reached that level in so short a time. By decade's end, Compaq was pushing $3 billion, with 45 percent of sales coming from abroad.

As they entered the 1990s, the inevitable scenario was unfolding: The copycat was tired of being a copycat. Compaq was developing their own computers instead of hitchhiking on IBM technology. Although they had yet to reach their 10th birthday by 1990, Compaq was counting on the culture they'd built during the 1980s to arm them in the battle against Big Blue. It's not exactly the "hang loose" culture of Silicon Valley. Compaq executives look like IBM clones—all dressed in dark suits and white shirts. No alcohol, including beer and wine, is allowed on Compaq premises. They use a "consensus management" process involving team meetings to iron out problems. Competence is not so important as teamwork. Loners are not welcome. Although they now have over 7,000 employees, Compaq tries to maintain the cohesiveness of a small company. Canion meets quarterly with all employees. There's an egalitarian streak, too. No reserved parking places at their Houston complex. And what is exceedingly rare in American companies: Every employee is eligible for stock options that, exercised during the 1980s, would have resulted in very tidy gains. Canion earned $2.1 million in 1989; his stock was worth $15 million in 1990.

Global presence.   Compaq has a distribution and training center in Eching, West Germany. The company markets products in 52 countries.

Stock performance.   Compaq stock bought for $1,000 in 1984 sold for $6,374 on January 2, 1990.

Compaq Computer Corporation, 20555 State Hwy 149, Houston, TX 77070; (713) 370-0670.

8

⊂⊖Ə CONTROL DATA CORPORATION

Employees: 25,800
Sales: $2.9 billion
Losses: $680 million
Founded: 1957
Headquarters: Minneapolis, Minnesota

Control Data limped into the 1990s as the virus-plagued giant of the computer industry. Why they stumbled so badly in the 1980s was not entirely clear, but Wall Street critics were quick to blame founder William C. Norris for pursuing social causes rather than paying attention to the bottom line. Under Norris, a crusty, autocratic leader, Control Data tried to harness their expertise to a variety of social ventures: opening plants in inner cities; launching programs to help small busi-

nesses and small farmers (Norris is a former Nebraska farmboy) and fielding PLATO (Programmed Logic for Automated Teaching Operations), a computer-based system of training and education. However, Norris always insisted these were not philanthropic programs but business opportunities to address "unmet social needs." He was a great advocate of public-private partnerships. *Fortune* editor Daniel Seligman undoubtedly spoke for the business community in 1983 when he called Norris "a business genius who unfortunately thinks he's a philosopher," an entrepreneur who talks "like a [Ralph] Naderite." Norris always gave back as good as he got. He derided his business colleagues as "predatory" and "indifferent to social needs," and in one interview he gave this assessment: "The average corporate executive, hell, he's never been to Woodlawn in Chicago, or the Bronx, or Liberty City in Miami. They read about it, but they read a lot of other horror stories that go in one ear and out the other."

What no one can deny is that Norris, a former Univac engineer, built from scratch a major computer company, succeeding where such giants as General Electric, RCA, Xerox and Bendix had failed. And then, in the 1980s, it all unraveled. At the start of 1986, Norris, then 74, stepped down as CEO of the company he'd founded 29 years earlier. Trouble had already set in. Control Data's initial franchise was the mainframe computer used for scientific applications. They'd also become a major supplier of data-processing services to companies that couldn't afford a big computer. A third major arm of the company was the manufacture of computer peripherals, especially disk drives. All these activities were undermined by developments in the late 1970s and early 1980s—the rise of powerful minicomputers, the introduction of personal computers, the growing incursion of workstations in offices and, of course, competition from Japanese makers of disk drives and other peripherals.

Control Data spent the last half of the 1980s hunkering down. From $5 billion in sales, they retreated to $3 billion. From employing 58,000, they dropped to 25,800. From 76 on the *Fortune* 500, they slid to 153. From profits of $161 million in

1983, they plunged into oceans of red ink. They lost $1.3 billion from 1984 to 1990. In 1986, Norris was replaced as CEO by Robert M. Price, a mathematician who joined the company in 1961 and rose through the programming and sales ranks. Under Price, Control Data's slide into financial ruin accelerated. In 1989 he surrendered the presidency to Lawrence Perlman; Perlman became CEO in January 1990.

In March 1990, Price retired from active employment with the company, and announced plans to retain the title of chairman. His severance pay totaled $4.24 million—after a four-year reign that produced $900 million in losses. But that's not all. He was slated to get $450,000 a year until 1993 ("consultation fees"); from then on he will receive a $300,000-a-year pension—lasting for the rest of his life. When stockholders and journalists heard of Price's golden parachute (by reading Control Data's stock proxy), many were enraged. The *Minneapolis Star-Tribune* called it an "obscene pile" of cash, and the company set up a telephone hotline to respond to complaints. In May 1990 Price resigned the chairmanship and Control Data announced that Price would no longer be a consultant.

As head of a crippled Control Data, 52-year-old Perlman (who has a law degree from Harvard) has few illusions. "Control Data is not working. The missing ingredient is a passion for winning. Too many people have become cynical, lost hope, stopped being committed." Perlman has been busy selling off much of Control Data's businesses: He was behind the sale of Control Data's finance business, Commercial Credit Co.; he auctioned off Imprimis, a disk-drive maker; ETA, the supercomputer arm; and founder Norris' baby, PLATO.

Still on board in 1990 were SAMI/Burke and Arbitron, leading suppliers of marketing research (including measurements of radio and TV audiences); and Ticketron, a computerized ticketing service and operator of state lotteries. Control Data itself badly needed to win the lottery. The consensus, as the 1990s began, was that Control Data was fighting for their life.

Stock performance. Control Data stock bought for $1,000 in 1980 sold for $734 on January 2, 1990.

Control Data Corporation, 8100 34th Avenue South, Box O, Minneapolis, MN 55440; (612) 853-8100.

9

Employees: 22,000
Sales: $2.6 billion
Losses: $511 million
Founded: 1951
Headquarters: Lowell, Massachusetts

The creation of an autocratic Chinese immigrant, An Wang, Wang Laboratories entered the 1980s flying high and by decade's end the company was very nearly turning in the wind. At the decade's start, they had sales of $500 million, the result of pioneering word-processing systems for offices. Wangs had replaced IBM typewriters in offices across the country, especially in law firms. Exiting the decade, Wang had sales of $2.6 billion but was losing money every day. They lost a staggering $511 million in 1989. In the era of the personal computer, Wang was invisible. They had resisted making their computers IBM compatible. And while An Wang had built a big company, he had never built a strong organization. Industry insider, editor Vincent Flanders, once scoffed that "Wang couldn't sell life jackets on the *Titanic.*"

Wang (known as "the Doctor" because of his Harvard PhD in physics) started out building radio transmitters for the army in his native China during World War II. In 1945 he emigrated to the U.S., earned his degree and founded Wang Laboratories with $600 in savings. He sold the patent to his one product, a data-storage device, to IBM for $500,000, and used the proceeds to manufacture electronic components. By the early 1970s, Wang's main product was programmable calculators. With great foresight, he switched to a low-priced, user-friendly word-processing system, which he introduced in 1976.

In 1986, even though they had sold stock to the public, Wang was still a family affair. The Wang family owned 78 percent of the Class C stock (which elects the majority of the board of directors). When Wang's eldest son Fred inherited the presidency that year, at age 36, a number of top executives resigned in protest. Ex-president John Cunningham bitterly predicted, "I bet Fred spends the next 30 years of his business career being compared unfavorably to his father."

In early 1989, as his father was recovering from cancer surgery and the company was reporting the $511 million loss, Fred Wang resigned and was replaced by ex-GEer Richard Miller, who immediately sold off lots of assets and fired thousands. In sales offices around the county, Wang people were given 15 minutes to clear out their desks and leave the premises. Security guards watched so they didn't get away with any company property. An Wang died on March 24, 1990, at age 70. Miller became chairman and CEO in his stead.

S*tock performance.* Wang stock bought for $1,000 in 1980 sold for $655 on January 2, 1990.

Wang Laboratories, Inc., One Industrial Avenue, Lowell, MA 01851; (617) 459-5000.

10

#1 *in supercomputers*

Employees: 5,000
Sales: $785 million
Profits: $89 million
Founded: 1972
Headquarters: Minneapolis, Minnesota

Cray Research has never run an advertisement. They don't have to. They dominate the supercomputer market so completely that scientists informally measure computer speed in units of "Crays." Cray used to sell most of their supercomputers—machines capable of at least 20 million calculations per second—to university scientists and Uncle Sam. They were used to test spacecraft designs, make weather forecasts and design nuclear bombs. But now Cray machines help Arco find petroleum, rock star Mick Jagger make videos and Boeing improve the fuel efficiency of their 767 airliner. The growing demand for supercomputers has in some ways been more curse than blessing. Cray now faces Japanese competition. And they also have to compete with their founder, who left in 1989 to form a separate company, called Cray Computer Corp.

Seymour Cray is the Greta Garbo of computer scientists. All he ever wants to be is alone. After he left Univac in 1957 with William Norris to found Control Data, Norris actually had to make special appointments to see him. "Even then his independence and reclusiveness were legendary," writes *Fortune.* Fed up with what one of his friends called "14 floors of bureaucracy," Cray left Control Data in 1972 to create Cray Research. He set up shop in an abandoned shoe factory modified to be as acoustically dead as possible. In silence he designed computers the same way he builds sailboats—obsessively. Every year Cray builds a new boat by hand, sails it all summer and then burns it at year's end to make way for a new, improved craft. Each of his supercomputers has in turn made its predecessor obsolete.

Cray Research's first computer, the Cray 1, was installed in 1976 at the Los Alamos weapons labs and cost $8 million. It was four times more powerful than anything previously built, but Cray sold only three in their first two years of business. The latest model, the $20 million Cray Y-MP, employs eight processors and has a computing speed 30 times that of the Cray-1. Time on a Cray computer can cost $7,500 an hour. The electric bill alone for operating the machine can run to $1 million a year. In mid-1990 they announced their cheapest machine—a $2.2 million version of the Y-MP.

For much of their early existence, Cray Research lacked any real competition. So the company stimulated it internally by pitting a research team Seymour Cray led against one led by Steve Chen, who came to Cray in 1979. The two worked in separate labs on the opposite sides of Chippewa Falls, Wisconsin, Cray's hometown. "Fiercely loyal to their leaders," noted the *Wall Street Journal*, "team members give up most fraternizing with other Cray colleagues." By most accounts, gregarious Chen and withdrawn Cray didn't get along. Chen left in 1987 when the company stopped funding his work on a machine 100 times faster and more powerful than any in existence. "The project was getting too far out in the ozone," said one senior Cray researcher. Two years later, Chairman John Rollwagen showed the door to founder Cray and his latest project, on which the company had already spent $50 million. Rollwagen (who had run the company since 1981) was no longer willing to gamble on Seymour Cray's brilliance.

Cray has always been an informal place to work. Employees wear blue jeans to work and can be found talking and joking in the halls. But chances are conversation is about work. Cray is as intense as they are informal. "We have little turnover," says Vice President Margaret Loftus. "Most who do leave do so because they can't cut it professionally. They leave because of the peer pressure. Peer pressure is very high here."

S*tock performance.* Cray Research stock bought for $1,000 in 1980 sold for $5,220 on January 2, 1990.

Cray Research, Inc., 608 Second Avenue South, Minneapolis, MN 55402; (612) 333-5889.

SOFTWARE

It's an amazing product. You can't really see it or touch it or feel it. Software is what makes a computer (the hardware) work, turning it into a useful tool for writers or business planners or investors or game players. The end product here is an operating system, or program, that can be slipped into a computer. WordStar or WordPerfect transforms the computer into a word-processing machine. Lotus 1-2-3 turns it into a manipulator of financial spreadsheets. Bill Gates called software "a combination of artistry and engineering." And he should know. He founded Microsoft, leader of this fledgling industry, whose other players include Lotus Development, Novell Inc., Oracle Systems and Ashton-Tate. Just about every one of them was born in the 1980s.

1

#1 *in personal computer software*

Employees: 3,400
Sales: $953 million
Profits: $210 million
Founded: 1975
Headquarters: Redmond, Washington

Workplace

A computer nerd when he was growing up in Seattle, William H. Gates III is recognized today as the most powerful man in the personal computer industry. That's because his company, Microsoft, is the leading independent supplier of the operating systems, languages and application programs (software) enabling users to effectively use computers (hardware). Bill Gates has become an industry standard setter—courted and feared.

He's courted because every personal computer maker wants him to write programs for their machines. He's feared by competitors who feel that he wants to own the entire software market. "Microsoft is like an elephant rolling around, squashing ants," observed Fred M. Gibbons, president of Software Publishing Corp., to *Business Week*.

When Bill Gates was in 10th grade, he wrote a computer program that plotted traffic patterns in Seattle, and it earned him $20,000. He dropped out of Harvard when he was 19 to start Microsoft with his high school crony, Paul Allen, another computer "hacker." Their mission from the start was to devise programs to drive personal computers. Their first project, in 1975, adapted the computer language, BASIC, for use in one of the very first personal computers, the Altair. Their breakthrough assignment, in 1980, was to devise an operating system for IBM's first personal computer. If you use an IBM personal computer (or one of the many clones) and see the MS-DOS symbol flash across the screen, you're looking at a Microsoft product. Since delivering DOS to IBM in 1981, Microsoft has developed variations of it for 300 other computers. DOS drives over 40 million personal computers worldwide.

Aside from operating systems and languages, Microsoft is a prime supplier of

America's youngest billionaire, Microsoft's Bill Gates, age 35, in 1990.

applications software such as Word (for word processing), Excel (for spreadsheets) and Windows (a new program said to make an IBM PC or clone as easy to use as an Apple Macintosh). While IBM has been their meal ticket, Microsoft has also developed software for Apple personal computers, IBM's chief competitor. Edward Esber, president of Ashton-Tate, the third largest independent software supplier for personal computers, said of Gates: "Bill isn't saying that everybody must wear a blue suit. But he is saying everybody must go to his tailor."

Microsoft derives nearly one-third of sales from products embedded as original equipment in computers. Every time a machine goes out the manufacturer's door, Microsoft gets a royalty payment. Computers are everywhere in the world—and in the late 1980s, Microsoft was getting nearly half their sales abroad.

Not every computer whiz likes to run a company. Bill Gates apparently does. In mid-1990 *Fortune* gushed over Gates, saying Microsoft's "clarity of purpose, competitiveness, tenacity, and technological self-confidence emanate from Gates." During the 1980s, as personal computers became hot sellers, Microsoft went from sales of $24 million (in 1982) to nearly $1 billion (in 1989). In 1986, after browbeating Goldman, Sachs into taking a low underwriting commission (a little over 6 percent), Bill Gates took Microsoft public, selling about 10 percent of the shares to the public for $59 million. Microsoft is an obscenely profitable company, regularly netting in profits more than 20 percent of sales—*after taxes.* That performance makes them one of the world's most profitable companies. In 1987, Gates became the first billionaire in the computer industry. The next year, he was the youngest member of *Fortune*'s roster of billionaires (net worth: $1.4 billion). By June 1990, his 36 percent of Microsoft stock was worth $2.8 billion. But his pay was a piddling $175,000 a year. Paul Allen, who left the company, still owned 17 percent of the shares. Most of Microsoft's 4,000 employees work in a 125-acre, campuslike setting in the Seattle suburb of Redmond. They can share in the spoils through stock purchase and stock option plans. Microsoft is one of the handful of U.S. companies offering stock options to all employees.

Gates seems to have the knack of hiring and keeping good people. In 1990 he hired 6 feet, 5 inch Michael R. Hallman away from neighbor Boeing to replace Jon A. Shirley as president. Shirley was recruited in 1984 from Tandy. Hallman, an ex-IBM salesman, left Big Blue because he was about to be transferred from Atlanta to IBM headquarters in Armonk, New York. He preferred Seattle and Boeing, where he headed up Boeing's $1.4 billion (bigger than Microsoft) computer services division. At Boeing, Hallman, 44 years old in 1990, was one of the youngest executives. At Microsoft, he is one of the oldest (the average employee is 30). Gates was 34 years old in 1990.

S*tock performance.* Microsoft stock bought for $1,000 in 1986 sold for $6,337 on January 2, 1990.

Microsoft Corp., One Microsoft Way, Redmond, WA 98052; (206) 882-8080.

OFFICE EQUIPMENT & SERVICES

No modern office is complete without a copier. Many have postage meters. Nearly all of them have file cabinets. And if it's big enough, it may have a cafeteria or vending machines dispensing food and drink. Most office workers are permanent employees, but some may be temporaries sent out by an outside company to fill in for a day, week or month. The office voraciously consumes products and services, and the five companies considered here—Xerox, Pitney Bowes, Steelcase, ARA and Kelly Services—all lead in their particular specialties.

1

XEROX

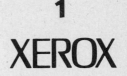

#1 *in copiers*

Employees: 112,300
Sales: $17.6 billion
Profits: $704 million
Founded: 1947
Headquarters: Stamford, Connecticut

People who grew up with copying machines don't realize what went on in the old offices: stacks of messy carbon paper—and hidden away in a back room, the foul-smelling mimeograph machine. Xerox, inventor of the copying machine, transformed the business office and in the process became one of the world's leading industrial corporations. In the 1980s, under the direction of David T. Kearns, an ex-IBMer, Xerox worked on their own transformation. They moved into financial services, rallied to defend their position in copying machines and edged into the growing market for computer workstations (another business they had almost invented).

Two books published in the 1980s captured the joy and agony of Xerox. One, *American Samurai*, by Gary Jacobson and John Hill Kirk, saluted the company for repelling the brutal Japanese assault on their core business: copiers. The second,

Fumbling the Future, by Douglas K. Smith and Robert Alexander, faulted the company for the opportunity they missed to pioneer personal computers. Xerox did, in fact, make a personal computer before the Apple computer was born. And, as the authors of *Fumbling the Future* detail, they had many of the leading brains of the computer industry assembled at their California think tank, the Palo Alto Research Center (PARC). However, fighting the Japanese on the one hand and besieged by a bunch of California computer nerds on the other hand, the Xerox bureaucracy somehow let the chance slip away. Other companies, notably Apple, picked up many of the ideas spawned at PARC. Xerox played nice guy about all of this. But they got tougher. They even sued Apple for using in the Macintosh computer the "window" screen Xerox claimed they developed for their ill-starred personal computer, the Star.

As the 1990s began, Xerox was a different company from the one they were in 1980. Copiers brought in less than half of sales. They had abandoned the publishing and medical imaging businesses. They had become a player in the new big game of the 1980s: financial services. They began with Xerox Credit, an in-house finance arm, to which they added the nation's 14th largest property casualty insurer, Crum & Forster, and two investment banking firms, Van Kempen Merritt and Furman Selz.

Perhaps the change that Kearns—and by proxy, Xerox—is most proud of was a restructuring that shook the company down to their roots. In the early 1980s Kearns fired 15,000 employees, cut the factory work force by 50 percent and launched a "Leadership Through Quality" program to retrain the remaining work force and rev them about the importance of product quality. As part of this program, Xerox eliminated 90 percent of their suppliers. Results: In 1982, 92 percent of the parts Xerox shipped were defect-free; by 1988, 99.97 percent. "The improvements," *Fortune* pointed out, "mean that when the customer pushes the button on a 50 Series copier today, he has about a 98 percent chance of getting good copies. In 1982 when he pushed the button on a 10 Series machine, he had only a 90 percent success rate." These corporate

THE POWER OF YOUTH OVER FAMILY PURCHASES

Parents Saying They Were Influenced by Child (Ages 6–17)	
Breakfast cereal	78%
Clothing	72%
Toys	68%
Ice cream	58%
Soft drinks	56%
Video movies	48%
Toothpaste	44%
Personal computers	10%
Automobile	8%

Source: Fortune, 8 May 1989.

improvements led to Xerox's selection for a 1989 Baldrige National Quality Award, an awards program Congress created in 1987 to honor the late Secretary of Commerce, Malcolm Baldrige (only one other company won an award in 1989). And aside from the honors, the program helped Xerox do something unprecedented in recent American business life: win back business lost to the Japanese.

History. Xerography, from the Greek words for *dry* and *writing*, is basically a process using static electricity to make copies instantly on plain paper. Chester Carlson, a patent attorney and amateur physicist, spent several years dabbling in his kitchen in New York City to discover the fundamental principles of what he called electrophotography. By 1937 he had enough of a process to patent it, and he set up a small lab behind a beauty parlor in nearby Astoria, Queens, to pursue his experiments. His breakthrough came on October 22, 1938, when he duplicated a glass slide on which he had written "10-22-38 Astoria."

Carlson spent six more years selling his invention. RCA, IBM, Remington Rand and General Electric all dismissed him. He finally sold it to Battelle Memorial Institute, a nonprofit research organization in Columbus, Ohio. Not until 1947 did a small photographic paper company in Rochester, New York, named the Haloid Company, begin to develop an electrophotography machine under license from Battelle.

In the 1940s, at company request, a Greek scholar at Ohio State University came up with a more distinctive name for the process: *xerography*. The machine itself, they decided, would be called Xerox, which later became the company's name.

They introduced their first copier in 1949, but it was slow and complicated. However, sure they were on the right track, they continued to tinker with the invention. The following year their big breakthrough came: the first dependable, easy-to-use document copier, the 914, so named because it could copy documents as large as 9 by 14 inches. The copier was a phenomenal success, and the company skyrocketed. Within three years they were one of the *Fortune* 500 companies.

Joseph C. Wilson, whose grandfather founded Haloid, became president in 1945. He believed strongly that a corporation had a duty to support the institutions of a free, healthy and educated society. In the 1960s Xerox came to be associated publicly with liberal political ideas. This stance was largely inspired by Wilson and Sol Linowitz, a Rochester lawyer who started representing the company in 1950 and eventually rose to board chairman. Linowitz later headed the U.S. negotiating team that worked out the 1978 treaty for the return of the Panama Canal Zone to Panama, and afterward became a special U.S. ambassador to the Middle East.

After wading into the financial services arena during the 1980s, Xerox found making money from money was not easy. In 1988, as they were rebuilding their copying business, financial services were stars, accounting for half of Xerox's profits. The next year, Xerox lost $400 million because of their investment in a floundering Chicago-based real estate outfit, VMS Realty, and they had to sock away money for expected insurance claims (1989 was the year of Hurricane Hugo and the northern California earthquake). As a result, Xerox ended the decade earning less money than they did in 1980.

Owners and rulers. In 1982, 52-year-old David Kearns became CEO. A former navy sailor, Kearns left IBM at age 41 to join Xerox. Six years later, in 1977, he

Between 1982 and 1988 the American workforce grew by 18 percent, while the temp workforce burgeoned 160 percent.

became president. He's a tough customer. Because of severe back problems, he stays on his feet all day—working at a stand-up desk. He has a reputation for fair-mindedness. In 1987 *Business Week* dubbed him "The Rejuvenator" for his work at Xerox. In 1989, Kearns earned $1.8 million, and Xerox picked up $56,640 of his expenses—the company plane, a financial planner, an accountant and a home security system. President Paul Allaire, 51, replaced Kearns as CEO in August 1990 while Kearns remains chairman. Allaire has spent his career at Xerox, joining the firm as a financial planner in 1966. Institutions like insurance companies and mutual funds own 70 percent of Xerox stock. The board of directors includes Vernon E. Jordan, Jr., former head of the National Urban League, and Joan Ganz Cooney, chairman of the Children's Television Workshop.

As a place to work. Leaner than they were in 1980 but committed to training, and working, with their people. Tony Costanza, international vice president of the Amalgamated Clothing and Textile Workers Union, called Xerox "far ahead of anybody else in this country in employee involvement." They remain a strong supporter of affirmative action. After Ronald Reagan was elected president, Kearns notified Xerox managers they would continue to be measured by the progress they make in this area and that while "national trends may fluctuate, this company's stance is unwavering." The road to the top at Xerox is through the sales force, and Xerox has tried to fill that pipeline with minorities and women. In 1986 *Black Enterprise* called Xerox the *best* company in America for blacks. In 1989, they had a dozen black officers, more than any other major U.S. manufacturer, and one of them, A. Barry Rand, headed the U.S. Marketing Group, the position once held by CEO Kearns.

Social responsibility. The founders of Xerox left a legacy in this area. David Kearns, more than any other American CEO, has become deeply involved in efforts to improve the nation's education system. In 1987 he addressed an open letter to presidential candidates proposing a six-point plan to reverse the decline in American schools. He believes both government and business must "push the schools for structural change." In 1986 Xerox funded with $5 million an Institute for Research on Learning to find better ways to teach children. They also funded other programs aimed at improving public education in inner cities. Since 1971 Xerox has given more than 350 employees social service leaves of up to a year to work for community groups (while continuing on full salary). Xerox's philanthropic budget in 1988 was $17 million. They have been a major funder of AIDS research and support programs.

Global presence. Xerox gets about one-third of sales abroad. Xerox's international arm is London-based Rank Xerox, of which they own 51 percent. Rank Xerox, in turn, owns 50 percent of Tokyo-based Fuji Xerox. To fight the Japanese in the low end of the copier market, Xerox is importing machines from—yes, you guessed it—Japan: Fuji Xerox and Sharp.

Stock performance. Xerox stock bought for $1,000 in 1980 sold for $1,671 on January 2, 1990.

Xerox Corp., P.O. Box 1600, Stamford, CT 16904; (203) 968-3000.

2

ARA services

#1 *in vending machines, uniform rentals*

Employees: 125,000
Sales: $4.2 billion
Profits: $82.6 million
Founded: 1959
Headquarters: Philadelphia, Pennsylvania

You never know where you might run into this company. You may have been born in a hospital—Mt. Zion in San Francisco, Emil Frei Medical Center in Tulsa, to name just two—where ARA runs the kitchen. Later on, you may have gone to a school where ARA serves lunch—they serve more than 650,000 schoolchildren in 175 school districts in 20 states. Then you may have gone on to a college where ARA operates the cafeteria—Boston University or the University of Virginia, for examples. Upon graduating, you may have wanted to celebrate at a fine restaurant—say, the Carnelian Room atop the Bank of America building in San Francisco or the "95th" in Chicago: Those are two of ARA's upscale restaurants. After you started work—say, at Dow Chemical or John Deere—you will run into ARA again: they run restaurants, stock vending machines or supply coffee service for most of the *Fortune* 500 companies. If you go out to the ballpark—Wrigley Field, Anaheim Stadium, Baltimore Memorial— that's ARA serving up those hot dogs, just as they do at the Las Vegas Convention Center and the Nashville Airport. If you run afoul of the law, you may end up in one of the 38 prisons where ARA dishes out the food or in one of the 79 jails where ARA is responsible for medical services. If you place your children in a day-care center operated by Children's World, that's ARA too. Finally, if you're a senior citizen or are handicapped, you may end up in one of the 270 Living Centers ARA operates. This company offers cradle-to-grave service. Their motto is: "Let ARA do it."

In addition to all the services mentioned above, ARA also operates the nation's largest uniform rental company (Aratex); distributes magazines, newspapers and books to thousands of retail customers; provides emergency medical care at more than 400 hospitals and other health-care facilities (Spectrum); and provides ground services (ramp, skycap and aircraft cleaning) at 20 airports. They have also provided the food and transportation services for each Olympic Games held since 1968. No wonder they call themselves the world's biggest service company. And it all began with vending machines—hence the original name, Automatic Retailers of America, since abbreviated to ARA. They're still the U.S.'s leading vending machine company.

ARA doubled sales during the 1980s and ceased being a publicly owned company. Faced with a takeover threat in mid-decade, ARA's managers took the company private, buying up all the shares from the public for $1.2 billion. Toward the end of the 1980s, some 350 top people at ARA owned over half of the stock (and controlled 93 percent of the votes). Unlike many other similar buyouts, ARA did not sell off pieces of the company to pay the lenders. On the contrary, ARA expanded their service portfolio during the 1980s. And they're now running restaurants for the British Army, Navy and Air Force.

ARA Services, The ARA Tower, 1101 Market Street, Philadelphia, PA 19107; (215) 238-3326.

3

Pitney Bowes

#1 *in postage meters, dictaphones*

Employees: 30,400
Sales: $2.9 billion
Profits: $187 million
Founded: 1920
Headquarters: Stamford, Connecticut

The first thing that pops into most people's minds when they hear about Pitney Bowes is postage meters. And well it should. Pitney Bowes not only invented the device businesses use instead of stamps but has also sold or rented more than 9 out of 10 of the meters in use. At the end of 1989, they had over 1 million postage meters in service in the U.S. and 100,000 or so in both Canada and Britain. In addition to meters, they make other mailing and shipping equipment, copiers, facsimile machines, bar-code markers (you see them on most of the packages you buy today), dictating machines and other voice-processing systems.

Pitney Bowes has 2 million customers—and two-thirds of their employees are in sales and/or service. Translation: Making the products is easier then selling them.

Pitney Bowes dominates their markets, but far from being fat and lazy, they are known for their technological innovations and an aggressive sales force backed by high-quality service. Some outsiders ascribe Pitney Bowes' edge to their unusual labor relations, such as their suggestion plan that pays those who put forth the suggestions 50 percent of the savings yielded from their ideas (up to $50,000).

History. Immortalized by a series of radio ads, the real Mr. Pitney was an inventor and the real Mr. Bowes an entrepreneur. Arthur Pitney was a wallpaper store clerk when he put together his first mailing device in 1901. The machine operated with a manual crank and put a stamp's imprint on parcels. But it was unwieldy—postal authorities had to reset the machine all the time—and was permitted only for third- and fourth-class mail. By 1919 the discouraged inventor was $90,000 in debt and his patents were expiring. Then a postal official suggested he get in touch with Walter Bowes of Stamford, Connecticut. Bowes made mail-canceling machines he sold to local post offices. He saw the potential for Pitney's machine if it could be used for first-class mail. So Bowes, the promoter, lobbied Congress for legislation to permit mechanically stamped first-class mail. He succeeded even before Pitney had perfected his machine. Bowes' 23-year-old stepson, Walter H. Wheeler, Jr., then offered design suggestions that perfected their Model M Postage Meter, and they got post office approval. The first piece of first-class mail using the new meter was sent from Stamford on November 16, 1920. Today about half of all mail is metered—that is, about 50 billion pieces of mail a year, most of which is imprinted by machines made either in Stamford or at other Pitney Bowes factories in nearby Connecticut towns.

Walter Wheeler put his own stamp on the company after he inherited the presidency from his stepfather in 1938. In 1947, he instituted the annual "jobholder meetings." Patterned on shareholder meetings where anybody who owns a share of stock is entitled to ask questions, Pitney Bowes' jobholder meetings are held every spring for all employees. These are no-holds-barred meetings. Tough questions are encouraged, and the best ones garner prizes of $50 savings bonds for making the managers squirm.

Pitney Bowes didn't make a major move outside of postage meters until 1979 when they bought Dictaphone, a Melbourne, Florida–based maker of dictating equipment. They use profits from their postage meter cash cow to get into new businesses. In 1988, mailing equipment represented about 53 percent of revenue; Dictaphone, 10 percent; copiers, another 10 percent; business forms and other supplies, 12 percent; and credit service (mostly to help businesses buy or rent their machines), 14 percent. From 1986 to 1990, Pitney Bowes spent $400 million on research and development, converting mechanical products into software-driven, high-tech, computerized devices. The mailroom of the future will still use lots of paper, but Pitney Bowes machines will be highly automated. For instance, a new system called Post Edge designed for huge mailings can stuff envelopes, read addresses on outgoing mail and assign a bar code (instead of a stamp) to the envelopes.

Owners and rulers. The founding families are long gone, and no one owns as much as 5 percent of the shares. George B. Harvey, who started as an accountant in 1957, became president in 1981 at age 50. A graduate of the Wharton Business School, Harvey led the company in the transition from electromechanical machines to electronic machines without laying off factory workers or setting up plants in the South or overseas. In 1984 Harvey issued a pronunciamento that henceforth at least 35 percent of all new administrative employees must be women and 15 percent minority. Pitney Bowes has two high-ranking women officers: Ann Pol, vice president–personnel, and Carole F. St. Mark, president of the business supplies and services unit. Of their dozen board members in 1990, three were women, one of them Eleanor Holmes Norton, former chief of the federal Equal Employment Opportunity Commission and a close adviser to Rev. Jesse Jackson.

As a place to work. One of America's exemplary employers. A generous profit-sharing plan has been in effect since 1946. Nineteen percent of quarterly operating profits are turned over to employees in the form of bonus checks, typically worth between 3 and 11 percent of their pay. A nonunionized company, Pitney Bowes maintains a unique Council of Personnel Relations to air out and resolve employee-management issues. The councils, made up of managers and elected employee reps, operate throughout the company and have procedures that allow unresolved issues to be bucked to the next level, the highest one being a council chaired by the CEO and an elected employee. At age 50 a Pitney Bowes employee begins to receive $300 a year from the company to help them prepare for retirement.

Social responsibility. In 1981 Pitney Bowes elected to build their new headquarters in the run-down part of Stamford, Connecticut, where they have long been based, rather than flee to an antiseptic, all-white enclave. In 1989 the Council on Economic Priorities awarded Pitney Bowes their annual corporate conscience award for their record of employee responsiveness.

Global presence. About 25 percent of Pitney Bowes' revenues come from abroad (mostly Europe and Canada). Not long after Pitney Bowes got their invention approved in the U.S., Wheeler was on a boat to England where, in 1922, British authorities approved the Pitney Bowes machine for their first-class mail. Some 6,000 Pitney Bowes employees work overseas.

Stock performance. Pitney Bowes stock bought for $1,000 in 1980 sold for $8,169 on January 2, 1990.

Pitney Bowes Inc., World Headquarters, Stamford, CT 06926; (203) 356-5000.

4

The Office Environment Company®

#1 *in office furniture*

Employees: 18,500
Sales: $1.8 billion
Profits: $120 million
Founded: 1912
Headquarters: Grand Rapids, Michigan

Workplace

If you fancy those old, clunky, wooden desks, then Steelcase is the enemy. This company, more than any other, is responsible for the look of the modern office. Since 1968, they've been the industry leader, earning a reputation as the General Motors of the office furniture industry.

Steelcase makes functional, durable furniture: chairs, desks and filing cabinets that last. They don't have the design reputation enjoyed by their Western Michigan neighbor, Herman Miller, but today Steelcase is trying to reverse that image. In 1990, they came out with a line of freestanding, modular furniture called Context. The sales brochure for the line declared, "The sleeping giants of the corporate world are not only awakening from their slumbers, they are learning to dance." Aetna Life and Casualty bought truckloads. Steelcase intends Context to be their first step from furniture maker to creative designer of complete office systems. The new corporate logo touts Steelcase as "The Office Environment Company," and they opened a striking white showroom in Los Angeles that *Interiors* asserted was "a tour de force of design intelligence." Vice Chairman Peter Wege admitted he was surprised to read that statement. He told *Forbes*, "When I read that, I said, 'Is this us?'"

Also surprising was that Wege, son of a Steelcase founder and head of one of the three families that control the company, had even talked to *Forbes*. A privately held company, Steelcase has traditionally been publicity shy. That's changing, too. By the end of the 1980s, Steelcase was regularly depicted in business magazines as a shining light of American industry. Sales more than tripled during the 1980s. And the articles invariably pointed to Steelcase's distinctive culture and good employee relationships as keys to their success.

History. Early in this century, office furniture was wooden—rolltop desks and heavy file cabinets. Fires were a major problem. It's no wonder. Rooms were lit with gas and heated with wood stoves or fireplaces. The furniture provided tinder. In 1912 Peter M. Wege came up with an idea: metal office furniture. Wege had worked as a supervisor at General Fireproofing and was also a talented sheet metal designer (with six U.S. patents to his credit). The Metal Office Furniture Company was born when Wege persuaded a Grand Rapids banker, Henry Idema, and 11 other investors to come up with $75,000 to back his idea. Grand Rapids was a natural place to launch the enterprise. It was known as "The Furniture City," home to nearly 60 furniture factories.

Wege started out making metal filing cabinets, safes, shelves and tables, emphasizing the safety and durability of

Where Steelcase's furniture artists design future office wares.

metal furniture. Business was slow at first because customers were accustomed to wood. But the U.S. government, never a stickler for fashion, was impressed with the safety aspect and, in 1915, Metal Office was awarded the first of many government contracts. Then Metal Office came up with a hit—the Victor, a steel wastebasket.

In 1921, to convince the public wooden office furniture was a thing of the past, Wege hired Jim Turner, a media wizard from Chicago. Turner coined a new trademark, a name as indestructible as the furniture: Steelcase. And he masterminded a series of magazine and newspaper ads featuring the Steelcase 601 desk withstanding great tests: supporting 6,000 pounds of sheet metal or being tipped on its side.

In 1937, Steelcase collaborated with world-famous architect Frank Lloyd Wright in the design and building of the "great workroom" for S. C. Johnson & Sons in Racine, Wisconsin. The Johnson Wax headquarters remains one of the most innovative office designs ever executed: a big, unpartitioned room, chairs with three legs, desks with three work surfaces and swinging doors.

During World War II many U.S. Navy ships had Steelcase furniture—cabinets, tables, desks and beds. When the Japanese surrendered to Gen. Douglas MacArthur in 1945, the ceremony took place aboard the *U.S.S. Missouri,* and the documents were signed on top of a Steelcase rectan-gular folding table (now exhibited at the Naval Academy Museum in Annapolis, Maryland). In the 1950s, Steelcase's sturdy, unglamorous furniture could be seen in the police station set of the TV series "Dragnet." And in 1973 Steelcase furnished 44 floors of the quarter-mile high Sears Tower in Chicago.

Steelcase spent $400 million in the late 1980s to refashion themselves into a more innovative, design-oriented company. As part of this make-over, they created the Steelcase Design Partnership. A consortium of six smaller companies purchased in recent years, the Partnership includes Atelier International (maker of lighting fixtures and reproductions of Frank Lloyd Wright furniture), Brayton International (European-styled executive and lounge chairs) and Designtex Fabrics.

Another part of the make-over was the 1989 construction, at a cost of $110 million, of a new research and development center, a seven-story pyramid set in the middle of the prairie in Caledonia, Michigan. Steelcase also considered employee make-overs, too. Organizational psychologists from MIT and Cornell came up with a series of gimmicks designed to stimulate worker creativity. The center is divided into "neighborhoods." There are 11 break areas, equipped with coffee, soft drinks, and marker boards to record "spontaneous" inspirations; outdoor terraces for working or eating; and "caves"—places where one person can retire to think in solitude. The atrium has ongoing art exhibits and a kinetic sculpture—a functioning 71-foot stainless-steel pendulum hanging from the center of the building to symbolize constant change. In the middle or "hub" of the pyramid sit the executive offices, where managers can look out on employees in the act of spontaneous creation.

Owners and rulers.   All of Steelcase's stock is held by descendants of the founders. Chairman Robert Pew is married to the daughter of banker Henry Idema. His successor as president and CEO, Frank Merlotti, worked his way up from the bottom. He started as a factory worker.

As a place to work.   Steelcase has annual turnover of 3 percent (three times better than national average) and a safety record five times better than the national average. They have never been unionized. Steelcase pays well (average wage more than $35,000) and offers great benefits: profit sharing; tuition reimbursement; a model child care counseling service; a minihospital staffed with 19 nurses, two physicians, a psychologist and two social workers; and Camp Swampy, a 1,700-acre recreation area 60 miles north of Grand Rapids with 42 campsites available free to all employees. In addition, they have an open-door policy (employees know the chairman will take phone calls at home to discuss a work-related or personal problem) and offer alternative work schedules. In 1990, 92 employees were sharing 46 jobs.

All that largess is coupled with strict discipline. The company puts out a 114-page handbook of employee rules and regulations. Employees are expected not to have friends or relatives call them during work hours, "except in case of emergency." Other restrictions: "You are entitled to two 10-minute break periods for each full shift"; "You may not leave your plant's parking area during break periods"; and "You are required to punch out on your daily and weekly time cards for lunch breaks when you leave the immediate plant area." Penalty points are assessed for various infractions ranging from failure to punch in or unauthorized use of a company telephone to assaulting a supervisor or drinking on the job. At 60 points, you get a verbal warning; at 120 points, a three-day disciplinary layoff; at 160 points, discharge.

Global presence.   More than 7,000 people work for Steelcase overseas in nine other countries. There are 20 factories outside the U.S.: 7 plants in France, 4 in England; others are in Spain, Portugal, Germany, Japan, Morocco and the Ivory Coast. Steelcase has sales offices serving 200 cities in 65 countries.

Steelcase Inc., P.O. Box 1967, Grand Rapids, Michigan 49501; (616) 247-2277.

5

#1 *in temporary services*

Employees: 3,800 permanent;
555,000 temporary
Sales: $1.4 billion
Profits: $1 million
Founded: 1946
Headquarters: Troy, Michigan

There's nothing temporary about Kelly Services. They made "Kelly Girl" part of the language by putting themselves squarely in the middle of this equation: Some companies need temporary help during a crunch while some people want the flexibility of temporary work. They now meet this demand with a temporary work force of over half a million women (and men). They're the oldest, largest and most well known of some 2,000 U.S. companies now offering this service. Others are Manpower (now British-owned and the biggest on a worldwide basis), Olsten and Uniforce.

History.   The "temp" business began shortly after World War II with a onetime auto salesman and accountant W. Russell Kelly. He figured American businesses needed skilled, dependable secretaries to help out in a crunch but not permanently burden fixed payrolls. So, in 1946, Kelly set up shop in Detroit with a staff of secretaries and clerks who worked in his office, performing tasks for other businesses. A year later, he began sending his secretaries out to clients' offices to fill in for sick or vacationing employees.

Over 1 million Americans work as temps every day for over 2,400 temporary help service agencies.

His idea caught on. Detroit businesses clamored for Kelly's girls to help with extra filing and typing chores. In 1954, Kelly opened an office in Louisville, Kentucky, and from there rapidly branched out to other U.S. cities. The cry, "Get me a Kelly Girl, she'll get the job done," was heard so frequently that Kelly changed the name of the company from Russell Kelly Office Service to Kelly Girl Service in 1959. They changed their name again in 1966 to Kelly Services after adding temporaries for light industrial, technical and marketing work.

The real boom in the temp industry started a decade later as businesses discovered they saved a bundle in benefit costs by hiring short-term workers. The industry grew 20 percent a year between 1975 and 1985, and temporary personnel companies began specializing in computer engineering, law, health care, accounting, word processing. New competitors chipped away at Kelly's dominance by being quicker to offer specialized temporaries and provide secretaries trained on the latest word-processing equipment. To catch up with Manpower, the world's largest temp agency, which had started a word-processing training program in 1982, Kelly introduced a system in 1986 to test and train temporary employees in a variety of word-processing programs. Kelly temps now go to their assignments armed with step-by-step reference books and can call an 800 number hot line if they get into trouble at the keyboard. Kelly also operates a homecare service for the elderly called Kelly Assisted Living.

Owners and rulers.   Kelly went public in 1962 but remains a family business. William Kelly, 90 in 1990, is the chairman and controls over half the stock—enough to place him on the *Forbes* list of America's 400 richest people (with wealth estimated at $550 million). Terrence Adderly, Kelly's stepson, became president in 1984. Kelly has increased cash dividends 23 times in 24 years.

As a place to work.   Kelly trains 6,000 temps a week. Temporary workers are largely an isolated lot, but Kelly tries to make them feel they're part of the club. Every year, offices throughout the U.S. celebrate "Kellyweek" with contests, lunches and breakfasts. Permanent employees are initiated into the organization at the Kelly Service School—the first stop for every new branch employee.

Global presence.   Kelly has offices in Britain, Canada, Australia, Europe and Puerto Rico, but the bulk of their business is in the U.S.

Stock performance.   Kelly stock bought for $1,000 in 1980 sold for $9,104 on January 2, 1990.

Kelly Services, Inc., 999 West Big Beaver Road, Troy, MI 48084; (313) 362-4444.

ACCOUNTING

For over half a century, eight large accounting firms dominated this industry. But the Big Eight (a nickname Fortune popularized in the 1960s) shrank to the Big Six during the 1980s because of two huge mergers. Two other firms became engaged during the decade, but succumbed to prenuptial jitters just before walking down the aisle. No one would be surprised if the 1990s reduces big accounting's ranks to the Big Five or Big Four or even Big Three.

Unlike H&R Block, the Big Six won't fill out your income tax forms. Big Six clients are strictly large and medium-sized corporations. The smallest of the Big Six does nearly three times as much business as next largest. As they enter the 1990s, these firms are relying increasingly on management consulting—supplying companies with expensive advice on how to better run their companies. One of the Big Six, Arthur Anderson, is the largest management consultant.

The Big Six are all partnerships, that is, owned by the firm's senior executives (who earn an average of about $200,000 a year), although they may report sales, they keep mum about profits. Typically it takes 11 to 13 years to become a partner in a Big Six firm. Each of these firms has hundreds of partners; KPMG Peat Marwick, for instance, has about 2,100 U.S. partners. The first step toward a partnership, taken by the thousands of undergraduates Big Six firms hire every year, involves the grunt work—long hours auditing financial records. The resulting job burnout translates into high turnover. The Big Six's collective record on promoting women to partnership is scandalous. Less than 5 percent of the Big Six partners are women, although this may change in the coming decade: As of 1990 over half of all accounting graduates and entry-level accountants were women, and a recent Supreme Court ruling forced Price Waterhouse to award a partnership to a woman.

1

Ernst & Young

#1 in accounting firms

Employees: 70,000
Sales: $4.3 billion
Founded: 1894
Headquarters: New York City, New York

Three plus six makes one. At least that's what happened when the third largest accounting firm, Ernst & Whinney, linked up with the sixth largest, Arthur Young, to become the world's largest accountancy. The 1989 merger was a good fit in many ways. Arthur Young's clients were mostly investment banks and high-tech firms on the East and West coasts, while Ernst & Whinney had more health-care and manufacturing clients concentrated in the Midwest and South. Arthur Young had more clients in Europe, while Ernst & Whinney had more in the Pacific Rim. Both had heavy-hitting clients: Arthur Young audited American Express, Mobil and Texas Instruments, while Ernst & Whinney did the books for BankAmerica, Time Inc. and Eli Lilly.

The similarities ended there. Although the two firms called it a merger, Ernst & Whinney had the upper hand, tightening their grip around Arthur Young's decentralized management. In the words of one observer, "Ernst & Whinney is treating this as an acquisition." Part of the imbalance resulted from Arthur Young's troubles during the 1980s. Once upon a time, Arthur Young's nickname was "Old Reliable"—so much so that they were the auditor's auditor, checking the books of other accounting firms. They could boast of a WASPish, clean (if stodgy) reputation among the Big Eight, far more conservative than the rest in interpreting tax laws. They published the second best-selling tax guide in America (Arthur Young Tax Guide). Former vice presidential candidate Geraldine Ferraro and her husband turned to Arthur Young to check their tax returns after they were accused of tax evasion (she told reporters she'd hired the "best" accountants in the country). In 1984, the former chairman of Coopers & Lybrand said with admiration, "They just don't take schlock clients."

That era ended in the late 1980s, when Arthur Young was plagued with financial problems. Federal regulators sued them for $560 million over their audit of Western Savings Association of Dallas. The feds charged Young had allowed Western to overstate net worth by more than $400 million. In 1988, the Bank of England sued them for negligence after a bank Arthur Young audited collapsed. That debacle cost Arthur Young $44 million. One observer commented, "Old, yes. I'm not sure about reliable."

The merger with Ernst & Whinney, a Cleveland-based firm whose audit paved the way for the 1979 government bailout of Chrysler, created a firm with 6,100 partners and two CEOs: Ray Groves from Ernst & Whinney and William Gladstone from Arthur Young. Gladstone, aged 59 in 1990, has been chairman and CEO of Arthur Young since 1985; he avidly collects baseball paraphernalia and peppers his speech with baseball analogies. "I believe the top man should sweat as hard as his team and feel as deeply as they do about winning," he told the *Wall Street Journal.*

The merged firm won't be checking the books of PepsiCo, however. An Arthur Young client since 1965, PepsiCo was dropped when Coca-Cola, an Ernst & Whinney client since 1924, forced the firm to choose. Ernst & Young said they picked Coke because Coke had been a client longer. They also disclosed Coke's annual audit fee was $14 million as opposed to Pepsi's $8.8 million.

With their huge client list, Ernst & Young has a formidable international presence. They can count themselves as one of the top three accounting firms in every European country save Finland and Italy—and they're number one in Japan.

While plenty of women get entry-level accounting jobs at Ernst & Young, the partnership ranks are still populated almost exclusively by men. In the San Francisco Bay Area, out of 52 partners, only 3 are women.

Ernst & Young, 787 Seventh Avenue, New York, NY 10019; (212) 830-6000.

2

KPMG Peat Marwick

#1 *in accounting firms outside the U.S.*
#2 *in accounting firms in the U.S.*

Employees: 68,000
Sales: $4.3 billion
Founded: 1883
Headquarters: Montvale, New Jersey

Telephone receptionists have to spit out a mouthful when they answer the phone for this company. KPMG Peat Marwick became the world's largest accounting firm in 1986 after New York–based Peat, Marwick, Mitchell & Co. merged with the Dutch–based Klynveld Main Goerdeler (known as KMG Main Hurdman in the U.S.). The first order of business was what to call this new amalgam. At first, the company's name in the U.S. was to be Peat Marwick, but auditors were to sign their statements with the name Peat Marwick Main. Worldwide, however, the company was to be called Klynveld Peat Marwick Goerdeler. After a while, they succumbed to the corporate love for alphabet soup and told everyone they were to be called KPMG Peat Marwick, which is redundant because the PM in KPMG stands for Peat Marwick. (Just to keep things interesting, their name varies overseas. In Britain, for instance, they're KPMG Peat Marwick Thomson.)

KPMG's stay at the top of the U.S. accounting heap was short-lived. In 1989 the newly merged Ernst & Young dislodged them from first place. But KPMG remains the biggest accounting firm outside the U.S. with more than 700 offices in 117 countries. Because of their strong European base, they're expected to benefit from the growing internationalization of the business world. Their other strength is that one-fourth of their clients are in the growing financial services field—banks, thrifts, insurance companies and the like. On the other hand, only 15 percent of KPMG's revenues come from management consulting, the biggest growth area in some Big Six firms. Like other accounting firms, KPMG has taken to scouring the ranks of smaller businesses for customers.

At one point in the late 1980s they ranked first in audits of new publicly owned companies, those selling stock to the public for the first time.

History. Peat Marwick Mitchell straddled the Atlantic from their inception. All three of the firm's namesakes—Sir William Barclay Peat, James Marwick and S. Roger Mitchell—were from Scotland, the motherland of modern accounting. Marwick and Mitchell, who knew each other at the University of Glasgow, set up an accounting firm in New York City in 1897. They both became U.S. citizens. In 1911 Marwick met Peat at the captain's table on board a transatlantic ship. Peat, who ran a London accounting firm, was receptive to a merger, and within a matter of weeks, the firm of Marwick, Mitchell, Peat & Co. was born. The next year the well-traveled, and, by then, well-connected Peat was made a Knight of the British Empire. Knighthood having its privileges, the Peat name found its way to the front in the renamed Peat, Marwick, Mitchell in 1925.

The firm merged in 1950 with Barrow, Wade, Guthrie & Co., which, because they were founded in 1883, lay claim to the title of having been the first accounting firm organized in the U.S. The transatlantic connections were evident here, too, as Wade and Guthrie were English, Barrow an American.

When Captain Roderick M. Peat stepped down as senior partner in 1966 after serving into his 80s, it marked the first time in 75 years a Peat had not at least partially controlled the firm. But William M. Black, an American-born, University of Glasgow–trained accountant, is credited as the architect of much of the firm's formative growth from the 1940s to the 1960s. Over the years, Peat earned a reputation for secrecy in a profession where secrecy and understatement are institutions. In 1966 *Fortune* described senior partner Black as "probably the best informed businessman in the world. As a member of 70 different partnerships, Black is privy to confidential and detailed information on business trends and developments from five continents—and tells none of it."

That secrecy was embarrassingly shattered in the early 1970s, when the firm, in response to lawsuits questioning their integrity, became the first of the Big Eight to submit to a review of their operations by another Big Eight firm. As might be expected, Big Eight member Arthur Young was "favorably impressed" with Peat's operations.

More strain followed the merger with KMG-Main Hurdman. The paint was hardly dry on the newly created company when it became clear the smaller Main Hurdman had been muscled out. Of 525 partners going into the deal, 175 remained in the ranks after three years. Several foreign divisions of KMG, accustomed to considerable autonomy, dropped out and went their own way.

Owners and rulers. Peat's most traumatic changing of the guard came in 1979 at the so-called Battle of Boca Raton. When partners gathered in Boca Raton in 1979 to vote on a successor, they shocked the accounting world by rejecting the former chairman's hand-picked choice and turned instead to Thomas L. Holton, a conservative CPA with a back-to-basics approach. Holton was succeeded in 1984 by Larry D. Horner, who remained chairman after the merger.

As a place to work. Of the Big Six, KPMG Peat Marwick may be the most hospitable environment for a woman accountant looking for success. There are instances of a woman partner working flextime, and a North Carolina office is equipped with a day-care facility. They say they have more women partners than any other Big Six firm in the U.S.: roughly 8 percent.

Social responsibility. The notion of public accountants checking the books of corporate clients has always generated controversy. In the 1920s, when directors of the Fitchburg Railroad wanted to confirm rumors of kickbacks, they hired Peat Marwick to audit the railroad's books. "While the audit was in progress, the chief

E ven going bankrupt costs money. To file Chapter 11, Manville Corporation shelled out $63.4 million in legal fees, $9.6 million in accounting fees and $9.5 million in investment banking fees.

company accountant committed suicide," said Peat Chairman Walter E. Hanson, as quoted by author Mark Stevens. "And, if that wasn't enough, the day that our report was delivered, the president dropped dead."

The firm didn't know it then, but they hadn't seen anything yet. Peat saw their share of lawsuits in recent years amidst a new wave of scrutiny of public accounting firms and the roles they play in examining corporate books. In 1982, the Federal Insurance Deposit Corporation (FDIC) sued them for $200 million for failing to spot serious problems with Oklahoma's Penn Square Bank. Five months after Peat Marwick issued them a clean bill of financial health, the bank collapsed. Consequently, Chase Manhattan dropped Peat Marwick and took their business to Price Waterhouse, saying they wanted another firm to take a "fresh look" at their books.

In another incident, the state of California sued KPMG Peat Marwick in 1987 for failing to disclose they were secretly negotiating a merger at a time the state had hired Main Hurdman to help them sue Peat Marwick for negligence in auditing the Western Community MoneyCenter, a thrift that went bankrupt in 1984. The lawsuit was settled for an undisclosed amount.

G*lobal presence.* KPMG gets over half their revenues from overseas clients, and over half their partners (2,900 of 5,300) work in foreign offices.

KPMG Peat Marwick, 3 Chestnut Ridge Road, Montvale, NJ 07645; (201) 307-7000.

3

#1 *in management consulting*

#3 *in accounting*

Employees: 51,400
Sales: $3.4 billion
Founded: 1913
Headquarters: Chicago, Illinois

Arthur Andersen refuses to march in lockstep with other big accounting firms. They were the first to work as management consultants, the first to publish their financial results, the first to sue government regulators.

Arthur Andersen is also distinguished as the only firm to maintain their own accounting college—the Center for Professional Education—complete with an 866-room training center with accommodations for 1,750 students on a 146-acre campus on the site of an old Catholic girls' school in St. Charles, Illinois. At this center they inculcate their professionals with a unique corporate culture some have called the Marine Corps of accounting.

H*istory.* The firm was founded in 1913 in a two-room Chicago office by namesake Arthur Andersen. They made a name for themselves during the Great Depression by untangling the snarled finances of Samuel Insull's Chicago-based utility empire. Utilities from around the nation enlisted Andersen's expertise, and the firm staked out a spot on accounting's map. The success also turned out to be the beginning of the firm's public role as accounting's nag. "Had there been a stronger accounting," founder Andersen lectured at the time, "there wouldn't have been a depression."

Andersen himself went so far as to have consulting engineers on staff to help him perform the auditing function more carefully when doing accounting work for a manufacturing company. In the early 1950s Andersen pioneered the field of management consulting when they advised General Electric how to set up their first computer system. Today, Andersen gets over 40 percent of revenues from their consulting business, still largely through helping companies set up computer and related information systems. Typical consulting projects net the company fees of up to $25 million, as opposed to $4 million for typical auditing jobs, according to *Washington Business.* Andersen now ranks as the biggest management consultant in the land, with consulting revenues greater than those of McKinsey and Booz, Allen combined.

Owners and rulers. Lawrence A. Weinbach became Andersen's CEO in 1989 at age 49. He's based in New York. An accounting major at the University of Pennsylvania's Wharton Business School, he became an Andersen partner after only nine years. Weinbach is known as a take-charge, self-assured executive in contrast to his predecessor, Duane R. Kullberg, who was unable to stop the dissension within Andersen's ranks of consulting partners.

As a place to work. For years Andersen was known for a tightly regimented management style. But conflicts between the consulting partners and the accounting/tax partners exploded in the late 1980s with wholesale defections of consulting partners. The friction revolved around money and power, the consultants arguing they didn't have enough of either in a firm long dominated by accountants. After filing lawsuits against some of the defecting partners and infiltrating meetings called by disaffected consultants, Andersen agreed in 1988 to split the firm into two divisions.

Social responsibility. Ironically, the accounting profession's self-proclaimed watchdog by the mid-1980's found themselves the target of a slew of lawsuits by shareholders and creditors of failed companies. They contended that Arthur Andersen should have foreseen that trouble loomed, and should have reported those problems to the public. In a two-month period in 1984 the firm paid out $65 million in out-of-court settlements and still faced a half dozen more major suits, including ones stemming from the failure or financial troubles of their clients: DeLorean Motor Co., Financial Corp. of America (American Savings & Loan),

the insurance broker Marsh & McLennan and Drysdale Government Securities Corp., which bought and sold government bonds and went out of business in one of Wall Street's more notorious failures.

Global presence. Although the last of the Big Eight to go abroad—in 1957—Arthur Andersen today runs a full complement of international operations, including a major presence in Europe and Asia. With 243 offices in 54 countries, they do 39 percent of their business abroad. Although foreign operations usually are autonomous at other Big Six firms, the Chicago office makes all the major decisions, causing complaints from foreign partners that Arthur Andersen is primarily an American firm run by Americans. In 1985, faced with growing competition for new business in the Far East, Arthur Andersen finally acquiesced to a major merger, adding Asia's largest accounting firm at the time, SGV Group, to their ranks.

Arthur Andersen & Co., 69 West Washington St., Chicago, IL 60602; (312) 580-0069.

4

Coopers &Lybrand

#2 *in number of female partners*
#5 *in accounting firms*

Employees: 50,000
Sales: $3 billion
Founded: 1973
Headquarters: New York City, New York

While many Big Eight accounting firms were courting and marrying during the 1980s, Coopers & Lybrand sat tight. Coopers was the only one of the Big Eight not to merge or propose a merger during the decade. As a result, what was accounting's biggest firm a decade ago now ranks fifth in the Big Six. An accounting consultant told the *New York Times*: "Coopers is left out in the cold. Twenty years from now, it will be clear they made a horrible, tragic mistake." But CEO Peter Scanlon defended sitting on the sidelines: "We're not opposed to mergers, but we're not going to do it because everyone thinks it's the right thing to do. It's insanity."

Scanlon's stiff-upper-lip response to criticism was characteristic. A Bronx native who attended Iona College, Scanlon was once described by the *New York Times* as a "blunt, heavy-smoking authoritarian." But Scanlon had solid business grounds for opposing mergers. Some clients don't subscribe to the bigger-is-better school of thought. Avon dropped Main Hurdman when they merged with Peat Marwick, saying "even if we had stayed with the same accounting firm, we would have been dealing with new faces anyway" because so many people and assignments get shuffled when two firms merge. Avon chose Coopers as their new accountants.

The firm traces their roots to Philadelphia in 1898 when William Lybrand, T. Edward Ross, Adam Ross and Robert Montgomery formed a partnership. Montgomery is well known to accounting professionals as the author of *Montgomery's Auditing*, first published in 1912. Now in its 11th edition, it's considered the definitive text on auditing technique. The modern firm of Coopers & Lybrand was formed in 1973 after a 15-year period during which a number of smaller well-established firms merged.

Coopers has a strong presence among the *Fortune* 500 companies, with clients ranging from Kroger and Ford Motor to AT&T and Arco. But Coopers doesn't project the blue-blooded image of a Price Waterhouse. An industry consultant noted: "I think of them as a hard-nosed, street-smart type of firm. They are a very proud firm. They may fight behind closed doors, but when the door opens, they say 'This is what we're going to do.' There's a lot of camaraderie at Coopers." They are also known for a shirt-sleeve atmosphere many young professionals find attractive.

Coopers & Lybrand, 1251 Avenue of the Americas, New York, NY 10020; (212) 536-2000.

5
Deloitte & Touche
#4 *in accounting*

Employees: 65,000
Sales: $3 billion
Founded: 1895
Headquarters: Wilton, Connecticut

A marriage of an odd couple. That's what the 1989 merger of Touche Ross with Deloitte, Haskins & Sells looked like from the outside. Touche Ross had a reputation as the most scrappy, least stuffy member of the Big Eight, and Deloitte was its "creaky old man."

Both had plenty of *Fortune* 500 clients. Touche audited Chrysler while Deloitte signed off on the General Motors reports. Long known for their contacts within the retailing industry, Touche did the books for Sears, Roebuck and Macy's, as well as Litton Industries and Pillsbury. In addition to working with the Wall Street buyout powerhouse of Kohlberg Kravis Roberts, Deloitte audited the books of Kimberly-Clark, Monsanto and Procter & Gamble.

Though the two firms were roughly the same size before the merger, the Deloitte half apparently took charge afterwards. J. Michael Cook, the head of Deloitte, became chairman and CEO of the combined firm, and Deloitte's headquarters became home for the top corporate officers. Cook, who became chairman of Deloitte, Haskins & Sells in 1986 at age 43, has a reputation as a tough-minded executive. A Miami native, Cook has spent his entire career with Deloitte. Touche Ross had the distinction of being the first accounting firm to have employees suspected of insider trading when three young accountants in their London office were charged with having profited from information obtained from a Touche audit of a British industrial conglomerate.

Outside the U.S., the company is known as Deloitte Ross Tohmatsu International. The Tohmatsu name comes from Tohmatsu Avoiki & Sanwa, Japan's largest audit firm, which was part of Touche Ross.

Only 52, or 3 percent, of Deloitte & Touche's 1,700 U.S. partners are women.

Deloitte & Touche, 10 Westport Road, P.O. Box 820, Wilton, CT 06897; (203) 761-3000.

6

Price Waterhouse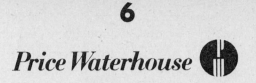

#6 *in accounting firms*

Employees: 40,770
Sales: $2.5 billion
Founded: 1849
Headquarters: New York, New York

He was there like a bad penny: at every Academy Awards ceremony, a dark-suited Price Waterhouse accountant laboriously explaining the voting rules and regulations. He was dropped from the 1990 show (as emcee Billy Crystal reminded everyone), but Price Waterhouse still has the distinction of counting the votes and sealing the envelopes for the Oscar winners. It's all in a day's work for the blue-blooded firm known as the "Tiffany" of the big accounting firms, with more *Fortune* 500 clients than any other (they count IBM and the World Bank as clients).

Price Waterhouse was founded in England in 1849, and in 1889 Edwin Waterhouse established an office in New York City. During the 1980s, they tried to merge with two other members of the Big Eight—Arthur Andersen and Deloitte, Haskins & Sells—and failed both times. In 1988, 52-year-old Shaun F. O'Malley, a graduate of the Wharton Business School of the University of Pennsylvania, became chairman and senior partner. He had previously headed the Philadelphia office. To become a partner takes 10 to 12 years, and of all the major accounting firms, Price Waterhouse has the fewest partners in proportion to the rest of the professionals, a 1-to-10 ratio (those making partner make more money because "they're diving into a large cake," according to one employee).

In 1987, Price raised entry-level salaries 20–35 percent (with a starting salary of over $35,000 in New York City). Price is reputedly a sweatshop. A tax accountant at a rival firm says, "They work you hard and pay you more. They want you to crunch numbers, not think."

Price Waterhouse reportedly has the fewest women of the major accounting firms—only 27 of 900 partners were women in 1990. In a highly publicized case, Ann B. Hopkins sued the firm for sexual discrimination, claiming she'd lost a promotion to partner because she failed to wear makeup or jewelry and didn't have her hair styled. Her evaluation noted she should take "a course in charm school before she is considered for admission." Price Waterhouse was convicted of illegal sex discrimination in making partnership decisions and ordered to make Hopkins a partner. According to federal judge Gerhard Gesell, Price Waterhouse maintained a partnership evaluation system that "permitted negative, sexually stereotyped comments to influence partnership selection."

Price Waterhouse, 1251 Avenue of the Americas, New York, NY 10020; (212) 489-8900.

7

H & R Block

#1 *in personal tax accounting*

Employees: 3,300
Sales: $975 million
Profits: $107 million
Founded: 1954
Headquarters: Kansas City, Missouri

You could look at H&R Block as the McDonald's of the tax preparation industry: a company that churns out a reliable service year after year, makes it cheap enough for almost everybody to afford and seems to be just around every corner.

In 1954, two brothers working together as accountants in Kansas City, Henry and Richard Bloch, hit on a simple, but majestic, idea: offer to do people's taxes for them. They offered tax preparation as a sideline to their other services, charging $5 a return. The business did so well they decided to become H&R Block, changing the *h* in their last name to a *k* so it wouldn't be mispronounced. H&R Block has become an American institution since then, especially just before April 15. They figure every year they complete 1 out of every 10 IRS forms individuals file—close to 10 million income tax returns, at an average price of $50. Unlike the Big Six, they cater to the masses, not corporations.

Satisfying 10 million customers every year with a service they need only once a year is no small feat. The key has been keeping turnover low among the 40,000 people that work for them only four months a year. As America's largest seasonal white-collar employer, they pay their people well, and pay them more for coming back. Every year for the first 10 years of service, Block's tax preparers receive an extra percentage point of the fees they generate, beginning at 20 percent and ending with 30 percent. Block also offers stock options (they were among the first companies to provide such a benefit for more than the top managers). They attract moonlighting bookkeepers, retired people, nurses, factory workers, women with children who don't want to work all year, "all kinds of people," says Henry Bloch, who still runs the company. They're the people who will fill out your form for you when you walk in the door, but their work is double-checked by a regional office to guarantee they don't make mistakes. With all that, H&R Block must be doing something right, because 75 percent of their workers, and 80 percent of their customers, come back the next year.

If you want to work for H&R Block, you have to take a tax class costing $180. The jobs go to the people who do best on the exam given at course end. Managers start out the same way: "To be a manager," says Henry Bloch, "you have to start at the bottom, no exceptions." Every January, office managers start from scratch in recreating the H&R recipe. They rent office space, arrange for advertising, hire and train people and get the office running.

If someone isn't satisfied, Block offers a free return the next year. Henry Bloch sees the only serious competition as the American who does his or her own taxes, which is why they offer to fill out tax forms for high school seniors for free: "Our aim is to get them started with us early—we don't want them to get into the habit of preparing their own tax returns.170

CEO Henry Bloch, who has gone in front of the TV cameras to hype the virtues of H&R Block, has stuck close to his roots in Kansas City; he and his wife live within a few miles of their four children and eight grandchildren. In homey Midwest fashion, they have a regular family Sunday dinner. Richard Bloch, the cofounder, withdrew from active work at H&R Block in 1969, and after surviving a bout with lung cancer, spends his time and money on cancer charity work in Fort Lauderdale, Florida.

H&R Block also owns CompuServe, a data network that personal computers can access through phone lines, with one-half million subscribers worldwide.

Stock performance. H&R Block stock bought for $1,000 in 1980 sold for $8,810 on January 2, 1990.

H&R Block, 4410 Main Street, Kansas City, MO 64111; (816) 753-6900.

MANAGEMENT CONSULTANTS

As companies in every industry went through the business convulsions of the 1980s—foreign competition, technological changes, deregulation, hostile takeover attempts—they clamored for advice from the soothsayers of big business: the management consultants. And consultants themselves became big businesses. The largest—the consulting arm of accounting firm Arthur Anderson—took in over $1 billion in revenue during 1989. Overall, management consultants sold over $10 billion worth of advice during 1989, as the industry grew at a healthy 10 percent a year in the U.S. and a spectacular 30 percent a year overseas during the 1980s.

1

McKinsey & Company, Inc.

#1 *in general business consulting*

Employees: 3,300
Sales: $600 million
Founded: 1925
Headquarters: New York City, New York

Workplace

The high priest of Big Business, McKinsey & Company, is sought after by governments as well as corporations. Among the firm's nonbusiness clients have been the government of Tanzania, the Roman Catholic Church and presidents Eisenhower and Kennedy (who paid for preinaugural studies of key appointive positions). One consulting outfit is bigger (Big Six accounting firm Arthur Andersen's consulting division, with revenues roughly double McKinsey's). Others are less stodgy (Boston Consulting Group and Bain & Co.). But none can match McKinsey's reputation at what *Forbes* called the "Big Picture consultant."

For up to $200,000 a month plus expenses, chairmen at one-third of Amer-

ica's 500 largest corporations (AT&T and Mobil Oil, for example) regularly retain McKinsey to devise new strategies for entire companies. In 1984, they were hired to reorganize the management of General Motors from top to bottom. At mammoth Citicorp, which has paid for more than two dozen studies, separate McKinsey teams have been known to bump into one another in the hallways. "Behind McKinsey's imposing mahogany doors on Manhattan's East 52nd Street," wrote *Forbes*, "are people who unabashedly think of themselves as secular versions of the Jesuits, uplifting the world of commerce with their vision."

History. If you don't like the idea of newly minted MBAs telling people how to run their businesses, blame Marvin Bower. As managing partner of McKinsey & Co., Bower took what the *New York Times* called "a revolutionary step" by deciding in 1953 to recruit consultants right out of business school. Under founder James O. McKinsey, a University of Chicago accounting professor, the firm had relied largely on experienced managers in their 40s. (McKinsey left the company in 1935 to become chairman of the Marshall Field department store.) Bower, a product of Harvard's schools of law and business, felt intellect was no less important in consultants than their practical experience. Moreover, he considered consulting as professional as doctoring or lawyering. Bower's beliefs still guide the firm. "We have a strong sense of ourselves as being part of a profession, not owners of a business," D. Ronald Daniel, managing director from 1976 to 1987, told the *New York Times*. Like many an old-time law firm, McKinsey regards talk of money-making as taboo. Jobs are called "engagements." McKinsey sells the services of two- to five-member consultant teams that typically spend up to six months poring over reams of financial data and interviewing employees. A recruiting brochure sternly proclaims "-McKinsey has never solicited clients nor advertised its services." They won't even itemize a monthly bill. "Daniel says that clients must 'trust McKinsey' to set a fair fee," reports *Forbes*. Said an executive at one of McKinsey's competitors: "People go to McKinsey because even if it doesn't work, they can claim that they've chosen the best."

One measure of McKinsey's success is the number of consultants eventually hired away by clients. PepsiCo's president, for example, was once the McKinsey partner in charge of the Pepsi account. Now Pepsi has more than a dozen ex-McKinseyites in its executive ranks. Other prominent McKinsey alumni have included the presidents of American Express, Dean Witter Financial Services and Sotheby's Holdings. "They know whom to call when their company has a big-league problem to solve," observes *Forbes*. But the close connection between client and consultant also suggests, as *Business Week* put it, "that McKinsey studies often told management what it wanted to hear."

McKinsey must now contend with a growing number of consulting "boutiques" (like Bain and Boston Consulting Group) and firms offering specialized services such as designing office computer networks. Given the Big Egos behind the firm's Big Picture approach, McKinsey is probably not about to change their ways. "We don't learn from clients," one partner told *Forbes*. "Their standards aren't high enough. We learn from other McKinsey partners."

Owners and rulers. McKinsey & Company is privately owned and run by the best and the whitest. As of 1986, none of McKinsey's primarily Harvard-educated partners was black, and only five were women. Other consulting firms have made small fortunes by selling out or going public. Not McKinsey. Their 270 partners still trade their shares among themselves at a price far below what they would command if the firm went public.

Presiding over the firm is a managing director McKinsey's senior partners elect once every three years. Like the election process itself, the eventual winner is low profile. Becoming a managing director is "not unlike the naming of a Pope, because no one runs for office and no one advocates or defends their positions," according to Alonzo McDonald (managing director from 1973 to 1976). Current managing director is Frederick W. Gluck, elected in 1988 at age 52. Gluck marks a departure from McKinsey's blue-blooded tradition as he neither went to an Ivy League college nor has an MBA degree. He

JOB STAYING POWER

A national survey by Gallup and Accountants on Call asked employed Americans how long they had been working for their present employer.

Number of Years Employed	Percentage of Americans Surveyed
1. 1 year or less	24%
2. 15 years or more	18%
3. 1–2 years	10%
4. 7–10 years	10%
5. 10–15 years	10%
6. 2–3 years	9%
7. 4–5 years	7%
8. 5–7 years	7%
9. 3–4 years	5%

Source: Journal of Accountancy, May 1990.

grew up in Bay Ridge, Brooklyn, the son of a nightclub dancer and high school dropout. The eldest of six children in a German Catholic family, he earned electrical engineering degrees from Manhattan College and New York University. "My background was so unusual they didn't know what to do with me [at McKinsey]," Gluck told *Business Week*.

As a place to work. The *New York Times* described McKinsey as something of a "post–business-school business school." Going to Harvard Business School first doesn't hurt. According to *Forbes*, about 10 percent of Harvard's first-year class are regularly offered summer jobs at McKinsey. Those who do well will land one of the 250 full-time associate slots McKinsey fills each year. Only one in five of the new hires will eventually make it (after about six years or so) to partner. Only 1 in 11 will become a senior partner. Despite (or perhaps because of) the stiff competition, McKinsey helps to place those who don't make the grade. And they keep in touch with them. McKinsey's in-house journal features news of alumni.

Those who do stay are on the road a lot. "On average, one or two weekday nights away from home may be considered normal. At times this may rise to three or four," states a recruiting brochure. Money in the pocket helps make up for the time away from home. Straight out of business school McKinsey associates can earn up to $100,000 in salary, benefits and bonuses in their first year on the job. Directors may make anywhere from $600,000 to $1 million a year.

Social responsibility. McKinsey has done extensive pro bono work for non-profit groups like the New York Philharmonic Symphony Orchestra. But don't expect the firm to talk about that—or anything else. Turning down a *Business Week* request for an interview, Daniel said, "We can't see how it serves the firm's interests. Besides, we're kind of a dull, anonymous bunch."

Global presence. In Great Britain, contracting for a management study is known as "doing a McKinsey." And in Germany, one publication called McKinsey "German industry's Number One secret holder." In 1986, McKinsey had twice as many offices overseas as in the U.S. (for a total of 35). Over half of McKinsey's senior partners are from abroad. The best known is Kenichi Ohmae, head of McKinsey's Tokyo office and author of *Triad Power: The Coming Shape of Global Competition* and other popular business books. *Business Week* called Ohmae "the most prominent and often-quoted consultant today."

McKinsey & Company, Inc., 55 East 52nd Street, New York, NY 10022; (212) 446-7000.

2

BOOZ·ALLEN & HAMILTON INC.

#1 *in government consulting*

Employees: 2,500
Sales: $340 million
Founded: 1914
Headquarters: New York City, New York

Booz, Allen & Hamilton is a department store in an age of boutiques. Unlike such firms as McKinsey or Bain, which offer advice on only a limited range of problems, Booz will advise corporate managers on almost anything—from big strategy questions such as whether to lop off a division, to minor technical questions about whether to install a new computer system.

Booz also attracts a different breed of advice-givers than the boutiques, which rarely look beyond the elite business schools like Harvard or Stanford to fill their professional ranks. A recent Booz recruiting brochure features new consultants from lowbrow schools like Rutgers and Ohio State as well as from highbrow Princeton and MIT. Booz doesn't force employees into a mold, either. As Booz vice president Ronald V. Coughlin told *Business Week*: "If you saw a group of McKinsey partners walk out of a movie theater, you'd say, 'The McKinsey meeting just broke up.' But if you saw a group of Booz Allen partners, you'd say, 'There goes the 8 o'clock show.'"

Booz has long dominated the field of consulting to governmental agencies. Fully one-third of the company's billings come from various federal, state, local or foreign governmental bodies. Booz's current chairman, R. Michael McCullough, also came from the government consulting side of the business. How he got the job in 1985 was a classic study of how a company should *not* choose a chief.

Previous chairman James Farley got taken with the idea that the new chairman should be selected democratically from among the firm's nearly 175 partners (who also own all of the privately held company). The election turned into a mud-slinging contest. One of the six unsuccessful candidates told *Forbes*: "It was like taking your clothes off in the middle of the street. It was very, very tough."

The winner, McCullough, was a relative unknown with few enemies. He wasted little time changing that situation. In short order, the new chairman decided to reorganize the business into industry groupings instead of geographically. Within a matter of months, approximately one-third of the partners quit. According to one former partner: "To say the process created bad feelings does not capture the essence."

Cynics might conclude Booz could have avoided the entire mess with some advice from a competent management consultant.

Booz, Allen & Hamilton, Inc., 101 Park Avenue, New York, NY 10178; (212) 697-1900.

3

◬ Arthur D. Little, Inc.

#1 *in contract research*

Employees: 2,600
Sales: $272 million
Profits: $6.8 million
Founded: 1886
Headquarters: Cambridge, Massachusetts

The granddaddy of the consulting business, Arthur D. Little straddles the line between the business world and academia. Headquartered near Harvard and MIT, ADL is the nation's preeminent industrial researcher. They have a thriving practice auditing environmental practices of corporate polluters. They also invented the field of contract research, where companies hire scientists and engineers to test products or solve technical problems. Often this work has been done in ADL's own labs. They worked on nonflammable motion picture film for Eastman Kodak and on Fiberglas for Owens-Illinois. They helped make Cream of Wheat instant (for Nabisco) and Cap'n Crunch crunchier (for Quaker Oats). ADL's researchers have earned over 3,000 patents, including one for a process to turn sows' ears into a silk purse. (Dr. Little, an MIT-trained chemist, performed this feat in 1921, using 100 pounds of sows' ears to make two silk purses, one of which sits outside ADL's corporate boardroom, while the other is on display at the Smithsonian in Washington, D.C.) The federal government has designated Dr. Little's "Research Palace" at 30 Memorial Drive in Cambridge a national historic site.

Today's Arthur D. Little gets nearly half their revenue from more conventional management consulting, competing head-to-head with such firms as McKinsey, BCG and Booz, Allen. But again, ADL can't shake their academic image. According to a Booz, Allen vice president who used to work at ADL: "If you characterize the people at ADL as pipe-smokers who wear tweeds, the people at Booz, Allen wear pinstripes and smoke cigars." ADL encourages this laid-back, academic culture. The corporate "limo" is a Checker cab, which upset a Ford Motor official who expected to be picked up in a Lincoln. And ADLers are forbidden to fly first class. As a result, ADL consultants rub shoulders with the middle managers in charge of research and development rather than the CEOs. Unfortunately for Little, whom you deal with makes a difference. According to *Business Week*, the average ADL consulting contract runs from $35,000 to $50,000 as opposed to $150,000 to $200,000 at Booz, Allen.

ADL is the only private company in America operating a business school. Called the ADL Management Education Institute, the school's students are from developing countries. And they own Opinion Research Corporation, one of the biggest pollsters in the country. Charles R. LaMantia is president and CEO; and John F. Magee, chairman. Magee succeeded Robert Kirk Mueller in that position; Mueller is the author of several books about corporate boards of directors. ADL is owned mostly by their own employees through an Employee Stock Ownership Program. The ESOP was set up to fend off an unwanted attempt by Plenum Publishing to take over the company in 1987.

ADL is a hard place to land a job. About 150 people were hired from more than 20,000 resumes received in a recent year. ADL is also a difficult place to leave, even though salaries are considerably lower than at competing consulting firms. One top ADL consultant explained why he turned down an offer that would have doubled his salary: "Why should I go there? Here I wear my sports shirt and slacks to work, and my time is my own. Who needs to play their game?"

Arthur D. Little, Acorn Park, Cambridge, MA 02140; (617) 864-5770.

C*hicago's Baker & McKenzie is the largest law firm in the world, with 1,400 attorneys in 46 offices around the world. The announcement for the opening of their 46th office—in Moscow—came on October 25, 1989.*

4
Boston Consulting Group

Employees: 1,000
Sales: 250 million
Founded: 1964
Headquarters: Boston, Massachusetts

In a field where intelligence—or the appearance thereof—is the most precious commodity, BCG appears to have more than their share. Founded by a former consultant with the brainy Arthur D. Little research consulting firm, BCG keeps their headquarters in Boston to be close to their main source of consultants—the Harvard School of Business. BCG picks out about a dozen of Harvard's smartest graduates and pays them starting salaries of about $100,000 a year to advise BCG's clients—100 or so big corporations.

Bruce Henderson founded the company with no more than a desk and a phone. But he had a couple of original ideas. One was the "growth matrix" or "product portfolio." Using this schema, managers can tag products as "stars," "cash cows" or "dogs." Managers of big companies juggling a variety of businesses found such ideas (which BCG calls their "bag of tools") useful because they help corporate strategists figure out whether to invest in, hold onto or dump a product or service.

Dozens of corporations (Texas Instruments, General Foods and Rockwell International, among them) brought in teams of Henderson's disciples, and BCG quickly became the biggest of what have been called management consultant "boutiques," specializing in one top-of-the-line consulting service: giving advice on corporate strategy.

BCG is no longer the star they were at the beginning of the 1980s. Other consulting boutiques have sprung up, notably Bain, created from a defection of BCGers. And Henderson's ideas have come under fire for being oversimplified. But BCG is no dog yet. Management consulting is still a growth industry.

Boston Consulting Group, Exchange Place, 31st Floor, Boston, MA 02109; (617) 973-1200.

5
Bain

Employees: 750
Sales: $200 million
Founded: 1973
Headquarters: Boston, Massachusetts

Not often is a company compared to a religious cult. But Bain is frequently likened to the Reverend Sun Myung Moon's Unification Church. Employees are referred to as "Bainies" and founder William W. Bain, Jr., as the "Reverend" Bain. And they're known for their cultlike secrecy. Some consulting firms list which companies seek them out for advice, considering it a form of advertising. Not Bain & Co. Bain not only refuses to disclose their clients, but they're known as the "KGB of Consulting," ready to punish any employee or former employee who dares to reveal clients' names.

According to writer Cassandra Jardine in her article "The Bain Cult," Bainies are a homogenous lot: "Bainies look perfectly at home in the 1980s world of fitter-than-thou upward mobility. They have the air of floating around Olympus—often absurdly young, all well dressed in the company uniform of dark suit, handmade shirt, red tie—or its female equivalent. A former Bainie remembers the communal shock when a fat person was employed in the computer department."

The Bainies (many of whom are MBAs from Harvard or Stanford) also have their own gospel—a nontraditional approach to management consulting. Bain insists on doing only "relationship consulting," not consulting on one-shot projects. So, a company wanting to hire Bain must sign a contract for a long period of time, say five years, rather than for work on specific problems. As a result, the Bainies aren't consultants in the usual sense of the term. They are "quasi-insiders."

This unconventional style made Bain the fastest-growing consulting firm of the 1980s. Their professional staff jumped from 100 in 1980 to about 750 by 1990, while fees from clients multiplied more than 10-fold. In the process, Bain surpassed Boston Consulting Group, from which founder William Bain defected in 1973 to form his own firm. Bain is now intent on topping McKinsey, the much older and prestigious leader of firms specializing in, among other things, strategic management consulting (giving advice to top managers about major policy issues).

While Bain refuses to tell who their clients are, ex-*Wall Street Journal* reporter Liz Roman Gallese flushed some out in a 1989 profile in the *New York Times Magazine*. Two of their big clients are Dun & Bradstreet, which was caught selling customers services they didn't need, and Chrysler, which was caught driving new cars with the odometers disconnected before they were sold to customers. Other corporate stalwarts taking Bain advice during the 1980s included Iowa Beef Processors, Hughes Tool and Burlington Industries, all caught up in the financial gyrations of the decade.

Another client—the British beer–and–liquor house, Guinness—became embroiled in a stock fraud scandal in the late 1980s that brought Bain's name into the pages of London tabloids. One of Bain's quasi-insiders, Olivier Roux, served as director of financial strategy for Guinness and a member of the company's board during their successful attempt to take over Distillers Co., the big Scotch whiskey producer. To bag Distillers, Guinness engaged in some highly questionable tactics to inflate the price of their stock (and thereby make the bid look stronger). In the end, Guinness did get Distillers but Ernest Saunders, the chairman of the company, was indicted on fraud charges, partially as a result of a letter the Bain consultant had written. Roux left both Guinness and Bain, leaving behind a very bitter ex-client, Saunders, who told Gallese: "It would appear that Bain would do anything to save its own neck. Isn't that, in fact, a hell of a warning both to client companies and other strategy consultants?"

Bain & Co., Two Copley Place, Boston, MA 02116; (617) 572-2000.

PART THREE

Tools: From High Technology to Heavy Metal

Chip Makers

Electrical and Industrial Equipment

Engineers

Garbage Collectors

THE CHIP MAKERS

There were computers before the microchip, or chip, arrived, but they were massive affairs, powered by thousands of transistors and miles of wiring. The chip places electronic circuits on silicon wafers as tiny as one-eighth by one-sixth of an inch. This new technology ushered in the era of modern electronics, increasing the power and speed of computing while sharply reducing the size of the computing device. It paved the way to everything from personal computers to programmable coffeemakers and the electronic wizardry built into the modern automobile. Two Americans, Jack Kilby of Texas Instruments and the late Robert Noyce (Fairchild Semiconductor and Intel), are credited with inventing the chip. But in the 1980s Japanese companies emerged as the leading suppliers. Of the world's 10 largest chip makers, only 3 are American. And the number one company is Japan's NEC. Motorola and Texas Instruments rank fourth and fifth, respectively, in worldwide sales of semiconductor chips.

When he died on June 3, 1990, the 62-year-old Noyce headed Sematech, a joint effort by the U.S. government and private industry to help American chip makers catch up with the Japanese.

1

MOTOROLA INC.

#1 *in U.S. semiconductors, cellular phones, two-way radios*

Employees: 103,000
Sales: $9.6 billion
Profits: $498 million
Founded: 1928
Headquarters: Schaumburg, Illinois

Workplace

They made the first car radio, the walkie-talkie and the equipment that carried Neil Armstrong's message from the moon—and they stand today as an authentic hero of American technology. Because they sold their Quasar TV plant to Matsushita in 1974, many people cited Motorola as just one more U.S. electronics company caving in to Japanese competition. In fact, the reverse is true. Motorola, a Chicago-area company for more than 60 years, has stood up to the Japanese—and won—in electronic areas far more sophisticated than the making of TVs. They rank among the world leaders in two-way radios and paging systems, cellular phones and—the essential component of computers and modern electronics—semiconductors. They have captured more than one-third of the U.S. market for cellular phones (and related equipment), a business expected to gross $2 billion for Motorola in 1990. Realizing Japanese companies were targeting U.S. electronics producers, Motorola beat them at their own game, launching a companywide crusade to improve product quality. Their success was recognized in 1988 when they became the first winner of the Malcolm Baldrige National Quality Award. During the 1980s Motorola tripled sales and profits, and increased staff by 50 percent.

History. Founder Paul Galvin returned to Illinois after serving in France during World War I to start a company that made storage batteries for radios. It went bust. So did another firm he formed to sell a device to enable radios to run on alternating current. Galvin's third venture—this time *making* radios—was about to go under when he heard of a New York company that was installing radios in cars. Galvin set to work. He and his engineers built and installed the first commercially manufactured car radio in time for the 1930 convention of the Radio Manufacturers' Association. Galvin named his company Motorola, a combination of *motor* and *victrola*.

Motorola made not only the first real car radio, but also the first FM two-way mobile radio (1940), which became standard equipment in police cars. During World War II, they supplied walkie-talkies and produced almost half the 70 million radio crystals the armed forces used. In the early days of TV, Motorola came out with the first black-and-white set priced under $200: the Golden View. It also pioneered the technology that made the automobile alternator possible. And Motorola equipment was part of every U.S. expedition into outer space.

By the 1970s, however, the all-American technology company was losing out to foreign rivals. Faced with increasingly stiff Japanese competition, Motorola sold their low-tech TV manufacturing and made a beeline for high-tech electronics. In 1983, Motorola made their last car radio. Today, they make such products as the microprocessors that are the "brains" behind many computers (including their own), copiers, videocassette recorders and the braking and fuel-injection systems in General Motors cars.

Motorola has long pursued policies that Japanese companies have become celebrated for. As far back as 1974 they adopted an employee involvement program designed to push decision making down to the lowest possible level. In the 1980s they were spending 2.4 percent of the annual payroll on training their work force—about double what other companies spend. They allocated over 8 percent of sales to research and development. And they became tigers on product quality. Robert Galvin, who succeeded his father as head of Motorola in 1959, has been described as a "quality fanatic." In 1981 he set a goal of reducing defects by 90 percent by 1986. They did it—and now they're aiming for similar improvements in the 1990s. Their goal for 1992 is to reduce product failures to fewer than 3.4 per million (in 1990 they were running 300 failures per million). As *Fortune* put it, "If Motorola gets there, you would have to buy one million of its pagers or cellular phones to find three or four that did not work, or had a cracked case or some other fault." Motorola's mania also extended to getting products made more rapidly. They used to ship pagers 27 days after receiving an order. Their new plant in Boynton Beach, Florida, now assembles pagers in two days or less.

Owners and rulers. The Galvins are a tough family. Founder Paul Galvin, a no-nonsense sort, headed the company until he died in 1959. His son Robert ruled from then until 1988, when he stepped down, at 65, in favor of George M. C. Fisher, an engineer and PhD mathematician who joined Motorola in 1976 after 10 years at

THE CONSUMER ELECTRONICS INVASION

In 1990 these percentages of American households owned the following products which were rare or nonexistent in 1980.

1.	VCR	68%
2.	Answering machine	31%
3.	Home computer	23%
4.	CD player	19%

Source: The *New York Times,* 29 March 1990.

Bell Labs. Fisher made $777,000 in 1989. Galvin is the largest stockholder, with 6 percent of the shares. Waiting in the wings is Christopher Galvin, Robert's son, who turned 40 in 1990. He's one of the three members of Motorola's office of chief executive (the other two are Fisher and Gary L. Tooker, president and chief operating officer). But don't presume Chris Galvin will automatically inherit the top spot. Fisher, who was 49 in 1990, told a *Forbes* reporter he plans to retire "in 15 or 20 years." In 1940, when he applied for a summer job at the company his father founded, Robert Galvin took a seat on a bench with other applicants. Offered a chance to step out of line, he refused, waiting from 7 to 10 A.M. for an interview. Galvin relished telling this story. "By 10 o'clock," he said, "half the people in the plant knew that the boss's son was willing to wait his turn. You are off and running when something like that happens."

As a place to work. Motorola has remained nonunion in a part of the country that has been a labor movement stronghold. They have long maintained a family atmosphere in which everyone is on a first-name basis. Benefits are good, and they maintain a pay-for-performance scheme that can bump up anyone's paycheck from 7 to 40 percent. They are also the largest U.S. company to screen all employees for presence of illegal drugs.

Social responsibility. After coming under heavy fire from antiapartheid activists for selling communications gear to South African security forces, Motorola sold the last of their factories in that country in 1985.

Global presence. Close to 40 percent of sales are abroad, and they have engaged the Japanese at home and abroad. At home they won a victory when the International Trade Commission upheld their complaint that the Japanese were dumping cellular phones in the U.S. at below-market prices. In 1982 they scored a breakthrough in Japan when their pocket pagers were accepted by Japan's giant Nippon Telegraph and Telephone (NTT). It marked the first time that a non-Japanese company had been admitted to the closed circle of NTT suppliers. Banzai!

Stock performance. Motorola stock bought for $1,000 in 1980 sold for $4,084 on January 2, 1990.

Motorola, Inc., 1303 East Algonquin Road, Schaumburg, IL 60196: (312) 3975000.

2

TEXAS INSTRUMENTS
INCORPORATED

#2 in U.S. semiconductors

Employees: 74,800
Sales: $6.5 billion
Profits: $292 million
Founded: 1930
Headquarters: Dallas, Texas

Texas Instruments is great at inventing. But they're not so great at selling their wizardry or converting their inventions into saleable products. One of the brainiest American companies, they suffered a horrendous fall from grace during the 1980s.

They lost their leadership in semiconductors, the bedrock electronic component in modern computer technology. They were forced to abandon the production of home computers and digital watches. They lost over $100 million in both 1983 and 1985. They had a mid-decade management crisis that resulted in the ouster of a CEO who had only recently taken over. They failed miserably to reach an announced goal of $15 billion in sales

by 1990 (1989 sales were $6.5 billion). They had to swallow their pride and form partnerships with other companies, not just American outfits like Intel and Sun Microsystems but Japanese companies like Hitachi, heretofore considered the enemy. In 1988, TI sold 80 percent of their subsidiary, Geophysical Service Inc. (GSI), to the Halliburton company. GSI plumbs the earth's surface, using seismic sound waves to detect the presence of crude oil. GSI was TI's original business.

Despite such losses, TI remains a technological powerhouse. They're the world's fifth largest maker of semiconductors (behind NEC, Toshiba, Hitachi and Motorola), and they're one of three American companies still making dynamic random access memory chips (DRAMS), the electronic devices that store computer data. TI is also a big defense contractor—one-third of total sales. Their HARM missile alone brings in 11 percent of sales.

History. Texas Instruments was born an oil exploration company called Geophysical Service, Inc. (GSI), founded in 1930 by Clarence Karcher and Eugene McDermott. Karcher had invented the technique of using sound waves to map underground strata. When the outbreak of World War II slowed oil exploration, GSI, which had been making electronic seismic equipment, got a contract to manufacture submarine-detecting devices for the Navy. After the war the company, renamed Texas Instruments, stayed in the electronics business.

Helped along by cold war military spending, Texas Instruments flourished. Their major breakthrough came in the 1950s, when TI became the first company to make transistors cheaply enough to be commercially useful in radios. Four years ahead of their competitors, they produced silicon transistors for military applications. In 1958 Jack St. Clair Kilby, a TI scientist, invented the integrated circuit, paving the way for miniaturized electronic systems by eliminating the need for masses of separate transistors joined by a maze of wiring. These inventions were the stepping stones to the electronic revolution.

While TI has not been adept at developing the end products based on this technology, toward the end of the 1980s their inventions began to yield a steady stream

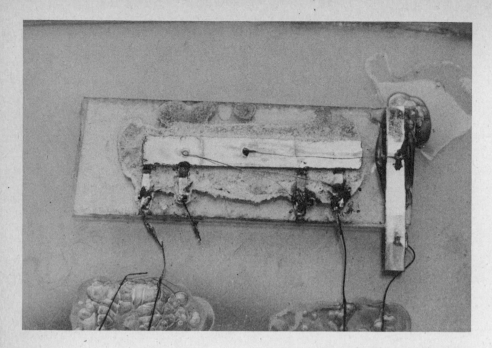

The first integrated circuit, created by Texas Instrument's Jack Kilby in 1958, was about one half the size of a paper clip and held only one transistor. Today's microchips can hold as many as one million transistors and are the basis of a $600 billion electronics

of income. TI succeeded in getting the Japanese to recognize the Kilby patent covering the integrated circuit. As a result, according to *Value Line*, they should now be receiving annual royalty payments ranging from $100 million to $600 million.

Owners and rulers. The board of directors is small: 10 people—all male, all white. The employee profit-sharing plan owns 11.7 percent of the stock, and each employee has voting rights over shares. Jerry Junkins, an Iowa-born engineer with an advanced degree from Southern Methodist, replaced J. Fred Bucy as CEO in 1985. With that change, said Wall Street analyst Daniel Klesken, "TI went from management by intimidation to management by inspiration."

As a place to work. Junkins will have to be awfully inspiring as TI is still an engineer-dominated company with a built-in rigidity. Employees wear badges whose colors tell how long the wearer has been with the company. Those with less than 5 years wear red; over 25 years, gold. Labor

unions are verboten. Everyone is tested for drug use. TI is the largest employer in the Dallas area, with a payroll of 32,000 (well over half of U.S. employees). And they are one of the few U.S. companies offering stock options to all employees. To give recognition to scientists, TI has an elite cadre known as "TI Fellows," people who have done outstanding work as measured by patents received or articles published or key contributions made. In the 1988 annual report, immediately following the listing of directors or officers, was a roster of 54 TI Fellows, from Robert Baboian to Ping Yang. Even here is a TI hierarchy: principal fellows, senior fellows and just plain fellows.

Global presence. TI intends to be a global player. They have factories in 15 countries (four in Japan) and do 31 percent of sales abroad. They link everyone together through 41,500 computer terminals—1 for about every two employees.

S*tock performance.* Texas Instruments stock bought for $1,000 in 1980 sold for $1,466 on January 2, 1990.

Texas Instruments Incorporated, 13500 North Central Expressway, Dallas, TX 75265; (214) 995-2011.

ELECTRICAL & INDUSTRIAL EQUIPMENT SUPPLIERS

A vast army of companies provide the muscle powering an industrial society. They make and sell such equipment as valves, electric motors, insulators, switches, relays, arc welders, turbines, generators, circuit breakers, fuses, robots, hydraulic systems. Their common denominator is that for the most part, they sell to other companies. This business is therefore, for most Americans, a behind-the-scenes operation. Even the industry giants are often unknown to consumers, although some of their wares will sometimes show up in hardware stores. The major electrical equipment companies belong to Washington-based National Electrical Manufacturers Association, which collects a wide range of statistical information about the industry. In the late 1980s a NEMA official explained that the best way for a company to get this information "is to join NEMA, pay its dues, and submit data. Only those members of the industry who give us numbers will get this information in return." So there.

1

ⓦ Westinghouse

#1 *in nuclear power plants, non-network radio stations*

Employees: 122,000
Sales: $12.8 billion
Profits: $922 million
Founded: 1886
Headquarters: Pittsburgh, Pennsylvania

No problem here with name recognition. Just about everyone has heard of Westinghouse, one of America's oldest companies. The problem is identifying what Westinghouse does. Refrigerators and toasters? They sold that business in 1975. Light bulbs? They stopped making them in 1985. Elevators? They sold that business to a Swiss company, Schindler, in 1989. Electrical transmission and distribution equipment like switches and trans-

f the price and technology of housing had kept pace with that of computer chips, the cost of the average American home would now be $12.

former (the original business of George Westinghouse)? They sold that business to another Swiss company, Asea Brown Boveri, also in 1989. Cable television? They sold that business in 1986.

All right, what does Westinghouse do? The firm is a changing mix (between 1985 and 1987 they sold or divested 70 businesses and bought 55), but the bottom line is they're engaged in a variety of unrelated activities: nuclear power generation (over half the capitalist world's nuclear power plants are based on Westinghouse technology), truck refrigeration (they own Thermo King), radar (for fighter planes and traffic control at airports), community development (Coral Springs on the east coast and Ft. Myers and Pelican Bay on the west coast of Florida), toxic and waste disposal (one of the top five companies in this burgeoning field), finance (over $6 billion worth of loans and leases outstanding), broadcasting (five TV stations and 22 radio stations), wholesaling of electrical supplies (inventory of more than 100,000 items sold through 230 Wesco stores and 1,500 independent distributors), office furniture systems and— in a hangover from a hectic buying spree of the 1970s—watches (they're the company behind Longines timepieces). They do about one-fifth of their sales abroad. Their biggest customer, accounting for another fifth of sales, is the Pentagon. They also operate six nuclear facilities for the Department of Energy, including the Savannah River Site at Aiken, South Carolina, where they took over from Du Pont in 1989. Former Secretary of Defense Frank Carlucci sits on the board.

Westinghouse managers are aware no one outside the company knows what they do. So in 1989 they authorized a major image-building ad campaign whose theme was: "The Best-Known Unknown Company in America." They also resurrected the theme first used in 1948 to promote their appliances: "You can be sure...if it's Westinghouse." (Remember Betty Furness opening that refrigerator door?)

History. George Westinghouse was one of the great inventors of the 19th century. At age 40, having already invented the air brake for trains, electric signals for railroads and a series of devices for the first practical transmission of natural gas, Westinghouse turned to the problem of transmitting electrical current over long distances. He settled on alternating current (AC) to accomplish this feat. Alternating current was the brainchild of Nikola Tesla, a former Edison associate who realized sending power over long distances would require high voltages, which would then have to be sent through transformers to reduce the voltage for home use. Westinghouse paid Tesla $1 million for his AC patents and electrified 130 towns in two years.

In the 20th century Westinghouse began to manufacture electrical products— everything from light bulbs to major appliances—and pioneered in atomic power and nuclear reactors for ship propulsion. They became the nation's number two utility supplier in the nation, second only to General Electric. But Westinghouse never quite got the hang of consumer appliances—and they gradually exited that business. In fact, they have entered, and left, a lot of businesses. No wonder they now have to remind people what Westinghouse stands for.

Owners and rulers. Westinghouse has been run since 1988 by John C. Marous and Paul E. Lego, both from working-class communities in western Pennsylvania (Marous from Pittsburgh, Lego from Johnstown) and both engineering graduates from the University of Pittsburgh. Marous' father was a house painter, Lego's a steelworker. Neither has ever worked for another company. Lego succeeded Marous as CEO in 1990. The previous year they paid themselves well—Marous took home $3.1 million, Lego $2.5 million.

As a place to work. A lot of people who worked for Westinghouse in the 1970s lost their jobs in the 1980s. The work force peaked at 199,000 in 1974; by the end of the 1980s, they were down to 122,000.

Social responsibility. Westinghouse wishes they had never set foot on Philippine soil. In 1976 they began constructing a $2.3 billion nuclear power plant there— and the Philippine government has been fighting with Westinghouse ever since. They claim the plant was overpriced and unsafe—built on the slope of an active volcano, in an area subject to both earthquakes and tidal waves. In 1989, Philippine President Corazon Aquino said Westinghouse bribed her predecessor (Ferdinand Marcos) and she refused to open the plant or pay Westinghouse $30 million in fees. Westinghouse still sponsors the famous Westinghouse Science Talent Search (begun in 1941), considered the oldest and most prestigious competition for high-school scientists. Winners get scholarships, and many go on to distinguished careers (five Westinghouse winners have earned Nobel prizes).

Stock performance. Westinghouse stock bought for $1,000 in 1980 sold for $11,044 on January 2, 1990.

Westinghouse Electric Corporation, West Building, Gateway Center, Pittsburgh, PA 15222; (412) 244-2000.

2

EMERSON

#1 in manufacturers of compressors

Employees: 72,600
Sales: $7 billion
Profits: $593 million
Founded: 1890
Headquarters: St. Louis, Missouri

Emerson Electric, a collection of companies making any number of electrical and electronic products, always ranks high in the annual *Fortune* survey of America's "most admired corporations," as they do whenever business executives are asked to name their favorite companies. That's probably because you can almost set your clock by the metronomic advances Emerson makes. In 1989 sales and profits went up for the 32nd consecutive year; dividends to shareholders were increased for the 33rd consecutive year. The holiest of

the holy at Emerson Electric is to beat last year's record.

The enforcer of this code is Charles F. Knight, who took charge of Emerson in 1973 when he was 37 and who is on everybody's list of "best managers" as well as on everybody's list of "toughest bosses." From headquarters in St. Louis, Knight rides herd over more than 50 businesses, most of which he has bought, making sure they'll eclipse last year's performance. Few of these businesses bear the Emerson name. They operate under their original names, such as Skil, Copeland, Liebert, Unmimount, XOMOX, Rosemount, Ridge, Branson, Alco Controls, Hazeltine, Micro Motion.

And few of the goods these firms produce are familiar. Skil power tools and In-Sink-Erator food waste disposers do find their way into the consumer marketplace. But most of Emerson products are bought by other companies. They make meters, pumps, valves and other instruments to help companies run factories; they turn out electric motors, gears, bearings, sprockets, threaders, components for appliances and communications equipment, electronic warfare products, lighting fixtures. A good example of an Emerson company is Copeland, acquired in 1986. They're the world's largest maker of compressors, the essential component in refrigerators and air conditioners. Still another is Liebert, acquired in 1987. They make products to cool computer rooms.

The bottom line to all this activity is always the bottom line: make more money than last year. Tied to that goal is a relentless drive to be number one. Emerson boasted in 1989 that 84 percent of their products held the number one position in their markets (compared to 76 percent in 1978).

History. Founded in 1890 in St. Louis, Emerson sold the first electric fan in America. They remained a leader in electric motors and fans until World War II, when they branched out into aircraft armaments. But little of note happened at the electric motor manufacturer until 1954. That year, a dynamic former football coach and electrical engineer from Cleveland, 44-year-old Wallace R. "Buck" Persons, took over.

Persons' first move was to institute a ruthless philosophy called the Southern

Strategy. He relocated Emerson factories out of St. Louis and into small plants in the deep rural South, where labor costs were considerably cheaper. He then consolidated Emerson's strong antiunion stance and decentralized the company, operating each plant as if it were a separate entity. And Persons began buying companies left and right—22 from 1957 to 1973.

From 1954 to 1973, sales increased from $40 million to $938 million and Persons was ready to retire. For a successor Persons chose Charles F. Knight, a former Cornell football player who'd been an Emerson consultant with his father's firm, Lester B. Knight & Associates, for 10 years and had worked for four years in Germany. In his first 12 years at the helm, Knight acquired 46 different businesses and abandoned 29 product lines. In 1976, Persons told *Business Week*, "Chuck has exceeded all our expectations." Emerson entered 1990 with sales above the $7 billion mark.

Owners and rulers. No one doubts the master of this company is Chuck Knight, described by *Fortune* as "driven, calculating and willing to body-punch when he gets in close," who was paid $1.8 million in 1989 and who owned 480,000 shares of stock worth about $19 million in early 1990. W. R. Persons at age 80 was still on the board in 1990. Judging from the composition of Emerson's board and management, no women, blacks, Hispanics or Asians need apply here. Board members include the heads of Anheuser-Busch, Baxter International and British Petroleum, on all of whose boards Knight holds a seat.

As a place to work. Demanding. Knight's obsession is always to be a low-cost producer. He rules by plans and budgets, keeping close tabs on his line managers. *Fortune* reported that he spends a lot of time "in his personnel command post, a room in which the names, photos, current positions, expertise and experience of his top 700 executives are arrayed on magnetic boards, by division and business." To get lower costs, Knight has moved plants offshore and to nonunion areas of the South. He boasted in 1988 that in the previous five years Emerson had "closed 49 plants and moved 6,000 jobs" in the quest for lower

THE 10 LARGEST PUBLIC BANKRUPTCIES

Company	Assets
1. Texaco	$35.9 billion
2. Financial Corporation of America	$33.9 billion
3. MCorp	$20.2 billion
4. Gibraltar Financial	$15.0 billion
5. Imperial Corporation of America	$12.3 billion
6. Campeau Allied/Federated	$11.4 billion
7. Baldwin-United	$9.4 billion
8. Southmark	$9.2 billion
9. Integrated Resources	$7.9 billion
10. Penn Central	$6.9 billion

Source: *The Bankruptcy DataSource*, Boston, 20 June 1990.

costs, including the transfer of 250 union jobs from St. Louis (where Emerson is based) to nonunion plants in Mexico and Florida. "We pay less per hour than we did five years ago," said Knight. "I don't know how many other companies in corporate America can say that."

Social responsibility. Emerson keeps a low profile. They are not generous to communities where they operate. During the 1980s they were engaged in two hassles with the Pentagon. In 1985 they were fined $325,000 for overcharging on defense contracts. And in 1989, Hazeltine, a company they acquired in 1986, was temporarily barred from new Defense Department contracts after a consultant they used was found guilty of bribing a Navy official as part of a scheme to obtain contracts.

Global presence. One of Knight's mandates was to move Emerson into overseas markets—and he has done that. They now get 30 percent of sales internationally. Of the 202 Emerson plants operating at the end of 1988, 70 were located in 15 countries outside the U.S. In 1989 they teamed up with one of Europe's electronic wizards, Robert Bosch of West Germany, to buy the Louisville power-tool maker, Vermont American. And in 1990 they plunked down $460 million to buy Leroy-

Somer, a French maker of electric motors and generators.

Stock performance. Emerson Electric stock bought for $1,000 in 1980 sold for $4,816 on January 2, 1990.

Emerson Electric Co., 8000 West Florissant Avenue, St. Louis, MO 63136; (314) 553-2000.

3

#1 *in car coatings*
#2 *in fiberglass, flat glass*
#3 *in chlorine/caustic soda*

Employees: 35,500
Sales: $5.7 billion
Profits: $465 million
Founded: 1883
Headquarters: Pittsburgh, Pennsylvania

PPG is difficult to classify. *Business Week* places them in the building materials industry. *Forbes* lodges them in automotive parts. And *Fortune* puts them in chemicals. They're all right, of course. As a major producer of glass and paints, PPG sells to residential and commercial builders. As a major producer of windshields and coatings, PPG counts automakers as some of their biggest customers (GM alone accounts for 10 percent of sales). And as the world's fourth largest producer of chlorine and caustic soda, PPG has a $1 billion-plus chemical business, selling basic chemicals to other industrial manufacturers and specialty chemicals such as silica compounds to companies making tires and shoes.

Formerly known as Pittsburgh Plate Glass, they changed their name to PPG Industries in 1968 to signal what had long been true: They made a lot more than glass. Yet PPG is still the world's second largest producer of glass (Pilkington of Britain is first)—and glass accounts for 42 percent of sales. They have 19 glass plants in the U.S., producing flat glass, automotive glass, fiberglass and glass used in

buildings. They're the world's largest producer of automotive coatings or finishes—and coatings and resins account for 34 percent of sales. Each one of the 45 million cars produced annually in the world requires about $100 worth of coatings, which adds up to an enormous market. One reason for PPG's preeminence in this business was their development, in 1963, of catonic electrodisposition coatings, a primer that provided superior resistance to corrosion. Two out of every three cars made in the world today are coated with these primers, supplied by PPG or their licensees.

History. In 1883, Scottish-born former railroad worker John Pitcairn joined with an Ohio River boat operator, John Baptiste Ford, to open a plate glass factory in Creighton, Pennsylvania—the nation's first such commercially successful plant. In seeking to make better and cheaper glass, they got into chemicals (in 1899, to supply the alkali needed for glass production, they built a soda ash plant in Ohio); paints and brushes (in 1900, as part of their glass-distribution system); oil (by mistake in 1933 when drilling for natural gas to produce alkali); and fiberglass (in 1953, because the government ordered Owens-Corning to license their technology).

But no one need accuse PPG of being a go-getter company. They never borrowed money and rarely modernized their equipment or technology. During the 1950s, the company seemed to be gathering dust—an impression confirmed by the extreme old age of their management. In 1955, most of the directors were over 65 and an 86-year old CEO was replaced by a 73-year-old CEO. His successor stayed at the top until he was 73. They lumbered through the 1970s, keeping intact what one employee called a "prim and proper American Gothic atmosphere," mainly by making generic products no one else bothered with—like acrylic coating for aluminum siding.

In 1984, a scrappy new CEO, Vincent Sarni, took over and revamped PPG's hallowed management system. "For those who don't perform, we will either change their job or get rid of them," he declared to *Business Week*. In the old days, top executives rose through one division and were essentially ignorant of the other divisions. Under Sarni, promising managers

Six out of every 100 engineers are women.

were shuffled all over the company—glass executives learning the chemicals business, and chemicals people reading up on coatings and resins. Sarni brought in two vice presidents from other companies—Honeywell and Mueller Brass—and in 1988 he eliminated an entire level of upper management. "He's set himself up as the ultimate dictator," one disgruntled former executive told *Business Week*. Sarni also sold off $400 million of PPG's low-profit generic businesses—a Canadian fertilizer company, for example—and created a new division, Biomedical Systems. In 1986 he paid $100 million to buy the medical electronics businesses of Honeywell and Litton Industries. "There's been enough change at this company to need a scorecard," one analyst told the *Wall Street Journal* in 1988.

Owners and rulers. The son of an Italian immigrant, Vincent A. Sarni grew up in New Jersey, attended the University of Rhode Island and played semipro football before going to work as a senior accountant for Rheem Manufacturing. He joined the PPG chemicals division in 1968. The blunt-spoken Sarni is fond of strolling through PPG factories and sharing lunch with production-line workers. Sarni made $2 million in 1989. The board of directors are all white and all male. Employees own 14 percent of the company through an Employee Stock Ownership Plan.

As a place to work. Changing under Sarni from authoritarian to more participative. PPG has a legacy of stodginess and antiunion attitudes that Sarni is trying to reverse with new incentives and programs. A new program that hands out bonuses pegged to the company's profits awarded $600 to 30,000 employees in 1989. In the chemical division, seven employees each received $1,000 in PPG stock. PPG has also established the PPG Collegium to honor scientists, researchers and others who have made important contributions over a period of not less than 10 years. In early 1989 the Collegium had 14 members.

Social responsibility. PPG's headquarters has been likened to a cathedral (complete with turrets and arches) made of reflective glass. The 42-story tower is the centerpiece of PPG Place, a downtown Pittsburgh complex built between 1981 and 1984. Many residents consider it central to Pittsburgh's renaissance. In 1985, PPG said they would donate $120 million over the next five years to the Scripps Research Clinic. The San Diego lab studies plant cells to develop environmentally safe herbicides to increase crop yield. PPG said their donation would aid in "bringing more food to the world's table." The donation will also benefit PPG. They have first dibs on patents of lab results.

Global presence. PPG more than tripled their sales in Europe during the 1980s and entered the 1990s with more than 30 percent of revenues coming from abroad. They have 48 plants in 12 countries and one-third of their employees are outside the U.S. Through acquisitions of companies in Italy and France, PPG is now the third largest glass maker in Europe behind France's Saint Gobain and Britain's Pilkington. PPG is also one of Europe's largest makers of automotive coatings, with three plants in Italy, three in Spain, two in France and one each in England and Germany.

Stock performance. PPG stock bought for $1,000 in 1980 sold for $8,345 on January 2, 1990.

PPG Industries, Inc., One PPG Place, Pittsburgh, PA 15272; (412) 434-3131.

4
Siemens

#1 in PBXs (private telephone exchanges)

Employees: 305,000 (27,000 in the U.S.)
Sales: (World), $34 billion (U.S.), $3.2 billion
Founded: 1847
Headquarters: Munich, Germany
U.S. Headquarters: New York City, New York

This 143-year-old German electronics giant (imagine a combination of General Electric and IBM) has mounted a strong putsch in the American market through subsidiaries, affiliates and joint ventures whose operations include 47 manufacturing plants, 400 sales and service locations and 35 research-and-development labs. Siemens owns 10 percent of semiconductor maker Advanced Micro Devices. They also joined with IBM to try to turn around the Silicon Valley company, ROLM, manufacturer of PBX systems (private telephone exchanges). Back home in Germany, Siemens is the largest supplier of telecommunications equipment to the state-owned telephone company—and is now the world's largest supplier of PBXs.

Siemens AG, Wittelsbacher Platz, 8000 Munich 1, Germany.

Siemens Corp., 767 Fifth Avenue, New York, NY 10153; (212) 832-6601.

5

#1 *in industrial hose fittings, piston equipment for aerospace*

Employees: 21,900
Sales: $1.9 billion
Profits: $32 million
Founded: 1916
Headquarters: Maumee, Ohio

This company emerged from the 1980s completely transformed. Trinova is the old Libbey-Owens-Ford company. In 1986 they sold the original business, glass making, and with it went the Libbey-Owens-Ford name. Some people claim they never got over the shattering experience of supplying window panes for the infamous John Hancock Building in Boston. The panes kept breaking after the building was finished in 1976. Meanwhile, General Motors, the company that kept LOF in business for 50 years, started buying from PPG (formerly known as Pittsburgh Plate Glass). Fortunately, LOF had acquired some nonglass businesses—Aeroquip (flexible hoses) in 1968, Vickers (hydraulic systems) in 1984 and Sterling Engineered Products (plastics) in 1988—and with the help of a New York corporate identity firm, Anspach, Grossman & Portugal, they regrouped under the name

Trinova, moving headquarters from Toledo to the suburb of Maumee.

Trinova's products (made by Aeroquip and Vickers) are all over the insides of cars, trucks and airplanes: fuel pumps, oil seals, power-steering pumps, hose lines, brake steering reservoirs, valves, air-conditioning assemblies, spring brakes, generators, piston motors, hydraulic controls that lower and retract landing gears—any product using oil or some other fluid for transmitting power. Trinova's third leg, plastics, yields decorative laminates, molded furniture, instrument panels, wheel covers, bumper strips, side moldings on cars. Trinova constantly acquires companies all over the world and says proudly that the word *foreign* is not in their vocabulary. "For the true global supplier, home is wherever he can best utilize his customers," said President Darryl F. Allen at the end of the climactic 1980s, pointing out that "Frankfurt, West Germany, has the largest concentration of Trinova employees of any metropolitan area in the world." (Take that, Toledo!) Trinova heroically defines their mission as one of seeking out investments "that will enhance our long-term cash flow." They do 40 percent of sales abroad. Only white, male Americans sit on Trinova's board.

Trinova sold Libbey-Owens-Ford to the big British glass maker, Pilkington—and in 1989 Pilkington sold 20 percent of their newly acquired American subsidiary to Nippon Sheet Glass of Japan. It represented a double power play. The British will now get their glass windows into Japanese cars, and the Japanese will now be able to get their windows into American cars. All thanks to the reshuffling that created Trinova.

Stock performance. Trinova stock bought for $1,000 in 1980 sold for $4,224 on January 2, 1990.

Trinova Corporation, 1705 Indian Wood Circle, Maumee, OH 43537; (419) 891-2200.

6

GRACO

Graco Inc.

#1 *in spray-painting robots*

Employees: 2,100
Sales: $300 million
Profits: $15 million
Founded: 1926
Headquarters: Minneapolis, Minnesota

If you drive a Ford Taurus or a Chrysler LeBaron, chances are that it was spray-painted by a Graco robot. Graco specializes in machines—pumps, spray guns, valves, robots—that apply fluids and semisolid substances to various surfaces. For example, they pump tomato paste onto frozen pizzas, lubricants into automobiles and paint onto just about anything. They even applied the adhesive holding down the artificial turf at the Minneapolis Metrodome. "Fluid handling" brings in almost half of Graco's revenues. But spray-painting robot arms—which accounted for one-quarter of revenues—have also made Graco a leader among U.S. robotics firms. Graco supplies robots to Ford, Chrysler, Ferrari, Rolls Royce, Audi and Mazda. They do 44 percent of sales abroad.

Like many other wholesome sagas of American success, Graco's story begins with two brothers in a gas station. In 1926, Leil and Russell Gray were mechanics at a downtown Minneapolis garage when they devised a grease gun run by air pressure. They gave up being "grease monkeys"—a nickname for mechanics coined during the 1920s—to start the Gray Company, which supplied service stations with pumps to move grease, oil and transmission fluid. In the 1980s the rising cost of oil-based paints convinced them to do two things: move into electrostatic painting, which uses electrical charges to help make paint stick, and develop a more efficient way to apply that paint. Graco got into robotics in 1981 when they bought 50 percent of GRI, a firm just getting started in Michigan. After losing money for two years, GRI landed spray-painting contracts with Chrysler and Ford. Sales doubled twice from 1984 to 1986. Graco now owns all of GRI.

The largest single Graco shareholder is a trust in the name of Clarissa L. Gray, deceased wife of one of the founders, with 36 percent. The Equitable Life Assurance Society owns another 6 percent, and members of the board of directors own 5 percent.

David Koch, son-in-law of one of the founders, became the company's third chairman in 1962. He has loosened the family reins by bringing in outside talent. He recruited President Walter Weyler and others from General Electric.

The members of Graco's nonunionized work force average more than 15 years employment with the company. When Graco shares began trading on the New York Stock Exchange, Koch defied Wall Street tradition by buying the first shares not for himself but for the Employee Stock Ownership Plan.

S*tock performance.* Graco stock bought for $1,000 in 1980 sold for $4,871 on January 2, 1990.

Graco, Inc., 4050 Olson Memorial Highway, P.O. Box 1441, Minneapolis, MN 55440; (612) 623-6000.

ENGINEERS

Engineering companies build dams, highways, tunnels, harbors, bridges, power plants, airports—even entire cities. They thrive when infrastructures are being built or rebuilt. And government contracts are clearly important to the big firms in this industry. The big companies also operate globally, building a skyscraper in one country, clearing a jungle in another. The international panoply of engineering giants includes France's Bouygues, Italy's Snamprogetti, Britain's John Laing, Sweden's Alex Johnson, South Korea's Hyundai, Japan's Kumagai Gumi and Ohbayashi and America's Bechtel and Fluor.

1

#1 *in engineering*

Employees: 26,100
Sales: $4.5 billion
Founded: 1898
Headquarters: San Francisco, California

In *Friends in High Places* (Simon & Schuster, 1988) journalist Laton McCartney profiled the family-owned Bechtel Group, depicting the giant engineering and construction firm as prospering by virtue of their high-level contacts with political leaders. If there were substance to this scenario, Bechtel should have been riding high during the 1980s. Their former president, George P. Shultz, was Secretary of State in the Reagan cabinet; their former legal counsel, Caspar W. Weinberger, was Secretary of Defense; their former vice president for nuclear development, W. Kenneth Davis, was Deputy Secretary of Energy. These connections notwithstanding, Bechtel took a severe beating in the 1980s when they had all these "friends in high places." From $13.6 billion in 1982, revenues declined to

$4.5 billion in 1989. From 42,000 employees, the payroll shrank to 17,500. It was Bechtel's worst slump since the Depression.

A triple whammy did it. Bechtel was the leading builder of nuclear power plants—and this business dried up during the 1980s. Bechtel was a leading builder of the new infrastructure in the Middle East (buildings, pipelines, highways, ports, entire cities)—but when oil prices plunged, the oil-producing nations in the Arab world cut back on construction projects. Finally, Bechtel faced new and tough competition from construction companies based in Japan and South Korea.

Even so, Bechtel still qualifies as the world's biggest engineer. At the start of 1990, they were working on 1,650 projects for 550 clients around the world. Included were the Eurotunnel between France and England; two international airports in Saudi Arabia; the SEMASS waste-to-energy project in Massachusetts; decontamination of the Three Mile Island Unit 2 reactor; a 170-mile stretch of the Trans-National highway system in Turkey; and the ambitious creation of an industrial city, Jubail, in the middle of the Saudi Arabian desert. According to the *Guinness Book of World Records*, Jubail is the largest construction project in history. Engineers have had to raise the site's elevation by more than 2 meters and move more than 340 million cubic meters of earth. On the drawing boards is a project to build two geothermal power plants in southern Japan.

History. Bechtel's success has been closely tied to the growth and power of big government in the U.S. The company began in 1898, when Warren A. Bechtel left his Kansas ranch and hired out with his mule team to grade a stretch of railroad in Oklahoma. Bechtel followed the rails to Oakland, California, where he continued contracting for railroad construction and added new projects like irrigation canals,

Every year only 3 percent of engineering and science degrees are conferred on blacks and Hispanics.

highways and pipelines. Bechtel's three sons grew up among tractors and steam shovels and were running field projects in their early 20s.

By the time they incorporated in 1925, Bechtel was one of the West's biggest construction outfits. In 1931 a consortium of six companies Bechtel organized won the contract to build Hoover Dam, the biggest in history. More huge projects followed: another dam on the Colorado River, Bonneville Dam on the Columbia and the foundations for the San Francisco Bay Bridge. Warren Bechtel died in 1933, but his son Steve expanded the business and was primed when World War II brought a flood of contracts. Bechtel turned out almost 600 ships for the war effort.

After the war Bechtel followed the government into new areas. Benefiting from America's role in the Middle East, Bechtel began an extensive involvement there when they contracted to build the 1,100-mile Trans-Arabian pipeline. Bechtel also built the first electricity-generating nuclear plant in Arco, Idaho, in 1951, and constructed a nuclear fuel reprocessing plant at the same site. Alone or in concert with other companies, Bechtel has built the subway systems for Washington, D.C., and the San Francisco Bay Area and half of America's nuclear power plants. They also have the distinction of being the first company to rehabilitate a nuclear power plant after an accident: They contracted to clean up Three Mile Island at an estimated cost of $400 million over four years.

Owners and rulers. Stephen Bechtel, Jr., grandson of the founder, stepped down as CEO and chairman of Bechtel in 1990. *Forbes* estimates he is worth $1.2 billion, mostly from his family's 50 percent ownership of the company (senior managers own the balance). His son, Riley Bechtel, took his place. When Riley became president in 1989 at age 37, he succeeded Alden Yates, president from 1983 to 1989, one of only two nonfamily members to hold the presidency (the other was George Shultz). Yates died of cancer in 1989. After leaving the Reagan cabinet, Shultz rejoined the Bechtel board.

As a place to work. Bechtel has a reputation as an ingrown, stuffy place to work, one with an engineering mentality. But at least these days they seem to be aware of

it. They even created a human resources department in 1988.

Social responsibility. Being privately owned, Bechtel doesn't have to disclose any information about themselves, but they bristle at the frequent designation, "secretive," and as each year goes by more veils are dropped. The annual report they issue to employees is made available to the press. And when McCartney's book appeared in 1988, labeling them on the cover as "the most secret corporation," Bechtel didn't turn the other cheek. They labeled the book "trash" and issued a point-by-point rebuttal. They also circulated an editorial from the industry publication, *Engineering News-Record*, that answered McCartney's main point as follows: "Having friends in high places is no sin. In fact, being in the right place at the right time and knowing the right people can be called entrepreneurship. Bechtel's relationships with the Armand Hammers and Ibn Sauds, and its abilities to attract the Weinbergers and Shultzes have the stuff that Bechtel competitors have envied through the years. It is and remains the real power behind the company. This book won't change that."

Global presence. Less than before. Besides the Eurotunnel, Bechtel is working on the Trans-Tokyo Bay Bridge and a new rapid transit system for Taipei. But the international portion of their business, close to 80 percent in 1980, was down to 43 percent in 1988.

Bechtel Group, Inc., P.O. Box 3965, 50 Beale Street, San Francisco, CA 94119; (415) 768-1234.

GARBAGE COLLECTORS

The U.S., world leader in many economic categories, also leads in garbage. According to one estimate, Americans generate 150 million tons of solid waste every year. According to another estimate, New York City "produces" 4 lbs. of garbage per person every day, compared to 3 lbs. for Tokyo (as in everything, Japan is catching up), 2.5 lbs. for Paris and 1.6 lbs. for Rome. The proliferation of waste has presented a golden opportunity to garbage-collecting companies. Previously, they were, for the most part, local scavengers, collecting the garbage in their communities. But the big companies have followed their noses and crisscrossed the country buying up local garbage collectors, looking to extract dollars from the colossal pileup of our wastes.

1

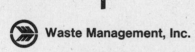 **Waste Management, Inc.**

#1 *in garbage collection, recycling*

Employees: 39,400
Sales: $4.4 billion
Profits: $562 million
Founded: 1968
Headquarters: Oakbrook, Illinois

Not every company can hold their annual meeting near a garbage landfill. Waste Management, the nation's biggest garbage collector, can. In 1989 they invited shareholders to troop to their new groundwater analysis lab in the Settler's Hill Sanitary Landfill Complex in the Chicago suburb of Geneva. Two 18-hole golf courses were also being built on the landfill, illustrating Waste Management's thesis that garbage dumps can serve some useful purposes.

With the country about to be buried by garbage, Waste Management is in the right business at the right time. At the end of 1988 they were picking up garbage in 46 states and the District of Columbia, serving 7.6 million households (through contracts with 1,200 municipalities) and 655,700 businesses. They were also operating 125 landfills for garbage disposal—and looking for more sites. Waste

Management is interested in every phase of garbage. They own 79 percent of Chemical Waste Management, which disposes of hazardous materials, including radioactive wastes and asbestos, and they operate incinerators throughout the U.S. to burn infectious wastes collected from hospitals. They run the Recycle America program, which picks up bottles, cans and paper at the curbsides of 1.2 million households. At 14 of their landfills they're converting organic waste into methane gas to generate electricity. And they have joined with two other companies, Du Pont and Jefferson Smurfit, to recycle plastic and paper. Their goal is "helping the world dispose of its problems." They also gained control of Wheelabrator Technologies in 1990.

Waste Management grew along with the garbage by zealously buying up local waste collectors. Their starting point was Chicago's first garbage business, Ace Scavenger Service, founded in 1894 and run by the Huizenga family. Dean Buntrock, an insurance salesman, married Elizabeth Huizenga and they were living in Boulder, Colorado, when her father, the head of Ace Scavenger, died in 1956. Buntrock moved to Chicago to take the helm at Ace. In 1968 he joined with his wife's cousin, Wayne Huizenga, who ran a garbage collection company in Florida, to form Waste Management. They sold stock to the public in 1971, the same year the Environmental Protection Agency was born. And then they went around the country buying up garbage companies. During the 1980s they scooped up more than 470 of them. Waste Management's 1980 sales were $560 million. In 1989 they were $4.5 billion. They have captured an estimated 25 percent of the private garbage collection business.

Waste Management has also been a feverish collector of citations, complaints, court convictions and fines stemming from the way they do business. The

> **E**ach year, Americans create 150 million tons of solid waste, enough to bury 26,000 football fields under a layer of garbage 10 feet deep.

News/Sun-Sentinel of Orlando, Florida, found that during the 1980s the EPA cited Waste Management for pollution violations more than 600 times. Another report said that between 1980 and 1988 they were fined $46 million for such practices as bribery and illegal waste handling. Still another report, in *Forbes*, said that between 1983 and 1988 18 grand juries investigated them. Waste Management has also been hauled into courts across the country on charges of conspiring with competitors to fix prices and allocate territories. In 1989 the company entered a no contest plea to a price-fixing charge in Los Angeles and was fined $900,000. A year later two other Waste Management companies in California pleaded guilty to price-fixing and paid a fine of $1.5 million. Such has been the outcry against Waste Management that in 1988 the Arlington, Virginia–based Citizens Clearinghouse for Hazardous Wastes published a 76-page manual detailing the company's record so local communities could battle the company. They concluded Waste Management's "rise to the top of the garbage heap is a testament to how an enterprising group of profit-minded businessmen can break laws, be convicted and still make a profit and grow. The history of this company is a tribute to the dark side of the American Dream."

Waste Management has undertaken a large-scale campaign to clean up their image and position themselves as an environmentally sensitive company. They have made substantial contributions to environmental organizations, and Dean Buntrock, who was still CEO of Waste Management in 1990, joined the board of one of these groups, the National Wildlife Federation. They also hired people away from environmental groups and the EPA. In fact, an EPA official once complained: "Sometimes the EPA acts as if it were a wholly owned subsidiary of Chem-Waste Management." In 1988 Waste Management brought onto their board former U.S. senator and White House chief of staff, Howard H. Baker, Jr. In early 1990 a Waste Management official conceded the company may have had problems in the early 1980s, but he said that "people fail to understand that we are part of the solution, we are managing the waste generated by others."

One group Waste Management has not won over is Greenpeace. At the company's 1987 annual meeting, held at the Drury Lane Theatre near Chicago, Greenpeace activists delivered a half ton of horse manure to the front door an hour before the meeting began and hung out a banner reading, "WASTE MANAGEMENT STINKS." Then, as Buntrock welcomed shareholders, a loud voice interrupted him, shouting, "Welcome to the annual stockholders meeting... We are proud to announce that our company is racked by a series of investigations relating to bribery, insider trading and environmental violations... We are especially pleased to announce that we have reached a record-breaking level of environmental fines..." The taped message came from a black briefcase chained to a chair, and it went on for several minutes before an employee cut the chain and carried off the talking briefcase. Waste Management thought they had the last laugh. A year later the company newsletter reported that when the Greenpeace ship, *Gondwana*, pulled into Auckland, New Zealand, after engaging Japanese whalers in the Antarctic, they asked the local waste management company to dispose of nine liters of waste in their storage tank. The local company is owned by the ubiquitous Waste Management.

Stock performance. Waste Management stock bought for $1,000 in 1980 sold for $21,747 on January 2, 1990.

Waste Management, Inc., 3003 Butterfield Road, Oakbrook, IL 60521; (708) 572-8800.

New Yorkers generate 27,000 tons of trash each day, most of which is dumped at the Fresh Kills landfill on Staten Island. Already the highest mountain on the eastern sea board, Fresh Kills will be 500 feet high by 1997 when it's scheduled to close. (It can't go any higher because it would interfere with planes flying to and from Newark International Airport.)

2

LAIDLAW
TRANSPORTATION LIMITED

#1 *in school buses*
#2 *in garbage collection*

Employees: 30,000
Sales: $1.4 billion
Profits: $199 million
Founded: 1958
Headquarters: Burlington, Ontario

Almost everyone is familiar with those yellow school buses. Here's the biggest operator—a Canadian company doing three-quarters of their sales in the U.S. Laidlaw operates 20,000 school buses. In addition to picking up kids, they now also collect garbage, ranking as the second largest solid and chemical waste management company in North America. Garbage is increasing faster than kids, so Laidlaw is in a good position. Canada's largest company, Canadian Pacific, obviously thinks so too. In early 1989 they acquired a 47 percent interest in Laidlaw. Michael DeGroote, chairman of Laidlaw, received 12 million shares worth about $240 million as part of this sale. He promptly sold half his shares, pocketing $118 million. When the *Wall Street Journal* asked why DeGroote had sold the shares, Laidlaw's general counsel, Ivan Cairns, responded: "He had his own reasons for selling, and I'm certainly not about to comment on them."

S*tock performance.* Laidlaw stock bought for $1,000 in 1980 sold for $18,140 on January 2, 1990.

Laidlaw, Inc., 3221 North Service Road, Burlington, Ontario, Canada L7N 3G2; (416) 336-1800.

PART FOUR

Earthly Goods
and
Basic Materials

Miners

Oil & Gas

Oilfield Services

Forest & Paper

Steel

Aluminum

Chemicals

MINING

Mining companies no longer play the prominent roles they once did even though the minerals that are dug out of the ground are still vital to a modern industrial economy. Seventy years ago 10 mining companies ranked among the 100 largest U.S. manufacturers, including Anaconda in eighth place, Kennecott in 19th and American Smelting & Refining (Asarco) in 34th. Today, no mining company gets into the top 100. AMAX is the closest—it ranks 120th.

The reason their rankings fell during the 1980s: prices of most metals, copper especially, were depressed to the floor. It didn't even pay for most copper miners to take the ore out of the ground. In the previous decade, oil companies, enriched by soaring prices for their product, bought mining outfits—ARCO absorbed Anaconda, Sohio (now BP) took over Kennecott. These takeovers were not beneficial to mining, according to Plato Malozemoff, longtime head of Newmont Mining, who noted in 1989 that they had "led to the destruction of great companies" or "affected them to the point of debility." Another change that has affected U.S. mining companies: the need to be in compliance with environmental regulations governing emissions into air and discharges into waterways, rules that may not have to be observed by their foreign competitors.

Any way you look at it then, this is an industry with its back to the wall, hence their appeal to Washington, D.C., for protection.

AMAX

#1 in molybdenum production

#3 in coal production

#4 in aluminum production

Employees: 20,000
Sales: $3.9 billion
Profits: $360 million
Founded: 1887
Headquarters: New York City, New York

AMAX, a producer of coal, aluminum, gold and molybdenum (an ore used to harden steel), is glad to have the 1980s behind them. They're also glad to have a folksy Coloradan steering them into the 1990s as opposed to an erudite French engineer who almost ran the enterprise aground. AMAX entered the decade in seemingly superb shape, mining, refining and fabricating 16 different metals and minerals, activities that yielded a rich lode of profits. Chevron (then called Standard Oil of California) was certainly impressed. They had latched onto 21.7 percent of AMAX's shares in 1975, and in 1981, when AMAX stock was trading at $38 a share, they offered to buy all the rest for $78.50 a share. The AMAX board of directors, whose members included such luminaries as former President Gerald Ford, former Secretary of Defense Harold Brown, and former Transportation Secretary William T. Coleman, Jr., rejected the offer on the advice of Pierre Gousseland, a French mining engineer who had taken command of AMAX a few years earlier. Gousseland said the company was worth $100 a share. That rejection must be etched firmly in the minds of AMAX shareholders. Soon thereafter metals prices plunged to their lowest levels in 50 years, yanking AMAX into four consecutive years of horrendous losses and sending AMAX stock to a low of $10.50 in 1985. The AMAX shares Chevron was willing to buy for $78.50 in 1981 never rose above $30 after 1983.

While AMAX was hemorrhaging (losses totaled $1.4 billion between 1982 and 1985), Gousseland's pay increased 50 percent to more than $600,000 a year; and the company continued to maintain, for top executives, two condominiums at Keystone, Colorado; a fishing camp in Canada; and a corporate plane. In addition, according to *Business Week*, Gousseland "raised hackles because of his friendship with Erika Tordjman, the president of Paris-based AMAX Europe." Although AMAX supposedly had a policy prohibiting executives from flying first-class, Tordjman made frequent transatlantic trips on the Concorde. Air France gave her an award for being the biggest buyer of Concorde tickets during 1982.

Into this breach, in mid-decade, stepped the "Durango Kid," Allen Born, who grew up in the mining town of Durango, Colorado, following his father and grandfather into the mining business. He became a metallurgist and worked for AMAX for 14 years before leaving in 1981 to go to a Canadian mining company, Placer Development, now Placer Dome. In 1985, his back to the wall, Gousseland persuaded Born to return to AMAX. On January 1, 1986, with Gousseland's retirement (and a 10-year, $10,860-a-month consulting contract), Born became CEO (1989 pay: $1.2 million).

A straight-talking, folksy westerner, Born took AMAX out of a lot of businesses: nickel, copper, zinc, potash, lead, silver, phosphates. He made coal, gold, aluminum and molybdenum the core of the company. He raised cash and reduced debts by selling off huge chunks of the business. His attitude toward a loser is "fix it, sell it or shoot it." He reduced AMAX's payroll by one-third, letting go all of Gousseland's top lieutenants, including Ms. Tordjman. He is also a much more accessible leader than was Gousseland, meeting regularly with nonmanagement employees and insisting they call him by his first name. In 1989 he granted stock options to 5,000 salaried employees.

Born had AMAX making money again by 1987. He's also a bit of a wheeler-dealer, ready to sell off businesses for a good price and buy others when he senses an opportunity. In 1989 he tried to buy one of Canada's biggest mining companies, Falconbridge, for $2.4 billion but was unsuccessful. Asked why he would buy a company that mined copper, nickel and zinc—businesses Amax had recently opted out of—Born said: "Hey, I don't hate any commodity. I mean, when quality comes your way, you have to jump at it." After expanding gold mining in the U.S., he sold off AMAX's Australian gold mines because the price was so good. In mid-1990 Born entered a bidding war against Hanson to buy Peabody Coal, the nation's largest coal producer. He once told a meeting of security analysts in London: "Listen, if you want my grandmother, for the right price I'd probably sell her to you." That, according to *Fortune*, "flummoxed the Britishers. But Born had a longer view of the matter, later confiding with a wink that he would just wait until the price dropped, then buy her back again."

An era ended at AMAX in 1983 when Walter Hochschild died at the age of 82. (His son Adam Hochschild was a founder of the left-liberal monthly *Mother Jones*.) He had a 63–year assocation with the company cofounded by his father. In 1987 AMAX celebrated their centennial, dating from the formation of American Metal, a metal-trading company, in New York in 1887. They combined with Climax Molybdenum in 1957 and became AMAX in 1974. Entering the 1990s, no descendants of the founding families are active in the company, not even to the extent of holding a board seat.

Stock performance. AMAX stock bought for $1,000 in 1980 sold for $611 on January 2, 1990.

AMAX Incorporated, 200 Park Avenue, New York, NY 10166; (212) 573-8800.

2

Pittston

Employees: 14,600
Sales: $1.6 billion
Profits: $3.8 million
Founded: 1930
Headquarters: Greenwich, Connecticut

They're headquartered in one of the most affluent suburbs of New York City, but they dig coal out of the Appalachian seams of Virginia, West Virginia and Kentucky. Pittston differs from other major coal producers in that they sell 70 percent of their black ore abroad. Forty percent of Pittston's coal is sold as coking fuel to Japanese steelmakers, who have helped to decimate the U.S. steel industry. In that kind of arena, Pittston coal competes against coal dug in Australia, Poland and China. It's the world market.

Citing that competitive scene, Pittston pulled out of the Bituminous Coal Operators Association in 1987 and asked for a different contract with their workers, members of the United Mine Workers. One of the first consequences, once the old contract ran out, was that 1,500 retirees who had expected lifetime health insurance benefits were stripped of their coverage. For the workers still in the mines, Pittston asked that they shoulder some health insurance costs and accept new work rules that would keep the mines open 24 hours a day, seven days a week. Those demands provoked one of the most bitter strikes of the 1980s.

It began on April 5, 1989, and ended nearly 11 months later, on February 26, 1990, when some 1,700 striking Pittston workers returned to the mines under a settlement reached on the last New Year's Eve of the decade. This strike stirred the juices. Pittston CEO Paul W. Douglas accused the miners of leaving "behind the rule of reason," and they characterized him as a traitor to his late father, Illinois Senator Paul Douglas, long identified with the liberal wing of the Democratic Party. The strike was a throwback to the confrontations of the organizing days of the 1930s except this time the UMW borrowed the nonviolent, activist strategies of the civil rights movement. They blockaded roads, staged sit-ins at mines, excoriated replacement workers as scabs, put pressure on banks and institutional investors to break their ties with Pittston, mobilized women and children, rallied the clergy to their cause and gained such wide support from the entire labor movement it led to the readmission of the UMW to the AFL-CIO. Refrains long familiar to the Appalachian hills were heard again: "We Shall Overcome," "Solidarity Forever," "Which Side Are You On?"

A busload of miners traveled to the Pittston annual meeting (held on May 10, 1989, in their headquarters building in Greenwich, Connecticut) to confront Douglas directly. Harry Whitaker, a veteran of 31 years in Pittston mines, said to Douglas: "I loaded 100 tons of coal in 32 minutes, 1,500 tons in eight hours. I worked in dust, water and mud. I've crawled around. I was promised I would get health benefits for life. My disability is pneumoconiosis... I don't know how long it's been since I've slept at night like you fellows do every night. I have nine pillows propping me up. I gave my life to you fellows. I'm just like the slag that comes out of the mines. You dump it over the hill. That's what you did to me." John Olsen, president of the Connecticut AFL-CIO, rose to support the miners, telling Douglas: "You have brought dishonor on Connecticut and we plan to broadcast that at every opportunity."

The strike crippled Pittston's coal production and knocked down 1989 profits by more than 50 percent. In the new contract, both sides gave up something. Pittston agreed to continue 100 percent medical coverage for employees and retirees in return for getting flexible work rules allowing them to operate the mines around the clock. The UMW hailed the settlement as a victory. Pittston said the new contract will save them $30 million a year in costs.

In addition to mining coal, Pittston owns the Brink's armored car business and an air freight forwarder, Burlington Air Express.

Stock performance. Pittston stock bought for $1,000 in 1980 sold for $1,005 on January 2, 1990.

Pittston, Co., One Pickwick Plaza, P.O. Box 8900, Greenwich, CT, 06836; (203) 622-0900.

OIL & GAS

It's not true that everything always goes up. The price of oil went down during the 1980s—and that slide was reflected in the declining fortunes of the giant petroleum companies. To be sure, they have not been reduced to pygmies—oil companies hold three of the Top 10 slots on the Fortune 500 and four more in the next tier (11 to 20)—but just about all the major oil companies had smaller profits in 1989 than they did in 1980. Fewer people work for the oil companies today than they did in 1980.

The 1980s also saw a major restructuring of this industry. The number of gasoline stations continued to dwindle (many of them are also selling hot dogs and popcorn these days)—and so did the number of big players. Of the 25 biggest oil and gas companies at the start of the 1980s, 11 were either acquired, merged or sold off. Companies whose status changed during the decade were: Shell Oil (absorbed by Big Daddy, Royal Dutch/Shell); Superior Oil (now part of Mobil); Conoco (Du Pont); Sohio (British Petroleum); Getty Oil (to Texaco, which had to pay a $3 billion premium to Pennzoil); Gulf (Chevron); Tenneco (Chevron, Amoco, others); Cities Service (Occidental); General American Oil (Phillips); Marathon (USX); and Texas Oil & Gas (USX).

1

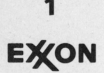

#1 *in oil production, refinery runs and sales (worldwide)*

#2 *in gas production*

Employees: 102,500
Sales: $86.7 billion
Profits: $3 billion
Founded: 1870
Headquarters: Houston, Texas

Social Conscience

Exxon, America's largest oil company, is so big even their oil spills are done up in grand style. On March 24, 1989, one of their 70 tankers—the 978-foot *Exxon Valdez*—ran into a reef, ruptured and emptied 11 million gallons of crude oil into Prince William Sound off the Alaskan coast. Exxon then spent millions of dollars cleaning up more than 1,000 miles of oil-contaminated beaches. The worst oil spill in U.S. history brought down on Exxon's head a firestorm of criticism from environmentalists, some of whom showed up at the company's annual meeting bearing placards reading "Exxon Greed Kills Animals" and "Make Exxon Pay." The criticism has had an effect on Exxon employees. One manager told *Fortune*, "Whenever I travel now, I feel like I have a target painted on my chest." The spill also led to the formation of a new watchdog group, the Coalition for Environmentally Responsible Economics (CERES), which drafted a set of principles, the Valdez Principles, to govern corporate environmental practices (*à la* the Sullivan Principles in South Africa).

The massive Alaskan cleanup effort nicked Exxon's profits by nearly $2 billion, enough to pulverize most companies but not this one. As Lawrence G. Rawl, chairman and CEO, assured shareholders: "I am confident that Exxon's traditional financial strength will not be impaired by this major accident."

That financial strength was much in evidence during the 1980s when the one event that could shatter Exxon happened: a sharp decline in crude oil prices. Exxon met that crisis head-on. While revenues declined by over $20 billion during the decade, profits held up fairly well because Exxon took a meat ax to costs. They sold off nonoil businesses—electric motors (Reliance Electric), nuclear fuels, computerized office equipment (Zilog, Qyx)—and streamlined operations. The big savings were in payroll. In 1982, they had 182,000 employees; by decade's end 102,000. People who thought joining Exxon meant lifetime employment were shocked.

While Exxon's U.S. operations have long been run out of Houston, New York City remained corporate headquarters, functioning as the command post for operations in 79 countries. But that, too, changed during the 1980s. The Exxon Tower in Rockefeller Center was sold to the Japanese. And then, as the decade closed, Exxon announced they would move corporate headquarters to Houston. Significantly, about 100 of the 300 top executives and staffers refused to move to Texas. One manager opined: "The company is going down the poop chute." Exxon had been based in New York City since 1885 when John D. Rockefeller established the offices of the Standard Oil Trust at 26 Broadway. There they remained until 1933 when they moved uptown to Rockefeller Center.

After the *Valdez* spill, some activists urged Exxon creditcard holders to cut up their cards and send them to the company as a protest against the despoiling of Prince William Sound. Some 10,000 cardholders did so—out of a total of 7 million. That was just a blip on a screen for Exxon, which derives no more than 10 percent of their sales from gasoline pumped at service stations. Most people who pull up at Exxon stations are probably not aware that this company not only derives most of their revenues elsewhere—exploration of oil—but they also get most of their sales and profits from abroad.

Still, Exxon is Big Oil, a monster no matter where you look at them. On each day they pumped an average of 4.2 million barrels of oil. Their chemical company ranks as one of the 10 largest in the world, one of the 5 biggest in the U.S. They rank third in retail sales of gasoline behind Amoco and Shell.

History. John D. Rockefeller was born in 1839 to a con-artist father and a Calvinist mother. After graduating from high school, he worked as a bookkeeper for a commodity merchant in Cleveland. After three years, young John started his own commodity business, the firm of Clark & Rockefeller. In 1863, Rockefeller invested $4,000 in a Cleveland oil refinery. At first, he thought his investment was an unimportant sideline, but as the oil boom continued he began to devote more attention to it. In 1865, at age 26, he bought out the other refinery investors and took control of the business.

Rockefeller realized the big money was not in owning wells, since prices collapsed every time someone struck a new find, but in controlling oil refining and transportation. So Rockefeller leased all the available railroad cars he could, preventing competitors from moving their oil out of Cleveland, and in 1870, formed his new company: Standard Oil. Several railroads came up with a new plan: They would secretly combine with the largest refiners, to the benefit of both parties. Freight rates would go up, and refiners in on the scheme would get their money back through rebates on shipments. Rockefeller told his younger brother Frank, a partner in a firm competing with Standard Oil: "We have a combination with the railroads. We're going to buy out all the refiners in Cleveland. We well give everyone a chance to come in... Those who refuse will be crushed." Within three months, Rockefeller bought up all but 3 of his 25 competitors in Cleveland (including brother Frank, who remained bitter for the rest of his life) and controlled one-quarter of the nation's refining capacity. Then he convinced independent refiners in New York and Pennsylvania to join Standard Oil. By 1880, Rockefeller was refining 95 percent of the nation's oil. A ruthless operator, Rockefeller bribed state legislators, undercut competitors' prices and devised an oil trust to pretend the companies under Standard Oil's umbrella were independent.

As the extent of Rockefeller's power became known, several states passed antitrust laws. Rockefeller reorganized the trust as a holding company, called Standard Oil (New Jersey), which owned shares of all the other companies. The government brought suit against Standard Oil in 1906, under the Sherman Anti-Trust Act of 1890, and in 1911 the Supreme Court declared Standard Oil an illegal monopoly. Standard Oil was split into 34 separate companies, including Standard Oil of New York (later Mobil), Standard Oil of California (later Chevron), Standard Oil of Ohio (Sohio, now BP), and Standard Oil of Indiana (now Amoco).

The branch of Standard Oil that eventually became Exxon was Standard Oil of New Jersey (often called Jersey Standard). Jersey Standard and Mobil joined with British and French oil companies to participate in the Red Line Agreement of 1928, in which a group of companies divided up among themselves Middle East oil reserves. Jersey Standard contin-

mported oil was responsible for 40 percent of the 1989 trade deficit.

ued to prosper, but occasionally came under fire—once during World War II, when the Justice Department discovered Jersey had a deal with Hitler's Germany in the 1930s. Jersey had supplied Germany with patents for a lead vital to the production of aviation fuel and in exchange, Germany was to develop a formula for synthetic rubber and share it with Jersey.

After World War II, Jersey Standard's supply of oil and wealth grew sharply as a result of operations in Iran and Saudi Arabia. They went on to discover oil in many other places—Libya, the Netherlands, Alaska, the North Sea—but nothing matched their flow from the Middle East. Standard Oil of New Jersey became Exxon in 1972. They use the Esso brand name to sell gas abroad.

The late 1980s were a trying time for Exxon; in addition to the *Exxon Valdez* spill, a refinery in Baton Rouge, Louisiana, exploded and a pipeline leaked 500,000 gallons of heating oil into an estuary. By some estimates, Exxon has spent $3 billion to clean up these disasters. Many see CEO Larry Rawl as part of the problem. In 1986, Rawl restructured Exxon, with a massive reduction in the work force (28 percent of employees lost their jobs), creating a system one former employee called "overworked and undermanned." These cutbacks have been blamed for everything from low morale at Exxon to the *Valdez* oil spill itself (the crews manning oil tankers were also cut) to the disorganized cleanup efforts (many senior employees with experience in oil spill response were laid off). Exxon is virtually the only major oil company that *decreased* spending on research and development—by 20 percent from 1985 to 1990.

Owners and rulers. In January 1987, 59-year-old Lawrence G. Rawl became chairman of the board and CEO, succeeding Clifton C. Garvin, Jr. Rawl, the son of an Irish-American truck driver, earned extra money as a teenager in Ridgewood, New Jersey, by pumping gas at an Exxon station (known as Esso in those days). He earned a degree in engineering from the

University of Oklahoma on the GI bill and joined Humble Oil of Texas, which became part of what is now Exxon. Rawl likes to put his feet up on chairs and tables, chews cigars and is known for his "wise-ass remarks," a former colleague told *Business Week* (his 1989 pay: $1.4 million). Lee R. Raymond, age 51 (1990), is president; the youngest Exxon president since the legendary Walter C. Teagle in 1917. He joined the company in 1963 after getting a Ph.D in chemical engineering at the University of Minnesota. In response to demands Exxon appoint an environmentalist to their board, they named John H. Steele, a marine scientist at Woods Hole Oceanographic Institution. Many environmental activists were dismayed with the appointment. John Bell, an official representing 15 environmental organizations, said, "being a marine scientist doesn't mean he's an environmentalist."

As a place to work. Exxon used to be famous for job security, a legion of "womb-to-tombers." During the Great Depression of the 1930s, they didn't lay off one employee—largely because of a work-sharing program. They were also famous for their stuffy bureaucracy and for the cachet of the Exxon name— "There's instant prestige when you say you work for Exxon." All of that ended dramatically in the late 1980s. Prestige went out the window after the *Valdez* spill, and many workers were shown the door. Under Rawl, entire layers of bureaucracy vanished—and thousands of employees over 50 were forced to retire, others were fired outright and some took salary cuts. "Some people won't be promoted—that's just life," Rawl told the *Wall Street Journal*. Staff at Exxon headquarters shrank from 1,500 to 300. In the words of one Exxon employee, "I don't know anyone who is happy, and I know a lot of people who are looking to leave." A pipe fitter at Exxon's refinery in Billings, Montana, said after the *Valdez* spill: "Morale is as low as I've seen it in my 14 years here."

Social responsibility. "The name Exxon has become a household word for environmental irresponsibility," the environmental protection commissioner of New York City told the *Wall Street Journal* in 1990. In March of 1990, a jury found the captain of the ill-fated *Exxon Valdez* not guilty of a felony. Joseph J. Hazelwood, whose drunkenness was rumored to have caused the worst oil spill in the nation's history, was instead convicted of misdemeanor negligence. But now Exxon may have to stand trial. In February 1990, Exxon was indicted on five felony and misdemeanor charges related to the *Valdez* disaster.

Global presence. Massive. U.S. operations bring in less than 20 percent of Exxon's revenues. They operate in 79 countries. Even their chemical operations are worldwide. Exxon Chemical people work in 51 countries—and U.S. plants employ 7,840 of the worldwide total of 18,000.

Stock performance. Exxon stock bought for $1,000 in 1980 sold for $7,333 on January 2, 1990.

Exxon Corporation, 800 Bell Street, Houston, TX 77002; (713) 656-3636.

2

Mobil

#2 *in oil sales*
#3 *in refinery runs*

Employees: 68,800
Sales: $50.2 billion
Profits: $1.8 billion
Founded: 1866
Headquarters: Fairfax, Virginia

The most pugnacious of the big oil companies, Mobil will joust with their critics any time, as evidenced by editorials they run as advertisements on newspaper op ed pages. In the mid-1980s Mobil anointed a new leader, Allen E. Murray, a Brooklyn-born accountant said to be in the Mobil mold of a New York City streetfighter. That reputation notwithstanding, Mobil sold their skyscraper on 42nd Street in New York City and as the 1980s closed began moving their headquarters—not to Texas, where Exxon and Shell went—but to Fairfax, Virginia,

where they will be within easy rifle range of the bureaucrats in Washington, D.C. The move was climactic for a company whose name when they were part of the Rockefeller Standard Oil Trust was Socony (Standard Oil Company of New York).

Mobil has always been better at selling oil than finding it. Even today they run much more oil through their refineries than they take out of the ground. During the 1980s, along with other oil companies, they reduced the number of service stations selling Mobil gasoline. They now have about 11,000 U.S. stations (down from 19,000), and they're getting 85 percent of their gasoline sales from 14 states, mostly along the eastern seaboard (in 1980 Mobil had service stations in 46 states). But the new stations are bigger and sleeker, pumping 50 percent more gasoline than the old ones, enabling Mobil to push their national market share to 7 percent, ranking them among the top five sellers.

Recognizing the need to shore up oil and gas reserves, Mobil, in 1984, plunked down $5.7 billion to buy Superior Oil, one of the last of the big independent drillers. They also stepped up exploration in 20 countries, notably Indonesia, Norway and Nigeria. Mobil relies on overseas wells for 55 percent of their supplies. During the 1970s, when oil prices skyrocketed, Mobil used their newfound wealth to buy Marcor, which put them in the packaging (Container Corp. of America) and merchandising (Montgomery Ward) businesses. They were harshly criticized at the time for not using their oil profits to find new oil, especially in the U.S. Mobil thumbed their noses at the critics, pointing out how difficult the government was making it for oil companies to earn money. However, in the 1980s Mobil sold both Container Corp. (1986) and Montgomery Ward (1988), deciding after all they should stick to what they know best: oil and gas.

History. In 1866 a carpenter in Rochester, New York, devised a method for making kerosene by distilling crude oil in a vacuum. His Vacuum Oil Company was soon manufacturing various lubricants, especially Vacuum Harness Oils used for tanning leather. Thirteen years after Vacuum was formed, John D. Rockefeller bought the company, and in 1882 he made

Vacuum part of his newly organized Standard Oil Trust. That same year he also set up the Standard Oil Company of New York (Socony) as the trust's administrative arm. Socony refined and sold gasoline in New York and New England, which soon became known as Soconyland because the company was supplying 92 percent of the area's oil needs.

In 1911, the Supreme Court broke up Rockefeller's oil trust into 34 companies, including Vacuum and Socony. Because Socony never owned any oil wells of their own under the Rockefeller trust, much of Mobil's subsequent history has been a mad scramble to get their own supplies. Socony developed a huge market in China in the early 1900s by introducing kerosene lamps (called *mei foo*, from the Chinese symbols for Socony, meaning "beautiful confidence"). In 1931 they joined forces with Vacuum, their former sibling in the Standard Oil Trust.

Socony-Vacuum began selling their oil and gasoline under the Mobil brand name, using a flying red horse as their symbol. (They changed their company name to Socony-Mobil in 1955 and to Mobil in 1966.) In 1933, they joined with Jersey Standard (now Exxon) in a venture called Stanvac. Using Jersey Standard's oil wells and refinery in Indonesia and Socony-Vacuum's huge marketing apparatus in the Far East, Stanvac built an oil-selling operation in 50 countries that spread from the Africa's east coast to New Zealand. Federal trustbusters broke up Stanvac in 1962, leaving each company with half the assets. Socony-Vacuum's most productive effort to secure a steady oil supply came in 1948 when they bought a 10 percent interest in the Arabian American Oil Company (Aramco), the Saudi Arabian company then owned jointly by Standard Oil of California and Texaco.

Owners and rulers. When Allen Murray joined Mobil in 1952 as an accountant, few predicted he would make it to the top, as he did in 1986. More plebeian than patrician, Murray is noted for his wit and tough guy image: the kind of guy, says someone at Mobil, that "you'd be more inclined to see at a hockey game than a symphony." At Mobil, Murray attracted the attention of longtime President William Tavoulareas. According to

one Mobil executive, the two men are "cut from the same street-smart mold." During his reign at Mobil, Murray has sold off everything not relating to what he calls "the basics": oil and gas. In the first 6 months of 1986, he also trimmed 6 percent of Mobil's work force, amounting to 10,000 jobs, without blinking an eye. However, he gets good marks from his fellow executives for generating "a lot more discussion of various ideas and alternatives." With Murray, "People are not afraid to speak up." He earned $1.7 million in 1989.

Mobil's board has 18 members, two of them women: Jewel Lafontant, a black Chicago lawyer and Eleanor Sheldon, former president of the Social Science Research Council.

As a place to work. The 1980s were stressful for Mobil employees. Secretaries and managers alike were fired by the dozens. Nearly 20 percent of the work force was zapped during the decade. Older executives were asked to retire early. The *Wall Street Journal* reported that one manager came to work and, before his morning coffee cooled, was told to be gone by the afternoon. The attitude of those in charge of this mayhem can be inferred from a no-holds-barred question-and-answer session between Chairman Murray and a group of employees selected by the company magazine, *Mobil World*. One female employee asked whether Murray considered reassigning especially good workers rather than simply laying them off when cutbacks were necessary. Murray responded that they did reassign at upper levels of the company, but he was unaware of what his company did for those at lower levels.

Mobil's had their share of safety-related incidents during the 1980s. In 1984, a laboratory worker in Plainsboro, New Jersey, collapsed after being exposed to nerve gas. Mobil fired the biologist who tried to report it. The courts later decided it was a wrongful firing. A Mobil refinery in Torrance, California, had an alarming series of accidents between 1987 and 1989. One worker fell to his death, another was killed in an explosion, four were badly burned, and eight injured. A company hired to study the plant blamed Mobil's lax enforcement of their own safety rules. Mobil paid $88,000 for the study and rejected the findings.

In their annual report, Mobil brags they're "the first major oil company to have a national contract with a child care referral service." They also "have contracted" with a service to help spouses find work in a new city when they relocate people.

Social responsibility. Mobil is a major supporter of TV's Public Broadcasting System (some wags now call PBS the "Petroleum Broadcasting Service). Mobil has always had a testy relationship with the press, made worse by their habit of press bashing in "advertorials"—advertising space used to air their opinions to the public. In December 1984, Mobil began boycotting the *Wall Street Journal*—refusing to advertise in the paper or send press releases. The reason: The *Journal* took information from a Mobil proxy statement and implied Mobil's president William Tavoulareas used Mobil resources to set up his son Peter in the shipping business. Mobil also charged that for five years the *Journal* had been blatantly biased against Mobil. In 1987, CEO Murray said the *Wall Street Journal* was "a gossip column." The boycott ended, however, that year.

Global presence. Mobil operates wells and refineries in Indonesia, Nigeria, Norway and the U.K.

Stock performance. Mobil stock bought for $1,000 in 1980 sold for $4,337 on January 2, 1990.

Mobil Corporation, 3225 Gallows Road, Fairfax, VA 22037; (703) 846-3000.

3

#1 *in gas production*
#3 *in oil production*
Employees: 39,400
Sales: $32.4 billion
Profits: $2.4 million
Founded: 1902
Headquarters: White Plains, New York

Texaco likes to call themselves "the star of the American road." In the 1980s they looked more like a falling star as they lost the biggest lawsuit in American history and filed for protection under bankruptcy laws.

It was quite a comedown for a company whose arrogance was once a byword in the oil industry. Once Texaco was proud of having Texaco stations in every state in the Union, selling more gasoline to American motorists than any other company and squeezing more profits out of a barrel of oil than any other producer. Those marks of distinction have all been erased. Texaco emerged from the 1980s a diminished force, unlikely ever again to assert the dominance they once had.

Strong as they appeared coming into the 1980s, Texaco had one weakness: a lack of oil reserves. They decided to solve that deficiency by, as one oilman put it, drilling for oil on Wall Street. Egged on by investment banker Bruce Wasserstein, Texaco offered $10.1 billion to buy Getty Oil. But Texaco bid for Getty on January 6, 1984, two days after Getty had announced an agreement in principle to merge with Pennzoil. However, since no contract had been signed, Getty accepted Texaco's higher offer. The Getty purchase doubled Texaco's oil reserves overnight. But Pennzoil sued, charging Texaco had illegally interfered with a done deal. And Pennzoil won. On November 19, 1985, a Houston jury awarded them damages totaling (with interest) an incredible $11.1 billion. Texaco was shell-shocked.

This crushing defeat changed Texaco's life—for good. They appealed the decision but won only a minor reduction in the damages. To avoid posting a $10 billion bond, they entered Chapter 11 bankruptcy on April 12, 1987—the biggest bankruptcy filing in U.S. history. Meanwhile, raider Carl Icahn accumulated nearly 15 percent of Texaco's shares and used his position as the company's largest shareholder to force Texaco to the bargaining table with Pennzoil. In the closing days of 1987, Texaco settled the litigation by agreeing to pay Pennzoil $3 billion. They were then free to emerge from bankruptcy proceedings.

Texaco spent the rest of the decade restructuring themselves. They sold their German and Canadian companies (they had owned 99 percent of Deutsche Texaco and 78 percent of Texaco Canada) plus some 600 U.S. oil-producing properties. They cut $50 million out of their overhead, shoving thousands of employees out of the company. Finally, Texaco gave up sole ownership of two-thirds of their U.S. refinery and distribution system by setting up a new entity, Star Enterprise, which is 50-50 owned by Texaco and their old Middle Eastern partner, Saudi Arabia. Roped into Star Enterprise are Texaco refining and marketing facilities in 23 East and Gulf Coast states, including the big refinery at Port Arthur, Texas, 50 distribution terminals and over 11,000 service stations. So now if you fill up at the man with the star in New York, Pennsylvania, Florida, Texas and 19 other states, half of what you pay will go to the Saudis. The gasoline your car gets is also likely to have been refined from the Saudi crude because part of the deal calls for Saudi Arabia to supply 600,000 barrels of oil a day for 20 years.

All of these deals netted Texaco nearly $6 billion—and in early 1989, despite their need for cash to reinvest in the business, they bowed once again to Carl Icahn's pressure and paid shareholders a special dividend of $8 a share or a total of $1.9 billion

---

So far, *General Public Utilities has spent $960 million over 10 years to clean up the Three Mile Island nuclear accident, and the plant is still unsafe.*

Despite this comeuppance, Texaco remained a potent force in the oil industry, producing about 1.4 million barrels of oil a day and running nearly 2 million barrels through their refineries. They entered the 1990s with debt of $6.5 billion, down from the horrendous $10.4 billion of 1985, and they were even talking about a "new Texaco," which they plan to build into "one of the most admired companies in the industry."

History. In 1902, feisty former Standard Oil employee Joseph Cullinan joined with New York investment banker Arnold Schlaet to form the Texas Fuel Company. Cullinan had a nose for crude oil. The new company hit a gusher almost immediately, on land outside of Beaumont, Texas, near Spindletop Hill. Within a year, Cullinan had 36 storage tanks full of Spindletop oil and a 20-mile pipeline to the deep-water port at Port Arthur, Texas.

Most of Texaco's oil was sold for home lamps, to run the boilers of Southern sugar planters or to power locomotives. When the automobile era came in, Texaco's far-flung sales and marketing network formed the basis for an extensive chain of service stations. Texaco became an international company in one bold leap in 1936 when they joined with Standard Oil of California (now Chevron) in a share-the-pie venture that endures to this day: Caltex, a joint marketing company to transport and sell Middle Eastern oil outside the U.S.

Texaco has a past they would just as soon forget. In 1937 they outraged President Roosevelt by supplying oil to Spanish dictator Francisco Franco. Texaco president Torkild Rieber shipped oil to Germany after the outbreak of World War II, and in 1940 he served as courier for Goering's peace plan, which required the surrender of Britain. He also celebrated the fall of France to Hitler's invaders at a party at the Waldorf-Astoria. Rieber was forced to resign after the *New York Herald Tribune* revealed Texaco had harbored a Nazi spy at their New York headquarters. Texaco then began sponsoring the Metropolitan Opera broadcasts, an act of atonement continuing to this day.

Under the leadership of Augustus C. ("Gus") Long, Texaco expanded their operations into every state. Texaco advertised on national radio and TV, "You can trust your car to the man who wears the star." Gus Long started a tradition of paying the lowest salaries possible—at all levels—at Texaco. When they moved headquarters from New York City to suburban White Plains, they neglected to inform employees they'd be working an extra 45 minutes per day at the same salary.

Owners and Rulers. James W. Kinnear became CEO in January 1987 at age 59. An Annapolis graduate, he served in the Korean War and has spent his entire career at Texaco. Kinnear's hobbies include collecting fine china, growing orchids and raising spaniels (1989 pay: $1.8 million).

As a place to work. Texaco has been notorious for their bureaucracy. But in 1989, as part of a companywide restructuring resulting from bankruptcy, Texaco announced plans to cut 12 of their 26 layers of bureaucracy.

Social responsibility. In 1989, a federal judge fined Texaco $750,000 because the company did not perform a safety test on one of their oil platforms—and then falsified records to cover up. The safety test was designed to prevent a blowout, an explosion of oil, gas or water from a well. "It could have blown everyone to kingdom come," the judge commented. In 1988, Texaco agreed to pay $8.95 million to clean up drums of hazardous waste at their refinery in Bakersfield, California.

Global presence. Texaco and Chevron operate a joint-venture called Caltex operating wells and refineries in over 50 countries in the Far East, Middle East and Africa.

Stock performance. Texaco stock bought for $1,000 in 1980 sold for $4,834 on January 2, 1990.

Texaco, 2000 Westchester Avenue, White Plains, NY 10650; (914) 253-4000.

4

Chevron

#1 in U.S. oil refining and natural gas

Employees: 54,300
Sales: $29.4 billion
Profits: $251 million
Founded: 1913
Headquarters: San Francisco, California

Imagination has never been Chevron's strong suit. The biggest company in the West, they're known as a stuffy bastion of conservatism with a long history of aloofness and indifference to public opinion. A Wall Street analyst, speaking in 1986 to Scripps Howard News Service, put it this way: "The problem with Chevron is that it's a West Coast company run by very provincial people."

In the 1980s Chevron had their head handed to them. They didn't do as miserably as their international partner, Texaco, but it was bad enough. In the decade's first year, they cranked out sales of $40 billion and profited $2.4 billion. It was the biggest year the company—then called Standard Oil of California—ever had. And it still is. Coming out of the decade, Chevron's sales were below $30 billion and profits were way below what they were in 1980.

The amazing aspect of this slide is that it came after they paid $13.4 billion to buy Gulf Oil in 1984 and after they paid $2.5 billion for Tenneco's oil and gas operations in 1988. It all goes to show how important the price of oil is. In 1980, when the price was $34 a barrel, money rolled into San Francisco in such torrents Standard Oil of California didn't know what to do with it. One of their ideas was to buy up the mining company, AMAX, an overture, fortunately for them, rebuffed. So they bought Gulf. In 1986, when the price of oil dropped to as low as $12 a barrel, Chevron's profits nosedived.

Standard Oil of California changed their name—but not their operating style—in 1984. After buying Gulf, Chevron dismantled it. When the two compa-

THE DECADE'S BIGGEST CEO MONEY-MAKERS

Executive	Company	1980s Earnings
1. Charles Lazarus	Toys 'R' Us	$156.2 million
2. Steven Ross	Time Warner	$84.6 million
3. Craig McCaw	McCaw Cellular Comm.	$76.9 million
4. Lee Iacocca	Chrysler	$65.9 million
5. Michael Eisner	Walt Disney	$61.9 million
6. T. Boone Pickens Jr.	Mesa Petroleum	$56.9 million
7. Frederick Smith	Federal Express	$55.9 million
8. Paul Fireman	Reebok International	$54.5 million
9. Donald Pels	Lin Broadcasting	$49.8 million
10. Jim Manzi	Lotus Development	$47.9 million

Source: Business Week, 7 May 1990.

nies were joined in 1984, they had a combined payroll of 79,000. That was reduced to 54,000. Gulf headquarters in Pittsburgh was sold along with their 60 percent interest in Gulf Canada. And hundreds of Gulf service stations in 18 states were sold. In 1989 Chevron began rebranding the 3,000 Gulf service stations flying the Orange Disc banner in Texas, Louisiana, Arkansas and New Mexico into Chevron stations. To motorists in those states, Chevron delivered this message: "Welcome to the oil company you already know."

Chevron sells gasoline through 12,800 service stations in 33 states. However, 60 percent of their sales come from six states: Texas, California, Florida, Alabama, Georgia and Kentucky.

Chevron's nickname is "the good, gray Chevron." But Chevron isn't just gas. They also make chemicals—for industry, agriculture and consumer products—with 26 plants in 14 states and facilities in Brazil, Ecuador, Japan and France. Products include fertilizers and Ortho brand lawn and garden chemicals. In addition, Chevron mines and sells coal, uranium, platinum and palladium and supplies hot water to geothermal plants in California, Nevada and Utah. In 1989, Chevron's real estate subsidiary bought the 5,600-acre Gauer Ranch in Sonoma Valley, California—400 acres of vineyards and a winery called Vinwood Cellars. This foray into the wine business won't produce a Chateau Chevron label, though—the oil company's wine is sold under the Gauer Estate Vineyard label.

History. In 1879, a nomadic oilman from Pennsylvania named Demetrius Scofield and some partners formed the Pacific Coast Oil Company in California. At that time John D. Rockefeller's Standard Oil Company was shipping oil around the Horn to California. After oil was discovered under Los Angeles, Rockefeller waged a ruthless price war and forced Scofield to sell his company to Standard in 1900. When the Supreme Court broke up the Standard Oil trust in 1911, Scofield came back to head Standard Oil Company of California, one of 34 companies that emerged from the Rockefeller empire.

In 1932, Standard of California struck oil on the Persian Gulf island of Bahrain. They then paid King Ibn Saud (a desert warrior and ruler of the new country he named Saudi Arabia) 50,000 British pounds in gold for the rights to the Arabian oil fields. Texaco, Exxon and Mobil bought into the deal, and everyone made millions until the 1970s when the OPEC nations banded together to boost the price of oil. The Saudis then announced they wanted their fields back.

Owners and rulers. In 1989, Kenneth T. Derr, aged 52, became Chevron's sixth CEO and chairman of the board (1989 pay $948,000). Frequently described as low-key, tall, heavyset Derr (who graduated from Cornell) succeeded the more outspoken George M. Keller. Chevron's top executives and directors are white men. Former Secretary of State George Shultz sits on Chevron's board. He replaced Carla Hills, who went to work for the Bush administration. An employee stock trust owns 15 percent of stock; Pennzoil owns 10 percent.

A*s a place to work.* Chevron has a reputation as a bureaucratic, dull workplace. In 1986, they fired 4,500 employees, most of them middle managers. It amounted to a near 9 percent reduction of the work force. After the cutback, however, Chevron opened 10 resource centers and set up a job search program to help ex-employees find new jobs. Some workers are alienated by what they claim is a racist atmosphere at Chevron plants. In 1988, a jury awarded $165,000 in damages to a black plant worker, who charged he was fired because he had complained about racism and harassment. "There was evidence of offensive symbols and pictures of blacks with exaggerated features on the walls," he told the *Contra Costa Times.* "Chevron did attempt to clean up the walls at times, but it kept reappearing."

S*ocial responsibility.* In 1989, Chairman Kenneth Derr complained he was faced with "the curious situation of the city boycotting its biggest company." The city was San Francisco, which boycotts any company doing business in South Africa. Chevron owns half of Caltex Petroleum, operator of a South African refinery. A proxy resolution requiring them to get out of South Africa garnered more than 10 percent of the votes at the 1990 shareholders' meeting. Wilderness advocates were outraged in 1988 when the company tried to drill for petroleum in a Montana site inhabited by grizzly bears, mountain goats and wolves. Minorities were angry in 1989 when a Chevron oil refinery exploded in Richmond, north of San Francisco, a black, working-class town. Townspeople accused Chevron of "industrial racism" when the company allowed the fire to burn out of control for four days. The explosion came after years of complaints from workers and the town about a series of fires, toxic emissions (clouds and fumes), and the lack of safety precautions for employees. But there are

signs that Chevron is cleaning up their act—in 1988 they reduced by 90 percent the amount of pollutants released into the San Francisco Bay.

In 1990 they began to run ads showing their concern for endangered species, threatened habitats and wildlife at a cost of $6 million a year. The ads are also airing in the Soviet Union to reassure environmentalists opposing a possible Chevron drilling project there.

G*lobal presence.* Chevron has plants in France, Japan, Brazil and Ecuador, and they operate in 80 countries. In 1936, Chevron, along with Texaco, formed Caltex, which develops wells and refineries in over 50 countries in the Far East, Middle East and Africa.

S*tock performance.* Chevron stock bought for $1,000 in 1980 sold for $4,256 on January 2, 1990.

Chevron Corporation, 225 Bush Street, San Francisco, CA, 94104; (415) 894-7700.

5

#1 *in retail sales of gasoline*

Employees: 53,500
Sales: $24 billion
Profits: $1.6 billion
Founded: 1889
Headquarters: Chicago, Illinois

Social Conscience

Amoco is the oil company of middle America, established by John D. Rockefeller in Indiana to refine Ohio oil for midwestern farmers. Even their name means American Oil Company. For nearly 100 years their corporate name was Standard Oil (Indiana). They scrapped it in 1985, four years short of their 100th birthday, in favor of Amoco, the brand name under which much of their gasoline is sold. They sell their fuel at 11,400 service stations in 30 states. In the heart of their territory—the Midwest—their stations still fly the Standard name and reign as kings of the road. They sell nearly 14 percent of the gas in the midwest. Nationally, Amoco supplied 8.7 percent of the gasoline sold in 1988. Their stations in the East stretch from Massachusetts to Florida.

Amoco still views the world with midwestern eyes, although they now operate in 40 countries and drill for oil in the North Sea, Egypt, Gabon, Argentina and the South China Sea, among other places. Compared with other giant oil pumpers, Amoco remains largely a domestic company. In 1988 they derived 77 percent of their revenues from the U.S. Throw in Canada and the percentage hits 85 percent. Amoco became a much bigger Canadian player when they paid $4.2 billion in 1988 to acquire financially strapped Dome Petroleum. That made Amoco North America's largest natural gas company.

Like other big oil producers, Amoco has an important stake in petrochemicals. They're major suppliers of PTA (purified terephtalic acid), the raw material for polyester, and polypropylene resins and fibers, now widely used in carpets. Their synthetic carpet yarn, Genesis, is guaranteed for five years not to fade or stain. In 1988 chemicals accounted for one-third of Amoco's profits.

From a central control point in Tulsa, Oklahoma, Amoco controls 15,000 miles of pipelines that transport crude oil to refineries and chemical feedstocks from refineries to chemical plants. It's the nation's largest pipeline network. Amoco also transports crude oil in 14 tankers. One of their tankers, the *Cadiz*, broke up off the coast of France in 1978, discharging 223,000 tons of crude oil over 130 miles. The suit brought by the French government was finally settled in 1989 when Amoco was ordered to pay $85 million.

Amoco gets high marks from activists who monitor corporate social responsibility programs. They have been a bulwark of support for community rebuilding in their hometown, Chicago, where their skyscraper overlooks Lake Michigan. They elected to stay in Chicago rather than retreat to the suburbs. They were the first company in the nation to take seriously a program to buy products and services from minority-owned companies. They have had a vice president for environmental affairs and safety since 1987. Entering the 1980s, they had an all-white, male board. Exiting the decade, they had one woman director (retired Equitable Insurance executive Ruth Block) and one black (Argonne National Laboratory research director Walter Massey). In 1987 the Council on Economic Priorities gave their first Corporate Conscience Award for community involvement to Amoco. In 1989 Amoco reported to the CEP they had 294 women and 303 minorities earning $50,000 or more per year.

Stock performance. Amoco stock bought for $1,000 in 1980 sold for $4,568 on January 2, 1990.

Amoco Corporation, 200 East Randolph Drive, Chicago, IL 60601; (312) 856-6111.

6

Shell Oil

#2 *in retail sales of gasoline*

Employees: 31,300
Sales: $21.7 billion
Profits: $1.4 billion
Founded: 1907
Headquarters: Houston, Texas

Most people think Shell is an American company. And why not? They have been operating in the United States for over 75 years. They bring up crude oil in 17 states, the Gulf of Mexico and offshore California. They refine this oil and natural gas liquids in refineries in seven states, operate 10 chemical plants in five states and own a pipeline system covering 8,800 miles (plus interests in other pipeline networks). What's more, they have 10,800 service stations in 40 states, pumping more gas into American cars than any other oil company except Amoco (and

LARGEST MERGERS OF THE 1980s

	Acquiring Company	Cost	Year
1. SmithKline Beckman	Beecham Group	$16.1 billion	1989
2. Gulf Oil	Chevron	$13.3 billion	1984
3. Kraft	Philip Morris	$13.0 billion	1988
4. Squibb	Bristol-Myers	$12.0 billion	1989
5. Warner Communications	Time	$11.7 billion	1989
6. Getty Oil	Texaco	$10.2 billion	1984
7. Conoco	Du Pont	$8.0 billion	1981
8. Sohio	British Petroleum	$7.8 billion	1987
9. Marathon Oil	USX	$6.6 billion	1981
10. RCA	General Electric	$6.4 billion	1986

this lead switches back and forth between Amoco and Shell).

But no, they're not an American company. In fact, the last vestiges of American ownership were eliminated during the 1980s. Houston-based Shell Oil entered the 1980s with a listing on the New York Stock Exchange, representing 30.5 percent of their shares. The other 69.5 percent was held by the Anglo-Dutch combine, Royal Dutch/Shell Group, which runs neck and neck with Exxon for the title of the world's largest oil company. In the mid-1980s the Anglo-Dutch parent decided to buy up all the shares of the American company they didn't already own. The independence the American company enjoyed was evident in the bickering that followed the bid from Europe. Royal Dutch/Shell offered $55 a share. The board of directors of the American company rejected it. In the end the parent company upped their offer to $60 a share. So now you can no longer buy shares in Shell Oil of the United States.

However, the U.S.-based Shell Oil continues to issue an annual report covering their operations and has a board of directors in which Americans predominate. In the 1988 report the only mention of their Anglo-Dutch parent is the reference that Shell Oil researchers "have access to certain research conducted around the world by the Royal Dutch/Shell Group of Companies."

John Bookout retired as Shell's president in 1988 after 12 years at the helm. He is credited with vastly improving Shell's U.S. position: finding new sources of oil, resisting the temptations to diversify or pull off a mega-merger and keeping open only those service stations that pumped a lot of gasoline. In an interview with the *Wall Street Journal* on the eve of his retirement, Bookout said: "You don't have to go back too far ago that Texaco was still bragging that they were marketing in 50 states when we were leaving as fast as we could." Bookout is a geologist. His replacement, Frank H. Richardson, is also a geologist. After leaving Shell, Bookout was elected to the board of the parent company, which means monthly trips to either London or The Hague.

History. In 1907 Shell Transport & Trading—an oil company founded by Marcus Samuel, a Jewish merchant in London—merged with Royal Dutch Petroleum, an East Indies oil company headed by a xenophobic Dutchman, Henri Deterding. Samuel named his company Shell after the cargoes of seashells—popular in the Victorian era—he brought back from the Far East in the mid-1800s. Samuel's eldest son bought kerosene made from Russian crude oil and shipped it in tankers to the Far East. After the merger, Deterding took over, intent on fighting rival Rockefeller's

Standard Oil all over the globe. In 1912, a year after the Supreme Court had broken up the Standard Oil Trust, Deterding moved into the U.S. Before long Shell had made major oil discoveries in California, and by 1929 Shell gasoline was being sold in all 48 states. Deterding's erratic behavior was not an asset to Shell, though. He wrote in his memoirs that "if I were dictator of the world—and please, Mr. Printer, set this in larger type—I would shoot all idlers on sight." After running the company for 36 years, Deterding retired, moved to Germany and was a major supporter of the Nazi Party (Hitler sent a wreath to his funeral).

Owners and rulers. The British and the Dutch but shares of the two parents—Royal Dutch and Shell Transport—trade on the New York Stock Exchange. The days of Deterding are long gone. Many of the brightest professionals in the oil business run Shell.

As a place to work. One of the best. They may be the least narrow-minded of all the oil giants—and in the U.S. they have a strong pay-and-benefits package. During the 1980s, when oil companies took a meat ax to their work forces, Shell more or less held the line.

Social responsibility. Shell tries to be a good citizen in the U.S., but their parent's massive involvement in South Africa has put them on an international boycott list. Boston and other cities refuse to allow municipal-owned vehicles to fill up with Shell gas. Although Shell has never had a spill to rival Exxon's *Valdez*, they have had numerous problems at their refinery in Martinez, California, including a massive spill there in 1988. In 1989, the company agreed to pay $20 million in claims.

Global presence. The bright yellow, scalloped shell is everywhere. Shell has companies in 103 countries. They do 46 percent of their sales in Europe, 18 percent in the Far East, 24 percent in the U.S., and 12 percent elsewhere in North and South America.

Stock performance. Shell stock bought for $1,000 in 1980 sold for $5,836 on January 2, 1990.

Shell Oil Company, One Shell Plaza, Houston, TX 77002; (713) 241-4083.

7

BP The British Petroleum Company p.l.c.

#1 *in U.S. oil production*

Employees: 47,850
Sales: $15.4 billion
Profits: $1.6 billion
Founded: 1909
Headquarters: Cleveland, Ohio

The largest U.S. oil producer is—surprise—British. Cleveland-based BP America is actually the old Standard Oil of Ohio company, except they're now 100 percent-owned by British Petroleum, the world's third largest oil company (behind Exxon and Shell). Sohio, as the company used to be called, entered the 1980s with their own stock market listing even though BP already owned 53 percent of the shares. The British secured this stake in a 1969 swap that gave Sohio access to BP's newly found oil reserves on Alaska's North Slope. For 17 years the British allowed Americans to continue to run Sohio. They only asked for three seats on Sohio's 16-member board of directors. Then, in 1986, the people in London decided the Americans were making a mess of things. They sacked the top managers and replaced them with Brits. And the following year they got their hands on $7.9 billion and bought up all remaining Sohio shares. They might as well be flying the Union Jack on the Standard Oil skyscraper that dominates the Cleveland skyline.

The BP flag is being hoisted wherever the British can find a flagpole. More than 1,000 U.S. service stations were renamed BP during 1989, including former Mobil stations on the West Coast and Gulf service stations in Nashville. In 1990 BP will haul down the Boron name on stations in Ohio and neighboring states, replacing it with BP. At the same time, they'll substitute BP for Gulf on service stations in the Southeast. That will still leave the Sohio name on service stations in Ohio. Changing Sohio to BP is a little trickier because they're the brand leader in the state, but the British have served notice that Sohio, too, will eventually fall to the BP juggernaut. All 7,700 stations in 26 states will eventually be required to fly the BP name. British Petroleum wants one global brand. So much for the original John D. Rockefeller company.

BP America is the largest domestic oil producer by virtue of their Alaskan output of 826,000 barrels a day, roughly 40 percent of all the oil coming out of Alaska. BP owns or has interests in 12,000 miles of pipeline that can carry 2 million barrels of oil a day. They also own 50 percent of the 800-mile Trans-Alaskan Pipeline System.

At one point, the British government was the principal owner of British Petroleum, a company midwifed by Winston Churchill in 1914 and known as the Anglo-Persian Oil Company and the Anglo-Iranian Oil Company before adopting BP in 1954. However, Margaret Thatcher sold all the government shares, and the Middle Eastern kingdom of Kuwait has emerged as the largest holder, with 9.9 percent of the shares. One could argue that Arabs are the major owners of the U.S.'s most productive oil field.

Back in Cleveland, BP makes a special effort to be a good corporate citizen. Their philanthropic contributions totaled $10.7 million in 1988, and they pumped another $500,000 into low-income housing investments.

BP America ranks as one of America's 25 largest companies by almost any financial measurement. Over half of British Petroleum's assets are now located in the U.S. Among these are Purina Mills, the nation's largest animal feed producer, which BP bought from Ralston Purina, and a chemical division that is the world's largest producer of acrylonitrile, used in the production of synthetic fibers and plastics.

BP America employs more than 40,000 people, which means Americans make up the biggest nationality in the entire British Petroleum work force (including the British). As of 1990, Americans held only 6 percent of British Petroleum shares.

BP America, 200 Public Square, Cleveland, OH 44114; (216) 586-4141.

8

AtlanticRichfieldCompany ◆

#7 *in convenience stores*

Employees: 26,526
Sales: $15.3 billion
Profits: $1.9 billion
Founded: 1866
Headquarters: Los Angeles, California

Social Conscience

Millions of oil credit cards are stuffed in the wallets of American motorists, but not one bears an Arco logo. Arco, formally known as Atlantic Richfield, abolished the cards in 1982, saying they would concentrate on delivering low prices—a typical move for a company proud of being a maverick. Arco used to be bogged down in staid Philadelphia as Atlantic Refining, an almost forgotten remnant of the Rockefeller oil empire; now they're based in glitzy Los Angeles—and on the West Coast Arco pumps more gasoline than anybody else and operates a string of am/pm convenience stores to boot. Between 1965 and 1980 Arco transformed themselves into one of the nation's major natural resource companies under the inspired leadership of Robert O. Anderson, a Stetson-hatted, bow–tie wearing, cowboy–boot shod oilman with a strong interest in modern art. Since 1986 Arco has been transformed again, selling off businesses and unwanted gas stations, becoming leaner and meaner. Measured by how much profit they make on their sales, they emerged from the 1980s as the most profitable company in the oil industry.

History. Atlantic Petroleum Storage Company, later known as Atlantic Refining, was founded in 1866 by Charles Lockwood, James S. Wright and other early pioneers of the Pennsylvania oil industry. Atlantic became part of Standard Oil in 1874 and was set loose by the 1911 Supreme Court decree breaking up the Rockefeller-owned trust. Atlantic was handicapped from the start because

Actor Edward Olmos (right) plays the role of real-life teacher Jaime Escalante (left) in "Stand and Deliver," a film about a math teacher who inspired unmotivated Los Angeles minority students to academic achievement. Arco provided crucial funding for the film.

they'd served as the refinery arm of the Standard Oil Trust—and therefore had no oil reserves.

As big as Arco is today, they bear the stamp of Robert Orville Anderson, said to be most comfortable when riding horseback on his 100,000-acre spread in New Mexico. An associate once recalled Anderson sitting in a meeting on Wall Street, looking at his watch, noting it was 4:00 P.M. and muttering, almost automatically, "Well, it's time to saddle up." Anderson no longer has anything to do with Arco, but no one can gainsay that he built this oil company. A great success as an independent oil operator, first in the refinery business and then as a wildcatter, Anderson sold his Hondo Oil Company to Atlantic Refining of Philadelphia in 1962, receiving 500,000 shares of Atlantic stock. At that point, at age 44, Bob Anderson was ready to retire from the oil business. He was slated to succeed Walter Paepcke as director of the Aspen Institute for Humanistic Studies at Aspen, Colorado, a center where businessmen could be exposed to humanistic values. The place was made to order for Bob Anderson, and he has remained close to it.

What brought Bob Anderson back into the petroleum business? His Atlantic Refining shares made him the company's largest stockholder and gave him a board seat. Sitting on that board, he quickly realized Atlantic Refining was a poorly managed affair, with no great chances of surviving unless they had better direction. So in 1965 Bob Anderson came down off the mountain and went to Philadelphia to give that direction. "I figured," he said in an interview, "that I would get in there when I was 47—and get the hell out on my 50th birthday." However, that scenario didn't unfold in Philadelphia.

Bob Anderson made his first big move in 1965. He reached clear across the country to acquire Richfield Oil, a Los Angeles-based company that was, after Chevron, California's largest oil producer.

The new company was called Atlantic Richfield.

The merger was a strange one. An East Coast company acquired a West Coast company. Neither had much business between the two coasts. But Bob Anderson made it work. He filled in the middle part of the country by buying the assets of Sinclair Oil, including a big petrochemical complex in Houston and service stations in the East and Midwest. But what really fueled Arco's growth was a Richfield drilling team that struck it big on Prudhoe Bay on Alaska's North Slope in 1968. The field ranked as the largest in North America. Some 1.6 million barrels of oil flowed *daily* from Prudhoe in 1987, representing 20 percent of U.S. oil production.

In 1972, Anderson, never fond of the East, moved Arco's headquarters to Los Angeles, where they were closer to the source of the company's oil supply. They were also closer to Anderson's Diamond A ranch in Roswell, New Mexico.

Helping Anderson transform the company was Thornton F. Bradshaw, an ex-Harvard Business School professor who joined Atlantic Refining in 1956, becoming president in 1964. Bradshaw articulated a public affairs philosophy that made Arco sound, at times, like the oil industry's flaming radical.

For a while, in the 1970s, it seemed Arco—and Anderson—could do no wrong. And indeed it's difficult to trip up when the basic product you deal in enters the decade selling at $3 a barrel and moves out of it heading for $30 a barrel. Arco was awash in money, which they used to buy Anaconda, one of the great names in American copper history. Arco began mining copper and silver and producing aluminum.

When oil prices broke in the 1980s, Arco was far more alert than other oil producers to the consequences. They quickly hunkered down. They fled the metals businesses and stopped selling gasoline in 12 eastern states, giving up 2,000 service stations, leaving them with 1,700 stations in four Western states (California, Arizona, Nevada and Oregon). They even sold the refinery in Philadelphia that was virtually their birthright, as well as nearly 1,000 U.S. oil properties. In retrenching, Arco halved the company payroll. The result was a much more sharply focused company (sales dropped from $28 billion in 1981 to $15 billion in 1986). The massive restructuring included taking on a heavy load of debt and the buying up of big chunks of stock to make themselves less attractive to hit-and-run raiders.

Owners and rulers. When Robert O. Anderson left Arco in 1986, he was the largest individual shareholder, but he held less than 1/2 of 1 percent of the stock. His stock and real estate were worth about $200 million, enough to earn him a place on the *Forbes* list of the 400 richest Americans. Lodwrick M. Cook, who grew up on a farm in Grand Cane, Louisiana, and who joined Arco fresh out of engineering school, became CEO in 1985. He's a folksy character who instituted a new series of face-to-face meetings with employees called PrimeTime. He made $2.3 million in 1989.

As a place to work. How can a company that reduced their payroll from 54,433 in 1981 to 26,526 in 1986 be a good place to work? It depends, of course, on how the cutbacks were handled. Arco generally got good marks. Many of the 6,300 employees who opted for early retirement walked out with fat bundles of cash. Don Murray, Arco's employee relations vice president, called it "the most generous enhanced retirement package for its time in industry." For those who remained, it was clear that Arco was turning into a no-frills, cost-conscious company. The pay-and-benefit package is still super, though slightly diluted.

Arco is exemplary in other areas. They've long been the industry leader in the hiring and promotion of minorities and women. During the restructuring of the 1980s, the percentage of women and minorities in Arco's total work force, and in professional positions, increased sharply. The company also speaks forthrightly to its employees through a newspaper, *The Spark*, which reflects a vivacity and sense of humor all too rare in corporate literature. Looking back on the retrenchment of the 1980s, Phoebe Wood, manager of corporate finance, put it this way: "Arco is leaner but it isn't meaner."

Social responsibility. While Anderson is gone, his legacy lingers. Arco rates as the most interesting of all the major oil companies because they do the unexpected. They broke ranks with the industry by opposing the oil depletion allowance. They were the first major oil company to support diversion of highway tax funds for mass transit uses. Arco issues the best corporate report in the country on "do good" activities. Called "To Make a Difference: Arco and Society," the report runs to 100 pages and details the myriad of programs in which Arco is involved, including a listing of all the grants their foundation makes.

Global presence. Small—but growing. In 1986, for the first time, foreign production of crude oil and natural gas liquids accounted for 10 percent of the company total. Eighty-four percent of that foreign production came from the offshore waters of Indonesia, but Arco is now drilling for oil in Gabon, the Congo, Egypt, New Zealand, Ecuador, Turkey and Syria.

Stock performance. Atlantic Richfield stock bought for $1,000 in 1980 sold for $4,761 on January 2, 1990.

Atlantic Richfield Company, 515 South Flower Street, Los Angeles, CA 90071; (213) 486-3511.

9

Employees: 21,400
Sales: $12.4 billion
Profits: $219 million
Founded: 1917
Headquarters: Bartlesville, Oklahoma

What price freedom? Under attack in the mid-1980s by two corporate raiders, T. Boone Pickens, Jr., and Carl C. Icahn, Phillips fought them off by going deeply into hock to buy up their own stock. Their debt quadrupled to $8.9 billion, and they disposed of their uranium mines, oil-shale projects and geothermal fields. The result is a leaner Phillips, but they still pack a big punch. Their three refineries at Borger and Sweeney, Texas, and Woods

Cross, Utah, feed 11,000 service stations in 28 states, primarily in the Midwest. Phillips is also one of the largest producers of natural gas liquids, which are refined and used to make plastics (ethylene, propylene, polyethylene and polypropylene) at 21 plants (10 of them in Texas). In 1988 these petrochemical operations were so strong they earned nearly as much profit as the entire oil and gas activities. Ekofisk, the North Sea oilfield Phillips discovered in 1969, was still going strong 20 years later, accounting for one-fifth of the company's crude oil supplies.

The 1980s were traumatic for Phillips because of an explosion at Phillips' Pasadena, Texas, polyethylene plant that killed 23 people and caused $500 million in damages. The federal goverment fined Phillips $5.7 million for 575 violations connected with the explosion.

History. Frank Phillips was born in Scotia, Nebraska, in 1873 and worked as a ranch hand and barber (he had his own rainwater-based cure for baldness, "Phillips' Mountain Sage"). After marrying the local banker's daughter in 1897, Phillips sold the three barber shops he owned and became a traveling bond salesman. In a few years, he'd earned commissions of $75,000 and began investing in speculative oil leases in Oklahoma. In 1903, he set up Anchor Oil and began drilling; his first two holes were dry, but the next 80 were gushers.

In 1917, Frank and his brother L. E. incorporated Phillips Petroleum Company to replace Anchor. Under the leadership of "Uncle Frank" (as his employees called him) and his almost evangelical faith in research and development, Phillips rapidly took the lead in airplane fuel and discovered a new process for the conversion of waste gas into gasoline. The first Phillips gas station opened in Wichita, Kansas, in 1927 and the gasoline was called Phillips 66 after U.S. Highway 66 (which runs from Texas to Chicago). Frank Phillips remained chairman until his retirement in 1949, earning a reputation for rugged individualism and eccentric egoism. Among other things, he constructed a 4,000-acre retreat near Bartlesville named Woolaroc, complete with a lodge modeled after his Nebraska birthplace and stocks of exotic birds and animals.

While other oil companies were heavily invested in Middle Eastern oil fields, Phillips got most of their oil from sources in the U.S., Egypt and the Alaskan North Slope. In the 1970s, Phillips drilled the first successful oil fields in the Norwegian section of the North Sea, where production almost doubled from 1988 to 1989. Today over half of Phillips' oil comes from abroad. Chairman and CEO C. J. Silas took home $1.3 million in 1989.

Phillips came out of the decade with about 20,000 employees instead of the 30,000 they had in 1980. But for those remaining, their stake in the company was much bigger as Phillips has adopted an Employee Stock Ownership Plan that held 20 percent of the company's shares at decade's end.

Stock performance. Phillips stock bought for $1,000 in 1980 sold for $2,728 on January 2, 1990.

Phillips Petroleum, Phillips Building, Bartlesville, OK 74004; (918) 661-6600.

10

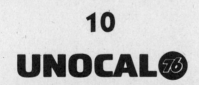

UNOCAL 76

Employees: 17,800
Sales: $10.1 billion
Profits: $260 million
Founded: 1890
Headquarters: Los Angeles, California

Social Conscience

No one ever fills up at a Union 76 service station to save money. Their prices are usually the highest around. And, if you're driving an older automobile that takes leaded gasoline, forget about Union—they don't offer it, although they have three grades of unleaded gas. On the other hand, Union 76, Unocal's retail face, is not to be discounted. They go their own way, emphasizing full-service in an era of self-service, spending their advertising dol-

lars featuring a folksy service station manager called Murph and preaching that their gasoline is better. The appeal is old-fashioned but has worked. In areas where they operate—Unocal has 10,600 stations and 340 truck stops, mostly in the West—they're tough competitors. In California, their home state, they rank right behind the two leaders, Arco and Chevron.

The emphasis on Victorian virtues stemmed from the long reign of crusty Fred L. Hartley, who joined the company as a refinery laborer in 1939, became CEO in 1964 and ruled the roost for the next 24 years. An autocrat with no use for government regulations or environmental critics, Hartley had Unocal sponsor newscaster Paul Harvey on radio because he approved of Harvey's conservative political views. After Arco captured first place in the California market by stressing low prices, high volume, convenience stores and no credit cards, Hartley had this observation: "We know all about Arco. They sell hamburgers and hot dogs, and they give their gasoline away. Anybody can do that." Unocal gets just over half their crude from offshore fields located throughout the world; two-thirds of their oil comes from the U.S. Unocal's refineries are located near Los Angeles, San Francisco, Chicago and Beaumont, Texas.

Questioned for years about the lack of women on Unocal's board of directors, Hartley responded by citing the scarcity of engineering and technical skills among women. After he stepped down as CEO in 1988 in favor of Richard J. Stegemeier (who made $1.1 million in 1989), Unocal named their first female director: Ann McLaughlin, former Secretary of Labor. Unocal's executive vice president and vice chairman is Reagan's former Transportation Secerataty Claude Brinegar.

In the mid-1980s raider Boone Pickens made a run at Unocal. Hartley repulsed him by borrowing $4.3 billion to buy up one-third of Unocal's stock. "The purpose of our company is to run it," said Hartley. "We're not for sale." Through an Employee Stock Ownership Plan, Unocal employees own 8.6 percent of the company.

In 1979, a massive toxic spill at the Unocal refinery in Rodeo, California, released phenol, a lysol like chemical. Unocal never reported the spill and refused to spend money to prevent other

A Sun Company tank wagon in 1907.

such spills from occurring. Tom Billecci, a plant supervisor, took this allegation and others like it to 13 federal and state agencies. The Sierra Club joined forces with Billecci and filed additional suits against Unocal. In early 1990, a judge approved an agreement requiring Unocal to pay $4.2 million for illegally dumping pollutants from the Rodeo refinery from 1977 to 1986.

S*tock performance.*   Unocal stock bought for $1,000 in 1980 sold for $3,645 on January 2, 1990.

Unocal Corporation, P.O. Box 7600, Los Angeles, CA 90051; (213) 977-7600.

11

Employees: 21,500
Sales: $9.8 billion
Profits: $98 million
Founded: 1886
Headquarters: Radnor, Pennsylvania

Sun, an oil company that celebrated their centennial in 1986, spent the 1980s undoing their 1970s' attempt to convert them-

selves into a conglomerate. They entered the 1980s organized into 14 companies operating in a bunch of nonoil businesses like trucking, industrial distribution, fish farms and convenience stores. At one time they even made an abortive bid for a medical supply outfit, Becton, Dickinson. Then came the early 1980s and superhigh oil prices, prompting Sun to scrap this strategy and return to their oil-and-gas heritage. Because they were supplying little of the crude oil that ended up as gasoline sold at Sunoco stations, they decided to buy themselves some oil producing fields. In 1982 they bought Texas Pacific Oil from Seagram for $2.3 billion. In 1984 they spent $350 million to acquire oil fields in California's Kern County. "There's no question," said Robert McClements, Jr., Sun president in the early 1980s, "that this is the heart of our business."

However, in 1988, by which time he was Sun chairman and CEO, McClements had a change of heart. Now the venerable Sun Company decided they really didn't need to drill for oil in the U.S. Presto, in 1989 they created a separate company out of their oil and gas operations. (At birth Oryx Energy was the U.S.'s largest independent oil and gas producer.) The old Sun Company kept their refineries and service stations. They will buy their crude oil on the open market. (Perhaps Oryx will sell them some.) But wait a minute, Sun is not completely out of oil and gas production—that's only in the U.S. They continue to pump, and explore for, oil in other places, especially Canada and the North Sea. However, their 1988 ouput of 42,000 barrels a day was well below the needs of their 7,000 U.S. service stations (including the 1,000 stations added in 1988 when Sun bought Atlantic Petroleum).

As the 1980s were winding down, McClements assured shareholders: "I want to confirm to you that we will remain dominantly an oil company." But of course who knows what the 1990s will bring? (McClements took home $1.6 million in 1989.)

Sun started life in 1886 when former schoolteacher Joseph Newton Pew told his young nephew Robert to buy two oil leases in Ohio. Three years later, Newton joined with his friend Edward Emerson to found the Sun Oil Line Company. Pew later bought out his business partner and various male members of the Pew family ran the company for many years. R. Anderson ("Andy") Pew, a great-grandson of the founder, is the only Pew still visible at Sun; he sits on the board of directors and is president of the Helios Capital Corporation, Sun's real estate investment arm.

Sun's 1968 merger with Tulsa-based Sunray DX had its genesis in 1967 at an oil industry dinner held in Midland, Texas. Company representatives were seated alphabetically—so Sun's president, Robert G. Dunlop, found himself seated next to the chairman of Sunray DX. "We got to talking," Dunlop later recalled, "and it seemed there might be an opportunity for us to put the companies together." And so they did. Twenty years later Sun took down the DX signs from the stations in the midsection of the country and replaced them with Sunoco banners. So much for dinner conversation.

Sun has extensive coal operations in Virginia, Kentucky, West Virginia, Wyoming and Utah, and operates seven ocean tankers and a fleet of tugs and barges. Sun also has a real estate firm, Radnor Corporation, which develops properties for commercial and private use.

Stock performance. Sun stock bought for $1,000 in 1980 sold for $3,515 on January 2, 1990.

Sun Inc., 100 Matsonford Road, Radnor, PA 19087; (215) 293-6000.

12

OXY

Occidental Petroleum Corporation

Employees: 53,000
Sales: $20.1 billion
Profits: $256 million
Founded: 1920
Headquarters: Los Angeles, California

This company's CEO is better known than the company. Known to friends and enemies as Oxy, Occidental Petroleum is one of the giants of American business, but the name doesn't mean much to most people. They're big in the oil business—but they have no refineries or gasoline stations. They're also big in chemicals—but they don't make any finished products. They're one of the U.S.'s leading coal producers—but the coal is sold to electric utilities and steel foundries. They're the major owner of the country's biggest beef and pork producer—but they ship it in boxes to supermarkets and their name doesn't appear on the plastic-wrapped meats you see in refrigerated cases. On the other hand, Oxy is Dr. Armand Hammer's company—and even if you haven't the foggiest notion of what Oxy does, you're likely to have heard of him.

As he entered the 1980s, Armand Hammer was 81 years old. Time to retire? Not on your life. All that Occidental Petroleum did during the 1980s was double their sales (from $9.6 billion to more than $20 billion); buy the nation's largest beef packer, IBP, for $900 million (and then sell, at a $100 million profit, 49 percent of the firm); buy the nation's 18th largest oil company, Cities Service, for $4 billion (and then sell their refineries and service stations); scoop up, for $3 billion, one of the nation's biggest natural gas pipeline companies, MidCon; buy, for $3.1 billion, the chemical businesses of Diamond Shamrock and Cain Chemical (making Oxy the largest producer of automotive brake fluids and the third largest maker of ethylene, a raw material for plastics); discover a huge oil field in a flooded plain east of the Andes mountains in Colombia;

and begin mining, with Chinese partners, what promises to be the biggest open pit coal mine in the world in mainland China.

That business activity was aside from the personal ventures of Dr. Hammer, who went to Moscow numerous times to meet with one leader after another to arrange deals and seek release of political prisoners, traveled to China to make deals with the leaders of that country, launched a campaign to raise $1 billion for cancer research and, using $86 million of corporate funds, began construction of a museum to house the three Hammer art collections next to Occidental headquarters on Wilshire Boulevard in Los Angeles.

History. In 1956, Dr. Armand Hammer and his third wife moved to Los Angeles, intending to lead quiet lives as retirees. Hammer began looking for a good tax shelter, and he settled on Oxy. The company had a few oil leases in California and assets of $78,000. They had not paid a stockholder dividend since 1934. Hammer and his wife each loaned the company $50,000 to drill wells on the leases. The unexpected happened—Oxy struck oil in Fresno county, about 200 miles north of Los Angeles. Hammer came out of retirement and entered the oil business.

Hammer's father was a radical socialist physician in New York City, and his leftist contacts in America had given young Armand a toehold in Russia after the Bolshevik triumph there. After World War I, Hammer went to Russia with a medical degree and much-needed medical supplies. He met Lenin, who thanked him and suggested a trade: America's wheat for Russian furs and caviar. Later he offered Hammer a concession on a Russian asbestos mine. By 1930, Hammer had made several million dollars in Russian-American trade.

When Stalin came to power, Hammer fled to the U.S. with an enormous cache of Russian Czarist and Soviet art, which he sold for a fortune. He then dabbled in bourbon and beer-barrel manufacturing, and sold Angus bull semen to breeders.

Hammer brought his wheeler-dealer techniques to Occidental when he convinced the Libyans to give an oil concession to Oxy, and Oxy made a major oil strike in 1966. Hammer continued to enjoy an excellent rapport with the Soviets; in the mid-1970s, he struck a $20 billion, 20-year fertilizer deal with them. In 1970, after Muammar al Qaddafi led a coup d'etat in Libya, Hammer was forced to sell 51 percent of Oxy's oil operation to Libya. After years of being mistakenly connected with Arm & Hammer baking soda, Armand Hammer bought a stake in its maker, Church & Dwight, in the 1980s and got a board seat.

Owners and rulers. As 1990 opened, Armand Hammer remained chairman and CEO of the company he had built from a couple of unpromising oil leases. Oxy now ranks as the nation's 16th largest industrial company based on sales. On May 21, 1990, as Occidental Petroleum held their annual meeting on his birthday, Dr. Hammer turned 92. Two heirs apparent—former Dow Chemical president Zoltan Merszei and former First National Bank of Chicago president A. Robert Abboud—were dispatched by Dr. Hammer during the 1980s and replaced by Dr. Ray Irani, a PhD in chemical engineering who joined Oxy in 1983 and was named president in 1984. He is the seventh president since 1968. Dr. Hammer's grandson, Michael A. Hammer, serves as secretary of Oxy and is the youngest board member (he was 34 in 1990). Armand Hammer's 1989 pay was $2.3 million.

The 1981 acquisition of IBP (once known as Iowa Beef Processors) made Los Angeles real estate developer David Murdoch the largest Oxy shareholder—he then tried to dump Dr. Hammer. However, Oxy's board of directors, known as the oldest board in America (10 are over the age of 70), rallied behind Hammer and bought out Murdoch, paying a premium for his shares to get rid of him.

Social responsibility. The federal government finally succeeded during the 1980s in getting Oxy to assume some responsibility for Hooker Chemical's dumping of toxic wastes in Love Canal near Niagara Falls (Oxy acquired Hooker in 1968). A North Sea drilling platform owned by Oxy exploded on July 6, 1988, killing 166 people in the worst disaster in 25 years of oil exploration in the North Sea. In summer 1989 Dr. Hammer won an important personal victory when President George Bush pardoned him for making illegal political contributions to

President Richard Nixon's 1972 reelection campaign. His conviction had resulted in a sentence of one year's probation and a $3,000 fine.

Stock performance. Occidental Petroleum stock bought for $1,000 in 1980 sold for $2,704 on January 2, 1990.

Occidental Petroleum, 10889 Wilshire Boulevard, Los Angeles, CA 90224; (213) 208-8800.

13

PENNZOIL COMPANY

#1 *in motor oil*

Employees: 10,400
Sales: $2.3 billion
Profits: $104 million
Founded: 1889
Headquarters: Houston, Texas

Talk about hitting the jackpot. This small oil company received a check for $3 billion from Texaco in 1988 as settlement of a suit won in a Houston courtroom. The suit charged Texaco with interfering in an agreement Pennzoil had to acquire Getty Oil. Three billion dollars exceeded Pennzoil's total annual sales. And it was nearly double all the profits Pennzoil made during the 1980s. Pennzoil's lawyer Joseph Jamail pocketed a fee estimated at $420 million, thrusting him onto *Forbes'* list of the 400 richest Americans.

The question immediately became: What would Pennzoil's tough leader, J. Hugh Liedtke, do with all that money? In early 1990 he put up $2.1 billion to buy about 9 percent of Chevron and another $43 million to pick up 80 percent ownership of the Jiffy Lube chain.

Burly J. Hugh Liedtke is considered the father of Pennzoil. He was born in 1922 in Tulsa, Oklahoma—the petroleum capital of the world at that time. His father was a judge and a lawyer for Gulf Oil, and young Hugh spent his summers working in the oil fields. He attended Amherst College, served in the Navy during World War II and then went to the University of Texas law school where he rented a room from then-congressman Lyndon B. Johnson.

After graduating, Liedtke befriended an oil-field equipment salesman named George Bush. In 1953, Hugh and his younger brother Bill joined with Bush to found Zapata Petroleum. They borrowed $1 million to finance an oil-drilling scheme that paid off handsomely: Out of 137 holes drilled, not one was dry. In two years, they had revenues of $86 million and profits of $12 million. Bush sold his shares and eventually became president of the U.S.

Liedtke stayed in the oil business and in 1962 bought control of J. Paul Getty's South Penn Oil Company which he merged with Zapata to create Pennzoil. The new name was designed to cash in on the name recognition of South Penn's big product, a yellow can of lubricant oil. Pennzoil is the nation's best-selling motor oil and has used Arnold Palmer as a TV advertising spokesman. In 1972 a Pennzoil jet flew almost $750,000 in Nixon campaign funds from Texas to Washington, and some of the money turned up in a Watergate burglar's bank account. In the end, Pennzoil was not charged with criminal violations. In 1990 James L. Pate became president and CEO while Leidtke remained chairman. Pate, an economist and former advisor to President Gerald Ford, joined Pennzoil in 1976.

Stock performance. Pennzoil company stock bought for $1,000 in 1980 sold for $3,680 on January 2, 1990.

Pennzoil Company, P.O. Box 2967, Houston, TX 77252; (713) 546-4000.

OILFIELD SERVICES

The business of exploring and drilling for oil requires an enormous supporting cast of companies, suppliers of rigs, drills, helicopters, pipes, barges, trucks and miscellaneous services such as movies and Thanksgiving turkeys for those working on offshore drilling platforms. Great fortunes have been made in supplying oilfield services. The Howard Hughes fortune derived from his father's 1908 invention of a rotary rock bit that, placed at the end of drill, enabled drillers to penetrate rock and go down deep into the earth. The wire log that used electricity to test for the presence of oil was the foundation of one of the most profitable companies of recent times, Schlumberger.

However, suppliers of these services are crucially dependent on activities in the oilfields. When no one is drilling for oil, they are out of business. And the 1980s were very lean for these companies. Both Schlumberger and Halliburton took tremendous hits, depressing their profits. And nine of the industry's major companies spent the second half of the 1980s mired in red ink. They were: Global Marine, McDermott, Parker Drilling, Reading & Bates, Tidewater, Smith International, Rowan, Zapata and Western Company of North America.

1

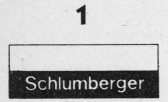

#1 *in oilfield services*

Employees: 50,000
Sales: $4.92 billion
Profits: $454 million
Founded: 1919
Headquarters: New York City, New York

It sounds simple. You drop an electrical probe into a hole drilled in the earth's surface—and by measuring electrical resistances you get a log indicating the presence or absence of oil. Called wireline logging, it's the closest thing to taking an X-ray of an oil well, and is now used wherever oil exploration goes on. Schlumberger (pronounced "Schloombear-zhay") invented wireline logging and began selling it commercially in 1927. For the first 30 years, that was the only service they offered. Today they supply every type of oilfield service—seismic surveys, cementing, drilling, pumping. Having learned how to measure underground for the presence of oil, Schlumberger moved into a number of other measurement and testing businesses. They operate 79 plants in 17 countries where they make electricity, water and gas meters. They have also developed automatic testing equipment to locate and diagnose flaws in the production of semiconductors and printed-circuit boards.

Schlumberger has set their cap on being a multinational, a company whose nationality is difficult to detect. Incorporated in the Netherlands Antilles, they have a corporate staff of 200 people located in three places: Paris, New York and Houston. They're proud of their diversity. Not every company sets as a goal the development of a "multiracial culture inside our company."

Schlumberger has always been profitable, but even for them, the 1980s were trying. When the price of oil is low, there's not a great incentive to drill for more or to use Schlumberger services to find out where oil is. In addition, Schlumberger unfortunately purchased semiconductor maker Fairchild Camera & Instrument in 1979. They were no more able to turn the company around than any of the previous owners—and in 1985 they sold off the firm at a loss. The write-offs from Fairchild and the erosion of their oilfield business led to a loss of $1.6 billion in 1986. For other companies, that might be a disaster. But not Schlumberger. They don't owe any money, and they hoard a couple of billion dollars of cash reserves. They pay a quarterly dividend of 30 cents a share—and not once was that dividend payment interrupted.

History. Conrad Schlumberger, a physics professor in Paris, discovered minerals could be identified by their degree of resistance to electricity. With support from his father, Paul, and help from his brother, Marcel, a civil engineer, he pursued this idea through a partnership the

Schlumbergers formed in 1919. It led, in 1927, to the development of the first practical device for plumbing the earth's surface to detect the presence of oil. Called a sonde, the device itself was designed by Henri Doll, an engineer married to Conrad's daughter. In 1929 Shell Oil hired the Schlumbergers to probe wells in Venezuela and California. By 1938 they were running probes on 1,000 wells a month around the world.

Conrad died in 1936, leaving Marcel in charge until the early 1950s, when his son Pierre took over and moved headquarters to Houston, Texas. To prevent inbreeding and stagnation, Pierre announced that from then on, Schlumberger family members could not be company officers. In 1965 Pierre was succeeded by an extraordinary manager, Jean Riboud, who moved headquarters to New York City. Born in France, Jean Riboud had joined the French Resistance during World War II, was captured by the Germans and spent two years in Buchenwald. He emerged from the concentration camp ridden with tuberculosis and weighing 98 pounds. After recovering his health, Riboud moved to New York, where the aging Marcel Schlumberger offered him a job. Riboud died of cancer in 1985, and the next year Euan Baird became the first American to head the company. His pay in 1989 was $1.1 million.

Owners and rulers. Of the 11 members of the board, 6 are French, 4 are Americans and 1 is Japanese (Eiji Umene, managing director of Nippon Steel). Three board members—Nicolas Seydoux, Didier Primat and Paul LePercq—are related to the Schlumberger family, and they hold some 7.2 million shares of stock, worth about $350 million in early 1990. More than 440 institutions held 40 percent of the stock at the end of 1988. Schlumberger's stock trades all over the world—on the New York Stock Exchange, the Paris Bourse, London, Amsterdam, Frankfurt and all the Swiss exchanges.

As a place to work. They run a decentralized operation where on-site managers have wide responsibilities. Their 50,000 employees include people of 75 nationalities. For their oilfield services crews, they recruit engineers from the best universities in the oil-producing na-

tions of Asia, Africa and Latin America. In 1987, their wireline, seismic and testing operations were headed by a Frenchman; a Dane ran seismic activities; an American headed up research and engineering; an Ecuadoran was in charge of U.S. operations and a German was in charge of those overseas. Schlumberger people are also expected to be mobile. The wireline assignment policy has been described as: "Any place, any time, no choice."

Social responsibility. Outside of the oil patch they're not well known. However, they have a strong following on Wall Street, where they ranked 49th in market value at the end of 1988, well ahead of such companies as J. P. Morgan, H. J. Heinz, Chrysler, Aetna Life & Casualty, Xerox, General Mills, CBS and Campbell Soup. One of the major additions to the art world during the 1980s was the opening of a new museum in Houston, the Menil Collection, housing 10,000 works of 20th-century art. The museum was a gift to Houston from Dominque de Menil, daughter of Conrad Schlumberger. She and her late husband, Jean de Menil, collected the works over 40 years after fleeing Paris in 1941 and moving to Houston, where Schlumberger had an office close to the Texas oil fields.

Global presence. Schlumberger does business in over 100 countries. Of their $4.9 billion of revenues in 1988, $1.5 billion—less than one-third—came from the U.S. Europe accounted for $2 billion (including $920 million from France).

Stock performance. Schlumberger stock bought for $1,000 in 1980 sold for $1,524 on January 2, 1990.

Schlumberger N.V., 277 Park Avenue, New York, NY 10172; (212) 350-9400.

2

Halliburton Company

#2 *in oilfield services*

Employees: 63,500
Sales: $5.7 billion
Profits: $134 million
Founded: 1919
Headquarters: Dallas, Texas

For a polar opposite of Schlumberger, take Halliburton. They square off against each other in the oilfields, vying to supply services and equipment to companies exploring and drilling for oil and gas, but there the similarity ends. Schlumberger has a rather refined, scientific, exotic aura, but Halliburton bubbles up from the muck and mire of rough-and-tumble Texas politics.

Buried in the formation of Halliburton are four legendary bootstrap entrepreneurs. One was Erle P. Halliburton, a short roustabout from the hills of Tennessee who was born dirt poor and spent four years in the Navy before venturing into the oilfields, where he learned how to cement wells. It was backbreaking, dangerous work. Halliburton, an engineer by aptitude, invented better ways to cement oil wells. In 1924 he started a company financed by seven major oil companies that had been his customers and had confidence in him. They were right. Halliburton eventually became the largest supplier of oilfield services—and Erle P. Halliburton headed the company until his death in 1957. He crafted the company in his image. As late as 1959, a company historian reported, "every major official except one started as a truck driver." The exception was the then chairman of Halliburton, an accountant who had been hired, the founder of the company used to say, "because we had to have somebody who could read and write."

The other branch of Halliburton is the Brown & Root construction company, started by Herman Brown and his brother-in-law, Dan E. Root, in 1919 to build roads in central Texas. Brown's younger brother, George, joined the company in 1921, and the Brown brothers became sole owners in 1929 when Dan Root died. The rise of Brown & Root into one of the world's largest construction companies was linked with the ascension of Lyndon B. Johnson in Texas and then national politics. This symbiotic relationship is sketched in detail in Robert A. Caro's book, *The Years of Lyndon Johnson: The Path to Power*. The Browns were Johnson's principal financial backers during his early political career. And they then persuaded other Texan businesses to support him. In return, Johnson, as Congressman and then Senator, saw to it that major construction projects were awarded to Brown & Root. In 1937, Johnson's first year in Congress, Brown & Root received the government contract to build the Marshall Ford Dam on the Colorado River in Blanco County, Texas, the first of many government building contracts to come their way. "We always believed in good government and keeping good people in office," George Brown once told an interviewer. "Those things go hand in hand. There's a place for both."

When Herman Brown died in 1962, the construction company was sold to Halliburton. George Brown died in 1983 at age 88. He was a major benefactor of Houston institutions, especially his alma mater, Rice University. When he became chairman of the Rice board of trustees in 1943, the school had 1,400 students, four buildings and a $14 million endowment. At his death Rice had 21 buildings, 3,600 students and an endowment of over $400 million. Houston's new convention center, opened in 1987, was named for him.

Today's Halliburton no longer has any Browns or Roots or Halliburtons. Their leader since 1983 has been Thomas H. Cruikshank, an accountant, a lawyer and an 11-handicap golfer. When the oil patch went dry in the early 1980s, he sliced Halliburton's payroll from 115,000 to 48,000. He took home $1.3 million in 1989.

Stock performance. Halliburton stock bought for $1,000 in 1980 sold for $1,508 on January 2, 1990.

Halliburton Company, 3600 Lincoln Plaza, 500 North Akard Street, Dallas, TX 75201; (214) 978-2600.

FOREST & PAPER PRODUCTS

The forests have been around for a long time but the industry that rests on this natural resource went through some profound changes during the 1980s. By one count, about 35 percent of the paper capacity in the U.S. changed hands during this decade.

One company that was a giant at the start of the 1980s—the Continental Group, with annual sales of $3.9 billion— disappeared. Two companies that were minor players at the beginning of the decade emerged as new giants. James River Corp. multiplied its sales by 10 times (from $560 million to $5.9 billion) to become one of the largest paper producers in the world. Stone Container, a company specializing in cardboard boxes, paper bags and sacks (so called "brown paper") did even better, ballooning from sales of $380 million to $5.3 billion.

Atlanta-based Georgia-Pacific (they began the decade in Portland, Oregon) emerged as the undisputed champion of this industry in early 1990 when they acquired, after some skirmishing, Great Northern-Nekoosa. The acquisition should lift them to leadership positions in lumber, paper, forest acreage owned and total sales.

1

Georgia·Pacific

#1 *in paper and wood products*

Employees: 60,000
Sales: $10.2 billion
Profits: $661 million
Founded: 1927
Headquarters: Atlanta, Georgia

T. Marshall Hahn, Jr., a former nuclear physics professor, has led Georgia-Pacific into undisputed possession of first place in the forest products industry. That mission was accomplished in early 1990 when Hahn completed a $3.8 billion takeover of Great Northern Nekoosa, whose management had strongly opposed the

combination. Their 1990 sales are expected to come in above $14 billion, more than 40 percent higher than Weyerhaeuser's.

Hahn, who became chief executive in 1983, also led Georgia-Pacific out of the Pacific Northwest, where they had been headquartered for three decades, and back to Georgia, where they were born. That move brought G-P closer to their forestlands in the Southeast and to their main customers. Southern pine grows much more quickly than the Douglas fir of the Pacific Northwest. So G-P loggers can now cut twice as often.

Even before the Great Northern Nekoosa gambit, G-P was a giant. They ranked as the largest producer of soft plywood (22 percent of U.S. output), and they accounted for 5 percent of U.S. lumber output (second only to Weyerhaeuser). G-P was also a big producer of disposable diapers and coffee filters. With Great Northern in tow, G-P became the biggest papermaker—newsprint, copier, computer and writing paper.

Hahn brought the company back to their roots in the 1980s, getting out of furniture, chemicals, oil and gas. Prior to Great Northern, he bought 18 companies, including U.S. Plywood in 1987 and American Forest Products and Brunswick Pulp & Paper in 1988.

History. Many of the players in the forest products industry started with a strong base: they owned a lot of tree-filled lands. That wasn't the case with Georgia-Pacific. Owen Cheatham, a descendant of Benjamin Franklin, founded the Georgia Hardwood Lumber Company in Augusta, Georgia, in 1927. He didn't own any land; he bought lumber from southern mills and resold it. Cheatham was a wily salesman. During World War II his company became the largest supplier of lumber to the armed forces operated five sawmills. A turning point came in 1947, when the company bought a plywood mill in Washington state. And in plywood the company made their mark. For nearly a century, furniture makers had been using veneers (thin layers of wood) to make tables and chairs, but the invention of plywood in the 1930s changed the industry. Plywood is composed of alternating sheets of veneer tightly glued together, with the grain of each adjacent ply run-

The eruption of Mount St. Helens on May 18, 1980, destroyed 68,000 acres of a Weyerhaeuser tree farm. Two-thirds of it had been successfully reforested by 1990.

ning in a different direction. The resulting "plywood" resists warping and splitting and is structurally stronger than steel of the same weight.

After buying more plywood mills in Washington and Oregon, the company changed their name to Georgia-Pacific Plywood Lumber Company and moved their headquarters to the Pacific Northwest in 1953. In the 1950s they borrowed over $160 million to invest in timberland in the West and South. Overnight they became an industry giant. Between 1955 and 1965 they multiplied their size by seven times. In fact, they became so big that in 1972 the Federal Trade Commission forced them to sell 20 percent of their assets. Thus was born Louisiana-Pacific, which now does $2 billion a year in sales.

In 1959 Georgia entered the chemical business, intending to produce the resins used in gluing plywood. They soon branched out into chemicals for lumber, pulp and paper, and started producing formaldehyde, ammonia, chlorine and other chemicals. As the 1970s dawned, only two companies were bigger: Weyerhaeuser and International Paper. In the early 1980s, when Georgia-Pacific moved their headquarters back to the South, an angry Portland resident told the *Los Angeles Times*, "There's a feeling that they came up from the South, liked our trees, cut them down and now they're going back."

Owners and rulers. Hahn came aboard in 1975, plucked fresh from the academic world. He earned a doctorate in nuclear physics from MIT at age 23, and became president of Virginia Polytechnic Institute at 35. While making the rounds pitching corporations for money, he caught the eye of Robert Pamplin, then G-P's chairman, who persuaded him to switch to the corporate world. Pamplin liked the way Hahn had called in the cops to arrest some anti-Vietnam War protesters at VPI in 1970 and then kicked the students out of school when they were released from jail. Hahn proved to be a decisive leader, buying and selling dozens of businesses. In his free time, Hahn works on his 600-acre cattle ranch in Virginia, where the scientist in him comes out to play: He does genetic breeding on his herd. He made $1.7 million in 1989.

Georgia-Pacific has one woman on their board, Norma Pace, an economist and former official of the American Paper Institute.

As a place to work. A big question mark hung over the heads of people working at Georgia-Pacific headquarters in the early 1980s: Stay or go? As the company prepared to move from Portland, Oregon, to Atlanta in 1982, they invited all 600 employees to go along, offering various incentives, including free house-hunting trips and help in selling old homes and buying new ones. In the end, half the headquarters employees stayed put in Oregon at the cost of losing their jobs.

Georgia-Pacific has long been known as a highly decentralized company that has little bureaucracy. Managers are expected to work long hours and meet high standards—or else. One manager told *Fortune*: "That's good—but also frightening. If you're producing, fine. If you keep having problems, Hahn will fire you without taking the smile off his face."

Social responsibility. Environmental activists have targeted G-P because the company imports millions of pounds of wood from the rainforests of Brazil, Indonesia, Malaysia and the Philippines. G-P was also the target of organizers of Redwood Summer in 1990 because of G-P's logging of old growth forests in Northern California.

Stock performance. Georgia-Pacific stock bought for $1,000 in 1980 sold for $2,647 on January 2, 1990.

Consumer brands.

   Tissue paper: MD, Angel Soft, Cormatic, Mr. Big Bath

   Paper towels: Sparkle, Delta, Mr. Big Paper

Paper napkins: Coronet, Hudson, Soft Ply.

Georgia Pacific Corporation, 133 Peachtree Street Northeast, Atlanta, GA 30303; (404) 521-4000.

2

Weyerhaeuser

#1 *in timber*

Employees: 46,100
Sales: $10.1 billion
Profits: $341 million
Founded: 1900
Headquarters: Federal Way, Washington

Workplace

Weyerhaeuser, the self-styled "tree-growing company," lost their lead position in the forest products industry during the 1980s. They fell to second place, behind Georgia-Pacific, because of a combination of factors. A fickle housing market played havoc with their basic business, lumber. They entered other businesses—building houses, running a California savings and loan (talk about a death wish), selling suntan oil and pet supplies—that didn't pan out. And they watched helplessly as Georgia-Pacific bought a bunch of companies in the paper and wood products field.

Each year Weyerhaeuser (pronounced *ware-houser*) plants 200 million new trees, thins out forests and fertilizes them. As a result, they claim to get twice as much growth per acre than they did in 1966, the year they began their aggressive replanting programs. Also, one-half of all their forestlands are intensively managed tree plantations. They sell seedlings from their nurseries—120 million a year—to other would-be tree planters. In short, they're in the business of making sure they'll have plenty of trees to cut down in the future.

History Frederick Weyerhaeuser came to the U.S. from Germany in 1852, at age 18. After a stint as a brewer's apprentice in Pennsylvania, he noticed "brewers became confirmed drunkards" and moved to Illinois, where he worked in a sawmill and lumberyard. His boss went broke in the panic of 1858, and Weyerhaeuser bought the yard at a sheriff's auction. Over the next 40 years he built a prosperous lumber business, heading a syndicate that bought up sawmills and timberlands in Wisconsin and Minnesota. In 1881 he moved his family to St. Paul, where his next-door neighbor was James J. Hill, the Burlington Northern railroad tycoon. Hill sold Weyerhaeuser 900,000 acres in Washington for $6 an acre, and the Weyerhaeuser timber company was born. Weyerhaeuser soon picked up another 200,000 acres in Oregon for $5 an acre. When he died in 1914, he owned nearly 2 million acres of timberland in the Northwest. (When Mount St. Helens erupted early in the 1980s, it was on Weyerhaeuser land.)

In the 1930s Weyerhaeuser adopted the slogan "Timber is a crop" and pioneered the concept of maintaining a perpetual harvest on the land, in contrast to the prevailing practice of "cut and run." In 1941 they dedicated the nation's first tree farm, in Washington state. The company's main weakness has always been the cyclical nature of the timber industry. "The Big W," as Weyerhaeuser is known, has dealt with this pattern by buying into a variety of businesses. By 1989 they were making disposable diapers; selling suntan oil, milk cartons, garden equipment and pet supplies; building homes. And they owned (among other things) a California savings and loan and a securities firm. But all these nonforest companies contributed only 7.5 percent of operating profits, a dismal record prompting a critical article from *Forbes* entitled, "Lost in the Woods." Weyerhaeuser announced in April 1989 they would sell everything but their core businesses: forest products (harvesting and selling lumber, plywood, hardwood, veneer, logs, chips) and paper (including newsprint, packaging products, pulp and paperboard). The company owns 5.8 million acres of forest in the U.S., divided equally between the South and the Pacific Northwest, and owns licenses covering 13 million acres in Canada. Over half of the lands are tree plantations (which are twice as productive as natural forests).

O*wners and rulers.*   The great-grandson of the founder, George H. Weyerhaeuser, was CEO in 1990 at age 63. He joined the firm fresh out of Yale in 1947 and became CEO in 1966. In 1988, John W. Creighton, Jr., 55, was named president and appears to be Weyerhaeuser's chosen successor. He's a former tax lawyer who rose in the company through the real estate operations (now being disbanded). The family flavor remains—the Weyerhaeusers own 12 percent of the stock (worth nearly $1 billion), and George's two sons have followed him into the business.

A*s a place to work.*   Weyerhaeuser has long been considered the class act of the timber industry, known for their humane attitudes toward the environment and their employees. They have one of the most spectacular corporate headquarters in America. The five-story building between Seattle and Tacoma overlooks a 10-acre lake and, beyond an expanse of forest, commands a view of majestic Mt. Rainier. Its rooftop terraces are covered with ivy, and inside are tapestries of forest scenes, a jungle of potted plants and plank floors everywhere—even in the elevators. There are virtually no doors in the place.

During the 1980s, however, Weyerhaeuser laid off thousands of employees and experienced a 38-day strike in 1986. About 70 percent of their work force is unionized.

G*lobal presence.*   In 1987, exports from Weyerhaeuser mills were a hefty $1.5 billion—21 percent of sales. Paper accounts for half of these exports, and Weyerhaeuser is a leading exporter of logs to Japan.

S*ocial responsibility.*   Although some environmental groups slam Weyerhaeuser for clear-cutting forests (denuding patches of forestlands), Weyerhaeuser has also won praise for sensitivity to environmental issues. They were one of the first forest products companies to *have* an environmental policy. And *Audubon* once called them "the best of the SOBs."

S*tock performance.*   Weyerhaeuser stock bought for $1,000 in 1980 sold for $1,972 on January 2, 1990.

Weyerhaeuser Company, 33663 Weyerhaeuser Way South, Federal Way, WA 98003; (206) 924-2345.

3

INTERNATIONAL PAPER COMPANY

#2 *in paper*
Employees: 59,500
Sales: $11.4 billion
Profits: $864 million
Founded: 1898
Headquarters: Purchase, New York

Until Georgia-Pacific made their run in the late 1980s and early 1990s, International Paper, slow-moving behemoth of the forest products industry, ranked as the world's largest paper producer. They make all kinds of paper, from fine writing papers to coarse industrial grades. They supply one out of every four pieces of paper used in American copiers.

This unknown giant spent over $5 billion during the 1980s modernizing their decrepit plants. They also spent a couple of billion dollars buying other companies—Hammerhill Paper in mid-decade was the big one. They also raised a couple of billion dollars selling off their Canadian newsprint mills and some oil-and-gas properties. And they cut costs wherever they could, especially in the work force. They even moved out of their digs in New York City, where they'd been since their founding as a paper monopoly in 1898. They moved most of their operating staff (1,000 employees) to what the New Yorkers considered the boondocks (Memphis) while their small corporate headquarters staff of 125 relocated to Purchase, a Westchester County suburb.

By any standard, IP is huge. They own 28 pulp and paper mills and control 7.2 million acres of timberland. They boast that they sell "almost every kind of paper product imaginable"—packaging materials (containers, cartons and paper bags), coated and uncoated paper for magazines and publications, pulp products (for use in yarn, car tires, disposable diapers).

History. International Paper was formed in 1898 through the merger of 20 New England and New York paper mills. While other companies innovated and experimented, International just bought more mills and more land, moving ahead by sheer weight. From 1943 through the 1960s, the Hinman family ran IP. Edward Hinman, who took over in 1966, was the last family member to run the place. One former executive told Forbes, "I never once heard him

make a decision. He'd say, 'That's very interesting,' and leave the room."

In 1970 IP enraged environmentalists by running a two-page magazine ad describing "the disposable environment—the kind of fresh thinking we bring to every problem." During that decade, a series of outsiders (executives lured away from AT&T, General Electric and Du Pont) headed the company. The flashiest of these was Edwin A. Gee, who during his time at Du Pont made his mark by zipping around town in Jaguars and Porsches. He appeared at International Paper's New York office in 1980 clad in a cardigan sweater and golf socks. Gee was succeeded in 1985 by another Du Ponter, John A. Georges, who led an expansion into photographic materials (the 1989 purchase of Ciba-Geigy's Ilford Group) and composite wood products (buying Masonite in 1988). Georges took home $1.4 million in 1989.

During the 1980s IP transferred 6.2 million acres of forestlands to a partnership, IP Timberlands, which has a separate listing on the New York Stock Exchange. IP owns 84 percent of IP Timberlands. This maneuver was meant to realize the value of the lands; namely, they hoped investors would bid up the price of this entity. But, as Georges admitted in a report to security analysts, the ploy didn't work.

As a place to work. During 1986–87, three IP plants were on strike and a lockout was on at a fourth. The biggest strike

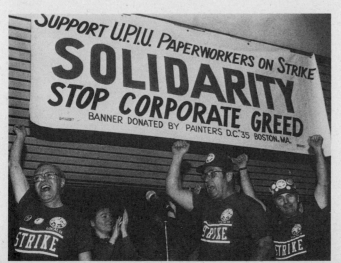

Striking workers from International Paper's Jay and Lock Haven, Maine, paper mills at a rally in 1988.

was in Jay, Maine, where 1,250 workers went on strike for 16 months, protesting the loss of 178 jobs and the elimination of double pay on Sundays. The strike was led by Ray Rogers, the union activist involved in the 1985 Hormel strike in Austin, Minnesota. IP's management did not back down. They claimed that since the paper plant was open seven days a week, premium pay on Sundays was unnecessary. The strike was one of the most bitter of the 1980s: Townspeople carried guns and baseball bats in their cars. In the end, the union backed down, and IP made no concessions.

Stock performance.   International Paper stock bought for $1,000 in 1980 sold for $4,695 on January 2, 1990.

International Paper Company, 2 Manhattanville Road, Purchase, NY 10577; (914) 397-1500.

PAPER PRODUCTION
(In metric tons)

1.	U.S.	69.5 million
2.	Japan	24.6 million
3.	Canada	16.6 million
4.	China	12.6 million
5.	U.S.S.R.	10.8 million
6.	W. Germany	10.6 million
7.	Finland	8.7 million
8.	Sweden	8.2 million
9.	France	6.3 million
10.	Italy	5.4 million

Source: American Paper Institute cited figures from *Pulp and Paper International,* July 1989.

4

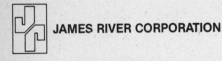

JAMES RIVER CORPORATION

#3 *in paper*

Employees: 40,500
Sales: $6.1 billion
Profits: $245 million
Founded: 1969
Headquarters: Richmond, Virginia

Twenty-five years ago no one had heard of the James River Corporation—and for a good reason: They didn't exist. But James River entered the 1990s producing enough pulp and paper to rank second in the world in that category. During the 1980s they multiplied sales *tenfold*. And they performed this amazing upward spiral in a low-tech industry dominated by old-timers.

The James River story stands as a commentary on the slothfulness that runs through the paper and wood industries. Populated by companies blessed with large forestlands and mills they allowed to deteriorate, these industries became bloated and inefficient. They were never known for go-ahead thinkers. Two engi-neers who worked for a Richmond company, Ethyl Corp., knew in their bones they could take the measure of these lazy giants. Using borrowed funds, they bought a mill on the James River in Richmond that their employer didn't want— and then proceeded to buy mills and forestlands from major companies that thought they were dumping money-losing entities. They bought from Gulf + Western (Brown), American Can (Dixie/Northern), Champion International, Crown Zellerbach, Scott Paper, Phillips Petroleum and Monsanto. And they're still buying. In 1987 they acquired a 50 percent stake in a Scandinavian paper company, Kayserberg.

The two founders, Brenton Halsey and Robert Williams, still run the show, and are multi-millionaires by virtue of their stockholdings. Employees, through stock ownership plans, own 9 percent of the stock. Their nearly all-Southern board of directors includes the president of the University of Virginia. One outsider represents their banker: Citicorp.

James River's mission statement reads: "James River Corporation exists for the purpose of increasing the standard of living of the Corporation's shareholders and employees and otherwise contributing to the economic well-being of its customers, suppliers and the nations in which the Corporation is doing business."

They've certainly improved the standard of living of shareholders, who saw the value of their stock increase sixfold during the 1980s.

James River has become one of the nation's largest producer of sanitary paper products (Northern bathroom tissue and Brawny paper towels, disposable diapers, baby wipes, medical uses); supplies paper for businesses, catalogs and magazines; and makes paper and plastic cups, plates and bowls (under the names Dixie and Paper Maid), paperboard packages and containers.

Stock performance. James River stock bought for $1,000 in 1980 sold for $5,902 on January 2, 1990.

James River Corporation, Tredegar Street, Richmond, VA 23219; (804) 644-5411.

5

SCOTT

#1 in toilet paper, napkins and paper towels

Employees: 28,200
Sales: $5.7 billion
Profits: $376 million
Founded: 1879
Headquarters: Philadelphia, Pennsylvania

Like Kimberly-Clark, Scott Paper converts timber into some of the essential products of modern civilization: toilet tissue, paper napkins and paper towels. They are, in fact, the world's largest supplier of these products. Toilet tissue put Scott on the map. As indoor plumbing spread during the early part of the 20th century, two brothers who sold bags from a pushcart in the streets of Philadelphia— E. Irvin and Clarence Scott—began to make up rolls of toilet paper for home use. Their first brand name, Waldorf, was introduced in 1902. Scott Paper became a missionary for soft tissues and were not above advertising them as a preventative for hemorrhoids. One ad used in the 1930s had a small boy saying, "They have a pretty house, Mother, but their bathroom paper hurts." For 39 years, beginning in 1927, Scott was run by Thomas B.

McCabe, a Swarthmore College fraternity brother of Irvin Scott's son, Arthur. He later became a major patron of Swarthmore, a college just outside Philadelphia.

Philip E. Lippincott joined Scott in 1959, fresh from the Army and Dartmouth College. One of Lippincott's marketing assignments was Viva, the two-ply towel, which went on to become an industry hit. Lippincott became president in 1980, when he was 44, CEO in 1982 and chairman in 1983. He engineered Scott's success in the 1980s by zapping diversions (a clutch of home furnishing companies) and concentrating on two core businesses: Sanitary papers and the coated papers turned out by its S.D. Warren division for printers and publishers. Their one new diversion was acquisition of several food-service companies producing plastic cups, paper napkins, placemats and other disposable products.

Scott is the only U.S. paper company with a major presence overseas. They have 43 mills abroad and do $1 billion in sales overseas. In Europe Scott sells twice as many paper products as their nearest competitor.

Scott faded from the advertising limelight in the 1980s. Prior to 1980, they ranked regularly as one of the nation's 100 leading advertisers. Now they're never in that group. Sometimes they don't even make the top 200! They seem to have conceded to Procter & Gamble the top brand position in toilet tissue (Charmin) and paper towels (Bounty), but Scott still sells more because they have a variety of brands and they are also busy stocking washrooms in restaurants and offices.

Social responsibility. In 1989, Scott made plans to set up a eucalyptus tree plantation and pulp mill in rural West Papua, Indonesia, that would destroy thousands of acres of tropical rainforest. The Indonesian government awarded Scott the concession without consulting any of the 15,000 members of the Auyu tribe. Felling of the forests would halt the tribe members' fishing, hunting and gathering. Scott has announced plans for an $8 million environmental and social study, but they're currently operating a 150-acre test plantation to see which eucalyptus varieties grow best.

Consumer brands.

Baby care products: Wash a-bye Baby wipes, Baby Fresh.

Bathroom tissue: Cottonelle, ScotTissue, Waldorf.

Facial tissue: Scotties, Scotties Accents.

Paper towels: ScotTowels, Job Squad, Viva.

Health care products: Promise bladder control pads and pants.

Stock performance. Scott Paper stock bought for $1,000 in 1980 sold for $7,422 on January 2, 1990.

Scott Paper Company, Scott Plaza, Philadelphia, PA 19113; (215) 522-5000.

6

✺

Kimberly-Clark Corporation

Employees: 39,000
Sales: $5.7 billion
Profits: $424 million
Founded: 1872
Headquarters: Dallas, Texas

It may seem ridiculous to think of a stand of trees turning into Kleenex tissues and Huggies disposable diapers, but that's pretty much what Kimberly-Clark does. Most of the big forest products companies convert felled trees into lumber, plywood, boxes and papers sold, for the most part, to other companies. Kimberly-Clark does some of that, too—they're a major supplier of newsprint and they make cigarette papers and thin papers for bibles. But they focus mainly on consumer products, even more so today than in 1980 when 60 percent of sales came from items sold in supermarkets and drugstores. By the end of the 1980s that figure was nearing 80 percent. They make toilet tissue, household towels, sanitary napkins and paper towels. Among their well-known brands are Kotex, Delsey, New Freedom and Hi-Dri—all products consumers buy and eventually throw away: disposables.

In the mid-1980s, Darwin Smith, K-C's leader since 1971, grew irritated with what he perceived as Wisconsin's anti-business attitude (reflected in the tax code), and so he moved the corporate headquarters from its historic place in Neenah, Wisconsin, to Dallas. The move shocked Wisconsinites even though the mills, and most of the employees, remained there. Kimberly-Clark now has two operations centers—one in Neenah, the other in Roswell, outside of Atlanta. Corporate headquarters in Dallas has only 45 people.

K-C doubled sales and nearly tripled profits during the 1980s, largely because they successfully fronted mighty Procter & Gamble on the disposable diaper front, coming away with a 33 percent market slice for their Huggies brand. Huggies became the top selling product in their stable, eclipsing the old leader, Kleenex.

The company was named for John A. Kimberly and Charles B. Clark, who, along with two other young men living in Neenah, Wisconsin, invested $7,500 apiece in 1872 to establish a business making newsprint from linen and cotton rags. In 1920 they introduced Kotex sanitary napkins (sold in plain brown wrappers and un-advertiseable until the 1970s, when Kimberly-Clark began a series of taboo-busting TV commercials for sanitary napkins). In 1924, executives were unsure whether to introduce a disposable diaper or a cold cream remover. They opted for the cold cream remover, calling it Kleenex. Kotex and Kleenex became so successful many people use them as generic terms for sanitary napkins and facial tissue.

Darwin Smith, 64 in 1990, was slated to continue as CEO until April 1992 (1989 pay: $1.3 million). Smith's heir apparent is Wayne R. Sanders, 42 in 1990. Sanders has degrees in civil engineering and business administration. He worked as a financial analyst at Ford for three years before joining Kimberly-Clark. Kimberly-Clark has one of the most diverse boards of directors in America, including two women (Pastora San Juan Cafferty, a public policy professor at the University of Chicago, and Evalyn Stolaroff Gendel, a physician), a priest (Father John P. Raynor, who is also president of Marquette University); a former astronaut (Walter M. Schirra) and the head of the company's Mexican operations (Claudio X. Gonzalez).

THE UNKINDEST CUT
(Most Dangerous Places to Work)

Injury/Illness per 100 Workers per Year

1.	Meatpacking Plants	33
2.	Mobile Home Manufacturing	30
3.	Vending Machine Manufacturing	28
4.	Manufacture of Wooden Roof Support	27
5.	Processing of Raw Cane Sugar	26
6.	Prefabricated Wood Buildings	26
7.	Reclaiming Scrapped Rubber	26
8.	Special Sawmill Products	25
9.	Boat Building and Repairing	24
10.	Manufacture of China Plumbing Fixtures	24

Source: The *New York Times,* 21 August 1988. Statistics are for 1986.

One day in 1987, Kimberly-Clark closed headquarters (located in the Las Colinas office park outside Dallas) and bussed corporate staffers to a diaper plant in Paris, Texas—90 miles away—to show them how a plant worked. CEO Smith also harbored the hope that the white-collar executives would return with ideas on how to improve office productivity.

Because of their location in small Wisconsin towns, K-C started an airline ferry service that blossomed into Midwest Airlines, a company subsidiary. They also have a special program at Marquette University where they provide scholarships for South African blacks denied an opportunity to go to college in South Africa.

S*tock performance.* Kimberly-Clark stock bought for $1,000 in 1980 sold for $11,225 on January 2, 1990.

C*onsumer brands.*

Kleenex, Huggies, Kotex, New Freedom, Lightdays, Anyday, Profile, Depends, Delsey.

Kimberly-Clark Corporation, P.O. Box 619100, Dallas, TX 75261; (214) 830-1200.

7

Stone Container Corporation

#1 *in container boards, corrugated containers, grocery bags*

Employees: 27,800
Sales: $5.3 billion
Profits: $186 million
Founded: 1915
Headquarters: Chicago, Illinois

Stone Container has come a long way since 1926 when the Stone brothers founded J. J. Stone & Company on Chicago's south side. They're now the world's largest maker of brown paper bags and boxes. Their specialty lies in combining linerboard with corrugated paper to make containers used in storage and shipping. These containers are made in small plants scattered all over the U.S.—140 plants in 40 states—because it's too costly to transport a container more than 125 miles.

Roger W. Stone, grandson of the founder, propelled the company forward during the 1980s by going deeply into debt to buy the "brown" goods that major paper companies didn't want. The paper business divides into white, meaning printing papers, and brown, meaning papers used for packages (cartons, boxes). Stone Container was a relatively small outfit coming into the 1980s with sales of $280 million in corrugated containers and cardboard boxes. Move the clock ahead 10 years and Stone Container has sales of over $5 billion, nearly 20 times what they had in 1980. Their mills and plants annually turn out 750,000 tons of bags and sacks and 34.5 billion square feet of corrugated boards. As the decade ended, they moved into newsprint and "market pulp" (a substance used to make fine paper) by acquiring Canada's Consolidated Bathurst for $2.2 billion. Bathurst, in turn, owns Europa Carton, the largest German packaging company, and Bridgewater Ltd., the largest producer of newsprint in Britain. Stone Container does more than one-quarter of sales abroad, and they're not afraid of a little debt. They owed about $4 billion in early 1990. Of the 14 members of the board of directors, 5 are Stones and 1 (Richard J.

Raskin) is a son-in-law of a Stone. Stone family members hold 24 percent of the stock, worth an estimated $400 million.

Stock performance. Stone Container stock bought for $1,000 in 1980 sold for $7,216 on January 2, 1990.

Stone Container Corporation, 150 North Michigan Avenue, Chicago, IL 60601; (312) 346-6600.

8

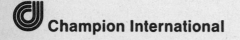

Champion International

Employees: 30,000
Sales: $5.2 billion
Profits: $432 million
Founded: 1891
Headquarters: Stamford, Connecticut

Champion is a reborn paper company. Their mills in Bucksport, Maine, Deferiet, New York, and Sartell, Minnesota, turn out paper for magazines and catalogs. Mills in Sheldon and Lufkin, Texas, turn out newsprint. Mills in Canton, North Carolina, Courtland, Alabama, Hamilton, Ohio, and Pensacola, Florida, turn out paper used in envelopes, computer forms, brochures, annual reports and copiers. To supply these mills, Champion owns or controls 6.4 million acres of U.S. timberland, plus another 2.5 million in Canada.

Andrew C. Sigler, Champion's CEO since 1974, who earned $2.1 million in 1989, pursued a three-pronged strategy during the 1980s: (1) get out of wood products and packaging, (2) invest heavily in paper mills to modernize them, (3) reduce payroll and introduce teamwork on the mill floor. An outspoken critic of Wall Street raiders, he had the company adopt a "Champion Way Statement" and a "Champion Way in Action" to articulate philosophies and values. These manifestos emphasized change and new ways of working: "Ours is a capital-intensive industry in which the competence and dedication of people make the difference. All employees need to become better problem solvers, learn to work more closely with others, and have the informa-

tion to make informed decisions. The company, in turn, will support these efforts by spending capital dollars for profit-improvement projects which make strong economic sense."

How this philosophy worked out can be seen in Champion's 1984 acquisition of another big paper company, St. Regis. Coming into the 1980s, Champion had sales of $3.9 billion, profits of $247 million and 43,000 employees; St. Regis had sales of $2.5 billion, earnings of $158 million and 31,000 employees. After the Champion-St. Regis combination and subsequent sell-offs, the new Champion International came into the 1990s with sales of $5.2 billion, profits of $432 million and 30,000 employees (only 21,000 in the U.S.). It's known as the disappearing work force.

In 1988, Champion became the first company in the paper industry—and the first in Connecticut's Fairfield County (home to many of the nation's top corporations)—to open an on-site child-care center for children of their employees. The center at Champion's headquarters in downtown Stamford serves 60 children, aged three months to five years, and in 1990 was accredited by the National Academy of Early Childhood Programs. CEO Sigler said: "A society is responsible for its children. Currently we're letting a lot of them down. That's terribly shortsighted. Business must make child care its business."

Stock performance. Champion International stock bought for $1,000 in 1980 sold for $1,846 on January 2, 1990.

Champion International, 1 Champion Plaza, Stamford, CT 06921; (203) 358-7000.

9
mead

#1 *in paper-based school and office supplies*

Employees: 21,400
Sales: $4.6 billion
Profits: $216 million
Founded: 1846
Headquarters: Dayton, Ohio

If you remember your school days, you'll remember Mead. They're the number one supplier of notebooks, pads and other paraphernalia that go into schoolbags. Remember those spiral books that produced ragged sheets when you yanked out the pages? Now Mead has attacked this problem with a line of "Wireless Neatbooks" where pages are perforated for less messy removal. No more ragged edges. Of such is progress in the paper industry.

Mead turns out these office and school supplies from their vast horde of mills and trees covering 688,000 acres on Michigan's Upper Peninsula; 118,000 acres in Ohio and Kentucky; and 559,000 acres in the South. Mead is very midwestern, with origins going back to 1846 when Colonel Daniel Mead cofounded a company in Dayton, Ohio, to make printing papers. They're still based in Dayton, still make paper and still have a Mead on the board—Nelson S. Mead, age 68 in 1990. In addition to school supplies (and the Ampad legal pads omnipresent in offices), they make many of the cardboard packages used to carry beverages out of supermarkets.

Mead had a rocky time in the 1980s. After beating back a takeover attempt by Occidental Petroleum in 1979, CEO James McSwiney went on a $1.5 billion spending spree—increasing Mead's white paper capacity by 47 percent and buying a host of unrelated businesses: rubber products (Murray Rubber), pipes and valves (Gulf Consolidated Services), truck and auto parts castings (Lynchburg Foundry). This strategy backfired into a loss of $85.8 million in 1982—Mead's first losing year since 1938.

Mead was also on the losing end of a price-fixing case brought by the Justice

The timber industry gets over 20 percent of its business from remodeling and repair needs and a little below 30 percent from homebuilding needs.

Department against 37 makers of corrugated containers. Every company except Mead settled out of court, each paying a fine of $9 million. Mead fought on, and after McSwiney stepped down as CEO in 1982, his successor, Burnell Roberts, had to swallow a $45 million settlement. In 1989 Roberts took home $918,000.

Mead recovered in the mid-1980s by concentrating on their old standbys—school and office supplies—and expanding their new electronic database systems. Mead has a mega hit in Lexis, an electronic law library, and they also supply Nexis, a data base for news media. In 1988, over 200,000 subscribers paid $300 million to tap into the information on Lexis and Nexis. And Mead is currently developing a new system called EDGAR, which will provide a data base for the Wall Street crowd—recording the Securities & Exchange Commission's filings. Mead expects to profit in two ways from the data base systems: After you get information from the data base you can print out the data on—what else?—Mead paper.

Stock performance. Mead stock bought for $1,000 in 1980 sold for $4,500 on January 2, 1990.

Mead Corporation, Courthouse Plaza Northeast, Dayton, OH 45463; (513) 495-6323.

10

Boise Cascade Corporation

Employees: 19,700
Sales: $4.3 billion
Profits: $268 million
Founded: 1957
Headquarters: Boise, Idaho

The go-go years at Boise Cascade are over. Under the command of John B. Fery, a Bellingham, Washington, native and a graduate of the Stanford Business School, Boise Cascade has developed into a solid, if boring, peddler of paper and paper products. Fery became CEO in 1972 when he was 42 and was still there in 1990, by which time he had refashioned Boise from a miniconglomerate to one doing nearly two-thirds of their business in paper products of all kinds.

Boise owns or controls 6.5 million acres of timberlands, which feed 14 paper mills. Boise's end products include writing paper, copier paper, checks, lottery tickets, pages of *Time, Newsweek* and *National Geographic*, and pages in paperback books. In addition, Boise wholesales thousands of office products, everything from their own paper to paper clips and furniture. They distribute to dealers and directly to big companies. And finally, what with all those forests, they're still in the wood business, operating 16 lumber mills and 12 plywood mills.

Boise was formed in 1957 by the merger of two regional lumber producers—Boise Payette of Boise and Cascade Lumber of Yakima, Washington. Boise Cascade was basically a harvester of wood—they didn't even own a pulp mill to make paper. Robert Hansberger, a Harvard Business School graduate with grandiose ideas, led the company through some halcyon years between 1957 and 1972. A proponent of "free-form management," he hired managers from the nation's top business schools and turned them loose. (One of them, William Agee, went on to run Bendix, where—following his Boise Cas-

cade rulebook—he tried to take over a bigger company with the help of wife-to-be Mary Cunningham, only to find his own company swallowed.) Hansberger's boys pulled off 33 mergers and acquisitions in a dozen years, building Boise into a $1 billion giant and putting them into a host of businesses they knew nothing about, especially real estate development, where their investments in California backfired so badly the whole company almost went under. That's when John Fery took over. He reversed those policies. In one 18-month stretch in the mid-1980s he bought, sold and closed 90 different properties.

Fery's restructuring pushed sales from $3 billion to $4.3 billion during the 1980s while profits doubled to about $270 million. On the other side of the ledger, he reduced the number of employees from 35,000 to 19,000. Not without trauma. Boise's attempt to introduce flexible work rules so workers could be assigned to different jobs met stiff resistance from the unionized work force. In summer 1986 workers at the Boise mill in Rumford, Maine, struck for 76 days before they finally gave up and accepted the company's terms. The strike was bitter. The *New York Times* reported that the people who crossed the picket lines— management, salaried people and replacements imported from other towns—were "subjected to abusive language. Homes were vandalized, nails were spilled on roads and driveways, gunshots were fired into the mill and into a car." After the strike ended, a sign posted on a major highway running through Rumford said: "Lincoln freed the slaves, Boise wants them back."

In 1987 Robert H. Waterman, coauthor of *In Search of Excellence*, joined the board of directors. Fery earned $1 million in 1989.

S*tock performance.* Boise Cascade stock bought for $1,000 in 1980 sold for $3,363 on January 2, 1990.

Boise Cascade Corporation, 1 Jefferson Square, Boise, ID; 83728; (208) 384-6161.

STEEL

The golden age of American steelmaking is over. Foreign producers started to land steel in the U.S. at prices lower than steel turned out in American mills, and by 1984 they had captured one-quarter of all steel sold in the U.S. That's when voluntary restraint agreements went into effect, holding imports to 20 percent of U.S. consumption.

These quotas saved the industry. But much of the damage had already been done—and this industry will never be the same. Over 400 mills closed during the 1980s. Over 200,000 steelworkers lost their jobs. Two big producers—LTV (parent of Jones & Laughlin, Republic and Youngstown Sheet & Tube) and Wheeling-Pittsburgh—entered Chapter 11 bankruptcy. National Steel, the sixth largest producer, sold their big Weirton mill to employees, sold half of the remaining steel business to Nippon Kokan and is now planning to sell the remaining share also to the Japanese. Two other big producers, Armco and Inland Steel, have joint projects going with Japanese steelmakers. Bethlehem Steel closed their big mill at Lackawanna, New York, and reduced payroll from 90,000 to 30,000. And industry leader, U.S. Steel, rushed pell-mell for other businesses, particularly oil and gas, so now steel accounts for less than 30 percent of their sales—and, in a symbolic act, they changed their name to the nondescript USX.

1

#1 *in steel*

#3 *in convenience stores*

Employees: 53,600
Sales: $17.5 billion
Profits: $965 million
Founded: 1901
Headquarters: Pittsburgh, Pennsylvania

Workplace   Social Conscience

David M. Roderick became chairman of U.S. Steel in 1979, and when he retired 10 years later he could claim he'd changed the company, right down to their very name. Roderick closed more than 140 steel facilities and sold off $6 billion worth of assets. Meanwhile, he bought Marathon Oil, Texas Oil & Gas, Husky Oil, Western Gas and Rock Island Refining, and these aquisitions made them the nation's third largest convenience store operator. In mid-decade, to signify the company's new thrust, the name, U.S. Steel Corporation, adopted at their founding in 1901, was changed to USX. U.S. Steel began the 1980s with 166,000 employees (down from the 201,000 the steelmaker once had on the payroll). USX exited the decade with fewer than 55,000 employees. USX now gets nearly two-thirds of sales and profits from oil and gas.

To Roderick, this transformation saved the company. He explained his philosophy in a 1982 interview: "I think that many people don't fully appreciate that the primary role and duty of management really is to make money. And in our case, our primary objective is not to make steel but to make steel profitably."

Roderick was replaced at decade's end by Charles A. Corry. One man Corry will have to answer to, whether he likes it or not, is corporate raider Carl Icahn, the largest USX shareholder. In 1986 Icahn tried, without success, to take over The Corporation, as USX is called on Wall

SULTANS OF STEEL

Company	Country	Output in Metric Tons
1. Nippon Steel	Japan	28.4 million
2. Usinor Sacilor	France	22.9 million
3. Sidebras	Brazil	17.1 million
4. Posco	S. Korea	15.5 million
5. British Steel	U.K.	14.2 million
6. US Steel (USX)	U.S.	12.9 million
7. NKK	Japan	12.3 millin
8. Thyssen	W. Germany	11.9 million
9. Ilva	Italy	11.4 million
10. Bethlehem	U.S.	11.1 million

Source: Metal Bulletin, 1989.

Street. Nonetheless, he ended up with the biggest block of stock, 13.3 percent. Roderick met with Icahn once a month between 1986 and 1989, but their meetings didn't smooth over their differences. In spring 1990, Icahn launched a battle to split USX into two companies again—a steel company and an energy company—arguing the stock would be more valuable that way. He spent $10 million in newspaper and TV ads and mailings to persuade other USX stockholders to back his plan, but he failed to garner a majority of votes.

History. U.S. Steel traces their roots to two legends of American business—Andrew Carnegie and J. P. Morgan. Carnegie was born to a weaver in Dunfermline, Scotland, in 1835. The family moved to the U. S. in 1848, and Andrew started working at age 13. Most things the young entrepreneur touched seemed to turn to gold. He speculated successfully on some oil in Pennsylvania. He bought into and reorganized the Keystone Bridge Company. He set up the Cyclops Iron Company. And after watching a demonstration of the steelmaking technique in France, he converted his plants from iron to steel and proclaimed, "The day of iron has passed—steel is king!"

Carnegie's industrial empire soon outstripped all rivals, making him the world's Steel King. By the turn of the century Carnegie Steel made more steel than the entire British steel industry. How did he do it? With the help of powerful inside connections in critical industries; buying or merging with other companies; sharp dealing; and, of course, plain fraud, as when Carnegie Steel sold the U.S. government a batch of inferior, overpriced steel armor plate.

Carnegie kept an iron grip on every phase of his company's operation, refusing even to sell stock in Carnegie Steel lest it weaken his control. But at a December 1900 dinner speech by Carnegie's president, Charles W. Schwab, who spoke glowingly about steel prospects, financier J. P. Morgan said, "Well, if Andy wants to sell, I'll buy. Go and find his price." Schwab went to Carnegie, who, after a day's deliberation, agreed. He asked for $480 million. Carnegie picked up a piece of paper, scribbled a few of his company's vital statistics on it, and handed it to Schwab. Schwab took the paper to Morgan, who looked at it and said simply, "I accept this price." That was it—the biggest deal to date in American industry. Carnegie said he left business because he wanted to retire and devote his life to education and philanthropy. He eventually gave away 90 percent of his wealth, or $324 million. (The U. S. is dotted with public libraries established with Carnegie money.)

Morgan added other steel companies to the empire, and the result was a monolith that controlled 65 percent of the U.S. steel industry. But Morgan was a banker, not a steelmaker. The obsolete mills and unmanageable mixture of divisions and subdivisions began to take a toll. By 1930 U.S. Steel's share of the market had fallen to 40 percent. In his memoirs, writer Dwight MacDonald describes his conclusion after doing a four-part series on U.S. Steel for *Fortune* in the mid-1930s: "The more research I gathered, the more it became evident that the biggest steel company in the world benefited neither its workers (wages were low...), its customers (prices were kept high...), nor its owners (who got slim dividends)."

Some would argue that not much has changed.

Owners and rulers. USX entered the 1990s with a new CEO, Charles Corry, Roderick's handpicked successor. The contrast with Roderick, an ex-marine sergeant whom the *Wall Street Journal* described as a "bulldog of a man," couldn't be clearer. Roderick was known for quotability, like "the steel business isn't Camelot anymore," and "the economic hammer has dropped." Corry, a Cincinnatian who joined the company in 1959 as a tax attorney, is more understated. "At first blush, he can seem jejune," noted the *Wall Street Journal*. But Corry, not Roderick, scouted opportunities outside steel for USX. In 1981, he persuaded Roderick to go after Marathon Oil, which USX acquired for $6 billion. Corry is no sentimentalist about steel lasting forever at USX. Calling it a "marginal industry," he says, "the jury is still out on steel." Corry took home $1.3 million in 1989.

As a place to work. In a *Pittsburgh Post-Gazette* cartoon after the company changed their name, one steelworker says to another, "I think we're the 'EX' in USX." There was good reason to feel this way: A USX steelworker in the 1980s stood a better-than-even chance of losing his job. Add to that the worst labor relations in the industry, and no wonder the work force is bitter. "Can't nobody say nothing good about them," one steelworker in Gary, Indiana, told a reporter. Those that kept their jobs faced longer hours, smaller crews, bigger workloads and a greater risk of on-the-job accidents. Roderick became known for his contemptuous attitude toward unions. He once called union leaders "the do-nothings of this world." Throughout the 1980s, USX refused to open their company books and

records to unions during negotiating sessions, a practice other companies in the industry had adopted. This only fueled the bad blood between USX and their workers. In John Hoerr's book, *And the Wolf Finally Came*, a union man says, "To the average union man, they're always crying wolf. And the wolf finally came." Laid-off or striking steelworkers found it hard to get another job; one said when he told a would-be employer he worked at USX, "They laughed in my face... They just laughed in my face." USX wasn't any kinder or gentler toward the thousands of white-collar workers they laid off; they just told them, "Clean out your desk, this is your last day." The executive ranks were demoralized, too; a 1984 survey of executives showed they thought top management put profits first and employees last. The traditions once characterizing life in steel communities—softball games, choral groups, plant newspapers—vanished at USX during the 1980s. "These events drew us together...and gave us a sense of belonging," one former labor relations executive said. "In effect, the company has cut out everything that doesn't make a profit."

Social responsibility. In the 1980s, USX was the focal point of a great deal of human misery, shutting down steel mill after steel mill, from Utah to Pennsylvania, forcing thousands upon thousands of steelworkers to move on—if they could. Many shutdowns made the evening network news. The statistics start to tell the story. In three years, 1983 to 1986, the employee rolls were cut from 74,681 to 30,718. But those numbers can't capture the fact that entire towns, like Clairton in the Mon Valley near Pittsburgh, turned into ruins, with alcoholism and suicide climbing way above national rates. USX didn't make the pain any easier, maintaining a stiff upper lip through it all. The closest Roderick came to any public expression of regret was, "It's unfortunate, but that's the way it is," as he announced USX would close four more plants in 1987, laying off 3,700 workers—just after

The steel industry cut 60 percent of its work force in the 1980s.

union steelworkers agreed to come back to work after a six-month strike, the longest in company history since 1959.

G*lobal presence.* One reason U.S. Steel made a comeback in the decade's latter half was the voluntary restraints President Reagan worked out with foreign governments in which steel companies in Japan and Korea agreed to hold back on their exports. U.S. Steel also adopted a new policy of cooperating with foreign companies—they have joint operations with a South Korean company in Pittsburg, California, and in the Midwest with Kobe Steel of Japan.

S*tock performance.* USX stock bought for $1,000 in 1980 sold for $3,444 on January 2, 1990.

C*onsumer brands.*

Marathon Oil, Husky Oil.

USX Corporation, 600 Grant Street, Pittsburgh, PA 15230; (412) 433-1121.

2

#2 *in steel*
Employees: 30,500
Sales: $5.3 billion
Profits: $246 million
Founded: 1905
Headquarters: Bethlehem, Pennsylvania

When the going got tough in the U.S. steel industry, a lot of steel companies got going—right out of the steel business. Not Bethlehem. While U.S. Steel was buying oil companies, and National Steel was selling out to the Japanese and to their workers, "Bessie" stuck with steel and took a beating. They barely survived the early 1980s when companies controlling one-fifth of the nation's steel capacity went bankrupt. From 1980 to 1987—the year Bethlehem contemplated filing for Chapter 11—the company slashed their work force by more than half (a cut of

roughly 50,000 jobs) and lost over $2 billion. Yet they also plowed $3 billion into their steel plants, and actually made a profit in 1988. But after sticking with steel for so long, Bethlehem may now be in an industrial deadend. Asked *Business Week,* "Is Bethlehem investing in a future it doesn't have?"

H*istory.* Bethlehem has always ranked behind U.S. Steel, but they've never behaved as if they were second best. After all, Charles M. Schwab, creator of the modern-day Bessie, was the first president of U.S. Steel. Schwab had worked his way up from mill hand to president of Carnegie Steel and then U.S. Steel. After a highly publicized dispute with U.S. Steel's chairman, Schwab struck out on his own and took control of Bethlehem Steel in 1904. At the time, the company had an iron mill in Bethlehem, Pennsylvania, an ore mine in Cuba, and seven other small facilities. Together they accounted for less than 1 percent of U.S. steel capacity.

Schwab built his company largely on two products: revolutionary flange-shaped steel girders used in the first modern skyscrapers and munitions. Even prior to the First World War, one New York newspaper noted Bethlehem was "equipped to turn out every instrument of warfare used on land or sea." But if guns and I-beams made Bethlehem grow, "money was the great motivator for Schwab," wrote *Mother Jones.* "He spent it ardently, using it to build, among other structures, the most lavish private residence in Manhattan—and money was the key to his management system." Schwab's deputy, Eugene G. Grace, received a bonus of $1,636,000 in 1929—the year of the Wall Street crash. His $500,000 bonuses thereafter regularly made him the U.S.'s highest paid corporate executive.

Grace took over Bethlehem in 1939 when Schwab died. By then, the company had become the world's second largest steelmaker. Not only did they control 14 percent of U.S. steel capacity, but also their famed steel fabricating division had put up the Golden Gate Bridge, the Waldorf Astoria hotel, the Holland and Lincoln tunnels and countless other structural landmarks. During the war, Bethlehem's plants in Lackawanna, New York; Sparrows Point, Maryland; Bethle-

n 1946, the United States produced half the world's steel. Today, the U.S. share is 10 percent.

hem and elsewhere turned out 1,121 ships, enough tinplate to create a 1.5 million mile long string of tin cans and enough wire to fence in the moon's orbit around the earth.

For almost two decades, Grace ran the company *Fortune* once called "the archetype of the U.S. industrial image" as a one-man show. Bethlehem under Grace developed a reputation for two things: technological excellence and insular management. "Grace wanted corporate uniformity," writes John Strohmeyer, author of *Crisis in Bethlehem*. "He not only created an inbred board consisting only of officers employed within the company, but also established the precedent for board behavior: lunch together in the corporate dining room, golf together in the afternoon, socializing together in the evening. His word was law. It prevailed in all decisions from building new open hearths to installing a new sand trap on the tenth hole of the Saucon Valley Country Club's old course." A series of strokes finally forced "Mr. Grace," as he was known to all, to step down at age 80. When he died three years later in 1960, he was buried in a grave surrounded by a rotunda, complete with a semicircular granite bench for seating 20 mourners.

The good times lasted through 1974, when Bethlehem had a record $342 million in profits. It was all downhill from there. In 1977, Bethlehem posted their first year in the red since 1933. They also hired Donald Trautlein, a former Price-Waterhouse auditor, as comptroller. Promoted two years later to company head, he became what *Bethlehem Globe-Times* editor Strohmeyer called "the most resented and ruthless chairman in Bethlehem's history, but also the man most determined to save the U.S. steel industry."

Trautlein inherited a company losing money because of high labor costs ($16 an hour versus $9 an hour in Japan) to produce steel in greater quantities than American industry needed. Trautlein began by cutting the little things—the

country club subsidies, the private security force used to patrol executive neighborhoods. Then he put down the scalpel and picked up the axe. In one fell swoop, he chopped 7,300 jobs (in a community of 22,701) by closing most of Bethlehem's Lackawanna mill. More cuts followed at Bethlehem's other plants. He scrimped and saved for new equipment, convinced that "sooner or later we are going to have capital spending in this country." At the same time, Trautlein and several other top executives gave themselves huge salary increases and severance packages in case of a takeover.

Bethlehem continued to bleed red ink. With little left to shut down or sell, Trautlein left in 1986 and was succeeded by Walter Williams. Ironically, Trautlein's program of modernization and massive cuts paid off a year after he resigned. When demand for steel picked up in 1987–88, Bethlehem staged what the *Wall Street Journal* called "the most impressive turnaround" among the nation's steelmakers. The long-term outlook for Bethlehem, however, may be bleaker because of foreign competition.

As a place to work. The U.S. steel industry may be dying off, but not before it takes a few more steelworkers with it. In just one year (1979) at just one of Bethlehem's mills (Sparrows Point), major accidents caused six deaths, one coma, seven amputations, 70 eye injuries, 86 back injuries and hernias, 181 burns, 205 fractures and dislocations and 395 large cuts and puncture wounds.

Bethlehem's white-collar workers faced the more mundane horrors of conformity and hierarchy. "The definition of intelligence or ability was to do things the Bethlehem way," said one Bethlehem executive. And the Bethlehem way covered all aspects of life. One company speechwriter was forced to resign from the board of the local American Red Cross chapter because Bethlehem hadn't been notified beforehand. Hierarchy ruled even in the country club locker room, "where ranking officers received shower priority," reports Strohmeyer.

Today, labor relations may be at an all-time low. According to Mark Reutter, author of *Sparrows Point*, workers there thought the thinning of executive ranks in the early 1980s would loosen things up.

However, faced with rising employee dissatisfaction and recalcitrant management, United Steelworkers Union district director Dave Wilson said in 1988, "We are reliving the past." The Sparrows Point plant manager refused to even meet with union officers to work out differences on work rule revisions, and in 1988 a record 2,600 unresolved employee grievances were filed.

Social responsibility. In 1989, the mayor of Lackawanna, New York, a city practically created by Bethlehem Steel, told Bessie to "get out. Let Bethlehem take its coke gas and benzene emissions and its water pollution to where it has clearly staked its future." Mayor Thomas Radich worked for Bethlehem Steel for 30 years, but now that 22,000 jobs have become 1,300, he and others feel only the pollution is left.

Bethlehem agreed in 1989 to pay $92 million toward cleaning up pollutants discharged into the Chesapeake Bay by the Sparrows Point mill, pinpointed as a leading industrial source of acid rain ingredients and cancer-causing air pollutants in Maryland.

Stock performance. Bethlehem Steel stock bought for $1,000 in 1980 sold for $1,164 on January 2, 1990.

Bethlehem Steel Corporation, Bethlehem, Pennslyvania. 18016; (215) 694-2424.

3

#3 *in steel*

Employees: 38,000
Sales: $6.4 billion
Profits: $295 million
Founded: 1947
Headquarters: Dallas, Texas

LTV has been one of the great high-wire acts of American Big Business. As one of the country's first giant conglomerates, their debt-defying financial feats regularly left Wall Street analysts on the edge

of their seats—and the company on the edge of bankruptcy. In 1978 LTV took on so much debt to become the nation's third largest steelmaker that *Business Week* called the deal a "suicide pact." Three years later, LTV posted record profits.

In 1984, when they bought Republic Steel to become, briefly, the country's second biggest steelmaker, Chairman Raymond Hay called the deal "a landmark in the annals of America's basic industries." It was a landmark all right. Two years later, LTV became the largest industrial company ever to file for bankruptcy.

LTV is still America's third biggest steelmaker, one of the leading producers of steel for autos and appliances, a major manufacturer of aircraft parts and missiles and one of the largest suppliers of oil field equipment and supplies. But the company's trapeze artist days are over. LTV is still operating under the watchful eye of the federal bankruptcy court.

History. The saga of James Ling and the company he started make the TV series "Dallas" seem dull by comparison. In just 20 years, the man *Fortune* called "part prestidigitator, part brooding genius, part wunderkind" turned a $2,000 electrician's business into a $1 billion conglomerate. Not bad for an Oklahoma boy who dropped out of school at 14. Before joining the Navy as a 21-year-old electronics technician in 1944, he had worked as a bank messenger, busboy, cashier and bookkeeper. He never made over $10,000 a year. Determined to escape his penny-ante existence, and with two children and a wife to support, Ling used his Navy training to start the Dallas-based Ling Electric Company. After that, he never made under $100,000 a year.

Ling's business approach was unconventional. Investment bankers laughed at his plan to take his company public in 1955. So he went to the Texas State Fair, rented a booth and hawked shares in Ling Electric at $2 a pop. After buying Temco Electronics (the *T* in LTV) in 1960, he shocked Dallas by going after Chance-Vought, the nation's second oldest producer of military aircraft and one of the city's most venerable firms. A bitter battle ensued. Relations between Ling and the city's upper crust weren't helped by the ostentatious $3 million Dallas mansion he built, complete with tennis court, two-hole golf course and $12,000 bathtub. But Ling won. Chance-Vought became the *V* in LTV.

Ling's buying days had just begun. Using a technique he called Project Redeployment, Ling would purchase a company, split it up and sell shares in each new division to the public, greatly increasing the firm's dollar value in the process. After LTV bought meatpacker Wilson & Co. in 1967, the company became Wilson & Co. (the meats), Wilson Sporting Goods Co. (the world's largest sporting goods manufacturer) and Wilson Pharmaceutical & Chemical Corp.— promptly dubbed Meat Ball, Golf Ball and Goof Ball. His 1968 purchase of Greatamerica Corp. brought in Braniff International and National Car Rental. In one year (1967 to 1968), LTV jumped from 168th on the *Fortune* 500 to 38th. By then, LTV had amassed 25 companies that manufactured 15,000 products—from bacon to guided missiles and baseballs to marshmallow gelatin. *Fortune* raved about "Jimmy Ling's Wonderful Growth Machine," calling it "the creature of an extraordinary intelligence."

But after Ling bought Jones & Laughlin, the nation's sixth largest steelmaker in 1968, the Justice Department decided LTV had grown big enough. An antitrust suit forced LTV to sell Braniff and other holdings. By then LTV's buying binge had left them nearly bankrupt. Stock fetching $167 a share in 1967 went for $20 in 1970, when Ling was ousted as chairman and replaced by LTV Aerospace head Paul Thayer. The hodgepodge Thayer inherited prompted him to remark, "I don't think anyone would deliberately start out to build a company like this one." He stripped LTV down to aerospace, food and steel, and got rid of extravagances like LTV's 6,423-acre west Texas game preserve.

That didn't mean abandoning the dealmaking. In 1978, Thayer launched what the *New York Times* called "one of the largest industrial consolidations in years" by taking over Lykes Corp., parent of Youngstown Sheet & Tube, the nation's eighth biggest steelmaker. Three years later, LTV sold Wilson Foods, which once brought in almost half its sales. The U.S. steel industry was facing tough times, but Thayer forged blindly ahead, buying Republic Steel in 1984. In theory the

It now takes about one-third the time to produce a ton of steel it took in 1981. Steel industry profits rose 27.4 percent between 1981 and 1986.

creation of the nation's second largest steelmaker would make a stronger whole from two weak parts. The reality: an even bigger money-loser. In 1986, when LTV filed for bankruptcy, they lost $3.25 billion—the most of any U.S. company that year. That year their top executives took home $1 million in "performance-related" pay. While LTV was chopping steelmaking jobs left and right, Chairman Raymond Hay received a "bonus" of $130,000. Of course, even if Hay himself had been fired, LTV would have had to pay him 150 percent of his salary for two years. Chapter 11 enabled LTV to cancel their labor contracts and freeze all their bills. Even with that breathing space, the company is in a bind. They can't sell their steel mills—no one will buy them. With demolition costs at $200,000 an acre, they can't even afford to destroy them. So Hay's plan is to cut steelmaking costs and capacity and rely on LTV's perennially profitable defense division (Star Wars systems for the Pentagon and parts for Boeing airliners) to keep the company alive.

Owners and rulers. These days, the people who really own and run LTV are their creditors. Ex-Xerox executive Hay may be chairman, but two committees made up of unsecured creditors call the shots. They approve everything from possible plant shutdowns to the CEO's salary.

As a place to work. The only thing worse than working for a bankrupt company is retiring from one. LTV "has lost a raft of managers uneasy about working for a company in bankruptcy-law proceedings," reported the *Wall Street Journal* in 1987. Retired steelworkers and steel executives are worried about their pensions. When LTV filed for Chapter 11, they said they could cover only one-third of their pension obligations to 101,000 active and retired steelworkers, with a shortfall of $2 billion. LTV tried to turn over the pensions to the federally funded Pension

Benefit Guaranty Corp., but the agency refused. The Supreme Court upheld the agency in 1990, placing the burden of paying the retirees back on LTV's shoulders.

Social responsibility. When former chairman Paul Thayer, a World War II ace fighter pilot who once flew his plane under the Golden Gate Bridge, left in 1982 to become U.S. Deputy Secretary of Defense, he gave himself some nice going-away gifts—$1 million in stock, two pensions totaling $424,000 a year, a car and club memberships worth $144,000. Thayer resigned from his government position in 1984 after the Securities and Exchange Commission accused him of helping a Dallas stockbroker friend earn $1.9 million from insider stock tips.

Lawyers reach for their calculators when they read the "Legal Proceedings" section of LTV's 10-K form: a horn of plenty brimming with environmental offenses, sex discrimination cases and securities litigation—not to mention the tangle of lawsuits brought on by their 1986 bankruptcy filing.

The LTV Corporation, 2001 Ross Avenue, Dallas, TX 75201; (214) 979-7711.

4

#1 in tinplate, majority employee-owned industrial firms

#7 in steel

Employees: 8,000
Sales: $1.3 billion
Profits: $16 million
Founded: 1909
Headquarters: Weirton, West Virginia

Workplace

The nation's seventh largest steelmaker became an employee-owned company in 1984 when workers realized the only way to save their jobs was to buy the mill. Weirton is the largest private employer in West Virginia and America's largest majority employee-owned industrial firm. Weirton is the leading U.S. producer of tinplate, accounting for nearly one-quarter of domestic production. Almost 90 percent of Weirton's tinplate is bought by 15 can manufacturers, mostly for food canning.

History. A former general manager at U.S. Steel's Monessen, Pennsylvania, plant, Ernest T. Weir had two worries when he started his own steel and tinplate company: that mammoth U.S. Steel would cut off his supply of raw materials, and that strikes by organized labor would disrupt his mills. Expansion would solve the first problem; the creation of a company town would solve the second. He hoped his new steel mill at Holiday Cove (incorporated as Weirton in 1947), in that strip of West Virginia between the Ohio and Pennsylvania borders, would be a community where "workers and managers lived near each other, ...belonged to the same churches and fraternal organizations, and in many cases were family members, relatives, and friends." In 1919, when strikes wracked the rest of the U.S.

Four of Weirton Steel's 8,100 worker-owners.
By 1990 there were 11.5 million employees of
companies that are owned by their workers,
including Avis and Publix Supermarkets.

steel industry, 186 Wobblies (members of the Industrial Workers of the World) at Weirton Steel were rounded up, forced to kneel and kiss the American flag and then run out of town.

In 1929, Weir combined the Hanna Mining Company and Great Lakes Steel with Weirton Steel to form National Steel, the nation's fifth largest steelmaker. Weirton's work force—represented by an independent union—produced high-quality tinplate that went into one out of every five cans used in America. Higher-than-average wages and job security took some of the sting out of being known by other steelworkers as "the Weirton scabs." "When you were going through school in this area," said one local minister, "you never really worried about what you wanted to be. You thought, 'Gee, I'd like to be a doctor, gee, I'd like to be an engineer.' But if that didn't work out, you knew you had a lifetime job in the mill."

That certainty began to fade during the late 1970s. Cheap foreign steel, inflation and the increasing use of aluminum for beverage containers cut sharply into National's profits. National responded with a move that no doubt made Weir roll over in his grave. In 1980, they bought First Nationwide Savings & Loan of Cali-

fornia. Almost overnight, the nation's fourth largest steelmaker became the nation's fourth largest savings and loan holding company. To boost steel revenues, National tried to raise productivity—not by buying new equipment but by hiring more supervisors. "They had hundreds and hundreds of extra bosses around, pushing and pushing," said one Weirton worker. Although Weirton posted a 1 percent profit in 1981—when most mills were deep in the red—National cut employment from 11,000 to 7,500. One year later, headquarters announced they would "substantially limit" new investment in Weirton and that they were considering "various possibilities for the future."

"We had a gun to our heads," said one worker. "We had to buy the mill. It was either that or nothing." A $500,000 feasibility study was performed, financed in part by voluntary contributions of $60 each by management people and $390,000 by the Independent Steelworkers Union from their strike fund. Later, Weirton-area communities raised $1.5 million through a telethon and various fund-raisers to help pay the $5 million tab for lawyers, bankers and consultants who assisted with the buyout negotiations.

In July 1982, Weirton's joint labor-management committee ironed out a deal enabling them to buy the mill from National for $386 million plus taking on certain debts. The rank and file approved the pact on September 23, 1983, by an eight to one margin. To secure bank credit, Weirton's workers took a cut in their hourly wages that dropped them from the highest in the U.S. steel industry ($24 an hour) to among the lowest ($19). In return, they would get one-third of the company's profits if and when they reached $100 million in net worth, and half when they reached $250 million.

As of 1989, Weirton had made money every year since the buyout. Productivity had risen remarkably. In the first year of employee ownership, for example, Weirton shipped 20 percent more steel than the previous year—with only a 5 percent increase in the number of "employee-owners." The first profit-sharing checks (averaging $2,000) were issued on March 6, 1986. That pumped more than $20 million into the grocery stores, barber shops and auto dealerships of Weirton and its neighbors. "Employee ownership was the best thing that could have happened to us," commented Walter Bish, president of Weirton's largest union. But Weirton's biggest hurdles were yet to come. In 1988, company president Herbert Elish said Weirton needed to invest $500 million over the next few years to upgrade equipment. That raises an old question for Weirton's new owners. "Will the workers behave like responsible capitalists, ready to postpone money today for money tomorrow?" asked Forbes. They were—and voted to reduce profit sharing and make other changes allowing Weirton to raise $740 million for modernization. Additionally, employee-owners supported a proposal to sell about 23 percent of their stock in 1989. Weirton now is listed on the New York Stock Exchange.

Owners and rulers. When Weirton's workers voted to buy their plant, they launched America's biggest Employee Stock Ownership Plan (ESOP). Strictly speaking, the ESOP is a trust that has taken out a loan to buy the company's stock. Every year part of the company's income goes to the ESOP trust that pays off the loans used to buy the stock. Each time a payment is made, stock equal to the amount of that payment is allocated to employees. So employees don't have to put up their own cash to get stock in the ESOP. "Since the buyout," reported Forbes in 1988, "the workers have...allocated to themselves $158 million worth of Weirton Stock—about $19,000 of stock per employee."

Although Weirton's workers are majority owners of their company, they don't necessarily run the firm. Under the terms of the 1983 agreement, direct worker representation on the company's 12-member board is limited to three seats. The rest are open to management (one to three seats) and "independent" directors (six to eight). Shareholders elect the latter. However, Weirton's hourly workers account for about 85 percent of total payroll, thus they receive about 85 percent of the allocated stock and actually control voting power.

CEO Herbert Elish came to Weirton in 1987 from Dreyfus, a financial services firm, where he was a senior vice president. Elish made $400,000 in 1988. One of the all-male board of directors is Irving Bluestone, a former official of the United Auto Workers union.

As a place to work. "When I came to Weirton in 1981," said Father Charles Schneider of Weirton's St. Joseph the Worker Church, "there was an appalling lack of pride. [Workers] felt Weirton Steel owed them a job because their fathers and grandfathers worked for the company. Now that they own the company, that attitude is gone." No doubt about it, Weirton has been a happier place to be since the buyout. One of the first things president Robert Loughhead did when he was appointed in 1983 was to get rid of the executive dining room and reserved parking places. He also established "participation teams" that meet twice weekly to look for ways to make production more efficient and improve communication between management and labor. Workers have found ways to double their output. "We're ten times more interested in doing the job," a Weirton executive told U.S. News & World Report. "Welders who used to throw a welding rod away when it got down to 4 inches now wait until it's 2 inches." Some tension remains between hourly workers and the supervisors National brought in in the bad old days. One 12-year veteran complained in 1984 that "it's still too much of the same regime." Corey Rosen, executive director of the National Center for Employee Ownership, admitted "Weirton is not a perfect example of workplace democracy," but "it is vastly more democratic than any other steel company."

Social responsibility. Since the ESOP formation in 1984 through 1989, Weirton has spent about $85 million on new air and water quality controls.

Weirton Steel Corporation, 400 Three Springs Drive, Weirton, WV 26062; (304) 797-2000.

ALUMINUM

A dozen companies fabricate aluminum in the U.S., but four account for about 60 percent of the production. A lightweight metal refined from bauxite ore, aluminum has found its way into more and more products, but its biggest use is as a beverage container. Although steel cans are still widely used to pack vegetables, fruits and sauces, aluminum has conquered the beverage market, with a 95 percent market share. The U.S. is both the biggest aluminum producer and consumer.

Fortunately, since a lot of electricity is needed to produce aluminum, recycling has taken hold in this industry. Both Alcoa and Reynolds Metals have nationwide networks of recycling centers where they pay for used cans. The number of cans recycled goes up every year. Over half the cans shipped in the 1980s were recycled.

1

#1 in aluminum

Employees: 59,800
Sales: $10.9 billion
Profits: $945 million
Founded: 1888
Headquarters: Pittsburgh, Pennsylvania

Once a company has experienced monopoly power, it's difficult to enter the real world. After they found out how to make aluminum, Alcoa—short for Aluminum Company of America—had it all to themselves for the first 50 years of their life. The second 50 years, which ended in 1988, were different. Although Alcoa remained on top of the aluminum heap, they faced stiff competition from resourceful newcomers like Reynolds Metals and Kaiser Aluminum and from a former satellite, Alcan of Canada. In the early 1980s, under the direction of Alcoa veteran Charles W. Parry, the company began to say they didn't want to stay trapped in the aluminum business for the

The aluminum industry recycled over half the cans produced in the 1980s—more than 232 billion containers.

rest of their life. Parry talked about space age materials, predicting that by 1995 Alcoa would be getting half of revenues from nonaluminum sources. It sounded great, but the strategy never got very far. In 1987 Alcoa's board of directors, still under the influence of former CEO W. H. Krome George, ousted Parry and brought in a non-Alcoan, Paul H. O'Neill, who repudiated Parry's vision. He quickly sold off the nonaluminum businesses (natural gas drilling, aerospace materials) and said Alcoa would stick with—surprise—aluminum as their meal ticket.

O'Neill had luck riding with him. Parry's reign had coincided with a slump in the aluminum market, with prices declining to rock-bottom levels. Mighty Alcoa posted a loss in 1982. O'Neill's reign coincided with a resurgence of the aluminum market. Nothing like a doubling of the price of aluminum bumps up the profits of the industry's largest producer.

Alcoa mines bauxite in Australia, Brazil, Guinea, Jamaica, Suriname and Bauxite, Arkansas, and smelts it into aluminum to make numerous products—everything from industrial components (rods, wires, tubes and castings for aircraft and automobiles, for example) to aerospace and defense system components (helicopter blades and missile domes) to finished products, like memory disks for computers. Their biggest product is the sheet aluminum used in beverage cans, but Alcoa has found a way to profit from every angle. They sell the refined bauxite itself in products as diverse as sandpaper and toothpaste. Alcoa of Australia mines gold.

History. Although aluminum is the most plentiful metal in the world, comprising one-twelfth of the earth's crust, it was virtually unmarketed little more than 100 years ago, and could only be had at exorbitant cost. The first aluminum object ever made was a toy rattle for Napoleon's son. And the metal was so rare French emperor Napoleon III had his artisans design an aluminum table service for guests who deserved something better than mere gold.

A 22-year old Oberlin College graduate, Charles Martin Hall, found an inexpensive way to separate aluminum from its oxide. In October 1885, Hall found he could produce aluminum cheaply by dissolving alumina in a bath of molten cryolite, a salt compound, and passing an electrical current through the solution. Hall immediately applied for a patent, and in 1888 he got some backers in Pittsburgh to help him set up the Pittsburgh Reduction Company.

Their first products were aluminum pots, but few merchants took a chance on the metal. In 1889, the company needed $4,000 to pay a debt. Company president Arthur Vining Davis went to Pittsburgh's Mellon Bank, where Andrew W. Mellon paid the debt in exchange for stock. The Mellons soon gained effective control of the company.

With a patent-insured monopoly on the aluminum refining process (and therefore the entire industry), Alcoa staged an aggressive campaign to convince makers of metal products to switch to aluminum. By 1907, when the company adopted their present name, aluminum had been used in buildings, boats, automobiles, kitchen utensils, surgical instruments, electrical transmission wires and the Wright Brothers' airplane. Aluminum foil followed in 1910.

Alcoa's early monopoly prevented genuine competition. The company had begun mining their own bauxite in 1903 and effectively controlled the major known sources of the ore in the U.S. by 1910. But not until 1946 did the Justice Department finally force Alcoa to break up and yield many of their aluminum-processing patents and plants to competitors, including Reynolds Metals. At that time, Alcoa controlled 90 percent of the U.S.'s primary aluminum business. In addition, Alcoa was forced to sell off Aluminium Ltd. (later Alcan), their Canadian subsidiary.

Owners and rulers. Although Michael Patrick Allen's 1987 book, *The Founding Fortunes*, states that Mellon family members still hold 17 percent of Alcoa's stock, no tangible evidence of these holdings exists. Mellon family members no longer sit on the board; nor do any representatives of the Mellon Bank, whose trust department used to hold big chunks of the Mellon fortune. The one link to the old era is Paul L. Miller, who joined the Alcoa board in 1965 after becoming president of First Boston, an investment banking firm once in the Mellon orbit. The 69-year-old Miller was still on the board in 1989. The 1980s saw the passing of the Hunts from Alcoa. Alfred M. Hunt, whose grandfather cofounded Alcoa and whose father was president from 1928 to 1951, retired as vice president and secretary in 1984. O'Neill, 51 when he took over in 1987, was previously president of International Paper. He had just joined Alcoa's board in 1986. O'Neill is a director of a New York-based, nonprofit research organization, Manpower Demonstration Research Corp., and in 1988 he brought the MDRC president, Dr. Judith M. Gueron, onto the Alcoa board. She's the first female director the company has had.

As a place to work. How do you change a culture that's over 100 years old and rife with management-labor hostility? O'Neill is trying. He junked the corporate limo, doesn't join country clubs, lives frugally, spends endless time travelling and talking to employees and started a drive for workplace safety that cut injuries by 30 percent.

Social responsibility. In 1983 Alcoa paid $1.5 million to clean up more than 1.8 million gallons of waste oil and sludge they illegally dumped outside of Olney, Illinois, from 1975 to 1977. With assets of $223 million, the Alcoa Foundation is the country's largest corporate foundation, but that doesn't mean that they lead in philanthropic contributions. In 1988 they made 2,560 grants totaling $10.8 million, well under the 1 percent of pretax profits many outsiders take as a minimum commitment for a concerned company. The $10.8 million also included $1.2 million mandated by the company's matching gift program. Alcoa matches employee contributions to educational institutions on a 2-for-1 basis (for every dollar the employee gives, Alcoa gives two). Alcoa maintains 240 recycling centers, and in 1989 they paid $232 million to collect 17.1 billion used aluminum beverage containers.

Global presence. When Alcoa set up Alcan in Canada in 1928, they put all their foreign operations in 11 countries under the aegis of the Canadian company. After World War II, when ties with Alcan were severed, Alcoa had to start from scratch in the international arena. By 1990 Alcoa was deriving 25 percent of revenues abroad. Their two main outposts are in Brazil and Australia, where they have full-scale aluminum mining and production facilities.

Stock performance. Alcoa stock bought for $1,000 in 1980 sold for $4,072 on January 2, 1990.

Aluminum Company of America, 1501 Alcoa Building, Pittsburgh, PA 15219; (412) 553-4707.

2

Alcan Aluminium Limited

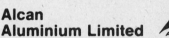

Employees: 56,000
Sales: $8.8 billion
Profits: $835 million
Founded: 1928
Headquarters: Montreal, Canada
U.S. headquarters: Cambridge, Massachusetts

Once an offshoot of Alcoa, Alcan Aluminium (they use the British spelling) has been on their own since 1945 and ranks as one of Canada's largest companies. Excluding U.S.S.R. production, they account for an estimated 12 percent of the worldwide output of aluminum, second only to Alcoa's 17 percent slice. Alcan is also known as the most efficient aluminum producer because they generate their own hydroelectric power. Massive jolts of electricity are required to process aluminum from bauxite ore—and Alcan has a decided edge over companies buying electricity. Hardly known to Americans because they make no consumer products, Alcan nevertheless has a strong U.S. presence, with plants in Oswego, New York; Fairmont, West Virginia; Warren, Ohio; and three Kentucky towns—Seebree, Berea and Logan. They supply aluminum sheets for beverage containers and other aluminum parts for industrial manufacturers, including automakers.

The race is on to come up with advanced versions of aluminum that can substitute for steel. For that reason Alcan moved their U.S. headquarters from Cleveland to Cambridge, Massachusetts, in 1985. "We want to tap top minds," a company official told the *Wall Street Journal*. Alcan reached a milestone in 1988 when they earned $931 million after taxes—the biggest profit a Canadian company ever made.

Alcan Aluminium Limited, 1188 Sherbrooke Street West, Montreal, Quebec H3A 3G2, Canada; (514) 848-8000.

3

REYNOLDS ALUMINUM

#1 *in aluminum foil*

Employees: 30,500
Sales: $6.1 billion
Profits: $533 million
Founded: 1919
Headquarters: Richmond, Virginia

They've been the evangelists of the aluminum business, promoting new uses for this lightweight metal. While Alcoa sat on the biggest capacity in the industry, Reynolds developed aluminum-based consumer products like foil wrap and beverage cans. As a result, although Alcoa is bigger, Reynolds is better known.

During the 1980s Reynolds sought complete control of the packaging area at the supermarket, cashing in on consumer loyalty to Reynolds tinfoil. Reynolds Wrap was launched in 1947 and for 35 years was Reynolds' only consumer product. But starting in 1982 came a bombardment—plastic wrap, wax paper, cooking bags, colored plastic wrap (in red, green, yellow and blue) and triple-seal food storage bags in 1989. By decade's end these products accounted for $500 million in sales. Reynolds entered these areas by buying established packaging companies—Presto Industries (the number three producer of food wrap and plastic bags),

Cut-Rite wax paper, Baker's Choice baking cups and trays and Mt. Vernon plastic packaging products.

Besides packaging, Reynolds aluminum is used in everything from cans to wheels, electrical cable and chemicals. They also supply packaging, vinyl building materials and products made from copper, nickel and stainless steel. Reynolds has interests in real estate, oil, gas, coal, minerals and Eskimo Pie ice creams.

H*istory.* In summer 1902, wealthy tobacco magnate R. J. Reynolds convinced his young nephew, R. S. Reynolds, to leave law school and enter the family tobacco business, which R. J.'s father had founded. R. S. soon became the tobacco company's master merchandiser, largely responsible for turning Prince Albert loose tobacco and Camel cigarettes into industry leaders.

In 1919, R. S. saw that cigarette consumption had increased dramatically during World War I, until demand for the tinfoil used in cigarette packs far outstripped supply. Striking out on his own, he borrowed $100,000 from the tobacco company and founded U.S. Foil in a small one-story building in Louisville, Kentucky. R. S. was the first manufacturer to recognize the advantages of lighter, cheaper aluminum over the traditional lead-tin alloy. In 1928 he built the first aluminum foil plant in Louisville, and after buying out the shares the tobacco company held, formed Reynolds Metals. In 1935 the company pioneered rotogravure printing on aluminum, and thus, entered the aluminum packaging field. And in 1937 R. S. borrowed $15 million to buy the company's first smelting plant. Reynolds introduced aluminum siding for residential housing. But their real success flowed from a 1946 antitrust ruling that forced Alcoa to sell patents and factories to competitors.

A*luminum recycling saved 10 billion kilowatt-hours of electricity in one year, enough energy to light New York City's residences for over six months.*

THE TOP 10 BLACK-OWNED COMPANIES

Company	Employees	Sales
1. TLC Beatrice (Food)	6,000	$1.5 billion
2. Johnson Publishing (Media/Cosmetics)	2,300	$241 million
3. Philadelphia Coca-Cola Bottling (Soft-drink bottling)	985	$240 million
4. H. J. Russell (Media/Food)	668	$133 million
5. The Gordy Co. (Entertainment)	70	$100 million
6. Soft Sheen (Cosmetics)	565	$87 million
7. Trans Jones (Transportation)	1,264	$78 million
8. The Bing Group (Steel)	170	$74 million
9. The Maxima Corp. (Computers)	918	$58 million
10. Dick Griffey Prod. (Entertainment)	86	$50 million

Source: *Black Enterprise*. June 1990.

The 67-year-old R. S. began to yield control to his four sons—R. S., Jr., David, William and J. Louis—in 1948. R. S. died in 1955, and his namesake became chairman until 1976, when David Reynolds took over. The brothers expanded overseas and pushed into big new markets like the aluminum beverage can. In response to environmentalist protests, Reynolds introduced in 1976 what is now the standard tab for aluminum cans, Reynolds' patented Stay-On-Tab. Environmentalists had protested the traditional detachable ring-pull tabs as a source of litter. By the mid-1980s, 30 states had mandated use of the Stay-On-Tab for environmental reasons.

In the early 1980s, however, aluminum's crusader was tired and tarnished. Reynolds reported losses in 1982 and 1983. So, management took up the axe. Between 1983 and 1985, the company shut down 11 plants, closed down four smelters and fired a whopping one-third of all employees—both salaried and hourly. But they also spent over $1 billion on capital improvements, mostly on upgrading outdated plants. Reflecting on the situation, CEO William Bourke later told the *Richmond News Leader:* "We were either going to get the weight off or were going to die. And that weight was too many people and too many old, high-cost plants. So we had to get rid of it. That's a painful process. I mean, nobody wants to preside at a wake."

Owners and rulers. In 1985 58-year-old William O. Bourke became the first non-Reynolds family member to run the company. Bourke had run up an impressive record as head of Ford Motor's North American operations for five years. Explaining what he does in his leisure time, Bourke told the *Wall Street Journal:* "I enjoy growing vegetables. It gets me off my butt." He also tends cattle.

When he retired in 1988 at age 72, David Reynolds was the last surviving son of the company's founder and had been with the company since dropping out of Princeton at 21. He and other family members still hold at least 4 percent of the stock, just under 2 million shares, worth over $100 million in early 1990.

Social responsibility. Reynolds is at the forefront of the recycling movement; in 1968 they founded the nation's first consumer-oriented aluminum recycling business. Through their consumer aluminum recycling network of over 1,500 locations nationwide, Reynolds buys used aluminum from consumers. In 1988, they recycled a record 433 million pounds of aluminum used by consumers, paying out $173 million. That year, Reynolds recycled more cans than they produced.

Global presence. Reynolds does 21 percent of sales abroad. In November 1989 they announced a joint venture with an Italian company (Fata European Group) and a group of Soviet organizations to build an aluminum foil factory in Siberia. Reynolds will hold a 13.5 percent interest in the factory, which will cost $200 million to build.

Stock performance. Reynolds Metals stock bought for $1,000 in 1980 sold for $4,954 on January 2, 1990.

Reynolds Metals Company, 6601 West Broad Street, P.O. Box 27003, Richmond, Virginia 23261; (804) 281-2000.

4

KAISER ALUMINUM & CHEMICAL CORPORATION

Employees: 11,250
Sales: $2 billion
Founded: 1931
Headquarters: Oakland, California

Yes, there's still a Kaiser Aluminum. They remain the U.S.'s third largest aluminum producer, accounting for 9 percent of industry output, even though they were kicked around like a football during the 1980s. They're also a shrunken version of the company that went under the Kaiser name at the decade's start. They no longer have a chemicals business. They're no longer real estate developers in California and Hawaii. They no longer have an operating company in Europe. And they've gone from 27,000 employees to about 11,000.

Still based in Oakland, historic home of the Kaiser companies, they went through two ownership changes during the 1980s. First, after a protracted struggle that started in 1985, they fell under the control of British wheeler-dealer Alan E. Clore, who set up a company, Kaiser Tech, as a holding company for Kaiser Aluminum. When the stock market crashed on October 19, 1987, Clore was forced to sell many of his holdings. His 27 percent stake in Kaiser Tech went to Houston corporate raider, Charles E. Hurwitz, who then acquired all remaining shares and lodged his new acquisition in Maxxam Inc., the resting place for another of Hurwitz's northern California acquisitions, Pacific Lumber. So, Kaiser Aluminum is owned by Kaiser Tech, in turn owned by Maxxam, whose shares trade on the New York Stock Exchange.

Owners and rulers. Hurwitz fired Kaiser Tech CEO James Pasmun in January 1989 and replaced him with a Houston crony, John Seidl—without consulting the board of directors. Pasmun had spent his career in the aluminum industry and had led Kaiser to a nice profit in 1988. Seidl was an aluminum virgin, having spent his career with a natural gas producer. But Seidl is politically well-connected; he was deputy assistant secretary in the Department of the Interior and the Department of Health, Education and Welfare in the Nixon administration. Another Hurwitz crony who sits on Kaiser Tech's board is former Texas Governor John Connally.

Hurwitz is undoing the legacy of Henry J. Kaiser, last of the great self-made American industrialists. He differed from predecessors like Rockefeller and Carnegie by becoming a liberal Democrat with a strong sense of social responsibility. Kaiser assembled a remarkable group of enterprises from construction and engineering to cement, steel and autos (the short-lived Henry J.) in the western U.S. during the first half of this century. With five other large firms Kaiser helped build the Hoover, Bonneville and Grand Coulee dams. After World War II (when he was one of the biggest shipbuilders), Kaiser augmented his construction business by picking up several aluminum-processing plants in Washington state and Louisiana for a song from the federal government because Alcoa was being forced to sell them in the wake of an antitrust case. The largest of the remnants of the Kaiser empire is the Oakland-based health maintenance organization (HMO), Kaiser Permanente. The father of all HMOs, nonprofit Kaiser Permanente delivers comprehensive health care to more than 5 million people.

Kaiser Aluminum & Chemical Corporation, Kaiser Center, 300 Lakeside Drive, Oakland, CA 94643; (415) 271-3300.

CHEMICALS

Chemicals have insinuated themselves into every aspect of modern life, from the clothes we wear to the materials we use, and the big chemical companies are the alchemists of our times. Not everyone appreciates alchemists. Some prefer what they call "natural" elements, cotton rather than polyester, ceramics rather than plastic, organically grown foods rather than those grown with pesticides. But chemistry inexorably marches on, driven by the economics of mass production. Coming into this century, German companies dominated this industry. Two world wars, with Germany on the losing side, did wonders for the U.S. chemical industry, which now has three world-class players, although the German companies have come back from the devastation of World War II to take over the top spots in this industry. And the Big Three of the German chemical industry— Bayer, BASF and Hoechst—have steadily expanded their U.S. base. Meanwhile, both Du Pont, Dow Chemical and Monsanto have entered the international arena in a major way.

1

#1 *in chemicals*

Employees: 141,000
Sales: $35.5 billion
Profits: $2.5 billion
Founded: 1801
Headquarters: Wilmington, Delaware

Workplace

If the big corporation is dead, somebody better tell Du Pont. The nation's largest chemical producer is credited with having invented the modern corporation— they did it first in their own company, devising a divisional system allowing managers to operate a diverse organization, and then transplanted the system to reorganize General Motors, which they controlled during the first half of this century. If not for Du Pont, GM might have foundered. In the 1980s, as the big corporation, with layers of bureaucracy, fell into disfavor in many quarters, Du Pont sailed through the choppy waters, nearly tripling sales (from $13.6 billion to $35.2 billion) but barely increasing the number of employees (from 134,000 to 140,000). A neat trick.

However, the 1980s marked, in many ways, the end of an era for Du Pont. In 1987 they stopped making explosives, their original product and for their first 30 years their *only* product. The du Pont family has less and less to do with the company, and a Canadian liquor company now owns the largest chunk of stock. Also, lifetime employment is no longer a Du Pont benefit.

And although they're still the nation's premier chemical producer, during the 1980s they made a slew of acquisitions that changed the character of the business. First, they swallowed a huge oil company, Conoco, which also made them the nation's second largest coal producer. They built up a $1 billion pharmaceutical business. They bought Shell Oil's herbicide and pesticide lines, making them the second largest U.S. agricultural chemicals producer.

Du Pont produces a vast array of chemicals—for everything from papermaking to crop protection, for use in construction, metals mining, apparel, electronics and agricultural products. Du Pont makes polymers (for building products, automotive paints, separation systems), fibers (nylon, polyester, acrylic and Lycra for clothes, carpets and furnishings), imaging systems and medical products (diagnostics, pharmaceuticals, laser systems), synthetic rubber and resins. During the 1980s, Du Pont celebrated the 50th birthdays of both nylon and teflon. Nylon is made today in 15 plants around the world and in 1987, its 50th year, was still accounting for one-tenth of Du Pont's total sales and *one-quarter* of profits. Another hot product is the stain-resistant carpet, Stainmaster, introduced in 1986, which helped make Du Pont the largest maker of carpet fiber. Still another is Lycra, the fiber in Spandex athletic wear and Gortex swim suits —it brings in more than $500 million a year.

History. In 1797, Pierre Samuel du Pont and his son Eleuthère Irénée du Pont de Nemours fled the political turmoil in France. Their friend Thomas Jefferson advised them to settle on Delaware's Brandy-wine River. There, in 1801, they founded a gunpowder business called E. I. du Pont de Nemours. During the early years, the company sold black powder to the U.S. government, eventually expanding into smokeless powder, dynamite and nitro-glycerine. Until the turn of the century, Du Pont (headed by succeeding generations of the family) functioned as a gigantic one-family show, with various arms and branches making different products.

In the 20th century, although the du Ponts remained a presence, the company evolved into the epitome of the professionally managed corporation. Their family-tree style of organization, giving managers responsibility for their areas, became the model for the running of a big company. In 1917 Du Pont remodeled General Motors using the same principles.

Du Pont moved into synthetics after World War I, making artificial fibers and plastics. They developed cellophane and a clothing fiber called rayon. The most important Du Pont discovery was the 1930 creation of nylon. Made from coal, water and air, the new fiber was used for women's stockings, tire cord, auto parts and brushes. Lucite, a clear, tough plastic resin, soon followed, and in 1938 Du Pont scientists invented teflon, a resin used primarily in cookware. Other ground-breaking products coming out of Du Pont's research labs were Orlon, Dacron polyester, Mylar and Freon, a refrigerator coolant. Du Pont did not entirely forget their first business—explosives. They built and operated the world's first pluto-nium plant to fuel the atomic bombs dropped over Japan in 1945.

Owners and rulers. In 1951 there was opposition at Du Pont to hiring a Jewish lawyer, Irving Shapiro, to work in the legal department at $12,000 a year. Shapiro was not only hired but rose, in 1974, to become Du Pont's CEO, a selection *Fortune* characterized as "wildly im-

> **D**u Pont spends $800 million a year to operate their pollution control equipment, and another $240 million in salaries and benefits for 3,000 environment specialists on staff.

probable" because he had no technical background and "astonishing" in that "the son of a poor Jewish shopkeeper should move to the top of the most family-dominated of the nation's major corporations." Today, in an extension of this scenario, a Jewish family—the Bronfmans, leaders of Canada's Seagram company—controls more Du Pont stock than anyone else, including the du Ponts themselves. As a by-product of Du Pont's acquisition of Conoco, Seagram ended up with 24 percent of Du Pont. The liquor company has 6 representatives on Du Pont's 24-member board of directors. Four du Pont family members still sit on the board, but no du Ponts work in the upper management—and their stockholdings appear to be declining. According to *Forbes*, du Ponts held 15 percent of Du Pont stock in 1988, down from the 35 percent estimated in 1979.

Du Pont had four CEO's during the 1980s. After Shapiro stepped down in 1981, British-born chemist Edward B. Jefferson became chairman. In 1986 Jefferson was succeeded by Richard E. Heckert, a Ph.D chemist and veteran of Du Pont's research labs (he followed his brother into the company). In 1989 the mantle went to a North Carolinian, Edgar Smith Woolard, Jr., an industrial engineer whose forté is management rather than science. He was paid $2.7 million that year.

As a place to work. Du Pont's employee benefits have always been progressive; they came out with a pension and retirement plan in 1904, company-paid life insurance in 1919, paid vacations in 1934, health insurance in 1936 and a disability pay plan in 1937. The Du Ponters are a close bunch. Of the U.S. work force of 100,000 in 1984, nearly 7,000 were married to another Du Ponter, and the company has led in the implementation of benefits helping working parents

TOP CHEMICAL COMPANAIES

Company	Sales
1. Du Pont	$13.0 billion
2. Dow Chemical	$10.8 billion
3. Exxon	$7.2 billion
4. Union Carbide	$6.2 billion
5. Monsanto	$5.2 billion

Source: Chemical and Engineering News,
20 June 1988

balance a career and a family. Du Pont remains a good place to work even though they trimmed the ranks by 11,000 in 1986 with an early retirement package. One Du Pont executive told the *Washington Post* in 1986: "There are people out there who think if they got a job with Du Pont, they've got a job for life. We'd better damn well change their minds." Other companies come to Du Pont to learn how to implement safety programs. If an accident occurs in a Du Pont plant anywhere in the world, the report must be on the CEO's desk the next morning. A lot of people say a Bhopal-type accident (see Union Carbide profile) would be impossible at Du Pont.

Social responsibility. In 1974, when scientists first theorized that chlorofluorocarbons (CFCs) might be piercing the ozone layer that shields the earth from harmful ultraviolet rays, Du Pont dismissed the idea as "speculative." However, they also promised that if scientists could demonstrate CFCs were harmful to public health, they would stop making them. That moment came on March 24, 1988, when Du Pont, reacting to a new study by a National Aeronautics and Space Administration panel, said they would phase out production of CFCs by the century's end. CFCs are used as coolants in refrigerators and air conditioners; they're also used to make plastic foam and as cleaning agents. The Du Pont brand, Freon, had annual sales of $600 million. Du Pont held 50 percent of the U.S. market and 25 percent of the world market. Du Pont set out immediately to develop substitutes for the CFCs.

In 1988, Du Pont came under criticism for an aging nuclear facility they designed, built and operated on the Savannah River in South Carolina. A Congressional hearing reported allegations that Du Pont failed to report accidents at the plant. In October 1988, CEO Richard E. Heckert took out a full page in the *New York Times* and set forth his argument, entitled, "Safety and the Savannah River." Heckert explained that Du Pont operated the plant for 38 years as a public service, earning no profit. He agreed safety "incidents" had occurred, but said all of them had been reported and none had ever led to personal injury.

Global presence. Major. Du Pont expects to be doing half their sales abroad by the mid-1990s (up from 40 percent in 1988). They have 200 plants in 40 countries. One out of every four employees works abroad. Europe is, by far, Du Pont's biggest overseas market, with sales there reaching $9.5 billion in 1988, 60 percent of that volume attributable to Conoco, which drills for oil in the North Sea and sells gasoline in 10 European countries.

Stock performance. Du Pont stock bought for $1,000 in 1980 sold for $5,096 on January 2, 1990.

E. I. du Pont de Nemours and Company, 1007 Market Street, Wilmington, DE 19898; (302) 774-1000.

2

#2 *in chemicals*

Employees: 58,800
Sales: $17.6 billion
Profits: $2.5 billion
Founded: 1897
Headquarters: Midland, Michigan

No more Mr. Tough Guy? Is Dow Chemical turning into a softie? That was the impression left by Dow's image-building commercials running on network evening news shows in 1985. To the theme, "Dow Lets You Do Great Things," they featured heart-warming stories of college graduates who joined Dow because there they could help the world become a better place.

Each year 60 million tons of hazardous chemical wastes are produced.

Dow, more than ever before, seemed concerned about what people thought about them. Keith R. McKennon, president of Dow Chemical U.S.A., told *New York Times* reporter Claudia Deutsch: "We had been a proud group who felt that people who knew nothing were telling us what to do. It took us a long time to realize that regulators, legislators, even environmentalists had a right to ask questions." In the mid-1980s a Dow conducted survey concluded: "The current reputation of Dow with its many publics may be at an all-time low. We are viewed as tough, arrogant, secretive, uncooperative and insensitive." Toward decade's end Dow conducted another survey to determine whether to drop the word, *Chemical,* from their corporate name. After looking at the results, they decided that *chemical* was not perceived as a dirty word.

Announcing the name would go unchanged, Dow's president, Frank Popoff, said: "We are, and will be, a company based primarily on chemistry. We must do a much better job of helping the general public understand the contributions of chemistry."

The 1985 image-building campaign was designed to erase the reputation Dow earned by making napalm bombs during the Vietnam War. They haven't made this product for years, but people still associate them with this flaming jellied gasoline that adhered to its victims skin as it burned.

Dow, second to Du Pont in the U.S. and sixth in the world chemical industry, makes over 2,000 products. They rank among the world leaders in plastics, including polyethylene, polyurethane and polystyrene. They're a formidable producer of basic, building-block chemicals—caustic soda, chlorine, hydrogen chloride, magnesium hydroxide, vinyl chloride—other companies use to make all kinds of products. Long known as "the chemical company's chemical company," selling generic chemicals by the ton, Dow engineered a series of deals in the 1980s that made them important direct sellers to consumers and farmers as well. Prior to 1980, consumers knew Dow mainly through Saran Wrap and Ziploc storage bags. Today, Dow's muscle is behind Citrucel laxative ("It's not gritty, like Metamucil"), Cepacol mouthwash, Nicorette gum (to stop smoking), Yes detergent, Spray 'N Wash stain remover, Spiffits cleaning towels, Freezloc wrap, Fantastik cleaner, Lamaur hair-care products and herbicides such as Spike, Starane and Verdict. Their antihistamine Seldane racked up worldwide sales of nearly $400 million in 1989.

History. Herbert Henry Dow, born in 1866, grew up in Derby, Connecticut (until he was 12), and Cleveland, the son of a master mechanic and inventor and scion of a family that came to America from England in 1637. Herbert's father, Joseph Dow, worked at Cleveland's Chisholm Steel Shovel Works, and he developed what may have been America's first steam turbine. From his father, Herbert learned about manufacturing and the process of invention; chemistry he learned at Cleveland's Case School of Applied Science, the forerunner of Western Reserve University. There he first experimented with extracting bromine from brine—and learned about the rich deposits of prehistoric brine trapped underground at Midland, Michigan, 125 miles north of Detroit. He repaired to Midland in the 1890s, backed by Cleveland money, to extract bromine from brine by electricity. His first successful product, chlorine bleach, was made in 1897, the year Dow Chemical Company was formed. Other products, most of them derived from the brine deposits, followed: chloroform, ethylene, phenol, magnesium. Dow became one of the pioneer companies of the American chemical industry. They got a big boost during World War I when chemical supplies from Germany were no longer available. Companies such as Dow and Monsanto filled the void. The chemists were necessary for the munitions industry. Dow even turned out a mustard gas during World War I.

Dow got another big boost during World War II when they were the prime supplier of magnesium (used in bombs and in plane manufacture) and chemicals such as styrene and butadience (used in the production of synthetic rubber). They put this experience to good use after the war, developing new families of plastics. Styrofoam emerged from Dow before the war was over. Saran Wrap debuted in 1952, although Dow had produced it during the war (one of its uses was as an insect screen). With sales of $200 million in 1949, Dow was already a big company, but they quadrupled sales in the next 10 years. They borrowed to finance their growth (unusual in those days), and they were quicker than Du Pont to put chemical plants in Europe and Asia.

During the 1980s, Dow grew by buying other businesses. In 1981 they bought the Merrell pharmaceutical business (mostly prescription drugs) from Vicks. In 1985 they doubled their consumer business by purchasing Texize cleansers from Morton Thiokol. In 1988 they bought Essex Chemical, a leading producer of auto sealants and adhesives. In 1989 they made two big deals. First, they joined their insecticides with Eli Lilly's fungicides to create a new company, Dow Elanco, which is now the largest U.S. producer of agricultural chemicals (and the sixth largest in the world). Dow Chemical owns 60 percent of Dow Elanco. Then, they combined their pharmaceutical business with Marion Laboratories to create another new company, Marion Merrell Dow, with sales in excess of $2 billion (see profile on Page 000.) Dow Chemical owns two-thirds of Marion Merrell Dow.

O*wners and rulers.* For more than 65 years Dow family members headed this company. Frank Popoff became CEO in December 1987 at age 52. Popoff, born in Sofia, Bulgaria, immigrated to Indiana when he was five years old. He succeeded Paul Orrefice, a native of Italy, who became chairman of the board. Popoff's leadership style is more laid-back than Orrefice's. One former manager said, "Paul could intimidate me just by looking at me. Frank just isn't like that." Popoff made $2.2 million in 1989. The board of directors includes one black (Willie Davis, former football star of the Green Bay Packers), one woman (Barbara H. Franklin) and the president of Princeton University (Harold T. Shapiro). Two Dows are also on the board—cousins Herbert H. Dow and Michael L. Dow.

A*s a place to work.* In 1987, CEO Popoff told the *New York Times,* "Dow is at peace with itself, and we want our people to feel good about the company, too." Dow is still a haven for tough-minded chemical engineers. Headquarters employees call the buildings by number, rather than name (the research and development building is number 1776), and everyone— from the CEO to the new recruit—eats at the austere company cafeteria, which is equipped with plastic trays. A former chairman confides, "Dow's personality has always been very technical, very small town, very sure of ourselves." Dow is the main industry in Midland, a town of 37,000 people located in central Michigan.

S*ocial responsibility.* Dow's greatest about-face has come in the area of environmental protection, where they changed from a zealous defender of everything they did (including the production of the dioxin-laden defoliant Agent Orange) to a company concerned about the side effects of their products and processes. In the last half of the 1980s Dow spent $860 million on environmental health and safety improvements. One result: a better than 50 percent cut in air emissions from U.S. plants. In the 1970s when the Environmental Protection Agency wanted to inspect Dow's power plant in Midland, the company said "nothing doing" and after the EPA flew a reconnaissance plane over the facility, Dow sued them. In the 1980s Dow lined up with the Sierra Club to ask for bigger appropriations for EPA. Dow's 1989 annual report noted the company "has learned through experience that it cannot exist—much less prosper—without public acceptance. The company must be accountable to the public and willing to listen to the public's view, open its doors to seek ideas and gain the support of its

A *bout 45 percent of U.S. chemical employees work for foreign-owned companies. In 1980 that number was only 20 percent. Four of the 10 largest U.S. chemical companies have foreign parents.*

neighbors." Now there's a different Dow Chemical Company.

G*lobal presence.* Chairman Paul Orrefice has said a global company "has a lot of funny accents at headquarters, and we do." Of Dow's 22-member management committee, 10 were born in foreign countries, including Orrefice and Popoff, and 17 have worked abroad. Dow operates 179 plants in 31 countries and sells over half of their products abroad—mostly in Europe, which buys one-third of all of Dow's products. They strengthened their European consumer business in 1989 by acquiring the plastic wrap, food and garbage bags and aluminum foil products sold under the Glad and Albol brand names.

S*tock performance.* Dow stock bought for $1,000 in 1980 sold for $5,405 on January 2, 1990.

Dow Chemical Company, 2030 Dow Court, Midland, MI 48640; (517) 636-1000.

3

#3 *in chemicals*

Employees: 45,000
Sales: $8.7 billion
Profits: $573 million
Founded: 1886
Headquarters: Danbury, Connecticut

Social Conscience

Union Carbide just made it out of the 1980s—no longer the chemical powerhouse of 1980, but still big enough to rank third in the industry. More than 3,400 residents of Bhopal, India, a city 360 miles south of New Delhi, did not survive the decade. They died as a result of a poison gas leak from a pesticide plant 50.9 percent owned by Union Carbide. Thousands of other residents were injured by the noxious fumes escaping from the plant on December 3, 1984. Victims were still dying at the rate of one a day in 1990. Believed to be the worst industrial accident in history, it consumed Carbide for the rest of the decade.

The legal struggle over the disaster did not end until February 14, 1989. During that siege Carbide's chairman, Warren M. Anderson, was arrested when he visited Bhopal immediately after the leak. Meanwhile, Carbide claimed the leak resulted from an act of sabotage—a finding others disputed. After years of minimizing their responsibility for the accident, Carbide agreed to pay $470 million to the Indian government to settle all claims. The new government of V. P. Singh announced in 1990 it may refile criminal liability charges against Carbide if the Indian Supreme Court upholds legal challenges to the settlement.

H*istory.* Union Carbide's parent was a carbon company, founded in 1886, that produced the first dry cell battery and originated the Eveready trademark. In 1917 a group of New York financiers patched the carbon company together with four other companies to form Union Carbide and Carbon Corporation. When the U.S. entered World War I, the company expanded into gases and chemicals. During World War II, Carbide chemists learned how to refine and produce uranium, and the company's research labs helped develop the atom bomb.

Chemistry can lead to all manner of enterprise, but Carbide could never figure out where to go. They knew how to make bulk chemicals, but weren't adept at finished products, especially those sold directly to consumers. During the 1970s they fiddled around with Chaste, a feminine deodorant; Tight Spot, a foot deodorant; Drydees, a disposable diaper; and Stud, an oil additive. All flopped. In 1979 the *Wall Street Journal* described them as "an unwieldy giant run amok, plunging into often mindless ventures." And this was *before* Bhopal. After the Indian disaster, they were even more of a basket case and attracted the attention of financiers who saw an opportunity to pick up good assets at cheap prices. To avoid being taken over, Union Carbide retrenched. They sold off all their consumer businesses (Eveready batteries, Prestone anti-freeze, Glad plastic bags), their agricultural chemicals and even their headquarters in Danbury, Connecticut. In 1989, CEO Robert D. Kennedy revamped Carbide by setting up the firm as a holding company for three separate businesses—chemicals and plastics, industrial gases and carbon. Today's Carbide makes graphite electrodes and other carbon products; industrial gases such as oxygen, nitrogen, hydrogen, helium and argon; and a long line of chemicals and plastics, including ethylene glycol, polyethylene and polycrystalline silicon. In short, they're back to square one: making bulk chemicals.

Owners and rulers. Kennedy, a 31-year veteran at Carbide, became CEO in 1986, succeeding Warren Anderson, who never recovered from Bhopal. Kennedy took home $1.4 million in 1989.

As a place to work. When Kennedy took over in 1986, he had a whopping morale problem. "Everyone was so sick and tired of being beaten up all the time," he told the *New York Times*. Carbide has long been known for their insularity and bureaucracy, but Kennedy is trying to change that. *Business Week* reported in 1988 that workers at Carbide's Texas City, Texas, plant are encouraged to take initiatives such as spreading mats on the plant floor for a daily workout.

Social responsibility. Living down the legacy of Bhopal is hard, but Carbide is giving it a try. In the late 1980s they became a major advocate of business involvement in education, urging companies to work toward the improvement of American school systems. CEO Kennedy also urged colleagues in the chemical industry to report regularly to plant communities about progress made to reduce polluting emissions. This voice was not the one Carbide had prior to Bhopal. In 1990 the Council of International and Public Affairs published a book, *Abuse of Power*, which traced a Carbide legacy: America's worst industrial disaster (an estimated 700 deaths at Hawk's Nest, West Virginia, in 1930), the U.S.'s largest mercury spill (Oak Ridge, Tennessee, 1970), the U.S.'s most polluting plant during the 1970s (Alloya, West Virginia) and willful violations of health and safety standards that in 1985 drew a fine of $1.4 million from the federal Occupational Safety & Health Administration. Lucinda Wykle, coauthor of the book, said: "Union Carbide's Bhopal disaster was not an isolated incident for a corporation with an otherwise clean environment, health and safety record."

Global presence. Union Carbide derives about one-third of sales abroad.

Stock performance. Carbide stock bought for $1,000 in 1980 sold for $2,993 on January 2, 1990.

Union Carbide Corporation, 39 Old Ridgebury Road, Danbury, CT 06817; (203) 794-2000.

4
Monsanto

#4 in chemicals
Employees: 43,900
Sales: $8.7 billion
Profits: $679 million
Founded: 1901
Headquarters: St. Louis, Missouri

Never underestimate a CEO's power. No matter how big the company, a CEO has the opportunity to change the firm's directions and fortunes. Richard J. Mahoney seized that opportunity after becoming Monsanto's boss in 1983. He transformed this colossus of the chemical industry, getting rid of oil and gas operations and petrochemicals, abandoning commodity chemicals once Monsanto mainstays—and buying into a whole new area: pharmaceuticals.

As a result, today's Monsanto is a different animal than the one that prowled in 1980. They're still the world's largest herbicide maker under the brand names Roundup and Lasso, but they gave up another leadership position when they stopped making acetylsalicylic acid—good old aspirin—which they sold to other companies in bulk. They also sold off their AstroTurf business. And their vanillin business. And their polystyrene plastics business. They still have a fiber business (Wear-Dated and Acrilan are

Monsanto is one of the many big American industrial corporations to experiment with worker involvement programs during the 1980s.

Monsanto brand names), but they no longer make raw materials like acrylonitrile that go into man-made fibers. Their big new businesses, accounting for nearly one-quarter of sales, are drugs and the artificial sweetener Nutrasweet, which they acquired in 1985 when they bought G. D. Searle for $2.8 billion. They're looking to widen this business in the 1990s with their fat substitute, Simplesse.

But the biggest change—or at least *attempted* change—is in the corporate culture. A driven man itching to make his mark, Mahoney has been trying to stamp out old habits that go with a lazy, commodity business where external forces dictate how well the company does. In lopping off old businesses and adding new ones, Mahoney has crusaded tirelessly for policies and practices that empower employees while measuring (and rewarding) them by achievement of goals. To rally the troops to his cause, Mahoney wrote a "bible," an 89-page inspirational book, *A Commitment to Greatness*, which he had disseminated throughout the company in 1988. In it he pronounced dead the old Monsanto "culture of forgiveness." His Monsanto, he said, would be a company that made their own luck: "Managers and subordinates will be judged and rewarded by performance...

There must be a sense of urgency... Make the numbers, hit the targets, get the results on time—without excuses."

Mahoney also offered a salvation-through-work vision. He told employees that in a society where so many traditional institutions have been eroded, "the place where we work has become increasingly important in defining who we are and what we stand for. People who work for companies perceived to be superior in purpose and achievement share some of that aura." And the bottom line to this vision is: "Weekends and vacations are too short to be the total focus of one's lifetime."

Mahoney's own bottom line is to make more money. He's frank about that. He wants to do it both short-term and long-term. Monsanto's 1989 profits were five-fold 1979's. Of course not everyone shares in this bonanza. Over that same period Mahoney chopped the Monsanto payroll from 63,000 to under 42,000. Mahoney himself took home $1.7 million in 1989.

Dick Mahoney yearns to have his Monsanto recognized as one of the "most admired corporations" in the annual *Fortune* survey. But in 1989 *Fortune* singled him out for another distinction: one of America's "toughest bosses." The magazine said Mahoney "has a tendency to lecture and is prone to idealistic pronouncements," but that others see him as someone with a "big ego" who "listens to others but doesn't understand." *Fortune* said after Mahoney began selling off businesses, bumper stickers began showing up at Monsanto with the advice: "Dick Mahoney before he dicks you."

Monsanto was founded in 1901 by John Francisco Queeny, the son of Irish immigrants. He named the company after his wife's maiden name. The first products were saccharin, vanillin and caffeine. They made their first big growth spurt during World War I when the U.S. was deprived of chemical supplies from Germany.

Monsanto entered a lot of chemical businesses, including textile fibers and plastics, but their biggest success came in agricultural chemicals, where they rank among the world leaders. They were one of the major producers of Agent Orange, the dioxin-laden defoliant used in the Vietnam War and suspected of causing permanent damage to GIs who fought there. Veterans of that war later sued Monsanto and seven other manufacturers. In 1984, a year after Mahoney became CEO, Monsanto and the other chemical companies settled the case for $180 million just as it was about to go to trial.

Monsanto's big bet for the future is biotechnology. Under the direction of chief scientist Howard A. Schneiderman, they have taken the lead in the chemical industry in the development of gene-altered crops that are immune to viruses (and, incidentally, to Monsanto herbicides).

Stock performance. Monsanto stock bought for $1,000 in 1980 sold for $6,055 on January 2, 1990.

Monsanto Company, 800 North Lindbergh Boulevard, St. Louis, MO 63166; (314) 694-1000.

5
GRACE

Employees: 46,400
Sales: $6.1 billion
Profits: $253 million
Founded: 1854
Headquarters: New York City, New York

Defining W. R. Grace is like trying to hit a moving target. Their normal operating mode is change. Since the end of World War II, they have bought over 100 companies—and sold more than 70. In 1980 they owned regional home improvement stores such as Channel, Handy Dan, Handy City and Orchard Supply plus a bunch of restaurant chains—Coco's, Moonraker, El Torito, Del Taco, La Fiesta, Houlihan's, Reuben E. Lee and Annie's Santa Fe. They also owned a chain of stores specializing in leather goods and western wear: Shepler's and Berman's. And they'd built up Herman's into the nation's biggest sporting goods chain. All told, Grace had in tow some 1,500 retail establishments across the country. They also made fertilizers. All of that stuff is gone now—the restaurants, the stores, the fertilizers. In their place have come other operations. They're now the world's largest cocoa processor. They control National Medical Care, the leading U.S. provider of kidney dialysis services. And they own Baker & Taylor, the book wholesaler.

One constant at Grace is specialty chemicals, especially Cryovac, the plastic used to vacuum pack meats and vegetables. They sell more than $1 billion worth of Cryovac every year. The other constant is J. Peter Grace, chairman, president, CEO and grandson of the founder.

History. William Russell Grace fled the potato famine in Ireland by sailing to Peru as the ship's candlemaker. There he started a business charting ships to haul guano (bird droppings) for fertilizer. He invested in Peruvian land, cotton mills, sugar, tin and nitrates. Grace left Peru in 1865 because of poor health and moved to New York, where he went into shipping. He set up a triangular trade between Peru, the U.S. and Europe—what would eventually become the famous Grace Line. He died in 1904 (after serving two terms as the first Catholic mayor of New York).

In 1945, J. Peter Grace inherited the throne from his father Joseph (W. R.'s son), who'd had a stroke. Peter Grace was 32, and his grandfather's guano business had grown into a transportation, trading and agricultural mammoth. Young Grace had no reverence for tradition. He rapidly transformed the company beyond recognition by leaving South America and expanding into chemicals and consumer businesses. His strategy, or lack of it, led to a bloated hodgepodge, everything from taco stands to coal mines and cowboy clothes, shrimp farms and automobile clutches. Many of the consumer businesses were sold, and by 1990 the chemical business accounted for the biggest chunk of income.

O*wners and rulers.* J. Peter Grace, who remains at the helm at age 77 in 1990, is obsessed with time: He wears a watch on both wrists (one set to New York time, the other to the time zone where he is at the moment). He carries a pistol, a Berretta, in a holster tucked under his belt because of threats from Latin American terrorists (although Grace is almost entirely gone from that region now). And although he was brought up in Gatsby-like indulgence, he sent all five of his sons and four daughters to parochial schools and Catholic universities. After President Reagan selected Grace to head a commission to study waste in government, Grace became a tireless crusader on the lecture and talk show circuit. He made $3.3 million in 1989.

S*tock performance.* Grace stock bought for $1,000 in 1980 sold for $2,883 on January 2, 1990.

W. R. Grace & Company, Grace Plaza, 1114 Avenue of the Americas, New York, NY 10036; (212) 819-5500.

6

BFGoodrich

#1 *in polyvinyl chloride*

Employees: 12,100
Sales: $2.4 billion
Profits: $172 million
Founded: 1870
Headquarters: Akron, Ohio

Goodrich always seems to be explaining what they are not. This founding member of the U.S. tire industry used to be confused so often with Goodyear they began advertising themselves as the "one without the blimp." Then, in 1986, Goodrich decided that being number four in the tire industry wasn't good enough—and so they joined with another also-ran, Uniroyal, a major supplier to General Motors, to form a 50–50 partnership, the Uniroyal Goodrich Tire Company, into which they merged their respective tire operations. Then, a year later, in a typical Goodrich flip-flop, the company decided on second thought they didn't even want this peripheral involvement in the business that gave them life—and so sold off their 50 percent interest in UGTC. That prompted Goodrich to start running ads headlined, "No blimp, no tires," explaining to a thoroughly confused public: "We won't be famous as the tire company without the blimp much longer. Not because we got a blimp. But because we don't make tires anymore."

Oh, motorists can still find and buy Goodrich tires. They just aren't made by B. F. Goodrich, which has hunkered down into a maker of plastics, specialty chemicals and aerospace products such as aircraft brakes, emergency-evacuation systems, helicopter flotation devices, sonar domes and life rafts. Goodrich's biggest business, accounting for nearly half of 1989 sales, is polyvinyl chloride (PVC), a plastic with a wide range of uses in building materials (house sidings, pipes, flooring), automotive parts, packaging film, bottles. Goodrich is the world's largest PVC producer, which is, by volume, the U.S.'s second largest selling plastic.

Stock performance. B. F. Goodrich stock bought for $1,000 in 1980 sold for $3,468 on January 2, 1990.

The B. F. Goodrich Company, 3925 Embassy Parkway, Akron, OH 44313; (216) 374-4595.

7

#**1** in age

Employees: 5,400
Sales: $848 million
Profits: $43 million
Founded: 1767
Headquarters: Windsor Locks, Connecticut

The U.S.'s oldest company, Dexter originally operated a New England paper mill. Today they're a chemical and plastics business, turning out such products as adhesives, coatings, urethane moldings and filters. They're still based in the place they started—Windsor Locks, Connecticut. In 1989, K. Grahame Walker became president and CEO, marking the first time in 17 generations that a member of the founding family was not at the helm. Dexter's status as a senior corporate citizen didn't keep the state of Connecticut and the federal Environmental Protection Agency from bringing a suit in 1989 charging Dexter with violating "virtually every provision" of the U.S. Clean Water Act. Dexter was accused of fouling the Connecticut River with illegal waste discharges. Fish were killed. It was one of the largest water-pollution cases ever brought in New England.

Stock performance. Dexter stock bought for $1,000 in 1980 sold for $3,324 on January 2, 1990.

The Dexter Corporation, 1 Elm Street, Windsor Locks, CT 06096; (203) 627-9051.

PART FIVE

Weaponry and Aerospace

Boeing

McDonnell Douglas

Rockwell International

Huges Aircraft

Lockheed

General Dynamics

Raytheon

Textron

Northrop

GenCorp

WEAPONS

Defense budgets doubled during the 1980s, but at decade's end, as the cold war began to wind down, the nation's weapons makers were scrambling to adjust to the new environment. Speculation centered on which weapons systems were most likely to be abandoned. Surveying the scene in mid-1990, the British weekly, The Economist, divided the top 10 U.S. military contractors into three classes:

*1. **The hawks:** General Dynamics, Raytheon and Martin Marietta. They're not ready to give up their dependence on the military. "Bigger and better guns," they say.*

*2. **The doves:** General Motors (Hughes), Boeing, United Technologies and General Electric. They have substantial activities outside the defense area—and so they're not worried. They're ready for cuts in military spending.*

*3.**The turkeys:** McDonnell Douglas, Grumman and Lockheed. They "haven't a clue."*

1

THE *BOEING* COMPANY

#1 *in commercial aircraft*
#9 *in defense contracting*

Employees: 159,200
Sales: $20.3 billion
Profits: $675 million
Founded: 1916
Headquarters: Seattle, Washington

The one American product that's as ubiquitous around the world as Coca-Cola and McDonald's is the Boeing jet airplane. Boeing jets fly for more than 160 airlines. They've built more than half the jets ever flown. And—will wonders never cease—all these planes have been built in the U.S., specifically in two Seattle-area plants. One is in Renton, 12 miles south of Seattle. The other, at Everett, 30 miles north of Seattle, is the world's largest enclosed space—taller than an 11-story building, one-half-mile wide and the length of 40 football fields. To see what's going on, supervisors need binoculars. To light this 780-acre complex requires the power used to electrify 32,000 average American homes.

The Boeing family of jets began with the 707 in 1954 and grew to include the 727, 737, 747, 757 and 767. The biggest selling plane in Boeing's history is the 737, which flies short- to medium-range distances. As of September 1988, over 2,100 737s had been sold to 141 airlines. The biggest plane in Boeing's fleet is the 747-400, which Northwest Airlines put into service in 1989. The 747-400 has a wing span of 211 feet and can carry 412 passengers from San Francisco to Bangkok without refueling. Price tag: $130 million.

Boeing is the aerospace industry's largest employer (and also the state of Washington's), and they indirectly employ thousands of others through subcontracts. Boeing buys from nearly 4,000 companies. To build the 757, they used 1,300 subcontractors, but just 4 of them—Pratt & Whitney, Rolls-Royce, Rockwell and Honeywell—supplied 53 percent of the plane.

This jet-plane pioneer added propeller planes to their fleet in 1986 when they paid $155 million to buy Canada's de Havilland company, builder of the Dash 8 and Triton turboprop aircraft for commuter runs (but they were looking for a buyer of it in 1990). It was Boeing's first acquisition since buying the Vertol helicopter company in 1960. Philadelphia-based Vertol makes the world's biggest helicopters. Their olive-colored Chinooks were used extensively in the Vietnam War, virtually symbolizing that conflict.

Aside from building planes, Boeing produces missiles, rockets and sophisticated electronic systems. They're also a major supplier of computer information services. They would be a $5.6 billion company without the airplanes. Boeing derives 26 percent of sales from the U.S. government.

History. Boeing started out as a rich timberman's hobby. William Edward Boeing, a Yale graduate, came to Washington early in this century from Wisconsin to acquire timber properties. He learned to fly and bought the second pontoon plane built by aviation pioneer Glenn L. Martin. Boeing wanted the seaplane because he liked to fish, and it gave him quick access to lakes and rivers in British Columbia. After finding it took six months to get replacement parts, the impatient Boeing decided to make his own plane. In 1916 he set up his "factory" in a boathouse on the shores of Lake Union near downtown Seattle. His stick-and-wire seaplane was built in six months—the first of thousands of Boeings.

In 1919 Boeing and a World War I pilot, Edward Hubbard, organized an airmail service between Seattle and Victoria, British Columbia. Later they won the U.S. Post Office contract to carry mail between San Francisco and Chicago. In other words, Boeing was both building planes and operating them—and by decade's end he and his associates, mainly Frederick B. Rentschler, had brought into being what would be recognized today as a conglomerate. Lumped into a New York–based holding company called United Aircraft were Boeing, the Seattle plane builder; Pratt & Whitney, the aircraft engine builder; Northrop, a maker of military planes; the Sikorsky airplane works (they built amphibians); and a bunch of regional airlines merged into a system called United Air Lines. It all came unglued in 1934 after a government investigation into collusion in the awarding of airmail contracts. Plane builders were then separated from plane operators. United Airlines emerged as an independent company based in Chicago. Pratt & Whitney still makes engines as part of United Technologies.

Boeing remained in Seattle to build planes. They made the P-12 fighters, the Stratoliner (the first four-engine plane to operate on transcontinental runs) and the famous Clipper flying boats used by Pan Am on international routes. Their B-17, the Flying Fortress, dropped 640,000 tons of bombs on German targets, more than all the bombs dropped by all other Allied planes. The B-17 was followed by the B-29, the Super Fortress, the biggest airplane ever built up to that time. A B-29 dropped the atomic bombs on Hiroshima and Nagasaki in 1945. After the war, Boeing continued to make bombers—the B-47, the B-50 and the famous B-52.

In 1952, when Douglas Aircraft's DC series dominated the commercial plane market, Boeing invested $16 million to develop a jet-powered prototype. This move sent them to the head of the class. Boeing's jet lifted into the air for the first

TOP 10 DEFENSE CONTRACTORS

Company	1989 Contracts
1. McDonnell Douglas	$8.6 billion
2. General Dynamics	$6.9 billion
3. General Electric	$5.7 billion
4. Raytheon	$3.7 billion
5. General Motors/Hughes	$3.6 billion
6. Lockheed	$3.6 billion
7. United Technologies	$3.5 billion
8. Martin Marietta	$3.3 billion
9. Boeing	$2.8 billion
10. Grumman	$2.3 billion

time in 1954. American Airlines, always first with the latest Douglas equipment, was impressed enough to place orders. The first scheduled flight of a jetliner took place on January 25, 1959. American Airlines Flight #2 left Los Angeles and swept across the country to New York in four hours and three minutes. The plane, which cost $5.5 million, was a Boeing 707. It put Boeing into a leadership position they've yet to give up.

Not that there wasn't turbulence along the way. In the late 1960s and early 1970s Boeing was in a slump. They'd opted to make the 747 jumbo jet, and when the planes were ready, the airline industry had no great need for them. From 1969 to 1972 Boeing didn't get a single order for a 747. Congress then halted Boeing's work on the controversial SST (Supersonic Transport). Boeing's work force was slashed from 105,000 to 38,000. Seattle's unemployment rate soared to 13 percent. A billboard appeared in the city: "Will the last one to leave Seattle please turn off the lights?"

They entered the 1980s with Seattle-area employment of 80,000. That dropped to 73,700 in 1985, but hit 153,000 in 1990, after record-breaking orders poured into Seattle. In the first six months of 1990, Boeing received new orders for 214 planes worth $19.3 billion, giving them a backlog (1,760 jets) big enough to keep the production lines going until century's end. One remarkable aspect of Boeing is lack of debt, despite the billions they gamble in developing new planes.

Owners and rulers. They've had only six CEOs in 74 years. William M. Allen, a lawyer known for his gentle demeanor, took command after World War II and bet the company on jet aircraft. He was succeeded in 1969 by a no-nonsense, blunt-speaking aeronautical engineer, Thornton A. Wilson, known inside Boeing as "T." He worked 43 years for Boeing before retiring on January 1, 1988. Another Boeing veteran, Frank Shrontz, became CEO in 1986. Shrontz, an Idahoan who holds a law degree and a Harvard MBA, interrupted his 32-year Boeing career twice—to serve as assistant secretary of the Air Force in 1973 and assistant secretary of defense in 1976. He took home $1.1 million in 1989. Over half of Boeing's stock is held by big institutional investors like insurance companies. The combined holdings of all directors and officers (66 persons) come to less than 1 percent of total shares. Boeing has a heavyweight, all-male, all-white board of directors whose members include former Secretary of State George P. Shultz, the former heads of Chevron (two of them), Prudential Insurance and Caterpillar, and the heads of three of the biggest companies in the Pacific Northwest: Weyerhaeuser, PACCAR and Boise Cascade.

As a place to work. Boeing runs a tight ship. No freewheeling here. They drove a hard bargain during the 1980s, putting in a two-tier wage system (new employees get less money than old employees doing the same job) and paying lump-sum bonuses in lieu of wage increases. In 1989 production was sharply curtailed by a 48-day work stoppage. Nevertheless, employees are loyal. "That's the peculiar thing about Boeing," an official of the International Association of Machinists once said. "Workers take great pride in their work here. They like to think they are making a contribution, helping build the best airplanes in the world." Look at any issue of the weekly company newspaper, *Boeing News*, and you will see long listings of employees who have retired or are celebrating anniversaries of 45 years, 40 years, 35 years, 30 years and 25 years. Each issue also carries pages listing jobs open throughout the company.

Social responsibility. Boeing makes the front pages more often than most companies. Every time a plane goes down, they're in the limelight. Hailed by *Time* in a 1980 cover story for "innovation, reliability and plain downright engineering excellence that is unmatched in the industry," Boeing had some rocky times in the 1980s. A Japan Air Lines 747 crashed on a domestic flight in 1985, killing 520 people in the worst single-plane accident in history. Boeing later took responsibility for the crash, attributing it to faulty repair of the plane's rear pressure bulkhead. Then a series of accidents involving the 737 and the discovery of poor wiring and plumbing on 757s and 767s occurred. As a result, the Federal Aviation Administration issued a directive in 1989 for inspections of all Boeing planes built since 1980. An analysis of these incidents in the *New York Times* speculated they may have resulted from an inexperienced work force (Boeing added 22,000 employees in Seattle between 1985 and 1988) and/or from the fatigue of a work force constantly working overtime. Boeing denied they had any quality control problems, but admitted that "it is very clear that we can be doing better than we are doing."

Global presence. Wherever there's an airport, you'll find Boeing. Boeing planes

Boeing's 747 and 767 manufacturing plant in Everett, Washington, is the largest enclosed space in the world, 291 million cubic feet.

touch down somewhere in the world every four and a half seconds every day. They're the nation's second largest exporter—$7.8 billion in 1988 or 46 percent of their total revenues. Some of these exports are weapons. In 1988 Boeing's European military sales were $478 million, in Asia $225 million.

Stock performance. Boeing stock bought for $1,000 in 1980 sold for $5,575 on January 2, 1990.

The Boeing Company, 7755 East Marginal Way South, Seattle, WA 98108; (206) 655-2121.

2

#1 *in defense contracting*

Employees: 124,700
Sales: $14.6 billion
Losses: $40 million
Founded: 1967
Headquarters: St. Louis, Missouri

McDonnell Douglas prospered during the 1980s. Under President Ronald Reagan, the Pentagon budget doubled, and McDonnell Douglas rode the crest, getting more defense orders than any other defense firm. Their problem, as the decade ended, was how to adjust to what seemed to be the winding down of the cold war. How can a maker of fighter planes do well when nations decide not to fight one another? Their major products are among the most expensive new weapons systems —fighters, helicopters and missiles—and all seem likely targets for congressional budget slashers. The company was preparing to slash the workforce by 10 percent in 1990.

McDonnell Douglas' specialty has been combat planes that can wreak destruction. They make the F-15 Eagle, a supersonic fighter, for the Air Force; the F/A/ Hornet, a multimission attack plane for the Navy and the Marine Corps; and the AV-8B Harrier, a vertical and short takeoff and landing plane, for the Marine Corps. With

the blessing of the U.S. government, they also sell these planes to other governments. The world's largest builder of combat planes, they passed General Dynamics during the 1980s to become number one on the Pentagon buying list. In addition to planes, McDonnell Douglas makes the Harpoon and Tomahawk missiles, the Apache attack helicopters (they bought Hughes Helicopters in 1984), guns and ammunition, and the Delta expendable launch vehicles to boost satellites into orbit. McDonnell Douglas does two-thirds of their sales with the U.S. government.

The Douglas part of the company makes jet planes for airlines, running a distant second to Boeing. In 1988 airlines in the noncommunist world placed orders for 1,068 passenger jets. McDonnell Douglas snared 246—or 23 percent—of those orders, below the 58 percent Boeing garnered but comfortably above the 14 percent that went to the European consortium, Airbus. The bulk of those orders were for the MD-80, a midrange jet going head-to-head with the Boeing 737s.

McDonnell Douglas has two other businesses. One is information services, a byproduct of the computer expertise they developed in making planes and missiles. This branch includes Tymnet, a data transmission network supplying such services as credit card authorization and hotel reservations. The second is financial services, a by-product of financing their customers airplane purchases. McDonnell now leases cars, trucks and heavy machinery, engages in real estate lending and leases small planes built by others to commuter airlines. This business is extremely profitable, unlike the building of jet planes.

History. McDonnell Douglas was created in 1967 by the merger of a military plane builder, McDonnell Aircraft, with a commercial plane builder, Douglas Aircraft. Both were family-run outfits. Both were Scottish families. It was a cross-country merger; McDonnell's base was St. Louis; Douglas Aircraft's, Long Beach, California. But if anyone dominated, McDonnell did. They were going great guns selling planes to the military. Douglas, after a brilliant run in aviation's early days, had been beaten to the punch in the jet age by Boeing.

Douglas' most famous series of planes was the Douglas Commercial—called DC and followed by a number, beginning with the DC-2 in 1933. The DC-3 became a legend. Known as the immortal, it was so perfect aerodynamically that engineers claimed it could glide if the engines failed. Airlines eventually bought 448 DC-3s—and they were steady sellers on the used market for years. The DC-7 became the first commercial plane to fly nonstop across the U.S. Their leadership ended in the late 1950s when Boeing's jet was introduced. Douglas' first jet, the DC-8, was still in the test stage.

After the 1967 merger, McDonnell Douglas began building the DC-10, one of the most controversial planes in history because of several crashes, including one in 1979 that killed 250 American Airlines passengers during a takeoff from Chicago's O'Hare Airport.

McDonnell Douglas thought they'd overcome their DC-10 troubles, but airplane design problems resurfaced in 1989 with the crash of a United Airlines plane in Iowa that killed 110 people, followed eight days later by the crash, killing 75 people, of a Korean Air DC-10 attempting to land in Libya in poor weather. That the crashes resulted from structural defects was unclear, but the possibility was raised that Douglas Aircraft might have to redesign the hydraulic system of the MD-11, their new entry in the wide body market. The MD-11 is based largely on the DC-10 design.

In early 1989, the *last* plane bearing the DC designation, a DC-10, was delivered to Nigeria Airways. Now it's MD (for McDonnell Douglas).

The two company founders died within six months of each other in the early 1980s. James Smith McDonnell, an irascible, tenacious, domineering entrepreneur, died in 1980—at age 81. Known as Mr. Mac, he started his company in 1939 with a staff of one in a rented office at St. Louis' Lambert Field. Donald Wills Douglas, an engineer who began building planes in California in the 1920s and then built an enormous company around them (during World War II he had 157,000 employees), died at 88 in 1981.

Owners and rulers. The McDonnells are still in charge here. The bearded John F. McDonnell, son of the founder, serves as chairman and CEO (1989 pay: $1.2

One of the few bearded CEOs in America, John F. McDonnell, chairman and son of the founder of McDonall Douglas.

million), while his brother James sits on the board and is a vice president. Uncle Sanford McDonnell, who served as CEO after his brother (the founder) retired, is on the board. The McDonnell family owns about 15 percent of the stock, worth an estimated $400 million. But the biggest owners are the employees. Over 86,000 of the nearly 125,000 people working at MDC own 30 percent of the stock through savings plans.

As a place to work. Changing. When James McDonnell ran the company, he talked about the employees as a team, but he made all the major decisions and presided over a hierarchical company with many management layers. The McDonnell uncle and nephew—Sanford and John— in charge during the 1980s tried to renew the company by emphasizing participative management by employees. In annual reports, advertisements and company magazines they're talking today about the contributions made by rank-and-filers. John McDonnell addresses them as "teammates" and in the 1988 annual report he admits "culturally" the company used to be "a hierarchical organization of people with a fierce pride—bordering on arrogance." (He could be talking about his father.) McDonnell also began stripping away layers of management. At Douglas Aircraft, California's largest employer, McDonnell compressed 11 management layers into and reduced management ranks from 5,000 to 2,800. He also replaced the old Douglas Aircraft management with new people dispatched from St. Louis (for the first time since the 1967 merger McDonnell people are running Douglas Aircraft). One of the imports was Joel D. Smith, once with the United Auto Workers, where he observed the team approaches used at the Toyota–General Motors joint venture in Fremont, California. In 1983, when workers at Douglas Aircraft walked out in a four-month strike, Smith walked the picket line. Now he's in charge of quality control at Douglas.

Social responsibility. With the cold war thawing, they're keenly aware that support for defense spending is weakening, but feel the programs they have in the pipeline equip them "to compete in a declining market." At every annual meeting during the 1980s, a coalition of religious orders presented a resolution requiring the company to reduce dependence on military spending. In 1989 the resolution garnered 3.5 percent of shareholder votes even as the company said they were "proud to be in the forefront of corporations providing products and technologies used in the defense of the free world."

McDonnell Douglas is one of 30 companies to celebrate United Nations Day with a paid holiday for all employees.

Global presence. You bet. They do 23 percent of sales abroad, mostly combat planes sold to foreign governments— these sales must be cleared through the U.S. government. The F-15 Eagle flies for the armed forces of Israel, Japan and Saudi Arabia; the F/A Hornet for Spain, Kuwait and Switzerland; the Harrier for Spain and Britain's Royal Air Force.

Stock performance. McDonnell Douglas stock bought for $1,000 in 1980 sold for $2,256 on January 2, 1990.

McDonnell Douglas Corporation, P.O. Box 516, St. Louis, MO 63116; (314) 232-0232.

3

Rockwell International

#1 *in space contracts*

Employees: 110,400
Sales: $12.5 billion
Profits: $721 million
Founded: 1919
Headquarters: Pittsburgh, Pennsylvania

There's an old Rockwell boast, "If it moves, we probably made something on it." One of the high-tech giants of American business, Rockwell makes the space shuttle, bombers and fighter planes, satellites, control instruments on the flight decks of jet planes, fiber optic lines that carry telephone conversations, electronic automation systems to run factories, printing presses, gas meters and a long line of automotive components such as truck axles, air disc brakes, universal joints, suspension rings, power window regulators and plastic body panels. That's just a small sampling of the thousands of products produced in over 100 Rockwell plants in the U.S., Canada, Mexico, Europe, Australia, Brazil and the Far East.

With all these products, the one that mattered to Rockwell the most in the 1980s was the B-1 bomber, which had a tortured political history. First proposed by President Richard Nixon in 1970, the B-1 was scrapped by President Jimmy Carter and revived by President Ronald Reagan, a decision that was a bonanza for Rockwell. By the time the last B-1 rolled out of Rockwell's Palmdale, California, plant in 1988, 100 had been produced at a total cost of $16 billion—and for six years in the 1980s the B-1 contract accounted for 25 percent of Rockwell's total sales.

The end of the B-1 work sharply reduced Rockwell's dependency on the Pentagon. Whereas the U.S. government accounted for 58 percent of sales in 1987, by 1989 Pentagon contracts accounted for only 28 percent of Rockwell's revenues. However, they remain the largest contractor to the National Aeronautics & Space Administration, a position held since 1973. One of their sad moments in the 1980s was the January 28, 1986, explosion that destroyed the *Challenger* shuttle (and killed seven people aboard) shortly after it rocketed off from Cape Canaveral. Rockwell, whose work on the shuttle was never faulted, served as prime contractor for *Challenger*. Before decade's end, they'd supplied NASA with another shuttle.

Rockwell's major move of the 1980s was the acquisition of Milwaukee's Allen-Bradley for $1.7 billion in 1985. They produce electronic control systems that help manufacturers run factories. As a result, Rockwell now has more business in commercial electronics than in aerospace. Rockwell installs more than 1 million gas and water meters every year in the U.S. and makes axles and brakes for one-half of all U.S. heavy-duty trucks and tractors. Their Goss presses print two out of every three newspapers in the country.

Rockwell is always obsessed with defining themselves. For a good part of the 1980s they used the line, "Where science gets down to business." Then, toward decade's end, they began singing, "Let's reach a little higher." CEO Donald Beall is aware of the identity problem. He told the *Wall Street Journal*: "What we do is not fully understood. It drives me up the wall."

History. Rockwell's schizophrenia is rooted in a convoluted history. They were put together pell-mell by the company's founder, Al Rockwell, who hoped to create another General Electric. Robert Anderson, who reshaped the company during the 1970s and 1980s, called them "the most ill-conceived company ever conceived."

Rockwell-Standard began in 1919 by making truck axles in Oshkosh, Wisconsin. Col. Willard F. Rockwell and his son, Willard Jr. collected 50 companies before 1967 when they merged with North American Aviation, an aerospace company that once owned Eastern Airlines and almost went belly up during the depression before being rescued by General Motors.

Nine months before the merger, on January 27, 1967, three astronauts—Virgil Grissom, 40, Edward White II, 36, and Roger Chaffee, 31—burned to death in a fire that broke out inside an Apollo space capsule at Cape Kennedy, Florida. The ghastly accident touched off a barrage of criticism of North American Aviation, Apollo's builder. Of the two companies, North American was much the larger—

Through mid-1990, Boeing had received orders for 284 of its 747–400 jumbo jets, a monster plane that can seat 600 people and fly 8,400 miles nonstop. The leading customer is Japan Air Lines, with 40 orders. Each plane sells for $130

with sales of $2 billion to Rockwell-Standard's $635 million. But from the outset of this merger the shots were clearly called by the Rockwells: Col. Willard F. Rockwell and son, Willard Jr. *Fortune* once described Col. Rockwell as someone who picks up and discards companies "like a gin-rummy player." The colonel himself once prophesied: "By 1980, 200 companies will control 60 to 75 percent of the world's gross national product, and we intend to be one of them." Two years after the merger, Rockwell took over Miehle-Goss-Dexter, the big printing-press manufacturer.

Shortly after merging with North American, the Rockwells lured Robert Anderson away from Chrysler to bring order to their industrial melange. Anderson had been general manager of the Chrysler-Plymouth division and became unhappy when his subordinate at Chrysler, John Riccardo, was promoted over him. "It's not that I have to be on top," Anderson told the *Wall Street Journal*. "I just hate to be shafted."

Owners and rulers. Today's Rockwell is largely the handiwork of Robert Anderson, who came aboard in 1968 after leaving Chrysler. He became CEO in 1974, reshaped the company, tripled sales and stayed in the catbird's seat until 1988 when he stepped down in favor of his handpicked successor, a hard-driving, 49-year-old engineer, Donald R. Beall, who was paid $1.3 million in 1989. Reviewing his 20 years with the company, Anderson said he was most proud of the "quality of management" at Rockwell. One of the largest stockholders on the Rockwell board—even though the amount is only one-tenth of 1 percent of the shares—is Bruce M. Rockwell, the son of Al Rockwell, who works for the Detroit investment banking firm, First of Michigan. The biggest chunk of Rockwell shares, 40 percent of the total, is held by the employee savings plan. Each employee has voting rights over his (this company is largely male) shares.

As a place to work. Many Rockwell companies—Allen-Bradley in Milwaukee, Goss in Chicago, Collins in Cedar Rapids, Iowa—have cultures of their own, predating their acquisition, but under Anderson, and now Beall, the thrust has been to Rockwellize them. While sales doubled in the 1980s, U.S. employees declined by over 10,000. According to Rockwell, 1 out of every 10 managers is a minority group member. Rockwell has plants all over the U.S., but the big concentration of employees is in the aerospace plants around Los Angeles. They had 35,000 employees in southern California at the end of 1989. Some 20,000 Rockwell employees are scientists and engineers. The big employee stockholding flows from a savings plan under which Rockwell people may salt away 8 percent of their pretax pay, with the company putting in 75 percent of what the employee saves (and the company has the option of making their contribution entirely in stock). This plan is for salaried people or nonunionized employees. As of 1988, 42,000 of Rockwell's employees were participants.

Social responsibility. Like other defense contractors, Rockwell was plagued during the 1980s by discoveries of overcharging—at one point the Air Force suspended the company from receiving new contracts—but their worst moment came at decade's end when the Department of Energy replaced Rockwell as the manager of the plutonium weapons plant at Rocky Flats, Colorado, just as two years earlier the company had lost their contract to operate the plutonium-producing facility at Hanford, Washington. A front-page story in the Wall Street Journal disclosed the government had faulted Rockwell for a variety of sloppy and dangerous practices at Rocky Flats, including the dumping of cancer-causing chemicals into streams, the burning of hazardous waste in a closed incinerator and the exposure of employees to possibly hazardous materials such as beryllium. The Journal reported that on one raid at Rocky Flats, FBI agents found that for over a decade a Rockwell manager ran a model shop where such trinkets as baseball caps, coffee mugs, foot massagers and cuff links were made and then given as gifts to Department of Energy officials. Paperweights turned out there bore the legend: "Would we lie to you?"

Global presence. Rockwell greatly expanded their overseas operations during the 1980s to 22 percent of total revenues, up from 13 percent in 1983. They now get half their automotive component sales abroad.

Stock performance. Rockwell International stock bought for $1,000 in 1980 sold for $5,450 on January 2, 1990.

Rockwell International, 600 Grant Street, Pittsburgh, PA 15219; (412) 565-2000.

4

GM Hughes Electronics

#1 *in satellites, weapons-related electronics, automotive-related electronics*

#5 *in weapons making*

Employees: 97,000 (weapons: 72,000)
Sales: $11.2 billion (weapons: $7.4 billion)
Profits: $750 million (weapons: $160 million)
Founded: 1932 (weapons)
Headquarters: Detroit, Michigan (weapons: Los Angeles, California)

Long known as the Cadillac of military contractors, Hughes Aircraft hopes to avoid becoming a run-of-the-mill Chevy now that General Motors owns them. Before GM bought them in 1985, Hughes Aircraft had built up a sterling reputation for making the most technologically advanced and highest quality electronic equipment in the weapons business, with products ranging from missiles and radar systems to microwave transmitters and space satellites. Scientific wizardry is what Hughes is all about, although their reputation was not enhanced in 1990 when the $1.5 billion Hubble Space Telescope built by their Perkin-Elmer subsid-

30 year-old Howard Hughes with his company's most famous aircraft, the H-1 racer. The original H-1 is on permanent display at the Smithsonian's National Air and Space Museum in Washington, D.C.

iary was shot into orbit and failed miserably because of a microscopic flaw in its mirror. Previously, Hughes had boasted that the Hubble was "the greatest leap in astronomy since Galileo first gazed into a telescope in 1609."

The tradition of quality stems from their founder, the legendary Howard Hughes. Hughes set up the company to build state-of-the-art experimental airplanes, including the H-1 racer, which he piloted to several world speed records, and the huge flying boat, the Spruce Goose, now a tourist attraction in Long Beach (it only flew once). After World War II, Hughes Aircraft stopped building planes to concentrate on high-tech military electronics gear, such as the Falcon, the world's first air-to-air, radar-guided missile. Hughes transferred his company's stock to the Howard Hughes Medical Institute, and the company was then run by a succession of engineers free from the usual profit-making constraints. Howard Hughes gave up control of Hughes Aircraft after the Air

Force became fed up with his erratic behavior. They hired the best and the brightest engineers, paid them well and let them make the best equipment they could. As one House Armed Services Committee aide said in 1981: "Buying a product from Hughes is more like buying a Cadillac than a Volkswagen... They are the top in military systems. They are expensive, but they are a first-rate operation."

When General Motors bought Hughes Aircraft, they were one of the country's largest privately held companies, with sales of $8 billion. GM quickly merged Hughes with their Delco auto electronics division, brought in three former GM or Delco managers to fill top slots, and began pressuring Hughes to improve profitability, leading to a rare reduction in the size of Hughes' payroll. Meanwhile, another Hughes legacy reared its ugly head—executive in-fighting. The Los Angeles Times reported various Hughes executives had referred to one another in press interviews as "jug head," "showboat," "hypocrite," "bigot," "loose cannon" and "back-stabber." In 1988, a new CEO abruptly resigned after only two weeks. To the surprise and delight of Hughes veterans, GM did not bring in an auto executive as CEO. Instead they installed Malcolm Currie, a doctorate in engineering from the University of California at Berkeley, and a Hughes Aircraft employee since 1954, where he has obtained several patents. Currie, who also served as Under Secretary of Defense in the Ford administration, hopes to reduce the company's reliance on the Pentagon from 80 percent of sales to 60 percent by bolstering the commercial satellite business, pushing flight simulators to train airline pilots and getting contracts for air-traffic control systems.

GM Hughes Electronics Corporation, General Motors Building, 3044 West Grand Boulevard, Detroit, MI 48202; (313) 556-5000.

Hughes Aircraft Company, P.O. Box 45066, Los Angeles, CA 90045; (213) 568-6111.

5

Lockheed

#1 *in Star Wars contracts*

Employees: 84,700
Sales: $9.9 billion
Profits: $2 million
Founded: 1916
Headquarters: Calabasas, California

Some of the nation's brainiest people work for Lockheed, developing weapons of destruction and devising systems to repel weapons of destruction that might be aimed at the U.S. They make the submarine-launched Trident missiles, huge military transport planes, rocket boosters to send satellites into orbit, antisubmarine aircraft and a galaxy of top-secret, airborne equipment that serves, in effect, as "spies in the sky." Much of their work is classified, and it's therefore difficult to determine precisely what Lockheed does. Barbed wire surrounds many of their plants, and dense, complicated language in their literature blocks understanding.

Their original business—plane building—was carried out in Burbank until May 1990 when Lockheed decided to move from their original location. Most plane building will now take place in Marietta, Georgia, though Lockheed's headquarters remains in southern California. Their aerospace and missile businesses are carried out in northern California from their Silicon Valley base in Sunnyvale.

One thing they don't do anymore is build airliners. The Electra turboprop introduced in 1959 did so poorly—two of them crashed within months of going into service—that they stopped making them in 1961 after 170 were built. (One of the Electras still flying crashed near Reno in 1985, killing 64 people.) The L-1011 Tri-Star jet introduced in the 1970s also did poorly—airlines preferred the Boeing and Douglas widebodies—and Lockheed stopped making them in 1981. (In 1983 Kakuei Tanaka, Japan's former prime minister, was sentenced to four years in jail for taking a $2 million bribe from Lockheed as part of their TriStar sales effort.)

Lockheed's number one customer, accounting for 88 percent of their sales, is the U.S. government. They're the number one contractor for the Strategic Defense Initiative (SDI) or Star Wars program President Ronald Reagan launched. One of their projects is a missile described as a "kinetic energy vehicle." Lockheed claims it will be "so precisely guided that it can intercept an incoming ballistic warhead traveling at 23,000 miles per hour and destroy it through collision rather than by setting off a nuclear blast." (They don't explain why the collision won't also set off a nuclear blast.) Another of their projects, tracked down by *San Francisco Examiner* reporter John Markoff, involves a Big Brother satellite dubbed Keyhole. This satellite will circle the globe, capable of zeroing in on any small object on the earth, producing instant TV pictures or three-dimensional digital photographs. They will also be able to pick up radio and telephone conversations. Lockheed will know what

Currently the defense industry employs 40 percent of America's engineers and scientists.

TOP NUCLEAR WEAPONS CONTRACTORS

		Value of Contracts*
1.	McDonnell Douglas	$3.9 billion
2.	General Electric	$3.4 billion
3.	General Dynamics	$2.8 billion
4.	Westinghouse	$2.7 billion
5.	Lockheed	$2.7 billion
6.	United Technologies	$2.1 billion
7.	University of California	$2.0 billion
8.	Martin Marietta	$1.8 billion
9.	Rockwell International	$1.5 billion
10.	DuPont	$1.2 billion
11.	AT&T	$1.2 billion
12.	Boeing	$1.1 billion
13.	Allied Signal	$.8 billion
14.	Raytheon	$.8 billion
15.	EG & G	$.6 billion

*These are contracts awarded by the Dept. of Defense and Dept. of Energy in fiscal year 1988.

Source: Nuclear Free America.

you're doing. Lockheed will know what everybody is doing.

Spectacular as these scientific feats appear to be, Lockheed limped through the 1980s, running late on deliveries and going over budget on fixed-price contracts, which meant they ate the losses. That performance attracted a raider, Houston's Harold Simmons, who accumulated 19 percent of Lockheed's shares and appealed to other shareholders to turn out the board of directors and replace them with his slate, whose members included a former deputy administrator of NASA, a former Air Force general, a former chief of Naval Operations and former Texas Senator John G. Tower, President George Bush's defeated nominee for Secretary of Defense. At their annual meeting on March 29, 1990, Lockheed shareholders rejected the Simmons slate.

H*istory.* In 1913, brothers Allan and Malcolm Loughhead (who later changed the spelling of their name) flew their seaplane over San Francisco Bay. Three years later they established an aircraft company in Santa Barbara, working with designer Jack Northrop. Malcolm and Northrop left, but Allan scored a hit in 1926 with the Vega plane, which Amelia Earhart later used in her transatlantic solo flight. The company moved to Los Angeles but went bankrupt in 1931.

In 1932, Lockheed was resurrected by Boston bankers Robert and Courtlandt Gross—without Allan Lockheed, but with his name. Six years later the company entered the weapons industry, producing the Hudson bomber for the British. Lockheed has depended on military contracts ever since. The Korean War in the 1950s made Lockheed the country's biggest defense company, as they churned out Shooting Star fighters and Constellation transports. A major try at commercial airline business flopped with the Electra propjet.

Alas, scandal and mismanagement became a way of life at Lockheed for many years. In 1959, the company sold Starfighters to Germany; 175 of the planes crashed, killing 85 pilots, including the son of Germany's minister of defense. Then, in 1969, Lockheed posted a loss of $32 million and advised the Pentagon that unless they received a $600 million transfusion, they would have to stop work on four military projects. In 1971, the U.S. Senate voted (by a one-vote margin) to guarantee up to $250 million in loans to keep Lockheed alive. In 1975, congressional investigations discovered Lockheed had paid $25.5 million in bribes to foreign powers, among them a Middle Eastern wheeler-dealer and the former prime minister of Japan. In Japan, the word *Lockheed* became a household word standing for corruption of public officials.

O*wners and rulers.* Employees, through their savings plans, own 19 percent of the shares—about what Simmons owned. Most of the rest is owned by institutions like insurance companies and state pension plans. Daniel Tellep, a graduate of the engineering school at University of California at Berkeley, is CEO (1989 pay: $813,000). His appointment was significant because he came up from the missiles and space end of the business, not plane building.

As *a place to work.* A little uptight, as befitting a military contractor. Just about everybody needs a security clearance. In Silicon Valley, home of the missiles and space division, they're the largest employer, with a work force of 25,000, but they don't have the informality and perks found in neighboring high-tech firms. Their work force is older and more stable. Lockheed is one of the few unionized Silicon Valley firms. When they moved their aerospace operations north from Los Angeles, the International Association of Machinists made the move too.

Social responsibility. In February 1990, Lockheed was fined $1 million by air pollution regulators in Los Angeles. Most of the fine was for record-keeping violations, but Lockheed also agreed to buy more equipment to reduce the air pollution generated by paint spraying at their aerospace plants. Lockheed has been accused of hiding their problems behind the cloak of "national-security." For example, in 1988, 160 Lockheed plant workers building a top-secret fighter plane claimed they became ill after chemical exposure, but security regulations prevented them from seeking medical care. In 1986, the Pentagon accused Lockheed of overcharging them $175 million for a contract involving C-5B cargo planes. That same year, Congress accused Lockheed of losing over 1,000 classified documents crucial to national security. Former CEO Lawrence Kitchen told the *New York Times*, "Our internal laxness is inexcusable." In 1988, Lockheed closed their plant in the Los Angeles ghetto of Watts. They had opened the plant after the riots of the late 1960s and created thousands of jobs in the community for 18 years.

Global presence. For a military contractor, not major. In 1987 4 percent of sales came from foreign governments—and another 8 percent came from commercial customers overseas.

Stock performance. Lockheed stock bought for $1,000 in 1980 sold for $3,925 on January 2, 1990.

Lockheed Corporation, 4500 Park Granada Boulevard, Calabasas, CA 91399; (818) 712-2000.

6

GENERAL DYNAMICS

#2 *in weapons making*

Employees: 102,800
Sales: $9.6 billion
Profits: $379 million
Founded: 1899
Headquarters: St. Louis, Missouri

A lot of people in the U.S. government became angry with General Dynamics during the 1980s, but it was like getting mad at a child who misbehaves. Before long the child is forgiven—and the parent hopes a lesson has been learned. But the child is not going to be expelled from the family anymore than General Dynamics is going to be permanently debarred from defense contracts. They have expertise the Pentagon needs. They hold, for example, a monopoly on the building of nuclear-powered submarines for the U.S. Navy. And so, even though the Secretary of Defense and the Secretary of the Navy both blew their gaskets at GD practices, the company ended the decade in good shape, now taking in nearly $10 billion a year and working on programs less likely to be cut than ongoing projects at other defense contractors. In addition to nuclear subs, GD makes tanks for the Army (the 55-mile-per-hour M-1), the F-16 fighter planes for the Air Force, and missiles and gun systems for all military branches (the sea-launched Tomahawk and SM-1 missiles and Phalanx gun system, the air-launched Sparrow missile Afghan guerrillas used against Soviet jets).

GD lost their number one defense contracting rank to McDonnell Douglas during the 1980s, but they still get 87 percent of revenues from the government.

History. John Jay Hopkins hoped to create the General Motors of the weapons industry. So, shortly after World War II, the former Wall Street lawyer began buying up a variety of arms makers. When he started buying, Hopkins was president of the Electric Boat company of Groton, Connecticut, the nation's biggest submarine maker. Electric Boat had a colorful history dating to the turn of the century. Their eccentric founder was Irish immigrant

John P. Holland, father of the modern submarine. In an early effort to sell his machine, Holland held a press conference just after the outbreak of the Spanish-American War and offered to sink the Spanish fleet in a Cuban harbor. All he needed was for the Navy to tow his sub down to Cuba where Holland said he would personally take charge of dispatching the Spaniards. The Navy ignored the offer, but the newspapers had a field day. A famous cartoon appeared showing Holland with a derby sticking his head out of a sub asking, "What? Me worry?"—which some believe was the model for *Mad* magazine's mascot Alfred E. Neuman. Eventually, the Navy took Holland seriously, and Electric Boat went on to produce hundreds of subs for both world wars.

With Electric Boat as the cornerstone of his arms-making conglomerate, Hopkins bought an electronics company, Stromberg-Carlson, and two plane makers—Canadair, Canada's biggest airplane maker, and San Diego–based Consolidated Vultee Aircraft, better known as Convair. Aviation pioneer Reuben Fleet started Convair in 1923 by building trainers and seaplanes (known then as flying boats). During World War II, Convair made more B-24 bombers and Catalina patrol bombers than any other company.

Hopkins created General Dynamics in 1952 as the umbrella company for his holdings. In 1959, Henry Crown targeted GD for a takeover and, in effect, took them over by merging his concrete manufacturing company with GD—and coming away with 20 percent of the stock. Henry Crown and his family have remained the effective power behind the GD throne for over 25 years.

Not long after Crown got on the GD board, the company nearly went bankrupt. By trying to make commercial jet airliners (the Convair 880 and 990), GD lost almost $500 million between 1959 and 1962. *Business Week* noted then that the venture "ranks as the most unprofitable move any U.S. company has made. The $490 million that went down the drain was almost $50 million more than Ford Motor Co. dropped on bringing to market and producing the Edsel."

As GD's largest shareholder, Henry Crown was not amused. In the first of many such maneuvers over the years,

Crown got the board to push out the company's president and install in his place a former Pan Am executive, Roger Lewis. The ultimate ingrate, Lewis pushed Crown off the board several years later and repossessed all of Crown's stock, which was nonvoting. But a few years later Lewis got dumped after Crown accumulated enough voting stock to oust him. Crown brought in David Lewis (no relation), then president of McDonnell Douglas. David Lewis attached one condition to taking the job: He wanted GD to shift their headquarters from New York City to St. Louis so he wouldn't have to move. The Crowns, based in Chicago, didn't object. GD didn't have any business in New York City anyway. So Lewis set up shop in St. Louis, from where he kept a tight rein on the far-flung operations. By the end of the 1970s, he had established GD as the number one defense contractor.

The 1980s were traumatic for General Dynamics. Ronald Reagan came into the White House determined to boost the defense budget, but GD got caught up in one fracas after another. In his first year in office, Defense Secretary Caspar Weinberger berated GD's performance on the first Trident nuclear submarine, the *U.S.S. Ohio*, then two years behind schedule, as "an extraordinarily poor piece of work." Navy Secretary John F. Lehman, Jr., went to the mat with General Dynamics over and over again between 1981 and 1985. He was irate not only at the delays at the Electric Boat yard in Groton but also over "sloppy workmanship" resulting in thousands of faulty welds and messy management resulting in subs having "steel that was not acceptable for use." Takis Veliotis, in charge of the Groton yard, was booted upstairs, at Lehman's insistence,

T*he F-16 fighter plane built in Fort Worth by General Dynamics has become the workhorse of air forces around the world. The U.S. Air Force has 1,500 of them, and another 1,000 fly for 14 other countries, including the Netherlands, Israel, Egypt, Norway, Pakistan, Thailand, Turkey and Greece. Sticker price: $20 million.*

TOP NASA CONTRACTORS

Company	1989 Sales
1. Rockwell	$1.69 billion
2. Lockheed	$550 million
3. McDonnell Douglas	$510 million
4. Thiokol	$420 million
5. Martin Marietta	$350 million

to the GD board of directors, and then, in a bizarre turn of events, Veliotis fled to Greece in 1982 after being indicted for illegal business practices. There he regaled journalists with stories about how General Dynamics knowingly set out to defraud the government on the nuclear sub program. Among the tidbits he disclosed were almost $68,000 worth of gifts bestowed by General Dynamics on Admiral Hyman Rickover. Veliotis has yet to return to the U.S. to face the charges against him. In May 1985 Navy Secretary Lehman, reacting to all these disclosures, barred General Dynamics from new orders for what he called "a pervasive corporate attitude that we find inappropriate to the public trust." Shortly afterwards, David Lewis, who had reached retirement age, resigned—a move apparently pleasing to Lehman. In August 1985 the ban on GD was lifted.

The 1980s were climactic for GD in other ways as well. They bought Chrysler's tank division and Cessna Aircraft. Cessna makes small propeller planes and corporate jets in Wichita, Kansas. They also closed their big shipyard in Quincy, Massachusetts, bought from Bethlehem Steel in 1963.

Owners and rulers. After Lewis resigned in 1985, the Crowns brought in Stanley C. Pace as CEO. A World War II bomber pilot who spent nine months in a German POW camp, Pace was a 31-year veteran at TRW where he had a Mr. Clean reputation. He immediately imposed a new code of ethics at GD so strict employees can't accept gifts worth more than $5. The in-house ethics squad fired 27 employees in 1987 alone for infractions such as altering time cards. The Crown family still owns 22 percent of the stock. Henry's

son Lester sits on the board as chairman of the executive committee.

As a place to work. A collection of many ·different fiefdoms, General Dynamics has never had an esprit de corps, an identifying culture. Nearly half the employees are unionized. The Electric Boat Yard has been a tough workplace, the scene of many pitched battles between labor and management. In 1984 the United Auto Workers, representing draftsmen at the yard, got into a nasty scrap with management and charged the company with poor safety conditions. They also said, incidentally, that GD sold Allen wrenches to the Air Force for $9,600 apiece.

Social responsibility. Pace has been trying to instill some sense of responsibility at GD. Shortly after he took over, he convened a first-ever meeting of community relations directors from different plant sites. And in the late 1980s General Dynamics seemed to be keeping out of trouble.

Stock performance. General Dynamics stock bought for $1,000 in 1980 sold for $1,776 on January 2, 1990.

General Dynamics Corporation, Pierre Laclede Center, St. Louis, MO 63105; (314) 889-8200.

7

Raytheon

#4 in defense contracting

Employees: 76,900
Sales: $8.8 billion
Profits: $529 million
Founded: 1957
Headquarters: Lexington, Massachusetts

Based in historic Lexington, Massachusetts, where the revolutionary Minutemen took on the British redcoats more than 200 years ago, Raytheon thrives on war products. During World War II they supplied radar warning systems to the armed forces and designed the fuse for the first atomic bomb. Today, they're the nation's largest missile maker, turning out the Patriot, Sparrow and Hawk weapons. The largest factory employer in Massachusetts, Raytheon used the profits from Pentagon work to diversify into consumer appliances (Amana, Caloric, Modern Maid, Speed Queen), book publishing (D. C. Heath), small airplanes (Beech Aircraft) and power plant construction (United Engineers).

But selling weapons to the military is still by far the biggest business. In 1989, weapons accounted for over half of sales (55 percent) and an even higher percentage of profits (82 percent). Appliances and Beech aircraft accounted for about 12 percent of sales. Despite the reliance on Pentagon contracts, Raytheon has, for the most part, avoided the scandals from payoffs or dubious political contributions that have marred the reputations of many competitors. Their rectitude may be due in part to an unusually stable top management. Only three men, all native Bostonians, have run Raytheon since their founding 66 years ago. One was a descendant of two American presidents, John and John Quincy Adams. The current CEO is a born-again Christian from a working-class family.

The pair of entrepreneurs who founded Raytheon would fit right into Silicon Valley today. Vannevar Bush and Laurence Marshall roomed together as engineering students at Tufts University in Boston, and started the American Appliance Company in 1922 to experiment with radio, then the nation's newest phenomenon. At the time, radios operated only on large batteries. American Appliance developed a tube that allowed radios to use power from wall sockets. An enterprising salesman suggested marketing the tubes under the name raytheon, a combination of French and Greek words that mean, roughly, "light from the gods."

The tubes were a big hit. By 1926, Raytheon's sales topped $1 million and the company attracted a steady stream of bright young engineers from Harvard, Tufts and MIT, where Bush was a professor. Marshall led Raytheon until 1948. He kept a copy of the children's book, *The Little Engine That Could*, in his office. Whenever others suggested a goal was impossible, he pointed to the book. Radio set sales got an unexpected boost during the depression when President Franklin D. Roosevelt began broadcasting his famous Fireside Chats. The reliance on the

U.*S. companies sold $120.6 billion of the world's most expensive toys—aircraft, missiles and space vehicles in 1989—60 percent of the worldwide total of aerospace products.*

government soon became more direct. Prior to World War II, Raytheon stepped up experiments with radar systems for ships, planes and submarines, and when war broke out, they had a near monopoly on the new technology. They grew from fewer than 1,000 employees before the war to over 16,000. Raytheon never returned completely to civilian life. They profited from the cold war, as Raytheon's engineers designed the next generation of military products: missile guidance systems. In 1950, a Raytheon-designed Lark missile scored history's first interception and destruction of an aircraft.

Tom Phillips, the product of a working-class neighborhood in Boston, took over in 1964 from Charles Adams, the aristocratic financier who led the company after Marshall. Phillips thought the company was too dependent on government contracts. The year after he took over, he bought Amana Refrigeration. (See Raytheon profile in Home Appliances chapter, page 0000.) After that, he added many other companies, ranging from electronics and appliances to road construction and geophysical exploration for oil companies. Most of the acquisitions have paid off, but some have flopped. Lexitron, a California maker of word-processing equipment, lost more than $100 million before the firm was dumped after six years. And Beech Aircraft seemed to be an albatross—they lost money every year until 1988, when they first turned a profit. Beech was bought in 1980, partly because Raytheon's number two executive, D. Brainerd Holmes, was a flying fanatic who piloted a Beech Baron.

Stock performance. Raytheon stock bought for $1,000 in 1980 sold for $2,803 on January 2, 1990.

Raytheon Company, 141 Spring Street, Lexington, MA 02173; (617) 862-6600.

8

#1 *in electric golf carts,
helicopters*

*Employees: 59,000
Sales: $7.4 billion
Profits: $269 million
Founded: 1943
Headquarters: Providence, Rhode Island*

About the only thing that hasn't changed over Textron's 47-year history is the name. And now even that bears no relation to Textron's business. Originally named *Tex* for textiles and *tron* for synthetics, Textron now makes just about everything *but* synthetic fibers. Among their products are Bell helicopters, wings for the B-1B bomber, engines for the M-1 tank, Homelite chain saws, E-Z-Go golf carts and Speidel watchbands. Other subsidiaries sell life insurance, provide personal loans and operate airports. Aerospace and defense products accounted for nearly half of 1989 sales.

Textron's founder was Royal Little, an indefatigable entrepreneur and nephew of Arthur D. Little, who started the Cambridge, Massachusetts, consulting firm bearing his name. Little launched Textron in 1943 as a successor to a business he had started 20 years earlier: processing rayon yarns. Now he planned to make clothing and fabrics from synthetic materials. It was a good idea but subject to the rollercoaster whims of the fashion world. In 1952 Textron lost $6.4 million on sales of $98 million—and Royal Little was ready for something else. The something else turned out to be stringing together companies in unrelated fields. Between 1953 and 1960, Little bought nearly 50 companies—and Textron became the first conglomerate.

Little left Textron in 1962 to run a venture capital firm, Narragansett Capital. A conservative New England banker, Rupert Thompson, once described as "less a chief executive than an asset manager," took over. And he was succeeded in 1968 by G. William Miller, who tried and failed to take over a series of big companies (United Fruit, Kendall, Lockheed) before he went off

in 1977 to become Treasury Secretary (and later Federal Reserve Board chairman) in the Carter administration.

Companies come and go at Textron, so consult the roster to see which ones are on board. Subsidiaries report to Providence headquarters, and units failing to meet goals are candidates for expulsion from the family. Expelled during the 1980s were Polaris snowmobiles and Talon zippers, the world's number one zipper producer.

Doing the expulsion (and acquiring) these days is Beverly Dolan, who became part of the company by selling his company, E-Z-Go golf carts, to Textron in 1960. Dolan became CEO in the mid-1980s. He's also chairman and president. In 1989 he made $2.3 million, twice as much as senior vice president William Anders, who was a crew member of the *Apollo 8* mission that orbited the moon.

In 1988 Textron's Bell helicopters subsidiary was forced to return $90 million for fraudulently overcharging the army for helicopter parts.

Stock performance. Textron stock bought for $1,000 in 1980 sold for $3,082 on January 2, 1990.

Textron Inc., 40 Westminster Street, Providence, RI 02903; (401) 421-2800

9

NORTHROP

*Employees: 42,800
Sales: $5.2 billion
Losses: $81 million
Founded: 1939
Headquarters: Los Angeles, California*

Founded by Jack Northrop, a U.S. aviation pioneer, Northrop flew through the 1980s in characteristically maverick fashion. They actually put up their own money, $1 billion, to develop a new jet fighter, the F-20 Tigershark. Only no one wanted to buy it. So they stopped making it. By decade's end, Northrop had a large number of eggs in one basket: the B-2 Stealth bomber. The advantage of the B-2, being developed for the Air Force, is that radar screens cannot track it. According to Northrop, detecting the B-2 would be as difficult as finding someone you know in the Rose Bowl when it's filled, the lights are out and all you have is a flashlight. The problem with the B-2—one, anyway—is the cost at a time when the cold war was thawing. At $500 million a pop, it may be the most expensive piece of weaponry ever devised. The Air Force still wants it. Northrop still wants to build it. In 1989 the B-2 was already accounting for one-half of Northrop's sales. Interviewed by the *Wall Street Journal* in June 1990, Congressman John Kasich, an Ohio Republican, said: "This plane is going to bankrupt America."

Apart from the Stealth aircraft, Northrop makes the F-18 fighters, sophisticated avionics systems for missiles and planes, and fuselages for the Boeing 747. Their F-5 became the world's most widely used supersonic fighter.

Northrop is not an aerospace supergiant, but they've always had a fierce pride in what they do, a legacy from their founder. Jack Northrop designed the Vega that Amelia Earhart flew across the Atlantic in 1932, and he introduced the metal body construction that replaced wood. Donald Douglas, founder of Douglas Aircraft, once said: "Every major airplane in the skies today has some Jack Northrop in it." The company he started in 1939 has always gone their own way. They're one of the few southern California aerospace companies where unions have failed to organize workers. Northrop's a less bureaucractic place than other defense contractors—and a company where members of families work. Northrop has also enjoyed stability at the top—only three CEOs in their first 50 years: Jack Northrop from 1939 to 1952, O. P. Echols to 1959, Thomas V. Jones from 1959 to 1989. As the 1990s opened, 51-year-old Kent Kresa was at the helm. He's an MIT-trained engineer who previously ran the B-2 program.

Northrop has even had a way with scandals. Jones, a brilliant salesman, thought nothing in 1972 of stashing $50,000 in his desk drawer and handing it to a Nixon reelection campaign manager. Jones compounded his indiscretion by falsifying documents and lying to a grand jury. He eventually pleaded guilty to a felony charge and was fined close to $200,000. In

The United States exported $32.1 billion worth of aerospace products in 1989—$25.6 billion in civil aircraft, $6.5 billion in military planes.

the mid-1970s Northrop also admitted paying over $2 million to curry favor with government officials in Indonesia, Saudi Arabia, Iran and other countries.

Jones was considered too valuable to boot out, so he stayed on, although a court suit by an angry stockholder resulted in the addition of four independent directors to the board and a permanent rule that 60 percent of the board be people outside the company. Although he has given up the CEO's position, Jones continues as chairman. He's the company's largest shareholder, holding 4.5 percent of the stock, worth over $50 million in early 1990.

Northrop was in hot water again in 1990 when they pleaded guilty to 34 felony counts for falsifying test results. They were fined $17 million, believed to be one of the largest penalties ever assessed against a military contractor. However, Northrop doesn't take anything lying down. When syndicated columnist Richard Reeves, trained as a mechanical engineer, blasted the company for violating the "professional religion" of engineers—respect for numbers—Northrop's senior vice president Les Daly fired off this retort to the *Los Angeles Times*:

"He [Reeves] might have avoided smearing a lot of engineers at Northrop and elsewhere if he had reported that the failure to perform certain tests was the failure of three or four people, as the record shows; that when Northrop discovered what they had done, they were fired; that Northrop promptly disclosed the problem to the public and reported in great detail to the military services using the equipment; that Northrop offered to redo the tests and repay the government for the cost of the tests which weren't performed... The company pleaded guilty because under the law it accepted responsibility for the unauthorized and unacceptable acts of three or four of its employees—even though they had acted on their own and even though it had fired them nearly three years before when their behavior was discovered."

Stock performance. Northrop stock bought for $1,000 in 1980 sold for $1,759 on January 2, 1990.

Northrop Corporation, 1800 Century Park East, Los Angeles, CA 90067; (213) 553-6262.

10

GenCorp

#1 *in tennis balls*

Employees: 15,400
Sales: $1.9 billion
Profits: $210 million
Founded: 1915
Headquarters: Fairlawn, Ohio

Remember General Tire & Rubber? This company was the sprawling conglomerate assembled by freewheeling entrepreneur William O'Neil. They made General tires, owned the old Howard Hughes company (RKO Pictures), operated four TV stations and 12 radio stations (RKO Broadcasting), made Penn tennis balls, designed and built rocket motors and liquid rocket propulsion systems (Aerojet), produced wallpapers and plastic car bodies and bottled and canned Pepsi-Cola, Dr. Pepper and other soft drinks at plants in Indiana, Ohio, Tennessee, Virginia and West Virginia.

After O'Neil died in 1960, three of his sons—Michael, Thomas and John—ran different sectors of the company as separate fiefdoms. Michael sat in Akron as CEO; he was interested in the tire business. Thomas, designated chairman, ran the RKO broadcasting operations from New York. And John, the chief financial officer, lived in Washington, D.C., but refused to come to Akron headquarters (even for board meetings) because he didn't like to fly, even though the company owned 45 percent of Denver-based Frontier Airlines.

In Akron, Michael kept a cash box from which he doled out $350,000 of illegal political contributions between 1968 and 1973. General Tire also slipped $500,000 to a Moroccan agent to prevent Goodyear from doing business in that country. Other companies had engaged in this kind of hanky-panky, but they didn't operate broadcasting stations. Presented with these stories and later evidence that the RKO radio network had billed advertisers for commercials that never ran, the Federal Communications Commission moved to strip General Tire of their station operating licenses. The fight lasted 23 years, ending only in 1988 when the last station left the corral. Most of the stations had to be sold at distress prices. For example, in 1980, after the FCC revoked their license to operate WNAC-TV in Boston, General Tire netted only $22 million for the station. In 1985 a comparable Boston TV station sold for $450 million.

General Tire steamed into the 1980s under these storm clouds and emerged a different company. In 1984 they changed their name to GenCorp. In 1985 a former head of TRW's automotive parts division, A. William Reynolds, became the first non-O'Neil to head the company. And he restructured GenCorp. The tire business was sold to German tire maker, Continental A.G. The soft drink bottlers were sold to IC Industries. RKO Pictures was sold to the managers who had been running the firm. And the remaining radio and TV stations were peddled as fast as possible, the biggest sale being the 1987 transfer of WOR-TV, New York, to MCA for $387 million.

Coming into the 1990s then, GenCorp no longer made tires, which once accounted for over 40 percent of revenues. In 1989, they had sales of $1.9 billion (down from $2.3 billion in 1979) and 15,400 employees (down from 42,000 in 1979). They were still making rocket fuels and ammunition, wallpapers and plastic car body panels and a variety of vinyls, laminates, films and latex for use as coatings. And they were, under the Penn name, the world's largest producer of tennis balls. Two O'Neils—John and Michael—were still on the board.

Stock performance. GenCorp stock bought for $1,000 in 1980 sold for $2,868 on January 2, 1990.

GenCorp Incorporated, 175 Ghent Road, Fairlawn, OH 44313; (216) 869-3300.

PART SIX

Conglomerates: An Endangered Species

General Electric
ITT
United Technologies
Tenneco
3M
Allies-Signal
TRW
Hanson Industries
Litton Industries
Teledyne
Greyhound Dial
National Intergroup
Figgie International

CONGLOMERATES

The word, conglomerate, *came into vogue during the 1960s as a term for a hodge-podge of different companies operating under the same parent. It's derived from the Latin verb,* conglomerare, *to roll together into a ball. The word has always had a somewhat pejorative connotation, witness the Mel Brooks film,* Silent Movie, *where greedy, power-mad executives run a company called Engulf & Devour. Conglomerates have not, however, taken over the world, as critics predicted. Some of the high-flying conglomerates of the 1960s and 1970s—ITT, Litton Industries, Gulf+Western Industries (now Paramount Communications)—have instead narrowed their vision and reduced their size.*

We classify as conglomerates companies whose business operations are so diversifed that they don't fit easily into any other category. Since our basic way of organizing this book is by industry, we also include divisions of some of these conglomerates in their industry settings. Ergo, while we lead off this section with General Electric, easily the nation's largest conglomerate, we profile GE units in home appliances and broadcasting (NBC).

1

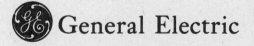

General Electric

#1 *in major appliances, electric motors, nuclear reactors, light bulbs, network TV, hard plastics, power generators, circuit breakers, locomotives, medical diagnostic imaging*

#2 *in factory automation, aircraft engines*

#3 *in defense contracting*

Employees: 295,000
Sales: $54.6 billion
Profits: $3.9 billion
Founded: 1878
Headquarters: Fairfield, Connecticut

After 112 years in American life, GE found people no longer knew what they stood for. When we used to think of General Electric, we immediately thought of light bulbs, refrigerators and a host of electric appliances. But today's company even downplays the name General Electric, preferring the designation, GE. And under that rubric they engage in a host of activities, which may change from time to time. In addition to refrigerators, ranges, dishwashers and washing machines, they make jet aircraft engines; X ray machines, CAT scanners and nuclear imagers that lay bare the inner body; thermoplastics to replace glass in bottles and steel in car panels; and aerospace gear such as satellites, space platforms and radar defense systems.

Today's GE has also roamed beyond manufacturing. Thanks to buying RCA in 1986, they became proprietor of the nation's leading TV network (NBC) and the owner of seven major TV stations. In addition, GE has become a potent force in the world of finance through three subsidiaries: GE Capital (formerly General Credit Corp.), Employers Reinsurance (bought from Texaco for $1 billion) and Kidder, Peabody (80 percent-owned). If these financial services separated out, their assets (more than $60 billion) would rank them as the nation's fifth largest diversified financial company, behind American Express, Federal National Mortgage Association (Fannie Mae), Salomon and Aetna Life, but ahead of Merrill Lynch, CIGNA and Morgan Stanley. GE finances commercial real estate development and lends money to a variety of businesses including those engaged in takeovers. Only eight commercial banks have more money out in loans than GE ($32 billion at the end of 1987). In 1987 GE derived nearly 15 percent of pretax profits from their role as a money supplier.

GE remains a potent manufacturer with perhaps the most visible national presence of any industrial company. Even after reducing payroll by 100,000 during the 1980s, GE was still operating 213 manufacturing plants in 34 states. And in city after city—Louisville, Philadelphia, Schenectady, Pittsfield, Cleveland—they remain the largest employer. Only four companies—General Motors, Sears, IBM and Ford—have larger U.S. payrolls.

H*istory.* GE began in October 1878 when the Edison Electric Light Company was organized to support Thomas Alva Edison's experiments to develop an incandescent lamp at his lab in Menlo Park, New Jersey—experiments crowned with success a year later. Money from the J. P. Morgan banking house fueled the growth of Edison Electric, whose sales reached $10 million by 1890.

Tom Edison the inventor had difficulty playing the role of Tom Edison the industrialist. Complicating his problems were legal fights over patents and his stubborn insistence that the electrical future belonged to direct current despite the rapidly accumulating evidence that alternating current was a more efficient path to follow. In 1892, the bankers bypassed Edison and merged his company with a competitor, Thomson-Houston of Lynn, Massachusetts, to form General Electric. Edison's biographer, Robert Conot, author of *A Streak of Luck*, said the disappearance of his name from the corporate flag was "a stunning blow" to Edison. Two years later he sold all his GE shares, though he remained tied to the company as a consultant, collector of royalties on patents and a director (he retained his board seat for 10 years but went to only one meeting, in August 1892).

The avenues that opened for Edison's successors were broad, fast moving and seemingly limitless. The first skyscraper to use electric elevators went up in Chicago in 1885. In 1890 the electric chair was introduced. Electric trolleys were built in every big American city. Electric motors made factories more productive.

And everywhere homes were being lit up. Night was being abolished.

To consolidate their position at the forefront of this revolution, GE established a corporate research lab at Schenectady, New York, in 1900. One of the first scientists to work there was Charles Steinmetz, the brilliant hunchbacked immigrant from Germany, nicknamed "the wizard of electricity."

Not all of GE's history has been so bright. Antitrust lawsuits have been a problem for GE during most of their corporate life. Between 1911 and 1967 they were a defendant in 65 antitrust actions. One of them, settled in 1949, found GE had effective control of 85 percent of the light bulb business (55 percent from their own output, 30 percent from licensees); the settlement forced GE to open up their patents to others. This dominance in the lamp market financed GE's entry into the appliance business. GE made a fan as early as 1894, an iron in 1905, a toaster in 1908 and a waffle iron in 1915, but between the two world wars, under the leadership of Owen D. Young and Gerard Swope, the company moved aggressively into electrical home appliances, beginning with the hermetically sealed "Monitor-top" refrigerator, which signaled the beginning of the end for the old icebox.

The most devastating of the antitrust actions was one brought by the Justice Department after World War II. It charged that GE, along with other electrical equip-

---

Top 10 Ways To Make A GE Executive Very Angry*

10. Play "keep away" with his company hat.
9. Bring in Sylvania bulbs from home.
8. Use plenty of 2-syllable words in conversation.
7. Tell him there is no Reddy Kilowatt.
6. Ask him not to yell "whee" when riding the elevator.
5. Clip out article from *USA Today* on "America's Love Affair with Candles."
4. Ask if GE's guided missiles come in "avocado" or "harvest gold."
3. Use his "lucky pencil" without permission.
2. Ask him what letters GE stand for.
1. Tell him you can't actually mate with cartoon characters.

*As heard on the "David Letterman Show" on the GE-owned NBC television network

ment makers, agreed among themselves to set prices on a wide range of products sold to utilities, everything from $2 insulators to multimillion-dollar turbine generators. The conspiracy was so well documented all the defendants pleaded guilty or no contest to the charges. The fines and damages GE paid did not crimp their balance sheet, but they did sully their reputation. Three GE executives were given 30-day jail sentences, others were forced to leave the company. And all this took place as GE's message, "Progress Is Our Most Important Product," was being delivered every week on TV by a former actor, Ronald Reagan, who also toured GE plants warning against the scourge of socialism, which he said "was engulfing America, held back only by a few brave businessmen."

But history is circular. After World War I GE, at the behest of the U.S. government, launched Radio Corp. of America (RCA) as successor to the British-owned Marconi Wireless Telegraph company. GE, on their own, opened one of the country's first radio stations, WGY in Schenectady, in 1922, while RCA went on to pioneer U.S. broadcasting. In 1931, after the antitrust implications of this arrangement became clear, the bureaucrats in Washington, D.C., changed their minds, and GE sold the RCA holdings. As a consolation prize GE came away with the Art Deco skyscraper at 50th Street and Lexington Avenue that served for many years as their corporate headquarters and was known as the GE Building. In 1986, 55 years later, in the biggest non-oil merger up to that time, GE "reacquired" a now much bigger RCA for $6.3 billion. By then GE, was headquartered in Fairfield, Connecticut. But they soon took down the RCA name from 30 Rockefeller Plaza and rechristened the skyscraper The GE Building (a source of endless jokes for David Letterman, late night host on GE's NBC network).

Modern leaders of GE have not always agreed about what the company should be doing. In 1976, General Electric, as they were pleased to call themselves in those days, made the biggest acquisition in U.S. corporate history up to that time, paying $2.3 billion for Utah International. That put GE in the natural resources business (mostly in Australia): mining coal, copper, uranium and iron ore, and producing natural gas and oil. Seven years later, after

John F. Welch, Jr., became the eighth CEO in GE's history, most of Utah International was sold off. In 1983 GE also sold seven radio and TV stations as well as their houseware division, which means GE no longer makes toasters or irons or fans—no small appliances of any kind. The next year, 1984, GE bought Employers Reinsurance, and two years later, in addition to scooping up RCA, GE bought 80 percent of the investment banking house, Kidder Peabody, just in time to become part of the insider trading scandal on Wall Street.

One of Jack Welch's prescriptions is that GE must be either number one or two in any field in which they compete. If not, out they go. The combined RCA-GE business in consumer electronics—radio and TV sets, VCRs, stereos—did meet that test, but in 1987 Welch threw that entire passel of products to the French electronics giant, Thomson S.A., in exchange for Thomson's medical diagnostic business, where GE was already a U.S. leader. In 1989, when one looked back over the carnage of the 1980s, the balance sheet showed GE had disposed of over 250 businesses for $9 billion while acquiring over 350 businesses for $16 billion. This frenetic activity flowed from the rallying cry of Chairman Jack Welch: "I want to shake people and say, 'Wait a minute, the world's a different place.'" And yet, in 1989, after seven years of furious buying and selling, GE leaders expressed surprise the financial community didn't seem to understand what was going on. The company was chastened to discover people were, horror of horror, beginning to use the *C* word, *conglomerate*, to describe GE, coupling this description with the pejorative question: "Who knows what they will buy or sell next?"

Owners and rulers. No matter how big the company, the man in the catbird's seat can still change the firm's course. Jack Welch has certainly left his mark, having done more to reshape GE than any previous CEO. When he took over in April 1981, Welch was, at 45, the youngest chief executive GE has ever had. A chemical engineer, he was also the first PhD to hold that position. While Welch has spent his entire working career with GE, he has not been averse to bringing in outsiders to head up important departments. He recruited Benjamin W. Heineman, Jr., as

THE 10 MOST VALUABLE COMPANIES IN AMERICA*

Company	Market Value
1. IBM	$62.4 billion
2. Exxon	$59.3 billion
3. General Electric	$57.9 billion
4. AT&T	$45 billion
5. Philip Morris	$35.8 billion
6. General Motors	$28.8 billion
7. Merck	$27.9 billion
8. Bristol-Myers Squibb	$27.8 billion
9. Amoco	$27.4 billion
10. Du Pont	$26.9 billion

*Based on what their stock was selling for on March 16, 1990.

Source: Business Week, 13 April 1990

legal counsel, installed Joyce Hergenhan as corporate public relations director and in 1989 reached down into the ranks to select 37-year-old Teresa M. LeGrand as director of the 120-strong corporate audit staff at Schenectady. LeGrand is the first woman to hold this post, which was the launching pad for Welch's predecessor, Reginald Jones. Institutions like pension funds and insurance companies hold nearly half of GE's stock. Welch has been widely praised for being a scrappy leader who faces reality. Inside GE he's also known as an enemy of bureaucracy and mediocrity. Not everyone admires him. Tom Peters, who became a management guru after coauthoring In Search of Excellence, is certainly not a Welch fan. He expressed dismay that the best use Welch could find for GE's money was to buy RCA, and he gave this assessment to Business Week: "If Mad Jack hasn't bought or sold one or two businesses in a day, it's a crappy day for him." Welch took home $3.6 million in 1989. Talk about prestigious boards, GE's is the heavyweight of the heavyweights, including a former Chairman of the Joint Chiefs of Staff, retired Air Force General David C. Jones; a former U.S. Attorney General, William French Smith; the president of Cornell University, Frank H. T. Rhodes; the chairman of J. P. Morgan, Lewis T. Preston; and—the oldest director in terms of service (1962)—Walter B. Wriston, retired chairman of Citicorp. Two women—Gertrude Michaelson, senior vice president of Macy's, and Barbara Scott Preiskel, a lawyer—are directors.

As a place to work. GE entered the 1980s with 400,000 employees and exited with 300,000. Unsurprisingly then, Welch is called, "Neutron Jack," meaning he's like the neutron bomb—whenever he visits a plant, the buildings are left standing but the people disappear. Although GE has a long history of adversarial labor relations, they've succeeded in recent years in renegotiating union contracts without incurring strikes. About 68,000 of their U.S. manufacturing employees are unionized. Welch has been candid about his mission as GE's leader. He wants to shake up the place, get rid of 112 years of accumulated bad habits, push decision making down in the ranks and get people to have a sense of ownership about the business. Stock options now go to 3,000 people, up from 400 in 1980. There's no lifetime job security in Jack Welch's GE. "Jobs at GE," he said, "are the best in the world for people who want to compete." As a result, many employees work long hours. In an article in Fortune in 1989, Welch said GE workers who put in 90-hour weeks are doing "something terribly wrong. I go skiing on the weekend, I go out with my buddies on Friday and party." In response, Mark Markovitz, a GE engineer in Schenectady, New York, said GE managers work 90 hours a week because "many of our colleagues were nuked by Welch."

Social responsibility. You name it—and GE has been accused of it. Supplying faulty nuclear power plants. Price fixing. Racism and sexism in hiring and promotion policies. Cheating the Pentagon on military contracts. In 1987, INFACT, the activist organization that brought Nestlé to their knees over the issue of infant formula marketing in Third World countries, targeted GE for a worldwide boycott to protest their production of nuclear weapons. Claiming GE puts "profits before people," the INFACT indictment charged that just as the company used Ronald Reagan to sell Americans on the all-electric home, they now sell Americans on "the permanent war economy and the nuclear arms race." GE did not fall into the Nestlé trap of suing their critics or violently denouncing them. Although they didn't exactly turn the other cheek, GE spokespersons trod softly, agreeing to open a dialogue with the protesters, saying they shared with them a desire for peace and emphasizing that by supplying the Defense Department they were only carrying out the wishes of a democratically elected government. The Pentagon is GE's most important customer, accounting for 24 percent of sales. One practice spreading at GE is manager-manned volunteer projects by managers to rehabilitate rundown inner-city areas. It began in San Diego, where 480 managers in the plastics business spent a day refurbishing a seedy YMCA instead of on the golf course. The idea has since been picked up in other wings of GE as a regular part of business meetings.

In December 1989, NBC's "Today" show reported on the use of substandard materials in American industry in which GE was supposed to be one of the companies featured. However, NBC News officials deleted a portion of the report—the only reference to GE—that described the GE purchase and use of substandard bolts in their airline engines.

Global presence. GE is not a major brand name overseas, but the company's international sales are impressive and growing rapidly, accounting for 27 percent of total sales. In 1987, GE logged exports of $4 billion. GE's jet engines power passenger planes of Air France, Alitalia and Lufthansa as well as fighter planes of Egypt and Bahrain. GE locomotives roll on tracks in China and Gabon. GE's foreign affiliates had 1987 revenues of $5.2 billion meaning that, combined with exports, the company's international operations came to $9.2 billion that year. GE sees themselves as the defender of American turf, holding the fort against the multinational superpowers of other countries: Siemens, Toshiba, Philips, Hitachi, Matsushita. After the convulsions in Eastern Europe at the end of the 1980s, GE took over a light bulb factory in Hungary.

Stock performance. GE stock bought for $1,000 in 1980 sold for $7,455 on January 2, 1990.

General Electric Co. 3135 Easton Turnpike, Fairfield, CT 06431; (203) 373-2211.

2

ITT
International Telephone and Telegraph Corporation

#1 *in industrial pumps and valves*
#2 *in hotels (by rooms available)*
#8 *in property/casualty insurance*

Employees: 118,000
Sales: $20.1 billion
Profits: $922 million
Founded: 1920
Headquarters: New York City, New York

When a company runs ads explaining what they do, chances are good they've gone through a reorganization trauma. ITT launched such an informational campaign in 1987 and continued it in 1988 and 1989 to tell people which businesses they operated. The campaign was an appropriate response to what has happened at ITT. The company spent the 1980s going down the roller coaster they went up during the previous two decades.

Harold S. Geneen, a relentlessly hardworking accountant, assumed command of ITT in 1959 and touched off one of the most feverish buying sprees in corporate history. In 20 years Geneen grabbed 350 companies for ITT, turning a stagnant telephone company whose operations were mostly abroad into a sprawling conglomerate with mostly U.S. sales.

After Geneen retired, the baton passed to Rand Vincent Araskog, a West Point graduate and Russian expert who worked at Honeywell before joining ITT in 1968. Whereas Geneen was an acquirer, Araskog was a discarder—and consolidator. He sold off over 100 of the companies Geneen had bought. Araskog's pruning culminated in 1987 when ITT exited the business that had given them birth: telecommunications. He sold the telephone business for $1 billion and a 37 percent interest in Alcatel, an offshoot of France's Compagnie Generale d'Electricite. In 1990 he sold off another 7 percent of Alcatel for $640 million.

As a result, ITT has slimmed down to eight basic businesses: (1) auto parts components (exhaust systems, antilock brake systems), (2) electronic components, (3) pumps and valves, (4) defense technology (radar controls, surveillance systems), (5) insurance (Hartford), (6) lending (ITT Consumer Finance and ITT Commercial Finance), (7) information operations (foreign "Yellow Pages") and (8) hotels (Sheraton). ITT also owns 17 percent of Western Union.

To maintain the fiction this is a family of companies, ITT now insists subsidiaries designate ITT as part of their name. So it's ITT Sheraton, ITT Hartford, ITT Fluid Technology and so on (until the unit is sold).

History. Sosthenes Behn and Harold Geneen, the two dominant figures in ITT's first 60 years, were not at all alike. Both were builders, but they had different visions for ITT—and their styles were quite different. However, they did share an obsessive, single-minded devotion to the company, so much so that in both of their regimes ITT had an unsavory reputation for pursuing their own ends without much regard for other interests such as love of country or social justice.

Behn's task, in the period between the two world wars, was to make ITT into a worldwide company that produced telephones, switches and other telephone equipment and also provided telephone service. Considering ITT was an *American*-based company operating public utilities in *other* countries, this was as much a diplomatic mission as a business venture. And Colonel Behn, a Signal Corps officer during World War I, was equal to the task. Aristocratic in bearing and tastes (he lived for many years in the Plaza Hotel in New York City), multilingual, happy to flit from country to country, at ease at formal banquets, Sosthenes Behn succeeded in establishing ITT as a prime supplier of the equipment needed to make telephone systems work (especially in Germany and Britain) as well as an operator of telephone utilities (especially in Latin America). He got his first big break in 1923—a contract to provide phone service in Spain. In 1925, in the wake of an antitrust action that forced AT&T's manufacturing subsidiary, Western Electric, to sell their overseas operations, he bought a network of European plants. The colonel then turned to Latin America, acquiring telephone companies in Uruguay, Chile, Argentina and Brazil. Germany was also a major outpost for ITT, and shortly after Adolf Hitler came to power, Behn met with him and soon installed Nazis on the boards of his German companies. One of them was Kurt von Schroeder, later an SS general and major financial supporter of the Gestapo. He became a leading force in ITT's German operations. Under his direction, ITT bought a 28 percent stake in Focke-Wulf, a manufacturer of bomber planes.

According to British journalist Anthony Sampson, whose book, *The Sovereign State of ITT*, became a best-seller in the 1970s, ITT was a company so obsessed with profits they were above such considerations as patriotism or morality. "If the Nazis had won," Sampson wrote, "ITT in Germany would have appeared impeccably Nazi; as they lost, it reemerged as impeccably American." Another biographer, Robert Sobel, disagrees, claiming that Behn cooperated with the U.S. State Department during World War II. However, it's clear even from Sobel's sympathetic account in *ITT:The Management of Opportunity*, that Behn had a foot in every camp. His main goal was the salvation of his company, which was always teetering on the brink of bankruptcy.

While Sosthenes Behn grew up in affluent and sophisticated circumstances, Harold Geneen had a more Spartan upbringing. His father left the family before Harold was five. Harold was forced to leave school at 16, becoming a page at the New York Stock Exchange, where he worked for six years. Meanwhile, for eight years, off and on, he went to night school at New York University, finally in 1935 at age 25 getting his degree in accounting. Thus armed, he joined one of the big accounting firms and after six years moved over to the client side, successively with American Can (packaging), Bell & Howell (photography), Jones & Laughlin (steel) and Raytheon (electronics). He became adept at figuring out from the numbers what was wrong and what was right, a skill that never left him. When he finally got a chance to be ITT's CEO in 1959, he was ready.

In his 1984 book, *Managing*, Geneen related how uncomfortable he felt when he first sat in the penthouse office that was once Sosthenes Behn's in the old International Telephone & Telegragh building at 67 Broad Street in New York's financial district. It was a "European-style" office with "a large ornate desk...large oriental rugs on the floor, a stone fireplace on one wall" and "an enormous crystal chandelier" that "swayed overhead as the wind outside caught the top of the building." Geneen replaced the Old World artifacts with modern furniture—and two years later moved the headquarters uptown to a new, nondescript building at 320 Park Avenue, where it still is.

Geneen brought to ITT an accountant's passion for financial controls, logic and hands-on management. Essential to him was that he know *everything* going on in the company, and he built a system of "open communications" to ensure nothing would be hidden from him. To Geneen, management was a religion, and while he acquired company after company—Avis (car rentals), Continental Baking (Wonder bread, Twinkies), Sheraton (hotels), Grinnell (fire-alarm systems), Canteen Corp. (vending machines, cafeterias in factories and offices), Bobbs-Merrill (publishing), Levitt (homebuilding), Hartford (insurance), Eason Oil (heating oil), Burpee (seeds), O. M. Scott (lawn and garden products), Bell & Gossett (pumps), Teves (German automotive components supplier)—his game was not acquisition-for-acquisition's-sake; that is, he didn't buy companies merely to inflate sales. His intent all along was to *manage* them to greater glory. Harold Geneen's favorite maxim was, "Managers must manage," by which he meant they must push their units to perform—to increase sales and

profits methodically. And if they didn't do it, they had Harold Geneen to answer to.

But attention to the numbers blindsided Geneen to social and political problems. In the early 1970s, just prior to the Watergate scandal, ITT was transfixed in the public spotlight as a company that would stop at nothing to achieve their ends, even meddling in the presidential politics of two nations to do so. In the U.S., the company was accused of making a deal to get a favorable settlement of an antitrust suit by offering the Republican Party $400,000 to finance their convention in San Diego, where Sheraton had three hotels. In Chile, where the ITT-owned utility faced possible nationalization, the company offered the CIA $1 million to fund a campaign to block the election of left-wing candidate Salavador Allende as president. The offer was made by John McCone, former CIA director who happened to be a director of ITT.

These two episodes put ITT's name on the front pages of newspapers and in the lineups of the network evening newscasts. Geneen and other top ITT officials were called to testify before Congress and generally confirmed biographer Anthony Sampson's impression of the company as "arrogant" and "two-faced." On the domestic side, as a result of an antitrust suit, ITT was allowed to keep Hartford Insurance in return for giving up four companies (Avis, Levitt, Canteen and Grinnell) and agreeing not to acquire any more big companies (assets over $100 million) for the next 10 years. So, in the final years of his stewardship, Geneen made no major acquisitions. The company he had built was turned over to others.

The new leader, Araskog, declared at first that ITT would reemphasize their original business, telecommunications, and go head-to-head with AT&T in the U.S. market. That plan never worked. In-

Women Directors

Among large corporations only two have as many as four women serving on their board of directors. They are Gannett, owner of the nation's largest newspaper chain, and Ogden, which cleans buildings, incinerates garbage and operates racetracks. Seven companies have three female directors: Avon, Consolidated Edison, Baxter, Philip Morris, New York Times, Pitney Bowes and Sears, Roebuck.

stead, Araskog shed a slew of companies and finally gave up the telecommunications business by merging the firm into Alcatel. Geneen's last big acquisition, Hartford, has proved to be a jewel. Hartford now generates premiums of $9 billion a year, and accounts for over one-third of ITT's profits.

Owners and rulers. ITT has a long history of one-man rule—and since 1979 that man has been Rand Araskog, who was 59 in 1989 (and made $3.8 million). Institutions (mutual funds, insurance companies, pension funds) are major holders of ITT stock. An Employee Stock Ownership Plan owns 11 percent of the stock. The members of ITT's board of directors (12 are outsiders) are the highest paid directors in American business, each receiving, on average, $86,000 a year. Dr. Benjamin F. Payton, president of Tuskegee University, was elected a director in 1987. The lone woman, Bette B. Anderson, undersecretary of the Treasury Department during the Carter administration, was elected in 1981.

As a place to work. Any company that goes from 379,000 employees to 118,000 in 10 years cannot inspire enthusiasm among job seekers. Minorities make up 24 percent and women 45 percent of the U.S. work force.

Social responsibility. In the mid-1980s a trio of corporate raiders—Jay Pritzker, Philip Anschutz and Irwin Jacobs—drew a bead on ITT. Araskog beat them off—and emerged from the fight a zealous opponent of the takeover game, sentiments he put into print in a 1989 book, *The ITT Wars*, where he declaimed against Boone Pickens ("People who should have known better lapped up his rhetoric"), Gillette and Goodyear (for paying greenmail), SEC chairman John Shad (for letting convicted stock manipulator Ivan Boesky sell his stock at a profit) and the *New York Times* and the *Wall Street Journal* (for running "editorial after editorial supporting the raiders' goals"). The head of a company built by hundreds of acquisitions (all friendly, to be sure) said: "We are in danger of reversing the meaning of industrial capitalism, which was created to produce jobs, profits, goods and services. The financial world has its place, but if we allow it to manipulate, dominate, and control legitimate business interests, the tail will be wagging the dog."

Global presence. ITT is one of the few companies where overseas sales have declined in importance. Whereas they were doing 65 percent of sales abroad 20 years ago, they now do only 30 percent. ITT indirectly maintains a strong presence overseas through their 30 percent holding in France's Alcatel, which vies with AT&T, Siemens, Philips, NEC, Ericsson and Northern Telecom in the world telecommunications market. Thus, in any fight between AT&T and Alcatel for a piece of business from a national telephone company, ITT will be on France's side. ITT's automotive components business (annual sales of $2.5 billion) is largely European-based.

Stock performance. ITT stock bought for $1,000 in 1980 sold for $3,871 on January 2, 1990.

ITT Corp., 320 Park Avenue, New York, NY 10022; (212) 752-6000.

3

⚙ UNITED TECHNOLOGIES

#1 *in elevators, air-conditioning, aircraft engines*

#2 *in helicopters*

#9 *in defense contracting*

Employees: 194,100
Sales: $19.5 billion
Profits: $702 million
Founded: 1925
Headquarters: Hartford, Connecticut

Some important names in American industrial history—Pratt & Whitney, Carrier, Otis, Sikorsky—are buried in this amorphous conglomerate. Their names are more familiar than the corporate name, United Technologies, adopted in 1975 to reflect the company's growing diversity.

This diversity was engineered by Harry Gray, who arrived in 1971 from Litton Industries, the company that invented the genre, conglomerate. Gray bought company after company, whether they wanted to be acquired or not, and in less than a decade quadrupled the size of what used to be called United Aircraft.

Gray relinquished the CEO's post in 1986, and his successor, Robert F. Daniell, quickly began to discard companies. "Harry Gray was brought here to grow the company," said Daniell after he was named chairman. "But now the company is built, the blocks are in place and growth will be a secondary objective."

With sales nearing $20 billion in 1989, United Technologies packs a big punch. Pratt & Whitney, their biggest business, builds engines powering many of the world's commercial and fighter aircraft, and has been locked in a dogfight with General Electric for worldwide leadership of this business. Otis builds more elevators and escalators than any other company. Carrier leads the world in air-conditioning. Sikorsky vies with Textron's Bell for top position in helicopters. Hamilton Standard makes sophisticated aerospace gear such as flight control and space guidance systems, and supplies the space suits astronauts wear. With annual sales approaching $1 billion, UT's automotive group ranks as one of the leading parts suppliers to auto manufacturers; their products include electric wire assemblies, small electric motors, electrical switches, hose assemblies, and plastic components for interior trim. The number one customer is Ford Motor, accounting for over half of the group's sales.

Prior to Gray's arrival, the company did over half of their business with the U.S. government. Because of acquisitions outside the defense area, the government's share is now 27 percent. UT's four most important customers are the Pentagon, Ford, Boeing and McDonnell Douglas.

History. United Technologies emerged from a long series of mergers, acquisitions and restructurings (and the series is ongoing). During the 1920s a bunch of fledgling aviation companies banded together to form United Aircraft & Transportation Corporation. This was a vertical combination linking airplane builders (Boeing, Chance Vought, Sikorsky), airlines (five carriers which combined into United Airlines), propeller makers (Hamilton Aero and Standard Steel) and an engine maker (Pratt & Whitney, a Hartford tool company). Fearing monopolization of the emerging aviation industry, Congress, in 1934, forced airplane builders out of the airline business. Boeing and United Airlines were split off into separate companies while the rest of the operation continued as United Aircraft.

From the Pratt & Whitney base in Hartford, United Aircraft soared into the future with the aircraft industry. More often than not, the federal government was priming the pump. The first engine they built, the Wasp, was for the U.S. Navy. During World War II Pratt & Whitney engines powered half of the U.S. planes. After the war Pratt & Whitney built the J57 jet engine, which powered the first U.S. supersonic fighter, the F-100, and the first commercial jetliner, the Boeing 707.

Pentagon orders also helped Igor Sikorsky develop the helicopter at United Aircraft. Sikorsky designed planes for the Russian czar before coming to the U.S., and after becoming part of United Aircraft in 1928 he developed the amphibians that opened up transoceanic air travel. Sikorsky put a helicopter into the air (actually just inches off the ground) for the first time in 1939, and during World War II, with orders from the Army Air Corps, he switched exclusively to building these whirlybirds.

Pratt & Whitney dominated the aircraft engine market through the 1960s and well into the 1970s. However, in the late 1960s problems surfaced. Engines designed for the Boeing 747 jumbo jet malfunctioned, and the U.S. Navy experienced breakdowns with a Pratt & Whitney engine supplied for the F-14 fighter. In 1971, these problems led to a $43 million loss for the entire company. Realizing they were in trouble, United Aircraft brought in Harry Gray, and he changed the company's course.

Gray was controversial from the time he arrived in Hartford. Six days before he accepted the job, Gray visited General Electric's engine plant at Evendale, Ohio. As the number three man at Litton Industries, he was a welcome visitor. Litton, a shipbuilder, was a prime customer—and according to the GE folks, they rolled out the red carpet for Gray, showing him their long-range plans. When GE's engine builders read a couple of weeks later that Gray had taken the top post at their archcompetitor, they hit the ceiling, writing a letter to protest Gray's actions.

At United Aircraft, Gray brushed off the criticism as unjustified. He said he'd told GE not to show him anything of a proprietary nature. The ruckus takes on added interest because from this time on GE set their cap on becoming the leader in the aircraft engine business. Pratt & Whitney's problems opened the door—and GE rushed in. Fourteen years later, in 1985, GE did, in fact, displace Pratt & Whitney as the main supplier of jet engines to the U.S. Navy and Air Force. In a review of this 14-year combat, the business magazine *Dun's Review* attributed the outcome to "dogged determination" by GE and "arrogance" by United Technologies.

Although Pratt & Whitney is still the biggest unit, United Technologies no longer has all their eggs in the aerospace basket. Harry Gray diversified the company. His two biggest acquisitions were both hostile, that is, the companies he targeted had to be dragged kicking and screaming to the altar. The first, Otis Elevator, was conquered in 1975 after a three-month skirmish. The second, Carrier, was roped in 1979 after a bitter seven-month struggle that saw the Justice Department try to block the acquisition and Carrier management accuse Harry Gray of "unconscionable" conduct.

Both Otis and Carrier have illustrious histories antedating United Aircraft. Elisha Graves Otis invented the safety elevator (it wouldn't fall even with a severed hoisting cable), and he opened a shop in Yonkers, New York, to make this newfangled device in 1853. It made the high-rise building possible. Today, Otis builds, installs and services elevators, escalators and moving sidewalks all over the world. In 1987, they had contracts to service, every month, 580,000 elevators and escalators. (Otis derives over half their income from these service contracts.) Willis Haviland Carrier was an engineer who developed the world's first air-conditioning system in 1902, just eight months after he'd graduated from Cornell. In 1915, he and six friends started the company bearing his name. Seven years later Carrier introduced the first air-conditioning system using a centrifugal compressor with a safe refrigerant—and that invention made possible the air-conditioning of offices, stores and homes.

TOP 10 U.S. EXPORTERS

Company	1989 Export Sales
1. Boeing	$11 billion
2. General Motors	$10.1 billion
3. Ford Motor	$8.6 billion
4. General Electric	$7.2 billion
5. IBM	$5.4 billion
6. Du Pont	$4.8 billion
7. Chrysler	$4.6 billion
8. United Technologies	$3.3 billion
9. Caterpillar	$3.2 billion
10. McDonnell Douglas	$2.8 billion

Source: *Fortune,* 16 July 1990

Many observers wondered whether Harry Gray would ever relinquish the levers of control. Doing so was, as Fortune suggested in 1984, difficult because "in 13 years he has refashioned" the company "so completely, even down to its name, that it has become his creation." Nevertheless, in 1986, he did step down. His successor, Robert Daniell, reminded shareholders in the annual report that "United Technologies is one of the great corporations of the world because of Harry J. Gray's leadership for the past 15 years." Daniell then began the dismantling. Wire and cable maker Essex Wire, semiconductor supplier Mostek and printing ink manufacturer Inmont were sold off. Next on the chopping block was Norden Systems, which became famous during World War II for bombsights and was acquired by United Aircraft in 1958. Harry Gray used to boast of the radar expertise Norden contributed to UT, but when the division began spouting red ink in the 1980s as a result of fixed-income contracts with the Pentagon, Daniell appeared ready to dump the firm. In a news briefing in 1989, John A. Rolls, UT's chief financial officer, said, "We're not so sure that we're the best guys to run Norden. We're not a systems house"—words that no doubt bucked up the Norden ranks.

Owners and rulers. Getting Harry Gray out of the cockpit took time, but the board of directors finally did force the selection of Daniell, an engineer who rose to the top through the ranks of the Sikorsky division. He made $1.8 million in 1989. His style has frequently been contrasted with Harry Gray's. For example, the *New York Times* reported that in 1981, after straightening out late delivery problems at Sikorsy, Daniell spent three days "on a round-the-clock basis to shake the hand of each of the division's 1,200 employees, working on three shifts." Harry Gray, still on the board in 1989, owned only 100 shares. Management reports to a heavyweight board of directors whose members, in 1988, included John S. Reed, boss of Citicorp; Pehr Gyllenhammar, charismatic head of Sweden's Volvo; Charles W. Duncan, Jr., former secretary of the Department of Energy; Jacqueline G. Wexler, former president of Hunter College; and Antonia Handler Chayes, former undersecretary of the U.S. Air Force. An Employee Stock Ownership Plan owns 8 percent of the stock.

As a place to work. United Technologies, Connecticut's largest employer, has never won high marks from labor. When UT moved to take over Carrier, the United Auto Workers, in an unusual action, tried to block the takeover with appeals to banks and the attorney general of New York State, alleging UT had treated workers harshly and shown "hostility to unions." Harry Gray ran the company in an autocratic fashion. Daniell promised under his regime the company would have "participatory management." UT has a poor record in promoting women. Of 47 top officers, none are female.

Social responsibility. Social activists regularly criticize UT for their elevator factories in South Africa, where they're the country's fifth biggest employer, for their auto parts factory in Northern Ireland, where they refuse to sign the antidiscrimination MacBride Principles and for their work as a major Pentagon supplier. During the 1970s the city of Yonkers, New York, where the Otis elevator company was born, literally "declared war" against United Technologies, charging the company "betrayed a trust" by deciding to close the Otis plant there after the city spent $14 million redeveloping land to accommodate a plant expansion by Otis. In 1986, UT announced plans to build a new rocket motor plant on little-used farmland in California's Central Valley. A coalition of farmers, ranchers, environmentalists, students and ministers opposed the plant. Some objected to having an arms factory. Others were concerned about safety and pollution problems. Despite the high unemployment the plant was supposed to address, the coalition forced UT to abandon the idea. The coalition's initial organizer was John Holmes, an orthopedic surgeon who practices in Merced. After investigating United Technologies, he concluded the company was nothing but a "bunch of hoodlums wrapping themselves in the flag."

Global presence. UT does 29 percent of their total business abroad. Otis, particularly, is a worldwide force, with plants in over 30 countries. In 1986, UT's Sikorsky unit teamed up with Italy's Fiat to buy a 32.4 percent interest in British helicopter maker Westland.

Stock performance. United Technologies stock bought for $1,000 in 1980 sold for $3,719 on January 2, 1990.

United Technologies Corp., United Technologies Buildings, Hartford, CT 06101; (203) 728-7000.

4

#1 *in auto exhaust systems, shock absorbers*
#2 *in shipbuilding, farm equipment*
#4 *in natural gas delivery*

Employees: 92,000
Sales: $14.1 billion
Profits: $584 million
Founded: 1943
Headquarters: Houston, Texas

Tenneco is an old-fashioned conglomerate—they run all kinds of businesses having nothing to do with one another—and to keep current, check the roster regularly because the cast of characters keeps changing. In 1988, for example, the company decided to sell their oil and gas operations, a business big enough to rank Tenneco 14th in the petroleum industry. In 1987, they sold Tenneco West (formerly called Kern County Land), which encompassed some 1 million acres of farmland, mostly in California, and had made Tenneco one of the nation's largest suppliers of table grapes and almonds. In 1986, they sold off their insurance business (Philadelphia Life) and their precious metals operations. In 1985, they sold their polyvinyl chloride business.

Those sales didn't decimate Tenneco. Their Newport News shipyard at Newport News, Virginia, builds aircraft carriers and submarines for the U.S. Navy and is the world's largest privately owned shipyard. Their agricultural equipment division, operating as J I Case, is the world's second largest maker of farm machines (after John Deere). Tenneco is also one of the world's major automotive parts suppliers, making shock absorbers, struts and suspension systems under the Monroe name and exhaust systems under the Walker name. Their Packaging Corp. of America unit is one of the leading producers of paperboard, molded fiber, aluminum foil and plastic packaging, with more than 50 U.S. plants; this company also owns 450,000 acres of forestland.

And then there's Tenneco's original business, not yet discarded: gas pipelines. The Tenneco Gas Pipeline Group operates an 18,000-mile network of pipelines delivering natural gas to customers in 26 states stretching from Texas to New England and accounting for 12 percent of U.S. natural gas consumption.

History. The company began life in 1943 as the Tennessee Gas and Transmission Company, their mission then to lay a gas pipeline from Louisiana to Tennessee. That project didn't work out, but founder Gardiner Symonds was not easily deterred. He built his first pipeline from south Texas through Tennessee and into Appalachia. The business grew, but Symonds chafed at being regulated by the Federal Power Commission, which set prices for natural gas. He went searching for businesses "where when you make a dollar, you can keep it."

He found plenty of them—chemicals, insurance, packaging, oil and gas exploration. In 1961, he merged Tennessee Gas with Bay Petroleum to form Tenneco, and during the turbulent 1960s Symonds went about his business, acquiring one company after another. His two biggest catches were Kern County Land, in 1967, and Newport News Shipbuilding, in 1968. Symonds died in 1971 while he was still Tenneco chairman. In just over 25 years, starting from scratch, he had assembled a company that ranked, with sales of $2.5 billion, 34th on the *Fortune* 500.

Along with California's Kern County Land came two Wisconsin manufacturing companies. One was Walker Manufacturing, a maker of auto exhaust systems; the other was J. I. Case, a farm and construction equipment company founded in 1842 by Jerome Increase Case. And Case contributed another unexpected dividend: James L. Ketelsen, a hardworking accountant who started at Case in 1959 as an assistant controller. Tenneco installed him as president of the Case unit and brought him to Houston headquarters in 1972. Six years later, at 48, he became CEO, a position he still held in 1990.

Some say that Ketelsen, an Iowan, is just a "tractor man at heart." He certainly has patience. Case has been losing money for as long as anyone can remember. And in 1984 he stunned Wall Streeters, for whom he has little regard, by paying $430 million to buy distressed farm equipment business, International Harvester. One analyst cracked, "It's like doubling up your losses." His sale of the oil and gas properties underlined his determination to give John Deere a run for their money. Deere holds about 45 percent of the farm equipment market. Case's share is about 35 percent. One ex-Tenneco executive told *Business Week* in 1986: "He's willing to sacrifice one of America's largest corporations to be No. 1 in tractors."

The International Harvester unit now part of Tenneco descends from a company Cyrus Hall McCormick founded in 1847. McCormick's reaper revolutionized American agriculture. The company known as International Harvester was formed in 1902 by the amalgamation of McCormick's company with four other machinery makers. In seeing International Harvester pass from the scene in 1984, Chairman Donald D. Lennox conceded it was an emotional wrench, add-

In 1978 Fortune *found only 10 women among the 6,400 highest-paid officers and directors on its list of leading American companies. They redid the survey in 1990, checking out the 4,012 highest-paid officers and directors of 799 publicly held companies—and found 19 women or less than one-half of 1 percent.*

ing: "But you can only pay so much for tradition and history, and you have to let your emotions stand aside and let your good business judgment take over."

Owners and rulers. Institutions (banks, mutual funds, insurance companies) own 48 percent of Tenneco's stock. All the directors and officers as a group own less than three-tenths of 1 percent of the shares. Ketelsen is a stubborn leader who disdains investment bankers and follows his own hunches. Analysts were amazed when he sold the oil and gas properties in 1988. And when he bought International Harvester's farm equipment business in 1985, *Business Week* headlined the move: "Will Tenneco's Harvester Deal Turn Out to 'the Corporate Equivalent of Vietnam?'" Ketelsen took home $1.6 million in 1989. The board of directors has one woman, M. Kathryn Eickhoff, head of her own economic consulting firm and formerly associate director for economic policy in the Office of Management and Budget.

As a place to work. Tenneco is known as one of the best places to work in Houston, where headquarters staff numbers 3,700. Amenities include a lavish fitness center in downtown Houston and a country club outside the city. The emphasis on fitness may stem from Ketelsen, a zealous jogger, an activity he continued after triple bypass heart surgery. In 1987, Case signed a contract with the United Auto Workers guaranteeing all workers at their farm equipment plants job security even during economic downturns. In July 1990 Tenneco brought 100 top women managers to Houston for a conference exploring how they might advance in businesses long dominated by men.

Social responsibility. In the late 1970s and early 1980s, when crude oil prices went through the roof, Tenneco signed take-or-pay contracts with companies supplying them with natural gas. In these contracts, Tenneco agreed to pay a minimum price ($3.75 per thousand cubic feet) for a set volume of natural gas—and was obligated, under these contracts, to pay for this natural gas even if they didn't need it. When prices nosedived, Tenneco was in the embarrassing position of having to pay more for gas than they could sell it for. Ketelsen's solution: cancel the contracts. He did so in 1983, causing an uproar in the energy industry. Tenneco renegotiated many of their supplier contracts and also secured a ruling from the Federal Energy Regulatory Commission allowing them to bill customers for 50 percent of the costs of these renegotiations. Other suppliers sued Tenneco for breach of contract, and some of these suits were still in the courts in 1989.

Tenneco adopted a Houston inner-city school, Jefferson Davis High, and pledged that from the class of 1992 on, they'll offer *every* graduate a $4,000 college scholarship. The dropout rate at Jefferson High had been running at 66 percent.

Global presence. Tenneco does 27 percent of business abroad. Their main overseas unit is British chemical company, Albright & Wilson.

Stock performance. Tenneco stock bought for $1,000 in 1980 sold for $3,255 on January 2, 1990.

Tenneco Inc., Tenneco Building, Houston, TX 77002; (713) 757-2131.

5

#1 *in data recording products, overhead projectors, pressure-sensitive tapes*

Employees: 86,600
Sales: $12 billion
Profits: $1.2 billion
Founded: 1902
Headquarters: St. Paul, Minnesota

Social Conscience | Workplace

Their most famous product is Scotch tape but that just scratches the surface of this remarkable, sprawling company which has evolved from a maker of sandpaper to a multimarket, multitechnology, multiproduct, multinational company whose diversity defies classification. By their own count, 3M makes 6,800 *kinds* of products and services. The actual number, counting all the permutations, tops 50,000. Every year 3M publishes a product directory. The 1987 version ran to 258 pages. According to one estimate, each day nearly one-half of the world's population makes use of—or benefits from—a 3M product. The users could be a TV viewer watching a program recorded on Scotch videotape, motorists finding their way with the help of Scotchlite reflective road signs, a gift box wrapper reaching for the Scotch tape, a reader looking at a magazine that has been printed on 3M lithographic plates, a personal computer owner slipping in a 3M diskette, a patient taking Tambocor to control an irregular heartbeat.

3M has, from time to time, acquired other companies, but unlike other conglomerates most of their growth has been internal. 3M's peculiar talent is an ability to take a particular technology and find an abundance of commercial uses for it or develop a single product into dozens of marketable forms. They like to say at 3M that one thing leads to another. Scotch cellophane tape spawned a vast array of tapes. One avenue led to audio- and videotapes, another to surgical tapes. Once

hospitals became a market, a line of health-care products was not far behind. After 3M takes on a particular technology, they'll go to the ends of the earth to discover uses. So Scotchlite reflective materials not only find their way into traffic signs and license plates but into road stripes and onto bicycles and vests and shoes. 3M makes a lot of products that stick, seal and protect—and they can be found in various places in the home, office and factory. One tape, for example, attaches moldings and trim to cars; another adhesive, Scotch-melt, bonds vinyl, wood and plastic; and still another fastens disposable diapers. To make their 747 jetliners, Boeing buys about 1,000 3M products, including Post-it notes, structural adhesives, masking tapes, microfilm printers, cleaning compounds, Safety-Walk antislip surfacing material, abrasive discs and Scotchcal drag resistant tapes.

Although outsiders have difficulty defining what this corporate animal is, 3M likes to feel they're *one* company whose business breaks down into four broad sectors:

1. Industrial and electronic (36 percent of sales)—tapes, abrasives, wires and cables, roof granules, fiber-optics, fluorochemicals.

2. Information and imaging technologies (28 percent of sales)—lithographic plates, X-ray films, overhead projectors, diskettes.

3. Life sciences (22 percent of sales)—surgical drapes and masks, surveillance and monitoring devices, drugs, dental fillings and braces, stethoscopes, wound closures.

4. Commercial and consumer (14 percent of sales)—household cleaning devices, carbonless paper, caulks, window insulators, Post-its, outdoor advertising displays.

One thread tying the parts together is this companywide goal: shoot for 25 percent of sales coming from products and services introduced in the past five years. The goal is not always met, but it's not for want of trying. 3M is a company ceaselessly and shamelessly on the prowl for new products, a mission supported by one of the biggest research and development budgets in American industry. 3M invested $700 million in research in 1988, equivalent to 6.6 percent of sales, nearly double the average for U.S. industrial companies. And 3M has 6,400 engineers, technicians and scientists working in research labs.

H*istory.* Minnesota Mining and Manufacturing is the company's legal name, even though everyone calls them 3M—and the company prefers the 3M designation. They've just never changed the name from the one the founders adopted in 1902. How *manufacturing* ever got into the title in the first place is a mystery. The company was started to mine a very hard mineral, corundum, at a site near Two Harbors, a town on the northwest bank of Lake Superior, midway between Silver Bay and Duluth. The mining business turned out to be a bust—there were no corundum deposits—but the company survived thanks to investors from St. Paul. St. Paul, built on the bluffs overlooking the Mississippi River, was a bustling port city in the early part of the century, full of entrepreneurs on the make. The 3M investors—principally Edgar B. Ober and Lucius P. Ordway—converted the company into a sandpaper manufacturer and in 1910 relocated the firm to St. Paul, 3M headquarters ever since.

Although the money people from St. Paul saved the company from going under, two farm boys—William L. McKnight and Archibald Granville Bush—developed 3M into Minnesota's largest and most valuable company. McKnight joined the company in 1907 as an assistant bookkeeper. Two years later Bush replaced McKnight, who moved up to cost accountant. Both were graduates of Duluth Business University, where they'd studied penmanship, business letter writing and bookkeeping.

McKnight and Bush formed a team that stayed intact for over 50 years. McKnight came to head up the company while Bush drove the sales force. They introduced principles that became permanently embedded in 3M's operating style. The principles stressed the importance of quality control, research to develop new products and attention to customer needs. Early on 3M developed the knack of improving an existing product or combining old products into new ones. 3M was the first to make a waterproof sandpaper. Their first nonabrasive product, masking tape, appeared in 1925. And the celebrated Scotch tape, which involved taking the cellophane Du Pont had invented and backing it with stickum, was introduced in 1930.

While 3M, with their 50,000–plus products, qualifies as a conglomerate, the company points out that many of these products were derived from the coating-and-bonding technology involved in their original product, sandpaper.

While 3M was successful before World War II, they exploded afterwards. 3M had plants in only three cities at war's end. In 1952, on their 50th birthday, sales had just nudged past the $100 million mark, and employment stood at 10,000. Subsequent leaps were mighty as 3M followed the serendipitous path of letting one thing lead to something else. The amazing part of the growth is that through it all 3M remained pretty much themselves. For that tenacity, they're one of America's most widely admired companies.

One reason for this endurance may have been the long tenure of the early leaders, McKnight and Bush. Their careers at 3M spanned both world wars. Bush ended up chairing the company's executive committee from 1949 to 1966, when he died at age 78. McKnight retired as company chairman in 1966 but served on the board until 1978 when he died at age 90. A half mile from 3M's headquarters in St. Paul, McKnight Road crosses Bush Avenue.

O*wners and rulers.* 3M has been such a consistent performer—they've been paying cash dividends since 1916 and in 1989 increased the dividend for the 31st consecutive year—that their stock is a big favorite of institutional investors (bank trust departments, pension funds, insurance companies). They hold over half of the outstanding shares. The largest single shareholder is John G. Ordway, Jr., grandson of the Ordway who saved the company from going bankrupt in 1905. His three-tenths of 1 percent of the total shares was worth $40 million in 1990. Allen Jacobson, a chemical engineer who joined 3M in 1947, became the sixth CEO in 1986, the latest in a long line of straight-talking, no-nonsense, technically oriented 3M leaders. Jacobson has spent a good deal of time visiting 3Mers at their workplaces. "This is a company that is run by personal interaction, not the book," he told an interviewer in 1987. Jacobson made $2.2 million in 1989. Of 3M's 37 corporate officers, only 1—assistant secretary JoAnn J. Bohne—is a woman. Of 3M's 91 top line executives—the people who manage business units—only 1, Juilanne H. Prager, head of technical planning and coordination in the consumer products group, is a woman. And of the 14 white board members, only 1—economist Norma T. Pace—is a woman.

As a place to work.   One of the best. 3M is known as a company that gives people room to develop their own ideas. It is acceptable for researchers to spend 15 percent of their time on unauthorized projects, a practice called "institutionalized lawlessness" or "bootlegging." If a

3M's Arthur Fry came up with the idea for Post-it notes while trying to create a bookmark that wouldn't fall out of church hymnals.

3Mer does come up with an idea for a new product, he or she is free to move about the company lining up a team of people to develop it. 3M is a great believer in decentralization and small towns. In the U.S., they operate 100 plants in 37 states—and only 5 of those plants have over 1,000 employees. 3M plants can be found in such places as Honeoye, New York; Wahpeton, North Dakota; Cynthiana, Kentucky; and Praire du Chien, Wisconsin. However, the biggest concentration is at the 425-acre, campuslike headquarters complex in St. Paul, where 22 buildings house some 12,000 workers. 3M rarely fills a position from the outside. Headhunters always cite 3M as the company that's the toughest in the country to pry anyone away from.

S*ocial responsibility.* The two largest foundations in Minnesota—the McKnight Foundation and the Bush Foundation— resulted from 3M's extraordinary success. 3M has a reputation as a generous giver. They had a contributions budget of nearly $30 million in 1988, and in St. Paul company and employee donations represent close to 15 percent of the money raised by United Way. Since 1975 3M has had a "Pollution Prevention Pays" program that has sharply reduced plant emissions and drawn praise from environmental organizations. In 1988, folk singer Pete Seeger presented 3M with the Corporate Conscience Award from the Council on Economic Priorities for environmental initiatives.

Although 3M prides themselves on respect for employees, the company aroused the ire of workers in Freehold Township, New Jersey, when they closed the audio- and videotape plant there in 1985, throwing 360 people out of jobs. The dispute over the closing received high visibility because Freehold is the hometown of rock star Bruce Springsteen, who joined in the protest and contributed $20,000 to the futile campaign waged by the workers and their union, the Oil, Chemical and Atomic Workers.

G*lobal presence.* Major. Although 3M didn't enter the international arena until 1951, foreign sales now account for 45 percent of business. 3M ranks as the 29th largest U.S. multinational. They operate 89 plants in 37 foreign countries. And they do overseas what they do here. Some

2,000 scientists work in 38 research labs abroad.

S*tock performance.* 3M stock bought for $1,000 in 1980 sold for $4,809 on January 2, 1990.

Minnesota Mining and Manufacturing Company, 3M Center, St. Paul, MN 55144; (612) 733-1110.

6

#1 *in automotive turbochargers, turboprop engines, hydrofluoric acid and fluorine, process technology for petroleum plants*

#3 *in nylon*

Employees: 108,300
Sales: $11.9 billion
Profits: $528 million
Founded: 1920
Headquarters: Morristown, New Jersey

Allied-Signal is another perfect example of a company whose constitutent parts— Bendix brakes, Fram filters, Garrett turbochargers, Autolite spark plugs, Anso carpet yarns—are more well known than the corporate parent. But that's hardly surprising because the elements go back many years whereas Allied-Signal is a child of the 1980s, spliced together from many different pieces and reassembled again and again as parts are splintered off.

The pivotal character in this corporate morality play is Edward L. Hennessy, Jr., an ex-seminarian who apprenticed at a trio of conglomerates (Textron, ITT, and United Technologies) before getting his first command post in 1979 at Allied Chemical, a commodity chemicals producer. One of his first moves was to rename the company Allied Corporation. He was not going to be mired in a sluggish chemical backwater. Indeed, Hennessy seems to have a strong aversion to the word *chemical.* He has excised it from the company literature. Activities normally considered chemical are grouped under the heading "engineered materials."

The chemistry Hennessy practices is buying and selling. He has bought and sold dozens of companies in deals totaling over $10 billion, transforming Allied into a behemoth three times pre-Hennessy size. The two biggest acquisitions were Bendix, in 1983, and Signal, in 1985. Bendix put Allied into the aerospace industry and made them one of the world's largest suppliers of automotive parts: brakes, steering systems, seat belts, turbochargers, spark plugs, filters. Automotive accounts for one-third of Allied-Signal's sales. The number one customer: Ford Motor, which bought nearly $700 million worth of equipment from Allied in 1987.

Signal turned Allied into a much bigger aerospace supplier, making hundreds of products found on planes, including gas turbine engines, air-conditioning units, radar devices, communications gear, flight control systems, hydraulic components. Aerospace accounts for 42 percent of Allied-Signal's sales. The number one customer: the U.S. government, which bought $2.4 billion worth of equipment from Allied in 1987.

The third foundation of the house Hennessy built, accounting for one-quarter of sales, is what he calls engineered materials, including chemicals, plastics, fibers and an old Signal unit, UOP, which has the know-how to set up oil-refining, petrochemical and food-processing plants. More than 4,000 plants in 110 countries run on UOP processes.

History. Allied-Signal, only five years old in 1990, has some venerable roots. Allied Chemical, organized in 1920, was an American effort to end dependence on the big German dyestuff manufacturers, and it combined five companies: Barrett, General Chemical, National Aniline & Chemical, Semet-Solvay Process and Solvay Process. A giant at birth, they ranked behind only Du Pont and Union Carbide in the U.S. chemical industry. Wall Street financier Eugene Meyer, who later bought the *Washington Post*, helped form Allied Chemical, and in 1973 his daughter, Katharine Graham, became the first woman to sit on Allied's board. The oldest of the five founding companies was Barrett, started in Chicago in 1854 by Samuel Barrett, who became known as the father of tarred roofing paper. After the Chicago fire of 1871, Barrett supplied the roofing for the rebuilt South Side.

Over the years, Allied Chemical remained a stalwart of the chemical industry, but never won any prizes for daring. In the late 1970s they were traumatized when the Justice Department prosecuted them for the prolonged dumping of a highly toxic pesticide, Kepone, into the James River in Virginia. The lawsuit cost the company $20 million in fines, settlements and legal fees.

Signal began in 1922 as the bootstrap operation of a 29-year-old avocado and lemon grower, Samuel B. Mosher. He operated on the fringes of one of the biggest oil strikes ever made—the Signal Hill field northeast of Long Beach in southern California. Mosher essentially dealt with a by-product, contracting with drillers to draw off from their wells the wet gas that lifted the crude oil to the surface. Well operators, interested only in the crude, usually let this gas escape into the air or burned it at the end of a flare stack. Mosher borrowed $4,000 from his father to build a plant to extract natural gas from this by-product. From this humble beginning Signal Oil & Gas became an integrated oil company, and eventually the largest independent operator in the West. In 1962, when Signal was 40 years old, they ranked 166th on the *Fortune* 500 list.

Forrest N. Shumway, a lawyer and Mosher's nephew, became president in 1964, and he transformed Signal from an oil and gas operator to a miniconglomerate that bought, or made major investments in, other companies. Shumway, only 37 in 1964, didn't buy companies for keeps. In fact, in 1974 he sold off his uncle's original business, pocketing $480 million from Britain's Burmah Oil for the Signal oil and gas properties. Shumway had already renamed the company Signal Companies. And because he didn't like the traffic and smog of Los Angeles, he moved Signal's headquarters to a low-slung, Spanish-style building on the Torrey Pines mesa overlooking the Pacific Ocean at La Jolla, outside San Diego.

Shumway's Signal had fingers in many pies—Mack Trucks, Golden West Broadcasters (KTLA in Los Angeles and the California Angels baseball team), Garrett, Ampex, UOP, Natomas—but the two biggest deals came in the 1980s. With a one-two punch, Forrest Shumway went out in a burst of glory. First, in 1983, he merged Signal, which then had sales of $5.4 billion, with New Hampshire-based Wheelabrator-Fry, a conglomerate with sales of $1.5 billion, put together by an extraordinary wheeler-dealer, Michael D. Dingman. Then, in 1985, he merged Signal with Allied. On January 1, 1988, after 30 years with the company, Shumway retired. He took with him two lump sum payments, one for $4.3 million, another for $3.5 million, and he began collecting his monthly pension of $9,843.

While Sam Mosher was struggling on the West Coast to get his company off the ground, the Bendix company was founded in Detroit in 1924 to serve the automotive industry. The founder was Vincent Bendix, inventor of the Bendix Starter Drive, the device that eliminated the old hand-cranked starter for cars. Bendix also made the first reliable four-wheel braking system for cars. Later they moved into aircraft components. By 1980, they were a major industrial company, with sales of $4 billion, ranking 114th on the Fortune 500. Two years later, in a bizarre episode, their independence ended.

William M. Agee was Bendix's CEO in 1982 at the ripe age of 44. His wife, business strategist Mary Cunningham, was at his side. They decided to buy aerospace company Martin Marietta, which not only spurned their attentions but also adopted the Pac-Man defense: Eat your enemies before they eat you. So, in fall 1982, Wall Streeters were treated to the spectacle of Bendix taking a big bite out of Martin Marietta while Martin Marietta, true to their word, started buying up Bendix shares. Martin Marietta also invited master accumulator, Harry Gray of United Technologies, to join in the Bendix carve-up. Agee, foiled in his takeover attempt, then brought in Ed Hennessy's Allied Corp. as his white knight. And that's how Bendix ended up in Allied-Signal's garage.

Of course, the companies parked in this garage are always moving around. For example, in fall 1985, only two months after the Signal-Allied merger, Hennessy announced at a press conference at New York's Pierre Hotel that he was shedding 30 companies, a mixed bag of engineering and construction service, chemical, scien-

Johnson Products of Chicago, the only black-owned company with a listing on a major stock exchange (the American), changed hands in 1989 when 49.5 percent of all the shares were acquired by Joan B. Johnson, increasing her holdings to 54 percent. Mrs. Johnson got the shares as part of a divorce settlement with George E. Johnson, founder of the cosmetics company.

tific instruments and real estate development firms, all adding up to annual sales of $3.2 billion. However, instead of dumping them one by one, Allied-Signal spun all of them off into a new entity headed by Michael Dingman, who only two years earlier had moved his Wheelabrator-Frye entourage into Signal. The new entity, the Henley Group, sold stock to the public in 1986 for $1.2 billion, the largest new issue of stock in U.S. business history. (Dingman is even more restless than Hennessy. In 1989, he split the Henley Group into two parts, one called the Wheelabrator Group, the other retaining the Henley Group name. The new Henley is headquartered in the old Signal Companies' hacienda in La Jolla.)

Meanwhile, back in New Jersey, Ed Hennessy was still struggling to dispel the image left by a spate of stories in the business press to the effect that Allied-Signal has been so busy making deals it's hard to tell what they stand for or where they're going.

Owners and rulers. Employee savings and stock purchase plans held nearly 15 percent of Allied-Signal shares at the start of 1988. Hennessy rules with an iron hand. He is the only corporate officer to hold a board seat. In 1987, *Fortune* quoted a person close to the company: "Ed is incapable of operating anything. While he's buying and selling parts, the company is run by staff. They have a mess of corporate airplanes and five layers of presidents and vice presidents before you get down to the operating levels." And, also in 1987, an unidentified Allied-Signal executive said this to *Business Week* about Hennessy: "He intimidates people."

Hennessy made $2.9 million in 1989. On Allied-Signal's board are former astronaut Thomas Stafford, former Marine Corps commandant Paul X. Kelley, former Mobil chairman Rawleigh Warner, Jr., former Time Inc. chairman Ralph P. Davidson and academic luminaries from MIT, the University of Tennessee, the Wharton School at the University of Pennsylvania and California State University (Jewel Plummer Cobb, the only woman and the only black on the board).

As a place to work. Uneasy. Allied-Signal employees are never sure their unit will not be severed from the corporate body next week. Benefits are not uniform because different subsidiaries have different programs. Many people have been lopped from the payroll in cost-cutting moves to appease Wall Street.

Social responsibility. Allied-Signal is such a moving target it's difficult for anyone to draw a bead on them. The company has a foundation, but issues no information about disbursements—not even to shareholders requesting such information.

Global presence. Allied-Signal does 19 percent of sales abroad. They have partnerships with companies in various countries, including Rolls-Royce in Britain, Crouzet in France and Nitto Boseki in Japan.

Stock performance. Allied stock bought for $1,000 in 1980 sold for $1,656 on January 2, 1990.

Allied-Signal Corporation, Columbia Road and Park Avenue, P.O. Box 400R, Morristown, NJ 07960; (201) 455-2000.

7

#1 *in car seat belts and airbags, power steering systems, engine valves for cars, consumer credit reports*

Employees: 73,800
Sales: $7.3 billion
Profits: $263 million
Founded: 1901
Headquarters: Cleveland, Ohio

TRW is a manufacturer for manufacturers; that is, they make products that end up as parts in the final products of other companies. For example, TRW boasts there's scarcely a car anywhere that doesn't have at least one TRW part, whether it's rack and pinion steering gears or seat belts or engine valves or electrical relays that turn the dome light on when the car door is opened. They're expected to benefit greatly during the 1990s from government-mandated seat belts or airbags in all cars.

Making car parts, specifically valves, was the launching pad for this company in the early 1900s. Originally called the Cleveland Cap Screw Company, they became Electric Welding Company (1908), Steel Products Company (1915) and Thompson Products (1926), after Charles E. Thompson, a welder whose idea to make valves by welding the head to the stem (instead of shaving down a rod of metal) propelled the company into the world's largest valve maker.

The company entered the world of high technology after World War II when they backed two brilliant engineers, Simon Ramo and Dean Wooldridge, to form their own company, Ramo-Wooldridge, that pioneered the ballistic missile program for the U.S. Air Force. Thompson Products formally merged with Ramo-Wooldridge in 1958, using the corporate name Thompson Ramo Wooldridge until 1965, when it was abbreviated to TRW.

The merger also brought into the company another scientist, Ruben F. Mettler, who, like Ramo and Wooldridge, got a PhD at the California Institute of Technology, the MIT of the West Coast, and served

COMPANIES GETTING MORE THAN HALF OF SALES OUTSIDE THE UNITED STATES

	Outside U.S.
Gillette	65%
Colgate	65%
IBM	59%
NCR	59%
CPC International	56%
Coca-Cola	54%
Digital Equipment	54%
Dow Chemical	54%
Xerox	54%
Caterpillar	53%
Hewlett-Packard	53%

as technical supervisor for the Atlas, Titan, Thor and Minuteman missile programs. Mettler became TRW president in 1969 and chairman and CEO in 1977. He has imparted to TRW a concern for ethics not always present at other defense contractors. Mettler stepped down in 1988 and was replaced by Joseph T. Gorman, who has been with the company for 22 years. Gorman made $1.2 million in 1989.

TRW was the first company to build a spacecraft, *Pioneer 1*, and now has built over 170 of them. They're also one of the major builders of satellites, the largest contractor in Ada (the Defense Department's standard computer language), one of the world's largest producers of software and a prime contractor in the Defense Department's "Star Wars" program.

The company's expertise in computer software has translated into another business, credit reporting. They track the credit ratings of 138 million consumers (over half the U.S. population). More than 500,000 people have enrolled in TRW Credentials, a service allowing consumers to access their credit file. TRW used to be a model of privacy. Since 1984, however, when Richard Whilden took over the Information Systems Group, TRW has repeatedly violated their own ethics code. They're using computer analyses to discover customers for mailing lists—the kind of "noncredit information" they promised not to collect in their ethics code, according to *Business and Society Review*. TRW's tarnished reputation continues to tarnish. In 1988, they pleaded

guilty to federal charges of conspiring to overcharge the government on contracts for military aircraft engines. TRW agreed to pay $14.8 million in penalties and refunds.

TRW has been shedding old-line manufacturing units to concentrate on the high technology and information systems areas. The company's largest concentration of people (17,000) is at the Space Center in Redondo Beach, California. The other major concentration (10,000) is in the headquarters city of Cleveland. TRW maintains 89 manufacturing facilities in 17 states, does 45 percent of business with the U.S. government and 26 percent abroad.

Stock performance. TRW stock bought for $1,000 in 1980 sold for $3,769 on January 2, 1990.

TRW Inc., 1900 Richmond Road, Cleveland, OH 44124; (216) 291-7000.

8

Hanson Industries

#1 *in portable typewriters, whirlpool baths, fireman's boots*

#3 *in titanium dioxide (whitening agent)*

#5 *in cement, shoes*

Employees: 70,000
Sales: $5.9 billion
Profits: $761 million
Founded: 1973
Headquarters: Iselin, New Jersey

The Value Line Investment Survey has a succinct definition of this company: "Hanson makes money by buying and selling companies." Hanson Industries is the U.S. subsidiary of London-based Hanson PLC (PLC stands for public limited company, meaning, in Britain, you can buy stock in the company, as opposed to a private limited company, which uses Ltd.). In 25 years Hanson PLC became one of Britain's 10 biggest companies. And in 17 years, Hanson Industries became one of the U.S.'s 100 biggest industrial companies. The strategy was the same on both sides of the Atlantic: buy companies, sell off pieces to defray the purchase price and make the remainder yield super profits (or else throw them out of the house).

Two Yorkshiremen are the principal players in this Anglo-American conglomerate. James Hanson (now Lord Hanson) looks out for the British side, Gordon White (now Sir Gordon White) runs the American operation. Sir Gordon bought so many companies that Hanson Industries accounts for more than half the total sales of Hanson PLC ($11.3 billion in 1989). He was the model for the British corporate raider depicted in the movie *Wall Street*. The British parent, Hanson PLC, has a listing on the New York Stock Exchange, and American investors own 15 percent of the company.

Sir Gordon bought not one but two U.S. conglomerates: U.S. Industries and Kidde Inc., each with dozens of businesses of their own. Among the businesses Hanson Industries owned at the start of 1990 were Smith Corona typewriters, Carisbrook textiles, Kaiser Cement, the Jacuzzi whirlpools, Faberware cookware, Ames tools, shoemaker and shoe store operator Endicott Johnson (Nettleton, Liberty, Trimfoot), and Ground Round restaurants.

Sir Gordon never visits any of the companies he buys. In fact, he hardly ever sets foot in the U.S. command post at Iselin, New Jersey. He stays across the Hudson River on Park Avenue where he studies which company to buy next. Hanson is as adept at selling companies as buying them. They especially like to sell companies whose operations and profits have been improved during their tenure at Hanson. In 1989, Sir Gordon sold one of his first U.S. acquisitions, Hygrade, the maker of Ball Park Franks. Sara Lee bought the firm for $140 million.

Hanson has a way with arithmetic. In 1986, after buying SCM despite a ferocious attempt by management and Merrill Lynch to defeat the bid, Sir Gordon deftly disposed of Glidden paints (which went to Britain's Imperial Chemical Industries for $580 million), Durkee's Famous Foods (which went to another British company, Reckitt & Colman, for $120 million) and several other units for a total cash-in of $926 million. The takeover price for the whole enterprise was $930 million, which meant that Hanson acquired the rest of SCM (Smith-Corona, titanium oxide, industrial chemicals, Durkee's institutional food business) for nothing.

In 1990 Hanson became the U.S.'s largest coal producer by acquiring Peabody Holdings. To get Peabody, they outbid American mining company, AMAX. As the bidding got under way, Sir Gordon White said: "Anyone who wants to bid against us for Peabody is going to find it difficult. It's going to have to be a very attractive price because we really do want Peabody." Sir Gordon's takeover of Peabody came on the heels of Lord Hanson's purchase of Consolidated Gold Fields for $5.7 billion, the largest deal in the U.K.'s history.

Stock performance. Hanson PLC stock bought for $1,000 in 1980 sold for $1,854 on January 2, 1990.

Hanson Industries, 99 Wood Avenue South, Iselin, NJ 08830; (201) 549-7050.

Hanson PLC, 1 Grosvenor Place, London SW1X7JH, England.

Sir Gordon White (if you want to sell a company): 410 Park Avenue, New York, NY 10022; (212) 826-0098.

9

LITTON INDUSTRIES, INC.

#1 *in electronic surveillance systems, aircraft guidance systems, missile cruisers*

#2 *in oil well logging*

#3 *in shipbuilding*

Employees: 52,900
Sales: $5.1 billion
Profits: $179 million
Founded: 1953
Headquarters: Beverly Hills, California

No longer is Litton Industries the quintessential conglomerate. That was their early mission in life, as they went about buying up companies, in helter-skelter fashion. But then they discovered an odd thing: Those companies, once bought, had to be somehow managed. Many were mismanaged to oblivion. In the 1980s Litton Industries shrunk, selling 14 major divisions with sales over $1 billion. They gave up their most visible product, the microwave oven, and exited a host of other businesses—office furniture, medical products, business machines (Royal typewriters, Sweda cash registers, Monroe calculators) and publishing (*Medical Economics, Physicians Desk Reference, McGuffey's Reader* and other Van Nostrand–Reinhold titles).

Litton has retreated to their roots as a developer of highly sophisticated electronic products and systems, primarily for the military. "We've become what we started out to be," observed Fred O'Green, a former Lockheed engineer who joined Litton in the glory days of 1962 and was CEO from 1981 to 1986.

From being interested in anything and everything, Litton has narrowed their fields of endeavor to four:

1. Advanced electronics: systems for tracking and controlling aircraft and products such as laser gyros and gallium arsenide for use in electronic warfare (missile guidance).

2. Resource exploration services: seismic analyses to determine whether it's worth drilling for oil and gas—on land or underwater.

3. Industrial automation: computerized systems to automate factory production and material handling.

4. Marine engineering and production: Ignalls shipyard at Pascagoula, Mississippi, one of the nation's largest, builds amphibious assault ships and guided missile cruisers.

Litton management oversees these operations from an enclave in Beverly Hills featuring a columned headquarters resembling a southern antebellum plantation house. Those operations include plants in 52 cities in 28 states, with the two biggest concentrations being California and Texas. The government is Litton's most important customer, accounting for 48 percent of sales. Litton does 23 percent of their business abroad: The whole world clamors for their electronic warfare products.

An executive perk at Litton is low-cost borrowing. The top 50 people get to borrow money at 4 percent interest without putting up any security. At the start of 1988, $4 million were lent out under this program. CEO Orion L. Hoch borrowed $1 million at 6 percent interest to buy a house. His note is due when he leaves the company or on October 14, 2012, whichever comes first. He also took home $1.2 million in 1989.

On Litton's board in 1989 were Charles B. Thornton, Jr., son of Litton's founder, Charles B. "Tex" Thornton. He is the largest single stockholder, with nearly 2 percent of the total shares. Arjay Miller, former dean of the Stanford Business School and former president of Ford Motor, was elected to the board in 1986— and that was a throwback to Litton's founding. Tex Thornton and Miller were members of the famous World War II Air Force team known as the Whiz Kids (they were systems people before anyone had heard of systems) who offered themselves as a package to Ford Motor after the war ended. Another member of the group was Robert McNamara, who also became pres-

Whatever Happened To...

Max Factor cosmetics? They're now part of Revlon.

Eversharp? They're now Schick Safety Razor — and they belong to Warner-Lambert.

Schlitz beer? They're now part of Stroh.

Beech-Nut baby foods? They're now part of Ralston Purina.

Bulova watches? They're now part of Loews.

Goodrich tires? They're now part of Michelin.

Colt firearms? They were sold in 1990 to an investor group headed by the State of Connecticut.

Bumble Bee seafoods? They were bought in 1989 by the Uni Group of Thailand.

Jergens lotion? They were sold to a Japanese company.

ident of Ford and then Defense Secretary and head of the World Bank. Thornton spent two years at Ford, gravitating to Hughes Tool before starting Litton.

Litton was the great spawner of other conglomerates. Among the conglomerate builders who came out of Beverly Hills to fashion "Littons" of their own were Harry Gray (United Technologies), Fred Sullivan (Walter Kidde), George Scharffenberger (City Investing) and Dr. Henry Singleton, who founded Teledyne, which now holds the biggest chunk of Litton stock (29 percent of all shares).

Stock performance. Litton Industries stock bought for $1,000 in 1980 sold for $2,294 on January 2, 1990.

Litton Industries Inc., 360 North Crescent Drive, Beverly Hills, CA 90210; (213) 859-5000.

10

◤◥TELEDYNE, INC.

#1 *in dental irrigators, swimming pool heaters, zirconium*

Employees: 35,100
Sales: $3.5 billion
Profits: $150 million
Founded: 1960
Headquarters: Los Angeles, California

What does the Water Pik, a dental cleaning device, have to do with the Model 324 Unmanned Air Vehicle, a remote-controlled plane used in military reconnaissance? They're both made by units of Teledyne, an eccentric conglomerate whose stock qualifies as one of the greatest investments of the second half of the 20th century. One thousand dollars invested in Teledyne during their early days in the 1960s would have grown, if left alone, to over $50,000 by 1990.

An assemblage of over 100 companies, Teledyne was largely the creation of Dr. Henry E. Singleton, a Texan who went to the Naval Academy at Annapolis for three years before switching to MIT, where he took BS, MA and PhD degrees in electrical engineering. He worked at Hughes Aircraft and Litton Industries before bolting

in 1960 with another Litton colleague, George Kozmetsky, to form Teledyne.

Singleton the scientist turned out to be a wizard at finance. In addition to buying a lot of companies and keeping careful track of them, he discovered that by acquiring insurance companies he could, by using their funds, play the stock market. Over 25 years he bought and sold shares in over 24 major companies, invariably making money for Teledyne. He also built up huge positions in some companies: Curtiss Wright and his old employer, Litton Industries, for examples. Coming into the 1990s, Litton's largest shareholder, with 29 percent of the stock, was Teledyne, founded by one of the Lidos (Litton Industries dropouts).

Singleton carried out his mission in an almost solitary fashion, disdaining conventional ways of doing business. Not until 1987 did he bother to pay a cash dividend. He kept his board of directors a small, tight group of people he knew. The company president for many years was his Annapolis roommate, George Roberts, who holds a PhD in metallurgy and who replaced Singleton as CEO in 1987. Teledyne may have been the only American company where the two top officers both held doctorates. Teledyne had another distinction. They were one of the highest priced stocks on the New York Stock Exchange, selling for $358 a share in mid-1989.

In 1989, as he surveyed, from his Century City offices in Los Angeles, the domain he built from scratch, Henry Singleton could see an array of companies stretching over five broad sectors:

1. Aviation and electronics—microcircuits the size of postage stamps, electronic guidance and navigation systems, piston and turbine engines and remotely piloted planes built by Teledyne Ryan Aeronautical, whose predecessor company, Ryan Aeronautical, built the *Spirit of St. Louis* for Charles Lindbergh.

2. Industrial products—many kinds of engines, machine tools, giant welding machines, offshore oil platforms, rubber urethane tires.

3. Specialty metals—Teledyne is the leading U.S. producer of zirconium and its byproduct, hafnium, essential metals in the production of nuclear reactors. Tung-

TOP EMPLOYEE-OWNED COMPANIES*

Company	Type of Business	Number of Employees
1. Publix Supermarkets	Supermarkets	65,000
2. HealthTrust	Hospital management	30,000
3. Avis	Car rental	13,500
4. EPIC	Hospitals	10,000
5. Science Applications	R&D & computers	10,000
6. Parsons	Engineering, mining, constr.	10,000
7. Charter Medical	Hospitals	9,000
8. Amsted Industries	Manufacturing	8,300
9. Weirton Steel	Steel	8,100
10. Avondale	Shipbuilding	7,500
11. Wyatt Cafeterias	Cafeterias	6,500
12. Austin	Construction	6,500
13. Milwaukee Journal	Newspaper, communications	6,200
14. W.L. Gore Associates	Textiles, electronics	5,000
15. Republic Engineered Steel	Steel	4,900
16. Simmons	Furniture	4,900
17. Graybar	Electrical equipment	4,700
18. Treasure Chest Advertising	Printing	4,000
19. National Steel & Shipbuilding	Shipbuilding	4,000
20. Stebbings Engineering	Engineering	4,000
21. Davey Tree Expert Company	Tree service	3,800
22. Lifetouch	Photography studios	3,000
23. Arthur D. Little	Consulting	2,600
24. Northwestern Steel & Wire	Steel	2,300
25. CH2M Hill	Engineering	2,300

* At least 50 percent owned by their employees.

Source: National Center for Employee Ownership.

sten, molybdenum, tantalum and various alloys are also produced by Teledyne.

4. Consumer products—Water Pik, Shower Massage, AR speakers.

5. Finance—United Insurance, Trinity Universal Insurance and Fireside Thrift, a California savings and loan.

Singleton turned 73 in 1990. He is the largest single shareholder, holding 13 percent of the stock, and since the company started in 1987 to pay a cash dividend of $4 a share per year, that gave him an annual dividend payout of $6 million. He's worth $670 million. Singleton finally decided to retire from day-to-day management in April 1989. He continues as chairman. Dr. Singleton has never had much to do with the press, and he has never allowed his picture to appear in an annual report. Teledyne watchers are therefore always wondering what he will do next—and in early 1990 they got some answers. Teledyne spun off one segment of their business—financial services (the insurance companies and Fireside Thrift)—to shareholders and named a new president, 48-year-old William T. Rutledge, onetime foreman at Bethlehem Steel who joined Teledyne in 1986. The Litton stock Teledyne held was lodged in the portfolios of the insurance companies—and what this means is unclear except that because Henry Singleton was indisputably the largest Teledyne shareholder, he automatically became the largest shareholder in Unitrin Inc., the holding company formed through the spinoff of the financial services units. In short, Dr. Henry Singleton may not be ready yet to hang up his financial scalpel.

Teledyne was doing one-quarter of their business with the Defense Department, and in 1989 one unit, Teledyne Electronics, was temporarily barred from receiving federal contracts after an investigation determined their marketing rep in Washington had bribed a government official to steer to Teledyne a $24 million Air Force contract for electronic test devices. After pleading guilty to charges brought by the Justice Department, Teledyne was fined $4.4 million and, in an unusual penance, agreed to forego profits on another Pentagon contract.

In January 1989 two Teledyne vice presidents were convicted of conspiracy and wire fraud for bribing a Navy contracting officer to win a $24 million electronics contract for aircraft radar test kits. Both officials were sentenced to a year in prison, and Teledyne paid a settlement of $8 million.

Stock performance. Teledyne stock bought for $1,000 in 1980 sold for $5,343 on January 2, 1990.

Teledyne Inc., 1901 Avenue of the Stars, Los Angeles, CA 90067; (213) 277-3311.

11

#1 *in deodorant soaps, bus manufacturing, trade show decorating, money orders*

#2 *in airline catering*

Employees: 36,800
Sales: $3.5 billion
Profits: $109 million
Founded: 1914
Headquarters: Phoenix, Arizona

Workplace

Greyhound used to implore us to "Take the bus and leave the driving to us." They don't do that anymore. They sold off the business that gave the company life 65 years ago, although, as of mid-1990, they continued to hold a 22.5 percent interest in Dallas-based GLI Holding, which took over the intercity bus operation. In 1990, however, they changed their name—from Greyhound to Greyhound Dial—to signal they're really more interested in getting people to smell better than in busing them.

Greyhound Dial still makes buses, both intercity coaches and the transit buses rolling on the streets of New York and other cities. They feed people on airlines and in airline terminals, handle baggage and fueling at airports, build trade exhibits, run a cruise line, lend money and market consumer products, among them Dial soap, Purex detergents, Brillo soap pads, Armour Star canned meats and Lunch Bucket microwave meals.

History. John W. Teets, Greyhound's current leader, probably doesn't like to be reminded of the company's origin as a bus company that transported miners across Minnesota's Mesabi Iron Range. When Carlton Jackson, a history professor at Western Kentucky University, began researching his history of the Greyhound bus company, (*Hounds of the Road*, Bowling Green University Press, 1984), he received little help from the corporate folks in Phoenix. He concluded, as he mentions

THE 10 HIGHEST-PAID WOMEN EXECUTIVES*

	Job	Salary**
1. Robin Burns	CEO, Estée Lauder USA	$1.3 million
2. Linda Allard	Director of Design, Ellen Tracy Inc.	$1 million
3. Verna Gibson	President, CEO, The Limited Stores	$1 million
4. Karen Anderegg	President, Clinique (Estée Lauder)	$850,000
5. Andrea Robinson	President, Ultima II (Revlon)	$650,000
6. Cathleen Black	Publisher, USA Today	$600,000
7. Claire Gargalli	President, CEO, Equimark Corp.	$597,730
8. Barbara Bass	President, CEO, Emporium (Carter Hawley Hale)	$550,000
9. Jill Barad	President, Mattel USA	$504,923
10. Mary Moore	Chief Creative Officer, Wells Rich Greene	$500,000

*This list does not include founders and co-founders of firms, or executives of companies founded by a member of their immediate family.

**Salaries only, not including stock options, bonuses or other extras.

Source: Savvy, June/July 1990.

in his introduction, that "the present Greyhound management is simply not historical-minded." Of course, as Jackson was writing his book, Greyhound was reshaping itself, which meant repudiating the past. The Armour meatpacking plants, part of Greyhound since 1970, were sold to ConAgra in 1983 (though they still make canned meats under the Armour Star label). And the bus company was lopped off in 1987. Meanwhile, Greyhound acquired other companies to expand their presence in airline and airport catering (Dobbs and Carson International), laundry products (Boraxo, 20 Mule Team) and bus manufacturing (the RTS modular bus formerly made by General Motors).

The restructuring began with the selection of John W. Teets as CEO in 1982. Teets had no allegiance to the old bus company. One of his favorite sayings is management must "see the company not as it is, but as it can grow to be."

Owners and rulers. One of the few CEOs who does not hold a college degree, John Teets is clearly the man in charge. In 1989, he held the positions of chairman, president and CEO. He was also the only member of management with a board seat. Greyhound's oldest board member is John

H. Johnson, publisher of *Ebony* and head of one of America's largest black-owned businesses. He joined the board in 1974 when Joe Black, former ace relief pitcher for the Brooklyn Dodgers, was working full-time for Greyhound as ambassador to the black communities where the bus company got a lot of passengers—and employees.

Social responsibilty. Under Teets, Greyhound gained the reputation of being tough on labor. At both Armour and the bus company, he demanded wage concessions—and when they weren't forthcoming, replaced the work force with nonunionized employees. And then he got rid of these operations entirely.

Although they're the biggest company in Phoenix, Greyhound has not earned high marks there for corporate citizenship, which may be in line with an older company tradition. Carlton Jackson interviewed one bus driver who told him: "I have never seen any contribution ever given by Greyhound Lines to any charity in the United States in the 33 years I have been employed."

Global presence. Negligible, although Greyhound retained ownership of the Canadian bus line after selling the U.S. business.

Stock performance. Greyhound stock bought for $1,000 1980 sold for $3,811 on January 2, 1990.

Consumer brands

Tone, Pure & Natural, Purex soaps and detergents; Brillo scouring pads; Sno bol toilet bowl cleaner; Borateem bleach, Boraxo and 20 Mule Team soaps; Dobbs Houses; Aeroplex newsstands; Premier Cruise Lines.

The Greyhound Dial Corporation, III West Clarendon, Phoenix, AZ 85077; (602) 248-4000.

12

National Intergroup

#4 in drug wholesaling

Employees: 6,500
Sales: $3 billion
Profits: $26 million
Founded: 1926
Headquarters: Pittsburgh, Pennsylvania

Confronted with hard times in the steel industry, what does a steelman do? Howard M. "Pete" Love's answer was: cut and run. Love, a Harvard Business School graduate, became CEO of National Steel, the nation's sixth largest steelmaker, in 1980, following in the footsteps of his father, George Love, a former vice chairman of the steel company. But the times were different. Foreign-made steel had captured one-quarter of the American market, and the U.S. steel industry was in disarray.

Love moved to reposition National Steel to make it less dependent on the business that was its raison d'être: steelmaking. He hoped to become a major national player in the savings and loan field, using as his base the California thrift institution, First Nationwide, acquired in 1980. He sold the Weirton plant to the workers, and 50 percent of the rest of the steelmaking operations to Nippon Kokan, Japan's second largest steelmaker. He bought an independent oil distributor, Permian, and a drug wholesaler, Foxmeyer, and became a variety store operator by bringing the Ben Franklin stores into the fold.

Clearly, National was no longer just a steelmaker. And to reflect the new diversity, Love renamed the company his fa-ther once headed to the nondescript National Intergroup, a perfect title for a conglomerate: It could stand for anything (or nothing).

And so it did. By decade's end, to raise money Love sold off First Nationwide to Ford Motor for $425 million and one-half of Permian to the public. Squeezing any profit out of this motley collection was still difficult—and their troubles attracted the attention of a Wall Street group, Centaur Partners, which accumulated 16.5 percent of the shares and told Love he should dissolve National Intergroup completely by selling off everything and giving the proceeds to the shareholders.

Howard Love ignored this advice, and in mid-1990, prior to the company's annual meeting, he proposed his own radical surgery:

1. Sell the remainer of National Steel holdings to Nippon Kokan.
2. Sell the Permian shares.
3. Sell the Ben Franklin stores.
4. Keep Foxmeyer, the sole remaining unit.
5. Change the company name to Foxmeyer.

Love's strategy was rejected by shareholders, who elected three Centaur partners to the board with a mandate to dissolve the company.

So ends the short, sweet saga of National Intergroup.

National Intergroup Inc., 20 Stanwix Street, Pittsburgh, PA 15222; (412) 394-4100.

13

#1 *in team sporting goods, self-propelled work platforms,electrical relays for airplanes*

Employees: 17,400
Sales: $1.4 billion
Profits: $70 million
Founded: 1963
Headquarters: Willoughby, Ohio.

Figgie is an old-fashioned conglomerate fashioned by their founder, Harry E. Figgie, Jr., whose importance to the company cannot be underestimated. The holder of two engineering degrees, a law degree and an MBA from the Harvard Business School, Figgie raised $5.8 million in 1963 to buy Cleveland-based Automatic Sprinkler Corp., maker of fire protection sprinklers, and from that small base (annual sales were $23 million) he cooked up a melange of companies whose activities range from making baseballs and baseball bats to selling casualty insurance to supplying the Pentagon with electronic missile-tracking equipment. Figgie rules the roost. In 1981, he changed the corporate name from A-T-O Inc. to Figgie International. In 1982, he moved the corporate headquarters to Richmond, Virginia, because he didn't like what he called the "very anti-business climate" in Cleveland—and besides, he was developing a 1,600-acre tract in the Richmond area. In 1989, he went back to Ohio when Cleveland, along with the state of Ohio, offered him a 630-acre tract for a headquarters site. While the Cleveland site is being developed, their temporary headquarters are in a suburb. In 1989, *Fortune* named Figgie one of "America's toughest bosses." Figgie served under Gen. George Patton during World War II and admits to knowing "how to chew ass." He puts it this way: "You don't build a company like this with lace on your underwear."

Since 1963 Figgie has bought 60 companies. They include Rawlings Sporting Goods of St. Louis, Fred Perry Sportswear, Advance Security (10th largest private guard supplier), Consolidated Packaging Machinery (they put the caps on bottles), Huber Essick (construction equipment), Scott Aviation (oxygen masks) and American LaFrance (oldest maker of aerial ladder fire trucks). Figgie worries a lot about free enterprise, and has therefore endowed four chairs of free enterprise—two at the University of Virginia, one at Baldwin-Wallace College in Berea, a Cleveland suburb, and one at his alma mater, the Harvard Business School. Harry Figgie turned 66 in 1989. In May 1989 he appointed Vincent Chiarucci, a CPA with Figgie for only three years, president. The post had been vacant since 1982.

S*tock performance.* Figgie stock bought for $1,000 in 1980 sold for $9,720 on January 2, 1990.

Figgie International Inc., 4420 Sherwin Road, Willoughby, OH 44094; (216) 946-9000.

PART SEVEN

Maintaining the Flow: The Circulation System

Travel & Transportation
Airlines
Railroads
Delivery Services
Truckers

Telephone
Telephone

Money
Banks
Insurance
Financial Services
Investment Bankers

TRAVEL & TRANSPORTATION

AIRLINES

Airplanes and airports are more crowded than ever. Nearly twice as many fares are sold today as a decade ago—450 million a year in 1989 versus 250 million in 1980. In that same period the U.S. has opened no major airports. But not all U.S. airlines have benefitted from this huge explosion in air travel. Much of the turmoil in the airline industry stemmed from deregulation in 1979, which forced airlines to compete against each other instead of having fares and routes regulated by the federal government. Many older, well-established airlines no longer exist—Western, Ozark, PSA, Frontier, Piedmont, National. They were bought out by the megacarriers that dominate the industry as the new decade opens. The top eight airlines now carry 90 percent of all airline traffic.

1

AmericanAirlines

#1 *in airlines*

Employees: 69,800
Sales: $10.5 billion
Profits: $455 million
Founded: 1930
Headquarters: Fort Worth, Texas

In December 1988, Robert Crandall, feisty boss of American Airlines, rushed to the public address system at the airline's Dallas–Fort Worth headquarters to let his troops know: "We're Number One." For the first time in 28 years American Airlines had bested United Airlines in the measurement the industry uses, revenue passenger miles, to recapture first place in domestic air travel. If the 1980s belonged to any airline, it was American. They started the decade losing $75 million. They emerged with annual profits of nearly a half billion dollars. This swing left competitors whiffing American Airlines' exhaust.

American has combined competitive zeal with an ability to outsmart rivals. Ask Braniff Airways. They filed for bankruptcy in 1983 and accused American of waging a "dirty tricks" campaign to force them out of business. American is clearly the industry's innovator, having introduced Super Saver fares, frequent-flyer bonuses, a two-tier wage structure and an advanced computerized reservation system. American expanded rapidly during the 1980s, introducing flights to Europe and Japan, and buying Air Cal, a West Coast airline, in 1987. In 1990 they were poised to take over TWA's Chicago-London run and Eastern's Latin American routes. In the U.S. they fly to 162 airports in 41 states.

History. American likes to trace company origins back to Charles Lindbergh. In 1926 Lindbergh, then a little-known barnstormer, flew a load of mail from Chicago to St. Louis in a World War I surplus biplane, a model nicknamed "The Flaming Coffin." Airmail was the chief commercial use of airplanes at the time, and the federal government heavily subsidized the service. Lindbergh worked for Robertson Aircraft, one of a hodgepodge of 85 aircraft-related companies consolidated into American Airways in 1930.

American Airways flew a weird assortment of Fords, Lockheeds, Condors and half a dozen other types of planes. In 1931 they became the first airline to have a plane built to their own specifications: a nine-passenger, single-engine Pilgrim 100-A. But the airline really took off after 1934, when C. R. Smith, a tall, gruff Texan, became president. Believing aviation's future lay in carrying passengers, not mail, Smith introduced a Curtiss Condor plane with sleeping berths, a flying Pullman car, and stewardesses, and adopted the name American Airlines.

Smith viewed air transportation as a marketable product, something "like a box of Post Toasties." Selling it, in his opinion, was "fully as important as producing it." Until then most airline advertising had consisted of a schedule and a picture of an airplane. Smith confronted the big taboo of airline advertising head-on: "Afraid to fly?" read the headline on a 1937 ad. American's routes to California flew over the deserts of the Southwest— The Sunshine Route, they called it, implying safer flying weather than on United's flights across the Rockies. When a United plane crashed in the mountains near Denver, American's ads boasted of "The Low-Level Routes to the West."

Nevertheless, the early years were unprofitable for American, as well as other airlines, because of high costs and low passenger volume. The dominant transport plane in the mid-1930s was the 14-seat Douglas DC-2. C. R. Smith thought a bigger plane would probably make money, so he had Douglas Aircraft design the 21-passenger DC-3, destined to become one of the most famous commercial planes in history. American had DC-3s in the air by 1936; they also turned their first profit that year: $4,600. By decade's end, they were the country's number one airline.

Smith married Elizabeth Manget, a Dallas Junior Leaguer, in 1938, but the marriage had to compete with his love for American Airlines. After a four-day honeymoon Smith dropped his bride off at their apartment and disappeared to his office for the next day and a half. Ultimately the airline won. They were divorced, and from then on Smith lived in a bachelor apartment in New York decorated with paintings of Western scenes by Frederic Remington and Charles Russell.

After World War II Smith outfitted the airline with all new planes, which represented the biggest outlay of money any airline had ever made. In 1949, while United was still flying DC-3s, Smith had a good laugh on his chief competitor by donating American's last DC-3 to a museum. In 1953 American offered the first nonstop, coast-to-coast flights aboard their 80-seat DC-7s. That same year they surpassed the Pennsylvania Railroad as the world's largest passenger carrier in terms of sales. In 1959 they ushered in the jet age with their Boeing 707s.

Smith left the airline in 1968 to become Secretary of Commerce during fellow Texan Lyndon Johnson's last year in the White House. He was succeeded at American by George A. Spater, a quiet professorial lawyer who collected first editions of Virginia Woolf, lunched with the New

AIRLINE LEADERS
(Ranked by revenue passenger miles flown in 1989)

Airline	RPMs* (billions)
1. American	78.3
2. United	69.6
3. Delta	59.3
4. Northwest	45.7
5. Continental	38.8
6. TWA	35.0
7. Pan Am	29.4

* A revenue passenger mile (RPM) is one paying passenger flown one mile.

York literati and shunned the company limousine to commute by train. Spater became one of Watergate's earliest casualties when he announced in 1973 he'd made an illegal $55,000 corporate contribution to Nixon's reelection campaign. American had been turned down repeatedly in their requests for new routes, and Spater was led to believe his donation would bring more favorable treatment from the Civil Aeronautics Board.

Under C. R. Smith, American was known for years to traveling businessmen as one of the country's most professional and efficient airlines. After he left, things got so bad in the early 1970s one American vice president sent a note to 140,000 regular passengers apologizing for the poor service. By the late 1980s American had recovered their old reputation and began to rival Delta Airlines, the traditional favorite, in surveys of passenger satisfaction.

American's revival can be traced largely to Robert Crandall, who joined the company in 1973 as chief financial officer and became president in 1980. Crandall invested in a computerized reservations system, called SABRE, used by travel agents. Not only did SABRE become a cash cow for the airline (earning profits in 1985 of $143 million on sales of $336 million), it opened the way to other innovations. SABRE tracked unfilled seats, making it possible for American to introduce special fares for nonbusiness travelers. In 1977 American introduced the Super Saver coast-to-coast fare to fill their big jets. American then introduced the first frequent-flier program, using the computerized system's ability to track a passenger's mileage with the airline. In 1982 they changed their corporate name to AMR.

Owners and rulers. Crandall's personal intensity is legendary (a two-pack-a-day smoker, he runs four miles every morning before showing up at the office by 7 A.M.). Crandall, who turns 53 in 1990, has been known to order staffers to appear at predawn meetings. One executive arrived for one of Crandall's 5 A.M. meetings in his pajamas. A fanatic cost cutter, Crandall once heard the company had two security guards at an airline facility in the Virgin Islands. First he eliminated one of the guards, then had the other replaced with a German shepherd. Finally, he had a tape made of a barking dog to be played from time to time to scare away intruders. A Wharton Business School graduate, Crandall worked as head of Hallmark Cards' computer programming division and later as senior financial officer at Bloomingdale's department store before American hired him. Crandall made $2.1 million in 1989.

As a place to work. American is seen as a tough employer. They're the only airline without flexible weight policies for flight attendants—and they have more stringent standards for women employees than for men. In his first three years as airline head, Crandall laid off 7,000 of the company's 41,000 employees. In 1983 he demanded the mostly unionized work force accept contracts dictating a two-tier wage scale, whereby newly hired workers would be paid at a substantially lower rate than those hired earlier. Rather than forcing a confrontation, Crandall went throughout the company, holding employee meetings, arguing his case for the need to reduce labor costs so American could compete effectively with the lower-cost airlines in the newly deregulated environment. He also coupled the demand with a profit-sharing plan and an irrevocable promise of job security, or as he told *Fortune*: "We have simply renounced our ability to lay people off." Much to everyone's surprise, the company's appeal worked, and employees ratified the two-tier contract against the recommendation of the union leadership. Crandall has continued regular employee meetings and instituted a quality of work life program which increases employee involvement in decisions affecting how their jobs are performed.

Social responsibility. American got a black eye in 1979 when the Federal Aviation Administration fined the company $500,000 for improper maintenance of their DC-10 jumbo jets, including one that crashed that year in Chicago killing all 273 passengers.

Three years later, Crandall's zeal caused more public relations problems in Dallas when he suggested to Braniff's president that the two firms raise fares by 20 percent in a phone conversation Braniff's president secretly recorded. The tape wound up in the hands of the Justice Department, which sued American and Crandall for illegal monopoly practices. American also paid publisher William Morrow $150,000 to recall 25,000 copies of a 1984 book about Braniff called *Splash of Colors, the Self-Destruction of Braniff International* by John Nance, former Braniff pilot. Morrow came out with a revised edition that stated the case had been dropped (after Crandall agreed to pay a fine). Crandall still refuses to discuss the subject.

Stock performance. AMR stock bought for $1,000 in 1980 sold for $5,782 on January 2, 1990.

AMR Corporation, Inc., 4200 American Blvd., Dallas–Fort Worth Airport, Fort Worth, TX 76155; (817) 355-1234.

2

#2 *in airlines*

Employees: 68,000
Sales: $9.8 billion
Profits: $342 million
Founded: 1926
Headquarters: Chicago, Illinois

United frittered away their lead in the airline business during the 1980s, and wound up on the auction block. In mid-1990 the airline seemed about to be taken over by employees, who reasoned they couldn't do any worse than the managers in the cockpit during this hectic decade.

United, which flies to all parts of the U.S. from hubs in Chicago, Denver, San Francisco and Washington, D.C. (they operate a fleet of 434 planes), was run for most of the 1980s by an ex-hotel man intent on creating a huge travel empire. On paper the idea made sense. Passengers getting off a plane often head straight for the car rental desk. Then, after piling into their car, they head for a hotel. So, United went out and bought the Hertz car rental agency, expanded their Westin hotel chain, added the 88-hotel Hilton International chain, and developed a travel reservations service (Covia). Other airlines enjoyed watching the industry's giant dabble in other fields. In 1988 United discovered American had seized the top spot United had enjoyed for the previous quarter-century, even though United had entered the 1980s nearly 50 percent larger than their nearest rival. By decade's end, United had sold off all its nonairline ventures and concentrated again on convincing people to "Fly the Friendly Skies" (United's famous advertising slogan crafted by the Leo Burnett agency). The task is enormous. United has long been a cold, impersonal airline, especially to employees. As one flight attendant puts it: "You're just a number."

History. United Airlines began as just that—an amalgamation of several companies, all started by aviation pioneers. In his comprehensive history of U.S. air carriers, *The Sky's the Limit*, Patrick Kelly traces United's origins to 1926, when Varney Air Lines started flying a 460-mile route between Pasco, Washington, and Elko, Nevada—a stretch of unlikely territory for American commercial air transport to begin. Several other carriers were getting off the ground then: Bill Boeing of Seattle was building planes and flying sacks of mail between Chicago and San Francisco; Frederick Rentschler of Hartford, Connecticut, was making airplane engines for Pratt & Whitney; Vernon Gorst's Pacific Air Transport was flying mail between Seattle and Los Angeles; Clement Keys, a Wall Street promoter, organized National Air Transport and won the airmail contract between Chicago and Dallas; and Bill Stout, backed by Henry and Edsel Ford, built the Ford trimotor airplane and flew passengers between Detroit, Chicago and Cleveland on Stout Air Services.

By 1931 all these companies had fused into one: United Air Lines. (Not until the 1970s did they make *Airlines* one word.) They flew the first coast-to-coast passenger flights along a route they called the Main Line—from New York to San Francisco via Chicago. They were also the first airline to hire stewardesses. The first one, in 1930, was Ellen Church, who convinced the airline's PR man to hire women rather than men, saying: "Don't you think it would be better psychology to have women up in the air? How is a man going to say that he's afraid to fly when a woman is working on the plane?"

In 1934 Congress decided airlines had to be separated from airplane manufacturers to inhibit monopolization. Boeing and Pratt & Whitney were split off, and the presidency of United Air Lines devolved upon 34-year-old William "Pat" Patterson, a former loan officer for Wells Fargo Bank in San Francisco. Headquarters moved from New York to Chicago.

When Patterson took over in 1934, United Air Lines was three times as big as nearest competitor, American Airlines. Over the next 32 years Patterson ran United with a banker's go-slow approach. They started with a virtual monopoly on the Chicago–New York, route flying Boeing 247s, but TWA and American soon fielded faster Douglas DC-2s and took away much of their business. By 1938 American was taking in twice as much money as United. United's competitors edged further ahead in the late 1950s when the airlines were placing their orders for jet planes. American ordered Boeing 707s, which became available two years earlier than Douglas's DC-8s, but Patterson doggedly held out for Douglas because of a supposed advantage in the seating layout.

United regained their long-lost position as the nation's top airline in 1961 not by attracting more passengers or changing policies, but simply by taking over financially weak Capital Airlines. Through the merger United gained a vast network of north-south routes in the East. In 1985, United became the first U.S. carrier to fly to all 50 states.

Four years after Patterson's 1966 retirement, United entered the hotel business by buying the Western International Hotel chain (renamed Westin Hotels in 1981; among Westin's locations were such venerable hotels as San Francisco's St. Francis and New York's Plaza). The airline also got their next two presidents from the hotel subsidiary: Eddie Carlson in 1970 and his protégé, Richard Ferris, who was only 38 when he was picked in 1975. Ferris fashioned the strategy of a travel conglomerate.

Ferris also antagonized the pilots and other United employees by prolonging a strike in 1985 for a month after the issues had been settled by refusing to rehire some 500 trainees who had not crossed the picket lines. Relations degenerated to the point that Ferris traveled on private jets whenever possible to avoid contact with the pilots. Ferris also alienated employees by buying the Hertz car rental business in 1986 for nearly $600 million with cash that came partly from the employees' overfunded pension fund. That acquisition was part of Ferris' grand design to create the world's premiere air travel organization. Also part of the plan were the purchases the following year of Pan American's Pacific air routes and the Hilton International Hotel chain. Commenting on the Hilton acquisition, United pilots' union head F. C. Dubinsky said, "It's our belief that they've been buying hotels so they can have more rooms for dissatisfied passengers." Ferris' vision required a new name, so he hired Lippincott & Marguilies,

which had come up with such corporate names as Nynex, Amtrak and RCA. In early 1987 Lippincott came up with Allegis—a combination of allegiance and aegis. Employees and stock analysts thought the name was a joke, suggesting it sounded like a medicine for sniffles.

Others on Wall Street were not impressed. They thought Ferris' grand design shortchanged the airline, which was losing ground to other carriers. The pilots themselves offered $4.5 billion to buy the airline (but not the other subsidiaries). The company's board of directors rejected the pilots' bid and fought off several other suitors. In short order, the board threw out Ferris, sold off Hertz (to Ford Motor, Volvo and their managers), Westin (to a Japanese investor), and Hilton. It appeared United was going to be an airline again. And the hoard got rid of the Allegis name, after using it all of 11 months.

Owners and rulers. When United's board hired Stephen Wolf to run the company in late 1987, they turned to a man with a reputation as a turnaround artist. Wolf did wonders at both Republic Airlines and Tiger International when both were on the brink of bankruptcy. In contrast to the high-flying Ferris years, Wolf told the New York Times: "The ultimate success of United rests on the company's relationship with its employees." But Wolf, who made $1.2 million in 1989, managed to alienate employees when he tried to lead a group of investors to buy out the company in fall 1989. Wolf stood to make a quick $77 million from the deal. Partly because of union opposition, Wolf and his backers failed to get financing, and the deal collapsed in October 1989. The collapse touched off a major stock market tumble. In April 1990, United's directors agreed to sell the company to employees for $14.4 billion, making United one of the U.S.'s largest employee-owned companies—if they could get the financing. Gerald Greenwald, who left the number two spot at Chrysler to lead the employee buyout, was to be paid at least $9 million, even if the deal doesn't go through.

As a place to work. United has long had difficult relations with the major unions of pilots, mechanics, and flight attendants, which represent nearly two-thirds of the airline's work force. After the

1985 strike, flight attendant Linda Schoonhoven told a union publication: "I don't feel much for the company, just indifference. The company is to be endured, like a looney relative. Occasionally, I feel pity for it; it's a pity that it chooses to waste the great potential of our talents and abilities and it's even a greater pity that it seems to thrive on antagonizing us." Still, United employees are paid well by industry standards, particularly in comparison with carriers like Continental and Braniff. And, like all airline employees, they enjoy the terrific side benefit of free air travel passes.

A top United financial executive was dismissed in the late 1980s after he told Boston security analysts that labor costs on their new Pacific routes would be low because the company hires foreign nationals, who, "as you know, work for rice bowls."

Social responsibility. United has never been a generous giver, and in the 1980s they closed all their regional public relations offices.

Global presence. In addition to Pacific service, United began flying to Paris and Frankfurt in early 1990 and plans to extend transatlantic service in 1990 by flying to Milan and Rome and eventually to London, Budapest and Warsaw.

Stock performance. United stock bought for $1,000 in 1980 sold for $8,224 on January 2, 1990.

UAL Corporation, 1200 Algonquin Road, Elk Grove Township, Illinois (P.O. Box 66919, Chicago, IL 60666); (708) 952-4000.

3

#3 *in airlines*

Employees: 56,900
Sales: $8.6 billion
Profits: $473 million
Founded: 1926
Headquarters: Atlanta, Georgia

Workplace

The good ol' boy of the airline industry is fast becoming a world traveler. With air routes in 42 states, Delta now also flies to 10 countries (including France, Mexico and Japan), and hopes to open routes to the Soviet Union. Their far-flung outposts are a long way from their roots in the south's red soil. Delta still holds the annual stockholders meetings in Monroe, Louisiana, where Delta was born over 60 years ago. There are now as many Delta employees as residents of that small city near the Mississippi River delta, which gave the airline its name. And employees still talk of the close-knit Delta "family," an anomaly in the post deregulation era of intense competition, mergers and labor turmoil.

History. Like many families, Delta had a strong father in founder Collett Everman Woolman, who worked as a government agricultural agent in Louisiana. An aviation buff, he believed aerial cotton spraying would wipe out the boll weevil and got an airplane manufacturer to invest in the enterprise. Soon Woolman's operation was crop dusting throughout the South and even had planes spraying in Peru during the winter months. While in Peru, Woolman saw the possibilities of carrying passengers by air. The first passenger flight of Woolman's Delta Air Service took off from Dallas in 1929 bound for Shreveport and Monroe, Louisiana, and Jackson, Mississippi.

Keeping an airline aloft in the impoverished South during the depression years, especially an undercapitalized one, required considerable attention to small details. According to W. David Lewis and Wesley Phillips Newton in *Delta: The History of an Airline*, Woolman scavenged discarded rubber bands and paper clips and had old rags found around the hangar laundered so they could be reused. Even today, Delta's top eight managers meet every Monday morning to approve any company expenditures over $1,000. One Monday morning not long ago, the top management committee approved two items at Chicago's O'Hare airport—a $1,252 door to a washroom and $1,447 for upholstery cleaning of the Delta Crown Room. But the penny-pinching has paid off. During the 1970s, Delta was the nation's most profitable airline, making more money than much larger rivals like United and American. Though they lost money in the recession years of 1982 and 1983, Delta is back on track as a money machine.

Many of Delta's early employees continued with the company for the next 40 years, forming the core of the Delta family. Employees called Woolman The Boss, but the phrase was as much an endearment as an indication of his undisputed control of the organization until his death in 1966. He was a gentle autocrat who took a sincere personal interest in individual employees. He could recall names and details of family lives of any employee he ever met. Woolman also pointedly singled out employee contributions made at the lowest ranks. When visiting a station, he always talked first with the ramp personnel before meeting with the bigwigs. Delta continues that tradition with regular meetings between top management and small groups of individual employees. In the monthly employee magazine, a column cites employees who performed services "Above & Beyond." One column related the story of flight attendant Debbie Moller, who drove three passengers from New Orleans to Baton Rouge after they missed a connecting flight.

During Woolman's long tenure, Delta grew slowly, adding outposts throughout the South during the 1930s and 1940s. In 1953, Delta merged with another early aviation pioneer, Chicago & Southern Air Lines, expanding their routes in the Midwest. In 1972 Delta picked up routes along the Atlantic seaboard by buying another old-timer, Northeast Airlines, headquartered in Boston. Fifteen years later, in 1987, Delta filled in the last major gap in their U.S. routes by buying for almost $900 million Western Airlines. Before their acquisition, Western held the title of America's oldest airline, with the first flight delivering mail between Los Angeles and Salt Lake City on April 17, 1926. In May of the same year, the first passengers rode from Salt Lake City to Los Angeles on folding chairs in the mail compartment.

Owners and rulers. Promotion from within is gospel at Delta since Woolman's day. All of the company's top managers started at the bottom and worked their way up. Current CEO Ron Allen started in the personnel department in 1963. His predecessor, David Garrett, began as a reservations clerk in 1946. Allen made $1.4 million in 1989. Only one time in the company's history did a top officer come from outside the fold. He'd been an executive at General Dynamics and lasted less than a year. Employees own 14 percent of the company stock. Swissair and Singapore Airlines each own 5 percent.

As a place to work. Over 250,000 people have job applications on file at Delta's

No Layoffs Here

According to Fred Foulkes, a researcher at Boston University, only 13 U.S. companies employing more than 1000 people adhere to a non-layoff policy, meaning they will never institute a general employee layoff. He identified them as: Delta Airlines, Digital Equipment, Federal Express, IBM, S. C. Johnson, Lincoln Electric, Mazda Motor, Motorola, National Steel, New United Motor (joint General Motors-Toyota operation), Nissan Motor, Nucor and Xerox.

The average flight of the top ten airlines is about one-third empty.

headquarters. Few will get to work for the carrier: Turnover is a minuscule 0.3 percent a year, and the company has long had a no-layoff policy. In 1982, three stewardesses led a drive to buy a $30 million Boeing 767 with money entirely raised by employees themselves, who pledged nearly a thousand dollars each. When the plane was delivered in December that year, 7,000 employees were there to christen it *The Spirit of Delta*.

Not everyone fits in well in a close-knit family. One former Western machinist told the *Los Angeles Times* he was annoyed at having to cut off his beard and remove an earring from his left ear to conform to Delta regulations. Delta president Ron Allen explained: "We keep pretty tough standards here. There's a certain presentation we want to make. And that's a very clean-cut, straightforward presentation, one that makes the passenger comfortable traveling with Delta." Delta did go out of their way to welcome Western employees, however. They offered all former Western employees jobs with Delta and raised their wages to match Delta's higher rates. The former Western employees showed their appreciation by abandoning their unions. Except for pilots, who are members of the Air Line Pilots Association and a small group of flight dispatchers, Delta's employees are nonunion—an anomaly in a highly organized airline industry.

The largest concentration of employees is in Atlanta. With 17,300 employees in Georgia, Delta is the state's second largest private employer. They also have hubs in Cincinnati, Dallas–Fort Worth, Salt Lake City and Los Angeles.

Social responsibility. The airline has long trumpeted their employees as Delta Professionals. That's why two bizarre incidents in mid-1987 stung so badly. In a period of six weeks, a Delta pilot landed at the wrong airport, and another pushed the wrong button, causing his craft to plunge 25,000 feet before stabilizing only 1,500 feet above the Pacific Ocean. Red-faced, the company sent a letter to all frequent fliers, apologizing for the incidents.

Global presence. A standing joke among air passengers in the South is "Regardless of whether a man is bound for heaven or for hell, he has to change planes in Atlanta." As the largest airline at the Atlanta airport (382 daily departures, carrying over 10 million passengers yearly), Delta has long used Atlanta as a hub, meaning Delta passengers going between two other points in the South often change planes in Atlanta. The same can now be true for southerners traveling abroad. Except for Mexican routes inherited from Western, Delta's foreign destinations (Tokyo, Korea, Ireland, London, Paris, Germany, Puerto Rico, Bermuda and the Bahamas) are all served by flights from Atlanta.

Stock performance. Delta stock bought for $1,000 in 1980 sold for $4,389 on January 2, 1990.

Delta Air Lines, Inc., Hartsfield Atlanta International Airport, Atlanta, GA 30320; (404) 765-2600.

4
Continental Airlines Holdings

Employees: 68,000
Sales: $6.7 billion
Losses: $886 million
Founded: 1969
Headquarters: Houston, Texas

Workplace

Frank A. Lorenzo's moment of glory came in early 1987 when he looked up and found he'd assembled the country's largest airline operation, offering the American flying public 20 percent of all the available seats. His holding company, Texas Air, had two principal spokes, Eastern Airlines and Continental Airlines, which included what used to be New York Air, Peoples Express, Frontier Airlines and Rocky Mountain Airways. *Fortune* dubbed Lorenzo "master of the skies." The names union leaders had for him are mostly unprintable.

His was a brief moment in the sun. His confrontations with Eastern's unions precipitated a strike in 1989. But the tactic backfired after Eastern filed for Chapter 11 bankruptcy and the courts removed Lorenzo from control. Then in mid-1990 Lorenzo was out completely, selling nearly all his stock in Continental Airline Holdings (Texas Air's new name) to Scandinavian Airlines System for $31 million, promising not to compete in the airline business for seven years. A machinists union official quipped: "Our condolences to whatever industry he stalks next."

History. Frank Lorenzo was born Francisco Anthony Lorenzo in 1940 in Queens, New York, the son of Spanish immigrants. His father ran a beauty parlor, playing the stock market on the side, and young Frank was more interested in stocks and bonds than hair spray. At age 15, he bought his first stock: TWA. His bedroom was cluttered with model planes, the walls festooned with airplane posters. Lorenzo sold ties at Macy's and drove a truck to pay his way through Columbia, where his nickname became Frankie Smooth Talk. After graduating from Harvard Business School and spending time in the army, Lorenzo worked as a financial analyst for TWA and then Eastern.

In 1969, 29-year-old Lorenzo quit his analyst's job and joined a Harvard classmate, Robert Carney, to found Jet Capital Corporation. They sold stock to the public to raise $1 million to invest in airline ventures. Two years later Jet Capital bought floundering Texas International Airlines (known in an earlier incarnation as Trans-Texas, nicknamed Teeter Totter Airlines). As Texas International's president Lorenzo immediately established an anti-union reputation, making few concessions when employees struck for four months in 1974. In 1978, Lorenzo became the first to try to buy an airline against the wishes of the firm's management when he began buying stock in National Airlines, a large, but financially precarious, airline. Lorenzo's overture was rebuffed, and the Civil Aeronautics Board told him to stop buying stock to avoid breaking federal law. Although Lorenzo failed to get National, he made a profit of $46 million by selling his National stock to Pan Am. He then set up a holding company, Texas Air

Corporation, which included Texas International and New York Air, a cheap, non-union carrier in the Northeast.

In 1981 Lorenzo launched his second hostile takeover: Continental Airlines. Continental was created by Robert Six, last of the old scarf-and-goggles aviators in the airline business, who bought the Southwest Division of Varney Speed Lines in 1937. Six changed the airline's name to Continental, and they went national during his tenure, 1938 to 1975. In the 1980s, Alvin Feldman was president. He did not take kindly to Frank Lorenzo's takeover bid. Unions tried to thwart it with an Employee Stock Ownership Plan. When the plan failed, and it became clear Continental had fallen to Lorenzo, Feldman committed suicide.

After swallowing Continental, Texas Air became the nation's seventh largest airline. But the air traffic controllers went on strike, and competition between airlines was fierce. In 1981, Texas Air took a huge loss; and in 1983, Lorenzo filed bankruptcy for Continental. Two-thirds of the work force (8,000 people) were fired. Because of a Supreme Court ruling, bankrupt firms did not have to honor "burdensome" union contracts—so Continental started flying again almost immediately, but with cheap, nonunion labor, bringing Lorenzo undying labor enmity.

From the moment he took over Eastern, it was war between Lorenzo and the unions. In 1989 the bankruptcy court removed Eastern from Lorenzo's control. Many observers doubted whether Eastern would ever emerge from bankruptcy.

Lorenzo bought Eastern Airlines for $600 million in April 1986. Eastern began in 1928 by transporting U.S. mail between cities on the East Coast. The man who built the airline was Eddie Rickenbacker, the nation's top flying ace in World War I (he shot down 26 German planes and won the Congressional Medal of Honor), who bought Eastern from General Motors in the 1930s and established them as a leading carrier from New York to Miami and on to the Caribbean and Latin America. Eastern introduced the Boston-New York-Washington shuttle. They were always a no-frills airline with a strong unionized work force that meant nothing but trouble for Frank Borman, the former astronaut who tried to guide Eastern through the new, deregulated airline skies of the 1980s. Borman never won the confidence of Eastern workers, and, in 1986, tired of fighting them, he sold the airline to their worst enemy, Frank Lorenzo.

Owners and rulers. Scandinavian Airlines System now owns 16.8 percent of the company. To run Continental, SAS lured Hollis L. Harris from Delta Air Lines, where he had risen, over 36 years, from gate agent to president.

As a place to work. Whew! What can you say? Lorenzo has sacked thousands and reduced the pay of thousands more, hired new people willing to work for less money and dismantled the unions at two of the country's biggest airlines. Managers also come and go. Continental Airlines has had seven presidents in seven years. Texas Air was rated worst in quality of products and service in a 1988 *Fortune* survey of 306 companies.

Global presence. With the sale of Latin American operations, Eastern no longer has a non-U.S. presence. Continental flies over both the Pacific and the Atlantic oceans with daily flights to London, Paris, Japan, the Philippines, Central America, the Pacific Islands, New Zealand and Australia.

Stock performance. Texas Air stock bought for $1,000 in 1980 sold for $1,317 on January 2, 1990.

Continental Airlines Holdings Inc., 333 Clay Street, Suite 4040, Houston, TX 77002; (215) 698-2000.

5

NORTHWEST

Employees: 40,000
Sales: $6.5 billion
Profits: $355 million
Founded: 1926
Headquarters: Minneapolis, Minnesota

Northwest flew into the 1990s with a crew of ex-hotel people in the cockpit. They bought Northwest for $3.6 billion in July 1989. The new team, headed by Al-

fred Cecchi, had no experience running an airline—and neither does the new CEO, Frederick Rentschler, who came from Beatrice. But they've brought a new style to an airline long known for slow service, long delays and frequent labor disputes and strikes.

Even before the takeover, Northwest had begun to change. They carry more passengers across the Pacific Ocean than any other U.S. airline, but they dropped Orient from their name in 1986, shortly after purchasing Republic Airlines, a merger that doubled their size. Northwest now flies to over 135 cities in 39 states, as well as to Asia and Europe, Mexico and the Caribbean.

History. Shortly before Checchi's crew took over, Northwest had moved into a new headquarters on 154 acres near the Minneapolis–St. Paul airport. Employees can look out their windows and watch ducks floating on three ponds. By contrast, *Fortune* magazine once called the airline's former headquarters "a dreary, windowless bunker that would make a bomb shelter look plush."

The man responsible for that austere tone was Donald Nyrop, who ran the airline from 1955 until 1979. The *Wall Street Journal* called him "the Vince Lombardi of airline executives." He was devoted to the bottom line. If he found a paying customer unable to get a seat on a crowded Northwest flight, he would get off himself and wait for the next plane. Nyrop even had the doors to the stalls in the men's room at the old headquarters removed because he wanted to make sure executives wouldn't spend too much time there reading.

After merging with Republic Airlines, Northwest insisted former Republic workers accept about 25 percent less than Northwest workers were getting for comparable jobs. In the resulting chaos, Northwest's service got so bad (delayed flights, lost baggage) passengers were wearing buttons saying "Fly Northwest if your only option is walking."

Engineering the Republic merger was a man cut from the Nyrop mold. On the day the merger was approved, CEO Frederick Rothmeier greeted the former Republic headquarters workers with the following memo: "The workday begins at 8 a.m. for all Northwest managers, supervisors, clerks... There are no exceptions. This is the kickoff time. No one starts cold, so I expect the officers and department heads to be here before 8 o'clock in the morning to prepare their departments for the work-day... No one is required to work on Saturdays. However, given the structure of our management team, it is virtually impossible to get the job done without Saturday work."

Since taking control, Checchi has spent time getting acquainted with employees. He meets with groups of 40 to 50 employees, gives a presentation and then invites questions. Checchi thinks his experience as a hotelier will improve Northwest's image with passengers. Soon after the takeover, he was telling reporters he wanted to redesign cabins so they would include quiet, well-lighted places for those who want to work, and television and high-tech sound systems for those who want to be entertained.

Owners and rulers. The three men who spearheaded the group of investors that bought Northwest all joined Marriott in the mid-1970s. Harvard MBA Checchi and Gary Wilson worked on intricate financing strategies that helped Marriott save money by selling hotels to local partnerships. Checchi left to be a financial advisor to Fort Worth oil heir Sid Bass, helping him buy one-quarter of Walt Disney's stock and then changing the management. Checchi personally made $50 million from his Disney stock. With Bass' backing, Wilson went to Disney as chief financial officer, leaving, after the Northwest deal, with Disney stock options and bonuses worth almost $65 million. Meanwhile, Frederic Malek, a former aide to President Nixon, rose in Marriott's management ranks to head the hotel chain between 1981 and 1988. A personal friend of George Bush, Malek managed the 1988 Republican National Convention, but didn't get an appointment in the Bush administration.

NWA, Inc.: Box E-5270 Minneapolis–St. Paul International Airport, St. Paul, MN 55111; (612) 726-2111.

6

Employees: 53,700
Sales: $6.3 billion
Losses: $63 million
Founded: 1939
Headquarters: Arlington, Virginia

An airline with a lot of short hops, USAir grew sixfold during the 1980s to become a national presence. They now fly to 135 airports in 36 states as well as to the Bahamas, Canada, Britain and West Germany. They have more flights per day than any other airline. Not bad for an airline that began as a mail deliverer across the mountains of West Virginia. USAir is headquartered in a cramped, antiquated hangar at Washington's National Airport. For many years their main hub was Pittsburgh, capital of the so-called Rust Belt. While avoiding the flashy frills often associated with airlines, USAir made money, being the most consistently profitable airline in an industry noted for companies that make profits irregularly at best. As one USAir executive explained, "Everything we do is to make money." Yet their conservative financial approach did not mean they shortchanged their employees. They never had a strike, paid the highest wages in the industry and enjoyed generally amicable relations among their mostly unionized work force.

When 1990 dawned, however, USAir was in large part a different carrier. They entered the ranks of the surviving megacarriers in 1987, buying California-based PSA and North Carolina–based Piedmont. They're still a puddle jumper, but they now go head-to-head with United and other carriers on one of the most heavily traveled routes in the airline world: San Francisco–Los Angeles.

History. Richard C. du Pont, a glider buff and scion of the Delaware du Ponts, started the company in 1939 as All American Aviation to deliver mail in Pennsylvania and West Virginia. The company pioneered a method by which a plane, through a system of hooks and ropes, could swoop down to treetop level, drop off a container of mail and snatch up the outgoing mail without landing. During World War II the U.S. Army Air Corps adapted this method to rescue stranded fliers. Richard du Pont, while supervising this program, was killed in a glider crash in California in 1943.

The company became Allegheny Airlines in 1953 and grew as a regional carrier, subsidized by the federal government to shuttle passengers from the small cities of the East and "feed" them into the routes of the major airlines. In the mid-1960s, Allegheny switched their fleet to jet planes and concentrated on longer, more profitable flights. Under Civil Aeronatics Board regulations, however, they had to continue to provide service to the smaller towns on their routes—towns like Hagerstown, Maryland, and Philipsburg, Pennsylvania. To satisfy the federal requirements, they spun off many of their puddle-jumper flights to independent pilots with smaller planes.

One of the directors is George Goodman, author of popular articles and books on financial matters under the pen name of Adam Smith.

In 1978 Allegheny Airlines surveyed air passengers to find out what they thought of different airlines, including one that didn't exist: USAir. USAir scored highly. In fact, it was preferred over Allegheny. In 1979, Allegheny changed their name to USAir.

S*tock performance.*   USAir stock bought for $1,000 in 1980 sold for $5,090 on January 2, 1990.

USAir Group, Inc., 2345 Crystal Drive, Arlington, VA 22227; (703) 418-7000.

7

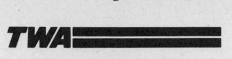

#1 *among transatlantic airlines*
#7 *among domestic airlines*

Employees: 30,000
Sales: $4.6 billion
Losses: $298 million
Founded: 1928
Headquarters: Mount Kisco, New York

TWA used to be Howard Hughes' airline. Now they're Carl Icahn's. The contrast between the two men speaks volumes about the biggest U.S. trans-Atlantic carrier.

For starters, Hughes was an aviation buff. He bought control of TWA (then called Transcontinental and Western Air) in 1939. Under Hughes TWA became the world's most technically advanced airline. They pioneered pressurized planes that could fly passengers over bad weather rather than through it. They were first with four-engine planes that could cross the Atlantic. But Hughes was an eccentric. He would hold up major business decisions for weeks while fretting over minute details of airplane design. He once disappeared with a new Lockheed Constellation from the TWA fleet and took it to the Bahamas, where he practiced landings for days on end. Hughes' antics and frequent firings of top managers helped him lose the confidence of Wall Street bankers he needed to purchase a fleet of jet aircraft. In 1960, the Wall Streeters forced Hughes to give up control of the airline, though he kept a majority of the stock for another six years.

The Hughes years had an important impact on the company. Robert Serling, the preeminent airline historian, once wrote: "TWA is a carrier built on a foundation of loyalty that has withstood the terrible buffeting of decisions, deeds and circumstances beyond the control of officers and employees alike.... [Employee loyalty] was a simple yet powerful weapon of survival amid constant management instability. There was more than one occasion when loyalty was the only glue that held TWA together."

The airline's new owner, Carl Icahn, has eroded that loyalty. Icahn is neither an

The average passenger airplane is about 13 years old.

eccentric nor particularly interested in aviation. A product of Princeton and Wall Street, he has devoted his life to making money. He got his start as a stockbroker about the time Hughes was fighting the bankers. By the late 1970s, Icahn became one of the new breed of corporate raiders who would buy stock in a company, threatening to buy the rest. Generally, it was a bluff. Icahn and other raiders (T. Boone Pickens, Victor Posner, Saul Steinberg) typically went away when the company's management offered to buy back the raider's stock at a premium—a practice called greenmail. Icahn played this game well, making millions from raids on such companies as Saxon Industries, Hammermill Paper, Marshall Field, American Can, Owens-Illinois and Phillips Petroleum.

In 1985 corporate raiders zeroed in on TWA, which was then in bad shape, losing money every day. Management had ventured into other fields, creating a miniconglomerate called Trans World Corporation, owning Hilton Hotels International, Canteen Corp. of America (vending machines) and Century 21 (real estate), as well as the airline. Company management agreed to a takeover by Texas Air. But TWA's pilots' and machinists' unions refused to go along because they distrusted Texas Air chairman Frank Lorenzo. They encouraged Carl Icahn to bid for the airline, to become a white knight, in takeover parlance.

Not only did Icahn bid, he surprised everyone when he actually bought the airline and became chairman, vowing to run TWA to make money. He took over Ozark Airlines in 1986, giving TWA about 80 percent of the flights out of St. Louis. He sold the reservation system to Delta and then sold the Chicago-London route to American. He also demanded big pay cuts from the unions. Icahn stood firm when the flight attendants refused. The flight attendants lost the ensuing bitter strike and their jobs. Most were replaced with new hires making about $12,000 a year.

Icahn's obsessive drive to lower costs did not create a winning airline. TWA is a major carrier over the Atlantic but has a weak domestic route system. However, Icahn has used the airline as one of his toys. For example, he acquired 13 percent of USX through TWA. In 1990, with TWA still losing money, Icahn was exploring ways to unload the airline.

Trans World Airlines, Inc., 101 South Bendford Road, Mount Kisco, NY 10549; (914) 242-3000.

8

#8 *among airlines:*

Employees: 23,300
Sales: $3.6 billion
Profits: $337 million
Founded: 1927
Headquarters: New York City, New York

One might compare Pan Am to an aging star athlete who hobbles around on bad knees. Everybody recalls what he once represented, but that memory makes today's reality all the more painful to contemplate.

Until 1969 Pan Am was a one-man show. The man was Yale-educated Juan Trippe, who put together the backers to finance a small mail-carrying operation in the 1920s and built it into the world's largest air transport company by 1930. The 1930s were Pan Am's golden years. Their Clipper flights to Europe and across the Pacific featured hot meals served on china by white-jacketed stewards. The airline pioneered commercial transoceanic flying. They even built airfields on small Pacific islands so amphibious aircraft could refuel on the seven-day, 8,200-mile trip between San Francisco and Manila.

After World War II, Pan Am had to contend with an unheard of phenomenon—competition—at home and abroad. Trans World Airlines started to fly the Atlantic, United Airlines extended their routes to Hawaii. Worse yet for Pan Am, every nation in the world wanted to have an airline of its own, and the rules of the game specified if a country allowed a foreign airline to land, they could then demand their airline be allowed reciprocal landing rights. Pan Am—and Trippe—were unsuited for this kind of melee. The years of unchallenged supremacy had lent Pan Am an air of arrogance that earned them a reputation for being one of the world's most unfriendly airlines.

As their market share eroded, Pan Am continued to do business the way they'd always done it. They did change planes, however. Trippe, a tiger for new equipment, was one of the first to give Boeing a jumbo order for the 747 jumbo jet. The expense of the jumbo jets and heightened competition were too much: Pan Am was unprofitable for most of the 1970s.

After deregulation in 1978, the financially weak company also faced the problem of having no domestic routes to feed their international routes. So, they bought National Airlines in 1979. National was known as the "Fly Me" company because of their ad campaign in the 1970s featuring seductive stewardesses that angered the feminists of the day. The merger didn't help much in any case because National mostly carried passengers between Florida and New York. Pan Am still had no access to passengers coming from the interior cities to connect with their international flights.

The 1980s brought little good news. Pan Am lost money in 8 of 10 years, despite major concessions by unionized workers. Worse, they had to sell off assets to staunch the flow of red ink. The New York headquarters atop Grand Central Station went in 1980. The Intercontinental hotel chain was sold in 1981. The Pacific routes, once their crown jewel, were sold to United Airlines in 1985. However, with all their financial woes, the most searing blow Pan Am took in the decade came on December 21, 1988, when New York–bound Flight 103 blew up over Lockerbie, Scotland, killing 270 people, many of them American college students returning home. Later determined an act of sabotage, the crash touched off highly charged emotional responses, ranging from praise for Pan Am for the way they handled the crisis (U.S. Ambassador to Britain Charles H. Price II said they "ren-

WHAT THEY SPEND TO FEED YOU:
The Cost of Airline Food

Airline	Cost Per Passenger
1. Pan Am	$6.54
2. American	$5.21
3. TWA	$5.02
4. United	$4.90
5. Delta	$4.17
6. Northwest	$4.02
7. Eastern	$3.78
8. Continental	$3.52
9. Piedmont	$2.48
10. USAir	$1.93
Industry Average	**$4.21**

Source: The Wall Street Journal, 7 April 1988.

dered a great humanitarian service") to denunciation of the airline for not informing the public a bomb threat had been received. Phyllis Rosenthal, mother of a 23-year-old woman who died in the crash, rebuked Pan Am in the Wall Street Journal, declaring: "By denying Andrea access to information she might have used, and by failing to provide the best security possible, the airline broke faith with my family and denied Andrea the fundamental right to take care of herself."

On December 21, 1989, Pan Am bought full-page ads in American newspapers to deliver this message:

"One year ago today, 270 lives were lost in one senseless, barbaric act. At 2:02 P.M. (E.S.T.) today, we ask you to join us in pausing for a moment of prayer for these and all other victims of terrorism all over the world.

"The People of Pan Am."

In 1990, still losing money, Pan Am put up for sale their routes inside Germany and the Washington–New York–Boston shuttle service. They had been seeking a merger partner but found no one willing to link up with the airline that was the country's first flag carrier to the rest of the world.

Stock performance. Pan Am stock bought for $1,000 in 1980 sold for $439 on January 2, 1990.

Pan Am Corp., 200 Park Avenue, New York, NY 10166; (212) 880-1234.

RAILROADS

"I've been workin' on the railroad" is a refrain sung by fewer and fewer Americans. Fifty years ago, over 1 1/2 million people worked on the railroads; today the figure is slightly above 250,000, or one-sixth as many employees. In the past decade alone, the major railroads halved their work forces.

Behind rail's decline are planes and trucks. Travelers prefer flying to taking the train. Fifty years ago, nearly 80 percent of all public intercity travel was by train (most of the rest was on buses). Today, nearly 90 percent is by air and nearly 7 percent by bus, leaving the trains with just over 3 percent. And the private railroad companies gave up on their passenger service, causing the federal government to jump in and create Amtrak in 1971.

A similar story holds for freight transportation, where railroads now compete head-to-head with trucks, river barges and oil pipelines. Big railroads have fought back by buying up major truck lines, shipping companies and oil pipeliners. Several corporations running the rails today wouldn't be caught dead referring to themselves as mere railroads. Today, they're transportation companies.

1

#1 *in railroad revenues*

Employees: 53,100
Sales: $7.7 billion
Profits: $452 million
Founded: 1828
Headquarters: Richmond, Virginia

Created in 1980 by the merger of Chessie System (*C*) with Seaboard Coast Line (*S*), CSX no longer calls themselves a railroad. They prefer global transporter, with the *X* in their name standing for the related businesses they've acquired: Sea-Land, the largest U.S. container ship operator, and American Commercial the largest operator of barges on the nation's inland waterway system. Two other acquisitions made in the 1980s—Texas Gas Resources, operator of the sixth largest natural gas pipeline, and Lightnet, second largest transmitter of fiber-optics data—were discarded in 1989. The CSX inventory includes 110,000 containers; 2,365 barges; 2,850 locomotives; 200,000 railroad cars; and 44 ships. Thanks to Sea-Land, CSX operates in 64 countries. (The barge line became part of CSX with the Texas Gas acquisition in 1983.)

These statistics suggest railroading is just one of many transportation activities for CSX. But in fact, hauling freight by rail still brings in nearly 70 percent of revenues. CSX has 19,800 miles of track in 21 states, connecting the East and Midwest and Canada with the Southeast. No one carries more coal than CSX—175 million tons in 1989. In revenues, CSX ranks as the nation's largest railroad. Or as the company likes to put it: "We move more merchandise to more places than anyone else in the world."

CSX sold off their coal properties and mineral rights to concentrate on transportation. They do, however, have real estate holdings that generated $180 million in revenue in 1989, and they still operate the 6,500-acre Greenbrier resort in White Sulfur Springs, West Virginia, one of the plush watering holes for American business executives and the setting for the CSX annual meeting.

History. America's oldest railroad died on CSX's watch. In October 1986, CSX announced that the Baltimore & Ohio Railroad, known to generations of Americans as the B&O, would be consolidated with CSX's two other railroads under their transportation division. That ended 158 years of American railroading begun on July 4, 1828, when Charles Carroll, last surviving signer of the Declaration of Independence, presided over the B&O's groundbreaking ceremonies just west of Baltimore. Once seen on plush Pullman coaches and coal trains running from Baltimore to Chicago, the B & O name now survives on a few rusting railway bridges and millions of Monopoly boards.

Many other rail lines are buried in CSX history. The B&O lost their independence in 1962 when they were acquired by the Chesapeake & Ohio, a railroad founded in 1868. The Western Maryland line,

founded in 1852, was acquired by the C&O in 1973—and the amalgamation of these three railroads (B&O, C&O and Western Maryland) formed the Chessie System in 1973. The Seaboard Coast Line was also the end result of a series of mergers that united the Seaboard, the Atlantic Coast Line and the Louisville & Nashville.

Making money in the railroad business is not easy. CSX's profits in the 1980s zig-zagged from $280 million in 1980 to $465 million in 1984 to $350 million in 1989. They are, in many ways, a mirror of U.S. industry, being major carriers of cars, chemicals and forest products. When CSX was created in 1980, the railroad had 27,000 miles of track and 76,000 employees. By decade's end, they had 19,800 miles and 38,000 employees. Meanwhile, rail revenues have leveled out at about $5 billion a year.

Owners and rulers. Chairman Hays Watkins isn't one to get sentimental about the fading of the railroad business. "Never should you let your emotions overrule or cloud strategic business sense," he told *The Journal of Commerce*.

The romance of the rails has always paled before Watkins' passion for numbers. After joining C&O as an accountant in 1949, he rose to head the Chessie System. According to the *Wall Street Journal*, the Chessie under Watkins kept "the fastest ledgers in big business." Quarterly financial results were released the day after the quarter ended—sooner even than those of most banks. "I'm what you call a bean-counter and proud of it," says Watkins. His successor, John Snow, named president and CEO in 1989, also came up from the "wrong" side of the tracks. As a lawyer, economist and former Department of Transportation official, he's seen the inside of more Washington hearing rooms than locomotives. He made $1.3 million in 1989.

As a place to work. CSX may be expanding their reach, but they're shrinking their railroad work force in the process. The company broke ranks with other railroad companies in 1988 by beginning separate talks with 15 labor unions on a company proposal to cut back their work force by 25 percent (10,000 employees). Proposing severance payments of $50,000 to $75,000 to each departing worker, CSX also offered to share the savings (estimated at $475 million) 50-50 with remaining railroad employees. The company failed, however, to convince the unions, forcing the firm to revert to a more conventional attempt to buy out lifetime employment contracts. This tactic cost the company $778 million. CSX pays workers considerably more than other carriers to win a union agreement to cut freight train crews from five to three people.

Social responsibility. CSX thinks they have too many railroad employees. The Federal Railroad Administration thinks they have too few. The agency stated in a 1988 report "that the training, equipping, and numerical strength of the maintenance of work forces in [the District of Columbia and Maryland] are inadequate." Prompting their report were nine "serious" CSX derailments in the District of Columbia in 1987, including two (heaven forbid) that disrupted commuter service into D.C. More disturbing was a July 1986 derailment in Miamisburg, Ohio, of a freight train carrying a load of phosphorus. The chemical ignited on contact with the outside air, releasing a cloud of poisonous gas that forced the evacuation of 40,000 people from their homes—the largest evacuation ever caused by a derailment. In the following blizzard of lawsuits, CSX faced damage claims totaling $1 billion.

Stock performance. CSX stock bought for $1,000 in 1980 sold for $5,542 on January 2, 1990.

CSX Corporation, One James Center, Richmond, VA 23219; (804) 782-1400.

2

BURLINGTON NORTHERN

#1 *in railroad mileage*

Employees: 32,700
Sales: $4.6 billion
Profits: $243 million
Founded: 1849
Headquarters: Fort Worth, Texas

Burlington Northern became a railroad again in 1988. They have always been a railroad, of course, but thanks to all the land they picked up alongside their tracks, they also became a powerful natural resources company. These properties included the country's largest private coal reserves, one of the biggest oil and natural gas reserves and 1.5 million acres of forestlands. Richard M. Bressler, hard-driving BN chairman, packaged all these nonrail operations into a separate company, Burlington Resources, and spun the firm off to shareholders. That left Burlington Northern in the singular position of being in one business: railroading, which is where they started out. Burlington has more track than any other railroad—25,504 miles connecting the Midwest, the Pacific Northwest and the Gulf of Mexico. They're the largest carriers of grain and other agricultural products, but their biggest freight category is coal. In 1989 their railcars carried record amounts of coal out of Wyoming's Powder River Basin.

History. The Burlington Northern story is one of the most convoluted in American railroad history, involving four separate major railroads—Great Northern, Northern Pacific, Burlington (named for a town in Iowa) and Frisco lines.

The Great Northern was the brainchild and labor of love of James J. Hill, a burly, one-eyed empire builder largely responsible for the development and population of a stretch of America between Minnesota and Washington state. Known as one of the 19th century's great robber barons, Hill was described in Matthew Josephson's classic book by the same name in these terms: "His unique exterior—like a 'grim old lion'—reinforced by a naturally stern manner, give him a formidable reputation in his territory... He carried everything in his head, worried, systematized, labored himself or drove others around him with unflagging energy. He had no small scruples; rough-hewn throughout, intolerant of opposition, despotic, largely ruling by fear, his contemporaries said, he was also given to personal violence in the department offices of his road.'"

Hill assembled a vast network of railroads over unfriendly terrain without benefit of the land grants that had made the Union Pacific and Central Pacific possible. Once he completed his road in 1893, he advertised widely for farmers, lumberjacks and businessmen to move out into Montana and the states of the Pacific Northwest and turn the wild, desolate terrain into something resembling a civilization.

Hill built his railroad along a 1,500-mile route roughly paralleling Northern Pacific's, completed a few years earlier. Both roads began in the northern Midwest and ran through Minnesota, North Dakota, Montana and Idaho, out to Seattle. Distinguished journalist Henry Villard, who had reported the famous Lincoln-Douglas debates and major battles of the Civil War for Horace Greeley's *New York Tribune*, supervised the railroad construction for Hill. And for a while in the 1870s General George Custer helped protect Villard's construction crews from Indian attacks as they made their way across Montana territory. The Northern Pacific was also the beneficiary of land grants President Lincoln signed in 1864. In addition to granting the railroad a right-of-way through public lands, following the trail blazed by Lewis and Clark in 1804–1806, Lincoln gave the railroad large parcels of land the company could sell to finance construction along the way. The Lincoln land grants made the contemporary Burlington Northern one of the West's richest landowners.

Just after the turn of the century Burlington Northern, Northern Pacific and Chicago, Burlington and Quincy wanted to merge but couldn't because of a Supreme Court ruling. Nevertheless, they continued to function almost as though the merger had gone through—even occupying the same headquarters in St. Paul, Minnesota, in 1915, with a wall down the center of the building to keep them in technical compliance with the Court's ruling. The wall finally came down in 1970, when Chief Justice Earl Warren approved the merger. In 1980 Burlington Northern merged with the St. Louis–San Francisco Railway. Popularly known as the Frisco, the line never got farther west than Tulsa, Oklahoma. But they became an important road connecting the Midwest with the South and Gulf of Mexico. With the merger of Frisco into Burlington Northern, the longest railroad in U.S. history was created with a direct rail route between the coalfields of Montana and the industrial plants of the Deep South, such as those around Birmingham, Alabama.

O*wners and rulers.* An oil man ran Burlington Northern through the 1980s. Before coming to Burlington in 1980, Richard Bressler was Atlantic Richfield's chief financial officer. He stays out of the limelight and dislikes long meetings—annual meetings have been known to last less than half an hour. One of his first acts after coming to Burlington was to eliminate a big corporate image ad campaign. The following year he moved Burlington Northern's corporate headquarters from St. Paul to Seattle. In 1984 he moved the railroad's headquarters to Fort Worth and in 1988, after splitting off Burlington Resources, he also moved the corporate headquarters to Texas. As one former Burlington executive told *Business Week*: "Dick judges strictly on results, and he's not slow to replace people—even personal friends—when he's not satisfied." The president and CEO at Burlington Northern, located in Fort Worth, Texas, is Gerald Grinstein, a lawyer. Grinstein made $1.5 million in 1989. Bressler remains chairman of both Burlington Northern and Burlington Resources.

A*s a place to work.* The railroad has not been a fun place to work since Bressler took over. He has nearly halved railroad employment. And he has taken a hard line toward what he considers restrictive and antiquated union work rules (89 percent of the company's railroad employees are unionized), nearly provoking a strike in 1987. He told *Forbes*: "Railroad labor is basically overpaid and underworked."

Burlington lost one of the largest race bias suits in U.S. history when in 1983 they agreed to pay $50 million in back pay and other compensation to 4,000 current and former black employees. According to the Equal Employment Opportunity Commission, Burlington had discriminated against blacks in hiring, discipline, termination, initial assignment, transfer, promotion and training. For instance, blacks were almost never hired as engineers, so only two out of thousands of Burlington engineers were black.

In 1986, BN's women employees won a class action suit against Burlington Northern and 13 unions. BN worker Margaret Holden filed the suit in 1981 after being passed over for promotion 14 times. According to the suit, BN denied women advancement opportunities and accepted seniority and transfer rules that locked women in particular departments and low-paying jobs.

Stock performance. Burlington Northern stock bought for $1,000 in 1980 sold for $11,373 on January 2, 1990.

Burlington Northern, Inc., 777 Main Street, Fort Worth, TX 76102; (817) 878-2000.

3

#2 *in railroad revenues*
#3 *in railroad mileage*

Employees: 45,000
Sales: $6.5 billion
Profits: $595 million
Year Founded: 1862
Headquarters: Bethlehem, Pennsylvania

Union Pacific—a name etched deeply in American history as the railroad that opened the West—fired up the Iron Horse again during the 1980s. Going into the 1980s over half their profits were from oil, gas and mining, and they'd dropped to eighth place in the railroad industry. Coming into the 1990s, they were getting ready to sell off their energy and real estate companies, and they now ranked a strong third in the railroad industry.

This change in direction began early in the decade when UP bought two western railroads, the Missouri Pacific and the Western Pacific. In the mid-1980s they hitched up another road, the Missouri-Kansas-Texas Railroad, known as the Katy. Acquisitions are nothing new in railroading: They're as much a part of the business as timber ties are to tracks. But the big change at UP was the arrival of a new engineer at the controls.

In 1981, when Ronald Reagan moved into the White House, his Transportation Secretary was Drew Lewis, who drew the enmity of organized labor by firing 11,000 striking air traffic controllers. By the decade's end, Lewis was boss of Union Pacific. And he didn't come in, cap in hand, asking how to run a railroad. His mission has been to cut away layers of people—at both management and train crew levels—and change the culture of a company the *Wall Street Journal* described as "notoriously hidebound even by railroad standards." In 1988, in a message that traveled through the company like a bolt of lightning, the Philadelphia-born Lewis moved UP's headquarters from their posh digs on Park Avenue in New York City to Bethlehem, Pennsylvania, an hour from his farm. The holding company for the railroad had been based in New York for 90 years.

Uncle Pete, as the railroad is called, operates 23,000 miles of track in 19 states, nearly all of them west of the Mississippi River, their historic stage. They run 2,800 locomotives on those tracks carrying 84,000 freight cars. They're major haulers of new automobiles, chemicals and grain plus coal from their own mines in Wyoming. They also own Overnite Transportation, the nation's fifth largest (and largest nonunion) trucker, acquired in 1986, and USPCI, a landfill operator and disposer of hazardous wastes, acquired in 1988.

History. The Union Pacific Railroad was created in 1862 by an act of Congress. President Abraham Lincoln had his hands full fighting the Civil War, but he quickly signed into law the bill setting up a company whose mandate was to lay a rail and telegraph line from the Missouri

*On May 10, 1869, in Promentory, Utah,
Union Pacific and Central Pacific, which
later became Southern Pacific, completed
America's first transcontinental railroad
with a golden spike.*

River to the California border where it was
to link up with the Central Pacific (predecessor of the Southern Pacific), authorized under the same act to build a line
eastward from Sacramento. The Union
Pacific was to raise capital from private
investors, and the government provided
inducements in the form of bonds or loans
(about $25,000 worth for every mile of
track built) and land grants (10 square
miles or 6,400 acres for every mile of
track). It might seem like a cushy arrangement today—and in the eyes of muckrakers who looked back later, it *was*—but the
task was daunting and investors were not
clamoring for a piece of the action. By
1864 not a mile of track had been laid and
Congress liberalized the inducements—
the land grants, for example, were *doubled*.

The Union Pacific set out from Omaha
in 1865, using an army of 10,000 men to
lay track over a region once known as
"The Great American Desert," now
known as Kansas, Nebraska, Wyoming
and Colorado. The UP work gangs, Stewart Holbrook recounted in *The Story of
American Railroads*, were made up of
ex-soldiers, "hundreds of Irishmen from
New York, ex-convicts from everywhere,
and a scattering of plains mule skinners,
mountain men, and dubious bushwhack-
ers. They had hardly turned up a mile of

sod before a whole raft of gamblers, sellers
of grog, and female harpies had set up
shop near the railhead." Meanwhile, the
Central Pacific set out from Sacramento to
go through the Sierras with the aim of
meeting the westward-bound UP to form
the first transcontinental railroad. Their
track layers were largely Chinese, 6,000 of
them eventually, many brought directly
from Canton. It took them a year to bore
the Summit Tunnel through the solid
granite of the Sierra range. The UP and the
CP hooked up on May 10, 1869, the day
of the Golden Spike. In a well-orches-
trated ceremony, the last spike was driven
to link the two roads at Promontory Point,
a shack town 60 miles west of Ogden,
Utah. It's a triumph celebrated in Cecil B.
DeMille's 1939 movie for Paramount Pictures, *Union Pacific*, starring Joel McCrea
and Barbara Stanwyck. The Union Pacific
may be the only company whose name is
the title of a major motion picture.

UP's first 35 years were marked by one
upheaval after another, including bankruptcy and scandals reaching into the
halls of Congress. The only time they
seemed to function well was during the
11-year stewardship (1873–1884) of Jay
Gould, one of America's celebrated robber
barons. He reassumed control of the railroad in 1890, but after he died in 1892, the
Union Pacific crumbled, falling into

bankruptcy in 1893, along with four other big lines: Philadelphia & Reading, the Erie, Northern Pacific and Atchison, Topeka & Santa Fe. So the first phase of UP's history ended in financial ruin.

The next phase was the Harriman era. The Union Pacific was auctioned off in November 1897 at their freight depot in Omaha. A syndicate organized by the Wall Street firm of Kuhn, Loeb & Co. paid about $75 million for the railroad (the government got all the money owed to it)—and the central figure in that investor group turned out to be Edward Henry Harriman, son of an Episcopal minister, who had begun his career on Wall Street as an office boy when he was 14 years old. Before he died in 1909, Harriman had spent $98 million on equipment and another $62 million on new lines. He engaged in his share of fights and had to bear up under Teddy Roosevelt's description of him as a "wealthy corruptionist" and "enemy of the Republic," but he built the railroad, leaving a legacy carried on by his sons, W. Averell and E. Roland Harriman, and by his trusted lieutenant, Judge Robert Scott Lovett, a Texas-born railroad lawyer, and his son, Robert Abercrombie Lovett.

Harriman's son Averell ran the railroad company in the 1930s (during that time he built from scratch the Sun Valley resort in Idaho—it was on the UP line) and then went off to a public service career whose posts included ambassadorships to Britain and the Soviet Union, Secretary of Commerce and Governor of New York. His younger brother, Roland Harriman, took over as UP chairman in 1946 and headed the company for the next 20 years in tandem with his boyhood chum, Bob Lovett, who returned to the company in 1953 after serving as Secretary of Defense in the Truman administration. But when Harriman died in 1978, Lovett left the board—and for the first time in this century the Union Pacific had neither Harrimans nor Lovetts as directors.

During all this time the Union Pacific railroad was run out of Omaha. The line never had tracks in the East. The New York headquarters simply reflected where the owners lived and where they obtained the capital needed to keep the railroad in good shape.

In 1970 Union Pacific pushed heavily into oil and gas. Frank Barnett, a tax lawyer, headed the company then, and one day—as detailed by Maury Klein in *Union Pacific*—he had breakfast with a friend who told him Celanese Corp. wanted to sell their oil companies, Champlin Petroleum and Pontiac Refining. Barnett bought them in 1969 for $240 million. That's not the kind of breakfast you can have in Omaha—or Bethlehem, for that matter.

O*wners and rulers.* The Goulds, Harrimans and Lovetts have nearly all stepped off the Union Pacific train. The sole surviving passenger is Elbridge T. Gerry, Jr., a partner in Brown Brothers Harriman, the family's Wall Street banking firm, and a great-grandson of E. H. Harriman. He joined the board in 1986, taking the seat his father once held. Neither Gerry had ever worked for the railroad. And the Harriman holdings in UP are no longer significant. Uncle Pete has always been important to the Mormon community of Salt Lake City. Brigham Young once served on the board, and that constituency is now represented by Spencer F. Eccles, chairman of First Security Bank, who has been a director since 1976. Drew Lewis is intent on shaking up the ranks. He introduced an incentive scheme under which the top 30 executives will share in a $17 million bonus pool if UP's stock ever trades above $100 a share for 60 consecutive days. As of early 1990, the stock had never traded over $86.60. Lewis' 1989 compensation (salary, bonus and stock awards) came to $3.5 million, ranking him as the nation's 49th highest paid CEO. He owned 1/2 of 1 percent of UP stock, worth $3.3 million in 1990. Lewis is the only UP officer on the board, whose ranks he has broadened by adding former Secretary of State Henry A. Kissinger and—the first female director—Judith Richards Hope, senior partner in the Washington, D.C., law firm, Paul, Hastings, Janofsky & Walker.

A*s a place to work.* UP's shrinking, but for the people still aboard, the firm may be more exciting. Less hierarchical. Less formal. Interested in change. At the start of the 1980s the different railroads now joined under the UP banner—the Union Pacific, the Missouri Pacific, the Western Pacific and the Katy—had well over 50,000 employees. By 1990 the work force had been reduced to 30,000—and Lewis was looking to cut another 6,000 by getting unions to agree to new work rules. To run the railroad, Lewis brought in a non-railroad man, Michael Walsh, a pepperpot from Cummins Engine who has dashed around Uncle Pete, meeting face-to-face with rank and filers to tell them he's an enemy of bureaucracy. In Omaha he had a fitness center built on the first floor of the headquarters building after observing to a local newspaper reporter that "a lot of these guys are disproportionately overweight."

S*tock performance.* Union Pacific stock bought for $1,000 in 1980 sold for $2,987 on January 2, 1990.

Union Pacific Corporation, Martin Tower, Eighth & Eaton Aves., Bethlehem, PA 18018; (215) 861-3273.

4

**NORFOLK
SOUTHERN**

Employees: 33,300
Sales: $4.5 billion
Profits: $606 million
Founded: 1982
Headquarters: Norfolk, Virginia

Observers always note this railroad seems to run by gravity: They send empty railcars up the Appalachian hills and roll them down loaded with coal. It's a monopoly route that translates into handsome profits. Norfolk is the nation's second largest coal carrier—and coal accounts for one-third of their freight revenues. Formed in 1982 by the merger of the Norfolk & Western Railway and the Southern Railway, Norfolk Southern operates over 15,900 miles of track in 20 states and the Canadian province of Ontario, stretching from their eastern headquarters in Norfolk, Virginia, as far west as Kansas City, as far north as Ontario and south to New Orleans and Jacksonville, Florida. In addition to coal, they carry chemicals, paper and automobiles. From the standpoint of trackage or revenues,

they're not the country's largest railroad, but they consistently make more money than other lines. They've done it by having a monopoly on Appalachian coal. In 1989, when their chief competitor, CSX, took in $7.7 billion in revenues, they logged revenues of $4.5 billion; but whereas CSX earned $351 million after taxes, Norfolk Southern came through with profits of $606 million.

Railroads compete with truckers for freight shipments—and the Norfolk decided in 1985 they ought to learn more about the trucking business. So they bought North American Van Lines, the nation's fourth largest truck operator. Toward decade's end they developed the Triple Crown trailer, which can travel on either the highway or railroad tracks.

During the early 1980s Norfolk made a shrewd investment by buying close to 20 percent of Piedmont Aviation. When USAir bought Piedmont in 1987, the railroad made $112 million on an investment of $151 million.

One reason Norfolk makes so much money is by keeping a tight rein on costs. In 1988–1989, they cut 2,700 miles of track from their system and reduced employment rolls by 5,000. At the time of the 1982 merger, combined employment of the two railroads was 42,000. By 1990, it was 30,000. This reduction was achieved through attrition and early retirement programs.

The histories of many railroads are submerged in these two lines. Southern Railway is the final product of 125 to 150 different railroads, beginning in 1827 with the South Carolina Canal & Rail Road, which ran their first regularly scheduled passenger train out of Charleston on Christmas Day 1830. Norfolk & Western resulted from over 200 railroad mergers stretching over more than 100 years. They began in 1838 with the Norfolk and Petersburg Railroad, a 10-mile line from Petersburg to City Point, Virginia.

S*tock performance.* Norfolk Southern stock bought for $1,000 in 1980 sold for $7,439 on January 2, 1990.

Norfolk Southern Corporation, One Commercial Place, Norfolk, VA 23510; (804) 629-2640.

5

CONRAIL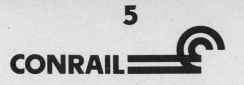

#5 *in railroads*

Employees: 32,600
Sales: $3.5 billion
Profits: $148 million
Founded: 1976
Headquarters: Philadelphia, Pennsylvania

Conrail picked an appropriate day for their first day of operations—April Fool's Day, 1976. On that day, Conrail seemed like a joke, perhaps even a cruel one, on American taxpayers. Created from the remains of six bankrupt railroads (including Penn Central, Reading and Erie Lackawanna), Congress pumped $2 billion into the new line just to get them moving.

For the next 11 years Conrail operated as a ward of the government. Estimates vary as to how much the rescue cost taxpayers—$7 billion on the low side, $10 billion on the high side. On March 26, 1987, Conrail was sold to the public—and the government got back about $1.8 billion. The sale constituted the largest new stock offering in Wall Street's history.

Today's Conrail bears little resemblance to the sickly child of a decade ago. Conrail makes money today by carrying chemicals, coal, cars, metals and other products over 13,000 miles of track that fan out from the Northeast to reach as far west as Chicago and St. Louis. Conrail's turning point was 1981, the first year they turned a profit. After that, they made money every year—and much of the credit for the turnaround goes to veteran railwayman Stanley Crane, who had been forced, in 1980, when he reached 65 years of age, to step down as chairman of Southern Railway. Taking the helm at Conrail in January 1981, Crane produced profits by chopping costs. He eliminated routes, got rid of commuter passenger lines and halved the work force, with departing workers receiving severance pay of up to $25,000, for a total of $130 million, courtesy of Uncle Sam.

If not for Crane, Conrail would probably not exist as an independent company. In 1982, his old company, Southern Railway, combined with Norfolk & Western to create Norfolk Southern. And three years later Transportation Secretary Elizabeth Dole proposed that Conrail be sold to Norfolk Southern for $1.2 billion. Crane opposed this plan, arguing Conrail was worth more and that a sale to NS would stifle competition. With the help of Wall Street investment banking house Morgan Stanley, Crane lobbied Congress against the Dole plan. For two years he and the Transportation Secretary didn't speak. And in the end, Congress came down on the side of Crane and a public sale. Crane stepped down as CEO in 1989. Conrail's current CEO is James A. Hagen, who made $305,000 in 1989. Hagen came to Conrail from rival CSX.

Everything, however, has not been smooth railing for Conrail since they became a private corporation. In 1988 the Federal Railroad Administration flunked Conrail in the first major safety investigation of a single railroad. Among hundreds of violations, the agency found over 100 instances where the railroad had underreported personal injuries and railroad equipment accidents. They also discovered 53 of 618 locomotives had defective warning whistles, certainly not the way to run a railroad.

Stock performance. Conrail stock bought for $1,000 in 1980 sold for $1,733 on January 2, 1990.

Consolidated Rail Corporation, 6 Penn Center Plaza, Philadelphia, PA 19104; (215) 977-4000.

6

#6 *in railroad revenues*

Employees: 19,100
Sales: $3 billion
Losses: $195 million
Founded: 1860
Headquarters: Chicago, Illinois

A famous name in American railroading—the Atchison, Topeka and Santa Fe—was frittered away in an orgy of mindless financial maneuvering that left this company in limbo as the last decade of the century began. Chicago-based Santa Fe announced a merger with San Francisco-based Southern Pacific in 1983, the resulting combination to be the nation's second largest railroad. There was only one hitch. The Interstate Commerce Commission had to approve it—and in 1986 the ICC said nothing doing, the merger would shrink competition. At the same time, Santa Fe, the owner of rich pieces of land, became the target of corporate raiders. To fend them off, the company took on a ton of debt to pay shareholders a special $30 dividend—and then began furiously selling off pieces of the company: SFP Timber, Robert E. McKee, Bankers Leasing, Kirby Forests, pipelines and, naturally, Southern Pacific.

They still have an 11,350-mile railroad, the Santa Fe, which connects Chicago with the Southwest, but in 1990 they announced that the company would be sliced into three parts: an energy company (Santa Fe Resources), a real estate company (Catellus Realty) and a railroad (Santa Fe).

History. Santa Fe's early history is interwoven with Kansas's. In the early 1870s, the Santa Fe's westernmost terminal was Dodge City. Dodge City became the end of the trail for the cowboys from Texas who drove their cattle north to be shipped by the Atchison, Topeka and Santa Fe line to packing houses to the east—and had their stories recounted in episodes of "Gunsmoke," "Bat Masterson" and countless other TV series and Hollywood movies about the Old West.

Not until 1882 did the railroad actually reach Santa Fe, New Mexico. A few years later, the line stretched to San Diego and San Francisco in the West, and to Chicago in the East. Today, those are still the railroad terminuses, along with a line extending through Texas to Houston.

One of Santa Fe's principal contributions to rail travel may well have been the introduction of decent food for travelers to the Wild West. Until Fred Harvey began operating the Santa Fe's whistle-stop food concessions in the 1870s, the trip by rail entailed greasy, expensive meals in a seemingly endless chain of hash-houses. Harvey, an Englishman with a penchant for fine linen and silverware, brought *haute cuisine* to the American prairie. His waitresses—known as Harvey Girls—were recruited from New England and the Midwest and lived in dormitories run by matrons. Nearly 5,000 lonely Westerners married Harvey Girls, celebrated in the 1946 Judy Garland movie, *The Harvey Girls*.

Santa Fe has no interest anymore in feeding people. They changed their corporate name to Santa Fe Industries in 1967 to reflect their growing interest in oil and gas. By 1980 the Value Line Investment Survey called them "an oil company which happens to own a railroad and some other transportation and natural resources businesses." Oil then accounted for nearly one-third of profits but less than 9 percent of sales.

Santa Fe turned their attention back to railroading in 1980 when they announced their intention to buy longtime competitor Southern Pacific. What followed was described by the *Wall Street Journal* as "one of the most disaster-prone acquisitions in business history."

To accomplish the merger, Santa Fe only needed to convince the Interstate Commerce Commission, seemingly a piece of cake since the ICC had routinely approved every big merger coming before it for 20 years. But Santa Fe blew it. They presented such a poor case one ICC commissioner called it "replete with self-contradictory testimony, omissions, and fuzziness." The ICC shocked the railroad industry by turning down the merger.

O*wners and rulers.* No one was more shocked at the ICC ruling than John Schmidt, a former lawyer who was Santa Fe's CEO at the time. Determined to get the ICC to reverse its ruling, Schmidt appealed the decision, but before his appeal could be heard, he was out on the street, the victim of a boardroom coup arranged by Benjamin Biaggini, SP's former head. After Biaggini had retired from Southern Pacific, Schmidt denied him use of the company jet and made him switch offices from a large one with a scenic view of the San Francisco Bay to a much smaller one looking out on a courtyard. Biaggini rallied enough board members to force out Schmidt in 1986. To ease the humiliation, the board gave him a going-away present of "a monthly consulting fee of $54,167 and additional compensation of $250,000" a year for five years plus an "additional incentive compensation" of up to $1.25 million—a total package worth nearly $6 million.

After the ICC reaffirmed its rejection of the merger shortly after Schmidt's ouster, Santa Fe sold Southern Pacific to Rio Grande Industries, parent of the Denver & Rio Grande Western Railroad. They then fought off hostile takeover bids by Henley Group and Olympia & York. But O&Y ended up with 20 percent of the stock and two board seats. Robert D. Krebs, former SP president, succeeded Schmidt as CEO. Krebs took home $1.5 million in 1989.

S*tock performance.* Santa Fe Pacific stock bought for $1,000 in 1980 sold for $2,126 on January 2, 1990.

Santa Fe Pacific, 224 South Michigan Avenue, Chicago, IL 60604; (312) 786-6000.

7

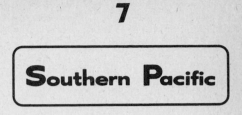

Southern Pacific

Employees: 22,900
Sales: $2.4 billion
Profits: $98 million
Founded: 1861
Headquarters: San Francisco, California

Here's a story about the little engine that could. In 1987 the Denver & Rio Grande Western Railroad consisted of only 3,400 miles of track extending from Kansas City to Salt Lake City. They were a midget compared with a big railroad, like Southern Pacific, which had more miles of track and carried much more freight. But the big railroad was on the auction block. The SP had been bought by the Santa Fe, and when the Interstate Commerce Commission nixed the deal, SP had to be sold.

Now Rio Grande may have been a small railroad, but their owner was one of America's richest men. According to *Forbes*, Philip Anschutz's fortune is worth over $1 billion. He started with his father's oil business, but made his fortune from an oil field in Utah—"the kind of field that gives oilmen goose pimples," he told *Forbes*. His other holdings include 11 million acres of ranches in the West and some prime real estate in Denver. (In mid-1990 he sued National Hog Farms for building an odorific farm close to his palatial duck preserve in Greeley, Colorado. He wants to force special environmental regulations that would cost the hog operation over $10 million.) Anschutz picked up Rio Grande in 1984 for a mere $500 million, saying, "It was a real steal." He couldn't pass up another bargain. So, in 1987 he offered to pay $1 billion in cash and assume $780 million in Southern Pacific debt—an offer Santa Fe couldn't refuse. Today, the little railroad owns the big one but lets the big one operate under their own name out of their old headquarters in San Francisco. And the orange-and-black Rio Grande logo has been rubbed off the locomotives, replaced with a big red-and-yellow SP.

When Anschutz bought the railroad he declared, "I want to reemphasize that we will be in the railroad business, first and foremost." But he acknowledged that "quite a bit of real estate came with Southern Pacific." That was an understatement. Southern Pacific still owns some of California's most valuable farmland, situated conveniently near the railroad's various rights-of-way. SP is the largest private landowner in California, Nevada and Utah, owning 2 percent of the land surface of California alone.

History. Southern Pacific's history is basically the story of the Far West, and the fates of the two are inextricably linked. SP was created by robber barons Leland Stanford, Mark Hopkins, Charles Crocker and C. P. Huntington, who functioned like a well-trained team of stage horses. They turned their railroad into the prototypical American monopoly through the time-honored techniques of graft, fraud and mendacity. In the process they built the state of California and inspired Frank Norris' muckraking 1901 novel, *The Octopus.*

By 1900 a map of California showing reclaimed desert land, telegraph lines, rail lines, ferry systems, farming areas and vital resources was largely a map of the SP empire. Where Southern Pacific went, so went civilization. The railroad created Reno, Nevada, as well as Fresno, Modesto, Truckee and Coalinga, California— all set up to encourage growth along Southern Pacific lines. From nothing, Southern Pacific created California tourism: building the Del Monte, Shasta Springs and Coronado hotels and advertising them across the country. They started *Sunset Magazine* in 1898 hoping to attract newcomers and settlers to California. People came to the Golden State in droves, and those who tilled the land soon made the state into the country's biggest agricultural producer—with Southern Pacific trains and tracks strategically placed to

Since 1981 the number of train-related injuries on trains each year has decreased 53 percent, but the amount of money awarded to victims has more than doubled to a total of $811 million.

haul California's fruits and vegetables to a hungry nation. Today food products are SP's principal cargo.

Southern Pacific achieved some unwanted notoriety in the late 1980s when they became the first company to lose a case involving random drug testing on the job. A SP computer programmer was fired in 1985 for refusing to submit to a urine test. She sued the company, and a jury ruled in her favor, awarding her $485,000.

Southern Pacific Transportation Company, One Market Plaza, San Francisco, CA 94105; (415) 541-1000.

8

#1 *in passenger rail service*

Employees: 20,000
Sales: $1.1 billion
Losses: $574 million
Founded: 1971
Headquarters: Washington, D.C.

Business is booming on Amtrak. It's standing-room only on peak-period trains on the routes between New York and Washington and between Los Angeles and San Diego. Sleeping berths are often sold out weeks in advance on long-distance trains such as the *California Zephyr* (Chicago to San Francisco) or the Silver Star (New York to Florida). In 1988 Amtrak carried more than 21 million passengers. That same year it collected over $1 billion in ticket sales for the first time in their history.

That's the good news. The bad news is this activity doesn't impress Amtrak's owners—the federal government. Congress created Amtrak in 1971 because the private railroads were gradually dismantling their unprofitable passenger lines in favor of money-making freight trains. Despite the recent upsurge in passengers and revenues, the government still has to subsidize Amtrak to the tune of nearly $600 million a year. Washington's politicians don't consider such losses the way to run a business, let alone a railroad. The result

Amtrak ridership on trains like the Super-liner (shown above) doubled during the 1980s—from 18.2 million in 1978 to 36.9 million in 1988.

is an ongoing and noisy political debate about the future of Amtrak, which runs all of the nation's intercity (that is, non-commuter) passenger trains with 24,000 miles of track through 44 states.

Amtrak's most vocal foes have been in the White House. When President Reagan submitted his first budget in 1981, he eliminated the Amtrak subsidy. But he didn't bank on Amtrak's popularity. One congressman reported pro-Amtrak mail ran "far more and far sooner than the complaints we heard on school lunches, Medicare cuts, even Social Security." Congress restored most of the subsidy and has done so every year since then despite the axe-wielding of Presidents Reagan and Bush.

Amtrak's ardent supporters—who cut across regional and political lines—claim almost all of Amtrak's problems are polit-ically inspired. When Amtrak's first pres-ident sought to rid the system of their most unproductive lines, he discovered he could only cut those in the districts of the least-powerful congressmen. Several little-used lines in West Virginia, a state represented by Senate Majority Leader Robert Byrd, are still with us today.

Worse, Washington has kept Amtrak from modernizing their trains and repair-ing their rails. "It was set up almost by design so it could collapse," former Amtrak VP Clark Tyler once explained: "It's a miracle it could survive at all." Amtrak now has fewer passenger cars (1,350) than in 1982 despite carrying one-quarter more passengers than they did then. What's more, nearly one-third of the cars are over 35 years old. Columnist Mike Royko once said he rode Amtrak because "the train would not be hijacked, at least not by anybody but a junk dealer."

Even worse, Amtrak has to share the rails with the much slower moving freight trains. Fifteen passengers were killed on January 4, 1987, when an Amtrak train collided with a Conrail freight train in Maryland. It was the worst accident in Amtrak's history. Such an accident never would have happened in France or Japan because freight trains don't move on the same tracks as passenger trains. Yet the government has been unwilling to appro-priate the money to give Amtrak their own tracks even for the so-called Northeast Corridor, the 443-mile stretch between

Boston and Washington, D.C., which accounts for over half of Amtrak passengers. In fact, Amtrak pays over $250 million a year to the private railroads just to use their tracks.

The bottom line, according to Amtrak's supporters, is nobody but Congress and the White House believe passenger service has to make money. No other passenger train service in the world does. Great Britain, France and Japan spend much more to subsidize their rail systems than does the U.S. Each year Japan spends more on buying new trains than Congress gives Amtrak for their entire budget.

By early 1990, however, things were looking up for Amtrak. Passenger complaints are down, and the reliance on government money is declining. Fares now account for 72 cents out of every dollar Amtrak spends, up from 40 cents in 1980. President W. Graham Claytor expects by the year 2000 Amtrak may cover all operating costs, something no national railroad system in the world does. One new feature he also wants to introduce by the decade's end is "tilt trains," which maintain speed and comfort on curves by leaning into them and reducing trip time. Amtrak stays alive, and the U.S. keeps their second-rate passenger railroad running with more passengers—on increasingly older trains.

Amtrak, National Railroad Passenger Corporation, 400 North Capitol Street, N.W., Washington, DC 20001; (202) 383-3000.

DELIVERY SERVICES

Americans no longer rely on the post office to get their letters and packages delivered. During the 1980s, business people came to depend on a variety of services promising fast delivery. Every day over 2 million documents and small packages are sent for overnight delivery, while over 10 million packages are sent via an express delivery service other than the post office. During the early 1980s, a host of companies got into the act, but competition reduced the ranks to a handful, with UPS dominating small package business, Federal Express overnight delivery.

1

#1 *in delivery services*

Employees: 117,000
Sales: $11 billion
Profits: $700 million
Founded: 1907
Headquarters: Greenwich, Connecticut

Workplace

"**W**e run the tightest ship in the shipping business," proclaim UPS TV ads. Indeed, UPS may be America's most efficient company. Nearly 50,000 of their familiar brown trucks carry a total of 9 million packages a day to every nook and cranny of America. UPS delivers more small packages than the U.S. Postal Service. Although UPS and the postal service compete for the same business, the two have little in common. The Postal Service generally loses money, UPS always makes money. Whereas the Postal Service is government owned, UPS is privately owned—by the managers and supervisors who work for the company. Whereas the

Postal Service has a monopoly on delivery to mailboxes, UPS picks up and delivers door-to-door. And whereas the Postal Service must accept all packages, UPS takes only packages weighing 70 pounds or less and shorter than 108 inches. It's more efficient that way. Dealing with small packages has enabled UPS to automate their sorting and loading. The weight limit also means one man can handle a UPS shipment. (Although more women are popping up in those brown uniforms, UPS drivers are still predominantly male.)

UPS has made a religion of efficiency. They employ over 1,000 efficiency experts, who time the moves of every employee down to tenths of a second, trying to find the quickest way to do every task. Drivers are supposed to walk at a rate of three feet per second, carry packages under the left arm, step into the van with the right foot while holding the van's key ring on the middle finger of the right hand. All UPS brown vans (called package cars) are washed daily. UPS does little or nothing to solicit customers. They employ few salespeople, and they did no advertising until 1982. But every day drivers call on 850,000 regular customers (mostly businesses) whether or not they have a package for delivery.

History. Serving business is how this company grew up. They were born in Seattle in 1907 when 19-year-old messenger boy Jim Casey founded the American Messenger company. He had six messengers, two bicycles and a telephone. He soon began delivering parcels for merchants in a Model T Ford refitted for carrying packages. A year later he added seven motorcycles. From the start, the drivers had to look neat: They wore suits, ties and caps. By 1918 Casey's company was handling all the deliveries for three of Seattle's largest department stores. In 1913 American Messenger became Merchants Parcel Company. After World War I, a renamed United Parcel Service specialized in delivering packages for stores. The company expanded to other cities on the West Coast and by 1930 to New York City. By the end of their first year there, UPS was delivering for 123 New York stores. By the early 1950s they were serving stores in 16 metropolitan areas; the ubiquitous brown trucks gave people the

impression UPS was an extension of the downtown department stores.

This department store image still clings to UPS even though the company radically changed course in 1953 by offering a door-to-door, parcel pickup-and-delivery service for wholesalers, manufacturers and others (translation: everybody). Today this service is by far the biggest part of their business. In 1953, UPS also got into the air express business, offering two-day (Blue Label) air service throughout the country.

Founder Jim Casey ran the company until 1962. He never married and lived in a two-room suite in New York's Waldorf Towers. He bequeathed the company a legacy of efficiency, using techniques developed by time-and-motion pioneer Frank Gilbreth. Company managers still like to quote Caseyisms contained in his book, *Determined Men*, or in the UPS Policy Book: "A leader does not have to remind others of authority by the use of a title." "You can't be a big man unless you have shown competence as a small man." In 1982, UPS entered the overnight delivery business in direct competition with this service's pioneer, Federal Express. Not only did the company begin their first ad campaign (they now spend $18 million a year on ads), they also went into debt for the first time. They sold $165 million worth of bonds in 1984 to buy planes and build an overnight transfer facility in Louisville, Kentucky. In 1987 they paid cash to buy 110 planes to become the 10th largest U.S. airline. They now own more than 300 aircraft, carrying over 600,000 documents a day.

Owners and rulers. UPS is completely owned by 20,000 managers and supervisors. Most, like CEO Kent C. "Oz" Nelson, started at the bottom. Once promoted into a supervisory position, the new "partner" can buy company stock, though most stock is awarded to them for their performance as profit producers. When UPS managers leave the company (and not many do) or retire, the stock has to be resold to the company. The top managers are multimillionaires from their UPS stock. Not many perks are associated with being a UPS official. Even top executives don't have reserved parking slots at the sedate company headquarters in Greenwich, Connecticut, and they have to stand in line to eat in company cafeterias along with the hourly workers. CEO Nelson doesn't even have his own secretary, and he does his own photocopying. The system breeds intense loyalty and a culture of hard work where only those who "bleed brown" get ahead.

As a place to work. UPS's mostly unionized (Teamsters) work force is well paid, about $16 an hour for the van drivers. But, as one employee told the *New England Monthly*: "It's the best delivery system in the world, but they're the most rotten bastards to work for." UPS requires rigid adherence to dress codes. Employees are expected to be neat—which means, in UPS terms, no pins on the uniform, no hair below the collar, no beards, nor "excessively bushy" sideburns or mustaches. And new hires are expected to join the team for good. Vice president Francis Erbich told *Business Week*, "I don't hire anybody I don't think will retire with us." Management's devotion to efficiency has created a climate some drivers claim is "medieval," like "a Roman galley." They complain about the way the company compares each driver's daily performance with computerized standards. Supervisors ride around with those who perform worst (termed the "least-best" driver), telling them how to save time. If the driver improves, the supervisor moves on to the next "least-best" driver, creating constant pressure on all drivers. Those who don't improve can be disciplined or fired.

The UPS passion for efficiency has provoked a number of labor disputes and strikes over the years and has given the company a black eye in the press. *New England Monthly* once described them as "New England's Meanest Employer." And some well-publicized lawsuits have been filed. For example, a UPS manager in New Jersey was fired for "adultery" because he moved in with a coworker after filing for a divorce from his wife. The coworker was not fired, however, because she was unmarried. UPS's lawyers contended that "Our society, rightly or wrongly, has distinguished steadily between fornication and adultery. Unless some law forbade this, UPS management was privileged to do likewise." UPS lost the case in court.

Global presence. Since 1985 UPS has gone worldwide. They now deliver to 145 countries. An industry executive told *Business Week*: "UPS moves slowly, but when it moves, it's the 900-pound gorilla."

United Parcel Service of America, Inc., 51 Weaver Street, Greenwich Office Park 5, Greenwich, CT 06830; (203) 622-6000.

2

#1 *in international air freight, overnight delivery*

#2 *in package delivery services*

Employees: 75,000
Sales: $6.8 billion
Profits: $114 million
Founded: 1971
Headquarters: Memphis, Tennessee

Workplace

Imagine doing business in America today without Federal Express. Their 29,000 white vans and cheerful couriers are familiar sights in business districts from Wall Street to Main Street. People in offices say "FedEx" to describe sending a document or package for overnight delivery.

Every business day Federal Express couriers pick up nearly 1 million packages or documents. Most are put on one of FedEx's 200-plus, purple-painted aircraft and flown to the Memphis Superhub where several thousand workers place them on planes bound for their final destinations and delivery by 10:30 A.M. the next day. An Overnight Letter from Minneapolis to Cleveland goes through Memphis as does one from Seattle to Phoenix. In recent years Federal Express has built regional sorting centers (in Oakland, Newark, Los Angeles and Chicago) to transport packages bound for nearby cities by truck (at one-sixth the cost of doing it by air).

History.   This story is one of the great entrepreneurial sagas of the second half of the 20th century. Young Yale college student writes a term paper describing a business opportunity: a nationwide overnight delivery service. Professor gives the student a *C*. Undeterred, the student launches an overnight delivery service several years after graduation. He raises millions of dollars from venture capitalists to buy a fleet of airplanes. The company turns a profit within three years, becoming the first service company in history to reach $1 billion in sales in 10 years. The student's personal stake in the enterprise (worth $250 million dollars) makes him one of America's wealthiest men.

Of course, there's more to the story. Founder Fred Smith spent two tours of duty in Vietnam, first as a Marine infantry officer participating in 27 offensive operations, and then as a forward air controller and spotter in a small plane picking targets for bombers just south of the DMZ, where some of the war's most intense fighting took place. By the time he left, Smith had won two Purple Hearts, the Silver and Bronze Stars, and the Vietnamese Cross of Gallantry.

After Vietnam Smith bought a used aircraft business in Little Rock, Arkansas, with some money inherited from his father (also an entrepreneur, having made a fortune from the Dixie Greyhound Bus Lines and the Toddle House restaurant chain). The younger Smith made money selling corporate jets, but his heart wasn't in it: "I really didn't like this business. It was full of shady characters." Besides, he was irritated at how difficult it was to get replacement parts: "I became infuriated that I could not receive on any timely and reliable basis air freight shipments from places around the United States." The

About 750,000 overnight packages are flown to Federal Express' Memphis superhub nightly where in 4 hours, 4,000 workers unload, sort, and reload them on 180 aircraft.

need he discovered as a small businessperson was, of course, the same need he'd already described in his Yale term paper.

Smith invested $4 million of his own money in the new enterprise, incorporated in 1971 as Federal Express, expecting his first customer to be the Federal Reserve Bank system. The bank deal fell through, but the name had a solid, patriotic ring to it, so he kept it. Like any good entrepreneur, Smith spent the next few years doing market research, hiring the best people he could find (a number came from UPS), getting equipment (airplanes, vans), lobbying Congress to eliminate restrictions on air cargo services and raising money. Lots of money. Though he eventually raised $80 million, there were plenty of rough times, such as the moment in 1973 when the General Dynamics board turned down his request for a loan. Instead of returning to Memphis, Smith took a plane to Las Vegas where he won $27,000 at the blackjack tables to help meet his payroll.

Everywhere he went, Smith preached the Federal Express gospel. "We're a freight service company with 550-mile-per-hour delivery trucks," he'd say. "This company is nothing short of being the logistics arm of a whole new society that is building up in our economy—a society that isn't built around automobile and steel production, but that is built up instead around service industries and high technology endeavors in electronics and optics and medical science. It is the movement of these support items that Federal Express is all about."

Federal Express proved reliable in their early years and grew rapidly. They stressed dependability in a series of memorable TV ads created by the Ally & Gargano agency in the early 1980s. In one, actor John Moschitta played a harried executive on several phones who spits out rapid-fire tongue-twisters, followed by an announcer who intones: "Federal Express. When It Absolutely Positively Has To Be There Overnight."

Like any success story, Federal Express has had some reverses. The worst was ZapMail, their attempt to enter the facsimile business. Federal Express lost an estimated $350 million before zapping the business in 1986. In 1989 they bought Flying Tiger, the world's biggest all-cargo carrier, for $880 million.

Owners and rulers. Fred Smith, who made $880,000 in 1989, holds about 9 percent of the stock, worth about $250 million in 1989. Employees own another 20 percent of the business. Like Smith, most top managers are in their 40s. The senior vice president and chief personnel officer, James Perkins, is one of the highest-ranking blacks in corporate America.

As a place to work. One of the best in America. Besides high wages and generous benefits (one of the best: passes to ride Federal Express planes), Federal Express has consciously tried to be a progressive workplace. They have a generous profit-sharing program, flextime provisions for clerical workers and a tuition reimbursement program that can even be used by part-time workers. Their grievance procedure, called the Guaranteed Fair Treatment process, has won plaudits from legal experts as the nation's best. In the final step of the GFT process, employees are judged by a jury of their own peers.

Global presence. Thanks to their purchase of Flying Tiger, they now have international service to 119 countries, and they fly to 160 airports around the world. However, they're having some trouble combining Tiger's unionized workers with Federal nonunion employees. Industry consultant Bernard La Londe said, "This merger will have to be handled like two porcupines making love: very carefully. Federal is playing big casino with big risks."

Stock performance. Federal Express stock bought for $1,000 in 1980 sold for $3,914 on January 2, 1990.

Federal Express Corporation, 2005 Corporate Ave., Memphis, TN 38132; (901) 369-3600.

3

AMERICAN PRESIDENT COMPANIES, LTD.

#1 *in transpacific shipping*

Employees: 4,800
Sales: $2.2 billion
Profits: $11.3 million
Founded: 1848
Headquarters: Oakland, California

This company picked the right ocean. The first shipping company to go around the world, American President Companies was in danger of sinking in the late 1970s. So, they shut down all their Atlantic ports, and as one executive put it, "We made the decision to put all our ships in one basket—the Pacific basket." That gambit worked out when trade between the U.S. and the Far East skyrocketed.

During the 1980s, American President also changed the way they do business. Formerly an old-fashioned steamship operator, they used to accept goods from port to port. Now they can pick up a load of VCRs in Japan and deliver them to a retailer in Ohio. To do so, American President has invested millions of dollars to buy hundreds of containers that can be loaded on railcars (including 900 double-stack railcars) or hitched up to a truck tractor. American President has nearly 100,000 such containers. By offering customers a coast-to-coast rail service, they could beat out their closest competitors' all-water Asia to New York service by 10 to 15 days. Today, American President is the largest carrier of containerized goods from Asia to New York even though none of their ships dock anywhere on the East Coast.

APC's best customer is the U.S. government, which ships military equipment to friends in the Pacific Rim. Other U.S. exports include scrap metal, lumber and cotton, all helpful to developing countries short of land. After the U.S., the countries giving APC the bulk of their business are Taiwan, Japan and Hong Kong. Reflecting the U.S. trade deficit, APC carries much more valuable cargo eastbound, from the Pacific Rim countries to the U.S. Imports into the U.S. tend to be "finished goods," clothing and already-assembled electronics such as Walkmans, TVs, and VCRs. As a U.S. flag carrier, American President also receives operating subsidies from the federal government.

History. This company's roots go back to the early days of steamship companies. They claim, in fact, to be "the oldest continuously operated steamship company in the U.S." The immediate predecessor was the West Coast–based Dollar Steamship Lines, founded in 1902. They in turn acquired an even older line, the Pacific Mail Steamship Company, founded in 1848 by a New York entrepreneur, William Aspinwall, who foresaw money was to be made from trade with the new western U.S. territories. Their ships initially sailed from East Coast ports to San Francisco via Cape Horn. Pacific Mail also started the first regular steamship service to China and Japan in 1867. In 1925 they started an around-the-world service. Pacific Mail became part of Dollar Steamship in 1925, and the company changed their name to American President Lines in 1938, when they began naming their ships after U.S. presidents. The first ship so named was the *President Hoover*. Before the days of air travel, APL had a fleet of ships plying the Pacific with passengers and cargo. During World War II the government requisitioned their fleet for use by the army and navy. The ships were returned to private hands after the war. Another shipper, American Mail Line, later became part of APL.

In 1952 APL came under the wing of Ralph K. Davies, a brilliant, adventurous oilman. Before World War II he became the youngest person ever to serve on the board of Standard Oil of California. Afterwards he split with Standard Oil (the stodgiest company in the West) and went off on his own. He and his associates took control of a virtually moribund company, Natomas, and built the firm into a thriving oil company, thanks largely to concessions Davies negotiated in Indonesia. Davies merged his controlling interest in APL into Natomas. When Dorman L. Commons, former chief financial officer at Occidental Petroleum, became CEO of Natomas in 1974, he had serious doubts about American President Lines. He didn't know anything about shipping, and he thought he would sell off the company. That never happened because (1) no one was interested in buying them and (2) he commissioned a study that indicated APL could, with proper management, make money. So APL stayed at Natomas. In fact, they became a wholly owned subsidiary, and Commons persuaded, with some difficulty, one of his Natomas executives, Bruce Seaton, to make the switch from energy to shipping.

Seaton is credited with turning APL around. He shut down the Atlantic port facilities, upgraded the fleet, purchased railcars and turned APL into a company that could deliver goods across the country as well as across the Pacific Ocean. In 1983, when the Texas oil company, Diamond Shamrock, mounted an ultimately successful hostile raid against Natomas, American President Lines was spun off to shareholders as a separate company, called American President Companies, with Seaton still at the helm.

During the 1980s, Seaton embarked on a $900 million expansion program, buying double-stack railcars and five new C10 container vessels, bringing their total to 23 container ships and one multipurpose ship. C10s are the largest vessels of their kind ever built, capable of holding nearly 4,000 twenty-foot containers. In ordering C10s, American President abandoned the Atlantic for good, as the C10s are too big to pass through the Panama Canal.

Owners and rulers. APC has been publicly owned since 1983, and their two biggest stockholders are Itel Corporation and First National Bank of Chicago. CEO Seaton turned 65 in 1990 but showed no sign of leaving.

As a place to work. American President has a unionized labor force, and generally seems to enjoy good relations with employees. One union official said, "They have a good track record. They seem to be just. Their wages are better than most."

Global presence. American President calls at ports in every major Asian country, including China, as well as ports in the Indian Ocean.

Stock performance. American President stock bought for $1,000 in 1983 sold for $2,016 on January 2, 1990.

American President Companies, Ltd., 1800 Harrison Street, Oakland, CA 94612; (415) 272-8000.

4

DHL Worldwide Express

#1 in international courier service
#5 in domestic overnight delivery

Employees: 20,000
Sales: $1.6 billion
Founded: 1969
Headquarters: Redwood City, California

While Federal Express, UPS, Emery, Airborne and others fought over the domestic overnight market, DHL quietly became the dominant courier of documents overseas. More than two-thirds of their sales come from international courier service, which numbered 50 million international shipments in 1989.

Founded by a trio of California lawyers, Adrian Dalsey, Larry Hillblom and Robert Lynn, to deliver documents between the West Coast and Hawaii, the company entered the international arena in 1972 when they recruited Hong Kong entrepreneur, Po Chung, to set up a global network. DHL International Ltd., headquartered in Hong Kong, has their own management and ownership, but the exact relationship between the two companies is unknown. DHL is fiercely private and publicity shy. Instead of relying on their own planes, DHL built their business by sending couriers ticketed as passengers who checked as excess baggage up to 150 green canvas "body bags" with as much as 70 pounds of documents (not subject to duties). Because airlines unload passenger baggage before cargo, DHL's canvas bags can be on their way to their final destinations without all the delays and red tape inherent in sending parcels as freight. Over the years, DHL has gained a reputation among corporate customers for fast, reliable service to overseas destinations, now including 160 countries.

As competitors like Federal Express and UPS began invading their international turf, DHL has fought back by raiding theirs. DHL didn't get into the domestic overnight delivery wars until 1983, but they have since bought their own fleet of planes and opened a sorting hub in Cincinnati. They have also launched a major advertising push to snare customers.

In October 1988, Patrick Foley was named CEO, succeeding Charles Lynch. Foley previously served as chairman of Hyatt Hotels and Braniff Airlines. In mid-1990, Japan Airlines, Lufthansa German Airlines and the Nissho Iwai Japanese trading company were negotiating an investment of $500 million to obtain an estimated 60 percent stake in DHL's international operations.

DHL Worldwide Express, 333 Twin Dolphin Drive, Redwood City, CA 94065; (415) 593-7474.

satisfy the bankers who'd loaned the money. To make matters worse, Emery began losing customers because of service problems and inability to integrate Purolator's network into their own. Emery's board ousted John Emery, Jr., and put the company up for sale. In early 1989, Emery found a buyer in Consolidated Freightways, the huge trucking company. The price tag, $230 million, was less than Emery had put up for Purolator two years earlier. Emery, fully owned by Consolidated, took over CF Air Freight, Consolidated's air freight service, and immediately began to dilute CF's profits. In early 1990 Emery was piling up such huge losses that their new parent was considering shutting them down for good.

Emery Air Freight Corporation, 3350 West Bayshore Road, Palo Alto, CA 94301; (415) 855-9100.

5

Emery Worldwide

#1 *in heavy freight delivery*

#3 *in overnight delivery*

Employees: 16,700
Sales: $1.4 billion
Founded: 1946
Headquarters: Palo Alto, California

This company had trouble seeing the opportunities existing in their own business. Founded just after the Second World War, Emery began life as an air freight forwarder, meaning they picked up and delivered a customer's freight, using the regularly scheduled airlines to fly the cargo. Their business was highly profitable with almost no overhead. When Federal Express bought their own aircraft, John Emery, Jr., the founder's son, scoffed, calling the fleet, "[Federal president Fred] Smith's expensive toy." By 1981 Emery was eating his own words. To get into the overnight game, he had to buy his own aircraft and space at the Dayton, Ohio, airport to serve as a sorting hub.

Six years later, still playing catch-up, Emery bought Purolator Courier, a company run for years by former Treasury Secretary Nicholas Brady. The $313 million price tag was high, and even selling off Purolator's oil filter business didn't

6

Employees: 9,000
Sales: $1.1 billion
Profits: $25 million
Founded: 1946
Headquarters: Seattle, Washington

Airborne specializes in serving large companies that do a lot of overnight shipping. By giving them huge discounts, they have bagged some of the country's biggest corporations, including IBM, which gives Airborne all their express packages weighing less under 150 pounds (at discount rates up to 84 percent below what Federal Express charges their infrequent shippers). The IBM contract is worth $40 million a year to Airborne. To win over big clients, Airborne has a 250-person army of salespeople knocking on doors. Airborne CEO Robert Cline uses an auto analogy to distinguish his firm: "Federal Express is the Cadillac of this business. High profile, lots of bells and whistles.

UPS is the Chevrolet. Less dramatic, less service-sensitive, less expensive for the infrequent user. We've tried to position ourselves in between."

Like Emery, Airborne began life as an air freight forwarder and ranked a poor third after Emery and Burlington Northern Air Freight. They jumped into overnight shipping in 1980 when they purchased a vacant Strategic Air Command base in Wilmington, Ohio, and a small airline that delivered checks for the Federal Reserve. The Wilmington hub now processes about 250,000 pieces every night with a fleet of about 50 planes. About one-quarter of Airborne's business involves overseas shipments. Airborne's executives—and about 500 of their underlings—run the operation from an unusual convex-shaped glass building on a bluff overlooking Puget Sound. Employees have dubbed the headquarters the "oil can."

Stock performance. Airborne Freight stock bought for $1,000 in 1980 sold for $1,920 on January 2, 1990.

Airborne Freight Corp., 3101 Western Avenue, P.O. Box 662, Seattle, WA 98611; (206) 285-4600.

TRUCKERS

Familiar highway names like Spector, Red Ball, McLean and Interstate no longer ride the roads. They, along with over 250 medium- to large-sized trucking companies, have gone out of business since 1980. During that same period, the 10 largest truckers consolidated their industry dominance. They now receive one out of every two dollars companies spend to truck goods. Before 1980, the top ten took less than one of every three freight dollars.

These developments illustrate the dramatic impact of the Motor Carrier Act of 1980, commonly known as deregulation. Before deregulation, truck companies applied to the Interstate Commerce Commission for the right to haul freight between two cities. The ICC also set their rates. Now truckers can ship freight anywhere and charge whatever they want. At first, the new rules caused a huge influx of new, small companies (more than 12,000 in the first few years). But most failed, as did many larger firms unable to adjust to the new environment. Winners have carved out niches for themselves. The biggest winners are nationwide giants capable of carrying freight anywhere. They've created hub-and-spoke systems similar to those of major airlines. Freight coming from smaller cities is transferred at huge sorting facilities onto express trucks going to major terminals. The top three—Consolidated Freightways, Roadway and Yellow Freight—now carry more than one-third of all U.S. freight.

1

CONSOLIDATED FREIGHTWAYS

#1 *in trucking*

Employees: 40,800
Sales: $3.8 billion
Profits: $8.6 million
Founded: 1929
Headquarters: Menlo Park, California

Consolidated's trucks are a familiar sight on the nation's highways. They ought to be. Over 37,000 roll on U.S. roads. Most

The percentage of trucks carrying a full load of freight has soared from 40 percent a decade ago to about 70 percent.

of their long-haul trucks are double-trailers, traveling an average 1,394 miles per trip. Consolidated's fleet carries freight in all 50 states from over 650 terminals, including 30 so-called consolidation centers serving as transfer points for the company's hub-and-spoke network. Besides their core business of long-haul trucking, Consolidated has four regional trucking companies, called Con-Way, specializing in overnight delivery within a 300-to-500-mile radius.

You won't see the hustle and bustle of the trucking business at Consolidated's Menlo Park headquarters, however. A *San Francisco Chronicle* reporter described the scene: "The two-story building is decorated with antiques, a collection of paintings, a flagstone lobby and carpeted offices. Employees wear suits and can polish their shoes on an automatic shoeshine machine in the restroom.

"[Company chairman Raymond] O'Brien...helps set the tone. He wears cufflinks and monogrammed shirts and often rides around town in a chauffeur-driven limousine. O'Brien shuns being pictured in the driver's seat of an 18-wheeler."

O'Brien stepped down as CEO in 1988 and returned to the helm in 1990 to continue reshaping Consolidated into more than a trucking firm. They started an air cargo service, CF AirFreight, in 1970, and O'Brien moved this arm into direct competition with Federal Express in 1985 by offering overnight delivery. Three years later, Consolidated bought Emery Air Freight, the third largest overnight deliverer, and combined them with CF Air Freight to form Emery Worldwide. However, Emery has been a drain on CF's earning power. They were losing money when CF bought them—and in 1990 they were still losing money. In early 1990 CF posted their first quarterly loss since 1961.

Consolidated began the 1980s by selling their Freightliner truck manufacturing division. Consolidated started making trucks in 1939 when they were still a small regional trucker operating out of Portland, Oregon. Consolidated's founder, Leland James, wanted to have lightweight, durable vehicles to handle the mountainous roads of the western states. Freightliner introduced trucks with cabs over the engines. They were also the first to use aluminum as their principal construction metal and to extensively use diesel engines.

Consolidated claims to have continued this innovative legacy through their extensive computerization since the mid-1960s. Consolidated also has the distinction of being one of the few trucking companies to *oppose* raising the 55-mile-per-hour speed limit. Consolidated insisted their big rigs would continue to drive at 55 mph even after Congress raised the speed limit on rural roads. Consolidated's computers told him the company had saved $2.1 million over a three-year period by operating at 55 mph rather than at 65 mph.

S*tock performance.* Consolidated stock bought for $1,000 in 1980 sold for $4,592 on January 2, 1990.

Consolidated Freightways, Inc., 175 Linfield Dr., Menlo Park, CA 94303; (415) 326-1700.

2

#2 *in trucking*

Employees: 33,500
Sales: $2.7 billion
Profits: $96 million
Founded: 1930
Headquarters: Akron, Ohio

Roadway fits the stereotype of a no-nonsense trucking company where managers are expected to be tough and workers are expected to toe the line. They also have a reputation for high-handedness with customers. A shippers' representative group explained: "At times, they've been arrogant. That's because they're good, and they know it."

From the outside, Roadway looks like their two major competitors, with a nationwide network of over 23,000 tractors, trailers and trucks operating from over 600 terminals as well as a hub-and-spoke system revolving around 31 hubs (called breakbulk facilities). Beneath the surface, however, Roadway is different. A long history of doing things their own way can be traced to founder Galen Roush, who started the company to transport tires made in Akron to auto plants in the Midwest and East. Roush died in 1976 and family members still control 30 percent of the stock (another 15 percent is owned by the employee Stock Ownership Trust), although none is active in day-to-day management. Roush's son and daughter have board seats.

Roush hired professional managers in the 1930s long before most other trucking firms even considered the need for management. He was a stickler for strict financial records. Terminal managers were given a lot of control. They could hire their own employees and set up their own work rules. At the same time, Roush rewarded efficient, profit-producing managers with cash bonuses and stock that made some of them millionaires.

Roush also shied away from publicity. Annual meetings frequently lasted only 15 minutes, and Roush refused any media contact, saying "A whale would never be harpooned if he didn't swim to the surface." In 1981, one of his successors granted *Forbes* a strict, one-hour interview but refused to be photographed: "Talk to our competitors," he said. "They're more photogenic." But even Roadway is beginning to change. They launched their first ad campaign in 1982, and their CEO as of 1990, Joseph W. Clapp, makes himself available for interviews.

Long a powerhouse in the Midwest and East, Roadway became a major factor in the West in 1988 with their purchase of California-based Viking Freight. Besides being California's biggest carrier, Viking was well known for progressive employment practices, such as having trucks equipped with AM/FM radios and cassette decks; off-duty rooms with pool tables, video games and color TVs with VCRs; and monthly meetings at each terminal attended by a senior company officer.

In 1985 Roadway took on United Parcel Service by launching a small package (less than 70 pounds) delivery service with their own trucks and terminals. By early 1990 Roadway Package System (RPS) had some 150 terminals spread throughout the East, Midwest and parts of the West. Each driver works a nine-hour day and picks up approximately 500 packages. RPS's drivers own their own trucks and pay for their own uniforms and insurance. As a result, RPS spends 20 to 30 percent less for labor costs than the unionized UPS.

S*tock performance.* Roadway Services stock bought for $1,000 in 1980 sold for $4,368 on January 2, 1990.

Roadway Services, Inc., 1077 Gorge Blvd., P.O. Box 88, Akron, OH 44309; (216) 384-8184.

3

YELLOW FREIGHT SYSTEM, INC.

#3 *in trucking*

Employees: 28,000
Sales: $2.2 billion
Profits: $69 million
Founded: 1924
Headquarters: Overland Park, Kansas

Run by a father-and-son team, Yellow Freight has been playing catch-up with their two bigger competitors by rapidly building new terminals and hubs since the company suffered a major setback in the early 1980s. In the 1970s Yellow had been the most profitable and fastest growing trucking company. They mushroomed by acquiring 65 truckers. But then they veered off the road. Trying to extend their network from their midwestern base, they paid $34.8 million for rights to run certain routes when Congress passed legislation that opened the roads to all comers, making this expensive purchase useless. As a result the company lost $13.8 million in 1980 and laid off 20 percent of their work force in early 1981.

In recent years Yellow's chairman, George Powell, Jr., and his son, George Powell III, who is president, have put the company back in gear. They now rival Roadway and Consolidated Freight in terms of terminals (over 600) and vehicles (over 30,000), and their service spans the nation. When George Powell III became president in 1987, he was following a family tradition. His father had run the company with his father, George Powell, Sr., a Kansas City banker, who had bought the nearly bankrupt Yellow Freight in 1952. The Powells own about 13 percent of Yellow's stock, and an employee profit-sharing and pension trust owns another 9 percent.

Stock performance. Yellow Freight stock bought for $1,000 in 1980 sold for $5,030 on January 2, 1990.

Yellow Freight System, Inc., 10990 Roe Ave., Overland Park, KS 66207; (913) 345-1020.

TELEPHONES

It was the most fateful decade of the century for the telephone industry, as American Telephone & Telegraph was carved up, creating seven Baby Bell companies to provide local service. Debate still rages as to the wisdom of this action. For most people, telephone charges went up sharply as local phone service had to stand on its own feet, no longer subsidized by long-distance. However, long-distance rates declined—and AT&T now had real competition in this area.

The phone business is a barn burner, generating total revenues—local and long-distance—of $141 billion in 1989, which makes it bigger than computers or aerospace. Telephone usage has grown three times as rapidly as the population, fed now by car phones, facsimile machines, information services, 800 and 900 numbers.

On one point, there's no argument: the Baby Bells, the companies providing local service, have done fabulously. And they are, in case anyone forgot to mention it, monopolies.

1

#1 *in long-distance telephone services*

Employees: 283,500
Sales: 36.3 billion
Profits: $2.7 billion
Founded: 1899
Headquarters: New York City, New York

We said goodbye to Ma Bell in the 1980s. The U.S.'s biggest company —measured by physical assets, after tax profits and number of employees—was broken up by the federal government in a classic violation of the principle, "If it ain't broke, don't fix it." American Telephone & Telegraph was shorn of 24 local telephone companies, which were divided into seven regional Baby Bells. AT&T retained the long-distance telephone business; the manufacturing of phones, switches, cables, integrated circuits, computers (although the old Western Electric name was dropped); and that peerless research subsidiary, Bell Laboratories, where the transistor and laser were invented.

The Bell System family members went into culture shock. Edward M. Block, who wrote the ad announcing the news—"To bring the benefits of the Information Age to America the Bell System had to be restructured"—said it "felt as though there had been a death in the family." The breakup went off as planned on January 1, 1984.

The mother company has hardly been reduced to nursing home status, however. Among all U.S. companies, the new AT&T ranks 10th in revenues and 7th in profit. They are still the undisputed long-distance leader. They handle 80 million calls *a day*, 77 percent of all long-distance calls, down from the 90 percent they commanded in 1984. The big difference now is they pay fees to the local companies they used to own to gain access to their lines. And never discount the power of inertia. For over 10 years, people have had the right to own their own phones as opposed to the old practice of renting them from AT&T. In 1988 AT&T still collected $3 billion from renting phones.

AT&T also has a strong computer presence, ranging from the hardware (the finished computer itself) to the software (the systems and programs that run the computer) to the innards (the semiconductor chips underlying this technology). When you order a pizza from Pizza Hut or make a reservation on an American Airlines flight, your orders are being processed on AT&T computer systems. Their UNIX operating system (operating systems allow computers to perform basic functions like storing information and displaying menus) was fast becoming an industry standard by 1989. UNIX is unique because it is an open system useable on different computer brands and on everything from personal computers to mainframes. In 1990 AT&T was toying with the idea of making UNIX a separate company, with shares held by other computer com-

THE LONG DISTANCE MARKET

Company	Market Share
1. AT&T	71.0%
2. MCI/Telecom USA	13.4%
3. US Sprint	8.0%
4. Others*	7.6%

*Others include Metromedia ITT, Allnet, Advance, Cable & Wireless, LiTel, Williams, Telecommunications Group and Telesphere Communications.

Source: The New York Times, 10 April 1990.

panies. UNIX got a big boost from AT&T's strategic alliance with Silicon Valley's Sun Microsystems, which emerged in the late 1980s as a leading supplier of UNIX-driven workstations. AT&T held 16.5 percent of Sun's stock at the end of 1989 and was preparing to bump that up to 20 percent in 1990. This investment alone has a stock market value of $850 million.

Whenever AT&T goes into the water, they make big waves. In 1990 they decided to go into the credit-card business. Out came their Universal card—available in either Visa or Mastercard versions—and in 80 days they had 1.7 million cardholders, ranking them among the leaders in this business, much to the irritation of the banking community. AT&T offered Universal cardholders a 10 percent discount on long-distance calls made with the card. AT&T is a big military contractor, too, with 6 percent of sales coming from the Pentagon, including operation of the nuclear weapons research center, Sandia Labs.

History. Alexander Graham Bell, Scottish-born inventor of the telephone, was the son and grandson of British elocution instructors (his father is believed to have been the inspiration for Professor Henry Higgins in George Bernard Shaw's play *Pygmalion*). At age 16, Bell built a speaking machine—an artificial skull that housed bits of tin, India rubber and a lamb's larynx. By blowing through it, he could make a "Ma-Ma!" cry. Bell also figured out how to manipulate his dog's mouth and vocal cords to make the pooch utter something that sounded like "How are you, Grandmama?" Glory came in 1876, when 29-year-old Bell was hard at

work in his Boston lab, tinkering with a device that became the telephone. Bell called for his assistant: "Mr. Watson, come here, I want you." Watson heard Bell's voice come over the wires.

Bell was not the only inventor working on the "speaking telephone"—and his patent was the subject of 600 separate challenges. The most celebrated came from Elisha Gray of Chicago, co-founder of Western Electric Manufacturing Company. In 1888 the U.S. Supreme Court sustained Bell's patent by a vote of 4 to 3. Bell perfected his invention and lived a quiet life as a tinkerer and instructor of the deaf until his death in 1922.

The Bell Telephone Company was founded in 1877 and expanded rapidly, controlled by a group of Boston bankers. They were challenged by Western Union Telegraph, which bought the rights to Elisha Gray's devices and hired a young inventor, Thomas Alva Edison, to build a better telephone. Edison did so, but the Bell company sued for patent infringement. Bell won and went through several reorganizations before becoming American Telephone and Telegraph in 1899, when they moved their headquarters from Boston to New York City. The move put them close to the wellsprings of money, an ingredient AT&T was going to be ever in need of in their zeal to spread telephones throughout the land. In particular, the move brought them within hailing distance of the era's dominant banker, J. P. Morgan—and indeed, during the first decade of the new century, Morgan gained effective control of AT&T.

After Bell's original patents expired in 1893 and 1894, thousands of independent companies sprang up from coast to coast. AT&T fought them by buying up some of them, undercutting their prices and refusing to connect their lines to the Bell System. The Morgan-controlled AT&T felt one telephone company was enough for the country. In 1909 they enhanced their near-monopoly position by annexing an old adversary, Western Union Telegraph. But that was one acquisition too much. Trust busters were alive and well in the U.S. at that time (they broke up both the Standard Oil and the American Tobacco trusts), and in 1913, to avoid a carve-up, AT&T struck a compromise with the federal government in the so-called

An AT&T telephone installer in 1911.
Courtesey of AT&T Archives

Kingsbury Commitment (named after an AT&T vice president, Nathan C. Kingsbury) that set the company's course for the next 70 years. AT&T agreed to sell off Western Union, buy no more phone companies without Interstate Commerce Commission approval and allow other phone companies to connect to the Bell System lines. The agreement virtually guaranteed AT&T a near-monopoly of U.S. phone services and made possible the Bell System. (Although they got rid of the telegraph business, AT&T continued, anachronistically, to keep Telegraph in their name. However, after the 1984 divestitures, the company stopped referring to themselves as American Telephone & Telegraph, preferring the designation AT&T.)

The galvanizing figure in AT&T's early history was Theodore N. Vail, who never went beyond high school. He first served as president from 1885 to 1887, left the company and then returned in 1907, at age 62, to steer the company for the next 12 years. He started the research function that became Bell Laboratories, and installed the policies and practices that set the tone for the Bell System. Vail grasped the idea that AT&T, as a regulated monopoly, could prosper by providing universal telephone service as long as they also recognized public service had to be embedded in their operations. As John Brooks, biographer of the company's first 100 years (*Telephone*), put it, Vail introduced the concept, now widely accepted, "that maximum private profit was not necessarily the *primary* objective of private enterprise." Vail also reversed the previous practice of management secrecy. In his 1911 annual report, he said: "If we don't tell the truth about ourselves, someone else will."

Bell Labs and Western Electric developed many of the technological milestones of the 20th century, including sound motion pictures (1926), TV transmission (1927), radio astronomy (1933), digital computers (1938), the transistor (1947), microwave relay (1948), the silicon solar cell (1954), lasers (1958) and satellite communications (1962). In World War II they built half the radar the U.S. armed forces used and after the war played a central role in the development of nuclear weapons.

Although AT&T was credited with introducing telephone service to most American homes, attacks on their monopoly position never ceased. The Bell System beat them all back until the latest assault, launched in 1974 during the early days of the Gerald Ford administration, when the Justice Department filed the antitrust suit that eventually resulted in the company's breakup. John deButts, then AT&T's chairman, vowed to fight to the bitter end, but he wasn't around when his successor, Charles Brown, threw in the towel in 1982. *Washington Post* reporter Steve Coll, author of *The Deal of the Century*, found deButts in 1984 at his country home in Virginia—and he was feeling what a lot of Bell System veterans were feeling. Coll reported deButts fought back tears to deliver this monologue: "I hear about it every single day from my friends. Friends from business, neighbors, even my family. I have a cousin around here who couldn't get phone service installed in his barn. Nobody could make up his mind about who was going to do what. He wanted service in several barns, with all the wires underground. He just wasn't getting to first base. So I finally called AT&T headquarters in New York and said, 'Why don't you get somebody down here who can take care of these problems?' And they did. But my cousin got a bill for $5,000. We never used to charge anybody for installation. It's unheard of. I even made them go back and check it to make sure it was right. It was.

"It pains me. It hurts me a lot. I've been used to saying, 'OK, Mr. Customer, if that's what you want, then that's what you're going to get.' What bothers me is that I see a deterioration of the service concept in the operating companies themselves. Profits are beginning to come first."

Owners and rulers. Owners: the same old army of widows and orphans (although their ranks are slightly smaller). Managers: the same old AT&T stalwarts (although outsiders are beginning to penetrate upper echelons). AT&T continues to have more shareholders than any other U.S. company: 2.6 million. They're also still a favorite holding of institutions like insurance companies, banks and mutual funds. Over 500 institutions hold nearly one-quarter of the AT&T shares. Robert E. Allen, who spent three decades at AT&T, beginning with Indiana Bell fresh out of Wabash College, became the company's 13th head in 1988, succeeding James E. Olson, who began his Bell career cleaning manholes in North Dakota. Allen was paid $2.8 million in 1989. During the 1980s AT&T began importing talent. Robert M. Kavner, AT&T's auditor at Coopers & Lybrand, joined the company in 1984 and is now president of the Data Systems Group (computers). John D. Zeglis, general counsel, also came aboard in 1984 from the Sidley & Austin law firm. And Gerald M. Lowrie, public affairs senior vice president, joined AT&T in 1985 from the American Bankers Association. Two blacks (Ford Foundation President Franklin A. Thomas and former U.S. Ambassador to the U.N. Donald F. McHenry) and two women (former Secretary of Commerce Juanita M. Kreps and economic consultant M. Kathryn Eickhoff) hold seats on AT&T's 19-member board of directors.

As a place to work. AT&T is now trying to become a "lean and mean" competitor while at the same time retaining the benevolence for which they were previously known. From 373,000 employees in 1984, AT&T went to 294,100 by decade's end, with more cuts in the offing. The frustration many old–timers felt bubbled to the surface in a letter sent by Dee Torrell, an employee with 12 years service, to the company magazine, *Focus*, in 1989. "I have seen," wrote Torrell, "a decline in our respect and caring for one another...we have forgotten how to interact with one another as people... The number of people who have expressed to me their disenchantment over the way we treat one another is overwhelming...competition is not synonymous with meanness toward our fellow human being." Torrell's letter drew a prompt handwritten response from Chairman Robert Allen, who commended it, saying: "Being competitive and caring about each other are not mutually exclusive. In fact, combining the two guarantees our success."

As a result of an agreement with unions in 1989, AT&T now courts the legions of mothers and fathers who work. The company has a $10 million fund for child-care facilities and offers up to one year of unpaid leave for family care. About 33 percent of managers are women.

Social responsibility.   The corporate watchdog, the Council on Economic Priorities, presented AT&T an award for environmental stewardship in 1990 to recognize the leadership role the company assumed in eliminating chlorofluorocarbons (CFCs), chemicals suspected of depleting the earth's ozone layer. AT&T pledged to halve consumption of CFCs by 1991 and phase them out entirely by 1994, the earliest target date for elimination any major electronics company has set. AT&T uses 4 million pounds of CFCs a year to make products like computer chips and circuit boards, accounting for one-third of all CFC use in the U.S. electronics industry.

AT&T is a major corporate philanthropist, giving away more than $30 million a year through their foundation. In recent years they have become a major arts supporter. They give $11 million a year to underwrite the "MacNeil-Lehrer News-Hour" on public TV.

Global presence.   In their former life, AT&T was restricted to the domestic front except for reaching all over the world with long-distance calling. Now they're trying to become an international giant overnight. They have 15,000 employees overseas in 41 countries. In 1989 they sold their 22 percent interest in Italian computer maker, Olivetti, but formed a joint venture with the state-owned Italian telephone company, Italtel, to make phones and other equipment for the European Common Market. They have a similar joint venture with Spain's national telephone company as well as joint ventures with Philips of the Netherlands, Ricoh of Japan and Lucky Goldstar in South Korea. Their goal is to get 20 percent of their equipment sales overseas by 1995. AT&T has also begun to manufacture overseas. Their first plant, making telephones, went

into Singapore in 1986. By 1989 they had produced 10 million telephones there.

Stock performance.   AT&T stock bought for $1,000 in 1980 sold for $6,338 on January 2, 1990.

American Telephone & Telegraph Company, 550 Madison Avenue, New York, NY 10022; (212) 605-5500.

2

#1 *in replaceable photoflash products*
#4 *in local telephone service*
#3 *in light bulbs*

Employees: 155,000
Sales: $17.5 billion
Profits: $1.4 billion
Founded: 1926
Headquarters: Stamford, Connecticut

Having lucked into some telephone operating companies about 70 years ago, GTE has been trying for a long time to get it right. But they never do. They went bankrupt once—and lived to tell the tale. They acquired a passel of companies—and yet remained just that, a collection of companies, a corporation with a blurred image. Ask most people what GTE is—and the likely response is a blank stare despite millions of dollars spent during the 1980s on a corporate identity campaign: "Gee! No, GTE." GTE was adopted as the corporate flag in 1971. It abbreviated General Telephone & Electronics, adopted in 1959 after General Telephone acquired Sylvania.

The heart of GTE, accounting for 75 percent of revenues, is telephone service to 15.1 million customers in 31 states. Their telephone companies operate in pockets not served by any of the ex-Bell companies. They're mostly in rural areas, although residents in the following cities have to rely on GTE: Long Beach and West Los Angeles; Tampa and St. Petersburg; Honolulu; Lexington, Kentucky; Fort Wayne, Indiana; and Erie, Pennsylvania.

Complaints about GTE service have been rampant. In southern California, their biggest market, their reputation was so bad people avoided renting an apartment or office in any area GTE served. During the 1980s GTE's service improved and customer complaints declined, but in 1989 California's Public Utility Commission ordered them to reduce static on their lines by 30 percent in the next three years. Even when it comes to making money, GTE lags. Their earnings record is erratic, and nearly all the Baby Bells run rings around them when it comes to squeezing profits from sales.

In 1990 they reached an agreement to merge with Atlanta–based Contel to create a company that would be number one in local telephone service and number two in cellular phones.

History. Founder Sigurd Odegard, owner of a small Wisconsin phone company, decided during a vacation to southern California he'd like to buy a small, independent telephone company in Long Beach. He set up Associated Telephone Utilities and was soon gobbling up other independent phone companies. During the depression, Odegard's company went broke and was reorganized under bankruptcy laws as General Telephone.

In the 1950s, they bought Automatic Electric Company, a telephone equipment manufacturer, and in 1958 merged with Sylvania, a large electronics company. The two buys gave GTE the factories and know-how to make the electronic switching systems a phone company needs.

After AT&T's monopoly on long-distance service was broken up, GTE bought Sprint from Southern Pacific Railroad in 1983. Sprint captured 5 percent of the long-distance toll market, third behind MCI's 8 percent, but GTE didn't know how to handle this success. They signed up so many customers they didn't have enough lines to handle the traffic—and so they began leasing lines from AT&T, which charged them a pretty penny. In addition, they didn't have a billing system to deal properly with so many customers. Sprint was soon throwing off losses of $500 to $600 million a year, and that was enough for GTE. They sold Sprint to a company that knew how to run this business. Kansas City–based United Telecommunications was soon making potfuls of money on Sprint service, so much so that they planned in 1990 to change their name to Sprint.

In 1989 GTE also moved to exit a business even more vital to telephone service—switching systems that route calls. GTE, in this instance, joined with AT&T in a joint venture to make these giant switches. Right now GTE owns 51 percent of the new company, AG Communication Systems, but AT&T will become 80 percent owner by 1994 and 100 percent owner by 2004. In other words, by the next century GTE telephone service will probably be much better, thanks to AT&T.

Owners and rulers. James L. ("Rocky") Johnson became CEO in 1988 at age 60. Johnson, a native Texan often described as "blunt," succeeded Theodore Brophy, a well-heeled, soft-spoken lawyer from Yale. Rocky Johnson probably won't win any popularity contests at GTE. Seven months into his new job, Johnson fired 7,000 GTE office workers (about 25 percent of the total) and another 7,000 maintenance workers. Johnson has been with GTE since he became a junior accountant at the company at 22. He told the *Los Angeles Times* in 1988 that if a line of business isn't working out, "we're going to see what the possibilities are in closing it or selling it…to somebody who can do better with it than we can." Johnson made $1.7 million in 1989.

Social responsibility. GTE's public image was not enhanced by events of the 1980s. In 1985, GTE pleaded guilty to possessing classified Pentagon documents and paid a $590,000 fine. They paid a defense consultant over $120,000 from 1979 to 1983 to give them information about the electronic weapons the Pentagon was planning to build and how much the government was willing to spend. In another government fiasco three years later, three GTE employees were accused of overcharging the U.S. Army for electronic warfare devices. That same year, the former head of GTE's Central American operations sued GTE. He claimed he was fired after refusing to bribe a Costa Rican government official. The former employee, who also accused GTE of illegal currency exchanges on the black markets in four Central American countries, was unanimously awarded $400,000 by a San Diego jury.

GTE also has a notoriously bad safety record at many plants. At GTE's subsidiary, Valenite Modco, factory workers at three U.S. tool plants developed debilitating and permanent lung scarring (fibrosis) after breathing cobalt dust. GTE promptly fired the workers, shut down the three U.S. plants and opened one in Mexicali, Mexico. In 1984, NBC's "Today" show ran a five-part Emmy Award-winning series on dying and diseased GTE Valenite workers. After the "Today" show, there were numerous other reports by Valenite workers of the lung disease, Hard Metals Disease. Workers at another GTE subsidiary, the Lenkurt plant in Albuquerque, New Mexico, were exposed to toxic chemicals resulting in neurological impairment (short-term memory loss, paralysis), cardiovascular disease, eye malformations and cancer of the female reproductive organs. GTE settled out of court in 1987 with 118 of the Lenkurt workers. GTE did, however, give $10 million in 1990 for education, making them one of the top 10 corporate contributors to education.

Global presence. GTE also provides telephone service in British Columbia and the Dominican Republic.

Stock performance. GTE stock bought for $1,000 in 1980 sold for $7,807 on January 2, 1990.

Consumer brands.

Sylvania.

GTE Corporation, One Stamford Forum, Stamford, CT 06904; (203) 965-2000.

3

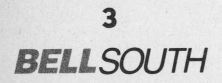

#1 *in local telephone service*

Employees: 101,200
Sales: $14 billion
Profits: $1.7 billion
Founded: 1984
Headquarters: Atlanta, Georgia

BellSouth was the biggest Baby Bell from the start of the breakup of the phone company in 1984, and they've lengthened their lead. They've also been the fastest growing Baby Bell, with sales and profits

both advancing about 50 percent during their first five years as an independent company.

Some of it was just luck. They're situated squarely in the South's booming economy, where their two operating companies, Atlanta-based Southern Bell, and Birmingham-based South Central Bell service 17 million telephone lines in nine states: Alabama, Kentucky, Louisiana, Mississippi and Tennessee (South Central); Florida, Georgia, South Carolina and North Carolina (Southern Bell). However, they have expanded from their telephone base to become one of the leading paging and cellular operators (they offer cellular phone service in 100 cities, including Chicago, New York, Los Angeles and Dallas), they publish over 900 telephone directories and they've established cellular and paging footholds in Argentina, Australia, Switzerland, Britain, Wales and France. They're the technological leader in fiber-optics cable, and they seem to have excellent labor relations. Robert Morris, a security analyst at Goldman Sachs, said, "BellSouth does almost everything right. It's been a consistent story. They never stumble." BellSouth earns considerably more money than any of the other Baby Bells, and they're the only one of the group to employ over 100,000 people. There's no confusion as to who's in charge here. John L. Clendenin, who hooked up with Illinois Bell right out of college in 1955 (he started at Swarthmore in the same class as Massachusetts Gov. Michael Dukakis but transferred to Northwestern to take journalism classes), has been chairman, president and CEO from the company's inception. He was paid $1.3 million in 1989. He presides over a board whose members include the presidents of the University of North Carolina and the University of Florida, former Federal Reserve board member Andrew F. Brimmer and Avon sales executive Phyllis Burke Davis.

BellSouth takes no chances with the press. In a bulletin issued to headquarters staff in 1989, the company advised them in the event of a call from a reporter, that they should take the caller's name and number and have someone in the media relations department return the call. BellSouthers picking up a phone and finding a reporter on the other end were told: "Do not divulge any information in any form. Do not admit, deny, confirm or acknowledge anything the reporter may say. In certain circumstances, virtually any comment may reveal information that could embarrass you and prove damaging to the company."

Stock performance. AT&T stock bought for $1,000 in 1980 was worth $8,648 in BellSouth stock on January 2, 1990.

BellSouth Corporation, 1155 Peachtree Street Northeast, Atlanta, GA 30367; (404) 249-2000.

4

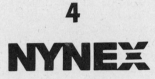

#5 *in local telephone service*

Employees: 96,400
Sales: $13.2 billion
Profits: $808 million
Founded: 1984
Headquarters: New York City, New York

When NYNEX was adopted in 1983 as the name for the holding company of New York Telephone and New England Telephone, it reminded some people of a disease. They just couldn't think which one it was. NYNEX (nigh-necks) did prove capable of raising the fever of their workers, whose numbers are just shy of 100,000. In 1986 all the Baby Bells negotiated new contracts with the Communications Workers of America, the principal union for telephone employees. The NYNEX employees were the last to settle—after an eight-day strike. The other six Baby Bells wrote profit-sharing plans into their contracts. NYNEX workers wanted none of that—they went for the traditional wage hikes geared to upward swings in the cost of living. In 1989 NYNEX workers were once again the last to settle a bitter strike against the phone companies. This time the NYNEX workers stayed out for four months, eventually winning continued company payment of the full cost of health insurance—in return for wage concessions. The walkout left bitter feelings in management and blue-collar ranks. *Business Week* quoted one union worker as saying: "If I see a problem coming, I'm not going to tell them about it."

NYNEX workers were lucky not to have a profit-sharing agreement because the company has been anemic in this area. In 1989, for example, they ranked third among the Baby Bells in revenues but last in profits.

Anyone who has to provide telephone service in New York City is asking for trouble. NYNEX serves over 11 million customers in seven Northeast states, but derives 60 percent of revenues from New York Telephone—and according to an estimate *Forbes* once made, "in lower Manhattan 0.33 percent of New York Telephone Co.'s customers generate 33 percent of that company's revenues." Aside from telephones, NYNEX has tried to become a computer maven for businesses. They design software programs for banks, insurance companies and brokerage houses, and they sell computer hardware and systems to businesses through 80 NYNEX Business Centers in 33 states (these were stores opened by IBM before they decided retailing was not for them). NYNEX also offers the ubiquitous cellular phone service.

This hard-pressed New York corporation has turned to midwesterners to help them out. NYNEX's first boss was Delbert (Bud) Staley, reared in Illinois Bell. He was paid $2.1 million in 1989, when he retired after 43 years of service. Staley was succeeded by William C. Ferguson, who spent his formative years in Michigan Bell.

Anyone unhappy with telephone service in New York and New England should not move to Gibraltar, where NYNEX stock owns 50 percent of the company operating the phone system.

Stock performance. AT&T stock bought for $1,000 in 1980 was worth $9,175 in NYNEX on January 2, 1990.

NYNEX Corporation, 335 Madison Avenue, New York, NY, 10017; (212) 370-7400.

5

⊕ **Bell Atlantic**

#2 *in local phone service*

Employees: 80,100
Sales: $11.4 billion
Profits: $1.1 billion
Founded: 1984
Headquarters: Philadelphia, Pennsylvania

They're known as the "bounciest Baby Bell" because they've moved aggressively to escape from their telephone box. As their own ads put it, "We're more than just talk." Bell Atlantic's vision is to become a leading player in the "information age," gobbledygook meaning they'd like regulations relaxed so they could become not just a carrier but also a supplier of video transmissions and computerized information services over their phone lines. During the 1980s Bell Atlantic muscled themselves into a variety of businesses (cellular phones, computer maintenance, distribution of computer parts, leasing of computers and other office equipment, real estate management) so now 25 percent of their revenue comes from non-telephone businesses, the highest percentage of any of the Baby Bells.

Not everything works out—in 1985 they retreated from computer retailing, shedding their CompuShop stores—but even so Bell Atlantic is ready to try new avenues. In their traditional phone business they also pioneered with services such as caller identification and Identa Ring, a service putting three telephone numbers on a single line, each with its own distinctive ring. While they're pushing their way into other businesses, Bell Atlantic's foundation business remains strong. They enjoy a monopoly of the local phone business in most parts of Delaware, Maryland, Virginia, West Virginia and Washington, D.C., territory covering only 3.6 percent of the U.S. land mass but holding more than 10 percent of the phones. At the end of 1989 Bell Atlantic was providing service to 17.1 million phone lines, second only to BellSouth. Telephone service is supplied by the traditional Bell operating companies: Chesapeake & Potomac, New Jersey Bell, Diamond State Telephone and Bell Company of Pennsylvania.

Bell Atlantic has used their new found freedom to become an aggressive player overseas. They lease and service computers in Western Europe and have teamed up with Ameritech to buy New Zealand's state-owned telephone company (at $2.5 billion the biggest commercial transaction in that country's history) and with U S West to build and operate a cellular phone network in Czechoslovakia. In addition, Bell Atlantic was negotiating in 1990 with various Latin American countries to buy into their phone systems.

This aggressiveness has a downside. In April 1990 Bell Atlantic agreed to pay a whopping $42 million fine to settle charges brought by the state of Pennsylvania that they'd used "deceptive techniques" to sell customers add-on services. It meant refunds of $36.4 million to 1.5 million residential customers. The fine came on the heels of an action by the U.S. Treasury Department barring Bell Atlantic from future business with the government because, said the feds, the phone company entered a misleading bid.

Bell Atlantic had one of the more visible CEOs of the phone business in Thomas E. Bolger, an AT&T career man who led the company out of the womb in 1984. Bolger retired at the end of 1988, succeeded by another career telephone man, Raymond W. Smith, who received $1.7 million in 1989. BA has only one female executive officer: Carolyn S. Burger, secretary and treasurer.

S*tock performance.* AT&T stock bought for $1,000 in 1980 was worth $9,744 in Bell Atlantic stock on January 2, 1990.

Bell Atlantic Corporation, 1600 Market Street, Philadelphia, PA 19103; (215) 963-6000.

6

AMERITECH
AMERICAN INFORMATION TECHNOLOGIES

#3 *in local telephone service*

Employees: 77,300
Sales: $10.2 billion
Profits: $1.2 billion
Founded: 1984
Headquarters: Chicago, Illinois

Despite their high-tech name, Ameritech (American Information Technologies) is the least diversified of the Baby Bells. Through their operating companies (Illinois Bell, Indiana Bell, Michigan Bell and Wisconsin Bell), they provide telephone service to 12 million customers in the Great Lakes region. They also publish telephone directories (27 billion pages in 1989), provide mobile phone service (242,000 lines) and own a company, Tigon, operating a voice-mailbox service. But phones remain Ameritech's heart and soul. In 1989 46 percent of their revenues came from local calls. In no other Baby Bell are local calls such heavy hitters. Ameritech's caution prompted one smart-aleck security analyst to characterize Ameritech as "dull" and "straightforward." But William L. Weiss, who led Ameritech out of AT&T's womb, has another way of putting it: "We have got one of the finest companies in the world in our basic telecommunications business. To the degree we take our eye off that and do too many other exotic things, we may very well begin to lose some of the thrust of our basic business." In one area—making money—Ameritech can't be faulted. Only 23 U.S. companies make more money after taxes than Ameritech. Illinois Bell used to be a training ground for AT&T presidents. But Weiss, who was still in command as the 1990s began, has nowhere else to go. He took home $1.3 million in 1989.

Stock performance. AT&T stock bought for $1,000 in 1980 was worth $9,505 in Ameritech stock on January 2, 1990.

American Information Technologies Corporation, 30 South Wacker Drive, Chicago, IL 60606; (312) 750-5000.

7

USWEST ®

#7 *in local phone service*

Employees: 70,00
Sales: $9.7 billion
Profits: $1.1 billion
Founded: 1984
Headquarters: Englewood, Colorado

Workplace

U S West is the most flamboyant of the Baby Bells. In fact, they prefer not to be known as an offspring of stodgy Ma Bell. In 1988 they became the first Baby Bell to strip *Bell* from their lexicon, changing the names of their phone companies (Mountain Bell, Northwestern Bell and Pacific Northwest Bell) to U S West Communications. They provide telephone service to 10 million customers in 14 western states. Their territory is bigger than that of any other Baby Bell, stretching from Canada to Mexico and from the Pacific Ocean to Minnesota, covering 45 percent of the Lower 48 states.

They were itching to go their own way even before they officially began life as a non-AT&T company on January 1, 1984. They were the first of the Baby Bells to choose a name (perversely omitting periods in U S), the first to select a board of directors (all from outside the company except for Chairman Jack MacAllister), the first to launch an image-building ad campaign—in which they characterized themselves as an aggressive, free-wheeling cowboy. Then they had to live up to the image. All the Baby Bells have lobbied for regulatory changes that would enable them to earn a higher return on their assets, but none has been as relentless and pugnacious in pursuing this end as U S West, so much so that the *Wall Street Journal* reported in 1987 that many people regard the company as "the bully of the Baby Bells." This characterization probably didn't bother Jack A. MacAllister, who led U S West out of AT&T land into the frontier of independence. The son of an Iowa schoolteacher who began his career with the phone company as a cable installer, MacAllister has instilled a rambunctious spirit in U S West ranks. For example, their employee newspaper, *U S West Today*, prints letters critical of the company. One such letter in 1989 (signed by the employee) expressed amazement MacAllister's pay had been hiked 40 percent (to $1.3 million). Through savings programs and pension plans, employees now own 14 percent of U S West's stock, up from 4.4 percent in mid-1985.

Like other Baby Bells, U S West has barged into other businesses, including cellular phones, lending and real estate development. In early 1989 they bought a full page in the *Wall Street Journal* to hype their BetaWest Properties unit, which they called one of North America's top 25 real estate developers, with 5 million square feet under management. A year later they announced they would sell the $1.4 billion worth of real estate BetaWest owned. U S West is big in the telephone directory business, publishing nearly 1,000 of them in 45 states, and they have moved overseas with cellular and cable TV ventures in Hong Kong, Britain, Hungary and France. They have also joined with six foreign companies to plan the construction of a fiber-optic cable to cross the Soviet Union and connect Asia with Europe.

U S West has pioneered in advancement of women and minorities. In 1989 women held two vice presidencies at corporate headquarters, 2 seats on the 14-seat board of directors and 45 percent of all positions classified as "officials and managers." Seven of 43 CEOs of U S West divisions were women. Minorities held 10.8 percent of "officials and managers" jobs. Especially notable, because it was the first effort of its kind in American business, was U S West's Accelerated Development Program for Women of Color, which targeted minority women for workshops and special training to equip them to move ahead in the company. The program was launched after minority employee groups, noting the absence of women of color in management ranks, asked the company to look at this problem. U S West recognizes and helps to fund the activities of seven employee support groups: EAGLE—for gays and lesbians; PAAN—for Pacific Asian Americans;

U S West Black Alliance—for blacks; U S West SOMOS—for Hispanics; U S West Veterans—for veterans; and Voice of Many Feathers—for native Americans.

Stock performance. AT&T stock bought for $1,000 in 1980 was worth $8,375 in U S West stock on January 2, 1990.

U S West Inc., 7800 East Orchard Road, Englewood, CO 80111; (303) 793-6500.

8

PACIFIC✸TELESIS.
Group

#6 *in local telephone service*

Employees: 68,500
Sales: $9.6 billion
Profits: $1.2 billion
Founded: 1984
Headquarters: San Francisco, California

It's hard to go wrong when you have over 13 million phones working for you in the nation's richest and most populous state. None of the Baby Bells is as dependent on one state as Pacific Telesis (PacTel) is on California, which boasts an economy on a par with Italy's or Britain's. Two metropolitan areas—Los Angeles and San Francisco—hold 62 percent of the phone lines serviced by Pacific Bell, one of PacTel's two telephone operating companies. The other, Nevada Bell, services 200,000 phone lines clustered mostly around the gambling den of Reno north of the California line. On a typical day Pac Bell will handle 57 million calls (18 million of them long distance), answer 2.3 million calls for directory assistance and mail 560,000 bills. And given that they service car-happy Los Angeles, no wonder PacTel has become one of the national leaders in cellular phone service and pagers. They also own 26 percent of a consortium bringing cellular phone service to West Germany.

When Pacific Telesis began their new life in 1984, the California connection was seen as a handicap because the state's Public Utilities Commission had been a tough regulator over the years. But the tables turned during the 1980s as PacTel became the first of the Baby Bells to wrest from the state regulatory body a new ruling removing the cap on profits routinely applied to telephone companies. To boost profits PacTel planned to lop 11,000 people from their payroll by 1995—and that's on top of cuts that nearly halved their work force between 1984 and 1990. When the Baby Bells were born in 1984, PacTel ranked near the bottom in profits. In 1989 they ranked second, behind BellSouth.

To shore up their image as a forward-looking company, PacTel has anted up big bucks for pompous and patronizing TV commercials explaining *Telesis* means "progress, intelligently planned." In addition to pruning their work force during the 1980s, PacTel tried to inculcate employees with a new culture, putting them through "leadership development" workshops designed to help them shed the "do-it-by-the-AT&T-manual" practices of the past in favor of new ways of thinking and acting based on self-reliance. Developed by management consultant Charles G. Krone, the training sessions had a dollop of eastern mysticism, raising in some people's minds the spectre of a cult, and they introduced an arcane language—"achieve closure," "path forward," "resistor," "align," "consciousness auditing"—that was quickly parodied. The program also cost a bundle, something like $30 million a year or $2.30 per customer. When the Public Utilities Commission heard about it, Pac Bell was informed they would have to eat the cost rather than pass it on to ratepayers. The program was soon disbanded.

The entire thrust at this Baby Bell has been to get new kinds of managers, not AT&T clones. In 1988, when Sam I. Ginn succeeded Donald E. Guinn (just had to drop the *u*) as CEO, a company executive told the *Wall Street Journal*: "Some of our people have not been able to cope with this new, competitive environment. The ones who can't adapt have been getting out.". Ginn's selection was a signal to the troops because even though he's an AT&T veteran, he rose to the top slot through management of nontelephone businesses. He took home $1.8 million in 1989. Pacific Telesis' heavyweight board of directors includes two former members of the Ronald Reagan cabinet: William French Smith, who was Attorney General, and William P. Clark, who was Secretary of the Interior and National Security Advisor.

All the Baby Bells have been trying to behave like entreprenuerial animals, but PacTel has led in shedding people from the payroll, causing deep resentment in the ranks. In 1990, 35 northern California employees signed a letter to Pac Bell President Philip Quigley saying top executives should "feel just a little guilty" taking down such high salaries (the three top officers each made over $1 million in 1989) when so many people were being severed. PacTel defended the high pay, pointing out it was tied to the performance of the company's stock, which soared 70 percent during 1989. Speaking in a special kind of language that has become lingua franca at PacTel, Quigley "explained" to *San Francisco Chronicle* reporter Carl T. Hall what the company was trying to do: "Many of our people were hired in a period in which they expected lifelong employment. We're in a transition now, in a hybrid state, moving from a homogenous customer-and-employee environment to more of a heterogenous customer-and-employee environment. And we're trying to get our employees to recognize this."

In 1986, as PacTel was in the midst of this transition, Caifornia's Public Utilities Commission ordered them to refund $35.6 million to customers who were sold optional services they didn't want.

Stock performance. AT&T stock bought for $1,000 in 1984 was worth $11,322 in Pacific Telesis stock on January 2, 1990.

Pacific Telesis Group, 130 Kearny Street, San Francisco, CA 94108; (415) 394-3000.

9

Southwestern Bell Corporation

#8 *in local telephone service*

Employees: 66,200
Sales: $8.7 billion
Profits: $1.1 billion
Founded: 1984
Headquarters: St. Louis, Missouri

Although they're headquartered in St. Louis, the ring that means the most to Southwestern Bell comes from Texas, where they generate nearly 60 percent of their phone revenues. Smallest of the Baby Bells, Southwestern Bell provides phone service to 7.8 million residential customers (and 1.4 million business customers) in five states—Missouri, Oklahoma, Kansas and Arkansas in addition to Texas. Their grasp of the business in that five-state territory is such that other phone companies control only 21 percent of the lines.

While they were trying to persuade regulators in those states to adopt new guidelines that would enable them to make more money in the phone business, Southwestern Bell borrowed $1.2 billion in 1987 so they could buy the *unregulated* cellular phone and paging businesses of Metromedia for $1.4 billion. That purchase made them a big player in both of those fields. Coming into the 1990s, Southwestern Bell was third nationally in the cellular phone business with 382,000 subscribers in 24 markets, including Chicago, Washington, D.C., Boston and Baltimore. And in the paging business they ranked number one, serving over 700,000 pagers in 32 markets. Physicians, detectives and drug traffickers are big users of pagers, but after discovering drug runners are about the only ones using over 1,000 pages a month, Southwestern Bell imposed a $1 charge on every page over that figure—and they also agreed to donate all revenues from this surcharge to TARGET, a nonprofit agency helping youths cope with drug addiction.

Southwestern Bell also publishes telephone directories (33.6 million copies in their five-state home base in 1988), distributes telephones and other telecommunications equipment (their Freedom Phone division sells phones in 16,000 stores and in 1988 they introduced Britain's first private pay phone), operates, as a minority partner, British and Israeli cable TV systems, and leads the industry in the deployment of Integrated Services Digital Network (ISDN) lines, a high-tech service carrying voice, data and video services over a single telephone line. They have sold customers over 17,000 ISDN lines.

Only 2 of SB's top 56 officers —Treasurer Cassandra Carr and Secretary Ann Goddard—are female. CEO Zane E. Barnes was awarded a whopping $2.5 million in stock in 1989 as a retirement present after 48 years with the company. Southwestern Bell neglected to disclose this payout to shareholders, an action which won them *Fortune*'s "1990 Proxy Obfuscation Award." Barnes was succeeded by Edward Edward Whitacre, Jr., with the company for 28 years. He made $1.5 million in 1989.

S*tock performance.* AT&T Bell stock bought for $1,000 in 1980 was worth $9,703 in Southwestern Bell stock on January 2, 1990.

Southwestern Bell, One Bell Center, St. Louis, MO 63101; (314) 235-9800.

10

MCI

#2 *in long-distance telephone service*

Employees: 19,200
Sales: $6.5 billion
Profits: $508 million
Founded: 1968
Headquarters: Washington, D.C.

MCI is the new kid on the telephone block. Cocky. But who wouldn't be after successfully challenging a powerful, government-sanctioned monopoly, AT&T? The nation's second largest long-distance

The Boston Telephone Despatch Company hired the first telephone operator, Emma M. Nutt, in 1878.

telephone company no longer has to lease their office equipment or fend off creditors with unsigned checks or wage the many lawsuits that made them known as "a law firm with an antenna on the roof." By mid-1990, MCI had 5 million customers, worldwide direct dialing and provided lines for 12 percent of all U.S. long-distance calls. In 1990, they also signed a deal to acquire Telecom USA, the fourth-ranked American long-distance company.

MCI owes most of their success to chairman and cofounder Bill McGowan. Scrappy and energetic, McGowan isn't easily put off. As an entrepreneur during the early 1960s, he once invited some navy officers to a demonstration of an ultrasonic beeper designed to repel sharks from downed aviators. The sharks ripped the device to shreds. "Never at a loss for words," reports *Newsweek*, "McGowan wondered aloud whether the Navy could use a shark aphrodisiac." His exuberant pep talks, often delivered in the speech of his working-class youth, prompt some employees to joke MCI will soon control 140 percent of the long-distance market. Breaking Ma Bell's monopoly has been his life's cause. He's fond of pointing out the cornerstone of his Washington, D.C., home, where a carving of the old Bell logo is cut in—with a crack right down the middle.

History. For want of an overcoat, a company was born. Jack Goeken, an absentminded electronics buff from Joliet, Illinois, was selling two-way radios to trucking companies to keep in touch with their drivers. He arrived in wintertime in New York minus his coat. To boost sales of his radio systems, Goeken was trying to extend their range by building a string of microwave towers from St. Louis to Chicago. He had come to New York naively hoping AT&T would let him look at a confidential report on the costs of owning and operating such a network. Since Ma Bell was then lobbying the FCC to deny Goeken an operating license, that seemed

unlikely. But when an AT&T receptionist saw Goeken come in from a winter storm wearing just a jacket, she assumed he was a Bell employee and gave him the document, with an extra copy to boot. Goeken used it to convince the FCC to grant his license, and Microwave Communications Inc., later MCI, was born.

The episode was typical. Until 1968, the good-natured but disorganized Goeken had relied mainly on credit cards, good luck and the kindness of strangers to pay his bills and keep MCI afloat. Then he met Bill McGowan, introduced as someone who could bring money and business experience to the new company.

The son of first-generation Irish immigrants, McGowan worked for Central Railroad in Wilkes-Barre, Pennsylvania, to put himself through college and then went on to Harvard Business School, a job in the film industry and a stint as a management consultant. After their first meeting in early 1968 Goeken had to borrow cash for cab fare from McGowan and Goeken's $10 check bounced. McGowan, however, knew a good idea when he saw one. He snapped up half of MCI in 1968 for $50,000 and agreed to manage the company. Goeken left the firm soon afterward. Believing that Goeken's plans were too modest, McGowan began filing licenses to build a nationwide network of towers linking 17 cities. When it came time to build MCI's microwave tower network, his roughneck crews put it up for about 40 percent less than AT&T could by using simple prefabricated materials, paying local farmers to bulldoze sites and spending the night in their trucks. To please one reluctant landowner, they even agreed to string one tower with Christmas lights.

With the microwave towers in place, MCI began offering business customers a variety of long-distance services. For instance, a Dallas company making a lot of calls to Chicago could get a special MCI hookup at rates much cheaper than the Bell system's. However, AT&T wasn't about to let a little upstart company steal customers. MCI claimed Ma Bell played unfairly by yanking the interconnections MCI needed to provide service and by undercutting their rates to drive MCI out of business. MCI filed an antitrust suit against AT&T, and the Justice Department, already seeking to break up the Bell

System, joined the fray on MCI's side in 1974. After years of wrangling, during which time MCI grew by offering a variety of long-distance services to businesses, a federal court decided against Ma Bell in 1980. The subsequent breakup of Ma Bell four years later, creating AT&T for long distance phone service and seven Baby Bells for local phone service, put MCI on an equal footing with AT&T in that no longer would MCI's customers have to dial a long sequence of code numbers to use MCI. In the ensuing competitive rush, MCI captured about 10 percent of all business and residential customers who were required to choose a primary long-distance carrier. MCI was no longer "a flea crawling up the leg of an elephant," as McGowan used to compare MCI's struggle against AT&T. They had become a baby elephant in their own right.

Owners and rulers. McGowan not only continues to run the company as chairman, but he's the biggest stockholder with almost 2 percent of the shares (worth some $150 million in mid-1989). He has slowed down a little since a heart attack and heart transplant in 1987 kept him out of the office for six months. A former workaholic, McGowan is reported to be putting in 40-hour weeks and has given up his three-pack-a-day smoking habit. He made $8.7 million in 1989. McGowan now shares the CEO's office with vice chairman V. Orville Wright. But he fully intends to work until his 70th birthday in 1998. He told *Fortune* the heart attack was "kind of thrilling" as he had "wild hallucinations and wonderful dreams, some of them very sexual."

As a place to work. McGowan wants people to work for MCI for the challenge of it, and he keeps them on their toes. Forty percent of all jobs are filled from outside, transfers are easy to obtain and managers are frequently shuffled. One frustrated former employee described MCI as "a nuthouse" with a "crazy, ferocious pace" and "no channels." That suits others just fine. The average age of employees is 30 and, according to *Business Week*, turnover is minimal.

MCI doesn't have employee gymnasiums, a credit union or Christmas parties. This is in line with McGowans' philosophy—he says, "MCI isn't going to take

care of your social and recreational needs, your entertainment. That's not our business." In fact, when one employee asked if MCI's new building would have a gym, McGowan exploded and told him if he wanted to exercise, he should "go climb a microwave tower."

Social responsibility. Although McGowan's father was a railroad union official, there's no love lost between McGowan and organized labor. He kept MCI union-free until the 1982 acquisition of Western Union International (WUI) brought with it a contingent of Teamsters. In 1984, a 97-day walkout at WUI over wages and pensions grew bitter after MCI started hiring permanent replacements and was settled only after protracted negotiations. As part of cost-cutting in late 1986, MCI shut down a Southfield, Michigan, branch with 450 workers on payroll, some 200 of whom had joined a union-organization drive led by the Communications Workers of America.

Global presence. MCI now has long-distance service to over 50 foreign countries, including Australia, Brazil, Canada, France, Greece, Italy and Japan.

Stock performance. MCI stock bought for $1,000 in 1980 sold for $29,102 on January 2, 1990.

MCI Communications Corporation, 1133 19th Street, NW, Washington, DC 20036; (202) 872-1600.

11

United Telecom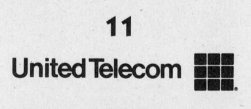

#3 *in long-distance telephone service*
#9 *in local telephone service*

Employees: 39,600
Sales: $7.5 billion
Profits: $363 million
Founded: 1899
Headquarters: Westwood, Kansas

William T. Esrey, an ex-AT&T man who pumps iron, changed the course of this company during the 1980s. And now he plans to change the name as well. United

Telecommunications previously hooked up small towns and rural villages to telephone wires. They still do that, but Esrey has entered the main ring with AT&T and MCI in the battle for the long-distance telephone market. He did that by having United Telecom buy 80 percent of US Sprint, a long-distance telephone service started by the Southern Pacific Railroad and bought by GTE in 1983. Esrey bought a 50 percent interest in Sprint in 1986, with GTE retaining the other half. In 1988, United Telecom took another 30 percent. Esrey wants to buy GTE's remaining 20 percent by the end of 1990 or early 1991— and then change the name of United Telecom to Sprint Corp.

The number three long-distance service provider (after AT&T and MCI), Sprint has about 8 percent of this $55 billion market. They're supported by a fiber-optic network they claim delivers sound of "pin drop" clarity. Sprint can also reach every dialable phone in the world. Sprint never made money for previous owners, but Esrey made the firm work for United Telecom, whose annual revenues jumped from $2.9 billion in 1986 to more than $7 billion in 1989, while the payroll expanded from 23,000 to nearly 40,000.

Sprint holds the telephone monopoly in some 3,000 communities in 19 states, the service provided by such operating companies as United Telephone of Florida (accounting for one-quarter of phone revenues), based in Altamonte Springs, Florida; Carolina Telephone & Telegraph (15 percent of revenues), based in Tarboro, North Carolina; United Telephone of Indiana, based in Warsaw, Indiana; and United Telephone of the Northwest, based in Hood River, Oregon. In 1989 the system controlled 3.7 million phone lines, less than one-third the lines serviced by Southwestern Bell, smallest Baby Bell. Sprint now brings in twice as much in revenue as all their local phone companies.

United Telecom retreated from the cellular and paging businesses in the 1980s, but they own North Supply, a wholesale distributor of telecommunications equipment; Directories America, a publisher of 260 telephone directories, and 9.3 percent of Southern New England Telephone. Only 1 of Sprint's 26 officers is a woman: M. Jeannine Strandjord, controller. Esrey was paid $1.7 million in 1989. Esrey's board includes one black, Harvard Business School professor James I. Cash, Jr.; one woman, management consultant Ruth M. Davis; Donald J. Hall of Hallmark Cards; and former U.S. ambassador to Britain, Charles H. Price II.

S*tock performance.* United Telecom stock bought for $1,000 in 1980 sold for $8,046 on January 2, 1990.

United Telecommunications, 2330 Shawnee Mission Parkway, Westwood, KS 66205; (913) 676-3000.

MONEY

BANKS

Banks sell money. When demand for it is great, the banks do well. In that sense, the 1980s were the greatest decade banks have ever seen as everybody—consumers, companies and governments—wanted to borrow more and more money. One simple indicator: in 1980 the balances on bank credit cards (Visa and Mastercard) totaled $55 billion; by 1988, $175 billion. The demand was also reflected in the loans on the books of major commercial banks. For instance, Citicorp's loans tripled during the 1980s. Of course, many of these loans—to countries in Latin America and real estate developers in Texas—were nonperforming (that is, borrowers were unable to meet the interest payments), and that caused significant losses for several big banks at decade's end.

1

CITICORP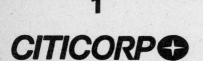

#1 *in bank loans, consumer credit cards, mortgage loans, student loans, foreign exchange trading*

Employees: 92,000
Assets: $231 billion
Profits: $498 million
Founded: 1812
Headquarters: New York City, New York

Workplace

Tough. Driving. Demonic. Citicorp has all those characteristics, at home and abroad, and undoubtedly they were banking's winner of the 1980s. Entering the decade in second place in U.S. banking, they emerged as number one. And not by an eyelash. They were twice as big as any other U.S. banking company.

Citicorp, parent of Citibank, is the biggest lender the U.S. has ever seen. They have customers in over 20 million American households, more than any other bank. They have issued more Visa and Mastercard credit cards than any other bank: 23 million. Plus 7 million more bearing the names Diners Club and Carte Blanche. They write more home mortgages than any other bank. They have made more student loans than any other bank. They have lent more money to Third World governments than any other bank.

U.S. banks have traditionally been restricted to one state and, in some instances, to one city, and in still other instances, to one office. The laws preventing interstate banking are coming down. But long before these barriers were lowered, Citibank pursued an aggressive strategy to become a national presence. Their main avenue was the credit card, which they issued with machine-gun rapidity to borrowers everywhere, meanwhile moving their credit card administrative offices to South Dakota to get around New York State's usury laws, which used to limit interest to 12 percent. Now they can charge nearly 20 percent interest, enabling them to run TV commercials that never mention the interest rate but convey the impression that even with over 20 million cards out there, someone at Citibank is sitting there checking transactions and letting cardholders know about any unusual activity. As the commercials say, "Not just Visa, Citibank Visa. Not just Mastercard, Citibank Mastercard." And then the commercials end with a tagline symbolizing the aggressive spirit of this company: "Because Americans want to succeed, not just survive."

History. When Broadway was still a cobblestone road lit by whale oil lamps, when the union had only 18 states, and the nation had only 88 banks, a group of New York merchants founded a new bank, City Bank of New York. For most of the 19th century the bank served the business interests of the owners. The bank almost went under in the panic of 1837, only to be rescued by the country's richest man, John Jacob Astor, who turned the firm

THE KINGS OF CREDIT

Bank	Market Share of Credit Card Debt
1. Citicorp	17%
2. Chase Manhattan	6%
3. Bank of America	5%
4. First Chicago	5%
5. Sears' Discover	4%
6. Optima	3%
7. Wells Fargo	3%
8. Manufacturers Hanover	3%
9. Bank of New York	2%
10. Maryland Bank	2%

Source: The Wall Street Journal,
4 October 1988.

over to Moses Taylor. Taylor ran the bank for the next 45 years, using the firm as a treasury for his many business interests, which included railroads, utilities and mining companies. In 1865, Taylor changed the bank's charter from a state to a national one, adopting the name, National City Bank. One of Taylor's companies was Western Union Telegraph, and when the first transatlantic cable was laid in 1866, the bank took Citibank as their cable address. Taylor's personal fortune, when he died in 1882, was assessed at $33 million. For the next nine years, the bank was run by his son-in-law, Percy Pyne. NCB was then New York City's 12th largest bank.

The seeds of Citibank's 20th century growth were planted in the Stillman era, 1891 to 1909, when James Stillman formed alliances with the period's leading industrialists—two of his daughters married sons of William Rockefeller, the brother of John D.—and turned Citibank into a prime lender to big corporations. By the time Stillman stepped down in 1909, National City was the country's largest bank. They also owned pieces of 12 other banks in New York and other cities, holdings that brought down on them the wrath of populists in Congress. National City disposed of these holdings just prior to the passage of the Federal Reserve Act of 1913, which created the Federal Reserve System, inaugurating the modern U.S. banking era.

In 1914 National City became the first U.S. national bank to open a foreign branch—in Buenos Aires—and in 1915 they became a worldwide banking empire when they bought the International Banking Corporation, with offices from London to Singapore.

City Bank was also the first "personal" banker. Until the 1920s commercial banks did most of their business with corporations. Few people had checking accounts, and individual savers went to saving banks. But in 1921 Citibank began opening new branches to attract individuals, and in 1928 became the first commercial bank to offer consumer loans. In 1961, under the guidance of Walter Wriston, who later became president, the bank invented the certificate of deposit, enabling depositors to earn a higher interest rate by locking up deposits for specified lengths of time.

In 1968 Citibank pioneered again when they created a "holding company," Citicorp, to take over ownership of the bank. Federal law barred banks from various activities (leasing, multistate consumer finance offices), but said nothing about holding companies that happened to hold a bank. Citibank grasped this way to get around these restrictions, and other banks soon followed suit, forming their own holding companies.

In the 1980s, Citicorp surged toward their goal of becoming the world's first global consumer bank, moving massively into the business of lending money to individuals. They beat other banks into the new technology of automated teller machines and thereby *doubled* their share of the deposit market in New York City. By 1989, they were lending more money to ordinary folks—to buy homes, cars and smaller purchases on credit cards—than they were to corporations. The key to their success has been the universal popularity of the credit card; in 1988 alone they issued an amazing 5 million new credit cards to customers around the world. They also developed fast financial services: If you want to buy a car in Madrid, they can approve your loan in a matter of minutes. A house loan in Germany might take up to two days, but no more.

Owners and rulers. Two-thirds of their stock is held by institutional investors

Every day computers are used to transfer over $1 trillion between financial institutions.

(pension funds, mutual funds, trust departments of other banks, insurance companies). The biggest individual shareholder on the board is John Reed, who succeeded Walter Wriston as CEO in 1984 and who has been called "America's most powerful businessman." An engineering graduate of MIT where he also got a master's in business (Citibank draws talent from places other banks don't even know about), Reed made his mark at Citibank in consumer banking. He owns 529,000 shares of stock, which represents a minuscule fraction of Citicorp's 327 million shares but was worth about $12.6 million in mid-1990. Citicorp is much more of a meritocracy than other banks—that, in fact, is their signature. One feature common to many of the senior managers is international experience. Another is youth. Three Citibankers on the board of directors in 1990—Richard S. Braddock, Michael A. Callen, Lawrence A. Small—were under 50. Reed became CEO when he was 45. The chairmen of Chevron, Kodak, General Motors, Du Pont, Boeing, and PepisCo all sit on Citicorp's board, as do the former chairmen of Union Pacific, Exxon, Xerox, Monsanto and J. C. Penney as well as the president of the Ford Foundation, the provost of MIT and a former dean of the Harvard Business School.

As a place to work.   Banks used to be known as dull places to work. Citibank changed that. They have attracted a hard-driving crew, people who relish action. "This is the only place in town where elevators are crowded at 11:30 at night," said one Citibanker at the New York headquarters. Two of Citicorp's 32 senior managers are women. That's a small cut but better than in other banks. Pamela Flaherty is the top human resources executive, and Nancy S. Newcombe is chief financial officer. She was named to this post in 1988 when she was 42. She had already put in 20 years at Citicorp.

Social responsibility.   They're the scrapper, not one to turn the other cheek.

They're recognized as the leader of the banking industry, not just because of their size but their innovations. They led the way with automatic teller machines. They crusaded against regulations preventing banks from operating across state borders and competing against brokerage houses. After Brazil stopped paying interest on its loans in 1987, Citicorp increased their reserves for possible loan losses by $3 billion. And after Citicorp acted, the other big money center banks followed in lockstep. In 1989, after Ecuador had gone for two years without paying interest on its loans, Citibank went to the bank account Ecuador had with Citibank—and seized $80 million. In 1990, after AT&T introduced their Universal credit card, Citibank began switching long-distance telephone service to MCI.

Global presence.   No one can touch them here. Although Japanese banks dominate the roster of the biggest banks in the world, that's a reflection of the high value of the yen and their position as national banks in their home country. None has the international reach of Citicorp, with 2,180 offices in 89 countries around the world. They have been at this longer than anyone, with foreigh offices dating to 1902 and a foreign exchange department started in 1897. Citibank has a presence in 67 developing nations.

Stock performance.   Citicorp stock bought for $1,000 in 1980 sold for $4,169 on January 2, 1990.

Consumer brands.

Citibank, Diners Club, Carte Blanche.

Citicorp, 399 Park Avenue, New York, NY 10043; (212) 559-0349.

2

CHASE

#2 *in banking, bank lending, consumer credit cards*

Employees: 41,600
Assets: $107.4 billion
Losses: $665 million
Founded: 1799
Headquarters: New York City, New York

Chase Manhattan is no longer David Rockefeller's bank. The youngest grandson of John D. Rockefeller left the bank in 1981 when he reached mandatory retirement age of 65. He not only retired as chairman but resigned from the board of directors as well. In the 1980s Chase Manhattan was Bill Butcher's bank. Willard C. Butcher, who joined Chase in 1947 after graduating from Brown, succeeded Rockefeller as CEO in 1980 and as chairman in 1981. He remained in command through the entire decade, a decade in which Chase suffered a serious loss of prestige and, in 1989, millions of dollars.

Solid and dull are adjectives commonly used to describe Chase Manhattan. But in the early 1980s, Chase was rocked by two financial debacles, the collapses of Penn Square Bank in Oklahoma and Drysdale Government Securities on Wall Street. At the start of the 1980s Chase ranked as the nation's third largest commercial bank, behind Bank of America and Citibank. At decade's end Chase was in second place behind Citibank, mainly because of reversals at Bank of America. The only bright spot for Chase during the 1980s was credit cards. They're now the second largest purveyor of credit cards, behind Citicorp. By 1990 Chase had 7 million pieces of Visa and Mastercard plastic in consumer's wallets—and they were carrying loans worth about $6 billion. Chase concentrated in the 1980s on being lean. They closed over 50 branches in New York City, mostly in less affluent neighborhoods. They also closed down operations in 18 countries, selling banks in Colombia,

Egypt, Belgium and the Netherlands. However, they're still in 55 countries, and overseas offices have 48 percent of Chase's deposits.

History. From their beginnings nearly two centuries ago, Chase has been as much a political as a financial institution. The Manhattan half of Chase Manhattan began in New York City in 1799 as the local water company. That year a group of civic leaders, headed by political rivals Alexander Hamilton and Aaron Burr, convinced the city council and the state legislature to authorize the creation of a private company, the Manhattan Company, to supply the city with pure water to combat an epidemic of yellow fever. But Burr, the schemer, was interested in more than just water. Unbeknownst to Hamilton, he slipped a clause into the law, authorizing the Manhattan Company to engage in other business if they had any surplus funds. What Burr had in mind was a bank to challenge the two banks Hamilton's Federalist friends operated. (Burr's duplicity fanned the fires of the Burr-Hamilton antagonism, which ended in 1804 when Burr killed Hamilton in a pistol duel in New Jersey.) Not surprisingly, the Manhattan Company almost immediately discovered the water system would not require their entire capital, and within six months the Bank of Manhattan Company opened on Wall Street.

The Chase National Bank, the other half of Chase Manhattan, was founded in New York in 1877 by a 75-year-old former schoolteacher who named the bank after Salmon P. Chase, Secretary of the Treasury under Abraham Lincoln. Albert H. Wiggin, who became president in 1911, masterminded a 20-year surge of growth and mergers that made Chase the leading lender to big industrial companies. Wiggin capped his career in 1930 by merging Chase with Equitable Trust, the nation's eighth-largest bank, owned by John D. Rockefeller, Jr., and run by his brother-in-law Winthrop Aldrich. Wiggin was made chairman of the new bank, then the world's biggest, but in 1934 he and his associates were disgraced when congressional investigators discovered they had used bank funds to speculate in Chase stock. Aldrich ended up at the helm and the Rockefellers took control, with the bank continuously identified as a lender to big business. When he lost the Republican nomination for president to Gen. Dwight D. Eisenhower in 1952, Senator Robert Taft complained: "Every Republican candidate for president since 1936 has been nominated by the Chase National Bank."

Chase merged in 1955 with the Bank of Manhattan whose 67 branches throughout New York City perfectly complemented Chase's branches in the borough of Manhattan. The chairman of the new Chase Manhattan bank was John J. McCloy, former U.S. high commissioner for occupied Germany, known on Wall Street as "the head of the Establishment." David Rockefeller became president and co-CEO in 1960 and chairman in 1969.

In 1982 Chase found themselves on the front pages a lot. In one case, they lost $146 million in loans originated by the Penn Square Bank in Oklahoma, which went bankrupt when the oil business went belly up. Chase didn't take the loss lying down. In a controversial and widely publicized move, they sued six of their own officers for $175 million claiming negligence and breach of duty. The suit was later settled out of court.

Worse for Chase's reputation was their connection with Drysdale Government Securities, a small Wall Street firm that specialized in buying and selling government treasury bonds. Chase, acting as a broker between Drysdale and various Wall Street firms, somehow didn't notice Drysdale was speculating with the millions of dollars in interest that the treasury bonds earned rather than passing the interest through Chase to Wall Street firms. When the scam was uncovered, Drysdale owed an estimated $270 million in interest payments, but had only $5 million. At first, Chase claimed they weren't responsible, an attitude that outraged Wall Streeters. An Irving Trust banker told *Newsweek*: "I can hardly think of another case where a bank has refused to pay up. Carried to its logical conclusion, Butcher should lose his Visa card." Reluctantly, Chase agreed to shell out the entire quarter-*billion* dollars worth of interest payments to prevent a collapse of the entire system. The episode hurt. Drysdale "was not followed as closely as if it had been a loan," a retired David Rockefeller admitted to *Forbes* in 1983.

After these disasters, Chase not only got leaner but meaner. "The troops understand what went wrong, and they're on guard," Thomas G. Labrecque, Bill Butcher's heir apparent, told *Business Week* in 1983. Chase clamped down with some of the tightest internal controls in banking, amounting to a system of double auditing.

Owners and rulers. The only Rockefeller link on the Chase board is Richard W. Lyman, president of the Rockefeller Foundation. The Rockefellers are also no longer the biggest shareholders. In 1990 the largest stockholders were two institutions—FMR Corp. with 9.3 percent, and S. C. Bernstein and Co. with 5.5 percent of the shares. Butcher was the largest single holder on the board, with 200,000 shares, worth about $8 million at the start of 1990, when he was approaching retirement. Butcher has his political involvements, too, serving as a trustee and at one time as chairman of the conservative think tank American Enterprise Institute. Slated to succeed him in October 1990 was Villanova graduate Labrecque, another career banker at Chase. Labrecque joined the bank as a management trainee in 1964. He made $1.5 million in 1989.

Global presence. Not as strong as under David Rockefeller, who was always gadding about the world and who once told *Wall Street Journal* reporter Julie Salamon: "If I go to make a courtesy call on the king or crown prince of Saudi Arabia, we don't particularly discuss banking business. But everyone down the line knows I've seen them, so my ability to get things done is clearly advanced by the fact that I have been to see the king." During the 1980s Chase shrunk their international operations and boosted their reserves for bad loans after two countries, Brazil and Ecuador, failed to pay interest due on their loans with Chase and other banks. The default by these two countries cost Chase $126 million after taxes in 1987. Their loss in 1989 of over $600 million resulted from bad loans in Arizona and several Third World countries.

The Chase Manhattan Corporation, 1 Chase Manhattan Plaza, New York, NY 10081; (212) 552-2222.

3

BANK OF AMERICA

#1 *in California banking*
#3 *in U.S. banking*

Employees: 61,020
Assets: $98.8 billion
Profits: $820 million
Founded: 1904
Headquarters: San Francisco, California

The first rule of banking is to avoid making bad loans. That's why the loan officer gives you such a hard time when you come in looking to borrow $2,500. However, if you ask for $250 million, your chances are probably much better. During the 1970s and 1980s Bank of America made a slew of bad big-ticket loans. They lost money lending to Greek shippers, California farmers and Texas real estate developers. They lost money issuing travelers checks in Indonesia. And, most of all, like other big money center banks, they were on the hook with shaky loans to Latin American countries. The once mighty Bank of America began the 1980s as the world's largest commercial bank. They ended the decade in third place, far behind the U.S. leader, New York's Citicorp. During this disastrous decade, the bank sold off huge chunks of assets to raise cash and nearly halved their payroll. In a humiliating retrenchment, they narrowed their focus to their home base, calling themselves a regional bank, competing with Wells Fargo and Security Pacific for California deposits and loans.

Still, Bank of America remains a banking power, especially in California, where they command at least 25 percent of the market. Trying to shore up shareholder morale in 1989, the bank presented this self-portrait: "In a typical working day, BankAmerica processes 12,100,000 checks, handles 995,000 credit and debit card transactions, completes 598,000 automated teller machine transactions, approves home loans worth $12,050,000, records 49,700 electronic funds transfers totaling $69,000,000 for clients around the world, takes in 220,000 business and 650,000 consumer deposits, prepares 534,000 statements, handles 1,112,000 pieces of mail, responds to 77,000 consumer inquiries through Teleservices centers, and redeems 3,600,000 individual travelers cheques." Such is the power of inertia.

History. It all started with a little savings bank in North Beach, hub of San Francisco's Italian neighborhood. A local fruit-and-vegetable wholesale dealer, Amadeo Peter Giannini believed San Francisco banks excluded smaller consumers from loans. So, in 1904, he set up the Bank of Italy and began to lend amounts as small as $25—often on no more collateral than his gut feeling about the debtor's intent to repay. His belief in the honesty of his clients paid off, and soon Bank of Italy was known as "The Little Fellow's Bank."

The great San Francisco earthquake of 1906 became a signal event in the bank's history. Giannini salvaged over $1 million in gold, currency and notes from the bank's vaults while raging flames from the huge fire that followed the quake were only three blocks away. He took the cash and paper to his house in the suburbs and buried the gold in his garden. While the major banks downtown could not gain access to their vaults for days after the catastrophe, Giannini set up a tent and desk on a pier and proclaimed Bank of Italy was open for business. The bank was in a marvelous position to lend money for the reconstruction of the 25,000 buildings destroyed by the quake and fire.

Giannini was, from almost the start of his career, an empire builder. In 1909, when California changed its banking laws to permit branches, Giannini immediately opened a branch in San Jose—and gradually dozens more. He bought banks all over the state, including the Bank of America of Los Angeles, which later became the banner under which all his California banks operated. And in 1928, looking beyond California and beyond the banking industry, Giannini established Transamerica as a holding company for all his business interests, which soon included insurance (Occidental Life was bought in 1930), real estate and banks in neighboring states (Oregon, Washington, Nevada and Arizona). In the late 1920s

Bank of America already ranked as the country's third largest bank behind the two New York biggies, National City (now Citicorp) and Chase. And at their peak, Transamerica had 645 banking offices that controlled 41 percent of all bank deposits and 50 percent of all loans in the West.

Attending one of his last board meetings in 1945, Giannini snapped at a vice-chairman who was reading a boring list of figures, "For God's sake, Franny, give 'em the big news!" That was the news that B of A had overtaken Chase Manhattan in assets, to become number one in the nation.

After A. P.'s death in 1949, son Mario took over and expanded the bank's operations overseas. In the 1950s, at the instigation of the big New York banks, the government forced B of A to shed their non-California and nonbanking operations, and Transamerica went their separate way. (See page 000 for Transamerica profile.) By 1970 B of A, with hundreds of California branches, was still the U.S.'s largest bank and a prime international lender as well, making them a natural target of anti–Vietnam War protesters. After a group torched a B of A branch near the University of California campus at Santa Barbara, one youth's explanation was: "Well, it was...the biggest capitalist establishment thing around." The violence rocked B of A's leaders. Chairman Louis Lundborg, in testimony before Congress, actually came out against the war, prompting newspaper headlines: "B of A Chairman—'War a Mistake.'" A year later, president A. W. ("Tom") Clausen scarcely mentioned financial news at the annual stockholders meeting, dwelling instead on the bank's "determination to aid minorities, preserve the environment...and be a catalyst for change in the 1970s."

Coming into the 1980s, Bank of America appeared to be riding high, with more assets, more deposits and higher profits than any other bank in the world. On the crest of this wave, Clausen left Bank of America to become president of the World Bank. Unfortunately, he left a legacy that would soon bring the mighty bank to their knees—a host of generous, poorly researched, risky loans. Clausen's successor, Samuel Armacost—known as a boy wonder when he took over at age 41—would spend much of the 1980s

cleaning up Clausen's mess. Losses from bad loans for the years 1980–1984 totaled a whopping $2.5 billion. Profits vanished.

Beginning in 1982, Armacost instituted sweeping changes—laying off employees, closing down branch offices. He also bought SeaFirst, Washington state's largest bank, and the Charles Schwab discount brokerage house. In the golden days of Bank of America, Giannini was famous for his benevolence, virtually guaranteeing lifetime employment for loyal workers. In 1985 Armacost issued a grim memo to managers, proclaiming that "if your subordinates aren't performing, replace them."

Armacost's turn was next. Amidst rumors Bank of America was on the verge of collapse, a desperate board of directors fired Armacost in 1986 and brought back 65-year-old Clausen, who had just retired from the World Bank. Clausen returned with a new crew culled from Wells Fargo. "These guys know how to make a buck," an executive vice president observed. The bloodletting continued. The Charles Schwab discount brokerage was sold, and Clausen axed 23,800 jobs in three years. From 1985 to 1988, Bank of America shed $27 billion in assets.

The retrenchments finally yielded profits in the late 1980s, but the company A. P. Giannini founded had changed for good.

There were various postmortems on what happened at B of A during the 1980s. Martin Mayer, a veteran observer of the banking scene, had this conclusion in the *New York Times Magazine*: "There are no black hats at Bank of America; it's just that in organizations of a certain size unforeseen problems seem to become unrecognized difficulties and then unmanageable losses. Perhaps the populists (of both parties) are right, and the time has come to resume the crusade against bigness itself."

But *Fortune* associate editor Gary Hector disagreed in the conclusion of his book, *Breaking the Bank*: "There were black hats at BankAmerica, men who sat idle for too long at the highest levels of one of the nation's best-known companies, men who accepted large salaries and tremendous responsibility for running a corporation and failed in their duties. They have gone on to other high-paying posts or retired with generous benefits. The people who paid most dearly for these mistakes are the shareholders and employees of BankAmerica, who lost their income, jobs, and, in many cases, their pride. These losses cannot be regained."

One irony of the 1980s was the attempt by First Interstate, a bank that came out of Transamerica, to take over Bank of America. It fizzled. When B of A was back on their feet, they were eyeing First Interstate.

Owners and rulers. Refugees from their San Francisco neighbor, Wells Fargo. Heading into the 1990s, the CEO and four vice chairmen—Frank Newman, Thomas Peterson, Lewis Coleman and Glenhall Taylor—had all been recruited from Wells Fargo, located just across the street in downtown San Francisco. The taciturn Clausen, back in the driver's seat, was being paid $1.5 million to hoist B of A out of the quicksand. His board of directors included nine men who had all been on the board in the 1970s, presided over the debacle in the 1980s and then summoned Clausen for an encore. In 1988 *California* magazine selected Clausen as one of the state's worst bosses, describing him as "unpredictable, autocratic, fond of both toadies and the most arcane bureaucratic routine." Gary Hector tells of a longtime bank client who described Clausen as "the only person I've ever met with a charisma bypass." Claire Giannini Hoffman, daughter of the founder, called Clausen "Der Führer." In 1990, Clausen stepped down, succeeded by Richard M. Rosenberg, who has a journalism degree from Boston's Suffolk University and spent 22 years at Wells Fargo. It's difficult to find a San Franciscan—in the business world or the press—who dislikes Dick Rosenberg. He's known particularly for his strong interest in community lending.

His first big move as CEO was taking over Western Savings and Loan of Arizona, with their $3 billion in deposits. The empire is being rebuilt. Rosenberg told *San Francisco Examiner* reporter Susan Burkhardt: "I'm absolutely convinced that what we are doing is exactly as Giannini would have it." Rosenberg made $1.3 million in 1989.

Social responsibility. As befitting their smaller size, the bank cut back their community support programs during the 1980s.

Global presence. In 1980 the bank had 400 offices in 94 countries. They're now down to 42 overseas offices, but foreign operations still accounted for 25 percent of 1988 income. They still had $18.8 billion in outstanding foreign loans, much of which was dubious Third World debt.

Stock performance. Bank of America stock bought for $1,000 in 1980 sold for $1,516 on January 2, 1990.

BankAmerica Corporation, P.O. Box 3700, San Francisco, CA 94137; (415) 622-3456.

4

J. P. Morgan & Co.

#4 *in banking*

Employees: 15,400
Assets: $89 billion
Losses: $1.3 billion
Founded: 1838
Headquarters: New York City, New York

Workplace

Morgan is one of the world's biggest and most powerful banks, but they're not the kind of bank where you pop in to get a car loan. For that matter, they don't encourage people to stop by. Morgan Guaranty Trust, J. P. Morgan's commercial banking arm, has only three U.S. offices—one at their imposing, two-story, limestone mansion on Wall Street across from the New York Stock Exchange (it's unmarked, you just have to know 23 Wall is Morgan Guaranty), the other two in midtown New York (at 5th Avenue and 44th Street and Madison Avenue and 58th Street). Opening a checking account there is difficult unless you're extremely well-heeled. And don't ask for a Visa or Mastercard credit card. They don't issue them. On the other hand, if you want to impress someone, J.P. Morgan is the way to go. No bank has more cachet.

The people who do come to see Morgan are treasurers of large corporations, finance ministers from governments around the world and very wealthy individuals. They deal in big money here. When World War I broke out, the governments of Britain and France appointed J. P. Morgan their joint U.S. financial rep and purchasing agent. In the 1980s, when Mexico found itself pressed to the wall by crushing debts owed to Morgan and other banks, Morgan came through with a refinancing plan.

Morgan is the conduit through which governments and large corporations raise huge sums of money, a business carried out on a global scale. Morgan doesn't even like to be identified as an American firm anymore. Their international business did get them in trouble in the late 1980s, however. They lost a whopping $1.3 billion in 1989—their first loss ever. Like many other big banks, Morgan made huge loans to Third World countries now unable to repay them.

Morgan is also one of the biggest players on the stock and bond markets by virtue of their big trust department. Morgan's portfolio managers invest the assets—$89 billion in 1990—of clients, which include big pension funds, universities, estates and corporations.

History. J. Pierpont Morgan, wrote E. L. Doctorow in *Ragtime*, "was that classic American hero, a man born to extreme wealth who by dint of hard work and ruthlessness multiplies the family fortune till it is out of sight. He controlled 741 directorships in 112 corporations. He had once arranged a loan to the United States Government that had saved it from bankruptcy. Moving about in private railroad cars or yachts he crossed all borders and was at home everywhere in the world. He was a monarch of the invisible, transnational kingdom of capital whose sovereignty was everywhere granted. Commanding resources that beggared royal fortunes, he was a revolutionist who left to presidents and kings their territory while he took control of their railroads and shipping lines, banks and trust companies, industrial plants and public utilities."

Morgan was not a self-made man. His father, Junius Spencer Morgan, made a fortune as a banker in the London firm that was predecessor of Morgan Grenfell. J. P. opened his own foreign exchange office in 1860, at age 24. According to Lewis Corey in *The House of Morgan*, his office grew successful not because he was a financial wizard and speculator like Andrew Carnegie and John D. Rockefeller, but because he knew how to organize and pick good partners. He believed that "men owning property should do as they like with it." What he liked to do was put together corporate monopolies. Among his creations were U.S. Steel, International Nickel, General Electric and AT&T. Morgan also liked to employ handsome young men in his bank, and to dally with pretty young women on his vacations. He was never at a loss for admirers despite an unfortunate physical characteristic: a bulbous red nose, the result of a chronic skin disease.

Pierpont's son, J. P. Morgan, Jr., took his father's place in 1913. The younger Morgan merged several public utilities into United Corporation and several food companies into Standard Brands in 1929. That same year, National Bank of Commerce of New York, founded in 1839 in a basement on Wall Street, merged into Guaranty Trust of New York. Guaranty Trust and J. P. Morgan later merged in 1959.

Owners and rulers. When Alan Greenspan was appointed chairman of the Federal Reserve in 1987, he had to resign from Morgan's board. Sitting on Morgan's board at the start of 1990 were the heads of MIT and the University of Chicago, former CEOs of Merck, IBM and Conoco, current CEOs of Tenneco, Procter & Gamble and Corning Glass. When George Shultz, Secretary of State in the Reagan cabinet, left Washington, he became chairman of Morgan's International Council, whose members included the CEOs of General Mills, Robert Bosch, Peugeot, Olivetti, Deere, Nestle, Akzo and Société Générale of Belgium. Dennis Weatherstone became chairman and CEO in January 1990, succeeding Lewis Preston. Weatherstone, a soft-spoken Englishman, began as a lowly clerk in Morgan's London branch.

As a place to work. Cushy. Morgan Guaranty pays the best salaries of any U.S. bank. The bosses get paid well, too: $2.2 million for CEO Lewis Preston in 1989. There's a free lunch every day and a profit-sharing plan.

Things are changing, however. Once, Morgan was a model of restraint and etiquette. There was an unforgiving dress code (no yellow socks); men had to wear jackets even in the bathroom; and tea was served at 4:30 daily in their racquet club. There are still free lunches, but much of Morgan's gentleman's club tradition is disappearing with the times. In August 1989, Morgan moved from staid stone headquarters at 23 Wall Street to a new $650 million, glass-and-stone tower 47 stories high at 60 Wall Street. (They still have a banking facility at 23 Wall.) In 1990, Morgan planned to cut their 15,400 work force by 10 percent to save money.

Social responsibility. Total 1989 company giving was over $9 million. They support housing and neighborhood rehabilitation programs. They gave $95,000 to AIDS research in 1988 and $65,000 to programs aiding disadvantaged young mothers with infants. Morgan offers six-month child-care leave for employees, both mothers and fathers, of newborn and newly adopted children.

Global presence. Enormous. Sixty-two percent of their loans are overseas, and over 47 percent of their revenue comes from international operations.

Stock performance. J. P. Morgan stock bought for $1,000 in 1980 sold for $6,206 on January 2, 1990.

J. P. Morgan & Co., Incorporated, 60 Wall Street, New York, NY 10015; (212) 483-2323.

5

SECURITY PACIFIC CORPORATION

#2 *in California branch banks*
#5 *in U.S. banking*

Employees: 41,000
Assets: $83.9 billion
Profits: $741 million
Founded: 1871
Headquarters: Los Angeles, California

Sometimes called Citicorp of the West, Security Pacific scored the biggest gains of the 1980s among the nation's largest banks. They nimbly avoided the pitfalls Bank of America and the big money center banks in New York and Chicago fell into. These firms were groaning under the weight of soured loans to Latin America, Texas and Oklahoma. Instead, Security Pacific expanded on a variety of other fronts, moving into banking in Oregon, Arizona, Washington and Nevada and into nonbanking activities such as leasing, insurance, new venture financing, foreign exchange trading and securities underwriting on an international scale. Entering the 1980s, Security Pacific ranked 11th in the standings of U.S. commercial banks with assets of $24.9 billion. Entering the 1990s, they ranked fifth with assets of over $83 billion. Left in the dust were Chemical, Manufacturers Hanover, First Interstate, Bankers Trust, Continental and First Chicago.

Born out of a series of intermarriages between banks in southern California, Security Pacific's oldest predecessor was the Farmer & Merchants Bank, the first incorporated bank in Los Angeles (founded in 1871). The bank's current name comes from a 1968 merger of L.A.-based Security First and San Francisco-based Pacific National Bank (founded in 1924).

Security Pacific operates California's second largest branch network (550 offices to B of A's 645), concentrated largely in southern California. During the 1980s they moved into neighboring states by buying the second largest bank in Washington (Rainier), the fourth largest bank in Oregon (Oregon Bank), the third largest bank in Arizona (Arizona Bank), the fourth largest bank in Nevada (Nevada National Bank) and northern California's Hibernia. All these banks were renamed Security Pacific. In 1990 they also added Gibraltar Savings of Beverly Hills, one of the largest S&Ls to go belly-up in the late 1980s.

Security Pacific has made their mark by behaving in unbankerly fashion. They were the first big bank with Spanish-language ATMs; they maintain public art galleries as part of their offices in Los Angeles and Costa Mesa; they introduced Japanese quality control circles; they supported a Black Officers' Support System for black employees; and they introduced incentive programs that showered people with bonuses for performing well (in 1988 bonuses were awarded to over 900 tellers in branch offices in Washington). Finally, in what may be a prelude to the future, they have established close ties with one of Japan's largest banks, Mitsui, through a series of interlocking agreements.

In mid-1990, Security Pacific pledged $2.4 billion in loans and donations over the next 10 years for low- to moderate-income housing and small and minority-owned businesses in California. This pledge to community development was the largest by any bank ever.

Leading Security Pacific through the 1980s was Richard Flamson, who became CEO in 1978 when he was 48. In 1990, Flamson designated his successor, Robert Smith, who turned 55 in 1990. Both have spent their entire careers with the bank. If you don't think this is a California institution, look at their board of directors. With the exception of two directors who came with the Rainier acquisition, they're all from the Golden State.

S*tock performance.* Security Pacific stock bought for $1,000 in 1980 sold for $5,868 on January 2, 1990.

Security Pacific Corporation, 33 South Hope Street, Los Angeles, CA 90071; (213) 345-4540.

6

CHEMICAL BANK

#6 *in banking*

Employees: 27,225
Assets: $67 billion
Losses: $482 million
Founded: 1824
Headquarters: New York City, New York

A stuffy New York bank far more used to dealing with companies than consumers, Chemical began and *ended* the 1980s as the nation's sixth largest commercial bank. That's not to say they stood still. In 1987 they made one of the biggest acquisitions in banking history, paying about $1 billion for Houston-based Texas Commerce, Texas' 3rd largest bank, the nation's 22nd largest. And they also bought Horizon Bank, New Jersey's fifth largest bank. In buying Texas Commerce,

Chemical was gambling they could turn the bank around. Like a lot of Texas banks, Commerce was burdened with a slew of bad energy and real estate loans. They had about $900 million of loans on which they were collecting zero interest. These sour loans made a nice fit with the $5 billion Chemical had out on loan to Third World governments. By the end of the 1980s Texas Commerce was still losing money, and Chemical was still not getting paid the interest Latin American debtors owed. Chemical hunkered down. They got out of leasing and processing stock certificates. They eliminated 2,000 employees.

Chemical is one of the country's oldest banks. They were founded in 1824 by a chemical company and stubbornly retained the name even though all chemical operations ceased in 1844. They even held on to the name after acquiring New York's Corn Exchange Bank in 1954. That made Chemical a major player on the streets of New York because Corn had 79 branch offices (to Chemical's 19). But Chemical, true to their heritage, was always more comfortable lending money to corporations than individuals. They're a leader in loans to mid-sized companies. Their affection for big corporate lending was demonstrated in 1969 when the Penn Central Railroad was going down the tubes. Most banks refused to lend the railroad any more money, but good old Chemical came through with a bridge loan of $50 million. Shortly thereafter Penn Central crashed into bankruptcy. Banking insiders then began to call the bank "Comical," a nickname that has stood the test of time.

S*tock performance.* Chemical stock bought for $1,000 in 1980 sold for $3,908 on January 2, 1990.

Chemical Banking Corporation, 277 Park Avenue, New York, NY 10172; (212) 310-6161.

7

MANUFACTURERS HANOVER

Employees: 21,600
Assets: $60.5 billion
Losses: $588 million
Founded: 1968
Headquarters: New York City, New York

When you lend $2.3 billion to Brazil, $1.9 billion to Mexico, $1.5 billion to Argentina, $1 billion to Venezuela and $820 million to Chile, you're asking for a lot of trouble. Manufacturers Hanover Trust—people in the banking business call them Manny Hanny—did precisely that. And they got into a lot of trouble. When Latin American countries found it difficult or impossible to meet interest payments during the 1980s and sought to refinance their loans, Manny Hanny was left holding the bag. They weren't alone, of course, but their exposure was very high relative to their size. In both Argentina and Chile, they were the largest lender. At the end of 1988 the bank had on their books $932 million of Argentine loans that were either not paying any interest or paying at a reduced rate. That nicked Manny Hanny's bottom line—profits after taxes—by $52 million. They were also one of Donald Trump's biggest lenders, and in mid-1990 had lost $4 million on the $158 million in outstanding loans they had made on the developer's casinos and other properties. During the 1980s Manny Hanny fell from fourth to seventh place in national bank standings.

An oldline New York bank, Manny Hanny was characterized by *Business Week* reporter Sarah Bartlett as follows in 1987:

"Manny Hanny, chock-full of convivial Irishmen, had long been considered a cozy place to work. Courting customers on the golf course was de rigueur, so much so, that as one analyst quips, 'the bank has the lowest handicap in New York.' Sure, there were the inevitable cliques, but consensus and committees were more the order of the day. One former employee comments that what little internal competition he was aware of focused on who would get to use the bank's boxes at Yankee and Shea Stadiums."

That culture was shattered during the turbulent 1980s. After John F. McGillicuddy took over as CEO in 1979, the bank went on a wild lending and acquisition spree. By the mid-1980s, the strategy backfired. Aside from the soft Latin American loans, there were other disasters. Manny Hanny bought C.I.T. Financial Corp., a commercial loan company, from RCA for $1.5 billion in 1983. By 1988, C.I.T. had chopped their work force by one-third, closed 35 field offices and was losing $20 million a year. C.I.T. had the bad loans to match Manny Hanny's. Chester Goss, a former C.I.T. executive, told the *Wall Street Journal*: "I spent 37 years of my life building a major financial company. Now, except for the name, you wouldn't recognize it."

Manny Hanny then went through their own bloodletting, selling off assets and dismissing 5,000 people. Said McGillicuddy: "It's a hell of a lot more fun building things than downsizing them." One of those who left was the president, John R. Torell III. In summer 1987, when Wall Street was awash with rumors about the trauma at Manny Hanny, Torell told a reporter—*Business Week*'s Sarah Bartlett—that the bank had found it difficult to retrench after making all those bad loans. "When you are on the top of the heap," he explained, "you really don't think about some of the things that you used to. I think the Greeks call it the sin of hubris." Seven months later Torell was out. McGillicuddy's heir apparent is Thomas S. Johnson, formerly president of rival Chemical Bank, who came aboard at the end of 1989. Known for his sharp tongue, Johnson was expected to continue shaking up the troops. McGillicuddy made $1.7 million in 1989.

Executives may be spending less time on the golf course these days, but Manny Hanny is still the firm of jolly jocks. Although the good old days of hosting the Westchester Golf Classic are gone, Manny Hanny is the undisputed sugar daddy of New York City sports. The firm holds a Yankees Hall of Fame Day every year. Manny Hanny sponsors the New York City Marathon, the Mets, the Giants, the Knicks, the Rangers and the Islanders. One of Manny Hanny's marketing tools is the Corporate Challenge Series—a 3.5 mile race they sponsor annually in 17 cities for corporate employees.

Although 60 percent of Manny Hanny's employees are women, they held only 9 of the 190 officer positions in 1989.

Stock performance. Manny Hanny stock bought for $1,000 in 1980 sold for $2,560 on January 2, 1990.

Manufacturers Hanover Corporation, 270 Park Avenue, New York, NY 10017; (212) 286-6000.

INSURANCE

The U.S. has over 2,200 companies selling life insurance policies. Another 3,500 companies offer property/casualty insurance (cars, homes, fire, theft). With that army of salespersons, no wonder the U.S. leads the world in insurance coverage. Insurance premiums add up. They have created financial gorillas. Prudential and Metropolitan Life both saw the amount of money they take in from annual premiums triple during the 1980s. Insurance is regulated, state by state, and arguments raged during the 1980s over the ever-escalating cost of automobile insurance. The insurance companies pleaded they were losing money writing it. Critics replied "nonsense." And toward decade's end, many insurance companies responded by pulling out of states where they complained they could not charge rates high enough to make a profit.

1

#1 *in life insurance companies*
#4 *in stock brokerages*

Employees: 69,600
Assets: $129.1 billion
Founded: 1873
Headquarters: Newark, New Jersey

Prudential likes to call themselves "rock solid." They had better be. If they went down, they would take a whole lot of the country with them. Prudential's base is life insurance—over $700 billion worth of policies—but they've become much more than a life insurance company. They're the largest health insurance company. They're the largest private owner of real estate, including the Empire State Building, Renaissance Tower in Dallas, Embarcadero Center in San Francisco, Hilton New York and Hilton Hawaiian Village in Honolulu and Gateway Center in their hometown, Newark, New Jersey. They own one of the largest real estate brokerage chains (they bought Merrill Lynch Realty in 1989). They're one of the largest players on Wall Street (through their own investments and their brokerage house, Prudential-Bache Securities). They use their money to arrange leveraged buyouts and finance new companies. They have 140 subsidiaries operating under the Prudential name, including Prudential-Bache Securities and Prudential Property and Casualty, which sells car and home insurance (the Pru was a latecomer to this field). Prudential generates over $30 billion a year in revenues. They have so many invested assets—and so much new money coming in—that every working day they have the problem of investing $100 million.

During the 1980s, Prudential's growth was remarkable. They started the decade neck-and-neck with Metropolitan Life, and now they're way ahead. Assets more than doubled, premium income nearly tripled and investment income went from $3 to $8 billion—with hardly any increase in employees (61,000 to 69,600).

In 1981 Prudential bought Bache, a Wall Street brokerage firm down on their luck. During the 1960s, Bache was second only to Merrill Lynch in the number of stockbrokers selling stocks to individual investors in 225 offices across the country. But during the ensuing decade, Bache made a series of missteps, most notably to get involved in the disastrous effort by Nelson and W. Herbert Hunt of Dallas to corner the silver market. Pru brought in George Ball, who had been president of E. F. Hutton, to build up Bache, which they renamed Prudential-Bache Securities. Ball pushed Pru-Bache into the investment banking business, hoping to grab the big fees corporate clients paid for help in raising money in buying or selling other companies.

By 1989 Pru-Bache had only managed to move to 18th place (from 35th) in the mergers and acquisitions field, and had lost money in three of the previous six years. So, Ball decided instead to make his mark by bolstering Pru-Bache's retail brokerage efforts, that is, selling stock and other investments to individuals. In 1989 Pru-Bache bought the failing Thomson McKinnon brokerage house, increasing Pru-Bache's number of brokers to 6,500. With Thomson McKinnon, Pru-Bache ranked fourth in numbers of stockbrokers, almost even with Dean Witter Reynolds,

but well behind Merrill Lynch and Shearson Lehman Hutton. Ball's push into the retail brokerage came under fire the next year, however. In an exposé in *Business Week*, Pru-Bache was said to have put considerable pressure on their brokers to sell clients various real estate investments, some of which had gone sour, causing clients to lose millions of dollars.

History. A young Yale dropout, John Fairfield Dryden, originally named this company the Widows and Orphans Friendly Society. He sold industrial insurance, low-cost policies for workers that paid off just enough money when they died to bury them, with maybe a little left over for their widows. Dryden changed the name to Prudential in 1875 to imitate a huge English insurer. At one point in their early history, cash was so tight a physician-director stayed up all night nursing a pneumonia patient who had insured herself for $500. The doctor reportedly later said, "A claim of $500 would very likely wreck the company. The way to save it was to save the patient." The patient lived.

Between 1876 and 1905, the value of industrial insurance policies in America grew from $500,000 to $2.5 billion. Industrial insurance was particularly lucrative because two-thirds of the workers who took out Prudential policies were unable to keep up payments. Prudential then pocketed the money they'd already received, not obliged to pay a cent when the policyholder died.

Dryden ran the company until 1911, continuing as president while serving in the U.S. Senate between 1902 and 1908. (One of his fellow senators was Morgan Bulkeley, head of Aetna.) The Pru's drive to the top was accomplished by bucking traditions. Beginning in 1946, they decentralized by setting up "home" offices: Chicago, Minneapolis, Boston, Houston, Los Angeles, Jacksonville, Toronto.

The old guard of the insurance business, the 33 companies in business for at least a century, command over half the industry's $1 trillion in assets.

On Pru's 20th anniversary, John Dryden commissioned the J. Walter Thompson ad agency to come up with a trademark. The rock of Gibraltar first appeared in 1896—and it's been running in every ad since.

Owners and rulers. The Prudential is a "mutual," which means they don't sell stock to the public. Rather, the owners are the people who own Prudential policies and pay Prudential premiums. So if you have Prudential insurance, you literally do own a piece of the rock. In 1987, 61-year-old Robert Beck unexpectedly resigned as CEO and chairman, after 9 years at the helm. He was replaced by 54-year-old Robert C. Winters, who has spent his entire career with the Pru, starting out as an actuary—calculating the odds of a given thing happening (such as accident or death) based on a set of characteristics (like the age and health of the insured).

As a place to work. Despite their size and clout, hardly anyone ever recommends Prudential as a good place to work.

Social responsibility. Prudential likes to think everything they do redounds to the public interest. They're proud of their social investment program, undertaken as part of an industrywide program, under which they have committed over $383 million to 88 projects since 1974, providing loans at below-market-rate interest and investing in health care and job-creating facilities. In addition, in 1977 they set up the Prudential Foundation as a philanthropic arm—and it gave grants of nearly $12 million in 1987. The foundation's major interest has been Newark, Pru's headquarters city.

The Prudential Insurance Company of America, Prudential Plaza, Newark, NJ, 07101; (201) 802-6000.

2

Metropolitan
Life Insurance Company

#2 *in life insurance companies*

Employees: 46,000
Assets: $93.7 billion
Founded: 1866
Headquarters: New York City, New York

During the 1980s, the 124-year-old insurer long known as the Old Lady of One Madison Avenue left her rocking chair and started eating everything in sight. Among her snacks were a real estate agency (Century 21), a money management firm (State Street Research and Management) and an international investment banker (10 percent of CS First Boston). By 1988 the Old Lady had gained serious poundage, weighing in with a massive $23 billion real estate portfolio, two health care subsidiaries (a health care consulting firm and a manager of health maintenance organizations, HMOs) and a British insurance company. The Met insures 45 million people and has 11,500 agents across the country.

The Met's former reputation as a stick-in-the-mud dowager was a legacy of the Eckers—Frederick, Sr. and Jr.—who dominated the place from 1929 to 1963. The Eckers were very, very cautious (and suspicious) people. They thought common stocks were too risky. They used to check how long female employees spent in the washrooms.

The Eckers stand in sharp contrast to the wheeler-dealer who founded the Met during the Civil War. Simeon Draper had the harebrained idea that with his extensive political and military contacts, his National Union Life and Limb Company could capture the market for insuring Yankee soldiers fighting in the Civil War. Unfortunately, soon after the company was started the Union Army suffered stunning losses, and Draper lost interest in the business. The Met finally got off the ground when they began selling industrial insurance in 1879. Industrial insurance was a capitalist version of the burial societies workers had set up among themselves to pay benefits to the wives and children of dead comrades. Noting the success of industrial insurance in England, the Met imported 500 English agents and sent them out to working-class neighborhoods to sell inexpensive policies for a few pennies a week. In the boom-and-bust cycle of the American economy in the late 19th and early 20th centuries, a high proportion of workers failed to meet their payments, which meant they couldn't collect on their policies and forfeited initial payments to Metropolitan. The Met's heavy emphasis on the lucrative industrial insurance business powered them to the top of the insurance world, a position they would not lose until the 1970s when Ecker-style cautiousness began to affect the business.

That conservatism changed under CEO John Creedon, who, during his tenure from 1983 to 1989, launched the Met's omnipresent ad campaign featuring characters from the cartoon strip "Peanuts" urging us to "Get Met—it pays." The Met's buying spree during Creedon's reign ruffled some feathers, however. A Texas hotelier charged the Met with a conflict of interest in 1988 after the big insurer threatened to foreclose on the mortgage of his hotel. He sued the Met for $7 million, claiming the Met intended to turn over the property to their Arizona-based hotel subsidiary, Doubletree (Doubletree was already managing two hotels the Met foreclosed). The Met was, the hotelier alleged, both creditor and competitor. "Do you really want to borrow money from a guy who might want to take over your business?" another hotel manager asked *Business Week*. The case was eventually settled, with the manager taking his settlement money from the Met to buy a different hotel.

On another front, the National Organization for Women (NOW) sued the Met for $20 million in 1985, charging their life insurance and disability income policies discriminate against women. Women pay less for insurance, NOW said, but their policies yield a lower value, while they pay relatively more for medical, disability and retirement income insurance.

In 1989, Creedon was succeeded by Robert Schwartz, aged 61, with the company since he was 21. A regional Boy Scout leader, Schwartz is an investment guru rather than an insurance salesman. In 1989, the Met tentatively stepped into Wall Street when they bid for the right to help a utility sell bonds. The Met lost the bid but declared they would bid again in the future.

The Met's board includes such luminaries as former U.S. Senator Russell Long, former Nixon Defense Secretary Melvin Laird, Children's Television Workshop's Joan Ganz Cooney and civil rights attorney Eleanor Holmes Norton.

Metropolitan Life Insurance Co., 1 Madison Avenue, New York, NY 10010; (212) 578-2211.

3

LIFE & CASUALTY

#3 *in property/casualty insurance*
#4 *in life/health insurance*

Employees: 45,500
Assets: $87.1 billion
Founded: 1853
Headquarters: Hartford, Connecticut

Coming into the 1980s, Aetna felt feisty enough to invest in a bunch of noninsurance businesses. They owned 32 percent of Geosource, a company that helps others find oil; 30 percent of the New England Whalers, an ice hockey team; and one-third of a telecommunications company, Satellite Business Systems (a three-way partnership with IBM and Comsat). By decade's end all these investments were wiped off their books. Back to Square One: insurance.

One of America's oldest insurance companies, Aetna writes insurance on anyone and anything—people, cars, homes, factories, ships. You name it and they'll insure it. They're the largest investor-owned insurance company, which means simply they're publicly owned (their shares trade

---

n 1989, Americans spent $89 billion on life insurance.

on the New York Stock Exchange) unlike mutual companies like Prudential and Metropolitan.

Aetna sells policies through their own sales force and through independent agents. Of 45,500 employees, over half work in the field. At the beginning of 1990, they had $280 billion of life and health insurance in force (that's the face value of all their policies). Only three other companies—Prudential, Metropolitan and Equitable—had more. They were collecting annual premiums of $8.6 billion on those policies. Their property and casualty policies bring in another $7 billion—and the biggest component here is automobile insurance. Aetna collects over $2.4 billion a year from insuring cars.

As is the case with other insurance companies, Aetna earns a considerable amount of money from investing the funds they receive from customers. About one-quarter of their revenues comes from investments. And they needed that infusion to stay above water. During the 1980s Aetna doubled revenues while profits went up by only one-third.

One of Aetna's strongest suits is group life and health insurance, the kind of coverage you get as an employee of a company. They therefore go head-to-head with such outfits as Blue Cross, Blue Shield and other providers of health and medical insurance. Pension programs are another employee benefit Aetna sells to companies. At the end of 1988 they were managing pension assets worth over $43 billion. They rank among the nation's 10 largest pension fund managers.

History.   In their early years, when a number of other insurers were going broke, Aetna survived because founder Eliphalet Bulkeley never sold more insurance than claims might force him to pay off. They also established a reputation for prompt payment of claims. The first claim was for a man who died of fever contracted in the jungles of Panama. It took nearly two months for news of his death to reach Hartford. But then, the claim was paid promptly.

Morgan Bulkeley, son of the founder, took over in 1879 and ran the firm for 43 years. Under his leadership, Aetna began writing accident insurance (1891), health insurance (1899), workmen's compensation (1902) and automobile insurance

(1907). Aetna and Morgan Bulkeley were also major factors in the history of Hartford and the state of Connecticut. While serving as president of Aetna, Bulkeley was mayor of Hartford for three terms, governor of Connecticut for four years and a U.S. Senator from Connecticut. Aetna's Hartford headquarters, with a tower similar to that of Independence Hall in Philadelphia, is the largest building of colonial design in the world.

During the 1960s, Aetna became known as a company concerned with social problems. They stirred up controversy in the late 1970s over ads criticizing juries for awarding huge amounts to plaintiffs in malpractice and accident suits. Aetna claimed these awards were responsible for the high cost of health and liability insurance premiums.

Owners and rulers.   Aetna started out the 1980s with John H. Filer as CEO, but in mid-decade, after a horrendous performance, the board of directors skipped over the battle-scarred veterans inside the company and replaced Filer with a corporate lawyer, genial James T. Lynn, who was Housing & Urban Development Secretary and director of the Office of Management & Budget during the Nixon-Ford administrations. What Lynn knew about insurance he had learned from six years on Aetna's board. Lynn made $2.1 million in 1989. Former tennis champion Arthur R. Ashe joined the board in 1982.

Social responsibility.   A leader in charitable contributions, they gave away nearly $12 million in 1989, about 2 percent of pretax profits, to about 700 beneficiaries, well above the corporate average.

Stock performance.   Aetna stock bought for $1,000 in 1980 sold for $3,012 on January 2, 1990.

Aetna Life & Casualty Company, 151 Farmington Avenue, Hartford, CT 06156; (203) 273-0123.

4

#7 *in life and health insurance*

#11 *in property and casualty insurance*

Employees: 48,600
Assets: $57.8 billion
Founded: 1792 (INA);
1865 (Connecticut General)
Headquarters: Philadelphia, Pennsylvania

The largest merger in the history of the insurance industry was hailed at the time as a "marriage made in heaven," bringing together a company strong in life and health insurance (Connecticut General) with one strong in property and casualty insurance (INA). That was 1982. A few years later, the marriage was on the rocks. Although CIGNA headquarters was in Philadelphia, where INA had been based, the company was Connecticut General-ized, with nearly all the top posts going to their people.

Even more traumatic was the 1985 disclosure, "Oops, we didn't realize these claims were going to be so high." The INA wing of the company had apparently miscalculated how much exposure they had in asbestos claims and a bunch of other areas—automobiles, workers' compensation, liability coverage for businesses, for example—and so they had to beef up reserves by a whopping $1.2 billion, throwing the whole company into the red to the tune of $733 million for 1985. The announcement stunned the industry—and Wall Streeters who follow the industry—because it came out of the blue.

CIGNA recovered from this disaster, heading into the 1990s with revenues approaching $20 billion. They are, after Aetna Life, the second largest stockholder-owned insurance company. (They also own 14 percent of Paine Webber, one of the largest stockbrokers.) CIGNA has carved out a place as a leader in what's called "managed health care," which involves prepaid medical insurance hooked into a system where costs are controlled either through a health maintenance orga-nization (HMO) or by a network of "preferred" providers (doctors and hospitals) who agree to charge CIGNA patients less than they charge regular patients. They're pitching this business hard to companies hit by rising health costs. If more and more companies opt for this kind of medical plan, CIGNA is sitting pretty as the early leader. In early 1990, CIGNA agreed to buy Equicor-Equitable HCA Corp. for $777 million, to establish themselves as the largest major provider of group health insurance. A few months later, they decided to pull out of the car and personal liability insurance businesses as part of their plan to become largely a commercial insurer, rather than insuring individuals.

The INA-CG merger brought under one roof two of America's oldest insurance writers. INA, an abbreviation of Insurance Company of North America, was founded in 1792 by a group of prominent Philadelphians meeting in Independence Hall, where the Declaration of Independence had been signed 16 years earlier. Their first policy insured a sea captain sailing from Philadelphia to London against piracy. After the San Francisco earthquake of 1906, INA paid out $4.7 million in claims. Connecticut General was founded in 1865. They pioneered in group life and health insurance.

The trauma of the 1980s ended with the passing of the old guard. Wilson H. Taylor became CEO in 1988 when he was 43. He joined Connecticut General in 1964.

CIGNA has more of an international presence than most U.S. insurance companies. Of their $17.8 billion of revenues in 1988, $2.3 billion came from abroad.

S*tock performance.* CIGNA stock bought for $1,000 in 1980 sold for $2,736 on January 2, 1990.

CIGNA Corporation, 1 Liberty Place, Philadelphia, PA 19192; (215) 523-4000.

5

The EQUITABLE
Financial Companies

#3 *in life insurance*

Employees: 23,000
Assets: $52.5 billion
Losses: $28.7 million
Founded: 1858
Headquarters: New York City, New York

MAMMOTH MALPRACTICE AWARDS

Year	Average Award	Largest Award	Number of Million Dollar Awards
1983	$887,938	$25.0 million	69
1984	$640,619	$27.6 million	71
1985	$1,179,09	$12.7 million	79
1986	$1,478,03	$15.8 million	92
1987	$924,416	$13.0 million	62
1988	$732,445	$8.1 million	54

Source: The *Wall Street Journal,*
28 April 1989.

The Equitable lost lots of money—and face—in the 1980s. They did so badly an influential investment service, Moody's, downgraded their claims-paying ability to a rating three full notches below competitors Metropolitan, Aetna and Prudential. Those ratings mean a lot in the insurance business. Their reputation among consumers and in the industry has slipp ed so much that by mid-1990 the *Wall Street Journal* reported "some agents complain they now have to spend as much time selling the company name as they do peddling Equitable's life insurance and financial products." Some critics claimed Equitable's problems stemmed from their status as a "mutual," an insurance company owned by policyholders rather than by stockholders, who are more inclined to monitor management. They said Equitable's management had a free reign until one day in 1988, when six outside directors blew the whistle on the company's chief operating officer, Leo Walsh.

Walsh's ill-fated baby was guaranteed investment contracts (GICs). Starting in the late 1970s, when inflation was high and people were reluctant to buy conventional life insurance, Walsh raked in billions from the pension funds of major corporations (like General Electric). His sales pitch: Equitable would invest their money and guarantee annual returns up to 18 percent for as long as 10 years. Equitable couldn't keep this promise. When interest rates dropped in the 1980s, Equitable couldn't pay up. By 1990 total losses on GICs approached $1 billion, and the company still had about $14 billion worth of them to honor. Nobody was sad to see Leo Walsh go when he quit in 1988. His time at Equitable has been likened to a reign of terror—between 1986 and 1988, 6 of the 16 executive vice presidents under Walsh quit or were fired.

Leo Walsh's GIC mania alone did not bring Equitable to their knees, however. They managed to lose nearly $100 million in a joint project, Equicor-Equitable HCA Corp. Other Equitable managers were swept up in the junk bond mania of the 1980s, leaving Equitable holding $2-$3 billion in the risky bonds Drexel Burnham Lambert issued. Other problems stemmed from their reaction to a New York law passed in 1983, allowing insurance companies to enter other industries. Equitable gleefully started sticking fingers into other people's pies, creating 26 new subsidiaries. When the soufflé fell, they sold off Equitable Life Leasing Corporation and the Relocation Management subsidiary and announced to the world they would stick to life insurance and related financial endeavors.

Equitable does more than push insurance. They own an array of financial service companies clustered under Equitable Investment Corporation: Equitable Capital Management, a private investment bank; Alliance Capital Management, which manages pension assets; and Equitable Real Estate, which has over $35 billion in real estate assets. In 1984, they boasted of pulling off the biggest real estate transaction in U.S. history, paying a staggering $700 million for 19 shopping centers. The Equitable Real Estate Group, created in 1985, accumulated a $27.5 billion portfolio of properties, and the Group's employees were getting rich— over 75 of them made more than $100,000. Among Equitable's holdings:

$1 billion invested in southern Florida projects, mostly malls, and over $1 billion in Manhattan real estate, including a half-ownership of Trump Tower and the city block where Equitable is headquartered.

Equitable moved into a 54-story, lime-stone-and-granite, $200 million head-quarters in 1988. Set in a seedy area of New York's Seventh Avenue, it contains lavish art works (art purchases went over budget at $7.5 million), including a monumental Roy Lichtenstein, *Mural with Blue Brushstroke*, and Thomas Hart Benton's 10-panel *America Today* murals. The headquarters also houses a branch of the Whitney Museum.

In 1984, unionized office workers at Equitable's Syracuse branch won the first-ever labor contract at Equitable. Among Equitable's concessions to the claims processors: wage increases, detachable keyboards, medical vision care for workers at video terminals, adjustable chairs and work breaks.

In 1987, 58-year-old Richard Jenrette became Equitable's chairman. Considered an outsider to the insurance business, Jenrette cofounded the brokerage house Donaldson, Lufkin & Jenrette in 1959. DLJ always served big institutions, and they were the first stock brokerage house to sell stock in their own company to the public. Equitable bought DLJ for $432 million in 1985. Equitable's chairman is traditionally a figurehead who makes speeches and lobbies in Washington. But Jenrette kept a close eye on Equitable's CEO, John Carter, who was fired in 1990—and replaced by Jenrette. Jenrette is no newcomer to the insurance business either. He financed his tuition at Harvard Business School by selling insurance for New England Mutual Life. His father was an agent for Prudential. He told the Wall Street Journal in 1987, "I grew up on premium income."

The Equitable Financial Companies, 787 Seventh Avenue, New York, NY 10019; (212) 554-2231.

6

Teachers Insurance and Annuity Association College Retirement Equities Fund

#1 *in pension funds*
#5 *in life insurance companies*

Employees: 3,500
Assets: $47.4 billion
Founded: 1918
Headquarters: New York City, New York

Social Conscience

TIAA-CREF, a cross between an insurance company and a pension fund, owns a huge chunk of America. We're talking about $17 billion worth of bonds issued by big companies and utilities, paying a fixed interest rate. Another $15 billion in mortgage loans. Over a $2.5 billion dollars in real estate holdings, including the Seagram Building on Park Avenue and One Liberty Place, Philadelphia's tallest building. Another $30 billion invested largely in stocks, such as Boeing, AMR (American Airlines), Citicorp, Rockwell International, Hewlett-Packard, Exxon, Wal-Mart, Hitachi and McDonald's.

Although virtually unknown to most Americans, TIAA-CREF is a familiar name on college campuses. They function as the pension system for teachers at colleges and universities. Other people who are employed in staff positions at these schools—administrators, researchers, athletic directors—are also covered. At the start of 1990 the TIAA-CREF pension system operated at over 4,000 schools and related research organizations and educational associations. About 1 million employees at these institutions were participating in the system, meaning they and their employers were salting away money in TIAA-CREF from every paycheck. Retirement benefits from this huge pool of money are already being paid to some 200,000 people, primarily ex-college teachers. Of this group, over 3,000 are over 90 years old; more than 50, over 100.

In 1987 1 million people, most of whom were black, Hispanic, or poor, were turned away from/by doctors or hospitals for financial reasons.

History. College teachers need to thank industrialist Andrew Carnegie for this retirement program. After selling his steel company at the turn of the century, he set about giving away his money. Communities wanting to build a library had only to write him. He eventually gave away $43 million for the construction of free public libraries. Shocked by the poor pay of college professors, Carnegie realized they could never save enough money for retirement. So he decided to do it for them. In 1905 he established the Carnegie Foundation for the Advancement of Teaching "to provide retiring pensions for the teachers of Universities, Colleges and Technical Schools" in the U.S., Canada and Newfoundland. It was funded initially with $10 million, to which Carnegie later added $5 million. Nearly 100 schools in the U.S. and Canada were enrolled in the plan. It soon became clear not even Andrew Carnegie's wealth could pension off all the college professors. That realization led, in 1918, to the formation of the Teachers Insurance and Annuity Association as a nonprofit entity to provide retirement income to teachers on a contractual basis, with the funding coming from the colleges and the teachers themselves. A key feature of the system from the start was portability; that is, a teacher can move from school to school without losing any pension benefits.

TIAA was organized in New York State under the laws applicable to insurance companies, and their funds were invested conservatively in bonds and mortgages— those instruments paying a fixed rate—so they guaranteed a certain pension level. Protests that this did not allow participants to participate in the advance of the economy (and the stock market) led in 1952 to the establishment of a companion vehicle, the College Retirement Equities Fund, that, in effect, bets on the stock market. In 1988 a third option, the CREF Money Market Fund, was offered to participants.

Owners and rulers. Clifton R. Wharton, Jr., became chairman and CEO in 1987 at age 61. A PhD in economics from the University of Chicago, Wharton is one of the few blacks to serve as CEO of a major U.S. company. TIAA-CREF trustees are an impressive bunch. Over half of them are faculty members or administrators at universities; Juanita Kreps, who served in the Carter cabinet, is one of nine female trustees. The trustees include two college presidents, a chancellor, and six deans; 19 trustees have doctorate degrees (most in finance or economics), and 7 trustees have law degrees. Trustees not in education tend to be former or current CEOs and presidents of corporations (about 12 were trustees in 1988).

Social responsibility. TIAA-CREF takes pride in being socially aware. In 1986, they voted their shares to urge companies to sign the antiapartheid Sullivan Principles or to get out of South Africa. The next year, TIAA-CREF told these companies to get out of South Africa altogether.

Teachers Insurance and Annuity Association of America, 730 Third Avenue, New York, NY 10017; (212) 490-9000.

7

#7 *in life insurance*
#9 *in property and casualty insurance:*

Employees: 36,000
Assets: $32.1 billion
Founded: 1864
Headquarters: Hartford, Connecticut

Like their Hartford neighbor, Aetna Life, Travelers will insure anyone and anything. Also like Aetna, they're a very old company. They celebrated their 125th birthday in 1989. And also like Aetna, they're an investor-owned insurance company—their shares trade on the New York Stock Exchange. Their original business was insuring people against traveling accidents—hence the name. Of course, while Travelers loves to sell insur-

OUR CONSTANT TRAVELING COMPANION.

A Travelers ad in the 1860s by cartooonist Thomas Nast who later created the Democratic Donkey and the Republican Elephant. Travelers also commissioned artists like Johann Keppler and Winslow Homer.

ance, they balk once in a while. In 1988, after California voters passed Proposition 103, mandating a rollback in car insurance rates, Travelers announced they would just as soon give up insuring automobiles in the country's most car-populous state. The state insurance commissioner forced them to continue servicing their 22,000 California policy-holders while they pursued an appeal in the courts.

Individual insurance is not as important to Travelers as it is to, say, Allstate or State Farm. In fact, they stopped selling major medical health insurance to individuals in early 1990. Travelers points out that over half of the *Fortune* 500 companies buy insurance services from them, which is a clue as to where their head is. Over half of their total premiums comes from sale of insurance and employee benefit programs to companies.

James Batterson founded Travelers on April Fools' Day in 1864. The year before, Batterson had gone before the Connecticut General Assembly and asked permission to form a company "for the purpose of insuring travelers against loss of life or personal injury while journeying by railway or steamboat." The first premium paid to Travelers was all of two cents—a

Connecticut businessman prankishly asked to be protected in case disaster befell him on a four-block walk from the post office to his house. During their first year, they sold insurance to a number of famous people, including circus-owner P. T. Barnum and writer Harriet Beecher Stowe. Another famous policyholder was Gen. George Custer; Travelers had to pay up after Custer was killed by Sioux warriors at Little Big Horn.

James Batterson was a Renaissance Man, despite an impoverished background (he had 11 siblings and his father was a poor stonecutter.) He translated the *Iliad* and *Odyssey* and was an architect for the Library of Congress, the National Capitol building, the Waldorf-Astoria Hotel in New York and two Vanderbilt mansions. He also chaired the Connecticut State Republican Committee and campaigned for Abraham Lincoln.

Travelers prides themselves on innovation. They were the first to come out with a retirement income contract in 1884 and the first to offer auto insurance in 1897. They were the first to insure aircraft in 1919, and in 1969 became the very first company to insure against accidents during space flights and moon explorations.

Insurance is a regulated industry, state by state, and Travelers has made it clear they won't do business where they can't raise rates to levels they feel are needed to earn a fair return. In 1990 they said they would stop writing car and home insurance in nine states: South Carolina, North Dakota, South Dakota, Wyoming, West Virginia, Nevada, Idaho, Arkansas and Oklahoma.

Stock performance. Traveler's stock bought for $1,000 in 1980 sold for $3,446 on January 2, 1990.

The Travelers Corporation, 1 Tower Square, Hartford, CT 06183; (203) 277-0111.

8

John Hancock

Financial Services

#9 *in life insurance companies*

Employees: 15,600
Assets: $30.9 billion
Founded: 1862
Headquarters: Boston, Massachusetts

The Boston Marathon is the oldest and most prestigious of the U.S. marathons, having been first run in 1896. But in the mid-1980s, it languished from lack of financial support. Whereas other 26-mile runs were offering cash prizes, the Boston Athletic Association was clinging to amateur status, giving winners medals and olive wreaths. To the rescue came the John Hancock Mutual Insurance Company, founded in Boston in 1862. They signed on in 1986 as sole sponsor of the Boston Marathon, promising to spend $10 million over the next 10 years, including annual prize money of $250,000. Pumping money into the Boston Marathon has made Hancock so happy they've become armchair jocks. They're now sponsoring the New York and Los Angeles Marathons, the Falmouth Road Race and the Sun Bowl (the first time a private company sponsored a college football game).

Hancock figured sports marketing was just the ticket for a company trying to reach upward-striving Americans with the news they weren't just an insurance company anymore. The move also fit in with the hard-edged advertising theme, "Real life, real answers," introduced in 1985 and continued through decade's end.

The fact is, venerable John Hancock, whose agents trudged the streets during the depression collecting premiums and passing out booklets on American history, is deemphasizing life insurance. They've set themselves apart from the rest of the life insurance industry by urging the abolition of boundaries in financial services. They believe banks should be allowed to enter the insurance business and vice versa—and they believe both banks and insurance companies should be free to compete with brokerage houses and investment bankers. They also believe federal regulation should replace state-by-state insurance.

Hancock has acted on those beliefs. Their agents now derive over 25 percent of income from noninsurance products like mutual funds. Eighty-five percent of their agents are registered to sell securities the way a stockbroker is. During the 1980s a Hancock subsidiary, John Hancock Freedom Securities, bought two regional stockbrokers, Tucker Anthony & R. L. Day of New York and Boston and Sutro & Co. of San Francisco. Hancock also formed a bank, First Signature Bank & Trust of North Hampton, New Hampshire. During the 1980s they also began offering new insurance policies—variable life and universal life—with returns linked to interest rates or the performance of investment accounts (stocks, bonds, money market funds). By 1987 these new policies accounted for 60 percent of the life insurance Hancock sold to individuals.

John Hancock might as well sing a new tune. In 1978, they were the nation's fifth largest life insurance company. By 1990 they had slipped to ninth place and were about to be passed by Northwestern Mutual.

John Hancock Financial Services, John Hancock Place, Post Office Box 111, Boston, MA 02117; (617) 572-6000.

9

Allstate®

#2 *in auto and home insurance*

Employees: 55,100
Assets: $11 billion
Founded: 1931
Headquarters: Northbrook, Illinois

It must be nice having a parent like Sears, Roebuck to bring you into the world. With sales offices in every Sears store and access to Sears' huge customer databases, Allstate Insurance today insures more than 1 out of every 10 U.S. cars and 1 out of every 10 homes, ranks among the top 10 life insurers (based on premiums collected), and is a bigger and bigger factor in writing insurance for small and medium-sized companies. By the same token, going into insurance was one of the smartest moves Sear ever made. Allstate now accounts for over half their profits. Based on revenues, Allstate ranks among the nation's 40 largest companies.

Allstate Insurance was born on a commuter train one autumn morning in 1930. Sears president, Gen. Robert E. Wood, was on his way to headquarters in Chicago, playing bridge with his buddy, insurance broker Carl Odell. In the midst of the game, Odell confided Sears could make a killing by selling auto insurance through the mail. Wood loved the idea. He convinced Sears' board of directors to finance the new company with $700,000 and dubbed the company Allstate, borrowing the brand name of Sears' tires (a name chosen in 1926 in a contest). Allstate sold policies through Sears catalogs until 1933, when they hired their first insurance agents to sell Allstate insurance in Sears stores.

For many years the only place to find an Allstate office was inside a Sears store. But now 70 percent of their sales force (4,000 agents) are in "neighborhood of-

fices," and their policies are also sold by Dean Witter, the brokerage house Sears now owns. The neighborhood salespeople are about 30 percent more productive than the agents set amidst the power tools and women's lingerie at Sears stores. But Allstate still benefits tremendously from their parent. In the late 1980s, Allstate Research & Planning Center, Sears' think tank, developed a huge database detailing various characteristics of Sears' customers—statistics like how much certain consumers earn in certain neighborhoods, what they buy and when they buy. Allstate is given access to this database—the "Household File"—and Allstate salespeople have an automatic leg up on their competitors.

Allstate's great growth came after World War II when cars began to clog American roads and crash into one another. Coming out of the war they were collecting premiums of $12 million a year from automobile owners; now they take in $8 billion—plus another $8 billion from people and businesses insuring their lives and properties. They began selling life insurance in 1957—and by 1963 they had $1 billion worth of insurance in force, the fastest growth in the history of the life insurance business. During the late 1950s they also started writing property and casualty insurance other than for automobiles.

With all their diversification into other lines, most people still regard Allstate as primarily an automobile insurer—and they've certainly been involved in all the battles on that front. For many years they had a reputation for low-cost insurance and poor claims service. They used to come in last or near the bottom of the list when *Consumer Reports* polled its readers on the service performance of car insurers.

On the other hand, they've lobbied Detroit for stronger bumpers and air bags, and they've offered discounts to safe drivers. They were among the companies that campaigned in 1988 against Proposition 103, the California initiative that mandated a rollback of automobile insurance rates, but they didn't try to pull out of the state when the proposition passed. They did, however, stop writing insurance in Massachusetts because of the state's no-fault system and regulatory climate. Allstate president Wayne Heiden told

---

B *lue Cross and Blue Shield*
cover the health-care costs of
77 million Americans.

employees: "We haven't made money in Massachusetts in a long time. We have no control over the kind of product we sell there, we have no control over the price, we have no control over who we sell it to. Very simply, it is not a free market."

Allstate Insurance Company, Allstate Plaza, North F3, Northbrook, IL 60062; (708) 402-5000.

10

#1 *in car and home insurance*

Employees: 49,000
Assets: $10.8 billion
Founded: 1922
Headquarters: Bloomington, Illinois

They insure more cars than any other American company, about one of every six on the road. They also insure more homes than any other company. And more pleasure boats. The result is a flood of money pouring into State Farm's headquarters in downstate Illinois. The torrent, in premiums and membership fees, comes to over $16 billion a year—and it's invested, mostly in bonds. On these investments State Farm makes close to $2 billion a year.

This is big money for a company that started out as a rebel against the insurance industry. They were founded in 1922 by a retired farmer, George J. Mecherle, who believed insurance companies were ripping off rural motorists by charging them the same rates for car insurance they charged motorists in Chicago and other cities. So he started State Farm, offering car insurance to farmers at rates 40 to 50 percent lower than the established companies quoted. To sell the insurance (all insurance *has* to be sold), he contracted with local chapters of the powerful Farm Bureau. They sold so many policies that in 20 years State Farm became the leading seller of car insurance, forcing the rest of

A ccording to Fortune, *corporate raider Carl Icahn's favorite* quote is: "If you want a friend, buy a dog."

the industry to charge different rates for different areas. In 1949 they set up their own agency force to sell the insurance. And now they sell in all 50 states—and in big cities, too.

State Farm began offering life insurance in 1929; home-owner and boat-owner insurance in 1935, low-value property insurance in 1962 and insurance for high-risk motorists in Texas starting in 1961.

Along the way the rebel became part of the Establishment. In 1988 State Farm fought shoulder to shoulder with other insurance industry members in a futile effort to defeat Proposition 103, the California initiative mandating a rollback in car insurance rates. After the proposition passed, State Farm posted a rate increase of 9.6 percent. They said they were losing $124 million a year insuring 2.7 million cars in the state. Harvey Rosenfield, chairman of the group that sponsored Prop. 103, said State Farm's proposed price increase was "the ultimate act of thumbing the industry's nose at the people of California."

In 1989, seven women filed suit against State Farm for discrimination against women and minorities in their hiring policies in Texas. The suit is closely patterned after one in California in 1988 in which State Farm paid $1.3 million to three female plaintiffs. Nevertheless, State Farm still has a folksy image centered around their own agents. Their longtime ad campaign always includes the refrain, "Like a good neighbor, State Farm is there." And they've apparently decided to keep the company's top positions in the family—the last three presidents have been Adlai Rust, his son Edward B. Rust and his son Edward B. Rust, Jr.

State Farm Insurance Companies, 1 State Farm Plaza, Bloomington, IL 61701; (309) 776-2311.

11

▼ Transamerica

Employees: 17,400
Assets: $7.7 billion
Founded: 1928
Headquarters: San Francisco, California

One of San Francisco's landmarks is the Transamerica Pyramid, rising 853 feet into the air at the north end of the financial district, on the edges of the city's Chinatown and North Beach districts. John Beckett, who ran Transamerica from 1960 to 1981, had the obelisklike structure built in the teeth of architectural critics and community activists who railed against it as another step in the Manhattanization of San Francisco. The building went up in 1971 and time seems to have borne out Beckett's prediction that the pyramid would make an aesthetic contribution to the city. On another of his predictions, however, the jury is still out. Beckett said: "Anybody who comes to San Francisco, at least, will know who we are." In 1971 most people had no idea who Transamerica was—and in 1990 they still hadn't the foggiest idea.

This ignorance prevails even though Transamerica popped in the mid-1980s for a $3 million, five-page, full-color, "pop-up" insert that ran as a centerfold advertisement in *Time*. When page turners reached the middle of the magazine, they came across a pop-up tableau usually found in children's books. The Pyramid popped up nine inches. The ad copy, if anyone bothered to read it, opened with this line: "Would the most innovative insurance company in America please stand up."

So, Transamerica is an insurance company? Well, not exactly. Coming into the 1990s, insurance was about half their business. The rest fell under the broad rubric, finance, which meant home equity loans, leasing of equipment like truck trailers and containers, advancing credit to appliance dealers, a real estate tax service sold to mortgage lenders, and management of mutual funds.

Of course, one reason Transamerica is hard to define is they keep changing the mix. Coming into the 1980s they looked like a conglomerate, owning United Artists (of Hollywood fame), Budget Rent-A-Car, Lyon Moving & Storage, Transamerica Airlines (a charter airline started by MGM/UA owner Kirk Kerkorian) and Delaval (a maker of steam turbines and diesel engines). All of those businesses were sold off during the decade (the airline, which Transamerica paid $90 million for in 1968, was actually shut down).

In addition, names that may have been familiar to people were wiped out in a massive effort to Transamericanize them. For example, they used to operate loan offices under the name Pacific Finance. And their main insurance company was Los Angeles–based Occidental, a leader in writing term insurance. But now everything is called Transamerica, with a little pyramid running next to the name.

The architect of the "new" Transamerica is James Harvey, who took over from Beckett in 1981 when he was 46 years old. Harvey, who joined Transamerica in 1965, remained in command throughout the 1980s. He made $1.9 million in 1989. He has a great view of San Francisco from the 24th floor of the Pyramid, which is just a few blocks away from the Bank of America building, an appropriate juxtaposition since the two companies were once joined by an umbilical cord. A. P. Giannini, founder of Bank of America, established Transamerica in 1928 as a holding company for his enterprises, which included B of A, Occidental Insurance and other banks operating in California, Oregon, Washington, Nevada and Arizona. By the 1950s, a combination of Washington, D.C., heavyweights—Congress, the Securities and Exchange Commission, and the Federal Reserve Board—had succeeded in breaking up this financial octopus. The Bank of America went their separate way. The other banks became what is now First Interstate (the country's ninth largest bank opera-

O*ver 37 million Americans have no health insurance.*

tion)—and Transamerica set out on their own erratic course.

S*tock performance.*   Transamerica stock bought for $1,000 in 1980 sold for $4,769 on January 2, 1990.

Transamerica Corporation, 600 Montgomery Street, San Francisco, CA 94111; (415) 983-4000.

FINANCIAL SERVICES

The 1980s were boom years for financial services of all kinds—witness the phenomenal growth of American Express into a smorgasbord of money-oriented activities: traveler's checks, credit cards, mutual funds, financial planning, buying and selling of stocks and bonds, raising money for companies and municipalities. Taking in $5 billion at decade's start, American Express was logging $25 billion in annual revenues by the end of the 1980s. In 1980 there were 500 mutual funds with assets totaling $100 billion. By decade's end there were over 2,000 such funds with assets well over $800 billion.

1

#1 *in credit cards, traveler's checks*
#2 *in stock brokerages*

Employees: 100,000
Sales: $23 billion
Profits: $1 billion
Founded: 1850
Headquarters: New York City, New York

American Express has perfected to a fine art the making of money by handling other people's money. This calling served them well during the Yuppie period of self-indulgence in the 1980s. Their revenues quadrupled, and their after-tax profits tripled to $1 billion, thereby placing them among a handful of financial services giants to earn so much in one year (Citicorp, Chase Manhattan and J. P. Morgan are the others).

Throughout the decade Karl Malden bellowed at us from the TV screen not to leave home without American Express traveler's checks. His warning was heeded (even though Henny Youngman said he wouldn't buy them "because they're always getting lost"). In 1988 American Express sold $24 billion worth of traveler's checks, double the 1980 level.

The key figure, though, is how many checks remain unredeemed. As long as they're not cashed, the monies already paid for the checks earn interest for American Express. In 1988, on any given day, this float of unredeemed checks averaged $4.1 billion. *Fortune* estimated traveler's checks generated revenues of $575 million for American Express in 1988, resulting in pretax profits of $120 million.

Traveler's checks are the number two profit maker at American Express. Number one is, of course, the American Express credit cards, sold with all the snob appeal the company can muster ("Membership has its privileges"). Going into the 1980s, American Express had 10 million cardholders, charging them $25 for the privilege of having the green card. Coming out of the decade, they had 32 million cardholders—and were charging them $55 for the Green Card, $75 for the Gold Card and $300 for the Platinum Card. American Express also introduced a new card during the 1980s, Optima, for people who wanted the option of paying only part of their charges, letting the rest convert into a loan. Some 4 million American Express cardholders also carry around Optima cards.

All told, people using American Express cards now charge about $100 billion worth of purchases a year on them. In addition to collecting membership fees that are double and triple what Visa and Mastercard charge, American Express discounts the bills sent in by merchants, taking an average of 3.3 percent off the top.

If you're an American Express cardholder, you know your monthly statement is always accompanied by fliers inviting you to buy various trinkets. Selling goods through the mail has become a big business for American Express, $600 million in 1988, more than is sold by the nation's biggest mail-order specialty house, L. L. Bean. American Express also uses their list of cardholders to sell subscriptions to the upscale magazines they began publishing in the 1980s: *Travel and Leisure, Food and Wine, New York Woman, L.A. Style* and *Atlanta*.

History. In 1850, Henry Wells, operator of an express delivery company in Buffalo, New York, joined forces with his two main competitors to form American Express. The new company quickly swallowed other competitors and expanded into the rapidly growing Midwest. But the board of directors balked when Wells and his vice president, William Fargo, proposed American Express extend their business to California, where the gold rush was in full swing. So the two men set up their own company: Wells, Fargo & Co. (Another partner, John Butterfield, set up the Overland Mail and Pony Express.)

Although they set up this outpost in the West, Wells and Fargo didn't leave American Express. On the contrary, they stayed in the East and took part in the internecine struggles that racked the company in its early years. By 1868 they had lost control of Wells, Fargo in San Francisco, which went on to become a famous banking house (minus the comma). Henry Wells left the company, but the Fargo family —and there were many of them—went on to rule American Express for nearly half a century. Cofounder William Fargo became a railroader, investing in the New York Central and the Northern Pacific before retiring to Buffalo. (A settlement named after him became the city of Fargo, North Dakota.) His younger brother, James C. Fargo, became president and ran American Express from 1881 to 1914, the longest tenure of any Amex CEO. He brought American Express into the business of making money on money by introducing the money order (1882) and Travelers Checques (1891). He also moved the company into Europe in the 1890s, establishing at the turn of the century the 11 Rue Scribe office in Paris that was to become a mecca for American tourists.

During World War I, the U.S. government ordered express companies to combine their operations into one big outfit—American Railway Express. It turned out to be a blessing in disguise. Shorn of their original business, American Express fell back on traveler's checks, and when American tourists flooded Europe after the war, the company prospered. So sound was their operation they cashed traveler's checks during the 1933 "Bank Holiday" when banks were closed and the nation's assets virtually frozen.

American Express kept headquarters at 65 Broadway in lower Manhattan for 101 years, then relocated to a new skyscraper in 1975 a few blocks away at One Liberty Plaza (165 Broadway). In 1985 they moved a little farther south to the new World Financial Center at the tip of Manhattan Island, where they bought one of the tower buildings for $490 million. Each move signified a bigger American Express as the company grew into a financial powerhouse. The growth was not without traumas. In 1929, American Express was acquired by the nation's third largest bank, Chase National, but they escaped with their independence in 1934 as a result of a U.S. government investigation of stock market manipulation. The probe flushed out the news that Chase's chairman, Albert H. Wiggin, had secretly engaged in various stock market shenanigans. One shining example: He profited $4 million by selling short the shares of Chase National (selling short means he was betting the stock would fall in price). Wiggin left Chase under this cloud, but his consolation prize was American Express, which he took in exchange for his Chase shares. In 1946, and again in 1949,the Rockefeller-controlled Chase bank tried to get American Express back in the fold, but they were rebuffed each time. And American Express went on to surpass Chase Manhattan Bank as a profit maker.

The 1980s brought good and bad news. The good news came with the 1984 purchase of Minneapolis-based Investors Diversified Services, the nation's largest personal financial planner through some 6,000 agents who sell a slew of IDS products: investment certificates, annuities, life insurance, mutual funds. They have 1.3 million clients and manage $47 billion worth of investments. However, two other acquisitions became messy embarrassments. One was Shearson Lehman Hutton, one of the nation's largest brokerage houses. Shearson, whose aim was to depose Merrill Lynch, got into so much trouble at the end of the 1980s that American Express had to bail them out with a massive infusion of money and new management. (see Shearson profile, p. 000). The other was the Geneva-based Trade Development Bank, acquired in 1983 from Lebanese businessman Edmond Safra, who stayed on until 1984 when he sold his Amex holdings and started all over again in the private banking business (handling the accounts of wealthy individuals).

Amex's reaction to Safra's defection is not something they're proud of. Once Safra was again a competitor, Amex people launched a smear campaign in newspapers in Latin America, Italy, France and Switzerland, linking him with illegal drug traffic, money laundering, organized crime and the Iran-Contra affair. None of the charges was ever substantiated. In 1989, American Express publicly apologized and donated $8 million to four charities of Safra's choosing (including the Anti-Defamation League of B'nai B'rith). In a letter to Safra, CEO Robinson decried the "unauthorized and shameful effort" to malign him—and executive vice president Harry Freeman resigned.

Owners and rulers. James D. Robinson III (known as Jimmy Three Sticks), whose father and grandfather ran First National Bank of Atlanta, is clearly the man in charge. He became CEO in 1977 when he was 41—and as 1990 dawned, he was still holding the reins. He was also the largest stockholder, with some 800,000 shares— only a fraction of the total (four-tenths of 1 percent) but worth about $30 million in late 1989. Robinson also made $3.5 million in 1989. Institutions (pension funds, insurance companies and the like) own over half of the shares. Former Secretary of State Henry A. Kissinger was elected to the board in 1984. His consulting company has contracts with American Express ($100,000 a year) and Shearson Lehman Hutton ($200,000 a year). Kissinger also made appearances on behalf of Shearson Lehman for which he was paid $120,000 a year.

As a place to work. Once known as a stuffy workplace, they're loosening up a bit. For one thing, they've moved a number of women into senior positions (42 percent of all managers are females). They also emerged during the 1980s as the largest employer in financial services. Their 1990 complement of 100,000 employees worldwide topped Citicorp by 15,000 and Prudential by 38,000. In 1989 they changed their bylaws to designate the company's top officer (Robinson right now) as the "chief quality officer," as well as the CEO, to impart the message that "quality is not merely a gospel to be preached but an ethic to be rigorously and continuously practiced."

Social responsibility. The debacles of the 1980s—Safra and Shearson Lehman Hutton—certainly didn't do Amex's public image much good, but they always seem to survive all manners of disaster. Robinson is the epitome of the genteel Southern aristocrat. He has a teflon surface that maintains his Boy Scout image. He is Vice Chairman of United Way's Board of Governors, and Amex contributes to a number of worthy causes—the Living With AIDS Fund in New York, the Academy Theatre of Atlanta, the Los Angeles Center for Independent Living for disabled people and the Philadelphia Coalition on Domestic Violence as well as various academies for disadvantaged high school students, who are trained for careers in financial services, travel and tourism.

Global presence. Thanks to 2,673 offices in 130 countries (Americans traveling abroad use them as mail drops) and the worldwide use of traveler's checks and credit cards, American Express is one of the world's most well known corporate names. Of the 32 million credit cards in force at the start of 1990, 10 million were held by people outside the U.S., half a million in Japan alone. Outside of the U.S., American Express is also a banker, operating the American Express Bank, primarily for rich people. They have 103 offices in 42 countries. In 1989 American Express charge cards were introduced into the Soviet Union, targeted for business people and Soviet government officials.

Stock performance. Amex stock bought for $1,000 in 1980 sold for $6,599 on January 2, 1990.

American Express Company, American Express Tower, World Financial Center, New York, NY 10285; (212) 640-2000.

2

DB The Dun & Bradstreet Corporation

#1 *in broadcast audience measurement, corporate credit ratings*

Employees: 70,500
Sales: $4.3 billion
Profits: $586 million
Founded: 1841
Headquarters: New York City, New York

Dun & Bradstreet makes a buck by collecting information and selling it. They keep tabs on 9.5 million U.S. companies to determine if they're credit-worthy. They also rate bonds and sell financial information through Moody's Investors Service. They're the largest printer of Yellow Pages telephone directories. And their A. C. Nielsen division is the arbiter of television program popularity, having enough electronic "spies" in American homes to tell which shows are being watched by the 77 million TV households.

As a company D&B has a reputation for caution and sticking to a game plan. In 1983, the company's senior executives drafted a 28-page corporate strategy document. For several years Chairman Charles Moritz, who helped write it, always carried a copy in his briefcase. For 15 years Moritz and his predecessors wooed A. C. Nielsen, the TV ratings and market research giant, before finally acquiring them in 1984. Since then, D&B has purchased over 45 other companies. But rather than branch out into new businesses, D&B makes deals they call "tuckunders." They buy companies that fit in well with existing divisions, and they sell off operations that no longer fit, however profitable. Recent castaways include six TV stations, the Official Airlines Guide, Funk & Wagnalls reference books and the publishing arm that puts out *Dun's Business Month*, now called *Business Month*. Credit reports, once their mainstay, now produce less than one-quarter of their profits. One of D&B's biggest problems is how to spend the cash hoard they've amassed over the years—about $760 million in 1989. Even here they show caution as they don't borrow money. In 1990 they didn't have a cent of long-term debt.

For all their information gathering, D&B is relatively unknown. "Typically, D&B refuses to comment," goes one *Business Week* account. Feature stories in the business press about the firm had been few and far between until 1989 when the *Wall Street Journal* published an exposé saying Dun had become more concerned with quantity than quality in their foundation business—giving credit ratings to businesses. According to the article, Dun's credit-rating employees were given extremely high quotas of companies to examine and, according to one former credit reporter, were told "not to be overly concerned about the quality" of their reports. So, information in the credit reports was either outdated or based on D&B employee "guesstimates." In addition, the *Journal* detailed how D&B had "churned" accounts, selling customers services they did not need. The company had to pay out tens of millions of dollars to settle lawsuits filed by customers who had been victimized.

History. The depression of 1837, which caused over 600 bank failures, convinced Lewis Tappan a great need existed to keep more systematic track of the creditworthiness of companies and individuals. He founded The Mercantile Agency in 1841 by inviting lawyers and others to give him information about companies with which they dealt. He got thousands of correspondents to give him reports. (D&B reporters included four future U.S. presidents—Lincoln, Grant, Cleveland and McKinley.) Banks and others interested in these reports either paid to have the agency send them report summaries on specific companies, or visited the New York office to peruse original reports in bulky sheepskin-bound ledgers. Tappan was also a social crusader, helping to found the New York Anti-Slavery Society, and he pledged his entire income of about $100,000 a year to Oberlin College and insisted the college admit blacks.

The Tappans left the company in 1849, and R. G. Dun joined the firm two years later and within a few years had renamed the company after himself. In 1857 John M. Bradstreet published the first book of commercial credit ratings. It was 110 pages long and listed 17,100 companies in nine different locations. Not to be outdone, *Dun Reference Book* appeared two years later with 519 pages and 20,268 businesses. The two publishers joined shortly thereafter and have dominated the field ever since.

Owners and rulers. The largest single shareholder is A. C. Nielsen, Jr., who received 3 percent of D&B's stock for selling A. C. Nielsen to D&B in 1984. Other acquisitions have provided D&B with top executives. Chairman Moritz, for example, started at Reuben H. Donnelley, the Yellow Pages publisher purchased in 1961. President Robert Weissman joined D&B from National CSS, a computer time-sharing firm snapped up in 1979.

Global presence. Dun & Bradstreet has recently been expanding their information network in Europe and the Far East. They now have operations in 34 different countries, including Argentina, France, Germany, Japan, Norway, the U.K. and Zimbabwe.

Stock performance. Dun & Bradstreet stock bought for $1,000 in 1980 sold for $5,687 on January 2, 1990.

The Dun & Bradstreet Corporation, 299 Park Avenue, New York, NY 10171; 212-593-6800.

INVESTMENT BANKERS

What a decade it was! The Dow Jones industrial average went to the highest level in its history; the stock market took the biggest one-day hit since 1929; Wall Street employment doubled; the Wall Street Journal celebrated its centennial; Michael Douglas played a ruthless Wall Street meglomaniac in Oliver Stone's film, Wall Street; RJR Nabisco was bought out in the biggest takeover in recorded history ($25.1 billion); high-flying investment banking house Drexel Burnham Lambert was driven out of business by the Justice Department; and hapless investment banker Sherman McCoy was the centerpiece of Tom Wolfe's first novel, The Bonfire of the Vanities, wherein his wife gallantly explains to their daughter what her daddy does—her damning analogy being: "Just imagine that a bond is a slice of cake, and you didn't bake the cake, but every time you hand somebody a slice of the cake a tiny little bit comes off, like a little crumb, and you can keep that."

1

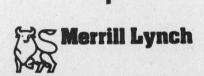 **Merrill Lynch**

#1 *in buying and selling stocks, raising money for companies, raising money for municipalities*

#2 *in mutual funds*

Employees: 41,500
Sales: $11.3 billion
Losses: $213 million
Founded: 1885
Headquarters: New York City, New York

Merrill Lynch used to pride themselves on being the stockbroker for the little guy. Now they want to serve the big guys too.

Anyone with money can buy stocks and bonds, but buying must be done through a broker. Merrill Lynch became the country's biggest broker by taking Wall Street to Main Street, servicing the small investor in offices throughout the nation. Now they have turned their attention to Wall Street itself, quickly becoming a leader in investment banking (raising money for companies, and arranging mergers and acquisitions).

The 1980s were memorable for Merrill:

◆ Their former chief, Donald Regan, left for Washington, D.C., to become Treasury Secretary and then chief of staff at the White House, where he clashed with the president's wife, Nancy Reagan. Upon returning to civilian life, he faulted his old company for becoming "fat" and "lazy," saying: "They got too used to limousines and perks. Look at the new headquarters. Mahogany paneling everywhere. The swish dining rooms. The chauffeured cars. See you in Boca Raton. See you at the Louvre. That attitude has permeated Merrill as well as the rest of Wall Street."

◆ Larry Speakes resigned as White House press secretary to become the $200,000-a-year communications chief for Merrill and then quit a year later after disclosures in his book, *Speaking Out*, that he had made up statements and attributed them to President Reagan.

◆ They set what may have been a record for a short-term trading loss, dropping $377 million in the course of three hectic days in April 1987 when Howard A. Rubin, a young trader, made some wrong bets on a newfangled, mortgage-backed security. Rubin had been hired away from Salomon Brothers in 1985 with a $1 million-a-year salary. After the 1987 debacle, he was fired (to be hired later by Bear Stearns).

◆ They moved their headquarters to the World Financial Center at the tip of Manhattan Island, where they took 25-year leases on two of the four towers, a move that turned out to be a financial disaster when costs of such basic amenities as heating and air-conditioning ran way over estimates and an overbuilt New York office building market made it difficult to sublease acres of expensive space. In early 1990 Merrill was paying rent (at $28 a square foot) on nine unoccupied floors in the South Tower.

◆ They celebrated their centennial in 1985 in very low-key fashion, issuing a varnished version of their history,

"A Legacy of Leadership," which reached very few people.

♦ They exited the real estate brokerage business they'd entered in the 1970s.

With all these conniptions, Merrill Lynch remains, because of sheer brute size, one of the most powerful forces in the economic life of Americans. They count as customers 6 million people who had, in mid-1989, assets of over $300 billion lodged with Merrill. They have 11,800 brokers (now they're called financial consultants). During 1989 they were buying and selling stocks at the rate of over $1 billion a week for their customers. They manage 47 mutual funds and 15 money market funds with combined assets of more than $100 billion. They raised $15 billion for 20 leveraged buyouts during the 1980s, making Merrill Lynch controller of such companies as Borg-Warner, Supermarkets General, Amstar, Jack Eckerd, Fruehaf and Denny's.

History. Charles Edward Merrill, according to a Merrill Lynch publication, "had the physique of a Plymouth Rock rooster, the savvy and courage of a horse trader, and the soul of a poet." As a youth in Jacksonville, Florida, Merrill made pots of money selling newspapers at the edge of the red-light district to gentlemen who wanted to cover their faces on the way out. He became a semipro baseball player and dabbled in law school and journalism before becoming a bond salesman. In 1914, 28-year-old Merrill opened his own Wall Street underwriting firm and within six months took on a partner, Edmund C. Lynch whom he met at the YMCA. (Merrill was a great promoter of grocery chains in the East, and in 1926 he went West to form, with M. B. Skaggs, the Safeway store chain that became, 50 years later, the nation's largest. Merrill's son-in-law, Robert A. Magowan, took the helm at Safeway in 1955—and today Merrill's grandson, Peter A. Magowan, heads the chain.)

Merrill Lynch made their greatest impact after World War II. They introduced the idea of salaried brokers to assure customers they were not simply interested in making a lot of trades to rack up commissions. Their biggest innovation was reaching the small investor through advertising and public relations that demystified the stock market for ordinary people. They became the largest retail

A *d agency Bozell, Jacobs, Kenyon & Eckhardt won the Merrill Lynch account after hiring a veterinary psychologist to advise them on the behavior of bulls.*

(i.e., selling to individuals) brokerage house by making an end run around the clubby Wall Streeters. As one critic said to the *New York Times*: "They're No. 1 because they never tried to become part of the Wall Street family. Their top men are mostly ex-office managers from Spokane or Buffalo or God knows where. They're brought here and they don't even try to develop relations outside the firm."

From their base as retail brokers, Merrill steadily expanded into other financial areas, notably investment banking, where they raise money for companies, municipalities and other government entities. And they were soon number one in these activities as well, thanks in great part to their distribution network. They have an army of salespersons selling for them. It's not for nothing they're known as the "Thundering Herd," although that also referred to the bulls that ran on their "Merrill Lynch is bullish on America" TV commercials. Investment banking was traditionally a relationship business going back many years (often to the right prep schools). Merrill didn't have that connection going for them. So they did it with muscle, overwhelming competitors with the sheer weight of their numbers, just as Daniel P. Tully, Merrill's president, explained to reporter Ellyn E. Spragins in 1990: "We therefore had to show municipalities and governments and institutions around the world that we were a factor."

Owners and rulers. After Donald Regan left in 1981, Roger E. Birk, age 50, became CEO and presided over three trying years for Merrill Lynch. He was succeeded by 56-year-old William A. Schreyer, who, almost immediately after assuming his post, had a heart attack and a triple-bypass operation—but it hasn't slowed him down. Schreyer, whose father worked for Merrill, is devoted to the firm: He told *Business Week*, "In high school, I wrote my senior-class paper on the New

York Stock Exchange. By the time I got into college, I knew exactly what I wanted to do. I wanted to come to Merrill Lynch." Schreyer took home $1.5 million in 1989, the same year that, for the first time in Merrill's 104-year history, they lost money. In 1985, Merrill got a new president and chief operating officer, Daniel P. Tully. The jovial Tully believes in the Optimist Creed (which includes an exhortation to "look on the sunny side of everything"), and he mounted a written version over the toilet in Merrill's executive bathroom.

Merrill's largest owners are other financial institutions: Templeton, Galbraith and Hansberger (8 percent of the stock), Batterymarch Financial (6.6 percent) and Metropolitan Life Insurance (5.1 percent).

As a place to work. It's a changing scene. Nearly 7,000 people were chopped from the payroll during the 1980s. And the number of branch offices was reduced from 510 to 470. While they moved their headquarters and trading rooms to the new World Financial Center in 1987, some 2,600 back-office people were shipped across the Hudson River to Jersey City, a decision that infuriated then Mayor of New York, Ed Koch, who said he would block Merrill Lynch from managing municipal bond offerings for the city. (The back-office people were not considered important enough to occupy such expensive space.)

Social responsibility. They live up to their Boy Scout image. While scandals swirled around a number of prestigious Wall Street firms in the 1980s, little of it adhered to Merrill Lynch. They did have a minor scandal. In 1989, stockbroker William Dillon was convicted of insider trading. He got advance copies of *Business Week* and then bought stocks favorably mentioned in the "Inside Wall Street" column. Prices of those stocks rose after the magazine appeared and Dillon sold his stocks at a profit; he made an estimated $118,000 on his scheme. In 1989 they announced a new program under which they told 250 first-grade students in 10 cities Merrill would pay for their college education if they hung in there. The program is patterned after one set up by industrialist Eugene Lang; it will cost Merrill an estimated $8 million.

Global presence. They have tried hard to position themselves as a global player, with over 500 offices in the U.S., Guam and Puerto Rico. Merrill Lynch was one of the first foreign firms to gain admission to the London and Tokyo Stock Exchanges. However, entering the 1990s, Merrill was still largely an American company, getting only 12 percent of revenues abroad and reeling from setbacks in London, Tokyo and Hong Kong.

Stock performance. Merrill Lynch stock bought for $1,000 in 1980 sold for $3,739 on January 2, 1990.

Merrill Lynch & Co., Inc., World Financial Center, New York, NY 10281; (212) 449-1000.

2

Shearson Lehman Brothers
#2 in buying and selling stocks

Employees: 42,000
Sales: $13 billion
Profits: $220 million
Founded: 1960
Headquarters: New York City, New York

What's in a name? With this outfit, you never know. A subsidiary of financial services giant, American Express, in 1989 they ranked as a stockbroker that rivaled Merrill Lynch in size. They had 600 U.S. offices, plus 22 more abroad. They had 40,000 employees and revenues over $12 billion. And yet they were a basket case. In mid-1990 they were changing their name from Shearson Lehman Hutton to Shearson Lehman Brothers, which is really not big news because they're always changing their name.

The ruins of at least a dozen Wall Street firms are buried in this company. They started out in 1960 as Carter, Berlind, Potoma & Weill. They progressed to Carter, Berlind & Weill and then—at the end of the 1960s—to Carter, Berlind, Weill & Levitt. Then they acquired Hayden Stone and changed their name to CBWL-Hayden Stone. But that was clumsy, so they dropped the CBWL (even though the people represented by those initials were the firm's principals) and adopted Hayden Stone in 1973. That year they also acquired 117-year-old brokerage house,

H. Hentz (without changing their name). In 1974 a 74-year-old firm, Shearson Hammill, was absorbed, and the name now became Shearson Hayden Stone. They ranked as wall Street's 10th largest brokerage house. That name lasted for five years until they took over prestigious, but down-on-its-heels, German-Jewish firm, Loeb Rhoades—and were renamed Shearson Loeb Rhoades. All these gyrations were orchestrated by Sandy Weill, who sold the firm to American Express in 1981 and was soon pushed out. Once again the name was changed, this time to Shearson/American Express.

In the 1980s two big Wall Street houses collapsed, their remains deposited in this maw. First, in 1984, came Lehman Brothers Kuhn Loeb, which was riven by discord. Shearson/American Express took them over and changed their name to Shearson Lehman Brothers. And in 1987 the E. F. Hutton firm was acquired for an incredible $1 billion. Hutton had pleaded guilty two years earlier to a gigantic check-kiting scheme, which meant 2,000 counts of mail and wire fraud, costing the firm $2 million in criminal fines and up to $8 million in victim compensation. Once again the name was changed, now to Shearson Lehman Hutton. That lasted for three years as the decade ended in a series of disasters for the firm. So, in 1990, American Express was preparing to buy back all the shares they'd sold to the public in 1987 (about 20 percent of the company)—and, yes, once again there was going to be a name change, or rather a reversion to an old one: Shearson Lehman Brothers.

Under the driving whip of an abrasive leader, Peter Cohen, Shearson seemed to do everything wrong during the 1980s. They were indicted for money laundering. They lost $140 million investing in a Texas bank, MCorp. They backed a hostile British bid for Pittsburgh-based Koppers, resulting in angry public officials of Pittsburgh and Pennsylvania tearing up their American Express cards as a protest. But the worst imbroglio was the 1988 battle over RJR Nabisco. Shearson, under Cohen's direction, put this company in play by devising a buyout package for Ross Johnson, RJR Nabisco's CEO, that was widely perceived as a management attempt to steal the company. Shearson

lost the deal to Kohlberg Kravis Roberts. It was a crushing defeat for Cohen, who was fired in 1990 with a severance contract worth $10 million.

To run Shearson Lehman Brothers, American Express installed their chief financial officer, Howard Clark, Jr., whose father was once Amex CEO. A Shearson insider told *Business Week*: "Amex has no confidence in Shearson's people to run the firm." According to the Value Line Investment Survey, American Express had already poured $1.5 billion into Shearson during the last two years of the decade and "may have to funnel that much over the next year or two."

A possible wild card is the big Japanese life insurance company, Nippon Life Insurance, which acquired a 13 percent stake in Shearson in 1987. Would you believe Nippon Shearson?

Stock performance. Shearson stock bought for $1,000 in 1980 sold for $479 on January 2, 1990.

Shearson Lehman Hutton, World Financial Center, American Express Tower, New York, NY 10285; (212) 298-2000.

3

SALOMON INC

Employees: 8,900
Sales: $9 billion
Profits: $470 million
Founded: 1910
Headquarters: New York City, New York

Salomon Brothers is the king of the bond traders, and they reaped a whirlwind during the 1980s. Beginning the decade as a partnership that ranked as Wall Street's fourth largest securities house, they emerged as a publicly traded corporation whose inner workings were exposed for all to see in the best-seller, *Liar's Poker*, by Michael Lewis, an ex-bond salesman at Salomon. What readers saw, through his eyes, was a scatalogical world populated by foul-mouthed, loud, vulgar screamers. Solly, as they are known on Wall Street, is the mother of all traders.

Salomon Inc., the corporate umbrella for a wide range of financial service activities (stock and bond trading, underwriting, commodities trading, foreign exchange, mergers and acquisitions), is a financial powerhouse. In 1990, when *Fortune* toted up the nation's 50 largest diversified financial companies, Salomon placed third with assets of $118 billion, exceeded only by the Federal National Mortgage Association ($124 billion) and American Express ($130 billion). In revenues ($9 billion in 1989), they ran third on Wall Street behind Shearson Lehman Hutton and Merrill Lynch.

Prior to 1980, Salomon's forte was trading bonds. In those days, this business was staid. That all changed in the 1980s when the Federal Reserve System, led by Chairman Paul Volcker, let interest rates float. Bond prices move in lockstep with interest rates—inversely. In other words, when the cost of money is high, bond prices decline; when interest rates go down, bond prices move up. As Lewis pointed out in his book, with interest rates free to fluctuate, bond prices would swing wildly: "Before Volker's speech, bonds had been conservative investments, into which investors put their savings when they didn't fancy a gamble in the stock market. After Volcker's speech, bonds became objects of speculation, a means of creating wealth rather than merely storing it. Overnight the bond market was transformed from a backwater into a casino. Turnover boomed at Salomon. Many more people were hired to handle the new business, on starting salaries of forty-eight grand."

Bonds are basically debt: They represent someone—a company, a government—borrowing money from someone else. And during the 1980s, led by the U.S. government, people, companies and governmental bodies borrowed more money than ever before. Salomon Brothers—sitting at the center of this whirlpool, matching buyer with seller and serving, in effect, as gatekeeper—made out like bandits.

Salomon, for example, invented the financial instrument known as the mortgage-backed security, which mushroomed into an enormous business during the 1980s and contributed to the downfall of many savings and loans. This security is a bond collateralized by hundreds or thousands of mortgages being paid off by home owners. Savings and loans, owners of many of these mortgages, were liberated during the 1980s to dabble in all kinds of nonsense—and they sold off mortgages to do that. Salomon was at the heart of this action. Lewis reports how he saw Salomon traders take advantage of witless S&L executives who "didn't know the mentality of the people they were up against. They didn't know the value of what they were selling. In some cases, they didn't know the terms (years of maturity, rates of interest) of their own loans... They might as well have written a check to Salomon Brothers."

Salomon's leader in the 1980s was John Gutfreund, the archetypal, cigar-stomping trader. He once said that to succeed on the Salomon trading floor, a person needed to wake up every morning "ready to bite the ass of a bear." Gutfreund also once said the partnership concept was the lifeblood of Salomon Brothers. However, in 1981, having recently remarried (to a former airline stewardess 18 years his junior), Gutfreund succeeded in disbanding the partnership by selling out to a commodities dealer, Phibro Corp., for $550 million, enabling him to extract $40 million to pursue the new social life his bride had in mind for him. Although Phibro had done the acquiring—the firm was called Phibro-Salomon—in three years Solly had cannibalized their acquisitor. In 1984, CEO David Tendler was fired, and Gutfreund ascended the throne. He discarded the Phibro name in 1986. In 1987, faced with a takeover threat from Ronald Perelman of Revlon Inc., Gutfreund responded by bringing in legendary investor Warren Buffett as a savior. In a deal that outraged many shareholders, Gutfreund arranged for Buffett to lend Salomon enough money, $700 million, to buy up their shares, thereby foiling the takeover threat. In return Buffett received a new issue of preferred stock that paid 9 percent interest, with a right to convert this stock into 13 percent of all Salomon Inc. shares. Buffet couldn't lose in the deal: He could just sit back and collect his 9 percent interest every year, or, if Salomon stock took off (which it didn't), he could convert the stock and reap a windfall. Gutfreund told Salomon's directors if they didn't approve this deal, he would quit, which occasioned this comment by Michael Lewis: "An aspect of the genius of Gutfreund was his ability to cloak his own self-interest in the guise of high principle. The two could be, on rare occasions, indistinguishable. (If there is one thing I learned on Wall Street, it's that when an investment banker starts talking about principles, he is usually defending his interest and that he rarely stakes out the high moral ground unless he believes there is gold under his campsite.)"

History.   Until 1970, Salomon was head-quartered at 60 Wall Street, site of the 1792 trade agreement that led to the founding of the New York Stock Exchange. Ironically, the firm had little to do with the wild and woolly stock market during their early history. Instead Salomon made their name on Wall Street as bond traders—a more esoteric activity dealing with smaller numbers of clients. For years they were the only Wall Street firm that maintained a New York Stock Exchange listing just so they could buy and sell certain bonds—interest-bearing debt certificates, or IOUs, sold to invest-ors by companies and governments through middlemen like Salomon.

Salomon had more humble beginnings, though.

Just past the turn of the century, Her-bert, Arthur and Percy Salomon were working for their father Ferd's business arranging bank loans for Wall Street firms. Ferd, an Orthodox Jew, wouldn't stay open on Saturdays, and in 1910 the ag-gressive brothers struck out on their own. The trio recruited Morton Hutzler, a free-lance bond trader. By the end of the 1920s, the firm was among Wall Street's promi-nent bond traders. The firm did not deal with individual investors, concentrating solely on so-called institutional invest-ors—the huge pension funds and compa-nies that buy and sell stocks, bonds and other securities in large quantities. In 1959 they started trading very large lots of stocks, called blocks, for their big clients (banks, insurance companies, etc.).

Appropriately Salomon Brothers chose the large-block business as their entry into the stock, or "equity," business. Salomon is known as a trader that will handle any deal, no matter how large. By the late 1960s, traders developed a new adjective for huge blocks of stocks bought and sold on the New York Stock Exchange:

"Salomon-sized." By the end of the 1960s, the firm was Wall Street's third-highest volume trader in stocks, behind Merrill Lynch and Bache.

Salomon used to lag far behind First Boston, Morgan Stanley and Goldman, Sachs in the highly profitable, prestigious business of underwriting the stocks and bonds issued by American's biggest com-panies issue when they needed to raise money. Much of that business derived from personal relationships going back to "old school" ties. "They have the compe-tence and the capital," Felix Rohatyn, a senior partner at Lazard Frerès, told *Busi-ness Week* in 1978. "But they may have to buy the three-piece suits."

But here, too, Salomon Brothers simply muscled their way in. Big changes on Wall Street and in the financial markets suddenly meant ties to prestigious com-panies were less important than the abil-ity to think and move with lightning speed, a Salomon forte. Seven years after his initial remarks, here was Rohatyn eat-ing his words in another *Business Week* interview: "When you are that competent and have that much capital, who needs three-piece suits?"

Owners and rulers.   Chairman and CEO John Gutfreund has dominated this com-pany to a greater extent than most Wall Street CEOs. Said Gutfreund in a recent interview: "People on the outside don't necessarily love us but I think now they respect us." In a management reorganiza-tion in 1986, Thomas W. Strauss was named vice chairman and emerged as heir apparent to Gutfreund, now in his late 50s. But control rests with investor War-ren Buffett.

As a place to work.   Winning at all cost has a price. In addition to the routine rigors of life on Wall Street—endless hours and crushing pressure—Salomon's rampant growth in the 1980s caused prob-lems and, ultimately, layoffs. Salomon historically has had a high turnover rate but they have served as the training ground for traders all over Wall Street.

Global presence.   Through the Salomon Brothers and Phibro subsidiaries, Salomon maintains commodities and se-curities trading and investment banking offices in London, Tokyo, Frankfurt and Zurich as well as throughout the U.S.

Stock performance. Salomon stock bought for $1,000 in 1980 sold for $2,396 on January 2, 1990.

Salomon Inc., One New York Plaza, New York, NY 10004; (212) 747-7000.

4

#1 *in mergers and acquisitions deals*

#2 *in raising money for companies*

Employees: 6,200
Sales: $3.4 billion
Founded: 1869
Headquarters: New York City, New York

Workplace

Goldman, Sachs is, arguably, the most admired firm on Wall Street. They trade stocks, bonds and Treasury notes, raise money for companies and governments, deal in foreign exchange and offer counsel on mergers and acquisitions. They are, in other words, a full-line securities house although they don't handle small investors. There are others in this class—Morgan Stanley comes to mind—but Goldman's reputation stems not so much from their prowess as a dealmaker as from the way they conduct business. They embody old-fashioned values—loyalty and integrity—with techniques and execution that are quite modern. Although they have brought many companies public—sold their shares to investors—Goldman has remained not only private, with no shares in the hands of the public, but also a partnership, meaning money put up for deals is their own money (the partners' money, that is).

The 128 partners run the place in a collegial fashion that is the envy of Wall Street. They don't seem to have giant egos

that need constant stroking. Understatement is the rule here. They're a major dealmaker, but they don't flaunt it. They give the impression they're in business to serve clients rather than to make potfuls of money (which of course they do anyway). Goldman, Sachs held to their course during the frenzied 1980s when the biggest mergers and acquisitions in the history of U.S. business were being mounted. They participated in many of these deals but on their own terms. They have a long-standing policy of not representing anyone attempting a hostile takeover—trying to acquire a company against the wishes of the firm's management. And they refused to bend that policy, which allowed them, in 1989, to run an advertisement directed to CEOs, which said: "When the phone rings Friday at 4:05, and you're informed that someone plans to make an offer for the company, 'Who do you want in your corner?'"

One of Goldman's oldest and strongest businesses is underwriting: raising money for a company by the sale of their stock. That's what it means to be an investment banker for a company. In the early part of this century they handled the initial stock offerings of Sears, Roebuck, F. W. Woolworth, May Department Stores and B. F. Goodrich. In 1956, when Ford Motor Company decided to sell stock to the public for the first time, Goldman got the call. In 1986, when software wunderkind Microsoft had their first stock offering, Goldman again led the underwriting.

One of the problems partnerships have is raising money for their operations. It has to be generated internally, from the partners, which is a disadvantage for an investment banker wanting to do very big deals. That problem was alleviated in 1986 when Japan's Sumitomo Bank paid $500 million in return for a 12.5 percent share in Goldman's profits through 1996. Aside from setting a value on Goldman ($4 billion), the deal was unusual in that the Federal Reserve Board, concerned about the separation of commercial banking (Sumitomo) from investment banking (Goldman), insisted Sumitomo have no say in the partnership. They didn't get any partnership seats, and they have no right to say anything about the way Goldman conducts business. They do have the right to send bright young men to Goldman to see how the "masters of the universe" operate. In an interview with writer Michael Schrage in *Manhattan, Inc.*, Sumitomo's managing director, Akira Kondoh, explained how they selected Goldman: "Solomon Brothers, too expensive; Merrill Lynch, too big; Bear Stearns was going public; First Boston—no, they already had a relationship with Crédit Suisse; Smith Barney—too retail. Kidder Peabody was an interesting candidate, but General Electric bought it while we were still looking. Shearson would have been good, but we didn't think American Express was looking for new investors. But Goldman, Sachs was our first choice from the beginning."

Sumitomo is one of Japan's largest banks, often compared in style to Citibank. When they first approached CEO John Weinberg with the idea, he joked that "we'd have to change our name to Goldman Sake."

History. Marcus Goldman didn't start out in finance. In 1848, he immigrated to the U.S. from Bavaria, where he had been a schoolteacher. After arriving in America, he sold dry goods door-to-door from a horse-drawn wagon (in New Jersey) and ran a clothing store (in Philadelphia). Goldman didn't find his calling until he was 49 years old and living in Manhattan. That year, in 1869, he opened a one-room basement office in New York's financial district.

In the beginning, Goldman had two employees, a bookkeeper and an office boy. His business was simple. Each day, wearing a black stovepipe hat, he bought promissory notes (called commercial paper) from jewelry and leather merchants, stowing the notes in his hat. As the day progressed, his hat would sit higher and higher on his head, proving to his neighbors business was good. Goldman would then go to commercial banks (the Chemical, the Park Bank) and sell the notes, making a profit on what was essentially a short-term loan to the merchants.

In 1882, Goldman's young son-in-law, Samuel Sachs, came aboard and the new company became "M. Goldman and Sachs." Three years later, Goldman's son and another son-in-law became partners, and the name was changed to "Goldman, Sachs and Co." In 1887, Goldman, Sachs developed an important relationship with a British merchant banking house,

Kleinwort Sons & Co., which enabled them to enter the foreign exchange and currency markets. Goldman, Sachs soon opened offices in Chicago and St. Louis (establishing an impressive roster of clients, like Sears, Roebuck and Cluett, Peabody) and joined the New York Stock Exchange in 1896. Ten years later, they entered the new field of investment banking. When a company offered stock to the public, Goldman, Sachs was willing to underwrite the company.

In 1927, Sidney J. Weinberg became the second partner not from the Goldman or Sachs families. He went on to head the firm as Senior Partner from 1930 until his death in 1969. The son of a liquor dealer from Brooklyn, Weinberg dropped out of school after the eighth grade and started at Goldman, Sachs when he was 16, cleaning spittoons and brushing the partners' silk hats. Under Weinberg's astute leadership during his long years at the firm Goldman, Sachs became a leader in domestic and international public offerings, project and real estate financing, commercial paper, block trading, mergers and acquisitions, investment research and foreign currency transactions. Weinberg was succeeded by Gustave Levy in 1969, who headed Goldman, Sachs until 1976 when "the two Johns"—John Weinberg and John Whitehead—headed the company together as cochairmen.

Owners and rulers. In 1984, at age 62, John Whitehead retired (becoming a diplomatic envoy for Ronald Reagan) and left Goldman, Sachs in the hands of cochair, 59-year-old John Weinberg. Weinberg, the younger son of Sidney Weinberg, was raised amidst wealth in Scarsdale, New York, but also put in time as a Marine during World War II. He joined Goldman, Sachs in 1950 after graduating from Princeton and getting an MBA from Harvard. In 1987 Stephen Friedman and Robert Rubin were both named vice chairmen and cochief operating officers—making them heirs apparent to Goldman, Sachs leadership. But Weinberg told the *New York Times* in 1987, "I'm going to work till I'm 99." In 1988, Weinberg was dropped from the *Forbes* list of America's 400 richest people, because of postcrash financial uncertainties, but he made $17 million in 1989.

As a place to work. Goldman has the reputation as the best place to work on Wall Street. Competition to get into the firm is intense, and once hired you're expected to pick a specialty and stick with it. "We do not coddle people around here," a Goldman, Sachs partner confided. Sixteen hour days are common. In early 1990, a confidential study at Goldman, Sachs was released to the *New York Times*, highlighting the firm's concern over greed and internal tensions. One partner told the *New York Times*, "We've become tougher in a more competitive world. Some would even say we've become ruthless." Another partner was quoted as saying in the study, "People have gotten rich very quickly. As they become financially independent, they tend to get more difficult." Another said, "In the old days, when you became a partner, you would feel free to give your wallet to another partner to hold for safekeeping. I do not think it is that way now." Also in early 1990, five female vice presidents quit the firm to open their own firm. Only 1 of the 128 Goldman partners is a woman.

Social responsibility. Goldman did not escape the 1980s without blemishes. Robert Freeman, a partner and senior stock trader, pleaded guilty in 1989 to insider trading charges brought by the Justice Department.

Goldman, Sachs & Co., 55 Broad Street, New York, NY 10004; (212) 676-8000.

5

Morgan Stanley

#3 *in mergers and acquisitions deals*

Employees: 6,600
Sales: $2.5 billion
Profits: $443 million
Founded: 1935
Headquarters: New York City, New York

If you wanted to buy 10 shares of stock in Campbell Soup, this would not be the place to come. But if you had built up a thriving, multimillion-dollar business and wanted to sell shares to the public, Morgan Stanley could arrange that for you. If you worked in the investment department of an insurance company and

Over 10,000 employees on Wall Street lost their jobs in 1989. At the beginning of 1990, the total number of employees is now about 225,000, 60,000 less than in 1987, but 165,000 more than in 1980.

needed to sell a huge block of bonds, Morgan Stanley could help you out. Not gratis, of course—they exact killer fees for their arcane services. Morgan Stanley is one of Wall Street's full-line securities houses: They raise money for companies; trade bonds, stocks, commodities and currencies (for well-heeled customers and themselves); arrange mergers and acquisitions; give financial advice. And they do this now on a global scale. They have, in fact, more offices (10) outside of the U.S. than inside (4). They maintain a big research department to analyze the securities in which they deal. The only thing they don't do is retail brokerage—that is, they aren't set up to service the small investor the way Merrill Lynch, Prudential Bache and Paine Webber are.

Morgan Stanley was known for years as the stuffiest of the stuffy. Jews were not hired, and blacks were seen on the premises only as shoeshine boys, women as secretaries. Customer relationships were cemented on the golf course. That era of WASP elitism is passing. In the 1980s Morgan Stanley scuffed their shoes to show Wall Street they too could play hardball—and they opened up their ranks to a more diverse group of employees.

If any firm was Wall Street's winner in the 1980s, it's Morgan Stanley. Previously, they did business only with the crème de la crème—AT&T, Coca-Cola, Exxon, General Motors. In the 1980s they waded in to some of the fiercest takeover battles, using, on behalf of their clients, every trick in the book, including helping corporate raiders take over companies against the wishes of management. When the decade's dust had cleared, many of Morgan Stanley's competitors were on the ropes or—like Drexel Burnham Lambert—had been knocked out. Morgan Stanley was stronger than ever. They had invested some of their own money in deals in which they were giving advice to others, thereby becoming majority owners of a raft of companies including Container Corp. of America, Burlington Industries, Colt Industries, Sterling Chemical and the Essex Group. At the start of the 1980s, Morgan Stanley was a privately held firm (owned entirely by their partners) with 1,800 employees, all but 50 of whom worked in the U.S. At decade's end, they were publicly owned (that is, their stock was sold on the stock exchange), and they had 6,600 employees, 2,000 of whom worked overseas (mostly in Tokyo and London). And they were a far richer firm—30 times richer: In 1980 the company was worth $88 million, compared with $2.65 billion 10 years later.

History. When Morgan Stanley announced they were selling stock to the public in March 1986, Wall Street gasped. Not that most patrician investment bank—not the bluest of bluebloods! Morgan Stanley's partners had first names that sounded like other peoples' last names. Their pedigrees included only the best colleges and clubs. The Morgan in their name came from the most patrician of all Wall Street families. Following the stock market crash of 1929 and subsequent disclosures of market manipulations by leading bankers, Congress passed the Glass-Steagall Act that gave banks this ultimatum: lend money or sell stock, you can't do both anymore. J. P. Morgan, Jr., chose banking (Morgan Guaranty); his youngest son, Henry, chose to raise money for companies (investment banking). So in 1935 Henry Morgan resigned from the family firm—along with two senior partners, Harold Stanley and William Ewing—to start their own business at 2 Wall Street, one block away from J. P. Morgan's offices. From day one, Morgan Stanley was a roaring success—mainly because they brought many of J. P. Morgan's former clients along.

The firm grew by serving as a banker to big corporations. They did big deals. In 1970 they helped AT&T raise money for expansion by selling bonds. In an offering that was the largest in U.S. corporate history—$1.6 billion—three times bigger than any previous undertaking. It took 4,000 workers just to handle the paperwork, which filled 20 boxcars. Two years later,

they moved their headquarters five miles north of Wall Street to the Exxon building in midtown Manhattan, where they're closer to their corporate clients.

Despite some changes during the 1970s, Morgan Stanley maintained their conservative ways. They insisted on handling underwriting deals (the selling of new stocks or bonds) by themselves. Or, if they worked with other investment bankers, Morgan Stanley insisted on top billing. When IBM needed to raise $1 billion in 1979, they asked Morgan Stanley to join with Salomon Brothers and Merrill Lynch in organizing a syndicate to sell the issue. Morgan Stanley declined, saying they had to be the lead underwriter—and lost multimillion-dollar fees.

The IBM sale marked a turning point. After that, Morgan Stanley would no longer play this aristocratic card. They were actually one of the first Wall Street firms to set up a mergers and acquisitions department, and in 1974 they helped International Nickel take over ESB in what is considered the first major hostile takeover—that is, a company bought out against management wishes. During the 1970s such deals were few and far between. Not so in the 1980s when Morgan's bankers helped corporate raider T. Boone Pickens try to take over General American Oil, turning around a year later to help Phillips Petroleum ward off a raid by Pickens and Carl Icahn. In other actions, Morgan's Joseph G. Fogg III helped Chevron buy Gulf Oil in 1984, netting $17 million in fees, and Eric Gleacher, another Morgan takeover advisor, helped Kohlberg Kravis Roberts engineer the $25 billion takeover of RJR Nabisco. Morgan's fee for that deal: $25 million.

Such fees, while extraordinary, pale by comparison with the money to be made by becoming a principal player in such deals. Morgan Stanley has their own capital to put up instead of just advising other companies on how to do deals. In just one deal, involving a Texas chemical company, Morgan made $120 million by selling the 10 percent of the company's stock they had purchased in a hostile takeover.

Morgan Stanley sold stock to the public in 1986 so they could have more capital to do bigger deals. Otherwise, the partners would have had to come up with the money.

Owners and rulers. Morgan Stanley is 80 percent owned by the firm's 254 managing directors and principals. (Only 20 percent of the company was offered to the public in 1986.) It's a pretty rich group. On average, each officer owns $5.5 million in stock. In 1990, S. Parker Gilbert, stepson of the founder, Harold Stanley, stepped down as chairman in favor of Richard B. Fisher.

As a place to work. The hours are long—and often include weekends—but Morgan Stanley pays well above the Wall Street average. It's a nice place to work if you like roll-top desks, ancestral portraits and wood paneling. Turnover is low.

It's still a stuffy place but less of a WASP enclave. They have a high-ranking Jewish member of their management committee, Lewis Bernard (he was the first Jewish partner at the firm), and the head of merchant banking is Donald Brennan, the son of an Irish–born steamfitter.

Global presence. Morgan Stanley wants to be a global player. They have offices in all the key places: London, Tokyo, Hong Kong. In 1989 13 percent of their revenues came from international operations.

Stock performance. Morgan Stanley stock bought for $1,000 in 1986 sold for $1,419 on January 2, 1990.

Morgan Stanley Group, Inc., 1251 Avenue of the Americas, New York, NY 10020; (212) 703-4000.

6

Bear Stearns

#8 in investment banking

Employees: 6,000
Sales: $2.4 billion
Profits: $140 million
Founded: 1923
Headquarters: New York City, New York

The Bear—their nickname on Wall Street—relishes their reputation as uncouth gunslingers who trade huge blocks of stocks, bonds, U.S. Treasury notes and other interest-bearing securities for institutions, well-heeled investors and themselves. On any given day they're likely to be holding trading positions of $12–$15 billion in fixed-income securities (bonds and other financial instruments paying a specified interest). One of their fortes is executing big trades before anyone knows what they're up to, a position enhanced by their sideline business as a "clearer" for other brokers and professional traders—that is, they execute buy and sell orders for others, handling all the bookkeeping chores. In 1989 they were performing this service for over 750 clients (brokers, market makers, specialists, arbitrageurs, hedge funds, money managers), thereby handling 8 percent of all trades done on the floor of the New York Stock Exchange. On October 16, 1989, the Monday after the big October 13 sell-off, The Bear processed 120,000 trades.

Bear Stearns became a bigger player during the 1980s, moving from a 1,000-person, private partnership with $46 million in capital to a 6,000-person, publicly traded company with $1.4 billion in capital. Under the whiplashing of cigar-smoking Alan C. "Ace" Greenberg, called by some the best trader on Wall Street, the Bear has been upgrading themselves into the services of investment banking where they raise money for corporations and have an outlook beyond 15 seconds. But old habits die hard. They're still regarded primarily as traders who will cut your heart out for an eighth of a point. Because of their scrappiness, some Wall Streeters still refer to them as "Boys Town." They once had a sign over their trading room that proclaimed: "Let's make nothing but money." When confronted in 1983 about the Bear Stearns' aggressiveness and their willingness to take anyone as a client, Greenberg told a New York Times reporter: "I'm depressed all the way to the bank with what they say."

Bear Stearns was founded in 1923, and according to Judith Ramsey Ehrlich and Barry J. Rehfeld, authors of The New Crowd, their early clients "were mainly rich Park Avenue German-Jewish widows." The Bear Stearns reputation as a big tough trading firm was established by Salim "Cy" Lewis, a burly, rambunctious autocrat who downed a bottle of Scotch a day and ruled over the trading floor for 40 years until he died of a heart attack in 1978. Lewis was known as an artist of the block trade and an indefatigable fundraiser for the United Jewish Appeal. He was succeeded by Ace Greenberg, who grew up in Oklahoma City, where his father ran a women's clothing store. He came to New York in 1949 armed with a bachelor's degree from the University of Missouri. He was turned down by six other brokerage firms before Bear Stearns hired him as a $37-a-week clerk. Greenberg, known for his nerves of steel, grew up in the Bear's trading room. Cy Lewis called him the man who "pissed ice water."

Greenberg has put his own mark on Bear Stearns, bringing them into the modern Wall Street era, although they retain the maverick flavor of their earlier life. He too, like Cy Lewis, is a great believer in charity. Bear Stearns is the largest per capita giver on Wall Street to the United Way. They're also the country's largest per capita giver to the United Jewish Appeal. All managing partners at Bear Stearns are required to give a percentage of pay and bonuses to charity. Goldman Sachs and Morgan Stanley may recruit at Harvard Business School—but not the Bear. During the 1980s Greenberg circulated this memo: "Our first desire is to promote from within. If somebody applies with an MBA degree, we will certainly not hold it against them. But we are really looking for people with PSD degrees. PSD stands for poor, smart, and a deep desire to become rich." Greenberg also doesn't believe in nepotism. One of his assistants, Edward Hirsch, once came to him to announce he had asked Greenberg's sister, DiAnne, to get married. Greenberg said: "Congratulations, you're fired."

The Bear sold stock to the public in 1985, but Greenberg and other partners still own half the shares. Their shares trade on the New York Stock Exchange.

Global presence. Amsterdam, Geneva, Hong Kong, London, Paris, Tokyo.

Stock performance. Bear Stearns stock bought for $1,000 in 1985 sold for $1,268 on January 2, 1990.

The Bear Stearns Companies Inc., 245 Park Avenue, New York, NY 10167; (212) 272-2000.

7
Charles Schwab

#1 *in discount brokerage firms*

Employees: 2,500
Sales: $553 million
Profits: $19 million
Founded: 1974
Headquarters: San Francisco, California

If you've ever looked at the financial pages, chances are you've seen Chuck Schwab's photogenic smile. The ads run regularly in major newspapers, featuring Schwab looking clean-cut and confident. He should be confident—he runs the nation's biggest discount brokerage. Schwab has over 100 offices across the country, and they service 1.3 million accounts. One-third of their customer accounts are in California.

For 183 years, there was no such thing as a discount brokerage. If you wanted to buy or sell stocks, the broker took a fixed commission for executing your order. Then, on May 1, 1975 ("Mayday"), the Securities and Exchange Commission abolished fixed commissions. Brokers could charge what they wanted. Enter Charles Schwab and his "no-frills" brokerage house. He would do no research. He would never offer customers advice. He would just take telephone calls, execute orders and charge up to 70 percent less than the conventional brokerage houses for the service. "Our passion is to make investors independent, not make them dependent on a commissioned salesman," Schwab told *Forbes*. To help his own cause, in 1984 Schwab wrote a book called *How To Be Your Own Stockbroker*.

Charles Schwab showed his stuff early. He grew up in a small farm community near Sacramento, California, the son of a district attorney. As a boy, he started a chicken farm (selling eggs and fertilizer), sold magazine subscriptions and harvested walnuts (gathering, sacking and selling them). By age 13, he was investing in the stock market. He took a BA and MBA from Stanford, published an investment newsletter for a while and started a mutual fund securities regulators shut down in 1972 because it wasn't properly registered. In 1974, when Schwab was 36, he set up shop in San Francisco with 10 people and a two-room office. A year later, "Mayday" arrived—and with it, the beginnings of Schwab's fortune. Ten years later, Schwab had a 28-story headquarters, over 1,500 employees and 92 offices around the world.

In 1981, Bank of America bought Charles Schwab's company for $53 million. Schwab himself joined the B of A board and became the bank's largest individual shareholder (his 32 percent stake at Schwab translated into $19 million worth of B of A stock). But Schwab wasn't happy for long. He had conflicts with B of A's CEO, Sam Armacost, and was upset over B of A's faltering stock price. Schwab was also an outsider at B of A: "I felt like the Lone Ranger," he told a friend. Schwab resigned in 1986 and bought his company back in 1987 for about $230 million. Back on his own, he was eager to make his mark again. In March 1989 Charles Schwab bought the country's fifth-largest discount broker, Rose & Co., for $37 million.

Despite the firm's great successes, there have been red faces in recent years. In 1988, *Business Week* published an article exposing a host of improper trading scams at Schwab. Chuck Schwab admitted that his company had made $2.4 million between 1985 and 1988 by trading with customers' accounts without permission of the customers themselves. Schwab repaid nearly $3 million to customers and the New York Stock Exchange censured and fined the firm $375,000—one of the stiffest fines in the exchange's history.

Stock performance. Charles Schwab stock bought for $1,000 in 1987 sold for $847 on January 2, 1990.

The Charles Schwab Corporation, 101 Montgomery Street, San Francisco, CA 94104; (415) 627-7000.

8
Kohlberg Kravis Roberts

#1 *in leveraged buyouts*

Employees: 24
Founded: 1976
Headquarters: New York City, New York

It's difficult to understand what happened in the business world during the 1980s without reference to Kohlberg Kravis Roberts. An investment banking firm, they became the central players in the buying and dismantling of big industrial companies. KKR was only four years old when the 1980s began, unknown even on Wall Street. When the decade ended, they ranked as a Wall Street superstar, enshrined as the greatest dealmaker of the times.

Founded by Jerome Kohlberg, Jr., Henry R. Kravis and George R. Roberts, KKR raised $62 billion to buy out 35 companies between 1976 and 1989. Among their deals were Owens-Illinois, Safeway Stores, Jim Walter, Beatrice, Red Lion Inns and Duracell. The capstone of their activities was RJR Nabisco, acquired at the end of 1988 for $25.1 billion in what was called "the deal of the century" and memorialized in the best-seller, *Barbarians at the Gate*, by Bryan Burrough and John Helyar. RJR Nabisco had ranked 19th on the *Fortune* 500 and their disappearance into a leveraged buyout signaled no company of any size was safe from a takeover.

1n 1988 *Fortune* called them "the second largest conglomerate," just a touch behind General Electric in annual revenues ($40 billion). A little later the *Washington Post* said KKR controlled "one of the largest industrial empires in the world, one that will probably have aggregate annual revenues greater than those of IBM ($50 billion)." These comparisons resulted from adding up all the revenues of the companies KKR had taken over. But KKR is really not an operating company, nor do they have a goal of building a giant holding company. They're a *transactional* company, buying companies only to restructure them and then sell them off at a profit. They are in-and-outers.

History. KKR's roots are in the hyperactive New York trading firm, Bear Stearns, known on Wall Street as the Bear. In 1976 Jerome Kohlberg left Bear Stearns where he was cohead of corporate finance, taking with him two up-and-coming colleagues, Henry Kravis and George Roberts, who were cousins and close friends. Ever since their boyhood, Kravis and Roberts had talked about going into business together, and this was their chance. Besides, said Kravis, "We weren't sure if we were successful at Bear Stearns because we were Bear Stearns or because we were us." Kohlberg, a gentlemanly, reserved character, called the shots at KKR the first 10 years or so.

At first, KKR did deals that were anything but glamorous, buying companies such as A. J. Industries, a brake-drum manufacturer, for $23 million. Then, in 1979, they did the largest buyout of a public company ever tried: Houdaille Industries, a machine tool maker, for the then-stunning sum of $355 million. Their tactic was the LBO, or leveraged buyout. In a leveraged buyout, a company is bought largely with borrowed funds. The collateral for the loans are the assets of the company being bought. It's as if someone knocked on your door and said they wanted to buy your house; when you asked how much money they intended to put up, they said "nothing" or "very little"; they explained the banks were willing to lend them the necessary funds, based on the value of the house; after buying it, they might sell off some of the land and make some improvements, and then, a few years down the road, resell the house at a profit.

KKR used very little of their own money in an LBO. First, they raised money from institutional investors who were promised higher returns on their investments than they could get in the stock market. Among the investors in KKR deals have been such institutions as Harvard, Yale, the Salvation Army and the pension funds of New York State, Oregon, Washington, Coca-Cola, Avon, Georgia-Pacific and United Technologies. These funds were supplemented by loans—often bridge loans that had to be repaid quickly—from big banks like Citibank, Bank of America, Bankers Trust and Manufacturers Hanover. And on top of that, the buyout package invariably included a slug of so-called junk bonds investment bankers assembled and sold. (Junk bonds are essentially funds loaned at very high interest rates. Throughout the 1980s the prime originator of "junk" was Drexel Burnham Lambert, but houses like Morgan Stanley and Salomon were peddling them fast and furiously before the decade ended.) KKR extracted their profits from these deals in three different cuts: they charged investors 1.5 percent for managing their funds; they took a fee (as high as 1 percent of the package) for doing the

deal; and then they kept 20 percent of the profits the deal generated when the acquired company was resold (often in pieces). Investors received 80 percent of the profits.

Gradually, as the investment pot grew, KKR did bigger and bigger leveraged buyouts, employing the same principles and practices Kohlberg laid down at the start, avoiding hostile deals. Then came the $6.2 billion acquisition of Beatrice in 1986. The ambitious Kravis and Roberts felt KKR could no longer play Mr. Nice Guy. In Wall Street parlance, the Beatrice buyout was a "bear hug," meaning KKR didn't leave the Beatrice board much choice in the matter. This time the drill wasn't to bail out existing management, since the CEO had just been fired, but to convince the board to let them buy the company. KKR's attitude was that if they didn't take over Beatrice, someone else would, since the company was floundering. It was "in play," as they say. So, without waiting for an invitation, KKR lined up their own team of managers and buyout package, pressing hard for a deal, which the Beatrice board finally accepted. Beatrice ended up being dismembered, with many of the pieces proving difficult to sell. Some were still on the auction block as the decade ended.

The Beatrice takeover wasn't exactly hostile, but it came too close for Kohlberg's comfort—and he left KKR. Kohlberg reportedly said: "I'll stick with deals where reason still prevails." Free to follow their own path, Kravis and Roberts pulled off "the deal of the century": RJR Nabisco.

Owners and rulers.   Both Kravis and Roberts grew up in the Southwest: Kravis in Oklahoma and Roberts in Houston. They went to college together at Claremont Men's College, and then Roberts went to law school, while Kravis went to business school at Columbia. Looking back, Kravis said, "In 1968, during the student riots...I left it to my liberal friends to do things like getting arrested. I had my mind on business." They both went to work for Bear Stearns, where they hooked up with Kohlberg, father of the LBO. George Roberts, who keeps to himself in San Francisco, is regarded as a "creative and conceptual" thinker, astute at valuing the companies KKR buys. Kravis, who lives in New York, more than makes up for his cousin's reticence. Married to fashion designer Carolyne Roehm, they are high on the list of guests at New York society events.

KKR has three other general partners: Paul E. Raether, Michael Michelson and Robert I. MacDonnell (Roberts' brother-in-law). Each oversees a group of companies. For their efforts they have been well compensated. Kravis and Roberts are each estimated to be worth over $300 million.

As a place to work. To die for if you want to make big money. Only two dozen employees generating millions of dollars of fees from deals.

Social responsibility. The debate has raged in the business press as to social benefits or social disasters for which KKR has been responsible. Supporters say the company is doing good work, getting companies to cut out the fat and run more efficiently. Detractors say KKR breaks up companies, destroys thousands of jobs and loads up companies with colossal amounts of debt. Others just see KKR as game players, engaged in the battle for the love of the game. Veteran *Fortune* editor Carol J. Loomis is in the latter camp. She said: "One thing is sure. They are not working for the love of restructuring corporate America. Chuck Schwab, head of the discount brokerage firm bearing his name, once spoke admiringly to Roberts of all KKR had done, as Schwab saw it, to improve U.S. business, taking companies out of the hands of uncaring boards and putting them in the hands of entrepreneurial owners. Roberts looked at Schwab sideways and said, 'That's not why we do it, Chuck.'"

Kohlberg Kravis Roberts, 9 West 57th Street, New York, NY 10019; (212) 750-8300.

9
Drexel Burnham

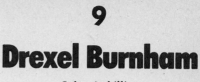

Sales: $4 billion
Founded: 1935
Died: 1990

The most successful and most profitable investment banking firm of the 1980s collapsed shortly after the decade ended. In a denouement hailed by many outsiders as a fitting epitaph to the 1980s, Drexel Burnham Lambert filed for protection of the bankruptcy court on February 13, 1990. No one expected them to emerge. Two months and 12 days later, Michael Milken, the man responsible for Drexel Burnham's meteoric rise, pleaded guilty to violating securities laws to settle a racketeering case brought by the Justice Department. Sentencing was scheduled for later in the year but he agreed to pay a fine of $600 million. Drexel Burnham had made a similar settlement in December 1988, paying a fine of $650 million.

The man and the firm so ignominiously downed—"Michael Milken is a crook," said the *New York Times* flatly—financed such companies as MCI, Mattel, McCaw Cellular, Fruit of the Loom, Warner Communications and Orion Pictures. They also helped to finance some of the biggest takeovers in the history of American business, including RJR Nabisco, Beatrice Companies, Storer Communications and Kaiser Tech. And the key element in this financing was the so-called junk bond. Never before has an abstruse financial term gained such common currency that it became a staple of the evening network TV news.

A junk bond is like any other bond in that it's simply an IOU from a company, which promises to pay a fixed rate of interest. Where they differ from other bonds—and this is why they're called junk—is that the company issuing them doesn't have the rock-solid financial structure of, say, an IBM or General Motors and hence has to pay a high rate of interest on this bond. The bond buyer gets a high interest—another, less pejorative term for these bonds is "high yield"—to compensate for what seems to be a bigger risk.

There is nothing new about junk bonds. Michael Milken didn't invent them. What he did do was analyze their past histories to determine that their record of repayment was very good and then launch them in quantities and values never seen before. In the process, he created a junk bond market of $200 billion and transformed Drexel Burnham from a characterless, third-tier investment firm into a combatative, super-profitable Wall Street powerhouse.

Bonds, like stocks, have market value— or at least their holders hope they do in the event they want to sell them. For high-grade corporate bonds, that's not a problem. They trade on the New York Stock Exchange, and you can look up their price every day. Junk bonds do not have the same kind of liquidity, meaning they may not always be instantly saleable. But Milken—and Drexel—provided that liquidity for their bonds. They matched buyer and seller. For example, if a company came to Milken looking to raise $200 million, he might get them $400 million backed by junk bonds. Then, six months later when he did a deal for another company and needed to find buyers for new junk bonds, he went back to the company he had previously overfunded, bringing them in as buyers of the new issue. It was a tight network—and he controlled it. "In most cases," *Fortune* said, "he was both the supply and the demand—the only buyer when customers wanted to sell their bonds, and the only seller when customers wanted to buy." In building this junk bond machine, Milken inevitably had dealings with the Wall Street wheeler-dealers of the 1980s. One of them, Ivan Boesky, was his undoing. A stock market player who paid for inside information with bundles of cash, Boesky was caught, paid a fine of $100 million and went to jail. As part of his plea bargaining, he fingered Milken.

The postmortems on Milken and Drexel have been numerous. In some circles, Milken is still regarded as a hero—someone who bucked the Wall Street establishment with a new financial product, helped many deserving companies get financing and forced lazy, complacent managements of old-line companies to streamline operations. To others, he is the devil incarnate, someone who lined his pockets at the expense of his clients and was responsible for loading up companies with so much debt they had to mutilate themselves. One example frequently cited was the Drexel-financed acquisition of Pacific Lumber by Maxxam—to meet the interest payments on their junk bonds, Pacific Lumber had to accelerate the chopping of trees in their northern California redwood forests. In the mid-1980s, when Drexel was riding high, *Business Week* placed Mike Milken in the same league as giants such as J. P. Morgan and Charles Merrill, declaring he had "altered the basic pattern of corporate finance in the U.S. and rocked the established order on Wall Street and throughout much of Corporate America." A few years later, writing in *Barron's*, Benjamin J. Stein labeled Milken the "betrayer of capitalism." Stein said if Milken was a "savior, he was the savior not of Main Street but of Wall Street and Rodeo Drive, not of the factory stiff but of the designers who sell fabric wallpaper at $200 a yard."

As Stein also noted, Milken made "the highest wage in the industrial history of mankind." In 1984, he made (including salary and bonus) $124 million; in 1985 $135 million; in 1986, $294 million; in 1987, $550 million; in 1988, $750 million. It was a pattern of enrichment typical of Drexel. Even as they were on the verge of bankruptcy at the end of 1989 (and Milken was no longer aboard), Drexel paid enormous year-end bonuses. Writing in *Vanity Fair*, Marie Brenner reported when Drexel's merger-and-acquisitions chief, Leon Black, learned his 1989 compensation was going to be $12 million, he hit the ceiling, considering that payout an insult in view of the work he had done on the RJR Nabisco buyout. So he squeezed another $3 million out of Drexel. In his book, *Liar's Poker*, Michael Lewis relates the story of a Salomon Brothers trader who defected to Drexel and found his first bonus was *several million dollars* more than he expected. While he sat there stunned, Milken leaned over and asked, "Are you happy?" When the former Salomon employee nodded, Milken asked: "How can we make you happier?"

The fat paychecks did not prevent Drexel Burnham from making more than than anyone else on Wall Street. In 1986, when they had 10,000 employees, they earned $1 billion. They still had 5,000 people on the payroll when they went down in 1990.

Drexel Burnham Lambert had three roots. One is I. W. (Tubby) Burnham, scion of a distinguished Jewish family—his father was a promiment Baltimore physician (he performed the first blood transfusion in the U.S.) and his grandfather was the distiller of I. W. Harper bourbon whiskey. Burnham opened his own brokerage house in 1935. The second is Drexel Firestone, an old-line Philadelphia investment banking house Burnham acquired in 1973. And the third was the Belgian banking house, Compagnie Bruxelles Lambert, which became a partner (and 25 percent owner) in 1976 when Drexel Burnham merged with their U.S. research arm (William D. Witter). Mike Milken came along with the Drexel Firestone acquisition. In a Founder's Day address in 1987, Tubby Burnham told the assembled Drexel troops: "Our firm has always known the rules and I believe we have lived by the rules. If we hadn't, there is no way we could have been in business for 52 years without so much as a censure. Insignificant, no, important, yes. Without these years of growth and experience we would be falling part under the avalanche of press, TV and radio attacks. Most of their information comes from our competitors, who delight at taking potshots at us while remaining as 'unnamed sources. '"

At the height of their powers, Drexel Burnham was an aggressive player. In her book, *The Predators' Ball*, Connie Bruck reports seeing a goal Drexel posted in big block letters: "TO BE AS BIG AS SALOMON SO WE CAN BE AS ARROGANT AS THEY ARE AND TELL THEM TO GO STUFF IT."

Index

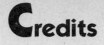redits

The individuals and corporations listed below granted permission to print the photographs or charts that appear on the following pages:

(8) Sara Lee Corporation; (14) General Mills, Inc.; (21, 22) The Quaker Oats Company; (32) Land O'Lakes, Inc.; (34) Cargill Incorporated; (46) Thomas J. Lipton, Inc.; (49) Gerber Products Company; (52) Hershey Foods Corporation; (56) Wm. Wrigley Jr. Company; (65) McDonald's Corporation; (69) Kentucky Fried Chicken; (71) Domino's Pizza, Inc.; (75) Fleming Companies, Inc.; (80) Safeway Inc.; (89) Levi Strauss & Company; (93) Liz Claiborne, Inc.; (96) Nike Inc.; (97) Brown Group, Inc.; (110) Springs Industries, Inc.; (114) Whirlpool Corporation; (121) Raytheon Company; (123) (c) Mark E. Jensen ; (126) Armstrong World Industries, Inc.; (134) Courtesy of The Procter & Gamble Company; (141) Courtesy of Beverly Labin; (143) S.C. Johnson & Son, Inc.; (151) The Gillette Company; (182) Marion Merrell Dow, Inc.; (190) Johnson & Johnson; (197) Sears, Roebuck and Company; (204) J.C. Penney Company, Inc.; (213) Montgomery Ward; (218) Toys R' Us; (222) Tandy Corporation; (237) Courtesy of Ford Motor Company; (247) Nissan Motor; (255) Deere & Company; (257) Goodyear Tire & Rubber Company; (266) Kevin Roche John Dinkeloo and Associates, courtesy of Cummins Engine Company, Inc.; (271) Budget Rent-a-Car Corporation; (276) Mattel, Inc.; (288) Disney Company; (295) MGM/United Artists Communications; (298) Marriot Corporation; (306) Eastman Kodak Company; (310) Hallmark Cards, Inc.; (318) RJR Nabisco Inc.; (327) Adolph Coors Company; (352) CBS; (365) New York Times Company; (369) The Washington Post Company; (374) The Reader's Digest Association, Inc.; (381) Random House; (393) Leo Burnett Company; (402) Courtesy of International Business Machines Corporation; (405) Digital Equipment Corporation; (407) Photo courtesy of Hewlett-Packard Company; (409) Unisys Corporation; (412) Courtesy of Apple Computer, Inc.; (418) Microsoft Corporation; (426) Steelcase Inc.; (476) Reprinted from May 7, 1990 issue of *Business Week* by special permission, copyright (c) 1990 by McGraw-Hill, Inc.; (448) Texas Instrument Incorporated; (482) (c) The ARCO Photography Collection, Los Angeles, CA; (486) Sun Company, Inc.; (494) Weyerhaeuser Company; (497) International Paper Company; (513) Weirton Steel Corporation; (528) Monsanto Company; (537) The Boeing Company; (543) GM Hughes Electronics Corporation; (570) Minnesota Mining & Manufacturing Company; (606) Southern Pacific Transportation Co.; (613) National Railroad Passenger Corporation; (617) Federal Express Corporation; (628) Courtesy of AT&T Archives; (663) The Travelers Corporation.

5525